INTERVIEWING AND CHANGE STRATEGIES FOR HELPERS

INTERVIEWING AND CHANGE STRATEGIES FOR HELPERS

Fundamental Skills and Cognitive Behavioral Interventions

FIFTH EDITION

SHERRY CORMIER
West Virginia University

PAULA S. NURIUS
University of Washington

THOMSON
BROOKS/COLE

Australia • Canada • Mexico • Singapore • Spain • United Kingdom • United States

THOMSON
BROOKS/COLE

Sponsoring Editor: *Lisa Gebo*
Marketing: *Caroline Concilla*
Marketing Assistant: *Mary Ho*
Assistant Editor: *Alma Dea Michelena*
Editorial Assistant: *Sheila Walsh*
Project Editor: *Kim Svetich-Will*
Production: *Matrix Productions*
Manuscript Editor: *Donald Pharr*

Permissions Editor: *Sue Ewing*
Cover Design: *John Edeen*
Cover Art: *Komra Moriko, Earth Mandalas*
Interior Design: *Patrick Devine*
Print Buyer: *Vena Dyer*
Compositor: *Carlisle Communications, Ltd.*
Printing and Binding: *Phoenix Color Corp*

COPYRIGHT © 2003 Brooks/Cole, a division of Thomson Learning, Inc. Thomson Learning™ is a trademark used herein under license.

ALL RIGHTS RESERVED. No part of this work covered by the copyright hereon may be reproduced or used in any form or by any means—graphic, electronic, or mechanical, including but not limited to photocopying, recording, taping, Web distribution, information networks, or information storage and retrieval systems—without the written permission of the publisher.

Printed in the United States of America
1 2 3 4 5 6 7 06 05 04 03 02

For more information about our products, contact us at:
Thomson Learning Academic Resource Center
1-800-423-0563

For permission to use material from this text, contact us by:
Phone: 1-800-730-2214 **Fax:** 1-800-730-2215
Web: http://www.thomsonrights.com

Cormier, L. Sherilyn (Louise Sherilyn)
  Interviewing and change strategies for helpers: fundamental skills and cognitive behavioral interventions / by Sherry Cormier and Paula S. Nurius.—5th ed.
    p. cm.
  Rev. ed. of: Interviewing strategies for helpers / Sherry Cormier, Bill Cormier, 1998
  Includes bibliographical references (p.) and indexes.
  ISBN 0-534-53739-1
  1. Counseling. 2. Helping behavior. 3. Interviewing. 4.Cognitive therapy. 5. Behavior therapy. I. Nurius, Paula. II. Cormier, L. Sherilyn (Louise Sherilyn, [date] Interviewing strategies for helpers. III. Title.
BF637.C6 C584 2003
158'.3—dc21   2002020530

ISBN 0-534-53739-1

Brooks/Cole-Thomson Learning
511 Forest Lodge Road
Pacific Grove, CA 93950
USA

Asia
Thomson Learning
5 Shenton Way #01-01
UIC Building
Singapore 068808

Australia
Nelson Thomson Learning
102 Dodds Street
South Melbourne, Victoria 3205
Australia

Canada
Nelson Thomson Learning
1120 Birchmount Road
Toronto, Ontario M1K 5G4
Canada

Europe/Middle East/Africa
Thomson Learning
High Holborn House
50/51 Bedford Row
London WC1R 4LR
United Kingdom

Latin America
Thomson Learning
Seneca, 53
Colonia Polanco
11560 Mexico D.F.
Mexico

Spain
Paraninfo Thomson Learning
Calle/Magallanes, 25
28015 Madrid, Spain

∼

In honor of Edith and Bill Keucher
and Gwyndolyn Garner, and in memory of
Lucille Medley, with grateful appreciation
and affection

∼

About the Authors

Sherry Cormier is a professor in the Department of Counseling, Rehabilitation Counseling and Counseling Psychology at West Virginia University, Morgantown, West Virginia. She is a licensed psychologist in the state of West Virginia. Her current research and practice interests are in counseling and psychology training and supervision models, and issues affecting girls and women. In her practice and supervision, she uses cognitive–behavioral, object-relations, and body-awareness approaches as well as Jungian and transpersonal psychology. She teaches the counseling techniques course in the CACREP master's program and the clinical supervision course in the APA Counseling Psychology doctoral program. She also supervises doctoral practicum, which is focused on the use of evidence-based helping strategies and the interface between research and practice. She is the mother of two twentysomething daughters. Her husband is a licensed professional counselor.

Paula S. Nurius is a professor in the University of Washington School of Social Work in Seattle, Washington. She brings master's and doctoral degrees in both psychology and social work to her teaching, practice, and research, with particular concern for vulnerable and traumatized populations. Her research has focused on the self-concept, clinical reasoning and critical thinking by service practitioners and coping with threats and stressors, particularly personal life stressors including intimate and acquaintance violence. Dr. Nurius teaches practice, theory, and research in master's and doctoral programs. She directs an NIMH-funded graduate training program in research to promote mental health and prevent mental health and behavioral disorders, and has long-standing interests in fostering linkages between practice and research and among allied disciplines committed to helping/human services. She enjoys the outdoor life of the Pacific Northwest with her husband and daughter.

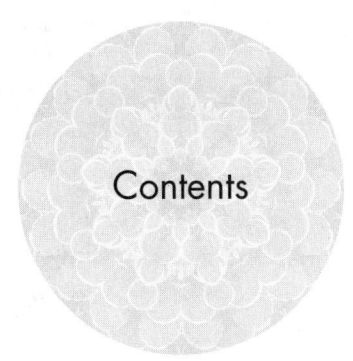

Contents

CHAPTER 1
ABOUT THIS BOOK 1

Envision This 1
A Practice Nexus for the Helping Professions 1
An Overview of Helping 6
Format of the Book 8
Globalization 13
Information Technology in the New Millennium 13
Infotrac Explorations 14
Suggested Resources 14

CHAPTER 2
BUILDING YOUR FOUNDATION AS A HELPER 16

Objectives 16
Characteristics of Effective Helpers: Self-Awareness, Interpersonal Awareness, and Critical Thinking 16
Issues Affecting Helpers: Values, Diversity, and Ethics 20
Summary 41
InfoTrac Explorations 41
Suggested Resources 41
Postevaluation 43
Postevaluation Feedback 44

CHAPTER 3
UNDERSTANDING NONVERBAL BEHAVIOR 45

Objectives 45
Client Nonverbal Behavior 46
How to Work with Client Nonverbal Behavior 54
Helper Nonverbal Behavior 56
Summary 58
InfoTrac Explorations 59
Suggested Resources 59
Postevaluation 60
Postevaluation Feedback 61

CHAPTER 4
INGREDIENTS OF AN EFFECTIVE HELPING RELATIONSHIP 63

Objectives 63
Facilitative Conditions 64
Emotional Objectivity: Transference and Countertransference 71
The Working Alliance 73
Relationship Variables and Resistance 76
Relationship Strategies for Involuntary Clients 79
Summary 80
InfoTrac Explorations 81

Suggested Resources 81
Postevaluation 82
Postevaluation Feedback 83

CHAPTER 5
LISTENING RESPONSES 84
Objectives 84
Listening to Clients' Stories 85
Four Listening Responses 86
Listening for Understanding: Paraphrasing, Reflecting, and Basic Empathy 89
Barriers to Listening 106
Listening with Diverse Groups of Clients 106
Summary 107
InfoTrac Explorations 107
Suggested Resources 108
Postevaluation 109
Postevaluation Feedback 112

CHAPTER 6
RELATIONSHIP ENHANCEMENT VARIABLES AND INTERPERSONAL INFLUENCE 113
Objectives 113
Strong's Model of Counseling as an Interpersonal Influence Process 113
The Interactional Nature of the Influence Process 114
Helper Characteristics or Relationship Enhancers 115
Summary 129
InfoTrac Explorations 130
Suggested Resources 130
Postevaluation 131
Postevaluation Feedback 133

CHAPTER 7
INFLUENCING RESPONSES 134
Objectives 134
Influencing Responses and Timing 135
What Does Influencing Require of Helpers? 135
Six Influencing Responses 135
Summary 163
InfoTrac Explorations 163
Suggested Resources 163
Postevaluation 166
Postevaluation Feedback 173

CHAPTER 8
CONCEPTUALIZING AND ASSESSING CLIENT ISSUES, CONCERNS, AND CONTEXTS 175
Objectives 175
What Is Assessment? 175
The Lazarus Model of Conceptualization: The BASIC ID 175
Our Assumptions About Assessment and Cognitive Behavior Therapy 178
The Person-in-Environment Model 181
The ABC Model of Behavior 185
Diagnostic Classification 190
Limitations of Diagnosis: Labels and Gender/Multicultural Biases 194
A Model Case 196
Summary 201
InfoTrac Explorations 201
Suggested Resources 201
Postevaluation 203
Postevaluation Feedback 205

CHAPTER 9
CONDUCTING AN INTERVIEW ASSESSMENT WITH CLIENTS 207
Objectives 207
Direct Assessment Interviewing 207
Intake Interviews and History 208
Mental-Status Examination 209
Cultural Issues in Intake and Mental-Status Interviews 211

Eleven Categories for Assessing Clients 212
Gender and Multicultural Factors in Interview Assessment 230
Limitations of Interview Leads in Assessment 230
Model Dialogue for Interview Assessment: The Case of Joan 230
Notes and Record Keeping 241
Client Self-Monitoring Assessment 242
Summary 244
InfoTrac Explorations 244
Suggested Resources 244
Postevaluation 247
Postevaluation Feedback 253

CHAPTER 10
IDENTIFYING, DEFINING, AND EVALUATING OUTCOME GOALS 255
Objectives 255
Outcome Goals and Their Purposes in the Helping Process 255
Cultural Issues in Outcome Goals 256
Change Issues in Outcome Goals 257
Resistance Issues in Outcome Goals 260
Interview Leads for Identifying Goals 262
Model Dialogue: The Case of Joan 267
Interview Leads for Defining Goals 271
Evaluation of Outcome Goals 280
Response Dimensions of Outcomes: What to Evaluate 281
Choosing Outcome Measures: How to Evaluate Outcomes 283
When to Evaluate Outcomes 287
Model Example: The Case of Joan 291
Model Dialogue: The Case of Joan 292
Summary 297
InfoTrac Explorations 298
Suggested Resources 298
Postevaluation 300
Postevaluation Feedback 306

CHAPTER 11
TREATMENT PLANNING AND SELECTION 307
Objectives 307
Treatment Planning: Common Factors and Specific Ingredients of Treatment 307
Factors Affecting Treatment Selection 308
Decision Rules in Planning for Type, Duration, and Mode of Treatment 314
Cost Effectiveness of Treatment 320
Multicultural and Gender Issues in Treatment Planning and Selection 322
The Process of Treatment Planning and Empowered Consent 331
Case Study: A Puerto Rican Woman Suffering from *Ataques de Nervios* 332
Termination Issues in Helping 335
Model Dialogue: The Case of Joan 338
Summary and Introduction to the Treatment Change Strategy Chapters 341
InfoTrac Explorations 341
Suggested Resources 342
Postevaluation 343
Postevaluation Feedback 344

CHAPTER 12
IMAGERY AND MODELING STRATEGIES 346
Objectives 346
Participant Modeling 348
Multicultural Applications of Modeling 351
Model Dialogue: Participant Modeling 353
Client Imagery: Assessment and Training 356
Multicultural Applications of Imagery 358
Guided Imagery 359
Model Example: Guided Imagery 363
Covert Modeling 364
Model Dialogue: Covert Modeling 370
Summary 376

InfoTrac Explorations 377
Suggested Resources 377
Postevaluation 379
Postevaluation Feedback 388

CHAPTER 13
REFRAMING, COGNITIVE MODELING, AND PROBLEM-SOLVING STRATEGIES 391

Objectives 391
The Process of Reframing 391
Multicultural Applications of Reframing 396
Model Case: Reframing 397
Cognitive Modeling with Cognitive Self-Instructional Training 397
Model Dialogue: Cognitive Modeling with Cognitive Self-Instructional Training 403
Problem-Solving Therapy 406
Multicultural Applications of Problem Solving 410
Stages of Problem Solving 413
Model Example: Problem-Solving Therapy 419
Summary 420
Postevaluation 423
Postevaluation Feedback 432
InfoTrac Explorations 421
Suggested Resources 421

CHAPTER 14
COGNITIVE CHANGE AND COGNITIVE RESTRUCTURING STRATEGIES 433

Objectives 433
Developments in Cognitive Therapy 434
Uses of Cognitive Restructuring 435
Multicultural Applications of Cognitive Therapy and Cognitive Restructuring 437
Six Components of Cognitive Restructuring 440
Model Dialogue: Cognitive Restructuring 454
Summary 459
InfoTrac Explorations 459
Suggested Resources 460

Postevaluation 461
Postevaluation Feedback 466

CHAPTER 15
STRESS MANAGEMENT STRATEGIES 467

Objectives 467
Stress and Coping 467
Cultural and Life Course Variations in Stress 470
The Physiology of Breathing and Stress 472
Steps for Breathing 475
Contraindications and Adverse Effects of Diaphragmatic Breathing 478
Model Example: Diaphragmatic Breathing 478
Stress Inoculation: Processes and Uses 479
Seven Components of Stress Inoculation 481
Model Dialogue: Stress Inoculation 490
Spirituality in Practice 492
Summary 497
InfoTrac Explorations 497
Suggested Resources 498
Postevaluation 499
Postevaluation Feedback 504

CHAPTER 16
MEDITATION AND MOVEMENT STRATEGIES 505

Objectives 505
Meditation: Processes and Uses 505
Applications of Meditation and Relaxation with Diverse Clients 508
Basic Meditation 508
Steps in Mindfulness Meditation 508
Steps for the Relaxation Response 511
Contraindications and Adverse Effects of Meditation 512
Model Example: Mindfulness Meditation 512
Muscle Relaxation: Process and Uses 514

Steps of Muscle Relaxation 521
Contraindications and Adverse Effects of Muscle Relaxation 522
Variations of Muscle Relaxation 522
Model Dialogue: Muscle Relaxation 525
Exercise Therapy 526
Summary 529
InfoTrac Explorations 529
Suggested Resources 530
Postevaluation 531
Postevaluation Feedback 542

CHAPTER 17
DESENSITIZATION STRATEGIES 543
Objectives 543
Reported Uses of Desensitization 544
Multicultural Variations of Anxiety and Use of Systematic Desensitization 548
Explanations of Desensitization 549
Components of Desensitization 549
Model Dialogue: Rationale for Desensitization 550
Model Dialogue: Identifying Emotion-Provoking Situations 551
Model Dialogue: Hierarchy Construction Using the Sud Scale 555
Model Dialogue: Selection of and Training in Counterconditioning Response 558
Model Dialogue: Imagery Assessment 560
Model Dialogue: Scene Presentation 562
Model Dialogue: Homework and Follow-Up 564
Problems Encountered During Desensitization 565
Variations of Systematic Desensitization 566
Summary 568
InfoTrac Explorations 568
Suggested Resources 569
Postevaluation 570
Postevaluation Feedback 572

CHAPTER 18
SELF-MANAGEMENT STRATEGIES: SELF-MONITORING, STIMULUS CONTROL, SELF-REWARD, SELF-AS-A-MODEL, AND SELF-EFFICACY 580
Objectives 580
Clinical Uses of Self-Management Strategies 581
Multicultural Applications of Self-Management 584
Characteristics of an Effective Self-Management Program 586
Steps in Developing a Client Self-Management Program 587
Self-Monitoring: Purposes, Uses, and Processes 589
Steps of Self-Monitoring 592
Model Example: Self-Monitoring 600
Stimulus Control 601
Model Example: Stimulus Control 605
Self-Reward: Processes and Uses 606
Components of Self-Reward 607
Model Example: Self-Reward 610
Self-as-a-Model 611
Model Dialogue: Self-as-a-Model 613
Self-Efficacy 615
Multicultural Applications of Self-Efficacy 622
Model Example: Self-Efficacy 629
Summary 630
InfoTrac Explorations 631
Suggested Resources 632
Postevaluation 636
Postevaluation Feedback 637
Appendix 639
References 640
Name Index 673
Subject Index 682

Preface

The fifth edition of *Interviewing and Change Strategies for Helpers* reflects a number of new changes! First and foremost is a new coauthor, Paula Nurius. Bill Cormier, who had been a coauthor from the original edition through the fourth edition, decided to devote all of his time to his Energy Flux company and to end his contributions to the book. We appreciate Bill's former efforts. Sherry Cormier is pleased that the new coauthor is Paula Nurius, and both found the process of collaboration mirrored their aims of complementarity and invigoration. This new edition of our book represents a blending of Sherry's research and expertise in counseling and psychology, and Paula's research and expertise in social work, human services, and psychology. This shared partnership in these interdisciplinary areas is reflected in a new conceptual foundation for this edition and also some changes in language. This edition is intended to be used by *helpers* who are trained in a variety of helping-oriented disciplines, including counseling, social work, psychology, human services, and related professions.

A NEW CONCEPTUAL MODEL

Our conceptual model, which is described in Chapters 1 and 2, reflects four critical areas for helpers from various disciplines—*core skills and resources, diversity and ecological models, effectiveness-based practice, and critical thinking and ethical judgment.* The core skills that we present cut across all helping disciplines and, in this edition, are still presented in Chapters 3–7, although we have reordered these chapters, beginning with Chapter 3, on nonverbal behavior, followed by ingredients of an effective relationship in Chapter 4 and associated microskills of listening responses in Chapter 5. Chapter 6 describes relationship enhancement variables and interpersonal influence, followed by associated microskills of influencing responses in Chapter 7. Diversity and ecological models and skills are presented in Chapters 2, 8, and 9, and are also integrated throughout the book. Effectiveness-based practice is introduced in Chapter 2 and again in Chapters 10 and 11, and is reflected in our cognitive–behaviorally oriented change strategies in Chapters 12–18.

We have added a new word to the title of this edition: *change.* This word is more descriptive of the goal-setting and treatment planning processes we describe in Chapters 10 and 11 and also in the change intervention strategies of Chapters 12–18. Layered across all of this is the fourth area of our conceptual model, critical thinking and ethical judgment. While we focus on this area specifically in Chapters 1 and 2, these topics are also explored again throughout the remainder of the book, for they permeate all of the decisions that helpers face at each phase of the helping process, from establishing the helping relationship to assessing client issues, setting treatment goals, and selecting, using, and evaluating change intervention strategies. Many users have indicated that combining major stages of the helping process with specific change strategies aids students' understanding.

SPECIFIC FEATURES OF THE BOOK

We have retained the specific features of the book that we have learned through feedback make it invaluable as a resource guide. First, we have retained and expanded the emphasis in the prior edition on multicultural and diversity issues. We have included in this new edition emphases on vulnerable, oppressed, and underserved populations. We also hope that we have drawn your attention to the effects that contextual and environmental factors have on clients and managed care related factors have on the helping services. The book balances attention to conceptual and empirical foundations with an emphasis on real-life factors in practice settings and ample use of examples and how-to guidelines. Chapters are guided by objectives and opportunities to practice with numerous learning activities and guided feedback. Model cases and dialogues are given in each chapter. Postevaluations with feedback designed to help assess chapter competencies are provided at the end of each chapter. Consistent with our theme of resources, in this edition, at the end of each chapter, we include a Suggested Resources section describing related readings and Web sites. New to this edition are activities using the Wadsworth InfoTrac technology. These are called InfoTrac Explorations and can also be found at the end of each chapter.

NEW TO THE FIFTH EDITION

In addition, specific new content for this edition includes the following:

1. Back by popular demand from the third edition, we have added much new material on client and helper resistance and involuntary clients. This new content is found in Chapters 4, 10, and 11.
2. Ethical decision-making models, confidentiality, multiple relationships, and ethics and technology are presented in Chapter 2.
3. Cultural implications of the helping relationship, interviewing skills, assessment, and treatment goals and strategies are presented in Chapters 3–11.
4. The person-in-environment/ecological model of assessment, including assessment of individual and environmental strengths and resources and environmental assessment tools such as ecomaps and social network maps, is described in Chapters 8 and 9.
5. The impact of managed care environments, referral and termination issues in the helping process, motivational interviewing, practice evaluation, uses and limitations of evidence-based treatments, and professional disclosure statements are described in Chapters 10 and 11.
6. In the change strategy Chapters, 12–18, updated research tables on evidence-based change strategies are included as well as discussion of use of these strategies with diverse clients.
7. Increased attention to cognitive schemas of clients has been added to Chapters 9 and 14.
8. A new chapter on stress management (Chapter 15), includes new material on stress and coping, cultural variations of stress, and spirituality.
9. Chapter 16 includes the addition of exercise therapy as a new evidence-based change intervention strategy.
10. Chapter 17 includes new content related to exposure therapies, with applications to clients with trauma histories.
11. Each chapter post evaluation will be available to download from a book-specific website accessible through http://info.wadsworth.com/0534537391. This site offers a host of resources for instructors and students, including a listing of related videos, web links, Infotrac® College Edition activities, online quizzes, and additional practice for Chapter 5 and 7 in addition to the post evaluations.
12. A manual offering test questions for each chapter and a booklet with quizzes for each chapter are also available through your Thomsom representative (1-800-423-0563; info@brookscole.com).

As a final change, we have updated many of the old references, including as much recent literature as possible. However, we have retained old, valuable references for which there is no newer edition or older articles that are classics and provide an important historical perspective.

PEOPLE WE ACKNOWLEDGE

Over the years, some have commented on the length and detail of the book and have asked, "What is it like to put together a book like this?" Our first response is always "It requires a lot of help." For this edition, we are indebted to a number of people for their wonderful help: Dan Fox for library research and Shirin Lee for additional practice exercises for microskills. Special thanks go to Victoria Railing and Linda Thurman for manuscript preparation and reference assistance; to Dr. Sam Maniar, who did mountains of research for updating our tables in chapters 12–18; and Rebecca Schacht, Betty Williams, and Jina Lee, who helped us scour for useful contemporary resources, keep track of it all, and establish useful ways to incorporate InfoTrac as a technology tool. We are grateful to Beth Robinson for preparation of our quizzes. We also acknowledge the support of Dr. Jeffrey K. Messing, Chairperson Emeritus, Department of Counseling, Rehabilitation Counseling and Counseling Psychology at West Virginia University. We are very grateful to all the staff at Brooks/Cole, particularly to our editor, Lisa Gebo, for her commitment and enthusiasm. We are indeed indebted to Lisa for her support, wisdom, and her wonderful sense of humor! We are also thankful for the support of our families, particularly our husbands, Jay and Michael, our daughters, and our friends; you are too numerous to name, but you know who you are! Finally, the final form of this book as you, the reader, now see it would not have been possible without the superb efforts of the entire production team, Merrill Peterson and Kim Svetich-Will, with the assistance of the copy editor, Don Pharr, the permissions editor, Sue Ewing, and the marketing manager, Caroline Concilla. Finally, we wish to acknowledge with gratitude the contribution of our reviewers, who include the following: Victor Barr, University of Tennessee, Knoxville; Kia Bentley, Virginia Commonwealth University; Susan Gray, Ellen Whiteside McDonnell School of Social Work, Barry University; Claudia Haferkamp, Millersville University; Geri Miller, Appalachian State University; Kaye Nelson, Texas A&M University, Corpus Christi; Barbara Shank, University of St. Thomas; M. Carolyn Thomas, Auburn University at Montgomery; and Frank Weathers, Auburn University. They probably do not fully realize the extent of their impact on the final form of this book. To all of you: Thank you. We could not have done this without each of your careful and detailed comments and suggestions.

Sherry Cormier & Paula S. Nurius

Instructions for Online Postevaluations

To our students:

For this edition, the postevaluations at the end of each chapter are also available for you to download and use in an electronic format. They are available on the book website at: http://info.wadsworth.com/0534537391.

We suggest several ways that you may want to use the electronic version of the postevaluations. **It is important to remember that since some parts of each postevaluation refer to tables, figures, and interview checklists that are found only in the book, you will need your book by your side in order to complete the postevaluations on line.** Also, the feedback for each postevaluation is in the book. Here are several ways you may wish to use the postevaluations on line:

1. Complete the postevaluation and e-mail it to your instructor for her or his review.
2. Complete the postevaluation and e-mail it to a predetermined peer group; your group can brainstorm various response alternatives on line, then bring this process to your class. (There is, of course, the in-person option of meeting with one or more peers or your instructor for discussion.)
3. Complete the postevaluation, then compare your responses on line with the responses listed in the Feedback for Postevaluation section in your book. Create a written journal around your responses—what responses are similar to the feedback? Which ones are different? What issues did completing this chapter postevaluation raise for you?

Each postevaluation is listed on line by chapter.

CHAPTER 1: ABOUT THIS BOOK

ENVISION THIS

Imagine yourself as the helper in the following four situations. Try to see, hear, and sense what is happening to you.

A 14-year-old boy who is accused of setting fire to his family home walks in defiantly to see you. He has been "mandated" to see you by the judge. He sits down, crosses his arms and legs in front of him, and stares at the ceiling. He is silent after your initial greeting.

A young woman in her twenties walks in and can't hold back her tears. After a while, she talks about how upset she is feeling. In the last year, three of her close friends have died of acquired immune deficiency syndrome (AIDS); she has also lost her parents' support because she has told them she is a lesbian.

A Latino and his teenage son come in together, but they are so at odds with each other that they initially refuse to be seen by you in the same room. According to the telephone intake report, they have repeatedly fought about the amount of freedom the son wants and the father is willing to give.

A middle-aged woman comes in. She has been escorted to your facility by her husband. She is so afraid to go out of her house that she does not drive anymore. In talking with her, you discover that she has confined herself to her home almost exclusively for the last year because of incapacitating anxiety attacks. Her husband has recently turned down a lucrative job offer to avoid having to move her into a new environment.

Now try to process exactly what it is like for you to imagine helping each of these four clients. How were you feeling? What thoughts were running through your head? How did you see or hear yourself responding? What things about yourself were you aware of that helped you in the interaction? What things hindered you? What skills did you use to deal with the client? What skills were you lacking? What did you observe about the client, and how did your observations affect your help giving? How did you know whether what you were doing was helpful?

Although responding to these kinds of questions may be difficult for you now, it will probably become easier as you go through the book and as you also acquire greater experience and more feedback. The specific emphases and purposes of the book are described in the following sections.

A PRACTICE NEXUS FOR THE HELPING PROFESSIONS

During the more than 20-year history of this book, we have learned from readers and the changing fields of practice, and our approach has evolved as a result. We illustrate the unique nature of this text in terms of today's *practice nexus,* the interrelation, connections, and interfaces of our field. As Figure 1.1 depicts, the areas of relatedness and connection among the major aspects of practice knowledge come together to define a central core of what you need for today's practice. So we focus on the center of things—symbolized here by the area of overlap among these components of practice knowledge—to provide a coherent and unifying foundation. As the figure shows, each component contains additional, more specialized content that each of you will pursue to greater or lesser degrees, depending on the need. And you will certainly find other components of practice that you will need to master as you further specialize. The totality of it all will develop over years of practice training and experience. To begin, however, you need core content, understanding of the interrelatedness, and practical as well as conceptual understanding.

We have found that having a sense of the organizing framework helps integrate the parts as you progress chapter by chapter, so let's briefly take a look.

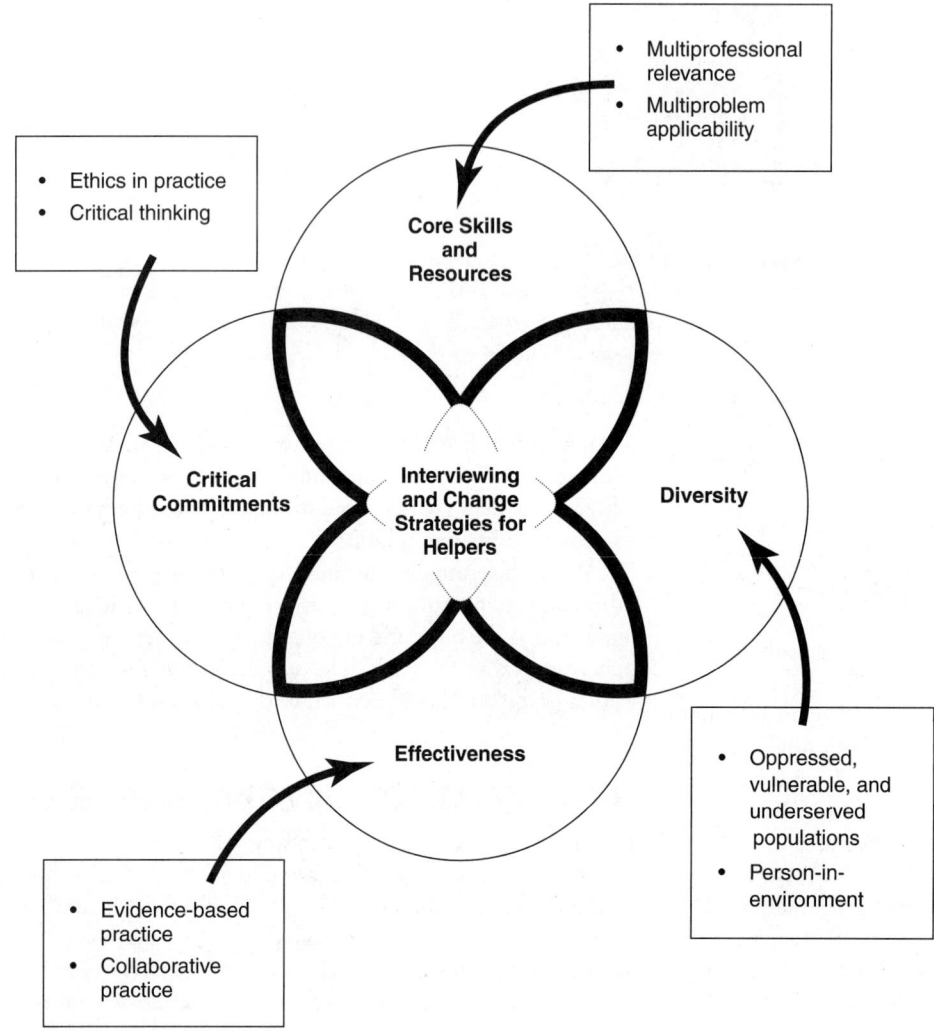

Figure 1.1 Today's Practice Nexus

BOX 1.1 — THE PRACTICE NEXUS IN ACTION: CENTRAL COMPONENTS

Core Skills and Resources

Multi-professional relevance

This book has long been adopted for courses in multiple disciplines. Thus, one goal is to support the growing multidisciplinary nature of today's practice by focusing on shared knowledge and skills. This provides practice training that is broadly relevant, bridges training backgrounds, and provides a solid foundation upon which to build specialized content. The range of settings within which helping services are provided is truly awesome—schools, health service facilities, social service and mental health centers, family service centers, correctional facilities, residential facilities, and independent practices, to name a few. We will interchangeably use terms such as *helper*, *practitioner*, and *clinician*, along with *client* and *service recipient*. These terms are sufficiently widely used to be applicable across a range of settings and service titles. We realize the terminology may be different in your own setting and practice philosophy, and we invite you to add to the learning exercises in ways that may more fully sculpt them for your needs.

BOX 1.1 THE PRACTICE NEXUS IN ACTION: CENTRAL COMPONENTS

The book is directed (but not restricted) to applying skills within a helper/client dyadic relationship. However, many of the skills and strategies can be used appropriately in other modalities, such as group work, case coordination and advocacy, couple and family counseling, and environmental or organizational interventions. Indeed, we anticipate that you will build on the core knowledge and skills of this book, adding proficiency in other modalities or specializations.

Multi-problem applicability

Evidence shows that our book stays in the personal libraries of students as they move into their practice careers, in part because the content has very broad applicability to populations, practice settings, and modalities (e.g., couples, families, groups). Our selection of models and strategies reflects a cognitive–behavioral framework. The practice strategies we include recognize that people are active meaning makers, continuously engaged in transactions with the people and places of their lives, and that this meaning making, contextual transaction, and "hot" factors such as goals, values, emotion, and motivation need to be taken into account.

The intervention strategies we have chosen to include share a consistent theory base about ways that people's thoughts, feelings, and behaviors are interrelated within their daily transactions with their life circumstances. It is useful to be aware of the broader array of theoretical orientations, so for your benefit we include below readings that provide overviews of major forces in counseling theories. We also include readings on cognitive–behavioral theory and interventions that show how it is evolving (e.g., more inclusive of hot factors, more contextualized, less rationalistic) as well as criticisms and limitations. Rather than duplicate this readily available reading, our aim is to focus on change strategies reflective of the practice nexus—that is, strategies that are widely used and recognized across disciplines; have broad applicability across types of problems, service settings, and diverse clientele; are amenable to teaching clients the reasoning and conduct of strategies to foster long-term self-help; have an empirical base that, although not perfect, indicates likely effectiveness and generalizability to helping situations (see Chapters 12–18).

Critical Commitments

Ethics in practice

The helping professions take their mission, roles, and responsibilities seriously by crafting guidelines in the form of standards for ethics in practice. We have included ethical standards web sites for several professions, which will help you better see what is common to and distinct among the perspectives. We speak directly to ethics (Chapter 2). But ethics is not so much a stand-alone factor as one that is interrelated to other critical commitments such as critical thinking as well as to other dimensions of practice, such as diversity, information technology, effectiveness, and practice contexts such as managed care. Thus, information on ethics is interspersed through the book as well as in Chapter 2.

The multifaceted nature of ethics in the practice nexus is illustrated in many of the frameworks developed to help practitioners sort through the various considerations in handling dilemmas, such as Hansen and Goldberg's (1999) seven-category matrix of moral principles and personal values; clinical and cultural factors; professional code of ethics; agency or employer policies; federal, state, and local statutes; rules and regulations; and case law. As with other critical commitments, we encourage a proactive, broad view of ethics and provide suggested readings, exercises, and examples to stimulate thought about grappling with ethical issues and to develop skills in anticipating and solving ethics-related problems.

Critical thinking

Recent years have underscored the importance of reflective, critical thinking not only in clinical decision making but also as it relates to the full spectrum of practice activities, both within one's own caseload and also as a team member engaged in collective considerations such as case conferencing, program development, and agency policy. Critical thinking involves careful examination of claims, arguments, beliefs, standards, information, interpretations, options, and actions to assess strengths and limitations and yield well-reasoned formulations and answers (Paul, 1993). Critical thinking is about critiquing (oneself, others, environments) but also about creativity, openness, and tolerance for complexity, ambiguity, and difference. This is part of why we provide examples and exercises, and urge skill- and reflection-building activities with your student and professional colleagues. Critical thinking may best be thought of as a skill (or rather, set of skills) that can be learned, but must be practiced with feedback to become honed and well-established.

Our own commitment to critical thinking is part of why we undertake massive literature updates to provide you with sources of evidence, theory, and perspective so that you can evaluate for yourself the strength and limitations of our and

(continued)

> **BOX 1.1   THE PRACTICE NEXUS IN ACTION: CENTRAL COMPONENTS** *CONTINUED*
>
> others' claims. Most all helpers bring profound caring and sincerity to their work, but history and research repeatedly show us that these are not sufficient to avoid bias or errors, ensure provision of helpful services, or guard against inappropriate or harmful practices (Gambrill, 1990; Gibbs & Gambrill, 1996). We also speak to the dimension of critical consciousness, a form of critical thinking directed to more explicit awareness of societal and environmental factors such as power relationships, commonalities, and differences among and within people (Reed, Newman, Suarez, & Lewis, 1997). Although critical consciousness requires engagement beyond what any one text or class can achieve, we will ask throughout that you be thoughtful about context, difference, and commonality.
>
> **Diversity**
>
> Oppressed, vulnerable, and underserved populations
>
> As societies become more pluralistic, the helping professions are more aware of the importance of attending to diversity than ever before. We build upon the real explosion of information related to diversity and divergent voices, including feminist and multicultural ones, to help increase awareness of inequities and how these affect us and our clients. In addition to being able to identify appropriate counseling strategies for diverse client problems, you should also be able to apply helping skills and strategies carefully and sensitively to a diverse group of clients. While you yourself may be a gay, Jewish man of middle socioeconomic level or an African American, straight, Protestant woman of upper socioeconomic level, your clients will invariably be somewhat different from you in terms of cultural background—factors such as age, culture, ethnicity, gender, language, disability, race, gender expression, sexual orientation, religion, and socioeconomic level. And even if you and your client share many similarities of background, he or she will still have unique characteristics that you must consider.
>
> Although we cannot be prescriptive about the best way to work with all diversity factors, it is important for us to recognize that they exist and that many of the counseling skills and strategies described in this book have been developed by Euro-American men in Western culture and may not be applicable to or sufficient for all clients. For these reasons, in the client descriptions used throughout the text as both model examples and practice ones, we often include cultural referent characteristics of the client such as race, ethnicity, sexual orientation, gender, age, and physical/mental status. Diversity is a focal topic in Chapter 2, but as part of the practice nexus, we interweave diversity throughout the book, such as examples and literature support regarding interviewing and change strategies with diverse clients.
>
> Person-in-environment
>
> Attention to diversity goes beyond differences of peoples. This book focuses on direct, clinical practice primarily with individuals—assisting them to gain a sense of mastery for dealing with stressful life circumstances and make use of personal and environmental resources to make desired changes in their lives. Although it is beyond the scope of this book to fully cover ecological processes or environmental interventions, we maintain a person-in-environment perspective. We cannot overstate the importance of continually being aware of ways in which problems are embedded within contexts and ways that environments are contributors to both problems and solutions. Throughout, we emphasize awareness that your clients are affected by the contexts in which they live—including familiar elements such as family, neighborhood, work, cultural and identificational groups, regional areas, and countries as well as differences in material, spatial, informational, and sociopolitical resources.
>
> We address issues of environment and transactions between people and their environments (see especially Chapters 8–11) and provide a wealth of suggested readings to further build your environment-changing skills. A person-in-environment commitment is also part of what shapes our focus on cognitive behavioral interventions. Increasingly, cognitive behavioral interventions reflect an ecological framing—connecting intrapersonal functioning (problematic thoughts, feelings) to individuals' historical and current contexts. This includes attention to factors such as perception and personal meaning, interpersonal transactions that can take on both adaptive and maladaptive forms, and use of learning principles and significant others to initiate and support contextually feasible change.
>
> **Effectiveness**
>
> Evidence-based practice
>
> Today's practice is highly influenced by regulatory requirements and ethical expectations regarding accountability. Use of empirically supported practice and evidence-based decision making has become part of training accreditation requirements as well as work-site expectations, although certainly not without issue. We anticipate that clinical practice in

> **BOX 1.1   THE PRACTICE NEXUS IN ACTION: CENTRAL COMPONENTS**
>
> coming years will increasingly be affected (positively and/or negatively) by pressures to demonstrate the evidence base of practice decisions and outcomes, development and use of practice guidelines, concern for generalizability (e.g., does an intervention appear effective across differing client and situation characteristics?), and efficiency.
>
> We speak to some of the factors to be balanced in this pursuit, particularly in Chapters 10 and 11. We also work to provide pragmatic aids to assist you—including interviewing and change strategies that have undergone empirical examination, providing behavioral descriptions of what the strategies entail, including updates on literature relevant to current interventions, and including concrete tools designed to prepare you to meet today's evidence requirements (see Chapters 12–18). At the same time, we also encourage you to recognize the realistic limitations on empirically demonstrable efficacy and the need for new tools (e.g., qualitative, contextually sensitive means of measuring) and emerging or evolving interventions that merit careful consideration.
>
> Collaborative practice
>
> Significant, sustainable change in people's lives requires much more than one can possibly transact within the limits of formal helping sessions. Collaboration reflects an ethical commitment to self-determination and informed participation, building on strengths toward problem solving, partnering with clients as well as other resource providers toward obtaining client goals, an educationally oriented approach that aids clients in their ongoing change efforts, and a pragmatic recognition that effective practice is not done to but with clients. We maintain that, realistically, clients are closest to their needs and situations. While this closeness can pose challenges, it nonetheless speaks to the importance of clients bringing their information, perspective, and networks to the table, serving as active agents toward realistic change for themselves as people-in-environments.
>
> These principles have guided many of the choices about what to include here, such as the strengths orientation in assessment (Chapters 8 and 9), emphasis on effective listening (Chapter 5), engagement of clients across the stages of helping (Chapters 3–7), and focus on change strategies that can feasibly be taught, tried out, and judiciously adapted as needed (Chapters 12–18). We also encourage you to consider ways that exercises, readings, and related resources within this book or other sources may be shared with clients. Collaboration applies also to how contemporary professionals work together in practice settings—which are commonly populated by practitioners of varying disciplinary and life experience backgrounds—and the need to be trained in the practice nexus to "work in the interface." Consider, for instance, the team of people needed in working with high-risk families—perhaps a child counselor, family therapy social worker, psychologist or psychiatrist if testing or medications are indicated, vocational worker, case coordinator, other specialists as needed (translation, disability, violence, chemical dependency, school liaison, etc.).

Today's Practice Nexus in Our Managed Care Context

The impact of the managed care movement on the helping professions is virtually unparalleled. Effects and implications reverberate throughout the practice nexus, raising new ethical dilemmas; diversity-related challenges; influences on core practice activities, including how a problem is articulated and interventions selected; and, of course, expectations regarding outcomes and effectiveness. This book responds to the realities of today's professional practice by attending to many of these issues and focusing on practice tools and strategies that you will need for defensible, sustainable practice within managed care and related systems of service delivery. Rather than being fixed, this approach involves wide-ranging balances (e.g., the use of short-term, empirically supported treatments balanced with the need to adapt interventions to be appropriate to the needs and environmental characteristics of a diverse clientele) common across the helping professions (see Chapter 11).

Let's consider a case example and the multiple levels of practice nexus consideration it may require:

> After a licensed psychologist has completed the initially allocated 10 sessions of treatment, the managed care organization (MCO) denies additional sessions for an indigent, adult, Native American client, with a history of severe sexual abuse and, at times, manipulative, suicidal gestures. Before the client is informed of this decision, she experiences a suicidal crisis and makes an emergency call to her psychologist, requesting a session later that day. Prior to meeting with the client, the psychologist attempts to obtain authorization from the MCO for at least one additional session. The regular case manager and departmental supervisor are both on vacation. On the basis of a limited understanding of the client, the interim case manager

insists that this suicidal crisis is a manipulative gesture and refuses to authorize additional sessions. (Hansen & Goldberg, 1999, p. 495)

Needless to say, there are many elements involved here. Critical commitments such as concern about ethical practice and critical consciousness intersect with diversity. For example, to what extent may factors be operating here that have historically resulted in lower-socioeconomic-status people of color being viewed in more pathological and decontextualized terms as well as underserved by mental health systems? Are there ways to engage the interim case manager toward a more complete understanding of the client that may result in a different interpretation? There are several current and earlier problems implicated. How might thinking in terms of multiple professional sources possibly expand the spectrum of resources to consider? How was the case originally framed in terms of primary problems to address and selected change strategies? Are there evidence-based alternatives or extensions to the original change strategies that can defensibly be argued toward addressing this multi-problem case? With a collaborative working philosophy in mind, are there ways to engage with the client and, possibly, her support network to solve the constraints, identify her strengths (including gains the client may have made in her therapeutic work thus far), and generate immediate or longer-term sources of assistance? Clearly, there are no simple solutions, but there are layers of connections. Awareness of these may aid you to think in different ways about clients and options, and work flexibly on the behalf of those who come to you for help.

AN OVERVIEW OF HELPING

A helping professional is someone who helps with the exploration and resolution of issues and problems presented by a client: the person seeking help. Helping interactions have four recognized components: (1) someone seeking help and (2) someone willing to give help who is also (3) capable of or trained to help (4) in a setting that permits help to be given and received (Hackney & Cormier, 2001, pp. 1–2).

We see four primary stages of helping (Egan, 1998; Hepworth, Rooney, & Larsen, 1997):
1. Relationship
2. Assessment and goal setting
3. Strategy selection and implementation
4. Evaluation and termination

The first stage of the helping process is *establishing an effective therapeutic relationship* with the client. This part of the process is based primarily on client- or person-centered therapy (Rogers, 1951) and more recently on social influence theory (Strong, Welsh, Corcoran, & Hoyt, 1992) and psychoanalytic theory (Gelso & Hayes, 1998; Safran & Muran, 2000). We present skills for this stage in Chapters 3–7. The potential value of a sound relationship base cannot be overlooked because the relationship is the specific part of the process that conveys the counselor's interest in and acceptance of the client as a unique and worthwhile person and builds sufficient trust for eventual self-disclosure and self-revelation to occur. For some clients, working with a counselor who stays primarily in this stage may be useful and sufficient. For other clients, the relationship part of therapy is necessary but not sufficient to help them with the kinds of choices and changes they seek to make. These clients need additional kinds of action or intervention strategies.

The second phase of helping, assessment and goal setting, often begins with or shortly after relationship building. In both stages, the practitioner is interested mainly in helping clients *explore* themselves and their concerns. Assessment is designed to help both the clinician and the client obtain a better picture, idea, or grasp of what is happening with the client and what prompted the client to seek the services of a helper at this time. The information gleaned during the assessment phase is extremely valuable in planning strategies and can also be used to manage resistance. We describe assessment strategies in Chapters 8 and 9. As the problems and issues are identified and defined, the practitioner and client also work through the process of developing outcome goals. Outcome goals are the specific results the client would like to occur as a result of counseling. Outcome goals also provide useful information for planning action strategies (see Chapter 10).

In the third phase of helping, strategy selection and implementation, the counselor's task is to help with client *understanding and related action*. Insight can be useful, but insight alone is far less useful than insight accompanied by a supporting plan that helps the client translate new or different understandings into observable and specific actions or behaviors. Toward this end, the counselor and client select and sequence a plan of action: intervention strategies that are based on the assessment data and are designed to help the client achieve the designated goals. In developing action plans, it is important to select plans that relate to the identified concerns and goals and that are not in conflict with the client's primary beliefs and values (see Chapters 11–18).

The last major phase of helping, evaluation, involves *assessing the effectiveness* of your interventions and the progress the client has made toward the desired goals (see Chapter 10). This kind of evaluation assists you in knowing when to terminate the process to revamp your action plans. Additionally, clients who can easily become discouraged during the change process, often find observable and concrete signs of progress to be quite reinforcing. Listing *assessment* evaluation as the last phase can inadvertently suggest that gauging effectiveness comes late or near the end of counseling. If, for example, we are not making effective progress in developing a collaborative, therapeutic relationship or understanding the perspective of our client, we need to be aware of this right away. In reality, we are and need to be explicitly assessing effectiveness throughout, and also sharing our observations as part of our collaborative relationship with clients.

Indeed, there is some flow and interrelationship among these four stages. In other words, all parts of these stages are present throughout the helping process, although not with the same degree of emphasis. As Waehler and Lenox (1994) point out, "Counseling participants do not go through a discrete state of relationship building and then 'graduate' to undertaking assessment as stage models imply" (p. 19). Each stage is interconnected to the others so that during the intervention phase, for example, the relationship process is still attended to, and termination may be discussed early in the relationship.

Just as there are stages and processes associated with helping, helpers also have stages and themes as they enter the helping profession, seek training, encounter clients, and gain supervised experience. In an award-winning study now summarized in a book, Skovholt and Ronnestad (1995) explored the development of helping professionals over the life span of their careers. They found that practitioners progress through a series of eight stages from the time they select helping as a career to the point where they are experienced practitioners. These eight stages of professional development can be described as follows. Skovholt (2001) expands on these stages and related factors in the development of practitioners, looking toward fostering "resilient practitioners."

1. Conventional stage
2. Transition to professional training stage
3. Imitation of experts stage
4. Conditional autonomy stage
5. Exploration stage
6. Integration stage
7. Individuation stage
8. Integrity stage

As with the stages of helping, these professional development stages are also interconnected. At each stage, certain themes most concern helpers. For example, an entry-level practitioner is necessarily more concerned with skill development than with individual identity as a helper. Entry-level helpers are also more likely to model the behaviors they see in expert teachers and supervisors. Further along the career path, different themes and concerns emerge.

We point this out as part of our reasoning for focusing on cognitive–behavioral theories and models of practice in this book. Evidence suggests that at earlier stages of development (as in courses for which this book is designed), detailed knowledge and the opportunity to achieve some initial depth of skills in applying and adapting practice methods match the learning needs and priorities of becoming an effective helper and feeling competent in one's work. Thus, while you will need to become familiar with the wider array of practice models and their relative strengths and limitations as part of your longer-range professional development, our emphasis at this stage is on core tools and skills.

We selected the cognitive–behavioral framework as the focus for change strategies for this reason and because of its consistency with priorities within the practice nexus. As two major practice theorists, John Prochaska and John Norcross (1999) have said (paraphrased from p. 354), cognitive–behavioral therapies are the fastest growing and most heavily researched orientations in the contemporary scene (Norcross, Alford, & DeMichele, 1992)—the "blue-chip" selection for the next five years in terms of its likelihood of growing. Some reasons for this popularity are the commitment of the cognitive–behavioral framework to psychotherapy integration, its dedication to empirical evaluation, and its psychoeducational approach, which makes it more accessible for direct use by clients (e.g., self-help formats, access through the Internet, and availability in computer-assisted mediums). Cognitive methods are commonly blended with other therapies (see Prochaska & Norcross, 1999, Chapter 14), a process consistent with current experimentation with integrative treatment models that build upon complementary strengths of differing approaches. This blended strategy is popular in societies outside the United States (providing a wider cultural and contextual base for evaluation) and is increasingly being used to treat serious and chronic disorders.

Although these factors have influenced our choice to focus on cognitive–behavioral strategies, every practice method has flaws and limitations, and we do not argue for a "card-carrying" adherence to a single perspective. Current estimates place the number of therapies in the hundreds—not a realistic number to review. However, there is a more limited set of therapies or therapy clusters commonly grouped as the central ones. Prochaska and Norcross (1999) provide a systematic review of the central tenets of each, including critiques and case examples. In their review, they include the following theoretical perspectives:

1. Psychoanalytic
2. Adlerian
3. Existential
4. Person-centered
5. Gestalt
6. Interpersonal
7. Exposure and flooding
8. Behavioral
9. Cognitive/cognitive–behavioral
10. Systemic
11. Gender and culture-sensitive
12. Constructivist
13. Integrative and eclectic

The Interweave of Interviewing and Change Strategies

Although interviewing and change strategies are often separated into different courses due to scheduling logistics, they are integrally related to each other, ebbing and flowing across the phases of the helping process. Rather than divide interviewing and change strategies into two books, this book aims for applied coherence by combining the two, as well as combining content on practice knowledge with exercises to enhance skill building.

In the first seven chapters of this book, we present what we call "fundamental skills." These include nonverbal behavior, relationship conditions, and verbal responses useful for practitioners of varying theoretical orientations. These include clinician and client nonverbal communication patterns and behaviors (Chapter 3); the facilitative relationship, conditions of empathy, genuineness, and positive regard (Chapter 4); and the microskills associated with listening and conveying basic (Egan, 1998) or reciprocal (Hepworth, Rooney, & Larsen, 1997) empathy (Chapter 5). These chapters also focus on helping as an interpersonal influence process and three relationship variables that enhance the influence base: expertness, attractiveness, and trustworthiness (Chapter 6). Expanding on the notion of helping as an influence process, we also present microskills associated with influencing (Ivey & Ivey, 1999b), challenging (Egan, 1998), and conveying advanced (Egan, 1998) or additive (Hepworth et al., 1997) empathy (Chapter 7).

Finally, we hope that in this book you will find training experiences that further your personal growth, develop your helping skills, and provide ways for you to evaluate your effectiveness. Personal growth is the most elusive and most difficult to define of these three areas. Although it is beyond the scope of this book to focus primarily on self-development, you may engage in self-exploration as you go through certain parts of the book, including refinement of your working model of practice and identity as a practicing professional. It is essential that you seek out additional experiences in which you can receive feedback from others about yourself, your strengths, and some behaviors that may interfere with counseling. These experiences might be field-based or classroom activities, feedback, growth groups, and personal counseling. It is well documented that a counselor's warmth, empathy, and positive regard can contribute to client change (see Chapter 4). We feel that your demonstration of these relationship conditions will enhance the way you use the skills and strategies presented in this book.

Above all, we want to convey that the book is about *practical application* of selected skills and strategies. Our coverage of theoretical and research concepts is limited because they are covered adequately in other texts; we believe that bringing together knowledge and skill building will be useful to your professional development.

FORMAT OF THE BOOK

We have used a learning format designed to help you demonstrate and measure your use of the helping competencies presented in this book. Each chapter includes a brief introduction; chapter objectives; content material interspersed with model examples, learning activities, and feedback; a postevaluation; and a role-play interview assessment. People who have participated in field testing this book have found that using these activities has helped them get involved and interact with the content material. You can complete the chapters by yourself or in a class. If you feel you need to go over an exercise several times, do so! If part of the material is familiar, jump ahead. We have taken care to include numerous references to assist you in further reading at any point. Throughout each chapter, your performance on the learning activities and self-evaluations will be a clue to the pace at which you can work through the chapter. To help you use the book's format to your advantage, we will explain each of its components briefly.

Objectives

As we developed each chapter, we had certain goals in mind for the chapter and for you. For each major topic, there are certain concepts and skills to be learned. After a short chapter introduction, you will find a section called "Objectives." The list of objectives describes the kinds of things that can be learned from the chapter. Using objectives for learning is similar to using goals in the helping process. The objectives

provide cues for your end results and serve as benchmarks by which you can assess your progress. As you will see in Chapter 10, an objective or goal contains three parts:
1. The behavior, or what is to be learned or performed
2. The level of performance, or how much or how often to demonstrate the behavior
3. The conditions of performance, or the circumstances or situations under which the behavior can be performed

Part 1 of an objective refers to what you should learn or demonstrate. Parts 2 and 3 are concerned with evaluation of performance. The evaluative parts of an objective, such as the suggested level of performance, may seem a bit hard-nosed. However, setting objectives with a fairly high mastery level may result in improved performance. In this book, the objectives are stated at the beginning of each chapter so you know what to look for and how to assess your performance in the activities and self-evaluations. If you feel that it would be helpful to see some objectives now, take a look at the beginning of Chapter 2.

Learning Activities

Learning activities that reflect the chapter objectives are interspersed throughout each chapter. These learning activities, which are intended to provide both practice and feedback, consist of model examples, exercises, and feedback. You can use the learning activities in several ways. Many of the exercises suggest that you write your responses. Your written responses can help you or your instructor check the accuracy and specificity of your work. Take a piece of paper, and actually write the responses down. Or you may prefer to think through an activity and just consider your responses.

Some exercises instruct you to respond by imagining yourself in a certain situation and doing certain things. We have found that this form of mental rehearsal can help you prepare for the kinds of counseling responses you might use in a particular situation. This type of responding does not require any written responses. However, if it would help you to jot down some notes after the activity is over, go ahead. You are the best person to determine how to use these exercises to your advantage.

Many of the exercises, particularly in the first seven chapters, are based on cognitive self-instruction. The objective of this type of activity is to help you not only to acquire the skill by providing you a description of it, but also to internalize the skill. Some research suggests that this approach may be an important addition to the more common elements of microtraining (modeling, rehearsal, feedback) found to be so helpful in skill acquisition (Morran, Kurpius, Brack, & Brack, 1995). The cognitive learning strategy is designed specifically to help you develop your own way to think about the skill or to "put it together" in a way that makes sense to you.

Another kind of learning activity involves a more direct rehearsal than the written or covert exercises. These "overt rehearsal" exercises are designed to help you apply your skills in simulated counseling sessions with a role-play interview. The role-play activities generally involve three persons or roles: a helper, a client, and an observer. Each group should trade roles so that each person can experience the role play from these different perspectives. One person's task is to serve as the helper and practice the skills specified in the instructions. The helper role provides an opportunity to try out the skills in simulated helping situations. A second person, the client, will be counseled during the role play.

We give a note of caution: Potentially conflicting aims must be balanced here. One is to strengthen training through supervised opportunities, such as role play, that approximate actual helping scenarios and provide input as well as application experience. However, ethical concerns must also be considered. For example, using a real concern or something a student feels strongly about and can readily envision may help augment the realism of portraying a client. On the other hand, self-disclosures in this context cannot be guaranteed to be held in confidence and may introduce discomfort or influence subsequent evaluation of the student/client by the instructor or student peers. Alternatives have been suggested, such as the use of actors as clients (see Levitov, Fall, & Jennings, 1999, for examples and discussion). This approach, of course, raises its own dilemmas and trade-offs.

We recommend group discussion of issues such as these prior to undertaking role play or other training exercises that raise issues such as privacy and vulnerability. Clear ground rules and safeguards need to be established, whatever the method. Evoking the part of a client reminds us of the difficulty and vulnerability that many clients feel with the self-disclosing and sorting out necessary for the helping process. We are not recommending required self-disclosure or inappropriate introduction of one's personal needs into the educational exchange, but judicious decisions about how to make optimal, appropriate use of experiential and other applied training exercises. Needless to say, we assume that you share a view of professionalism that maintains sensitivity and safeguards, whether as part of a role play, case conferencing, group supervision, or other such activity.

The third person in the role-play exercise is the "observer." This is a very important role because it develops and sharpens observational skills that are an important part of effective helping. The observer has three tasks to accomplish. First, this person should observe the process and identify what the client does and how the helper responds. When the helper is rehearsing a particular skill or strategy, the observer can also determine the strengths and limitations of the helper's approach. Second, the observer can provide consultation at any point during the role play if it might help the experience. Such consultation may occur if the helper gets stuck or if the observer perceives that the helper is practicing too many nonhelpful behaviors. In this capacity, we have often found it helpful for the observer to serve as a sort of alter ego for the helper. The observer can then become involved in the role play to help give the helper more options or better focus. However, it is important not to take over for the helper in such instances. The third and most important task of the observer is to provide feedback to the helper about his or her performance following the role play. The person who role-played the client may also wish to provide feedback.

Giving useful feedback is itself a skill used in some helping strategies. The feedback that occurs following the role play should be considered just as important as the role play itself. Although everyone involved in the role play will receive feedback after serving as the helper, it is still sometimes difficult to "hear" negative feedback. Sometimes, receptiveness to feedback will depend on the way the observer presents it. We encourage you to make use of these opportunities to practice giving feedback to another person in a constructive, useful manner. Try to make your feedback specific and concise. Remember, the feedback is to help the helper learn more about the role play; it should not be construed as the time to analyze the helper's personality or lifestyle.

The reverse can also be problematic. Feedback that is overly rosy or assumes too much (such as the helper's intent) is not inherently useful. Those playing observer or client can offer feedback in the way of questions about the reasoning or basis for a decision or direction that the helper took in the role play. This kind of walking through our practice judgments can be extremely useful to gaining skills in self-reflection and critical thinking. Establishing a respectful, specific, and constructive tone also furthers discussion of issues that naturally emerge through role playing, such as ethical conundrums or uncertainties.

Another learning activity involves having people learn the strategies as partners or in small groups by teaching one another. We suggest that you trade off teaching a strategy to your partner or the group. Person A might teach covert modeling to Person B, and then Person B will teach Person A muscle relaxation. The "student" can also receive feedback on his or her efforts to apply the new skill—for example, Person B would practice covert modeling (taught by A), and Person A would demonstrate the strategy learned from Person B. We learn in multiple ways, and techniques such as this capitalize on learning through teaching/modeling/feedback and learning through observing/applying/trying again with feedback.

The Role of Feedback in Learning Activities

Most of the chapter learning activities are followed by some form of feedback. For example, if a learning activity involves identifying positive and negative examples of a helping conversational style, the feedback will indicate which examples are positive and which are negative. We have also attempted in most of our feedback to give some rationale for the responses. In many of the feedback sections, several possible responses are included. Our purpose in including feedback is not for you to find out how many "right" and "wrong" answers you have given in a particular activity. The responses listed in the feedback sections should serve as a guideline for you to code and judge your own responses. With this in mind, we would like you to view the feedback sections as not only sources of information and alternatives, but also as aids to developing habits of "mindful," reflective practice reasoning and decision making that are part of critical thinking (e.g., "How did I arrive at that conclusion? What other pieces of information might I have sought or paid greater attention to?"). We hope you are not put off or discouraged if your responses are different from the ones in the feedback. We don't expect you to come up with identical responses; some of your responses may be just as good as or better than the ones given in the feedback—indeed, judicious adaptation is predicated on the recognition that specifics of individuals and circumstances must be taken into account to achieve appropriate and effective helping. Space does not permit us to list all the possibly useful responses in the feedback for each learning activity.

Locating Learning Activities and Feedback Sections in the Text

As we have indicated, each chapter contains a variety of learning activities and feedback for most but not all of the activities. Usually, a learning activity directly follows the related content section. We have placed learning activities in this way (rather than at the end of a chapter) to give you an immediate opportunity to work with and apply that content area before moving ahead to new material. Feedback on learning activities is usually separated by a page turn. This is done to encourage you to work through the learning activity on your own without concurrently scanning the same page to see how we have responded. We believe that this will help you work more independently and will encourage you to develop and rely more on your own knowledge base and skills. A potential problem with this format is difficulty in finding a particular learning activity or its corresponding feedback section. To minimize this problem, each learning activity and its corresponding feedback section are numbered. For example, the first learning activity in the book with feedback is found on page 26; it is numbered 2.2. Its corresponding feedback section, found on page 27, is also labeled 2.2.

Postevaluations and Web Site Resources

A postevaluation can be found at the end of each chapter. It consists of questions and activities related to the knowledge and skills to be acquired in the chapter. Postevaluations are also available on a book–specific Web site accessible through http://wadsworth.com/0534537391, as are InfoTrac activities, and chapter Web site resources. In addition, the Web site includes a listing of related videos, extra practice responses on interviewing skills, and multiple-choice quizzes for each chapter. These quizzes are designed to prepare you for post-degree certification testing.

Because you respond to the questions after completing a chapter, this evaluation is called *post;* that is, it assesses your level of performance *after* receiving instruction. The evaluation questions and activities reflect the conditions specified in the objectives. When the conditions ask you to identify a response in a written statement or case, take some paper and write down your responses to these activities. However, if the objective calls for demonstrating a response in a role play, the evaluation will suggest how you can assess your performance level by setting up a role-play assessment. Other evaluation activities may suggest that you do something or experience something to heighten your awareness of or information about the idea or skill to be learned.

The primary purpose of the postevaluation is to help you assess your competencies after completing the chapter. One way to do this is to check your responses against those provided in the feedback at the end of each postevaluation. If you find a great discrepancy, the postevaluation can shed light on those areas still troublesome for you. You may wish to improve in these areas by reviewing parts of the chapter, redoing the learning activities, or asking for additional help from your instructor or a colleague.

Role-Play Evaluation

In actual helping situations, you must demonstrate your skills orally—not just write about them. To help you determine the extent to which you can apply and evaluate your skills, we provide role-play evaluations at the end of most chapters. Each role-play evaluation consists of a structured situation in which you are asked to demonstrate certain skills as a helper with a role-play client. Your performance on a role-play interview can be assessed by using the role-play checklist at the end of the chapter. These checklists consist of steps and possible responses associated with a particular strategy. The checklist should be used only as a guideline. You should always adapt any helping strategy to the client and to the particular demands of the situation.

Here are two ways to assess your role-play performance. You can ask your instructor, a colleague, or another person to observe your performance, using the checklist. Your instructor may even schedule you periodically to do a role-play "checkout" individually or in a small group. If you do not have anyone to observe you, assess yourself. Audiotape or videotape your interview, and rate your performance on the checklist. Also, ask your "client" for feedback. If you don't reach the criterion level of the objective on the first try, you may need some extra work. The following section explains the need for additional practice.

Additional Practice

You may find some skills more difficult than others to acquire the first time around. People are often chagrined and disappointed when they do not demonstrate the strategy as well as they would like on their first attempt. We ask these individuals whether they hold similar expectation levels for their clients! You cannot quickly and simply let go of behaviors that you don't find useful and acquire others that are more useful. It may be unrealistic to assume that you will always demonstrate an adequate level of performance on *all* the evaluations on the first go-round. Much covert and overt rehearsal may be necessary before you feel comfortable with skill demonstration in the evaluations. On some occasions, you may need to work through the learning activities and postevaluations more than once.

Some Cautions About Using This Format

Although we believe that the format of this book will promote learning, we want you to consider several cautions about using it. As you will see, we have defined the skills and strategies in precise and systematic ways to make it easier for you to acquire and develop the skills. However, we do not intend that our definitions and guidelines be used like cookbook instructions, without thought or imagination. Similarly, one change strategy may not work well for all clients. As your helping experience accumulates, you will find that one client does not use a strategy in the same way, at the same pace, or with similar results as another client. In selecting helping strategies, you will find it helpful to be guided by the documentation concerning the ways in which the strategy has been used. But it is just as important to remember that each client may respond in an idiosyncratic manner to any particular approach or that conditions may require judicious adaptation. In short, you will need to identify the potential appropriateness of any given helping strategy but also fit the intervention to the client and context. After you have finished the book, we hope you will be able to select and use appropriate counseling strategies when confronted with a depressed client, an anxious client, a nonassertive client, and so forth. We also hope you will be aware of cases in which approaches and strategies included in this book may not be very useful.

Our definitions, descriptions, and examples will give you methodology and rationale for the various interviewing, relationship-building, and change strategies. But do not see this as formulaic, particularly in applying your skills in the interview process. If something does not seem to be working effectively or is not suited to the people or situation (including your own personality and work style), we hope you will make adjustments, adapting the procedure creatively and judiciously to provide the most appropriate and effective service. Finally, remember that almost anybody can learn and perform a skill as a routine. Similarly, almost anybody can fly by the seat of the pants or strictly adhere to a personal ideology that is resistant to critique. But not everyone shows the willingness and ability to synthesize qualities of the practice nexus—for example, balancing training in specific practice skills with sensitivity and ingenuity in order to continuously assess and collaborate with clients to establish well-suited forms of helping.

One of the most difficult parts of learning clinical helping skills seems to be trusting the skills to work and not being preoccupied with your own performance. Inordinate preoccupation with yourself, your skills, or a particular procedure reduces your ability to relate to and carefully attend to another person or circumstances of the moment. At first, it is natural to focus on the skill or strategy because it is new and feels a little awkward or cumbersome. But once you have learned and practiced a particular skill or strategy, the skills will be there when you need them. Gradually, as you acquire your repertory of skills and strategies, you should be able to change your focus from the procedure to the person. This is another example of what you will undergo as you are challenged, change, and grow as a helping practitioner, responding to the challenge and growth that clients undergo in their own learning and change efforts. New ways of thinking, feeling, relating, and behaving will inherently feel unnatural at first and will require considerable repetition and reinforcement before they become mastered, automatic, and synthesized as a smooth whole rather than a series of discrete steps. We will return to these issues in the chapters on change strategies.

Remember that helping is a complex process composed of many interrelated parts. Although different helping stages, skills, and strategies are presented in this book in separate chapters, in practice there is a meshing of all these components. As an example, the relationship does not stop or diminish in importance when a practitioner and client begin to assess issues, establish goals, or implement strategies. Nor is evaluation something that occurs only when formal helping sessions are terminated. Evaluation involves continual monitoring throughout the helping interaction. Even obtaining a client's commitment to use strategies consistently and to monitor their effects may be aided or hindered by the quality of the relationship and the degree to which client problems and goals have been clearly defined. In the same vein, keep in mind that most client problems are complex and multifaceted. Successful helping may involve changes in the client's feelings, observable behavior, beliefs, and cognitions. To model some of the skills and procedures you will learn, we have included cases and model dialogues in most chapters. These are intended to illustrate one example of a way in which a particular procedure can be used with a client. However, the cases and dialogues have been simplified for demonstration purposes, and the printed words may not communicate the sense of flow and direction that is normally present in practitioner/client interchanges. Again, with actual clients you will encounter more dimensions in the relationship and in the client's concerns than are reflected in the chapter examples.

Our third concern involves the way you approach the examples and practice opportunities in this book. Obviously, reading an example or doing a role-play interview is not as real as seeing an actual client or engaging in a live counseling interaction. However, some practice is necessary in any new learning program. Even if the exercises seem artificial, they probably will help you learn counseling skills. The structured practice opportunities in the book may require a great deal of discipline on your part, but the degree to which you can generalize your skills from practice to an actual helping interview may depend on how much you invest in the practice opportunities.

Options for Using the Book

We have written this book in its particular format because each component seems to play a unique role in the learning process. But we are also committed to the idea that each person must determine the most suitable individual method of learning. With this in mind, we suggest a number of ways to use this book. First, you can go through the book and use the entire format in the way it is described in this chapter. If you do this, we suggest that you familiarize yourself carefully with the format as described here. If you want to use this format but do not understand it, it is not likely to be helpful. Another way is to use only certain parts of the format in any combination you choose. You may want to experiment initially to determine which components seem especially useful. For example, you might use the postevaluation but not complete the chapter learning activities. Finally, if you prefer a "straight" textbook format, you can read only the content of the book and ignore the special format. Our intent is for you to use the book in whatever way is most suitable for your learning strategies.

You will also notice icons in the margins throughout the book. These correspond to chapter elements and are designed to help you quickly locate certain kinds of resources or learning activities at a glance. Specifically, you will see for Learning Activities, for Feedback on Learning Activity responses, for InfoTrac® Explorations, for Suggested Resources, for Postevaluations, and for Postevaluation Feedback.

GLOBALIZATION

"The fabled global community is now upon us" (Marsella, 1998, p. 1282). More than ever, the pluralism of our own nation in terms of cultural, racial, religious, and linguistic diversity is growing, yet so is our global interconnectedness, intensifying through our telecommunication, transportation, economic, environmental, political, and social welfare ties. Many of these developments provide new opportunities and productive changes. In addition, we also must increasingly grapple with problems that accompany this intricate web of forces as well as the pace and stresses of rapid change, such as culture shock and dislocation, migration, acculturation stress, identity confusion, social fragmentation, impoverishment and civil rights abuses, environmental degradation, critical health threats, and terrorism such as the September 11, 2001, attacks and beyond. Helping professionals are part of responding to the emergent concerns and needs caused by such factors and events, requiring tools not only for what is known and recognized today but also for continuing changes that we cannot anticipate.

You will see emphasis throughout this book on the use of system and contextual conceptualizations, cultural forces in people's lives and behaviors, cautions about national or ethnocentric bias, and recognizing the relevance of the world outside our borders. In the harried pace of our everyday lives, the global community can seem somewhat remote—compelling stories we hear on the news, but hard to see and feel in some practice arenas. This situation will change in the years to come, as many of the global forces forge ties both planned and unplanned that will illuminate our interconnections. We encourage a global perspective not only because it is realistic but also because we have as much to learn as to share with our international colleagues and neighbors.

INFORMATION TECHNOLOGY IN THE NEW MILLENNIUM

The surging growth of information technology since the first edition of this book is nothing short of phenomenal. You are likely a daily user of computer and related information technology—whether it be personal use such as word processing, e-mail, fax, and the Web, or the more-specialized uses in many service settings today, such as client case recording and management information systems that track and coordinate fiscal, administrative, and service activities. We are also seeing the growth of electronic tools for a variety of educational and therapeutic purposes, such as tutorials, interactive simulations, assessment and decision, case coordination or discharge planning, electronic referral and information sites and sources, multi-site conferencing and other distance technology, specialized tools aimed to reduce language and disability barriers, and a growing range of virtual technology and other computer-assisted tools intended for direct use with clients.

We encourage your participation both as a helping professional grounded in the knowledge and critical commitments of your discipline as well as a technologically savvy user. This approach will require hands-on skills that will allow you to judiciously evaluate the merits of technological tools and information (Nurius, 1995; 1999; Nurius & Hudson, 1993)—to query, for example, if any given computer product or information pulled from the Web has demonstrated effectiveness. Has this tool been assessed for its appropriateness with people of differing cultural backgrounds? Can it safely be applied in a manner consistent with ethical safeguards?

We have significantly updated the literature base of this fifth edition. But the pace of change in practice knowledge has never been greater. To help today's practitioner retain knowledge currency and access to information sources likely to be of the greatest value, we have added a technological resource—InfoTrac®, a searchable online database drawing from current scholarly and popular publications. In addition, we include some readings and exercises to help you develop your information search and evaluation skills. Be aware that no tool is complete. Infotrac has access to some but not all of the professional periodicals you will need. For example, it was not possible to include journals sponsored by some of the national organizations such as the American Psychological Association. Note that databases such as PsychLit or PsychInfo, available through most universities, will be essential sources in your information searches. We provide below Web sites for many of the national organizations where you can learn more about these organizations, including the journals that they sponsor.

INFOTRAC® EXPLORATIONS

1. Select one of the following practice nexus terms—*critical thinking, person in environment, evidence-based practice*—and explore issues that you find relevant to your helping practice.
2. Search for *information technology* and see what articles you can find that pertain to helping services. Do you see vulnerable or underserved populations represented in these articles?

SUGGESTED RESOURCES

Readings

Abreu, J. M., Chung, R. G., & Atkinson, D. R. (2000). Multicultural counseling training: Past, present, and future directions. *The Counseling Psychologist, 28,* 641–656.

Allen-Meares, P., & Garvin, C. (Eds.). (2000). *The handbook of social work direct practice.* Thousand Oaks, CA: Sage.

American Psychological Association. (1993a). Guidelines for providers of psychological services to ethnic, linguistic, and culturally diverse populations. *American Psychologist, 48,* 45–48.

Berlin, S. (2001). Clinical social work: A cognitive–integrative perspective. New York: Oxford University Press.

Brower, A. M., & Nurius, P. S. (1993). *Social cognition and individual change: Current theory and counseling guidelines.* Newbury Park, CA: Sage.

Chambless, D. L., & Hollon, S. D. (1998). Defining empirically supported therapies. *Journal of Consulting and Clinical Psychology, 66,* 7–18.

Corcoran, K., & Vandiver, V. (1996). *Maneuvering the maze of managed care: Skills for mental health practitioners.* New York: Free Press.

Egan, G. (2002). *The skilled helper* (7th ed.). Pacific Grove, CA: Brooks/Cole.

Fischer, A. R., Jome, L. M. & Atkinson, D. R. (1998). Reconceptualizing multicultural counseling: Universal healing conditions in a culturally specific context. *The Counseling Psychologist, 26,* 525–588.

Flynn, M. (2000). Computer-mediated communications in direct social work practice. In P. Allen-Meares & C. Garvin (Eds.), *The handbook of social work direct practice* (pp. 565–583). Thousand Oaks, CA: Sage.

Garvin, C. D., & Seabury, B. A. (1997). *Interpersonal practice in social work: Promoting competence and social justice* (2nd ed.). Boston, MA: Allyn & Bacon.

Gibbs, L., & Gambrill, E. (1999). *Critical thinking for social workers: Exercises for the helping profession* (2nd ed.). Thousand Oaks, CA: Pine Forge.

Hepworth, D. H., Rooney, R. H., & Larsen, J. A. (2002). *Direct social work practice: Theory and skills* (6th ed.). Pacific Grove, CA: Brooks/Cole.

Kemp, S. P., Whittaker, J. K., & Tracy, E. M. (1997). *Person–environment practice: The social ecology of interpersonal helping.* New York: Aldine de Gruyter.

Prochaska, J. O., & Norcross, J. C. (1999). *Systems of psychotherapy: A transtheoretical analysis* (4th ed.). Pacific Grove, CA: Brooks/Cole.

Skovholt, T. (2001). The resilient practitioner. Needham Heights, MA: Allyn & Bacon.

Spencer, M., Lewis, E., & Gutierrez, L. (2000). *Multicultural perspectives on direct practice in social work.* In P. Allen-Meares & C. Garvin (Eds.), *The handbook of social work direct practice* (pp. 131–150). Thousand Oaks, CA: Sage.

Sue, D. W., Bingham, R. P., Porche-Burke, L., & Vasquez, M. (1999). The diversification of psychology: A multicultural revolution. *American Psychologist, 54,* 1061–1069.

Waehler, C. A., Kalodner, C. R., Wampold, B. E., & Lichtenberg, J. W. (2000). Empirically supported treatments (ESTs) in perspective: Implications for counseling psychology training. *The Counseling Psychologist, 28,* 657–671.

Wright, J. H., & Wright, A. S. (1997). Computer-assisted psychotherapy. *Journal of Psychotherapy Practice and Research, 6,* 315–329.

Web Sites

American Association for Marriage and Family Therapy
http://www.aamft.org

American Association of Pastoral Counselors
http://www.aapc.org

American Counseling Association
http://www.counseling.org

American Psychiatric Association
http://www.psych.org

American Psychological Association
http://www.apa.org

American Psychological Society
http://www.psychologicalscience.org

Canadian Psychiatric Association
http://www.cpa-apc.org

Canadian Psychological Association
http://www.cpa.ca

Commission on Rehabilitation Counselor Certification
http://www.crccertification.com/index.html

Council on Social Work Education
http://www.cswe.org

National Assembly of Health and Human Service Organizations
http://www.nassembly.org

National Association of Social Workers
http://www.naswdc.org

National Organization for Human Service Education
http://www.nohse.com

Society for Social Work and Research
http://www.sswr.org

World Wide Web Resources for Social Workers (WWWRSW), developed by Gary Holden
http://www.nyu.edu/socialwork/wwwrsw

CHAPTER 2
BUILDING YOUR FOUNDATION AS A HELPER

We understand the importance of clear guidance in skill building and the pragmatic aspects of helping as you undertake professional training. In the chapters to come, you will see a heavy emphasis on the core skills and resources that you need. Before we begin systematically walking through these with you, we should take the time to reflect on some factors that permeate all phases of helping and that are crucial to insightful, sensitive, and appropriate service. Few professions rival helping practice in the importance of understanding oneself, the dynamics of human interaction, the complexity of implementing values and ethics in practice, and the ways that diversity among us as people contextualizes both problems and solutions. We see all of helping practice as grounded within a framework of the issues that we address in this chapter. Your personal work in sorting through these issues becomes a fundamental part of your professional identity and approach to practice. It is not easy work! But, using a building metaphor, it is part of a strong foundation on which you can build an enduring and well-constructed practice as a helping professional.

OBJECTIVES

After completing this chapter, you will be able to
1. Identify attitudes and behaviors about yourself that might aid in or interfere with establishing a positive helping relationship.
2. Identify issues related to values, diversity, and ethics in the context of contemporary service provision that might affect development of a helping relationship and appropriate services.

CHARACTERISTICS OF EFFECTIVE HELPERS

The relationship between client and practitioner is widely accepted today by persons of various theoretical orientations as an important part of the total helping process. According to Brammer, Abrego, and Shostrom (1993), the relationship is important not only because "it constitutes the principal medium for eliciting and handling significant feelings and ideas which are aimed at changing client behavior" but also because it often determines "whether counseling will continue at all" (p. 82). Without an effective relationship (whether defined in therapeutic terms or according to other forms of direct professional help), client change is unlikely to occur. One body of research indicates that the *quality* of the relationship "can serve as a powerful positive influence on communication, openness, persuasibility, and ultimately, positive change in the client" (Goldstein & Higginbotham, 1991, p. 22). Part of the effectiveness of the relationship depends on the helper's knowledge and use of himself or herself, appreciation of the complexity that accompanies diversity, and attentiveness to ways that the changing context of practice affects critical commitments (such as ethics and critical thinking) and effectiveness, as we discussed in the practice nexus.

The most effective helper is one who has not only developed the expertise and technical skills associated with help giving but has also recognized and worked with his or her own interpersonal issues. If you have excellent skills but lack insight about yourself, you are at higher risk of imposing errors or biases of which you are genuinely unaware. If you have good skills and you also know yourself (e.g., strengths, limitations, values, priorities, and challenges), you are more than a technician and are better able to learn, change, and adapt yourself and your helping strategies as needed. In this section of the chapter, we explore qualities and behaviors present in very effective helpers.

Self-Awareness and Interpersonal Awareness

As you grow in your helping profession and as you gain real-life counseling experience, you will become increasingly aware that you are affected by your practice experience. Clients and circumstances will trigger responses in you or push sensitive buttons that may cause you to react a certain way, to feel a certain way, or even to worry and lose sleep. This happens because we all carry effects from our personal histories and because we care about the well-being of people we work with and about the justness of systems we work within. None of us came from a perfectly healthy or fair past, and we have all learned ways of dealing with ourselves and other persons; some of these ways are healthy and productive, and some are unhealthy and defensive. We are not perfect or without weaknesses, and to be perfect is neither necessary nor realistic. The important point is that we are aware of our own biases and limitations. We are cognizant of the sensitivities that are opened up in us by working with clients, and we acknowledge that we must take responsibility for appropriately managing these. Otherwise, we may inadvertently be prioritizing our needs and risk diluting or misdirecting the capacity that our relationship and helping skills have for meeting *clients'* priorities.

Day (1995) has pointed out the importance of examining our motives for even entering the helping profession. He cites three of the most common motivations: (1) to do for others what someone has done for me, (2) to do for others what I wish had been done for me, and (3) to share with others certain insights I have acquired. Although these may be widespread reasons for becoming a helper, Day (1995) cautions that persons motivated in these ways "encounter several common problems that potentially convert their motivation to ill impact" (p. 109). Specifically, well-intentioned practitioners with such motives can become frustrated and discouraged. These feelings can then affect their behavior with clients and lead to pride rather than humility, insistence rather than invitation, telling rather than listening, "expert-ing" rather than collaborating, and making or coercing rather than assisting. Examining our motives for being a helper and the potential of these motives is another important facet of self-awareness.

Brems (2001) offers one way to think about self-awareness, both in terms of various dimensions within it as well as ways that it interfaces with knowledge and skills in development of competence. None of these dimensions of self-awareness are really independent or separate from others. For example, values and ethics are part of the personal or individual aspects that a practitioner brings to a helping encounter, but these certainly overlap with professional and cultural dimensions we bring as well. At this point in your professional development, there are three specific areas about yourself we invite you to explore in further depth: competence, power, and intimacy (see also Learning Activity 2.1). Depending on

---

LEARNING ACTIVITY 2.1

Exploring Personal Areas That Impact Your Counseling

This activity, adapted in part from Marianne and Gerry Corey (1992), is designed to help you explore areas of yourself that will, in some fashion, affect your helping. Take some time to consider these questions at *different points* in your development as a helper. There is no feedback for this activity, as the responses are yours and yours alone. You may wish to discuss your responses with a colleague or your own therapist.

1. Why are you attracted to the help-giving/counseling profession?
2. What was your role in your family when you were growing up, and what impact does it have on this attraction?
3. Who are you as a person?
4. What wounds or unfinished business do you carry with you into the counseling room?
5. In what way are you healing these wounds?
6. What do you notice or what do you think your work with clients will (does) trigger in you?
7. Do you honestly believe you *need* to be a counselor, or do you *want* to be a counselor?
8. With whom do you have unfinished business?
9. How do you handle being in conflict? Being confronted? Being evaluated? What defenses do you use in these situations?
10. What are repetitive or chronic issues for you? How might these affect your work with clients?
11. What do you see in other people that you consistently do not like? See whether you can find these same qualities in yourself and "own" them as also belonging to you.

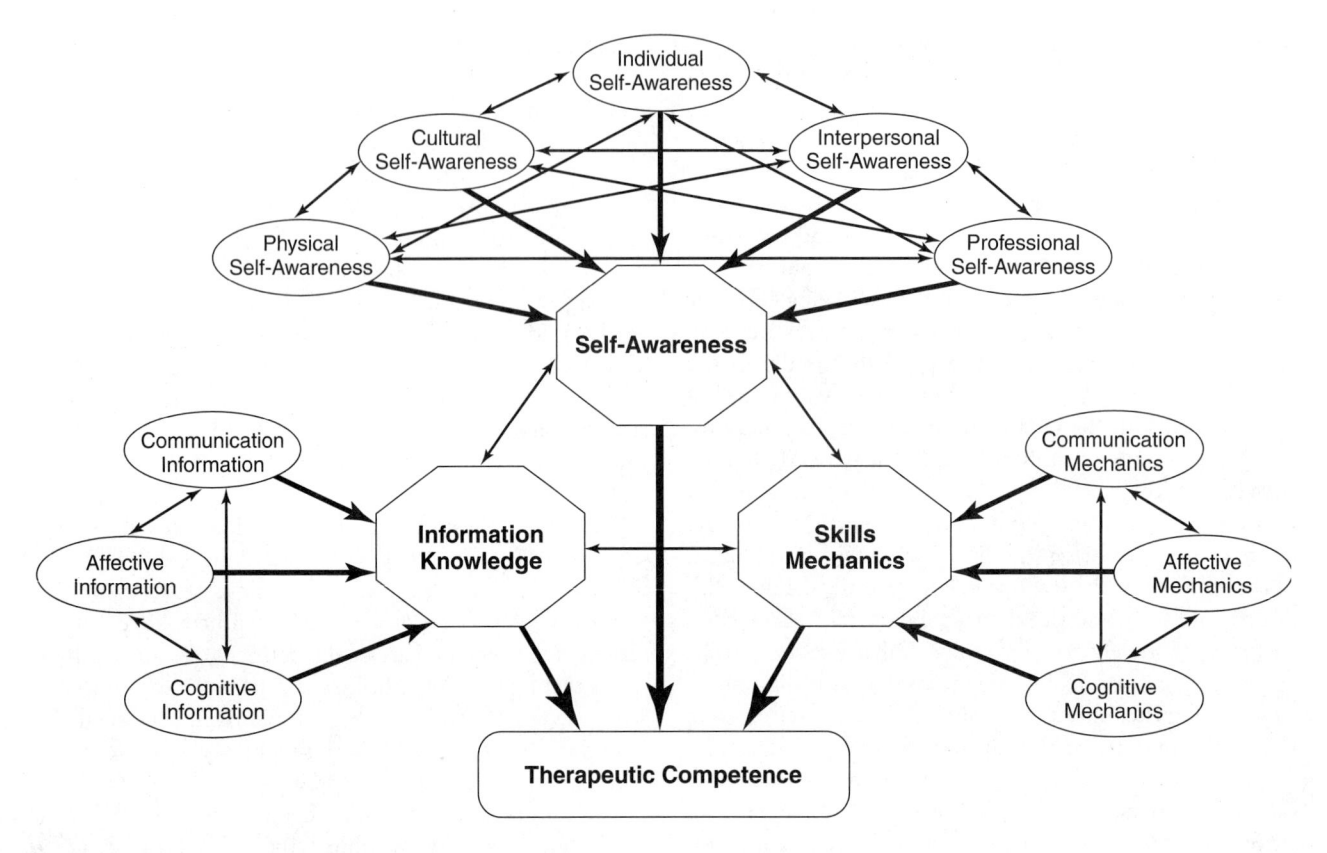

Figure 2.1 Diagram of Therapeutic Competence
Source: Basic skills in psychotherapy and counseling, (3rd ed.) by C. Brems, ©2001. Reprinted with permission of Brooks/Cole, an imprint of the Wadsworth Group, a division of Thomson Learning.

your specific professional discipline or field of practice, there are likely others to add to this early list—for example, the insight needed to assess how well suited one is to work in crisis services or with terminally ill people.

Competence

Competence, of course, involves training in the knowledge and skills outlined in Figure 2.1 and the connections illustrated in the practice nexus. Self-awareness involves a balanced assessment of our strengths and limitations in this regard. However, we also want to note the importance of our attitudes about ourselves and how these attitudes can significantly influence the way we behave. People who have negative views of themselves will "put themselves down" and will either seek out or avoid types of interactions with others that confirm their negative self-image. This behavior has serious implications for helpers. If we don't feel competent or valuable as people, we may communicate this attitude to the client. Or if we don't feel confident about our ability to counsel, we may inadvertently structure the helping process to meet our own self-image or ideological needs, or to confirm our negative self-pictures.

As Corey and Corey note, it is hard to be an effective helper if you have a "fragile ego" (Corey & Corey, personal communication, September 29, 1992). This is not to say that we don't all experience self-doubt at times, particularly in early stages of a new career. Rather, we are emphasizing that part of competence is knowing when it is time to seek supervision, consultation, or collegial support. Rather than being "bullet-proof," we underscore the importance of a generally sturdy self-esteem; the ability to handle complexity and discomfort, flexibility and openmindedness; a willingness to seek help as needed; and a commitment to lifelong learning (Brems, 2000; Egan, 1998; Kottler & Brown, 1992).

And, as we note in Chapter 1, critical thinking is a subtle yet crucial aspect of competence. Nickerson (1986) notes

BUILDING YOUR FOUNDATION AS A HELPER 19

> **BOX 2.1 CHARACTERISTICS OF CRITICAL THINKING**
>
> 1. It is purposeful.
> 2. It is responsive to and guided by *intellectual standards* (relevance, accuracy, precision, clarity, depth, and breadth).
> 3. It supports the development of intellectual *traits* in the thinker of humility, integrity, perseverance, empathy, and self-discipline.
> 4. The thinker can identify the *elements of thought* present in thinking about any problem, such that the thinker makes the logical connection between the elements and the problem at hand. The critical thinker will routinely ask the following questions:
>   - What is the *purpose* of my thinking (goal/objective)?
>   - What precise *question* (problem) am I trying to answer?
>   - Within what *point of view* (perspective) am I thinking?
>   - What *concepts* or ideas are central to my thinking?
>   - What am I taking for granted, what *assumptions* am I making?
>   - What *information* am I using (data, facts, observation)?
>   - How am I *interpreting* that information?
>   - What *conclusions* am I coming to?
>   - If I accept the conclusions, what are the *implications*? What would the consequence be if I put my thoughts into action?
>
> For each element, the thinker must consider standards that shed light on the effectiveness of her thinking.
>
> 5. It is *self-assessing and self-improving*. The thinker takes steps to assess her thinking, using appropriate intellectual standards. If you are not assessing your thinking, you are not thinking critically.
> 6. *There is an integrity to the whole system*. The thinker is able to critically examine her thought as a whole and to take it apart (consider its parts as well). The thinker is committed to be intellectually humble, persevering, courageous, fair, and just. The critical thinker is aware of the variety of ways in which thinking can become distorted, misleading, prejudiced, superficial, unfair, or otherwise defective.
> 7. It *yields a well-reasoned answer*. If we know how to check our thinking and are committed to doing so, and we get extensive practice, then we can depend on the results of our thinking being productive.
> 8. It is responsive to the social and moral imperative to enthusiastically argue from opposing points of view and to *seek and identify weakness and limitations in one's own position*. Critical thinkers are aware that there are many legitimate points of view, each of which (when deeply thought through) may yield some level of insight.
>
> Source: *Critical Thinking for Social Workers: Exercises for the Helping Profession (2nd ed.)*, by L. Gibbs & E. Gambrill, p. 4. Copyright 1999 by Pine Forge Press. Reprinted with permission of Sage Publications.

that self-awareness is one of three kinds of knowledge central to critical thinking (the others are domain-specific knowledge and knowledge about critical thinking itself). This aspect of self-knowledge involves awareness of human reasoning processes and conscious attention to one's own reasoning—for example, asking oneself "What do I believe, and why do I believe it? What biases or assumptions may I be working from? Can I make a well-reasoned argument for my position that includes attention to alternatives?" (Gibbs & Gambrill, 1999). Drawing from the work of Paul (1993), Gibbs and Gambrill (1999) outline characteristics of critical thinking. Take a few minutes to review Box 2.1. Although training in core knowledge and skills about helping practice contributes greatly to our competence, critical thinking helps shift from what we know to "how" we know.

Power

In helping, power can be misused in several ways. For example, a practitioner may try to be omnipotent or be convinced of the "right" direction. For this person, helping is manageable only when it is controllable or consistent with his or her beliefs. Such a practitioner may use a variety of maneuvers to stay in control, including persuading the client to do what she or he wants, becoming upset or defensive if a client is resistant or hesitant, and dominating the content and direction of the interview. The practitioner who needs to control the interview may be more likely to engage in a power struggle with a client.

In contrast, some practitioners may be afraid of power or wish to deny that they are exercising influence as part of their helping role. These practitioners may unwittingly attempt to escape from as much responsibility and participation in counseling as possible. Such a helper avoids forthrightly addressing roles or expectations and avoids expressing opinions. Professional relationships between helping practitioners and clients have aspects of unequal power of various types (e.g., authority, resources, and vulnerability). To deny or avoid acknowledgment of the power differential limits one's ability to manage this differential as honestly and productively as possible.

Another way that unresolved power needs can influence helping is seen in the "lifestyle converter." This person has very strong feelings about the value of one particular lifestyle or strategies for change. Such a helper may take unwarranted advantage—consciously or not—of the influence processes in a helping relationship by using counseling to convert the client to that lifestyle or ideology. In this case, counseling turns into a forum for the helping practitioner's views and pet peeves. As Woodman (1992) points out, it is quite easy to become addicted to the power of helping.

In reality, power is inherently a part of helping relationships and process. Part of our emphasis here is to include recognition of more subtle dimensions of power and choices about their use as part of one's self-awareness. For example, power can be differentiated in terms of that which is achieved or earned (for example, through an educational degree and demonstrated skills) and that which is ascribed or "inherited" in one sense or another. Ascribed power may stem from social structural characteristics of oneself or lineage such as gender, race, economic status, abledness, sexual orientation, or religion—with a multitude of ways of affecting helping practice (Reed et al., 1997). Power is an issue for practice not just at the individual level—between helper and client—but at other levels as well, such as the institutional power of the agency that a practitioner works within, power associated with regulatory bodies, and economic factors such as insurance coverage and managed care. As we will see in this chapter and throughout the book, power is very much a consideration in today's practice nexus and beyond.

Interpersonal Awareness and Intimacy

Needless to say, interpersonal habits, inclinations, and awareness are an important part of appropriate and effective helping. Brems (2001) notes a range of interpersonal patterns, with examples of levels or directions that are too high, are too low, or are fairly well balanced (healthy) relative to their likely impact in helping (see Table 2.1). It is natural for us all to wax and wane on these. Helpers are not hermetically sealed but are engaged in their own relationships, experiences, and ups and downs of life! At varying points, we will be more or less preoccupied with relationships, sensitive to approval from others, emotionally expressive, or comfortable with authority. The point is not to prescribe a narrow line of absolute correctness, but to stimulate ongoing self-assessment to help deal with excesses or insufficiencies as needed.

We will look at the first of these interpersonal patterns—intimacy—to illustrate the value of interpersonal awareness. A practitioner's unchecked intimacy needs can alter the direction and course of helping. As with power, certain degrees and forms of intimacy are inescapable and can be important elements of helping—consider, for instance, the depths of feeling involved through helping clients with painful experiences, losses, self-doubts, and worries. Clearly, there must be room for personality differences. We all know people for whom warmth takes on "Earth mother" or "father" proportions whereas others have a more reserved expressive style. Awareness of one's own style and that of clients can be important to accurately sensing and conveying empathy.

However, what we discuss here concerns more-extreme struggles with intimacy as a part of practice. A practitioner who is particularly sensitive to rejection or criticism may behave in ways that meet the need to be accepted and liked by the client. For example, the practitioner may routinely avoid challenging or confronting clients for fear the client may be "turned off." The practitioner may subtly seek positive client feedback as a reassurance of being valued and liked. Negative client cues may also be overlooked because the practitioner does not want to hear expressions of client dissatisfaction. Some practitioners have a high personal need for intimacy and may be at risk of bringing those needs into practice, crossing boundaries of appropriateness or comfort for the client.

Another kind of struggle involves helpers who are afraid of or uncomfortable with intimacy and intensity of expression, which may create excessive distance in the relationship. The helper may avoid emotional intimacy in the relationship by ignoring expressions of positive feelings from the client or by behaving in a gruff, distant, or aloof manner and relating to the client through the "professional" role. These kinds of responses may shut down the expression of feelings in clients or create feelings of not being valued or understood.

Many of the issues we have discussed here are common in human nature and human interaction. Achieving insight into our individual strengths or vulnerabilities in this regard requires an ongoing commitment. Although each helping relationship is defined somewhat idiosyncratically by the helping dyad or group, certain issues will affect many of the problem-solving or therapeutic relationships you will encounter. These include (but are not limited to) values, diversity, and ethics.

ISSUES AFFECTING HELPERS

Many issues affect helpers, but three crucial factors are values, diversity, and ethics.

TABLE 2.1 Interpersonal Patterns in Order to Explore to Gain Interpersonal Self-Awareness

Interpersonal Issue	Possible Patterns or Manifestations (excessive, insufficient, healthy)
Intimacy needs	Seeking excessive closeness; inability to establish intimate relationships; healthy capacity for intimacy
Need for approval from others	Excessive need for approval; indifference to others' level of approval; appreciation of approval from others but not dependent on it
Importance of relationships in life	Relationships unimportant; relationships the only priority; relationships ranked somewhere in the middle of the individual's list of priorities
Preoccupation with relationships	Thoughts dominated by occurrences in relationships; relationships and occurrence within them not given a second thought; relationships thought about to the extent necessary to keep them healthy and functional
Need for relationships	Inability to function outside of relationships; relationships dismissed as unnecessary to life; importance of relationships recognized without being incapacitated by their temporary absence
Level of trust	Inability to trust others; overly trusting and perhaps gullible; trusting within reasonable limits of exploration
Level of trustworthiness in relationships	Cannot be trusted because of violations of agreement and promises; always true to one's word even to the detriment of the self; generally trustworthy
Level of confidence in relationships	Self-doubt about own ability to relate well in intimate relationships; overly confident about being right and knowing what is best for relationships; confident that can remain healthy through collaboration relationships
Dependency needs	Excessively dependent to the point of not being able to function without the other; counterdependent denial of any interpersonal dependency needs; a balance of dependency needs and independence with mutuality in the relationship
Self-versus-other orientation in relationships	Preoccupied and concerned only with personal needs in relationships; preoccupied and concerned only about the needs of the relationship partner; aware of and concerned about the needs and wishes of both partners
Comfort with asking for help	Inability to ask for help under any circumstances: quick to ask for help without attempt to solve problems alone first; healthy balance of self-reliance and asking for assistance
Importance given to feedback from others	Dismisses feedback from relationship partners; overly concerned with and reactive to feedback; weighs feedback respectfully and carefully, then draws conclusions
Level of self-versus-other absorption	Completely self-absorbed and alienated; completely other absorbed and overinvolved; able to shift focus as needed for healthy relating
Approach-avoidance behaviors	Approach only; avoidance only; some approach, some avoidance as appropriate to the circumstances
Level of value granted to relationships	Overvalues all relationships; undervalues all relationships; realistically values relationships on their individual merit
Social skills	Absence of social skills with lack of self-efficacy about social relating: sense of overconfidence in social skills; appropriate social skills
Comfort in new relationships	Uncomfortable and self-conscious around strangers; overly confident and boisterous around strangers; comfortable but appropriately cautious in new relationships
Center of attention	Needs to be the center or focus of attention in social settings; always shrinks from being the center or focus of attention in social settings because of embarrassment; can shift in and out of focus or center of attention as dictated by healthy social relating
Self-disclosure in relationships	Never self-discloses, even in intimate relationships where disclosure is appropriate; self-discloses prematurely and inappropriately in all relationships or relationships where disclosure is not appropriate; carefully discriminates where and when self-disclosure is appropriate
Emotional expressiveness in relationships	Never expresses affect or tenderness; overly emotional and sympathetic in all relationships; can discriminate when and with whom expression of affect is appropriate and necessary
Identification with others	Overidentifies with everyone by losing sense of separate identity; stays entirely distanced, never being able to relate to anyone's experience; identifies as appropriate and fitting, and tailors expression to situation
Conflict with authority figures	Oppositional with and dismissive of superiors or perceived authority figures; overly submissive and guided by real or perceived authority figures; respectful of authority without compromising personal values and ethics
Stance toward equality in relationships	Always seeks to be one-up and in charge; always feels inferior and compelled to be one-down; views all humans as equal

Source: Basic Skills in Psychotherapy and Counseling, by C. Brems (3rd ed.), ©2001. Reprinted with permission of Brooks/Cole, an imprint of the Wadsworth Group, a division of Thomson Learning.

Values

The word *value* denotes something that we prize, regard highly, or prefer. Values are our feelings or attitudes about something and our preferred actions or behaviors. As an example, take a few minutes to think of (and perhaps list) five things you love to do. Now look over your list to determine how frequently and consistently you actually engage in each of these five actions. Your values are indicated by your frequent and consistent actions (Simon, 1995). If you say that you value spending time with friends but you hardly ever do this, then other activities and actions probably have more value for you. (See Learning Activity 2.2)

In interactions with clients, it is impossible to be "value free." Values permeate every interaction. Helpers cannot be "scrupulously neutral" in their interactions with clients (Corey, Corey, & Callanan, 1998). Okun (1997, p. 251) asserts that "in recent years, we have recognized that in any interpersonal relationship, whether a helping relationship or not, values are transmitted either directly or indirectly between the participants" (p. 233). Interviewers may unintentionally influence a client to embrace their values in subtle ways by what they pay attention to or by nonverbal cues of approval and disapproval (Corey et al., 1998). If clients feel they need the helper's approval, they may act in ways they think will please the helper instead of making choices according to their own value system.

Sometimes, helpers push values on a client because of a loyalty to their own perspective or a belief that their values are preferable to the client's. There are several problems with this approach. First, when we push a value onto a client, the client may feel pushed, too—either pushed toward or pushed away. Second, when we impose our own perspective, we undermine a collaborative relationship, convey a lack of appreciation or respect for differences, and often miss seeing or hearing something of the client's values and needs.

Obviously, not all of our values have an impact on the helping process. For example, the helper who values sailing can probably work with a client who values being a landlubber without any problem. However, values that reflect our ideas about morality, ethics, lifestyle, "the good life," roles, interpersonal living, and so forth have a greater chance of entering the helping process. The very fact that we have entered a helping profession suggests some of our values. There may be times when a referral is necessary because of an unresolved and interfering value conflict with a client. For example, a practitioner who views rape as the most terrible and sexist act a person can perform might have difficulty helping someone accused of rape. This practitioner might tend to identify more with the rape victim than with the client. From an ethical viewpoint, if a practitioner is unable to promote and respect the welfare of a client, a referral may be necessary (American Counseling Association, 1995; American Psychological Association, 1992; National Association of Social Workers, 1996).

Lum (1996) asserts that although social work values are oriented toward client rights, the collective values of other cultures should also be addressed—values in the areas of family, spirituality and religion, and multicultural identity. We agree with Lum, and we have found that a significant issue for many helpers is the capacity to work with clients whose values and lifestyles are different from their own.

Usually a helper's value system and level of respect for different values are developed during formative years and are influenced by such facts as family, religious affiliation, cultural and ethnic background, and geographic location. As adults, we bring to the helping situation varying levels of acceptance for difference. Generally, it is important to be able to expand our level of awareness to understand clients whose beliefs, values, lifestyle, and behaviors are quite different from our own. Otherwise, we run the risk of regarding clients with different values or lifestyles as somehow less sophisticated, knowledgeable, or "correct" than we are or, worse yet, as inferior to us. We do not mean to minimize the difficulty of these challenges. As earnest and open as we may feel, working with value and perspective differences can take subtle, confusing, and challenging forms.

A first step is to acknowledge honestly what your struggle is with this issue rather than deny your blind spots, your ignorance, or your feelings (frustration, anxiety, uncertainty, or anger). Thus, if you are adamantly opposed to abortion, you acknowledge your opposition and also your struggle when working with clients who are pro-choice, which may include referring them to other helping sources. We also believe it is particularly important for helpers to support the rights of those clients who—because of their physical or mental abilities, age, gender, race, gender expression, or sexual orientation—have traditionally been the recipients of prejudicial responses and often substandard treatment, ranging from negative stereotyping and emotional abuse to physical violence (Atkinson & Hackett, 1998).

For example, persons with disabilities suffer from economic and environmental discrimination, and children with disabilities are more likely to be physically, emotionally, and sexually abused. The elderly also suffer from economic discrimination, negative stereotyping, and also abuse; elder abuse is growing at an alarming rate in the United States. And despite the advances of women in the 20th century, many have been blocked or reversed because of recent maneuvering of conservative political forces. Faludi (1991) points out as an example that the Equal Employment Opportunity Commission (EEOC), the agency responsible for enforcing anti-sex discrimination laws, has been almost dismantled. Although attitudes toward women's work roles have changed, American women still earn comparatively less in wages than their male counterparts, are much less likely to be selected for management positions, are more-frequent victims of abuse and sexual harassment and assault, and are more likely to receive biased treatment from the mental health system.

Similar concerns exist with people of color who, despite civil rights legislation, continue to be the recipients of oppressive treatment and also harassment. It is a sad commentary on our times that racial profiling is evident in routine security monitoring, police detentions, border patrol activities, financial lending practices, residential rental and sale trends, and more. Unfortunately, harassment of persons of color appears to be on the upswing, if anything, and these groups continue to experience discrimination and exploitation in opportunities related to economics, education, and community inclusion, such as low rates of approval for bank loans, unfair treatment in employment, and so on. Even in the mental health field, there is an alarming equation of minority status and pathology. For example, Stevenson and Renard (1993) cite years of psychological research which assumes that the behaviors of African Americans are deficient instead of different. Turner (1993) has noted the destructive effects of a body of research that has used a "deficit" theoretical model and has also assumed that the Euro-American middle-class population in the United States represents the standard for measurement (p. 9).

Gay men and lesbian women also suffer from discriminatory treatment, including "social, legal, medical, psychological and religious" discrimination (Atkinson & Hackett, 1998, p. 100). Obviously, many persons in the world still view homosexuality as some pathogenic illness or see gay men and lesbian women as "perverted sinners." In addition to encountering homophobic attitudes from straight persons, lesbian women and gay men have to contend with the issue of "heterosexual privilege"—that is, the idea that heterosexuality is the more common and therefore the more acceptable sexual orientation. Generally, straight persons do not feel a need to hide their sexual orientation for fear of reprisal; for lesbian women and gay men, hiding or being "in the closet" for fear of the consequences is a pervading concern. In the mental health system, whereas treating the presenting problems of lesbian women and gay men is now customary, some practitioners still make the condition of homosexuality the focus of therapy. As Coleman and Remafedi (1989) point out, gay adolescents may be at particular risk and may have the most difficulty receiving affirmative counseling. Although practitioners often have more positive attitudes about gay men and lesbian women than does the public at large, much misinformation and stereotyping still appear to exist. These attitudes extend to variations in gender expression as well.

The American Psychological Association has developed guidelines for psychotherapy with lesbian, gay, and bisexual clients to provide helping practitioners with "(a) a frame of reference for the treatment of lesbian, gay, and bisexual clients and (b) basic information and further references in the areas of assessment, intervention, identity, relationships, and the education of psychologists" in particular and psychotherapeutic professional helpers more broadly (Committee on Lesbian, Gay, and Bisexual Concerns Joint Task Force, 2000, 1440). These guidelines are summarized as follows. We recommend the entire report as a resource for practice.

Attitudes Toward Homosexuality and Bisexuality

1. Helpers understand that homosexuality and bisexuality are not indicative of mental illness.
2. Helpers are encouraged to recognize their attitudes and knowledge about lesbian, gay, and bisexual issues may be relevant to assessment and treatment and seek consultation or make appropriate referrals when indicated.
3. Helpers strive to understand the ways in which social stigmatization (e.g., prejudice, discrimination, and violence) poses risks to the mental health and well-being of lesbian, gay, and bisexual clients.
4. Helpers strive to understand how inaccurate or prejudicial views of homosexuality or bisexuality may affect the client's presentation in treatment and the therapeutic process.

Relationships and Families

5. Helpers strive to be knowledgeable about and respect the importance of lesbian, gay, and bisexual relationships.
6. Helpers strive to understand the particular circumstances and challenges faced by lesbian, gay, and bisexual parents.
7. Helpers recognize that the families of lesbian, gay, and bisexual people may include people who are not legally or biologically related.
8. Helpers strive to understand how a person's homosexual or bisexual orientation may have an impact on his or her family of origin and the relationship to that family of origin.
9. Helpers are encouraged to recognize the particular life issues or challenges that are related to multiple and often conflicting cultural norms, values, and beliefs that lesbian, gay, and bisexual members of racial and ethnic minorities face.
10. Helpers are encouraged to recognize the particular challenges that bisexual individuals experience.
11. Helpers strive to understand the special problems and risks that exist for lesbian, gay, and bisexual youth.
12. Helpers consider generational differences within lesbian, gay, and bisexual populations and the particular

challenges that lesbian, gay, and bisexual older adults may experience.
13. Helpers are encouraged to recognize the particular challenges that lesbian, gay, and bisexual individuals experience with physical, sensory, and cognitive–emotional disabilities.

Education

14. Helpers support the provision of professional education and training in lesbian, gay, and bisexual issues.
15. Helpers are encouraged to increase their knowledge and understanding of homosexuality and bisexuality through continuing education, training, supervision, and consultation.
16. Helpers make reasonable efforts to familiarize themselves with relevant mental health, educational, and community resources for lesbian, gay, and bisexual people.*

Instances of heterosexual bias have been reported in psychology training programs as well as in mental health systems (Pilkington & Cantor, 1996). Similarly, guidelines have been developed to support nonsexist and gender-sensitive practice. One example of this is a set of 13 principles developed by the American Psychological Association's Committee on Women (see Fitzgerald & Nutt, 1986). Briefly, these principles can be summarized as a commitment by professional helpers to (1) be knowledgeable about biological, psychological, and social issues that have affected women; (2) be aware that practice theories may apply differently to women and men and be able to distinguish those limiting potential from those more useful to women; (3) be committed to sustained learning about issues and special problems relevant to women; (4) be aware of and recognize sexism and how it interacts with other forms of oppression; (5) be informed of verbal and nonverbal factors—particularly regarding power—as these affect women in work with helping practitioners; (6) use skills that are particularly helpful to women; (7) hold no preconceived limitations of potential changes or goals in counseling/therapy with women; (8) be sensitive to conditions where it may be advantageous for a woman to be seen by a male or female helper; (9) use nonsexist language; (10) not engage in sexual activity with their women clients under any circumstances; (11) review their own biases and values and the effects these can have on their women clients and their practice; (12) monitor their personal functioning so that it does not adversely affect their work with women clients; and (13) support the elimination of sex bias within institutions and individuals.

There are, of course, ongoing developments, refinements, and applications of guidelines that are valuable to practitioners. Sample resources in this regard include Brown, 1994; Crawford & Unger, 2000; Enns, 2000; and Yoder, 1999.

Diversity and Multicultural Competence

The helper's values are connected to values about diversity. As we mention in Chapter 1, because our world and our society are pluralistic, we cannot always expect to encounter clients who are like us. From a cultural context, there are many ways in which clients can be diverse: gender, gender expression, sexual orientation, race, ethnicity, socioeconomic level, religious or spiritual affiliation, disability status, age, and so on. By and large, we will use the term *multiculturalism* to include various dimensions such as these. However, we recognize that broadly defining multiculturalism may inordinately dilute its meaning, power, and utility—for example, obscuring fundamental factors related to race or blunting the kinds of needed awareness and change (Helms, 1994a, 1994b; Locke, 1990). Umbrella terms such as ALANAs (African, Latino/Latina, Asian and Pacific Islander, and Native American) and VREGs (visible racial/ethnic groups) are more often applied when discussing shared experiences of people of color (Cook & Helms, 1988; Helms & Cook, 1999).

Ho (1995) argues that practitioners need to pay more attention to the cultural influences that exist for any given client and "that shape personality formation and various aspects of psychological functioning" (p. 5). Ho's comment is applicable to variability within all cultural groups. As an example, consider that persons within various cultural groups may have preferences for how they are ethnically described. For example, a woman may prefer to be called a Hispanic rather than a Latina, but a man may wish to be known as a Hispanic rather than a Latino. For another person, the Hispanic referent may feel offensive. It is best not to make any assumptions. Instead, ask the client or follow the client's lead in the ethnic description he or she uses. The ethnic label a client chooses to use for self-identity is based on a number of cultural factors, such as age, acculturation level, generation, political consciousness, country of birth, region of the country, and socioeconomic status (Baker & Krugh, 1996).

As Table 2.2 shows, racial groups stem from a number of different national and cultural roots—which can vary along many dimensions, language and religion being among the most obvious, as well as by beliefs, customs, perspectives,

---

*Source: Adapted from "Guidelines for Psychotherapy with Lesbian, Gay, and Bisexual Clients," by Committee on Lesbian, Gay, and Bisexual Concerns Joint Task Force, *American Psychologist*, 55, pp. 1440–1451. Copyright 2000 by the American Psychological Association. Reprinted by permission.

TABLE 2.2 Ethnocultural Groups in the United States (1980, 1990, 1995)

White	Black	Hispanic Origin[a]	Asian	Native American
Subgroups:				

Anglo-Saxons
English
Celtics
  Welsh
  Scots
  North Ireland Irish
Swedes
Norwegians
Danes
Finns
Germans
Dutch
Appalachians
 	
White Ethnics
South and East Ireland
  Irish
Italians
Sicilians
Poles
Austrians
Hungarians
Czechs
Greeks
Portuguese
Russians
Yugoslavs
 	
Socioreligious Ethnics
Jews, Amish, Mormons
	African
	  Americans
	West Indians
	Haitians
		Mexicans
		Puerto Ricans
		Cubans
		Other Central and South Americans
		Spaniards
			Chinese
			Filipinos
			Japanese
			Koreans
			
			Indochinese
			Vietnamese
			Cambodians
			Lao
			
			Pacific Islanders
			Native
			  Hawaiians
			Guamanians
			Samoans
			Fijians
			
			Asia/Middle East
			Indians
			Arabs
			Ethiopians
			Iranians
			Egyptians
			Turks
			Pakistani
				American
				  Indians[b]
				Eskimos
				Aleuts

Source: Adapted from *Counseling and Development in a Multicultural Society* (3rd ed.), by J. A. Axelson, p. 31. ©1999. Reprinted with permission of Brooks/Cole, an imprint of the Wadsworth Group, a division of Thomson Learning. Data from Tables No. 19 and 51, *Statistical Abstract of the United States: 1996 (116th edition)* by U.S. Bureau of the Census.
[a]Persons who identified their origin or ancestry as "Spanish/Hispanic" also reported their "race" category (that is, White, Black or Negro, Asian or Pacific Islander, American Indian or Eskimo or Aleut, or other).
[b]550 federally recognized tribal entities, including about 226 village groups in Alaska; largest tribes are Cherokee and Navajo, followed by the Sioux and Chippewa; about 22% of all Native Americans, including Eskimos and Aleuts, lived on 287 reservations and trust lands in 1990.

and values. Differences exist both between and within cultural subgroups. For example, women of some ethnic groups are still socialized as a group to be "nice" and not to express anger; on the other hand, some men are socialized more to be strong and not to express tears or grief. However, within any given group of women, some express anger easily, just as within any group of men, some can express sadness easily. Similarly, people of varying spiritual faiths have different spiritual beliefs, practices, and rituals. If you are of the Christian faith, you may choose to celebrate Christmas; if you are Jewish, you may choose to celebrate Hanukkah. If you are Hindu or Buddhist, the concept of reincarnation is part of your religious framework, as is karmic theory—karmic referring to both good and bad deeds you do that follow you in future lives. You are also affected or shaped to some degree by your race and ethnic

LEARNING ACTIVITY 2.2   Personal Values

This learning activity presents descriptions of six clients. If you work through this activity by yourself, we suggest that you imagine yourself counseling each of these clients. Try to generate a very vivid picture of yourself and the client in your mind. If you do this activity with a partner, you can role-play the helper while your partner assumes the part of each client as described in the six examples. As you imagine or role-play the helper, try to notice your feelings, attitudes, values, and behavior during the visualization or role-play process. After *each* example, stop to think about or discuss these questions:

1. What attitudes and beliefs did you have about the client?
2. Were your beliefs and attitudes based on actual or presumed information about the client?
3. How did you behave with the client?
4. What values are portrayed by your behavior?
5. Could you work with this person effectively?

There are no right or wrong answers. A reaction to this learning activity can be found in the feedback section.

Client 1
This client is a young woman who is having financial problems. She is the sole supporter of three young children. She earns her living by prostitution and pushing drugs. She states that she is concerned about her financial problems but can't make enough money from welfare or from an unskilled job to support her kids.

Client 2
You have been assigned a client who is charged with rape and sexual assault. The client, a man, tells you that he is not to blame for the incident because the victim, a woman, "asked for it."

Client 3
This client is concerned about general feelings of depression. Overweight and unkempt, the client is in poor physical condition and smokes constantly during the interview.

Client 4
The client is a young white woman who comes to you at the college counseling center. She is in tears because her parents have threatened to disown her on learning that her steady male partner is an African American.

Client 5
The client is a gay man who is angry with his gay lover because he found out from a mutual friend that his lover recently slept with another man.

Client 6
The client is an elderly man who confides in you that he is on two kinds of medicine for seizures and "thought control." He states that occasionally he believes people are out to get him. Although he hasn't been employed for some time, he is now thinking of returning to the workforce and wants your assistance and a letter of reference.

---

group affiliation. Euro-Americans have traditionally favored a "rugged individualism"; many of the counseling approaches reflect an emphasis on the importance of the individual, individual rights, and individuation. Even this concept is shaped to some degree by learned gender roles. Some theories of the psychology of women have emphasized the "self in relation" and context sensitivity (Gilbert & Scher, 1999; Miller, 1991) although the direct applicability of this model to women of color is less clear (Enns, 1993). Within-group variations of cultural differences have not received as much emphasis as between-group differences. Learning Activity 2.2 offers an exercise to help illuminate and reflect on preconceptions, values, or reactions in different practice situations.

Acculturation and the Management of Diversity

Acculturation refers to the process by which individuals who belong to another cultural group accommodate to the attitudes, values, and behaviors of the host culture in which they live. The early models of acculturation assumed that some aspects of the indigenous culture are forgotten with time when aspects of the host culture are assimilated. Obviously, this rather narrow focus is limited because it seems to assume that the host culture is preferred and has more intrinsic value than the indigenous culture. A more recent model of acculturation has been developed by Szapocznik and Kurtines (1980) and is referred to as *biculturalism*. In this model, the individual is affected in some mutually inclusive way by forces and values within both the indigenous culture and another culture.

More recently, Szapocznik and Kurtines (1993) and Ho (1995) have expanded the bicultural model into a multicultural model that stresses the impact of multiple cultural environments upon an individual, recognizing the cultural pluralism that we discuss in Chapter 1. As an example of this, a Cuban American teenage boy may have been socialized to his Latino culture through his parents, to African American culture through a friend, and to Euro-American culture through school. Yeh and Hwang (2000) illustrate the challenges of "multidimensionality" of ethnic identity, relationships, goal pursuits, and everyday life for those balancing and integrating multiple heritages, value frameworks, world views, and networks. Using a case example of a young-adult first-generation Chinese American college student, Yeh and Hwang (2000) illustrate how cultural concepts such as an interdependent view of self and multiple selves can be useful in helping understand the shifting nature of "self" as one traverses sharply contrasting cultural spheres (e.g., to frame this as flexible and adaptive rather than fragmented or inauthentic). As Ho (1995) observes, this is an additive model in that people are able to gain competence in multiple cultures without inherently either losing their cultural identity or having to choose one culture over another (p. 14). This kind of additive approach suggests better physical and psychological health for both ethnic minority and ethnic majority persons (LaFromboise, Coleman, & Gerton, 1993).

Atkinson and colleagues (1998) point out that acculturation is related to the way that racial/ethnic minority clients view and respond to mental health services. They note that the research available suggests that "less acculturated racial/ethnic minorities are more likely to trust and express a preference for and a willingness to see an ethnically similar counselor than are their more acculturated counterparts" (p. 24). Acculturation and biculturalism seem to have important implications for the use of mental health services by racial/ethnic minority clients. Sue and Sue (1999) note that not only have racial/ethnic minority clients underused counseling services but that they have also tended to stop counseling often after only one contact with a therapist at a much higher rate than many Euro-American clients. Also, some ethnic minority clients receive lower quality and less frequent mental health services (Snowden & Cheung, 1990). Sue and Sue (1990) contend "that the reasons why minority-group individuals underutilize and prematurely terminate counseling/therapy lie in the biased nature of the services themselves," which "are frequently antagonistic or inappropriate to the life experiences" of clients from diverse cultural groups (p. 7).*

Smart and Smart (1995) point out that acculturation is pervasive, intense, of lifelong duration, and often results in various kinds of stress. Coleman (1995) concurs that learning to cope with diversity is stressful in and of itself and is augmented when variables such as race and ethnicity are added in. He notes that clients will use various strategies, varying from assimilation to separation, to cope with acculturation stress and also to manage the counseling relationship. If the helper and client use different strategies to cope with diversity, and the helper is not aware of or sensitive to the client's strategy, the helper runs the risk of using culturally inappropriate processes, goals, and strategies.

Acculturation and the Psychology of Oppression

Many clients have grown up in or have encountered in daily life an atmosphere of oppression—social, economic, and/or political. Traditionally, power has been held by Euro-American, upper-to-middle socioeconomic-level, non-disabled, heterosexual males, and clients who are outside this circle have encountered varying degrees of oppression. Das (1995) points out that in a multicultural or pluralistic society, cultures do not exist in isolation but influence one another. Therefore, contact with another culture leads to cultural change and a need for acculturation, although this acculturation "does not flow in a balanced way. Because of differences in power and status, people in the [United States] belonging to different racial and ethnic minorities are under greater pressure to acculturate to the more dominant (White) culture" (p. 49).

This pressure also applies to other groups, such as gays and lesbians, women, and persons with physical and mental challenges. As a result, not only are persons of the nondom-

---

FEEDBACK 2.2 — Personal Values

Perhaps your visualizations or role plays revealed to you that you may have certain biases and values about sex roles, age, cultures, race, physical appearance, and rape. Some of your biases may reflect your past experiences with a person or an incident. Most people in the helping professions agree that some of our values are communicated to clients, even unintentionally. Try to identify any values or biases you hold now that could communicate disapproval to a client or could keep you from "promoting the welfare" of your client. With yourself, a peer, or an instructor, work out a plan to reevaluate your biases or to help you prevent yourself from imposing your values on clients.

inant culture treated differentially and often denied equal access to opportunities, but they are also subject to both overt and covert forms of discrimination through oppression from the dominant group (see Freire, 1972). Oppression both widens the distance between various cultural groups and leads to conflict as well as intense feelings such as anger and hurt. Our experience has shown that well-meaning helpers of the mainstream cultural groups sometimes do not understand much about oppression and its effects on clients—such as the anger that the legacy of discrimination and oppression has created for some clients. As the writer Michael Dorris, who is of French, Modoc Indian, and Irish ancestry, notes,

> I think those who are tolerant and well-meaning have to realize that there is an enormous well of anger that must be expressed before the tolerance can become reciprocal. And that makes people from the dominant group wary and impatient.
>
> There is a long hiatus before trust comes and before the other side, the side that has borne the brunt of intolerance, can tolerate back. To expect that experience to accelerate just because the oppressors finally see the light is, I think, tremendously naive.
>
> We have to recognize that there needs to be a period of healing. Utopia is not just around the bend. What happens next is that the side that has been making the rules, defining the history, explaining conquered people to themselves in language that is not their own, has got to just shut up and listen. Ask questions, but don't just ask questions, because even the questions are ethnocentric. We must listen to what people say and not secretly think that they don't know what they're talking about. (1995, p. 15)

It is important for helping professionals to understand the psychology of oppression because it is part of the context that the client brings to counseling and other aspects of helping, and shapes part of the client's perceptions and views about the world, other people, and the helping process. Recognizing factors related to power, dominance, privilege, pressures to acculturate or conform, and institutionalized constraints or discrimination is part of developing critical consciousness. Reed and colleagues (1997, p. 51) offer the following definitions related to oppression-linked difference, relevant to today's practice. Assimilation emphasizes leaving one's "old" culture and blending into the new. Acculturation involves processes necessary to learn enough of the new culture to operate effectively and to "translate" and move successfully between the old and the new. Cultural relevance speaks to the degree of "fit" that a service or approach has to key aspects of another's culture. Cultural sensitivity involves levels of knowledge and skills that help people to understand cultures, especially those other than their own.

Cultural competence goes beyond this: having the skills necessary to assess situations and work across differences in culturally relevant ways. Cultural consciousness goes further still, with a recurring monitoring and scrutiny of our theory, language, thinking, and actions as they are culturally grounded. Critical consciousness includes not only culture but other dimensions of difference and dominance: embracing the need to continuously challenge and expand to move beyond our current knowledge and awareness towards multicultural knowledge and practice.

As part of the practice nexus, critical consciousness supports self-awareness of one's own values and assumptions as these relate to diversity and to including societal and environmental forces as targets for change in helping clients achieve their goals. These factors also come into play in the way that clients acquire a cultural identity, to which we turn next.

Cultural Identity Development

There appears to be a developmental process by which persons acquire an identity based on the particular racial/ethnic group or groups to which they belong. Although a number of specific ethnic-identity developmental models have been developed (Cross, 1971; Ruiz, 1990; Sue & Sue, 1971; Sue et al., 1998 provide excellent reviews), Atkinson and colleagues (1998) have summarized the process by which various racial/ethnic populations develop an identity. This is referred to as the "minority identity development" or MID model (Atkinson et al., 1998, p. 27). This model is based on a common experience of oppression and discrimination and helps explain how various ethnic groups see themselves and others in terms of their own culture and also the dominant culture. This is consistent with a definition of the term *minority* (Wirth, 1945; cited by Sue et al., 1998):

> a group of people who, because of physical or cultural characteristics, are singled out from the others in society in which they live for differential and unequal treatment, and who therefore regard themselves as objects of collective discrimination. (p. 347)

Thus, *minorities* refers to groups of people who share collective discrimination rather than to a numeric basis. The model has five stages. Although it is considered more a developmental process than a stage model, it is not irreversible, and not all persons move through it in the same way (Atkinson et al., 1998). These stages are summarized in Table 2.3.

White Americans also undergo cultural identity development. As with people of color, characteristics of white Amer-

TABLE 2.3 Summary of Minority Identity Development Model

Stage of minority development model	Attitude toward self	Attitude toward others of the same minority	Attitude toward others of different minority	Attitude toward dominant group
Stage 1: Conformity	Self-depreciating	Group-depreciating	Discriminatory	Group-appreciating
Stage 2: Dissonance	Conflict between self-depreciating and appreciating	Conflict between group-depreciating and group-appreciating	Conflict between dominant-held views of minority hierarchy and feelings of shared experience	Conflict between group-depreciating and group-appreciating
Stage 3: Resistance and Immersion	Self-appreciating	Group-appreciating	Conflict between feelings of empathy for other minority experiences and of culturo-centrism	Group depreciating
Stage 4: Introspection	Concern with basis of self-appreciation	Concern with nature of unequivocal appreciation	Concern with ethnocentric basis for judging others	Concern with the basis of group depreciation
Stage 5: Synergetic Articulation and Awareness	Self-appreciating	Group-appreciating	Group-appreciating	Selective appreciation

Source: Counseling American Minorities: A Cross-Cultural Perspective, (5th ed.), by Donald R. Atkinson, George Morten, and Derald Wing Sue. Copyright © 2002 The McGraw-Hill Companies. Reprinted with permission of the McGraw-Hill Companies.

icans' ethnic and/or socioreligious ancestry (e.g., English, Italian, Russian; Jewish, Amish, Mormon) may have substantial influence in construction of a personal or collective identity. In considering development of a racial identity, the experience of being white inherently brings with it socialization "in an environment in which members of their group (if not themselves personally) are privileged relative to others" (Helms & Cook, 1999, p. 89). Thus, cultural identity development for whites involves contending with racially ascribed privilege and entitlement. Helms and Cook (1999) present a process of development that takes into account individuals' recognition and struggle with sociopolitical dimensions of race in this society. A summary of this process in Box 2.2 depicts stages of development and evolution anchored at one end by relative obliviousness to or avoidance of racism or the sociopolitical implications of one's membership in the white group and, at the other end, informed positive socioracial group commitment and capacity to relinquish privileges associated with racism and one's membership in a "dominant" group.

Within a multicultural framework, there are a number of significant threads to be aware of. It is beyond the scope of this book to fully address socialization and related factors that differentially affect individuals and groups. For example, we know that there is a vast literature on sex and gender socialization and its impact on identity development—both positively and negatively. Unger and Crawford (1996; cited in Fassinger, 2000, p. 352) identified several overarching themes from this literature regarding persistent differences likely to affect gender-identity development. Males are consistently viewed and treated as the more valued sex. There is earlier and greater pressure for males to conform to gender roles than females, and this situation continues throughout childhood. Parents remain largely unaware of their differential treatment of daughters and sons. The different ways in which girls and boys are treated tend to produce patterns of nurturance, emotional sensitivity, and helplessness in girls, and efficacy and independence in boys. Children are not passive recipients of socialization but participate actively through expectations, behavioral choices, and views of the self. People are generally unaware of sociocultural mandates that dichotomize gender, dictate conformity, and punish deviance from social norms.

Understanding is also growing about ways that culture, minority status, and strains related to stigma affect lesbian, gay, and bisexual youths and adults. Cass (1979) and others have developed a homosexual-identity development model to describe the process by which gay men and lesbian women acquire their identity. Although framed in stage terms, this is not seen as fixed or absolutely universal,

BOX 2.2 SUMMARY OF WHITE RACIAL IDENTITY EGO STATUSES, EXAMPLES, AND INFORMATION PROCESSING STRATEGIES (IPS)

Status and Example

Contact Satisfaction with racial status quo, obliviousness to racism and one's participation in it. If racial factors influence life decisions, they do so in a simplistic fashion IPS: Obliviousness, denial, superficiality, and avoidance.

Example:
". . . the Balls have prided themselves on the ancestral image of compassion, emphasizing that masters tried as best they could not to separate slave families in sale; that no Ball masters perpetrated violence or engaged in master–slave sex. Ed Ball's research is viewed by some family members, especially the elderly ones, as a threat to long-held beliefs. Some would prefer not to know too many details about their ancestors' slave practices, one relative says" (Duke, 1994, p. 12).

Disintegration Disorientation and anxiety provoked by unresolvable racial moral dilemmas that force one to choose between own-group loyalty and humanism. May be stymied by life situations that arouse racial dilemmas. IPS: Suppression, ambivalence, and controlling.

Example:
"I was upset. I couldn't do anything for a couple of weeks . . . Was I causing more pain than healing? Was this somebody else's history, not mine? Was I an expropriator, as Stefani Zinerman [a Black woman newspaper editor] accuses me of being? Should I just stop [investigating my family's history of slave ownership] and let black [sic] people do their own history?" (Duke, 1994).

Reintegration Idealization of one's socioracial group; denigration and intolerance for other groups. Racial factors may strongly influence life decisions. IPS: Selective perception and negative outgroup distortion.

Example:
"When someone asks him, 'Don't you feel bad because your ancestors owned slaves?' his response is 'No, I don't feel bad because my ancestors owned slaves. I mean, get over it. If Ed wants to go around and apologize, Ed's free to go around and apologize. But quite frankly, Ed didn't own any slaves. He isn't responsible for slavery or anybody's misfortunes . . .' " (Duke, 1994, p. 24).

Pseudo-Independence Intellectualized commitment to one's own socioracial group and subtle superiority and tolerance of other socioracial groups as long as they can be helped to conform to White standards of merit. IPS: Selective perception, cognitive restructuring, and conditional regard.

Example:
"He has also said to them [the descendants of his family's slaves]: I am sorry . . . his mother, brother and a few other relatives believe the apology had a healing effect . . ." (Duke, 1994, p. 12).

Immersion The searching for an understanding of the personal meaning of Whiteness and racism and the ways by which one benefits from them as well as a redefinition of Whiteness. IPS: Hypervigilance, judgmental, and cognitive-affective restructuring.

Example:
"I'm interested to look at whiteness [sic] as carefully as white [sic] people look at blackness [sic]. As a white [sic] person, I'm interested to understand how my ethnicity [sic] has produced me as an individual . . . and how whiteness [sic] produces the majority experience of Americans. My plantation research might be a way for me to do this intellectually as a writer" (Duke, 1994, p. 12).

Emersion A sense of discovery, security, sanity, and group solidarity and pride that accompanies being with other White people who are embarked on the mission of rediscovering Whiteness. IPS: Sociable, pride, seeking positive group-attributes.

Example:
"But Ed's apology [for his family's ownership of slaves] produced positive reactions as well. Janet and Ted Ball, Ed's mother and brother, both were moved by [his apology]: 'I was crying too,' says Janet Ball . . . Ted Ball . . . says he whispered a private 'thank you' to his little brother. . . . He feels grateful to Ed 'for doing the hard work it took to get to the apology.' " (Duke, 1994, p. 24).

Autonomy Informed positive socioracial-group commitment, use of internal standards for self-definition, capacity to relinquish the privileges of racism. Person tries to avoid life options that require participation in racial oppression. IPS: Flexible and complex.

Example:
". . . It's [the exploration of his familial history of slave ownership] about me personally trying to find some way as a white [sic] person, quite apart from my family's history, to acknowledge what's happened in this country. I mean during the time that English-speaking people have been in this country, for more years were black [sic] people enslaved than not enslaved" (Duke, 1994, p. 25).

Note: Descriptions of racial identity statuses are adapted from Helms (1994). Racial identity ego statuses are listed in the order that they are hypothesized to evolve.
Source: Using Race and Culture in Counseling and Psychotherapy: Theory and Process, by J. E. Helms and D. A. Cook, pp. 90–91. Copyright 1999 Alyn & Bacon. Reprinted with permission.

but rather as illustrating some of the self/society contradictions and adaptation goals involved for lesbian, gay, and bisexual people.

People have multiple "statuses" and characteristics that make for multifaceted identity development. Some recent theorists are working to look at the combinations and intersections among factors such as race, ethnicity, gender, class, disability, and sexual orientation (Fouad & Brown, 2000; Robinson & Howard-Hamilton, 2000). These models are useful for practitioners in a number of ways. First, they help develop awareness of the role of stigma and oppression in the development of a client's cultural identity. As we discuss in Chapter 6, oppression is a major factor in the development of trust (and mistrust). Second, these models can help practitioners understand identity development issues for clients from historically disadvantaged, stigmatized, and/or underserved groups.

In a related vein, the models may be useful in helping clients to gain perspective about their identities, factors that have been influential, and choices that may not have been fully evident. For example, Vasquez (2000) cites a case of a young Chicano undergraduate she worked with clinically. In an effort to protect him from prejudice, his family had raised him in an upper-middle-class neighborhood and lifestyle, largely removed from the Chicano community. This seeming protective shield against prejudice was belied when the student was accused of cheating by a professor. It was eventually determined that a white student had cheated from the Chicano student and that the professor had based his accusation on an erroneous assumption. In counseling, the Chicano student noted feeling "better" than other Mexican American students and believed that to feel competent and successful, he needed detachment from "them" and his cultural group. Change strategies with him targeted his negative internalized stereotypes, "reformulating" his identification with his heritage, and participating in ethnic and cultural activities. Clearly, there is no one right answer or path to a healthy social identity. Ethnic identity is "part of a complex construct based on the social realms in which one interacts" (Vasquez, 2000, p. 121) and, in turn, is an important factor in the world views, self-construals, and well-being that each of us undertakes and experiences.

Cultural Competence and Guidelines for Working with Diverse Groups of Clients

Recent emphases in the training of helping professionals call for them to acquire a set of multicultural counseling competencies that include knowledge, attitudes and beliefs, and skills necessary to work effectively with diverse groups of clients (Das, 1995; Lum, 1996; Sue, Ivey, & Pedersen, 1996). A set of multicultural counseling competencies was developed in 1992 (Sue, Arredondo, & McDavis, 1992) and was recently operationalized (Arredondo et al., 1996). A summary of multicultural competencies applicable to a broad range of helpers and helping situations is provided by Hansen, Pepitone-Arreola-Rockwell, and Greene (2000), which also includes extensive literature citations supporting the specific competency guidelines.

There are many guidelines to consider in working effectively with issues of diversity. Space limits our ability to provide the breadth of what is available. We provide a few selected ones here, and we encourage you to pursue these and others to deepen your repertoire. Clearly, there is overlap, reflecting common themes of sensitivity when providing informed, effective practice to diverse groups of clients. However, also note some aspects of difference and oppression in the following guidelines, reflecting some of the unique components of diversity as they affect the helping process. We believe that these collectively provide constructive guides.

Kadushin and Kadushin (1997) identify characteristics of a culturally sensitive interviewer. These are broadly applicable to diversity, including but not limited to racial or ethnic culture, and are relevant across the spectrum of helping activities:

Culturally Sensitive Interviewer

1. The culturally sensitive interviewer approaches all interviewees of whatever cultural background with respect, warmth, acceptance, concern, interest, empathy, and due regard for individuality and confidentiality.
2. Culturally sensitive interviewers strive to develop an explicit awareness that they have a culture as a member of a particular racial or ethnic, gender, age, social class, occupational group as well as other characteristics and as such have been socialized to beliefs, attitudes, behaviors, stereotypes, biases, and prejudices that affect their behavior in the interview.
3. Having achieved such awareness, culturally sensitive interviewers are comfortably undefensive in their identity as a member of cultural groups.
4. Culturally sensitive interviewers are aware of the cultural factors in the interviewee's background that they need to recognize and accept as potential determinants of the interviewee's decision to come for help, the presentation and nature of the problem the client brings, and the choice of intervention.

5. The culturally sensitive interviewer is ready to acknowledge and undefensively and unapologetically raise for discussion cross-cultural factors affecting the interview.
6. Culturally sensitive interviewers recognize that the great variety of culturally distinct groups makes it impossible to have knowledge of all of them but accepts the obligation to study the cultural background of interviewees most frequently served.
7. Culturally sensitive interviewers are ready to acknowledge the limitations of their knowledge of an interviewee's cultural background and are ready to undefensively solicit help from the interviewee in learning what they need to know.
8. The culturally sensitive interviewer communicates an attitude that cultural differences are not better or worse but rather legitimately diverse, and respects such differences.
9. Culturally sensitive interviewers are aware of indigenous cultures' strengths, aware of culturally based community resources that might be a source of help, and aware that some kinds of help may be culturally inappropriate.
10. Culturally sensitive interviewers are aware of the problems of disenfranchisement, discrimination, and stigmatization frequently associated with minority group status.
11. Although sensitive to cultural factors that might be related to clients' problems, the culturally sensitive interviewer is aware that such factors may be central or peripheral to the situation of a particular client (a reminder of everyone's uniqueness). (adapted from the original list, pp. 347–348)

As we've noted, effective helping with diverse clients involves a critical consciousness of societal factors related to power and privilege, and a readiness to apply this understanding to practice goals such as empowerment and a collaborative work ethic. We find the following sets of guidelines instructive in their illustration of ways that these critical commitments translate into specific practice roles, skills, and attitudes along with the reality that people come with multiple forms of diversity and strengths as well as vulnerabilities. In GlenMaye's (1998) recommendations regarding empowerment of women, we can see not only deep understanding of gender issues but also relevance to other aspects of diversity:

- Practitioners must acknowledge and understand the role of oppression in the lives of women. This understanding will grow as practitioners themselves undergo the process of personal and political consciousness raising.
- The empowerment of women requires an environment of safety, trust, and support in which women are encouraged to believe in themselves and their own reality and to find their voice to speak their truth. The presence of other women is integral to the creation of this environment.
- Women must be given concrete opportunities to experience their own capability, strength, and worth. For instance, women who have experienced physical assault should be encouraged to find ways to experience bodily and emotional strength, and women who have experienced social indignities and assaults, such as homelessness, poverty, or racism, should be presented with opportunities to regain dignity and worth.
- Though empowerment for women is fundamentally related to autonomy and self-determination, women must also work together to change themselves and society. Rather than work merely for individual solutions to individual problems, practitioners must find ways to bring women together and to work with women clients toward social change.
- The many roles of the practitioner in empowerment practice include educator, supporter, advocate, activist, option clarifier, facilitator of concrete experiences of power, and model of lived empowerment. (pp. 49–50)

Finally, we offer principles for practice written specifically for empowerment practice with people who have severe and persistent mental disability (adapted from Manning, 1998). We find these guides a useful reminder that diversity takes many forms; one can see not only relevance for people with physical disabilities but also other characteristics that may serve to disempower or marginalize people. These guides remind us that people have "whole lives" to take into consideration and that collaborative, respectful helping can and should be a bedrock commitment although, clearly, neither simply or easily actualized. See if you can envision ways that these implications for helper attitudes, relationship, and roles will affect your own practice.

- *Attitudes.* Think of and interact with the person, not the label/diagnosis. Respect the person's right to self-determination. Be responsible to the "whole person," taking quality of life and environmental factors into account. Focus on a strength perspective rather than a deficit model for assessment and practice. Respect the diversity of skills and knowledge that consumers bring to the relationship. Let go of being the "expert." Trust consumers' internal

LEARNING ACTIVITY 2.3 Diversity

This activity, adapted from Wilson and Stith (1993), is designed to help you expand your awareness of your own cultural group and of other groups as well. You may wish to do this with a partner or in a small group.

1. Describe your awareness of the historical and current experience of your own cultural group and any of the following groups that are not representative of your cultural group:
    African American/Black
    American Indian/Native American
    Asian American/Asian
    Euro-American/White
    Latino/Latina

2. Describe the value systems and variations in family norms for your own cultural group and also for any of the following groups that are not representative of your cultural group:
    African American/Black
    American Indian/Native American
    Asian American/Asian
    Euro-American/White
    Latino/Latina

3. Describe current examples of *stereotyping* and *oppression* for your own cultural group and also for any of the above groups that are not representative of your cultural group.

---

motivation to learn and direct their lives. Respect consumers' ability and right to contribute—to you, to other consumers, to the agency/organization, and to the community. Recognize the individuality of people, respecting each person's unique qualities, values, and needs.

- *Relationship.* Practice according to a partnership model. Develop "power with and among" rather than "power over" in relationships with consumers. Allow time for a process of relationship building and growth. See the relationship as ongoing, not time limited. Deemphasize the professional role. Be genuine, spontaneous, and real. Work for active participation from consumer and practitioner. Share leadership; value the leadership the consumer brings to the role.

- *Helper role.* Develop a client-driven model of care focused on the goals and values held by the consumer. Emphasize building connections through roles, involvement, and community to replace lost culture, history, and identity. Develop opportunities for meaningful activities that help to build skills, knowledge, and reflexive thinking. Enhance consumers' ability to transform their environment rather than adapt to it. Engage consumers in taking risks, making decisions, and learning from them. Emphasize information, education, and skill-building that increases self-efficacy. Involve consumers and family members in decision-making roles in the relationship and within the organization. (adapted from Manning, 1998, pp. 105–106)

The importance of becoming familiar with the beliefs and practices of persons with backgrounds different from your own cannot be overestimated. For example, if you are working with a client who believes in reincarnation, or who believes his or her grades have brought shame to the family, or who is being silent and nondisclosive as a sign of respect, or whose life is affected daily by a chronic and limiting disability, you run the risk of alienating the client if you are either ignorant or nonempathic about such issues. See Learning Activity 2.3 for an exercise in this regard.

Some members of the helping professions now believe in culturally sensitive therapy so strongly that it has become part of ethical codes of behavior and guidelines for practice. For example, an American Psychological Association (APA) task force has produced "Guidelines to Providers of Psychological Services to Ethnic, Linguistic, and Culturally Diverse Populations" (APA, 1993). The newest American Counselors Association (ACA) code of ethics contains a separate section on respecting diversity (ACA, 1995). In spite of these advances, a recent survey of APA members who had completed doctoral programs in clinical, counseling, and school psychology showed that very few respondents felt competent to provide adequate counseling services to ethnic minority and diverse clients (Allison, Crawford, Echemendia, Robinson, & Knepp, 1994).

As Allison and colleagues (1994) note, "To expand the training of therapists beyond meeting the needs of YAVIS (i.e., young, attractive, verbal, intelligent, and successful) clients (Schoefield, 1964) and to prepare therapies to meet the mental health needs of an increasingly diverse population will require a continuing appreciation of the dimensions of human difference" (p. 793). At the end of this chapter, we provide a list of excellent multicultural readings and Web sites as Suggested Resources and have attempted to integrate a diversity focus throughout this book. You will reflect on and grapple with these and other complex issues throughout your professional career (not to mention your personal life). You are dynamic and continually evolving, as is our society. Thus, rather than static lists of "right answers" per se, we all need knowledge, skills, reflective capacity, and checks and balances external to ourselves to support sensitive, effective, and ethical decision making and action in contexts of change and complexity.

Ethical Issues

In some respects, this entire chapter is about ethical practice. Because ethics in the helping professions often refers to rules, standards, or principles applied to govern conduct, we now turn to some key ethical issues and resources that have wide relevance. As with other topics, we include resource information to aid you in locating further guidance.

Client Welfare

Attentiveness to ethical principles and adherence to ethical standards speak to critical commitments within the practice nexus. Helpers are obligated to protect the welfare of their clients. In most instances, this means putting the client's needs first. It also means ensuring that you are intellectually and emotionally ready to give the best that you can to each client—or to see that the client has a referral option if seeing you is not in the client's best interests.

The helping relationship needs to be handled in such a way as to promote and protect the client's welfare. There are many dimensions to protecting client welfare, including how the helping or therapeutic relationship is handled. As Brammer, Abrego, and Shostrom (1993) observe, ethical handling of client relationships is a distinctive mark of the professional helper/therapist.

All professional groups of helpers have a code of ethics adopted by their profession, such as the ethical standards of the American Counseling Association (1995), the American Psychological Association (1992), the National Association of Social Workers (1996), the National Organization for Human Service Education, and the National Board for Certified Counselors Standards for the Ethical Practice of WebCounseling. Marriage and family therapists, rehabilitation counselors, school counselors, health care providers, and other helping professionals have their own sets of ethical standards. In Chapter 1 we provide Web sites for a cross-section of professional helping groups. We encourage you to access these sites for the ethical guidelines and standards of practice.

The helper's value system is an important factor in determining ethical behavior. Behaving unethically can result in loss of membership in professional organizations or malpractice lawsuits. Of greatest consequence is the detrimental effect that unethical behavior can have on clients and on the helping relationship.

All helping practitioners should be familiar with the ethical codes of their profession. The following discussion highlights a few of the more critical issues and in no way is intended to be a substitute for careful scrutiny of existing ethical codes of behavior.

Ethical Decision-Making Models

Professional ethical codes provide one set of guidance about ethical expectations, roles, and responsibilities. Many practitioners have found that these do not always translate into clear decision making or problem solving when grappling with specific ethical dilemmas. Thus, there has been considerable effort to devise decision-making tools to assist in systematically sorting out issues, options, and priorities. For example, Kitchener (1984) argued for the need to move from a rule-bound approach to ethics to one that focuses on ethical principles, such as autonomy (respect for the right to make one's own decisions as long as competent to do so), nonmaleficence (do no harm), beneficence (helping others), justice (fairness), and fidelity (honesty, reliability). These and related principles have been the basis of several additional models and discussions (see Kitchener & Anderson, 2000, for a review), focusing largely on a critical–evaluative basis for determining what professional helpers ought to do. Recently, there has been considerable attention to issues of virtue or character—virtue ethics and how these may shape conceptions of moral behavior. For example, Meara, Schmidt, and Day (1996) focus on factors such as motivation, emotion, character, ideals, and moral habits, arguing for the need to go beyond models of ethics based on rules and principles of practice.

Our emphasis is on normative applied ethics, particularly topics widely encountered in various forms of helping practice. Drawing on the work of several ethicists, Kenyon (1999) has developed a pragmatic model for working through an ethical dilemma. Summarized in Table 2.4, this model walks a practitioner through assessment questions and planning, implementation, and evaluation steps designed to carefully undertake decision making with the best interests of client welfare in mind. As we have seen in this chapter, a commitment to ethics is critical to practice, but often complex and difficult. Although ethics involves high level abstraction about values, duties, and principles, we hope that this tangible tool will be useful in helping you hone your abil-

TABLE 2.4 An Ethical Decision-Making Model

Step	Considerations to be addressed
1. Describe the issue	Describe the ethical issue or dilemma.
	Who is involved? What is their involvement? How are they related?
	Whose dilemma is it?
	What is involved? What is at risk?
	What are the relevant situational features?
	What type of issue is it?
2. Consider ethical guidelines	Consider all available ethical guidelines and legal standards.
	Identify your own personal values relevant to the issue.
	Identify societal or community values relevant to the issue.
	Identify relevant professional standards.
	Identify relevant laws and regulations.
	Apply these guidelines.
3. Examine the conflicts	Examine any conflicts.
	Describe the conflicts you are experiencing internally.
	Describe the conflicts you are experiencing that are external.
	Decide whether you can minimize any of these conflicts.
4. Resolve the conflicts	Seek assistance with your decision if needed.
	Consult with colleagues, faculty, or supervisors.
	Review relevant professional literature.
	Seek consultation from professional organizations or available ethics committees.
5. Generate action alternatives	Generate all possible courses of action.
6. Examine and evaluate the action alternatives	Consider the client's and all other participants' preferences based on a full understanding of their values and ethical beliefs.
	Eliminate alternatives that are inconsistent with the client's and significant others' values and beliefs.
	Eliminate alternatives that are inconsistent with other relevant guidelines.
	Eliminate alternatives for which there are no resources or support.
	Eliminate remaining action alternatives that don't pass tests based on the ethical principles of universality, publicity, and justice.
	Predict the possible consequences of the remaining acceptable action alternatives.
	Prioritize (rank) the remaining acceptable action alternatives.
7. Select and evaluate the preferred action	Select the best course of action.
	Evaluate your decision.
8. Plan the action	Develop an action plan and implement the action.
9. Evaluate the outcome	Evaluate the action taken and the outcome.
10. Examine the implications	What have you learned? Are there implications for future ethical decision making?

Source: What Would You Do? (3rd ed.) by P. Kenyon, ©1999. Reprinted with permission of Brooks/Cole, an imprint of the Wadsworth Group, a division of Thomson Learning.

ity to undertake reasoning about ethical practice with increasing ease and confidence (See Learning Activity 2.4).

Confidentiality

Closely related to protecting client well-being is the issue of confidentiality. Helpers who breach client confidences can do serious and often irreparable harm to the helping relationship. Practitioners are generally not free to reveal or disclose information about clients unless they have first received written permission from the client. Exceptions vary from state to state but generally include the following, as summarized by Corey and colleagues (1998) and Vasquez (1993):

- If client poses a danger to self or others, including but not limited to duty to warn or protect
- If the client waives rights to privilege

- If the helper suspects abuse or neglect of a minor, an elderly or disabled person, or a resident of an institution
- If a court orders a helper to make records available
- If the client is deemed to have waived confidentiality by bringing a lawsuit
- If the client is involved in legal action and the client releases records
- If an emergency exists

Other types of exceptions in the course of providing services include clerical staff handling case documents, consultation, and supervision of the professional helper. All these limits should be addressed by helpers, and many require a disclosure statement, which the client is given at the beginning of helping services.

On June 13, 1996, in the United States Supreme Court case *Jaffee v. Redmond,* the concept of confidentiality was explored by the Court. It ruled that communications between therapists and their clients are privileged and therefore protected from forced disclosure in cases arising under federal law. Although this was an important affirmation, some see its practical impact as limited. As Shuman and Foote (1999) note, informing clients that helpers have valuable information, but that courts cannot have that information unless the clients say so, is unlikely to keep the courts at bay.

Jaffee reminds helpers to include discussion of likely contexts in which service providers may be expected to disclose information about clients to others. This is particularly salient in light of at least one study finding that, regardless of individual personality traits or demographic background, clients and students were less willing to be candid under a managed care context than in a standard fee-for-service setting due to confidentiality concerns (Kremer & Gesten, 1998). Confidentiality limits of managed care prompt these authors to offer the following practical suggestions in working with clients (Kremer & Gesten, 1998, p. 557):

- Provide your clients with a first session discussion of the information requirements and utilization review practices governing their therapy.
- Be certain your clients are informed by actively questioning their understanding of requirements and practices.
- If the managed care organization provides forms that delineate requirements and procedures, carefully review them with your clients before signing.
- Inform your clients about potential repercussions from disclosure of sensitive material.
- Plan for utilization review, provide only the necessary minimum of information required to secure appropriate treatment for your clients—avoid dramatic details and extensive explanations.
- Advocate for your clients by working to change managed care practices which limit or interfere with treatment.
- Always document interactions with utilization reviewers or managed care officials.

Although written with managed care in mind, these guides are relevant across a great many helping and institutional contexts.

A recent issue involving the limits of confidentiality has to do with whether the client who tests positive for the human immunodeficiency virus (HIV) is regarded as a danger to others. Consider the case example presented by Chenneville (2000):

> You have been seeing Michael Smith in therapy for the past 3 months. Michael is 33 years old and has been married for 8 years. He has two children, a boy and girl, ages 3 and 5, respectively. Michael admitted to you in the course of therapy that he had an affair with his neighbor several years ago. His wife never found out about the affair, which lasted approximately 6 months. Michael recently discovered that the woman with whom he had an affair died of AIDS. This prompted Michael to have an HIV test, the results of which were positive. Michael told you he has no intention of telling his wife about his test result. (p. 665)

What are the issues involved here? What questions need to be posed to fully assess the issues? Options for intervention? Ethical obligations? Would these issues be viewed differently if the client had different circumstances? If so, why, in what ways, and what would be the implications?

The ethical conflicts between duty to protect and duty to maintain confidentiality and work in the client's best interests take many forms. Because states vary as to their laws regarding HIV and confidentiality, and laws differ in what medical professionals and counseling or psychotherapy professionals are allowed, it is important to be informed about laws in your state. There are complex ethical, legal, and therapeutic issues surrounding this question as well as conflicting positions about how to interpret and apply legal criteria and ethical codes. For example, Schlossberger and Hecker (1996) conclude that although the therapist has a legal duty to warn specifically identifiable potential victims subject to a clear and imminent danger (based on a case known as the Tarasoff Case), the therapist has no duty to intervene when clients pose dangers that society, through law, grants them the right to pose unless state law requires seropositive clients to inform their partners. Corey and colleagues (1998) present an overview of positions, including a growing emphasis on the practitioner's responsibility to potential victims of clients' harmful acts along with negligence in failure to diagnose the potential for danger or to warn when an assessment of high danger has been made.

For those with interest in more detailed reading about practical steps to take, Corey and colleagues (1998) and Chenneville (2000) present recommendations for helpers, and Melchert and Patterson (1999) detail an assessment and intervention model based on integration of ethical and legal principles with information about the level of risk associated with clients' behavior (e.g., the HIV status of the client and the sexual or needle-sharing partners' awareness of the client's HIV status).

Confidentiality also has implications for effective multicultural practice. Lum (1996) points out that in a multicultural practice, the ethical value of confidentiality needs to be carefully explained to clients, for variations about the understanding of this principle exist within different cultural groups. In addition, today's context of managed care heightens the importance of informing clients about the limits of confidentiality. For example, clients may not be aware that insurance companies or HMOs do not necessarily maintain the same level of confidentiality as do professional helpers (Bennett, Bryant, VandenBos, & Greenwood, 1990).

Managed care reviewers are not necessarily bound by the same ethical codes or obligations as service providers, and they can also introduce vulnerabilities for breach of confidentiality in unsecured forms of communication, such as phone messages, e-mail, and fax. Although this subject is beyond the scope of this book, we urge you to explore ethical issues such as those related to confidentiality in your practice settings. To aid you, Cooper and Gottlieb (2000) provide a useful overview of challenging ethical issues within managed care.

Although managed care introduces serious challenges, we urge that you undertake a careful, critical assessment of any workplace. Woody (1999) reminds us that the risk of unintended violations of confidentiality affects us all. Whether you are in a home-based office or in work settings sharing space or equipment, consider the pitfalls associated with shared computers or LANS (local area networks), e-mail accounts, fax machines, mailboxes, and work spaces (whether the family dining table or a conference room) as well as accidental revelation by others (e.g., family members or nontherapist workers).

Multiple Relationships

Dual or multiple relationships arise when the practitioner is in a professional helping relationship with the client and simultaneously or consecutively has one or more other kinds of relationships with that same person, such as an administrative, instructional, supervisory, social, sexual, or business relationship. Multiple role relationships can be subtle and are significant sources of complaints regarding ethics. Such relationships are problematic because they can reduce the counselor's objectivity, confuse the issue, put the client in a position of diminished consent and potential abandonment, foster discomfort, and expose the client and practitioner to negative judgments or responses by others. Professional helpers should avoid becoming involved in dual relationships. If such involvement is unavoidable, make use of the referral option so that various relationships are not carried on simultaneously or consecutively.

Sometimes multiple relationships are unavoidable, such as in smaller communities where helpers in therapeutic or other roles are more likely to know clients in other contexts and are less likely to be able to refer clients elsewhere. Consider the many ways in which your life touches others—through children, neighbors, extended family, participation with various groups and organizations, and leisure pursuits—and you are likely to see how easy if not inescapable multiple role relationships can be at some point in time. Earlier we also pointed out that multiple role relationships may arise in instances in which a client's cultural and social values support multiple roles with a help-giving person. In instances when multiple role relationships cannot be avoided, it is important to seek face-to-face supervision and consultation about the issue. It is also important to document your discussion (Smith & Fitzpatrick, 1995).

Kitchener and Anderson (2000) identify factors to help gauge the relative danger or negative potential of various possible types of multiple role relationships. Using social theory (Kitchener, 1988), they note that when role expectations conflict or when the power differential is substantial, the potential danger of harm to clients is particularly high, however unintended it may be. For example, learning that a client's child is on the soccer team you coach involves one level of harm potential, contrasted to circumstances such as the client being a subordinate in an organizational hierarchy or in a role within one's religious organization or some other, more personal domain of each other's lives (e.g., financial investment partners or support group members). Multiple role relationship issues extend past therapy.

Drawing from several ethicists' work, Kitchener and Anderson (2000, adapted from p. 55) identify several reasons for avoiding posttherapy relationships. Although framed in therapeutic language, these extend to a range of types of helping practice and relationships: The former client may at some point wish to return to therapy with the therapist, which would be prohibited or at least unwise after a posttherapy relationship, depending on the specifics. The power differential may continue—leaving some clients vulnerable to exploitation after termination. Clients develop strong feelings toward their therapists that, along with the power differential, are a powerful combination that may lead to poor objectivity by the former client, which in turn can result in exploitation by the therapist. The posttherapy relationship could go poorly; thus, the former client might reevaluate his or her trust in psychology and/or helping practitioners. When the general public views posttherapy relationships, they may believe that professional boundaries are diffuse and casual. Therapist objectivity for future professional service, such as testifying in court on the former client's behalf, may be compromised by the posttherapy relationship. Clients may hold back information because they assume that some type of posttherapy relationship may ensue after termination. In some states, posttherapy relationships are illegal, depending on the nature of the relationship.

Under no circumstances should you agree to offer professional services when you can foresee clearly that a prior existing relationship would create harm or injury in any way. Obviously, sexual contact between practitioner and client is never warranted under any circumstance and is explicitly proscribed by all the professional codes of ethics. Smith and Fitzpatrick (1995) also address the failure to maintain appropriate treatment boundaries by the use of excessive self-disclosure on the practitioner's part. They note that this behavior is a common precursor to practitioner-initiated sexual contact: "Typically, there is a gradual erosion of treatment boundaries before sexual activity is initiated. Inappropriate therapist self-disclosure, more than any other kind of boundary violation, most frequently precedes therapist-patient sex" (p. 503). Sexual intimacy with former clients also raises ethical questions of exploitation. States vary in their positions regarding prohibition in terms of the amount of time following the termination of treatment.

Client Rights

Establishing an effective helping relationship entails being open with clients about their rights and options during the course of therapy. Nothing can be more damaging to trust and rapport than to have the client discover in midstream that the practitioner is not qualified to help with a particular issue, that the financial costs of therapy or other forms of helping are high, or that services involve certain limitations or nonguarantees of outcomes. At the outset, the practitioner should provide the client with enough information about therapy to help the client make informed choices (also called "empowered consent").

A general consensus is developing about what should be disclosed to clients, including (1) the kind of service, treatment, or testing being provided; (2) the risks and benefits of the service, treatment, or testing; (3) the logistics involved, such as length of appointments, number of sessions, canceling appointments, and costs; (4) information about the qualifications and practices of the helper; (5) risks and benefits of alternatives to the treatment, service, or test or of forgoing it; (6) the limits of confidentiality; and (7) emergency problems (Kitchener & Anderson, 2000). Depending on the diversity factors involved, we would add the importance of identifying available resources and sources of help that may be particularly relevant—for example, indigenous helpers, translators, consultants, and cultural or shared-experience networks or support groups.

Needless to say, an additional layer of considerations arises when children or other vulnerable groups are involved. For example, particular care is needed regarding consent when working with children or those with limited cognitive functioning. Laws are often unclear whether adolescents should be treated as adults or children when it comes to consent issues (Kitchener, 1999), and, of course, children and youth vary greatly as to their capacity to provide truly informed consent. Assent is less ambiguous in that it addresses children and young people's expressed willingness to participate in a described treatment or research activity. Kitchener and Anderson (2000) provide a useful overview of issues regarding informed consent not only with school-age youth and adolescents, but with other vulnerable populations as well.

Referral

We address referral more fully later in the book as part of goal selection and treatment planning. Here we speak to the importance of handling referral ethically and responsibly. Referring a client to another practitioner may be necessary when, for one reason or another, you are not able to provide the service or care that the client requires or when the client wants another helper (Cheston, 1991). However, careful referral involves more than just giving the client the name of another person or agency. The client should be given a choice among service providers who are competent and are qualified to deal with the client's problems or circumstances. In your recommendations and reasoning, you should respect your client's self-determination, along with the client's interest. The practitioner must obtain written client permission before discussing the case with the new service provider. Some clients may require assistance in understanding and/or taking steps to access the referral—with implications for the kinds of roles that helpers may need to undertake (such as advocacy or resource brokering). And to protect against aban-

LEARNING ACTIVITY 2.4 — Ethical Dilemmas

This activity, from Kenyon (1999), is designed to help you "walk through" an ethical dilemma relevant to your own practice, consider various dimensions, develop a plan for action, and discuss it with your student colleagues and instructor.

The issue. Describe one ethical dilemma that you find to be particularly troubling in your role as a student or professional in human services. Include as much detail (as many facts) as you can.

Ethical guidelines. What values, principles, and other guidelines are relevant?

Conflicts. Describe the conflicts. What makes it a dilemma?

Resolving the conflicts. What assistance have you sought with this decision? Did you get that assistance?

Action alternatives. What options are there?

Selecting and evaluating an action. Has this issue been resolved?

Implications. If it hasn't been resolved, why not? If it has been resolved, what do you think—ethically—of that resolution?

Class Discussion

1. Report the issues and dilemmas you've identified. There will probably be some that are shared among you.
2. On an issue-by-issue basis, explore the ethical guidelines, action alternatives, and selection and evaluation of action.
3. For each issue, is there substantial agreement among you, or do you disagree? Is that OK, or does it represent an ethical problem?

---

donment, the practitioner should follow up on the referral to determine whether impediments were encountered or assistance in making the contact is desired. Also, referrals are mandated in situations in which the services of the practitioner could be interrupted because of illness, death, relocation, financial limitations, or any other form of unavailability (Vasquez, 1994). Before we turn to emerging issues in ethics, it may be useful to walk through an ethical dilemma as preparation for your current practice (see Learning Activity 2.4).

Emerging Issues in Ethics

We are all aware of the many ways in which our society is changing, and ethical issues are part of these changes. Diversification in terms of racial demographics, immigrants from dissimilar parts of the world, the aging of the "baby boom" generation, new or growing types of counseling issues (e.g., associated with HIV/AIDS, violence, child welfare, the biomedical arena), and factors associated with managed care all contribute to complex ethical challenges. Cooper and Gottlieb (2000) summarize expected trends in systems of care in coming years that hold implications for ethics:

- larger, more multidisciplinary health care practices (and fewer independent practices)
- growing emphasis on business principles to guide decision making regarding use of health care resources
- fewer and larger managed care organizations
- increased use of outpatient mental health, in part due to increasing costs of inpatient care
- increased attention to preventive approaches
- increased use of group therapy, especially psychoeducational groups
- increased treatment planning, with focus on outcome measurement and attention to evidence base regarding which interventions appear to work best with whom, with what type of problem—"differential therapies"
- increased trend toward manualizing (detailing activities, sequences, time periods of specific therapeutic strategies) interventions and specifying those associated with diagnostic categories

Finally, no discussion of ethics is complete without attention to technology and the helping services. We address technology throughout the book, but it is important to note that as technology grows and evolves, so too must our capacity to ethically harness its use. McMinn, Buchanan, Ellens, and Ryan's (1999) survey of professional helpers to assess the occurrence and perceived ethicality of 40 technology uses is instructive in the extent of equivocal ratings of ethicality and the apparent need for guidelines and training (see Box 2.3). Consider how this will continue. For example, of these 40 technology uses, some may not yet have high levels of occurrence (such as using a computer to take notes during therapy or using computer-assisted therapy or other aids as an adjunct to traditional interventions), but will undoubtedly increase in the future, and others not yet foreseen will emerge (Schoech, 1999).

Ethical considerations related to technology can be particularly challenging in that emerging applications involve

BOX 2.3 EXAMPLES OF TECHNOLOGY USE IN PROFESSIONAL PRACTICE

1. Personally photocopying confidential client information
2. Having secretarial staff photocopy confidential client information
3. Retrieving audible messages from an answering machine in the presence of colleagues
4. Retrieving audible messages from an answering machine in the presence of support staff
5. Retrieving audible messages from an answering machine in the presence of clients
6. Failing to receive client messages due to equipment failure or technical problems
7. Providing regularly scheduled clinical services via telephone
8. Providing consultation for a colleague via telephone
9. Providing clinical supervision via telephone
10. Providing crisis intervention via telephone
11. Providing clinical services on telephone while charging via a 1-900 number
12. Faxing confidential information to another psychologist's office
13. Faxing client information to a hospital floor
14. Inadvertently faxing confidential client information to an incorrect location
15. Using a computer to take notes during therapy
16. Storing therapy records on a personal computer
17. Storing therapy records on a computer network
18. Storing clients' financial records on a personal computer
19. Storing clients' financial records on a computer network
20. Using a computer to generate client bills
21. Electronic (paperless) claim filing with insurance companies
22. Losing client records due to a computer failure
23. Allowing unauthorized access to confidential client records (e.g., by a computer hacker)
24. Leaving confidential client information displayed on a computer monitor where other clients might see it
25. Using computer-assisted therapy as an adjunct to traditional therapy
26. Using computer-assisted therapy in lieu of traditional therapy
27. Providing direct clinical services on the Internet
28. Advertising psychological services on the Internet
29. Providing direct clinical services via e-mail
30. Providing consultation for a colleague via e-mail
31. Providing clinical supervision via e-mail
32. Using computerized test administration software
33. Using computerized test-scoring software
34. Using computerized test interpretation software
35. Relying on computer software for diagnosis
36. Allowing professionals other than psychologists access to computerized assessment tools
37. Using teleconferencing for psychotherapy
38. Using teleconferencing for consultation
39. Using teleconferencing for clinical supervision
40. Using virtual reality in treating an anxiety disorder

Source: "Technology, Professional Practice, and Ethics: Survey Findings and Implications," by M. R. McMinn, T. Buchanan, B. M. Ellens, M. K. Ryan, *Professional Psychology: Research and Practice,* 30, p. 166, Table 1. Copyright 1999 by the American Psychological Association. Reprinted with permission of the publisher and author.

factors or circumstances without clear precedence or without an experience base to guide protections. We have included in the "Suggested Resources" for this chapter a Web site for a set of standards to guide Internet or Web counseling. There are now several such ethical codes among professional groups, reflecting heightened awareness and usage. In addition to online or "cybercounseling," there are techno–ethical considerations with quite a range of counseling-related activities at the individual helper level (such as use of computer-assisted assessment or therapy tools, use of assistive technology in professional helping, and information sharing across professional helpers) as well as at the institutional and macro levels (such as technology use in supervision, distance learning, virtual training, and data management and storage).

Peterson, Murray, and Chan (1998) provide a thoughtful overview of ethics and technology relative to professional helping in counseling and clinical roles. They note the dual importance of continuing vigilance regarding techno–ethical risks as well as opportunities for important advancements in effective and accessible helping. They present a case example of the potential of assistive technology: A school counselor is working with a child referred due to behavioral problems. The counselor discovered that a mobility impairment involving limited use of her arms was preventing the student from participating in many class activities. The counselor's knowledge of computer assistive technology—in this case a mouth stick and "sticky keys" software—opened up options for the student to participate, yielding a fuller and more rewarding communicative and learning experience. The student's class performance improved dramatically, and her behavioral problems diminished. Although important, this example is more obvious and perhaps more comfortable than some other applications that more deeply penetrate helper roles, relationships, or expertise. In addition to safeguarding client rights and protections, we as professional helpers also have the challenge of managing our own attitudes, anxieties, or vested interests should these pose unreasonable impediments to the appropriate use of technology in the service of clients and their needs. In following chapters, we will look at some specific examples with respect to interviewing and change strategies.

SUMMARY

Part of being an effective helper is knowing yourself so that you can use yourself as a creative, critical thinker who can work with clients toward meeting their goals. This self-awareness includes insight into one's values, strengths, and challenges but also extends to a fuller awareness of how you as an individual helper and change agent are part of the practice nexus—the idea that each of us brings a somewhat unique set of connections among knowledge, skills, commitments, diversity, and collaborative effectiveness. Ideally, this awareness enables you to respond to each client as a unique person, to develop understanding of clients who have different values from you, and to work in adaptive, collaborative ways with clients whose heritage may differ from your own in one or more significant ways. Finally, your self-awareness and context awareness should foster an appreciation of the balances to be struck in applying an ethical code of behavior in today's practice and pursuing an active role as a lifelong learner to contemporize and strengthen practice.

INFOTRAC® EXPLORATIONS

1. Search for the term *multicultural*. Select three to five articles that are relevant to helping practice, and examine how the articles refer to and use the term *multicultural*. What differences and similarities do you see? What components (attitude, comfort, skills, and knowledge) do you see most readily achievable? Which components would benefit from additional training or guidance?
2. Search for *ethics* in combination with an InfoTrac® option such as social science or science. Note the aspects of ethics highlighted in these articles. How do these ethical dimensions compare to what counseling professionals are most attuned to?

SUGGESTED RESOURCES

Readings

Arthur, G. L., & Swanson, C. P. (1993). *Confidentiality and privileged communication.* Alexandria, VA: American Counseling Association.

Atkinson, D. R., Morten, G., & Sue, D. W. (1998). *Counseling American minorities* (5th ed.). Boston, MA: McGraw-Hill.

Axelson, J. (1999). *Counseling and development in a multicultural society* (3rd ed.). Pacific Grove, CA: Brooks/Cole.

Bennett, B. E., Bryant, B. K., VandenBos, G. R., & Greenwood, A. (1990). *Professional liability and risk management.* Washington, DC: American Psychological Association.

Brems, C. (2001). *Basic skills in psychotherapy and counseling.* Belmont, CA: Brooks/Cole.

Corey, G., Corey, M., & Callanan, P. (1998). *Issues and ethics in the helping professions* (5th ed.). Pacific Grove, CA: Brooks/Cole.

Dworkin, S. H., & Gutiérrez, F. J. (1992). *Counseling gay men and lesbians.* Alexandria, VA: American Counseling Association.

Enns, C. Z. (2000). Gender issues in counseling. In S. D. Brown & R. W. Lent (Eds.), *Handbook of counseling psychology* (3rd ed., pp. 601–638). New York: Wiley.

Fouad, N. A., & Brown, M. T. (2000). Role of race and social class in development: Implications for counseling psychology. In S. D. Brown & R. W. Lent (Eds.), *Handbook of counseling psychology* (3rd ed., pp. 379–408). New York: Wiley.

Gilbert, L. A., & Scher, M. (1999). *Gender and sex in counseling and psychotherapy.* Boston: Allyn & Bacon.

Grohol, J. M. (2000). *The insider's guide to mental health resources online.* New York: Guilford (http://www.insidemh.com).

Ivey, A. E., Ivey, M. B., & Simek-Morgan, L. (1998). *Counseling and psychotherapy: A multicultural perspective.* Needham Heights, MA: Allyn & Bacon.

Kadushin, A., & Kadushin, G. (1997). *The social work interview: A guide for human service professionals* (4th ed.). New York: Columbia University Press.

Kenyan, P. (1999). *What would you do? An ethical case workbook for human service professionals.* Pacific Grove, CA: Brooks/Cole.

Kitchener, K. S., & Anderson, S. K. (2000). Ethical issues in counseling psychology: Old themes—new problems. In S. D. Brown & R. W. Lent (Eds.), *Handbook of counseling psychology* (3rd ed., pp. 50–82). New York: Wiley.

Lum, D. (2000). *Social work practice and people of color.* Pacific Grove, CA: Brooks/Cole.

Manning, S. S. (1998). Empowerment in mental health programs: Listening to the voices. In L. M. Gutiérrez, R. J. Parsons, & E. O. Cox (Eds.), *Empowerment in social work practice: A sourcebook* (pp. 89–109). Pacific Grove, CA: Brooks/Cole.

Marinelli, R., & Dell Orto, A. (Eds.). (1999). *The psychological and social impact of disability* (4th ed.). New York: Springer.

Perez, R. M., Debord, K. A., & Bieschke, K. J. (Eds.). (2000). *Handbook of counseling and psychotherapy with lesbian, gay, and bisexual clients.* Washington, DC: American Psychological Association.

Peterson, D. B., Murray, G. C., & Chan, F. (1998). Ethics and technology. In R. Cottone & V. M. Tarvydas (Eds.), *Ethical and professional issues in counseling* (pp. 196–235). Upper Saddle River, NJ: Prentice Hall.

Robinson, T. L., & Howard-Hamilton, M. F. (2000). *The convergence of race, ethnicity, and gender: Multiple identities in counseling.* Upper Saddle River, NJ: Merrill.

Ryan, C., & Futterman, D. (1998). *Lesbian & gay youth: Care & counseling.* New York: Columbia University Press.

Yoder, J. D. (1999). *Women and gender: Transforming psychology.* Upper Saddle River, NJ: Prentice Hall.

Web Sites

American Psychological Association—Ethics Information
www.apa.org/ethics

American Psychological Association ethical principles of psychologists and code of conduct
http://www.apa.org/ethics/code.html

Ask Your School Psychologist
http://www.bartow/k12.ga.us/psych/psych.html

Association for Multicultural Counseling and Development
http://www.bgsu.edu/colleges/edhd/programs/AMCD

Counselor's Corner—Multicultural Issues
http://members.aol.com/lacillo/multicultural.html

Ethical Standards for Internet On-Line Counseling
http://www.counseling.org/gc/cybertx.htm

International Society for Mental Health Online
http://www.ismho.org

National Association of Social Workers Code of Ethics
http://www.naswdc.org/Code/cdtoc.htm

TelehealthNet
http://www.telehealth.net

2 POST EVALUATION

Part One

According to Chapter Objective One, you will be able to identify attitudes and behaviors about yourself that could help or interfere with establishing a positive helping relationship. In this activity, we present a Self-Rating Checklist. This checklist refers to characteristics of effective helpers. Your task is to use the checklist to assess yourself *now* with respect to these attitudes and behaviors. If you haven't yet had any or much contact with actual clients, try to use this checklist to assess how you believe you would behave in actual interactions. Identify any issues or areas you may need to work on in your development as a helper. Discuss your assessment in small groups or with an instructor, colleague, or supervisor. There is no written feedback for this part of the postevaluation.

Self-Rating Checklist

Check the items that are most descriptive of you.

A. Competence Assessment

____ 1. Constructive negative feedback about myself doesn't make me feel incompetent or uncertain of myself.
____ 2. I tend to put myself down frequently.
____ 3. I feel fairly confident about myself as a helper.
____ 4. I am often preoccupied with thinking that I'm not going to be a competent helper.
____ 5. When I am involved in a conflict, I don't go out of my way to ignore or avoid it.
____ 6. When I get positive feedback about myself, I often don't believe it's true.
____ 7. I set realistic goals for myself as a helper that are within reach.
____ 8. I believe that a confronting, hostile client could make me feel uneasy or incompetent.
____ 9. I often find myself apologizing for myself or my behavior.
____ 10. I'm fairly confident I can or will be a successful helper.
____ 11. I find myself worrying a lot about "not making it" as a helper.
____ 12. I'm likely to be a little scared by clients who would idealize me.
____ 13. A lot of times I will set standards or goals for myself that are too tough to attain.
____ 14. I tend to avoid negative feedback when I can.
____ 15. Doing well or being successful does not make me feel uneasy.

B. Power Assessment

____ 1. If I'm really honest, I think my helping methods are a little superior to other people's.
____ 2. A lot of times I try to get people to do what I want. I might get pretty defensive or upset if the client disagreed with what I wanted to do or did not follow my direction in the interview.
____ 3. I believe there is (or will be) a balance in the interviews between my participation and the client's.
____ 4. I could feel angry when working with a resistant or stubborn client.
____ 5. I can see that I might be tempted to get some of my own ideology across to the client.
____ 6. As a helper, "preaching" is not likely to be a problem for me.
____ 7. Sometimes I feel impatient with clients who have a different way of looking at the world than I do.
____ 8. I know there are times when I would be reluctant to refer my client to someone else, especially if the other counselor's style differed from mine.
____ 9. Sometimes I feel rejecting or intolerant of clients whose values and lifestyles are very different from mine.
____ 10. It is hard for me to avoid getting into a power struggle with some clients.

C. Intimacy Assessment

____ 1. There are times when I act more gruff than I really feel.
____ 2. It's hard for me to express positive feelings to a client.
____ 3. There are some clients I would really like to have as friends more than as clients.
____ 4. It would upset me if a client didn't like me.
____ 5. If I sense a client has some negative feelings toward me, I try to talk about it rather than avoid it.
____ 6. Many times I go out of my way to avoid offending clients.
____ 7. I feel more comfortable maintaining a professional distance between myself and the client.
____ 8. Being close to people is something that does not make me feel uncomfortable.
____ 9. I am more comfortable when I am a little aloof.
____ 10. I am very sensitive to how clients feel about me, especially if it's negative.
____ 11. I can accept positive feedback from clients fairly easily.
____ 12. It is difficult for me to confront a client.

Part Two

According to Chapter Objective Two, you will be able to identify issues related to values, ethics, and diversity that could affect the development of a therapeutic relationship, given six written case descriptions. In this activity, read each case description carefully; then identify in writing the major kind of issue reflected in the case by matching the type of issue with the case descriptions listed below. There may be more than one issue reflected in each case. Feedback follows the postevaluation (p. 44).

(continued)

POST EVALUATION

(continued)

Type of Issue

A. Values conflict
B. Values stereotyping
C. Ethics—breach of confidentiality
D. Ethics—client welfare and rights
E. Ethics—referral
F. Diversity issue

Case Description

____ 1. You are counseling a client who is in danger of failing high school. The client states that he feels like a failure because all the other students are so smart. In an effort to make him feel better, you tell him about one of your former clients who also almost flunked out.

____ 2. A 58-year-old man who is having difficulty adjusting to life without his wife, who died, comes to you for counseling. He has difficulty in discussing his concern or problem with you, and he is not clear about your role as a counselor and what counseling might do for him. He seems to feel that you can give him a tranquilizer. You tell him that you are not able to prescribe medication, and you suggest that he seek the services of a physician.

____ 3. A fourth-grade girl is referred to you by her teacher. The teacher states that the girl is doing poorly in class yet seems motivated to learn. After working with the girl for several weeks, including giving a battery of tests, you conclude that she has a severe learning disability. After obtaining her permission to talk to her teacher, you inform her teacher of this and state that the teacher might as well not spend too much more time working on what you believe is a "useless case."

____ 4. You are counseling a couple who are considering a trial separation because of constant marital problems. You tell them you don't believe separation or divorce is the answer to their problems.

____ 5. A Euro-American helper states in a staff meeting that "people are just people" and that he does not see the need for all this emphasis in your treatment facility on understanding how clients from diverse racial/ethnic/cultural backgrounds may be affected differently by the therapy process.

____ 6. A client comes into a mental health center and requests a helper from his own culture. He also indicates that he would consider seeing a helper who is not from his culture but who shares his world view and has some notion of his cultural struggles. He is told that it shouldn't matter who he sees because all the therapists on the staff are value-free.

POST EVALUATION FEEDBACK

PART TWO

Chapter Objective Two

1. C: Ethics—breach of confidentiality. The helper, broke the confidence of a former client by revealing his grade difficulties without his consent.

2. E: Ethics—referral. The helper did not refer in an ethical or responsible way, because of failure to give the client names of at least several physicians or psychiatrists who might be competent to see the client.

3. B: Values stereotyping. The helper is obviously stereotyping all kids with learning disabilities as useless and hopeless (the "label" is also not helpful or in the client's best interest).

4. A: Values conflict. Your values are showing: Although separation and divorce may not be your solution, be careful of persuading clients to pursue your views and answers to issues.

5. F: Diversity issue. The Euro-American helper is obviously ignorant and also at Stage 1 (contact) of the white racial identity scale (racial naivete).

6. F and B: Diversity issue and values stereotyping. The response to this client ignores the client's racial identity status and also responds in a stereotypical way to his or her request.

CHAPTER 3

UNDERSTANDING NONVERBAL BEHAVIOR

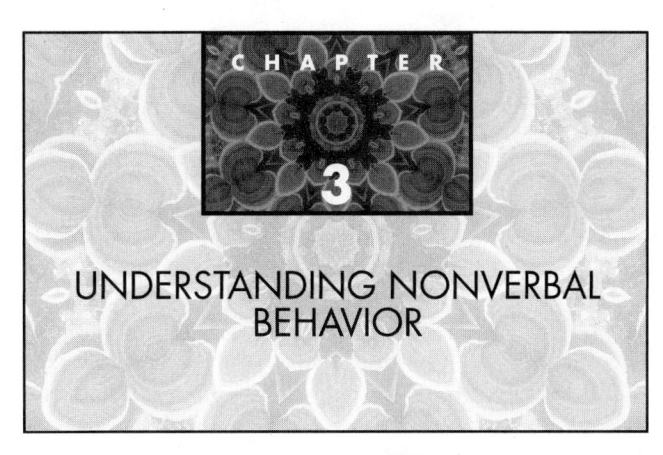

OBJECTIVES

After completing this chapter, the student should be able to
1. From a list of client descriptions and nonverbal client behaviors, describe one possible meaning associated with each nonverbal behavior.
2. In an interview situation, identify as many nonverbal behaviors of the person with whom you are communicating as possible. Describe the possible meanings associated with these behaviors. The nonverbal behaviors you identify may come from any one or all of the categories of kinesics, or body motion; paralinguistics, or voice qualities; proxemics, or room space and distance; and the person's general appearance.
3. Demonstrate effective use of helper nonverbal behaviors in a role-play interview.
4. Identify at least three out of four occasions for responding to client nonverbal behavior in an interview.

Nonverbal behavior plays an important role in our communication and relationships with others. In communicating, we tend to emphasize the spoken word. Yet much of the meaning of a message, 65 percent or more, is conveyed by our nonverbal behavior (Birdwhistell, 1970). Nonverbal behavior is an important part of helping because of the large amount of information it communicates. Knapp and Hall (1997, p. 32) define nonverbal behavior as "all human communication events that transcend spoken or written words." Of course, many nonverbal behaviors are interpreted by verbal symbols. Separating nonverbal from verbal behavior is somewhat artificial because in real life these two dimensions of communication are inseparable, dependent upon each other for meaning and interpretation. The nonverbal behaviors we discuss in this chapter are supported by and support the verbal behaviors and skills we describe in the remainder of the book.

Clients from some cultural groups may place more emphasis on their own nonverbal behavior and that of their helpers. In part, these clients have learned to rely more on nonverbal communication and less on verbal elaborations to explain something or to get a point across (Sue & Sue, 1999, p. 38). Also, some clients of color have learned that verbal messages of white people are often less trustworthy than their nonverbal behavior (Sue & Sue, 1999, p. 38).

Helpers learn much about a client by becoming sensitized to the client's nonverbal cues. Also, the helper's nonverbal behavior affects the client. One of the primary kinds of client verbal messages—the affective message—is highly dependent on nonverbal communication. Ekman and Friesen (1969, p. 88) have noted that much of the information that can be gleaned from the words of clients is derived from their nonverbal behavior. In addition to the expression of affect or emotions, nonverbal behavior in person-to-person communication is also used to help present oneself to others, to convey interpersonal attitudes such as liking or disliking, to convey information about turn taking in communication, and to establish rituals such as those used at the beginning and end of a helping session (Knapp & Hall, 1997).

Five dimensions of nonverbal behavior with significant effects on communication are *kinesics, paralinguistics, proxemics, environmental factors,* and *time*. Body motion, or kinesic behavior, includes gestures, body movements, posture, touch, facial expressions, and eye behavior (Knapp & Hall, 1997). Associated with the work of Birdwhistell (1970), kinesics also involves physical characteristics that remain relatively unchanged during a conversation, such as body physique, height, weight, and general appearance. In addition to observing body motion, helpers must identify nonverbal vocal cues called paralanguage—the "how" of the message. This includes voice qualities and vocalizations (Trager, 1958). Silent pauses and speech errors can be considered part of paralanguage as well (Knapp & Hall, 1997, p. 428). Also of interest to helpers is the area of proxemics (Hall, 1966)—that is, one's use of social and personal space. As it affects the helping relationship, proxemics involves the size of the room, seating arrangements, touch, and the distance between helper and client.

Perception of one's environment is another important part of nonverbal behavior because people react emotionally to their surroundings. Environments can cause clients to feel arousal or boredom and comfort or stress, depending on the degree to which an individual tunes into or screens out relevant parts of the surroundings. A fifth aspect of nonverbal behavior involves perception and use of time. Time can be a significant factor in helping, including promptness or delay in starting and ending sessions, as well as the amount of time spent in communicating with a client about particular topics or events. All these aspects of nonverbal behavior are affected by cultural affiliation.

CLIENT NONVERBAL BEHAVIOR

An important part of a counselor's repertory is the capacity to discriminate various nonverbal behaviors of clients and their possible meanings. Recognizing and exploring client nonverbal cues is important in counseling for several reasons. First, clients' nonverbal behaviors are clues about their emotions. Even more generally, nonverbal behaviors are part of clients' expressions of themselves. As Perls states, "Everything the patient does, obvious or concealed, is an expression of the self" (1973, p. 75). Much of a client's nonverbal behavior may be obvious to you but hidden to the client. Passons (1975, p. 102) points out that most clients are more aware of their words than of their nonverbal behavior. Exploring nonverbal communication may give clients a more complete understanding of their behavior.

Nonverbal client cues may represent more "leakage" than client verbal messages do (Ekman & Friesen, 1969). Leakage is the communication of messages that are valid yet are not sent intentionally. Passons (1975) suggests that because of this leakage, client nonverbal behavior may often portray the client more accurately than verbal messages (p. 102). A client may come in and *tell* you one story and in nonverbal language convey a completely different story (Erickson, Rossi, & Rossi, 1976).

Knapp and Hall (1997, p. 32) point out that nonverbal and verbal behavior are interrelated to such a degree that considering each of them as a separate facet of communication is difficult since both are involved in sending messages and receiving and interpreting the meaning of messages.

Recognizing the ways that nonverbal cues support verbal messages can be helpful. Knapp and Hall identify six such ways:

1. *Repetition:* The verbal message is to "come in and sit down"; the hand gesture pointing to the room and chair is a nonverbal repeater.
2. *Contradiction:* The verbal message is "I like you," communicated with a frown and an angry tone of voice. Although in this situation the nonverbal behavior often carries more weight than the verbal message, this may vary according to the age and familiarity with the verbal language of the client.
3. *Substitution:* Often a nonverbal message is used in lieu of a verbal one. For example, if you ask a client "How are you?" and you get a smile, the smile substitutes for a "Very well today."
4. *Complementation:* A nonverbal message can complement a verbal message by modifying or elaborating the message. For example, if someone is talking about feeling uncomfortable and begins talking faster with more speech errors, these nonverbal messages add to the verbal one of discomfort. When the nonverbal and verbal behaviors are complementary rather than contradictory, communication goes more smoothly, especially in the accuracy with which messages are decoded. In helping interviews in which clarity of communication is important, helpers need to be attentive to the ways that nonverbal messages and verbal messages complement each other.
5. *Accent:* Nonverbal messages can emphasize verbal ones and often heighten the impact of a verbal message. For example, if you are communicating verbal concern, the verbal message may come through stronger with nonverbal cues such as furrow of the brows, a frown, or tears. The kind of emotion one conveys is detected best by facial expressions. The body conveys a better description of the intensity of the emotion (Ekman, 1964; Ekman and Friesen, 1967).
6. *Regulation:* Nonverbal communication helps to regulate the flow of conversation. Have you ever noticed that when you nod your head at someone after he or she speaks, the person tends to keep talking? But if you look away and shift your body position, the person may stop talking, at least momentarily. Whether we realize it or not, we rely on certain nonverbal cues as feedback for starting or stopping a conversation and for indicating whether the other person is listening.*

---

*Excerpt adapted from Nonverbal Communication in Human Interaction, (4th ed.), by Mark L. Knapp and J. A. Hall. Copyright 1997 by Harcourt, Inc. Adapted by permission of the publisher.

This has important implications in helping interviews, especially when helpers are needing to convey respect for clients and to listen carefully to client messages, because we make judgments about people based on these regulatory skills. As interviewers, it is important to remember that regulatory skills vary across clients—children are often less skilled in this area than most adult clients, and regulatory skills differ somewhat among various cultural groups.

Identifying the relation between the client's verbal and nonverbal communication may yield a more accurate picture of the client, the client's feelings, and the concerns that have led the client to seek help. In addition, the helper can detect the extent to which the client's nonverbal behavior and verbal behavior match or are congruent. Frequent discrepancies between the client's expressions may indicate ambivalence.

Nonverbal behavior has received a great deal of attention in recent years in newspapers, magazine articles, and popular books. These publications may have value in increasing awareness of nonverbal behaviors. However, the meanings that have been attached to a particular behavior may have become oversimplified. It is important to note that the meaning of nonverbal behavior will vary with people and situations (contexts). For example, water in the eyes may be a sign of happiness and glee for one person; for another, it may mean anger, frustration, or trouble with contact lenses. A person who has a lisp may be dependent; another may have a speech impediment. Twisting, rocking, or squirming in a seat might mean anxiety for one person and a stomach cramp for someone else. Further, nonverbal behaviors of one culture may have different or even opposite meanings in another culture. Watson (1970) reports significant differences among cultures in contact and noncontact nonverbal behaviors (distance, touch, eye contact, and so on). As an example, in some cultures, avoidance of eye contact is regarded as an indication of respect. As Sue and Sue (1999, p. 77) note, "the same nonverbal behavior on the part of an American Indian client may mean something quite different than if it was made by a White person."* We simply caution you to be careful not to assume that nonverbal behavior has the same meaning or effect for all. Also remember that for accuracy of interpretation, the nonverbal behavior(s) must be considered in conjunction with the verbal message as well. Examples of these nonverbal behaviors across cultures are found in Table 3.1. (See also Learning Activity 3.1)

---

*This and all other quotations from this source are from Counseling the Culturally Different by D. W. Sue and D. Sue. Copyright 1999 by John Wiley. This material is used by permission of John Wiley and Sons, Inc.

TABLE 3.1 Nonverbal attending patterns in European–North American culture compared with patterns of other cultures

Nonverbal dimension	European–North American pattern	Contrasting example from another culture
Eye contact	When listening to a person, direct eye contact is appropriate. When talking, eye contact is often less frequent.	Some African Americans may have patterns directly opposite and demonstrate more eye contact when talking and less when listening.
Body language	Slight forward trunk lean facing the person. Handshake is a general sign of welcome.	Certain Eskimo and Inuit groups in the Arctic sit side by side when working on personal issues. A male giving a female a firm handshake may be seen as giving a sexual invitation.
Vocal tone and speech rate	A varied vocal tone is favored, with some emotionality shown. Speech rate is moderate.	Many Latina/o groups have a more extensive and expressive vocal tone and may consider European–North American styles unemotional and "flat."
Physical space	Conversation distance is ordinarily "arm's length" or more for comfort.	Common in Arab and Middle-Eastern cultures is a six- to twelve-inch conversational distance, a point at which the European American becomes uncomfortable.
Time	Highly structured, linear view of time. Generally "on time" for appointments.	Several South American countries operate on a "being" view of time and do not plan that specified, previously agreed-upon times for meetings will necessarily hold.

Note: It is critical to remember that individuals within a single cultural group vary extensively.
Source: From *Counseling and Psychotherapy: A Multicultural Perspective,* (4th ed.), by A. E. Ivey, M. B. Ivey, and L. Simek-Morgan, p. 59. Copyright © 1997 by Allyn and Bacon. Reprinted by permission.

Kinesics

Kinesics involves eyes, face, head, gestures, touch, body expressions, and movements.

Eyes

Therapists who are sensitive to the eye area of clients may detect various client emotions, such as the following:

Surprise: Eyebrows are raised so that they appear curved and high.

Fear: Brows are raised and drawn together.

Anger: Brows are lowered and drawn together. Vertical lines show up between the brows. The eyes may appear to have a "cold stare."

Sadness: Inner corners of the eyebrows are drawn up until the inner corners of the upper eyelids are raised.

Also significant to counselor/client interactions is *eye contact* (also called "direct mutual gaze"). Eye contact may indicate expressions of feeling, willingness for interpersonal exchange, or a desire to continue or stop talking. Lack of eye contact or looking away may signal withdrawal, embarrassment, or discomfort (Exline & Winters, 1965). An averted gaze may serve to hide shame over expressing a particular feeling that is seen as culturally or socially taboo.

Excessive blinking (normal is 6 to 10 times per minute in adults) may be related to anxiety. Moisture or tears in the eyes may have contrasting emotional meanings for different people. Eye shifts—away from the helper to a wall, for example—may indicate that the client is processing or recalling material (Singer, 1975). Pupil dilation, which is an autonomic (involuntary) response, may indicate emotional arousal, attentiveness, and interest (Knapp & Hall, 1997, p. 341). Although pupil dilation seems to occur under conditions that represent positive interpersonal attitudes, little or no evidence supports the belief that the opposite (pupil constriction) is associated with negative attitudes toward people (Knapp & Hall, 1997).

In helping interviews, *more mutual gazing* seems to occur in the following situations:

1. Greater physical distance exists between the helper and client.
2. Comfortable, less personal topics are discussed.
3. Interpersonal involvement exists between the helper and client.
4. You are listening rather than talking.
5. You are female.
6. You are from a culture that emphasizes visual contact in interaction.

Less gazing occurs when

1. The helper and client are physically close.
2. Difficult, intimate topics are being discussed.
3. Either the helper or the client is not interested in the other's reactions.
4. You are talking rather than listening.
5. You are embarrassed, ashamed, or trying to hide something.
6. You are from a culture that has sanctions on visual contact during some kinds of interpersonal interactions.

Less eye contact may be desirable in situations where arousal levels are too high and need to be lowered—for example, when working with an autistic child or an agitated teenager in a "shame spiral."

Unfortunately, helpers all too often equate avoidance of eye contact with disrespect, shyness, deception, and/or depression, but for some clients of color, less frequent eye contact is typical of their culture and is not a sign of any of the above. The meanings and effects of eye contact vary both within and across cultural groups, involving not only frequency and duration of eye contact, but also "rules" about where and with whom to maintain eye contact (Knapp & Hall, 1997, p. 386). While most white U.S. persons make more eye contact when listening, and less eye contact when speaking, the reverse is true for some black American people (Sue & Sue, 1999, p. 80).

Mouth

Smiles can be associated with the emotions of happiness and joy. However, when some Asian clients smile, it may have more to do with feelings of embarrassment, discomfort, or shyness than happiness. Also, some Asian clients may refrain from smiling because they have learned from their cultural values that it is a sign of weakness (Sue & Sue, 1999, p. 78).

Tight lips may mean stress, frustration, hostility, or anger. When a person has a quivering lower lip or is biting the lips, these signs may connote anxiety or sadness. An open mouth without speech may indicate surprise or difficulty in talking.

Facial Expressions

The face of the other person may be the most important stimulus in an interaction because it is the primary communicator of emotional information (Ekman, 1982). Facial expressions are used to initiate or terminate conversation, provide feedback on the comments of others, underline or support verbal communication, and convey emotions. Most of the time, the face conveys multiple emotions (Ekman, 1982). For example, one emotion may be conveyed in one part of the face and another in a different area. It is rare for one's face to express only a single emotion at a time. More often than not, the face depicts a blend of varying emotions.

Different facial areas express different emotions. Happiness, surprise, and disgust may be conveyed through the lower face (mouth and jaw region) and the eye area, whereas sadness is conveyed with the eyes. The lower face and brows express anger; fear is usually indicated by the eyes. Although "reading" someone by facial cues alone is difficult, these cues may support other nonverbal indexes of emotion within the context of an interview.

Facial expressions conveying the basic emotions described above do *not* seem to vary much among cultures. In other words, primary or basic emotions such as surprise, anger, disgust, fear, sadness, and happiness do seem to be represented by the same facial expressions across cultures, although individual cultural norms may influence how much and how often such emotions are expressed (Mesquita & Frijda, 1992).

Head
The movements of the head can be a rich source for interpreting a person's emotional or affective state. When a person holds his or her head erect, facing the other person in a relaxed way, this posture indicates receptivity to interpersonal communication. Nodding the head up and down implies confirmation or agreement. Shaking the head from left to right may signal disapproval or disagreement. However, in Sri Lanka, shaking the head from side to side indicates agreement (Sue & Sue, 1999, p. 75). Shaking the head with accompanying leg movements may connote anger. Holding the head rigidly may mean anxiety or anger, and hanging the head down toward the chest may reflect disapproval or sadness.

Shoulders
The orientation of the shoulders may give clues to a person's attitude about interpersonal exchanges. Shoulders leaning forward may indicate eagerness, attentiveness, or receptivity to interpersonal communication. Slouched, stooped, rounded, or turned-away shoulders may mean that the person is not receptive to interpersonal exchanges. This posture also may reflect sadness or ambivalence. Shrugging shoulders may mean uncertainty, puzzlement, ambivalence, or frustration.

Arms and Hands
The arms and hands can be very expressive of an individual's emotional state. Arms folded across the chest can signal avoidance of interpersonal exchange or reluctance to disclose. Anxiety or anger may be reflected in trembling and fidgety hands or clenching fists. Arms and hands that rarely gesture and are stiffly positioned may mean tension, anxiety, or anger. Relaxed, unfolded arms and hands gesturing during conversation can signal openness to interpersonal involvement or accentuation of points in conversation. The autonomic response of perspiration of the palms can reflect anxiety or arousal.

Legs and Feet
If the legs and feet appear comfortable and relaxed, the person may be signaling openness to interpersonal exchange. Shuffling feet or a tapping foot may mean that the person is experiencing some anxiety or impatience, or wants to make a point. Repeatedly crossing and uncrossing legs may indicate anxiety, depression, or impatience. A person who appears to be very "controlled" or to have "stiff" legs and feet may be uptight, anxious, or closed to an extensive interpersonal exchange.

Touch
Touch is also a part of kinesics. As you might imagine, the use of touch is controversial. As of now, there are not many empirical data to guide our thinking about its use in the helping process. One of the issues is that touch itself can range on a continuum from less to more personal touch—see Figure 3.1. The meanings of an interpersonal touch in the helping context vary greatly, depending on "many environmental, personal, and contextual variables" (Knapp & Hall, 1997, p. 315). The type, location, and duration of touch can affect the meaning conveyed to clients. In Figure 3.1, touch falling in the middle part of the continuum (friendship, warmth) can be misconstrued by clients, and touch falling in the upper part of the continuum (love, sexual arousal) should always be avoided with clients because it is unethical. For example, Simon (1999) reported that physical contact such as hugging the client is a significant precursor to sexual dual relationships between helpers and clients. Touch that falls at the lower end of the continuum (functional, professional, social) such as a handshake between

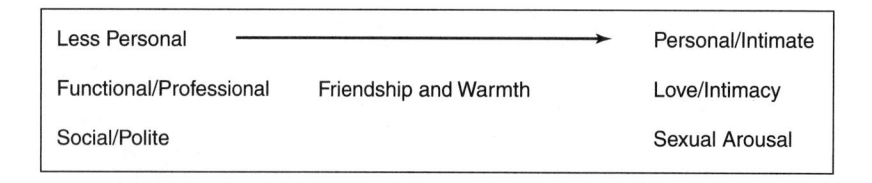

```
Less Personal  ———————————→  Personal/Intimate
Functional/Professional    Friendship and Warmth    Love/Intimacy
Social/Polite                                        Sexual Arousal
```

Figure 3.1 Continuum of touch
Source: Adapted from "Touch—A Bonding Gesture," by R. Heslin & T. Alper. In J. M. Wiemann & R. P. Harrison (Eds.), *Nonverbal Interaction.* Copyright © 1983 by Sage Publications.

helper and client is usually acceptable. Bear in mind, though, that some clients, especially those with a history of physical or sexual abuse, may shrink from all forms of touch, including a greeting such as a handshake. Also, cultural caveats come into play here as well. Shaking hands using the right hand may be seen as a "sign of peace" in some Muslim and Asian cultures, but touching anyone with the left hand may be seen as an "obscenity" (Sue & Sue, 1999, p. 79). Also, people from contact cultures may be more comfortable with touch than those from noncontact cultures.

Are there ever exceptions to this general rule? Yes! For example, consider the case of a female helper and a female client, both from a contact culture, or the situation of a person who is institutionalized, anxious, and lonely. And sometimes touch is initiated spontaneously by the client. Marguerite, a school counseling student, talked about working with a young girl whose mother had recently died unexpectedly. During the session with Marguerite, the little girl started to cry and, within a moment's time, climbed up on Marguerite's lap. In this situation, it would have been countertherapeutic and punitive to the young girl if Marguerite had immediately removed the child from her lap. She comforted her and waited until her crying had subsided, then gently lifted her onto the floor next to her, and they did some drawings. Consider the issues we discussed in Chapter 2—diversity, ethics, values, and the role of critical thinking in making therapeutic decisions such as the one faced by Marguerite. All of these factors come together in making a decision about the use of touch in the helping process. If, for example, you are a male clinician working with an adolescent female who wants to climb on your lap or hug you, different touch boundaries would be necessary than those present in Marguerite's situation.

Total Body and Body Movements

Most body movements do not have precise social meanings. Body movements are learned and culture-specific. The body movements discussed in this section are derived from analyses of (and therefore most applicable to) white adults from middle and upper socioeconomic classes in the United States.

Body movements are not produced randomly. Instead, they appear to be linked to human speech. From birth, there seems to be an effort to synchronize body movements and speech sounds. In adults, lack of synchrony may be a sign of pathology. Lack of synchrony in body movements and speech between two persons may indicate an absence of listening behavior by both.

One of the most important functions of body movements is *regulation*. Various body movements regulate or maintain an interpersonal interaction. For example, important body movements that accompany the counselor's verbal greeting of a client include eye gaze, smiling, use of hand gestures, and a vertical or sideways motion of the head (Krivonos & Knapp, 1975). Body movements are also useful to terminate an interaction, as at the end of a counseling interview. Nonverbal exit or leave-taking behaviors accompanying a verbal summary statement include decreased eye contact and positioning of your body near the exit. In terminating an interaction, particularly a therapeutic one, it is also important to display nonverbal behaviors that signify support, such as smiling, shaking the client's hand, and nodding your head. As Knapp and Hall (1997, p. 462) explain, "Supportiveness tends to offset any negativity which might arise from encounter termination signals while simultaneously setting a positive mood for the next encounter—that is, our conversation has terminated but our relationship has not."

Another way that body movements regulate an interaction involves *turn taking*—the exchange of speaker and listener roles within a conversation. As Knapp and Hall (1997) observe, "turn-taking behavior is not just an interesting facet of nonverbal communication"—it is important because data show that "we seem to base important judgments about others on how the turns are allocated and how smoothly exchanges are accomplished" (p. 459). Most of the time we take turns rather automatically: "Without much awareness of what we are doing, we use body movements, vocalizations, and some verbal behavior that often seems to accomplish this turn-taking with surprising efficiency" (Knapp & Hall, 1997, p. 458). Effective turn taking is important in a helping interaction because it contributes to the perception that you and the client have a good relationship and that, as the helper, you are a competent communicator. Conversely, ineffective turn taking may mean that a client perceives you as rude (too many interruptions) or as dominating (not enough talk time for the client).

The exchange of turns in a helping interview is not only the display of one or more of the signals we just described but also a "jointly negotiated process" between both helper and client (Knapp & Hall, 1997, p. 461). Also, keep in mind that "cultures with different conversational rules and specialized systems of communication like sign language will require somewhat different turn-exchange processes" (Knapp & Hall, 1997, p. 459). Sue and Sue (1999) provide an example of this idea:

> The cultural upbringing of many minorities dictates different patterns of communication that may place them at a disadvantage in counseling. Counseling initially demands that communication move from client to counselor. The client is expected to take the major responsibility for initiating conversation in the session, while the counselor plays a less active role.
>
> American Indians, Asian Americans, and Hispanics, however, function under different cultural imperatives that may make this difficult. These three groups may have been reared to respect elders and authority figures and "not to speak until spoken to.". . . A minority client who may be asked to initiate conversation may become uncomfortable and respond with only short phrases or statements. The counselor may be prone to interpret the behavior negatively, when in actuality it may be a sign of respect. (pp. 68–69)

In addition to regulation, body movements also serve the function of *adaptors*. Adaptors may include such behaviors as picking, scratching, rubbing, and tapping. In helping, it is important to note the frequency with which a client uses nonverbal adaptors because these behaviors seem to be associated with emotional arousal and psychological discomfort (Ekman, 1982). Body touching may reflect preoccupation with oneself and withdrawal from the interaction at hand. A client who uses adaptors frequently may be uncomfortable with the helper or with the topic of discussion. The helper can use the frequency of client adaptors as an index of the client's overall comfort level during the interview.

Another important aspect of a client's total body is his or her breathing. Changes in breathing rate (slower, faster) or depth (shallower, deeper) provide clues about comfort level, feelings, and significant issues. As clients relax, for example, their breathing usually becomes slower and deeper. Faster, more shallow breathing is more often associated with arousal, distress, discomfort, and anxiety (see also Chapter 15).

Paralinguistics

Paralinguistics includes such extralinguistic variables as voice level (volume), pitch (intonation), rate of speech, and fluency of speech. Pauses and silence also belong in this category. Paralinguistic cues are those pertaining to *how* a message is delivered, although occasionally these vocal cues represent *what* is said as well.

Vocal cues are important in helping interactions for several reasons. First, they help to manage the interaction by playing an important role in the exchange of speaker and listener roles—that is, turn taking. Second, vocal characteristics convey data about a client's emotional states. You can identify the presence of basic emotions from a client's vocal cues if you are able to make auditory discriminations. In recognizing emotions from vocal cues, it is also important to be knowledgeable about various vocal characteristics of basic emotions. For example, a client who speaks slowly and softly may be feeling sad or may be reluctant to discuss a sensitive topic. Increased volume and rate of speech are usually signs of anger or happiness, or may simply reflect cultural norms—for example, "many Arabs like to be bathed in sounds" (Sue & Sue, 1999, p. 81). Changes in voice level and pitch should be interpreted along with accompanying changes in topics of conversation and changes in other nonverbal behaviors.

Voice level may vary among cultures. Sue and Sue (1999) point out that some Americans have louder voice levels than people of other cultures. In working with a client, a helper should not automatically conclude that a louder voice means anger or that the client's lower voice volume indicates weakness or shyness (p. 81).

Vocal cues in the form of speech disturbances or aspects of *fluency* in speech also convey important information for therapists, for client anxiety or discomfort is often detected by identifying the type and frequency of client speech errors. Most speech errors become more frequent as anxiety and discomfort increase (Knapp & Hall, 1997).

Pauses and silence are another part of paralinguistics that can give the helper clues about the client. Unfilled pauses, or periods of silence, serve various functions in a helping interview. The purpose of silence often depends on whether the pause is initiated by the helper or the client. Clients use silence to express emotions, to reflect on an issue, to recall an idea or feeling, to avoid a topic, or to catch up on the progress of the moment. According to Sue and Sue (1999),

> cultures interpret the use of silence differently. The English and Arabs use silence for privacy, while the Russians, French, and Spanish read it as agreement among the parties (Hall, 1966, 1976). In Asian culture, silence is traditionally a sign of respect for elders. Furthermore, silence by many Chinese and Japanese is not a floor-yielding signal inviting others to pick up the conversation. Rather, it may indicate a desire to continue speaking after making a particular point. Often silence is a sign of politeness and respect rather than a lack of desire to continue speaking. (p. 80)

Helper-initiated silences are most effective when used with a particular purpose in mind, such as reducing the helper's level of activity, slowing down the pace of the session, giving the *client* time to think, or transferring some responsibility to the client through turn yielding or turn denying. When therapists pause to meet their own needs—for example, because they are at a loss for words—the effects of silence may or may not be therapeutic. As Cormier and Hackney (1999) observe, in such instances, when the effect is therapeutic, the counselor is apt to feel lucky rather than competent.

An example of when silence would *not* be useful is when a client discloses something very precious and significant, often revealing something that takes great vulnerability on the client's part. For example, Paul may share with you that he recently realized he is gay. Mariko may disclose something about the pain of being the only Japanese American student in her school. In instances like these, silence by the helper often makes the client feel ashamed of the revelation and misunderstood by the helper. Validation of the client's disclosure is essential.

Proxemics

Proxemics concerns the concept of environmental and personal space (Hall, 1966). As it applies to a helping interaction, proxemics includes use of space relative to the interviewing room, arrangement of the furniture, seating arrangements, and distance between helper and client. Proxemics also includes a variable that seems to be very important to any human interaction—territoriality. Many people are possessive not only of their belongings but of the space around them. It is important for therapists to communicate nonverbal sensitivity to a client's need for space. A client who feels that his or her space or territory has been encroached on may behave in ways intended to restore the proper distance. Such behaviors may include looking away or changing the topic to a less personal one.

In helping interviews, a distance of three to four feet between helper and client seems to be the least anxiety-producing and most productive, at least for adult, middle-class Euro-Americans (Lecomte, Bernstein, & Dumont, 1981). For these Americans, closer distances may inhibit verbal productivity, although females in this cultural group are generally more tolerant of less personal space than males, especially when interacting with other females. Disturbed clients also seem to require greater interaction distance. These spatial limits (three to four feet) may be inappropriate for clients of varying ages or cultures. The very young and very old seem to elicit interaction at closer distances. People from "contact" cultures (cultures where interactants face one another more directly, interact closer to one another, and use more touch and direct eye contact) may use different distances for interpersonal interactions than people from "noncontact" cultures (Watson, 1970). In short, unlike facial expressions, distance setting has no universals.

Sue and Sue (1999, p. 78) describe cross-cultural contrasts in proxemics as follows:

> For Latin Americans, Africans, Black Americans, Indonesians, Arabs, South Americans, and French, conversing with a person dictates a much closer stance than normally comfortable for Anglos. A Latin-American client may cause the [therapist] to back away because of the closeness taken. The client may interpret the [therapist's] behavior as indicative of aloofness, coldness, or a desire not to communicate. In some cross-cultural encounters, it may even be perceived as a sign of haughtiness and superiority. On the other hand, the [therapist] may misinterpret the client's behavior as an attempt to become inappropriately intimate, a sign of pushiness or aggressiveness. Both the [therapist] and the culturally different client may benefit from understanding that their reactions and behaviors are attempts to create the spatial dimension to which they are culturally conditioned.

Another aspect of proxemics involves seating and furniture arrangement. In some cultures, most helpers prefer a seating arrangement with no intervening desk or objects, although many clients like to have the protective space or "body buffer" of a desk corner. Eskimos may prefer to sit side by side.

Seating and spatial arrangements are an important part of family therapy as well. Successful family therapists pay attention to family proxemics such as the following: How far apart do family members sit from one another? Who sits next to whom? Who stays closest to the therapist? Answers to these questions about family proxemics provide information about family rules, relationships, boundaries, alliances, roles, and so on.

Environment

Helping occurs in an environment—typically an office, although other indoor and outdoor environments can be used. The same surroundings can affect clients in different ways. Surroundings are perceived as arousing or nonarousing (Mehrabian, 1976). Environments need to be moderately arousing so that the client feels relaxed enough to explore her or his problems and to self-disclose. If the client feels so comfortable that the desire to work on a problem is inhibited, the helper might consider increasing the arousal cues associated with the surroundings by moving the furniture around, using brighter colors, using more light, or even increasing vocal expressiveness. Therapists who talk louder and faster and use more expressive intonation patterns are greater sources of arousal for those around them (Mehrabian, 1976).

Environment is an important issue in working with clients from diverse cultural backgrounds. The idea of coming to an office with a scheduled appointment made in advance is a very Eurocentric notion. For some clients, a walk-in or drop-in visit may be more suitable. Also, for others, having sessions in an out-of-office environment may be desirable.

The environment also includes the structure and design of buildings and offices that serve clients and the placement of objects within these spaces. Accessibility and barrier-free environmental spaces are especially important in working with clients who may have physical challenges.

Time

Time has several dimensions that can affect a therapeutic interaction. One aspect has to do with the practitioner's and client's perceptions of time and promptness or delays in initiating or terminating topics and sessions. Many clients will feel put off by delays or rescheduled appointments and, conversely, feel appreciated and valued when extra time is spent with them. Clients may communicate anxiety or resistance by being late or by waiting until the end of a session to bring up a significant topic. Perceptions of time also vary. Some persons have a highly structured view of time, so being "on time" or ready to see the helper (or client) is important. Others have a more casual view of time and do not feel offended or put off if the helper is late for the appointment and do not

---

LEARNING ACTIVITY 3.1 — Client Nonverbal Communication

Part One

The purpose of this activity is to have you sample some nonverbal behaviors associated with varying emotions for different regions of the body. You can do this in dyads or in a small group. Act out each of the five emotions listed below, using your face, body, arms, legs, and voice:

1. Sadness, depression
2. Pleasure, satisfaction
3. Anxiety, agitation
4. Anger
5. Confusion, uncertainty

As an example, if the emotion to be portrayed were "surprise," you would show how your eyes, mouth, face, arms, hands, legs and feet, and total body might behave in terms of movement or posture, and you would indicate what your voice level and pitch would be like and how fluent your speech might be. After someone portrays one emotion, other members of the group can share how their nonverbal behaviors associated with the same emotion might differ.

Part Two

This activity will help you develop greater sensitivity to nonverbal behaviors of clients. It can be done in dyads or triads. Select one person to assume the role of the communicator and another to assume the role of the listener. A third person can act as observer. As the communicator, recall recent times when you felt (1) very happy, (2) very sad, and (3) very angry. Your task is to retrieve that experience *nonverbally*. Do *not say* anything to the listener, and do *not* tell the listener in advance which of the three emotions you are going to recall. Simply decide which of the three you will recall and tell the listener when to begin. The listener's task is to *observe* the communicator, to *note* nonverbal behaviors and changes during the recall, and, from these, to *guess* which of the three emotional experiences the person was retrieving. After about three to four minutes, stop the interaction to process it. Observers can add behaviors and changes they noted at this time. After the communicator has retrieved one of the emotions, switch roles.

expect the helper to be upset when they arrive later than the designated time.

Time is also a concept that is greatly shaped by one's cultural affiliation. Traditional U.S. society is often characterized by a preoccupation with time as a linear product and as oriented to the future; in contrast, some American Indians and African Americans value a "present-day" time orientation, Asian Americans and Hispanics focus on both past and present dimensions of time, reflecting these two cultures' traditions of strong respect for their ancestors and for the elderly in their societies. These differences in the way time is viewed and valued may contribute to discrepancies and misunderstandings in pace and scheduling.

HOW TO WORK WITH CLIENT NONVERBAL BEHAVIOR

In Chapter 1, we listed a variety of theoretical approaches used in the helping process. Many of these emphasize the importance of working with client nonverbal behavior. For example, behavioral practitioners may recognize and point out particular nonverbal behaviors of a client that constitute effective or ineffective social skills. A client who consistently mumbles and avoids eye contact may find such behaviors detrimental to establishing effective interpersonal relationships. Use of effective nonverbal behaviors also forms a portion of assertion training programs. Client-centered therapists use client nonverbal behaviors as indicators of client feelings and emotions. Gestalt therapists help clients recognize their nonverbal behaviors in order to increase awareness of themselves and of conflicts or discrepancies. For example, a client may say "Yes, I want to get my degree" and at the same time shake his head no and lower his voice tone and eyes. Body-oriented therapists actively use body language as a tool for understanding hidden and unresolved "business," conflicts, and armoring. Adlerian counselors use nonverbal reactions of clients as an aid to discovering purposes (often hidden) of behavior and mistaken logic. Family therapists are concerned with a family's nonverbal (analogic) communication as well as verbal (digital) communication. A tool based on family nonverbal communication is known as "family sculpture" (Duhl, Kantor, & Duhl, 1973). Family sculpture is a nonverbal arrangement of people placed in various physical positions in space to represent their relationship to one another. In an extension of this technique, family *choreography* (Papp, 1976), the sculptures or spatial arrangements are purposely moved to realign existing relationships and create new patterns.

Generally, irrespective of a particular theoretical orientation, there are several ways to respond to and work with clients' nonverbal behavior in a helping interview. These include the following:

1. Note or respond to discrepancies, or mixed verbal and nonverbal messages.
2. Respond to or note nonverbal behaviors when the client is silent or not speaking.
3. Use nonverbal behaviors to change the focus of the interview.
4. Work with changes in client nonverbal behavior that have occurred in an interview or over a series of sessions.

Nonverbal communication is also a useful way for helpers to note something about the *appropriateness* of a client's communication style and to observe *how* something is said, not just *what* is said (Sue & Sue, 1999, p. 80). Such observations may be especially important in working with clients belonging to various ethnic/cultural groups. For example, in traditional Asian culture, *subtlety* in communication versus directness is considered a "prized art" (Sue & Sue, 1999, p. 81). These "social rhythms" of communication style will vary among race, culture, ethnicity, and gender of clients. (See also Learning Activity 3.2.)

Mixed Messages

The helper can observe the client and see whether the client's words and nonverbal behavior send mixed messages. Contradictory verbal and nonverbal behavior would be apparent with a client who says "I feel really [pause] excited about the relationship. I've never [pause] experienced anything like this before" while looking down and leaning away. The helper has at least three options for dealing with a verbal/nonverbal discrepancy. The first is to note mentally the discrepancies between what the client says and the nonverbal body and paralinguistic cues with which the client delivers the message. The second option is to describe the discrepancy to the client, as in this example: "You say you are excited about the relationship, but your head was hanging down while you were talking, and you spoke with a lot of hesitation." (Other examples of confronting the client with discrepancies can be found in Chapter 7.) The third option is to ask the client "I noticed you looked away and paused as you said that. What does that mean?"

Nonverbal Behavior During Silence

The third way a practitioner can respond to the nonverbal behavior of the client is during periods of silence in the interview. Silence does not mean that nothing is happening! Also remember that silence has different meanings from one culture to another. In some cultures, silence is a sign of respect, not an indication that the client does not wish to talk more (Sue & Sue, 1999). The helper can focus on client nonverbal behavior during silence by noting the silence mentally, by describing the silence to the client, or by asking the client about the meaning of the silence (Itai & McRae, 1994).

Changing the Focus of the Interview

It may be necessary with some clients to change the flow of the interview, because to continue on the same topic may be unproductive. Changing the flow may also be useful when the client is delivering a lot of information or is rambling. In such instances, the helper can distract the client from the verbal content by redirecting the focus to the client's nonverbal behavior.

For "unproductive" content in the client's messages, the helper might say "Our conversation so far has been dwelling on the death of your brother and your relationship with your parents. Right now, I would like you to focus on what we have been doing while we have been talking. Are you aware of what you have been doing with your hands?"

Such responses can be either productive or detrimental to the progress of therapy. Passons (1975) suggests that these distractions will be useful if they bring the client in touch with "present behavior." If they take the client away from the current flow of feelings, the distractions will be unproductive (p. 105).

Changes in Client Nonverbal Behavior

For some clients, nonverbal behaviors may be indices of therapeutic change, of conflict, or of underlying emotions and physical reactions outside the client's awareness. Brems (2001) refers to these as "leaks"—that is, a client's gesture, facial expression, or other body movement that occurs while the client is discussing a particular issue (often in an unemotional or detached way). She provides the following examples of such nonverbal leaks in client communication:

- it is an unusual gesture, expression (facial or voice inflection), or movement that the clinician has not noted in the client before
- it is a quick gesture, expression, or movement that the client tries to hide as soon as it occurred
- it is a gesture, expression, or movement that occurs with some regularity, always in a predictable context
- it is a habitual gesture, expression, or movement that the client does not appear to be aware of and may even deny if asked about. (Brems, 2001, p. 360)

Once the helper observes a nonverbal leak, he or she must make a decision about whether to focus on the leak covertly or overtly, during the current session, or later.

The decision to respond to client nonverbal behavior covertly (with a mental note) or overtly depends not only on your purpose in focusing on nonverbal behavior but also on timing. Passons (1975) believes that helpers need to make overt responses to client nonverbal behavior early in the therapeutic process. Otherwise, when you call attention to something the client is doing nonverbally after the tenth session or so, the client is likely to feel confused and bewildered by what is seen as a change in your approach.

When responding to client nonverbal behavior with immediacy, it is helpful to be descriptive rather than evaluative and to phrase your responses in a tentative way. For example, saying something like "Are you aware that as you're talking, your neck and face are getting red splotches of color?" is likely to be more useful than evaluative and dogmatic comments such as "Why is your face getting red?" "You surely do have a red face," or "You're getting so red—you must feel very embarrassed about this." Brems (2001) provides a wonderful example of how one helper responded to leaks in her client's nonverbal behavior:

Clinician: Would you sit back the way you were sitting just a minute ago?
Client: Sit how? (*looks puzzled*)
Clinician: With your legs crossed like that (*models the position*) and your leg swinging....
Client: Why?
Clinician: I'd like to try something with you....
Client: Like that? (*shifts to the "leak" position*)
Clinician: Yeah, that was it. Now swing your lower leg, like that. (*models*)
Client: I really did that?
Clinician: Yes, you really did.
Client: Okay, so now what? (*swinging her leg*)
Clinician: When you were sitting like that you were talking about telling Amy that you would like to end the friendship. I got the feeling that you were communicating something else to her with the way you were holding your body. So I thought maybe you could sit like that again and listen to your body. See if you can identify any sensations you are aware of as you sit that way....
Client: Okay....
Clinician: Go ahead and start swinging your leg, like you did before.
Client: (*complies*)
Clinician: What do you notice in your body?
Client: I don't know.... (*tentative and unsure*)
Clinician: Hang in there with me for a moment. I really think this will help us out. Would you, just to give this a fair try, swing your leg a little harder?

Client: Swing harder?
Clinician: Yea, just put a little more "umph" in that movement.
Client: Okay.... (*grins and swings harder*)
Clinician: Okay, now what do you notice in your body?
Client: I'm not sure, but it seems like the right thing to do when I think about Amy right now. (*more forceful voice now*)
Clinician: What feels right about it?
Client: Well, it gives me something to do I guess. (*backs off the affect*) It occupies me with something because this is a tough thing to do, you know, to tell your friend you want out.
Clinician: What thoughts come to mind as you do it, as you swing your leg? (*allowing the detour away from obvious affect for now and going to the cognitive plane, which is more comfortable for the client*)
Client: Oh, I got it; it's like—"Hey Amy, I really wanna kick you out right now!"
Clinician: Were you aware of that thought before?
Client: No. But you know what, it's true. I would like to kick her.*

*From *Basic Skills in Psychotherapy and Counseling* (3rd ed.), by Christiane Brems © 2001. Reprinted with permission of Brooks/Cole, an imprint of the Wadsworth Group, a division of Thomson Learning.

HELPER NONVERBAL BEHAVIOR

As a helper, it is important for you to pay attention to your nonverbal behavior for several reasons. First, some kinds of helper nonverbal behavior seem to contribute to a facilitative relationship; other nonverbal behaviors may detract from the relationship. For example, "high," or facilitative, levels of such nonverbal behaviors as direct eye contact and body orientation and relaxed body posture can contribute to positive client ratings of counselor empathy even in the presence of a low-level, or detracting, verbal message (Fretz, Corn, Tuemmler, & Bellet, 1979). In addition, the degree to which clients perceive you as interpersonally attractive and as having some expertise is associated with effective nonverbal skills (Gazda et al., 1999).

Because much of the research on helper nonverbal behavior has been done with ratings of videotapes and photographs, it is difficult to specify precisely what nonverbal behaviors are related to effectiveness. Table 3.2 lists presumed effective and ineffective uses of nonverbal behaviors. In assessing this list, it is also important to remember that the effects of various helper nonverbal behaviors are related to contextual variables

---

LEARNING ACTIVITY 3.2 — Responding to Client Nonverbal Behavior

Part One

The purpose of this activity is to practice verbal responses to client nonverbal behaviors. One person portrays a client (1) giving mixed messages, (2) being silent, (3) rambling and delivering a lot of information, and (4) portraying a rather obvious change from the beginning of the interview to the end of the interview in nonverbal behavior. The person playing the helper responds verbally to each of these four portrayals. After going through all these portrayals with an opportunity for the role-play helper to respond to each, switch roles. During these role plays, try to focus primarily on your responses to the other person's nonverbal behavior.

Part Two

With yourself and several colleagues or members of your class to help you, use spatial arrangements to portray your role in your family and to depict your perceptions of your relationship to the other members of your family. Position yourself in a room, and tell the other participants where to position themselves in relation to you and one another. (If you lack one or two participants, an object can fill a gap.) After the arrangement is complete, look around you. What can you learn about your own family from this aspect of nonverbal behavior? Do you like what you see and feel? If you could change your position in the family, where would you move? What effect would this have on you and on other family members?

Part Three

In a role-play interaction or helping session in which you function as the helper, watch for some significant nonverbal behavior of the client, such as change in breathing, eye contact, voice tone, and proxemics. (Do not focus on a small nonverbal behavior out of context with the spoken words.) Focus on this behavior by asking the client whether she or he is aware of what is happening to her or his voice, body posture, eyes, or whatever. Do not interpret or assign meaning to the behavior for the client. Notice where your focus takes the client.

Part Four

Contrast the areas of client nonverbal behavior we describe in this chapter—kinesics, paralinguistics, proxemics, environment, and time—for Euro-American and non-Euro-American clients.

in helping, such as type of client, verbal content, timing in session, and client's perceptual style (Hill, Siegelman, Gronsky, Sturniolo, & Fretz, 1981). Thus, clients who subjectively have a favorable impression of the helper may not be adversely affected by an ineffective, or "low-level," nonverbal behavior such as tapping your finger or fiddling with your pen or hair. (We still recommend you avoid such distracting mannerisms.) Similarly, just engaging in effective use of nonverbal behaviors such as those listed in Table 3.2 may not be sufficient to alter the negative impressions of a particular client about you (see Learning Activity 3.3).

In addition to the use of effective nonverbal behaviors such as those listed in Table 3.2, there are three other important aspects of a therapist's nonverbal demeanor that affect a helping relationship: sensitivity, congruence, and synchrony.

Sensitivity

Presumably, skilled interviewers are better able to send effective nonverbal messages (encoding) and are more aware of client nonverbal messages (decoding) than are ineffective interviewers. There is some evidence that females of various cultures are better decoders—that is, more sensitive to other

TABLE 3.2   Effective and Ineffective Helper Nonverbal Behavior

Ineffective use	Nonverbal mode of communication	Effective use
Doing any of these things will probably close off or slow down the conversation		**These behaviors encourage talk because they show acceptance and respect for the other person**
Distant or very close	Space	Approximately arm's length
Away	Movement	Toward
Slouching; rigid; seated leaning away	Posture	Relaxed but attentive; seated leaning slightly toward
Absent; defiant; jittery	Eye contact	Regular
You continue with what you are doing before responding; in a hurry	Time	Respond at first opportunity; share time with the client
Used to keep distance between the persons	Feet and legs (in sitting)	Unobtrusive
Used as a barrier	Furniture	Used to draw persons together
Does not match feelings; scowl; blank look	Facial expression	Match your own or other's feelings; smile
Compete for attention with your words	Gestures	Highlight your words; unobtrusive; smooth
Obvious; distracting	Mannerisms	None or unobtrusive
Very loud or very soft	Voice: volume	Clearly audible
Impatient or staccato; very slow or hesitant	Voice: rate	Average or a bit slower
Apathetic; sleepy; jumpy; pushy	Energy level	Alert; stay alert throughout a long conversation

Source: Amity: Friendship in Action. Part 1: Basic Friendship Skills, by Richard P. Walters. Copyright © 1980 by Richard P. Walters, Christian Helpers, Inc., Boulder, CO. Reprinted by permission.

LEARNING ACTIVITY 3.3   Helper Nonverbal Behavior

The purpose of this activity is to have you experience the effects of different kinds of nonverbal behavior. You can do this in dyads or groups or outside a classroom setting.

1. Observe the response of a person you are talking with when
   a. You look at the person or have relaxed eye contact.
   b. You don't look at the person consistently; you avert your eyes with only occasional glances.
   c. You stare at the person.
   Obtain a reaction from the other person about your behavior.

2. With other people, observe the effects of varying conversational distance. Talk with someone at a distance of (a) 3 feet (about 1 meter), (b) 6 feet (2 meters), and (c) 9 feet (3 meters).
   Observe the effect these distances have on the person.

3. You can also do the same kind of experimenting with your body posture. For example, contrast the effects of two body positions in conversation: (a) slouching in seat, leaning back, and turning away from the person, compared with (b) facing the person, with a slight lean forward toward the person (from waist up) and with body relaxed.

persons' nonverbal cues—than are males (Sweeney, Cottle, & Kobayashi, 1980). Male practitioners may need to ensure that they are not overlooking important client cues. All of us can increase our nonverbal sensitivity by opening up all our sensory channels. For example, people who tend to process information through auditory channels can learn to pay closer attention to visual cues, and those who process visually can sensitize themselves to voice cues.

Congruence

Nonverbal behaviors in conjunction with verbal messages also have some consequences in the relationship, particularly if these messages are mixed, or incongruent. Mixed messages can be confusing to the client. For example, suppose a practitioner says to a client "I am really interested in how you feel about your parents" while the practitioner's body is turned away from the client with arms folded across the chest. The effect of this inconsistent message on the client could be quite potent. In fact, a *negative nonverbal* message mixed with a *positive verbal* one may have greater effects than the opposite (positive nonverbal and negative verbal). As Gazda and colleagues (1999, p. 85) point out, "When verbal and nonverbal messages are in contradiction, we usually believe the nonverbal message." The client may respond to inconsistent counselor messages by increasing interpersonal distance and may view such messages as indicators of counselor deception (Graves & Robinson, 1976). Further, mixed messages may reduce the extent to which the client feels psychologically close to the helper and perceives the helper as genuine. Lack of congruence between helper verbal and nonverbal messages can be especially detrimental in crosscultural helping interactions. Sue and Sue (1999) observe that many minority clients may intentionally challenge a helper "in order to assess the helper's nonverbal message rather than the verbal one. When topics related to racism are brought up in the session, what the therapist says may oftentimes be negated by his/her nonverbal communication. If this is the case, the minority client will quickly perceive the inconsistency and conclude that the therapist is incapable of dealing with cultural/racial diversity" (p. 140).

In contrast, congruence between helper verbal and nonverbal messages is related to both client and helper ratings of helper effectiveness (Hill et al., 1981). The importance of helper congruence, or consistency, among various verbal, kinesic, and paralinguistic behaviors cannot be overemphasized. Congruence between verbal and nonverbal channels seems especially critical when confronting clients (see Chapter 7) or when discussing personal, sensitive, or stressful issues. A useful aspect of congruence involves learning to match the *intensity* of your nonverbal behaviors with those of the client. For example, if you are asking the client to recall a time when she or he felt strong, resourceful, or powerful, it is helpful to convey these feelings by your own nonverbal behaviors. Become more animated, speak louder, and emphasize key words such as *strong* and *powerful*. Many of us overlook one of our most significant tools in achieving congruence—our voice. Changes in pitch, volume, rate of speech, and voice emphasis are particularly useful ways of matching our experience with the experience of clients.

Synchrony

Synchrony is the degree of harmony between the practitioner's and client's nonverbal behavior. In helping interactions, especially initial ones, it is important to match, or pace, the client's nonverbal behaviors. Mirroring of body posture and other client nonverbal behaviors contributes to rapport and builds empathy (Maurer & Tindall, 1983). Synchrony does not mean that the helper mimics every move or sound the client makes. It does mean that the practitioner's overall nonverbal demeanor is closely aligned with or very similar to the client's. For example, if the client is sitting back in a relaxed position with crossed legs, the helper matches and displays similar body posture and leg movements. Dissynchrony, or lack of pacing, is evident when, for example, a client is leaning back, very relaxed, and the helper is leaning forward, very intently, or when the client has a very sad look on her face and the helper smiles, or when the client speaks in a low, soft voice and the helper responds in a strong, powerful voice. The more nonverbal patterns you can pace, the more powerful the effect will be. However, when learning this skill, it is too overwhelming to try to match many aspects of a client's nonverbal behavior simultaneously. Find an aspect of the client's demeanor, such as voice, body posture, or gestures, that feels natural and comfortable for you to match, and concentrate on synchronizing this one aspect at a time. (See Learning Activity 3.4.)

SUMMARY

The focus of this chapter has been on helper and client nonverbal behavior. The importance of nonverbal communication in helping is illustrated by the trust (or lack of) that both helper and client place in each other's nonverbal messages. Nonverbal behavior may be a more accurate portrayal of our real selves. Most nonverbal behaviors are very spontaneous and cannot easily be faked. Nonverbal behavior adds significantly to our interpretation of verbal messages.

Five significant dimensions of nonverbal behavior were discussed in this chapter: kinesics (face and body expressions), paralinguistics (vocal cues), proxemics (space and

| LEARNING ACTIVITY | 3.4 | Observation of Helper and Client Nonverbal Behavior |

The purpose of this activity is to apply the material presented in this chapter in an interview setting. Using the Nonverbal Behavior Checklist at the end of the chapter, observe a helper and determine how many behaviors listed on the checklist she or he demonstrates. In addition, in the role play, see how much you can identify about the client's nonverbal behaviors. Finally, look for evidence of synchrony (pacing) or dissynchrony between the two persons and congruence or incongruence for each person.

distance), environment, and time. Although much popular literature has speculated on the meanings of "body language," in helping interactions, helpers must remember that the meaning of nonverbal behavior varies with people, situations, and cultures and, further, cannot be easily interpreted without supporting verbal messages.

This chapter also described various ways of working with client nonverbal behavior in an interview, including responding to discrepancies between verbal and nonverbal client behavior, responding to silence, using nonverbal behaviors to change the focus of an interview, and responding to client nonverbal "leaks" (changes in nonverbal behavior).

These categories of nonverbal behavior also apply to the helper's use of effective nonverbal behavior in the interview. In addition to using nonverbal behaviors that communicate interest and attentiveness, helpers must ensure that their own verbal and nonverbal messages are congruent and that their nonverbal behavior is synchronized with, or matches, the client's nonverbal behavior. Congruence and synchrony are important ways of contributing to rapport and building empathy within the developing relationship.

INFOTRAC® EXPLORATIONS

1. Search for *nonverbal communication,* and see what research you can find that pertains to interactions with clients.
2. Search for a research study or article on *gestures* that seems especially relevant to your field placement or work setting. Share the results of your search with your class, a fellow student, or a colleague.

SUGGESTED RESOURCES

Readings
Brems, C. (2001). *Basic skills in psychotherapy and counseling.* Belmont, CA: Wadsworth.

Ekman, P. (1993). Facial expression and emotion. *American Psychologist, 48,* 384–392.

Gazda, G., Asbury, F., Balzer, F., Childers, W., Phelps, R., & Walters, R. (1999). *Human relations development* (6th ed.). Needham Heights, MA: Allyn and Bacon.

Itai, G., & McRae, C. (1994). Counseling older Japanese American clients: An overview and observations. *Journal of Counseling and Development, 72,* 373–377.

Knapp, M. L., & Hall, J. (1997). *Nonverbal communication in human interaction* (4th ed.). Ft. Worth, TX: Harcourt Brace.

Pressly, P., and Heesacker, M. (2001). The physical environment and counseling: A review of theory and research. *Journal of Counseling and Development, 79,* 148–160.

Reed, J. R., Patton, M. J., & Gold, P. B. (1993). Effects of turn-taking sequences in vocational test interpretation interviews. *Journal of Counseling Psychology, 40,* 144–155.

Sue, D. W., & Sue, D. (1999). *Counseling the culturally different* (3rd ed.). New York: Wiley.

Web Sites
Center for Nonverbal Studies
http://members.aol.com/nonverbal2/index.htm

Exploring Nonverbal Communication
http://nonverbal.ucsc.edu

Kinesics
http://members.aol.com/doder1/kinesic1.htm

Nonverbal Communication
http://cbpa.louisville.edu/bruce/mgmtwebs/commun_f98/Nonverbal.htm

Proxemics
http://www.cs.unm.edu/~sheppard/proxemics.htm

3 POST EVALUATION

Part One

Describe briefly one possible effect or meaning associated with each of the following 10 client nonverbal behaviors (Chapter Objective One). Speculate on the meaning of the client nonverbal behavior from the client description and context presented. If you wish, write your answers on a piece of paper. Feedback follows the evaluation.

Observed Client Nonverbal Behavior	Client Description (Context)
1. Lowered eyes—looking down or away	Client has just described incestuous relationship with father. She looks away after recounting the episode.
2. Pupil dilation	Client has just been informed that she will be committed to the state hospital. Her pupils dilate as she sits back and listens.
3. Quivering lower lip or lip biting	Client has just reported a recent abortion to the helper. As she's finishing, her lip quivers, and she bites it.
4. Nodding head up and down	Helper has just described reasons for client to stop drinking. Client responds by nodding and saying "I know that."
5. Shrugging of shoulders	Helper has just informed client that he is not eligible for services at that agency. Client shrugs shoulders while listening.
6. Fist clenching or holding hands tightly	Client is describing recent argument with spouse. Her fists are clenched while she relates the incident.
7. Crossing and uncrossing legs repeatedly	Helper has just asked client whether he has been taking his medicine as prescribed. Client crosses and uncrosses legs while responding.
8. Stuttering, hesitations, speech errors	Client hesitates when helper inquires about marital fidelity. Starts to stutter and makes speech errors when describing extramarital affairs.
9. Moving closer	As helper self-discloses an episode similar to client's, client moves chair toward helper.
10. Flushing of face and appearance of sweat beads	Helper has just confronted client about racist remarks. Client's face turns red, and sweat appears on her forehead.

Part Two

Conduct a short interview as a helper and see how many client nonverbal behaviors of kinesics (body motion), paralinguistics (voice qualities), and proxemics (space) you can identify by debriefing with an observer after the session (Chapter Objective Two). Describe the possible effects or meanings associated with each behavior you identify. Confer with the observer about which nonverbal client behaviors you identified and which you missed.

Part Three

In a role-play interview in which you are the helper, demonstrate effective use of your face and body, your voice, and distance/space/touch (Chapter Objective Three). Be aware of the degree to which your nonverbal behavior matches your words. Also attempt to pace at least one aspect of the client's nonverbal behavior, such as body posture or breathing rate and depth. Use the Nonverbal Behavior Checklist at the end of the chapter to assess your performance from a videotape, or have an observer rate you during your session.

Part Four

Recall that there are four occasions for responding to client nonverbal behavior:

1. A client's "mixed" (discrepant) verbal and nonverbal message
2. Client's use of silence
3. Changes in client's nonverbal cues—or nonverbal "leaks"
4. Focusing on client's nonverbal behavior to change or redirect the interview.

Identify three of the four occasions presented in the following client descriptions, according to Chapter Objective Four:

1. The client says that your feedback doesn't bother him, yet he frowns, looks away, and turns away.

3 POST EVALUATION

2. The client has paused for a long time after your last question.
3. The client has flooded you with a great deal of information for the last five minutes.
4. The client's face was very animated for the first part of the interview; now the client's face has a very serious look.

3 POST EVALUATION FEEDBACK

PART ONE
Some of the possible meanings of these client nonverbal behaviors are as follows:

1. This client's lowering of her eyes and looking away probably indicates her *embarrassment* and *discomfort* in discussing this particular problem.
2. Dilation of this client's pupils probably signifies *arousal* and *fear* of being committed to the hospital.
3. In this example, the quivering of the client's lower lip and biting of the lip probably denote *ambivalence* and *sorrow* over her actions.
4. The client's head nodding indicates *agreement* with the helper's rationale for remaining sober.
5. The client's shrugging of the shoulders may indicate *uncertainty* or *reconcilement*.
6. In this case, the client's fist clenching probably denotes *anger* with her spouse.
7. The client's crossing and uncrossing of his legs may signify *anxiety* or *discomfort*.
8. The client's hesitation in responding and subsequent stuttering and speech errors may indicate *sensitivity* to this topic as well as *discomfort* in discussing it.
9. In this case, the client's moving closer to the helper probably indicates *intrigue* and *identification* with what the helper is revealing.
10. The client's sweating and blushing may be signs of *negative arousal*—that is, *anxiety* and/or *embarrassment* with the counselor's confrontation about the racist remarks.

PART TWO
Have the observer debrief you for feedback, or use the Nonverbal Behavior Checklist to recall which nonverbal behaviors you identified.

PART THREE
You or your observer can determine which desirable nonverbal behaviors you exhibited as a helper, using the Nonverbal Behavior Checklist.

PART FOUR
The four possible occasions for responding to client nonverbal cues as reflected in the postevaluation examples are these:

1. Responding to a client's mixed message—in this case the client's frown, break in eye contact, and shift in body position contradict the client's verbal message.
2. Responding to client silence—in this example the client's pause indicates silence.
3. Responding to client nonverbal behaviors to redirect the interview focus—in this example, to "break up" the flood of client information.
4. Responding to changes in client nonverbal cues or "leaks"—in this example, responding to the change in the client's facial expression.

NONVERBAL BEHAVIOR CHECKLIST
Name of Helper _____
Name of Observer _____

Instructions: Using a videotaped or live interview, use the categories below as guides for observing nonverbal behavior. The checklist can be used to observe the helper, the client, or both. The left-hand column lists a number of behaviors to be observed. The right-hand column has spaces to record a ✔ when the behavior is observed and to fill in any descriptive comments about it—for example, "Blinking—*excessive*" or "Colors in room—*high arousal.*"

(continued)

POST EVALUATION FEEDBACK

(continued)

Kinesics (✓) Comments

1. *Eyes*
Eyebrows raised, lowered, or drawn together
Staring or "glazed" quality
Blinking—excessive, moderate, or slight
Moisture, tears
Pupil dilation

2. *Face, mouth, head*
Continuity or changes in facial expression
Smiling
Swelling, tightening, or quivering lips
Changes in skin color
Flushing, rashes on upper neck, face
Appearance of sweat beads
Head nodding

3. *Body movements, posture, gestures, and touch*
Body posture—rigid or relaxed
Continuity or shifts in body posture
Frequency of body movements—excessive, moderate, or slight
Gestures—open or closed
Frequency of nonverbal adaptors (distracting mannerisms)—excessive, moderate, or slight
Body orientation: direct (facing each other) or sideways
Breathing—shallow or deep, fast or slow
Continuity or changes in breathing depth and rate
Crossed arms or legs
Greeting touch (handshake)

Paralinguistics
Continuity or changes in voice level, pitch, rate of speech
Verbal underlining—voice emphasis of particular words/phrases
Whispering, inaudibility
Directness or lack of directness in speech
Speech errors—excessive, moderate, or slight
Pauses initiated by helper
Pauses initiated by client

Proxemics
Continuity or shifts in distance (closer, farther away)
Position in room—behind or next to object or person

Environment
Arousal (high or low) associated with
   Furniture arrangement
   Colors
   Light
   Overall room

Time
Session started promptly or late
Promptness or delay in responding to other's communication
Continuity or changes in pace of session
Session terminated promptly or late

Synchrony and Pacing
Synchrony or dissynchrony between nonverbal behaviors and words
Pacing or lack of pacing between helper and client nonverbal behavior

Congruence
Congruence or discrepancies:
   Nonverbal—between various parts of the body
   Nonverbal/verbal—between nonverbal behavior and words

Summary

Using your observations of nonverbal behavior and the cultural/contextual variables of the interaction, what conclusions can you make about the helper? The client? The helping relationship? Consider such things as emotions, comfort level; deception, desire for more exchange, and liking.

CHAPTER 4

INGREDIENTS OF AN EFFECTIVE HELPING RELATIONSHIP

OBJECTIVES

After completing this chapter, you will be able to
1. Communicate the three facilitative conditions (empathy, genuineness, positive regard) to a client, given a role-play situation.
2. Identify issues related to transference and countertransference that might affect the development of the relationship and the working alliance, given four written case descriptions.

The quality of the therapeutic relationship remains the foundation on which all other therapeutic activities are built (Sexton & Whiston, 1994). The last several years have brought renewed acknowledgment of the significance of the most important components of that relationship (Gelso & Carter, 1994). Studies have been conducted to determine which factors in the relationship seem to be consistently related to positive therapeutic outcomes (Sexton & Whiston, 1994; Steenbarger, 1994; Whiston & Sexton, 1993), and three have emerged:

1. *Facilitative Conditions:* Empathy, positive regard, and genuineness. Conditions, especially empathy, which, if present in the helper and perceived by the client, contribute a great deal to the development of the relationship.
2. *Transference and Countertransference:* Issues of emotional intensity and objectivity felt by both client and helper. Usually related to unfinished business with one's family of origin, yet triggered by and felt as a real aspect of the therapy relationship.
3. *A Working Alliance:* A sense in which both therapist and client work together in an active, joint effort toward particular goals and outcomes.

The helping relationship is as important to the overall outcome of the helping process as any particular change or intervention treatment strategy. Indeed, some would argue that the helping relationship is more responsible for therapeutic outcomes than are particular treatment interventions (Hubble, Duncan, and Miller, 1999). Currently Division 29 (Psychotherapy) of the APA has completed a task-force investigation of empirically supported relationship (ESR) variables including, but not restricted to, the ones we described above—facilitative conditions, transference and countertransference, and the working alliance. In addition, this task force also reports effective and promising elements of customizing the therapeutic relationship to the individual client (Norcross, in press; Norcross, 2002).

Upon reviewing both the quantity and the quality of empirical research, this task force has characterized these empirically supported relationship variables as either *demonstrably effective, promising and probably effective,* or *insufficient to judge* (Norcross, in press). For example, both empathy and the working alliance have been classified as *demonstrably effective* relationship variables. Also considered *demonstrably effective* are cohesion in group therapy and goal consensus and collaboration. (We discuss goal collaboration in Chapter 10.) Positive regard, genuineness, management of countertransference, feedback, repair of ruptures in the working alliance, self-disclosure, and quality of relationship interpretations (the latter two discussed in Chapter 7) are designated as *promising and probably effective* relationship variables (Norcross, in press). The Division 29 Task Force is quick to point out that these conclusions are not intended to be practice standards, but rather to be used as a part of research-informed practice that helps practitioners make better informed choices about relationship variables with clients (Norcross, in press).

In summary, decades of research on the therapeutic relationship are leading away from the question "Does the therapeutic relationship work?" and toward the question "How does the therapeutic relationship work for this particular client with this set of issues and this kind of treatment?" These research-informed conclusions are designed to help practitioners answer the latter question with their clients and to integrate the therapist and the therapeutic relationship with the specific change interventions or treatment strategies used with clients (such as those we describe in Chapters 12–18). We briefly summarize some of the relationship research in this chapter, but for a complete discussion of these ESRs, we refer you to Norcross's excellent book, *Psychotherapy Relationships That Work* (in press).

In this chapter, we describe three components of the therapeutic relationship and how they are used with clients. Also, we discuss the way such variables as client gender and cultural status may be differentially affected by these conditions. Finally, we discuss how client and helper resistance may affect the relationship-building process.

FACILITATIVE CONDITIONS

Facilitative conditions have roots in a counseling theory developed by Rogers (1951), called *client-centered* or *person-centered* therapy. Because this theory is the basis of these fundamental skills, we describe it briefly in this section.

The first stage of this theory (Rogers, 1942) was known as the *nondirective* period. The helper essentially attended and listened to the client for the purpose of mirroring the client's communication. The second stage of this theory (Rogers, 1951) was known as the *client-centered* period. In this phase, the therapist not only mirrored the client's communication but also reflected underlying or implicit affect or feelings to help clients become more self-actualized or fully functioning people. (This is the basis of current concepts of the skill of empathy, discussed in the next section.)

In the most recent stage, known as *person-centered therapy* (Meador & Rogers, 1984; Raskin & Rogers, 1995), therapy is construed as an active partnership between two persons. In this current stage, emphasis is on client growth through *experiencing* of himself or herself and of the other person in the relationship.

Although client-centered therapy has evolved and changed, certain fundamental tenets have remained the same. One of these is that all people have an inherent tendency to strive toward growth, self-actualization, and self-direction. This tendency is realized when individuals have access to conditions (both within and outside therapy) that nurture growth. In the context of therapy, client growth is associated with high levels of three core, or facilitative, relationship conditions: *empathy* (accurate understanding), *respect* (positive regard), and *genuineness* (congruence) (Rogers, Gendlin, Kiesler, & Truax, 1967). If these conditions are absent from the therapeutic relationship, clients may not only fail to grow; they may also deteriorate (Carkhuff, 1969a, 1969b; Truax & Mitchell, 1971). Presumably, for these conditions to enhance the therapeutic relationship, they must be communicated by the helper *and* perceived by the client (Rogers, 1951, 1957). Clients have reported that these facilitative conditions are among the most helpful experiences for them in the overall helping process (Paulson, Truscott, & Stuart, 1999).

Rogers's ideas have had an enormous impact on the evolution of the counseling relationship, partly because of his emphasis on the client's capacity for growth and partly because his ideas were consistent with the cultural context of the times: permissiveness and antiauthoritarianism (Gelso & Fretz, 1992). However, as Lerman (1992) has observed, Rogers's humanistically oriented theory, while stressing growth, ignores the role of external influences and environmental constraints in a client's development. As she notes, studies of the lives of real women "have demonstrated that patriarchal institutions limit and severely constrict the possibilities for women" (p. 13). Ivey and Ivey (1999b) also note this issue as a limitation in working with some clients from African American, Native American, and Latin cultures, which focus less on the individual and more on the relationship and collective community.

Although Rogerian-based strategies for helping "are devoid of techniques that involve *doing* something to or for the client" (Gilliland & James, 1998, p. 119), in later writings Rogers (1977) asserts that these three core conditions represent a set of skills as well as an attitude on the part of the therapist. In recent years, a variety of persons have developed concrete skills associated with these three core conditions; much of this development is based on accumulating research evidence (Carkhuff, 1969a, 1969b; Egan, 1998; Gazda et al., 1999; Ivey & Ivey 1999b). This delineation of the core conditions into teachable skills has made it possible for people to learn how to communicate these core conditions to clients. As Wright and Davis (1994) note, aspects of the therapy relationship and technique are not separate domains but "are integrated aspects of a single process" (p. 29). In the following three sections, we describe these three important relationship conditions and associated skills in more detail. (We describe associated skills and verbal responses in Chapter 5.)

Empathy, or Accurate Understanding

Empathy may be described as the ability to understand people from their frame of reference rather than your own. Responding to a client empathically may be "an attempt to think *with*, rather than *for* or *about* the client" (Brammer, Abrego, & Shostrom, 1993, p. 98). For example, if a client says "I've tried to get along with my father, but it doesn't work out. He's too hard on me," an empathic response would be something like "You feel discouraged about your unsuccessful attempts to get along with your father." In contrast, if you say something like "You ought to try harder," you are responding from your frame of reference, not the client's.

Empathy has received a great deal of attention from both researchers and practitioners over the years. Current concepts emphasize that empathy is far more than a single concept or skill. Empathy is believed to be a multistage process consisting of multiple elements (Bohart and Greenberg, 1997; Ottens, Shank, & Long, 1995). A useful review of empathy is provided by Duan and Hill (1996). According to Hepworth, Rooney, and Larsen (1997), empathy plays "a vital role in nurturing and sustaining the helping relationship and providing the vehicle through which the practitioner becomes emotionally significant and influential in the client's life" (p. 99).

Ivey and colleagues (1993) distinguish between individual and multicultural empathy; the concept of multicultural empathy requires that we understand "different worldviews" from our own (p. 25). In cultural empathy, the helper responds not only to the client's verbal and nonverbal messages but also to the historical–cultural–ethnic background of the client. Misunderstandings or breaches of empathy are often not just a function of miscommunications but of differences in understanding styles, nuances, and subtleties of various cultural beliefs, values, and use of language (Sue & Sue, 1999). Constantine (2000) found that helpers' empathy represented some manifestation of their overall multicultural competence.

In an empathic misunderstanding, the helper should acknowledge it and take responsibility for it. Sue and Sue (1999) offer the following example of addressing a cultural misunderstanding: "I understand your worldview, and I know that what I do or say will appear very Western to you, but I'm limited in my communication style. I may or may not understand where you're coming from, but let's give it a try" (p. 99).

Research has abandoned the "uniformity myth" (Kiesler, 1966) with respect to empathy and seeks to determine when empathic understanding is most useful for particular clients and problems and at particular stages in the helping process. As Gladstein (1983, p. 178) observes, "In counseling/psychotherapy, affective and cognitive empathy can be helpful in certain stages, with certain clients, and for certain goals. However, at other times, they can interfere with positive outcomes." Generally, empathy is useful in influencing the quality and effectiveness of the therapeutic relationship. Empathy helps to build rapport and elicit information from clients by showing understanding, demonstrating civility (Egan, 1998), conveying that both helper and client are working "from the same side," and fostering client goals related to self-exploration (Gladstein, 1983).

Rogers's theory of client-centered therapy and his view of the role of empathy in the therapeutic process assume that at the beginning of counseling, a client has a distinct and already fairly complete sense of himself or herself, referred to as a self-structure. This is often true of clients with more "neurotic" or everyday features of presenting problems; that is, they bring problems of living to the helper and at the outset have an intact sense of themselves. Indeed, some recent research has suggested that empathy and the facilitative conditions in general may be more helpful for clients like this than for clients with a greater severity of presenting problems (Lambert & Bergin, 1992).

In contrast to the Rogerian view of the function of empathy—which is to help actualize the potential of an already established self-structure—is another view of empathy offered by the self-psychology theory of Kohut (1971b). This view assumes that many clients do not come into therapy with an established sense of self, that they lack a self-structure, and that the function of empathy in particular and of therapy in general is to build on the structure of the client's sense of self by completing a developmental process that was arrested at some time so that the person did not develop a whole sense of self.

Both Rogers (1951, 1957) and Kohut (1971b) have had an enormous impact on our understanding of the role that empathy plays in the development of a positive and authentic sense of self, not only in the normal developmental process but also in the helping relationship. Rogers's emphasis on understanding and acceptance helps clients learn that it is acceptable to be real, to be their true selves. Kohut's emphasis on empathy as a corrective emotional experience allows clients to discover parts of themselves that have been buried or split off and that in counseling can be integrated in a more holistic way. Both Rogers and Kohut

> ## LEARNING ACTIVITY 4.1 Validating Empathy
>
> Consider the following case descriptions of clients. What might be the effect on you on hearing each client's issue? What might you try to defend about yourself? How could you work with this to give a validating response to the client instead? Provide an example of such a response.
>
> 1. The client expresses a strong sexual interest in you and is mad and upset when she realizes you are not "in love" with her.
> 2. The client wants to be your favorite client and repeatedly wants to know how special he is to you.
> 3. The client is a man of Roman Catholic faith who wants to marry a Jewish woman. He is feeling a lot of pressure from his Latino parents, his priest, and his relatives to stop the relationship and find a woman of his own religious faith. He wants you to tell him what to do and is upset when you don't.

stress the importance of a nonjudgmental stance on the part of the helper (Kahn, 1991). It is our position that the views of both of these persons can be used together to create and sustain a facilitative helping relationship. Empathy is conveyed to clients by validating responses, by limit-setting responses, and by the provision of a safe-holding environment. In Chapter 5, we discuss the use of verbal responses to convey empathy.

Empathy and Validation of Clients' Experience

Both Rogers and Kohut developed their views on empathy from their work with various clients. For Kohut, the turning point was a client who came to each session with bitter accusations toward him. As he stopped trying to explain and interpret her behavior and started to listen, he realized these accusations were her attempts to show him the reality of her very early childhood living with incapacitated caregivers who had been unavailable to her. Kohut surmised that clients show us their needs through their behavior in therapy, giving us clues about what they did not receive from their primary caretakers to develop an adequate sense of self and also about what they need to receive from the helper.

It is important to remember that when a childhood need is not met or is blocked, it simply gets cut off but does not go away; it remains in the person in an often primitive form, which explains why some grown-up clients exhibit behaviors in therapy that can seem very childish. When these needs are chronically frustrated or repressed for the child, the child grows up with poor self-esteem and an impaired self-structure. Also, the self is split into a *true self*—the capacity to relate to oneself and to others—and a *false self*—an accommodating self that exists mainly to deny one's true needs in order to comply with the needs of the primary caregivers (Winnicott, 1958).

Kohut (1984) believes that empathy is at the core of providing a "corrective emotional experience" (in transactional analysis this is called *reparenting*) for clients. At the core of this is the therapist's acceptance of the client and his or her feelings. It means avoiding any sort of comment that may sound critical to clients. Because the lack of original empathic acceptance by caregivers has driven parts of the client's self underground, it is important not to repeat this process in helping interactions. Instead, the helper needs to create an opposite set of conditions in which these previously buried aspects of the self can emerge, be accepted, and integrated (Kahn, 1991, pp. 96–97). The way to do this is to let clients know that the way they see themselves and their world "is not being judged but accepted as the most likely way for them to see it, given their individual history" (Kahn, 1991, p. 97).

This is known as a validating response. Validating responses are usually verbal messages from the helper that mirror the *client's* experience. This sounds remarkably easy to do but often becomes problematic because of our own woundedness, which we discussed in Chapter 2. Too often we fail to validate the client because a button has been pushed in us, and we end up validating or defending ourselves instead. Kahn (1991) provides a wonderful illustration:

> Recently I had to close my office and see clients in a temporary place. One of my clients refused to meet me there because the parking was too difficult. She was angry and contemptuous that I would even ask her to do such a thing. I committed a whole list of Kohut sins. I told her that the parking was no harder there than anywhere else and that I assumed there was something else underlying her anger. She got angrier and angrier, and finally I did, too. It escalated into a near-disaster. Kohut would have felt his way into her situation and said with warmth and understanding, "I can really see how upsetting it

> **4.1 FEEDBACK: Validating Empathy**
>
> Here are some examples of validating responses. Discuss your emotional reactions and your response with a partner or in a small group.
>
> 1. I realize you are disappointed and upset about wanting me to have the same sort of feelings for you that you say you have for me.
> 2. It is important to you to feel very special to me. I understand this as your way of telling me something about what has been missing for you in your life.
> 3. I realize you feel caught between two things—your religious and cultural history and your love for this woman. You wish I could tell you what to do, and you're upset with me that I won't.

is for you to have the stability of our seeing each other disturbed. I think that figuring out where you'd park really is difficult, and I think there must be a lot of other upsetting things about our having to see each other somewhere else. And I can imagine some of those other things are even harder to talk about than the parking." Had she then kept the fight going, he might have said, "I think it must be really hard to have this move just laid on you without your having any say in the matter. It must seem like just one more instance where you get pushed around, where decisions get made for you, where you have to take it or leave it. It must be very hard."

Had I done that, I might have made it possible for her to explore other feelings—or I might have failed to do so. But whatever the outcome, she would have felt heard and understood. As it was, I became just one more in a long series of people telling her she was doing it wrong. (pp. 103–104)

Teyber (2000) notes that validating responses are especially important when working with clients of color, gay and lesbian clients, low-income clients, and any others who may feel different: "These clients will bring issues of oppression, prejudice, and injustice into the therapeutic process, and their personal experiences have often been invalidated by the dominant culture. These clients in particular will not expect to be heard or understood by the therapist" (p. 42).

The key to being able to provide validating responses is to be able to contain your own emotional reactions so that they do not get dumped out onto the client. This is especially hard to do when a client pushes your own buttons, and this is why working with yourself and your own "stuff" is so important.

We discuss this further in the section on countertransference later in this chapter. (See also Learning Activity 4.1)

Empathy and Limit-Setting Responses

As you can imagine, clients whose primary needs have not been met can present strong needs for immediate gratification to their helpers. As Kahn (1991) explains, "The most primitive side of clients wants to be gratified as *children;* that is, clients want to be hugged, to be told they're wonderful, to be reassured you will protect them and on and on" (p. 99). Part of providing an empathic environment is to reflect the client's wish or desire but not to actually provide the gratification. This constitutes a limit-setting response, and, combined with warmth and empathy, it contributes to the client's growth and also helps to create an atmosphere of safety. See whether you can tell the difference in the following two examples:

Client: I don't think I do anything very well. No one else seems to think I'm real special either.

Example One
Helper: Well, you are so special to me.

Example Two
Helper: I can see how that is a very hard thing for you—wanting to feel special and not feeling that way about yourself.

In the first example, the helper supplied reassurance and gratified the need, but in doing so, may have closed the door for more explanation of this issue by the client. In the second example, the helper reflected the client's pain and also the client's desire or wish and left the door open for a client response.

Wells and Glickauf-Hughes (1986) note that "for clients with backgrounds of deprivation and/or neglect, limit setting is a needed art of caring, protective containment" (p. 462). Limits may need to be set on behaviors with clients prone to acting out—not only because the client is distressed but also because the client's behavior violates your own limits as a helper. If a client repeatedly shouts at you, you may set limits by saying something like "I'm aware of how much you shout at me during our sessions. I know this is your way of showing me something about what has happened to you and how awful you feel about it. Still, in order for me to work effectively with you, I want you to talk to me about your distress without shouting."

We want to emphasize that throughout our discussion of the concept of empathy from the viewpoint of Kohut (1971a, 1984) and self-psychology, we have intentionally used the word *caregivers.* This is consistent with our personal stance that among various ethnic and cultural groups, mothers, fathers, and often grandparents and extended-family members represent the objects healthy children use to develop a cohesive sense of self; if self-esteem is impaired or the self needs are blocked, it is not the result of insufficient *mothering,* but rather insufficient and/or inconsistent caregiving in general. In Jungian terms, it is the absence of the feminine (or the "yang" of the "yin-yang") in both women and men and in predominantly patriarchal cultures that contributes to the lack of a "cherishing container" for the child (Woodman, 1993).

Helms and Cook (1999) add a cautionary note about exploring early childhood events for clients of color. They note that "where early childhood experiences are concerned, it is important for the therapist to remember that experiences that may sound like aberrations to the therapist may be normal for the client in the racial or cultural environment in which he or she was socialized" (p. 136). Moreover, it is important for therapists to be aware of different kinds of families and varying cultural and racial practices in familial roles and child rearing so that the Euro-American family is not used as the standard bearer for all clients.

Empathy and the Holding Environment

The empathic mirroring and limit-setting responses we have described are often referred to as the provision of a therapeutic *holding environment* (Winnicott, 1958). A holding environment means that the therapist conveys in words and/or behavior that he or she knows and understands the deepest feelings and experience of the client and provides a safe and supportive atmosphere in which the client can experience deeply felt emotions. As Cormier and Hackney (1999) note, it means "that the counselor is able to allow and stay with or 'hold' the client's feelings instead of moving away or distancing from the feelings or the client. In doing this, the counselor acts as a *container;* that is, the counselor's comfort in exploring and allowing the emergence of client feelings provides the support to help the client contain or hold various feelings that are often viewed by the client as unsafe" (pp. 99–100). The therapist as a container helps the client to manage what might otherwise be experienced as overwhelming feelings by providing a structure and safe space in having to do so.

Teyber (2000) has noted that the effective holding environment provided by a helper is usually dramatically different from what the young client is experiencing or what an adult client experienced while growing up. For example, if the child was sad, the parent may have responded by withdrawing, by denying the child's feelings, or by responding derisively (Teyber, 2000, p. 134). In all these parental reactions, the child's feeling was not heard, validated, or "contained"; as a result, the child learned over time to deny or avoid these feelings (thus constituting the "false self" we described earlier). Children are developmentally unable to experience and manage feelings on their own without the presence of another person who can be emotionally present for them and receive and even welcome their feelings. If the parent was unable to help the child hold feelings in this manner, it will be up to the helper to do so. In this way, the helper allows clients to know that he or she can accept their painful feelings and still stay emotionally connected to them (Teyber, 2000, p. 137).

Josselson (1992) points out that "of all the ways in which people need each other, holding is the most primary and the least evident," starting with the earliest sensations that infants experience—the sensation of being guarded by strong arms that keep them from falling and also help them to unfold as unique and separate individuals (p. 29). Not only is a child sufficiently nourished in such an environment, but just as important, the child also feels *real.* As Josselson notes in her seminal work on adult human relationships, this need for holding or groundedness does not disappear as we grow up, although the form of holding for adults may be with institutions, ideas, and words as much as with touch. Individuals who do not experience this sense of holding as children often grow up without a sense of groundedness in their own body as well as without a sense of self as a separate and unique person. Often their energy or "life force" is bound up and/or groundless, and they may seek to escape their sense of nothingness by becoming attached to any number of addictions. Josselson (1992) provides an excellent description of how the process of therapy can support clients' growth through the provision of this sort of holding environment:

> People often come to psychotherapy because they need to be held while they do the work of emotionally growing. They need a structure within which they can experience frightening or warded-off aspects of themselves. They need to know that this structure will not "let them down." They also need to trust that they will not be impinged upon by unwanted advice or by a therapist's conflicts or difficulties. Psychotherapy, because of clinicians' efforts to analyze what takes place, is one of the best understood of holding environments. Therapists "hold" patients as patients confront aspects of their memory and affective life that would be too frightening or overwhelming to face alone. (One of my patients once described her experience of therapy as my sitting with her while she confronts the mon-

sters inside.) Therapists continue to hold patients even as patients rage at them in disappointment, compete with them, envy them, or yearn for them. Adequate holding continues despite the pain of relatedness. (p. 36)

Note that in various cultures this sort of holding environment is supplied by indigenous healers as well.

Genuineness

Genuineness means being oneself without being phony or playing a role. Although most practitioners are trained to be *professionals,* a helper can convey genuineness by being human and by collaborating with the client. Genuineness contributes to an effective therapeutic relationship by reducing the emotional distance between the helper and client and by helping the client to identify with the helper, to perceive the helper as another person similar to the client. Genuineness has at least five components: supporting nonverbal behaviors, role behavior, congruence, spontaneity, and openness (see also Egan, 1998).

Supporting Nonverbal Behaviors

Genuineness is communicated by the helper's use of appropriate, or supporting, nonverbal behaviors. Nonverbal behaviors that convey genuineness include eye contact, smiling, and leaning toward the client while sitting. However, these two nonverbal behaviors should be used discreetly and gracefully. For example, direct yet intermittent eye contact is perceived as more indicative of genuineness than is persistent gazing, which clients may interpret as staring. Similarly, continual smiling or leaning forward may be viewed as phony and artificial rather than genuine and sincere. As we mentioned during our discussion of empathy, when establishing rapport the counselor should display nonverbal behaviors that parallel or match those of the client.

Role Behavior

Counselors who do not overemphasize their role, authority, or status are likely to be perceived as more genuine by clients. Too much emphasis on one's role and position can create excessive and unnecessary emotional distance in the relationship. Clients can feel intimidated or even resentful.

The genuine helper also is someone who is comfortable with himself or herself and with a variety of persons and situations and does not need to "put on" new or different roles to feel or behave comfortably and effectively. As Egan (1998, p. 50) observes, genuine helpers "do not take refuge in the role of counselor. Ideally, relating at deeper levels to others and to the counseling they do are part of their lifestyle, not roles they put on or take off at will."

Congruence

Congruence means simply that the helper's words, actions, and feelings match—they are consistent. For example, when a therapist becomes uncomfortable because of a client's constant verbal assault, she acknowledges this feeling of discomfort, at least to herself, and does not try to cover up or feign comfort when it does not exist. Practitioners who are not aware of their feelings or of discrepancies between their feelings, words, and actions may send mixed, or incongruent, messages to clients—for example, "Sure, go ahead and tell me how you feel about me" while fidgeting or tapping feet or fingers. Such messages are likely to be very confusing and even irritating to clients.

Spontaneity

Spontaneity is the capacity to express oneself naturally without contrived or artificial behaviors. Spontaneity also means being tactful without deliberating about everything you say or do. However, spontaneity does not mean that helpers need to verbalize every passing thought or feeling to clients, particularly negative feelings. Rogers (1957) suggests that helpers express negative feelings to clients only if the feelings are constant and persistent or if they interfere with the helper's ability to convey empathy and positive regard.

Genuineness does involve some self-disclosure by helpers, and we discuss this skill in Chapter 7 as an influencing response.

Positive Regard

Positive regard, also called respect, means the ability to prize or value the client as a person with worth and dignity (Rogers, 1957). Communication of positive regard has a number of important functions in establishing an effective therapeutic relationship, including the communication of willingness to work with the client, interest in the client as a person, and acceptance of the client. Egan (1998) has identified four components of positive regard: having a sense of commitment to the client, making an effort to understand the client, suspending critical judgment, and showing competence and care. Positive regard also involves expressing warmth to clients (Rogers, 1957).

Commitment

Commitment means you are willing to work with the client and are interested in doing so. It is translated into such actions as being on time for appointments, reserving time for the client's exclusive use, ensuring privacy during sessions, maintaining confidentiality, and applying skills to help the client. Lack of time and lack of concern are two major barriers to communicating a sense of commitment.

Understanding

Clients will feel respected to the degree that they *feel* the helper is trying to understand them and to treat their problems with concern. Helpers can demonstrate their efforts to understand by being empathic, by asking questions designed to elicit information important to the client, and by indicating with comments or actions their interest in understanding the client and the client's cultural heritage and values.

Helpers also convey understanding with the use of specific listening responses such as paraphrasing and reflecting client messages (see also Chapter 5).

Nonjudgmental Attitude

A nonjudgmental attitude is the helper's capacity to suspend judgment of the client's actions or motives and to avoid condemning or condoning the client's thoughts, feelings, or actions. It may also be described as the helper's acceptance of the client without conditions or reservations, although it does not mean that the helper supports or agrees with all the client says or does. A helper conveys a nonjudgmental attitude by warmly accepting the client's expressions and experiences without expressing disapproval or criticism. For example, suppose a client states "I can't help cheating on my wife. I love her, but I've got this need to be with other women." The helper who responds with regard and respect might say something like "You feel pulled between your feelings for your wife and your need for other women." This response neither condones nor criticizes the client's feelings and behaviors. In contrast, a helper who states "What a mess! You got married because you love your wife. Now you're fooling around with other women" conveys criticism and lack of respect for the client as a unique human being. The experience of having positive regard for clients can also be identified by the presence of certain (covert) thoughts and feelings such as "I feel good when I'm with this person" or "I don't feel bothered or uncomfortable with what this person is telling me."

A question that practitioners frequently face is how they can overcome personal and cultural biases to deal effectively with an individual who is perceived as unlikable, worthless, or offensive—such as a rapist, racist, or abuser of children.

A perspective on this situation is offered by Johanson and Kurtz (1991):

> It is difficult for therapists to help a rapist or racist if they have not made peace with the rapist or racist within themselves. If they do not do this first, their use of power will give rise to defenses against power in the offender, who will avoid change by playing whatever game is necessary to maintain the status quo. Therapists who recognize their own ability to manipulate, and who can employ power efficiently and dispassionately, are those with the best chance of transcending the manipulation and power plays of the offender. Therapists who can be honest and straightforward, communicating a sense of common human-beingness, are the ones who have the best chance of inviting offenders into the self-awareness of therapeutic processes. (p. 89)

Competence and Care

As helpers, we convey positive regard and respect by taking steps to ensure that we are competent and able to work with the clients who come to us for help. This means that we get supervision, consultation, and continuing education to maintain and improve our skills. It also means understanding that we are not a know-it-all and that we keep on learning and growing even after getting our degree and working in the field. It also means that we act in principled ways with clients. When we are confronted with a client we cannot work with, we use an ethical referral process. Above all else, we do not use clients for our own needs, and we are careful not to behave in any way that would exploit clients. We also are careful to pursue agendas of the client rather than our own (Egan, 1998, p. 45).

Warmth

According to Goldstein and Higginbotham (1991), without the expression of warmth, particular strategies and helping interventions may be "technically correct but therapeutically impotent" (p. 48). Warmth reduces the impersonal nature or sterility of a given intervention or treatment procedure. In addition, warmth begets warmth. In interactions with hostile or reluctant clients, warmth and caring can speak to the client's anger.

Nonverbal Cues of Warmth A primary way in which warmth is communicated is with supporting nonverbal behaviors such as voice tone, eye contact, facial animation and expressions, gestures, and touch. Johnson (2000) describes some nonverbal cues that express warmth or coldness (see Table 4-1). Remember that these behaviors may be interpreted differently by clients from various ethnic, racial, and cultural groups.

TABLE 4.1 Nonverbal Cues of Warmth and Coldness

Nonverbal cue	Warmth	Coldness
Tone of voice	Soft	Hard
Facial expression	Smiling, interested	Pokerfaced, frowning, disinterested
Posture	Lean toward other; relaxed	Lean away from other; tense
Eye contact	Look into other's eyes	Avoid looking into other's eyes
Touching	Touch other softly	Avoid touching other
Gestures	Open, welcoming	Closed, guarding oneself, and keeping other away
Spatial distance	Close	Distant

Source: Reaching Out: Interpersonal Effectiveness and Self-Actualization, (7th ed), by D. W. Johnson, p. 201. Copyright © 2000 by Allyn and Bacon. Reprinted by permission.

An important aspect of the nonverbal dimension of warmth is touch. In times of emotional stress, many clients welcome a well-intentioned touch. The difficulty with touch is that it may have a meaning to the client different from the meaning you intended to convey. In deciding whether to use touch, it is important to consider the level of trust between you and the client, whether the *client* may perceive the touch as sexual, the client's past history associated with touch (occasionally a client will associate touch with punishment or abuse and will say "I can't stand to be touched"), and the client's cultural group (whether touch is respectful and valued). To help you assess the probable impact of touch on the client, Gazda and colleagues (1999) recommend asking yourself the following questions:

1. How does the other person perceive this? Is it seen as genuine or as a superficial technique?
2. Is the other person uncomfortable? If the other person draws back from being touched, adjust your behavior accordingly.
3. Am I interested in the person or in touching the person? Whom is it for—me, the other person, or to impress those who observe? (p. 130).

Because of all the clients who present with trauma history, it is important to observe clear boundaries surrounding touch (Smith & Fitzpatrick, 1995). Check with the client and discuss these boundaries first.

Verbal Responses Associated with Warmth Warmth can also be expressed to clients through selected verbal responses. One way to express warmth is to use enhancing statements (Ivey et al., 1997) that portray some positive aspect or attribute about the client, such as "It's great to see how well you're handling this situation," "You're really expressing yourself well," or "You've done a super job on this action plan." Enhancing statements offer positive reinforcement to clients and to be effective must be sincere, deserved, and accurate.

Another verbal response used to express warmth is immediacy. Immediacy is a characteristic of a helper's verbal response describing something *as it occurs* within a session. (We discuss immediacy as a microskill in Chapter 7.)

EMOTIONAL OBJECTIVITY: TRANSFERENCE AND COUNTERTRANSFERENCE

The therapeutic relationship has the capacity to invoke great emotional intensity, often experienced by both the helper and the client. To some extent, practitioners need to become emotionally involved in the relationship. If they are too aloof or distant, clients will feel that the helper is cold, mechanical, and noncaring. However, if helpers are too involved, they may scare the client away or may lose all objectivity and cloud their judgment. The degree of emotional objectivity and intensity felt by practitioners can affect two relationship issues: transference and countertransference. (See Learning Activity 4.2.)

Transference

Transference is the

> process whereby clients project onto their therapists past feelings or attitudes toward significant people in their lives. . . . Through this process, clients' unfinished business produces a distortion in the way they perceive and react to the therapist. Their feelings are rooted in past relationships but are now directed toward the therapist. (Corey et al., 1998, p. 45)

LEARNING ACTIVITY 4.2 — Transference and Countertransference

In a small group or with a partner, discuss the likely transference and countertransference reactions you discover in the following three cases. Feedback is provided.

1. The client is upset because you will not give her your home telephone number. She states that although you have a 24-hour on-call answering service, you are not really available to her unless you give her your home number.
2. You are an internship student, and your internship is coming to an end. You have been seeing a client for weekly sessions during your year-long internship. As termination approaches, she becomes more and more anxious and angry with you and states that you are letting her down by forming this relationship with her and then leaving.
3. Your client has repeatedly invited you to his house for various social gatherings. Despite all you have said to him about "dual relationships," he says he still feels that if you really cared about him you would be at his parties.

Transference can occur very easily with helpers of all theoretical orientations when the emotional intensity has become so great that the client loses his or her objectivity and starts to relate to the helper as if he or she were some significant other person in the client's life. For example, a client may have been raised by a caregiver who was emotionally distant and unavailable to respond to the child's feelings. In therapy, the client may be reluctant to deal with feelings. When encouraged to do so by the helper, the client may react by becoming angry or withdrawn.

Gelso, Hill, Mohr, Rochlen, and Zack (1999) found that therapists view transference as a complex phenomenon in the course of therapy and that there does not seem to be any "single, uniform, or singular pattern" to it (p. 264). However, transference can easily be triggered by changes in the client's life and also by structural changes in therapy such as changes in fees, scheduling of sessions, location of sessions, and therapist availability.

Transference tends to occur regardless of the gender of the helper (Kahn, 1991) and, according to Kohut (1984), may occur because in the presence of an empathic helper, old unmet needs of the client resurface. For example, a recent qualitative study explored 11 dynamically oriented therapists and found that the content of client transference pertained to projections of the feared bad caregiver and the wished-for approving, good caregiver (Gelso et al., 1999). In addition, clients' transferential reactions can include any significant other, not just parents—such as siblings or anyone involved in an earlier and traumatic situation. Transference can be positive, negative, or mixed. At least part of the client's transference is unconscious—the client is not aware of it while it is actually occurring in the therapy process.

Often the transference (positive or negative) is a form of reenactment of the client's familiar and old pattern or template of relating. The value of it is that through the transference clients may be trying to help us see how they felt at an earlier time when treated in a particular way. Transference often occurs when the therapist (usually inadvertently) does or says something that triggers unfinished business with the client, often with members of the client's family of origin—parents and siblings or significant others. Helpers can make use of the transference, especially a negative one, by helping clients see that what they expect of us, they also expect of other people in their life; if, for example, a client wants to make the helper "look bad," that could be the client's intent with others as well.

Gelso and colleagues (1999) found five consistent ways that helpers worked with client transference:

1. focusing on the immediate relationship;
2. interpreting the meaning of the transference;
3. using questions to promote insight;
4. teaching, advising, and educating about the transference; and
5. self-disclosing.

Helpers can also work with transference issues in a helpful way by empathically reflecting on the client's desire or wish—for example, the wish to be loved, the wish to be important, and the wish to control. Often the transference acted out by the client not only includes a reenactment of an earlier important relationship but also a replay of how the client wishes it were (Kahn, 1991). Resolution of the transference process seems to occur with increased client insight, more realistic client expectations of the helper, and a more positive client view of himself or herself. Resolution of transference is also linked to what goes on in the actual relationship between ther-

> **FEEDBACK 4.2** — Transference and Countertransference
>
> 1. The transference is the client's emotional reaction to not having you available to her at all times. Possible countertransference reactions on your part include frustration, anger, and feelings of failure.
> 2. The transference is the client's feelings of abandonment as termination approaches. Potential countertransference includes sadness, irritation, and pressure.
> 3. The transference is the client's expectation for you to be socially involved with him. Possible countertransference includes feelings of letting him down, being upset, and impatience.

apist and client and to the quality of the working alliance between helper and client (Gelso et al., 1999). We discuss the working alliance in the last section of this chapter.

Helms and Cook (1999) have made an important contribution to the discussion of transference by their suggestion that transference can be racial–cultural as well as parental. They note that helpers should attend to the client's perceptions of the helper's race and culture as part of the potential transferential relationship (p. 138):

> It may be difficult for the client to develop transference related to parents (however "parents" are defined) if racial transference develops as an overriding concern. Under such circumstances, the therapist may come to symbolize whatever past traumatic experiences or socialization—personal or vicarious—that the client or the client's salient identity groups have had with members of the therapist's racial or cultural group(s). Sometimes it is necessary to work through this racial–cultural transference before the more mundane issue of parental transference can even be expected to occur. (p. 138)

Countertransference

Sheree, a beginning practicum student, finds herself working with Ronnie, a teenage boy who has been mandated to see a counselor. She has now seen Ronnie for six sessions. She describes him as "nonresponsive." She states that he sits with his cap down over his eyes so he can't really look at her directly and that he responds with "I don't know" to her inquiries. Sheree feels more and more frustrated. She states that she has tried so hard to establish a good relationship with Ronnie but feels that everything she tries is useless. It seems that Ronnie has succeeded in challenging her need to be helpful to him, and she is finding herself becoming more impatient with him in the sessions. This is an example of countertransference.

Countertransference includes feelings and attitudes the therapist has about the client. They may be realistic or characteristic responses, responses to transference, or responses to material and content that trouble the counselor (Kahn, 1991). As Kahn notes, a therapist's countertransference responses can be useful or damaging. He asserts that "at every moment deep characterological, habitual responses lie in wait, looking for an opportunity to express themselves as countertransference" (p. 121). Hurtful countertransference that comes from our own woundedness occurs when (1) we are blinded to an important area of exploration; (2) we focus on an issue more of our own than pertaining to the client; (3) we use the client for vicarious or real gratification; (4) we emit subtle cues that "lead" the client; (5) we make interventions not in the client's best interest, and, most important, (6) we adopt the roles the client wants us to play in his or her old script.

The findings of the Gelso and associates (1999) study suggest that countertransference reactions of helpers require careful management so they don't interfere with the work of helping. Countertransference responses originate in the unfinished business of the therapist and can be for better or for worse (Gelso and Hayes, 1998). Hayes and colleagues (1998) point out the importance of attending to cultural variables in understanding countertransference phenomena as well as "unfinished business" (family issues, helper needs), since unexplored biases often have a role in countertransferential reactions of helpers.

In order for us as helpers to manage our countertransference responses therapeutically, we must become aware of what they are and what they mean to us. This is one of the primary reasons that during and after training, helpers seek and receive individual and group consultation and supervision. In Box 4.1 we present examples of interpersonal process notes derived from M. Marshak (personal communication, May 11, 1999) that you may find useful in developing awareness of your own reactions to clients.

THE WORKING ALLIANCE

Sexton and Whiston (1994) point out that the therapeutic alliance has a "lengthy history" in psychotherapy, beginning with the work of Freud, although all therapeutic approaches considered the alliance to be very important (p. 35). The term *working alliance* was coined by Greenson (1967), who viewed the relationship as a sort of therapeutic collaboration

> **BOX 4.1 INTERPERSONAL PROCESS NOTES**
>
> Jot down during sessions: your thoughts, feelings, intuitions, sensations, dreams.
>
> How do feel when you're with this client?
>
> How and where are you blocked with this client?
>
> What is going on between the two of you?
>
> What is going on inside of you when there is a blockage or an issue?
>
> What keeps you from saying what you want to—what you feel?
>
> What keeps you from sitting still and being silent?
>
> How is your therapist activity maintaining the status quo—or moving the client?
>
> What stops the flow in your session?
>
> What disables you?
>
> How is the client using you?
>
> What are the client's expectations that "force" you into a certain mold or way of being with him or her?
>
> What are you doing to the client—are you "forcing" him or her into a certain way of being with you?
>
> What do your *imagination* and your *reveries* tell you about this client?
>
> What symbols come to your mind to describe the process with this client? (Draw something.)
>
> What about this client and session makes you come alive? Makes you "go dead"?
>
> How are you afraid of disappointing the client?
>
> What is lying behind the client's words?
>
> How do you create reflective space in and around the session for both you and the client?
>
> Where does "play" (in the best sense of the word) occur in this session?
>
> Does the language you use reflect your own voice, or does it reflect more of a textbook voice?
>
> What goes on in your body during this session with this client?
>
> What do you do to be seen as an "ideal" person, to avoid carrying "a shadow"?
>
> How are you taking care of yourself in this session with this client?
>
> *Source:* Abridged from a presentation on "The Person of the Analyst," by Mel Marshak, May 11, 1999, Pittsburgh Jung Society. Used with permission of Mel Marshak, Ph.D.

and partnership—a sense in which both counselor and client are working together in a joint fashion, like rowing a boat. If only one person pulls the oars, the boat doesn't move as well through the water. Bordin (1979) expanded Greenson's work and noted specifically that this alliance comprises three parts:

1. Agreement on therapeutic *goals* (more is said on this in Chapter 10)
2. Agreement on therapeutic *tasks*
3. An *emotional bond* between client and therapist

Gelso and Carter (1985, 1994) have expanded on Bordin's work as have others, including Mallinckrodt (1991, 1993). A meta-analysis found a stable and positive relationship between working alliance and therapy outcomes (such as client satisfaction and change) (Horvath & Symonds, 1991). Research also suggests that such an alliance needs to be founded early in therapy, may wax and wane over time but reemerge during times of crisis, and may be even more influential with more severe client issues (Sexton & Whiston, 1994). The working alliance is also affected by the kinds of bonds a client has established as a child with her or his parents and also by the client's social competence and social support (Mallinckrodt, King, & Coble, 1998; Mallinckrodt, Coble, & Gantt, 1995). These authors note that "therapists cannot rewrite a client's attachment history, but they can help a client acquire new social competencies. The therapist can become a stable quasi-attachment figure in the client's current life" (Mallinckrodt et al., 1995, p. 83). Patterns of attachment are observed in infants, and these patterns are believed to govern adult attachment as well. Attachment refers to the client's degree of comfort and trust in a close relationship such as the helping one and also to the extent that the client values relatedness with others (Kivlighan, Patton, & Foote, 1998).

Mallinckrodt, Gantt, and Coble (1995) have developed a client attachment to therapist scale (CATS) and have used this scale to identify patterns of attachment in therapy. Their results have implications for attachment theory and the working alliance. Clients who scored high on the CATS

LEARNING ACTIVITY 4.3	Working Alliance
With a partner or in a small group, discuss how the working alliance may be affected in working with various clients such as the following: 1. Children 2. Adolescents 3. Elderly	4. Persons with disabilities 5. Men 6. Women 7. Clients of color 8. Gay, lesbian, bisexual, and transgendered clients 9. Clients living in poverty

"securely attached" subscale perceived their therapist as responsive and accepting and reported a positive working alliance and good object-relations capacity. Clients who scored high on the CATS "preoccupied merger" subscale were more preoccupied with their therapist, wanted closer and more frequent therapist contact, had a number of serious object–relations deficits, and more readily formed a working alliance bond rather than coming to agreement in the goals and action phase of therapy. Clients who scored high on the "avoidant–fearful" CATS subscale tended to distrust their therapist, reported the poorest working alliance, and also had some object–relation deficits. These clients appeared to long for an emotional connection but feared their ability to engage in such a connection and also feared rejection by the therapist.

Client attachment and the experience of the helper appear to be related to the strength of the working alliance (Kivlighan et al., 1998). These authors found that clients who had a greater degree of comfort with intimacy formed a stronger working alliance with their helper; also for these clients, the experience level of the helper was not a factor in the strength of the working alliance. But for clients who were uncomfortable with intimacy, the experience level of the helper was closely linked to the strength of the bond that developed between helper and client (Kivlighan et al., 1998). Helpers who are experienced seem to retain clients longer in therapy than do inexperienced helpers—in part because they form the working alliance easily and more quickly.

Gelso and Carter (1994) point out that none of the relationship components we discuss in this chapter operate independently. For example, some part of the working alliance is influenced by both transference and countertransference, for a positive transference reaction may augment the therapy alliance and a negative transference reaction may erode it. Also, the stronger the alliance is, the safer the client usually feels in allowing and expressing the transferential reaction

and pattern. As Gelso and colleagues (1999) note, a strong working alliance serves as a buffer in "allowing often very difficult transference feelings to come out into the open and be resolved" (p. 165). A strong working alliance is critical for the resolution of transference issues, and the experience level of the helper plays a role in this process.

Practitioners obviously also need to pay attention to the ways in which this working alliance is formed with various clients, particularly clients from various cultural groups. As Berg and Jaya (1993) point out, proper attention to protocol may be very important in forming an initial alliance with some Asian American clients. They note that "paying proper respect to procedural rules is the first step in achieving a positive therapeutic alliance. *How* the client is shown respect is often more important than *what* the therapist does to help solve problems" (p. 33). Gender of clients may differentially affect the course of the working alliance. Ways to establish a productive working alliance with clients who have had few prior healthy attachments, have a history of sexual abuse, and have strong fears of abandonment also need attention (Mallinckrodt, Coble, & Gantt, 1995). (See Learning Activity 4.3.)

Helms and Cook (1999) describe how the working alliance may be affected in cross-racial therapy. They note that

> if a bond is formed in cross-racial therapy . . . , the client may have exaggeratedly positive reactions to the therapist because a cross-racial therapy bond may be the first significant nurturing experience that the client has had with a member of the therapist's race (p. 146).

Ruptures in the Working Alliance

There are times in the working alliance when tears and ruptures occur. These ruptures "highlight the tensions that are inherent in negotiating relationships with others" (Safran & Muran, 2000, p. 101). Indicators or markers of ruptures in the alliance often include the client's overt or indirect expressions of negative sentiments, disagreements about the goals or tasks of helping, and avoidance and nonresponsiveness (Safran, 1990). Also, as we indicated earlier, cross-racial tensions can also result in alliance ruptures.

Safran and Muran (2000) argue that ruptures are windows that let helpers see something about the client's interpersonal relationships rather than obstacles to overcome (p. 85). Moreover, ruptures in the alliance are a function of the interaction between the helper and client. As they explain, in the helping relationship clients often reenact an early, difficult, perhaps traumatic life experience and try to pull the helper into assuming the role of the perpetrator (p. 85). When this sort of rupture occurs, as well as ruptures resulting from lack of or inaccurate empathic understanding, or from countertransference responses, the ruptures can be repaired and begin to heal if the helper can recognize her or his contributions to the rupture and then acknowledge this directly to the client. This provides a new experience for the client (Safran & Muran, 2000, p. 88). For example, Francine, the client, has been describing her history with her depressed and unavailable caregiver as well as current events with the same caregiver. Her helper emotionally retreats, shuts down, and does not validate her feelings about these experiences. As a result, Francine does not show up for the next session. What does her helper do now about this rupture? First, she examines her responses to Francine in the last session. This exploration may occur alone or in consultation with a colleague, a supervisor, or her own therapist. When she realizes her contribution to the rupture, she decides to call, write, or e-mail Francine to let her know how much she hopes she will return. When Francine does return, the helper addresses the experience directly, saying something like "You know, in our last session several weeks ago when you were talking about all those times your parent was not there for you, I realized afterward that I went away from you and shut down, and in doing so, I also was not there for you. I am sorry about this." Helpers can also repair ruptures by empathizing with the client's experience of or reaction to the rupture (Safran & Muran, 2000, p. 102). For example with Francine, the helper could say "I can see why after you felt me also going away from you like your parent, you felt abandoned once more and didn't want to come in for our next session and go through the pain of that again." In order to respond effectively to ruptures, as helpers we need to remain open to ourselves and our own deepest feelings, both past and present, happy and difficult (Safran & Muran, 2000, p. 75). This process of staying open to ourselves requires finding or making enough space in our lives to stay attuned to ourselves and to feel our feelings. As well as creating time and space in our schedules, activities such as meditating, deep breathing, movement, and body scans also can assist in this process (see also Chapters 15 and 16).

RELATIONSHIP VARIABLES AND RESISTANCE

All of the relationship variables we discussed in this chapter—facilitative conditions, transference and countertransference, and the working alliance—are affected by the degree to which clients are interested in seeking help. However, some clients may feel coerced by a family member or an "official power structure" to seek help (Hepworth et al. 1997, p. 204). These clients are often referred to as involuntary clients. But at some point in the helping process, even voluntary and self-referred clients often engage in resistive behaviors simply because most clients are ambivalent about change and, as a result, manifest opposition to change in some ways (Hepworth et al. 1997, p. 570). Helpers can also demonstrate resistance, ambivalence, and lack of motivation to work with a particular client by such behaviors as being late for a session, ending the session early, canceling a session, and blocking out what a client says. Many of the countertransference responses we discussed earlier are examples of helper resistance and ambivalence. We define *resistance* simply as any client or helper behavior that interferes with or reduces the likelihood of a successful helping process and outcome. Although we discuss resistance and ambivalence to change in Chapters 10 and 11, in this section we describe strategies to use when resistance is specifically engendered by relationship variables.

Avoiding Personalizing Client Resistance

It is important for helpers to be accepting of themselves and of resistive client behavior when working with pessimistic or discouraged clients. Some helpers may personalize client resistance and feel as if they are the target of the client's resistive behavior. In such instances, acceptance of the client and of *yourself* is important. When a helper is unable or unwilling to accept a reluctant client and contracounseling behaviors, either the client, the helper, or both are often declared *persona non grata,* and the helper will experience failure in efforts to be helpful. Because therapists often experience client resistance as irritating, they may either give up on the client or subtly retaliate. Attempts to detach yourself from therapeutic and client outcomes may help you to be more accepting of yourself and of clients, especially when your own expectations are not met.

Encouraging Client Participation in Therapy

According to the theory of psychological reactance (J. W. Brehm, 1966; S. S. Brehm, 1976), individuals are likely to resist attempts by others to change them whenever their perception of freedom has been diminished or eliminated. Encouraging active client participation in the therapy process has a number of important benefits, all of which serve to counteract the effects of psychological reactance. First, active participation increases the client's sense of control, or perception of choice. Second, clients are in a better position to select strategies and tasks that work in *their* world. Third, clients may be more likely to comply and be less resistant in a cooperative rather than controlling helping environment. Oppositional behavior is less likely to occur if clients are *asked* to do something instead of *told* to (Lazarus & Fay, 1982).

There are a number of ways to encourage greater participation by clients. First, deemphasize your role in any changes made by the client. Focus on the client contributions instead. Avoid taking credit for success. Self-attributed change is more likely to be maintained than change attributed by the client to someone else, such as the therapist.

Second, actively attempt to reduce the visibility of your influence efforts. Take a low profile, and speak softly. The distinction between constructive influence, such as genuine efforts to help, and destructive influence, such as exploitation and coercion, is often blurred (Lazarus & Fay, 1982). Although a few clients respond positively to the use of authority or active influence, the majority of clients are either intimidated by or resistant to a great deal of therapeutic influence. Since the therapeutic relationship implies a position of presumed power, the therapist must take deliberate actions to engage in what Fisch, Weakland, and Segal (1982) call "one-downsmanship."

Third, solicit client input. Clients are often the best source of information about their intentions, problems, and proposed solutions. Take advantage of this resource in front of you!

Use of Timing and Pacing

Timing and pacing have to do with the speed with which a helper moves through an interview. If the helper proceeds too fast or paces too far ahead of the client, resistance may be engendered. Ways to decrease the resistance produced by timing and pacing include changing the pace, leaving a sensitive topic temporarily and returning to it later, or lessening the emotional intensity of the session (Brammer, Abrego, & Shostrom, 1993).

Timing and pacing also have to do with the process of taking small steps throughout therapy and assessing the client's reactions to each step before proceeding further or starting on a new task (Fisch et al., 1982, p. 27). The helper times and paces his or her comments and actions in accordance with client responses. If the client responds in any way other than a definite verbal or nonverbal acceptance of the therapist's lead, the therapist should change the pace or strategy. If the helper persists in using an approach or a strategy that is not working, there is a risk of increased resistance or reduced credibility (Fisch et al., 1982).

Another aspect of appropriate use of timing and pacing is to avoid taking a stand prematurely. The helper must first assess the client's views about problems, treatment, and outcome, then offer suggestions that are likely to fit the client.

Assessing and Using Patient Position

Fisch et al. (1982) have made a major contribution to the literature on change with the concept of patient position. *Patient position* refers to clients'

> strongly held beliefs, values, and priorities, which determine how they will act or not act. Thus, the importance of "position" is that it represents an inclination within patients which can be utilized to enhance the acceptance and carrying out of therapist directives.... Knowing what the client's position is allows one to formulate guidelines on how to couch—or frame—a suggestion in a way that the client is most likely to accept. (p. 90)

The helper must first listen carefully to what the client says in order to assess the client's important position statements. It is important to listen to the words that clients select and use, since clients indicate their positions in specific wording. The most useful positions are those strongly held by the client and, hence, repeated over and over during the sessions. For example, Tom, a 30-year-old male client, sought help from a helper about career choice. During the initial interview, the client said things about himself like "It is difficult for me to decide whether to go for a graduate degree or to get a good job and start earning some money. *I don't know how much you'll be able to help me* because I'm a very *complex* person. I've had an *unusual* background for someone my age. I've always been *on top* or *achieved* more than what was expected of me in school and in jobs I've held, and all at a young age. I now consider myself very *mature* and *experienced* about life. I've done a lot of things I wasn't supposed to have the ability to do. *I always rise to a challenge.* If someone says 'Tom, you can't do this,' *I set out to prove the person wrong. I guess I'm sort of a rebel.*"

In this brief example, Tom has revealed several "patient positions," such as the following:

1. He is somewhat pessimistic about whether the helper can help him or whether the process will benefit him ("I don't know how much you'll be able to help me").

2. He regards himself as someone special, unique, and complicated ("I'm a very complex person. I've had an unusual background. Mature and experienced, I've been on top and achieved.").
3. He functions best when told he can't do something; he may be likely to display oppositional behavior when told or asked to do something ("I rise to a challenge. I set out to prove the person wrong. I guess I'm sort of a rebel.").

"Patient positions" that have most bearing on the course of therapy include the client's notions about the nature of the issue and its assumed cause, about who is responsible for the issue, about how the issue can be resolved, and about the helping process itself and the client's role during therapy.

If the helper cannot detect these types of positions from listening to the client's words, selective questions such as the following can be an additional assessment tool:

"What is your interpretation of your concern?"

"If someone described your concern this way: ____, would you agree, or would that description be all wrong?"

"What is your best guess about why this problem exists?"

"Whom do you see as creating the issue?"

"How do you explain the fact that this issue has been so persistent [or gotten better or worse]?"

"Who do you feel needs to solve the concern?"

"This may or may not work for you, but have you tried ____?"

"How do you feel therapy will help you?"

"What is your thinking about my role [or your role] during therapy?"

"How would you describe yourself?"

After noting "patient position," the helper can use client position advantageously in several ways. First, the helper can avoid making any comments that might create resistance—comments that might be inflammatory to the client or might reduce your credibility because they are too discrepant from the client's values and beliefs. For example, with Tom, the helper would need to *avoid* inflammatory comments such as these:

1. "You have a very *simple* decision to make." (The word *simple* is likely to be inflammatory because it contradicts Tom's perception of himself and his concern as difficult and complex.)
2. "*Lots of people* find it hard to make this kind of career choice." (The phrase *lots of people* may be inflammatory because it is discrepant from Tom's view that he and his concern are unique.)
3. "It would be a good idea to make this decision in the next few months so you don't end up without a job or without a degree." (This statement is likely to be too "preachy" and may elicit oppositional behavior from Tom.)

Similarly, statements that might reduce the helper's credibility with Tom include

4. "I'm sure I can help you."
5. "If you work at it, counseling can be of great help to you." (These two statements do not match Tom's pessimistic view of the helper and of the value of the process.)

or

6. "Let's discuss the pros and cons of graduate school or employment, and you can find a solution *fairly easily.*" (This statement does not match Tom's view that his decision is a hard one that cannot easily be reached.)

It would be more helpful to make comments that match the views and positions of this client, such as the following ones:

1. "Since this is a *difficult* and *unique* issue, it will be important to *go slowly* and *take time* to work it through."
2. "Perhaps considering your *unusual background,* it would be best to start off by being a *little more skeptical* about counseling than the *average person* might be."
3. "This is an *important* and *weighty* dilemma. It is worthy of *careful analysis* and *attention.*"

The helper also needs to present suggestions and tasks in such a way that the client is likely to cooperate. To accomplish this, present tasks or actions in a way consistent with the client's position (Fisch et al., 1982, p. 101). Talk the client's language and suggest ideas that match the client's values and beliefs. Restate or reframe ideas in such a way that the client is likely to accept them (see also Chapter 13). For example, with Tom, the way the purpose or objective of therapy is framed can enlist or discourage his cooperation in working toward the purpose. Saying something like "It would be important to work toward a choice that will be satisfactory to you now and in the future, considering your background, achievements, and maturity" is likely to have more appeal to Tom than stating "You need to choose between school and a job." The strategies and actions suggested to Tom should also consider his perception of the issue and of himself. He is more likely to comply with strategies and tasks seen as unusual, grandiose, challenging, and risky, because they appeal more to his perception of himself as extraordinary and uncommon, than tasks that are relatively mundane, routine, and unobtrusive.

Acknowledging Anxiety/Discomfort About Your Competence

Resistance may be greater with inexperienced helpers who are concerned about their competence and effectiveness with clients. Competence anxiety has to do with commitment and is worsened, in fact, by the sense of overwhelming responsibility that beginning helpers take for their clients (Anderson & Stewart, 1983). An initial step useful for dealing with competence anxiety is to acknowledge it. Expressing your anxiety with a peer, colleague, or supervisor often diminishes it and reduces your preoccupation with yourself. Seeking consultation and supervision from supportive and knowledgeable persons is another strategy for dealing with concern about your effectiveness (Anderson & Stewart, 1983).

A third strategy is to establish your own limits in helping. Distinguish between things that you are legitimately responsible for and things that the client must be responsible for. Avoid doing work for the client! Weeks and L'Abate (1982) observe that a common myth surrounding counseling and therapy is that a helper is always responsible for producing change:

> The therapist is expected to be optimistic about the future. Therapists are expected to be supportive. When therapy is not proceeding smoothly, then the therapist works harder. The therapist may even work on one problem more as the client works on it less. This kind of approach may eventually lead to a dependency relationship, with the therapist assuming a rescuing role. (pp. 125–126)

Taking Care of Yourself: Avoid Compassion Fatigue

The axiom "Charity begins at home" has important implications for therapists. Therapist resistance is worse with helpers who are fatigued and overworked, who are so busy trying to take care of the lives of other people that they neglect their own needs. A more recent term for this phenomenon is *compassion fatigue*—the mental and physical exhaustion that results from taking better care of others than you do of yourself.

Eventually, what we refer to as "burnout" occurs. Signs of burnout include feeling relieved when a client cancels or postpones a session, having little energy available for sessions, lacking interest in client outcomes, and having persistent, recurring thoughts about whether you are in the right profession or about changing jobs (Anderson & Stewart, 1983). In severe cases of burnout, health problems may develop, and work may be missed. Tired and overworked therapists tend to show resistance by being slow to return a client's phone call or to reschedule a canceled session, by showing pessimism about outcomes, and by displaying less enthusiasm and intensity toward clients. Clients are very sensitive about whether the therapist wants to see them, and such resistive behaviors are easily transmitted to clients, even over the telephone. Thus, clients who show up late or postpone or cancel appointments may be reacting to helper resistance rather than to their own (Anderson & Stewart, 1983).

The best way to avoid resistance due to fatigue, overwork, and burnout is to prevent it. Arrange working and environmental conditions so that fatigue and burnout are unlikely to occur. For example, schedule short "breathing spaces" between clients, always take a lunch break, develop a support system with other colleagues, consult frequently with your supervisor, and arrange your office in a pleasing manner. When you're not working, learn to engage in relaxing activities, and don't bring your work home with you or dwell on what happened at work during leisure time.

Above all, remember not to jeopardize the needs of your clients because you haven't learned or cared enough to take care of your own. (See Learning Activity 4.4)

RELATIONSHIP STRATEGIES FOR INVOLUNTARY CLIENTS

As we noted earlier, involuntary clients who are under some pressure to seek help are likely to present more resistant behaviors than voluntary clients, at least initially. Although all

---

LEARNING ACTIVITY 4.4 — Compassion Fatigue

In dyads or small groups, discuss the problem of therapist resistance due to fatigue and burnout. Identify your own cognitive and behavioral signs of burnout and fatigue. Describe how you may communicate being resistant to clients. Identify ways to manage burnout or prevent it from occurring.

of the preceding strategies suggested to manage resistance also apply to involuntary clients, this section describes some special relationship skills that may be particularly useful for these clients.

Working with clients who are there under duress requires flexibility, creativity, and resourcefulness. Since an absent client can hardly be counseled, the helper needs to engage the client somehow, at least until the process makes a difference.

A useful beginning point is to start where the client is. <u>Show interest in what the client wants to talk about.</u> Since many involuntary clients are oriented toward self-protection, avoid demanding or even expecting that the client self-disclose or engage in other behaviors that rob him or her of any masks. Adapt your methods and style to the client's needs and style. If the client talks in a stilted and pedantic manner, a more formal approach is in order than if the client presents a casual interactional style.

Another initial strategy is to do something—anything—that is likely to be perceived as helpful by the client (Anderson & Stewart, 1983). Even a small intervention such as summarizing the situation or reflecting the client's resentment (Chapter 5) may enhance the client's expectations about therapy and may increase the helper's credibility. Sometimes a more involved intervention such as teaching the client relaxation, meditation (Chapter 14, Chapters 15 and 16), or a way to analyze irrational thinking may be immediately useful to this type of client.

Another strategy to use is to do anything that gives the client more control over what happens. When clients have little or no control over the process and outcome of therapy, they are more likely to view the helper as a representative of the referring agency or person, and resistance will increase (Anderson & Stewart, 1983). Discuss openly the pressures that have resulted in the client's being referred. If the court has ordered the client to have treatment, the therapist can restore the client's control by pointing out that the client can refuse therapy and accept the consequences. As Anderson and Stewart (1983, p. 241) observe, "While the consequences are usually serious enough to mean that this is not a desirable choice, it should be made clear that refusal is an option or [the client] will continue to resist the therapist at every turn."

Another way to increase the client's control and responsibility is to renegotiate the "contract" if possible. Ask clients whether they are bothered by anything in addition to what they were sent or referred for. The object of this approach is to come up with a complaint that the *client* is interested in changing (Fisch et al., 1982). If it is impossible to do this, an alternative is to negotiate an explicit treatment contract that meets the needs of the referring agency or person but also gives the client some control. It is also important not to exacerbate a client's loss of control by being vague about what you as the helper will or won't do, what you will and won't report to the referring agency, and so on (Anderson & Stewart, 1983). If you are required to write a report to the referring agency, part of the treatment contract you develop with the client might be that the report will be shared just with the client (Anderson & Stewart, 1983).

If all else fails, and the client is not interested in renegotiating a contract that reflects his or her other interests, a final strategy is to try to get the client interested in treatment. Fisch and colleagues (1982) describe this strategy as follows:

> If this can be accomplished, it will *not* be done by exhorting him to take his problem seriously, to buckle down to treatment, and the like. This is the one pitfall to avoid. The therapist has some chance of success, however, if he applies a different pressure by going the other way—by taking the position with the "client" that treatment probably is inadvisable. The identified patient now has the opportunity to convince the therapist why it could be in his own best interest to do something about *his* problem. (pp. 43–44)

If the identified client is still not interested in therapy, the helper has the option of terminating treatment and working with the complainant, who is usually the person pressuring the client to seek help. Often the complainant is more interested in solving the problem and more willing to make changes than the involuntary client (see also Chapter 10).

SUMMARY

This chapter has described three major components of the helping relationship: the facilitative conditions of empathy, genuineness, and positive regard; transference and countertransference; and the working alliance. None of these components operate independently from one another but, during the course of therapy, are connected to and influenced by one another. The components also are, to some degree, affected by client variables such as type and severity of problem, gender, race, and cultural affiliation. These components contribute to both the effective process and outcome of therapy and are considered important by almost all theoretical approaches to helping.

As King (1998) has observed, whatever else may happen in the helping process, the relationship between therapist and client is always present. One of the helper's biggest responsibilities is to attend to this relationship's quality and health.

King notes that client changes do not come from techniques as much from within the "crucible of human relationship" (King, 1998, p. 269). Resistance—either from clients or from helpers—if not recognized and explored, can threaten this crucible. When resistance is engendered from relationship variables, strategies to work with it include the following: avoid personalizing the resistance, encourage client participation in the helping process, use timing and pacing, assess and use "patient position," acknowledge anxiety about your competence, and take care of yourself as a helper.

INFOTRAC® EXPLORATIONS

1. Search for *empathy*. How many differing definitions and descriptions of empathy can you identify from your search?
2. Search for *transference*, and explore how this concept is related to the therapeutic relationship or working alliance.

SUGGESTED RESOURCES

Readings

Brammer, L. M., & MacDonald, G. (1999). *The helping relationship* (6th ed.). Needham Heights, MA: Allyn & Bacon.

Breggin, P. (1999). *The heart of being helpful: Empathy and the creation of a healing presence.* New York: Springer.

Constantine, M. (2000). Social desirability attitudes, sex, and affective and cognitive empathy as predictors of self-reported multicultural counseling competence. *The Counseling Psychologist, 28,* 857–872.

Dalenberg, C. (2000). *Countertransference and the treatment of trauma.* Washington, DC: American Psychological Association.

Duan, C., & Hill, C. (1996). The current state of empathy research. *Journal of Counseling Psychology, 43,* 261–274.

Egan, G. (2002). *The skilled helper* (7th ed.). Pacific Grove, CA: Brooks/Cole.

Gelso, C. J., Fassinger, R., Gomez, M., & Latts, M. (1995). Countertransference reactions to lesbian clients. *Journal of Counseling Psychology, 42,* 356–364.

Gelso, C. J., & Hayes, J. A. (1998). *The psychotherapy relationship.* New York: Wiley.

Gelso, C. J., Hill, C. E., Mohr, J., Rochlen, A., & Zack, J. (1999). Describing the face of transference: Psychodynamic therapists' recollections about transference in cases of successful long-term therapy. *Journal of Counseling Psychology, 46,* 257–267.

Glauser, A., & Bozarth, J. (2001). Person-centered counseling. The culture within. *Journal of Counseling and Development, 79,* 142–147.

Helms, J., & Cook, D. (1999). *Using race and culture in counseling and psychotherapy.* Boston: Allyn & Bacon.

Hepworth, D., Rooney, R., & Larsen, J. A. (2002). *Direct social work practice* (6th ed.). Pacific Grove, CA: Brooks/Cole.

Josselson, R. (1992). *The space between us: Exploring the dimensions of human relationships.* San Francisco: Jossey-Bass.

Kahn, M. (1991). *Between therapist and client: The new relationship.* New York: W. H. Freeman.

King, J. (1998). Contact and boundaries: A psychology of relationship. *Proceedings of the United States Association of Body Process Conference,* 267–272.

Kivlighan, D., Jr., Patton, M., & Foote, D. (1998). Moderating effects of client attachment on the counselor experience–working alliance relationship. *Journal of Counseling Psychology, 45,* 274–278.

Mallinckrodt, B., King, J., & Coble, H. (1998). Family dysfunction, alexithymia, and client attachment to therapist. *Journal of Counseling Psychology, 45,* 497–504.

Norcross, J. C. (Ed.) (in press). *Psychotherapy relationships that work: Therapist contributions and responsiveness to patient needs.* New York: Oxford University Press.

Paulson, B., Truscott, D., & Stuart, J. (1999). Clients' perceptions of helpful experiences in counseling. *Journal of Counseling Psychology, 46,* 317–324.

Safran, J., & Muran, J. (2000). *Negotiating the therapeutic alliance: A relational treatment guide.* New York: Guilford.

Teyber, E. (2000). *Interpersonal process in psychotherapy* (4th ed.). Pacific Grove, CA: Brooks/Cole.

Web Sites

Kidspeace: Healing magazine—play therapy
http://www.kidspeace.org/Healing/issue1/playther.html

POST EVALUATION

Part One

According to the first objective of this chapter, you will be able to communicate the three facilitative conditions to a client, given a role-play situation. Complete this activity in triads, one person assuming the role of the helper, another the role of client, and the third as the observer. The helper's task is to communicate the behavioral aspects of empathy, genuineness, and positive regard to the client. The client can share a concern with the helper. The observer will monitor the interaction, using the accompanying Checklist for Facilitative Conditions as a guide, and provide feedback after completion of the session. Each role play can last about 10–15 minutes. Switch roles so each person has an opportunity to be in each of the three roles. If you do not have access to another person to serve as an observer, find someone with whom you can engage in a role-played helping interaction. Tape-record your interaction, and use the accompanying checklist as a guide to reviewing your tape.

Checklist for Facilitative Conditions

Helper _____ Observer _____ Date _____

Instructions: Assess the helper's communication of the three facilitative conditions by circling the number and word that best represent the helper's overall behavior during this session.

Empathy

1. Did the helper indicate a desire to comprehend the client?
   1   2   3   4
   A little Somewhat   A great deal Almost always

2. Did the helper refer to the client's feelings?
   1   2   3   4
   A little Somewhat   A great deal Almost always

3. Did the helper discuss what appeared to be important to the client?
   1   2   3   4
   A little Somewhat   A great deal Almost always

4. Did the helper pace (match) the client's nonverbal behavior?
   1   2   3   4
   A little Somewhat   A great deal Almost always

5. Did the helper show understanding of the client's historical–cultural–ethnic background?
   1   2   3   4
   A little Somewhat   A great deal Almost always

6. Did the helper validate the client's experience?
   1   2   3   4
   A little Somewhat   A great deal Almost always

Genuineness

7. Did the helper avoid overemphasizing her or his role, position, and status?
   1   2   3   4
   A little Somewhat   A great deal Almost always

8. Did the helper exhibit congruence, or consistency, among feelings, words, nonverbal behavior, and actions?
   1   2   3   4
   A little Somewhat   A great deal Almost always

9. Was the helper appropriately spontaneous (for example, also tactful)?
   1   2   3   4
   A little Somewhat   A great deal Almost always

10. Did the helper demonstrate supporting nonverbal behaviors appropriate to the client's culture?
    1   2   3   4
    A little Somewhat   A great deal Almost always

Positive Regard

11. Did the helper demonstrate behaviors related to commitment and willingness to see the client (for example, starting on time, responding with appropriate intensity)?
    1   2   3   4
    A little Somewhat   A great deal Almost always

12. Did the helper respond verbally and nonverbally to the client without judging or evaluating the client?
    1   2   3   4
    A little Somewhat   A great deal Almost always

13. Did the helper convey warmth to the client with supporting nonverbal behaviors (soft voice tone, smiling, eye contact, touch) and verbal responses (enhancing statements)?
    1   2   3   4
    A little Somewhat   A great deal Almost always

Observer comments: _____
_____
_____
_____
_____

4 POST EVALUATION

Part Two

According to the second objective of the chapter, you will be able to identify issues related to transference and countertransference that might affect the development of the relationship and the working alliance, given four written case descriptions. In this activity, read each case carefully; then identify in writing the transference/countertransference issue that is reflected in the written case description. Feedback follows.

1. You are leading a problem-solving group in a high school. The members are spending a lot of time talking about the flak they get from their parents. After a while, they start to "get the leader" and complain about all the flak they get from you.

2. You are counseling a person of the other sex who is the same age as yourself. After several weeks of seeing the client, you feel extremely disappointed and let down when the client postpones the next session.

3. You find yourself needing to terminate with a client, but you are reluctant to do so. When the client presses you for a termination date, you find yourself overcome with sadness.

4. One of your clients is constantly writing you little notes and sending you cards basically saying what a wonderful person you are.

4 POST EVALUATION FEEDBACK

PART TWO

Chapter Objective Two

1. *Transference:* The group members seem to be transferring their angry feelings toward their parents onto you.
2. *Countertransference:* You are having a more than usually intense emotional reaction to this client (disappointment), which suggests that you are developing some affectionate feelings for the client and countertransference is occurring.
3. *Countertransference:* This is another example of your own countertransference—some emotional attachment on your part is making it hard for you to "let go" of this particular client (although termination does usually involve a little sadness for all parties).
4. *Transference:* The client is allowing herself to idealize you. At this point, this is a positive transference, although it could change.

CHAPTER 5

LISTENING RESPONSES

OBJECTIVES

After completing this chapter, the student should be able to
1. From a written list of 12 example listening responses, accurately classify at least nine of them by type: clarification, paraphrase, reflection, or summarization.
2. From a list of three client statements, write an example of each of the four listening responses for each client statement.
3. In a 15-minute helping interview in which you function as an observer, listen for and record five key aspects of client messages that form the basis of effective listening.
4. In a 15-minute role-play interview or a conversation in which you function as a listener, demonstrate at least two accurate examples of each of the four listening responses.

"Listening is the art by which we use empathy to reach across the space between us. . . . [G]enuine listening means suspending memory, desire, and judgment—and, for a few moments at least, existing for the other person" (Nichols, 1995, pp. 62, 64). According to Simpkinson and Simpkinson (1998), much of Western culture suffers from attention deficits in the sense that many of the clients we see are not getting enough attention and validation in their lives and are therefore psychologically malnourished. The Simpkinsons (1998) note that listening and being heard are "important psychological nutrients" that all of us need on a daily basis (p. 20). When these nutrients are missing, we lose a part of our identity and live in a state of "chronic psychological malnourishment" (p. 20).

Listening is a way to understand the client's frame of reference. As such, it is an important part of a "quiet and eliciting" helping style that through a process called *motivational interviewing* often motivates clients to change from within rather than from response to external pressure (Rollnick & Miller, 1995, p. 325).

Listening is a prerequisite for all other helping responses and strategies. Listening should precede whatever else is done. When a helper fails to listen, the client may be discouraged from self-exploring, the wrong issue may be discussed, or a strategy may be proposed prematurely.

We define listening as involving three processes: receiving a message, processing a message, and sending a message. These three processes are illustrated in Figure 5.1.

Each client message (verbal or nonverbal) is a stimulus to be received and processed by the helper. When a client sends a message, the helper receives it. Reception of a message is a covert process; that is, we cannot see how or what the helper receives. Failure to receive all the message may occur when the helper stops attending.

Once a message is received, it must be processed in some way. Processing, like reception, is covert, because it goes on within the helper's mind and is not visible to the outside world—except, perhaps, from the helper's nonverbal cues. Processing includes thinking about the message and pondering its meaning. Processing is important because a helper's cognitions, self-talk, and mental (covert) preparation and visualization set the stage for overt responding (Morran, Kurpius, Brack, & Brack, 1995). Errors in processing a message accurately often occur when helpers' biases or blind spots prevent them from acknowledging parts of a message or from interpreting a message without distortion. Helpers may hear what they want to hear instead of the actual message sent. Also, as Ivey, Gluckstern, and Ivey (1993) note, clients tend to talk about what they perceive you are able and willing to listen to.

The third process of listening involves the verbal and nonverbal messages sent by a helper. Sometimes a helper may receive and process a message accurately but have difficulty sending a message because of lack of skills. Fortunately, you

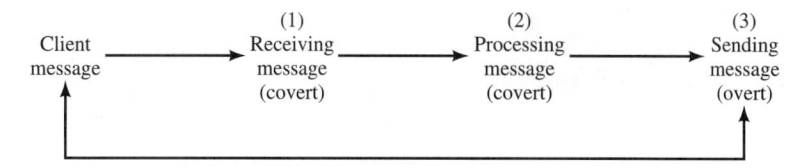

```
Client          (1)           (2)            (3)
message  →   Receiving  →  Processing  →  Sending
             message        message        message
             (covert)       (covert)       (overt)
     ↑_____|
```

Figure 5.1 Three processes of listening

can learn to use listening responses to send messages. Problems in sending messages can be more easily corrected than errors in the covert processes of receiving and processing messages. We hope that you are already able to receive and process a message without difficulty. Of course, this is a big assumption! If you think your own covert processes in listening are in need of further development, this may be an area you will need to work on by yourself or with someone else.

This chapter is designed to help you acquire four verbal listening responses that you can use to send messages to a client: clarification, paraphrase, reflection, and summarization. These responses are intended to convey that you are listening to and understanding client messages. This can be a hard process with any client. With clients who are culturally different from you, this process might be even more difficult because of varying cultural nuances in communication and expression. As Sue and Sue (1999) note, "While breakdowns in communication often happen between members who share the same culture, the problem becomes exacerbated between people of different races or ethnic backgrounds" (p. 58).

LISTENING TO CLIENTS' STORIES

Ivey, Ivey, and Simek-Morgan (1997) note that listening helps to bring out the client's story. Listening is healing because it helps clients tell their stories. Clients' messages represent stories about themselves—narratives about their histories and current experiences from which clients construct their identities and infuse their lives with meaning and purpose (White & Epston, 1990). Good therapists listen to these stories to help clients recognize how these narratives construct meaning and whether they help or hurt the development of the client's identity. Telling one's story can also provide emotional relief to clients who have suffered trauma, even for those clients who are very young or old (Terr, 1990). For clients who are suffering a loss such as a separation or divorce, loss of a job, or loss of a significant other, stories provide a way to make sense of the bereavement (Sedney, Baker, & Gross, 1994). For dying clients, stories represent a life that has been lived and is now coming to an end, but may not yet have been told. Healing is particularly evident for clients who tell their story when "hidden difficulties" or "shame" have been involved (Ostaseski, 1994).

Stories are also almost universally present and relevant in various ethnic cultural groups. Helpers can listen to many things about clients' stories. Ivey, Ivey, and Simek-Morgan (1997) recommend listening to the *facts* of the story, the client's *feelings* about the story, and the way the client *organizes* the story. Sedney and colleagues (1994) recommend listening to how the story is started, the sequences in the story, and "hints of anger, regret, and what ifs," as well as the client's understanding of the story and the role she or he plays in it (p. 291). Significant omissions also may provide clues. Ostaseski (1994) comments that as helpers, we must simply trust that some insight will arise for clients just from the telling of the story: "Often the story will deliver what is needed. So pay close attention to whatever you are presented with. Start with that. Take it. Believe it, and see where it leads you" (p. 11).

What Does Listening Require of Helpers?

When someone truly hears us, it is a special gift. We can all recall times when we felt wonderful—just because someone who means something to us stood or sat with us and really listened. Conversely, we can also remember instances in which we felt flustered because someone close to us was inattentive and distracted. Nichols (1995) has referred to listening as a "lost art," which he attributes partly to contemporary time pressures that distract our attention span and impoverish the quality of listening in our lives (p. 2). As a result, this lack of listening pervades our most prized relationships, contributes to interpersonal conflict, and leaves us with a sense of loss. Nichols (1995) observes that this loss is most severe when lack of listening occurs in relationships in which we counted on it to occur, such as in the helping relationship.

LEARNING ACTIVITY 5.1 Cultivating the Listening Mind

Part One

Obtain three small objects to eat, such as raisins or M&Ms. Sit in a comfortable position, close your eyes, and focus on your teeth. If wandering thoughts come, let them flow by. Starting with one raisin, slowly lift it to your mouth. Chew it very slowly. Observe your arm lifting the raisin to your mouth. . . . Think about how your hand holds it. . . . Notice how it feels in your mouth. . . . Savor it as you chew it ever so slowly. While doing this, notice your tongue and throat as you very slowly swallow the raisin.

Repeat this process with the next two objects. Afterward, notice what you realize about eating and raisins. What do you usually tune out?

Part Two

Lie still in a comfortable position. Scan your body, starting with your toes and moving very slowly up to the top of your head. Direct your attention to a spot that feels most tense or painful. Put your hand on that spot. Leave it there for a few minutes. Breathe with it. Just notice what happens as you go into this part of your body with your breathing and your awareness. You are not trying to change anything; just be aware of this place and accept it. Stay with this for a little while and see what happens to this spot.

In this chapter, we describe the use and purposes of four listening responses that, if acquired, will help you become a better listener. However, in addition to these responses, truly effective listening requires the capacity to be fully present to the client and free from distractions—both internal and external. In this way, the listening process provides the sort of "holding environment" we discussed in Chapter 4, and this requires a certain kind of *energy* on the helper's part—an energy that is highly involved and yet also quite contained.

Helpers who listen best usually have developed this sort of "mindfulness" about them that we discuss further in Chapter 16 in the meditation strategies. These helpers are also able to focus their energy very intently on the client with minimal intrusions—either from their own process or from the outer environment. This mindfulness quality is typically more highly developed in Eastern cultures, for example where persons rise at dawn to practice tai chi. Perhaps nowhere is this quality more evident than with those helpers who work with dying persons. Ostaseski (1994), director of the San Francisco Zen Hospice project, discusses this process in the following way:

> We sit at the bedside and we listen. We try to listen with our whole body, not just with our ears. We must perpetually ask ourselves, "Am I fully here? Or am I checking my watch or looking out the window?"
>
> At the heart of it, all we can really offer each other is our full attention. When people are dying, their tolerance for bullshit is minimal. They will quickly sniff out insincerity. Material may arise that we don't particularly like or even strongly dislike. Just as we do in meditation, we need to sit still and listen, not knowing what will come next, to suspend judgment—at least for the moment—so that whatever needs to evolve will be able to do so. (p. 11)

If you feel this is a quality you need to develop further in yourself, we encourage you to practice Learning Activity 5.1, adapted from Kabat-Zinn (1993), on a daily basis.

FOUR LISTENING RESPONSES

This chapter presents four kinds of listening responses: clarification, paraphrase, reflection, and summarization. *Clarification* is a question, often used after an ambiguous client message. It starts with "Do you mean that . . ." or "Are you saying that . . ." along with a repetition or rephrasing of all or part of the client's previous message. Similar to a clarification is the *paraphrase,* defined as a rephrasing of the content part of the message, which describes a situation, event, person, or idea. In contrast, *reflection* is a rephrasing of the client's feelings, or the affect part of the message. Usually the affect part of the message reveals the client's feelings about the content; for example, a client may feel discouraged (affect) about not doing well in a class (content). *Summarization* is an extension of the paraphrase and reflection responses that involves tying together and rephrasing two or more different parts of a message or messages.

Response	Definition	Intended purpose
Clarification	A question beginning with, for example, "Do you mean that" or "Are you saying that" plus a rephrasing of the client's message	1. To encourage more client elaboration 2. To check out the accuracy of what you heard the client say 3. To clear up vague, confusing messages
Paraphrase (responding to content)	A rephrasing of the content of the client's message	1. To help the client focus on the content of his or her message 2. To highlight content when attention to feelings is premature or self-defeating
Reflection (responding to feelings)	A rephrasing of the affective part of the client's message	1. To encourage the client to express more of his or her feelings 2. To help the client become more aware of the feelings that dominate him or her 3. To help the client acknowledge and manage feelings 4. To help the client discriminate accurately among feelings 5. To help the client feel understood
Summarization	Two or more paraphrases or reflections that condense the client's messages or the session	1. To tie together multiple elements of client messages 2. To identify a common theme or pattern 3. To interrupt excessive rambling 4. To review progress

TABLE 5.1 Definitions and Intended Purposes of Listening Responses

To illustrate these four responses, we present a client message with an example of each:

Client, a 35-year-old Latina widow, mother of two young children: My whole life fell apart when my husband died. I keep feeling so unsure about my ability to make it on my own and to support my kids. My husband always made all the decisions for me and brought home money every week. Now I haven't slept well for so long, and I'm drinking more heavily—I can't even think straight. My relatives help me as they can but I still feel scared.

Helper clarification: Are you saying that one of the hardest things facing you now is to have enough confidence in yourself?

Helper paraphrase: Since your husband's death you have more responsibilities and decisions on your shoulders, even with the support of relatives.

Helper reflection: You feel worried about having to shoulder all the family responsibilities now.

Helper summarization: Now that your husband has died, you're facing a few things that are very difficult for you right now . . . handling the family responsibilities, making the decisions, trying to take better care of yourself, and dealing with fears that have come up as a result.

Table 5.1 presents the definitions and the *intended* or hypothesized purposes of the four listening responses of clarification, paraphrase, reflection, and summarization. These responses may not have the same results for all clients. For example, a practitioner may find that reflecting feelings prompts some clients to discuss feelings, whereas other clients may not even acknowledge the counselor's statement (Uhlemann, Lee, & Martin, 1994). The point is that we are presenting some "modal" intentions for each listening response; there are exceptions. The listening responses will achieve their intended purposes most of the time. However, other dynamics within an interview may yield different client outcomes. Moreover, the effects of these verbal messages may vary depending on the nonverbal cues sent along with the message. It is helpful to have some rationale in mind for using a response. However, keep in mind that the influence a response has on the client may not be what you intended to achieve by selecting it. The guidelines in Table 5.1 should be used tentatively, *subject to modification by particular client reactions.*

The next three sections describe the listening responses and present model examples of each skill. Opportunities to practice each skill and receive feedback follow the examples.

Listening for Accuracy: The Clarification Response

Because most messages are expressed from the speaker's internal frame of reference, they may be vague or confusing. Messages that may be particularly confusing are those that include inclusive terms (*they* and *them*), ambiguous phrases (*you know*), and words with a double meaning (*stoned, trip*). When you aren't sure of the meaning of a message, it is helpful to clarify it.

According to Hutchins and Cole-Vaught (1997), a clarification asks the client to elaborate on "a vague, ambiguous, or implied statement." The request for clarification is usually expressed in the form of a question and may begin with phrases such as "Are you saying this . . ." or "Could you try to describe that . . ." or "Can you clarify that. . . ."

Purposes of Clarification

A clarification may be used to make the client's previous message explicit and to confirm the accuracy of your perceptions about the message. A clarification is appropriate for any occasion when you aren't sure whether you understand the client's message and you need more elaboration. A second purpose of clarification is to check out what you heard of the client's message. Particularly in the beginning stages of helping, it is important to verify client messages before jumping to quick conclusions. The following example may help you see the value of the clarification response:

Client: Sometimes I just want to get away from it all.

Helper: It sounds like you have to split and be on your own.

Client: No, it's not that. I don't want to be alone. It's just that I wish I could get out from under all this work I have to do.

In this example, the helper drew a quick conclusion about the initial client message that turned out to be inaccurate. The session might have gone more smoothly if the helper had requested clarification before assuming something about the client, as in the next example:

Client: Sometimes I just want to get away from it all.

Helper: Could you describe for me what you mean by getting away from it all?

Client: Well, I just have so much work to do—I'm always feeling behind and overloaded. I'd like to get out from under that miserable feeling.

In this case, the clarification helped both persons to establish exactly what was being said and felt. Neither the client nor the helper had to rely on assumptions and inferences that were not explored and confirmed. The skilled helper uses clarification responses to determine the accuracy of messages as they are received and processed. Otherwise, inaccurate information may not be corrected and distorted assumptions may remain untested.

Steps in Clarifying

There are four steps in clarifying for accuracy. First, identify the content of the client's verbal and nonverbal messages—what has the client told you? Second, identify any vague or confusing parts of the message that you need to check out for accuracy or elaboration. Third, decide on an appropriate beginning, or sentence stem, for your clarification, such as "Could you describe," "Could you clarify," or "Are you saying." In addition, use your voice to deliver the clarification as a question rather than a statement. Finally, remember to assess the effectiveness of your clarification by listening to and observing the client's response. If your clarification is useful, the client will elaborate on the ambiguous or confusing part of the message. If it is not useful, the client will clam up, ignore your request for clarification, and/or continue to make deletions or omissions. At this point, you can attempt a subsequent clarification or switch to an alternative response.

To help you formulate a clarification, decide when to use it, and assess its effectiveness, consider the following cognitive learning strategy:

1. What has this client told me?
2. Are there any vague parts or missing pictures in the message that I need to check out? If so, what? If not, decide on another, more suitable response.
3. How can I hear, see, or grasp a way to start this response?
4. How will I know whether my clarification is useful?

Notice how a helper applies this cognitive learning strategy in clarifying the client's message given in the previous example:

Client: Sometimes I just want to get away from it all.

Helper: [asked and answered covertly]:

1. *What has this client told me?*

That she wants to get away from something.

2. *Are there any vague parts or missing pictures in her message? If so, what?* (If not, I'll decide on a more suitable response.)

Yes—I need to check out what she means by "getting away from it all."

3. *How can I begin a clarification response?*

I can see the start of it, hear the start of it, or grasp the start of it. Something like "Well, could you tell me, or could you describe. . . ."

4. *How will I know that the response will be helpful?*
I'll have to see, hear, and grasp whether she elaborates or not. Let's try it. . . .

Suppose that, at this juncture, the helper's covert visualization or self-talk ends, and the following actual dialogue occurs:

Helper clarification: Could you describe what you mean by "getting away from it all"?

Client response: Well, I just have so much work to do—I'm always feeling behind and overloaded. I'd like to get out from under that miserable feeling.

From the client's response, the helper can determine that the clarification was effective because the client elaborated and added the missing parts or pictures from her previous message. The helper can covertly congratulate himself or herself for not jumping ahead too quickly and for taking the time to check out the client's deletion and the resulting ambiguity.

The following learning activity gives you an opportunity to try out this cognitive learning strategy to develop the skill of clarification.

LISTENING FOR UNDERSTANDING: PARAPHRASING, REFLECTING, AND BASIC EMPATHY

In addition to clarifying the accuracy of client messages, the practitioner needs to listen for information revealed in messages about significant situations and events in the client's life—and the client's feelings about these events. Ivey, Ivey, and Simek-Morgan (1997) talk about this as listening for (1) the main facts of the client's story and (2) the client's feelings about his or her story. Each client message will express (directly or indirectly) some information about client situations or concerns and about client feelings. The portion of the message that expresses information or describes a situation or event is called the *content*, or the cognitive part, of the message. The cognitive part of a message includes references to a situation or event, people, objects, or ideas. Another portion of the message may reveal how the client feels about the content; expression of feelings or an emotional tone is called the *affective* part of the message (Cormier & Hackney, 1999). Generally, the affect part of the verbal message is distinguished by the client's use of an affect or feeling word, such as *happy, angry,* or *sad*. However, clients may also express their feelings in less obvious ways, particularly through various nonverbal behaviors.

The following illustrations may help you distinguish between the content and affective parts of a client's verbal message:

Client, a 6-year-old first-grader: I don't like school. It isn't much fun.

The first sentence ("I don't like school") is the affect part of the message. The client's feelings are suggested by the words "don't like." The second sentence ("It isn't much fun") is the content part of the message because it refers to a situation or an event in this child's life—not having fun at school.

Here is another example:

Client, a 20-year-old woman: How can I tell my boyfriend I want to break off our relationship? He will be very upset. I guess I'm afraid to tell him.

In this example, the first two sentences are the content because they describe the situation of wanting to break off a relationship. The third sentence, the affect part, indicates the client's feelings about this situation—being *afraid* to tell the boyfriend of her intentions.

See whether you can discriminate between the content and affective parts of the following two client messages:

Client 1, a young man: I just can't satisfy my wife sexually. It's very frustrating for me.

In this example, the content part is "I can't satisfy my wife sexually." The affect part, or the client's feelings about the content, is "It's very *frustrating* for me."

Client 2, an institutionalized man: This place is a trap. It seems like I've been here forever. I'd feel much better if I weren't here.

In the second example, the statements referring to the institution as a trap and being there forever are the content parts of the message. The statement of "feeling better" is the affect part.

The skilled helper tries to listen for both content and affect parts of client messages because it is important to deal with significant situations or relationships *and* with the client's feelings about the situations. Responding to cognitive or affective messages will direct the focus of the session in different ways. At some points, the helper will respond to content by focusing on events, objects, people, or ideas. At other times, the helper will respond to affect by focusing on the client's feelings and emotions. Generally, the helper can respond to content by using a paraphrase and can respond to affect with a reflection.

Paraphrase

A paraphrase is a rephrasing of the client's primary words and thoughts. Paraphrasing involves selective attention given to the cognitive part of the message—with the client's key ideas

LEARNING ACTIVITY 5.2 — Clarification

In this learning activity, you are presented with three client practice messages.* For each client message, develop an example of a clarification response, using the cognitive learning strategy described earlier and outlined in the following example. To internalize this learning strategy, you may wish to talk through these self-questions overtly (aloud) and then covertly (silently to yourself). The end product will be a clarification response that you can say aloud or write down or both. An example precedes the practice messages. Feedback follows on page 91.

Example

Client, a 15-year-old high school student: My grades have really slipped. I don't know why; I just feel so down about everything.

Self-question 1: *What has this client told me?*
That she feels down and rather discouraged.

Self-question 2: *Are there any vague parts or missing pictures to the message that I need to check out? If so, what? (If not, decide on a different response.)*

Yes, several—one is what she feels so down about. Another is what this feeling of being down is like for her.

Self-question 3: *How can I hear, see, or grasp a way to start this response?*
"Are you saying there's something specific?" or "Can you describe this feeling. . . ?"

Self-question 4: *Say aloud or write an actual clarification response:*
"Are you saying there is something specific you feel down about?" or "Could you describe what this feeling of being down is like for you?"

Client Practice Messages

Client 1, a fourth-grader: I don't want to do this dumb homework anyway. I don't care about learning these math problems. Girls don't need to know this anyway.
Self-question 1: *What has this client told me?*
Self-question 2: *Are there any vague parts or missing pictures I need to check out? If so, what?*
Self-question 3: *How can I hear, see, or grasp a way to start my response?*
Actual clarification response: _____
_____
_____

Client 2, a middle-aged man: I'm really discouraged with this physical disability now. I feel like I can't do anything the way I used to. Not only has it affected me in my job, but at home. I just don't feel like I have anything good to offer anyone.

Self-question 1: *What has this client told me?*
Self-question 2: *Are there any vague parts or missing pictures I need to check out? If so, what?*
Self-question 3: *How can I hear, see, or grasp a way to start my response?*
Actual clarification response: _____
_____
_____

Client 3, an older person: The company is going to make me retire even though I don't want to. What will I do with myself then? I find myself just thinking over the good times of the past, not wanting to face the future at all. Sometimes retirement makes me so nervous I can't sleep or eat. My family suggested I see someone about this.

Self-question 1: *What has this client told me?*
Self-question 2: *Are there any vague parts or missing pictures I need to check out? If so, what?*
Self-question 3: *How can I hear, see, or grasp a way to start my response?*
Actual clarification response: _____
_____
_____

*Additional practice for the responses in this chapter is on the Brooks/Cole book Web site, http://info.wadsworth.com/0534537391

> ## 5.2 FEEDBACK
> ### Clarification
>
> **Client 1**
>
> 1. *What did the client say?*
>
> That she doesn't want to do her math homework—that she thinks it's not important for girls.
>
> 2. *Are there any vague parts or missing pictures?*
>
> Yes—whether she really doesn't care about math or whether she's had a bad experience with it and is denying her concern.
>
> 3. *Examples of clarification responses:*
>
> "Are you saying that you really dislike math or that it's not going as well for you as you would like?"
>
> "Are you saying that math is not too important for you or that it is hard for you?"
>
> **Client 2**
>
> 1. *What did the client say?*
>
> That he feels useless to himself and others.
>
> 2. *Are there any vague parts or missing pictures?*
>
> Yes—it's not clear exactly how things are different for him now and also whether it's the disability itself that's bothering him or its effects (inability to get around, reactions of others, and so on).
>
> 3. *Examples of clarification responses:*
>
> "Could you clarify exactly how things are different for you now from the way they used to be?"
>
> "Are you saying you feel discouraged about having the disability—or about the effects and constraints from it?"
>
> "Are you saying you feel differently about yourself now from the way you used to?"
>
> **Client 3**
>
> 1. *What did the client say?*
>
> He is going to have to retire because of company policy. He doesn't want to retire now and feels upset about this. He's here at his family's suggestion.
>
> 2. *Are there any vague parts or missing pictures?*
>
> Yes—he says he feels nervous, although from his description of not eating and sleeping it may be sadness or depression. Also, is he here only because his family sent him or because he feels a need too? Finally, what specifically bothers him about retirement?
>
> 3. *Examples of clarification responses:*
>
> "Would you say you're feeling more nervous or more depressed about your upcoming retirement?"
>
> "Are you saying you're here just because of your family's feelings or because of your feelings too?"
>
> "Could you describe what it is about retiring that worries you?"

translated into *your own words*. Thus, an effective paraphrase is more than just "parroting" the words of the client. The rephrasal should be carefully worded to lead to further discussion or increased understanding on the part of the client. It is helpful to stress the most important words and ideas expressed by the client. Consider the following example:

Client: I know it doesn't help my depression to sit around or stay in bed all day.

Helper: You know you need to avoid staying in bed or sitting around all day to help your depression.

In this example, the helper merely "parroted" the client's message. The likely outcome is that the client may respond with a minimal answer such as "I agree" or "That's right" and not elaborate further, or that the client may feel ridiculed by what seems to be an obvious or mimicking response. A more effective paraphrase would be "You are aware that you need to get up and move around in order to minimize being depressed."

Purposes of Paraphrasing

There are several purposes in using the paraphrase at selected times in client interactions. First, use of the paraphrase tells clients that you have understood their communication. If your understanding is complete, clients can expand or clarify their ideas. Second, paraphrasing can encourage client elaboration of a key idea or thought. Clients may talk about an important topic in greater depth. A third reason for use of paraphrases is to help the client focus on a particular situation or event, idea, or behavior.

Sometimes, by increasing focus, paraphrasing can help get a client "on track." For example, accurate paraphrasing can help stop a client from merely repeating a "story" (Ivey & Ivey, 1999).

A fourth use of paraphrase is to help clients who need to make decisions. As Ivey, Ivey, and Simek-Downing (1987, p. 73) observe, "Paraphrasing is often helpful to clients who have a decision to make, for the repetition of key ideas and phrases clarifies the essence of the problem." Paraphrasing is also useful when emphasizing content if attention to affect is premature or counterproductive.

Steps in Paraphrasing

There are five steps in paraphrasing content. First, attend to and recall the message by restating it to yourself covertly—what has the client told you? Second, identify the content part of the message by asking yourself "What situation, person, object, or idea is discussed in this message?" Third, select an appropriate beginning, or sentence stem, for your paraphrase. Paraphrases can begin with many possible sentence stems. Table 5.2 provides examples of phrases and sentence stems useful for beginning paraphrase and reflection responses. Next, using the sentence stem you selected, translate the key content or constructs into your own words and verbalize this into a paraphrase. Remember to use your voice as you deliver the paraphrase so it sounds like a statement instead of a question. Finally, assess the effectiveness of your paraphrase by listening to and observing the client's response. If your paraphrase is accurate, the client will in some way—verbally and/or nonverbally—confirm its accuracy and usefulness. Consider the following example of the way a helper uses the cognitive learning strategy to formulate a paraphrase:

Client, a 40-year-old Asian American woman [Said in a level, monotone voice]: How can I tell my husband I want a divorce? He'll think I'm crazy. I guess I'm just afraid to tell him.

1. *What has this client told me?*

That she wants a divorce and she's afraid to tell her husband, as he will think she's crazy.

2. *What is the content of this message—what person, object, idea, or situation is the client discussing?*

Wants divorce but hasn't told husband because husband will think she's crazy.

3. *What is an appropriate sentence stem?*

I'll go with a stem such as "You think," "I hear you saying," or "It sounds like."

4. *How can I translate the client's key content into my own words?*

TABLE 5.2	Examples of Phrases and Sentence Stems

Helper phrases

It seems like
It appears as though
From my perspective
As I see it
I see what you mean
It looks like
Sounds like
As I hear it
What you're saying is
I hear you saying
Something tells you
You're telling me that
You feel
From my standpoint
I sense that
I have the feeling that

Want a divorce = break off, terminate the relationship, split.

5. *How will I know whether my paraphrase is helpful?*

Listen and notice whether the client confirms its accuracy.

Suppose that at this point the helper's self-talk stopped and the following dialogue ensued:

Helper paraphrase: It sounds like you haven't found a way to tell your husband you want to end the relationship because of his possible reaction. Is that right?

Client: Yeah—I've decided—I've even been to see a lawyer. But I just don't know how to approach him with this. He thinks things are wonderful, and I don't want to dishonor him by divorcing him.

This is a paraphrase that has encouraged client elaboration and focus on a main issue. Learning Activity 5.3 gives you an opportunity to develop your own paraphrase responses.

Reflection of Feeling

We have just seen that the paraphrase is used to restate the cognitive part of the message. Although the paraphrase and the reflection of feeling are not mutually exclusive responses, the reflection of feeling is used to rephrase the *affective* part of the message, the client's emotional tone. A reflection is similar to a paraphrase but different in that a reflection adds an emotional tone or component to the message that is lacking in a paraphrase. Here are two examples that may illustrate the difference between a paraphrase and a reflection of feeling:

LEARNING ACTIVITY 5.3 Paraphrase

In this learning activity, you are presented with three client practice messages. For each client message, develop an example of a paraphrase response, using the cognitive learning strategy outlined in the example below. To internalize this learning strategy, you may wish to talk through these self-questions overtly (aloud) and then covertly (silently). The end product will be a paraphrase response that you can say aloud or write down or both. Feedback is given on page 94.

Example

Client, a middle-aged graduate student [said in a level, monotone voice]: It's just a rough time for me—trying to work, keeping up with graduate school, and spending time with my family. I keep telling myself it will slow down someday.

Self-question 1: *What has this client told me?*
That it's hard to keep up with everything he has to do.

Self-question 2: *What is the content of this message—what person, object, idea, or situation is the client discussing?*
Trying to keep up with work, school, and family.

Self-question 3: *What is an appropriate sentence stem?*
I'll try a stem like "It sounds like" or "There are."

Actual paraphrase response: It sounds like you're having a tough time balancing all your commitments *or* There are a lot of demands on your time right now.

Client Practice Statements

Client 1, a 30-year-old woman [said in a level tone without much variation in pitch or tempo]: My husband and I argue all the time about how to manage our kids. He says I always interfere with his discipline—I think he is too harsh with them.

Self-question 1: *What has this client told me?*
Self-question 2: *What is the content of this message? What person, object, idea, or situation is the client discussing?*
Self-question 3: *What is a useful sentence stem?*
Actual paraphrase response: _____

_____

Client 2, a 6-year-old boy [said in slow, soft voice with downcast eyes]: I wish I didn't have a little sister. I know my parents love her more than me.

Self-question 1: *What has this client told me?*
Self-question 2: *What is the content of this message—what person, object, idea, or situation is this client discussing?*
Self-question 3: *What is a useful sentence stem?*
Actual paraphrase response: _____

_____

Client 3, a college student [said in level, measured words with little pitch and inflection change]: I've said to my family before, I just can't compete with the other students who aren't blind. There's no way I can keep up with this kind of handicap. I've told them it's natural to be behind and do more poorly.

Self-question 1: *What has this client told me?*
Self-question 2: *What is the content of this message? What person, object, idea, or situation is the client discussing?*
Self-question 3: *What is a useful sentence stem?*
Actual paraphrase response: _____

_____

Client: Everything is humdrum. There's nothing new going on, nothing exciting. All my friends are away. I wish I had some money to do something different.

Helper paraphrase: With your friends gone and no money around, there is nothing for you to do right now.

Helper reflection: You feel bored with the way things are for you right now.

Note the helper's use of the affect word *bored* in the reflection response to tune into the feelings of the client created by the particular situation.

FEEDBACK 5.3
Paraphrase

Client 1

Question 1: *What has the client said?*
That she and her husband argue over child rearing.

Question 2: *What is the content of her message?*
As a couple, they have different ideas on who should discipline their kids and how.

Question 3: *What is a useful sentence stem?*
Try "It sounds like" or "Your ideas about discipline are."

Actual paraphrase response: *Here are examples; see whether yours are similar.*
It sounds like you and your husband disagree a great deal on which one of you should discipline your kids and how it should be done *or* Your ideas about discipline for your kids are really different from your husband's, and this creates disagreements between the two of you.

Client 2

Question 1: *What has this client said?*
He believes his little sister is loved more by his folks than he is, and he wishes she weren't around.

Question 2: *What is the content of his message?*
Client feels "dethroned"—wishes the new "princess" would go away.

Question 3: *What is a useful sentence stem?*
I'll try "It seems that" or "I sense that."

Actual paraphrase response: *Here are examples.*
It seems that you'd like to be "number one" again in your family *or* I sense you are not sure of your place in your family since your little sister arrived.

Client 3

Question 1: *What has this client said?*
He is behind in school and is not doing as well as his peers because he is blind—a point he has emphasized to his family.

Question 2: *What is the content of his message?*
Client wants to impress on his family that *to him* his blindness is a handicap that interferes with his doing as much or as well as other students.

Question 3: *What is a useful sentence stem?*
"It sounds like," "I hear you saying," or "You'd like."

Actual paraphrase response: *Here are some examples.*
It sounds like it's very important to you that your family realize how tough it is for you to do well in your studies here *or* You'd like your family to realize how difficult it is for you to keep up academically with people who don't have the added problem of being blind.

Purposes of Reflection

Reflecting feelings has five intended purposes. First, reflection is also used to encourage clients to express more of their feelings (both positive and negative) about a particular situation, person, or whatever. Some clients do not readily reveal feelings because they have never learned to do so, and other clients hold back feelings until the helper gives permission to focus on them. Expression of feelings is not usually an end in itself; rather, it is a means of helping clients and practitioners understand the scope of the issues or situation. Most if not all the concerns presented by clients involve underlying emotional factors to be resolved (Ivey, Ivey, & Simek-Morgan, 1997). For example, in focusing on feelings, the client may become more aware of lingering feelings about an unfinished situation or of intense feelings that seem to dominate his or her reaction to a situation. Clients may also become aware of mixed, or conflicting, feelings. Ambivalence is a common way that clients express feelings about problematic issues. Teyber (2000) notes that two common affective constructions with mixed components include anger-sadness-shame and sadness-anger-guilt. In the first sequence, the primary feeling is often anger, but it is a negative response to hurt or sadness. Often, the experiencing of the anger and sadness provokes shame. In the second sequence, the predominant feeling is sadness, but it is often connected to anger that has been denied because the expression of it produces guilt. These affective sequences are typically acquired in childhood and are a result of both the rules and the interactions of the family of origin. These affective elements are also strongly influenced by cultural affiliation. As Sue and Sue (1999) note, in Western cultures, which emphasize individualism, the predominant affective reaction following wrongful behavior is *guilt*. However, in some non-Western cultures, such as Asian, Hispanic, and Black, where the psychosocial unit is the family, group, or collective society, the primary affective reaction to wrongful behavior is not guilt but *shame*. Sue and Sue (1999) conclude that "guilt is an individual affect, while shame appears to be a group one" (p. 63). A review of cultural variations in emotions can be found in Mesquita and Frijda (1992).

A second purpose of reflection is to help clients manage feelings. Learning to deal with feelings is especially important when a client experiences an intense emotion such as fear, dependency, or anger. Strong emotions can interfere with a client's ability to make a rational response (cognitive or behavioral) to pressure. Also, when clients are given permission to reveal and release feelings, their energy and well-being is often increased. For example, during and after a crisis or disaster such as an earthquake, car bombing, or the disaster of the World Trade Center and the Pentagon on September 11, 2001, people feel overwhelmed by the intensity of their emotions. This feeling can persist for months or even years after the event. Practitioners who help clients in these sorts of situations do so in part by encouraging these clients to name, validate, and express their emotions in a safe context. At the end of this chapter we provide several Web sites related to communicating and responding to the emotions of a crisis and/or disaster.

A third use of reflection is with clients who express negative feelings about therapy or about the helper. When a client becomes angry or upset with you or with the help you are offering, there is a tendency to take the client's remarks personally and become defensive. Using reflection in these instances "lessens the possibility of an emotional conflict, which often arises simply because two people are trying to make themselves heard and neither is trying to listen" (Long & Prophit, 1981, p. 89). The use of reflection in these situations lets clients know that the helper understands their feelings in such a way that the intensity of the anger is usually diminished. As anger subsides, the client may become more receptive, and the helper can again initiate action-oriented responses or intervention strategies.

Reflection also helps clients discriminate accurately among various feelings. Clients often use feeling words like *anxious* or *nervous* that, on occasion, mask deeper or more intense feelings (Ivey, Gluckstern, & Ivey, 1993). Clients may also use an affect word that does not really portray their emotional state accurately. For instance, it is common for a client to say "It's my nerves" or "I'm nervous" to depict other feelings, such as resentment and depression. Other clients may reveal feelings through the use of metaphors (Ivey, Gluckstern, & Ivey, 1993). For example, a client may say "I feel like the person who rolled down Niagara Falls in a barrel" or "I feel like I just got hit by a Mack truck." Metaphors are important indicators of client emotion; as Ivey, Gluckstern, and Ivey (1993) note, they suggest that much more is going on with the client than just the "surface expression" (p. 71). Accurate reflections of feeling help clients to refine their understanding of various emotional moods.

Ivey, Gluckstern, and Ivey (1993) note that processing emotions does not always occur easily with some clients. As they suggest,

> In White, North American and other cultures, men are expected to hold back their feelings. You aren't a "real man" if you allow yourself to feel emotion. While many men can and do express their feelings in the helping interview, some should not be pushed too hard in this area in the first phases of counseling. Later, with trust, exploration of feelings becomes more acceptable.
>
> In general, women in all cultures are more in touch with and more willing to share feelings than men. Nonetheless, this will vary with the cultural group. Some cultures (for example, Asian, Native American) at times pride themselves on their ability to control emotions. However, this may also be true with those of British and Irish extraction.
>
> African Americans and other minorities have learned over time that it may not be safe to share themselves openly with White Americans. In cross-cultural counseling situations, trust needs to be built before you can expect in-depth discussion of emotions. (pp. 73–74)

Finally, this response, if used effectively and accurately, helps clients to feel understood. Clients tend to communicate more freely with persons whom they feel try to understand them. As Teyber (2000) observes, when understanding is present, "Clients feel that they have been seen and are no longer invisible, alone, strange, or unimportant. At that moment, the client begins to perceive the therapist as someone who is different from most other people and possibly as someone who can help" (p. 46).

As you will see in the following section, the reflection of feeling response is the primary verbal tool used to convey basic empathy.

Verbal Means of Conveying Empathy

Consider the following verbal tools for conveying empathy:

- *Show desire to comprehend.* It is necessary not only to convey an accurate understanding from the client's perspective but also to convey your *desire* to comprehend from the client's frame of reference.

Keeping in mind our discussion of cultural empathy, this desire includes an understanding not only of the individual, but also of the person's world view: his or her environmental and sociopolitical context and cultural group. McGill (1992) offers the idea of the *cultural story* as a way to open communication and develop understanding about the client's cultural group:

> The cultural story refers to an ethnic or cultural group's origin, migration, and identity. Within the family, it is used to tell where one's ancestors came from, what kind of people they were and current members are, what issues are important to the family, what good and bad things have happened over time, and what lessons have been learned from their experiences. At the ethnic level, a cultural story tells the group's collective story of how to cope with life and how to respond to pain and trouble. It teaches people how to thrive in a multicultural society and what children should be taught so that they can sustain their ethnic and cultural story. (McGill, 1992, p. 340)

Your desire to comprehend is evidenced by statements indicating your attempts to make sense of the client's world and by clarification and questions about the client's experiences and feelings.

- *Discuss what is important to the client.* Show by your questions and statements that you are aware of what is most important to the client. Respond in ways that relate to the client's basic problem or complaint. This should be a brief statement that captures the thoughts and feelings of the client and one that is directly related to the client's concerns.
- Use verbal responses that *refer to client feelings.* One way to define verbal empathy is through the reflection of feeling response, which reflects the client's feelings and conveys your awareness of the client's feelings. This response allows you to focus on the client's feelings by naming or labeling them. This is sometimes called *interchangeable* (Carkhuff, 1969a), *basic* (Egan, 1998), or *reciprocal* (Hepworth et al., 1997) empathy.
- Use verbal responses that bridge or *add on to implicit client messages.* Empathy also involves comprehension of the client's innermost thoughts and perspectives even when these are unspoken and implicit. According to Rogers (1977), "The therapist is so much inside the private world of the other that she can clarify not only the messages of which the client is aware but even those just below the level of awareness" (p. 11). The counselor bridges or adds on to client messages by conveying understanding of what the client implies or infers in order to add to the client's frame of reference or to draw out implications of the issue. This is sometimes called *additive* empathy (Carkhuff, 1969a; Hepworth et al. 1997) or *advanced* empathy (Egan, 1998).

At this level of empathy, the helper uses mild to moderate interpretations of the client's inferred feelings (Hepworth et al. 1997, p. 108). We discuss this skill for conveying advanced empathy in Chapter 7 as it is an influencing response rather than a listening one.

Carkhuff and Pierce (1975) have developed a Discrimination Inventory that presents a scale for assessing both basic and additive empathy messages. On this scale, helper responses are rated according to one of five levels; Level 3 is considered the *minimally* acceptable response. Level 3 responses on this scale correspond to Carkhuff and Pierce's concept of interchangeable empathy and Egan's (1998) concept of basic-level empathy; Level 4 corresponds to additive empathy (Carkhuff, 1969a) or advanced empathy (Egan), and Level 5 represents facilitating action. The scale can be used either to discriminate among levels of responses or to rate levels of helper communication. Here is an example of a verbal empathic response at each level of Carkhuff and Pierce's Discrimination Inventory:

Client: I've tried to get along with my father, but it doesn't work out. He's too hard on me.

Helper at Level 1: I'm sure it will all work out in time [reassurance and denial].

[or]

You ought to try harder to see his point of view [advice].

[or]

Why can't you two get along? [question].

Level 1 is a question, reassurance, denial, or advice.

Helper at Level 2: You're having a hard time getting along with your father.

Level 2 is a response to only the *content,* or cognitive portion, of the message; feelings are ignored.

Helper at Level 3: You feel discouraged because your attempts to get along with your father have not been very successful.

Level 3 has understanding but no direction; it is a reflection of feeling and meaning based on the client's explicit message.

In other words, a Level 3 response reflects both the feeling and the situation. In this response, "You feel discouraged" is the reflection of the feeling, and "because of not getting along" is the reflection of the situation.

Helper at Level 4: You feel discouraged because you can't seem to reach your father. You want him to let up on you.

Level 4 has understanding and some direction. A Level 4 response identifies not only the client's feelings but also the client's deficit that is implied. In a Level 4 response, the client's deficit is personalized, meaning the client owns or accepts responsibility for the deficit, as in "you can't reach."

Helper at Level 5: You feel discouraged because you can't seem to reach your father. You want him to let up on you. One step could be to express your feelings about this to your father.

A Level 5 response contains all of a Level 4 response plus at least one action step the person can take to master the deficit and attain the goal. In this example, the action step is "One step could be to express your feelings about this to your father."

In the following section, we present steps for reflecting feelings to convey *basic* empathy.

Steps in Reflecting Feelings

Reflecting feelings can be a difficult skill to learn because feelings are often ignored or misunderstood. Reflection of feelings involves six steps, which include identifying the emotional tone of the communication and verbally reflecting the client's feelings, using your own words.

The first step is to listen for the presence of feeling words, or affect words, in the client's messages. Positive, negative, and ambivalent feelings are expressed by one or more affect words falling into one of five major categories: anger, fear, conflict, sadness, and happiness. Table 5.3 presents a list of commonly used affect words at three levels of intensity. Becoming acquainted with such words may help you recognize them in client communications and expand your vocabulary for describing emotions. Table 5.4 describes affect words to use with children and teens. With very young children, using face symbols such as those depicted in Figure 5.2 is recommended.

A second way to identify the client's feelings is to watch the nonverbal behavior while the verbal message is being delivered. As you may remember from Chapter 3, nonverbal cues such as body posture, facial expression, and voice quality are important indicators of client emotion. In fact, nonverbal behavior is often a more reliable clue to client emotions because nonverbal behaviors are less easily controlled than words. Observing nonverbal behavior is particularly important when the client's feelings are implied or expressed very subtly.

After the feelings reflected by the client's words and nonverbal behavior have been identified, the next step involves reflecting the feelings back to the client, using different words. The choice of words to reflect feelings is critical to the effectiveness of this skill. For example, if a client expresses feeling annoyed, interchangeable affect words would be *bothered, irritated,* and *hassled.* However, words such as *angry, mad,* or *outraged* probably go beyond the intensity expressed by the client. With adult clients, it is important to select affect words that accurately match not only the type of feeling but also its intensity; otherwise, the helper makes an understatement, which can make a client feel ridiculed, or an overstatement, which can make a client feel put off or intimidated. Note the three major levels of intensity of affect words in Table 5.3—mild, moderate, and intense. You can also control the intensity of the expressed affect by the type of preceding adverb used—for example, *somewhat* (weak), *quite* (moderate), or *very* (strong) *upset*. With children, it works best to use a word or a symbol that captures their feelings as closely as possible.

Study Tables 5.3 and 5.4 carefully so that you can develop an extensive affect-word vocabulary. Overuse of a few common affect words misses the varied nuances of the client's emotional experience.

The next step in reflecting is to start the reflection statement with an appropriate sentence stem, such as one of the following:

"It *appears* that you are *angry* now."

"It *looks* like you are *angry* now."

"It is *clear* to me that you are *angry* now."

"It *sounds* like you are *angry* now."

"I *hear* you saying you are *angry* now."

"My *ears tell* me that you are *angry* now."

"I can *grasp* your *anger*."

"You are *feeling angry* now."

"Let's get in *touch* with your *anger*."

Refer also to Table 5.2 for sentence stems.

The next step in reflecting is to add the context, or situation, around which the feelings occur. This takes the form of a brief paraphrase. Usually the context can be determined from the cognitive part of the client's message. For example, a client might say "I just can't take tests. I get so anxious I

TABLE 5.3 Words That Express Feelings

Relative intensity of words	Feeling category				
	Anger	Conflict	Fear	Happiness	Sadness
Mild feeling	Annoyed	Blocked	Apprehensive	Amused	Apathetic
	Bothered	Bound	Concerned	Anticipating	Bored
	Bugged	Caught	Tense	Comfortable	Confused
	Irked	Caught in a bind	Tight	Confident	Disappointed
	Irritated	Pulled	Uneasy	Contented	Discontented
	Peeved			Glad	Mixed up
	Ticked			Pleased	Resigned
				Relieved	Unsure
Moderate feeling	Disgusted	Locked	Afraid	Delighted	Abandoned
	Hacked	Pressured	Alarmed	Eager	Burdened
	Harassed	Strained	Anxious	Happy	Discouraged
	Mad	Torn	Fearful	Hopeful	Distressed
	Provoked		Frightened	Joyful	Down
	Put upon		Shook	Surprised	Drained
	Resentful		Threatened	Up	Empty
	Set up		Worried		Hurt
	Spiteful				Lonely
	Used				Lost
					Sad
					Unhappy
					Weighted
Intense feeling	Angry	Coerced	Desperate	Bursting	Anguished
	Boiled	Ripped	Overwhelmed	Ecstatic	Crushed
	Burned	Wrenched	Panicky	Elated	Deadened
	Contemptful		Petrified	Enthusiastic	Depressed
	Enraged		Scared	Enthralled	Despairing
	Fuming		Terrified	Excited	Helpless
	Furious		Terror-stricken	Free	Hopeless
	Hateful		Tortured	Fulfilled	Humiliated
	Hot			Moved	Miserable
	Infuriated			Proud	Overwhelmed
	Pissed			Terrific	Smothered
	Smoldering			Thrilled	Tortured
	Steamed			Turned on	

Source: From *Helping Relationships and Strategies*, 3rd ed., (p. 72), by D. Hutchins and C. Cole Vaught. © 1997 by Brooks/Cole an imprint of the Wadsworth Group, a division of Thomson Learning.

just never do well even though I study a lot." In this message, the affect is anxiety; the context is test taking. The helper reflects the affect ("You feel uptight") *and* the context ("whenever you have to take a test").

The final step in reflecting feelings is to assess the effectiveness of your reflection after delivering it. Usually, if your reflection accurately identifies the client's feelings, the client will confirm your response by saying something like "Yes, that's right" or "Yes, that's exactly how I feel." If your response is off target, the client may reply with "Well, it's not quite like that," "I don't feel exactly that way," or "No, I don't feel that way." When the client responds by denying feelings, it may mean your reflection was inaccurate or ill-timed. It is very important for helpers to decide when to respond to emotions. Reflection of feelings may be too powerful to be used *frequently* in the very early stage of helping. At that time, overuse of this response may make the client feel uncomfortable, a situation that can result in denial rather than ac-

TABLE 5.4	Affect Words and Phrases for Children and Teens			
anxious	bored	childish	contented or fulfilled	curious
depressed	determined	disgusted	doubtful	embarrassed
empty	envious of others	excited	furious	guilty
hopeful	humble	hurt	irritated	jealous
lovable	mean and destructive	nervous	optimistic	proud
rebellious	sad	safe and secure	scared or afraid	silly
sorry	strong and capable	terrified	thrilled	warm and cozy
worried				

Source: Adapted from, *Group Activities for Counselors,* by Eliot, Inner Choice Publishing, 1994.

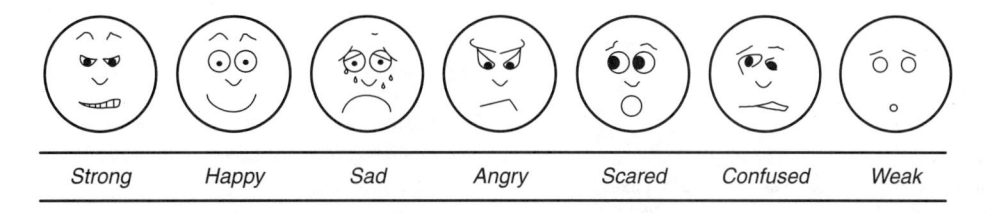

Figure 5.2 Feeling symbols for children
Source: From *Counseling Children,* 5th edition, by C. Thompson and L. Rudolph, © 2000. Reprinted with permission of Wadsworth, an imprint of the Wadsworth Group, a division of Thomson Learning.

knowledgment of emotions. But do not ignore the potential impact or usefulness of reflection later on, when focusing on the client's feelings would promote the goals of the session. In the following example, notice the way a helper uses a cognitive learning strategy (adapted from Richardson & Stone, 1981) to formulate a reflection of client feelings:

Client, a middle-aged man [said in loud, shrill, high-pitched voice, clenched fists]: You can't imagine what it was like when I found out my wife was cheating on me. I saw red! What should I do—get even—leave her—I'm not sure.

1. *What overt feeling words has this client used?*

None—except for the suggested affect phrase "saw red."

2. *What feelings are implied in the client's voice and nonverbal behavior?*

Anger, outrage, hostility.

3. *What is a good choice of affect words that accurately describe this client's feelings at a similar level of intensity?*

"Furious," "angry," "vindictive," "outraged."

4. *What is an appropriate sentence stem?*

From the client's use of words like "imagine" and "saw red," I'll try sentence stems like "It seems," "It appears," "It looks like."

5. *What is the context, or situation, surrounding his feelings that I'll paraphrase?*

His discovery that his wife was unfaithful.

6. *How will I know whether my reflection is accurate and helpful?*

Watch and listen for the client's response—whether he confirms or denies the feeling of being angry and vindictive.

Actual examples of reflection:

It looks like you're very angry now about your wife's going out on you.

It appears that you're furious with your wife's actions.

It seems like you're both angry and vindictive now that you've discovered your wife has been going out with other men.

Suppose that, following the reflection, the client said "Yes, I'm very angry, for sure—I don't know about vindictive, though I guess I'd like to make her feel as crappy as I do." The client has confirmed the helper's reflection of the feelings of anger and vindictiveness but has also given a clue that the word *vindictive* was too strong for the client to accept *at this time.* The helper picked up on the feelings, noting that the word *vindictive* might be used again later, after the client has sorted through his mixed feelings about his wife's behavior.

Learning Activity 5.4 will give you an opportunity to try out the reflection-of-feeling response.

LEARNING ACTIVITY 5.4 — Reflection of Feelings

In this learning activity, you are presented with three client practice messages. For each message, develop an example of a reflection-of-feeling response, using the cognitive learning strategy (Richardson & Stone, 1981) described earlier and outlined below. To internalize this learning strategy, you may wish to talk through these self-questions overtly (aloud) and then covertly (silently to yourself). The end product will be a reflection-of-feeling response that you can say aloud or write down or both. An example precedes the practice messages. Feedback is given after the learning activity (on page 102).

Example

Client, a 50-year-old steelworker now laid off [said in a loud, critical voice, staring at the ceiling, brow furrowed, eyes squinting]: Now look, what can I do? I've been laid off over a year. I've got no money, no job, and a family to take care of. It's also clear to me that my mind and skills are just wasting away.

Self-question 1: *What overt feeling words has the client used?*
None.

Self-question 2: *What feelings are implied in the client's nonverbal behavior?*
Disgust, anger, upset, frustration, resentment, disillusionment, discouragement.

Self-question 3: *What is a good choice of affect words that accurately describe the client's feelings at a similar level of intensity?*
Seem to be two feelings — anger and discouragement. Anger seems to be the stronger emotion of the two.

Self-question 4: *What is an appropriate sentence stem?*
Use stems like "I see you" or "It's clear to me that you" or "From where I'm looking, you." These are similar to the client phrases "now look" and "it's clear."

Self-question 5: *What is the context, or situation, surrounding his feelings that I'll paraphrase?*
Loss of job, no resources, no job prospects in sight.

Reflection-of-feeling response: I can see you're angry about being out of work and discouraged about the future *or* It looks like you're very upset about having your job and stability taken away from you.

Client Practice Statements

Client 1, an eight-year-old girl [said in level, measured words, glancing from side to side, lips drawn tightly together, flushed face]: I'm telling you I don't like living at home anymore. I wish I could live with my friend and her parents. I told my mommy that one day I'm going to run away, but she doesn't listen to me.

Self-question 1: *What overt feeling words has the client used?*
Self-question 2: *What feelings are implied in the client's nonverbal behavior?*
Self-question 3: *What are accurate and similar interchangeable affect words?*
Self-question 4: *What is a useful sentence stem?*
Self-question 5: *What is the context, or situation, concerning her feelings that I'll paraphrase?*
Actual reflection response: _____
_____
_____

Client 2, a middle-aged man in marital therapy [said in soft voice with downcast eyes]: As far as I'm concerned, our marriage turned sour last year when my wife went back to work. She's more in touch with her work than with me.

Self-question 1: *What overt feeling words did the client use?*
Self-question 2: *What feelings are implied in the client's nonverbal behavior?*
Self-question 3: *What are accurate and similar interchangeable affect words?*
Self-question 4: *What is a useful sentence stem?*
Self-question 5: *What is the context, or situation, surrounding his feelings that I'll paraphrase?*
Actual reflection response: _____
_____
_____

| LEARNING ACTIVITY | 5.4 | Reflection of Feelings |

Client 3, an adolescent [said in loud, harsh voice]: Now look, we have too damn many rules around this school. I'm getting the hell out of here. As far as I can see, this place is a dump.

Self-question 1: *What overt feeling words has this client used?*
Self-question 2: *What feelings are implied in the client's nonverbal behavior?*
Self-question 3: *What are accurate and similar interchangeable affect words?*

Self-question 4: *What is a useful sentence stem?*
Self-question 5: *What is the context, or situation, surrounding his feelings that I'll paraphrase?*
Actual reflection response: _____
_____
_____

Listening for Themes: Summarization

Usually, after a client has expressed several messages or has talked for a while, her or his messages will suggest certain consistencies or patterns that we refer to as *themes*. Themes in client messages are expressed in topics that the client continually refers to or brings up in some way. The helper can identify themes by listening to what the client repeats "over and over and with the most intensity" (Carkhuff, Pierce, & Cannon, 1977). The themes indicate what the client is trying to tell us and what the client needs to focus on in the helping sessions. Ivey, Ivey, and Simek-Morgan (1997) refer to this as listening to the way the client organizes his or her story (p. 63). The counselor can respond to client themes by using a summarization response. For example, suppose that you have been working with a young man who, during the last three sessions, has made repeated references to relationships with gay men yet has not really identified this issue intentionally. You could use a summarization to identify the theme from these repeated references by saying something like "I'm aware that during our last few sessions you've spoken consistently about relationships with gay men. Perhaps this is an issue for you we might want to focus on."

As another example, suppose that in one session a client has given you several descriptions of different situations in which she feels concerned about how other people perceive her. You might discern that the one theme common to all these situations is the client's need for approval from others, or "other-directedness." You could use a summarization such as this to identify this theme: "One thing I see in all three situations you've described, Juanita, is that you seem quite concerned about having the approval of other people. Is this accurate?"

Purposes of Summarization

One purpose of summarization is to tie together multiple elements of client messages. In this case, summarization can serve as a good feedback tool for the client by extracting meaning from vague and ambiguous messages. A second purpose of summarization is to identify a common theme or pattern that becomes apparent after several messages or sometimes after several sessions. Occasionally, a helper may summarize to interrupt a client's incessant rambling or "storytelling." At such times, summarization is an important focusing tool that brings direction to the interview.

A fourth use of summarization is to moderate the pace of a session that is moving too quickly. In such instances, summaries provide psychological breathing space during the session. A final purpose of a summary is to review progress that has been made during one or more interviews.

A summarization can be defined as a collection of two or more paraphrases or reflections that condenses the client's messages or the session. Summarization "involves listening to a client over a period of time (from three minutes to a complete session or more), picking out relationships among key issues, and restating them back accurately to the client" (Ivey, Gluckstern, & Ivey, 1993, p. 92).

A summarization may represent collective rephrasings of either cognitive or affective data, but most summarization responses will include references to *both* cognitive and affective messages, as in the following four examples:

1. Example of summarization to *tie together multiple elements* of a client message:

Client, a Native American medical student: All my life I thought I wanted to become a doctor and go back to work

> **5.4 FEEDBACK**
> Personal Values
>
> **Client 1**
>
> **Question 1:** *What overt feeling words did the client use?*
> "Don't like."
>
> **Question 2:** *What feelings are implied in the client's nonverbal behavior?*
> Upset, irritation, resentment.
>
> **Question 3:** *What are interchangeable affect words?*
> "Bothered," "perturbed," "irritated," "upset."
>
> **Question 4:** *What sentence stem will I use?*
> "Seems like," "It sounds like," or "I hear you saying that."
>
> **Question 5:** *What is the context, or situation, surrounding her feelings?*
> Living at home with her parents.
>
> **Actual examples of reflection:**
> It sounds like you're upset about some things going on at your home now *or* I hear you saying you're bothered about your parents.
>
> **Client 2**
>
> **Question 1:** *What overt feeling words did the client use?*
> No obvious ones except for phrases "turned sour" and "in touch with."
>
> **Question 2:** *What feelings are implied in the client's nonverbal behavior?*
> Sadness, loneliness, hurt.
>
> **Question 3:** *What are interchangeable affect words?*
> "Hurt," "lonely," "left out," "unhappy."
>
> **Question 4:** *What sentence stem is useful?*
> "I sense" or "You feel."
>
> **Question 5:** *What is the context, or situation, surrounding his feelings?*
> Wife's return to work.
>
> **Actual examples of reflection:**
> You're feeling left out and lonely since your wife's gone back to work *or* I sense you're feeling hurt and unhappy because your wife seems so interested in her work.
>
> **Client 3**
>
> **Question 1:** *What overt feeling words did the client use?*
> No obvious ones, but words like "damn," "hell," and "dump" suggest intensity of emotions.
>
> **Question 2:** *What feelings are implied in the client's nonverbal behavior?*
> Anger, frustration.
>
> **Question 3:** *What are interchangeable affect words?*
> "Angry," "offended," "disgusted."
>
> **Question 4:** *What sentence stem will I use?*
> Stems such as "It seems," "It appears," "It looks like," and "I can see."
>
> **Question 5:** *What is the context surrounding the feelings?*
> School rules.
>
> **Actual examples of reflection:**
> It looks like you're pretty disgusted now because you see these rules restricting you *or* It seems like you're very angry about having all these rules here at school.

on my reservation. Now that I've left home, I'm not sure. I still feel strong ties there that are pulling me back. I hate to let my people down, yet I also feel like there's a lot out here I want to explore first.

Summarization: You're away from the reservation now and are finding so much in this place to explore—at the same time, you're feeling pulled by your lifelong ties to your people and your dream of returning as a doctor.

2. Example of summarization to *identify a theme*:
Client, a 35-year-old male: One of the reasons we divorced was because she always pushed me. I could never say no to her; I always gave in. I guess it's hard for me just to say no to requests people make.

Summarization: You're discovering that you tend to give in or not do what you want in many of your significant relationships, not just with your ex-wife.

3. Example of summarization *to regulate pace of session and to give focus:*

Client, a young woman: What a terrible week I had! The water heater broke, the dog got lost, someone stole my wallet, my car ran out of gas, and to top it all off, I gained five pounds. I can't stand myself. It seems like it shows all over me.

Summarization: Let's stop for just a minute before we go on. It seems like you've encountered an unending series of bad events this week.

4. Example of summarization *to review progress* (often used as termination strategy near end of session):

Summary: Ronnie, we've got about five minutes left today. It seems like most of the time we've been working on the ways you find to sabotage yourself from doing things you want to do but yet feel are out of your control. This week I'd like you to work on the following homework before our next session. . . .

Helms and Cook (1999) note that for many clients of color, separation of feeling from content is not a "meaningful distinction" and is based on the Eurocentric cultural belief of mind–body dualism—that is, the notion that feelings and beliefs are separable (p. 178). It is necessary for you not only to learn interviewing skills, but also "to understand the cultural context in which the skill is appropriately expressed" (Helms & Cook, 1999, p. 178).

Steps in Summarizing

Summarizing requires careful attention to and concentration on the client's verbal and nonverbal messages. Accurate use of this response involves good recall of client behavior, not only within a session but over time—across several sessions or even several months of therapy. Developing a summarization involves the following four steps:

1. Attend to and recall the message or series of messages by restating these to yourself covertly—what has the client been telling you, focusing on, working on? This is a key and difficult part of effective summaries because it requires you to be aware of many, varying verbal and nonverbal messages you have processed *over time.*
2. Identify any apparent patterns, themes, or multiple elements of these messages by asking yourself questions like "What has the client repeated over and over" and "What are the different parts of this puzzle?"
3. Next, using the sentence stem you've selected, select words to describe the theme or tie together multiple elements, and say this as the summarization response. Remember to use your voice so that the summarization sounds like a statement instead of a question.
4. Assess the effectiveness of your summarization by listening for and observing whether the client confirms or denies the theme or whether the summary adds to or detracts from the focus of the session.

To help you formulate a summarization, consider the following cognitive learning strategy:

1. What was this client telling me and working on today and over time? That is, what are the *key content* and *key affect*?
2. What has the client repeated over and over today and over time? That is, what is the *pattern* or *theme*?
3. How will I know whether my summarization is useful?

Notice how a helper applies this cognitive learning strategy in developing a summarization in the following example:

Client, a middle-aged male fighting alcoholism (he has told you for the last three sessions that his drinking is ruining his family life but he can't stop because it makes him feel better and helps him to handle job stress) [said in low, soft voice, downcast eyes, stooped shoulders]: I know drinking doesn't really help me in the long run. And it sure doesn't help my family. My wife keeps threatening to leave. I know all this. It's hard to stay away from the booze. Having a drink makes me feel relieved.

Self-question 1: What has this client been telling me today and over time?

Key content: results of drinking aren't good for him or his family.
Key affect: drinking makes him feel better, less anxious.

Self-question 2: What has this client repeated over and over today and over time—pattern or theme?

That despite adverse effects and family deterioration, he continues to drink for stress reduction and "medicating" of feelings; that is, stress reduction through alcohol seems worth losing his family.

Suppose that at this time the helper delivered one of the following summarizations to the client:

"Jerry, I sense that you feel it's worth having the hassle of family problems because of the good, calm feelings you get whenever you drink."

"Jerry, you feel that your persistent drinking is creating a lot of difficulties for you in your family, and I sense your reluctance to stop drinking in spite of these adverse effects."

LEARNING ACTIVITY 5.5 — Summarization

In this learning activity, you are presented with client practice messages. For each message, develop a summarization response using the cognitive learning strategy described earlier and outlined below. To internalize this learning strategy, you may wish to talk through these self-questions overtly (aloud) and then covertly—that is, silently to yourself. The end product will be a summarization response that you can say aloud, write down, or both. An example precedes the practice messages. Feedback is given on page 105.

Example

Client, a 10-year-old girl

At beginning of the session [said in low, soft voice with lowered, moist eyes]: I don't understand why my parents can't live together anymore. I'm not blaming anybody, but it just feels very confusing to me.

Near the middle of the same session: I wish they could keep it together. I guess I feel like they can't because they fight about me so much. Maybe I'm the reason they don't want to live together anymore.

Self-question 1: *What has this client been telling me and looking at today in terms of key content and key affect?*
Key content: wants parents to stay together.
Key affect: feels sad, upset, responsible.

Self-question 2: *What has the client repeated over and over today or over time—that is, pattern or theme?* She's the one who's responsible for her parents' breakup.
Examples of summarization response: Joan, at the start of our talk today, you were feeling like no one person was responsible for your parents' separation. Now I sense you're saying that you feel responsible *or* Joan, earlier today you indicated you didn't feel like blaming anyone for what's happening to your folks. Now I'm sensing that you're feeling like you're responsible for their breakup.

Client Practice Messages

Client 1, a 30-year-old man who has been blaming himself for his wife's unhappiness [said in low, soft voice tone with lowered eyes]: I really feel guilty about marrying her in the first place. It wasn't really for love. It was just a convenient thing to do. I feel like I've messed up her life really badly. I also feel obliged to her.

Self-question 1: *What has this client been telling me and working on today?*
Key content:
Key affect:

Self-question 2: *What has this client repeated over and over today or over time in terms of patterns and themes?*
Summarization response: _____
_____
_____

Client 2, a 35-year-old woman who focused on how her life has improved since having children [said with alertness and animation]: I never thought I would feel this great. I always thought being a parent would be boring and terribly difficult. It's not, for me. It's fascinating and easy. It makes everything worthwhile.

Self-question 1: *What has this client been telling me and working on today?*
Key content:
Key affect:

Self-question 2: *What has this client repeated over and over today or over time in terms of patterns and themes?*
Summarization response: _____
_____
_____

Client 3, a 27-year-old woman who has continually focused on her relationships with men and her needs for excitement and stability:

First session [bright eyes, facial animation, high-pitched voice]: I've been dating lots and lots of men for the last few years. Most of them have been married. That's great because there are no demands on me.

Fourth session [soft voice, lowered eyes]: It doesn't feel so good anymore. It's not so much fun. Now I guess I miss having

LEARNING ACTIVITY 5.5 — Summarization

some commitment and stability in my life.

Self-question 1: *What has this client been telling me and working on today?*
Key content:
Key affect:

Self-question 2: *What has this client repeated over and over today or over time in terms of patterns and themes?*
Summarization response: _____
_____
_____

FEEDBACK 5.5 — Summarization

Client 1
Question 1: *What has the client told me?*
Key content: He married for convenience, not love.
Key affect: Now he feels both guilty and indebted.

Question 2: *What has the client repeated over and over now and before in terms of patterns and themes?*
Conflicting feelings—feels a strong desire to get out of the marriage yet feels a need to keep relationship going because he feels responsible for his wife's unhappiness.

Examples of summarization response:
I sense you're feeling pulled in two different directions. For yourself, you want out of the relationship. For her sake, you feel you should stay in the relationship *or* You're feeling like you've used her for your convenience and because of this you think you owe it to her to keep the relationship going *or* I can grasp how very much you want to pull yourself out of the marriage and also how responsible you feel for your wife's present unhappiness.

Client 2
Question 1: *What has the client told me?*
Key content: Children have made her life better, more worthwhile.
Key affect: Surprise and pleasure.

Question 2: *What has the client said over and over in terms of patterns and themes?*
Being a parent is uplifting and rewarding even though she didn't expect it to be. In addition, her children are very important to her. To some extent, they define her worth and value as a person.

Examples of summarization response:
It seems like you're feeling surprise, satisfaction, and relief about finding parenting so much easier and more rewarding than you had expected it would be *or* I hear feelings of surprise and pleasure in your voice as you reveal how great it is to be a parent and how important your children are to you *or* You seem so happy about the way your life is going since you've had children—as if they make you and your life more worthwhile.

Client 3
Question 1: *What has the client told me?*
Key content: She has been dating lots of men who have their own commitments.
Key affect: It used to feel great; now she feels a sense of loss and emptiness.

Question 2: *What has she repeated over and over in terms of patterns and themes?*
At first—feelings of pleasure, relief not to have demands in close relationships. Now, feelings are changing, feels less satisfied, wants more stability in close relationships.

Examples of summarization response:
Lee Ann, originally you said it was great to be going out with a lot of different men who didn't ask much of you. Now you're also feeling it's not so great—it's keeping you from finding some purpose and stability in your life *or* In our first session, you were feeling "up" about all those relationships with noncommittal men. Now you're feeling like this is interfering with the stability you need and haven't yet found *or* At first it was great to have all this excitement and few demands. Now you're feeling some loss from lack of a more stable, involved relationship.

"Jerry, I sense that, despite everything, alcohol feels more satisfying (rewarding) to you than your own family."

If Jerry confirms the theme that alcohol is more important now than his family, the helper can conclude that the summarization was useful. If Jerry denies the theme or issue summarized, the helper can ask Jerry to clarify how the summarization was inaccurate, remembering that the summary may indeed be inaccurate or that Jerry may not be ready to acknowledge the issue at this time. (See Learning Activity 5.5)

BARRIERS TO LISTENING

Egan (1998) discusses what he calls the "shadow side" of listening—that is, ways in which the listening process may fail. As he notes, active listening sounds good in theory but in practice is not without "obstacles and distractions" (p. 75).

We have observed three types of helpers who seem to have the most difficulty listening to clients. We identify these as follows:

1. *Frenetic* helpers: These helpers are so "hyper" and so much "in motion" (either internally, externally, or both) that they have great difficulty just sitting quietly and taking in clients' stories.
2. *Self-centered* helpers: These helpers are so in love with themselves and so "hell-bent" on getting their own ideas across that little opportunity exists for clients to tell their stories.
3. *Self-absorbed* helpers: These helpers often look physically present and attentive, yet there is so much "internal noise" going on inside that they aren't really emotionally available to hear clients.

Egan (1998) points out that one obstacle to listening effectively involves evaluations and filters. Although it is not possible to suspend judgment completely, most clients have finely tuned antennae that detect evaluative responses—perhaps because they have heard so much judgment in their lives. This seems particularly true for clients who have individual or cultural shame. When these clients hear evaluative listening from counselors, they are likely to shut down.

Filtered listening includes labels and biases (Egan, 1998, pp. 76–77). For example, if you are required to give your client a diagnosis, you may run through possible labels in your head while you are simultaneously trying to listen to the client. Or, in another scenario, perhaps the client you are seeing has already been labeled by someone else—the "borderline" client or the "dysthymic" client or the "oppositional" kid. An obstacle to listening in these instances is the temptation to look for corroborative behaviors while listening to the person. All of us use filters to structure our worlds, but these same filters, if very strong, can introduce biased listening into the helping process and can contribute to stereotyping (Egan, 1998, p. 76). Filters often come into play when we are listening to clients who are culturally different from ourselves in some way.

LISTENING WITH DIVERSE GROUPS OF CLIENTS

The listening process in a helping relationship varies depending on such things as the client's age, ethnicity, gender, and language(s). For example, active listening can be a useful way to establish rapport with children and adolescent clients (Thompson & Rudolph, 2000). Elderly clients who lack social contacts often long for a good listener in their lives.

With some clients of color, the listening process itself may conflict with their basic values. As Atkinson and colleagues (1993) observe,

> Often, in order to encourage self-disclosure, the counseling situation is intentionally designed to be an ambiguous one, one in which the counselor listens empathically and responds only to encourage the client to continue talking. This lack of structure in the counseling process may conflict with need for structure that is a value in many cultures. Racial/ethnic minority clients frequently find the lack of structure confusing, frustrating, and even threatening. (p. 53)

Gender differences also play a role, as some men tend to have a more directive style, asking more questions, and doing more interrupting and problem solving than some women, who may make more reflective statements (Ivey et al., 1997). For clients from some cultural groups, a more active style may be necessary. At the same time, however, the capacity to simply sit silently and be present can be useful with some Native American clients (Ivey et al., 1997, p. 202).

Another situation in which listening can pose special issues in the helping process is with clients who do not speak standard English, have English as a second language, or do not speak English at all. The counselor may feel that he or she has more trouble listening to the client in these situations, yet it is really the client who suffers the disadvantage. Sue and Sue (1999) note that "the lack of bilingual therapists and the requirement that the culturally different client communicate in English may limit the person's ability to progress in counseling/psychotherapy" (p. 72). Helms and Cook (1999) also address this issue. They recommend that when the helper and client are of different language origins, and when neither of them is at least partially competent in at least one of the other person's languages, a referral is needed (p. 194). If a referral is not possible, then the use of an interpreter is needed, although as Helms and Cook (1999) point out, this is less than ideal since the lack of language understanding by the helper may distort what the client says. If, on the other hand, the helper and client have different languages but both are at least somewhat able to understand a "marketplace" language, such as standard English, "then the therapist must learn to recognize some of the speech patterns of the client's at-home culture. This can be done by listening attentively to the client in an effort to discern when the client switches back and forth between the two cultural languages, as well as which emotions seem to accompany the shift" (p. 194).

SUMMARY

We often hear these questions: "What good does all this listening do? How does just rephrasing client messages really help?" In response, we will reiterate the rationale for using listening responses in helping.

1. Listening to clients is a very powerful reinforcer and may strengthen clients' desire to talk about themselves and their concerns. Not listening may prevent clients from sharing relevant information.
2. Listening to a client first may mean a greater chance of responding accurately to the client in later stages of helping, such as problem solving. By jumping to quick solutions without laying a foundation of listening, you may inadvertently ignore the primary issue or propose inadequate and ill-timed action steps (Sommers-Flanagan & Sommers-Flanagan, in press).
3. Listening encourages the client to assume responsibility for selecting the topic and focus of an interview. Not listening may meet your needs to find information or to solve problems. In doing so, you may portray yourself as an expert rather than a collaborator. Simply asking a series of questions or proposing a series of action steps in the initial phase of helping can cause the client to perceive you as the expert and can hinder proper development of client self-responsibility in the interview.
4. Good listening and attending skills model socially appropriate behavior for clients (Gazda et al., 1999). Many clients have not yet learned to use the art of listening in their own relationship and social contacts. They are more likely to incorporate these skills to improve their interpersonal relationships when they experience them firsthand through their contact with a significant other, such as a skilled helper.

All these guidelines have to consider both the gender and cultural affiliation of the client. Listening may have a differential effect depending on the client's gender and cultural affiliation.

Some helpers can articulate a clear rationale for listening but cannot listen in an interview because of blocks that inhibit effective listening. Some of the most common blocks to listening are these:

1. The tendency to judge and evaluate the client's messages.
2. The tendency to stop attending because of distractions such as noise, the time of day, or the topic.
3. The temptation to respond to missing pieces of information by asking questions.
4. The temptation or the pressure put on yourself to solve problems or find answers.
5. The preoccupation with yourself as you try to practice the skills. This preoccupation shifts the focus from the client to you and actually reduces, rather than increases, your potential for listening.

Finally, effective listening requires an involved yet contained sort of energy that allows you to be fully present to the client. Listening is a process that does not stop after the initial session but continues throughout the entire therapeutic relationship with each client.

Perhaps the best explanation of the inherent value of listening comes from Remen (1996), in her remarkable book *Kitchen Table Wisdom: Stories That Heal*:

> I suspect that the most basic and powerful way to connect to another person is to listen. Just listen. Perhaps the most important thing we ever give each other is our attention. And especially if it's given from the heart. When people are talking, there's no need to do anything but receive them. Just take them in. Listen to what they're saying. Care about it. (p. 143)

INFOTRAC® EXPLORATIONS

1. Mindfulness is a primary tool that you use when listening to clients. Search for *mindfulness*, and explore how the articles refer to and use this term.

2. Search for *listening technique* to see what you can find that applies to the helping process. You may wish to discuss this search and its results with a colleague or in a class discussion.

SUGGESTED RESOURCES

Readings

Atkinson, D. R., Morten, G., & Sue, D. W. (1998). *Counseling American minorities* (5th ed.). Madison, WI: Brown & Benchmark.

Brammer, L., Abrego, P., & Shostrom, E. (1993). *Therapeutic psychology* (6th ed.). Englewood Cliffs, NJ: Prentice Hall.

Carkhuff, R. R. (1993). *The art of helping VII.* Amherst, MA: Human Resource Development Press.

Cormier, S., & Hackney, H. (1999). *Counseling strategies and interventions* (5th ed.). Needham Heights, MA: Allyn & Bacon.

Egan, G. (2002). *The skilled helper* (7th ed.). Pacific Grove, CA: Brooks/Cole.

Ivey, A. E., Gluckstern, N., & Ivey, M. B. (1993). *Basic attending skills* (3rd ed.). North Amherst, MA: Microtraining Associates.

Nichols, M. P. (1995). *The lost art of listening.* New York: Guilford.

Remen, N. (1996). *Kitchen table wisdom: Stories that heal.* New York: Riverhead.

Sommers-Flanagan, J., & Sommers-Flanagan, R. (in press). *Clinical interviewing* (3rd ed.). New York: Wiley.

Teyber, E. (2000). *Interpersonal processes in psychotherapy* (4th ed.). Pacific Grove, CA: Brooks/Cole.

White, M., & Epston, D. (1990). *Narrative means to therapeutic ends.* New York: Norton.

Web Sites

AAP Offers Advice on Communicating with Children About Disasters
http://www.aap.org/advocacy/releases/disastercomm.htm

The Four Foundations of Mindfulness
http://www.buddhanet.net/4founds.htm

International Listening Association
http://www.listen.org

Psychworks, Inc.
http://www.psychworks.com

Satipatthana—The Foundations of Mindfulness
http://www.satipatthana.org

UCLA School Mental Health Project
http://smhp.psych.ucla.edu

5 POST EVALUATION

Part One

This part allows you to assess your performance on Chapter Objective One. On a sheet of paper, classify each of the listening responses in the following list as a clarification, paraphrase, reflection of feelings, or summarization. If you identify 9 out of 12 responses correctly, you have met this objective. You can check your answers against those provided in the feedback that follows on page 111.

1. **Client,** an older, retired person: How do they expect me to live on this little bit of Social Security? I've worked hard all my life. Now I have so little to show for it—I've got to choose between heat and food.
   a. Can you tell me who exactly expects you to be able to manage on this amount of money?
   b. All your life you've worked hard, hoping to give yourself a secure future. Now it's very upsetting to have only a little bit of money that can't possibly cover your basic needs.

2. **Client:** I'm having all these horrendous images that keep coming at me. I always thought I had had a happy childhood, but now I'm not so sure.
   a. Can you tell me what you mean by "horrendous images"?
   b. Recently you started to have some very scary memories about your past, and it's made you question how great your childhood really was.

3. **Client:** I feel so nervous when I have to give a speech in front of lots of people.
   a. You feel anxious when you have to talk to a group of people.
   b. You would rather not have to talk in front of large groups.

4. **Client:** I always have a drink when I'm under pressure.
   a. Are you saying that you use alcohol to calm you down?
   b. You think alcohol has a calming effect on you.

5. **Client:** I don't know whether I've ever experienced orgasm. My partner thinks I have, though.
   a. Are you saying that you've been trying to have your partner believe you do experience orgasm?
   b. You feel uncertain about whether you've ever really had an orgasm, even though your partner senses that you have.

6. **Client:** I haven't left my house in years. I'm even afraid to hang out the clothes.
   a. You feel panicked and uneasy when you go outside the security of your house.
   b. Because of this fear, you've stayed inside your house for a long time.

Part Two

Three client statements are presented. Objective Two asks you to verbalize or write an example of each of the four listening responses for each client statement.* In developing these responses, you may find it helpful to use the cognitive learning strategy you practiced earlier for each response. Feedback follows the evaluation.

Client 1, a 28-year-old woman [said in high-pitched voice, with crossed legs, lots of nervous "twitching" in hands and face]: My life is a shambles. I lost my job; my friends never come around anymore. It's been months now, but I still can't seem to cut down. I can't see clearly. It seems hopeless.
Clarification: _____
Paraphrase: _____
Reflection: _____
Summarization: _____

Client 2, an African American high school sophomore: I can't seem to get along with my mom. She's always harassing me, telling me what to do. Sometimes I get so mad I feel like hitting her, but I don't, because it would only make the situation worse.
Clarification: _____
Paraphrase: _____
Reflection: _____
Summarization: _____

Client 3, a 54-year-old man: Ever since my wife died four months ago, I can't get interested in anything. I don't want to eat or sleep. I'm losing weight. Sometimes I just tell myself I'd be better off if I were dead, too.
Clarification: _____
Paraphrase: _____
Reflection: _____
Summarization: _____

*These three client messages can be put on audiotape with pauses between statements. Instead of reading the message, you can listen to the message and write or say your responses during the pause.

(continued)

5 POSTEVALUATION

(continued)

Part Three

This part of the evaluation gives you an opportunity to develop your observation skills of key aspects of client behavior that must be attended to in order to listen effectively:
1. Vague or confusing phrases and messages
2. Expression of key content
3. Use of affect words
4. Nonverbal behavior illustrative of feeling or mood states
5. Presence of themes or patterns

Objective Three asks you to observe these five aspects of a client's behavior during a 15-minute interview conducted by someone else. Record your observations on the Client Observation Checklist that follows. You can obtain feedback for this activity by having two or more persons observe and rate the same session. Then compare your responses.

Client Observation Checklist

Name of helper _____

Name(s) of observer(s) _____

_____

Instructions: Given the five categories of client behavior to observe (left column), use the right column to record separate occurrences of behaviors within these categories as they occur during a short helping interview.*

Observed category of behavior	Selected key client words and nonverbal behavior
1. Vague, confusing, ambiguous phrases, messages	1. _____ 2. _____ 3. _____ 4. _____ 5. _____
2. Key content (situation, event, idea, person)	1. _____ 2. _____ 3. _____ 4. _____ 5. _____
3. Affect words used	1. _____ 2. _____ 3. _____ 4. _____

*If observers are not available, audiotape or videotape your sessions, and complete the checklist while reviewing the tape.

	5. _____
4. Nonverbal behavior indicative of certain feelings	1. _____ 2. _____ 3. _____ 4. _____ 5. _____
5. Themes, patterns	1. _____ 2. _____ 3. _____ 4. _____ 5. _____

Observer impressions and comments _____

_____

_____

Part Four

This part of the evaluation gives you a chance to demonstrate the four listening responses. Objective Four asks you to conduct a 15-minute role-play interview in which you use at least two examples of each of the four listening responses. Someone can observe your performance, or you can assess yourself from an audiotape of the interview. You or the observer can classify your responses and judge their effectiveness using the Listening Checklist that follows. Try to select a listening response to use when you have a particular purpose in mind. Remember, in order to listen, it is helpful to
1. Refrain from making judgments
2. Resist distractions
3. Avoid asking questions
4. Avoid giving advice
5. Stay focused on the client

Obtain feedback for this activity by noting the categories of responses on the Listening Checklist and their judged effectiveness.

Listening Checklist

Name of helper _____

Name of observer _____

Instructions: In the far left column, "Helper response," summarize a few key words of each statement, followed by a brief notation of the client's verbal and nonverbal response in the next column, "Client response." Then classify the message as a clarification, paraphrase, reflection of feeling, summarization, or other under the corresponding column. Rate the *effectiveness* of each helper response in

5 POSTEVALUATION

the far right column, "Effectiveness of response," on the following 1–3 scale:

1 = not effective. Client ignored helper's message or gave indication that helper's message was inaccurate and "off target."
2 = somewhat effective. Client gave some verbal or nonverbal indication that helper's message was partly right, accurate, "on target."
3 = very effective. Client's verbal and nonverbal behavior confirmed that helper's response was very accurate, "on target," or "fit."

Remember to watch and listen for the *client's* reaction to the response for your effectiveness rating.

Helper response (key words)	Client response (key words)	Type of helper response					Effectiveness of response (determined by client response) Rate from 1 to 3 (3 = high)
		Clarification	Paraphrase	Reflection of feelings	Summarization	Other	
1.							
2.							
3.							
4.							
5.							
6.							
7.							
8.							
9.							
10.							
11.							
12.							
13.							
14.							
15.							
16.							
17.							
18.							
19.							
20.							

Observer comments and general observations _____

POSTEVALUATION FEEDBACK

PART ONE
1. a. Clarification
   b. Summarization
2. a. Clarification
   b. Summarization
3. a. Reflection
   b. Paraphrase
4. a. Clarification
   b. Paraphrase
5. a. Clarification
   b. Reflection
6. a. Reflection
   b. Paraphrase

PART TWO
Here are some examples of listening responses. See whether yours are similar:

Client Statement 1
1. *Clarification:* "Can you describe what you mean by 'cutting down'?"
2. *Paraphrase:* "You seem to realize that your life is not going the way you want it to."
3. *Reflection:* "You appear frightened about the chaos in your life, and you seem uncertain of what you can do to straighten it out."
4. *Summarization:* "Your whole life seems to be falling apart. Your friends are avoiding you, and now you don't even have a job to go to. Even though you've tried to solve the problem, you can't seem to handle it alone. Coming here to talk is a useful first step in 'clearing up the water' for you."

Client Statement 2
1. *Clarification:* "Can you describe what it's like when you don't get along with her?"
2. *Paraphrase:* "It appears that your relationship with your mom is deteriorating to the point that you feel you may lose control of yourself."
3. *Reflection:* "You feel frustrated and angry with your mom because she's always giving you orders."
4. *Summarization:* "It seems like the situation at home with your mom has become intolerable. You can't stand her badgering, and you feel afraid that you might do something you would later regret."

Client Statement 3
1. *Clarification:* "Are you saying that since the death of your wife, life has become so miserable that you think of taking your own life?"
2. *Paraphrase:* "Your life has lost much of its meaning since your wife's recent death."
3. *Reflection:* "It sounds like you're very lonely and depressed since your wife died."
4. *Summarization:* "Since your wife died, you've lost interest in living. There's no fun or excitement anymore, and further, you're telling yourself that it's not going to get any better."

CHAPTER 6

RELATIONSHIP ENHANCEMENT VARIABLES AND INTERPERSONAL INFLUENCE

OBJECTIVES

After completing this chapter, the student should be able to
1. Given written descriptions of six clients, match the client description with the corresponding client "test of trust."
2. Given a role-play interaction, conduct a 30-minute *initial* interview in which you demonstrate behavioral aspects of attractiveness.
3. Given a role-play interaction, conduct a 30-minute *problem identification* interview in which you demonstrate verbal and nonverbal behaviors of expertness and trustworthiness.

In all human relationships, persons try to influence one another. The helping relationship is no exception. That helpers do influence clients is inescapable, and, according to Senour (1982, p. 346), the desire to avoid influence is "patently absurd [as] there would be no point to counseling if we had no influence on those with whom we work." Moreover, the influence process that operates in helping is a two-way street. Clients also seek to influence their helpers. As Dorn (1984, p. 343) observes, "Although the client has sought counseling because of dissatisfaction with personal circumstances, this same client will attempt to influence the counselor's behavior." Thus, the influence process in therapy is interpersonal—that is, between two persons—and reciprocal, or mutual.

In Chapter 4 we described the helping relationship in terms of the facilitative conditions of empathy, genuineness, and positive regard. In this chapter we focus on other dimensions of the helping relationship that make it a complementary influence process between helper and client. We also describe how helpers can best influence clients. The influence process in a helping relationship is important for achieving therapeutic outcomes. This influence base affects a client's decisions to seek help and to continue with the helper. It also affects the client's motivation to implement recommendations given by the helper, and it ultimately affects the therapeutic outcomes resulting from the helping relationship (Strong, Welsh, Corcoran, & Hoyt, 1992).

STRONG'S MODEL OF COUNSELING AS AN INTERPERSONAL INFLUENCE PROCESS

In 1968, Strong published what is now regarded as a landmark paper on counseling as a social influence process. He hypothesized that counselors' attempts to change clients precipitate dissonance in clients because of the inconsistency, or discrepancy, between the counselor's and the client's attitudes. This dissonance feels uncomfortable to clients, and they try to reduce this discomfort in a variety of ways, including discrediting the counselor, rationalizing the importance of their problem, seeking out information or opinions that contradict the counselor, attempting to change the counselor's opinion, or accepting the opinion of the counselor. Strong (1968) asserted that clients would be more likely to accept the counselor's opinions and less likely to discredit or refute the counselor if the clients perceive the counselor as expert, attractive, and trustworthy. These three helper characteristics (expertness, attractiveness, and trustworthiness) can also be called "relationship enhancers" (Goldstein & Higginbotham, 1991) because they have been identified as ways of making the therapeutic relationship more positive. As a pragmatic example of Strong's social influence model, a recent study found that client perceptions of the helper's influence predicted whether or not clients would implement the helper's recommendations (Scheel, Seaman, Roach, Mullin, & Blackwell Mahoney, 1999).

Strong (1968) initially suggested a two-stage model of counseling:

1. The counselor establishes a power base, or influence base, with the client through the three relationship enhancers of

expertness, attractiveness, and trustworthiness. This influence base enhances the quality of the relationship and also encourages client involvement in counseling. This stage of the model (drawing from social-psychology literature) assumes that counselors establish this influence base by drawing on power bases that can effect attitude change. Common power bases used by counselors include these:

- *Legitimate power:* power that occurs as a result of the counselor's role—a form that society at large views as acceptable and helpful.
- *Expert power:* power that results from descriptive and behavioral cues of expertness and competence.
- *Referent power:* power that results from descriptive and behavioral cues of interpersonal attractiveness, friendliness, and similarity between counselor and client (such as is found in "indigenous" helpers).

2. The counselor actively uses this influence base to effect attitudinal and behavioral change in clients. In this second stage of the model, it is important that clients perceive the counselor as expert, attractive, and trustworthy, as it is the *client's* perception of these counselor characteristics that determines, at least in part, how much influence counselors will have with their clients.

In the 1990s, Strong and colleagues (1992) added a third component to this social influence model: client responsiveness, describing this component as follows: "Client responsiveness to the ideas and recommendations presented by counselors is a function of their dependence on counselors. Dependence is a motivational factor that gets generated through the helping relationship" (p. 7).

We would add that all three components of the social influence model are greatly affected by cultural characteristics of the client, such as race, ethnicity, gender, and socioeconomic level.

THE INTERACTIONAL NATURE OF THE INFLUENCE PROCESS

As we noted at the beginning of this chapter, attempts at influence by helper and client are interdependent and interrelated. In considering helper attributes and behaviors (expertness, attractiveness, and trustworthiness) that contribute to influence, it is also important to consider client variables that may enhance or mediate influence effects of helpers (Hoyt, 1996).

Although most of this chapter focuses on the three helper characteristics that contribute most to the influence process in helping, remember that certain client characteristics may also enhance or mediate the helper's influence attempts. In other words, some clients may be more susceptible or less susceptible to helper influence, depending on such things as

- Attractiveness and social competence
- Conceptual level and cognitive style
- "Myths," beliefs, and expectations about helping
- Motivation
- Satisfaction with outcomes of helping
- Level of commitment required to change target behaviors
- Gender, race, and cultural background

With respect to issues of gender, sexual orientation, and racial/ethnic status, clients who perceive their helpers as more dissimilar from themselves may feel less safe and be more guarded, especially in initial interactions. Helpers in these situations may need to work more diligently and consistently to establish an influence base with more dissimilar clients. As Sue and Sue (1999) observe, the history of oppression faced by many minority clients contributes to their sense of discomfort with majority helpers. They note that in these situations, "what a counselor says and does in the sessions can either enhance or diminish his/her credibility and attractiveness" (p. 39).

Additionally, as helping is a *process* and involves distinctly different phases or stages, such as the ones mentioned in Chapter 1 (that is, relationship, assessment and goal setting, intervention and action, and evaluation and termination), it is also imperative to consider what kind of influence might be best suited for different phases of the process. For example, the descriptive aspects of expertness, such as role, reputation, education, and setting, are most useful and influential during the first part of helping, in which you are trying to encourage the client to continue by demonstrating your credibility. Yet, as helping ensues, these external trappings are *not* sufficient unless accompanied by behavioral demonstrations of expertness or competence that indicate the practitioner is skilled enough to handle the client's concerns successfully. As Whiston and Sexton (1993) state,

> Field studies indicated that factors that influence the counseling will vary on the stage of the counseling. Early in counseling, clients' ratings of counselor expertness, attractiveness, and trustworthiness may be high because of the *helping role* rather than because of any specific counselor behaviors (Heppner & Heesacker, 1982; LaCrosse, 1980). On the other hand, positive client ratings of counselor characteristics at the end of counseling were related to specific counselor behaviors (Heppner & Heesacker, 1982). [Further, in a review of 60 studies of the social influence model,] Heppner and Claiborn (1989) "concluded that the interaction between the client and counselor is not static, and to understand the relationship it is important to consider events as distinct times or stages during the counseling that influence this interaction." (p. 45)

However, it is important to note that almost all of these studies have used Euro-American participants as subjects. As Sue and Sue (1999) note, a caveat on the social influence model is that "findings that certain attributes contribute to a counselor's credibility and attractiveness may not be so perceived by culturally different clients. It is entirely possible that credibility, as defined by credentials indicating specialized training, may only mean to a Hispanic client that the White helper has no knowledge or expertise in working with Hispanics" (pp. 40–41).

The relationship of various aspects of helper expertness, attractiveness, and trustworthiness to stages of helping is depicted in summary form in Table 6.1. *Descriptive* cues associated with these three relationship enhancers refer to nonbehavioral aspects of the helper, such as demeanor, attire, and appearance; to situational aspects, such as the office setting; and to the helper's reputation, inferred from introductions, prior knowledge, and the display of diplomas and certificates. *Behavioral* aspects of these three variables refer to the helper's verbal and nonverbal behaviors or specific things the helper says and does. In the remainder of the chapter, we describe the behavioral components of these three variables and provide examples.

HELPER CHARACTERISTICS OR RELATIONSHIP ENHANCERS: EXPERTNESS, ATTRACTIVENESS, AND TRUSTWORTHINESS

Earlier we described the importance of three helper characteristics for establishing and using an influence base with clients: expertness, attractiveness, and trustworthiness. These three characteristics are also related and, in fact, intercorrelated (Hoyt, 1996; Zamostny, Corrigan, & Eggert, 1981) to the extent that helpers who are perceived by clients as competent are also likely to be viewed as interpersonally attractive and trustworthy. These three social influence variables are related to client satisfaction (Heppner & Heesacker, 1983;

TABLE 6.1 Relationship of Helper Expertness, Attractiveness, and Trustworthiness to Stages of Helping

Stage of helping	Purposes of influence efforts
Rapport and relationship (Stage 1) Descriptive aspects of *expertness*: education, role, reputation, setting Physical demeanor and *attractiveness* Interpersonal *attractiveness* conveyed by structuring Descriptive aspects of *trust*—role and reputation	Engage client to continue by communicating credibility Create initial favorable impression Reduce client anxiety, "check out" client expectations Encourage client openness and self-expression
Assessment and goal setting (Stage 2) Behavioral aspects of *expertness*: Verbal and nonverbal attentiveness Relevant and thought-provoking questions Behavioral aspects of *attractiveness*: Responsive nonverbal behavior Self-disclosure Behavioral aspects of *trustworthiness*: nonverbal acceptance of client disclosures, maintaining of confidentiality, accurate paraphrasing, nondefensive reactions to client "tests of trust"	Contribute to client understanding of self and of issues Obtain specificity Encourage relevant client self-disclosure and self-exploration Convey likability and perceived similarity to client Convey yourself as trustworthy of client communications so client will feel comfortable "opening up" and self-disclosing
Intervention strategies and action steps (Stage 3) Behavioral aspects of *expertness*: directness, fluency, confidence in presentation, and delivery; interpretations Behavioral aspects of *trustworthiness*: nonverbal dynamism, dependability and consistency of talk and actions, accurate and reliable information giving	Use of selected skills and strategies and display of confidence to demonstrate ability to help client resolve problems and take necessary action Demonstrate dynamism, congruence, and reliability to encourage client to trust your suggestions and ideas for action; also to diffuse any resistance to action, especially if target behaviors require high level of commitment or change
Evaluation, termination, and follow-up (Stage 4) Behavioral areas of *expertness*: Relevant questions Directness and confidence in presentation Interpersonal *attractiveness*: structuring Trustworthiness: reputation or demonstrated lack of ulterior motives or personal gain, honesty, and openness	Assess client progress and readiness for termination Contribute to client confidence in maintenance of change through self-directed efforts Reduce client anxiety about termination and dissolution of therapeutic relationship Increase client openness to dissolve relationship when appropriate and necessary

Zamostny et al., 1981), changes in client self-concept ratings (Dorn & Day, 1985), and less likelihood of premature client termination in therapy (McNeill, May, & Lee, 1987). Hoyt (1996) has concluded that the relationship between these three social influence variables and measures of outcome is complex. As well, more than 100 empirical investigations of the social influence model have found that responsive nonverbal behaviors and specific verbal responses can positively affect a client's perceptions of the helper's expertness, attractiveness, and trustworthiness (Heppner & Frazier, 1992).

Expertness

Expertness, also known as "competence" (Egan, 1999), is the client's perception that the helper will be helpful in resolving the client's concerns. Clients develop this perception from such things as the practitioner's apparent level of skill, relevant education, specialized training or experience, certificates or licenses, seniority, status, type of work setting, history of success in solving problems of others, and ascribed role as a helper. Clients appear to formulate these perceptions from aspects of the helper (language, attire, and so on) and of the setting (display of diplomas, certificates, professional literature, title) that are *immediately* evident to a client—that is, in initial contacts. Thus, in the initial stage of helping, in which the main goal is to establish an effective relationship and build rapport, descriptive cues such as those mentioned above (see also Table 6.2) associated with expertness play a predominant part in helping the practitioner establish an influence base with the client.

Initially, the *role* of helper also contributes to client perceptions of helper competence. In our society, a "helper" role is viewed as socially acceptable and valuable. Helpers convey legitimate power or influence simply by the role they hold. Thus, the "counselor role carries considerable initial

TABLE 6.2 Descriptive and Behavioral Cues of Expertness, Attractiveness, and Trustworthiness

Expertness	Attractiveness	Trustworthiness
Descriptive cues		
Relevant education (diplomas) Specialized training or experience Certificates or licenses Seniority Status Type of setting Display of professional literature Attire Reputation (past history of success in resolving problems of others) Socially validated role of helper	Physical demeanor; grooming, hygiene	Role as helper (regarded as trustworthy by society) Reputation for honesty and "straightforwardness," lack of ulterior motives
Behavioral cues		
Nonverbal behaviors Eye contact Forward body lean Fluent speech delivery	**Nonverbal behaviors (responsive)** Eye contact Direct body orientation facing client Forward body lean Smiling Head nodding	**Nonverbal behaviors** Nonverbal congruence Nonverbal acceptance of client disclosures Nonverbal responsiveness/dynamism
Verbal behaviors Relevant and thought-provoking questions Verbal attentiveness Directness and confidence in presentation Interpretations	**Verbal behaviors** Structuring Moderate level of self-disclosure Content of self-disclosure similar to client experiences and opinions	**Verbal behaviors** Accurate and reliable information giving Accurate paraphrasing Dependability and consistency of talk and actions Confidentiality Openness, honesty Nondefensive reflection of "tests of trust"

influence regardless of its occupant" (Corrigan, Dell, Lewis, & Schmidt, 1980, p. 425). Corrigan and colleagues believe that the legitimate power of our role is, in fact, so strong that demonstrated or behavioral cues of helper expertness are masked in the initial stage of helping because sufficient inherent power is ascribed to the role of a helper.

As shown in Table 6.1, in the initial stage of helping the practitioner wants to create a favorable initial impression and also to encourage the client into helping by communicating credibility (Whiston & Sexton, 1993). To some extent, such credibility will be conveyed for helpers by the inherent "power" of our roles. Additionally, helpers can seek to enhance evident and readily accessible descriptive cues associated with expertness by displaying diplomas, certificates, professional literature, titles, and so on. The helper's initial credibility is also enhanced when she or he has acquired a positive reputation (based on past history of helping others to resolve their problems) and the client is aware of this reputation.

However, role, reputation, and external or office "trappings" are insufficient to carry the practitioner through anything but the initial phase of helping. In subsequent phases, the helper must show actual evidence of competence through his or her behavior. This is especially important in working with clients from diverse groups. Role and reputation may not establish credibility with clients of color; in fact, in some cases these external trappings may reduce it. As Sue and Sue (1999) note, "Behavior-expertness, or demonstrating your ability to help a client becomes the critical form of expertness in effective multicultural counseling" (p. 45).

In effective multicultural helping, expertness means that the practitioner has some knowledge of the client's cultural values. It may be impossible for helpers to know everything about other cultural groups, but it is also myopic to stay centered within your own cultural group and not to develop awareness of the attitudes, beliefs, and practices of people from other cultures. At the very least, helpers can enhance their credibility with diverse groups of clients by acknowledging the limits of their knowledge and by being open to and interested in learning from clients. For example, a white male helper was working with a Latina. To his supervisor, he expressed frustration because he kept trying to get her to focus on herself, but she kept the focus on her children and their well-being. He lacked the understanding that for many Latinas, their role as mother and their relationship to their children are central to their own well-being. In trying to "get" her to focus on what he thought was best, he displayed cultural insensitivity and diminished her perception of his competence. If his supervisor also had lacked cultural sensitivity in this area, the process would have been perpetuated.

Behavioral expertness is measured by the extent to which the practitioner actually helps clients achieve their goals (Egan, 1998). Behavioral demonstrations of expertness are particularly crucial in the second and third stages of helping (assessment, goal setting, and intervention). These stages require great skill or actual technical competence if a helper is to make a thorough and accurate assessment of the client's concerns, help the client set realistic and worthwhile goals, and help the client take suitable action to reach those goals. Being able to accomplish these ends is extremely important because having charisma or being a "good person" will not get you through successive interactions with clients. As Corrigan and associates note, "In longer term counseling . . . continued evidence of a lack of expertise might negate the power conferred on a counselor by virtue of his/her role" (1980, p. 425).

Perceived expertness does not seem to be equivalent to practitioner experience—that is, experienced practitioners are not automatically perceived as more competent or expert than less experienced or even paraprofessional helpers (Heppner & Heesacker, 1982). Instead, expertness is enhanced by the presence or absence of selected nonverbal *and* verbal counselor behaviors that, together, interact to convey behavioral manifestations of competence (Barak, Patkin, & Dell, 1982). Nonverbal cues are especially important for enhancing the helper's credibility (Hoyt, 1996). *Nonverbal* behaviors associated with the communication of expertness include these:

1. Eye contact
2. Forward body lean
3. Fluent speech delivery (see also Chapter 3)

These nonverbal behaviors appear to contribute to perceived expertness by conveying attentiveness and spontaneity and lack of hesitancy in speech and presentation (see also Table 6.2).

Certain *verbal* behaviors seem to contribute to perceived expertness by establishing the helper as a source of knowledge and skill and by promoting credibility. These include the following:

1. Use of relevant and thought-provoking questions (see Chapter 7)
2. Verbal indications of attentiveness, such as verbal following, lack of interruptions, and listening responses (see Chapter 5)
3. Directness and confidence in presentation
4. Interpretations (see Chapter 7)
5. Concreteness (see also Learning Activity 6.1)

Concreteness

Because the skill of concreteness is not presented in any other part of the book, we describe it in some detail in this section. What clients say to you is often an incomplete representation of their experience. Their words and language (sometimes called "surface structure") do not really represent their experience or the meaning of their communication (sometimes called "deep structure"). Not only is the language of clients an incomplete representation of their experience; it is also full of various sorts of gaps—three in particular:

Deletions—when things are left out.

Distortions—when things are not as they seem or are misconstrued.

Generalization—when a whole class of things or people is associated with one feeling or with the same meaning, or when conclusions are reached without supporting data.

Because of these gaps, it is important for the helper to use some linguistic tools to make meaning of the client's words and to fill in these gaps. The most efficient linguistic tool for achieving these two objectives is questions—not just any questions, but particular questions designed to extract exactness and concreteness from clients. These questions also help ensure that you do not project your own sense of meaning onto the client, because your meaning may be irrelevant or inaccurate.

Consider the following example: A client says "I'm depressed." Therapist A responds by asking "About what, specifically?" Therapist B responds with "Depressed? Oh, yes, I know what that's like. How depressed?" The first therapist is likely to get a response from the client that leads to what depression is like for this client and eventually client responses that recover many missing pieces of the problem, as the client's initial statement is full of omissions. The second therapist assumes that her sensory experience or meaning of the word *depressed* is the same as the client's and fails to determine how the client's model of reality (or depression) may differ from her own and even from those of other clients.

Concreteness is a way to ensure that general and common experiences and feelings such as depression, anxiety, and anger are defined idiosyncratically for each client. Further, by requesting specific information from clients, you are relieved of having to search for your own equivalent meanings and interpretations. According to Lankton (1980, p. 52), "To translate a client's words into your own subjective experience, at best, results in valuable time and attention lost from the therapy session. At worst, the meaning you make of a client's experience may be wholly inaccurate."

Asking specific questions designed to elicit concreteness from clients is useful for assessing the client's current problems and also desired outcomes. Consequently, it is a facet of expertness that is particularly critical in the data-gathering and self-exploratory and understanding process characterized by the second stage of helping—assessment and goal setting. Moreover, it helps you to identify client limitations and resources that could contribute to or mitigate against effective solutions to issues. Thus, it is also an important part of expertness in the third phase of helping, in which action plans and intervention strategies are selected and applied.

Expertness Is Not "One Up"

It is extremely important to remember that expertness is not in any way the same as being dogmatic, authoritarian, or "one up." Expert helpers are those perceived as confident, attentive, and, because of background and behavior, capable of helping the client resolve concerns and work toward goals. Helpers misuse this important variable when they come across as "the expert" or in a one-up position with clients. This posture may intimidate clients, who might then decide not to return. In fact, particularly in initial sessions, helpers must do just the opposite: convey friendliness, equality, and likability. In later sessions, it is also important to deemphasize your influence efforts or make them inconspicuous in order to avoid engendering client resistance. In the next section, we describe how helpers exercise likability and friendliness through the variable of attractiveness.

Attractiveness

Attractiveness is inferred by clients from the helper's apparent friendliness, likability, and similarity to the client. As we mentioned earlier, the helper who is perceived as attractive by clients becomes an important source of referent power. The effects of attractiveness are apparently greatest when it is mutual—when the client likes the helper and the helper likes to work with the client (Heppner & Heesacker, 1982).

Attractiveness consists of both physical and interpersonal dimensions. Physical attractiveness is the primary descriptive cue associated with this relationship enhancer and, like the descriptive cues of expertness, appears to exert most influence in the *initial* stage of helping—during relationship and rapport building, when impression formation by clients is based on relatively apparent and accessible cues. During later stages of helping, the skills and competence, or behavioral manifestations, of expertness seem to outweigh the effects of physical attractiveness. In one study, clients did not want to return for sessions with helpers having poor skills even if the helpers were perceived as physically attractive (Vargas & Borkowski, 1982). Zlotlow and Allen (1981, p. 201) conclude that "although the physically attractive counselor may have a head start in developing rapport with clients as a result of widely held stereotypes about good-looking people, this advantage clearly is not an adequate substitute for technical skill or social competence." Harris and Busby (1998) found that both male and female participants—mostly white undergraduate college student volunteers—were more comfortable disclosing problems to physically attractive than to less attractive female helpers. These authors conclude that, consistent with earlier physical attractiveness research, this study demonstrates that attractiveness still has influence, "even though it has become politically correct to deemphasize physical attributes when judging others" (Harris & Busby, 1998, p. 255).

At the same time, it is important for helpers to remember that physical attractiveness is a "status variable": Those who are seen as physically attractive have more power and privilege than those who are not (Robinson & Howard-Hamilton, 2000, p. 149). Issues that arise in the helping relationship concerning physical attractiveness often have to do with body image of clients, able-bodiedness, and skin color. For example, as Robinson and Howard-Hamilton (2000) observe, able-bodied people carry more power: "Considerable silence surrounds the experiences of those who have disabilities" (p. 158). As well, attitudes toward those with disabilities are often degrading (p. 158). Skin color also has power and status, often with persons having lighter skin color being perceived as more desirable and powerful, although in the African American community this may be a double-edged sword "affecting those who are perhaps seen as 'too black' and those who may not be seen as 'black enough'" (Robinson & Howard-Hamilton, 2000, p. 151).

In effective multicultural counseling, attractiveness and credibility are related and are dependent on the practitioner's ability to understand the "psychological set or frame of reference for the culturally different client" (Sue & Sue, 1999, p. 41). Clients may be predisposed to use a particular set or frame of reference depending on their experiences with "race, ethnicity, and the experience of discrimination" (Sue & Sue, 1999, p. 41). For instance, some Puerto Rican and Asian American clients may use a problem-solving set with which they expect to receive information and direct suggestions from the helper. Helpers who are more "affectively oriented" and who do not value the problem-solving frame of reference for these clients will be perceived as less credible, attractive, and helpful than those who do (Sue & Sue, 1999, p. 42).

Selected nonverbal and verbal behaviors convey interpersonal attractiveness and also are quite important during the first two stages of helping—relationship/rapport and assessment and goal setting. Interpersonal attractiveness helps clients to open up and self-disclose by reducing client anxiety (through structuring and self-disclosure) and by creating the belief that this helper is someone with whom the client wants to work.

Nonverbal behaviors that contribute to attractiveness include eye contact, body orientation (facing client), forward body lean, smiling, and head nodding (Hermansson, Webster, & McFarland, 1988; see also Table 6.2). These and

---

LEARNING ACTIVITY 6.1 Expertness

Helper Competence

1. With a partner or in small groups, describe the ideal helping setting that would enhance most clients' initial impressions of helper competence. Be very specific in your descriptions.
2. With your partner or in small groups, discuss any clients who might not view your ideal setting described above as indicative of helper competence. Discuss the limitations of setting, role, and reputation as a means of enhancing the competence variable with these clients.
3. With your partner or in small groups, identify what you believe are the *three most important* things you can do behaviorally to enhance client perceptions of your competence. When you finish this part of the learning activity, you may want to share your descriptions of all three parts with another dyad or group, and vice versa.
4. Review these three things on your list, and explain how they may need to vary depending on the client's gender, race, and ethnicity.

other aspects of helper nonverbal behavior were discussed more extensively in Chapter 3.

Verbal behaviors that contribute to attractiveness include self-disclosure and structuring, discussed below. These behaviors appear to enhance the relationship by creating positive expectations, reducing unnecessary anxiety, and increasing the perceived similarity between client and practitioner. (See Learning Activity 6.2)

Helper Self-Disclosure

With respect to attractiveness, three factors related to self-disclosure are worth emphasizing:

1. Perceived attractiveness is related to a *moderate* level of helper self-disclosure (Edwards & Murdock, 1994). Too much or too little disclosure detracts from the client's perception of the helper as attractive.
2. The depth of personal material reflected in self-disclosure statements needs to be adapted to the stage of helping and the degree of the therapeutic relationship. In early sessions, self-disclosure of a factual nature is more useful; in later sessions, more personal or self-involving disclosures are more helpful (McCarthy, 1982).
3. Attractiveness is enhanced when helpers self-disclose problems and concerns previously experienced that are *similar* to the client's present problem. Similarity of self-disclosure may also promote the credibility and competence of the helper by suggesting that the helper knows about and can understand the client's concern (Corrigan et al., 1980). Accordingly, "disclosure of any prior problem (now successfully resolved) may confer on the counselor some 'expertise in problem resolution' or credibility accorded to 'one who has also suffered' " (Corrigan et al., 1980, p. 425). With clients of color, who may view helping as a "foreign experience," it can be useful for the practitioner to disclose something about his or her own past experiences in therapy—although not to the point of burdening or overwhelming the client (Helms & Cook, 1999, p. 191). We discuss the microskill of self-disclosure in greater detail in Chapter 7.

Structuring

Another way to maximize perceived similarity between helper and client is by the use of direct structuring. *Structuring* refers to an interactional process between helpers and clients in which they arrive at similar perceptions of the role of the helper, an understanding of what occurs in the helping process, and an agreement on which outcome goals will be achieved (Brammer, Abrego, & Shostrom, 1993; Day & Sparacio, 1980). Structuring enhances perceived helper/client similarity and interpersonal attractiveness and also fulfills an ethical obligation that requires helpers to inform clients of such things as the purposes, goals, techniques, and limitations of helping (American Counseling Association, 1995; American Psychological Association, 1995; National Association of Social Workers, 1996).

Direct structuring means that the helper actively and directly provides structure to the clients concerning the elements mentioned above. Direct structuring contributes to attractiveness by enhancing helper/client agreement on basic information and issues, thereby establishing some security in the relationship. Direct structuring is most important sometime in the first stage of helping (relationship and rapport), in which ambiguity and anxiety and lack of information about helping are likely to be greatest and the need to promote helper/client similarity is critical.

An example of the use of direct structuring with a new client in an initial interview follows:

Helper: Maria, I understand this is the first time you have ever been to see a counselor. Is that accurate or not?

Client: Yes, it is. I've thought about seeing someone for a while, but I finally got the courage to actually do it just recently.

Helper: I noticed you used the word *courage* as if perhaps you're feeling relieved you're here and also still somewhat uneasy about what happens in counseling.

Client: That's true. I'm glad I came, but I guess I'm also still a little unsure.

Helper: One thing that might help with the uncertainty is to talk for a few minutes about what goes on in counseling, what my role and your role are, and the kinds of things you may want to talk about or work on. How does that sound?

Client: Great. I think that would help.

Helper: OK. Many people come into counseling with something they need to get "off their chest"—sometimes they just need to talk and think about it. Later on, it is usually important to also do something about the issue. My role is to help you identify, talk about, and understand issues of concern to you and then to help you take any action that seems important to resolve the issue or to take your life in a different direction. This process can take several months or longer. At first, it usually is a little hard to open up and share some personal things with someone you don't know, but one thing that might help you do this is to know that, short of feeling strongly like you are going to harm yourself or someone else, whatever you tell me is kept in this room between us. Now—what are your questions or reactions?

Direct structuring is also very useful during the last stage of helping to ensure a smooth termination, to reduce client anxiety about dissolution of the therapeutic relationship, and to convey action expectations and information about what may happen after helping terminates. Consider the following example as a practitioner and client approach termination:

Helper: Jim, we started seeing each other every week six months ago; the last two months you've been coming in every other week. Several times you've mentioned recently how good you feel and how your relationships with women are now starting to take off in a direction you want. It seems to me that after about one or two more contacts we will be ready to stop seeing each other because you are able to handle these issues on your own now. What is your reaction to this?

Client: That sounds about right. I do feel a lot more confident in the way my relationships are going. I guess it does seem a little strange to think of not coming in here.

Helper: Yes. After you've been working together like we have, sometimes there's a little bit of strangeness or apprehension that accompanies the idea of finishing with counseling. However, I wouldn't suggest it at this time if I didn't feel very sure that you are ready to do this. It might help you to know that I'll be calling you several times after we finish to see how things are going, and, of course, if anything comes up in the future you want to talk over, just give me a call.

According to Day and Sparacio (1980), structure is also helpful at major transition points in helping, such as moving from one stage to another. This also reduces ambiguity, informs the client about any role and process changes in a different stage of therapy, and increases the likelihood that both helper and client will approach the forthcoming stage with similar rather than highly discrepant perceptions.

To provide structure effectively with clients, consider the following eight guidelines for structuring, adapted from Day and Sparacio (1980).

1. Structuring is not an ultimatum. It should be negotiated or requested, not coerced. Clients should be given the opportunity to respond and react to structure as well as be able to modify it.

LEARNING ACTIVITY 6.2 Attractiveness

Part One

Attributes of Attractive Persons

In a dyad or a small group, discuss the attributes of persons you know and consider to be "attractive" persons. Compile a written list of their attributes. Review your list to determine which attributes are descriptive ones, such as appearance and demeanor, and which attributes are behavioral—that is, things the person does. Explore whether your beliefs about attractiveness reflect any commonly held stereotypes—especially about dimensions of physical attractiveness such as able-bodiedness, body image and size, and skin color. How might your stereotypes affect your work with clients?

Part Two

Structuring

In this activity, write an example of the use of direct structuring for each of the following four examples. Feedback follows on page 122.

1. Write an example of structuring in an initial interview with a client who has never seen a helper before. Assume that this client is from a different culture than you.
2. Write an example of structuring in an initial interview with a client who is new to you but has seen three other helpers.
3. Write an example of structuring prior to starting the termination phase with a client who has never been in counseling before.
4. Write an example of structuring prior to starting the termination phase with a client who has been in counseling several times.

> **FEEDBACK 6.2**
> *Attractiveness*
>
> **Part Two**
> **Structuring**
>
> 1. "I notice that this is the first time you've been to see a helper. You may be uncertain about what to expect. In our work together, I'll try to understand you and your culture and to honor and respect your wishes and values. Also, I want to create an atmosphere in which you feel safe to express whatever is on your mind. Perhaps it would help for me to share with you something about myself and my own experiences in therapy before you tell me what's on your mind and what you're looking for from me."
> 2. "You probably know what goes on in this process generally. What I do might vary a little bit from the other helpers you've seen. I believe I'm here to listen to you, to help you understand some of your concerns, and to assist you in taking a course of action best for you to resolve these issues."
> 3. "I have the sense that you have really accomplished what you wanted to do. Let's take a few minutes to see . . . [reviews client's progress toward desired goals]. Since you also feel our work's about done, it seems like after two more sessions it will be time to close out our relationship for now. You may feel a little apprehensive about this, but I'll be calling you shortly after we finish to see how things are going. I imagine things will go quite smoothly for you. Once in a while, people find it's hard to start out on their own, but soon things start to fall into place. During these last three sessions, we'll also be working specifically on how you can take the things you've learned and done in our sessions out into your own world so things do fall into place for you out there."
> 4. "I believe after one or two more sessions, we're ready to finish. Since you've been through this before, do you have the same or a different opinion? [Time for client to respond.] One thing I want you to know about me is that I'll call you once or twice after we stop to see how things are going, and, of course, feel free to call me, too, if something comes up you need to discuss."

2. Structure, particularly restrictions and limitations, should not be applied for punitive reasons or in a punitive manner.
3. The helper should be aware of his or her rationale for structuring and should explain the reasons at the time of structuring or be prepared to provide a rationale in response to the client's request for explanation.
4. The helper should be guided by the client's readiness for structure and by the context of the relationship and process.
5. Too much or a too-rigid structure can be constraining for both the client and the helper (Pietrofesa, Hoffman, Splete, & Pinto, 1978).
6. Unnecessary and purposeless recitation of rules and guidelines can imply that the practitioner is more concerned with procedure than with helpfulness. In fact, a compulsive approach to structuring can be indicative of low levels of helper self-assurance (Hansen, Rossberg, & Cramer, 1994).
7. The helper must relate structure to the client's emotional, cognitive, and behavioral predisposition. For example, the highly independent individual or the isolate may be expected to resist what she or he interprets as personal threats or infringements. In such cases, structuring must be accomplished by sensitivity, tentativeness, and flexibility (Day and Sparacio, 1980).
8. Structuring must also be done in a way that is culturally sensitive. This means that both the expectations of the helper and the client are recognized and that there is an "attempt to generate a mutually satisfying set of procedures that honor the cultures inherent to the therapy, the therapist, and the client" (Helms & Cook, 1999, p. 169). Structuring is also an important factor when considering the age of the client. Structuring is very important in working with children because it defines the parameters of what you are doing, creating a sense of safety for the child. However, at the same time, structuring with child clients needs to be done in small doses.

Trustworthiness

According to Cohen and Cohen (1999, p. 71), "The bond of trust between therapist and client is a central value in counseling ethics. Where such a bond exists, the probability is good that the client will confide in the therapist. . . . Take away this bond of trust, and clients will be reluctant to disclose . . . thus, client welfare will likely not be served. . . ." In the interpersonal influence model, trustworthiness is perceived by clients from such factors as the helper's interest, competence, respect, and structuring (Edelstein & Semenchuk, 1996). Trust or mistrust is also greatly affected by the client's race, and ethnic and cultural affiliation.

Establishing Trust

In the initial stage of helping (relationship and rapport), clients are also dependent on readily accessible descriptive cues to judge the trustworthiness of helpers. For example, many clients are likely to find helpers trustworthy, at least initially, because of the status of their role in society. Clients also are more likely to perceive a helper as trustworthy if she or he has acquired a reputation for honesty and for ethical and professional behavior. Likewise, a negative reputation can erode initial trust in a helper. Thus, many clients may put their faith in the helper initially on the basis of role and reputation and, over the course of time, continue to trust the helping professional unless the trust is in some way abused. This is particularly true for clients from the dominant cultural group.

For clients who are not from the dominant cultural group, it may be the other way around. As LaFromboise and Dixon (1981, p. 135) observe, "A member of the minority group frequently enters the relationship suspending trust until the person proves that he/she is worthy of being trusted." For these and some other clients, helpers may have to earn initial trust. This is especially true as helping progresses. Trust can be difficult to establish yet easily destroyed. Initial trust based on external factors such as the helper's role and reputation must be solidified with appropriate actions and behaviors of helpers that occur during successive interactions (see also Table 6.2).

Johnson (2000) points out that it takes many successive consistent behaviors to establish trust but just one inconsistent behavior to destroy it; once destroyed or diminished, trust is extremely difficult to rebuild. Trust can also be damaged when the helper acts in any way that abuses the inherent power ascribed to the role as helper. For example, if the helper makes unilateral decisions about the client and the helping process and does not collaborate with the client, this abuse of power will diminish trust. Abuse of power may be particularly damaging when you are working with clients who are from nonmainstream cultural groups and who have been disempowered because of their race, income level, sexual orientation, religion, and so on. Helping professionals have a special responsibility to engage in "ethnic-sensitive practice" that attempts to empower disenfranchised clients and to "redress the oppression" that some clients from certain cultural groups have experienced (Zastrow, 1999, p. 302).

The helper's trustworthiness may also be an issue depending on the age of the client, the client's former history with other helpers, and the client's trauma history. Children often trust helpers very readily unless they have had a prior bad experience with a helper in which their trust was violated or unless they have a trauma history. Regardless of age, almost all clients who have trauma histories will have greater issues in trusting a helper than clients who do not.

During the second stage of helping, assessment and goal setting, trust is essential in order for the client to be open and revealing of very personal problems and concerns. Clients' self-exploration of issues during this phase can be limited by the amount of trust that has developed in the relationship prior to this time. Trust is also critical during the third and fourth stages of helping. In the third stage (action/intervention), the client often has to set in motion the difficult and vulnerable process of change. Trust can provide the impetus necessary for the client to do so. Trust is also critical to the fourth stage of helping (evaluation and termination). Effective termination ensues when the client trusts the helper's decision to terminate, trusts that it is not too early (leaving the client hanging) or too prolonged (creating excessive dependency for the client), and trusts that the helper is reliable and concerned enough to check in with the client on a periodic basis as a follow-up to therapy.

The behaviors that contribute most importantly to trustworthiness include helper congruence, or consistency, of verbal and nonverbal behavior, nonverbal acceptance of client disclosures, and nonverbal responsiveness and dynamism (see also Chapter 3). Incongruence, judgmental or evaluative reactions, and passivity quickly erode any initial trust.

Important verbal behaviors (see also Table 6.2) contributing to trust include accurate paraphrasing (see also Chapter 5), dependability and consistency between talk and actions, confidentiality, openness and honesty, accurate and reliable information giving (see also Chapter 7), and nondefensive reflections/interpretations of clients' "tests of trust." This last behavior is discussed in greater depth in the following section.

Client Tests of Helper Trustworthiness

According to Johnson (2000), trust between helpers and clients does not always develop automatically. Clients need to be assured that the helping process will be structured to meet their needs and that the helper will not take advantage of their vulnerability (Johnson, 2000). Often, clients do not ask about these issues directly. Instead, they engage in subtle maneuvers to obtain data about the helper's trustworthiness. Fong and Cox (1983) call these maneuvers "tests of trust" and liken them to trial balloons sent up to "see how they fly" before the client decides whether to send up the big one or the real one.* Brothers (1995) also describes successful and failed tests of trust in the therapy relationship.

Practitioners may be insensitive to such "tests of trust" and fail to identify that trust is the real concern of the client. Instead of responding to the trust issue, helpers may respond just to the content, the surface level of the message. Or the helper may view the client as "defensive, resistant, or hostile" and respond negatively (Fong & Cox, 1983, p. 163). If the trust issue is unresolved, the relationship may deteriorate or even terminate with the helper unaware that "the real issue was lack of trust" (Fong & Cox, 1983, p. 163).

Johnson (2000) observes that it is inappropriate to *never* trust or to *always* trust. We point this out because occasionally we have seen practitioners who seem to expect clients to trust them automatically and feel offended if clients don't trust them or if clients "test" their trustworthiness. We believe that trust has to be earned and that it is useful for clients to be a little skeptical and guarded about revealing too much too soon to a relatively unknown therapist.

We take the position that it may be particularly unwise for clients of color to trust a helper *initially* until the helper behaviorally *demonstrates* trustworthiness and credibility—specifically until the helper shows that (1) he or she will not recreate an oppressive atmosphere of any kind in the helping interaction; (2) he or she does not engage in discrimination, racist attitudes, and behaviors and (3) he or she has some understanding and awareness of the client's racial and cultural affiliation.

Fong and Cox observe that some client statements and behaviors are used repeatedly by many clients as "tests of trust." They state that "the specific content of clients' questions and statements is unique to individual clients, but the general form that tests of trust take—for example, requesting information or telling a secret—are relatively predictable" (p. 164). These authors have identified six common types of client "tests of trust," which we describe as follows.

Requesting information (or "Can you understand and help me?") Practitioners need to be alert to whether client questions are searches for factual information or for helper opinions and beliefs. Clients who ask questions like "Do you have children?" or "How long have you been married?" are probably looking for something in addition to the factual response. Most often, they are seeking verification from you that you will be able to understand, to accept, and to help them with their particular set of concerns. In responding to such client questions, it is important to convey your understanding and acceptance of the clients' concerns and of their need to feel understood. For example, a helper might say "Yes, I do have two children. I'm also wondering whether you believe that the fact that I have children means I can better understand your concerns."

Telling a secret (or "Can I be vulnerable or take risks with you?") Clients share secrets—very personal aspects of their lives—to test whether they can trust the helper to accept them as they really are, to keep their communications confidential, and to avoid exploiting their vulnerability after they have disclosed very personal concerns. Usually, this secret is not even relevant to the client's presenting concern but is related to something the client does that has "embarrassment or shame attached to it" (Fong & Cox, 1983, p. 164). And "if the counselor becomes perceptively defensive in reaction to the client's revelation or makes some statement that seems to be judgmental, the client is almost certain to decide that it is unsafe to be vulnerable with this person. The level of trust drops. And further self-disclosure of any depth may not be forthcoming, at least for a very long time" (p. 164).

Practitioners need to remember that clients who share secrets are really testing the waters to see how safe it is to self-disclose personal issues with you. Responding with nonverbal and verbal acceptance and listening assures clients that their private thoughts, feelings, and behaviors are safe with you. For example, suppose a client blurts out "I had an abortion several years ago. No one knows about this, not even my husband." The helper must respond to the entire message, especially acknowledging the "risk" involved: "That is your way of saying to me that this is secret between you and me."

---

*This and all other quotations from "Trust as an Underlying Dynamic in the Counseling Process: How Clients Test Trust," by M. L. Fong and B. G. Cox, *The Personnel and Guidance Journal, 62,* pp. 163–166, copyright 1983 by ACA, are reprinted with permission. No further reproduction authorized without written permission of the American Counseling Association.

LEARNING ACTIVITY 6.3 — Trustworthiness

Part One

Identification of Trust-Related Issues

With a partner or in a small group, develop responses to the following questions:

1. For clients belonging to the dominant cultural group or from racial/cultural backgrounds similar to your own:
   a. How does trust develop during therapeutic interactions?
   b. How is trust violated during therapeutic interactions?
   c. How does it feel to have your trust in someone else violated?
   d. What are ten things a helper can do (or ten behaviors to engage in) to build trust? Of the ten, select five that are most important and rank these from 1 (most critical, top priority to establish trust) to 5 (least critical or least priority to establish trust).
2. Complete the same four questions above for clients of color or from a racial/cultural background distinctly different from your own.

Part Two

Client Tests of Trust

Listed below are six client descriptions. For each description, (a) identify the content and process reflected in the test of trust, and (b) write an example of a helping response that could be used appropriately with this type of trust test. You may wish to refer to Table 6.3. An example is completed. Feedback follows.

Example

1. The client asks whether you have seen other people before who have attempted suicide.
   a. Test of trust (content): request for information
      (process): can you understand and help me?
   b. Example of helper response: "Yes, I have worked with other persons before you who have thought life wasn't worth living. Perhaps this will help you know that I will try to understand what this experience is like for you and will help you try to resolve it in your own best way."
2. The client's phone has been disconnected, and the client wants to know whether he can come ten minutes early to use your phone.
   a. Test of trust (content): _____
      (process): _____
   b. Example of helper response: _____
3. The client wonders aloud whether you make enough money as a helper that you would choose this occupation if you had to do it over again.
   a. Test of trust (content): _____
      (process): _____
   b. Example of helper response: _____
4. The client states that she must be stupid because she now has to repeat third grade while all the other kids in her class are going on to fourth grade.
   a. Test of trust (content): _____
      (process): _____
   b. Example of helper response: _____
5. The client has changed the appointment time at the last minute four times in the last several weeks.
   a. Test of trust (content): _____
      (process): _____
   b. Example of helper response: _____
6. The client is an Asian American male college student who indicates he is hesitant to speak openly and feels constrained by his concern that his family and friends do not discover he is coming to a counselor. He wonders whom you will tell about his visit to you.
   a. Test of trust (content): _____
      (process): _____
   b. Example of helper response: _____

Part Three

Mr. Hernández is a 38-year-old Mexican American who works as a gardener. He and his family are making an in-

(continued)

| LEARNING ACTIVITY | 6.3 | Trustworthiness *(continued)* |

quiry at the Family Service Association agency regarding a problem that one of the children is having in school. Mr. Hernández speaks some English in his business, because much of his clientele is middle- and upper-class whites. From morning to evening, he drives his truck and maintains the yards and landscapes of many wealthy professionals who live in exclusive sections of the city. Mr. Hernández works hard and is friendly to his customers. During the holidays, many customers give him extra money and gifts for his family. When he returns home after a hard day of work, Mr. Hernández is tired. He has a few friends in the barrio who visit him in the evenings. He enjoys playing cards with them at home and drinking beer. Mr. Hernández is reluctant to talk about personal and family problems to outsiders. Rather, he confides in his wife on the rare occasions when he is deeply troubled over a situation.

Respond to the following:

It is important to enter the world of a person of color. For 30 minutes you are to become Mr. Hernández. Role-play him getting up in the morning before dawn, eating his breakfast, and leaving for a full day of gardening. Imagine his feelings about his work, his gardening skills, his conversations with some of his customers during the day, and his evenings at home with family and friends.

Over the course of several months, Mr. Hernández tries to cope with a family problem that involves his eldest son, but he and his wife are unable to solve the problem. What would you do if you were Mr. Hernández?

- Would you approach a formal social-service agency with your problem?
- How would you feel during the opening session?
- What kind of worker would you like to have help you with your problem?
- What would you do to determine whether the worker is a person whom you can trust and in whom you are willing to confide?

Source: From *Social Work Practice and People of Color* (5th ed.) by D. Lum, p. 145. Copyright © 2000. Reprinted by permission of Brooks/Cole, an imprint of the Wadsworth Group, a division of Thomson Learning.

Asking a favor (or "Are you reliable?") Clients may ask helpers to perform favors that may or may not be appropriate. According to Fong and Cox (1983, p. 165), "all requests of clients for a favor should be viewed, especially initially, as potential tests of trust." When clients ask you to lend them a book, or call their boss for them, whether you grant or deny the favor is not as important as how you handle the request and how reliably you follow through with your stated intentions. It is crucial to follow through on reasonable favors you have promised to do. For unreasonable favors, it is important to state tactfully but directly your reason for not granting the favor. Efforts to camouflage the real reason with an excuse or to grant an unreasonable favor grudgingly are just as damaging to trust as is failure to follow through on a favor (Fong & Cox, 1983, p. 165). For instance, if a client asks you to see her at her home in order to save her time and gas money, you might tactfully deny her favor by saying "Jane, I can certainly appreciate your need to save time and money. I need to continue to see you in the office, however, because it is easier for me to concentrate and listen to you without any distractions I'm not used to." Asking favors is generally an indication that the client is testing your reliability, dependability, honesty, and directness. A good rule of thumb to follow is "Don't promise more than you can deliver, and be sure to deliver what you have promised as promised." Consistency is especially important to establish with clients who are not from the dominant cultural group. As Sue and Sue (1999) state, "Generally, minority clients who enter counseling with a White therapist will tend to apply a consistency test to what the counselor says or does" (p. 42).

Putting oneself down (or "Can you accept me?") Clients put themselves down to test the helper's level of acceptance. This test of trust is designed to help clients determine whether the helper will continue to be accepting even the parts of themselves that clients view as bad, negative, or dirty. Often this test of trust is conveyed by statements or behaviors designed to shock the helper, followed by a careful scrutiny of the helper's verbal and nonverbal reactions. Helpers need to respond neutrally to client self-putdowns rather than condoning or evaluating the client's statements and actions. As Fong and Cox note,

TABLE 6.3 Examples of Client Tests of Trust and Helpful and Nonhelpful Practitioner Responses

Test of trust	Client statement	Examples of nonhelpful responses	Example of helpful response
Requesting information (can you understand and help me?)	"Have you ever worked with anyone else who seems as mixed up as I am?"	"Yes, all the time." "No, not too often." "Once in a while." "Oh, you're not *that* mixed up."	"Many people I work with often come in feeling confused and overwhelmed. I'm also wondering whether you want to know that I have the experience to help you."
Telling a secret (can I be vulnerable with you?)	"I've never been able to tell anyone about this—not even my husband or my priest. But I did have an abortion several years ago. I just was not ready to be a good and loving mother."	"Oh, an abortion—really?" "You haven't even told your husband even though it might be his child, too?"	"What you're sharing with me now is our secret, something between you and me."
Asking a favor (are you reliable?)	"Could you bring this information (or book) in for me next week?"	Promises to do it but forgets altogether or does not do it when specified	Promises to do it and does it when promised
Putting oneself down (can you accept me?)	"I just couldn't take all the pressure from the constant travel, the competition, the need to always win and be number one. When they offered me the uppers, it seemed like the easiest thing to cope with all this. Now I need more and more of the stuff."	"Don't you know you could hurt yourself if you keep going like this?" "You'll get hurt from this—is it really a smart thing to do?"	"The pressure has gotten so intense it's hard to find a way out from under it."
Inconveniencing the helper (do you have consistent limits?)	"Can I use your phone again before we get started?"	"Of course, go ahead—feel free any time." "Absolutely not."	"Marc, the last two times I've seen you, you have started the session by asking to use my phone. When this happens, you and I don't have the full time to use for counseling. Would it be possible for you to make these calls before our session starts, or do we need to change our appointment time?"
Questioning the helper's motives (is your caring real?)	"I don't see how you have the energy to see me at the end of the day like this. You must be exhausted after seeing all the other people with problems, too."	"Oh, no, I'm really not." "Yes, I'm pretty tired."	"You're probably feeling unsure about how much energy I have left for you after seeing other people first. One thing about you that helps me keep my energy up is. . . ."

In responding to the client's self-putdowns, the counselor reflects to the client what the counselor has heard and then responds with statements of interest and acceptance. If the counselor makes the mistake of reacting either positively or negatively to the client's descriptions of their "bad" behavior early in the relationship, trust is unlikely to be built. Clients will see the counselor as potentially judgmental or opinionated. (1983, p. 165)

A client may say "Did you know I've had three abortions in the last three years? It's my own fault. I just get carried away and keep forgetting to use birth control." The helper needs to respond with nonverbal acceptance and may say something like "You've found yourself with several unwanted pregnancies."

Inconveniencing the helper (or "Do you have consistent limits?") Clients often test trust by creating inconveniences for the helper such as changing appointment times, canceling at the last minute, changing the location of sessions, or asking to make a phone call during the session. Practitioners need to respond directly and openly to the inconvenience, especially if it occurs more than once or twice. When the helper sets limits, clients may begin feeling secure and assured that the helper is dependable and consistent. Setting limits often serves a reciprocal purpose: The clients realize they also can set limits in the relationship. As an example of this test of trust, consider the client who is repeatedly late to sessions. After three consecutive late starts, the helper mentions "You know, Gary, I've realized that the last three weeks we've got off to quite a late start. This creates problems for me because if we have a full session, it throws the rest of my schedule off. Or if I stop at the designated time, you end up getting shortchanged. Can we start on time, or do we need to reschedule the appointment time?"

> **FEEDBACK 6.3** Trustworthiness
>
> **Part Two**
>
> **Client Tests of Trust**
>
> 2. a. Test of trust (content): Asking a favor (process): Are you reliable and open with me?
>   b. Example response: "I know how difficult it can be to manage without a telephone. Unfortunately, I see someone almost up until the minute you arrive for your session, so my office is occupied. There's a pay phone in the outer lobby of the building if you find you need to make a call on a particular day or time."
> 3. a. Test of trust (content): Questioning your motives (process): Do you really care, or are you just going through the motions?
>   b. Example response: "Perhaps, Bill, you're feeling unsure about whether I see people like yourself for the money or because I'm sincerely interested in you. One way in which I really enjoy [value] working with you is...."
> 4. a. Test of trust (content): Putting oneself down (process): Can you accept me even though I'm not too accepting of myself right now?
>   b. Example response: "You're feeling pretty upset right now that you're going to be back in the third grade again. I wonder if you're concerned, too, about losing friends or making new ones?"
> 5. a. Test of trust (content): Inconveniencing you (process): Do you have consistent limits?
>   b. Example response: "Mary, I'm not really sure anymore when to expect you. I noticed you've changed your appointment several times in the last few weeks at the last minute. I want to be sure I'm here or available when you do come in, so it would help if you could decide on one time that suits you and then just one backup time in case the first time doesn't work out. If you can give some advance notice of a need to change times, then I won't have to postpone or cancel out on you because of my schedule conflicts."
> 6. a. Test of trust (content): Information request [process]: Do you know enough about my cultural background and affiliation for me to be disclosive with you?
>   b. Example response: "I understand you are concerned right now about how much you can safely tell me. I respect your wish to keep the visit here just between us."

Questioning the helper's motives (or "Is your caring real?") As we mentioned earlier, one aspect of trustworthiness is sincerity. Clients test this aspect of trust by statements and questions designed to answer the question "Do you really care about me, or is it just your job?" Clients may ask about the number of other clients the helper sees or how the helper distinguishes and remembers all his clients or whether the helper thinks about the client during the week (Fong & Cox, 1983). Fong and Cox observe that "unless counselors are alert to the fact that this is a form of testing trust, they may fail to respond adequately to the crucial issue; that is, the client's need to be seen as a worthwhile human being in the counselor's eyes and not just as a source of income for the counselor" (p. 166). For instance, suppose a client says to her helping professional "I bet you get tired of listening to people like me all the time." The practitioner may respond with something that affirms her interest in the client, such as "You're feeling unsure about your place here, wondering whether I really care about you when I see so many other persons. Suzanne, from you I've learned..." (follow through with a personal statement directly related to this client).

Table 6.3 presents a summary of these six tests of trust with sample client statements and helpful and nonhelpful helper responses. (See Learning Activity 6.3)

Tests of Trust in Cross-Cultural Helping

Tests of trust may occur more frequently and with more emotional intensity in cross-cultural helping. This is often because clients from nondominant group membership have experienced past and current oppression, discrimination, and overt and covert racism. As a result, they may feel more vulnerable in interpersonal interactions, such as helping ones, that involve self-disclosure and an unequal power base. During initial helping interactions, clients with diverse backgrounds are likely to behave in ways that minimize their vulnerability and that maximize their self-protection (Sue & Sue, 1999). In U.S. culture, Euro-American helpers may be viewed automatically as members of the Establishment (Sue & Sue, 1999, p. 46). As Stevenson and Renard (1993) note, "The dynamics of hostile race relations still exist in our society. It is crucial that therapists question whether these relations are played out in the therapeutic context... sensitivity to oppression issues allows for the building of credibility for psychotherapists which becomes of supreme importance to cross-cultural relationships, especially in the early stages" (pp. 433–434). A therapist's disregard for issues of oppression only fuels a minority client's "legacy of mistrust" (Stevenson & Renard, 1993). Nickerson, Helms, and Terrell (1994) have recommended that helpers must understand and address the impact of cultural mistrust during the entire therapeutic process, from intake to termination.

Sue and Sue (1999) observe that perhaps more than anything else, challenges to the helper's trustworthiness will be a "frequent theme blocking further exploration/movement until the issue is resolved" to the client's satisfaction (p. 46). They provide several guidelines concerning trust issues with clients of color. First, clients from nondominant cultural groups are likely to test the helper's trustworthiness more often. Second, it is up to the helper, not the client, to establish trust. Third, to demonstrate trustworthiness requires self-disclosure by the helper. Helms and Cook (1999) also emphasize the importance of helper self-disclosure in establishing trust with clients of color. As they state, "if you want clients to tell you *all* about themselves, then you must tell them *something* about yourself"—but do so in a way that does not shift the focus from them to you (p. 191). Sue and Sue (1999) provide the following example of this test of trust and trust building in cross-cultural helping:

White Male Therapist: I sense some major hesitations . . . it's difficult for you to discuss your concerns with me.
Black Male Client: You're damn right! If I really told you how I felt about my coach [White], what's to prevent you from telling him? You Whities are all of the same mind.
White Therapist [*angry voice*]: Look, it would be a lie for me to say I don't know your coach. He's an acquaintance, but not a personal friend. Don't put me in the same bag with all Whites! Anyway, even if he was, I hold our discussion in strictest confidence. Let me ask you this question, what would I need to do that would make it easier for you to trust me?
Black Client: You're on your way, man! (pp. 46–47).

Sue and Sue (1999) conclude that

> That the therapist did not hide the fact that he knew the coach (openness), became angry about being lumped with all Whites (sincerity), assured the client he would not tell the coach or anyone about their sessions (confidentiality), and asked the client how he would work to prove he was trustworthy (genuineness) were all elements that enhanced his trustworthiness. (p. 47)

Johnson (2000) describes behaviors that *decrease* trust. Refusing to reciprocate in self-disclosure is one of them. Also, ridiculing the client, moralizing, and evaluating the client in any way will decrease trust, as will being nonresponsive and poker-faced. Another behavior that seriously diminishes trust is defensiveness (p. 99). Sue and Sue (1999) provide an example in which the helper displayed almost all of these behaviors and in doing so seriously impaired his trustworthiness:

Black Female Client: Students in my drama class expect me to laugh when they do "steppin fetchin" routines and tell Black jokes. . . . I'm wondering whether you've ever laughed at any of those jokes.
White Male Therapist [*Long pause*]: Yes, I'm sure I have. Have you ever laughed at any White jokes?
Black Client: What's a White joke?
White Therapist: I don't know [*nervous laughter*]; I suppose one making fun of Whites. Look, I'm Irish. Have you ever laughed at Irish jokes?
Black Client: People tell me many jokes, but I don't laugh at racial jokes. I feel we're all minorities and should respect each other. (p. 47)

In this example, the helper became defensive and failed to recognize the question behind the test of trust—e.g., "How open and honest are you about your own racism, and will it interfere with our session here?" (Sue & Sue, 1999, pp. 47–48).

Zastrow (1999) asserts that helping professionals need to accept that in cross-cultural helping, distrust is likely to be the norm. Helpers from the mainstream culture sometimes have trouble with this concept and wonder why it is so difficult for culturally different clients to trust them. Although this is a complicated process, one way to view it is that each cultural group has a "collective memory" (D. Cook, personal communication, April 10, 2000). This means that even if a specific client belonging to a particular cultural group has not had a personal experience with disempowerment and oppression that her or his cultural group has had, the memory of the collective culture will still permeate and affect the client's reactions to members of other cultural groups. Whaley (2001) explains that cultural mistrust seems to occur at a broader cultural level that extends beyond the interpersonal relationship with the helper. When cultural mistrust occurs, a culturally sensitive approach is for practitioners to address the mistrust issue directly with clients.

SUMMARY

In this chapter, we examined the social influence model of helping. In this model, the helper establishes an influence base with the client through the three relationship enhancers of expertness, attractiveness, and trustworthiness. The helper then uses this influence base to effect client change.

Helper characteristics contributing most to the influence process include expertness (or competence), attractiveness, and trustworthiness. Components of expertness include descriptive cues such as education and training, certificates and licenses, title and status, setting, reputation, and role.

Behavioral cues associated with expertness include responsive nonverbal behaviors such as fluent speech delivery, nonverbal and verbal attentiveness, relevant and thought-provoking questions, and interpretations. Nonverbal cues are especially significant.

Behavioral cues of attractiveness are responsive nonverbal behavior, moderate level of helper self-disclosure, similarity of the content of self-disclosure, and structuring.

Trustworthiness is based on one's role and reputation for honesty as well as nonverbal congruence, dynamism, and acceptance of client disclosures. Trustworthiness is also associated with accurate and reliable information giving, accurate paraphrasing, maintaining of confidentiality, openness and honesty, and nondefensive reactions to clients' "tests of trust."

Physical and interpersonal attractiveness and the role, reputation, and setting of the helper contribute to a client's early impressions that the helper is attractive, competent, and trustworthy. These aspects are most useful during the early sessions, in which the helper strives to establish rapport and to motivate the client to continue with the helping process. As therapy progresses, these aspects become less influential and must be substantiated by actual skills that demonstrate the practitioner's competence and resourcefulness toward resolving client concerns. Behavioral expressions of expertness and trustworthiness are particularly critical during all the remaining phases of helping-assessment and goal setting, intervention and action, and evaluation and termination.

Although expertness, attractiveness, and trustworthiness are important ingredients of a therapeutic relationship, practitioners engaged in cross-cultural helping cannot safely assume the existence of these variables. As Sue and Sue (1999) state, "The therapist working with a minority client is likely to experience severe tests of his/her expertness and trustworthiness before serious therapy can proceed. The responsibility for proving to the client that you are a credible therapist is likely to be greater when working with a minority client. How you meet the challenge is important in determining your effectiveness as a multicultural helping professional" (p. 48).

INFOTRAC® EXPLORATIONS

1. Search for *social influence*, and examine how the articles refer to and use this term.
2. Explore how many articles you can find that deal with *trust* in cross-cultural situations.

SUGGESTED RESOURCES

Readings

Brothers, D. (1995). *Falling backwards: An exploration of trust and self experience.* New York: Norton.

Cohen, D., & Cohen, G. (1999). *The virtuous therapist: Ethical practice of counseling and psychotherapy.* Belmont, CA: Wadsworth.

Harris, S., & Busby, D. (1998). Therapist physical attractiveness: An unexplored influence on client disclosure. *Journal of Marital and Family Therapy, 24,* 251–257.

Heesacker, M., Conner, K., & Prichard, S. (1995). Individual counseling and psychology: Applications from the social psychology of attitude change. *The Counseling Psychologist, 23,* 611–629.

Heppner, P., & Frazier, P. (1992). Social psychological processes in psychotherapy: Extrapolating basic research to counseling psychology. In S. D. Brown & R. Lent (Eds.), *Handbook of counseling psychology* (pp. 141–176). New York: Wiley.

Hoyt, W. T. (1996). Antecedents and effects of perceived therapist credibility: A meta-analysis. *Journal of Counseling Psychology, 43,* 430–447.

McNeill, B., & Stoltenberg, C. D. (1989). Reconceptualizing social influence in counseling. The elaboration likelihood model. *Journal of Counseling Psychology, 36,* 24–33.

Nickerson, K., Helms, J., & Terrell, F. (1994). Cultural mistrust, opinions about mental illness, and black students' attitudes toward seeking psychological help from white counselors. *Journal of Counseling Psychology, 41,* 378–385.

Robinson, T. L., & Howard-Hamilton, M. (2000). *The convergence of race, ethnicity, and gender: Multiple identities in counseling.* Upper Saddle River, NJ: Prentice Hall.

Scheel, M., Seaman, S., Roach, K., Mullin, T., & Blackwell Mahoney, K. (1999). Client implementation of therapist recommendations predicted by client perception of fit, difficulty of implementation, and therapist influence. *Journal of Counseling Psychology, 46,* 308–316.

Strong, S. R., Welsh, T., Corcoran, J., & Hoyt, W. (1992). Social psychology and counseling psychology: The history, products and promise of an interface. *Journal of Counseling Psychology, 39,* 139–157.

Sue, D. W., & Sue, D. (1999). *Counseling the culturally different* (3rd ed.). New York: Wiley.

Whaley, A. (2001). Cultural mistrust and mental health services for African Americans: A review and meta-analysis. *The Counseling Psychologist, 29,* 513–531.

Whiston, S. C., & Sexton, T. L. (1993). An overview of psychotherapy outcome research: Implications for practice. *Professional Psychology, 24,* 43–51.

Zastrow, C. H. (1999). *The practice of social work* (6th ed.). Pacific Grove, CA: Brooks/Cole.

Web Sites

Interpersonal Communication—Self Disclosure
http://www.abacon.com/commstudies/interpersonal/indisclosure.html

Interpersonal Influence Cluster
http://www.gov.sk.ca/psc/mdcentre/interpersonal_influence-dictionary.htm

Interpersonal Power and Influence in Organizations
http://www.mapnp.org/library/guiding/influenc/influenc.htm

6 POSTEVALUATION

Part One

Listed below are six written client descriptions. Your task is to match each description with the corresponding "test of trust" (Chapter Objective One). Feedback for this part follows on p. 133.

Test of Trust

1. Information request
2. Telling a secret
3. Asking a favor
4. Putting oneself down
5. Inconveniencing the helper
6. Questioning the helper's motives

Client Situation

1. The client asks you whether you get "burned out" or fatigued talking to people with problems all day. The client also asks you how many clients are in your current caseload, whether you really have enough time to see everyone, and whether you would see someone for a reduced fee.
2. The client is very nondisclosive and reticent but finally tells you that she has been sexually abused by her stepfather and that she has never told anyone about this before.
3. The client asks to borrow a novel she sees on your desk.
4. The client who presents with marital issues wants to know whether you are married or single.
5. The client wants you to see him on the weekend because that would make it easier for him to get to the session.
6. The client says she considers herself a whore because she sleeps around a lot.

Part Two

This part of the postevaluation is to be completed in triads; the first person assumes the role of helper, another takes the role of client, and the third assumes the role of observer. Trade roles so that each person has an opportunity to try out each of the three roles once. If triads are not available, an instructor can also observe you, or you can audiotape or videotape your interview for additional assessment.

Instructions to Helpers

Your task is to conduct a 30-minute *initial interview* with a client in which you demonstrate behavioral aspects of attractiveness listed in the Attractiveness Checklist that follows (Chapter Objective Two). Remember the purposes of trying to enhance your perceived attractiveness in initial interviews: to reduce client anxiety, to be perceived as likable and friendly and similar to the client, and to increase the probability of client disclosure.

Instructions to Clients

Present a real or hypothetical concern to the helper. Try to assume the role of a typical "new" client in an initial interview—somewhat apprehensive and a little reticent.

(continued)

POSTEVALUATION

(continued)

Instructions to Observers

Watch, listen, and assess the use of the helper's physical and interpersonal cues associated with attractiveness. Use the Attractiveness Checklist that follows as a guide for your observation and feedback.

Attractiveness Checklist

Behavioral Cues

Instructions: Check "Yes" if the helper demonstrated the following skills and behaviors; check "No" if they were not demonstrated.

1. Use of structure that is negotiated and is culturally sensitive
   Yes   No
2. Moderate level of self-disclosure
   Yes   No
3. Content of self-disclosure that matches client's concerns, experiences, and culture
   Yes   No
4. Disclosure of factual, nonintimate material (as this is an initial session)
   Yes   No
5. Responsive nonverbal behaviors
   a. Eye contact
      Yes   No
   b. Direct body orientation facing client
      Yes   No

Observer comments: _____
_____
_____

Part Three

This part of the postevaluation will also be conducted in triads so that each person can assume the roles of helper, client, and observer. For continuity, you may wish to stay in the same triads you used in Part Two of the postevaluation and trade roles in the same sequence.

Instructions to Helpers

You will be conducting a 30-minute *problem identification interview*—one in which you assess or explore the client's primary problems or concerns. During this interview, your task is to demonstrate behaviors associated with expertness and trustworthiness listed on the Expertness and Trustworthiness Checklist that follows (Chapter Objective Three). Remember, too, that the purposes of trying to enhance your perceived expertness and trustworthiness during this stage of helping are to contribute to the client's exploration and understanding of self and of issues, to work toward specificity and concreteness, and to encourage the client to share personal and relevant information with you.

Instructions to Clients

Be sure to have a particular "presenting issue" in mind to discuss with the helper during this role play. It will be helpful if the issue is something real for you, although it doesn't have to be "heavy." In addition to discussing your "presenting issue," try also to ask several questions related to at least one of the following "tests of trust"—requesting information, telling a secret, asking a favor, putting yourself down, inconveniencing the helper, or questioning the helper's motives.

Instructions to Observers

Watch, listen, and assess the use of the helper's behaviors associated with competence and trustworthiness. Use the Expertness and Trustworthiness Checklist that follows as a guide for your observation and feedback.

Expertness and Trustworthiness Checklist

Expertness

Instructions to observer: Check "Yes" if the helper demonstrated the behavior; check "No" if the helper did not.

1. Did the helper talk fluently and without hesitation?
   Yes   No
2. Did the helper use relevant and thought-provoking questions?
   Yes   No
3. Was the helper attentive to the client?
   Yes   No
4. Was the helper's presentation direct and confident?
   Yes   No
5. Did the helper accurately interpret any implicit client messages?
   Yes   No

Trustworthiness

6. Did the helper convey nonverbal and verbal acceptance of the client's disclosures?
   Yes   No
7. Was the helper's nonverbal behavior responsive, dynamic, and culturally sensitive?
   Yes   No

6 POST EVALUATION

8. Did the helper engage in accurate paraphrasing of the client's messages?
   Yes   No
9. Did the helper appear to safeguard and respect confidentiality of the client's communication?
   Yes   No
10. Did the helper seem open, honest, and direct with the client?
    Yes   No
11. Was the information the helper gave "checked out" (or promised to be checked out) for accuracy and reliability?
    Yes   No
12. Were the helper's verbal messages consistent with overt actions or behaviors?
    Yes   No
13. Did the helper respond to any client "tests of trust" appropriately and nondefensively?
    Yes   No
14. Did the helper show some understanding and awareness of the client's racial/ethnic/cultural affiliation?
    Yes   No
15. Did the helper disclose something about herself or himself?
Observer comments: _____
_____

6 POST EVALUATION FEEDBACK

PART ONE

1. f. Questioning your motives to see whether you really care.
2. b. Telling you a secret, something she perhaps feels embarrassed about.
3. c. Asking you a favor; in this case, it is probably a reasonable one.
4. a. Requesting information overtly—but covertly wondering whether your personal life is together enough to help the client or whether you have enough significant life experiences similar to his own to help him.
5. e. Trying to inconvenience you to see whether you have limits and how you set them and follow through on them.
6. d. Putting herself down by revealing some part of herself she feels is "bad" and also something that will test your reaction to her.

CHAPTER 7

INFLUENCING RESPONSES

OBJECTIVES

1. From a written list of 12 counselor influencing responses, identify the 6 influencing responses by type, with at least 9 accurate classifications.
2. With a written list of three client statements, write an example of each of the six influencing responses for each client statement.
3. In a 30-minute helping interview in which you are an observer, listen for and record six key aspects of client behavior that form the basis for influencing responses.
4. Conduct at least one 30-minute helping interview in which you integrate the core skills and knowledge you have acquired so far: ethics, critical commitments (Chapter 2), multicultural competencies (Chapter 2), nonverbal behavior (Chapter 3), relationship variables (Chapters 4 and 6), listening responses (Chapter 5), and influencing responses (Chapter 7).

Listening responses involve responding to client messages primarily from the client's point of view, or frame of reference. There are times in the helping process when it is legitimate to move beyond the client's frame of reference and to use responses that include clinician-generated data and perceptions. These *influencing responses* are active rather than passive and reflect helper-directed more than a client-centered style (Ivey and Ivey 1999b). Whereas helper listening responses influence the client indirectly, influencing responses exert a more direct influence on the client. Influencing responses are based as much on the helper's perceptions and hypotheses as on the client's messages and behavior. As Ivey and Ivey (1999b) note, these influencing responses "take a more proactive approach to human change" in that "they provide several alternatives for action and restorying that can promote change more rapidly and, sometimes, more permanently" (p. 276). In this chapter, we present six influencing responses: questions, interpretations (also called additive or advanced empathy), information giving, immediacy, self-disclosure, and confrontation.

The general purpose of influencing responses, according to Egan (1998), is to help clients see the need for change and action through a more objective frame of reference.

INFLUENCING RESPONSES AND TIMING

The most difficult part of using influencing responses is the timing, the point at which these responses are used in the interview. As you recall from Chapter 5, some helpers tend to jump into influencing responses before listening and establishing rapport with the client. Listening responses generally reflect clients' understanding of themselves. In contrast, influencing responses reflect the helper's understanding of the client. Influencing responses can be used a great deal in the interview as long as the helper is careful to lay the foundation with attending and listening. The listening base can heighten the client's receptivity to an influencing message. If the helper voices his or her opinions and perceptions too quickly, the client may respond with denial, with defensiveness, or even with dropping out of counseling. When this happens, often the helper needs to retreat to a less obtrusive level of influence and do more listening, at least until a strong base of client trust and confidence has been developed.

On the other hand, some clients from various cultural groups may actually be less defensive with a more active and directive communication style because it is more consistent with their needs and values. Further, some clients of color may feel more comfortable with the use of directive and active skills because these responses provide them with data about "where the therapist is coming from . . . to many minority clients, a therapist who expresses his/her thoughts and feelings may be better received" in a helping situation (Sue & Sue, 1999, p. 93).

WHAT DOES INFLUENCING REQUIRE OF HELPERS?

In the previous chapter, we discussed what listening requires of helpers. We noted that accurate and effective listening depends on the ability of helpers to listen to the client and to restrain some of their own energy and expressiveness. In contrast, influencing responses require the helper to be more expressive and more challenging. Egan (1998) describes the use of influencing responses as the responding to "sour notes" present in the client's communication and behavior. To use influencing responses effectively, helpers must first provide a supportive and safe environment by listening carefully, and then they must feel comfortable enough with themselves to provide feedback or amplification to the client that the client may not like. Helpers who have esteem issues of their own may find the use of influencing responses difficult as these responses carry the risk of upsetting a client by what is said or challenged. Ultimately, the use of effective influencing responses requires helpers to feel secure enough about themselves to have their own voice and to tolerate client disapproval and disagreement.

Some helpers prefer to stay in the "safety net" of a more passive attending style. This may be acceptable to some clients, but it may also mean that the helper and client have entered into a covert collusion with each other not to say anything that expresses displeasure or disappointment. Ironically, as we noted earlier, staying in the more passive listening mode can evoke guardedness and mistrust for some clients of color, creating even-more-disappointing outcomes.

SIX INFLUENCING RESPONSES

We have selected six influencing responses to describe in this chapter. *Questions* are open or closed queries that seek elaboration or information from clients. *Interpretations* are responses that identify themes and patterns, make implied client messages explicit, and are often based on the helper's ideas or hunches about the client. Interpretations are sometimes referred to as advanced empathic responses (Egan, 1998) or as additive empathy (Hepworth et al., 1997). *Information giving* is the communication of data or facts about experiences, events, alternatives, or people. *Immediacy* is a verbal response that describes something as it is currently occurring within the helping interview. *Self-disclosure* involves sharing of personal information or experiences with the client. *Confrontation* responses (also called challenging responses by Egan [1998]) describe patterns of discrepancies and inconsistencies in client behavior and communication.

Look at the way these six influencing responses differ in this illustration:

Client, a 35-year-old Latina widow, mother of two young children: My whole life fell apart when my husband died. I keep feeling so unsure about my ability to make it on my own and to support my kids. My husband always made all the decisions for me. Now, I haven't slept well for so long, and I'm drinking more heavily—I can't even think straight. My relatives help me as much as they can, but I still feel scared.

Helper questions: What sorts of experiences have you had in being on your own—if any?

What feels most scary about this?

Helper interpretation: When your husband was alive, you depended on him to take care of you and your children. Now it's up to you, but taking on this role is uncomfortable and also unfamiliar. Perhaps your increased drinking is a way to keep from having to face this. What do you think?

Helper information giving: Perhaps you are still grieving over the loss of your husband. I'm wondering whether there are rituals in your culture as well as certain people who might be helpful to you in your loss.

Helper immediacy: I can sense your vulnerability as you share this with me, and I'm glad you feel comfortable enough with me to let me in on some of it. I think that might help ease some of the burden you are carrying.

Helper self-disclosure: I think I can really understand what you are facing and trying to cope with since your husband died. I also went through a period in my life when I was on my own and responsible for the well-being of me and my two children, and it was a tough time—lots to deal with at once.

Helper confrontation: It seems as if you're dealing with two things in this situation: first, the experience of being on your own for the first time, which feels so new and scary you're unsure you can do it, and second, the reality that, although your relatives help out, the responsibility for you and your children does now rest on your shoulders.

Table 7.1 describes the definitions and intended purposes of these six influencing responses. Remember, these intended purposes are presented only as tentative guidelines, not as "the truth." Remember also that the critical commitment aspect of the practice nexus (Chapter 1) emphasizes your own thinking about and judicious adaptation of these responses.

TABLE 7.1	Definitions and Intended Purposes of Helper Influencing Responses	
Response	**Definition**	**Intended purpose**
Questions	Open-ended or closed query or inquiry	*Open-ended questions* 1. To begin an interview 2. To encourage client elaboration or to obtain information 3. To elicit specific examples of client's behaviors, feelings, or thoughts 4. To motivate client to communicate *Closed questions* 1. To narrow the topic of discussion 2. To obtain specific information 3. To identify parameters of a problem or issue 4. To interrupt an overtalkative client—for example, to give focus to the session
Interpretation (Advanced/Additive Empathy)	Mirroring of client behaviors, patterns, and feelings, based on implied client messages and the helper's hunches	1. To identify the client's implicit messages 2. To examine client behavior from alternative view 3. To add to client's self-understanding and influence client action
Information giving	Communication of data or facts	1. To identify alternatives 2. To evaluate alternatives 3. To dispel myths 4. To motivate clients to examine issues they may have been avoiding
Immediacy	Description of feelings or process issues as they are occurring within the helping interview	1. To open up discussion about covert or unexpressed feelings or issues 2. To provide feedback about process or interactions as they occur 3. To help client self-exploration
Self-Disclosure	Purposeful revelation of information about oneself through verbal and nonverbal behaviors	1. To build rapport, safety, and trust in the therapeutic alliance 2. To convey genuineness 3. To model self-disclosure for the client 4. To instill hope and promote feelings of universality 5. To help clients consider other and different alternatives and views
Confrontation	Description of discrepancy/distortions	1. To identify client's mixed (incongruent) messages or distortions 2. To explore other ways of perceiving client's self or situation 3. To influence client to take action

The remainder of the chapter describes and presents model examples of these skills. You will have an opportunity to practice each skill and receive feedback about your responses.

Questions

Questions are an indispensable part of the interview process. Their effectiveness depends on the type of question and the frequency of their use. Questions have the potential for establishing a desirable or undesirable pattern of interpersonal exchange, depending on the skill of the therapist. Beginning interviewers err by assuming that a helping interview is a series of questions and answers or by asking the wrong kind of question at a particular time. These practices are likely to make the client feel interrogated rather than understood. Even more-experienced helpers overuse this potentially valuable verbal response. Unfortunately, asking a question is all too easy to do during silence or when you are at a loss for words. Questions should not be asked unless you have a particular purpose for the question in mind. For example, if you are using a question as an open invitation to talk, realize that you are in fact asking the client to initiate a dialogue; allow the client to respond in this way.

Open and Closed Questions

Most effective questions are worded in an open-ended fashion, beginning with words such as *what, how, when, where,* or *who.* According to Ivey, Ivey, and Simek-Morgan (1997), the particular word used to begin an open-ended question is important. Research has shown that "what" questions tend to solicit facts and information, "how" questions are associated with sequence and process or emotions, and "why" questions produce reasons. Similarly, "when" and "where" questions solicit information about time and place, and "who" questions are associated with information about people. The importance of using *different* words in formulating open-ended questions is critical.

Open-ended questions have a number of purposes in different situations (Cormier & Hackney, 1999; Ivey & Ivey, 1999b):
1. Beginning an interview
2. Encouraging the client to express more information
3. Eliciting examples of particular behaviors, thoughts, or feelings so that the helper can better understand the conditions contributing to the client's concerns
4. Developing client commitment to communicate by inviting the client to talk and guiding the client along a focused interaction

In contrast to open-ended questions, closed (focused) questions can be useful if the practitioner needs a particular fact or seeks a particular bit of information. These questions begin with words such as *are, do, can, is,* and *did,* and can be answered with a yes, a no, or a very short response. As we see in Chapter 9, questions are a major tool for obtaining information during the assessment process. These are examples of closed questions:
1. Of all the issues we discussed, which bothers you the most?
2. Is there a history of depression in your family?
3. Are you planning to look for a job in the next few months?

The purposes of closed questions include the following:
1. Narrowing the area of discussion by asking the client for a specific response
2. Gathering specific information
3. Identifying parameters of concerns
4. Interrupting an overtalkative client who rambles or "storytells"

Closed questions must be used sparingly within an interview. Too many closed questions may discourage discussion and may subtly give the client permission to avoid sensitive or important topics. An exception to this general rule of thumb is provided by Hepworth and colleagues (1997). They note that it may be necessary to use more closed questions if the client "has limited conceptual and mental abilities" (p. 153).

Shainberg (1993) observes that "the point of a question is to open a person to [his or her] own process . . . to come in from a different angle than the client" (p. 87). She notes that it is all too easy for helpers to become sloppy or to lack creativity in formulating truly effective questions. For her, the difference between an effective and a poor question is whether the question enables the client to look at things in a new way or at a deeper level. She notes that "for many clients, being asked a good question is like having some new energy" (p. 88). Shainberg (1993) also describes other issues involved in using questions effectively:
1. The *frequency* of questions—more does not mean better.
2. The *timing* of a question—"stock" questions such as "How does this make you feel?" or "What was that like for you?" usually yield "pat" answers.

Examples of thought-provoking questions suggested by Shainberg can be found in Box 7.1.

Guidelines for the Use of Questions

Questions will be used more effectively and efficiently if you remember some important guidelines for their use.

First, develop questions that center on the concerns of the client. Effective questions arise from what the client has already said, not from the helper's curiosity or need for closure.

> **BOX 7.1 SAMPLE QUESTIONS**
>
> "What sorts of experiences do you have with this issue?"
>
> "Do you have some understanding of how painful this is—or is it painful?"
>
> "This feeling you describe—does this happen in any particular part of your body?"
>
> "Have you ever really let yourself experience this feeling?"
>
> "What can you tell me about your readiness to heal?"
>
> "What is scary (or painful, sad, etc.) about this?"
>
> "What is the prize that will unlock the puzzle as things stand right now?"
>
> "What is it that you don't want to see (feel or do)?"
>
> "How can you come alive in your life?"
>
> "Is there something from the past, some wound from the past that keeps you where you are right now?"
>
> "What do you find yourself longing (wishing) for?"
>
> "How is it that you create some of your own unhappiness?"
>
> "What is your relationship with your own pain (fear, sadness)? Do you fight it, dread it, turn against yourself in it, or think someone else will fix it—or believe it will go on forever—or take good care of yourself when you have it?"
>
> "What is your relationship with your family?"
>
> "What is important to you? To your family? To your culture?"
>
> "What is it time for right now in your life?"
>
> *Source:* Adapted from *Healing in Psychotherapy*, by D. Shainberg. Copyright 1993 by Gordon & Breach Science Publishers. Reprinted by permission.

Second, after a question, use a pause to give the client sufficient time to respond. Remember that the client may not have a ready response. The feeling of having to supply a quick answer may be threatening and may encourage the client to give a response that pleases the helper.

Third, ask only one question at a time. Some interviewers tend to ask multiple questions (two or more) before allowing the client time to respond. We call this "stacking questions." It confuses the client, who may respond only to the least important of your series of questions. This guideline is especially important in working with children and the elderly, for these clients may need more information-processing time.

Fourth, avoid accusatory or antagonistic questions. These are questions that reflect antagonism either because of the helper's voice tone or because of use of the word *why*. You can obtain the same information by asking "what" instead of "why." Accusatory questions can make a client feel defensive.

Finally, avoid relying on questions as a primary response mode during an interview (an exception would be when doing an intake, a history, or an assessment session). Remember that for some cultural groups, questions may seem offensive, intrusive, and lacking in respect. In any culture, consistent overuse of questions can create a number of problems in the therapeutic relationship, including creating dependency, promoting yourself as an expert, reducing responsibility and involvement by the client, and creating resentment (Gazda et al., 1999). The feeling of being interrogated may be especially harmful with "reluctant" clients. Questions are most effective when they provoke new insights and yield new information. To determine whether it is really necessary to use a question at any particular time during a session, ask the question covertly to yourself, and see whether you can answer it for the client. If you can, the question is probably unnecessary, and a different response would be more productive.

Steps in the Use of Questions

There are four steps in formulating effective questions. First, determine the purpose of your question—is it legitimate and therapeutically useful? Often, before probing for information, it is therapeutically useful to demonstrate first that you have heard the client's message. Listening before questioning is particularly important when clients reveal strong emotions. It also helps clients to feel understood rather than interrogated. For this reason, before each of our example questions, we use a paraphrase or reflection response. In actual practice, this "bridging" of listening and influencing responses is very important because it balances the aspects of attending and action modes in the interview. Second, depending on the purpose, decide what type of question would be most helpful. Remember that open-ended questions foster client exploration, whereas closed or focused questions should be reserved for times when you want specific information or you need to narrow the area of discussion. Make sure that your question centers on concerns of the client, not issues of interest only to you. Finally, remember to assess the effectiveness of your questioning by determining whether its purpose was achieved. A question is not useful simply because the client answered or responded to it. Additionally, examine how the client responded and the overall explanation, inquiry, and dialogue that ensued as a result of particular questions.

These steps are summarized in the following cognitive learning strategy:

1. What is the purpose of my question, and is it therapeutically useful?
2. Can I anticipate the client's answer?
3. Given the purpose, how can I start the wording of my question to be most effective?
4. How will I know whether my question is effective?

Notice how the helper applies this cognitive learning strategy in the following example:

Client: I just don't know where to start. My marriage is falling apart. My mom recently died. And I've been having some difficulties at work.

Helper:

1. *What is the purpose of my question—and is it therapeutically useful?*
   To get the client to focus more specifically on an issue of most concern to her.
2. *Can I anticipate the client's answer?*
   No.
3. *Given the purpose, how can I start the wording of my question to be most effective?*
   "Which one of these?"
   "Do you want to discuss ____?"
4. *How will I know whether my question is effective?*
   Examine the client's verbal and nonverbal response and resulting dialogue, as well as whether the purpose was achieved (whether client starts to focus on the specific concern).

Suppose that at this time the helper's covert visualization or self-talk ends, and the following dialogue ensues:

Helper question: Things must feel overwhelming to you right now [reflection]. Of the three concerns you just mentioned, which one is of most concern to you now? [question].

Client response: My marriage. I want to keep it together, but I don't think my husband does [accompanied by direct eye contact; body posture, which had been tense, now starts to relax].

From the client's verbal and nonverbal responses, the helper can conclude that the question was effective because the client focused on a specific concern and did not appear to be threatened by the question. The therapist can now covertly congratulate herself or himself for formulating an effective question with this client.

Learning Activity 7.1 gives you an opportunity to try out this cognitive learning strategy in order to develop effective questions.

Interpretive Responses and Additive/Advanced Empathy

Interpretation is a skill that involves understanding and communicating the meaning of a client's messages. In making interpretive statements, the helper uses her/his hunches or ideas to identify patterns and to make implied client messages more explicit (Egan, 1998). Interpretive responses can be defined in a variety of ways. We define an interpretation as a statement that—based on the helper's hunches—identifies behaviors, patterns, goals, wishes, and feelings that are suggested or implied by the client's communication.

An interpretation differs from the listening responses (paraphrase, clarification, reflection, summarization) in that it deals with the *implicit* part of a message—the part the client does not talk about explicitly or directly. As Brammer and colleagues (1993) note, when interpreting, a helper will often verbalize issues that the client may have felt only vaguely. Our concept of interpretation is similar to what Egan (1998) calls "advanced accurate empathy," or what Hepworth and associates (1997) refer to as additive empathy. Hepworth and colleagues (1997) note that at this level of empathy, the practitioner uses mild to moderate interpretive responses that accurately identify "implicit underlying feelings and/or aspects of the problem. The practitioner's response illuminates subtle or veiled facets of the client's message, enabling the client to get in touch with somewhat deeper-level feelings and unexplained meanings and purposes of behavior" (pp. 109–110). Further, these interpretive responses may also identify "implied goals" or actions desired by but perhaps unacknowledged by the client (p. 110). These interpretive responses go beyond the expressed meaning of client messages to partially expressed and implied messages, hence the use of the term "additive" empathy. If these responses are accurate and well timed, clients will gain a new and fresh perspective (Egan, 1998).

LEARNING ACTIVITY 7.1 — Questions

In this learning activity, you are given three client practice statements.* For each client message, develop an example of a question, using the cognitive learning strategy described earlier and outlined below. To internalize this learning strategy, you may wish to talk through these self-questions overtly (aloud) and then covertly. The end product will be a question that you can say aloud or write down or both. An example precedes the practice messages. Feedback is at the end of the learning activity on page 141.

Example

Client 1, a middle-aged Latina woman: I just get so nervous. I'm just a bunch of nerves.

Self-question 1: What is the purpose of my question—and is it therapeutically useful?

To ask for examples of times when she is nervous.

This is therapeutically useful because it contributes to increased understanding of the problem.

Self-question 2: Can I anticipate the client's answer? No.

Self-question 3: Given the purpose, how can I start the wording of my question to be most effective? "When" or "what."

Actual questions: You say you're feeling pretty upset [reflection]. When do you feel this way? [probe] or What are some times when you get this feeling? [question].

Client Practice Messages

The purpose of the question is given to you for each message. Try to develop questions that relate to the stated purposes. Remember, too, to precede your question with a listening response such as paraphrase or reflection.

Client 1, a retired Euro-American woman: To be frank about it, it's been pure hell around my house the last year.

*Additional practice for the responses in this chapter can be found on the Brooks/Cole book Web site, http://info.wadsworth.com/0534537391

Self-question 1: What is the purpose of my question? To encourage client to elaborate on how and what has been hell for her.

Self-question 2: Can I anticipate the client's answer?

Self-question 3: Given the purpose, how can I start the wording of my question(s) to be most effective?

Actual question(s): _____

_____

Client 2, a 40-year-old physically challenged man: Sometimes I just feel kind of blue. It goes on for a while. Not every day but sometimes.

Self-question 1: What is the purpose of my question? To find out whether client has noticed anything that makes the "blueness" better.

Self-question 2: Can I anticipate the client's answer?

Self-question 3: Given the purpose, how can I start the wording of my question to be most effective?

Actual question(s): _____

_____

Client 3, a 35-year-old African American woman: I just feel overwhelmed right now. Too many kids underfoot. Not enough time for me.

Self-question 1: What is the purpose of my question? To find out how many kids are underfoot and in what capacity client is responsible for them.

Self-question 2: Can I anticipate the client's answer?

Self-question 3: Given the purpose, how can I start the wording of my question to be most effective?

Actual question(s): _____

_____

> ### 7.1 FEEDBACK — Questions
>
> **Client 1**
> Sample questions based on defined purpose: It sounds like things have gotten out of hand [paraphrase]. What exactly has been going on that's been so bad for you? [question] *or* How has it been like hell for you? [question].
>
> **Client 2**
> Sample questions based on defined purpose: Now and then you feel kind of down [reflection]. What have you noticed that makes this feeling go away? [question] *or* Have you noticed anything in particular that makes you feel better? [question].
>
> **Client 3**
> Sample questions based on defined purpose: With everyone else to take care of, there's not much time left for you [paraphrase]. Exactly how many kids are underfoot? [question] *or* How many kids are you responsible for? [question].

Egan (1998) calls these responses "advanced empathy" because they challenge clients to look deeper.

There are many benefits and purposes for which interpretation can be used appropriately in a helping interview. First, effective interpretations can contribute to the development of a positive therapeutic relationship by reinforcing client self-disclosure, enhancing the credibility of the therapist, and communicating therapeutic attitudes to the client (Claiborn, 1982, p. 415). Another purpose of interpretation is to identify patterns between clients' explicit and implicit messages and behaviors. A third purpose is to help clients examine their behavior from a different frame of reference in order to achieve a better understanding of the problem. Finally, almost all interpretations are offered to promote insight. Johnson (2000) observes that interpretation is useful for clients because it leads to insight, and insight is a key to better psychological living and a precursor to effective behavior change.

Here is an example that may help you understand the nature of the interpretation response more clearly:

Client 1, a young woman: Everything is humdrum. There's nothing new going on, nothing exciting. All my friends are away.

Interpretation: You are tired of the same old, same old, the monotony of it all—you feel bored by it, and lonely—perhaps even restless. . . . You wish something new, something different, something exciting would happen in your life. Does this fit with what you are saying?

Sometimes the implicit response may have to do with a cultural aspect of the client's message. Consider the voice of Thad, the only African American student in his communications class: "This is the first class I have ever had to stand up and give a real speech to. And I just feel like I can't do it, it won't be good enough, it won't meet standards, it won't be as good as the other speeches are. . . . It just won't be good enough." The sensitive helper may hear the implied cultural aspect of Thad's message and give an interpretive response similar to the following: "Giving this speech is a first for you, and you feel gripped with doubt and fear about it—in part because this is a new experience for you and also perhaps because you're the only person of color in the room and you're holding yourself to a higher standard."

What Makes Interpretations Work?

During the last few years, a variety of research studies have explored the interpretive response, although conclusive evidence on this response is limited because of variations in definitions, designs, client differences, timing of the interpretation, and so on (Spiegel & Hill, 1989). Claiborn (1982) has proposed three ways that account for how interpretations work with clients. One is the *relationship* model, which assumes that interpretations work by enhancing the therapeutic relationship. Another is the *content* model, which assumes that the meaning and wording of the interpretive response effect subsequent change. The third is the *discrepancy* model; this assumes that the discrepancy between the helper's ideas and the client's ideas motivates the client to change. Spiegel and Hill (1989) conclude that all three of these models are relevant in considering the use and impact of an interpretive response, each model describing "an aspect that is operative in the process of intervention" (p. 123). Stated another way, all three models have some clinical relevance to offer. We describe this further in the next section.

Ground Rules for Interpreting

From the *relationship model,* we learn that the overall quality of the therapeutic relationship affects the degree to which an interpretation is likely to be useful to the client. As Spiegel and Hill (1989) observe, "The relationship serves as both a *source* of interpretations and is also enhanced by them" (p. 126). Interpretations need to be offered in the context of a safe and empathic contact with the client. From the *content* model, the *quality* of the interpretation is as important as the *quantity*. As Spiegel and Hill (1989) note, "More is not always better" (p. 125).

Another aspect of the *content* involves making sure your interpretation is based on the client's actual message rather than your own biases and values projected onto the client. This requires that you be aware of your own blind spots. As an example, if you have had a bad experience with marriage and are biased against people's getting or staying married, be aware of how this could affect the way you interpret client statements about marriage. If you aren't careful with your values, you could easily advise all marital-counseling clients away from marriage, a bias that might not be in the best interests of many of them.

A third aspect of the *content* concerns the way the helper phrases the statement and offers it to the client. Although preliminary research suggests there is no difference between interpretations offered with absolute and with tentative phrasing (Milne & Dowd, 1983), we believe that in most cases the interpretation should be phrased tentatively. Using tentative rather than absolute phrasing helps avoid putting the counselor in a one-up position and engendering client resistance or defensiveness to the interpretation. After an interpretation, check out the accuracy of your interpretive response by asking the client whether your message fits. Returning to a clarification is always a useful way to determine whether you have interpreted the message accurately.

Finally, the *content* of an interpretation must also be congruent with the client's cultural affiliations. Because many of our counseling theories are based on Eurocentric assumptions, this can be a thought-provoking task. It is most important *not* to assume that simply because an interpretation makes sense to you, it will make the same sort of sense to a client whose racial, ethnic, and cultural backgrounds vary from your own.

The *discrepancy* model involves the *depth* of the interpretation you offer to the client. Depth is the degree of discrepancy between the viewpoint expressed by the helper and the client's beliefs. Presenting clients with a viewpoint discrepant from their own is believed to facilitate change by providing clients with a reconceptualization of the problem (Strong et al., 1992). An important question is to what extent the helper's communicated conceptualization of the issue should differ from the client's beliefs. A study by Claiborn and associates (1981) addressed this concern. The results supported the general assumption that highly discrepant (that is, very deep) interpretations are more likely to be rejected by the client, possibly because they are unacceptable, seem too preposterous, or evoke resistance. In contrast, interpretations that are either congruent with or only slightly discrepant from the client's viewpoint are most likely to prompt change, possibly because these are "more immediately understandable and useful to the clients" (Claiborn et al., 1981, p. 108; Claiborn & Dowd, 1985).

The depth of the interpretation also has some impact on the time at which an interpretation is offered—both within a session and within the overall content of treatment. The client should show some degree of readiness to explore or examine himself or herself before you use an interpretation. Generally, an interpretation response is reserved for later, rather than initial, sessions because some data must be gathered as a basis for an interpretive response and because the typical client requires several sessions to become accustomed to the type of material discussed in counseling. The client may be more receptive to your interpretation if she or he is comfortable with the topics being explored and shows some readiness to accept the interpretive response. As Brammer and colleagues (1993, p. 181) note, a helper usually does not interpret until the time when the client can almost formulate the interpretation for herself or himself.

Timing of an interpretation within a session is also important. If the helper suspects that the interpretation may produce anxiety or resistance or break the client's "emotional dam," it may be a good idea to postpone it until the beginning of the next session (Brammer et al., 1993).

Client Reactions to Interpretation

Client reactions to interpretation may range from expression of greater self-understanding and release of emotions to less verbal expression and more silence.

Generally, the research on interpretation has not *systematically* explored differential client reactions. Research conducted in this area has yielded varying results (Spiegel & Hill, 1989). Based on these studies, Spiegel and Hill (1989) have speculated that an individual client's receptivity to an interpretation has to do with the "client's self-esteem, severity of disturbance, level of cognitive complexity, and psychological mindedness" (p. 1240). To their list, we would also add the client's cultural affiliation as an important moderating variable.

Although the concept of promoting insight, a goal of interpretation, is compatible for some Euro-American clients, insight may not be so valued by other clients. As Sue and Sue (1999) note, "When survival on a day-to-day basis is important, it seems inappropriate for the therapist to use insightful processes" (p. 65). Also, some cultural groups simply do not feel the need to engage in contemplative reflection. Indeed, the very notion of thinking about oneself or one's issues too much is inconsistent for some clients, who may have been taught not to dwell on themselves and their thoughts. Other clients may have learned to gain insight in a solitary manner, as in a "vision quest," rather than with another person such as a helper. In actual practice, you can try to assess the client's receptivity by using a trial interpretation, bearing in mind that the client's initial reaction may change over time.

If interpretation is met initially with defensiveness or hostility, it may be best to drop the issue temporarily and introduce it again later. Repetition is an important concept in the use of interpretations. As Brammer and colleagues observe, "Since a useful and valid interpretation may be resisted, it may be necessary for the counselor to repeat the interpretation at appropriate times, in different forms, and with additional supporting evidence" (1993, p. 183). However, don't push an interpretation on a resistant client without first reexamining the accuracy of your response (Brammer et al., 1993).

Steps in Interpreting

There are three steps in formulating effective interpretations. First, listen for and identify the *implicit* meaning of the client's communication—what the client conveys subtly and indirectly. Listen for behaviors, patterns, and feelings, as well as for implied goals, actions, and wishes. Second, make sure that your view of the issue, your frame of reference, is relevant to the client's cultural background, keeping in mind some of the precautions we addressed earlier. Finally, examine the effectiveness of your interpretation by assessing the client's reaction to it. Look for nonverbal "recognition" signs such as a smile or contemplative look as well as verbal and behavioral cues that indicate the client is considering the issue from a different frame of reference or that the client may not understand or agree with you.

To help you formulate an effective interpretation and assess its usefulness, consider the following cognitive learning strategy:
1. What is the implicit part of the client's message?
2. Is my view of this issue culturally relevant for this client?
3. How will I know whether my interpretation is useful?

Notice how a therapist applies this cognitive learning strategy in the following example:

Client, Euro-American woman: I really don't understand it myself. I can always have good sex whenever we're not at home—even in the car. But at home it's never too good.

Helper:
1. *What is the implicit part of the client's message?*

That sex is not good or fulfilling unless it occurs in special, out-of-the-ordinary circumstances or places. Also that the client doesn't understand what exactly is going on with her sexually and perhaps wishes she could have good sex at home as well as in other places.
2. *Is my view of this issue culturally relevant for this client?* This client seems relatively comfortable in talking about and disclosing information about her sexual feelings and behaviors. However, be careful not to make any assumptions about the client's sexual orientation. At this point we do not know whether this person is lesbian, bisexual, or straight.

Suppose that at this point the helper's covert visualization or self-talk ends and the following dialogue ensues:

Helper interpretation: Ann, I might be wrong about this—it seems that you get psyched up for sex only when it occurs in out-of-the-ordinary places where you feel there's a lot of novelty and excitement. You don't quite understand this yet and perhaps wish you could have great sex at home, too. Does that sound accurate?

Client [lips part, slight smile, eyes widen]: Well, I never thought about it quite that way. I guess I do need to feel like there are some thrills around when I do have sex—maybe it's that I find unusual places like the elevator a challenge.

At this point, the practitioner can conclude that the interpretation was effective because of the client's nonverbal "recognition" behavior and because of the client's verbal response suggesting the interpretation was on target. The therapist might continue to help the client explore whether she needs thrills and challenge to function satisfactorily in other areas of her life as well.

Learning Activity 7.2 gives you an opportunity to try out the interpretation response.

Information Giving*

There are many times in the helping interview when a client may have a legitimate need for information. For instance, a client who reports being abused by her partner may need

---

*Although this section focuses on delivery of information within a helping interview, providing clients with informational sources outside the interview is also important. A useful compendium is the Authoritative Guide to Self Help Resources in Mental Health (Norcross et al., 2000). This book provides descriptions and ratings of more than 600 books, movies, and Web sites for many mental health problems and issues.

LEARNING ACTIVITY 7.2 — Interpretation

Three client practice statements are given in this learning activity. For each message, develop an example of an interpretation, using the cognitive learning strategy described earlier and outlined below. To internalize this learning strategy, you may want to talk through these self-questions overtly (aloud) and then covertly. The end product will be an interpretation that you can say aloud, write down, or both. An example precedes the practice messages. Feedback follows the learning activity (on page 145).

Example

Client, a young Asian American woman: I don't know what to do. I guess I just never thought I'd ever be asked to be a supervisor. I feel so content just being a part of the group I work with.

Self-question 1: What is the implicit part of the client's message?

That the client feels afraid to achieve more than she's presently doing. She feels uncertain and perhaps overwhelmed by the thought of this job transition—and perhaps is concerned about losing her place in the group if she moves out of it to become a supervisor.

Self-question 2: Is my view of this issue culturally relevant for this client?

With her Asian American background, the client may feel more comfortable working in and for a collective group of people.

Actual interpretation response: Despite your obvious success on the job, you seem to be reluctant to move up to a position that requires you to work by yourself. I'm wondering whether you're responding in part to your cultural background, which stresses belonging to a group and working for the good of the group rather than promoting yourself.

Client Practice Statements

Client 1, a young, Native American woman: I can't stand to be touched anymore by a man. And after I was raped, they wanted me to go see a doctor in this hospital. When I wouldn't, they thought I was crazy. I hope you don't think I'm crazy for that.

Actual interpretation response: _____
_____
_____

Client 2, a 50-year-old Jordanian man: Sure, I seemed upset when I got laid off several years ago. After all, I'd been an industrial engineer for almost 23 years. But I can support my family with my job supervising these custodial workers. So I should be very thankful. Then why do I seem down?

Actual interpretation response: _____
_____
_____

Client 3, a young Euro-American man: I have a great time with Susie [his girlfriend], but I've told her I don't want to settle down. She's always so bossy and tries to tell me what to do. She always decides what we're going to do and when and where and so on. I get real upset at her.

Actual interpretation response: _____
_____
_____

> **FEEDBACK 7.2**
> **Interpretation**
>
> **Client 1**
>
> *Interpretation example:* I'm guessing that not only has the rape affected your trust of other men—even doctors—but also that your cultural background is having some effect, too. I'm wondering if you would feel safe going to a traditional healer, and one that you know, instead.
>
> **Client 2**
>
> *Interpretation example:* It sounds as though when you lost your job as an engineer, you also lost some parts of the role you have learned from your culture about being a man, a husband, and a father. Even though you're glad to have a job, you're sad about these losses and what they mean for you as a man, and as a husband, father, and provider for your family. Does that seem accurate?
>
> **Client 3**
>
> *Interpretation example:* You like spending time with Susie, but you feel pressured to settle down with her and are also put off by her bossiness. It sounds like you wish you had more of the control in the relationship. Does that fit with what you are saying?

information about her legal rights and alternatives. A client who has recently become physically challenged may need some information about employment and about lifestyle adaptations such as carrying out domestic chores or engaging in sexual relationships. Information giving is an important tool of feminist therapy approaches. For example, feminist therapists may give information to clients about gender role stereotyping, the impact of cultural conditioning on gender roles, strategies for empowerment, and social/political structures that contribute to disempowerment (Devore & Schlesinger, 1999). Recent research has found that helpers tend to provide information about the helping process and about facts concerning client behaviors, as well, when conducting consultation sessions (Lin, Kelly & Nelson, 1996).

We define information giving as the communication of data or facts about experiences, events, alternatives, or people. As summarized in Table 7.1, there are four intended purposes of information giving. First, information is necessary when clients do not know their options. Giving information is a way to help them identify possible alternatives. For example, you may be counseling a pregnant client who says she is going to get an abortion because it is her only choice. Although she may eventually decide to pursue this choice, she should be aware of other options before making a final decision. Information giving is also helpful when clients are not aware of the possible outcomes of a particular choice or plan of action. Giving information can help them evaluate different choices and actions. For example, if the client is a minor and is not aware that she may need her parents' consent for an abortion, this information may influence her choice. In the preceding kinds of situations, information is given to counteract ignorance. Information giving can also be useful to correct invalid or unreliable data or to dispel a myth. In other words, information giving may be necessary when clients are misinformed about something. For example, a pregnant client may decide to have an abortion on the erroneous assumption that an abortion is also a means of subsequent birth control.

A final purpose of information giving is to help clients examine issues they have been successfully avoiding (Egan, 1998). For example, a client who hasn't felt physically well for a year may be prompted to explore this problem when confronted with information about possible effects of neglected treatment for various illnesses.

Differences Between Information Giving and Advice

It is important to note that information giving differs from advice. In giving advice, a person usually recommends or prescribes a particular solution or course of action for the listener to follow. In contrast, information giving consists of presenting relevant information about the issue or problem, and the decision concerning the final course of action—if any—is made by the client. Consider the differences between the following two responses:

Client, a young mother: I just find it so difficult to refuse requests made by my child—to say no to her—even when I know they are unreasonable requests or could even be dangerous to her.

Helper (advice giving): Why don't you start by saying no to her just on one request a day for now—anything that you feel comfortable with refusing—and then see what happens?

Helper (information giving): I think there are two things we could discuss that may be affecting the way you are handling this situation. First, we could talk about what you feel might happen if you say no. We also need to examine how your requests were handled in your own family when you were a child. Very often as parents we repeat with our children the way we were parented—in such an automatic way we don't even realize it's happening.

In the first example, the practitioner has recommended action that may or may not be successful. If it works, the client may feel elated and expect the helper to have other magical solutions. If it fails, the client may feel even more discouraged and question whether counseling can really help her resolve this problem. Appropriate and effective information giving is presented as what the client *could* ponder or do, not what the client *should* do, and what the client *might* consider, not *must* consider.

Several dangers are associated with advice giving that make it a potential trap for helpers. First, the client may reject not only this piece of advice but any other ideas presented by the helper in an effort to establish independence and thwart any conspicuous efforts by the helper to influence or coerce. Second, if the client accepts the advice and the advice leads to an unsatisfactory action, the client is likely to blame the helper and may terminate therapy prematurely. Third, if the client follows the advice and is pleased with the action, the client may become overly dependent on the practitioner and expect, if not demand, more "advice" in subsequent sessions. Finally, there is always the possibility that an occasional client may misinterpret the advice and may cause injury to himself or herself or others in trying to comply with it.

Ground Rules For Giving Information

Information giving is generally considered appropriate when the need for information is directly related to the client's concerns and goals and when the presentation and discussion of information are used to help the client achieve these goals.

To use information giving appropriately, a helper should consider three major guidelines: when to give information, what information is needed, and how the information should be delivered. Table 7.2 summarizes the "when," "what," and "how" guidelines for information giving in counseling. The first guideline, the "when," involves recognizing the client's need for information. If the client does not have all the data or has invalid data, a need exists.

To be effective, information must also be well timed. The client should indicate receptivity to the information before it is delivered. A client may ignore information if it is introduced too early in the interaction.

The helper also needs to determine what information is useful and relevant to clients. Generally, information is useful if it is something clients are not likely to find on their own and if they have the resources to act on the information. The helper also needs to determine whether the information must be presented sequentially in order to make the most sense to the client. Because clients may remember initial information best, presenting the most significant information *first* may be a good rule of thumb in sequencing information. Finally, in selecting information to give, be careful not to impose information on clients, who are ultimately responsible for deciding what information to use and act on. In other words, information giving should not be used as a forum for the helper to subtly push his or her own values on clients (Egan, 1998).

One of the critical facets of giving information has to do with the cultural appropriateness of the information being

TABLE 7.2 The "When," "What," and "How" of Information Giving in Helping

When—recognizing client's need for information	What—identifying type of information	How—delivery of information in interview
1. Identify information presently available to client.	1. Identify kind of information useful to client.	1. Avoid jargon.
2. Evaluate client's present information—is it valid? Data-based? Sufficient?	2. Identify reliable sources of information to validate accuracy of information, including computer sources.	2. Present all the relevant facts; don't protect client from negative information.
3. Wait for client cues of readiness to avoid giving information prematurely.	3. Identify any sequencing of information (option A before option B).	3. Limit amount of information given at one time; don't overload.
	4. Identify cultural relevance of information.	4. Ask for and discuss client's feelings and biases about information.
		5. Know when to stop giving information so action isn't avoided.
		6. Use paper and pencil to highlight key ideas or facts.

given. As Lum (2000) observes, "Much cross-cultural contact involves communicating with people who do not share the same types of information" (p. 144). Also, some research suggests that people in different cultures vary in the types of information they attend to (Basic Behavioral Science Task Force of the National Advisory Mental Health Council, 1996). In the United States, practitioners working with non-Euro-American clients too easily and too frequently provide them with information that is based on Eurocentric notions. For example, providing information to a sick client about a traditional physician and medical care setting may be useful if the client is Euro-American. However, for many non-Euro-American clients, such information may be so removed from their own cultural practices regarding health and illness that the information is simply not useful to them.

Other mismatches between Eurocentric and non-Eurocentric information abound in family therapy. Enmeshment—the concept of a family system lacking clear boundaries between and among individuals—is a prime example. For some Euro-American families, enmeshment is considered a sign of pathology because in enmeshed families, the autonomy of individual members is considered hampered. However, for many Asian families and also for some rural Euro-American families, enmeshment is so completely the norm that any other structure of family living is foreign to them; in many of these families, the prevailing culture dictates that the good of the family comes before the individual members' needs and wishes (Berg & Jaya, 1993). Boundaries in these families are blurred in ways that do not usually occur in some Euro-American families. For example, young Asian children may be carried on their mothers' backs until they are three or four years of age. Toilet training also occurs later, and often there is a practice of "co-sleeping" in which the children sleep in the same room as the parents (Itai & McRae, 1994). If the helper assumes that this behavior is pathological and gives the client information about becoming more "individuated" or "establishing clearer boundaries," the client may feel misunderstood and also greatly offended. Therefore, a very important question to be addressed in effective information giving is this: What cultural biases are reflected in the information I will give the client, based on the client's ethnic, racial, and cultural affiliations, and is this information culturally relevant and appropriate? If you are not careful to assess the assumptions reflected in the information you share with clients, not only may your information seem irrelevant but your credibility in the client's eyes may also be diminished. Remember from the practice nexus (Chapter 1) that because of the effects of globalization, we cannot afford to be culturally encapsulated regarding the kinds of information we make available to clients.

Information Giving Via Technology

It is important to note that information is not just given to clients during sessions, but is also available electronically. For example, a client who is struggling with having just learned that he or she has a malignant brain tumor can benefit from electronic information as well as what the helper provides during the session. We don't believe that all information should be given to clients electronically, but we do feel that electronic information will become an increasingly important information-giving tool in the helping process. Many useful Web sites are now available for clients; also, many community services, referral sources, and information services are now available online (Schoech, 1999). In addition, many types of support groups are available online and may be especially useful for "homebound" clients (Garvin and Seabury, 1997; Schoech, 1999).

For diverse groups of clients, a number of Web sites are available that deal with information that may be especially pertinent (Gorski, 2001). However, many clients who are outside of mainstream groups, such as some rural, low-income clients and clients of color, do not have ready access to computer technology, for this technology has not been "shared evenly across all segments of society or in the world" (Garvin & Seabury, 1997, p. 269). In addition to these social justice issues, there are also emerging ethical issues related to providing information via computers. As Bloom (2000) points out, "there is no one central repository and distribution point of technological information. . . . [T]he traveler of the information highway is still urged to exercise caution" (p. 188). The quality and accuracy of Web sites vary tremendously. Some Web sites may not be suitable for child clients, and many chat rooms contain offensive language. This is a prime example of a situation in the practice nexus (see Chapter 1) in which practitioners need to apply their core knowledge and skills to think critically about the judicious use of information giving via electronic means. Will it be effective for a given client, what are the ethical implications, and what kind of access do oppressed, vulnerable, and underserved clients have?

As Nurius (1999) points out, because there are "no reviewers, editors, or institutional overseers of psychological resources that anyone who cares to can put on-line, each individual must be his or her own judge to a greater extent" in sorting out issues of quality, appropriateness, and accessibility (p. 63). However, the American Psychological Association has created a Web site to help people evaluate material online at dotcomsense.com.

Schoech (1999) summarizes a number of advantages and disadvantages of computer-based information. Advantages include convenience and flexibility, self-paced time frame, and provision of an educational service to clients. Disadvantages include the lack of regulations and ethical standards, the lack of current research on effectiveness, and procedures that may be overly structured and too mechanical for some clients (p. 129). Now, some professional organizations in human services have begun to provide standards on the use of information technology in the helping process (American Psychological Association, 1995b). In Chapter 2, we referred to an initial set of standards for the ethical practice of Web counseling. We have also found an excellent resource on online mental health resources by Grohol (2000). This reference book is usually updated every year so that it contains very current information. For online updates, see the Web site http://www.insidemh.com. Also, three recent special issues of *The Journal of Technology in Human Services* have been devoted to current and future issues in Web-based human services (Finn & Holden, 2000). Finally, a book by Schoech (1999) on human services technology provides many useful Web sites for (1) computer-assisted and assistive technology instruction, (2) computer software programs and professionally monitored support groups, and (3) computer-assisted treatment applications for crisis management, cognitive therapy, sex therapy, couples therapy, and phobias. As Schoech (1999) notes, "the largest number of client internet technology applications involves education and information," including information about mental health and mental illness, various treatment interventions, and medications (p. 133).

In the interview itself, the actual delivery of information, the "how" of information giving, is crucial. The information should be discussed in a way that makes it usable to the client and encourages the client to hear and apply the information (Gazda et al., 1999). Moreover, information should be presented objectively. Don't leave out facts simply because they aren't pleasant. Watch out, too, for information overload. Most people cannot assimilate a great deal of information at one time. Usually, the more information you give the clients, the less they remember. Clients recall information best when you give no more than several pieces at one time.

Be aware that information differs in depth and may have an emotional impact on clients. Clients may not react emotionally to relatively simple or factual information such as information about a helping intervention, an occupation, or a résumé. However, clients may react with anger, anxiety, or relief to information that has more depth or far-reaching consequences, such as a biopsy or an HIV test. Ask about and discuss the client's reactions to the information you give. In addition, make an effort to promote client understanding of the information. Avoid jargon in offering explanations. Use paper and pencil as you're giving information to draw a picture or diagram highlighting the most important points, or give clients paper and pencil so they can write down key ideas. Remember to ask clients to verify their impression of your information either by summarizing it or by repeating it to you. Try to determine, too, when it's time to stop dealing with information. Continued information giving may reinforce a client's tendency to avoid taking action.

Steps in Information Giving

There are six steps in formulating the what, when, and how of presenting information to clients. First, assess what information the client lacks about the issue. Second, determine the cultural relevance of information you plan to share. Third, decide how the information can be sequenced in a way that aids client comprehension and retention. Fourth, consider how you can deliver the information in such a way that the client is likely to comprehend it. Keep in mind that in cross-cultural helping situations, effective delivery requires you to communicate in a language and style that the client can understand. Fifth, assess the emotional impact the information is likely to have on the client. Finally, determine whether your information giving was effective. Note client reactions to it and follow up on client use of the information in a subsequent session. Remember, too, that some clients may "store" information and act on it at a much later date—often even after therapy has terminated. If you have provided information via technology, remember to follow up on it and to ask for the client's reactions, questions, and concerns about it.

To help with your use of information giving, we have put these six steps in the form of questions that you can use as a cognitive learning strategy:

1. What information does this client lack about the issue?
2. Based on the client's ethnic, racial, and cultural affiliations, is this information relevant and appropriate?
3. How can I best sequence this information?
4. How can I deliver this information so that the client is likely to comprehend it?
5. What emotional impact is this information likely to have on this client?
6. How will I know whether my information giving has been effective?

LEARNING ACTIVITY 7.3   Information Giving

In this learning activity, three client situations are presented. For each situation, determine what information the client lacks and develop a suitable information-giving response, using the cognitive learning strategy described earlier and outlined below. To internalize this learning strategy, you may want to talk through these self-questions overtly (aloud) and then covertly. The end product will be an information-giving response that you can say aloud, write down, or both. An example precedes the practice situations. Feedback follows the learning activity (on page 150).

Example

The clients are a married couple in their thirties: Gus is a Euro-American man, and his wife, Assani, is an Asian American woman. They disagree about the way to handle their four-year-old son. The father believes the boy is a "spoiled brat" and thinks the best way to keep him in line is to give him a spanking. The mother believes that her son is just a "typical boy" and that the best way to handle him is to be understanding and loving. The couple admit that there is little consistency in the way the two of them deal with their son. The typical pattern is for the father to reprimand him and swat him while the mother stands, watches, comforts him, and often intercedes on the child's behalf.

Self-question 1: What information do these clients lack about this issue?

Information about effective parenting and child-rearing skills.

Self-question 2: Based on the clients' ethnic, racial, and cultural affiliations, is this information relevant and appropriate?

I have to recognize that there are probably different cultural values brought to this parenting situation by the mother and father. I'm going to have to find information that is appropriate to both value systems, such as the following:

1. All children need some limits at some times.
2. There is a hierarchy in parent/child relationships; children are taught to respect parents, and vice versa.
3. Children function better when their parents work together on their behalf rather than disagreeing all the time, especially in front of the child.

Self-question 3: How can I best sequence this information?

Discuss item 3 first—working together on the child's behalf—and note how each parent's approach reflects his or her own cultural background. Stress that neither approach is right or wrong, but that the approaches are different. Stress points of common agreement.

Self-question 4: How can I deliver this information so that the clients are likely to comprehend it?

Present the information in such a way that it appeals to the values of both parents. The mother values understanding, support, and nurturing whereas the father values authority, respect, and control.

Self-question 5: What emotional impact is this information likely to have on these clients?

If I frame the information positively, it will appeal to both parents. I have to be careful not to take sides or cause one parent to feel relieved while the other feels anxious, guilty, or put down.

Self-question 6: How will I know whether my information giving has been effective?

I'll watch and listen to their nonverbal and verbal reactions to it to see whether they support the idea and also follow up on their use of the information in a later session.

Example of information-giving response: You know, Assani and Gus, I sense that you are in agreement on the fact that you love your child and want what is best for him. So what I'm going to say next is based on this idea that you are both trying to find a way to do what is best for Timmy. In discussing how you feel about Timmy and his behavior—and this is most important—remember that Timmy will do better if you two can find a way to agree on parenting. I think part of your struggle is that you come from cultures where parenting is viewed in different ways. Perhaps we could talk first about these differences and then find areas where you can easily agree.

Client Practice Situations

Client 1 is a young Native American man who has had his driver's license taken away because of several arrests for

(continued)

LEARNING ACTIVITY 7.3 — Information Giving (continued)

driving under the influence of alcohol. He is irate because he doesn't believe drinking a six-pack of beer can interfere with his driving ability. After all, as he says, he has never had an accident. Moreover, he has seen many of his male relatives drive drunk for years without any problem. He believes that losing his license is just another instance of the white man's trying to take away something that justifiably belongs to him.

Information-giving response: _____

_____

_____

Client 2 is an African American male who has been ordered by the court to come in for treatment of heroin addiction. At one point in your treatment group, he talks about his drug use with several of his sexual partners. When you mention something about the risk of AIDS, his response is that it could never happen to him.

Information-giving response: _____

_____

_____

Client 3 is a 35-year-old Euro-American woman with two teenage daughters. She is employed as an executive secretary in a large engineering firm. Her husband is a department store manager. She and her husband have had a stormy relationship for several years. She wants to get a divorce but is hesitant to do so for fear that she will be labeled a troublemaker and will lose her job. She is also afraid that she will not be able to support her daughters financially on her limited income. However, she indicates that she believes getting a divorce will make her happy and will essentially solve all her own internal conflicts.

Information-giving response: _____

_____

_____

FEEDBACK 7.3 — Information Giving

Client 1
Example of information-giving response:
I realize this seems to you to be just another example of what white men do to people of your nation that is unjust and unfair. I also realize that you are following what you've seen many of your male relatives do. So I'm sure, based on all this, it does seem hard to believe that drinking a six pack of beer can interfere with the way you drive. In fact, it can and does affect how you judge things and how quickly you react. So far, you're accident-free. I'm sure if you thought *you* could be in danger or could put someone else's life in danger from drinking and driving, you might think about it differently. Would you be willing to watch a short film clip with me or check out a Web site?

Client 2
Example of information-giving response:
Kevin, when you say this could never happen to you, it makes me wonder what you know about HIV. Do you know any black men who have tested positive for HIV? And are you aware that the virus can be spread easily through shared needles and also through semen?

Client 3
Example of information-giving response:
Leslie, in discussing your situation with you, there are a couple of things I want to mention. First, it might be useful for you to consider seeing a competent lawyer who specializes in divorce mediation. This person could give you detailed information about the legal effects and processes of a divorce. Usually, a person does not lose a job because of a divorce. Besides, in most instances, the husband is required to make support payments as long as the children are of minor age. I would encourage you to express these same concerns to the lawyer. The other thing I'd like to spend some time discussing is your belief that you will feel very happy after the divorce. That might be very true. It is also important to remember, though, that just the process of ending a relationship—even a bad relationship—can be very unsettling and can bring not only relief but often some feelings of loss and maybe sadness for you and for your children.

Consider the way a helper uses this cognitive learning strategy in the first example of Learning Activity 7.3.

Immediacy

Immediacy is a characteristic of a helper verbal response describing something *as it occurs* within a session. Immediacy can also be thought of as authenticity (Hepworth et al., 1997) or direct, mutual talk (Egan, 1998). Immediacy involves self-disclosure but is limited to self-disclosure of *current* feelings or what is occurring at the present in the relationship or the session. When persons avoid being immediate with each other over the course of a developing relationship, distance sets in.

In using immediacy in counseling, the therapist reflects on a current aspect of (1) some thought, feeling, or behavior of the *counselor;* (2) some thought, feeling, or behavior of the *client;* or (3) some aspect of the *relationship.* Here are some examples of these three categories of immediacy:

1. *Helper immediacy*

The helper reveals his or her own thoughts or feelings in the helping process as they occur "in the moment."

"I'm glad to see you today."

"I'm sorry, I am having difficulty focusing. Let's go over that again."

2. *Client immediacy*

The practitioner provides feedback to the client about some client behavior or feeling as it occurs in the interview.

"You're fidgeting and seem uncomfortable here right now."

"You're really smiling now—you must be very pleased about it."

3. *Relationship immediacy*

The helper reveals feelings or thoughts about how he or she experiences the relationship.

"I'm glad that you're able to share that with me."

"It makes me feel good that we're getting somewhere today."

Relationship immediacy may include references to specific "here and now" transactions or to the overall pattern or development of the relationship (Egan, 1998). For example, "I'm aware that right now as I'm talking again, you are looking away and tapping your feet and fingers. I'm wondering if you're feeling impatient with me or if I'm talking too much" (specific transaction). Consider another example in which immediacy is used to focus on the development and pattern of the relationship: "This session feels so good to me. I remember when we first started a few months ago, and it seemed we were both being very careful and having trouble expressing what was on our minds. Today, I'm aware we're not measuring our words so carefully. It feels like there's more comfort between us."

Immediacy is not an end but, rather, a means of helping the practitioner and client work together better. If allowed to become a goal for its own sake, it can be distracting rather than helpful. It is primarily used to address issues in the relationship that, if left unresolved, would interfere with the helping relationship and the therapeutic alliance. Examples of instances in which immediacy might be useful include the following (Egan, 1998):

1. Hesitancy or "carefulness" in speech or behavior ("Mary, I'm aware that you [or I] seem to be choosing words very carefully right now—as if you [or I] might say something wrong").
2. Hostility, anger, resentment, irritation ("Joe, I'm feeling pretty irritated now because you're indicating you want me to keep this time slot open for you but you may not be able to make it next week. Because you have not kept your appointment for the last two weeks, I'm concerned about what might be happening in our relationship").
3. Feeling of being "stuck"—lack of focus or direction ("Right now I feel like our session is sort of a broken record. We're just like a needle tracking in the same groove without really making any music or going anywhere").
4. Tension and trust ("I'm aware there's some discomfort and tension we're both feeling now—about who we are as people and where this is going and what's going to happen").

Immediacy can also be used to deal with the issues of transference and countertransference described in Chapter 4.

Immediacy has three purposes. One purpose is to bring out in the open something that you feel about yourself, the client, or the relationship that has not been expressed directly. Generally, it is assumed that covert (unexpressed) feelings about the relationship may inhibit effective communication or may prevent further development of the relationship unless the helper recognizes and responds to these feelings. This may be especially important for negative feelings. In this way, immediacy may reduce the distance that overshadows the relationship because of unacknowledged underlying issues.

A second purpose of immediacy is to generate discussion or to provide feedback about some aspects of the relationship or the interactions as they occur. This feedback may include verbal sharing of the helper's feelings or of something the helper sees going on in the interactive process. Immediacy is not used to describe every passing feeling or observation to the client. But when something happens in the process that influences the client's feelings toward counseling, then dealing openly with this issue has high priority. Usually it is up to the helper to initiate discussion of unresolved feelings or issues (Patterson & Welfel, 2000). Immediacy can be a way to begin such discussion and, if used properly, can strengthen the working alliance.

A third purpose of immediacy is to help clients gain awareness of their relationships to other people and of issues that cause problems for them with other people. Teyber (2000) has described this as the client's *interpersonal style* and notes that there are three predominant kinds of interpersonal styles: moving toward others, moving away from others, and moving against others. The rationale for this use of immediacy is that clients usually respond to helpers the way they respond to other people in their lives. For example, if José is oppositional with the therapist, he is perhaps also oppositional with significant others in his life. If Catherina idealizes the helper, she probably also idealizes other people in her life who are important to her. If Jorge goes out of his way to please the therapist, he most likely works hard to please other people as well. Immediacy can be a model for clients of how to address and resolve problems in their interpersonal relationships outside of therapy. Individual clients, as well as couples, families, and groups, usually follow the interpersonal model set by the practitioner (Hepworth et al. 1997).

Ground Rules and Client Reactions

Several rules can help practitioners use immediacy effectively. First, the helper should describe what she or he sees *as it happens*. If the helper waits until later in the session or until the next interview to describe a feeling or experience, the impact is lost. In addition, feelings about the relationship that are discounted or ignored may build up and eventually be expressed in more intense or distorted ways. The helper who puts off using immediacy to initiate a needed discussion runs the risk of having unresolved feelings or issues damage the relationship.

Second, to reflect the "here-and-nowness" of the experience, any immediacy statement should be in the present tense—"I'm feeling uncomfortable now," rather than "I just felt uncomfortable." This models expression of current rather than past feelings for the client.

Further, when referring to your feelings and perceptions, take responsibility for them by using the personal pronoun *I, me,* or *mine,* as in "I'm feeling concerned about you now" instead of "You're making me feel concerned." Expressing your current feelings with "I" language communicates that you are responsible for your feelings and observations, and this may increase the client's receptivity to your immediacy expressions. Hepworth and colleagues (1997) note that "I" messages are also effective in group work in that they can "profoundly affect the quality of group processes" (p. 23).

Also, as in using all other responses, the helper should consider timing. Using a lot of immediacy in an early session may be overwhelming for some clients and can elicit anxiety in either helper or client.

Cultural differences also play a role in the decision to use immediacy. Some clients may feel awkward discussing personal feelings or be unwilling to give feedback if solicited by the helper.

As Gazda and associates (1999, p. 222) observe, "It is highly desirable that a strong base relationship exist before using the dimension of immediacy." If a helper uses immediacy and senses that this has threatened or scared the client, then the helper should decide that the client is not yet ready to handle these feelings or issues. And not every feeling or observation a helper has needs to be verbalized to a client. The session does not need to turn into a "heavy" discussion, nor should it resemble a confessional. Generally, immediacy is reserved for initiating exploration of the most significant or most influential feelings or issues. Of course, a helper who never expresses immediacy may be avoiding issues that have a significant effect on the relationship.

Finally, in using immediacy, even if it is well timed, helpers have to be careful that the immediacy response is based on what is actually happening in the relationship rather than being a reflection of their countertransference response to something occurring with the client. For example, Joe is a beginning helper who has just seen one of his very first clients, Maria. Maria is very depressed, so he suggests a consultation with the staff psychiatrist. Maria is receptive to this idea, and Joe schedules this consultation for her after their session the following week. When the time arrives for the consultation, Joe takes Maria over to the psychiatrist's waiting room, and she is told that due to some scheduling problems she will have to wait at least an hour or longer before the consultation. Maria becomes upset and lashes out at Joe, saying that she has taken extra time off of work for this consultation and is losing money because of it. Joe reacts based on his first impulse: "Well, if that's the way you feel, you might as well not come back to see me next week." Fortunately, Joe has a safe and trusting relationship with his supervisor and brings this situation up. His supervisor helps Joe to see that what he blurted out was more a reflection of his countertransference and not truly based on what he really felt about Maria and their relationship. In fact, he likes working with Maria very much, and she is important to him, but his response was based on his own feeling that he and the helping process were, in his eyes, not more important to her.

One way to prevent a situation like Joe's is to reach for feelings that underlie your immediate experiencing—for example, you may have a superficial level of a feeling such as dislike or boredom but, reaching underneath, discover curiosity or compassion. In another example, you may feel annoyed at the client for being late but, reaching deeper, feel disappointment that the client isn't more committed to the helping process (Hepworth et al., 1997).

Steps in Immediacy

Immediacy is a complex set of skills and requires both critical thinking and judicious adaptation. The first part of immediacy—and an important prerequisite of the actual verbal response—is awareness, or the ability to sense what is happening in the interaction (Egan, 1998). To do this, you must monitor the flow of the interaction to process what is happening to you, to the client, and to your developing relationship. Awareness also implies that you can read the clues without a great number of decoding errors and without projecting your own biases and blind spots into the interaction. After awareness, the next step is to formulate a verbal response that somehow shares your sense or picture of the process with the client. Sometimes this may include sharing more than one feeling or sharing conflicting feelings (Hepworth et al., 1997). The critical feature of immediacy is its emphasis on the here and now—the present.

The third step is to describe the situation or targeted behavior in neutral or descriptive rather than evaluative terms (Hepworth et al., 1997). The fourth step is to identify the specific effect of the problem situation, the relationship issue, or the client's behavior on others and on you (Hepworth et al., 1997). This helps clients take action by authentically sharing how the client affects you rather than cajoling, pleading, or directing the client to change, which usually backfires. The last step is to get the client's reactions to your immediacy response. For example, you can ask the client something like "What is your reaction to what I just shared?" If your response is not helpful, clients will most likely shut down, retreat, or even lash out at you. If immediacy is helpful, clients will provide feedback and engage in more exploration.

To help you formulate an effective immediacy response, consider the following cognitive learning strategy:
1. What is going on right now—in me—with the client—in the process and interaction between us—that needs to be addressed?
2. How can I formulate an immediacy response that addresses this issue in the "here and now"?
3. How can I describe the situation or behavior in a descriptive rather than an evaluative way?
4. How can I identify the specific effect of this situation or behavior?
5. How will I know if my immediacy response is useful to the client?

Notice how the helper uses this cognitive learning strategy for immediacy in the following example:

Client: Isabella is struggling with a decision about whether to get a job or go back to school. She has been inundating you with e-mails and phone calls between your weekly sessions. This has gone on for several weeks. You are feeling put off by this. You decide during the session to use immediacy to respond because she is also talking about how much difficulty she seems to have in making connections with other people—who just don't seem to be responsive to her.

Helper:

Self-question 1: What is going on right now that needs to be addressed? With me—my feelings of moving away from Isabella.

With her—her pattern of inundating me with e-mails and phone calls during the week, which I suspect may be happening with other people in her life—underneath this are probably feelings of anxiety and uncertainty.
With the interaction between us—as she increases her requests for my time and energy, I find myself pulling back and giving less.

Self-question 2: How can I formulate an immediacy response that addresses this issue in the "here and now"?

Use the present tense and start first with what I'm aware of, such as "I'm aware of some feelings I'm having that might be related to your experiences in connecting with other people."

Self-question 3: How can I describe the situation or behavior in a descriptive (versus evaluative) way?

Take responsibility for my feelings by using an "I" message, describing her behaviors with the e-mails and phone calls without blaming her.

Self-question 4: How can I identify the specific effect of this situation or behavior?

Describe what I see happening in the process—as she requests more of my time and energy with the e-mails and phone calls, I find myself pulling back, giving less, and wondering if this is part of her difficulty in connecting with other people as well.

Self-question 5: How will I know if my immediacy response is useful to her?

I will ask for her feedback at the very end of my immediacy response.

Immediacy response: Isabella, I'm aware of some feelings I'm having that may relate to both your school and work decision and also to your feeling a lack of responsiveness from other people you try to connect with. If you feel willing to hear them, I'd like to share them with you now [pause to get an indicator of her willingness, which often may be nonverbal]. OK? Well, I'm finding myself pulling back from you and giving you less of my time and energy as you are making more requests of my time through daily e-mails and phone calls asking me what you should do. I'm guessing you're feeling a lot more anxious about this decision than I know. As a result, you are moving toward me with such intensity that I am actually moving back from you when this happens. I wonder if this might also be going on with some of the people in your life you are having trouble connecting to? [pause] What's your reaction to this?

Isabella's response: Well, that's a lot to digest. I guess I never thought of it that way, and I didn't realize it would have that effect. You are right in that I am feeling very uncertain about what step to take next. I've never had much

---

LEARNING ACTIVITY 7.4 — Immediacy

In this learning activity, you are given three client practice statements. For each client message, develop an example of *immediacy*. Apply the cognitive learning strategy and the five self-questions below to each example. Feedback follows on page 155.

Example

The client has come in late for the third time, and you have concerns about this for several reasons. One is that it affects your schedule, and another is that you feel concerned about the client's commitment to the helping process.

Immediacy response: I'm aware that you're having difficulty getting here on time, and I'm feeling uncomfortable about this. I feel uncertain now about when or whether to expect you for your session. I guess I'm also wondering about your commitment to being here. What is your take on this?

Apply the five self-questions to the following client examples in formulating your immediacy response.

Self-question 1: What is going on right now that needs to be addressed?

Self-question 2: How can I formulate an immediacy response that addresses this issue in the "here and now"?

Self-question 3: How can I describe the situation or behavior in a descriptive versus an evaluative way?

Self-question 4: How can I identify the specific effect of this situation or behavior?

Self-question 5: How will I know if my immediacy response is effective?

1. The client stops talking whenever you bring up the subject of her academic performance.
Your immediacy response:_____
_____
_____

2. The client has asked you several questions about your competence and qualifications.
Your immediacy response:_____
_____
_____

3. You experience a great deal of tension and caution between yourself and the client; the two of you seem to be treating each other with kid gloves. You notice physical sensations of tension in your body, and signs of tension are also apparent in the client.
Your immediacy response:_____
_____
_____

> ### 7.4 FEEDBACK
> #### Immediacy
>
> Here are some expressions of immediacy. See how these compare with yours.
>
> 1. Every time I mention academic performance, like now, you seem to back off from this topic.
>
> I'm aware that, during this session, you stop talking when the topic of your grades comes up.
>
> Am I hitting a nerve there, or is there something else going on that would help me understand this better?
>
> 2. I'm aware that right now it seems very important to you to find out more about me and my background and qualifications. I'm sensing that you're concerned about how helpful I can be to you and how comfortable you're feeling with me. What's your reaction to this? Maybe you have something you want to share, and, if so, I'd like to hear it.
>
> 3. I'm aware of how physically tight I feel now and how tense you look to me. I'm sensing that we're just not too comfortable with each other yet. We seem to be treating each other in a very fragile and cautious way right now. I'm not sure what this is about. What reactions do you have to this?

confidence in my ability to make decisions. When I was growing up—I think maybe because I was the "baby" of the family, lots of decisions were made for me. Now, with my parents both dead, it's all up to me, and that feels scary.

Isabella's response suggested she has benefited from the helper's immediacy response in that she is able to begin to explore the idea of having trouble relying on herself for decisions. Although she did not respond to the part about the other people in her life, this may come at a later time in the session or in a subsequent session. Learning Activity 7.4 gives you the opportunity to develop and practice the skills of immediacy using the cognitive learning strategy described earlier.

Self-Disclosure

Self-disclosure can be direct or indirect (Egan, 1998). Direct self-disclosure is the "conscious and intentional revelation of information about oneself through both verbal expressions and nonverbal behaviors" (Hepworth et al., 1997, p. 121). Indirect or unintentional self-disclosure also occurs through every word, look, movement, and emotional expression that the helper makes. As we mentioned in Chapter 3, this is one reason why awareness of our nonverbal behavior as helpers is so important. Our focus in this chapter is on the use of purposeful and direct self-disclosure as a verbal intervention tool to achieve certain purposes in the helping process.

Direct self-disclosure is used with clients for several reasons (Egan, 1998; Hepworth et al., 1997; Simone, McCarthy, & Skay, 1998). First, conscious use of self-disclosure can build rapport and foster the therapeutic alliance by increasing the helper's authenticity, by promoting feelings of universality, and by increasing trust. This purpose of self-disclosure is important with all clients and is perhaps critical with clients from various racial and ethnic groups who may depend upon some helper self-disclosure in order to feel safe (Helms & Cook, 1999). The whole idea of self-disclosing intimate aspects of one's life to a stranger such as a therapist may seem "absurd and inappropriate" to clients from some cultural groups, such as American Indians and Hispanics, who stress friendship as a precondition to self-disclosure (Sue & Sue, 1999, p. 67). Helms and Cook (1999) provide a useful guideline in the use of self-disclosure in cross-racial helping situations: "If you want clients to tell you *all* about themselves, you must disclose *something* about yourself," but of course do so in a way that does not shift the focus from them to you (p. 191). In this situation, self-disclosure is used to aid client disclosure through modeling by the practitioner. Another purpose of self-disclosure is to instill hope in clients and to help clients who may feel alone. Finally, self-disclosure can be used to help clients consider other and different alternatives and views, and may be especially suitable to move clients who are in a rut to take some action.

Ground Rules and Client Reactions

Self-disclosure is a complex skill. There are ethical issues surrounding the use of it, requiring critical thinking and judicious adaptation (see the practice nexus in Chapter 1), perhaps more so than with any of the other listening and influencing responses we discuss in the book. In part, this is because it is often very tempting for helpers to disclose something about themselves that meets more of their needs for expression and validation than the client's needs, constituting a sort of role reversal. There is also a risk of overidentifying with a client and projecting your own experiences and feelings onto the client in the material you self-disclose. For example, a client comes in and reports she is in a second marriage and comments "Aren't second marriages great?" The helper self-discloses in response and says "Yes, I think so, too. I have no regrets about having divorced my first husband. What about you?" The client looks sad and puzzled by this: "Well, my first husband died in a car wreck." In an example such as this, the thoughtless use of self-disclosure could get the helper into a lot of difficulty. As Simone, McCarthy, and Skay (1998) note, effective self-disclosure ultimately requires an "awareness of the ethical and clinical issues related to maintaining professional boundaries and staying focused on the client and the client's needs" (p. 181). In the following section, we provide guidelines to help you think critically about this skill.

The first guideline refers to the timing or the decision about *when* to self-disclose to a client. Hepworth and colleagues (1997) suggest that in most instances, self-disclosure is not useful until rapport has been established with the client: "the danger in premature self-disclosure is that such responses can threaten clients and lead to emotional retreat at the very time when it is vital to reduce threat and defensiveness" (p. 121). Remember that self-disclosure is classified as an influencing response, so building a good preliminary base of listening responses with clients is usually a good idea.

The second ground rule has to do with the "breadth" of the disclosure or *how much* disclosure to provide: the amount of information disclosed. Most of the evidence indicates that a moderate amount of disclosure has more positive effects than a high or low level (Edwards & Murdock, 1994). Some self-disclosure may indicate a desire for a close relationship and may increase the client's estimate of the helper's trustworthiness. Some self-disclosure can provide role modeling for clients from cultures with a low level of emotional expressiveness (Lum, 2000). Helpers who disclose very little could add to the role distance between themselves and their clients. At the other extreme, too much disclosure may be counterproductive (Goodyear & Schumate, 1996). The helper who discloses too much may be perceived as lacking in discretion, being untrustworthy, seeming self-preoccupied, or needing assistance. A real danger in overdisclosing is the risk of being perceived as needing as much help as the client. This could undermine the client's confidence in the helper's ability to be helpful. Also, too much self-disclosure can lead clients who are from cultures unaccustomed to personal sharing to retreat (Lum, 2000).

Excessive self-disclosure may represent a blurring of good treatment boundaries. Greenberg, Rice, and Elliott (1993) have referred to the process of too much helper self-disclosure and not enough attention to boundary issues as promiscuous self-disclosure. They note that effective use of self-disclosure is based on the helper's accurate awareness of his or her own inner experience (Greenberg et al., 1993). Also, as we noted in Chapter 2, excessive self-disclosure is the most common boundary violation that precedes unethical sexual contact between therapist and client (Smith & Fitzpatrick, 1995).

Another ground rule concerns the *duration* of self-disclosure—the amount of time used to give information about yourself. Extended periods of helper disclosure will consume time that could be spent in client disclosure. As one person reveals more, the other person will necessarily reveal less. From this perspective, some conciseness in the length of self-disclosive statements seems warranted. Another consideration in duration of self-disclosure involves the capacity of the client to use and benefit from the information shared. As Egan (1998) observes, helpers should avoid self-disclosing to the point of adding a burden to an already overwhelmed client. Of course, if the client doesn't seem to respond positively to the self-disclosure, it is best not to use any more of it (Egan, 1998). And after the self-disclosure, it is wise to make sure that the focus doesn't stay on you but goes back to the client.

A fourth ground rule to consider in using self-disclosure concerns the *depth,* or intimacy, of the information revealed. You should try to make your statements similar in content and mood to the client's messages. Ivey, Gluckstern, and Ivey (1997) suggest that the practitioner's self-disclosure be closely linked to the client's statements. For example:

Client: I just feel so down on myself. My husband is so critical of me, and often I think he's right. I really can't do much of anything well.

Helper (parallel): There have been times when I've also felt down on myself, so I can sense how discouraged you are. Sometimes, too, criticism from a male has made me feel even worse, although I'm learning how to value myself regardless of critical comments from my husband or a male friend.

Helper (nonparallel): I've felt bummed out, too. Sometimes the day just doesn't go well.

The final guideline to think about involves *with whom* self-disclosure may or may not be feasible. The nature of the client's problems, the client's ego strength, and any diagnoses are all relevant factors to consider. Hepworth and associates (1997) recommend very limited and concrete self-disclosure with clients who are psychotic or have severe and ongoing mental illness. Similarly, Simone and colleagues (1998) have found that self-disclosure is not used much with clients diagnosed with personality disorders (Axis II on a DSM-IV diagnosis—see Chapter 8 for more information). In particular, clients with a narcissistic personality disorder are unlikely to respond positively to helper self-disclosure. It takes the focus away from them and constitutes a narcissistic wound, a likely reenactment of their old history with significant caregivers. Unfortunately, helpers who themselves have unhealed narcissistic issues may be most likely to use self-disclosure inappropriately and excessively. Self-disclosure is also used less with clients who have been diagnosed with impulse control and conduct disorders (Simone et al., 1998).

On the other hand, for some clients the use of self-disclosure is highly indicated. These include clients who are adolescents and some clients of color, who may feel more comfortable and trusting of practitioners who self-disclose. Self-disclosure is also a primary action tool in both individual and group counseling for clients with substance abuse problems (Egan, 1998). Finally, Simone and colleagues (1998) found that self-disclosure is used most often with clients who have adjustment, anxiety, post-traumatic stress, and mood disorders.

Steps in Self-Disclosure

There are four steps in developing a self-disclosure response. First, assess the purpose of using self-disclosure at this time, and make sure that you're disclosing for the client's benefit and not your own. Simone and colleagues (1998) suggest a series of questions to help you think through the benefits and risks of self-disclosure with a client:

> Will my disclosure pull the focus from the client? Will it blur boundaries? Will it make the client focus on my needs or feel frightened about my vulnerability? Will my disclosure cause the client concern about my ability to help? Will this disclosure improve or diminish our rapport? Will it help the client look at different viewpoints, or will it confuse the client? Will the disclosure help the client feel more hopeful and less alone, or could it demoralize the client? Does this client need me to model disclosure behavior? (p. 182)

Second, assess whether you know enough about the client (and/or the client's diagnosis) to determine if this client can use your self-disclosure to add to insight and to take action. Consider the nature of the client's problems and diagnoses and how this situation may affect the client's ability to use your self-disclosure effectively. Third, assess the timing of the self-disclosure. Note what indicators you have that suggest whether the client is ready to accept your self-disclosure or be put off by it. Fourth, remember to assess the effectiveness of your self-disclosure. You can follow up on the client's reactions by paraphrasing and reflecting and by open questions. Observe whether the client is receptive to your self-disclosure or seems shut down by it. If the client seems uncomfortable with your self-disclosure or doesn't acknowledge any similarity with his or her own situation, it is best not to make additional self-disclosures—at least in this session and perhaps not with this client.

To help you formulate an effective self-disclosure response, consider the following cognitive learning strategy:

1. What is my reason for disclosing now? Is it linked to the client's needs and statements rather than to my own needs and projections?
2. What do I know about this client and the nature of the client's problems and diagnoses. Can this client use the self-disclosure?
3. How do I know if the timing is right for using self-disclosure with this client?
4. How will I know if my self-disclosure is effective?

Notice how the practitioner uses this cognitive learning strategy for self-disclosure in the following example:

Client, a 45-year-old gay man whose partner recently left him: My partner of 20 years has recently left me for another man. I can't help but wonder if he didn't find me attractive anymore. I have been feeling so disgusted with myself. I keep wondering if I should have been doing things differently—if somehow it was all my fault. It just makes me feel that I must have done something wrong. I keep thinking if only I had done this or done that, he wouldn't have left.

Helper:

Self-question 1: What is my reason for disclosing now?

My reason for disclosing now is to instill hope in this discouraged client. It is linked to his statements of feeling totally responsible for the breakup of his relationship.

Self-question 2: What do I know about this client and the nature of his problems? Can he effectively use the self-disclosure?

The client is not psychotic or severely mentally ill and does not appear to have an impulse or conduct disorder. I will keep my response short and get the focus back to the client after it.

Self-question 3: How do I know if the timing for self-disclosure is right?

The timing seems OK because the client seems very discouraged and stuck in his discouragement and self-blame.

Self-question 4: How will I know if my self-disclosure is effective?

I will follow up my self-disclosure with a response that returns the focus to him and checks out his reaction to the self-disclosure.

LEARNING ACTIVITY 7.5 — Self-Disclosure

Respond to the following three client situations with a self-disclosing response, using the cognitive learning strategy described earlier and outlined below. Make sure you reveal something about yourself. It might help you to start your statements with "I." Also try to make your statements concise and similar in content and depth to the client messages and situations. An example is given first, and feedback is provided on page 159.

Example

The client is having a hard time stating specific reasons for seeking counseling, and you have the feeling that a big part of this may be due to cultural differences between you and the client.

Self-question 1: What is my reason for disclosing now? Is it linked to the client's needs and statements rather than my own needs and projections?

Self-question 2: What do I know about this client and the nature of the client's problems? Can this client use the self-disclosure?

Self-question 3: How do I know if the timing is right for using self-disclosure with this client?

Self-question 4: How will I know if my self-disclosure is effective?

Actual self-disclosure: I know it takes time to get started. I'm reluctant at times to share something that is personal about myself with someone I don't know, and we come from different ethnic groups. I'm wondering if you feel this way, too?

Client practice messages

Client 1: The client, Monita, is feeling like a failure because nothing seems to be going well. She states that she "works herself to death" but never feels like she measures up.

Actual self-disclosure: _____

Client 2: The client is hinting that he or she has some concerns about sex but does not seem to know how to introduce this concern in the session.

Actual self-disclosure: _____

Client 3: The client has started to become aware of feelings of anger for the first time and is questioning whether such feelings are legitimate or whether something is wrong with him or her.

Actual self-disclosure: _____

Helper self-disclosure: Rich, I have been in a similar situation, and it took me a long time to realize that it wasn't my fault, that no matter what or how much I did, my partner still would have left. Does my experience have any usefulness for you?

Client response: Well, I'm surprised something like this has happened to you. You seem to have it together. I guess if it could happen to someone like you, maybe it isn't all because of me.

Rich's response seems to confirm the helper's intent of instilling hope and moving him out of his discouragement. In this situation, the use of self-disclosure seemed to be effective.

Learning Activity 7.5 gives you the opportunity to develop and practice the skill of self-disclosure.

Confrontation

A confrontation is a verbal response in which the helper describes discrepancies, conflicts, and mixed messages apparent in the client's feelings, thoughts, and actions. Hepworth and associates (1997) describe the confrontation response in this way: "Similar to interpretation and additive empathy it is a tool to enhance clients' self-awareness and to promote change. Confrontation involves facing clients with some aspect of their thoughts, feelings, or behaviors that is contributing to or maintaining their difficulties" (p. 546).

7.5 FEEDBACK: Self-Disclosure

Here are some possible examples of counselor self-disclosure for these three client situations. See whether your responses are *similar;* your statements will probably reflect more of your own feelings and experiences. Are your statements fairly concise? Are they similar to the client messages in content and intensity?

Client 1: Monita, I sense how difficult it is for you to work so hard and not feel successful. I have also struggled at times with my own high standards and gradually have learned to be more gentle and easier on myself. Is this something you can relate to?

Client 2: Sometimes I find it hard to start talking about really personal things like sex. I wonder if this is what's happening to you right now.

Client 3: I can remember when I used to feel pretty afraid of admitting I felt angry. I always used to control it by telling myself I really wasn't angry. Does this feel like what is happening with you?

Confrontation has several purposes. One purpose is to help clients explore other ways of perceiving themselves or an issue, leading ultimately to different actions or behaviors. Egan (1998) refers to this purpose as challenging the client's "blind spots," the "self-limiting ways of thinking and acting that clients fail to see or don't want to see" (p. 150). This may involve challenging distortions as well as discrepancies. These distortions may be cognitive ones (often the result of inaccurate, incomplete, or erroneous beliefs and information) or affective ones, involving attributions made from inaccurate or erroneous perceptions (Hepworth et al., 1997).

A second and major purpose of confrontation is to help the client become more aware of discrepancies or incongruities in thoughts, feelings, and actions. This is important since discrepancies can be indicators of unresolved, contradictory, or suppressed feelings. With both of these purposes, challenging clients, if done well, can influence clients to change.

There are many instances within an interview in which a client says or does something that is inconsistent. For example, a client may say she doesn't want to talk to you because you are a male but then goes ahead and talks to you. In this case, the client's verbal message is inconsistent with her actual behavior. This is an example of an inconsistent, or mixed, message. The purpose of using a confrontation to deal with a mixed message is to describe the discrepancy or contradiction to the client. Often the client is unaware or only vaguely aware of the conflict before the helper points it out. In describing the discrepancy, you will find it helpful to use a confrontation that presents or connects *both* parts of the discrepancy.

Six major types of mixed messages and accompanying descriptions of confrontations are presented as examples (see also Egan, 1998; Ivey & Ivey, 1999b).

1. *Verbal and nonverbal behavior*
    a. The client says "I feel comfortable" (verbal message) and at the same time is fidgeting and twisting her hands (nonverbal message).
       Helper confrontation: You say you feel comfortable, and you're also fidgeting and twisting your hands.
    b. Client says "I feel happy about the relationship being over—it's better this way" (verbal message) and is talking in a slow, low-pitched voice (nonverbal message).
       Helper confrontation: You say you're happy it's over, and at the same time your voice suggests you have some other feelings, too.
2. *Verbal messages and action steps or behaviors*
    a. Client says "I'm going to call her" (verbal message) but reports the next week that he did not make the call (action step).
       Helper confrontation: You said you would call her, and as of now you haven't done so.
    b. Client says "Counseling is very important to me" (verbal message) but calls off the next two sessions (behavior).
       Helper confrontation: Several weeks ago you said how important counseling is to you; now I'm also aware that you called off our last two meetings.
3. *Two verbal messages* (stated inconsistencies)
    a. Client says "He's sleeping around with other people. I don't feel bothered [verbal message 1], but I think our relationship should mean more to him than it does" [verbal message 2].
       Helper confrontation: First you say you feel OK about his behavior; now you're feeling upset that your relationship is not as important to him as it is to you.
    b. Client says "I really do love little Georgie [verbal message 1], although he often bugs the hell out of me" [verbal message 2].
       Helper confrontation: You seem to be aware that much of the time you love him, and at other times you feel very irritated toward him, too.

4. *Two nonverbal messages* (apparent inconsistencies)
   a. Client is smiling (nonverbal message 1) and crying (nonverbal message 2) at the same time.
      Helper confrontation: You're smiling and also crying at the same time.
   b. Client is looking directly at helper (nonverbal message 1) and has just moved chair back from helper (nonverbal message 2).
      Helper confrontation: You're looking at me while you say this, and at the same time, you also just moved away.
5. *Two persons* (helper/client, parent/child, teacher/student, spouse/spouse, and so on)
   a. Client's husband lost his job two years ago. Client wants to move; husband wants to stick around near his family.
      Helper confrontation: Edie, you'd like to move. Marshall, you're feeling family ties and want to stick around.
   b. A woman presents anxiety, depression, and memory loss. You suggest a medical workup to rule out any organic dysfunction, and the client refuses.
      Helper confrontation: Irene, I feel it's very important for us to have a medical workup so we know what to do that will be most helpful for you. You seem to feel very reluctant to have the workup done. How can we work this out?
6. *Verbal message and context or situation*
   a. A child deplores her parents' divorce and states that she wants to help her parents get back together.
      Helper confrontation: Juanita, you say you want to help your parents get back together. At the same time, you had no role in their breakup. How do you put these two things together?
   b. A young couple have had severe conflicts for the past three years, and still they want to have a baby to improve their relationship.
      Helper confrontation: The two of you have separated three times since I've been seeing you in therapy. Now you're saying you want to use a child to improve your relationship. Many couples indicate that having a child and being parents increases stress. How do you put this together?

Ground Rules for Confronting

Confrontation needs to be offered in a way that helps clients examine the consequences of their behavior rather than defend their actions (Johnson, 2000). In other words, confrontation must be used carefully in order not to increase the very behavior or pattern that the helper feels may need to be diminished or modified. The following ground rules may assist you in using this response to help rather than to harm. First, be aware of your own motives for confronting at any particular time. Although the word itself has a punitive or emotionally charged sound, confrontation in the helping process is not an attack on the client or an opportunity to badger the client (Patterson & Welfel, 2000). Confrontation is also not to be used as a way to ventilate or "dump" your frustration onto the client. It is a means of offering constructive, growth-directed feedback that is positive in context and intent, not disapproving or critical (Patterson & Welfel, 2000). To emphasize this, Egan (1998) uses the word *challenge* in lieu of *confront*. Ivey and Ivey (1999b) describe confrontation as a "supportive" kind of challenge and a "gentle skill that involves listening to the client carefully and respectfully, and then seeking to help the client examine oneself or the situation more fully . . . it is not going against the client, it is going with the client" (p. 196).

To avoid blame, focus on the incongruity as the problem, not on the person, and "allow your nonjudgmental stance to be reflected in your tone of voice and body language" (Ivey & Ivey, 1999b). In describing the distortion or discrepancy, the confrontation should cite a *specific example* of the behavior rather than make a vague inference. A poor confrontation might be "You want people to like you, but your personality turns them off." In this case, the practitioner is making a general inference about the client's personality and also is implying that the client must undergo a major "overhaul" in order to get along with others. A more helpful confrontation would be "You want people to like you, and at the same time you make frequent remarks about yourself that seem to get in the way and turn people off."

Moreover, before a helper tries to confront a client, rapport and trust should be established. Confrontation probably should not be used unless you, the helper, are willing to maintain or increase your involvement in or commitment to the helping relationship (Johnson, 2000). The primary consideration is to judge what your level of involvement seems to be with each client and adapt accordingly. The stronger the relationship, the more receptive the client may be to a confrontation.

The *timing* of a confrontation is very important. As the purpose is to help the person engage in self-examination, try to offer the confrontation at a time when the client is likely to use it. The perceived ability of the client to act on the confrontation should be a major guideline in deciding when to confront (Johnson, 2000). In other words, before you jump in and confront, determine the person's attention level, anxiety level, desire to change, and ability to listen. A confrontation is most likely to be heard when the client feels safe with you and is less likely to be heard when it occurs early in the relationship (Hepworth et al., 1997). An exception to this general ground rule is in instances of legal violations and danger to self or to others, when confrontation would be mandated earlier in the helping process (Hepworth et al., 1997).

Appropriate use of timing also means that the helper does not confront on a "hit and run" basis (Johnson, 2000). Ample time should be given after the confrontation to allow the client to react to and discuss the effects of this response. For this reason, helpers should avoid confronting near the end of a session.

It is also a good idea not to overload the client with confrontations that make heavy demands in a short time. The rule of "successive approximations" suggests that people gradually learn small steps of behaviors more easily than trying to make big changes overnight. Initially, you may want to confront the person with something that can be managed fairly easily and with some success. Carkhuff (1987) suggests that two successive confrontations may be too intense and should be avoided. According to Hepworth and associates, "Overuse and abusive use that does not convey caring for the client as a person is unethical and ineffective" (1997, p. 545). With clients who are fragile or clients who are experiencing severe stress or emotional strain, it is wise to avoid using confrontation altogether (Hepworth et al., 1997).

Gender and cultural affiliations of clients also have an impact on the usefulness of the confrontation response. This response may be more suitable for Euro-American male clients, particularly manipulative and acting-out ones (Ivey & Ivey, 1999b). Some traditional Asian and Native American clients may view confrontation as "lacking in respect," "a crude and rude form of communication," and "a reflection of insensitivity" (Sue & Sue, 1999, p. 76). For *all* clients, it is important to use this response in such a way that the client views you as an *ally*, not an adversary (Patterson & Welfel, 2000).

Finally, acknowledge the limits of confrontation. Confrontation usually brings about client awareness of a discrepancy or conflict. Awareness of discrepancies is an initial step in resolving conflicts. Confrontation, as a single response, may not always bring about resolution of the discrepancy without additional discussion or intervention strategies (see Chapters 12–18). Genuine client awareness is often difficult to detect because it may not be an immediate reaction but one that occurs over a period of time (Ivey & Ivey, 1999b).

Client Reactions

Sometimes helpers are afraid to confront because they are uncertain how to handle the client's reactions to the confrontation. Even clients who hear and acknowledge the confrontation may be anxious or upset about the implications.

Hill and Nutt-Williams (2000) note that the empirical evidence surrounding client reactions to confrontation is mixed. For clients who have reasons (often cultural ones) to distrust helpers or for clients such as some adolescents, who may be oppositional, confrontation can produce resistance and lead to poorer client outcomes. Some evidence suggests that in these cases, a process called motivational interviewing, which is based on the client-centered listening responses and basic empathy, may yield better client outcomes (Miller, 2000). Motivational interviewing has been especially useful in chronic problems such as substance abuse (see Chapter 10). However, another recent study involving substance abuse showed similar and comparable improvement for both confrontational and motivational interviewing styles (Schneider, Casey, & Kohn, 2000).

Generally, a practitioner can expect four types of client reaction to a confrontation: denial, confusion, false acceptance, or genuine acceptance.

In a denial of the confrontation, the client does not want to acknowledge or agree to the helper's message. A denial may indicate that the client is not ready or tolerant enough to face the discrepant or distorted behavior. Egan (1998, pp. 165–166) lists some specific ways the client might deny the confrontation:

1. Discredit the helper (for example, "How do you know when you don't even have kids?").
2. Persuade the helper that his or her views are wrong or misinterpreted ("I didn't mean it that way").
3. Devalue the importance of the topic ("This isn't worth all this time anyway").
4. Seek support elsewhere ("I told my friends about your comment last week, and none of them had ever noticed that").
5. Agree with the challenger but don't act on the challenge ("I think you're right. I should speak up and tell how I feel, but I'm not sure I can do that").

At other times, the client may indicate confusion or uncertainty about the meaning of the confrontation. In some cases, the client may be genuinely confused about what the practitioner is saying. This may indicate that your confrontation was not concise and specific. At other times, the client may use a lack of understanding as a smokescreen—that is, as a way to avoid dealing with the impact of the confrontation.

Sometimes the client may seem to accept the confrontation. Acceptance is usually genuine if the client responds with a sincere desire to examine her or his behavior. Eventually such clients may be able to catch their own discrepancies and confront themselves. But Egan (1998) cautions that false acceptance also can occur, which is another client game. In this case, the client verbally agrees with the helper. However, instead of pursuing the confrontation, the client agrees only to get the helper to leave well enough alone. The risk of having confrontation rejected is greatest among clients who need to be confronted the most but, because they are less likely to engage in self-confrontation and may have lower self-esteem, are more likely to read criticism or blame into this response when none is intended (Hepworth et al., 1997).

There is no set way of dealing with client reactions to confrontation. However, a general rule of thumb is to follow up with basic empathy and go back to the client-oriented listening responses of paraphrase and reflection. A helper can use these responses to lay the foundation before the confrontation and return to this foundation after the confrontation. The sequence might go something like this:

Helper: You seem to feel concerned about your parents' divorce [reflection].

Client [said with low, sad voice—mixed message]: Actually, I feel pretty happy—I'm glad for their sake they got a divorce.

Helper: You say you're happy, and at the same time, from your voice I sense that you feel unhappy [confrontation].

Client: I don't know what you're talking about, really [denial].

Helper: I feel that what I just said has upset you [reflection].

Steps in Confronting

There are four steps in developing effective confrontations. First, observe the client carefully to identify the type of discrepancy, or distortions, that the client presents. Listen for a period of time so that you can detect several inconsistencies before jumping in immediately with a confrontation response.

Second, assess the purpose of your confrontation. Make sure that it is based on the client's need to be challenged in some way and not on your need to challenge. Assess whether the relationship is sufficiently safe enough for the client to be able to benefit from the confrontation. Also assess whether the confrontation is appropriate based on the client's race and ethnicity, gender, and age.

Third, summarize the different elements of the discrepancy. In doing so, use a statement that *connects* the parts of the conflict rather than disputes any one part, as the overall aim of confrontation is to resolve conflicts and to achieve integration. A useful summary is "On the one hand, you _____, and on the other hand, _____." Note that the elements are connected with the word *and* rather than *but* or *yet*. This approach helps you present your confrontation in a descriptive rather than a judgmental way.

Make sure that your tone of voice and nonverbal behavior convey concern and caring for the client as well.

Fourth, remember to assess the effectiveness of your confrontation. A confrontation is effective whenever the client acknowledges the existence of the incongruity or conflict. However, keep in mind that the effectiveness of your confrontation might not be immediate. Watch also for signs that the client may feel defensive or signs indicating indirect reactions to your confrontation. Remember that the client may be adept at masking an overt negative reaction but may subtly withdraw or shut down in the rest of the session if the confrontation has not been well received.

To help you formulate a confrontation, consider the following cognitive learning strategy:

1. What discrepancy or distortions do I see, hear, or grasp in this client's communication?
2. What is my purpose in confronting the client, and is it useful for this client at this time?
3. How can I summarize the various elements of the discrepancy or distortion?
4. How will I know whether my confrontation is effective?

Notice how a helper uses this cognitive learning strategy for confrontation in the following example:

Client [said in low, soft voice]: It's hard for me to discipline my son. I know I'm too indulgent. I know he needs limits. But I just don't give him any. I let him do basically whatever he feels like doing.

Helper:

1. *What discrepancy or distortion do I see, hear, or grasp in this client's communication?*

    A discrepancy between two verbal messages and between verbal cues and behavior: Client knows son needs limits but doesn't give him any.

2. *What is my purpose in confronting the client, and is it useful for this client at this time?*

    My purpose is to challenge the inconsistencies between what this parent actually does with his son and what he wants to do but has not yet been able to, and to support him in this action. There doesn't appear to be anything about the client that would make him more defensive with the use of this response at this time.

3. *How can I summarize the various elements of the discrepancy or distortion?*

    Client believes limits would help son; at the same time, client doesn't follow through.

4. *How will I know whether my confrontation is effective?*

   Observe the client's response and see whether he acknowledges the discrepancy.

Suppose that at this point the helper's self-talk or covert visualization ends, and the following dialogue occurs:

Helper confrontation: William, on the one hand, you feel like having limits would really help your son, and at the same time, he can do whatever he pleases with you. How do you put this together?

Client response: Well, I guess that's right. I do feel strongly he would benefit from having limits. He gets away with a lot. He's going to become very spoiled, I know. But I just can't seem to "put my foot down" or make him do something.

From the client's response, which confirmed the discrepancy, the helper can conclude that the confrontation was initially useful (further discussion of the discrepancy seems necessary to help the client resolve the conflict between feelings and actions).

Learning Activity 7.6 gives you an opportunity to apply this cognitive learning strategy to develop the skill of confrontation.

SUMMARY

Listening responses reflect clients' perceptions of their world. Influencing responses provide alternative ways for clients to view themselves and their world. A change in the client's way of viewing and explaining things may be one indication of positive movement in counseling. According to Egan (1998), helper statements that move beyond the client's frame of reference are a "bridge" between listening responses and concrete change programs. To be used effectively, influencing responses require a great deal of helper concern and judgment.

In the last two chapters, we have described these two different sorts of helper communication styles. Part of the decision about the timing of these responses involves the helper's awareness of the client's cultural affiliations. As Sue and Sue (1999) note, it is important for helpers to be able to shift their communication style to meet the unique cultural dimensions of every client.

In Chapters 1 and 2, you learned about foundations for being a helper, including self-awareness, attention to diversity, and critical thinking and ethics. In Chapter 3, you discovered valuable reasons for attending to and working with client nonverbal behavior as well as important aspects of your own nonverbal behavior, including kinesics, paralinguistics, proxemics, environment, and time variables. In Chapters 4 and 6, you learned about important relationship variables such as empathy, genuineness, positive regard, competence, attractiveness, and trustworthiness. In Chapters 5 and 7, you acquired a base of various verbal responses to use in helping interactions to aid client exploration, understanding, and action. These responses included clarification, paraphrase, reflection, summarization, questions, interpretation, information giving, immediacy, self-disclosure, and confrontation. All of this has occurred within a context of cultural pluralism. You have learned, for example, that the impact of the facilitative conditions and the social influence factors will vary with clients from differing cultural/ethnic groups. Similarly, we have pointed out that various aspects of nonverbal behavior are culture bound and that the effectiveness of verbal communication styles also depends somewhat on the cultural affiliation of both helper and client. You have also had various types of practice in which you have demonstrated each set of skills in role-play interactions. In actual counseling, these skills are blended together and used in a complementary fashion. In Part Four of the postevaluation, we structure a practice opportunity that simulates an actual initial helping interview with a client. The purpose of this activity is to help you put the skills together—that is, integrate them for yourself in some meaningful, coherent fashion. It is analogous to learning anything else that requires a set of skills for successful performance. To swim, for example, you have to learn first to put your face in the water, then to float, then to kick, then to move your arms in strokes, and finally to do it all at once. Initial attempts feel awkward, but out of such first steps evolve championship swimmers.

INFOTRAC® EXPLORATIONS

1. Search for *self-disclosure,* and discuss the results of your search in class or with another student or colleague.
2. Search for *confrontation,* and explore the many meanings of this term. Contrast articles that use this term in a punitive manner with those that use it in a challenging, helpful manner.

SUGGESTED RESOURCES

Readings

Bloom, J. (2000). Technology and web counseling. In H. Hackney (Ed.), *Practice issues for the beginning counselor* (pp. 183–202). Boston: Allyn & Bacon.

Brammer, L. M., Abrego, P. J., & Shostrom, E. I. (1993). *Therapeutic psychology* (6th ed.). Englewood Cliffs, NJ: Prentice Hall.

LEARNING ACTIVITY 7.6 — Confrontation

We give you three client practice statements in this learning activity. For each message, develop an example of a confrontation, using the cognitive learning strategy described earlier and outlined below. To internalize this learning strategy, you may wish to talk through these self-questions overtly (aloud) and then covertly. The end product will be a confrontation that you can say aloud or write down or both. An example precedes the practice messages. Feedback follows the learning activity (on page 165).

Example

Client, a Latino college student: I'd like to get through medical school with a flourish. I want to be at the top of my class and achieve a lot. All this partying is getting in my way and preventing me from doing my best work.

Helper:

Self-question 1: What discrepancy or distortions do I see, hear, or grasp in this client's communication?

A discrepancy between verbal message and behavior; he says he wants to be at the top of his class and at the same time is doing a lot of partying.

Self-question 2: What is my purpose in confronting the client, and is it useful for this client at this time?

My purpose is to help him explore the two different messages in his communication and to do so with sensitivity and respect.

Self-question 3: How can I summarize the various elements of the discrepancy or distortion?

He wants to be at the top of his class and at the same time is doing a lot of partying, which is interfering with his goal.
Actual confrontation response: You're saying that you feel like achieving a lot and being at the top of your class and also that you're doing a lot of partying, which appears to be interfering with this goal *or* Eduardo, you're saying that doing well in medical school is very important to you. You have also indicated you are partying instead of studying. How important is being at the top for you?

Client Practice Messages

Client 1, an Asian American graduate student: My wife and child are very important to me. They make me feel it's all worth it. It's just that I know I have to work all the time if I want to make it in my field, and right now I can't be with them as much as I'd like.

Actual confrontation response: _____

Client 2, a 13-year-old African American girl: Sure, it would be nice to have Mom at home when I get there after school. I don't feel lonely. It's just that it would feel so good to have someone close to me there and not to have to spend a couple of hours every day by myself.

Actual confrontation response: _____

Client 3, a Euro-American high school student: My dad thinks it's terribly important for me to get all A's. He thinks I'm not working up to my potential if I get a B. I told him I'd much rather be well rounded and get a few B's and also have time to talk to my friends and play basketball.

Actual confrontation response: _____

Brown, J. (1997). The question cube: A model for developing repertoire in training couple and family therapists. *Journal of Marital and Family Therapy, 23,* 27–40.

Cormier, S., & Hackney, H. (1999). *Counseling strategies and interventions* (5th ed.). Needham Heights, MA: Allyn & Bacon.

Egan G. (2002). *The skilled helper* (7th ed.). Pacific Grove, CA: Brooks/Cole.

Erdman, P., & Lampe, R. (1996). Adapting basic skills to counsel children. *Journal of Counseling and Development, 74,* 374–377.

Garvin, C., & Seabury, B. (1997). *Interpersonal practice in social work: Promoting competence and social justice* (2nd ed.). Boston: Allyn & Bacon.

Gazda, G. M., Asbury, F. S., Balzer, F. J., Childers, W. C., Phelps, R. E., & Walters, R. P. (1999).

7.6 FEEDBACK
Confrontation

Client 1

Examples of confrontation responses: David, on the one hand, you feel your family is very important, and on the other, you feel your work takes priority over them. How do you put this together? *or* You're saying that your family makes things feel worthwhile for you. At the same time you're indicating you must make it in your field in order to feel worthwhile. How do these two things fit for you?

Client 2

Examples of confrontation responses: Denise, you're saying that you don't feel lonely and also that you wish someone like your mom could be home with you. How do you put this together? *or* It seems as though you're trying to accept your mom's absence and at the same time still feeling like you'd rather have her home with you. I wonder if it does feel kind of lonely sometimes?

Client 3

Examples of confrontation responses: Gary, you're saying that doing a variety of things is more important than getting all A's whereas your father believes that all A's should be your top priority. *or* Gary, you're saying you value variety and balance in your life; your father believes high grades come first. *or* Gary, you want to please your father and make good grades, and at the same time, you want to spend time according to your priorities and values.

(*Note:* Do not attempt to confront both discrepancies at once!)

Human relations development (6th ed.). Boston, MA: Allyn & Bacon.

Grohol, J. M. (2002). *The insider's guide to mental health resources.* New York: Guilford.

Hepworth, D. H., Rooney, R. H., & Larsen, J. (2002). *Direct social work practice* (6th ed.). Pacific Grove, CA: Brooks/Cole.

Hill, C. E., & Williams, S. E. (2000). The process of individual therapy. In S. D. Brown & R. W. Lent (Eds.), *Handbook of counseling psychology* (pp. 670–710). New York: Wiley.

Ivey, A. E., Gluckenstern, N., & Ivey, M. B. (1997). *Basic influencing skills.* North Amherst, MA: Microtraining Associates.

Jacobs, E. (1994). *Impact therapy.* Odessa, FL: Psychological Assessment Resources.

Johnson, D. W. (2000). *Reaching out: Interpersonal effectiveness and self actualization* (7th ed.). Boston: Allyn & Bacon.

Schneider, R., Casey, J., & Kohn, R. (2000). Motivational vs. confrontational interviewing: A comparison of substance abuse assessment practices at employee assistance programs. *Journal of Behavioral Health Services and Research, 27,* 60–74.

Schoech, D. (1999). *Human services technology* (2nd ed.). New York: Haworth.

Simone, D. H., McCarthy, P., & Skay, C. (1998). An investigation of client and counselor variables that influence likelihood of counselor self-disclosure. *Journal of Counseling and Development, 76,* 174–182.

Web Sites

Common Sense Ways to Protect Your Privacy and Access Online Mental Health Information
http://www.dotcomsense.com

Multicultural Pavilion
http://curry.edschool.Virginia.edu/go/multicultural

The Insider's Guide to Mental Health Resources Online
http://www.insidemh.com

University of Maryland Diversity Database
http://www.inform.umd.edu/Diversity

7 POSTEVALUATION

Part One

This part is designed to help you assess your performance on Objective One. Using the written list of client statements and helper responses below, identify and write the type of influencing response—question, interpretation, information giving, immediacy, self-disclosure, and confrontation—reflected in each helper response. There may be more than one kind of influencing response in each option. If you can accurately identify nine out of twelve responses, you have met this objective. You can check your answers against those provided in the feedback that follows the postevaluation.

1. **Client** [talking rapidly, with pressured speech]: The pressure from my job is starting to get to me. I'm always in a constant rush, trying to hurry and get several things done at the same time. There's never enough time.
   a. Yeah, it sounds like that saying of "the hurrieder I go, the behinder I get." And in your situation, the more you rush, the more pressure you feel, and the more pressure you feel, the more you rush. So you're sort of caught in this ongoing process, and it barely feels tolerable. You'd like to find a way out of it.
   b. It's important you are aware of this. Continued anxiety and stress like this can lead to health problems if they go unchecked.
   c. Now that you are mentioning this, I'm noticing how pressured you seem with me, partly from how fast you're talking and also from how you seem to be hurrying through the session. Does that feel accurate to you?

2. **Client:** I'm tired of sitting home alone, but I feel so uptight when I ask a girl for a date.
   a. You seem to be saying that you feel lonely and also that you're not willing to risk asking a girl to go out with you.
   b. What makes you so anxious when you speak with girls?
   c. I can relate to what you are saying in that I too have had to deal with some fears of my own in meeting new people. One thing that helped me was to join a couple of social and community groups where everyone was new to each other. This helped me practice meeting new people in a low-risk situation—if they didn't like me, I didn't lose much. Although this example isn't specific to dating, I think some of the principles are similar. What do you think?

3. **Client:** I don't know why I tolerate his abuse. I really don't love him.
   a. On the one hand, you say that you don't love him, and on the other hand, you remain in the house and allow him to beat you. How do you put these two things together?
   b. You may be caught up in a vicious cycle about whether your feelings for him, even though they're not love, outweigh your regard for yourself. Does this seem to fit you?
   c. It might be helpful for you to know the process that other women in your shoes go through before they finally get enough courage to leave for good. I'd like to give you the name of someone to talk to at our local domestic violence agency. Also, there are several Web sites I can give you if you have access to and would like to use the Internet.

4. **Client:** I don't know why we ever got married in the first place. Things were fine for a while, but since we moved, things have just started to fall apart in our marriage.
   a. What qualities attracted you to each other originally?
   b. You're having a difficult time right now, which has led you to question the entire marriage. I wonder whether you would react this way if this present problem wasn't causing such distress.
   c. I, too, have been in situations like this. When one thing goes wrong, it makes me feel like throwing the whole thing away. Is this something you can relate to in what you are experiencing now with your marriage?

Part Two

For each of the following three client statements, Objective Two asks you to say or write an example of each of the six influencing responses. In developing these responses, it may be helpful to use the cognitive learning strategy you practiced earlier for each response. Example responses are given in the Postevaluation Feedback.

Client 1, a Euro-American parent [spoken with loud sighs]: My house looks like a mess. I can't seem to get anything done with these kids always under my feet. I'm afraid that I may lose my temper and hit them one of these days. I just feel so stressed out.

7 POSTEVALUATION

Question: _____
Interpretation: _____
Information giving: _____
Immediacy: _____
Self-disclosure: _____
Confrontation: _____

Client 2, an African American graduate student: I feel so overwhelmed. I've got books to read, papers to write. My money is running low, and I don't even have a job. Plus, my roommate is thinking of moving out. I just can't seem to get a break—no one goes out of their way to lift a finger to help me.

Question: _____
Interpretation: _____
Information giving: _____
Immediacy: _____
Self-disclosure: _____
Confrontation: _____

Client 3, a young, Native American man: I haven't gotten hooked on this stuff. It doesn't make me feel high, though, just good. All my bad thoughts and all the pain go away when I take it. So why should I give it up? You're not here to make me do it, are you?

Question: _____
Interpretation: _____
Information giving: _____
Immediacy: _____
Self-disclosure: _____
Confrontation: _____

Part Three

This part of the postevaluation gives you an opportunity to develop your skills in observing key aspects of client behavior that must be attended to in order to develop effective and accurate influencing responses:

1. Issues and messages that need more elaboration, information, or examples
2. Implicit messages and themes
3. Myths and inaccurate information
4. Feelings and process issues
5. Distorted perceptions and ideas
6. Discrepancies and incongruities

Objective Three asks you to observe these six aspects of client behavior during a 30-minute interview. Record your observations on the Client Observation Checklist that follows. You can obtain feedback for this activity by having two or more persons observe and rate the same session—then compare your responses.

Client Observation Checklist

Name of helper _____
Name(s) of observer(s) _____
_____

Instructions: Given the six categories of client behavior (left column), use the right column to record separate occurrences of behaviors within these categories as they occur during a 30-minute helping interview.

Observed category	Selected key client words and behavior
1. Issues and messages that need more elaboration, information, or examples	1. _____ 2. _____ 3. _____ 4. _____
2. Implicit messages and themes	1. _____ 2. _____ 3. _____ 4. _____
3. Myths or inaccurate information	1. _____ 2. _____ 3. _____ 4. _____
4. Client and/or helper feelings and process issues presently occurring within the session	1. _____ 2. _____ 3. _____ 4. _____
5. Distorted perceptions and ideas	1. _____ 2. _____ 3. _____ 4. _____
6. Discrepancies and incongruities	1. _____ 2. _____ 3. _____ 4. _____

Part Four

Chapter Objective Four provides you with an opportunity to integrate the core skills and knowledge you have acquired so

(continued)

7 POST EVALUATION

(continued)

far in working with this book. To begin this process, conduct one 30-minute role-play interview. You may want to consider this an initial helping interview in which you are creating rapport and getting to know the "client." Here are the specific tasks for this integrative helping session:

1. Be alert to ethical situations and issues that arise and how you resolve them.
2. Assess the degree to which you are able to conduct this interview in a culturally competent way.
3. Assess the key aspects of your nonverbal behavior in the interview.
4. Pay attention to the quality of the helping relationship and specifically to your demonstration of the facilitative conditions of empathy, genuineness, and positive regard, and to the relationship enhancers of expertness, attentiveness, and trustworthiness.
5. Use as many of the listening and influencing verbal responses as seem appropriate within the time span of this session.

Try to regard this interview as an opportunity to get involved with the person in front of you, not as just another practice. If you feel some discomfort, you may wish to do several more interviews with different kinds of clients. To assess the overall effectiveness of your interview, use the Interview Inventory that follows. You may wish to copy the inventory or superimpose a piece of paper over it for your ratings.

Interview Inventory
Interview Number: ____ Helper: ____
Client: ____ Rater: ____ Date: ____

Instructions for rating: This rating form has five parts. "Ethical Issues" assesses any ethical issues that were present and how these were resolved. "Multicultural Competencies" assesses ten aspects of culturally competent interview behaviors. "Nonverbal Behavior" evaluates your use of various nonverbal behaviors. "Relationship Variables" measures aspects of establishing and enhancing a therapeutic relationship. "Verbal Behavior" assesses listening and influencing responses. To use the Interview Inventory for rating, follow the instructions found on each part of the inventory that follows.

Overall Effectiveness

After all the ratings are completed, look at your ratings in the light of these questions:

1. What ethical dilemmas arose for you, and how did you resolve these?
2. What aspects of multicultural competence do you feel most comfortable with? What parts are still hard for you?
3. Which nonverbal skills were easiest for you to demonstrate? Which ones did you find most difficult to use in the interview?
4. Which relationship variables were easiest for you to demonstrate? Hardest?
5. Examine the total number of verbal responses you used in each category. Did you use responses from each category with the same frequency? Did most of your responses come from one category? Did you seem to avoid using responses from one category? If so, for what reason?
6. Was it easier to integrate the verbal responses or the nonverbal skills?
7. What have you learned about the effectiveness of your interview behavior so far? What do you think you need to improve?

Ethical Issues

Instructions: Note any ethical issues that came up during the interview and how the helper responded to these issues.

Ethical Issue	Helper Response
1. _____	_____
2. _____	_____
3. _____	_____
4. _____	_____

Cultural Impact of Your Helping Style

Using the 6-point scale, indicate the number on the scale that best represents the helper's behavior during the observed interaction. Circle the appropriate number on the chart found below. Then, based on the observations made from your practice session and also your own observations, consider the following questions about your helping style, adapted from Sue and Sue (1999):

1. What is my predominant helping/communication style?
2. What does my style suggest about my values and biases regarding human behavior and people?
3. How might my nonverbal behaviors reflect stereotypes, fears, or preconceived ideas about various racial/ethnic groups?
4. In what way does my helping style hinder my ability to work effectively with a culturally different client?

7 POSTEVALUATION

Multicultural Competence[*]

The helper	Rarely		Sometimes		Consistently	
1. Displayed awareness of his or her own racial and cultural identity development and its impact on the helping process.	1	2	3	4	5	6
2. Was aware of his or her own values, biases, and assumptions about other racial and cultural groups and did not let these biases and assumptions impede the helping process.	1	2	3	4	5	6
3. Exhibited a respect for cultural differences among clients.	1	2	3	4	5	6
4. Was aware of the cultural values of each client as well as of the uniquenesses of each client within the client's racial and cultural group identification.	1	2	3	4	5	6
5. Was sensitive to nonverbal and paralanguage cross-cultural communication clues.	1	2	3	4	5	6
6. Demonstrated the ability to assess the client's level of acculturation and to use this information in working with the client to implement culturally sensitive helping.	1	2	3	4	5	6
7. Displayed an understanding of how race, ethnicity, and culture influence the treatment, status, and life chances of clients.	1	2	3	4	5	6
8. Was able to help the client sort out the degree to which the client's issues or problems are exacerbated by limits and regulations of the larger society.	1	2	3	4	5	6
9. Was able to help the client deal with environmental frustration and oppression.	1	2	3	4	5	6
10. Was able to recognize and work with the client dealing with multiple oppressions.	1	2	3	4	5	6

[*]Adapted from *Pathways to Multicultural Counseling Competence: A Developmental Journey* (5th ed.), by B. Wehrly, pp. 240–241. Copyright 1996 by Brooks/Cole an imprint of the Wadsworth Group, a division of Thomson, Learning. Adapted with permission.

Nonverbal Behavior

Instructions: This part of the inventory lists a number of significant dimensions of nonverbal behavior. Check (✔) any that you observe of the helper, and provide a brief description of the key aspects and appropriateness of the behavior. An example is given on the chart below.

Behavior	Check (✔) if observed	Key aspects of behavior
Example Body posture	✔	Tense, rigid until last part of session, then relaxed
1. Eye contact 2. Facial expression 3. Head nodding 4. Body posture 5. Body movements 6. Body orientation		

(continued)

POST EVALUATION

(continued)

Behavior	Check (✔) if observed	Key aspects of behavior
7. Gestures		
8. Nonverbal adaptors		
9. Voice level and pitch		
10. Rate of speech		
11. Verbal underlining (voice emphasis)		
12. Speech errors		
13. Pauses, silence		
14. Distance		
15. Touch		
16. Position in room		
17. Environmental arousal		
18. Time in starting session		
19. Time in responding to messages		
20. Time in ending session		
21. Autonomic response (for example, breathing, sweat, skin flush, rash)		
22. Congruence/incongruence between helper verbal and nonverbal behavior		
23. Synchrony/dissynchrony between helper/client nonverbal behavior		
24. Other		

Relationship Variables

Instructions: Using the 5-point scale, indicate which number on the scale best represents the helper's behavior during the observed interaction. Circle the appropriate number on the chart below.

1. Conveyed accurate understanding of the client.

1	2	3	4	5
Not at all	Minimally	Somewhat	A great deal	Almost always

2. Conveyed support and warmth without approving or disapproving of the client.

1	2	3	4	5
Not at all	Minimally	Somewhat	A great deal	Almost always

3. Focused on the person rather than on the procedure or on helper's "professional role."

1	2	3	4	5
Not at all	Minimally	Somewhat	A great deal	Almost always

7 POSTEVALUATION

4. Conveyed spontaneity, was not "mechanical" when responding to client.

1	2	3	4	5
Not at all	Minimally	Somewhat	A great deal	Almost always

5. Responded to feelings and issues as they occurred within the session (that is, "here and now").

1	2	3	4	5
Not at all	Minimally	Somewhat	A great deal	Almost always

6. Displayed comfort and confidence in working with the client.

1	2	3	4	5
Not at all	Minimally	Somewhat	A great deal	Almost always

7. Responded with dynamism and frequency; was not "passive."

1	2	3	4	5
Not at all	Minimally	Somewhat	A great deal	Almost always

8. Displayed sincerity in intentions and responses.

1	2	3	4	5
Not at all	Minimally	Somewhat	A great deal	Almost always

9. Conveyed friendliness and goodwill in interacting with client.

1	2	3	4	5
Not at all	Minimally	Somewhat	A great deal	Almost always

10. Informed client about expectations and what would or would not happen in session (that is, structuring).

1	2	3	4	5
Not at all	Minimally	Somewhat	A great deal	Almost always

11. Shared similar attitudes, opinions, and experiences with client when appropriate (that is, when such sharing added to, not detracted from, client focus).

1	2	3	4	5
Not at all	Minimally	Somewhat	A great deal	Almost always

12. Other significant relationship aspects: _____
_____
_____
_____

(continued)

7 POST EVALUATION

(continued)

Verbal Behavior

Instructions: Check (✓) the type of verbal response represented by each helper statement in the corresponding category on the rating form. At the end of the observation period, tally the total number of checks associated with each verbal response on the chart below.

	Listening responses				Influencing responses						
	Clarification	Paraphrase	Reflecting feeling (basic empathy)	Summarization	Open question	Closed question	Interpretation (advanced empathy)	Information giving	Immediacy	Self-disclosure	Confrontation
1											
2											
3											
4											
5											
6											
7											
8											
9											
10											
11											
12											
13											
14											
15											
16											
17											
18											
19											
20											
Total:											

POSTEVALUATION FEEDBACK

PART ONE

1. a. Interpretation
   b. Information giving
   c. Immediacy and closed question
2. a. Confrontation
   b. Open question
   c. Self-disclosure and open question
3. a. Confrontation
   b. Interpretation and closed question
   c. Information giving
4. a. Open question
   b. Interpretation
   c. Self-disclosure and closed question

PART TWO

Here are some examples of influencing responses. Are yours similar?

Client statement 1

Question: What exactly would you like to be able to accomplish during the day?
or
How could you keep the kids occupied while you do some of your housework?
or
When do you feel most like striking the children?
or
How could you control your anger?

Interpretation: I wonder whether you would be able to accomplish what seems important to you even if the kids weren't always underfoot. Perhaps it's easy to use their presence to account for your lack of accomplishment.

Information giving: If you believe your problem would be solved by having more time alone, we could discuss some options that seemed to help other women in this situation—things to give you more time alone as well as ways to cope with your anger.

Immediacy: I can tell from the way you're talking and breathing right now that this stress is very much with you—not just at home but even as we are working together here today.

Self-disclosure: I know what it is like to feel like your life is spinning out of control, and it's not a pleasant state to be in—for me, it's pretty stressful. How about for you?

Confrontation: On the one hand, you seem to be saying the kids are responsible for your difficulties, and on the other, it appears as if you feel you are the one who is out of control.

Client statement 2

Question: How could you organize yourself better so that you wouldn't feel so overcome by your studies?
or
What kind of work might you do that would fit in with your class schedule?
or
How might you cope with these feelings of being so overwhelmed?

Interpretation: You seem to feel so discouraged with everything that I imagine it would be easy now to feel justified in giving it all up, quitting grad school altogether.

Information giving: Perhaps it would be helpful if we talked about some ways to help you with your time and money problems.

Immediacy: I'm sensing how frustrated you're feeling right now as you talk and wondering if you're seeing me as someone unwilling to help you.

Self-disclosure: Wow. I think I know something about what you are saying, how it feels to have the whole world cave in on you at once. It's an awful lot to try to handle.

Confrontation: You've mentioned several reasons that you feel so overwhelmed now, and at the same time I don't think you mentioned anything you're doing to relieve these feelings.

Client statement 3

Question: What do you feel comfortable sharing with me about your pain?

Interpretation: Even though you don't feel hooked on this substance, it seems as if using it helps you avoid certain things—do you think this is so?

Information giving: I'm wondering what you would think of the idea of our spending some time talking about other ways to deal with the pain—such as practices and rituals consistent with your own cultural and ethnic background.

Immediacy: I'm wondering if there is something I'm saying or doing to make you feel like I'm going to be policing your actions as we work together.

Self-disclosure: I went through a similar way of thinking when I gave up smoking. Cigarettes were always there for

(continued)

POST EVALUATION FEEDBACK

(continued)
me—when nothing else was, they were. In that way, it was hard for me to see what could be so bad about continuing to smoke. Does this fit with what you're feeling in your situation?
Confrontation: You're telling me that you're pretty sure you're not hooked on this and at the same time you recognize it seems to medicate your pain. How do you put these two things together?

CHAPTER 8

CONCEPTUALIZING AND ASSESSING CLIENT ISSUES, CONCERNS, AND CONTEXTS

Institutionalized patient: Why are people always out to get me?

Student: I can't even talk to my mom. What a hassle!

Physically challenged person: Ever since I had that automobile accident and had to change jobs, I don't seem to be able to get it together.

Older person: I never feel like I can do anything well anymore. And I feel so depressed all the time.

These client statements are representative of the types of concerns that clients bring to helpers every day. One thing these clients and others have in common is that their initial problem presentation is often vague. A helper can translate vague client concerns into specific problem statements by using certain skills associated with assessment. This chapter presents a conceptual framework that a helper can use to assess clients. Chapter 9 demonstrates a way for the helper to implement this framework in the interview setting.

OBJECTIVES

After completing this chapter, the student should be able to identify, in writing, using two client case descriptions,
1. The client's behaviors
2. Whether the behaviors are overt or covert
3. The client's individual and environmental strengths
4. The antecedent contributing conditions
5. The consequences and secondary gains
6. The way each consequence influences the behaviors
7. The sociopolitical context of the issue

WHAT IS ASSESSMENT?

Assessment consists of procedures and tools used to collect and process information from which the entire helping program is developed. Interviewing the client and having the client engage in other assessment procedures are only part of the overall assessment process in counseling and therapy. Equally important is the helper's own mental (covert) activity that goes on during the process. The helper typically gathers a great amount of information from clients during this stage of helping. Unless the helper can integrate and synthesize the data, they are of little value and use. The helper's tasks during the assessment process include knowing what information to obtain and how to obtain it, putting it together in some meaningful way, and using it to generate clinical hunches, or hypotheses, about client issues, hunches that lead to tentative ideas for treatment planning. This mental activity of the helper's is called "conceptualization"—which simply means the way the helper thinks about the client's problem configuration. A recent study assessed the relationship of counselors' hypothesis formation skill levels and counseling effectiveness (Morran et al., 1994). The results of this study found that a higher level of hypothesis formation skill was associated with more positive client assessment of the helper.

The assessment methods we describe later in this chapter and in Chapter 9, and our interview assessment model particularly, are based on a model of conceptualization we have used over the years in our teaching and in clinical practice. The origins of this model were first described by Richmond (1917) and by Kanfer and Saslow (1969). Before describing our model in detail, we would first like to describe a current model of client or case conceptualization proposed by Lazarus (1976, 1989) that has influenced the development of our own clinical model of problem conceptualization.

THE LAZARUS MODEL OF CONCEPTUALIZATION: THE BASIC ID

According to Lazarus (1989), who is associated with broad-spectrum behavior therapy, there are seven modalities to explore in assessment and intervention with clients. To refer to these seven areas of assessment and treatment in abbreviated fashion, Lazarus uses the acronym BASIC ID. A brief discussion of each component of the BASIC ID follows. In using this model of conceptualization, remember that each modality described by Lazarus interacts with the other modalities and should not be treated in isolation.

B: Behavior. Behavior includes simple and more complex psychomotor skills and activities such as smiling, talking, writing, eating, exercising, and having sex. In most clinical interviewing, the therapist has to infer what the client does or does not do on the basis of client self-report, although occasionally other measures of behavior can corroborate client verbal report. Lazarus (1989) notes the importance of being alert to behavioral excesses and deficits—things the client does too much or too little.

A: Affect. Affect includes felt or reported feelings and emotions. According to Lazarus (1989), this is perhaps the most overworked area in psychotherapy and also one of the least understood. Included in this category would be the presence or absence of particular feelings as well as hidden or distorted feelings.

S: Sensation. Sensation includes five major senses with respect to sensory processing of information: visual (sight), kinesthetic (touch), auditory (hearing), olfactory (smell), and gustation (taste). A focus on sensory elements of experience is important in developing personal fulfillment. As well, presenting complaints are sometimes described as felt body sensations such as stomach distress or dizziness (Lazarus, 1989). Therapists need to be alert to pleasant and unpleasant reported sensations as well as sensations of which clients seem unaware.

I: Imagery. According to Lazarus, imagery comprises various mental pictures that exert influence on a client's life (1989). For example, a husband who was nagged by what he called repetitive ideas that his wife was having an affair (apparently with no realistic basis) was actually troubled because he generated constant pictures or images of his wife in bed with another man. Lazarus (1989) believes that imagery is especially useful with clients who tend to overuse the cognitive modality and intellectualize their feelings.

C: Cognition. Cognitions are thoughts and beliefs, and Lazarus is most interested in exploring the client's mistaken beliefs—the illogical or irrational ones. He usually looks for three faulty assumptions that he believes are common and also potentially more damaging than others:
1. The tyranny of the SHOULD—a belief that often can be inferred from the client's actions and behaviors as well as from self-report. This belief often places unreasonable demands on self and others.
2. Perfectionism—expecting infallibility, often not only of themselves but of others as well.
3. External attributions—the myths that clients verbalize when they feel they are the victims of outside persons or circumstances and have no control over or responsibility for what is happening to them.

I: Interpersonal Relationships. Many therapists (including Sullivan, Horney, and Fromm) have stressed the importance of interpersonal relationships, or "social interest" (Adler, 1964). Lazarus (1989) notes that problems in the way clients relate to others can be detected not only through self-report and role playing but also by observation of the helper/client relationship. Assessment of this modality includes observing the way clients express and accept feelings communicated to them by others as well as the way they behave and react to others.

D: Drugs. Lazarus asserts that drugs represent an important nonpsychological modality to assess (and potentially treat) because neurological and biochemical factors can affect behavior, affective responses, cognitions, sensations, and so on. In addition to specific inquiries about psychotropic medications, assessment of this modality includes the following:
1. Overall appearance—attire, skin or speech disturbances, tics, psychomotor disorders.
2. Physiological complaints or diagnosed illnesses.
3. General health and well-being—physical fitness, exercise, diet and nutrition, avocational interests and hobbies, and leisure time pursuits.

This modality may often require consultation with or examination by a physician or other health professional.

Lazarus (1976) asserts that most helpers, including eclectic ones, fail to assess and treat these seven basic modalities. Instead, they deal with only one or two modalities, depending on their personal preferences and theoretical orientation, even though "durable results are in direct proportion to the number of specific modalities deliberately invoked by any therapeutic system" (p. 13).

The BASIC ID model of case conceptualization is applied to the following case and summarized in the modality profile (Lazarus, 1989) shown in Table 8.1.

TABLE 8.1	Modality Profile of Client Case Using BASIC ID (Lazarus, 1976, 1989)
Modality	Observations
B: Behavior	Passive responding; some withdrawal from conversation
	Slow rate of speech
	Frequent shrugging of shoulders
	Overeating
A: Affect	Alone—loneliness
	Unloved
	Denies concern or upset over weight
S: Sensation	Muscular tension—upper torso particularly
I: Imagery	Frequent fantasies of a move and different lifestyle
	Persistent dreams of being rescued
C: Cognition	Negative self-verbalizations and perceptions
	Self-perfectionistic standards
	Attributes her issues to forces outside herself
I: Interpersonal relationships	Is exploited by ex-husband, daughters, boss
	Submissive in interactions with others
D: Drugs	Well groomed
	Well dressed
	50–75 pounds overweight
	Articulate
	Stomach distress—weekly
	Good health—mostly sedentary activity
	Little leisure time

The client is a 35-year-old female who looks about 50 to 75 pounds overweight, though well groomed, well dressed, and articulate. The client states that she is in generally good health, does little exercise, works either on the job or at home, and has little free time. Free time is spent mainly in sedentary activities such as reading or watching TV. The client is divorced and has two school-age daughters. She does report occasional stomach distress—often as much as once or twice weekly. The client's presenting issue is overall "dissatisfaction with myself and my life." The client notes that she lives in a small town and has been unable to meet many available partners. She would like to have a good relationship with a male. She was divorced four years ago and states that her husband became interested in another woman and "took off." She says that she also has poor relationships with her two daughters, whom she describes as "irresponsible and lazy." On inquiry, it appears that the client is easily exploited and rather submissive in most of her relationships with significant others. In her job, she agrees to take work home with her even though she receives no overtime pay. She describes herself as feeling alone, lonely, and sometimes unloved or unlovable. She also reports that she often has thoughts that her life has been a failure and that she is not the kind of person she could be, although she portrays herself as a victim of circumstances (divorce, job, small town) beyond her control. However, she also reports rather frequent fantasies of moving and living in a different town and having a different job. She also describes repetitive dreams in which she can recall vividly the image of being rescued. She behaves very passively in the session—talks slowly, shrugs her shoulders, and occasionally withdraws from the conversation. Some muscular tension is apparent during the interview, particularly in her upper body. She states that overeating is a major concern, one that she attributes to not having her life go the way she wants it to and being unable to do much about it. At the same time, she appears to deny any concern about her weight, stating that if she's not worried about it, then it shouldn't matter to anyone else either.

In treatment planning, the first areas of focus would be the two modalities about which the client is most concerned—affective and interpersonal. If the interpersonal modality is selected as the initial area of focus, changes in this modality will likely lead to changes in the affective one also, for the client's feelings of loneliness are a direct result of lack of effective interpersonal relationships. From a feminist therapy perspective, part of the focus in the interpersonal and affective modalities would be on the way society's expectations of her as a woman have contributed to her feelings of distress and isolation. Skill training programs such as assertion training and social skills training are likely to be most effective in helping the client establish new relationships and avoid further exploitation in her present ones. Such skill training could also be directed toward some of her overt behaviors that may interfere with establishing new relationships, such as her speech rate and her style of responding in conversations. Strengths such as her good health and visualizations of change would also be areas of focus. Although the client denies any concern about her weight, she may also allow her weight to prevent her from engaging in the very kind of social interactions and relationships she finds absent from her life. Strategies such as Gestalt dialoguing and TA redecision work may help her examine her conflicting feelings about being overweight. If and when she decides to make weight reduction a goal, cognitive strategies (such as cognitive restructuring, Chapter 14) aimed at modifying any cognitive misperceptions would be useful, as would behavioral strategies (such as self-management, Chapter 18) targeted toward helping her modify her overeating behavior and supporting environmental contingencies. See Table 8.1 for a summary of this case.

OUR ASSUMPTIONS ABOUT ASSESSMENT AND COGNITIVE BEHAVIOR THERAPY

Like the previously described case conceptualization models, our model of assessment in helping is based on several assumptions about clients, issues, and behavior. These assumptions are drawn from the cognitive–behavioral approach to counseling. Cognitive behavior therapy includes a variety of techniques and strategies that are based on principles of learning and designed to produce constructive change in human behaviors. This approach was first developed in the 1950s under the term *behavior therapy* by, among others, Skinner, Wolpe, Lazarus, and Krumboltz. Early behavior therapists focused on the importance of changing clients' observable behavior. Since the 1950s, there have been significant developments in behavior therapy. Among the most important is the emergence of cognitive behavior therapy, which arose in the 1970s as a result of the work of such persons as Meichenbaum and Beck. Cognitive behavior therapy emphasizes the effects of private events such as cognitions, beliefs, and internal dialogue on resulting feelings and performance. This orientation to change now recognizes that both overt responding (observed behavior) and covert responding (feelings and thoughts) are important targets of change as long as they can be clearly specified (Rimm & Masters, 1979, p. 1).

Thyer and Myers (2000) articulate two additional assumptions of a cognitive–behavioral and social learning model of assessment:

1. Similar learning processes taking place in different environments, within an individual's life span, have given rise to the diversity of expressions we call the human experience and
2. Assessment of clients involves an analysis of past and present learning experience that may be responsible for giving rise to problematic situations. This is called a functional assessment. By definition, social learning theory takes into account the person-in-environment. (p. 201)

Follette and Hayes (2000) describe a functional assessment as "the assessment and conceptualization of clinically relevant problem behaviors and their current and historical context to aid in selecting an appropriate intervention, to provide a means to monitor treatment progress, and to aid in the evaluation of the effectiveness of an intervention" (p. 391). They also point out that in actual practice, the primary feature of doing a functional assessment with a client is "treatment utility," meaning "the demonstration that improved outcomes are achieved by the use of assessment as compared to its nonuse" (p. 391). Although data that show how functional assessment improves treatment outcomes are currently limited, it is still considered better to conduct this kind of thorough assessment of client issues than no assessment at all. We explore these assumptions and explain their role in assessing clients in the following section.

Most Behavior Is Learned

Undesired (maladaptive) behavior is developed, maintained, and subject to alteration or modification in the same manner as normal (adaptive) behavior. Both prosocial and maladaptive, or self-defeating, behaviors are assumed to be developed and maintained either by external situational events or cues, by external reinforcers, or by internal processes such as cognition, mediation, and problem solving. For the most part, maladaptive behavior is not thought to be a function of physical disease or of underlying intrapsychic conflict. This fundamental assumption means that we do not spend a great deal of time sorting out or focusing on possible unresolved early conflicts or underlying pathological states. However, it does not mean that we rule out or overlook possible organic and physiological causes of undesired behavior. For example, clients who complain of "anxiety" and report primarily somatic (body-related) symptoms such as heart palpitations, stomach upset, chest pains, and breathlessness may be chronic hyperventilators (Lum, 1976), although hyperventilation can be considered only after the client has had a physical examination to rule out cardiopathy. Physical examinations also may reveal the presence of mitral valve heart dysfunction for some individuals who complain of "panic attacks." Other somatic symptoms suggesting anxiety, such as sweating, tachycardia, lightheadedness, and dizziness, could also result from organic disorders such as hypoglycemia, thyroid or other endocrine disorders, or a low-grade infection.

Physiological variables should always be explored, particularly when the results of the assessment do not suggest the presence of other specific stimuli eliciting the problem behavior. Many psychological disorders have a biological component as well as a learning component. For example, the neurotransmitter serotonin is implicated in both depression and anxiety disorders. Further, the cycling rate of serotonin is affected by genetic markers. Some disorders such as alcoholism and schizophrenia have both genetic and biochemical markers that can increase a person's vulnerability to such a disorder. This is one reason why medical history is assessed during an initial interview (see Chapter 9). In these situations, evaluation of the client by a physician is warranted.

It is also important to recognize the need for occasional physiological management of psychological issues—for example, in the kinds of disorders mentioned above. Medications may be necessary in addition to psychological intervention. Antidepressants are typically recommended for some forms of depression, particularly the endogenous type as distinct from the more reactive (situational) type. They have been found helpful as a supplement to psychological treatment for some instances of agoraphobia, a disorder typified by a marked fear of being alone or in public places. Anxiety or panic attacks are also often managed with antidepressants but additionally with beta blockers and/or other antianxiety agents. Furthermore, a biological element, such as biochemical imbalance, seems to be present in many of the psychoses, such as schizophrenia, and these conditions usually require antipsychotic drugs to improve the client's overall level of functioning.

Some clinical disorders such as dementia, delirium, amnesia, and substance-related disorders are associated with organic damage or brain pathology such as senility, drug effects, brain diseases, injuries, and poisons. (Sometimes this organic brain pathology is also referred to as "central nervous system impairment," or CNSI.) A well-known example of a brain disorder is senile dementia, a mental impairment in older persons caused by brain degeneration such as Alzheimer's disease or a serious stroke or circulatory problems in the body. In instances where the practitioner believes there may be organic damage or deterioration, it is wise to have the client evaluated by a neuropsychologist or neurologist. It is easy, for example, to confuse dementia with depression or with the symptoms of normal aging in an elderly client (Zarit & Zarit, 1998).

Causes of Client Issues and Therefore Treatments/Interventions Are Multidimensional

Rarely is a client concern caused by only one factor, and rarely does a single, unidimensional treatment program work in actual practice. For example, with a client who reports depression, we may find evidence of organic contributing factors such as Addison's disease (dysfunction of the adrenal gland), of environmental contributing conditions such as being left by his partner after moving to a new town, and of internal contributing factors such as self-deprecatory thoughts and images. Causes and contributing conditions of most client problems are multiple and include overt behavior, environmental events and relationships with others, covert behavior such as beliefs, images, and cognitions, feelings and bodily sensations, and possibly physiological/organic conditions. Intervention is usually more effective when directed toward all these multiple factors. For the client described above, his endocrine balance must be restored and maintained, he must be helped to deal with his feelings of rejection and anger about his partner's departure, he needs to develop alternative resources and supports, including self-support, and he needs help in learning how to modify his self-deprecating thoughts and images. Additionally, he may benefit from problem-solving skills in order to decide the direction he wants his life to take. Also, a focus on his own strengths and coping skills may help give him the confidence he needs to implement this new direction. We also need to consider the effect of his environment. What kind of environmental context (family, community, social and cultural environment) did he leave? What sort of environmental context does he find or has he not found in his new city? How does this affect his level of depression? Would treatment interventions be solely psychological ones, or does he also need physiological interventions made by a health care practitioner to treat his depression? The more complete and comprehensive the treatment, the more successful the helping process tends to be, and also the less chance of relapse.

Issues Are to Be Viewed Operationally

We suggest a way to view client issues that defines the client's present undesired behaviors and some contributing conditions. This approach is called defining the problem "operationally," or "concretely." An operational definition functions like a measure, a barometer, or a "behavioral anchor." Operational definitions indicate some very specific behaviors; they do not infer vague traits or labels from the client's statement. Mischel (1973, p. 10) has contrasted these two approaches to conceptualization: "The emphasis is on what a person *does* in situations rather than on inferences about what attributes he *has* more globally."

Consider the following example of a way to view a client's concern operationally. In working with the "depressed" client, we would try to define precisely what the client means by "depressed" in order to avoid any misinterpretation of this self-report feeling statement. Instead of viewing the client's issue as "depression," we would try to specify some thoughts, feelings, actions, situations, and persons that are associated with the client's depression. We would find out whether the client experiences certain physiological changes during depression, what the client is thinking about while depressed, and what activities and behaviors occur during the depressed periods.

In other words, the helper, in conjunction with the client, identifies a series of referents that are indicative of the state of being depressed, anxious, withdrawn, lonely, and so on. The advantage of viewing the issue this way is that vague phenomena are translated into specific and observable experiences. When this occurs, we not only have a better idea of what is happening with the client, but we also have made the issue potentially measurable, allowing us to assess progress and outcome (see also Chapter 10).

Most Issues Occur in a Social Context

Client issues do not usually occur in a vacuum but are related to observable events (verbal, nonverbal, and motoric responses) and to less visible covert or indirect events (thoughts, images, moods and feelings, body sensations) that precipitate and maintain the problem. These internal and external events are called "antecedents" or "consequences." They are functionally related to the issue in that they exert control over it, so a change in one of these variables often brings about a change in related variables. For example, a child's inability to behave assertively with his teacher may be a function of learned fears, a lack of social skills, and the fact that he has moved, is in a new school, and also has his first male teacher. Changing one part of this overall concern—for example, helping him reduce and manage his fears—will exert an effect on all other variables in the situation.

In Chapter 10, in the discussion on goals, we learn that the helper must be alert not only to the way different parts of the issue are related but also to the impact that change in one variable may have on the others. Occasionally, a symptom may perform a very useful function for the client, and removing it could make things worse. For example, in the above illustration, add to the case the fact that the child had on one occasion been sexually abused by a male house intruder. The symptom of fear may be serving the function of protection in his relationships with unknown males. Removal of the fear without consideration of the other parts of the issue could make the presenting problem worse or could bring about the onset of other issues.

The functional relationship of behavior and the environment reflects a systemic/ecological view; it was articulated as early as 1979 and again in 1993 by Bronfenbrenner. In a social–ecological view of mental health treatment, the individual client and his or her environment are linked together, so assessment includes not only an individual focus but a contextual focus, including key social settings, events, and resources (Rosado & Elias, 1993).

In the Bronfenbrenner style, practitioners need to examine the social and cultural contexts of relationships among these key social settings, events, and resources. Whereas the ecological context of issues is important to consider for all clients, some writers have noted that the sociopolitical context surrounding the client is especially important for clients who feel marginalized, such as clients of color and women (Axelson, 1999; Brown, 1994; Garvin & Seabury, 1997; Rogoff & Chavajay, 1995). For example, Brown (1994) asserts that in feminist therapy, the first and foremost client is the cultural context; thus "feminist therapy concerns itself not simply with individual suffering but with the social and political meaning of both pain and healing. . . . Feminist therapy aims to deprivatize the lives of both therapists and the people with whom they work by asking, out loud and repeatedly, how each life and each pain are manifestations of processes operating in a larger social context" (p. 17). As an example, it is not enough just to help a female client with her stated feelings of "depression"; you must also explore how the culture's expectations of her gender contribute to her depression (Ivey, Ivey, & Simek-Morgan, 1997).

A similar focus on the cultural and political context with Native American clients has been described by LaFromboise and Low (1989):

> traditionally, Indian people live in relational networks that serve to support and nurture strong bonds of mutual assistance and affection. Many tribes still engage in a traditional system of collective interdependence, with family members responsi-

ble not only to one another but also the clan and tribe to which they belong. The Lakota Sioux use the term *tiospaye* to describe a traditional community way of life in which an individual's well-being remains the responsibility of the extended family.... When problems arise among Indian youth, they become problems of the community as well. The family, kin, and friends join together to observe the youth's behavior, draw the youth out of isolation, and integrate that person back into the activities of the group. (p. 121)

Ivey, Ivey, and Simek-Morgan (1997) point out that in working with some clients, such as the Lakota Sioux described in the above example, the helper should extend the focus of the assessment from the individual to the *mitwelt*—that is, the immediate family, extended family, and community.

Stated another way, in a social–ecological view of mental health treatment, the individual client and his or her environment are linked together, so assessment covers not only an individual focus but a contextual focus also, including key social settings, events, and resources (Rosado & Elias, 1993). In the practice nexus described in Chapter 1, we referred to this as the person-in-environment model, and in the following section we explain how this model is used in assessing clients.

THE PERSON-IN-ENVIRONMENT MODEL

In Chapter 1, we described the person-in-environment as a central feature of the growing edge of practice today. Sometimes this model is also referred to as an "ecological" model. This model of conceptualizing clients is based on the following two notions:
1. Client concerns do not reside solely within an individual but are embedded within cultural, environmental, and social systems or contexts.
2. There is movement away from a focus on individual pathology and toward a focus on strengths, past successes, resources, and coping skills of clients. (Freeman, 2000; McAuliffe & Eriksen, 1999)

These two assumptions are consistent with current and emerging policy guides on psychology, social work, counseling, and human services curricula as well as the multicultural competencies we referred to in Chapter 2. Further, they suggest a model of client assessment based on the following two levels:

The individual client or *Who* and

The client's environmental and cultural context or *Where* (see also Figure 8.1; McAuliffe & Eriksen, 1999).

When assessment is conducted on both of these two levels, practitioners obtain a "balanced view" of the client (Summers, 2001, p. 60). In the following section we describe the guiding principles of each of these two levels of client assessment in greater detail. Specific interviewing and related tools for gathering information for each level are described in Chapter 9.

The Individual Client or *Who*

The individual client brings personal attributes to therapy consisting primarily of covert, internal experiences and overt behaviors. In conceptualizing the client's issues, we assess for four specific dimensions:

- Feelings or affective dimensions
- Physiologic sensations or somatic dimensions
- Thoughts, beliefs, schemas, or cognitive dimensions
- Actions or behavioral dimensions

We describe these dimensions in greater detail later in this chapter. We look both for excesses and deficits in these areas, as recommended by Lazarus (1997), and specific clinical disorders reflected by these excesses and deficits. We also assess for previous solutions and successes, and client strengths, resources, and coping skills. A focus on client strengths and resources furthers collaboration between helper and client, deemphasizes stigmas associated with client problems and diagnostic labels, and enhances the client's sense of self-efficacy (Hepworth et al., 1997). Cowger (1994) summarizes this well when he notes that "clinical practice based on empowerment assures that client power is achieved when clients make choices that give them more control over their presenting problem situations and in turn their own lives" (p. 263). Summers (2001) provides two cases illustrating how the individual characteristics of two different clients affected their prison stay (see Box 8.1).

The Client's Environmental and Cultural Context or *Where*

Individual clients also bring ecological and cultural variables to helping that affect the client's presenting issues. Ecological variables are ones that involve the relationship between individuals and their environment (Triandis, 1994). For example, a client is a member of some kind of a family system. Depending on the client's culture, the family system has its own structure and values. As well, clients may belong to specific social groups, spiritual groups, educational groups, and community groups.

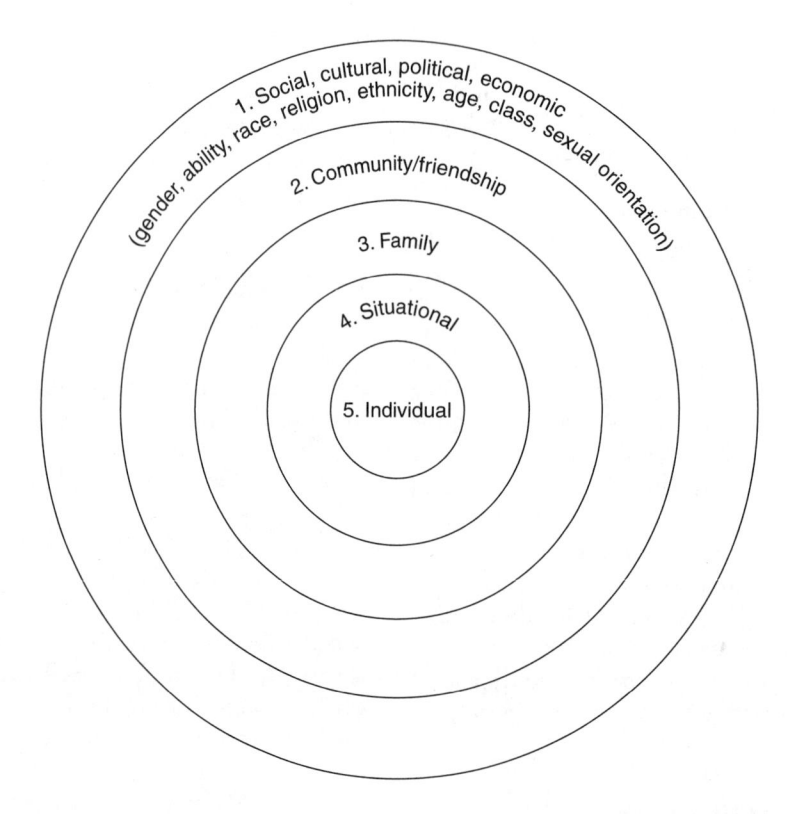

Figure 8.1 Levels of Assessment
Source: "Toward a Constructivist and Developmental Identity for the Counseling Profession: The Context–Phase–Stage–Style Model," by G. McAuliffe and K. Ericksen. *Journal of Counseling and Development, 77,* pp. 279–280. © 1999 ACA. Reprinted with permission. No further reproduction authorized without written permission.

Circles from outer to inner:
1. Social, cultural, political, economic (gender, ability, race, religion, ethnicity, age, class, sexual orientation)
2. Community/friendship
3. Family
4. Situational
5. Individual

Client problems are affected by the larger society and community in which the client lives, such as the government, economy, geography, and faith heritage. Clients are also members of one or several cultural groups and are influenced by the structure, socialization, and values of these groups. We refer to ecological variables that affect client issues as *contextual and relational* dimensions. It is important to assess the impact of these dimensions since "the reason for the client's problems may lie in the *context* rather than with the client" (Summers, 2001, p. 63). The larger social context may also have affected the client's presenting concerns. For example, one client may have experienced loss of employment, disenfranchisement in voting, a poor health care system, and a barely adequate school system. Another client may have experienced a boom in the stock market, preferential political treatment, a first-rate health care system, and a private school (Summers, 2001).

In assessing for *contextual and relational* dimensions of the client's issues, we look for areas of environmental supports and barriers, including places, settings, events, and people who are sources of empowerment and disempowerment (Kemp, Whittaker, & Tracy, 1997). For example, what is the extent and availability of family and community resources? If the client is an immigrant or refugee, how has his or her status been affected by the move? We cannot overemphasize the importance of assessing the contribution of these environmental variables to identified issues. This sort of assessment helps clients determine, for example, whether an issue may stem from racism and prejudice in *other persons* so that clients or helpers do not inappropriately personalize their concerns.

Consider the same two individuals, Ralph and Edwardo, who were described (see Box 8.1). Now they are in different environmental settings, and with different con-

> **BOX 8.1 THE CASES OF RALPH AND EDWARDO**
>
> Ralph had been in prison for some youthful gang activity. While he was there, he took advantage of every opportunity to change. He went to church regularly, developed a personal relationship with a minister who came to the prison often, and obtained his high school diploma. Ralph was a warm, humorous person who attracted many friends. His outgoing personality attracted people to him who ultimately encouraged him and gave him support. During his time in prison, his mother wrote to him often, pleading with him to change his ways. Ralph felt bad about the trouble he had caused his mother, particularly in view of the fact that she had raised him after his father left home, and he saw her letters as a reason to do better. When he left prison, he enrolled in college courses and attached himself to the church, where he was warmly welcomed.
>
> Edwardo was in the same prison for youthful gang activities. He was quiet and retiring and did not attract the attention and support that Ralph had secured for himself. Edwardo attempted to get his high school diploma while in prison, but had trouble asking for help when he needed it and eventually gave the project up in frustration. Preferring not to join groups, he did not go to church or any other group activity that promoted independence and responsibility. Because Edwardo spoke so little and rarely smiled, he was often misunderstood as being hostile. In fact, he felt shy and awkward around other people. Edwardo's mother wrote him regularly, and she too pleaded with him to do better and "turn his life around"; but Edwardo tended to see these letters as nagging and to blame his mother for the fact that his father left when he was very young. He rarely answered her mail. When Edwardo left prison, he moved back with his old friends and resumed his former criminal activities.
>
> This illustration demonstrates how individual characteristics play a role in the outcome for the client. Part of developing a balanced understanding of the client is being able to see what the client brings to the situation and how that interacts with the larger context of his or her life. Ralph brought a personality that attracted others to assist him. He brought a good relationship with his mother and a motivation to do things more constructively. Edwardo brought a more retiring personality, one that was less attractive to others and often misunderstood. Edwardo's interpersonal skills were not as developed as Ralph's. The individual characteristics of Edwardo and Ralph affected the outcome of their prison time.
>
> Source: "Fundamentals of case management practice," by N. Summers, p. 60. Copyright © 2001 Reprinted with permission of Brooks/Cole, an imprint of the Wadsworth Group, a division of Thomson Learning.

textual and relational variables, even though both are still incarcerated (see Box 8.2).

Another aspect of assessing the context includes a cultural analysis of client issues. We concur with Ridley, Li, and Hill (1998) that assessing for cultural data directly from clients is an ethical responsibility of helpers. And, further, while it may be necessary to ask clients to clarify cultural data for your own understanding, it is important to do so in a way that doesn't burden the client.

A broad-based perspective by which to conceptualize clients from a cultural perspective has been developed by Sinacore-Guinn (1995). This model, which she calls "the diagnostic window," is depicted in Figure 8.2. It involves assessment of four categories:

1. *Cultural systems and structures,* including "Community structure, family, schools, interaction styles, concepts of illness, life-stage development, coping patterns, and immigration history" (p. 21).
2. *Cultural values,* including the five value orientations of *time, activity, relational orientation, person–nature orientation,* and *basic nature of people.*
3. *Gender socialization,* including cultural, ethnic, and racial variations in prescribed gender roles, meaning and attitudes assigned by clients to gender, and also preferred sexual orientation.
4. *Trauma,* including direct, indirect, and insidious trauma, as well as the social environmental and sociopolitical context surrounding the trauma.

The helper's task is to understand, in a culturally sensitive way, the client's presenting issues regarding these four areas that, as shown in Figure 8.2, fall outside the window. This understanding prevents an automatic labeling of issues in these areas as necessarily pathological, even though they may be troubling or conflict arousing for the client. It is *within* the window "that pathology exists and it is from the presence of pathology that the diagnosis is made" (Sinacore-Guinn,

> **BOX 8.2** **THE CASES OF RALPH AND EDWARDO** *CONTINUED*
>
> Now we will look at Edwardo and Ralph differently. For our purposes, let us suppose that Ralph and Edwardo are both warm, humorous people. Both make friends easily and enjoy the company of other people. Each of them is sent to prison for youthful gang activities, but the context is different. Edwardo goes to a prison upstate. It was recently built and the focus is on rehabilitation. There Ed is provided with high school and college classes as well as religious and self-improvement activities. He is able to take advantage of many different programs to further his goals. A supportive counselor works with him to come up with a good set of goals and helps Ed implement these. They meet on a weekly basis. The location of the prison has another advantage. Edwardo is now closer to his father, who lives only a few miles from the prison. His father begins to visit, offering his support and a place for Ed to live when his sentence is completed. Edwardo leaves the prison on a solid footing and continues his work toward a college degree.
>
> Ralph, on the other hand, is sent to an ordinary prison where the counseling staff is overwhelmed. His counselor sees Ralph's potential, but has trouble getting Ralph into high school courses because they are crowded. During the time Ralph is at the prison, the education staff experiences a number of turnovers and layoffs. Ralph never can get into the program and stick to it. He rarely sees his counselor because of the number of inmates with whom the counselor must work. No family member comes to visit Ralph, partly because he has been sent so far from them and partly because they blame him for his incarceration and have lost interest in him. Ralph's mother, sick with severe chronic asthma, rarely writes. There are church services, which Ralph attends regularly, but the prison does not allow inmates to meet the pastors before or after services because of a strict schedule, and the pastors who have formed relationships with inmates come irregularly at other times. When Ralph leaves the prison, he has not completed his high school diploma. He moves near some people he knew in prison, and soon he takes up the criminal activities in which he participated before his incarceration.
>
> Here it is the context that is different. Edwardo finds himself in a supportive context: a counselor who focuses on his goals and sees that these are implemented, plenty of self-improvement opportunities, a warm relationship with his father, a prison committed to education. Ralph, however, finds himself confronted with indifference, lack of supportive programs and activities, an overwhelmed counselor, and a family too distant to give encouragement.
>
> *Source:* "Fundamentals of case management practice," by N. Summers, p. 60. Copyright © 2001 Reprinted with permission of Brooks/Cole, an imprint of Wadsworth, a division of Thomson Learning.

1995, p. 25). Using this model, not all clients will have material inside the window. As Sinacore-Guinn (1995) asserts, "The key is for the counselor to carefully limit the frame of that window against overinclusion. Presenting problems that reside outside the window are not pathological and should be given a V code" (pp. 25–26). (See also the "Diagnostic Classification" section of this chapter.)

Specific cultural dimensions that we assess for include such things as suggested by Hays's (2001) ADRESSING framework:

A—age and generational history; acculturation
D—disability status
R—race; religious and spiritual affiliations and values
E—ethnicity, cultural identity
S—social status and socioeconomic status or class
S—sexual orientation
I—indigenous heritage
N—national origin
G—gender

Also, any key symptoms, markers of distress, stressors, and trauma must be assessed for their cultural as well as clinical meaning (Castillo, 1997). For example, how is the client's overall level of stress related to any of the aspects on the ADRESSING framework, such as acculturation, race, gender, or sexual orientation? Have the client's experiences with anything on this framework produced trauma? What are the psychological and physiological signatures that suggest trauma? What are the effects for this client from historical trauma of the client's primary ethnic group, such as the enslavement of African Americans, the dislocation of Native Americans, the Holocaust, or the imprisonment of Japanese Americans during World War II? (Root, 1992, p. 258). And what about cultural strengths and values? Just

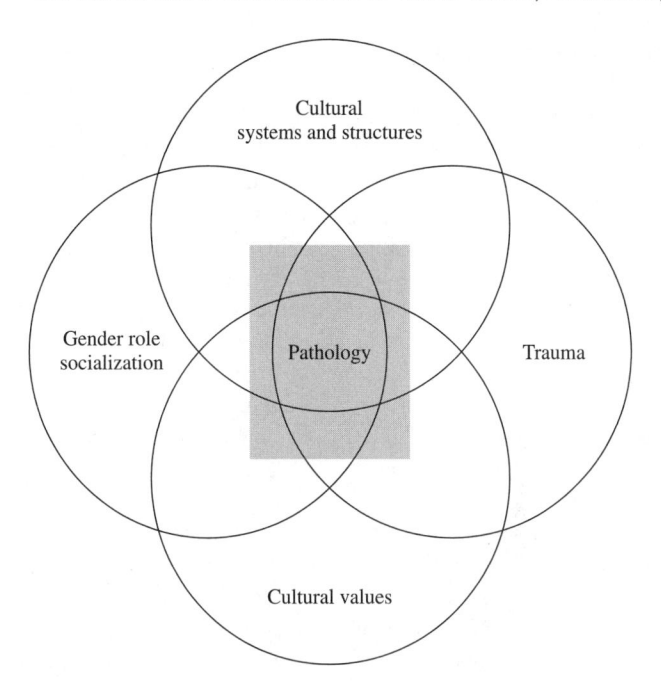

Figure 8.2 The diagnostic window.
Source: "The diagnostic window: Culture- and Gender-Sensitive Diagnosis and Training," by A. L. Sinacore-Guinn, Counselor Education and Supervision, 35, pp. 18–31. © 1995 ACA. Reprinted with permission. No further reproduction authorized without written permission of the American Counseling Association.

as cultural variables can be related to trauma, aspects of the ADRESSING framework can also produce strengths, resources, and ways to cope. For example, clients may come from cultural communities whose sociopolitical histories model resistance or from communities where there are extended kinship systems to increase connections (Iglesias and Cormier, in press).

In the following section of the chapter, we expand this model and elaborate on the way in which both individual and environmental aspects of client concerns can be identified in a functional analysis of the antecedents, behaviors, and consequences.

THE ABC MODEL OF BEHAVIOR

One way to identify the relationship between behavior and environmental events is with the ABC model (Bellack & Hersen, 1998; O'Leary & Wilson, 1987). The ABC model of behavior suggests that the behavior (B) is influenced by events that precede it, called antecedents (A), and by some types of events that follow behavior, called consequences (C). An antecedent (A) event is a cue or signal that can tell a person how to behave in a situation. A consequence (C) is defined as an event that strengthens or weakens a behavior. Note that these definitions of antecedents and consequences suggest that an individual's behavior is directly related to or influenced by certain events. For example, a behavior that appears to be caused by antecedent events such as anger may also be maintained or strengthened by consequences such as reactions from other people. Assessment interviews focus on identifying the particular antecedent and consequent events that influence or are functionally related to the client's defined behavior.

As a very simple example of the ABC model, consider a behavior (B) that most of us engage in frequently: talking. Our talking behavior is usually occasioned by certain cues, such as starting a conversation with another person, being asked a question, or being in the presence of a friend. Antecedents that might decrease the likelihood that we will talk may include worry about getting approval for what we say or how we answer the question or being in a hurry to get somewhere. Cultural norms can also serve as antecedents that occasion talking behavior—for example, in some cultures, there is a hierarchy from elders to youth, and younger persons do not initiate conversation out of respect for the elders. Our talking behavior may be maintained by the verbal and nonverbal attention we receive from another person, which is a very powerful consequence, or reinforcer. Other positive consequences that might maintain our talking behavior may be that we are feeling good or happy and engaging in positive self-statements or evaluations about the usefulness or relevance of what we are saying. We may talk less when the other person's eye contact wanders, although the meaning of eye contact varies across cultures, or when he or she tells us more explicitly that we've talked enough. These are negative consequences (C) that decrease our talking behavior. Other negative consequences that may decrease our talking behavior could include bodily sensations of fatigue or vocal hoarseness that occur after we talk for a while, or thoughts and images that what we are saying is of little value to attract the interest of others. As you will see in the next three sections, not only do the components of undesired behavior often vary among clients, but what functions as an antecedent or consequence for one person in one environment is often very different for someone else in a different environment.

Behavior

Behavior includes things a client does as well as things a client thinks about. *Overt* behavior is behavior that is visible or could be detected by an observer, such as verbal behavior (talking), nonverbal behavior (for example, gesturing or smiling), or motoric behavior (engaging in some action such as walking). *Covert* behavior includes events that are usually internal—inside the client—and are not so readily visible to an observer, who must rely on client self-report and nonverbal behavior to detect such events. Examples of covert behavior include thoughts, beliefs, images, feelings, moods, and body sensations.

As we indicated earlier, behavior that clients report rarely occurs in isolated fashion. Most reported undesired behaviors are typically part of a larger chain or set of behaviors. Moreover, each behavior mentioned usually has more than one component. For example, a client who complains of anxiety or depression is most likely using the label to refer to an experience consisting of an *affective* component (feelings, mood states), a *somatic* component (physiological and body-related sensation), a *behavioral* component (what the client does or doesn't do), and a *cognitive* component (thoughts, beliefs, images, or internal dialogue). Additionally, the experience of anxiety or depression may vary for the client, depending on *contextual* factors (time, place, concurrent events, gender, culture, sociopolitical climate, and environmental events), and on *relational* factors such as the presence or absence of other people. All these components may or may not be related to a particular reported concern. For example, suppose our client who reports "anxiety" is afraid to venture out in public places except for home and work because of heightened anxiety and/or panic attacks.

She is an adult, single woman who still lives at her parental home, and she provides care to her elderly mother, whom she also describes as dependent and helpless. She has lived all of her life in a small, rural community. She reports mistrust of strangers, especially those whom she did not know while growing up. She states she would like to leave and be out on her own and move away, but she is too afraid. As Fodor (1992) notes, she is metaphorically engaged in some sort of sit-in strike, making a statement about her own limited role (as well as her mother's). Her reported concern of anxiety seems to be part of a chain that starts with a cognitive component in which she thinks worried thoughts and produces images in which she sees herself alone and unable to cope or to get the assistance of others if necessary. These support her underlying cognitive "schema" or structure of limited autonomy (see also Chapter 14).

The cognitive component leads to somatic discomfort and tension and to feelings of apprehension and dread. These three components work together to influence her overt behavior—for the last few years, she has successfully avoided almost all public places. Consequently, she depends on the support of family and friends to help her function adequately in the home and at work and particularly on the few occasions when she attends public activities. These people form her relational network.

At the same time that you see these apparent behaviors of concern, bear in mind there also will be both overt and covert behaviors of this client that represent strengths, resources, and coping skills. The very act of courage it takes to come and see you is an overt behavioral strength and action of initiative. Her recognition of some conflicting feelings and beliefs about her life choices is a covert behavioral strength. Her support network of friends and her steady work situation are examples of environmental strengths; being a part of a small, close-knit community can be a cultural strength.

It is important to determine the relative importance of each component of the reported behavior in order to select appropriate intervention strategies (see also Chapter 11). In Chapter 9 we describe ways to obtain descriptions of these various components with an interview assessment method. It is often valuable to list, in writing, the various components identified for any given behavior.

Antecedents

According to Mischel (1973), behavior is situationally determined. This means that given behaviors tend to occur only in certain situations. For example, most of us brush our teeth in a public or private bathroom rather than during a concert or a spiritual service. Antecedents may elicit emotional and physiological reactions such as anger, fear, joy, headaches, or elevated blood pressure. Antecedents influence behavior by either increasing or decreasing its likelihood of occurrence. For example, a child in a first-grade class may behave differently at school than at home or differently with a substitute than with the regular teacher.

Antecedent events that occur immediately before a specific behavior exert influence on it. Events that are not in temporal proximity to the behavior can similarly increase or decrease the probability that the behavior will occur. Antecedents that occur in immediate temporal proximity to the specified behavior are technically called *stimulus events* (Bijou & Baer, 1976) and include any external or internal event or condition that either cues the behavior or makes it more or less likely to occur under that condition. Antecedents that are temporally distant from the specified behavior are called *setting events* (Kantor, 1970) and include circumstances that the person has recently or previously passed through. Setting events may end well before the behavior and yet, like stimulus events, still aid or inhibit its occurrence. Examples of setting events to consider in assessing client issues are the client's age, developmental stage, and physiological state; characteristics of the client's work, home, or school setting; multicultural factors; and behaviors that emerge to affect subsequent behaviors (Wahler & Fox, 1981). Both stimulus and setting antecedent conditions must be identified and defined individually for each client.

Antecedents also usually involve more than one source or type of event. Sources of antecedents may be *affective* (feelings, mood states), *somatic* (physiological and body-related sensations), *behavioral* (verbal, nonverbal, and motoric responses), *cognitive* (schemas, thoughts, beliefs, images, internal dialogue), *contextual* (time, place, multicultural factors, concurrent environmental events), and *relational* (presence or absence of other people). For example, with our client who reported "anxiety," there may be a variety of antecedent sources that cue or occasion each aspect of the reported behavior, such as fear of losing control (cognitive/affective), negative self-statements about autonomy and self-efficacy (cognitive), awareness of apprehension-related body sensations, fatigue, and hypoglycemic tendencies (somatic), staying up late and skipping meals (behavioral), being in public places (contextual), and absence of significant others such as friends and siblings, and the demands of her elderly mother (relational).

There are also a variety of antecedent sources that make components of the client's anxiety less likely to occur. These include feeling relaxed (affective), being rested (somatic), eating regularly (behavioral), decreased dependence on her friends (behavioral), decreased fear of separation from mother (affective), positive appraisal of self and others (cognitive), expectation of being able to handle situations (cognitive), absence of need to go to public places or functions (contextual), and being accompanied to a public place by a significant other (relational).

The influence that antecedents have on our behavior may vary with each of us, depending on our learning history. It is also important to keep in mind that antecedents are overt or covert events that in some way influence the specific behavior either by cuing it or by increasing or decreasing the likelihood that it will occur under certain conditions. In other words, not everything that precedes a behavior is automatically considered an antecedent—only those things that influence a behavioral response in some manner. However, undesired behavior may also be affected by other situational factors (props) that are usually present in the situation but do not directly influence the behavior. This is especially observable if any of these situational factors changes dramatically (Goldiamond & Dyrud, 1967). For instance, a child's behavior in school may be at least temporarily affected if the child's only sibling is hospitalized for injuries received in an automobile accident or if the child's father, who has been a household spouse for ten years, starts to work full time outside the home.

During the assessment phase of the helping process, it is important to identify those antecedent sources that prompt desirable behaviors and those that are related to inappropriate responses. The reason is that during the intervention (treatment) phase, it is important to select strategies that not only aid the occurrence of desirable behavior but also decrease the presence of cues for unwanted behavior. In Chapter 9 we describe and model ways to elicit information about antecedent sources and their effects on behavior by using an interview assessment approach.

Consequences

The consequences of a behavior are events that follow a behavior and exert some influence on the behavior, or are functionally related to the behavior. In other words, not everything that follows a behavior is automatically considered a consequence. For example, suppose you are counseling a woman who tends occasionally to go on drinking binges.

She reports that, after a binge, she feels guilty, regards herself as a bad person, and tends to suffer from insomnia. Although these events are *results* of her binge behavior, they are not consequences unless in some way they directly influence her binges, either by maintaining or by decreasing them. In this case, other events that follow the drinking binges may be the real consequences. For instance, perhaps the client's binges are maintained by the feelings she gets from drinking; perhaps they are temporarily decreased when someone else, such as her partner, notices her behavior and reprimands her for it or refuses to go out with her.

Consequences are categorized as positive or negative. Positive consequences can be referred to technically as *rewards* or *reinforcers;* negative ones can be labeled *punishers.* Like antecedents, the things that function as consequences will always vary with clients. By definition, positive consequences (rewarding events) will maintain or increase the behavior. Positive consequences often maintain or strengthen behavior by positive reinforcement, which involves the presentation of an overt or covert event following the behavior which increases the likelihood that the behavior will occur again in the future. People tend to repeat behaviors that result in pleasurable effects.

People also tend to engage in behaviors that have some payoffs, or value, even if the behavior is very dysfunctional (such payoffs are called *secondary gains*). For example, a client may abuse alcohol and continue to do so even after she loses her job or her family because she likes the feelings she gets after drinking and because the drinking helps her to avoid responsibility. Another client may continue to verbally abuse his wife despite the strain it causes in their relationship because the abusive behavior gives him a feeling of power and control. In these two examples, the behavior is often hard to change, because the immediate consequences make the person feel better in some way. As a result, the behavior is reinforced, even if its delayed or long-term effects are unpleasant. In other words, in these examples, the client "values" the behavior that he or she is trying to eliminate. Often the secondary gain, the payoff derived from a manifest problem, is a cover for more severe issues that are not always readily presented by the client. According to Fishman and Lubetkin (1983), it is important for therapists to be alert to this fact in order to focus on the core issue that, when ameliorated, will generalize to other areas as well. For example, consider a client who is overweight and wants to "lose weight" as her goal for therapy. Yet assessment of this presenting concern reveals that the client's obesity allows her to avoid looking for suitable employment and allows her to live at home with her parents. Successful therapy would need to be targeted not only to the manifest concern (weight and overeating) but also to the core, or underlying, issue that the weight masks—namely, avoidance of assuming responsibility for herself. Part of successful helping would also involve acceptance of her own unique body image in a cultural context that values thinness. Similarly, the client described above who uses alcohol to avoid responsibility will need a treatment program targeted not only toward eliminating alcohol abuse but also toward changing her pattern of avoiding responsibility. As Fishman and Lubetkin note, many cognitive behavior helpers "are too wedded to the 'prima facie' problems that clients bring to therapy. We have observed from our own clinical experience that 'under material' may often be responsible for maintaining the manifest behavior" (1983, p. 27). Clients may not always know why they engage in a behavior. Part of therapy involves making reasons or secondary gains more explicit.

Positive consequences can also maintain behavior by negative reinforcement—removal of an unpleasant event following the behavior, increasing the likelihood that the behavior will occur again. People tend to repeat behaviors that get rid of annoying or painful events or effects. They also use negative reinforcement to establish *avoidance* and *escape* behavior. Avoidance behavior is maintained when an *expected* unpleasant event is removed. For example, staying at home stops agoraphobia fears. Avoidance of public places is maintained by removal of these expected fears. Escape behavior is maintained when a negative (unpleasant) event *already occurring* is removed or terminated. For example, punitive behavior toward a child temporarily stops the child's annoying or aversive behaviors. Termination of the unpleasant child behaviors maintains the parental escape behavior.

Negative consequences weaken or eliminate the behavior. A behavior is typically decreased or weakened (at least temporarily) if it is followed by an unpleasant stimulus or event (punishment), if a positive, or reinforcing, event is removed or terminated (response cost), or if the behavior is no longer followed by reinforcing events (operant extinction). As an example, an overweight man may maintain his eating binges because of the feelings of pleasure he receives from eating (a positive reinforcing consequence). Or his binges could be maintained because they allow him to escape from a boring work situation (negative reinforcing consequence). In contrast, his wife's reprimands or sarcasm or refusal to go out with him may, at least temporarily, reduce his binges (punishing consequence). Although using negative contingencies to modify behavior has many disadvantages, in real-life settings such as home, work, and school, punishment is widely used to influence the behavior of others. Helpers must be alert to the presence of negative consequences in a client's life and its effects on the client. Helpers must also be careful to avoid the use of any verbal or nonverbal behavior that may seem punitive to a client, because such behavior may contribute to unnecessary problems in the therapeutic relationship and subsequent client termination of (escape from) therapy.

Consequences also usually involve more than one source or type of event. Like antecedents, sources of consequences may be *affective, somatic, behavioral, cognitive, contextual,* and/or *relational*. For example, with our client who reports "anxiety," her avoidance of public places and functions is maintained because it results in a reduction of anxious feelings (affective), body tension (somatic), and worry about more autonomy (cognitive). Additional consequences that may help to maintain the problem may include avoidance of being in public (behavioral) and increased attention from family and friends (relational). Contextual consequences may include reinforcement of cultural and gender values of being tied to her family of origin, being the family caregiver, and being able to "stay in the nest."

It would be inaccurate to simply ask about whatever follows the specified behavior and automatically classify it as a consequence without determining its particular effect on the behavior. As Cullen (1983, p. 137) notes, "If variables are supposed to be functionally related to behavior when, in fact, they are not, then manipulation of those variables by the client or therapist will, at best, have no effect on the presenting difficulties or, at worst, create even more difficulties."

Occasionally, students seem to confuse consequences as we present the concept in this chapter with the kinds of consequences that are often the results of a behavior—for example, Julie frequently procrastinates on studying and, as a consequence, receives poor grades. Although poor grades are the result of frequent procrastination, they are not a consequence in the way we are defining it unless the poor grades in some way increase, decrease, or maintain the procrastination behavior. Otherwise, poor grades are simply the result of studying too little. One way to distinguish consequences from mere effects of behavior is to remember a rule of thumb termed "gradient of reinforcement." This term refers to the belief that consequences that occur soon after the behavior are likely to have a stronger impact than consequences that occur after a long time has elapsed (Hull, 1980). Poor grades can be so far removed in time from daily studying (or lack of it) that they are unlikely to exert much influence on the student's daily study behavior.

During the assessment phase of helping, it is important to identify those consequences that maintain, increase, or decrease both desirable and undesirable behaviors related to the client's concern. In the intervention (treatment) phase, this information will help you select change strategies that will maintain and increase desirable behaviors and will weaken and decrease undesirable behaviors such as behavioral excesses and deficits. Information about consequences is also useful in planning treatment approaches that rely directly on the use of consequences to help with behavior change, such as self-reward (see also Chapter 18). In Chapter 9 we describe and model ways to elicit information about consequences with an interview assessment approach.

It is important to reiterate that antecedents, consequences, and components must be assessed and identified for each particular client. Two clients might complain of anxiety or "nerves," and the assessments might reveal very different components of the behavior and different antecedents and consequences. A multicultural focus here is also important; the behaviors, antecedents, and consequences may be affected by the client's cultural affiliations and social–political context. Also remember that there is often some overlap among antecedents, behavior, and consequences. For example, negative self-statements or irrational beliefs might function in some instances as both antecedents and consequences for a given component of the identified concern. Consider a college student who reports depression after situations with less than desired outcomes, such as asking a girl out and being turned down, getting a test back with a B or C on it, and interviewing for a job and not receiving a subsequent offer of employment. Irrational beliefs in the form of perfectionistic standards may function as an antecedent by cuing, or setting off, the resulting feelings of depression—for example, "Here is a solution that didn't turn out the way I wanted. It's awful; now I feel lousy." Irrational beliefs in the form of self-deprecatory thoughts may function as a consequence by maintaining the feelings of depression for some time even after the situation itself is over—for example, "When things don't turn out the way they should, I'm a failure." At the same time, keep in mind this client has rational and coping beliefs as well as irrational ones, and behavioral, environmental, and cultural strengths as well. These may be less obvious to him than the presenting issues, but part of your task is to help him "uncover" what they are. It is also important to note that most issues presented by clients involve both multiple and complex chains of behavior sequences, so an ABC analysis is conducted on more than one factor. We illustrate this later in the chapter in our model case of Joan.

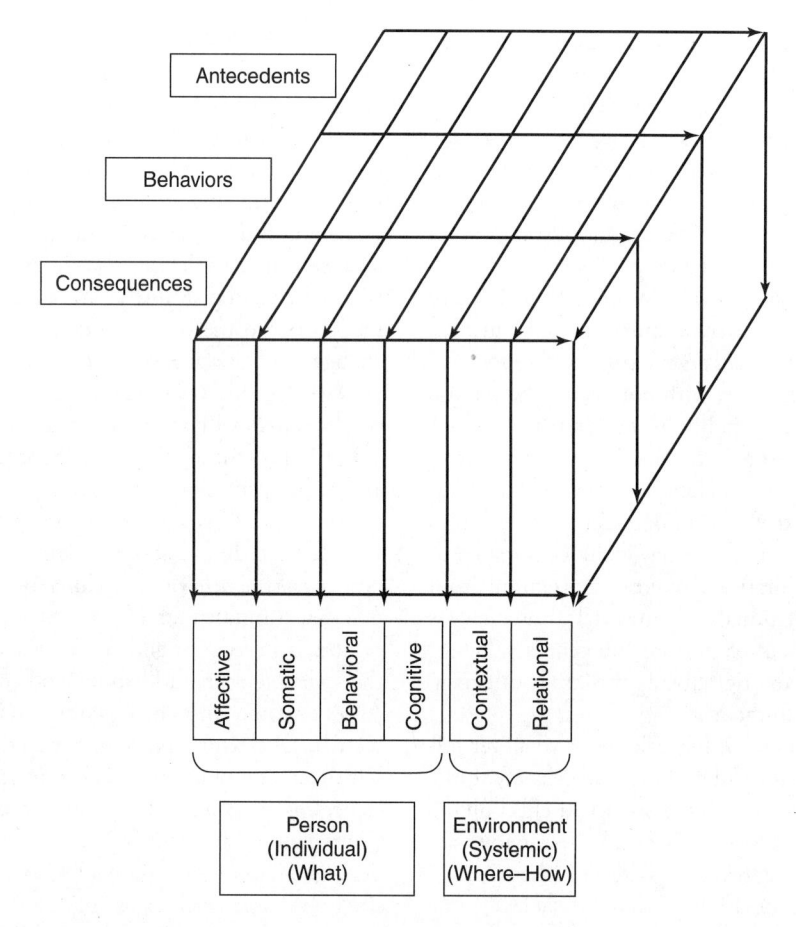

Figure 8.3 ABC and Person-in-Environment Assessment Model

A visual summary of the person-in-environment and ABC models of assessment is depicted in Figure 8.3. We also suggest you work with the material presented in these two models by going through the case presented in Learning Activity 8.1.

DIAGNOSTIC CLASSIFICATION

Our emphasis throughout this chapter is on the need to conduct a thorough and precise assessment with each client to be able to define client issues in very concrete ways. In addition, helpers need to be aware that client behaviors can be organized in some form of diagnostic taxonomy (classification).

The official classification system is found in the American Psychiatric Association's *Diagnostic and Statistical Manual of Mental Disorders,* fourth edition (*DSM-IV,* 1994). The reader is urged to consult the manual as well as the *DSM-IV Casebook* (Spitzer, Gibbon, Skodol, Williams, & First, 1994). Web sites keyed to these *DSM-IV* categories can be found in a handbook by Stamps and Barach (2001). A useful *DSM-IV* resource for child clients has been compiled by Morrison and Anders (1999).

Our interest is simply to summarize the basic diagnostic codes and categories found in *DSM-IV* so that the reader will not be caught off guard if a colleague or supervisor begins talking about "Axis I, II," and so on. Obviously, this short explanation is not a substitute for a thorough study of the *DSM-IV* system.

DSM-IV consists largely of descriptions of various mental and psychological disorders broken down into 17 major diagnostic classes, with additional subcategories within these major categories. Specific diagnostic criteria are provided for

LEARNING ACTIVITY 8.1 Case Conceptualization

Using the case of Mrs. Oliverio, described later in this Learning Activity, complete the following four questions:

1. Based on the case and based on your clinical hunches or hypotheses, list what you think are the major issues for Mrs. Oliverio.
2. Next examine the issues you named—do they reflect something about Mrs Oliverio as an individual, something about Mrs. Oliverio's environment, or both?
3. Using the information in the case description, complete as many of the windows shown in Figure 8.2 as you can. After doing this, what windows seem to be more predominant for Mrs. Oliverio based on what you know from the case description? What pieces of information do you still need to discover about her in order to complete all the windows?
4. Go through the case again. Complete as much of the grid in Figure 8.3 as you can based on the information you have about the client. Discuss your responses with a classmate or your instructor.

The Case of Mrs. Oliverio

Mrs. Oliverio is a 28-year-old married woman who reports that an excessive fear that her husband will die has led her to seek therapy. She further states that because this is her second marriage, it is important for her to work out her problem so that it doesn't ultimately interfere with her relationship with her husband. However, her husband is a sales representative and occasionally has to attend out-of-town meetings. According to Mrs. Oliverio, whenever he has gone away on a trip during the two years of their marriage, she "goes to pieces" and feels "utterly devastated" because of recurring thoughts that he will die and not return. She states that this is a very intense fear and occurs even when he is gone on short trips, such as a half day or a day. She is not aware of any coping thoughts or behaviors she uses at these times. She indicates that she feels great as soon as her husband gets home. She states that this was also a problem for her in her first marriage, which ended in divorce five years ago. She believes the thoughts occur because her father died unexpectedly when she was 11 years old. Whenever her husband tells her he has to leave, or actually does leave, she reexperiences the pain of being told her father has died. She feels plagued with thoughts that her husband will not return and then feels intense anxiety. She is constantly thinking about never seeing her husband again during these anxiety episodes. According to Mrs. Oliverio, her husband has been very supportive and patient and has spent a considerable amount of time trying to reassure her and to convince her, through reasoning, that he will return from a trip. She states that this has not helped her to stop worrying excessively that he will die and not return. She also states that in the past few months her husband has canceled several business trips just to avoid putting her through all this pain.

Mrs. Oliverio also reports that this anxiety has resulted in some insomnia during the past two years. She states that as soon as her husband informs her that he must leave town, she has difficulty going to sleep that evening. When he has to be gone on an overnight trip, she doesn't sleep at all. She simply lies in bed and worries about her husband dying and also feels very frustrated that it is getting later and later and that she is still awake. She reports sleeping fairly well as long as her husband is home and a trip is not impending.

Mrs. Oliverio reports that she feels very satisfied with her present marriage except for some occasional times when she finds herself thinking that her husband does not fulfill all her expectations. She is not sure exactly what her expectations are, but she is aware of feeling anger toward him after this happens. When she gets angry, she just "explodes" and feels as though she lashes out at her husband for no apparent reason. She reports that she doesn't like to explode at her husband like this but feels relieved after it happens. She indicates that her husband continues to be very supportive and protective in spite of her occasional outbursts. She suspects the anger may be her way of getting back at him for going away on a trip and leaving her alone. She also expresses feelings of hurt and anger since her father's death in being unable to find a "father substitute." She also reports feeling intense anger toward her ex-husband after the divorce—anger she still sometimes experiences.

Mrs. Oliverio has no children. She is employed in a responsible position as an administrative assistant and makes $28,500 a year. She reports that she enjoys her work, although she constantly worries that her boss might not be pleased with her and that she could lose her job, even though her work evaluations have been satisfactory. She reports that another event she has been worried about is the health of her brother, who was injured in a car accident this past year. She further reports that she has an excellent relationship with her brother and strong ties to her church.

each category. These criteria are supposed to provide the practitioner with a way to evaluate and classify the client's concerns. The particular evaluation system used by *DSM-IV* is called *multiaxial* because it consists of an assessment on five codes, or *axes:*

Axis I   Clinical disorders and other disorders that may be a focus of clinical attention
Axis II   Personality disorders and mental retardation
Axis III   General medical conditions
Axis IV   Psychosocial and environmental problems
Axis V   Global assessment of functioning

Axis I comprises the clinical disorders as well as any other disorders that the helper decides are an important focus of clinical attention. A new category in the *DSM-IV* also coded on Axis I is that of religious and spiritual problems. These issues are viewed as a phase of life problem rather than a particular clinical disorder (Faiver, Ingersoll, O'Brien, & McNally, 2001). If no clinical disorder is present, Axis I is coded as V71.09. Remember from our earlier discussion on the diagnostic window (Sinacore-Guinn, 1995) that not all clients will have a pathological or clinical disorder. If the clinician suspects there is a clinical disorder but needs more information about the client before deciding conclusively, then Axis I is coded in the interim as 799.9, which means "diagnosis deferred."

Axis II is used for reporting both personality disorders and mental retardation. The contributors to the *DSM-IV* note that these two listings were given a separate axis to help ensure that either condition would not be overlooked. Axis II may also be used to record information about the presence of client defensive mechanisms and maladaptive personality features that are present but not in sufficient strength to warrant a diagnosis of personality disorder. If no diagnosis on Axis II is present, the helper uses the code of V71.09. Axis III is used to note current medical conditions of the client that are relevant to the understanding and/or management of the client's clinical disorders. For example, a client with hypothyroidism may suffer from some sort of depression (coded on Axis I), and the recording of hypothyroidism on Axis III notes the link between the two conditions.

Axis IV is used "for reporting psychosocial and environmental problems that may influence the diagnosis, treatment and prognosis of the mental disorder(s)" reported in Axis I and II (American Psychiatric Association, 1994, p. 29). These include nine general categories relating to negative life events, environmental and familial stresses, and lack of social support (identified by the helper). They are grouped in the following categories:

Issues with primary support group
Issues related to the social environment
Educational issues
Occupational issues
Housing issues
Economic issues
Issues with access to health care services
Issues related to interaction with the legal system/crime
Other psychosocial and environmental issues

Axis V is used to report the helper's assessment of the client's overall level of functioning. This rating is useful in planning treatment and assessing treatment goals. This evaluation is coded on a Global Assessment of Functioning (GAF). The assessment ranges from 0 (inadequate information) to 100 (superior functioning). Descriptions for all other ratings are as follows:

91–100	Superior functioning in a wide range of activities; life's problems never seem to get out of hand
81–90	Absent or minimal symptoms
71–80	Symptoms, if present, are transient and expectable reactions to stressors
61–70	Some mild symptoms
51–60	Moderate symptoms
41–50	Serious symptoms
31–40	Some impairment in reality testing or communication
21–30	Behavior considerably influenced by delusions or hallucinations or serious impairment in communication or judgment
11–20	Some danger of hurting self or others
1–10	Persistent danger of severely hurting self or others

Examples of this multiaxial evaluation system can be found following the analyses of the client cases in this chapter. Box 8.3 describes the 17 major diagnostic categories of *DSM-IV* that are classified on Axis I and Axis II.

Barron (1998) observes that, in spite of apparent conceptual and practical limitations of diagnosis, the process can aid helpers in assessing target behaviors and in selecting appropriate interventions for treatment. For instance, knowledge about selected features of various types of clinical pathology, such as the usual age of the patient at the onset of some disorder or whether the disorder is more common in men or in women, can aid in assessment. A very useful addition to the *DSM-IV* is its routine inclusion of discussions of age, gender, and cultural implications of

BOX 8.3 THE 17 MAJOR *DSM-IV* CLASSIFICATIONS

Disorders usually first diagnosed in infancy, childhood, or adolescence—mental retardation Axis II, learning disorders, motor skills disorders, communication disorders, pervasive developmental disorders, attention-deficit and disruptive behavior disorders, feeding and eating disorders of infancy or early childhood, tic disorders, elimination disorders. Axis I

Delirium, dementia, and amnestic and other cognitive disorders—different types of delirium, dementia, and amnestic disorders. Axis I

Mental disorders due to a general medical condition not elsewhere classified—catatonic disorder and personality change. Axis I

Substance-related disorders—alcohol-related disorders; amphetamine (or amphetaminelike)-related disorders, caffeine-related disorders, cannabis-related disorders, cocaine-related disorders, hallucinogen-related disorders, inhalant-related disorders, nicotine-related disorders, opioid-related disorders, phencyclidine (or phencyclidinelike)-related disorders, sedative-, hypnotic-, or anxiolytic-related disorders, polysubstance-related disorder. Axis I

Schizophrenia and other psychotic disorders—schizophrenia (paranoid, disorganized, catatonic, undifferentiated, or residual types), schizophreniform disorder, schizoaffective disorder, delusional disorder, brief psychotic disorder, shared psychotic disorder due to delusions or hallucinations, substance-induced psychotic disorder. Axis I

Mood disorders—depressive disorders, bipolar disorders. Axis I

Anxiety Disorders—panic disorder without agoraphobia, panic disorder with agoraphobia, agoraphobia without history of panic disorder, specific phobia, social phobia, obsessive-compulsive, posttraumatic stress disorder, acute stress disorder, generalized anxiety disorder. Axis I

Somatoform disorders—somatization disorder, undifferentiated somatoform disorder, conversion disorder, pain disorder, hypochondriasis, body dysmorphic disorder. Axis I

Factitious disorders—with predominantly psychological signs and symptoms, with predominantly physical signs and symptoms, with combined psychological and physical signs and symptoms. Axis I

Dissociative disorders—amnesia, fugue, identity and depersonalization disorders. Axis I

Sexual and gender identity disorders—sexual dysfunctions (due to desire, arousal, orgasmic or pain disorders), sexual dysfunction due to a general medical condition, paraphilias (due to exhibitionism, fetishism, frotteurism, pedophilia, sexual masochism, sexual sadism, transvestic fetishism, voyeurism, or paraphilia), gender identity disorders. Axis I

Eating disorders—anorexia nervosa, bulimia nervosa. Axis I

Sleep disorders—primary sleep disorders (dyssomnias, parasomnias), sleep disorders related to another mental disorder (insomnia, hypersomnia), other sleep disorders. Axis I

Impulse-control disorders not elsewhere classified—intermittent explosive disorder, kleptomania, pyromania, pathological gambling, trichotillomania. Axis I

Adjustment disorders—with depressed mood, with anxiety, with mixed anxiety and depressed mood, with disturbance of conduct, with mixed disturbance of emotions and conduct. Axis I

Personality disorders—paranoid, schizoid, schizotypal, antisocial, borderline, histrionic, narcissistic, avoidant, dependent, obsessive-compulsive. Axis II

Other conditions that may be a focus of clinical attention—psychological factors affecting medical condition, medication-induced movement disorders, other medication-induced disorder. **The following are classified with V codes:** relational issues, issues related to abuse or neglect, additional conditions that may be a focus of clinical attention (noncompliance with treatment, malingering, adult antisocial behavior, child antisocial behavior, borderline intellectual functioning, age-related cognitive decline, bereavement, academic problem, religious or spiritual issue, acculturation issue, phase of life issue, occupational issue, identity issue). Axis I

---

the various disorders. As an example, under panic attacks, it notes that in some cultures a panic attack may involve an intense fear of witchcraft or magic, and under agoraphobia, it reports that in some cultural or ethnic groups the participation of women in public life is restricted (see also Fodor, 1992).

Selected features of *DSM-IV* are useful for suggesting additional information about behaviors and the controlling variables. For example, the operational criteria found in *DSM-IV* often indicate further target behaviors associated with a particular disorder that should be assessed, and the associated features of a disorder often suggest controlling or contributing variables to be assessed. For instance, if a client describes behaviors related to depression, the helper can use the operational criteria for major depressive episodes to ask about other target behaviors related to depression that the client may not mention. Helpers can also be guided by the associated features of this disorder to question the client about possible controlling variables typically associated with the disorder (for depression, events such as life changes, loss of reinforcers, and family history of depression).

Nelson and Barlow (1981) also observe that diagnoses may be useful in suggesting treatments that have been found effective with similar concerns. For example, clients with phobias typically benefit from modeling (see Chapter 12) or from fear-reduction approaches such as systematic desensitization (see Chapter 17) and may also require antianxiety medication. Reports from a Division 12 (APA) task force describe empirically supported treatments for specific diagnostic categories such as desensitization for phobias and cognitive therapy for depression, anxiety, and pain. (We present a further discussion of this subject in Chapter 11.)

LIMITATIONS OF DIAGNOSIS: LABELS AND GENDER/MULTICULTURAL BIASES

Diagnostic classification presents certain limitations, and these are most apparent when a client is given a diagnostic classification without the benefit of a thorough and complete assessment. The most common criticisms of diagnosis are that it places labels on clients, often meaningless ones, and that the labels themselves are not well defined and do not describe what the clients do or don't do that makes them "histrionic" or "a conduct disorder" and so on.

Also, the process of making diagnoses using the current edition of the diagnostic and statistical manual has come under sharp criticism from members of feminist therapy groups, from persons of color, and from those who are advocates for clients of color (Sinacore-Guinn, 1995). For example, feminist therapists assert that the development of clinical disorders in women almost always involves a lack of both real and perceived power in their lives (Brown & Ballou, 1992). These therapists have noted that the concept of "distress," which permeates the traditional diagnostic classification system, reflects a "highly individualized phenomenon" and overlooks distress as "a manifestation of larger social and cultural forces" (Brown, 1992, p. 113). Root (1992) observes that "one of the contributions of the feminist perspective is to depathologize normal behavior" (p. 248). As an example, behavior that may be viewed in the traditional diagnostic classification as "regressive, signs of instability, or impaired traditional functioning, may be viewed from a feminist perspective as healthy strategies for staying alive and sane in dangerous and insane places" (Brown, 1992, p. 113) and as self-preservation behaviors (Root, 1992). Gender bias in the assignment of several different *DSM* disorders has been found in various studies (Becker & Lamb, 1994; Ford & Widiger, 1989). Brown (1992) argues that a feminist perspective of psychopathology must include the pathology of oppression. The theoretical foundations of psychiatry and psychology underpinning traditional diagnosis "have limited contexts and tend to be ahistorical . . . making invisible the experiences of large segments of the population who have been historically oppressed" (Root, 1992, p. 258). In this model, health is defined not just as an absence of distress "but also as the presence of nonoppressive attitudes and relationships toward other humans, animals, and the planet" (Brown, 1992, p. 112). A feminist model of psychopathology and health also examines the existence and the meaning of particular symptom patterns that may emerge with certain cultural groups. As Root (1992) observes, "For many minority groups, the repeated and/or chronic experience of traumatic events makes it difficult for the individual to believe in anything but unique vulnerability"; this sort of vulnerability "is reinforced in persons who are subject to repeated discrimination or threat, such as anti-gay/lesbian violence, racist-motivated violence, anti-Semitic violence, chronic torture experienced by many Southeast Asian refugees, and repeated interpersonal sexual assault and violence" (p. 244).

In addition to the social–political context described above, a feminist view of psychopathology and health also involves an examination of the social–political context surrounding an individual's expressed behavior. As Fodor (1992) notes, in an earlier time and in a different social context, not leaving the house was considered appropriate behavior for women; now this condition has become pathologized as "agoraphobia." Similarly, Ross (1990) observes that hearing voices or seeing ghosts is not viewed as a pathological symptom and a sign of psychosis in those cultures that consider such experiences to be indications of *divine favor*. A feminist conception of diagnosis includes cultural relativity and ascertains what is normal for *this* individual, in *this* particular time and place (Brown, 1992, p. 113). Feminist practitioners would ask a client "What has happened to you?" rather than "What is wrong with you?"

Similar concerns about bias in diagnosis have been raised by cross-cultural researchers and practitioners. Snowden and Cheung (1990) found bias in diagnosis by practitioners when they were diagnosing clients of color. Atkinson and colleagues (1996) found bias by the fact that Euro-American psychologists rated specific *DSM-IV* disorders as more appropriate for an African American female client than did the African American psychologists. They concluded that the differential diagnosis could be based on negative racial bias by white psychologists, positive racial bias by black psychologists, or biases on the parts of both groups of helpers (p. 504). They conclude that helpers must continually examine their rationale for their diagnoses of clients of color (p. 504). Mwaba and Pedersen (1990) found that in many cases, clinicians misinterpret culturally appropriate behaviors as pathological.

Sinacore-Guinn (1995) cautions that within any cultural system, variables such as coping styles have specific meanings. In making gender- and culture-sensitive diagnoses, helpers must also ascertain the cultural meanings of symptoms, behaviors, and presenting issues for each client. As she notes, "Clients may be struggling with a structure within their culture or a conflict between two (or more) cultures of which they are a part. What may be misconstrued as an adjustment disorder may in fact be a cultural conflict in which the client is trying to negotiate and satisfactorily meet the demands of separate cultural systems" (p. 21). Immigration history is another example of a cultural variable that must be understood from the perspective of the client's cultural affiliations. As Sinacore-Guinn (1995) observes, "It is not uncommon in some cultures for children to be raised by a relative while one or both of the parents are establishing themselves, and thus ultimately the family, in a new country. If the counselor does not understand this situation from a cultural perspective, he or she may inappropriately attempt to diagnostically apply a Western notion of abandonment where it does not apply" (p. 22).

Sue (1991) points out that helpers may make two kinds of errors in the assessment process with clients of color. First, they may assume that ethnic differences exist when they do not—or the reverse assumption, that all clients will exhibit the same symptomatology. Sue (1991) recommends that in instances when the helper is unfamiliar with a particular cultural group, the aid of a consultant be sought. Sue and Sue (1999) point out that the history of oppression (described earlier by Brown for women) also affects resulting diagnoses made for clients of color who, because of this history, may be reluctant to self-disclose and, as a result, may be labeled *paranoid*. Sue and Sue (1999), like Brown, argue that diagnosis of clients of color must be understood from a larger social–political perspective. Otherwise, these clients may receive a diagnosis that overlooks the survival value of their behaviors in a racist society.

Itai and McRae (1994) observe that misdiagnoses can easily occur when English is not the primary language of the client. They also note that cultural practices that may seem psychotic to Euro-American practitioners may be typical for some non-Euro-American clients. For example, an older Japanese American woman may say that she speaks with her dead husband. They also caution Euro-American practitioners to be careful about assigning a diagnosis of certain personality disorders to older Japanese American clients. They note, for example, the Asian value of collectivity versus the Euro-American value of self-sufficiency. Because they value interdependence and collectivity, some Asian American clients tend to agree with most other persons, regardless of their own point of view. As Itai and McRae (1994) observe, "These behaviors do not suggest a diagnosis of Dependent Personality Disorder but show differences of cultural emphasis regarding interdependence, respect, and conformity" (p. 376). Bauermeister and others (1990) observe that the same phenomenon may occur in the diagnosis of attention deficit-hyperactivity disorder for some Puerto Rican clients whose behaviors, although similar to some ADHD behaviors, simply reflect a different time and activity orientation, not pathology or overactivity.

In response to these concerns, the contributors to the *DSM-IV* recognize that accurate diagnosis can be challenging "when a clinician from one ethnic or cultural group uses the *DSM-IV* classification to evaluate an individual from a different ethnic or cultural group" (p. xiv). They observe that helpers who are not cognizant of the nuances of a client's cultural frame of reference "may incorrectly judge as psychopathology those normal variations in behavior, belief, or experience that are particular to the individual's culture" (p. ix). In the *DSM-IV*, in addition to very brief discussions of age, gender, and cultural features of many of the clinical disorders, there is an appendix that includes a glossary of 12 "culture-bound" syndromes—that is what the *DSM-IV* (APA, 1994) defines as "localized, folk, diagnostic categories that frame coherent meanings for certain repetitive, patterned, and troubling sets of experiences and observations" (p. 844). Although there is not usually an equivalent found in the *DSM-IV* clinical categories, associated relevant *DSM-IV* categories are also cross-listed with these syndromes. In addition to this glossary, the appendix also includes an outline for a supplemental "cultural formulation" to be used in addition to the multiaxial system. The categories to be included in the helper's cultural formulation include (1) cultural identity/affiliation of the client, (2) any cultural explanations of the client's "illness," (3) cultural factors related to psychosocial environment and levels of functioning,

(4) cultural elements of the relationship between the helper and client, and (5) overall cultural assessment that may affect diagnosis and treatment of the client.

Smart and Smart (1997) conclude that although the *DSM-IV* shows improvement in the area of cultural sensitivity, "work remains to be done" (p. 396). In particular, they recommend an awareness of the threats to cultural sensitivity that arise from "pigeonholing" people from different backgrounds based on a classification system such as the one used in clinical diagnosis (p. 397). They assert that although the *DSM-IV* "reflects a great deal of careful thought and preparation," it is still "biased toward the North American culture in which it has arisen" (p. 397). An excellent compendium for exploring culturally sensitive diagnoses of clinical disorders is Castillo's (1997) book, *Culture and Mental Illness*. We strongly recommend that all practitioners familiarize themselves with this book as a supplement to the more limited cultural material found in the *DSM-IV*.

Despite the apparent disadvantages of diagnosis, many practitioners find themselves in field placement and work settings in which they are required to make a diagnostic classification of client behaviors. Often, even clients request a diagnosis in order to receive reimbursement from their health insurance carrier for payment made for helping services. This situation is becoming more common with the growth of managed care/HMOs (health maintenance organizations). We believe that when the *DSM-IV* system of classification needs to be used, it should be applied within the context of a complete multifactor and multicultural approach and should not be used as a substitute for an idiographic assessment. (See Learning Activity 8.2)

A MODEL CASE

To assist you in conceptualizing client concerns with the models from this chapter, we provide a case illustration followed by two practice cases for you to complete. The conceptual understanding you should acquire from this chapter will help you actually define client issues and contributing variables with an interview assessment, described in Chapter 9. Extensions of this case will be used as illustrations in remaining chapters of the book.

The Case of Joan

Joan is a 15-year-old Euro-American student completing her sophomore year of high school and presently taking a college preparatory curriculum. Her initial statement in the first counseling session is that she is "unhappy" and feels "dissatisfied" with this school experience but feels unable to do anything about it. On further clarification, Joan reveals that she is unhappy because she doesn't think she is measuring up to her classmates and that she dislikes being with these "top" kids in some of her classes, which are very competitive. She reports particular concern in one math class, which she says is composed largely of "guys" who are much smarter than she is. She states that she thinks about the fact that "girls are so dumb in math" rather frequently during the class and she feels intimidated. She reports that as soon as she is in this class, she gets anxious and "withdraws." She states that she sometimes gets anxious just thinking about the class, and when this happens, she gets "butterflies" in her stomach, her palms get sweaty and cold, and her heart beats faster. When asked what she means by "withdrawing," she says she sits by herself, doesn't talk to her classmates, and doesn't volunteer answers or go to the board. Often, when called on, she says nothing. As a result, she reports, her grades are dropping. She also states that her math teacher has spoken to her several times about her behavior and has tried to help her do better. However, Joan's nervousness in the class has resulted in her cutting the class whenever she can find any reason to do so, and she has almost used up her number of excused absences from school. She states that her fear of competitive academic situations has been there since junior high, when her parents started to compare her with other students and put "pressure" on her to do well in school so she could go to college. When asked how they pressure her, she says they constantly talk to her about getting good grades, and whenever she doesn't, they lash out at her and withdraw privileges, like her allowance and going out with her friends. She reports a strong network of girlfriends with whom she "hangs out a lot." She reports that during this year, since the classes are tougher and more competitive, school is more of a problem to her, and she feels increasingly anxious in certain classes, especially math. Joan also states that sometimes she thinks she is almost failing on purpose to get back at her parents for their pressure. Joan reports that all this has made her dissatisfied with school, and she has questioned whether she wants to stay in a college prep curriculum. She has toyed with the idea of going into the military or to culinary school instead of going to college. However, she says she is a very indecisive person and does not know what she should do. In addition, she is afraid to decide this because if she changed her curriculum, her parents' response would be very negative. Joan states that she cannot recall ever having made a decision without her parents' assistance. She feels they have often made decisions for her. She says her parents have never encouraged her to make decisions on her own because they say she might not make the right decision without their help. Joan is an only child. She indicates that she is constantly afraid of making a bad or wrong choice.

Analysis of Case

There are three related but distinct concerns for Joan. Her "presenting" issue is an academic one (note the corresponding diagnosis on the *DSM-IV* Axis I)—she feels anxious about her performance in competitive classes at school, primarily math, and is aware that her grades are dropping in this class. Second, she is generally unsure about her long-term goals and career choice and whether the college prep curriculum she is in is what she wants. (Note the diagnosis of identity problem on Axis I of the *DSM-IV* classification.) She feels indecisive about this particular situation and regards herself as indecisive in many other situations as well. These two concerns are exacerbated by her relationship with her parents. This is coded as a psychosocial and environmental issue on Axis IV of the *DSM-IV* classification. This coding notes the potential influence of this relational situation on the academic and decision-making/identity issues mentioned above. Next, we analyze these two situations according to the ABC model we presented earlier in the chapter.

Analysis of School Issue

1. Relevant Behaviors

Joan's behaviors at school include
   a. Self-defeating labeling of her math class as "competitive" and of herself as "not as smart as the guys."
   b. Sitting alone, not volunteering answers in math class, not answering the teacher's questions or going to the board, and cutting class.

Her self-defeating labels are a covert behavior; her sitting alone, not volunteering answers, and cutting class are overt behaviors.

2. Individual and Environmental Strengths

These include Joan's level of insight about her behavior and the support of her math teacher.

3. Context of Issue

   a. *Antecedent Conditions*

Joan's behaviors at school are elicited by anxiety about certain "competitive" classes, particularly math. Previous antecedent conditions would include verbal comparisons about Joan and her peers made by her parents and verbal pressure for good grades and withholding of privileges for bad grades by her parents. Note that these antecedent conditions do not occur at the same time. The antecedent of the anxiety in the "competitive" class occurs in proximity to Joan's problem behaviors and is a "stimulus event." However, the verbal comparisons and parental pressure began several years ago and probably function as a "setting event."

   b. *Consequences*

Joan's behaviors at school are maintained by
   1. An increased level of attention to her by her math teacher.
   2. Feeling relieved of anxiety through avoidance of the situation that elicits anxiety. By not participating in class and by cutting class, she can avoid putting herself in an anxiety-provoking situation.
   3. Her poorer grades, possibly because of two "payoffs," or secondary gains. First, if her grades get too low, she may not qualify to continue in the college prep curriculum. This would be the "ultimate" way to avoid putting herself in competitive academic situations that elicit anxiety. Second, the lowered grades could also be maintaining her behaviors because she labels the poor grades as a way to "get back at" her parents for their pressure.

Analysis of Decision-Making Issue

1. Relevant Behaviors

Joan's behavior can be described as not making a decision for herself—in this case, about a curriculum change. Depending on the client, issues in making decisions can be either covert or overt. In people who have the skills to make a decision but are blocking themselves because of their "labels" or "internal dialogue" about the decision, the behavior would be designated as covert. A related covert aspect of the decision-making problem may have to do with an underlying cognitive "schema" of impaired autonomy (see Chapter 14). Joan's indecisive behavior seems based on her past learning history of having many decisions either made for her or made with parental assistance. The lack of opportunities she has had to make choices suggests she has not acquired the skills involved in decision making. This would be classified as overt.

2. Individual and Environmental Strengths

Strengths include Joan's awareness of autonomy issues within herself and with her parents. Another strength is her strong social support network of close girlfriends.

LEARNING ACTIVITY 8.2 Assessment Models

To help you in conceptualizing a client's issue from the two models (person-in-environment and ABC), we provide the following two cases. We suggest that you work through the first case completely before going on to the second one. After reading each case, respond to the questions following the case by yourself or with a partner. Then check your responses with the feedback.

The Case of Ms. Weare and Freddie

Ms. Weare and her nine-year-old son, Freddie, have come to Family Services after Ms. Weare said she had reached her limit with her son and needed to talk to another adult about it. Their initial complaint is that they don't get along with each other. Ms. Weare complains that Freddie doesn't get ready himself in the morning, and this makes her mad. Freddie complains that his mother yells and screams at him frequently. Ms. Weare agrees she does, especially when it is time for Freddie to leave for school and he isn't ready yet. Freddie agrees that he doesn't get ready himself and points out that he does this just to "get mom mad." Ms. Weare says this has been going on as long as she can remember. She states that Freddie gets up and usually comes down to breakfast not dressed. After breakfast, Ms. Weare always reminds him to get ready and threatens him that she'll yell or hit him if he doesn't. Freddie usually goes back to his room, where, he reports, he just sits around until his mother comes up. Ms. Weare waits until five minutes before the bus comes and then calls Freddie. After he doesn't come down, she goes upstairs and sees that he's not ready. She reports that she gets very mad and yells "You're dumb. Why do you just sit there? Why can't you dress yourself? You're going to be late for school. Your teacher will blame me, since I'm your mother." She also helps Freddie get ready. So far, he has not been late, but Ms. Weare says she "knows" he will be if she doesn't "nag" him and help him get ready.

When asked about the option of removing her help and letting Freddie get ready on his own, she says he is a smart kid who is doing well in school and that she doesn't want this factor to change. She never finished high school herself, and she doesn't want that to happen to Freddie. She also says that if he didn't have her help, he would probably just stay at home that day, and she wouldn't get any of her own work done. On further questioning, Ms. Weare says this behavior does not occur on weekends, only on school days. She states that as a result of this situation, while she's never punished him physically, she feels very nervous and edgy after Freddie leaves for school, often not doing some necessary work because of this. Asked what she means by "nervous" and "edgy," she reports that her body feels tense and jittery all over. She indicates that this does not help her high blood pressure. She reports that since Freddie's father is not living at home, all the child rearing is on her shoulders. Ms. Weare also states that she doesn't spend much time with Freddie at night after school because she does extra work at home at night, for she and Freddie "don't have much money."

DSM-IV Diagnosis for Ms. Weare

Axis I   V61.20 parent–child relational issue
Axis II V71.09, no diagnosis
Axis III 401.9 (hypertension, essential)
Axis IV None
Axis V GAF = 75 (current)

Respond to these questions. Feedback follows the Learning Activity.

1. What behaviors does Freddie demonstrate in this situation?
2. Is each behavior you have listed overt or covert?
3. What individual and environmental strengths do you see for Freddie?
4. What behaviors does Ms. Weare exhibit in this situation?
5. Is each behavior you have listed overt or covert?
6. What individual and environmental strengths do you see for Ms. Weare?
7. List one or more antecedent conditions that seem to bring about each of Freddie's behaviors.
8. List one or more antecedent conditions that seem to bring about each of Ms. Weare's behaviors.
9. List one or more consequences (including any secondary gains) that influence each of Freddie's behaviors. After each consequence listed, identify how the consequence seems to influence his behavior.
10. List one or more consequences that seem to influence each of Ms. Weare's behaviors. After each consequence listed, identify how the consequence seems to influence her behavior.
11. Identify aspects of the socio–political context that appear to affect Ms. Weare's behavior.

LEARNING ACTIVITY 8.2   Assessment Models

The Case of Mrs. Rodriguez

Mrs. Rodriguez is a 34-year-old Mexican American woman. She was brought to the emergency room by the police after her bizarre behavior in a local supermarket. According to the police report, Mrs. Rodriguez became very aggressive toward another shopper, accusing the man of "following me around and spying on me." When confronted by employees of the store about her charges, she stated "God speaks to me. I can hear His voice guiding me in my mission." On mental-status examination, the counselor initially notes Mrs. Rodriguez's unkempt appearance. She appears unclean. Her clothing is somewhat disheveled. She seems underweight and looks older than her stated age. Her tense posture seems indicative of her anxious state, and she smiles inappropriately throughout the interview. Her speech is loud and fast, and she constantly glances suspiciously around the room. Her affect is labile, fluctuating from anger to euphoria. On occasion, she looks at the ceiling and spontaneously starts talking. When the helper asks to whom she was speaking, she replies, "Can't you hear Him? He's come to save me!" Mrs. Rodriguez is alert and appears to be of average general intelligence. Her attention span is short. She reports no suicidal ideation and denies any past attempts. However, she does express some homicidal feelings for those who "continue to secretly follow me around." When the family members arrive, the helper is able to ascertain that Mrs. Rodriguez has been in psychiatric treatment on and off for the last 10 years. She has been hospitalized several times in the past 10 years during similar episodes of unusual behavior. In addition, she has been treated with several antipsychotic medicines. There is no evidence of organic pathology or any indication of alcohol or drug abuse. Her husband indicates that she recently stopped taking her medicine after the death of her sister and up until then had been functioning adequately during the past year with not much impairment.

DSM-IV Diagnosis for Mrs. Rodriguez

Axis I   295.30, Schizophrenia, Paranoid Type
Axis II V71.09, no diagnosis
Axis III None
Axis IV Issues with primary social support system (recent death of sister)
Axis V   GAF = 25 (current)

Respond to these questions. Feedback follows.

1. List several of the behaviors that Mrs. Rodriguez demonstrates.
2. Is each behavior you have listed overt or covert?
3. List any individual and environmental strengths you observe.
4. List one or more antecedents that seem to elicit Mrs. Rodriguez's behaviors.
5. List one or more consequences that appear to influence the behaviors, including any secondary gains. Describe how each consequence seems to influence the behavior.
6. Identify aspects of the socio–political context that affect her behavior.

---

3. *Context of Issue*

   a. *Antecedent Conditions*

Joan's previous decision-making history is the primary antecedent condition. This consists of (1) having decisions made for her and (2) a lack of opportunities to acquire and use the skills of decision making.

   b. *Consequences*

The consequences that seem to be maintaining her behavior of not deciding include

1. Getting help with her decisions, thereby avoiding the responsibility of making a choice.
2. Anticipation of parental negative reactions (punishment) to her decisions through her self-talk.
3. Absence of positive consequences or lack of encouragement for any efforts at decision making in the past.
4. In the specific decision of a curriculum change, her low grades, which, if they get too bad, may help her avoid making a curriculum decision by automatically disqualifying her from the college prep curriculum.

   c. *Social–Political Context*

This part of the assessment addresses the question of how Joan's presenting issues are a manifestation of the social-political context and structure in which she lives. Joan's concerns appear to be shaped by a context in which she has been reinforced (and punished) for what she does (or doesn't do). This pattern has led to a devaluing and uncertainty of who

FEEDBACK 8.2
Assessment Models

The Case of Ms. Weare and Freddie

1. Freddie's behavior is sitting in his room and not getting ready for school.
2. This is an overt behavior, as it is visible to someone else.
3. Strengths for Freddie include his being smart, doing well in school, and having a mom who believes in him and wants to see him do well academically.
4. Ms. Weare's behaviors are (a) feeling mad and (b) yelling at Freddie.
5. (a) Feeling mad is a covert behavior, as feelings can only be inferred; (b) Yelling is an overt behavior that is visible to someone else.
6. Strengths for Ms. Weare include her decision to seek help and her recognition of not trying to cope with this situation alone anymore.
7. Receiving a verbal reminder and threat from his mother at breakfast elicits Freddie's behavior.
8. Ms. Weare's behavior seems to be cued by a five-minute period before the bus arrives on school days.
9. Two consequences seem to influence Freddie's behavior of not getting ready for school: (a) he gets help in dressing himself, and this influences his behavior by providing special benefits; (b) he gets some satisfaction from seeing that his mother is upset and is attending to him. This seems to maintain his behavior because of the attention he gets from her in these instances. A possible secondary gain is the control he exerts over his mother at these times. According to the case description, he doesn't feel that he gets much attention at other times from his mother.
10. The major consequence that influences Ms. Weare's behavior is that she gets Freddie ready on time and he is not late. This result appears to influence her behavior by helping her avoid being considered a poor mother by herself or someone else and by helping him succeed in school.
11. This parent–child relational issue is undoubtedly affected by the fact that Ms. Weare is raising her son alone and appears to be living in a fairly isolated social climate with little social support. She also is the sole economic provider for Freddie, and her behavior and her child rearing are affected by her lack of financial resources. Overall, she appears to feel disempowered in her ability to handle her parental and financial responsibilities.

The Case of Mrs. Rodriguez

1. There are various behaviors for Mrs. Rodriguez: (a) disheveled appearance, (b) inappropriate affect, (c) delusional beliefs, (d) auditory hallucinations, (e) homicidal ideation, (f) noncompliance with treatment (medicine).
2. Disheveled appearance, inappropriate affect, and noncompliance with treatment are overt behaviors—they are observable by others. Delusions, hallucinations, and homicidal ideation are covert behaviors as long as they are not expressed by the client and therefore not visible to someone else. However, when expressed or demonstrated by the client, they become overt behaviors as well.
3. Strengths include a lack of reported suicide ideation and support and care from her extended family.
4. In this case, Mrs. Rodriguez's behaviors appear to be elicited by the cessation of her medication, which is the major antecedent. Apparently, when she stops taking her medicine, an acute psychotic episode results.
5. This periodic discontinuation of her medicine and the subsequent psychotic reaction may be influenced by the attention she receives from the mental health profession, her family, and even strangers when she behaves in a psychotic, helpless fashion. Additional possible secondary gains include avoidance of responsibility and of being in control.
6. Identify the socio–political context of the issue. In this case it is important to note the potential influence of the cultural–ethnic affiliations of Mrs. Rodriguez. Ideas that may seem delusional in one culture may represent a common belief held by very many persons in another culture. Delusions with a religious thread may be considered a more typical part of religious experience in a particular culture, such as a sign of "divine favor." The skilled helper would take this into consideration in the assessment before settling on a final diagnosis.

she is—and what she wants and needs. She appears to feel powerless in her current environment, partly, we suspect, because of the power her parents have exerted over her; partly because of the power exerted by a school system that emphasizes college-prep values, and partly because of lessons she has learned from her cultural groups about men, women, and achievement. In her math classroom, the gender context plays a big role. She is literally in the gender minority. She compares herself negatively to the boys in the classroom who hold the power, and is shut down by her negative comparison. Brown and Gilligan (1992), Pipher (1994), and others have noted the onset of adolescence as a turning point in girls' lives—especially those of white girls—in which, in order to achieve and to relate, girls seem to lose a sense of their true self and become tentative in their expressiveness and unsure of their identity. Both the overt and covert behaviors we describe in #1 above appear to be tools Joan is using to cope with this loss and sense of powerlessness as well as ways to attempt to increase the power she has and decrease the power held by other sources of authority.

DSM-IV Diagnosis

Axis I	V62.3 academic issue
	313.82 identity issue
Axis II	V71.09, no diagnosis
Axis III	None
Axis IV	Issues with primary support system
Axis V	GAF = 65 (current)

SUMMARY

Assessment is the basis for development of the entire helping program. Assessment has important informational, educational, and motivational functions in therapy. Although the major part of assessment occurs early in the helping process, to some extent assessment, or identification of client concerns, goes on constantly.

An important part of assessment is the helper's ability to conceptualize client concerns. In this chapter we described two models of case or problem conceptualizations: These two models are the person-in-environment model and the ABC model. Conceptualization models help the practitioner think clearly about the complexity of client issues.

The models of assessment described in this chapter are based on several assumptions, including these:
1. Most behavior is learned, although some psychological issues may have organic (biological) causes.
2. Causes of issues are multidimensional.
3. Issues need to be viewed operationally, or concretely.
4. Issues occur in a social and cultural context and are affected by internal and external antecedents that are functionally related to or exert influence in various ways.
5. Components of the issue as well as sources of antecedents and consequences can be affective, somatic, behavioral, cognitive, contextual, and relational.
6. In addition to assessment of client issues, a focus on clients' individual and environmental resources and strengths is also important.

Another part of assessment may involve a multiaxial diagnosis of the client. Current diagnosis is based on the *Diagnostic and Statistical Manual,* fourth edition, and involves classifying the disorders, medical conditions, and psychosocial and environmental issues, and making a global assessment of current functioning. Diagnosis can be a useful part of assessment. For example, knowledge about selected features of various types of clinical syndromes can add to understanding of a client's concern. However, diagnosis is not an adequate *substitute* for other assessment approaches and is not an effective basis for specifying goals and selecting intervention strategies unless it is part of a comprehensive treatment approach in which issues are identified in a concrete, or operational, manner for each client. Research has shown that both assessment and diagnosis are subject to gender and cultural bias. The skilled practitioner conducts a multidimensional assessment process that includes an awareness of the current and historical sociopolitical context in which the client lives and also the client's gender and cultural referent groups.

INFOTRAC® EXPLORATIONS

1. Search for *behavioral assessment,* and see what you can find about doing a CBT assessment. Share the results of your search with your class.
2. Search for articles on *psychological diagnosis,* and see what articles you can find that discuss the variations, effects, and implications of diagnosis.

SUGGESTED RESOURCES

Readings

Berg-Cross, L., & Chinen, R. (1995). Multicultural training models and the person-in-culture interview. In J.

Ponterotto, J. Casas, L. Suzuki, & C. Alexander (Eds.), *Handbook of multicultural counseling* (pp. 333–356). Thousand Oaks, CA: Sage.

Canino, I., & Spurlock, J. (2000). *Culturally diverse children and adolescents: Assessment, diagnosis, and treatment* (2nd ed.). New York: Guilford.

Cuéllar, I., & Paniagua, F. (Eds.). (2000). *Handbook of multicultural mental health: Assessment and treatment of diverse populations.* San Diego, CA: Academic.

Edelstein, B., Drozdick, L., & Kogan, J. (1998). Assessment of older adults. In A. Bellack & M. Hersen (Eds.), *Behavioral assessment* (pp. 378–406). Needham Heights, MA: Allyn & Bacon.

Hays, P. (2001). *Addressing cultural complexities in practice.* Washington, DC: American Psychological Association.

Hepworth, D., Rooney, R., & Larsen, J. (2002). *Direct social work practice* (6th ed.). Pacific Grove, CA: Brooks/Cole.

Kemp, S., Whittaker, J., & Tracy, E. (1997). *Person–environment practice: The social ecology of interpersonal helping.* New York: Aldine de Gruyter.

Mitchell, R. W. (2000). *Documentation in counseling records.* Washington, DC: American Counseling Association.

Morrison, J. (1995). *The first interview: A guide for clinicians.* New York: Guilford.

Morrison, J., & Anders, T. (1999). *Interviewing children and adolescents.* New York: Guilford.

Okun, B., Fried, J., & Okun, M. (1999). *Understanding diversity.* Pacific Grove, CA: Brooks/Cole.

Pedersen, P. B., & Ivey, A. (1993). *Culture-centered counseling and interviewing skills.* New York: Praeger.

Sarwer, D., & Sayers, S. (1998). Behavioral interviewing. In A. Bellack & M. Hersen (Eds.), *Behavioral assessment* (pp. 63–78). Needham Heights, MA: Allyn & Bacon.

Sommers-Flanagan, J. & Sommers-Flanagan, R. (in press). *Clinical Interviewing* (3rd ed.). New York: Wiley.

Tracey, E. M., & Whittaker, J. K. (1990). The social network map: Assessing social support in clinical social work practice. *Families in Society, 71,* 461–470.

Web Sites

A Guide to Psychology and Its Practice—Diagnosis in Clinical Psychology
http://members.aol.com/avpsyrich/diagnos.htm

Centre for Multimodal Therapy
http://members.tripod.co.uk/Stress_Centre/index.html.htm

DSM-REPORT
http://www.psychreport.com

Functional Behavioral Assessment and Behavioral Intervention Plans
http://www.naswdc.org/sections/SSW/schclark.htm

8 POSTEVALUATION

Read the case descriptions of Mr. Huang and of Mr. Robinson that follow, and then answer the following questions:

1. What are the client's behaviors?
2. Are the behaviors overt or covert?
3. What are the client's individual and environmental strengths?
4. What are the antecedent conditions of the client's concern?
5. What are the consequences of the behaviors? Secondary gains?
6. In what way do the consequences influence the behaviors?
7. In what ways are the behaviors manifestations of the social–political context?

Answers to these questions are provided in the Feedback section that follows the Postevaluation.

The Case of Mr. Huang

A 69-year-old Asian American man, Mr. Huang, came to counseling because he felt his performance on his job was "slipping." Mr. Huang had a job in a large automobile company. He was responsible for producing new car designs. Mr. Huang revealed that he noticed he had started having trouble about six months before, when the personnel director came in to ask him to fill out retirement papers. Mr. Huang, at the time he sought help, was due to retire in nine months. (The company's policy made it mandatory to retire at age 70.) Until this incident with the personnel director and the completion of the papers, Mr. Huang reported, everything seemed to be "OK." He also reported that nothing seemed to be changed in his relationship with his family. However, on some days at work, he reported having a great deal of trouble completing any work on his car designs. When asked what he did instead of working on designs, he said "Worrying." The "worrying" turned out to mean that he was engaging in constant repetitive thoughts about his approaching retirement, such as "I won't be here when this car comes out" and "What will I be without having this job?" Mr. Huang stated that there were times when he spent almost an entire morning or afternoon "dwelling" on these things and that this seemed to occur mostly when he was alone in his office actually working on a car design. As a result, he was not turning in his designs by the specified deadlines. Not meeting his deadlines made him feel more worried. He was especially concerned that he would "bring shame both to his company and to his family who had always been proud of his work record." He was afraid that his present behavior would jeopardize the opinion others had of him, although he didn't report any other possible "costs" to him. In fact, Mr. Huang said that it was his immediate boss who had suggested, after several talks and lunches, that he use the employee assistance program. Mr. Huang said that his boss had not had any noticeable reactions to his missing deadlines, other than reminding him and being solicitous, as evidenced in the talks and lunches. Mr. Huang reported that he enjoyed this interaction with his boss and often wished he could ask his boss to go out to lunch with him. However, he stated that these meetings had all been at his boss's request. Mr. Huang felt somewhat hesitant about making the request himself. In the last six months, Mr. Huang had never received any sort of reprimand for missing deadlines on his drawings. Still, he was concerned with maintaining his own sense of pride about his work, which he felt might be jeopardized since he'd been having this trouble.

DSM-IV Diagnosis

Axis I   309.24, Adjustment disorder with anxiety
Axis II V71.09, no diagnosis
Axis III None
Axis IV Issues related to the social environment: adjustment to life cycle transition of retirement.
Axis V   GAF = 75 (current)

The Case of Mr. Robinson

This is a complicated case with three presenting issues: (1) work, (2) sexual, and (3) alcohol. We suggest that you complete the analysis of Questions 1–6 listed at the beginning of this postevaluation separately for each of these three concerns. Question 7 can be completed at the end of the third issue.

Mr. Robinson, a 30-year-old African American business manager, has been employed by the same large corporation for two years, since his completion of graduate school. During the first session, he reports a chronic feeling of "depression" with his present job. In addition, he mentions a recent loss of interest and pleasure in sexual activity, which he describes as "frustrating." He also relates a dramatic increase in his use of alcohol as a remedy for the current difficulties he is experiencing.

(continued)

8 POST EVALUATION

(continued)

Mr. Robinson has never before been in counseling and admits to feeling "slightly anxious" about this new endeavor. He appears to be having trouble concentrating when asked a question. He traces the beginning of this to the completion of his master's degree a little over two years ago. At that time, he states, "Everything was fine." He was working part time during the day for a local firm and attending college during the evenings. He had been dating the same woman for a year and a half and reports a great deal of satisfaction in their relationship. Drinking occurred infrequently, usually only during social occasions or a quiet evening alone. On completion of his degree, Mr. Robinson relates, "Things changed. I guess maybe I expected too much too soon." He quit his job in the expectation of finding employment with a larger company. At first there were few offers, and he was beginning to wonder whether he had made a mistake. After several interviews, he was finally offered a job with a business firm that specialized in computer technology, an area in which he was intensely interested. He accepted and was immediately placed in a managerial position. Initially, he was comfortable and felt confident in his new occupation; however, as the weeks and months passed, the competitive nature of the job began to wear him down although he still loves working with computers. He relates that he began to doubt his abilities as a supervisor and began to tell himself that he wasn't as good as the other executives. He began to notice that he was given fewer responsibilities than the other bosses, as well as fewer employees to oversee. He slowly withdrew socially from his colleagues, refusing all social invitations. He states that he began staying awake at night obsessing about what he might be doing wrong. Of course, this lack of sleep decreased his energy level even further and produced a chronic tiredness and lessening of effectiveness and productivity at work. At the same time, his relationship with his girlfriend began to deteriorate slowly. He relates that "She didn't understand what I was going through." Her insistence that his sexual performance was not satisfying her made him even more apprehensive and lowered his self-esteem even further. After a time, his inhibition of sexual desire resulted in inconsistency in maintaining an erection throughout the sexual act. He then saw a doctor, who said nothing was physically wrong and suggested he talk to someone about the erectile problem. This resulted in an even greater strain on their relationship, so she threatened to "call it quits" if he did not seek treatment for his "problem." He reports that it was at this time that he began to drink more heavily. At first, it was just a few beers at home alone after a day at the office. Gradually, he began to drink during lunch, even though, he states, "I could have stopped if I had wanted to." However, his repeated efforts to reduce his excessive drinking by "going on the wagon" met with little success. He began to need a drink every day in order to function adequately. He was losing days at work, was becoming more argumentative with his friends, and had been involved in several minor traffic accidents. He states he has never abused alcohol before, although his grandfather, who helped raise him, was a recovering alcoholic when he was in his later years. Mr. Robinson has gone to a couple of Al Anon meetings. He points out that he has never felt this low before in his life. He reports feeling very pessimistic about his future and doesn't see any way out of his current difficulties. He's fearful that he might make the wrong decisions, and that's why he's come to see a helper at this time in his life.

DSM-IV Diagnosis

Axis I 305.00 Alcohol abuse
        302.72 Male erectile disorder
        311.00 depressive disorder NOS (not otherwise specified)
Axis II V71.09, no diagnosis
Axis III None
Axis IV Issues with primary social support system and occupational problems
Axis V GAF = 55 (current)

POST EVALUATION FEEDBACK

The Case of Mr. Huang

1. Mr. Huang's self-reported behaviors include worry about retirement and not doing work on his automobile designs.
2. Worrying about retirement is a covert behavior. Not doing work on designs is an overt behavior.
3. Individual and environmental strengths include his prior job success and the support of his boss and family.
4. One antecedent condition occurred six months ago, when the personnel director conferred with Mr. Huang about retirement, and papers were filled out. This is an overt antecedent in the form of a setting event. The personnel director's visit seemed to elicit Mr. Huang's worry about retirement and his not doing his designs. A covert antecedent is Mr. Huang's repetitive thoughts about retirement, getting older, and so on. This is a stimulus event.
5. The consequences include Mr. Huang's being excused from meeting his deadlines and receiving extra attention from his boss.
6. Mr. Huang's behaviors appear to be maintained by the consequence of being excused from not meeting his deadlines, with only a "reminder." He is receiving some extra attention and concern from his boss, whom he values highly. He may also be missing deadlines and therefore not completing required car designs as a way to avoid or postpone retirement; that is, he may expect that if his designs aren't done, he'll be asked to stay longer until they are completed.
7. The anxiety that Mr. Huang is experiencing surrounding the transition from full-time employment to retirement is a fairly universal reaction to a major life change event. However, in addition to this, Mr. Huang is also affected by his cultural/ethnic affiliation in that he is concerned about maintaining pride and honor, not losing face or shaming the two groups he belongs to—his family and his company. This recognition is an important part of the assessment because it will also be a focus in the intervention phase.

The Case of Mr. Robinson: Analysis of Work Issue

1. Mr. Robinson's behaviors at work include (a) overemphasis on the rivalry that he assumes exists with his fellow administrators and resulting self-doubts about his competence compared with that of his peers and (b) missing days at work because of his feelings of depression as well as his alcohol abuse.
2. His discrediting of his skills is a covert behavior, as is much of his current dejection. Avoiding his job is an overt behavior.
3. Individual and environmental strengths include the fact that he still likes working with computers—and that he still has his job.
4. The antecedent conditions of Mr. Robinson's difficulties at work are his apparent perceptions surrounding the competitiveness with his co-workers. These perceptions constitute a stimulus event. This apprehension has led him to feel inadequate and fosters his depressive symptomatology. It should be recognized that his occupational concerns arose only after he obtained his present job, one that requires more responsibility than any of his previous positions. Acquisition of this job and its accompanying managerial position is a setting event.
5. The consequences that maintain his difficulties at work are (a) failing to show up for work each day and (b) alcohol abuse.
6. Failing to show up for work each day amounts to a variable-interval schedule of reinforcement, which is quite powerful in maintaining his evasion of the workplace. A possible secondary gain of his absenteeism is the resulting decrease in his feelings of incompetence and depression. His abuse of alcohol provides him with a ready-made excuse to miss work whenever necessary or whenever he feels too depressed to go. It should be noted that alcohol as a drug is a central nervous system depressant as well. Alcohol abuse is also a common complication of depressive episodes.

Analysis of Sexual Issue

1. His behavior in the sexual area is an apparent loss of interest in or desire for sexual activity, which is a significant change from his previous behavior. His feelings of excitement have been inhibited so that he is unable to attain or maintain an erection throughout the sexual act.
2. The inability to achieve and/or sustain an erection is an overt behavior. We may also assume that whatever he is telling himself is somehow influencing his observable behavior. His self-talk is a covert behavior.

(continued)

POST EVALUATION FEEDBACK

(continued)

3. Individual and environmental strengths include the fact that he saw a doctor and that nothing was wrong physically to produce the sexual dysfunction.
4. There are apparently no organic contributing factors. Therefore, it appears likely that the antecedent conditions of Mr. Robinson's current sexual problem are the anxiety and depression associated with the work situation.
5. The consequences maintaining his sexual problem appear to be (a) the lack of reassurance from his girlfriend and (b) his current alcohol abuse. The girlfriend's ultimatum that he begin to regain his normal sexual functioning is creating psychological stress that will continue to prevent adequate sexual response. Although alcohol may serve as a relaxant, it also acts to physiologically depress the usual sexual response.

Analysis of Alcohol Issue

1. Relevant behavior is frequent consumption of alcoholic beverages during the day as well as at night.
2. Although alcohol abuse is certainly an overt behavior, we might also assume that Mr. Robinson is engaging in some self-defeating covert behaviors to sustain his alcohol abuse.
3. Individual and environmental strengths include his reporting of no prior history of substance abuse, his reported familiarity with Al Anon and 12-step programs, and, most importantly, the fact that he recognizes he has an alcohol issue and is seeking help.
4. It is quite apparent that Mr. Robinson's maladaptive use of alcohol occurred only after his difficulties with his job became overwhelming. It also appears to be linked to the onset of his sexual disorder. There is no history of previous abuse of alcohol or other drugs.
5. Consequences include the payoffs of avoidance of tension, responsibility, and depression related to his job as well as possible increased attention from others.
6. By abusing alcohol, Mr. Robinson has been missing days at work and thus avoids the tension he feels with his job. Alcohol abuse is serving as a negative reinforcer. Moreover, his use of alcohol, which is a depressant, allows him to maintain his self-discrediting behavior, which, owing to the attention he derives from this, may also be maintaining the alcohol abuse. Finally, alcohol may also provide a ready-made excuse for his poor sexual functioning with his girlfriend.
7. His issues appear to be affected by the socio–political climate in which he works, his particular life stage of development, and also probably by the history of oppression he has undoubtedly experienced as an African American male. Mr. Robinson made a fairly rapid transition from being a student and working part time to being a manager in a competitive firm. This progress occurred at a time in which he was also concerned developmentally with issues of identity and intimacy. The difficulties he has encountered have challenged both his concept of himself and his intimate relationship with his girlfriend. Although his firm is competitive, his own sense of vulnerability and his mistrust of himself and of his colleagues have no doubt been affected by his societal experiences of discrimination and oppression. (It is important to recognize that any cultural suspiciousness he feels has been for him an adaptive and healthy mechanism of coping with a host culture different from his own.)

His increasing use of alcohol to self-medicate has further exacerbated both his work functioning and his sexual relationship with his girlfriend. His girlfriend appears to be responding to him with threats and intimidation, perhaps in an attempt to control or gain power in the relationship. Indeed, their relationship appears to lack a power base that is shared equally between both partners.

CHAPTER 9

CONDUCTING AN INTERVIEW ASSESSMENT WITH CLIENTS

OBJECTIVES

1. Given a written description of a selected client, outline in writing at least 2 questions for each of the 11 assessment categories that you would ask during an assessment interview with this person.
2. In a 30-minute role-play interview, demonstrate leads and responses associated with 9 out of 11 categories for assessing the client. An observer can rate you, or you can rate your performance from a tape, using the Assessment Interview Checklist at the end of the chapter. After the interview, identify orally or in writing some hypotheses about antecedent sources that cue the issue, consequences that maintain it, secondary gains, or "payoffs," and client and environmental strengths and resources that might be used during intervention.
3. Given a written client case description, construct in writing a self-monitoring assessment plan for the client and an example of a log to use for self-recording the data.
4. Given a role-play interview, help the client complete a social network map and an ecomap.

In Chapter 8 we described a number of important functions of assessment in the helping process and noted that assessment is a way of identifying and defining a client's concerns in order to make decisions about therapeutic treatment. A variety of tools or methods are available to the practitioner that can help identify and define the range and parameters of client issues. These methods include standardized tests, such as interest and personality inventories; psychophysiological assessment, such as monitoring of muscle tension for chronic headaches with an electromyograph (EMG) machine; self-report checklists, such as assertiveness scales or anxiety inventories; observation by others, including observation by the helper or by a significant person in the client's environment; self-observation, in which the client observes and records some aspect of the issue; imagery, in which the client uses fantasy and directed imagery to vicariously experience some aspect of the issue; role playing, in which the client may demonstrate some part of the issue in an in vivo yet simulated enactment; and direct interviewing, in which the client and helper identify concerns through verbal and nonverbal exchanges. All these methods are also used to evaluate client progress during the helping process, in addition to their use in assessment for the purpose of collecting information about clients. In this chapter we concentrate on direct interviewing, not only because it is the focus of the book but also because it is the one method readily available to all helpers without additional cost in time or money. However, we will also mention ancillary use of some of the other methods of assessment named above. In actual practice, it is very important not to rely solely on the interview for assessment data but to use several methods of obtaining information about clients.

DIRECT ASSESSMENT INTERVIEWING

According to cognitive–behavioral literature, the interview is the most common behavioral assessment instrument (Nelson, 1983). As Sarwer and Sayers point out,

> The behavioral interview is the foundation of the behavioral assessment process. Despite the technological advances in behavioral assessment such as observational coding and analysis, the interview is still the most essential step in examining the reasons for and planning the treatment of patients' difficulties. It is still guided by the need for a clinician to start from the patient's complaints and discover the relations between the person's environment and his or her individual responses to it. (1998, p. 63)

Despite the overwhelming evidence confirming the popularity of the interview as an assessment tool, some persons believe it is the most difficult assessment approach for the helper to enact. Successful assessment interviews require specific guidelines and training in order to obtain accurate and valid information from clients that will make a difference in treatment planning (Duley, Cancelli, Kratochwill, Bergan, & Meredith, 1983; Edelstein & Semenchuk, 1996).

In this chapter we describe a structure and some guidelines to apply in assessment interviews in order to identify and define client issues. This chapter and other chapters in this book describe interview leads that in applied settings are likely to elicit certain kinds of client information. However, as Sarwer and Sayers (1988) observe, little research on the effects of interview procedures has been conducted. The leads suggested in this chapter are supported more by practical considerations than by empirical data. As a result, you will need to be very attentive to the effects of using these questions with each client. Edelstein and colleagues (1998) note that since the clinical assessment interview relies on client self-report, its accuracy and reliability are very much dependent on the accuracy and veracity of what the client says to the clinician (p. 383).

INTAKE INTERVIEWS AND HISTORY

Part of assessment involves eliciting information about the client's background, especially as it may relate to *current* concerns. Past, or historical, information is not sought as an end in itself or because the helper is necessarily interested in exploring or focusing on the client's "past" during treatment. Rather, it is used as a part of the overall assessment process that helps the practitioner fit the pieces of the puzzle together concerning the client's presenting issues and current life context. Often a client's current issues are precipitated and maintained by events found in the client's history. In no case is this more valid than with clients who have suffered trauma of one kind or another. For example, a 37-year-old woman came to a crisis center because of sudden onset of extreme anxiety. The interviewer noticed that she was talking in a "little girl" voice and was using gestures that appeared to be very childlike. The clinician commented on this and asked the client how old she felt right now. The client replied, "I'm seven years old," and went on to reveal spontaneously an incident in which she had walked into a room in an aunt's house and found her uncle fondling her cousin. No one had seen her, and she had forgotten this until the present time. In cases such as this one, history may serve as a retrospective baseline measure for the client and may help to identify cognitive or historical antecedent conditions that still exert influence on the current issue and might otherwise be overlooked. With elderly clients who show symptoms of mood fluctuations and forgetfulness, interviewing a caregiver about historical events may be especially important (Sloane and Gleason, 1999).

The process of gathering this type of information is called "history taking." In many agency settings, history taking occurs during an initial interview called an "intake interview." An intake interview is viewed as informational rather than therapeutic and, to underscore this point, is often conducted by someone other than the practitioner assigned to see the client. In these situations, someone else, such as an intake worker, sees the client for an interview, summarizes the information in writing, and passes the information along to the helper.

In managed care and some state and federally funded mental health programs, intakes are often required before reimbursement for services is given. Sometimes these mandated intake interviews come with a lengthy standardized format that the practitioner must complete with the client in its entirety.

An example of a computer-assisted intake interview is the "computerized assessment system for psychotherapy evaluation and research," called CASPER (Farrell & McCullough-Vaillant, 1996). In this system, 122 intake interview questions appear on a computer screen covering a wide range (18) of content areas. Once the client identifies certain areas of concern he or she then rates the severity and duration of each concern, as well as the extent to which the client wants to focus on a concern in treatment.

In other places, the helpers conduct their own intakes. For helpers who work either in private practice or in a school or agency in which intakes are not required, it is still a good idea to do some history taking with the client. A number of specific interview protocols for areas such as affective disorders, substance abuse, eating disorders, and attention deficit disorders are reported in Rogers' (2001) book on diagnostic and structured interviewing. A semi-structured intake and assessment protocol for child and adolescent clients is the CAFAS—Child and Adolescent Functional Assessment Scale—developed by Hodges (1997). An advantage of this interview protocol is that it assesses for strengths and goals as well as problems in performance in school, work, home, community, behavior toward others, moods, self-harm, substance use, and thinking. Other examples of interview protocols for child and adolescent clients are found in Morrison and Anders (1999). Edelstein and Semenchuk (1996) provide examples of interview protocols suitable for older adults.

Various kinds of information can be solicited during history taking, but the most important areas are the following:
1. Identifying information about the client
2. General appearance and demeanor
3. History related to the presenting concerns
4. Past psychiatric and/or counseling history
5. Educational and job history
6. Health (medical) history
7. Social/developmental history (including religious and cultural background and affiliations, predominant values, description of past problems, chronological/developmental events, military background, social/leisure activities, present social situation)
8. Family, marital, sexual history
9. Assessment of client communication patterns
10. Results of mental status; diagnostic summary

Box 9.1 presents specific questions or content areas to cover for each of these ten areas.

The sequence of obtaining this information in a history or intake interview is important. Generally, the interviewer begins with the least threatening topics and saves more sensitive topics (such as VI, VII, and VIII) until near the end of the session, when a greater degree of rapport has been established and the client feels more at ease about revealing personal information to a total stranger.

Not all of this information may be required for all clients. Obviously, this guide will have to be adapted for use with different clients—especially those of varying ages, such as children, adolescents, and the elderly, who may need a simpler way to provide such information and in a shorter amount of time.

Handling Sensitive Subjects in the Interview Assessment Process

Morrison (1995) has pointed out that some important subjects that come up in intake and assessment interviews can be sensitive for both helpers and clients. Yet this potential sensitivity does not mean that such subjects should be overlooked or discarded. However, it does mean that the helper should proceed with good judgment and seek consultation about when it is appropriate to assess these areas. For example, as one of our reviewers so aptly observed, it may be regarded as voyeuristic if a male counselor asks a young female presenting with an academic/career issue about her sexual practices and activity. On the other hand, if a client comes in and discusses problems in dating persons of the opposite sex and feelings of attraction to same-sex people, not pursuing this is an important omission.

Specific subjects that may fall into the category of sensitive topics include questions about (1) *suicidal thoughts and behavior;* (2) *homicidal ideas and violent behavior;* (3) *substance use,* including alcohol, street drugs, and prescribed medications; (4) *sexual issues,* including sexual orientation, sexual practices, and sexual problems; and (5) *physical, emotional, and sexual abuse,* both historic and current. As it is beyond the scope of this book to provide you with the specific information necessary to assess these five areas in an interview, we refer you to Morrison's (1995) excellent guide.

MENTAL-STATUS EXAMINATION

If, after conducting an initial interview, you are in doubt about the client's psychiatric status or suspicious about the possibility of an organic brain disorder, you may wish to conduct (or refer the client for) a mental-status examination. According to Kaplan and Sadock (1998), the mental-status exam is one that classifies and describes the areas and components of mental functioning involved in making diagnostic impressions and classifications. The major categories covered in a mental-status exam are general description and appearance of the client; mood and affect; perception; thought processes; level of consciousness; orientation to time, place, and people; memory; and impulse control. Additionally, the examiner may note the degree to which the client appeared to report the information accurately and reliably. Of these categories, disturbances in consciousness (which involves ability to perform mental tasks, degree of effort, degree of fluency/hesitation in task performance) and orientation (whether or not clients know when, where, and who they are and who other people are) are usually indicative of organic brain impairment or disorders and require neurological assessment and follow-up as well. Examples of specific mental status exams for the elderly are given in Hill, Thorn, and Packard (2000), and examples of ones for child and adolescent clients can be found in Morrison and Anders's (1999) excellent guide.

It is important for practitioners to know enough about the functions and content of a mental-status exam to refer those clients who might benefit from this additional assessment procedure. A summary of the content of a brief mental-status exam is given in Box 9.2. For additional information about mental-status examinations and neurophysiological assessment, see Kaplan and Sadock (1998) and Morrison (1995).

BOX 9.1 HISTORY-TAKING INTERVIEW CONTENT

1. *Identifying information* Client's name, address, home, and work telephone numbers; name of another person to contact in case of emergency.

    Age
    Gender
    Culture
    Ethnicity and indigenous heritage
    Race
    Languages
    Disabilities
    Marital status
    Occupation
    Citizenship status

2. *General appearance*
Approximate height
Approximate weight
Brief description of client's dress, grooming, overall demeanor

3. *Presenting concerns* (do for each concern that client presents)
Note the presenting concern (quote client directly):
When did it start? What other events were occurring at that time?
How often does it occur?
What are thoughts, feelings, and observable behaviors associated with it?
Where and when does it occur most? Least?
Are there any events or persons that precipitate it? Make it better? Make it worse?
How much does it interfere with the client's daily functioning?
What previous solutions/plans have been tried and with what result?
What made the client decide to seek help at this time (or, if referred, what influenced the referring party to refer the client at this time)?

4. *Past psychiatric/counseling history* Previous counseling and/or psychological/psychiatric treatment.
Type of treatment
Length of treatment
Treatment place or person
Presenting concern
Outcome of treatment and reason for termination
Previous hospitalization
Prescription drugs for emotional/psychological issues

5. *Educational/job history* Trace academic progress (strengths and weaknesses) from grade school through last level of education completed
Relationships with teachers and peers
Types of jobs held by client and socioeconomic history, current status
Length of jobs
Reason for termination or change
Relationships with co-workers
Aspects of work that are most stressful or anxiety-producing
Aspects of work that are least stressful or most enjoyable
Overall degree of current job satisfaction

6. *Health/medical history* Childhood diseases, prior significant illnesses, previous surgeries
Current health-related complaints or illnesses (for example, headache, hypertension)
Treatment received for current complaints: what type and by whom
Date of last physical examination and results
Significant health problems in client's family of origin (parents, grandparents, siblings)
Client's sleep patterns
Client's appetite level
Current medications (including such things as aspirin, vitamins, birth control pills, recreational substance use)
Drug and nondrug allergies
Disability history
Client's typical daily diet, including caffeine-containing beverages/food; alcoholic beverages
Exercise patterns

7. *Social/developmental history* Current life situation (typical day/week, living arrangements, occupation and economic situation, contact with other people)
Social/leisure time activities, hobbies
Religious affiliation—Childhood and current
Spiritual beliefs and concerns
Contacts with people (support systems, family, friends)
Community and cultural affiliations
Military background/history
Significant events reported for the following developmental periods:
Preschool (0–6 years)
Childhood (6–13 years)
Adolescence (13–21 years)
Young adulthood (21–30 years)
Middle adulthood (30–65 years)
Late adulthood (65 years and over)

8. *Family, marital, sexual history* Presence of physical, sexual, and/or emotional abuse from parent, sibling, or other
How well parents got along with each other

> **BOX 9.1 HISTORY-TAKING INTERVIEW CONTENT** *CONTINUED*
>
> Identifying information for client's siblings (including those older and younger and client's birth order, or position in family)
> Which sibling was most favored by mother? Father? Least favored by mother? Father?
> Which sibling did client get along with best? Worst?
> History of previous psychiatric illness/hospitalization among members of client's family of origin
> Use of substances in family of origin
> Dating history
> Engagement/marital history—reason for termination of relationship
> Current relationship with intimate partner (how well they get along, problems, stresses, enjoyment, satisfaction, and so on)
> Number and ages of client's children
> Other people living with or visiting family frequently
>
> Description of previous sexual experience, including first one (note whether heterosexual, homosexual, or bisexual experiences are reported)
> Present sexual activity
> Any present concerns or complaints about sexual attitudes or behaviors
> Current sexual orientation
>
> 9. *Diagnostic summary (if applicable)* Axis I. Clinical disorders. *DSM-IV* code
> Axis II. Personality disorders and mental retardation
> Axis III. General medical condition
> Axis IV. Psychosocial and environmental problems (note: sociopolitical factors can be included here as well)
> Axis V. Global assessment of functioning (0 to 100 scale)

> **BOX 9.2 SUMMARY OF BRIEF MENTAL STATUS EXAM**
>
> Note the client's physical appearance, including dress, posture, gestures, and facial expressions.
>
> Note the client's attitude and response to you, including alertness, motivation, passivity, distance, and warmth.
>
> Note whether there were any client sensory or perceptual behaviors that interfered with the interaction.
>
> Note the general level of information displayed by the client, including vocabulary, judgment, and abstraction abilities.
>
> Note whether the client's stream of thought and rate of talking were logical and connected.
>
> Note the client's orientation to four issues: people, place, time, and reason for being there (sometimes this is described as "orientation by four").
>
> *Source: Adapted from Hackney and Cormier, 2001, pp. 78–79.*

History taking (and mental-status exams, if applicable) usually occur near the very beginning of the helping process. After obtaining this sort of preliminary information about the client as well as an idea of the range of presenting complaints, you are ready to do some direct assessment interviewing with the client in order to define the parameters of concerns more specifically. We present guidelines for assessment interviews after Learning Activity 9.1.

CULTURAL ISSUES IN INTAKE AND MENTAL-STATUS INTERVIEWS

It is important to note and account for sources of cultural bias within a traditional intake interview and mental-status exam, since culture is an important determinant of "how one experiences, identifies, interprets, and communicates psychic function" (Foulks, 1982, p. 240). Canino and Spurlock (2000) point out that "in some cultures disturbed behavior may be viewed as related to a physical disorder or willfulness"; thus, talking about the behavior is not expected to help (p. 75). In some cultural groups, there is a sanction against revealing personal information to someone outside the family or extended-family circle. Also, clients' perceptions of what is socially desirable and undesirable behavior as well as perceptions of psychological distress may reflect different values than the ones you hold: "Certain cultural factors must be considered in determining the normalcy or pathology of a response. For example, 'hearing the Lord speak' may be a culture-specific impression and therefore nonpathological for some religious groups. An inner-city

> ### LEARNING ACTIVITY 9.1 — Intake Interviews and History
>
> To give you a sense of the process involved in doing an intake or history interview (if you don't already do lots of these on your job!), we suggest you pair up with someone else in your class and complete intake/history interviews with each other. Conduct a 30–45-minute session, with one person serving as the helper and the other taking the client's role; then switch roles. As the helper, you can use the format in Box 9.1 as a guide. You may wish to jot down some notes. After the session, it might be helpful to write a summary of the session, using the major categories listed in Box 9.1 as a way to organize your report. Review your report with your instructor. As the client in this particular activity, rather than playing a role, be yourself. Doing so will allow you to respond easily and openly to the helper's questions, and both of you can more readily identify the way in which your particular history has influenced the current issues in your life.

African American adolescent's statement 'All Whites are out to get us' may actually represent the thinking of the community in which he lives rather than qualify as a sign of paranoia" (Canino & Spurlock, 2000, p. 80). In interpreting the information received from an intake interview and mental-status exam, remember that some information can have cultural meanings that are unknown to you. For example, some cultures view the child as a year of age at the time of birth; other cultures may favor the use of culturally sanctioned healing remedies instead of traditional Western medical or psychological treatment (Canino & Spurlock, 2000, p. 54). Also, cultures have different practices regarding discipline of children and adolescents, so what you may view as either indulgent or harsh may not be seen that way by the client and the client's collective community. What constitutes a "family" also varies among cultures; in assessing for family history, it is important to ask about extended-family members who may live outside the household as well as about a parent's significant other (Canino & Spurlock 2000, p. 67). Clients might also report religious and spiritual beliefs that are unfamiliar to the helper, and these can affect the client's help-seeking behavior and perceptions of distress. An example of an assessment interview protocol that is designed to be "sensitive to cultural issues without stereotyping any particular individual" is the Person-in-Culture-Interview (Berg-Cross & Chinen, 1995, pp. 339–340).

ELEVEN CATEGORIES FOR ASSESSING CLIENTS

To help you acquire the skills associated with assessment interviews, we describe 11 categories of information you need to seek from each client. This information is based on the case conceptualization models presented in Chapter 8. These 11 categories are illustrated and defined in the following list and subsections. They are also summarized in the Interview Checklist at the end of the chapter.

1. Explanation of *purpose* of assessment—presenting rationale for assessment interview to the client.
2. Identification of *range* of concerns—using leads to help the client identify all the relevant primary and secondary issues to get the "big picture."
3. *Prioritization* and *selection* of issues—using leads to help the client prioritize issues and select the initial area of focus.
4. Identification of *present behaviors*—using leads to help the client identify the six components of current behavior(s): affective, somatic, behavioral, cognitive, contextual, and relational that are issue–related.
5. Identification of *antecedents*—using leads to help the client identify sources of antecedents and their effect on the current issue.
6. Identification of *consequences*—using leads to help the client identify sources of consequences and their influence on the current issue.
7. Identification of *secondary gains*—using leads to help the client identify underlying controlling variables that serve as payoffs to maintain the issue.
8. Identification of *previous solutions*—using leads to help the client identify previous solutions or attempts to solve the issue and their subsequent effect on the issue.
9. Identification of *client individual and environmental strengths and coping skills*—using leads to help the client identify past and present coping or adaptive behavior and how such skills might be used in working with the present issue.

10. Identification of the *client's perceptions* of the concern—using leads to help the client describe her or his understanding of the concern.
11. Identification of *intensity*—using leads and/or client self-monitoring to identify the impact of the concern on the client's life, including (a) degree of severity and (b) frequency or duration of current behaviors.

The first three categories—explanation of the purpose of assessment, identification of the range of concerns, and prioritization and selection of concerns—are a logical starting place. First, it is helpful to give the client a rationale, a reason for conducting an assessment interview, before gathering information. Next, some time must be spent in helping the client explore all the relevant issues and prioritize issues to work on in order of importance, annoyance, and so on.

The other eight categories follow prioritization and selection. After the helper and client have identified and selected the issues to work on, these eight categories of interviewing leads are used to define and analyze parameters of the issue. The helper will find that the order of the assessment leads varies among clients. A natural sequence will evolve in each interview, and the helper will want to use the leads associated with these content categories in a pattern that fits the flow of the interview and follows the lead of the client. It is very important in assessment interviews not to impose your structure at the expense of the client. The amount of time and number of sessions required to obtain this information will vary with the concerns and with clients. It is possible to complete the assessment in one session, but with some clients, an additional interview may be necessary. Although the practitioner may devote several interviews to assessment, the information gathering and hypothesis testing that go on do not automatically stop after these few sessions. Some degree of assessment continues throughout the entire helping process.

Explaining the Purpose of Assessment

In explaining the purpose of problem assessment, the helper gives the client a rationale for doing an assessment interview. The intent of this first category of assessment is to give the client a "set," or an expectation, of what will occur during the interview and why assessment is important to both client and helper.

Explaining the purpose of the interview assessment is especially important in cross-cultural helping since "culturally based attitudes weigh heavily in a person's related expectations regarding assessment." Explaining the purpose, goals, and process of assessment to culturally different clients may ease misunderstandings between clients and helpers "so that a meaningful assessment interview can be conducted" (Ridley et al., 1998, p. 842).

One way the helper can communicate the purpose of the assessment interview is "Today I'd like to focus on some concerns that are bothering you most. In order to find out exactly what you're concerned about, I'll be asking you for some specific kinds of information. This information will help both of us identify what you'd like to work on. How does this sound [or appear] to you?" After presenting the rationale, the helper looks for some confirmation or indication that the client understands the importance of assessing issues. If client confirmation or understanding is not forthcoming, the helper may need to provide more explanation before proceeding to other areas. It is also important in initial interviews with clients to create expectations that inspire hope (Lazarus, 1989). Most clients are so focused on their pain that they are unable to see, hear, or grasp much beyond it. So you need to be in touch not only with their pain but also with their potential, their possibilities, and their future.

Identifying the Range of Concerns

In this category, the practitioner uses open-ended leads to help clients identify all the major issues and concerns in their life now. Often clients will initially describe only one concern, and on further inquiry and discussion, the helper discovers a host of other ones, some of which may be more severe or stressful or have greater significance than the one the client originally described. If the helper does not try to get the "big picture," the client may reveal additional concerns either much later in the helping process or not at all.

These are examples of range-of-concerns leads:

"What are your concerns in your life now?"
"Could you describe some of the things that seem to be bothering you?"
"What are some present stresses in your life?"
"What situations are not going well for you?"
"Is there anything else that concerns you now?"

After using range-of-concerns leads, the practitioner should look for the client's indication of some general areas of concern or things that are troublesome for the client. An occasional client may not respond affirmatively to these leads. Some clients may be uncertain about what information to share, or may be from a cultural group in which it is considered inappropriate to reveal personal information to a stranger. In such cases, the helper may need to use a different approach from verbal questioning. For example, Lazarus (1989) has recommended the use of an "Inner Circle" strategy to help a client disclose concerns. The client is given a picture like this:

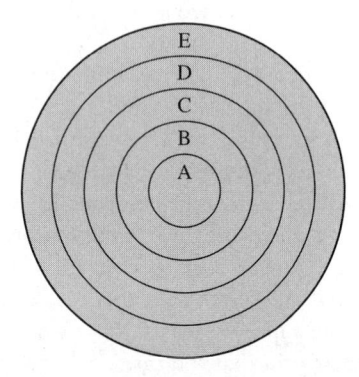

The helper points out that topics in circle A are very personal, whereas topics in circle E are more or less public information. The helper can provide examples of types of topics likely to be in the A circle, such as sexual concerns, feelings of hostility, intimacy problems, and dishonesty. These examples may encourage the client to disclose personal concerns more readily. The helper also emphasizes that progress takes place in the A and B circles and may say things like "I feel we are staying in Circle C" or "Do you think you've let me into Circle A or B yet?" (Lazarus, 1989). Sometimes the helper may be able to obtain more specific descriptions from a client by having the client role-play a typical situation. Another client might provide more information by describing a fantasy or visualization about the concern. This last method has been used by Meichenbaum (1994), who asks the client "to run a movie through your head" in order to recall various aspects of the concern. Throughout all of these methods it is important to communicate respect for the client's cultural values and to provide assurance of confidentiality.

Exploring the range of concerns is also a way to establish who is the appropriate client. A client may attribute the concern to an event or to another person. For instance, a student may say "That teacher always picks on me. I can never do anything right in her class." Because most clients seem to have trouble initially "owning" their role in the issue or tend to describe it in a way that minimizes their own contribution, the helper will need to determine who is most invested in having it resolved and who is the real person requesting assistance. Often it is helpful to ask clients who feels it is most important for the concern to be resolved—the client or someone else. It is important for practitioners not to assume that the person who arrives at their office is always the client. The client is the person who wants a change and who seeks assistance for it. In the example above, if the student had desired a change and had requested assistance, the student would be the client; if it were the teacher who wanted a change and requested assistance, the teacher would be the client. (Sometimes, however, the helper gets "stuck" in a situation in which a family or a client wants a change and the person whose behavior is to be changed is "sent" as the client.)

The question of who is the appropriate client is also tricky when the issue involves two or more persons, such as a relationship, marital, or family issue. In rehabilitation counseling, for example, the client may be not only the individual with a disability, but also the client's employer. Many family therapists view family issues as devices for maintaining the status quo of the family and recommend that either the couple or the entire family be involved, rather than one individual. Although this is a great concept in theory, in practice it is sometimes difficult to implement.

Prioritizing and Selecting Issues

Rarely do clients or the results of assessment suggest only one area or issue that needs modification or resolution. Typically, a presenting concern turns out to be one of several unresolved issues in the client's life. For example, the assessment of a client who reports depression may also reveal that the client is troubled by her relationship with her teenage daughter. History may reveal that this adult woman was also physically abused as a child. After the client describes all of her or his concerns, the practitioner and client will need to select the issues that best represent the client's purpose for seeking help. The primary question to be answered by these leads is "What is the specific situation the client chooses to start working on?"

Prioritizing issues is an important part of assessment and goal setting. If clients try to tackle too many issues simultaneously, they are likely to soon feel overwhelmed and anxious and may not experience enough success to stay in therapy. Selection of the issue is the client's responsibility, although the helper may help with the client's choice. If the client selects a problem that severely conflicts with the helper's values, a referral to another helper may be necessary. Otherwise, the helper may inadvertently or purposely block the discussion of certain client areas by listening selectively to only those issues that the helper can or wants to work with.

The following guidelines form a framework to help clients select and prioritize issues to work on:

1. Start with the presenting issue, the one that best represents the reason the client sought help. Fensterheim (1983, p. 63) observes that relief of the presenting concern often improves the client's level of functioning and may then make other, related issues more accessible to treatment. Leads to use to help determine the initial or presenting issue include "Which issue best represents the reason you are here?" and "Out of all these concerns you've mentioned, identify the one that best reflects your need for assistance."
2. Start with the issue that is primary or most important to the client to resolve. Often this is the one that causes the client the most pain or discomfort or annoyance or is most interfering to the client. Modifying the more important issues seems to lead to lasting change in that area, which may then generalize to other areas (Fensterheim, 1983). Responses to determine the client's most important priority include "How much happiness or relief would you experience if this issue were resolved?" "Of these concerns, which is the most stressful or painful for you?" "Rank-order these concerns, starting with the one that is most important for you to resolve to the one least important." "How much sorrow or loss would you experience if you were unable to resolve this issue?"
3. Start with the concern or behavior that has the best chance of being resolved successfully and with the least effort. Some issues/behaviors are more resistant to change than others and require more time and energy to modify. Initially, it is important for the client to be reinforced for seeking help. One significant way to do this is to help the client resolve something that makes a difference without much cost to the client.

    Responses to determine what issues might be resolved most successfully include "Do you believe there would be any unhappiness or discomfort if you were successful at resolving this concern?" "How likely do you think we are to succeed in resolving this issue or that one?" "Tell me which of these situations you believe you could learn to manage most easily with the greatest success."
4. Start with the issue that needs resolution before other issues can be resolved or mastered. Sometimes the presence of one issue sets off a chain of other ones; when this issue is resolved or eliminated, the other ones either improve or at least move into a position to be explored and modified. Often this concern is one that, in the range of elicited ones, is central or prominent.

    Questions to ask to help determine the most central issue include "Out of all the issues we've discussed, which is the most predominant one?" and "Out of all the issues we've discussed, describe the one that, when resolved, would have the greatest impact on the rest of the issues."

If, after this process, the helper and client still have difficulty prioritizing issues and selecting the initial area of focus, try the procedure recommended by Goldfried (1983). The client asks the following question about each identified issue: "What are the consequences of my *not* doing anything therapeutically to handle this particular issue?"

Understanding the Present Behaviors

After selecting the initial area of focus, it is important to determine the components of the present behavior. For example, if the identified behavior is "not getting along very well with people at work," with an expected outcome of "improving my relationships with people at work," we would want to identify the client's *feelings* (affect), *body sensations* (somatic phenomena), *actions* (overt behavior), and *thoughts and beliefs* (cognitions) that occur during the situations at work. We would also explore whether these feelings, sensations, actions, and thoughts occurred with *all* people at work or only *some* people (relationships) and whether they occurred only at work or in *other* settings, at what *times,* and under what *conditions* or with what *concurrent events* (context). Without this sort of exploration, it is impossible to define the behavior operationally (concretely). Furthermore, it is difficult to know whether the client's work concerns result from the client's actions or observable behaviors, from covert responses such as feelings of anger or jealousy, from cognitions and beliefs such as "When I make a mistake at work, it's terrible," from the client's transactions with significant others that suggest an "I'm not OK—they're OK" position, from particular events that occur in certain times or situations during work, as during a team meeting or when working under a supervisor, or from toxic people or environmental conditions in the workplace.

Without this kind of information about when and how the present behavior is manifested, it would be very difficult and even presumptuous to select intervention strategies or approaches. The end result of this kind of specificity is that the behavior is defined or stated in terms such that two or more persons can agree on when it exists. In the following sections, we describe specific things to explore for each of these six components and suggest some leads and responses to further this exploration with clients.

Affect and Mood States

Affective components of behavior include self-reported feelings or mood states, such as "depression," "anxiety," and "happiness." Feelings are generally the result of complex interactions among behavioral, physiological, and cognitive systems rather than unitary experiential processes (Basic Behavioral Science Research for Mental Health, 1995). Clients often seek help because of this component—that is, they feel bad, uptight, sad, angry, confused, and so on and want to get rid of such unpleasant feelings.

One category of things to ask the client about to get a handle on feelings or mood states is feelings about the present behavior. After eliciting them, note the content (pleasant/unpleasant) and level of intensity. Example leads for this are the following:

"How do you feel about this?"

"What kinds of feelings do you have when you do this or when this happens?"

"What feelings are you aware of?"

A second category is concealed or distorted feelings—that is, feelings that the client seems to be hiding from, such as anger, or a feeling like anger that has been distorted into hurt. Below are example responses for this:

"You seem to get headaches every time your husband criticizes you. What feelings are these headaches masking?"

"When you talk about your son, you raise your voice and get a very serious look on your face. What feelings do you have—deep down—about him?"

"You've said you feel hurt and you cry whenever you think about your family. What other feelings do you have besides hurt?"

"You've indicated you feel a little guilty whenever your friends ask you to do something and you don't agree to do it. Try on resentment instead of guilt. Try to get in touch with those feelings now."

The practitioner can always be on the lookout for concealed anger, which is the one emotion that tends to get "shoved under the rug" more easily than most. Distorted feelings that are common include reporting the feeling of hurt or anxiety for anger, guilt for resentment, and sometimes anxiety for depression, or vice versa. It is also important to be aware that exploration of the affective component may be very productive initially for clients who process information easily in a kinesthetic manner. For clients who do not, however, asking "How do you feel?" can draw a blank, uncomprehending look accompanied by an "I don't know what you mean" statement. Like any other response, "How do you feel?" is not equally productive with all clients and tends to be a tremendously overused lead in helping sessions. Remember also that clients from some cultures may be reluctant to share feelings, especially vulnerable ones, with someone they don't yet know or trust.

Somatic Sensations

Closely tied to feelings are body sensations. Some clients are very aware of these "internal experiencings"; others are not. Some persons are so tuned into every body sensation that they become hypochondriacal, while others seem to be switched off "below the head" (Lazarus, 1989). Neither extreme is desirable. Somatic reactions are quite evident in problems such as sexual dysfunction, depression, anxiety, and trauma. Some persons may describe complaints in terms of body sensations rather than as feelings or thoughts—that is, as headaches, dizzy spells, back pain, and so on. Behavior can also be affected by other physiological processes, such as nutrition and diet, exercise and lifestyle, substance use, hormone levels, and physical illness. Usually, when this is the case, some form of physiological treatment is warranted as well as psychological intervention. The helper will want to elicit information about physiological complaints, about lifestyle and nutrition, exercise, substance use, and so on and about other body sensations relating to the behavior. Some of this information is gathered routinely during the health history portion of the intake interview, but bear in mind that the information obtained from a health history may vary depending on the client's cultural affiliation. For clients who have trouble reporting somatic sensations, helpers can ask them to focus on their nonverbal behavior (Chapter 3) or to engage in a period of slow, deep breathing and then to conduct a "body scan" (see Chapter 16).

Useful leads to elicit this component of the present behavior include these:

"What goes on inside you when you do this or when this happens?"

"What are you aware of when this occurs?"

"What sensations do you experience in your body when this happens?"

"When this happens, are you aware of anything that feels bad or uncomfortable inside you—aches, pains, dizziness, and so on?"

Overt Behaviors or Motoric Responses

Clients often describe a behavior in very nonbehavioral terms. In other words, they describe a situation or a process without describing their actions or specific behaviors within that event or process. For example, clients may say "I'm not getting along with my partner" or "I feel lousy" or "I have a hard time relating to authority figures" without specifying what they do to get along or not get along or to relate or not relate. In this part of the assessment interview, you are interested in finding out precisely what the client does and doesn't do related to the issue. Examples of overt behaviors might be compulsive handwashing, crying, excessive eating, stealing, and making deprecatory or critical comments about self or others.

When inquiring about the behavioral domain, the helper will want to elicit descriptions of both the presence and absence of concrete overt behaviors connected to the issue—that is, what the client does and doesn't do. The helper also needs to be alert to the presence of behavioral *excesses* and *deficits*. Excesses are things that the person does too much or too often or that are too extreme, such as binge eating, excessive crying, or assaultive behavior. Deficits are responses that occur too infrequently or are not in the client's repertory or do not occur in the expected context or conditions, such as failure to initiate requests on one's behalf, inability to talk to one's partner about sexual concerns and desires, or lack of physical exercise and body conditioning programs. Again, it is important to keep a cultural context in mind here—what might be considered a behavioral excess or deficit in one culture may be different in another. The helper may also wish to inquire about "behavioral opposites" (Lazarus, 1989) by asking about times when the person does *not* behave that way.

These are examples of leads to elicit information about overt behaviors and actions:

"Describe what happens in this situation."

"What do you mean when you say you're 'having trouble at work'?"

"What are you doing when this occurs?"

"What do you do when this happens?"

"What effect does this situation have on your behavior?"

"Describe what you did the last few times this occurred."

"If I were photographing this scene, what actions and dialogue would the camera pick up?"

Occasionally the practitioner may want to supplement the information gleaned about behavior from the client's oral self-report with more objective assessment approaches, such as using role plays or accompanying clients into their environments. These additional assessment devices will help practitioners improve their knowledge of how the client does and doesn't act in the situation and in the environmental setting. Additionally, when such observations are coupled with the interview data, the helper can develop more reliable hunches about how the issue manifests itself and how the client may respond to treatment.

Cognitions, Beliefs, and Internal Dialogue

In the last few years, helpers of almost all orientations have emphasized the relative importance of cognitions or symbolic processes (Bandura, 1969; Ellis, 1984) in contributing to, exacerbating, or improving situations that clients report. Unrealistic expectations of oneself and of others are often related to presenting issues, as are disturbing images, self-labeling and self-statements, and cognitive distortions. When the cognitive component is a very strong element of the concern, part of the resulting treatment is usually directed toward this component and involves altering unrealistic ideas and beliefs, cognitive distortions and misconceptions, and dichotomous thinking.

Not all clients process cognitions or symbolic processes in the same way. Therefore, the helper has to be sensitive to how this component may manifest itself with each client and respond accordingly. For example, some clients can easily relate to the term *irrational ideas;* others, particularly adolescents, seem to be offended by such terminology and prefer phrases like "clean up your thinking" (Baker, 1981). Clients who process information kinesthetically may have a great deal of difficulty exploring the cognitive component because they typically don't "think" this way. In contrast, people who process information visually may report cognitions as images or pictures. For example, if you ask "What do you *think* about when this happens?" the client may say "I *see* my wife getting into bed with someone else." Imagery may be a very useful supplemental assessment device with such clients. Clients who process in an auditory modality may report cognitions as "talking to myself" or "telling myself" and can probably verbalize aloud for you a chain of internal dialogue connected to the issue.

Assessment of the cognitive component is accordingly directed toward exploring the presence of both irrational and rational beliefs and images related to the identified issue. Irrational beliefs will later need to be altered. Rational beliefs are also useful during intervention. Although irrational beliefs take many forms, the most damaging ones seem to be related to automatic thoughts or self-statements and maladaptive assumption such as "shoulds" about oneself, others, relationships, work, and so on, "awfulizing" or "catastrophizing" about things that don't turn out as we expect, "perfectionistic standards" about ourselves and often projected onto others, and "externalization," the tendency to think that outside events are responsible for our feelings and problems. The practitioner will also want to be alert for the presence of cognitive distortions and misperceptions, such as overgeneralization, exaggeration, and drawing conclusions without supporting data. Underlying these automatic thoughts and assumptions are cognitive schemas—a schema is a deep-seated belief about oneself, others, and the world that takes shape in the client's early developmental history and confirms the client's core belief about oneself, others, and the world (see also Chapter 14). For example, depressed or anxious clients often focus selectively on cognitive schemas "that mark their vulnerability" (Leahy & Holland, 2000, p. 296).

Although clients may have difficulty verbalizing specific cognitions and beliefs, their nonverbal cues may be important indicators that core beliefs and schemas are being activated in the assessment process. Linscott and DiGiuseppe (1998) note that

> when the therapist has touched on a core-disturbed belief system, the client will frequently exhibit emotional and behavioral reactions. The client who was previously actively engaged in the conversation with the therapist may abruptly begin to avoid the therapist's questions, make little eye contact, evidence disturbed facial expressions, and work to change the subject. Or the client may become enlivened, as if a light bulb has been illuminated by the therapist's inquiries. . . . In addition, the client's sudden anger and confrontational arguments with the therapist may also signal that a core belief has been elicited. (p. 117)

Leads to use to assess the cognitive component include the following:

"What beliefs [or images] do you hold that contribute to this concern? Make it worse? Make it better?"

"Complete the following sentences for me:

I should . . .

People should . . .

My husband [or mother, and so on] should . . .

Work [or school] should . . .

Sex should . . ."

"When something doesn't turn out the way you want or expect, how do you usually feel?"

"What data do you have to support these beliefs or assumptions?"

"What are you thinking about or dwelling on when this [issue] happens?"

"Can you describe what kinds of thoughts or images go through your mind when this occurs?"

"What do you say to yourself when this happens?"

"What do you say to yourself when it doesn't happen [or when you feel better, and so on]?"

"Let's set up a scene. You imagine that you're starting to feel a little upset with yourself. Now run through the scene and relate the images or pictures that come through your mind. Tell me how the scene changes [or relate the thoughts or dialogue—what you say to yourself as the scene ensues]."

"What are your mental commentaries on this situation?"

"What's going through your mind when _____ occurs? Can you recall what you were thinking then?"

"If you had a rule book about yourself and the world, what would the rules be?"

Context: Time, Place, Concurrent Events and Environment

Behaviors occur in a social context, not in a vacuum. Indeed, what often makes a behavior a "problem" is the context surrounding it or the way it is linked to various situations, places, and events. For example, it is not a problem to undress in your home, but the same behavior on a public street in many countries would be called "exhibitionism." In some other cultures, this same behavior might be more commonplace and would not be considered abnormal or maladaptive. Looking at the context surrounding the issue has implications not only for assessment but also for intervention, because a client's cultural background, lifestyle, and values can affect how the client views the issue and also the treatment approach to resolve it.

Assessing the context surrounding the issue is also important because most issues are "situation-specific"—that is, they are linked to certain events and situations, and they occur at certain times and places. For example, clients who say "I'm uptight" or "I'm not assertive" usually do not mean they are *always* uptight or nonassertive but, rather, in particular situations or at particular times. It is important that the helper not reinforce the notion or belief in the client that the feeling, cognition, or behavior is pervasive. Otherwise, clients are even more likely to adopt the identity of the "problem" and begin to regard themselves as possessing a particular trait such as "nervousness," "social anxiety," or "nonassertiveness." They are also more likely to incorporate this trait into their lifestyle and daily functioning.

In assessing contextual factors associated with the issue, you are interested in discovering
1. *Situations* or *places* in which the issue usually occurs and situations in which it does not occur (*where* the issue occurs and where it does not).
2. *Times* during which the issue usually occurs and times during which it does not occur (*when* the issue occurs and when it does not).
3. *Concurrent events*—events that typically occur at or near the same time as the issue. This information is important because sometimes it suggests a pattern or a significant chain of events related to the issue that clients might not be aware of or may not report on their own.
4. Any *cultural, ethnic, and racial affiliations,* any particular *values* associated with these affiliations, and how these values affect the client's perception of the issue and of change.
5. *Sociopolitical factors*—that is, the overall Zeitgeist of the society in which the client lives, the predominant social and political structures of this society, the major values of these structures, who holds power in these structures, and how all this affects the client.

These are example responses to elicit information about contextual components of the issue—time, place, and concurrent events:

"Describe some recent situations in which this issue occurred. What are the similarities in these situations? In what situations does this usually occur? Where does this usually occur?"

"Describe some situations when this issue does not occur."

"In what situations does this not occur?"

"When does this usually occur? Not occur?"

"Can you identify certain times of the day [week, month, year] when this is more likely to happen? Less likely?"

"Does the same thing happen at other times or in other places?"

"What else is going on when this problem occurs?"

"Describe a typical day for me when you feel 'uptight.' "

"Are you aware of any other events that normally occur at the same time as this issue?"

Assessing the context surrounding the client's problems includes exploring not only the client's "immediate psychosocial environment" but also wider environmental contexts such as cultural affiliation and community (Kemp et al., 1997, p. 89). Part of your intervention approach often involves helping clients to feel more empowered to act on their behalf in their environment. Typically, the kinds of environmental systems you assess for during the interview include ones such as neighborhood and community, institutions and organizations, socio-cultural-political systems, and person–family support networks (Kemp et al., 1997, p. 93). The last one—social networks—we discuss in the next section on relational aspects of the issue. Within each system, it is important to assess the extent to which the system adds to the client's concerns—as well as the availability of resources within the system to help the client resolve the concerns.

A frequently used tool for assessing context and environment is an ecomap, shown in Figure 9.1. An ecomap is a useful supplement to the interview and a method "for visually documenting the client's relationship with the outside world, including the flow of energy and the nature of relationships experienced" (Kemp et al., 1997, p. 102). To complete an ecomap, a client first circles all systems that are part of his or her current environment. Next, the client draws a solid line ____ from himself or herself to circles that represent a positive or strong connection, followed by a broken line ------- to circles that represent a negative or stressful connection. Finally, the client draws a wavy line ∼∼∼ to circles that are needed but not available. We illustrate this process in the model dialogue with our client Joan later in this chapter.

After completing the ecomap, the practitioner can use interview leads like the following ones to complete the picture about the environmental events surrounding the client's concerns:

"How would you describe the relationship between yourself and all these systems and structures in your current environment?"

"How do you experience your current environment? How has this experience been affected by your gender, race, ethnicity, income status, and so on?"

"What is the relationship between you and these larger systems in your ecomap—what has this relationship been like so far in your life? How has this affected your current concerns?"

"Do you feel that you need more relationships with any of these larger systems in your ecomap? If so, what has made it difficult for these to develop?"

"How would you describe the sociopolitical and socioeconomic environment you are in—how has this affected your concerns?"

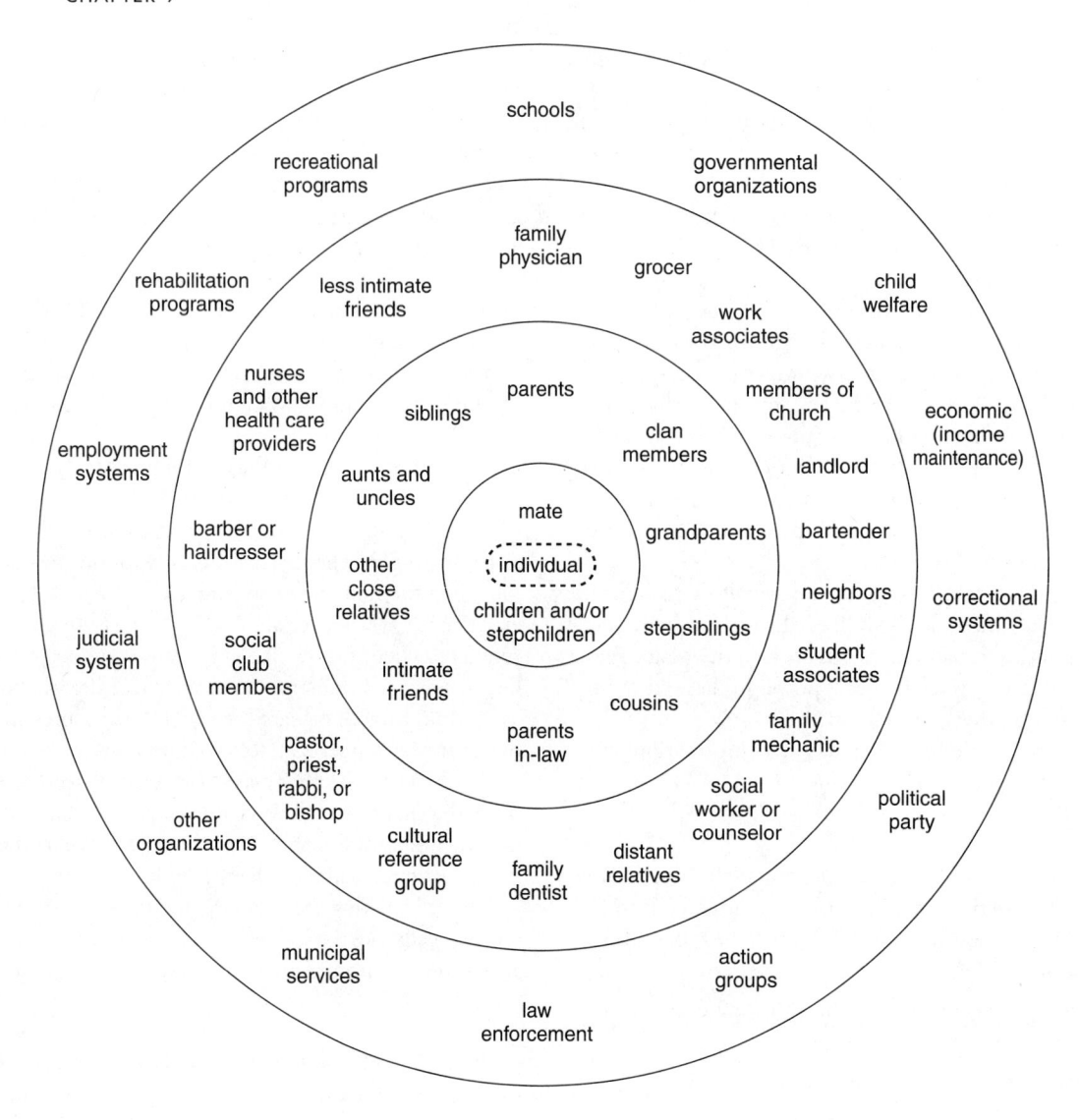

Figure 9.1 Ecomap
Source: Direct Social Work Practice: Theory and Practice (5th ed.), by D. Hepworth, R. Rooney, & J. Larsen, p. 267. Copyright © 1997 by Brooks/Cole, an imprint of the Wadsworth Group, a division of Thomson Learning. Reprinted by permission.

"How much has your concern been affected by oppression, prejudice, and discrimination in your environment?"

"How has your environment fostered empowerment? Or disempowerment? How has this affected the concerns you are bringing to me?"

"What kinds of opportunities do you have in your environment to share cultural or spiritual beliefs and practices?"*

*Adapted from Kemp, Whittaker, and Tracy, 1997, pp. 103–106.

To familiarize yourself with assessing an individual in relationship to her or his environment, complete Learning Activity 9.2.

Relationships, Significant Others and Social Support

Just as issues are often linked to particular times, places, events, and environmental conditions, they are also often connected to the presence or absence of other people. People around the client can bring about or exacerbate a concern. Someone temporarily or permanently absent from

| LEARNING ACTIVITY | 9.2 | Ecomaps |

1. Using the ecomap in Figure 9.1, circle everything that is a part of your current environment.
2. Now draw a solid line ——— from yourself to any circles that represent positive or strong connections to you.
3. Now draw a broken line ----- from yourself to any circles that represent stressful or negative situations to you.
4. Now draw a wavy line ~~~ from yourself to any circles that are needed by you but not available to you.
5. Look over your drawings. What can you summarize from them? You may wish to share your conclusions with a classmate.

the client's life can have the same effect. Assessing the client's relationships with others is a significant part of many theoretical orientations to counseling, including dynamic theories, Adlerian theory, family systems theory, and behavioral theory.

Interpersonal issues may occur because of a lack of significant others in the client's life, because of the way the client relates to others, or because of the way significant others respond to the client. Consider the role of "other people" in the development of Mario's "school phobia":

Mario, a 9-year-old new arrival from Central America, had moved with his family to a homogeneous neighborhood in which they were the first Spanish-speaking family. Consequently, Mario was one of the few Latino children in his classroom. He soon developed symptoms of school phobia and was referred to an outpatient mental health clinic.

A clinician sensitive to cultural issues chose to work very closely with the school, a decision that facilitated access for Mario to a bicultural, bilingual program. The clinician also realized that Mario was a target of racial slurs and physical attacks by other children on his way to and from school. The school responded to the clinician's request to address these issues at the next parent–teacher conference. With the ongoing support of a dedicated principal, Mario's symptoms abated, and he was able to adjust to his new environment. (Canino & Spurlock, 2000, p. 74).

Other persons involved in the issue often tend to discount their role in it. It is helpful if the practitioner can get a handle on what other persons are involved in the issue, how they perceive the issue, and what they might have to gain or lose from a change in the issue or the client. As Gambrill (1990) observes, such persons may anticipate negative effects of improvement in an issue and covertly try to sabotage the client's best efforts. For example, a husband may preach "equal pay and opportunity" yet secretly sabotage his wife's efforts to move up the career ladder for fear that she will make more money than he does or that she will find her new job opportunities more interesting and rewarding than her relationship with him. Other people can also influence a client's behavior by serving as role models (Bandura, 1969). People whom clients view as significant to them can often have a great motivational effect on clients in this respect.

An important aspect of the relational context of the client's concern has to do with availability and access to resources in the client's social and interpersonal environment, including support from immediate and extended family, friends, neighbors, and people affiliated with the client in work, school, and community organizations. One specific tool that can supplement the interview leads to understand more about a client's social support system is the social network map (Tracy & Whittaker, 1990). This tool has been used empirically with a variety of client problem situations (Kemp et al., 1997). The social network map involves a graphic tool (see Figure 9.2) designed to identify both the type and amount of support the client receives from seven social systems:

1. household
2. other/family
3. work/school
4. clubs/associations/faith and church groups and organizations
5. friends
6. neighbors
7. formal services and programs, such as community-based ones

This list can be modified for any given client, with categories of social support added or deleted. Using the map displayed in Figure 9.2, "clients are encouraged to write in the people in their social network that fit in each sector.

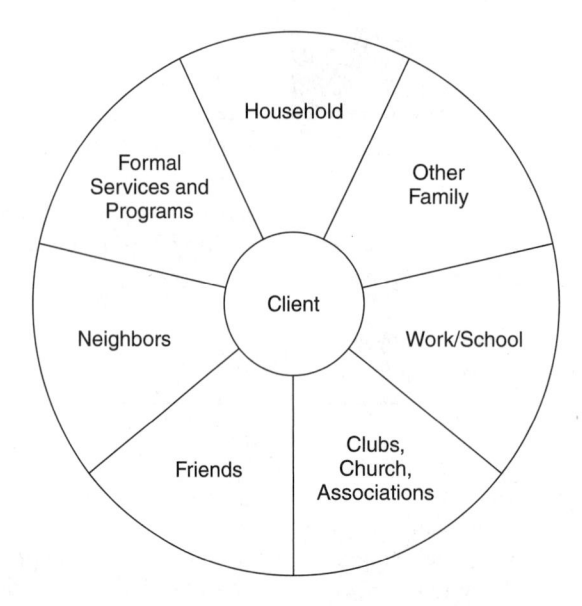

Figure 9.2 Social Network Map
Source: Interpersonal Practice in Social Work (2nd ed.), by C. Garvin & B. Seabury, p. 197. Copyright © 1997 by Allyn & Bacon. Reprinted by permission.

This can be accomplished by drawing in small circles with names to represent women and small squares with names to represent men, or the gender symbols for male and female may be used" (Garvin & Seabury, 1997, p. 197). If necessary, the map can be enlarged for more room. Clients can also use symbols such as arrows to indicate closeness or distance between themselves and their identified circles, as well as the type and direction of help received. Also, as noted by Kemp and associates (1997), clients sometimes list deceased network people or religious or spiritual leaders on the map (p. 117).

Information gleaned from the social network map can be used in goal setting (see Chapter 10) and in planning useful intervention strategies (see Chapter 11). For example, are people in the network draining the client, or is the client a drain on the network? (Kemp et al., 1997, p. 117). Are there responsive and dependable people in the network whom the client can involve in an intervention plan? (Kemp et al., 1997, p. 118). Does the client feel "surrounded by a network that is perceived as negative, non-supportive, or stress-producing?" Or does the client or the network lack skills to access people in the network effectively? (Kemp et al., 1997, p. 118).

Example leads to use to assess the relational component of the issue include the following:

"How many significant close relationships or friendships do you have in your life now?"

"What effects does this issue have on your relationships with significant others in your life?"

"What effects do these significant others have on this concern?"

"Who else is involved in this issue besides you? How are these persons involved? What would their reaction be if you resolved this issue?"

"From whom do you think you learned to act or think this way?"

"What persons *present* in your life now have the greatest positive impact on you? Negative impact?"

"What persons *absent* from your life have the greatest positive impact on you? Negative impact?"

"Whom do you know and respect who handles this issue in a way that you like?"

"What feelings do you have about your relationship?"

"How confident do you feel in relating to this person?"

"How much comfort do you have being close to this person?"

"How often do you need his or her approval?"

"What is the level of trust that you experience with this person?"

"How much anxiety and worry do you experience with this person?"

"How much do you feel this person is controlling your emotions?"

"How dependent are you on this person?"

"How often do you feel confused about how to act with this person?"

"How easy is it to regulate your own emotions when you are with or think about this person?"

"How much independence do you experience with this person?"

"What types of social support do you have available in your life right now—too much support or too little?"

"What or who do you think you need in your life right now that isn't available to you?"

"Who are the main people in this social support system?"

"Which of these people are there for you? Which of these people are critical of you?"

"What people and social support systems in your life empower you? Disempower you?"

"What things get in your way of using these social support systems and the effective people in them?"

"What people in your life are nourishing to you? Toxic or depleting to you?"

"What people in your life do you look up to? What qualities do they have that help you in your current situation?"

Identifying Antecedents

You may recall from Chapter 8 that there are usually certain things that happen before or after an issue that contribute to it. In other words, people are not born feeling depressed or thinking of themselves as inadequate. Other events may contribute to the issue by maintaining, strengthening, or weakening the undesired behaviors, thoughts, or feelings. Much of the assessment process consists in exploring contributing variables that precede and cue the issue (antecedents) and things that happen after the issue (consequences) that, in some way, influence or maintain it.

To review our previous discussion of the ABC model, remember that, like behaviors, the sources of antecedents and consequences are varied and may be affective, somatic, behavioral, cognitive, contextual, or relational. Further, antecedents and consequences are likely to differ for each client. Antecedents are both external or internal events that occasion or cue the behaviors and make them more or less likely to occur. Some antecedents occur immediately before; other antecedents (setting events) may have taken place a long time ago.

In helping clients explore antecedents, you are particularly interested in discovering (1) what *current* conditions (covert and overt) exist *before* the issue that make it *more likely* to occur, (2) what *current* conditions (covert and overt) exist that occur *before* the issue that make it *less likely* to occur, and (3) what *previous* conditions, or setting events, exist that *still* influence the issue.

Example leads to identify antecedents follow and are categorized according to the six possible sources of antecedents, described in Chapter 8:

Affective

"What are you usually feeling before this happens?"

"When do you recall the first time you felt this way?"

"What are the feelings that occur before the issue and make it stronger or more constant?"

"What are the feelings that occur before the issue that make it weaker or less intense?"

"Are there any holdover feelings or unfinished feelings from past events in your life that still affect this issue?"

"What do you know of the roots of this feeling?"

Somatic

"What goes on inside you just before this happens?"

"Are you aware of any particular sensations in your body before this happens?"

"Are there any body sensations that occur right before this issue that make it weaker or less intense?"

"Is there anything going on with you physically—an illness or physical condition—or anything about the way you eat, smoke, exercise, and so on that affects or leads to this issue?"

Behavioral

"If I were photographing this, what actions and dialogue would I pick up before this happens?"

"Can you identify any particular behavior patterns that occur right before this happens?"

"What do you typically do before this happens?"

"Can you think of anything you do that makes this more likely to occur? Less likely to occur?"

Cognitive

"What kinds of pictures or images do you have before this happens?"

"What are your thoughts before this happens?"

"What are you telling yourself before this happens?"

"Can you identify any particular beliefs that seem to set the issue off?"

"What do you think about [see or tell yourself] before the issue occurs that makes it stronger or more likely to occur? Weaker or less likely to occur?"

Contextual

"Has this ever occurred at any other time in your life? If so, describe that."

"How long ago did this happen?"

"Where and when did this occur the first time?"

"How do you see those events related to your concern?"

"What things happened that seemed to lead up to this?"

"When did the issue start—what else was going on in your life at that time?"

"What were the circumstances under which the issue first occurred?"

"What was happening in your life when you first noticed this?"

"Are there any ways in which your cultural affiliation and values contribute to this issue? Make it more likely to occur? Less likely?"

"Are you aware of any events that occurred before this issue that in some way still influence it or set it off?"

"Do you see any particular aspects or structures in your community that have contributed to this issue?"

Relational

"Can you identify any particular people who seem to bring on this issue?"

"Are you usually with certain people right before or when this occurs?"

"Whom are you usually with right before this occurs?"

"Can you think of any person or any particular reaction from a person that makes this more likely to occur? Less likely?"

"Are there any people or relationships from the past that still influence or set off or lead to this issue in some way?"

"Do you think the way people in your social network hold power has contributed to this issue? How?"

Identifying Consequences

Recall from Chapter 8 that consequences are external or internal events that influence the current issue by maintaining it, strengthening or increasing it, or weakening or decreasing it. Consequences occur after the issue and are distinguished from results or effects by the fact that they have direct influence on the issue by either maintaining or decreasing it in some way.

In helping clients explore consequences, you are interested in discovering both internal and external events that maintain and strengthen the undesired behavior and also events that weaken or decrease it.

Example leads to identify consequences follow and are categorized according to the six sources of consequences described in Chapter 8.

Affective

"How do you feel after ____?"

"How does this feeling affect the issue (for example, keep it going, stop it)?"

"Are you aware of any particular feelings or emotions that you have after it that strengthen or weaken it?"

Somatic

"What are you aware of inside you just after this happens? How does this affect you?"

"Are there any body sensations that seem to occur after the issue that strengthen or weaken it?"

"Is there anything you can think of about yourself physically—illness, diet, exercise, and so on—that seems to occur after this? How does this affect it?"

Behavioral

"What do you do after this happens, and how does this make the issue worse? Better?"

"How do you usually react after this is over? In what ways does your reaction keep the issue going? Weaken it or stop it?"

"Can you identify any particular behavior patterns that occur after this? How do these patterns keep the issue going? Stop it?"

Cognitive

"What do you usually think about afterward? How does this affect the issue?"

"What do you picture after this happens?"

"What do you tell yourself after this occurs?"

"Can you identify any particular thoughts [or beliefs or self-talk] during or after the issue that make it better? Worse?"

"Are there certain thoughts or images you have afterward that either strengthen or weaken the issue?"

Contextual

"What happened after this?"

"When does the issue usually stop or go away? Get worse? Get better?"

"Where are you when the issue stops? Gets worse? Gets better?"

"Can you identify any particular times, places, or events that seem to keep the issue going? Make it worse or better?"

"Are there any ways in which your cultural affiliations and values seem to keep this issue going? Stop it or weaken it?"

"Do you think the particular social and political structures of your society or community maintain this issue? How?"

Relational

"Are you usually with certain people during and afterward? When it gets worse? Better?"

"Can you identify any particular people who can make the issue worse? Better? Stop it? Keep it going?"

"Can you identify any particular reactions from other people that occur after the issue? In what ways do these reactions affect the issue?"

"How do you think this issue is perpetuated by the persons in your social network who hold power?"

Identifying Secondary Gains: A Special Case of Consequences

As we mentioned in Chapter 8, occasionally clients have a vested interest in maintaining the status quo of the concern because of the payoffs that the issue produces. For example, a client who is overweight may find it difficult to lose weight, not because of unalterable eating and exercise habits, but because the extra weight has allowed him to avoid or escape such things as new social situations or sexual relationships and has produced a safe and secure lifestyle that he is reluctant to give up (Fishman & Lubetkin, 1983). A child who is constantly disrupting her school classroom may be similarly reluctant to give up such disruptive behavior even though it results in loss of privileges, because it has given her the status of "class clown," resulting in a great deal of peer attention and support.

It is always extremely important to explore with clients the payoffs, or secondary gains, they may be getting from having the issue because often during the intervention phase such clients seem "resistant." In these cases, the resistance is a sign the payoffs are being threatened. The most common payoffs include money, attention from significant others, immediate gratification of needs, and avoidance of responsibility, security, and control.

Questions you can use to help clients identify possible secondary gains include these:

"The good thing about _____ is . . ."

"What happened afterward that was pleasant?"

"What was unpleasant about what happened?"

"Has your concern ever produced any special advantages or considerations for you?"

"As a consequence of your concern, have you got out of or avoided things or events?"

"What are the reactions of others when you do this?"

"How does this issue help you?"

"What do you get out of this situation that you don't get out of other situations?"

"Do you notice anything that happens afterward that you try to prolong or to produce?"

"Do you notice anything that occurs afterward that you try to stop or avoid?"

"Are there certain feelings or thoughts occurring afterward that you try to prolong?"

"Are there certain feelings or thoughts occurring afterward that you try to stop or avoid?"

Exploring Previous Solutions

Another important part of the assessment interview is to explore what things the client has already attempted to resolve the concern and with what effect. This information is important for two reasons. First, it helps you to avoid recommendations for resolution that amount to "more of the same." Second, in many instances, solutions attempted by the client either create new concerns or make the existing one worse.

Garvin and Seabury (1997) note that while some clients have the skills and resources to resolve problems, other clients such as "oppressed clients may not have the same resources to cope" (p. 195). If clients cannot find resources or successful solutions, they "may frantically and repeatedly apply unsuccessful strategies" (p. 195). This kind of "amplifying loop results in a vicious cycle of attempts and failures, which ultimately propels the individual into active crisis" (p. 195).

Leads to help the client identify previous solutions include the following:

"How have you dealt with this or other concerns before? What was the effect? What made it work or not work?"

"How have you tried to resolve this concern?"

"What kinds of things have you done to improve this situation?"

"What have you done that has made the concern better? Worse? Kept it the same?"

"What have others done to help you with this?"

"What has kept the issue from getting worse?"

Identifying the Client's Coping Skills, Individual and Environmental Strengths, and Resources

When clients come to helpers, they usually are in touch with their pain and often only with their pain. Consequently, they are shortsighted and find it hard to believe that they have any internal or external resources that can help them deal with the pain more effectively. In the assessment interview, it is useful to focus not solely on the issues and pains but also on the person's positive assets and resources (which the pain may mask). This sort of focus is the primary one used by feminist helpers; that is, an emphasis is placed on the client's strengths rather than the client's weaknesses (Brown & Ballou, 1992). Recent cognitive–behavioral therapists have also placed increasing emphasis on the client's self-efficacy (Wilson, 1995)—the sense of personal agency and the degree of confidence the client has that she or he can do something. This focus is also consistent with brief therapy models that recommend finding "at least one thing to like or respect about each client or his or her coping and call attention to it" (Cooper, 1995, p. 38). Helpers also should remember that, like many variables, coping skills are culture and gender specific; some men and women may not report using the same coping strategies, just as "effective coping" defined in one cultural system may be different in another one (Sinacore-Guinn, 1995). The coping styles of clients who experience stress related to discrimination, oppression, and "other environmental conditions may be taxed" (Canino & Spurlock, 2000, p. 65). When these kinds of stressors are ongoing and persistent, coping styles that you consider maladaptive may be adaptive for the client as a way to survive his or her environment (Canino & Spurlock, 2000, p. 66).

Focusing on the client's positive assets achieves several purposes. First, it helps convey to clients that in spite of the psychological pain, they do have internal resources available that they can muster to produce a different outcome. Second, it emphasizes wholeness—the client is *more* than just his or her "problem." Third, it gives you information on potential problems that may crop up during an intervention. Finally, information about the client's past "success stories" may be applicable to current concerns. Such information is extremely useful in planning intervention strategies that are geared to using the kind of problem-solving and coping skills already available in the client's repertoire. As LeShan (1995) notes, focusing on what is right with a person or what has happened to the person rather than on what is wrong and how it can be fixed creates a paradigm shift for clients who can then begin to regard themselves with greater care.

Narratives with particular sources of adversity can be revised with the practitioner's help. For example, clients who have experienced trauma can help to heal themselves by telling or drawing the story of the trauma and its key events. It is also important for these clients to put an ending on the story. Clients with trauma histories usually feel helpless in the face of the trauma. As these clients co-construct their stories, they can also narrate strengths and resources they used to help cope with the trauma. Images of strength are especially important in healing stories of adult survivors. By focusing on strengths rather than solely on problems, "we can discover partially forgotten strategies from the past that individuals already know that can help them solve current issues" (Ivey & Ivey, 1999a, p. 38).

Information to be obtained in this area includes the following:

1. Behavioral assets and problem-solving skills—at what times does the client display adaptive behavior instead of

problematic behavior? Often this information can be obtained by inquiring about "opposites"—for example, "When don't you act that way?" (Lazarus, 1989).
2. Cognitive coping skills—such as rational appraisal of a situation, ability to discriminate between rational and irrational thinking, selective attention and feedback from distractions, and the presence of coping or calming "self-talk" (Meichenbaum & Cameron, 1983).
3. Self-control and self-management skills—including the client's overall ability to withstand frustration, to assume responsibility for self, to be self-directed, to control undesired behavior by either self-reinforcing or self-punishing consequences, and to perceive the self as being in control rather than being a victim of external circumstances (Lazarus, 1989).
4. Environmental strengths and resources—in addition to the three "individual" client strengths described above, it is increasingly important to assess the strengths and resources available within the client's environment. These include not only the support network we mentioned earlier but also such things as availability of adequate employment, housing, and health care. A listing of these is provided in Box 9.3. Environmental strengths also include cultural strengths of belonging to a collective community, such as community cohesiveness, community racial identity, and community resources, groups, and organizations (Kemp et al., 1997). Cultural affiliations can give clients certain "protective" factors that serve as sources of strength when clients experience adversity (Canino & Spurlock, 2000, p. 71).

In addition to these more-concrete aspects of the community, other, less-tangible factors such as "community identity, degree of attachment to the community, and shared community values, . . . as well as the community's ability to relate to other groups and institutions, are important domains of a strengths-based assessment. Finally cultural narratives and folklore are extremely important sources of strength, including cultural accounts of origins, migrations, and survival" (Kemp et al., 1997, p. 99).

The following leads are useful in identifying these kinds of individual and environmental strengths and resources:

"What skills or things do you have going for you that might help you with this concern?"

"Describe a situation when this concern is not interfering."

"What strengths or assets can you use to help resolve this concern?"

"When don't you act this way?"

"What kinds of thoughts or self-talk help you handle this better?"

"When don't you think in self-defeating ways?"

"What do you say to yourself to cope with a difficult situation?"

"Identify the steps you take in a situation you handle well. What do you think about and what do you do? How could these steps be applied to the present issue?"

"In what situations is it fairly easy for you to manage or control this reaction or behavior?"

BOX 9.3 ENVIRONMENTAL RESOURCES

1. Adequate social support systems (e.g., family, relatives, friends, neighbors, organized groups).
2. Access to specialized health care services (e.g., physicians, dentists, physical therapists, hospitals, nursing homes).
3. Access to day-care services (for working parents and single-parent families).
4. Access to recreational facilities.
5. Mobility to socialize, utilize resources, and exercise rights as a citizen.
6. Adequate housing that provides ample space, sanitation, privacy, and safety from hazards and pollution (both air and noise).
7. Adequate police and fire protection and a reasonable degree of security.
8. Safe and healthful work conditions.
9. Adequate financial resources to purchase essential resources.
10. Adequate nutritional intake.
11. Predictable living arrangements with caring others (especially for children).
12. Opportunities for education and self-fulfillment.
13. Access to legal resources.
14. Access to religious organizations.
15. Employment opportunities.

Source: Direct Social Work Practice: Theory and Skills (5th ed.), by D. Hepworth, R. Rooney, & J. Larsen, p. 266. Copyright © 1997. Reprinted with permission of Brooks/Cole, an imprint of the Wadsworth Group, a division of Thomson Learning.

"Describe any times you have been able to avoid situations in which these issues have occurred."

"To what extent can you do something for yourself in a self-directed way without relying on someone else to prod you to do it?"

"How often do you get things done by rewarding yourself in some way?"

"How often do you get things done by punishing yourself in some way?"

"What kind of resources in any aspect of your community or environment are you currently using?"

"What aspects of your community and overall environment do you find helpful?"

"What kinds of things in your community and environment would you describe as strengths or assets?"

"What strengths and resources in your community and environment are available that you need to use more often?"

Practitioners can help clients see how they can find meaning from their concerns by drawing attention to patterns and themes represented in the clients' narratives (Ivey & Ivey, 1999a). One strategy for doing this is to use client narratives and stories that focus on images of strength from the client's collective community. Ivey and Ivey (1999a, p. 38) suggest the following interview leads:

1. "Could you tell me a positive story from your culture and community?"
2. "What positive image representing that story comes to mind? What are you seeing, hearing, feeling?"
3. "Could you tell me another positive story from your culture and community?"
4. "How do these positive stories and images represent a pattern in your present life? How could you draw from these strengths to deal with current issues?"
5. "As you reflect back on your community as a whole, how do these systems (family, church, culture) affect your development? How are you part of a living community? How have you been changed by history, and how will you change history?"

Exploring the Client's Perception of the Concern

Most clients have their own perception of and explanation for their concern. It is important to elicit this information during an assessment session for several reasons. First, it adds to your understanding of the concern. The helper can note which aspects of the concern are stressed and which are ignored during the client's assessment of the issue. Second, this process gives you valuable information about "patient position." *Patient position* refers to the client's strongly held beliefs and values—in this case, about the nature of the issue (Fisch et al., 1982). Clients usually allude to such "positions" in the course of presenting their perception of the concern. Ignoring the client's position may cause the therapist to "blunder into a strategy that will be met with resistance" (Fisch et al., 1982, p. 92). You can get clients to describe their view of the concern very concisely simply by asking them to give it a one-line title as if it were a movie, play, or book. Another way to elicit the client's perception of the concern that Lazarus (1989) recommends is to describe the concern in only one word and then to use the selected word in a sentence. For example, a client may say "guilt" and then "I have a lot of guilt about having an affair." The same client might title the concern "Caught Between Two Lovers." This technique also works extremely well with children, who typically are quick to think of titles and words without a lot of deliberation. It is also important to recognize the impact of culture, ethnicity, and race on clients' perceptions and reports of concerns. As Rosado and Elias (1993) note, some Latino clients report the cause of concerns in terms of external factors, supernatural forces, or both. Helpers must not minimize or ridicule such explanations; also, they should incorporate such explanations into the assessment and treatment process.

In the change phase of helping, successful interventions often depend on recognizing and validating the client's "perception of the problem" (Sloane & Gleason, 1999, p. 30). This emphasis on the client's perspective has made a dramatic impact on the care of elderly clients, but the principle extends to all clients: When clients speak out about their perspective, there is more collaboration and shared investment in the change process (Sloane & Gleason, 1999, p. 30).

Leads to help clients identify and describe their view of the concern include these:

"What is your understanding of this issue?"

"How do you explain this concern to yourself?"

"What does the issue mean to you?"

"What is your interpretation [analysis] of this concern?"

"What else is important to you about the concern that we haven't mentioned?"

"Give the issue a title."

"Describe the issue with just one word."

Ascertaining the Frequency, Duration, and Severity of the Concern

It is also useful to determine the intensity of the concern. You want to check out how much the concern is affecting the client and the client's daily functioning. If, for example, a client says "I feel anxious," does the client mean a little anxious or very anxious? Is this person anxious all the time or only some of the time? And does this anxiety affect any of the person's daily activities, such as eating, sleeping, or working? There are two kinds of intensity to assess: the degree of intensity or severity and the frequency (how often) or duration (how long) of it.

Degree of Intensity

Often it is useful to obtain a client's subjective rating of the degree of discomfort, stress, or intensity of the concern. The helper can use this information to determine how much the concern affects the client and whether the client seems to be incapacitated or immobilized by it. To assess the degree of intensity, the helper can use leads similar to these:

"You say you feel anxious. On a scale from 1 to 10, with 1 being very calm and 10 being extremely anxious, where would you be now?"

"How strong is your feeling when this happens?"

"How has this interfered with your daily activities?"

"How would your life be affected if this issue were not resolved in a year?"

In assessing degree of intensity, you are looking for a client response that indicates how strong, interfering, or pervasive the concern seems to be.

Frequency or Duration of Undesired Behaviors

In asking about frequency and duration, your purpose is to have the client identify how long (duration) or how often (frequency) the current behaviors occur. Data about how long or how often these occur *before* a change strategy is applied are called baseline data. Baseline data provide information about the *present* extent of the problem. They can also be used later to compare the extent of the problem before and after a treatment strategy has been used (see also Chapter 10).

Leads to assess the frequency and duration of the current behavior include the following:

"How often does this happen?"

"How many times does this occur?"

"How long does this feeling usually stay with you?"

"How much does this go on, say, in an average day?"

Some clients can discuss the severity, frequency, or duration of the behavior during the interview rather easily. However, many clients may be unaware of the number of times the behavior occurs, how much time it occupies, or how intense it is. Most clients can give the helper more accurate information about frequency and duration by engaging in self-monitoring of the behaviors with a written log. Use of logs to supplement the interview data is discussed later in this chapter.

Box 9.4 provides a review of the 11 categories of client assessment. This table may help you conceptualize and summarize the types of information you will seek during assessment interviews.

BOX 9.4 REVIEW OF 11 ASSESSMENT CATEGORIES

1. *Purpose* of assessment
2. *Range* of concerns
3. *Prioritization* of issues
4., 5., 6., 7. Identification of

Antecedents	Behaviors	Consequences and secondary gains (payoffs)
Affective	Affective	Affective
Somatic	Somatic	Somatic
Behavioral	Behavioral	Behavioral
Cognitive	Cognitive	Cognitive
Contextual	Contextual	Contextual
Relational	Relational	Relational

8. *Previous solutions*
9. *Coping skills and individual and environmental strengths*
10. *Client perceptions* of issue
11. *Frequency, duration, severity* of issue

GENDER AND MULTICULTURAL FACTORS IN INTERVIEW ASSESSMENT

Assessment interviews based on the ABC model may not be compatible with all clients, especially some women and some non-Euro-American clients. This model of an interview-based assessment reflects a sort of specificity that is both Eurocentric and androcentric. Some women and clients from some cultural groups may not think in these specific ways. They may have difficulty relating to these kinds of questions and have trouble in providing particular responses. The helper who is sensitive to this difficulty will not regard such clients as resistant or uncooperative but rather will recognize that "many people have a style of cognitive processing that differs from white, middle-class masculine norms" (Kantrowitz & Ballou, 1992, p. 80). Belenky, Clinchy, Goldbeyer, and Tarule (1986) have found that women's cognitive processing styles or "ways of knowing" are often circular or nonlinear, intuitive, and based on connection. Jackson (1987) has noted a difference in the cognitive processing style of African Americans and Euro-Americans. He states that African Americans tend to use inferential reasoning based on contextual, interpersonal, and historical factors whereas Euro-Americans tend to rely on either inductive or deductive reasoning (p. 233).

Other clients may have difficulty responding to these sorts of interview leads because their cultural affiliation does not advocate the use of immediate self-disclosure, particularly to nonfamily members or strangers. Clients of color who have experienced discrimination and oppression from the host culture may also be reluctant to self-disclose too much in assessment interviews, and self-exploration may be discouraged in some families because it is considered an individual rather than a collective approach (Sue & Sue, 1999).

Language is another factor that can affect the usefulness of the assessment interview. Often helpers in the United States will encounter clients for whom English is not the primary language. With them, the helper should make efforts to allow them to speak in their primary language to enhance their feelings of ease and also to aid the assessment process.

LIMITATIONS OF INTERVIEW LEADS IN ASSESSMENT

The leads we present in this chapter are simply tools that the helper can use to elicit certain kinds of client information. They are designed to be used as a road map to provide some direction for assessment interviews. However, the leads alone are an insufficient basis for assessment because they represent only about half the process at most—the helper responses. The other part of the process is reflected by the responses these leads generate from the client. A complete interview assessment includes not only asking the right questions but also synthesizing and integrating the client responses.

A useful way to synthesize client responses during assessment interviews is to continue to build on and use all the fundamental helping skills presented earlier in this book. Think of it this way: In an assessment interview, you are simply *supplementing* your basic skills with some specific leads designed to obtain certain kinds of information. Many of your leads will consist of open-ended questions. However, even assessment interviews should not disintegrate into a question-and-answer or interrogation session. You can obtain information and give the information some meaning through other verbal responses, such as summarization, clarification, confrontation, and reflection. Demonstrating sensitivity is especially important because sometimes during assessment, a client may reveal or even reexperience very traumatic events and memories. Handling the assessment interview in an understanding and empathic way becomes critical. It is also extremely important to clarify and reflect the information the client gives you before jumping ahead to another question. The model dialogue that follows will illustrate this process. (See Learning Activity 9.3.)

MODEL DIALOGUE FOR INTERVIEW ASSESSMENT: THE CASE OF JOAN

To help you identify how these assessment leads are used in an interview, read the following dialogue from the case of Joan (from Chapter 8). An explanation of the helper's response and the helper's rationale for using it appear before the responses.

Helper response 1 is a *rationale* to explain to the client the *purpose* of the assessment interview.

1. **Helper:** Joan, last week you dropped by to schedule today's appointment, and you mentioned you were feeling unhappy and dissatisfied with school. It might be helpful today to take some time just to explore exactly what is going on with you and school and anything else that concerns you. I'm sure there are ways we can work with this dissatisfaction, but first I think it would be helpful to both of us to get a better idea of what all the issues are for you now. Does this fit with where you want to start today?

LEARNING ACTIVITY 9.3 Interview Assessment

Part One

The following activity is designed to assist you in identifying assessment leads in an interview. You are given a helper/client dialogue from the case of Ms. Weare and Freddie (Chapter 8). This dialogue consists of an interview with the mother, Ms. Weare. For each helper response, your task is to identify and write down the type of assessment lead used by the helper. You may find it helpful to use the Interview Checklist at the end of the chapter as a guide for this learning activity. There may be more than one example of any given lead in the dialogue. Also, responses from previous chapters (listening and action) may be used. Other basic verbal interview responses are also included. Feedback follows the Learning Activity (on page 233).

Dialogue with Ms. Weare and Helper

1. **Helper:** Hello, Ms. Weare. Could you tell me about some things going on now that are concerning you?
   Client: Not too much. Family Services sent me here.
2. **Helper:** So you're here just because they sent you—or is there something bothering you?
   Client: Well, they don't think my kid and I get along too well. My kid is Freddie.
3. **Helper:** What do you think about the way you and Freddie get along?
   Client: Well, I yell at him a lot. I don't like to do that, but sometimes he gets me so mad. I don't like to, but he needs to learn.
4. **Helper:** So there are times when you get real mad at Freddie and then you yell at him. You don't like to do this, but you see it as a way to help him learn right and wrong.
   Client: That's it. I don't like to, but there are times when he needs to know something. Like yesterday, I bought him new pants, and he came home from school with a big hole in them. Now, I just don't have money to keep buying him new pants.
5. **Helper:** You just mentioned the incident with Freddie's pants. What are some other times that you get mad at Freddie?
   Client: Every morning. Freddie's in fourth grade now. But he still doesn't dress himself in the morning. I want to be a good mother and get him to school on time, and he tries to be late. He waits around not getting dressed.
6. **Helper:** Any other times you can remember getting mad?
   Client: Well, not too long ago he was playing outside and broke a window. I got mad then. But that doesn't happen every day like his not getting dressed does.
7. **Helper:** So one thing that really bothers you is what goes on in the mornings. Could you tell me exactly what does happen each morning at your house?
   Client: Well, I call Freddie to get up and tell him to dress before he comes down for breakfast. He comes down all right—in his pajamas. I warn him after breakfast to get ready. Usually about five minutes before the bus comes, I'll go up. He'll just be sitting in his room! He's still not dressed. I'll yell at him and then dress him so he's not late.
8. **Helper:** And your main feeling at this point is that you're mad. Anything else you feel?
   Client: No, just very mad.
9. **Helper:** And what exactly do you do when you go upstairs and he's not dressed?
   Client: I yell at him. Then I help dress him.
10. **Helper:** What kinds of things do you usually say to him?
    Client: I tell him he's dumb and he's going to be late for school, and that I have to make sure he won't be.
11. **Helper:** You mentioned this happens in the morning. Does this situation go on every morning or only some mornings?
    Client: Just about every morning except weekends.
12. **Helper:** When did these incidents seem to begin?
    Client: Ever since Freddie started going to school.
13. **Helper:** So it appears that this has been going on for about five years, then?
    Client: Yes, I guess so.
14. **Helper:** OK, now let's go back over this situation. You told me you remind Freddie every morning to get dressed. He never dresses by breakfast. You remind him again. Then, about five minutes before the bus comes, you go upstairs to check on him. When do you notice that you start to feel mad?
    Client: I think about it as soon as I realize it's almost time for the bus to come and Freddie isn't down yet. Then I feel mad.
15. **Helper:** And what exactly do you think about right then?
    Client: Well, that he's probably not dressed and that if I don't go up and help him, he'll be late. Then I'll look like a bad mother if I can't get my son to school on time.

(continued)

| LEARNING ACTIVITY | **9.3** | Interview Assessment *(continued)* |

16. **Helper:** So in a sense you actually go help him out so he won't be late. How many times has Freddie ever been late?
    Client: Never.
17. **Helper:** You believe that helping Freddie may prevent him from being late. However, your help also excuses Freddie from having to help himself. What do you think would happen if you stopped going upstairs to check on Freddie in the morning?
    Client: Well, I don't know, but I'm his only parent. Freddie's father isn't around. It's up to me, all by myself, to keep Freddie in line. If I didn't go up and if Freddie was late all the time, his teachers might blame me. I wouldn't be a good mother.
18. **Helper:** Of course, we don't *really* know what would happen if you didn't go up and yell at him or help him dress. It might be so different for Freddie after the first day or two he would dress himself. It could be that he thinks it's easier to wait and get your help than to dress himself. He might think that by sitting up there and waiting for you to help, he's getting a special advantage or attention from you.
    Client: You mean like he's getting a favor from me?
19. **Helper:** Sure. And when we find a way to get a favor from someone, we usually do as much as we can to keep getting the favor. Ms. Weare, I'd like to ask you about something else. Do you think maybe that you see helping Freddie out as a way to avoid having Freddie be late and then not having someone blame you for this?
    Client: Sure. I'd rather help him than get myself in hot water.
20. **Helper:** OK, so you're concerned about what you think might happen to you if he's late. You see getting him ready on time as a way to prevent you from getting the heat for him.
    Client: Yes.
21. **Helper:** How do you usually feel after these incidents in the morning are over?
    Client: Well, it upsets me.
22. **Helper:** OK, you feel upset. Do these feelings seem to make you want to continue or to stop helping Freddie?
    Client: Probably to stop. I get worn out. Also, sometimes I don't get my work done then.
23. **Helper:** So helping Freddie so he won't be late and you won't be blamed sort of makes you want to keep on helping him. Yet when you feel upset and worn out afterward, you're tempted to stop helping. Is this right?
    Client: I guess that could be true.
24. **Helper:** Gee, I imagine that all the responsibility for a 9-year-old boy would start to feel like a pretty heavy burden after a while. Would it be right to say that it seems like you feel very responsible for Freddie and his behavior?
    Client: Yeah. I guess a lot of the time I do.
25. **Helper:** Those may be feelings we'll want to talk about more. I'm also wondering whether there are any other things in your life causing you any concern now?
    Client: No, this is about it.
26. **Helper:** Ms. Weare, we've been talking a lot about some problem situations you've had with Freddie. Could you tell me about some times when the two of you get along OK?
    Client: Well, on weekends we do. Freddie dresses himself whenever he gets up. I sleep later.
27. **Helper:** What happens on weekends when the two of you get along better?
    Client: Sometimes I'll take him to a movie or a game. And we eat all our meals together. Usually, weekends are pleasant. He can be a good boy, and I don't scream all the time at him.
28. **Helper:** So you realize it is possible for the two of you to get along. How do you feel about my talking with Freddie and then with both of you together?
    Client: That's OK.

Part Two

To incorporate the interview leads into your verbal repertory. We suggest that you try a role-play interview of the case of Ms. Weare (Chapter 8) or the case of Mr. Huang (Chapter 8) with a triad. One person can take the role of the client (Ms. Weare or Mr. Huang); another can be the helper. Your task is to assess the client's concerns using the interview leads described in this chapter. The third person can be the observer, providing feedback to the helper during or following the role play, using the Interview Checklist at the end of the chapter as a guide.

9.3 FEEDBACK: Interview Assessment

Part One

Identifications of the responses in the dialogue between Ms. Weare and the helper are as follows:

1. Open-ended question
2. Clarification response
3. Open-ended question
4. Summarization response
5. Paraphrase response and behavior lead: exploration of context
6. Behavior lead: exploration of context
7. Paraphrase response and behavior lead: exploration of overt behavior
8. Reflection-of-feeling response and behavior lead: exploration of affect
9. Behavior lead: exploration of overt behavior
10. Behavior lead: exploration of overt behavior
11. Paraphrase and behavior lead: exploration of context
12. Antecedent lead: context
13. Clarification response
14. Summarization response and antecedent lead: affect
15. Behavior lead: exploration of cognitions
16. Paraphrase and open question responses
17. Consequences: overt behavior
18. Consequences: secondary gains for Freddie
19. Consequences: secondary gains for Ms. Weare
20. Summarization response and exploration of secondary gains for Ms. Weare
21. Consequences: affect
22. Consequences: affect
23. Summarization (of consequences)
24. Reflection-of-feeling and interpretation responses
25. Range-of-concerns lead
26. Coping skills
27. Coping skills
28. Paraphrase and open-ended question

Client: Yeah. I guess school is the main problem. It's really bugging me.

Helper response 2 is a lead to help Joan identify the *range* of her concerns.

2. **Helper:** OK, you just said school is the *main* concern. From the way you said that and the way you look right now, I have the feeling school isn't the *only* thing you're concerned about in your life.

Client: Well, you're right about that. I'm also kind of not getting along too well with my folks. But that's kind of related to this school thing, too.

In the next response, the helper will simply *listen* to Joan and synthesize what she's saying by using a *paraphrase* response.

3. **Helper:** So from your point of view, the school thing and the issue with your parents are connected.

Client: Yeah, because I'm having trouble in some of my classes. There's too much competition. I feel the other kids are better than I am. I've thought about changing from this college prep program to the work-study program, but I don't know what to do. I don't like to make decisions anyway. At the same time, my folks put a lot of pressure on me to perform well, to make top grades. They have a lot of influence with me. I used to want to do well, but now I'm kind of tired of it all.

In the next response, the helper continues to listen to Joan and *reflect her feelings.*

4. **Helper:** It seems like you're feeling pretty overwhelmed and discouraged right now.

Client: Yeah, I am [lowers head, eyes, and voice tone].

Helper senses Joan has strong feelings about these issues and doesn't want to cut them off initially. *Instructs* Joan to continue focusing on the feelings.

5. **Helper:** [Pause]: Let's stay with these feelings for a few minutes and see where they take you.

Client [Pause—eyes fill with tears]: I guess I just feel like all this stuff is coming down on me at once. I'd like to work something out, but I don't know how—or where, even—to start.

Helper continues to *attend,* to *listen,* and to *reflect* the client's current experience.

6. **Helper:** It seems like you feel you're carrying a big load on your shoulders—

Client: Yeah.

In response 7, the helper *summarizes* Joan's concerns, followed by a lead to determine whether Joan has *prioritized* her concerns.

7. **Helper:** I think before we're finished I'd like to come back to these feelings, which seem pretty strong for you now. Before we do, it might help you to think about not having to tackle everything all at once. You know you mentioned three different things that are bothering you—your competitive classes, having trouble making decisions, and not getting along with your parents. Which of these bothers you most?

Client: I'm not really sure. I'm concerned right now about having trouble in my classes. But sometimes I think if I were in another type of curriculum, I wouldn't be so tense about these classes. But I'm sort of worried about deciding to do this.

Helper response 8 is a *clarification*. The helper wants to see whether the client's interest in work-study is real or is a way to avoid the present issue.

8. **Helper:** Do you see getting in the work-study program as a way to get out of your present problem classes, or is it a program that really interests you?

Client: It's a program that interests me. I think sometimes I'd like to get a job after high school instead of going to college, or maybe just go to culinary school or even into the Army. *But I've been thinking about this for a year, and I can't decide what to do. I'm not very good at making decisions on my own.*

Helper response 9 is a *summarization* and *instruction*. The helper goes back to the three areas of concern mentioned in "Identifying the Range of Concerns." Note that the helper does not draw explicit attention to the client's last self-deprecating statement.

9. **Helper:** Well, your concerns of your present class problems and of making this and other decisions are somewhat related. Your parents tie into this, too. Maybe you could explore all concerns and then decide later about what you want to work on first.

Client: That's fine with me.

Helper response 10 is a lead to *identify some present behaviors* related to Joan's concern about competitive classes. Asking the client for examples can elicit specificity about what does or does not occur during the situation of concern.

10. **Helper:** OK, what is an example of some trouble you've been having in your most competitive class?

Client: Well, I withdraw in these classes. I've been cutting my math classes. It's the worst. My grades are dropping, especially in math class.

Helper response 11 is a *behavior* lead regarding the *context* of the concern to see whether the client's concern occurs at other *times* or other *places*.

11. **Helper:** Where else do you have trouble—in any other classes, or at other times or places outside school?

Client: No, not outside school. And, to some degree, I always feel anxious in any class because of the pressures my parents put on me to get good grades. But my math class is really the worst.

Helper response 12 is a lead to help the client identify *overt behaviors* in math class (*behavioral* component of concern).

12. **Helper:** Describe what happens in your math class that makes it troublesome for you [could also use imagery assessment at this point].

Client: Well, to start with, it's a harder class for me. I have to work harder to do OK. In this class I get nervous whenever I go in it. So I withdraw.

Client's statement "I withdraw" is vague. So helper response 12 is another *overt behavior* lead to help the client specify what she means by "withdrawing." Note that since the helper did not get a complete answer to this after response 8, the same type of lead is used again.

13. **Helper:** What do you do when you withdraw? [This is also an ideal place for a role-play assessment.]

Client: Well, I sit by myself; I don't talk or volunteer answers. Sometimes I don't go to the board or answer when the teacher calls on me.

Now that the client has identified certain overt behaviors associated with the concern, the helper will use a *covert behavior* lead to find out whether there are any predominant *thoughts* the client has during the math class (*cognitive* component of issue).

14. **Helper:** What are you generally thinking about in this class?

Client: What do you mean—am I thinking about math?

The client's response indicated some confusion. The helper will have to use a more specific *covert behavior* lead to assess cognition, along with some *self-disclosure,* to help the client respond more specifically.

15. **Helper:** Well, sometimes when I'm in a situation like a class, there are times when my mind is in the class and other times I'm thinking about myself or about something else I'm going to do. So I'm wondering whether you've noticed anything you're thinking about during the class?

Client: Well, some of the time I'm thinking about the math problems. Other times I'm thinking about the fact that I'd rather not be in the class and that I'm not as good as the other kids, especially all the guys in it.

The client has started to be more specific, and the helper thinks perhaps there are still other thoughts going on. To explore this possibility, the helper uses another *covert behavior* lead in response 16 to assess *cognition.*

16. **Helper:** What else do you recall that you tell yourself when you're thinking you're not as good as other people?

Client: Well, I think that I don't get grades that are as good as some other students'. My parents have been pointing this out to me since junior high. And in the math class I'm one of four girls. The guys in there are really smart. I just keep thinking how can a girl ever be as smart as a guy in math class? No way. It just doesn't happen.

The client identifies more specific thoughts and also suggests two possible antecedents—parental comparison of her grades and cultural stereotyping (girls shouldn't be as good in math as boys). The helper's records show that the client's test scores and previous grades indicate that she is definitely not "dumb" in math. The helper will *summarize* this and then, in the next few responses, will focus on these and on other possible *antecedents,* such as the nervousness the client mentioned earlier.

17. **Helper:** So what you're telling me is that you believe most of what you've heard from others about yourself and about the fact that girls automatically are not supposed to do too well in math.

Client: Yeah, I guess so, now that you put it like that. I've never given it much thought.

18. **Helper:** Yes. It doesn't sound like you've ever thought about whether *you, Joan,* really feel this way or whether these feelings are just adopted from things you've heard others tell you.

Client: No, I never have.

19. **Helper:** That's something we'll also probably want to come back to later.

Client: OK.

20. **Helper:** You know, Joan, earlier you mentioned that you get nervous about this class. When do you notice that you feel this way—before the class, during the class, or at other times?

Client: Well, right before the class is the worst. About ten minutes before my English class ends—it's right before math—I start thinking about the math class. Then I get nervous and feel like I wish I didn't have to go. Recently, I've tried to find ways to cut math class.

The helper still needs more information about how and when the nervousness affects the client, so 21 is another *antecedent* lead.

21. **Helper:** Could you tell me more about when you feel most nervous and when you don't feel nervous about this class?

Client: Well, I feel worst when I'm actually walking to the class and the class is starting. Once the class starts, I feel better. I don't feel nervous about it when I cut it or at other times. However, once in a while, if someone talks about it or I think about it, I feel a little nervous.

The client has indicated that the nervousness seems to be more of an antecedent than a problem behavior. She has also suggested that cutting class is a consequence that maintains the issue, because she uses this to avoid the math class that brings on the nervousness. The helper realizes at this point that the word *nervous* has not been defined and goes back in the next response to a *covert behavior* lead to find out what Joan means by *nervous* (affective component).

22. **Helper:** Tell me what you mean by the word *nervous*— what goes on with you when you're nervous?

Client: Well, I get sort of a sick feeling in my stomach, and my hands get all sweaty. My heart starts to pound.

In the next response, the helper continues to *listen* and *paraphrase* to clarify whether the nervousness is experienced somatically.

23. **Helper:** So your nervousness really consists of things you feel going on inside you.

Client: Yeah.

Next the helper will use an *intensity* lead to determine the *severity* of nervousness.

24. **Helper:** How strong is this feeling—a little or very?

Client: Before class, very strong—at other times, just a little.

The client has established that the nervousness seems mainly to be exhibited in somatic forms and is more intense before class. The helper will pursue the relationship between the client's nervousness and overt and covert behaviors described earlier to verify that the nervousness is an *antecedent*. Another *antecedent* lead is used next.

25. **Helper:** Which seems to come first—feeling nervous, not speaking up in class, or thinking about other people being smarter than you?

Client: Well, the nervousness. Because that starts before I get in the class.

The helper will *summarize* this pattern and confirm it with the client in the next response.

26. **Helper:** Let's see. So you feel nervous—like in your stomach and hands—before class and when math class starts. Then during class, on days you go, you start thinking about not being as smart in math as the guys and you don't volunteer answers or don't respond sometimes when called on. But after the class is over, you don't notice the nervousness so much. Is that right?

Client: That's pretty much what happens.

The helper has a clue from the client's previous comments that there are other antecedents in addition to nervousness that have to do with the client's concern—such as the role of her parents. The helper will pursue this in the next response, using an *antecedent* lead.

27. **Helper:** Joan, you mentioned earlier that you have been thinking about not being as smart as some of your friends ever since junior high. When do you recall you really started to dwell on this?

Client: Well, probably in seventh grade.

The helper didn't get sufficient information about what happened to the client in the seventh grade, so another *antecedent* lead will be used to identify this possible *setting event*.

28. **Helper:** What do you recall happened in seventh grade?

Client: Well, my parents said when you start junior high, your grades become really important in order to go to college. So for the last three or four years they have been telling me some of my grades aren't as good as other students'. Also, if I get a B, they will withhold a privilege, like going out with my friends.

The helper has no evidence of actual parental reaction but will work with the client's report at this time, since this is how the client perceives parental input. If possible, a parent conference could be arranged later with the client's permission. The parents *seem* to be using negative rather than positive consequences with Joan to influence her behavior. The helper wants to pursue the relationship between the parents' input and the client's present behavior to determine whether parental reaction is eliciting part of Joan's present concerns and will use a lead to identify this as a possible *antecedent*.

29. **Helper:** How do you think this reaction of your parents' relates to your present problems in your math class?

Client: Well, since I started high school, they have talked more about needing to get better grades for college. And I have to work harder in math class to do this. I guess I feel a lot of pressure to perform—which makes me withdraw and just want to hang it up. Now, of course, my grades are getting worse, not better.

The helper, in the next lead, will *paraphrase* Joan's previous comment.

30. **Helper:** So the expectations you feel from your parents seem to draw out pressure in you.

Client: Yes, that happens.

In response 31, the helper will explore another possible *antecedent* that Joan mentioned before—thinking that girls aren't as good as boys in math.

31. **Helper:** Joan, I'd like to ask you about something else you mentioned earlier that I said we would come back to. You said one thing that you think about in your math class is that you're only one of four girls and that, as a girl, you're not as smart in math as a boy. Do you know what makes you think this way?

Client: I'm not sure. Everyone knows or says that girls have more trouble in math than boys. Even my teacher. He's gone out of his way to try to help me because he knows it's tough for me.

The client has identified a possible consequence of her behavior as teacher attention. The helper will return to this later. First, the helper is going to respond to the client's response that "everyone" has told her this thought. Helpers have a responsibility to point out things that clients have learned from stereotypes or irrational beliefs rather than actual data, as is evident in this case from Joan's academic record. The helper will use *confrontation* in the next response.

32. **Helper:** You know, studies have shown that when young women drop out of math, science, and engineering programs, they do so not because they're doing poorly, but because they don't believe they can do well.* It is evident to me from your records that you have a lot of potential for math.

Client: Really?

Helper response 33 is an *interpretation* to help the client see the relation between overt and covert behaviors.

33. **Helper:** I don't see why not. But lots of times the way someone acts or performs in a situation is affected by how the person thinks about the situation. I think some of the reason you're having more trouble in your math class is that your performance is hindered a little by your nervousness and by the way you put yourself down.

In the next response, the helper *checks out* and *clarifies* the client's reaction to the previous interpretation.

34. **Helper:** I'm wondering now from the way you're looking at me whether this makes any sense or whether what I just said muddies the waters more for you?

Client: No, I guess I was just thinking about things. You mentioned the word *expectations*. But I guess it's not just that my parents expect too much of me. I guess in a way I expect too little of myself. I've never really thought of that before.

35. **Helper:** That's a great observation. In a way the two sets of expectations are probably connected. These are some of the kinds of issues we may want to work on if this track we're on seems to fit for you.

Client: Yeah. OK, it's a problem.

---

*From studies conducted at Wellesley College's Center for Research on Women.

The helper is going to go back now to pursue possible consequences that are influencing the client's behavior. The next response is a lead to identify *consequences*.

36. **Helper:** Joan, I'd like to go back to some things you mentioned earlier. For one thing, you said your teacher has gone out of his way to help you. Would you say that your behavior in his class has got you any extra attention or special consideration from him?

Client: Certainly extra attention. He talks to me more frequently. And he doesn't get upset when I don't go to the board.

Helper response 37 will continue to explore the teacher's behavior as a possible *consequence*.

37. **Helper:** Do you mean he may excuse you from board work?

Client: For sure, and I think he, too, almost expects me *not* to come up with the answer. Just like I don't expect myself to.

The teacher's behavior may be maintaining the client's overt behaviors in class by giving extra attention to her and by excusing her from some kinds of work. Declines in achievement in math and science among girls after seventh grade have been linked to teachers' differing expectations for girls and boys and their subsequent behavior in the classroom. Teachers often pay less attention to girls than boys in the classroom, and when they do pay attention to girls, it is more in the form of protecting girls by solving problems for them (DeAngelis, 1994). A teacher conference may be necessary at some later point. The helper, in the next two responses, will continue to use other leads to identify possible *consequences*.

38. **Helper:** What do you see you're doing right now that helps you get out of putting yourself through the stress of going to math class?

Client: Do you mean something like cutting class?

39. **Helper:** I think that's perhaps one thing you do to get out of the class. What else?

Client: Nothing I can think of.

The client has identified cutting class as one way to avoid the math class. The helper, in the next response, will suggest another *consequence* that the client mentioned earlier, though not as a way to get out of the stress associated with the class. The helper will suggest that this consequence functions as a *secondary gain,* or *payoff,* in a tentative *interpretation* that is checked out with the client in the next three responses:

40. **Helper:** Well, Joan, you told me earlier that your grades were dropping in math class. Is it possible that if these grades—and others—drop too much, you'll automatically be dropped from these college prep classes?

Client: That's right.

41. **Helper:** I'm wondering whether one possible reason for letting your grades slide is that it is almost an automatic way for you to get out of these competitive classes.

Client: How so?

42. **Helper:** Well, if you became ineligible for these classes because of your grades, you'd automatically be out of this class and others that you consider competitive and feel nervous about. What do you think about that?

Client: I guess that's true. And then my dilemma is whether I want to stay in this or switch to the work-study program.

In the next response, the helper uses *summarization* and ties together the effects of "dropping grades" to math class and to the earlier-expressed concern of a curriculum-change decision.

43. **Helper:** Right. And letting your grades get too bad will automatically mean that decision is made for you, so you can take yourself off the hook for making that choice. In other words, it's sort of a way that part of you has rather creatively come up with to get yourself out of the hassle of having to decide something you don't really want to be responsible for deciding about.

Client: Wow! Gosh, I guess that might be happening.

44. **Helper:** That's something you can think about. We didn't really spend that much time today exploring the issue of having to make decisions for yourself, so that will probably be something to discuss the next time we get together. I know you have a class coming up in about ten minutes, so there's just a couple more things we might look at.

Client: OK—what next?

In the next few responses (45–52), the helper continues to demonstrate *listening responses* and to help Joan explore *solutions* she's tried already to resolve the issue. They look together at the *effects* of the use of the solutions Joan identifies.

45. **Helper:** OK, starting with the nervousness and pressure you feel in math class—is there anything you've attempted to do to get a handle on this concern?

Client: Not really—other than talking to you about it and, of course, cutting class.

46. **Helper:** So cutting class is the only solution you've tried.

Client: Yeah.

47. **Helper:** How do you think this solution has helped?

Client: Well, like I said before—it helps mainly because on the days I don't go, I don't feel uptight.

48. **Helper:** So you see it as a way to get rid of these feelings you don't like.

Client: Yeah, I guess that's it.

49. **Helper:** Can you think of any ways in which this solution has not helped?

Client: Gee, I don't know. Maybe I'm not sure what you're asking.

50. **Helper:** OK, good point! Sometimes when I try to do something to resolve a concern, it can make the issue better or worse. So I guess what I'm really asking is whether you've noticed that your "solution" of cutting class has in any way made the problem worse or in any way has even contributed to the whole issue?

Client: [Pause]: I suppose maybe in a way. [Pause] In that, by cutting class, I miss out on the work, and then I don't have all the input I need for tests and homework, and that doesn't help my poor grades.

51. **Helper:** OK. That's an interesting idea. You're saying that when you look deeper, your solution also has had some negative effects on one of the issues you're trying to deal with and eliminate.

Client: Yeah. But I guess I'm not sure what else I could do.

52. **Helper:** At this point, you probably are feeling a little bit stuck, like you don't know which other direction or road to take.

Client: Yeah.

At this point, the helper shifts the focus a little to exploration of Joan's *assets, strengths, and resources.*

53. **Helper:** Well, one thing I sense is that your feelings of being so overwhelmed are sort of covering up the resources and assets you have within you to handle the issue and work it out. For example, can you identify any particular skills or things you have going for you that might help you deal with this issue?

Client: [Pause]: Well, are you asking me to brag about myself?

Clients often talk about their pain or limitations freely but feel reluctant to reveal their strengths, so in the next response, the helper gives Joan a specific *directive* and *permission* to talk about her *assets*.

54. **Helper:** Sure. Give yourself permission. That's certainly fine in here.

Client: Well, I am pretty responsible. I'm usually fairly loyal and dependable. It's hard to make decisions for myself, but when I say I'm going to do something, I usually do it.

55. **Helper:** OK, great. So what you're telling me is you're good on follow-through once you decide something is important to you.

Client: Yeah. Mm-hmm. Also, although I'm usually uptight in my math class, I don't have the same feeling in my English class. I'm really doing well in there.

In response 56, the helper will pick up on these "pluses" and use another *coping skills* lead to have the client identify particular ways in which she handles positive situations, especially her English class. If she can demonstrate the steps to succeed in one class, this is useful information that can be applied in a different area. This topic is continued in response 57.

56. **Helper:** So there are some things about school that are going OK for you. You say you're doing well in your English class. What can you think of that you do or don't do to help you perform well in this class?

Client: Well, I go to class, of course, regularly. And I guess I feel like I do well in reading and writing. I don't have the hangup in there about being one of the few girls.

57. **Helper:** So maybe you can see some of the differences between your English and math classes—and how you handle these. This information is useful because if you can start to identify the things you do and think about in English that make it go so well for you, then you potentially can apply the same process or steps to a more difficult situation, like math class.

Client: That sounds hopeful!

Joan and the helper have been talking about *individual strengths*. Next (in responses 58–62), the helper will explore any *environmental and cultural strengths and resources* that can help Joan in this situation.

58. **Helper:** So far we've been talking about your own individual assets. Can you think of any assets or resources—including people—in your immediate environment that could be useful to you in dealing with these concerns?

Client: Well, I mentioned my math teacher. He does go out of his way to help me. He even has given all of us his e-mail address to use if we get stuck on a homework problem, and he has a tutoring session after school every Thursday too. But I haven't used his help too much outside of class.

59. **Helper:** So you rely on him more during class?

Client: Yup.

60. **Helper:** Are there any other people or resources available to you that you may or may not be using?

Client: Hmm.

61. **Helper:** Earlier you mentioned your friends. Do you ever do homework with them or have study groups with them?

Client: No—we mainly just go out on weekends to do things. But I think that might be a good idea, and I think my parents would be in favor of that one too.

62. **Helper:** Anything else you can think of?

Client: Well, I'm kind of stuck; I don't see anything else that could help me right now. To help Joan explore contributing conditions of her environment, the helper uses an *ecomap* in responses 63–69.

63. **Helper:** One thing we could start today and finish next time is kind of a chart or drawing. It is actually called an ecomap, and what it does is help us to get a picture about your world and the ways that other people and systems in it can either contribute to your concerns or can be used to help resolve them. Would you like to see what this map looks like?

Client: Sure. [Helper shows Joan ecomap such as the one in Figure 9.1.]

64. **Helper:** Now, not everything that you see in this set of circles will pertain to you and your world—you don't

have any children yet or in-laws, for example. But for ones that are in your world—let's start by drawing around each of them.

Client: So you draw a circle around things like parents, aunts and uncles—grandparents?

65. **Helper:** Mm-hmm, do that for any and all that apply to you now. [Joan draws circles around the things she sees in her life now.]

Client: Is that it?

66. **Helper:** Not quite. Next I'd like you to draw a solid line from yourself to anything you've circled that is positive or represents a strong connection for you.

Client: OK [draws several solid lines].

67. **Helper:** Almost there. Next, I'd like you to draw a broken line from yourself to anything that feels like a negative or stressful connection to you.

Client: OK [continues drawing—this time, broken lines].

68. **Helper:** Last thing—now draw a wavy line from yourself to anything that you need that is not available to you.

Client: OK, here goes [draws several wavy lines].*

Client: That was kind of fun.

69. **Helper:** It *is* fun, and it is also surprising how much information you can get from this.

In the next few responses, the helper tries to elicit *Joan's perception and assessment of the main issue.*

70. **Helper:** Right. It is. I feel hopeful, too. Just a couple more things. Changing the focus a little now, could you think about the issues that you came in with today—and describe the main issue in one word?

Client: Ooh—that's a hard question!

71. **Helper:** I guess it could be. Take your time. You don't have to rush.

Client: [Pause]: Well, how about "can't?"

72. **Helper:** OK, now, to help me get an idea of what that word means to you, use it in a sentence.

Client: Any sentence?

73. **Helper:** Yeah. Make one up. Maybe the first thing that comes in your head.

---
*See Joan's ecomap in Figure 9.3.

Client: Well, "I can't do a lot of things I think I want to or should be able to do."

Next, the helper uses a *confrontation* to depict the incongruity revealed in the sentence Joan made up about her concern. This theme is continued in response 75.

74. **Helper:** OK, that's interesting too, because on the one hand, you're saying there are some things you *want* to do that aren't happening, and on the other hand, you're also saying there are some things that aren't happening that you think you *should* be doing. Now, these are two pretty different things mixed together in the same sentence.

Client: Yeah. [Clarifies.] I think the wanting stuff to happen is from me and the should things are from my folks and my teachers.

75. **Helper:** OK, so you're identifying part of the whole issue as wanting to please yourself and others at the same time.

Client: Mm-hmm.

In response 76, the helper identifies this issue as an extension of the *secondary gain* mentioned earlier—avoiding deliberate decisions.

76. **Helper:** I can see how after a while that would start to feel like so much trouble that it would be easier to try to let situations or decisions get made for you rather than making a conscious or deliberate choice.

In the next two responses, the helper explores the *context* related to these issues and sets up some *self-monitoring* homework to obtain additional information. Note that this is a task likely to appeal to the client's dependability, which she revealed during exploration of *coping skills.*

77. **Helper:** That's something else we'll be coming back to, I'm sure. One last thing before you have to go. Earlier we talked about some specific times and places connected to some of these issues—like where and when you get in the rut of putting yourself down and thinking you're not as smart as other people. What I'd like to do is give you sort of a diary to write in this week to collect some more information about these kinds of problems. Sometimes writing these kinds of things down can help you start making changes and sorting out the issues. You've said that you're pretty dependable. Would doing this appeal to your dependability?

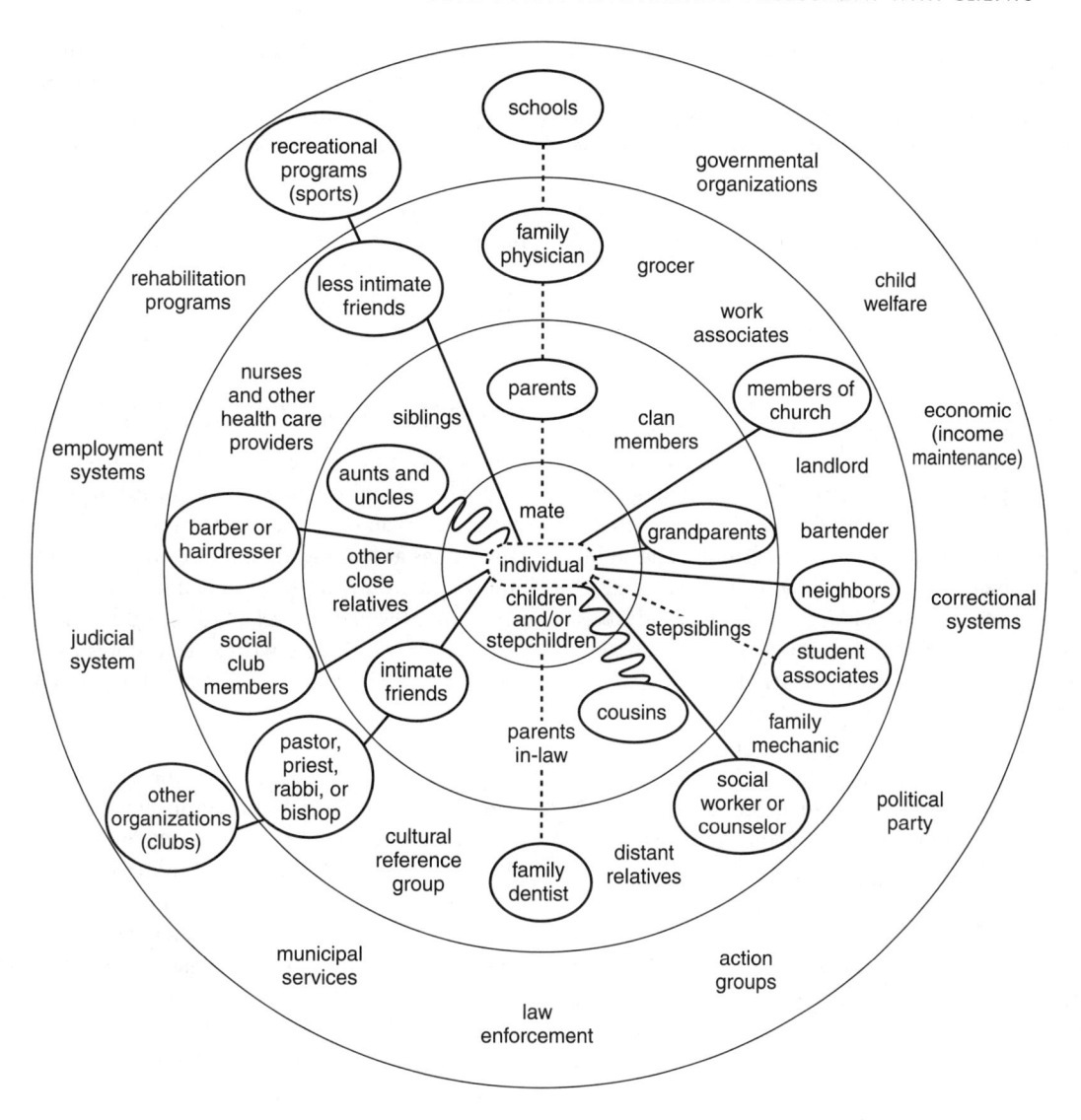

Figure 9.3 Ecomap of Joan
Source: Adapted from *Direct Social Work Practice: Theory and Skills (5th ed.),* by D. Hepworth, R. Rooney, & J. Larsen, p. 267. Copyright © 1997 by Brooks/Cole, an imprint of The Wadsworth Group, a division of Thomson Learning. Reprinted by permission.

Client: Sure. That's something that wouldn't be too hard for me to do.

78. **Helper:** OK, let me tell you specifically what to keep track of, and then I'll see you next week—bring this back with you. [Goes over instructions for Joan's log sheet—see section of chapter titled "Client Self-Monitoring Assessment."]

At this time, the helper also has the option of giving Joan a history questionnaire to complete and/or a brief self-report inventory to complete, such as an anxiety inventory or checklist.

NOTES AND RECORD KEEPING

Generally, some form of written record is started at the time the client requests an appointment. According to Mitchell (2001), helpers must keep timely and accurately written records for three primary reasons: fiscal, clinical, and legal accountability. Ethical codes such as the ones mentioned in

Chapter 2 also mandate the need for accurate and timely record keeping.

Increasingly, with both government-funded agencies and private health maintenance organizations, written records are becoming a tool for billing as well as for keeping track of client progress. Mitchell (2001) points out that if you don't have records to verify services rendered, both government-funding sources and insurance companies may not pay, or if they do, they may want their money returned until verification of services can be provided. Swenson (1997) notes helpers now tend to keep records on computers, and while this makes record keeping easier, data stored in electronic form are copied "more easily and [are] harder to protect than paper data" (p. 93). It is important to remember that duties to maintain confidentiality apply just as much to electronic data as to written records. Identifying data about the client are recorded initially, as well as appointment times, cancellations, and so on. The intake or initial history-taking session is recorded next. In writing up an intake or history, it is important to avoid labels, jargon, and inferences. If records were subpoenaed, such statements could appear inflammatory or slanderous. Be as specific as possible. Don't make evaluative statements or clinical judgments without supporting documentation. For example, instead of writing "This client is homicidal," you might write "This client reports engaging in frequent (at least twice daily) fantasies of killing an unidentified or anonymous victim," or instead of "The client is disoriented," consider "The client could not remember where he was, why he was here, what day it was, and how old he was."

It is also important to keep notes of subsequent treatment sessions and of client progress. These can be recorded on a standardized form such as the Sample Treatment Planning Form (Figure 9.4) or in narrative form. (See also Chapter 11 for further discussion.) Generally, treatment notes are brief and highlight only the major activities of each session and client progress and improvement (or lack of it). These notes are usually started during intakes, with additional information added from the assessment interviews. As interviews progress, notations about goals, intervention strategies, and client progress are also included. Again, labels and inferences should always be avoided in written notes and records. Mitchell (2001) advocates the use of client participation in record keeping. He notes that reading your progress notes back to clients at the end of the sessions can encourage teamwork and reduce client stress and discontent.

It is also important to document in detail anything that has ethical or legal implications, particularly facts about case management. For example, with a client who reports depression and suicidal fantasies, it would be important to note that you conducted a suicide assessment and what its results were, that you consulted with your supervisor, and whether you did anything else to manage the case differently, such as seeing the client more frequently or setting up a contract with the client.

Many practitioners who are people-oriented persons complain about paperwork. If you fall into this group, be aware of Mitchell's (2001) dictum: "Write with pride." Mitchell (2001) points out that often we are judged by the kind of written record and paper trail we leave behind us.

CLIENT SELF-MONITORING ASSESSMENT

The data given by the client in the interview can be supplemented by client self-monitoring outside the interview. Self-monitoring can be defined as the process of observing specific things about oneself and one's interaction with others and the environment. In using self-monitoring as an assessment tool, the client is asked to record her or his observations in writing. These written recordings can be entered on a log or a daily record sheet. The future will surely involve the use of hand-held computers for collecting self-monitoring data (Haynes, 1998).

One purpose of client self-monitoring is to help the practitioner and client gain information about what actually occurs with respect to the issues in real-life settings. Another purpose is to validate the accuracy of the client's oral reports during the interviews. Client self-monitoring of situations and behaviors outside the interview should add more accuracy and specificity to the information discussed in the interview. As a result, client self-monitoring may accelerate treatment and enhance the client's expectations for change. Self-monitoring is also a useful way to test out hunches about the issue and to identify relations between classes of events such as thoughts, feelings, and behaviors.

As we mentioned earlier, a client can record observations on some type of written record, or log. Two types of logs can be used for different observations a client might make. A *descriptive log* can be used to record data about identification and selection of client concerns and strengths (see Figure 9.5). A *behavior log* can be used to record information about the behaviors and their antecedents and consequences or the relation between these classes of events (see Figure 9.6 for an example).

Silverman and Serafini (1998) observe that children have successfully used self-monitoring logs in a number of ways. If a more open-ended behavioral log is too difficult for any given child client, they recommend the use of a structured checklist instead.

MENTAL HEALTH NETWORK: OUTPATIENT TREATMENT REPORT (OTR)   Provider: _____

Client Name: _____ Birthdate: _____ Age: ____ Sex: M   F

A. ASSESSMENT

1. Presenting Problem (Client's Perspective): _____
   _____
   _____

2. Precipitating Event(s) (Why Help-seeking Now?): _____
   _____
   _____

3. Relevant Medical History (Medications, Drug/ETOH use, Illness, Injury, Surgery, etc.): _____
   _____
   _____

4. Prior Psychiatric/Psychological Conditions & Treatments: _____
   _____

5. Other Relevant History (Vocational/School, Relationship/Sexual, Social/Legal): _____

6. Brief Mental Status Evaluation: (Check as necessary)

APPEARANCE/DRESS	INTELLIGENCE	JUDGMENT/INSIGHT	DELUS./HALLUCIN.	THOUGHT DISORDER	RECENT MEMORY	REMOTE MEMORY
__ appropriate	__ high	__ intact	__ absent	__ absent	__ intact	__ intact
__ inappropriate	__ average	__ impaired	__ present	__ present	__ impaired	__ impaired
__ not assessed	__ low	__ not assessed	__ not assessed	__ not assessed	__ not assessed	__ not assessed

7. Mood/Affect: (Describe) _____

8. Suicide Assessment: (Risk, priors, plan) _____ Homicide Assessment: (Victim, violence, plan) _____

9. Clinical Formulation (Explanation of symptoms; include strengths/resources, obstacles to treatment/hidden agendas): Please be specific yet brief and clear ____
   _____
   _____

10. Code Nos. & Names DSM-4 Axis II: _____   Diagnostic Impressions: DSM-4 Axis I: _____

B. TREATMENT PLAN:

1. Focused, Targeted, Behavior & Measurable GOALS (Prioritize) Specifically Addressing Presenting Problems(s): Use as many rows as needed.

2. TYPE OF TREATMENT: Cognitive/Behavioral Interpersonal/Insight/Emotional Awareness Other: _____

3. DURATION: Service dates this OTR: _____ \# Sessions expected for DISCHARGE: _____ \# Discharge by (DATE): _____

4. MODE: Individual   Couple   Family   Individual/Family combination   Medication management   Group (if available)   Other (___)
          (90806)   (90847)   (90862)   (90853)   CPT Code___

PROBLEM(S)	GOALS	MEASURABLE SUCCESS CRITERION	SELECTED INTERVENTIONS
1. _____	_____	_____	_____
2. _____	_____	_____	_____
3. _____	_____	_____	_____

Therapist Signature & Phone: _____   Lic. No.: _____   Date: _____

Client Comments:

Figure 9.4 Sample Treatment Planning Form
Source: Adapted from the Treatment Planning Form, by Mental Health Network, Inc., 771 Corporate Drive, Suite 410, Lexington, KY. Reprinted by permission.

DAILY RECORD SHEET					
Date	Time	Place	Activity	People	Observed behavior

Figure 9.5 A Descriptive Log

SUMMARY

This chapter focused on the use of direct interviewing to assess client concerns. In many settings, initial assessment interviews often begin with an intake interview to gather information about the client's presenting issues and primary symptoms as well as information about such areas as previous counseling, social/developmental history, educational/vocational history, health history, and family, relationship, and sexual history. This interview often yields information that the practitioner can use to develop hypotheses about the nature of the client's issues. History interviews also serve as a retrospective baseline of how the client was functioning before and what events contributed to the present concerns and coping styles. For occasional clients, intakes or history interviews may be followed by a mental-status exam, which aids the helper in assessing the client's psychiatric status.

The model presented in this chapter for direct assessment interviewing is based on the person-in-environment and ABC models described in Chapter 8. Specifically, practitioners are interested in defining six components of behavior—affective, somatic, behavioral, cognitive, contextual, and relational. They also seek to identify antecedent events that occur before the issue and cue it, and consequent events that follow the issue and in some way influence it or maintain it. Consequences may include "payoffs," or secondary gains, that give value to the dysfunctional behavior and thus keep the issue going. Antecedent and consequent sources may also be affective, somatic, behavioral, cognitive, contextual, and relational. Contextual and relational ABCs form the basis of an environmental assessment to determine the ways in which clients' social network (or lack thereof) and environmental barriers and resources affect the issue.

Gender and multicultural factors must also be considered in the assessment interview. Other important components of direct assessment interviewing include identifying previous solutions the client has tried for resolving the issue, exploring individual and environmental strengths, exploring the client's perceptions of the issue, and identifying the frequency, duration, or severity of the concern.

In addition to direct assessment interviewing, other assessment tools include ecomaps, social network maps, role playing, imagery, self-report measures, and self-monitoring. All these techniques can be useful for obtaining more specific information about the identified concerns.

INFOTRAC® EXPLORATIONS

1. Search for articles on *clinical and behavioral interviewing,* and summarize one of these articles for your class.
2. Search for *social support systems,* and see what you can find about the research on social networks.

SUGGESTED RESOURCES

Readings

Barron, J. (Ed.). (1998). *Making diagnosis meaningful.* Washington, DC: American Psychological Association.

Bellack, A., & Hersen, M. (1998). *Behavioral assessment.* Needham Heights, MA: Allyn & Bacon.

Castillo, R. J. (1997). *Culture and mental illness.* Pacific Grove, CA: Brooks/Cole.

For Joan
Week of Nov. 6–13

Behavior observing	Date	Time	Place	(Frequency/ duration) Number or amount	(Antecedents) What precedes behavior	(Consequences) What follows behavior
1. Thinking of self as not as smart as other students	Mon., Nov. 6	10:00 A.M.	Math class	IIII	Going into class, know have to take test in class.	Leaving class, being with friends.
	Tues., Nov. 7	10:15 A.M.	Math class	IIII IIII	Got test back with a B.	Teacher consoled me.
	Tues., Nov. 7	5:30 P.M.	Home	IIII II	Parents asked about test. Told me to stay home this weekend.	Went to bed.
	Thurs., Nov. 9	9:30 A.M.	English class	II	Thought about having to go to math class.	Got to math class. Had substitute teacher.
	Sun., Nov. 12	9:30 P.M.	Home	III	Thought about school tomorrow.	Went to bed.
2. a. Not volunteering answers	Tues., Nov. 7	10:05 A.M. 10:20	Math class	II	Felt dumb.	Nothing.
b. Not answering teacher questions	Thurs., Nov. 9	10:10 A.M. 10:20 10:40	Math class	III	Felt dumb.	Nothing.
c. Not going to board	Thurs., Nov. 9	10:30 A.M.	Math class	I	Teacher called on me.	Nothing.
	Fri., Nov. 10	10:10 A.M. 10:35 A.M.	Math class	II	Teacher called on me.	Nothing.
	Thurs., Nov. 9	10:45 A.M.	Math class	I	Didn't have a substitute teacher.	Nothing.
	Fri., Nov. 10	10:15 A.M.	Math class	I	Teacher asked girls to go up to board.	Teacher talked to me after class.
3. Cutting class	Wed., Nov. 8	9:55 A.M.	School	1 hour	Didn't want to hassle with class or think about test.	Cut class. Played sick. Went to nurse's office for an hour.

Figure 9.6 Example of Behavior Log

Edelstein, B., & Semenchuk, E. (1996). Interviewing older adults. In L. Carstensen, B. Edelstein, & L. Dornbrand (Eds.), *The practical handbook of clinical gerontology* (pp. 153–173). Thousand Oaks, CA: Sage.

Follette, W., & Hayes, S. (2000). Contemporary behavior therapy. In C. Snyder & R. Ingram (Eds.), *Handbook of psychological change* (pp. 381–408). New York: Wiley.

Lazarus, A. (1997). *Brief but comprehensive psychotherapy: The multimodal way.* New York: Springer.

Linscott, J., & DiGiuseppe, R. (1998). Cognitive assessment. In A. Bellack & M. Hersen (Eds.), *Behavioral assessment* (pp. 104–125). Needham Heights, MA: Allyn & Bacon.

McAuliffe, G. J., & Eriksen, K. P. (1999). Toward a constructivist and developmental identity for the counseling profession: The context–phase–stage–style model. *Journal of Counseling & Development, 77,* 267–280.

Morrison, J. (1995). *DSM-IV made easy.* New York: Guilford.

Morrison, J. (1999). *When psychological problems mask medical disorders.* New York: Guilford.

Ridley, C., Li, L., & Hill, C. (1998). Multicultural assessment. *Counseling Psychologist, 26,* 827–910.

Smart, D. W., & Smart, J. F. (1997). DSM-IV and culturally sensitive diagnosis: Some observations for counselors. *Journal of Counseling & Development, 75,* 392–398.

Spitzer, R. L., Gibbon, M., Skodol, A. E., Williams, J. B., & First, M. B. (1994). *DSM-IV casebook.* Washington, DC: American Psychiatric Association.

Stamps, R., & Barach, P. (2001). *The therapist's Internet handbook.* New York: Norton.

Thyer, B., & Myers, L. (2000). Approaches to behavior change. In P. Allen-Meares & C. Garvin (Eds.), *Handbook of social work direct practice* (pp. 197–216). Thousand Oaks, CA: Sage.

Zarit, S., & Zarit, J. (1998). *Mental disorders in older adults.* New York: Guilford.

Web Sites

DSM-IV Diagnoses and Codes (Dr. Bob's Virtual En-psych-lopedia)
http://www.dr-bob.org/tips/dsm4a.html

Neurosciences on the Internet
http://www.neuroguide.com/

POSTEVALUATION

Part One

A client is referred to you with a presenting concern of "free-floating," or generalized (pervasive), anxiety. Outline the questions you would ask during an assessment interview with this client that pertain directly to her presenting component. Your objective (Chapter Objective One) is to identify at least 2 questions for each of the 11 assessment categories described in this chapter and summarized in Box 9.4. Feedback follows the postevaluation.

Part Two

Using the description of the above client, conduct a 30-minute role-play assessment interview in which your objective is to demonstrate leads and responses associated with at least 9 out of the 11 categories described for assessment (Chapter Objective Two). You can do this activity in triads in which one person assumes the role of helper, another the "anxious" client, and the third person the role of observer; trade roles two times. If groups are not available, audiotape or videotape your interview. Use the Interview Checklist at the end of the chapter as a guide to assess your performance and to obtain feedback.

After completing your interview, develop some hypotheses, or hunches, about the client. In particular, try to develop "guesses" about

1. Antecedent sources that cue or set off the anxiety, making its occurrence more likely
2. Consequences that maintain the anxiety, keep it going, or make it worse
3. Consequences that diminish or weaken the anxiety
4. Secondary gains, or payoffs, attached to the anxiety
5. Ways in which the client's "previous solutions" may contribute to the anxiety or make it worse
6. Particular individual and environmental strengths, resources, and coping skills of the client and how these might be best used during treatment/intervention
7. How the client's gender, culture, and environment affect the problem

You may wish to continue this part of the activity in triads or to do it alone, jotting down ideas as you proceed. At some point, it may be helpful to share your ideas with your group or your instructor.

Part Three

Devise a self-monitoring assessment procedure you could give to this client for homework in order to obtain information about the time, place, frequency, duration, and severity of her anxious feelings. Write an example of a log you could give to her to obtain this information (Chapter Objective Three).

Part Four

Conduct a role-play interview with this client in which you help her complete an ecomap using Figure 9.1 as a guide and a social network map using Figure 9.2 as a guide (Chapter Objective Four). If possible, continue with this activity in your triads, and obtain feedback from the observer.

Interview Checklist for Assessing Clients

Scoring		Category of information	Examples of helper leads or responses	Client response
Yes	No			
___	___	1. Explain purpose of assessment interview	"I am going to be asking you more questions than usual so that we can get an idea of what is going on. Getting an accurate picture about your concern will help us to decide what we can do about it. Your input is important."	___ (check if client confirmed understanding of purpose)
___	___	2. Identify range of concerns (if you don't have this information from history)	"What would you like to talk about today?" "What specifically led you to come to see someone now?" "Are there any other issues you haven't mentioned?"	___ (check if client described additional concerns)

(continued)

POST EVALUATION

(continued)

___ ___	3. Prioritize and select primary or most immediate issue to work on	"What issue best represents the reason you are here?" "Of all these concerns, which one is most stressful (or painful) for you?" "Rank-order these concerns, starting with the one that is most important for you to resolve to the one least important." "Tell me which of these issues you believe you could learn to deal with most easily and with the most success." "Which one of the things we discussed do you see as having the best chance of being solved?" "Out of all the things we've discussed, describe the one that, when resolved, would have the greatest impact on the rest of the issues."	____ (check if client selected issue to focus on)
___ ___	4.0. Present behavior		____ (check if client identified the following components)
	4.1. *Affective* aspects: feelings, emotions, mood states	"What are you feeling when this happens?" "How does this make you feel when this occurs?" "What other feelings do you have when this occurs?" "What feelings is this issue hiding or covering up?"	____ (check if client identified feelings)
___ ___	4.2. *Somatic* aspects: body sensations, physiological responses, organic dysfunction and illness, medications	"What goes on inside you then?" "What do you notice in your body when this happens?" "What are you aware of when this happens?" "When this happens, are you aware of anything that goes on in your body that feels bad or uncomfortable—aches, pains, and so on?"	____ (check if client identified body sensations)
___ ___	4.3. *Behavioral* aspects: overt behaviors/actions (excesses and deficits)	"In photographing this scene, what actions and dialogue would the camera pick up?" "What are you doing when this occurs?" "What do you mean by 'not communicating'?" "Describe what you did the last few times this occurred."	____ (check if client identified overt behavior)
___ ___	4.4. *Cognitive* aspects: automatic, helpful, unhelpful, rational, irrational thoughts and beliefs; internal dialogue; perceptions and misperceptions	"What do you say to yourself when this happens?" "What are you usually thinking about during this problem?" "What was going through your mind then?" "What kinds of thoughts can make you feel ____?" "What beliefs [or images] do you hold that affect this issue?" Sentence completions: I should ____, people should ____, it would be awful if ____, ____ makes me feel bad.	____ (check if client identified thoughts, beliefs)
___ ___	4.5. *Contextual* aspects: time, place, or setting events	"Describe some recent situations in which the issue occurred. Where were you? When was it?" "When does this usually occur?" "Where does this usually occur?" "Does this go on all the time or only sometimes?"	____ (check if client identified time, places, other events)

9 POST EVALUATION

CONDUCTING AN INTERVIEW ASSESSMENT WITH CLIENTS   249

	"Does the same thing happen at other times or places?"
	"At what time does this *not* occur? Places? Situations?"
	"What effect does your cultural/ethnic background have on this issue?"
	"What effects do the socio-political structures of the society in which you live have on this issue?"
	"How would you describe the relationship between yourself, your concerns, and your current environment? We could draw this relationship if you want to see it [using an ecomap]."
	"To what extent is your concern affected by oppression and discrimination that you experience in your environment?"
	"To what extent does your environment give or deny you access to power, privilege, and resources?"
	"What opportunities do you have in your environment for sharing spiritual and cultural values and activities?"

____ ____ 4.6. *Relational* aspects: other people "What effects does this concern have on significant others in your life?" ____ (check if client identified people)
"What effects do significant others have on this concern?"
"Who else is involved in the concern? How?"
"How does this person influence your life?"
"From whom do you think you learned to act or react this way?"
"How many significant close relationships do you have in your life now?"
"Whom do you know and respect who handles the issue the way you would like to?"
"What persons *present* in your life now have the greatest positive impact on this concern? Negative impact?"
"What about persons *absent* from your life?"
"Let's try filling out this drawing [social network map] to see what types of social support are available in your life right now."
"Who in your life empowers you? Disempowers you? Nourishes you? Feels toxic to you?"

____ ____ 5.0. Antecedents—past or current conditions that cue, or set off, the issue   ____ (check if client identified following antecedent sources)

____ ____ 5.1. *Affective* antecedents   "What are you usually feeling before this?"   ____ (feelings, mood states)
"When do you recall the first time you felt this way?"
"What are the feelings that occur before the issue and make it more likely to happen? Less likely?"
"Are there any holdover or unfinished feelings from past events in your life that still affect this issue? How?"

____ ____ 5.2. *Somatic* antecedents   "What goes on inside you just before this happens?"   ____ (body sensations, physiological responses)
"Are you aware of any particular sensations or discomfort just before the issue occurs or gets worse?"
"Are there any body sensations that seem to occur before the issue or when it starts that make it more likely to occur? Less likely?"

(continued)

POST EVALUATION

(continued)

____ ____		"Is there anything going on with you physically—like illness or a physical condition or in the way you eat or drink—that leads up to this issue?"	
____ ____	5.3. *Behavioral* antecedents	"If I were photographing this, what actions and dialogue would I pick up before this happens?" "Can you identify any particular behavior patterns that occur right before this happens?" "What do you typically do before this happens?"	____ (overt behavior)
____ ____	5.4. *Cognitive* antecedents	"What kinds of pictures do you have before this happens?" "What are your thoughts before this happens?" "What are you telling yourself before this happens?" "Can you identify any particular beliefs that seem to set the issue off?" "What do you think about [or tell yourself] before the issue occurs that makes it more likely to happen? Less likely?"	____ (thoughts, beliefs, internal dialogue, cognitive schemas)
____ ____	5.5. *Contextual* antecedents	"How long ago did this happen?" "Has this ever occurred at any other time in your life? If so, describe that." "Where and when did this occur the first time?" "How do you see those events as related to your concern?" "What things happened that seemed to lead up to this?" "What was happening in your life when you first noticed the issue?" "Are there any ways in which your cultural values and affiliations set off this issue? Make it more likely to occur? Less likely?" "How were things different before you had this concern?" "What do you mean, this started 'recently'?"	____ (time, places, other events)
____ ____	5.6. *Relational* antecedents	"Are there any people or relationships from past events in your life that still affect this concern? How?" "Can you identify any particular people that seem to bring on this concern?" "Are you usually with certain people right before or when this issue starts?" "Are there any people or relationships from the past that trigger this issue in some way? Who? How?" "How do the people who hold power in your life trigger this issue?"	____ (other people)
____ ____	6.0. Identify consequences—conditions that maintain and strengthen issue or weaken or diminish it		____ (check if client identified following sources of consequences)
____ ____	6.1. *Affective* consequences	"How do you feel after this happens?" "How does this affect the issue?" "When did you stop feeling this way?" "Are you aware of any particular feelings or reactions you have after the issue that strengthen it? Weaken it?"	____ (feelings, mood states)

9 POST EVALUATION

CONDUCTING AN INTERVIEW ASSESSMENT WITH CLIENTS 251

___ ___	6.2. *Somatic* consequences	"What are you aware of inside you—sensations in your body—just after this happens?" "How does this affect the issue?" "Are there any sensations inside you that seem to occur after the issue that strengthen or weaken it?" "Is there any physical condition, illness, and so on about yourself that seems to occur after this issue? If so, how does it affect the issue?"	____ (body or internal sensations)
___ ___	6.3. *Behavioral* consequences	"What do you do after this happens, and how does this make the issue better? Worse?" "How do you usually react after this is over?" "In what ways does your reaction keep the issue going? Weaken it or stop it?" "Can you identify any particular behavior patterns that occur after this?" "How do these patterns keep the problem going? Stop it?"	____ (overt responses)
___ ___	6.4. *Cognitive* consequences	"What do you usually think about afterward?" "How does this affect the issue?" "What do you picture after this happens?" "What do you tell yourself after this occurs?" "Can you identify any particular thoughts [beliefs, self-talk] that make the issue better? Worse?" "Are there certain thoughts or images you have afterward that either strengthen or weaken the issue?"	____ (thoughts, beliefs, internal dialogue)
___ ___	6.5. *Contextual* consequences	"When does this issue usually stop or go away? Get worse? Get better?" "Where are you when the issue stops? Gets worse? Gets better?" "Can you identify any particular times, places, or events that seem to keep the issue going? Make it worse or better?" "Are there any ways in which your cultural affiliation and values seem to keep this issue going? Stop it or weaken it?"	____ (time, places, other events)
___ ___	6.6. *Relational* consequences	"Can you identify any particular reactions from other people that occur following the issue?" "In what ways do their reactions affect the issue?" "Are you usually with certain people when the issue gets worse? Better?" "What happens to you after you have interacted with this person?" "Can you identify any particular people who can make the issue worse? Better? Stop it? Keep it going?" "How do the people who have power in your life situation perpetuate this concern?"	____ (other people)
___ ___	7. Identify possible secondary gains from issue	"What happened afterward that was pleasant?" "What was unpleasant about what happened?" "Has your concern ever produced any special advantages or considerations for you?" "As a consequence of your concern, have you got out of or avoided things or events?" "How does this concern help you?"	____ (check if client identified payoffs)

(continued)

9 POST EVALUATION

(continued)

____ ____	8. Identify solutions already tried to solve the issue	"What do you get out of this situation that you don't get out of other situations?" "Do you notice anything that happens afterward that you try to prolong or to produce?" "Do you notice anything that occurs after the problem that you try to stop or avoid?" "Are there certain feelings or thoughts that go on after the issue that you try to prolong?" "Are there certain feelings or thoughts that go on after the issue that you try to stop or avoid?" "The good thing about _____ [issue] is . . ." "How have you dealt with this or other issues before? What was the effect? What made it work or not work?" "How have you tried to resolve this concern?" "What kinds of things have you done to improve this situation?" "What have you done that has made the issue better? Worse? Kept it the same?"	____ (check if client identified prior solutions)
____ ____	9. Identify client coping skills, strengths, resources	"What have others done to help you with this?" "What skills or things do you have going for you that might help you with this concern?" "Describe a situation when this concern is not interfering." "What strengths or assets can you use to help resolve this?" "When don't you act this way?" "What kinds of thoughts or self-talk help you handle this better?" "When don't you think in self-defeating ways?" "What do you say to yourself to cope with a difficult situation?" "Identify the steps you take in a situation you handle well—what do you think about and what do you do? How could these steps be applied to the present issue?" "To what extent can you do something for yourself without relying on someone else to push you or prod you to do it?" "How often do you get things done by rewarding yourself in some way? By punishing yourself?" "What resources are available to you from your community and your environment?" "What kinds of things in your community and environment do you consider to be strengths and assets?" "What do you find meaning in from particular aspects of your culture?"	____ (check if client identified assets, coping skills)
____ ____	10. Identify client's description/assessment of the issue (note which aspects of issue are stressed and which are ignored)	"What is your understanding of this issue?" "How do you explain this concern to yourself?" "What does the issue mean to you?" "What is your interpretation [analysis] of the concern?" "What else is important to you about the concern that we haven't mentioned?"	____ (check if client explained issue)

9 POST EVALUATION

___ ___	11. Estimate frequency, duration, or severity of behavior/symptoms (assign monitoring homework, if useful)	"Sum up the issue in just one word." "Give the concern a title." "How often [how much] does this occur during a day—a week?" "How long does this feeling stay with you?" "How many times do you ____ a day? A week?" "To what extent has this interfered with your life? How?" "You say sometimes you feel very anxious. On a scale from 1 to 10, with 1 being very calm and 10 being very anxious, where would you put your feelings?" "How has this interfered with other areas of your life?" "What would happen if the issue were not resolved in a year?"	____ (check if client estimated amount or severity)

Other skills

Yes   No
___ ___ 12. The helper listened attentively and recalled accurately the information given by the client.
___ ___ 13. The helper used basic listening responses to clarify and synthesize the information shared by the client.
___ ___ 14. The helper followed the client's lead in determining the sequence or order of the information obtained.

Observer comments: _____
_____
_____

9 POST EVALUATION
FEEDBACK

PART ONE

See whether the questions you generated are similar to the following ones:

Is this the only issue you're concerned about now in your life, or are there other issues you haven't mentioned yet? (Range of concerns)

When you say you feel anxious, what exactly do you mean? (Behavior—affective component)

When you feel anxious, what do you experience inside your body? (Behavior—somatic component)

When you feel anxious, what exactly are you usually doing? (Behavior—behavioral component)

When you feel anxious, what are you typically thinking about [or saying to yourself]? (Behavior—cognitive component)

Try to pinpoint exactly what times the anxiety occurs or when it is worse. (Behavior—contextual component)

Describe where you are or in what situations you find yourself when you get anxious. (Behavior—contextual component)

Describe what other things are usually going on when you have these feelings. (Behavior—contextual component)

How would you describe the relationship between yourself and these concerns and your current environment? (Behavior—contextual component)

How does your cultural community and affiliation affect this issue? (Behavior—contextual component)

Can you tell me what persons are usually around when you feel this way? (Behavior—relational component)

How would you describe your support in your life right now? (Behavior—relational component)

Who in your life now empowers you? Disempowers you? (Behavior—relational component)

Are there any feelings that lead up to this? (Antecedent source—affective)

What about body sensations that might occur right before these feelings? (Antecedent source—somatic)

Have you noticed any particular behavioral reactions or patterns that seem to occur right before these feelings? (Antecedent source—behavioral)

(continued)

POST EVALUATION FEEDBACK

(continued)

Are there any kinds of thoughts—things you're dwelling on—that seem to lead up to these feelings? (Antecedent source—cognitive)

When was the first time you noticed these feelings? Where were you? (Antecedent source—contextual)

Can you recall any other events or times that seem to be related to these feelings? (Antecedent source—contextual)

Does the presence of any particular people in any way set these feelings off? (Antecedent source—relational)

Are you aware of any particular other feelings that make the anxiety better or worse? (Consequence source—affective)

Are you aware of any body sensations or physiological responses that make these feelings better or worse? (Consequence source—somatic)

Is there anything you can do specifically to make these feelings stronger or weaker? (Consequence source—behavioral)

Can you identify anything you can think about or focus on that seems to make these feelings better or worse? (Consequence source—cognitive)

At what times do these feelings diminish or go away? Get worse? In what places? In what situations? (Consequence source—contextual)

Do certain people you know seem to react in ways that keep these feelings going or make them less intense? If so, how? (Consequence source—relational)

As a result of this anxiety, have you ever gotten out of or avoided things you dislike? (Consequence—secondary gain)

Has this problem with your nerves ever resulted in any special advantages or considerations for you? (Consequence—secondary gain)

What have you tried to do to resolve this issue? How have your attempted solutions worked out? (Previous solutions)

Describe some times and situations when you don't have these feelings or you feel calm and relaxed. What goes on that is different in these instances? (Coping skills)

How have you typically coped with other difficult situations or feelings in your life before? (Coping skills)

What resources are available to you from your culture and community that you can use to help with this problem? (Individual and environmental strengths—coping)

What kinds of things in your community and environment do you feel are strengths and assets? (Individual and environmental strengths—coping)

If you could give this problem a title—as if it were a movie or a book—what would that title be? (Client perceptions of issue)

How do you explain these feelings to yourself? (Client perceptions of issue)

How many times do these feelings crop up during a given day? (Frequency of issue)

How long do these feelings stay with you? (Duration of issue)

On a scale from 1 to 10, with 1 being not intense and 10 being very intense, how strong would you say these feelings usually are? (Severity of issue)

PART THREE

To start with, you may want to obtain information directly related to the environmental conditions surrounding her experience of anxiety.

The log might look something like this:

Date   Time   Place   Activity   People

The client would be asked to record anxious feelings daily and to note the environmental events occurring at that time. Later, you may wish to add recording of information about duration and severity. You could add these two columns to the log:

How long   Intensity (1 to 10)

Although it might be valuable to ask the client also to observe and record cognitions (thoughts, beliefs), there is some evidence that many anxious clients fail to complete this part of self-monitoring because attending to cognitions is reactive and may cue, or increase, rather than decrease the anxiety (Hollon & Kendall, 1981).

CHAPTER 10

IDENTIFYING, DEFINING, AND EVALUATING OUTCOME GOALS

Pause for a few minutes to answer the following questions by yourself or with someone else.
1. What is one thing you would like to change about yourself?
2. Suppose you succeeded in accomplishing this change. How would things be different for you?
3. Does this outcome represent a change in yourself or for someone else?
4. What are some of the risks—to you or others—of this change?
5. What would be your payoffs for making this change?
6. What would you be doing, thinking, or feeling as a result of this change?
7. In what situations do you want to be able to do this?
8. How much or how often would you like to be able to do this?
9. Looking at where you are now and where you'd like to be, are there some steps along the way to get from here to there? If so, rank them in an ordered list from "easiest to do now" to "hardest to do."
10. Identify any obstacles (people, feelings, ideas, situations) that might interfere with the attainment of your goal.
11. Identify any resources (skills, people, knowledge) that you need to use or acquire to attain your goal.
12. How could you evaluate progress toward this outcome?

These steps reflect the process of identifying, defining, and evaluating goals for counseling. Goals represent desired results or outcomes and function as milestones of client progress. In this chapter we describe and model concrete guidelines you can use to help clients identify, define, and evaluate outcome goals for counseling.

OBJECTIVES

After completing this chapter, the student should be able to
1. Identify a situation about you or your life that you would like to change. Identify and define one desired outcome for this issue, using the Goal-Setting Worksheet in the Postevaluation as a guide.
2. Given a written client case description, describe the steps you would use with this client to explore and define desired outcome goals, with at least 11 of the 14 categories for selecting and defining goals represented in your description.
3. Demonstrate at least 11 of the 14 categories associated with identifying and defining outcome goals, given a role-play interview.
4. With yourself or another person or client, conduct an outcome evaluation of a real or a hypothetical counseling goal, specifying *when, what,* and *how* you will measure the outcome.

OUTCOME GOALS AND THEIR PURPOSES IN THE HELPING PROCESS

Treatment goals represent results or outcomes described by clients and are a direct outgrowth of the problems identified during the assessment process. Goals have six important purposes. First, they provide some directions for helping. Clearly defined goals reflect the areas of client concern that need most immediate attention. Establishing goals can also clarify the client's initial expectations. Goals may help both practitioner and client anticipate more precisely what can and cannot be accomplished through the helping process.

Although each theoretical orientation has its own direction, specifying goals individually for each client helps to ensure that helping is structured specifically to meet the needs of *that* client. Clients are much more likely to support and commit themselves to changes that they create than changes imposed by someone else. Without goals, the helping process may be directionless or may be based more on the theoretical biases and personal preferences of the helper (Bandura, 1969, p. 70). Some clients may go through counseling without realizing that the sessions are devoid of direction or are more consistent with the helper's preferences than the client's needs and aims. In other aspects of our lives, however, most of us would be quite aware of analogous situations. If we boarded a cruise ship destined for a place of our choice and the ship went around in circles or the pilots announced a change of destination that they desired, we would be upset and indignant.

Second, goals permit helpers to determine whether they have the skills, competencies, and interests for working with a particular client toward a particular outcome. Depending on the client's choice of goals and the helper's values and level of expertise, the helper decides whether to continue working with the client or to refer the client to someone else who may be in a better position to give services.

The third purpose of goals is their role in human cognition and problem solving. Goals help with successful performance and problem resolution because they are usually rehearsed in our working memory and because they direct our attention to the resources and components in our environment that are most likely to help with the solution of a problem (Dixon & Glover, 1984, pp. 128–129). This purpose of goals is quite evident in the performance of successful athletes, who set goals for themselves and then use the goals not only as motivating devices but also as standards against which they rehearse their performance over and over, often cognitively or with imagery. For example, running backs in football constantly "see themselves" getting the ball and running downfield, over and past the goal line. Champion snow skiers are often seen closing their eyes and bobbing their heads in the direction of the course before the race. In the case of helping goals, it is important for clients to be able to visualize and rehearse the target behaviors or end results reflected in their goals.

A fourth purpose of goals is to give the helper some basis for selecting and using particular change strategies and interventions. The changes that the client desires will, to some degree, determine the kinds of action plans and treatment strategies that can be used with some likelihood of success. Without an explicit identification of what the client wants, it is almost impossible to explain and defend one's choice to move in a certain direction or to use one or more change strategies. Without goals, the helper may use a particular approach without any rational basis (Bandura, 1969, p. 70). Whether the approach will be helpful is left to chance rather than choice.

A fifth and most important purpose of goals is their role in an outcome evaluation. Goals can indicate the difference between what and how much the client is able to do now and what and how much the client would like to do in the future. With the ultimate goal in mind, the helper and client can monitor progress toward the goal and measure effectiveness of a change intervention. These data provide continuous feedback to both helper and client. The feedback can be used to assess the feasibility of the goal and the effectiveness of the intervention.

Finally, goal-planning systems are useful because, like assessment procedures, they are often reactive; that is, clients make progress in change as a result of the goal-planning process itself. Goals induce an expectation for improvement, and purposeful goal setting contributes to a client's sense of hopefulness and well-being (Csikszentmihalyi, 1990). As Snyder (1995) notes, "Higher as compared to lower hope people have a greater number of goals, have more difficult goals, have success at achieving their goals, and perceive their goals as challenges" (p. 357).

CULTURAL ISSUES IN OUTCOME GOALS

Sue and Sue (1999) point out that "closely linked to the actual process of counseling are certain implicit or explicit goals . . . and that different cultural and subcultural groups may require different counseling processes and goals" (p. 220). They note that any given client may be exposed to one of four conditions in the helping process, as shown in Table 10.1.

We have commented in earlier chapters about the cultural relevance (or lack of relevance) of helping skills and processes for clients from varied cultural groups. In this chapter, we stress the importance of heeding Sue and Sue's (1999) concern about who determines the helping goals and the relevance of these goals for the client. These authors provide the following example to distinguish between appropriate and inappropriate helping goals:

An African American male student from the ghetto who is failing in school and getting into fights with other students can be treated by a school counselor in a variety of ways. Sometimes such a student lacks the academic skills necessary to get good

TABLE 10.1 Process and Goals in Counseling

Process	Goals
1. Appropriate	Appropriate
2. Appropriate	Inappropriate
3. Inappropriate	Appropriate
4. Inappropriate	Inappropriate

grades. The constant fighting is a result of peers' teasing him about his "stupidity." A counselor who is willing to teach the student study and test-taking skills as well as give advice and information may be using an appropriate process consistent with the expectations of the student. The appropriate goals defined between counselor and client, besides acquisition of specific skills, may be an elevation of grades. . . .

Often, a helping strategy may be chosen by the therapist that is compatible with the client's life experiences, but the goals are questionable. Again, let us take the aforementioned example of the African American ghetto student. Here the counselor may define the goal as the elimination of "fighting behavior." The chosen technique may be behavior modification. Since the approach stresses observable behaviors and provides a systematic, precise, and structured approach to the "problem," much of the nebulousness and mystique of counseling is reduced for the Black student. Rather than introspection and self-analysis, which some people of color may find unappealing, the concrete tangible approach of behavioral counseling is extremely attractive.

While the approach may be a positive experience for many minorities, there is danger here regarding control and behavioral objectives. If the Black student is being tested and forced to fight because he is a minority-group member, then the goal of "stopping fighting behavior" may be inappropriate. The counselor in this situation may inadvertently be imposing his or her own standards and values on the client. The end goals place the problem in the hands of the individual rather than society, which produced the problems (Sue & Sue, 1999, pp. 221–222).

Brown (1994) has offered a similar caveat with respect to gender-aware therapy for clients. She suggests that the particular way the helper conceptualizes the case will affect the client's choice of goals. A feminist and a systemic interpretation—which places emphasis on the contribution of external sociopolitical factors—allows clients to have different choices about helping outcomes: "Rather than compliantly taking on tasks assigned by the dominant culture—for example, 'Stop being depressed, become more productive'—a person furnished with this sort of knowledge may develop alternative goals for therapy such as 'Learn to get angry more often and see my connections to other people more clearly'" (Brown, 1994, p. 170). Werner-Wilson, Zimmerman, and Price (1999) discuss another way in which gender may affect selection of treatment goals. They note that in heterosexual-couples therapy, male and female clients may identify different problems and different desired outcomes. Influenced by gender socialization, helpers may not pursue the goals of women clients if they do not recognize the tendency of many women to accommodate (p. 254).

Rosado and Elias (1993) point out that mainstream practitioners often expect clients to develop long-range helping goals (p. 454). They note that these sorts of goals are inconsistent with the mind-set of some clients from urban and/or low-income areas. They recommend developing goals to meet "the pressing ecological need of these clients, even if they are of a short duration" (p. 454). As the authors note, financially indigent clients are concerned with survival issues and resolution of current problems. Similarly, Berg and Jaya (1993) note that for many Asian American clients, goals need to be developed that are short term, realistic, pragmatic, concrete, and oriented toward solutions.

In using cultural awareness to develop goals, the important point for helpers is to be aware of their own values and biases and to avoid deliberately or inadvertently steering the client toward goals that may reflect the norms and scripts of the mainstream culture rather than the client's expressed wishes (Burnett, Anderson, & Heppner, 1995; Chojnacki & Gelberg, 1995). A clear-cut example of this is in respecting a client's preferred sexual orientation when it is different from your own. It is also important to be attentive "to any possible conflicts between the client's own goals and the goals of others" in the client's immediate context, such as school, work, and family (Shiang, 2000, p. 176). For example, a son may define what it means to be a good son in a different way than his parents or his collective cultural group or his faith-based group.

CHANGE ISSUES IN OUTCOME GOALS

At the simplest level, an outcome goal represents what the client wants to happen as a result of the treatment process. Stated another way, outcome goals are an extension of the types of problems that the client experiences.

In change issues, the outcome goal is a change the client wants to make. The desired goals may reflect changes within the individual client, within the client's environment, or both. The desired changes may be in overt behaviors or situations, covert behaviors, or combinations of the two. These outcome goals may be directed at decreasing something, increasing something, developing something, or restructuring something. Furthermore, Lyddon (1995) distinguishes between first-order and second-order changes that clients make. First-order changes consist primarily of relatively simple linear movements whereas second-order changes are complex, nonlinear, and radical. First-order changes represent more or less minor adaptations a client makes; second-order change is core or deep—that is, "a radical restructuring of a person's core self, mode of being, or worldview" (Hanna & Ritchie, 1995, p. 176). As an example of these two kinds of changes, consider a client who presents with alcohol and sexual addictions. The client is a 30-year-old male who drinks a six-pack of beer daily and has had sex with over 200 women in the last 20 years. His first sexual experience occurred at age 10, when he was "seduced" by a 21-year-old woman. He noted that this experience felt good, so he continued to seek out multiple sexual partners. History reveals that he is an only child who grew up with two alcoholic parents and witnessed multiple instances of domestic violence between the two. He is also a self-professed workaholic who has come to counseling because he has developed a severe case of hypertension and because his physician has ordered him to slow down, work less, and cut back on his beer. He wants you to help him learn to take breaks from his work and to enjoy his leisure time when he does. He considers his childhood to have been relatively happy and normal, and shows no awareness of the relationship between his experiences in his family of origin and his current problems.

During the process of therapy, one of two things may happen: He may learn to cut back on his beer intake and on his work hours—a first-order change. It is also conceivable that he could begin to experience all the intense grief and rage that his addictions mask and experience change at a very deep, gut, or core level—a second-order change. However, it is important that his helper honor the level of change *he* requests. Mahoney (2000) cautions that the "cult of progress" reflected by client change—especially deeper-level change—is a "seductive" one and that it is "ethically irresponsible" to promise a client that anything can be permanently eliminated by therapy, particularly "old patterns" (p. 5).

Prochaska, DiClemente, and Norcross (1992) have developed a transtheoretical model of client change. Their model suggests that a client experiences five stages of change in moving toward a particular outcome:

1. *Precontemplation:* The client is unaware of a need for change or does not intend to change.
2. *Contemplation:* The client is aware of a need for change and thinks seriously about it but has not decided to make it.
3. *Preparation:* The client has decided to take some action in the near future and also has taken some action in the recent past that was not successful.
4. *Action:* The client has begun to engage in successful action steps toward the desired outcome but has not yet attained the outcome.
5. *Maintenance:* The client reaches his or her goals and now works both to prevent backslides and to consolidate changes made in the action phase.

A concrete example of this stage model of change is a person who exhibits verbally abusive behavior toward her or his colleagues. In the *precontemplation* phase, the client either doesn't recognize a need to change her or his abusive behavior or doesn't care; this person is content with things the way they are. The client moves into the *contemplation* phase as he or she becomes aware of some of the effects the abusive behavior has and starts to think about changing.

Next, the client attempts some change or problem-solution program but is unsuccessful—yet still plans to take additional action in the near future. This is the *preparation* stage. As the client finds successful ways of modifying his or her abusive behavior and commits to these, the *action* phase is initiated. Finally, he or she engages in behaviors to maintain the changes and to prevent recurrence of the abuse; this is the *maintenance* phase.

Over the last 15 years, clinical research has provided support for this model (Prochaska, 2000). These five stages have been found to relate to client self-managed change, treatment intervention, treatment outcome effectiveness, and persistence in therapy. In areas such as weight loss and substance abuse, smoking, hypertension management, and HIV/AIDS, clients who are in or use these stages have more positive treatment outcomes than those who do not (Prochaska, 2000). Further, the research suggests that clients in the first two stages are not as ready for change as those in later stages and that if they start, they may terminate the change process prematurely (Smith, Subich, & Kalodner, 1995).

This model has important implications for both goal setting and treatment selection because of several reasons. First, as practitioners, we need to have an understanding of what it means to change if we are to effect change in clients. Also, a client's readiness to change is a critical factor in developing outcome goals and selecting intervention strategies. Clients in Stage 1, *precontemplation* (see Table 10.2), come to counseling at someone else's request or under some sort of pressure: "Often the source of pressure is a system, such as the family, peer group, or organization of which the individual is a part" (Reid & Misener, 2000, p. 245). Clients in the precontemplation stage simply do not intend to change in the near future. As a result, they are uninterested and "avoid reading, talking, or thinking" about any change (Prochaska, 1999, p. 229). These clients *underestimate the benefits* of change and *overestimate the costs* of change and are *unaware* of this (Prochaska, 1999, p. 229). Some people stay stuck in the precontemplation stage of change for years and may get "unstuck" only after some sort of catalytic environmental, life, or developmental event. Initially, these clients may not participate in goal setting because they don't "own" the goal for change. The practitioner's task is to help these clients begin to contemplate the issue and their

TABLE 10.2	Stages of Change and Corresponding Interventions	
Stages of change	**Corresponding interventions**	**Role of helper**
Precontemplation	Be optimistic. Provide rationale for interventions and change. Convey respect and use active listening skills. Increase the "pros" of change.	Nurturing parent
Contemplation	Educate client about change process. Decrease the disadvantages or costs of change. Support client's ambivalence about change.	Socratic teacher
Preparation	Define, work toward, and evaluate selected outcomes. Present all alternatives. Encourage brief experiments with change.	Experienced coach
Action	Develop cognitions and skills to prevent relapse/setbacks prior to termination. Review action plan.	
Maintenance	Provide emotional support	Consultant

role in it as well as the possibility of a new response. Being optimistic and providing a good rationale for interventions and change can help in this process. Also, listening to the client's point of view and conveying respect are important. As the helper, it is important to "restrain" yourself, for trying to get the client to do something different will backfire. Prochaska (2000, p. 121) regards the role of the helper with clients at the precontemplation stage as a "nurturing parent." To help the client in precontemplation move to contemplation, the benefits of change must increase for the client. Prochaska (2000, p. 116) recommends asking these clients to make a list of the advantages of change, and then to double or triple it before the next session.

Clients in Stage 2, *contemplation,* may acknowledge the existence of a concern but may not see themselves as part of the solution, at least initially. Clients in this stage intend to change in the next six months, but not immediately (Prochaska, 1999). Clients who get stuck in this stage are often "chronic contemplators" who substitute thinking for action (Prochaska, 2000). Helpers have to be careful about reinforcing the client's contemplation. Part of the way in which the contemplation can be inhibiting action is that these clients contemplate their ambivalence—their uncertainty about whether the benefits of change are worth the assumed costs of it. With these clients, it is important to recognize their vacillation and to remember that ambivalence about change is common. All of us have what the Jungian approach refers to as "tension of the opposites" (as Mahoney [2000, p. 5] explains, "we all are trying to change and to stay the same"), with the need to hold on to what is familiar while testing out what is new. The therapist must first help these clients explore the advantages and disadvantages of working toward a specific outcome so they can find outcomes that are realistic and feasible and are likely to result in more benefits than costs. To help clients move from the contemplation stage to the preparation and action stages, the presumed costs for the client of change must decrease. Specifically, the benefits of change must be at least two times greater than the perceived and actual costs (Prochaska, 2000, p. 117). Prochaska (2000, p. 121) regards the role of the helper with clients in the contemplation stage as a "socratic teacher." As helpers, we need to be able to determine what stage of change our clients are in. Clients in the precontemplation and contemplation stages are simply not ready for the more traditional intervention strategies typically used in psychotherapy (such as the ones we describe in Chapters 12–18). If helpers treat clients in these two stages as if they were starting like those in the action stage, they will feel too pressured and are likely to drop out of therapy. Later in this chapter, we will describe one intervention useful for these first two stages called *motivational interviewing.*

Clients in the stages of *preparation* and *action* acknowledge that there is a problem, see themselves as part of the solution, and are committed to working toward specific outcomes (see Table 10.2). In general, as Smith and colleagues (1995) observe, "Persons further along in the stages seem more likely to progress and benefit from therapy" (p. 35). Clients in the preparation stage intend to take some action soon. They may have already tried something and they may have a plan (Prochaska, 1999). With these clients, the helper's task is to help them define their goals in specific ways so that progress toward outcomes can be determined. Outcome evaluation is important not only so that clients can see their actual progress but also to substantiate the effectiveness of the helping process. Increasingly, mental health providers working in agencies or receiving reimbursement from managed care companies are required to conduct outcome evaluations of the helping process. Specifically with clients in the preparation stage, practitioners can help them identify, try on, and experiment with change strategies, usually ones that are brief. Helpers can also present alternatives and possibilities. Prochaska (2000, p. 121) regards the role of the helper for clients in the preparation and action stages as an "experienced coach." Clients in the action stage are more self-directed and have made "specific, overt modifications in their lifestyle within the past 6 months" (Prochaska, 1999, p. 230). With these clients, the helper's tasks are to provide emotional support, review the client's action plan to see if it likely to be successful, and to maximize client choices (Prochaska, 1999).

Clients in Stage 5, *maintenance,* often face difficulties in maintaining changes acquired in the prior stages. It is often easier to prepare and act than to maintain. As clients reach this stage and before they terminate counseling, it is important to work on beliefs and actions to equip them to maintain changes as well as to prevent setbacks and relapses. Maintenance goals and skills are especially important in such areas as substance abuse, mood disorders such as depression, and chronic mental health problems such as schizophrenia. Prochaska (2000, p. 121) regards the role of helper with clients in the action and maintenance stages as a "consultant." An approach that seems particularly useful in working with clients at this last stage of the change model is Marlatt and Gordon's (1985) *relapse prevention* model. This model, which has been used frequently for relapse prevention in addictive behaviors (DeJong, 1994; MacKay & Marlatt, 1990), focuses on helping clients to

1. Identify high-risk situations for relapse
2. Acquire behavioral and cognitive coping skills
3. Attend to issues of balance in lifestyle

A recent meta-analysis on the relapse prevention model supported the overall effectiveness of relapse prevention in both reducing substance use—especially alcohol—and in improving psychological adjustment. These outcomes were consistent for both inpatient and outpatient settings and for individual, group, and couples treatment modalities (Irvin et al., 1999).

The model and processes we have described in this section are summarized in Table 10.2. As Cooper (1995) notes, it is important for therapists to recognize what stage of change is reflected by each client as different kinds of interventions are required depending on the particular style. Practitioners who are familiar with this change model can actively use it in the helping process by first identifying the stage a given client is in and then by applying the appropriate methods of change to move the client from one stage to another. Prochaska (1999) recommends that helpers set realistic goals for working with clients at each stage of the change model—with just the goal of trying to help a client move to the *next* stage. As he notes, helpers are increasingly under pressure to produce immediate results. If this pressure gets transferred to clients, many will get discouraged, become "resistant," and drop out of the helping process altogether (p. 227).

RESISTANCE ISSUES IN OUTCOME GOALS

The transtheoretical stages-of-change model has important implications for developing outcome goals with all clients, and particularly with clients who are uninterested in changing or are "involuntary" clients. Involuntary clients are in treatment under pressure, duress, or even coercion—for example, a client may be referred to substance abuse treatment instead of being sent to prison. When clients remain stuck in the precontemplation or contemplation stages of change, it is very easy for helpers to regard them as "unmotivated or resistant" to change. Yet, as Hubble, Duncan, and Miller (1999) assert, "the idea of an unmotivated client is not true . . . it is more correct to say the motivation of unmotivated clients may not match the therapist's goals and expectations" (p. 413). One approach that practitioners can use to help clients stuck in the precontemplation and contemplation stages of change (in addition to what we already have presented) is called *motivational interviewing,* or MI.

Motivational Interviewing

Motivational interviewing is an interviewing style defined as a direct yet client-centered helping style characterized by warmth, empathy, key questions, and reflective listening, designed to help clients explore and resolve ambivalence about change (Rollnick & Miller, 1995). MI seems to work especially well with involuntary clients who are not yet invested in identifying any outcome goals—usually because they don't believe that they have a problem or because they view someone else as the problem. In MI, the helper

carefully avoids a classic confrontational approach in which the therapist asserts the need for change while the client denies it. Instead of seeking to persuade directly, the counselor systematically elicits *from the client* and reinforces reasons for concern and change while maintaining a warm and supportive atmosphere for exploration of ambivalent feelings. Resistance is not confronted head-on but is skillfully deflected to encourage continued open exploration. (Miller, 1996, pp. 839–840)

MI has received a good deal of empirical support with a variety of different problems; it is especially effective with substance abuse (Miller, 1996). In one study, problem drinkers who participated in 4 weeks of MI treatment (called motivational enhancement training [MET] in this study) had comparable changes in the year after treatment to people who participated in a 12-week cognitive–behavioral treatment or a 12-week 12-step approach (Project MATCH, 1997). In addiction treatment, over 3 decades of MI research have produced the following conclusions:

1. Brief MI interventions can trigger significant client change.
2. Increasing the intensity of treatment does not consistently improve outcome.
3. Empathy of the helper is a potent predictor of client change.
4. A single MI session substantially augments the outcome of subsequent treatment. (Miller, 2000)

Rollnick, Mason, and Butler (1999) conclude that while there is evidence for the effectiveness of MI with some problems and in some settings, "our understanding of exactly why MI seems to work, and how to improve it, still needs a great deal of attention" (p. 210). Also, if skill deficits are present, clients at some point later in treatment will also benefit from skill training as well as MI (Baer, Kivlahan, & Donovan, 1999).

Classic MI involves the following five interviewing steps:

1. *Use empathy.* Use listening responses such as paraphrase and reflection (see Chapter 5) to show the client that you are attentive. Show interest by asking the client to tell you about a typical day (Killick & Allen, 1997). Avoid labels throughout the MI interviewing process, such as "your problem" (Killick & Allen, 1997).
2. *Develop discrepancy.* Wait until the client expresses a concern about his or her behavior. Then use this client state of concern to identify discrepancies between the client's current behavior and his or her important goals. Use open-ended questions (see Chapter 7) to explore their goals. Contrast the "cons" of the current behavior with the "pros" of change. The client may want to write down the pros and cons in a "balance sheet," with reasons for keeping the behavior in one column and reasons for giving it up in the other column (Hohmann, 1998). Ask the client to think about her or his life in five years, both with and without the current concern (Treasure & Ward, 1997). Be sure to reflect the reasons for change repeatedly so that the client hears this at least two times (Lawendowski, 1998). Do not confront in this process; instead, use summarization (see Chapter 5) to provide feedback about these pros and cons. As well, the summarization feedback can be written—in a letter the helper sends to the client after the MI interview (Treasure & Ward, 1997). Be very careful about the language you use in this process of developing the discrepancy. Inquire about good and "less good" things about the situation rather than "negative" or "bad" things about the "problem" (Rollnick, Heather, & Bell, 1992). Also, in the process of exploring pros and cons, be careful to limit the amount of information you provide (see Chapter 7). If the client is happy with things the way they are, no amount of information in the world is likely to be useful. When you do give information, soften your approach by asking something like "Would you be interested in learning about or hearing about ____?" (Killick & Allen, 1997, p. 39). If the client says no, honor the no!
3. *Avoid argumentation.* Do not get into a power struggle with the client. Don't push a client to change or to accept a label about himself or herself, such as alcoholic, abuser, wife beater, and so on. Labels are emotionally loaded and may arouse more defensiveness in the client (Hohmann, 1998). Although you may feel a strong desire to confront a client whose issues are especially difficult for others, this often leads to increased resistance—covert, if not overt (Treasure & Ward, 1997). Demanding change polarizes clients and may reinforce their "stuckness" in the precontemplation or contemplation stage of change.
4. *Roll with resistance.* When "resistance" surfaces, roll with it by acknowledging the validity of the client's concern and feelings. Keep emphasizing the client's power of choice. Shift the focus of the interview, and move to a less "loaded" topic (Hohmann, 1998). Remember that resistance often serves a necessary protective function and that clients are the best judge of their readiness to change.
5. *Support self-efficacy.* Provide support for what the *client* chooses even if it is not what you or someone else would have chosen (Hohman, 1998). Give credit to the client, not yourself, for any shifts or changes as they occur.

MI is an especially useful intervention for clients stuck at the precontemplation and contemplation stages of change. It is also useful in helping clients identify outcome goals. The discussion of a client's goals, specifically as they relate to

LEARNING ACTIVITY 10.1 — Stages of Change and Motivational Interviewing

Part One

Match the five client descriptions with the corresponding stage of change. Feedback follows.

Client Descriptions

1. The client wants to do something soon and may have already tried one plan of action. ___
2. The client doesn't want to change because of what he has to give up to do it. ___
3. The client feels ambivalent about changing in the near future. ___
4. The client has developed a plan of action. ___
5. The client has been successful in avoiding drugs over a long period of time. ___

Stages of Change to use in Matching

a. precontemplation
b. contemplation
c. preparation
d. action
e. maintenance

Part Two

Using the case description that follows, conduct a short (20-minute) motivational interviewing session, incorporating the five steps of motivational interviewing summarized below. You may wish to do this in triads, with one person assuming the role of helper, another the client, and the third the observer.

Steps of Motivational Interviewing

1. Use empathy.
2. Develop the discrepancy.
3. Avoid argumentation.
4. Roll with resistance.
5. Support self-efficacy.

The Case of John

John has been referred to you by his wife. His wife states that John's relationships with his colleagues have deteriorated over the last few months; several of them have called her to express concern. Recently in your session John has been obviously "clueless" about his behavior and clearly doesn't feel anything is wrong with him or his behavior at work. In fact, he tries to blame the problem on his colleagues and boss and their personalities and work ethic, which he says is not as good as his. He says he wants to get his wife "off his back."

---

the behavior of concern, is especially helpful in MI. It is critical to focus on which goals are important to the client. Once these have been elicited, the helper can contrast them with the client's actual behavior throughout the helping process (Draycott & Dabbs, 1998, pp. 359–360). In working with outcome goals, helpers need to remember that change is not so much a linear process but often more of a circular process, as clients vacillate back and forth between the stages of change—this is especially true for clients with chronic problems such as addictions. Prochaska and colleagues (1992) use the metaphor of a revolving door to describe this situation, with the client going around the revolving door several times before identifying and achieving his or her goals. In the remainder of this chapter, the model that we present for identifying and defining outcome goals is, for training purposes, a more linear and less intuitive process than what often occurs in the actual helping process.

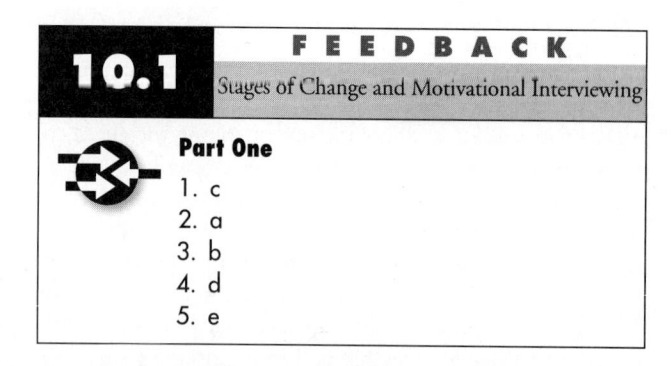

FEEDBACK 10.1 — Stages of Change and Motivational Interviewing

Part One

1. c
2. a
3. b
4. d
5. e

INTERVIEW LEADS FOR IDENTIFYING GOALS

In this section we discuss five categories of interview leads for identifying goals:

1. Providing a rationale
2. Eliciting outcome statements

3. Stating goals in positive terms
4. Determining what the goal is
5. Weighing advantages/disadvantages of the goal

The process of identifying goals and the associated interview leads are especially useful for clients at the first two stages of the Prochaska and associates change model: precontemplation and contemplation.

Providing a Rationale

The first step in identifying goals is to give the client a *rationale* for goals. This statement should describe goals, the purpose for having them, and the client's participation in the goal-setting process. The helper's intent is to convey the importance of having goals as well as the importance of the client's participation in developing them. An example of what the helper might say about the purpose of goals is "We've been talking about these two areas that bother you. It might be helpful now to discuss how you would like things to be different. We can develop some goals to work toward during our sessions. These goals will tell us what you want as a result of counseling. So today, let's talk about some things *you* would like to work on."

The helper might also emphasize the role that goals play in resolving problems through attention and rehearsal: "Paulo, you've been saying how stuck you feel in your marriage and yet how hopeful you feel, too. If we can identify specifically the ways that you want to relate differently, this can help you attend to the things you do that cause difficulty as well as the things you know you want to handle differently." Occasionally, offering examples of how other persons, such as athletes or dancers, use goal setting to aid performance may be useful to clients.

After this explanation, the helper will look for a client response that indicates understanding. If the client seems confused, the helper will need to explain further the purposes of goals and their benefits to the client or to clarify and explore the client's confusion. As we have indicated, this clarification is especially important for clients at the early stages of the Prochaska and associates change model.

Eliciting Outcome Statements

Interview leads are used to help clients identify goals. The following are examples of leads that can help clients define goals and express them in outcome statements:

"Suppose some distant relative you haven't seen for a while sees you after counseling. What would be different then from the way things are now?"

"Assuming we are successful, what would you be doing or how would these situations change?"

"What do you expect to accomplish as a result of counseling?"

"How would you like counseling to benefit you?"

"What do you *want* to be doing, thinking, or feeling?"

The helper's purpose in using these sorts of leads is to have the client identify some desired outcomes. The helper is looking for some verbal indication of the results the client expects. If the client does not know of desired changes or cannot specify a purpose for engaging in therapy, some time should be spent in exploring this area before moving on. The helper can assist the client in identifying goals in several ways: by assigning homework ("Make a list of what you can do now and what you want to do one year from now"), by using imagery ("Imagine being someone you admire. Who would you be? What would you be doing? How would you be different?"), by additional questioning ("If you could wave a magic wand and have three wishes, what would they be?"), or by self-report questionnaires or inventories. These sorts of leads and attitudes are useful in helping clients contemplate changes in their life and behavior.

Stating the Goal in Positive Terms

An effective outcome goal is stated in *positive* rather than negative terms—as what the client *does* want to do, not what the client *does not* want to do. This direction is very important because of the role that goal setting plays in human cognition and performance, as mentioned earlier. When the goal is stated positively, clients are more likely to encode and rehearse the things they want to be able to *do* rather than the things they want to avoid or stop. For example, it is fairly easy to generate an image of yourself sitting down and watching TV. However, picturing yourself *not* watching TV is difficult. Instead of forming an image of not watching TV, you are likely to form images (or sounds) related to performing other activities instead, such as reading a book, talking to someone, or being in the TV room and doing something else.

The practitioner will have to help clients "turn around" their initial goal statements, which are usually stated as something the person doesn't want to do, can't do, or wants to stop doing. Stating goals positively represents a self-affirming position and can be a helpful intervention for clients at the first two stages of the Prochaska and associates change model. If the client responds to the helper's initial leads with a negative answer, the helper can help turn this around by saying something like "That is what you *don't* want to do. Describe what you *do* want to do [think, feel]" or "What will you do instead, and can you see [hear, feel] yourself doing it every time?" or "What do you want things in your life to look like five years from now?"

Determining What the Goal Is

As we mentioned earlier, clients at the first stage, precontemplation, often want the goals to call for someone else to change rather than themselves—a teenager who says "I want my mom to stop yelling at me," a teacher who says "I want this kid to shut up so I can get some teaching done," or a husband who says "I want my wife to stop nagging." The tendency to project the desired change onto someone else is particularly evident in change problems that involve relationships with two or more persons.

Without discounting the client's feelings, the practitioner needs to help get this tendency turned around. The client is the identified person seeking help and services and is the only person who can make a change. When two or more clients are involved simultaneously in counseling, such as a couple or a family, all identified clients need to contribute to the desired change, not just one party or one "identified patient."

Who owns the change is usually directly related to the degree of *control* or *responsibility* that the client has in the situation and surrounding the change. For example, suppose that you are working with an eight-year-old girl whose parents are getting a divorce. The child says she wants you to help her persuade her parents to stay married. This goal would be very difficult for the child to attain, as she has no responsibility for her parents' relationship.

The practitioner will need to use leads to help clients determine whether they or someone else owns the change and whether anyone else needs to be involved in the goal-selection process. If the client steers toward a goal that requires a change by someone else, the practitioner will need to point this out and help the client identify his or her role in the change process.

Interview Leads to Determine Who Owns the Change

To help the client explore who owns the change, the helper can use leads similar to the following ones:

"How much control do you have over making this happen?"

"What changes will this goal require of you?"

"What changes will this goal require someone else to make?"

"Can this goal be achieved without the help of anyone else?"

"To whom is this goal most important?"

"Who, specifically, is responsible for making this happen?"

The intent of these leads is to have the client identify a goal that represents change for the client, not for others—unless they are directly affected. If the client persists in selecting a goal that represents change for others rather than himself or herself, the helper and client will have to decide whether to pursue this goal, to negotiate a reconsidered goal, or to refer the client to another helper, as we shall discuss shortly.

Weighing Advantages and Disadvantages of the Goal

It is important to explore the *cost/benefit* effect of all identified goals—that is, what is being given up (cost) versus what is being gained (benefit) from goal attainment (Dixon & Glover, 1984). We think of this step as the exploration of *advantages*, or positive effects, and *disadvantages*, or negative effects, of goal attainment. Exploration of advantages and disadvantages helps clients assess the feasibility of the goal and anticipate the consequences; then they can decide whether the change is worth the cost to themselves or to significant others.

Oz (1995) points out that most clients have already considered what is attractive about given alternatives and in fact may be "stuck" either because they want to preserve the benefits without incurring any costs or because the choice involves a values conflict, often between self-denial and costs to a relationship or to their image (Oz, 1995, p. 81). In identifying goals, the client needs to be aware of possible risks and costs and whether he or she is prepared to take such risks if, in fact, they do occur.

Oz (1995) also notes that although the cost factor most often affects a client's eventual choice, it is also the factor most often ignored by the client, and inadequate information about costs may lead to post-decisional regret (p. 79). The cost factor involved in change efforts also contributes frequently to client resistance to change, as we have seen in the Prochaska and associates change model.

Generally, the goals selected by clients should lead to benefits rather than losses. Remember from our discussion of the change model that the benefits of change need to outweigh the costs by at least two times in order for the client to move to the preparation and action stages. Advantages and disadvantages may be both short term and long term.

Desired changes	Immediate advantages	Long-term advantages	Immediate disadvantages	Long-term disadvantages
1.				
2.				
3.				

Figure 10.1 List for recording advantages and disadvantages of identified goals

The practitioner helps the client identify various kinds of short- and long-term advantages and disadvantages associated with goal attainment and then offers options to expand the client's range of possibilities (Gambrill, 1977). Sometimes it is helpful to write these in the form of a list that can be expanded or modified at any time, such as the one found in Figure 10.1.

Interview Leads for Advantages

Most clients can readily identify some positive consequences associated with their desired changes. Nevertheless, it is still a good idea with all clients to explore positive consequences of the change, for at least four reasons: to determine whether the advantages that the client perceives are indicative of actual benefits, to point out other possible advantages for the client or for others that have been overlooked, to strengthen the client's incentive to change, and to determine to what degree the identified goal is feasible given the client's overall functioning. These are examples of leads that can be used to explore advantages of client change:

"In what ways is it worthwhile for you to pursue a change?"

"What do you see as the benefits of this change?"

"Who would benefit from this change, and how?"

"What are some positive consequences that may result from this change?"

"How would attaining this goal help you?"

"In what ways will your life improve by achieving this goal?"

"What are the good things that may result from pursuing this goal or making this change in your life now?"

In using these leads, the helper is looking for some indication that the client is pursuing a goal on the basis of the positive consequences the goal may produce. If the client overlooks some advantages, the helper can describe them to add to the client's incentive to change.

If the client is unable to identify any benefits of change for herself or himself, this may be viewed as a signal for caution. Failure to identify advantages of change for oneself may indicate that the client is attempting to change at someone else's request or that the identified goal is not very feasible, given the "total picture." For instance, if a client wants to find a new job while she is also fighting off a life-threatening illness, the acquisition of a new job at this time may not be in the best interests of her desire to regain her health. Further exploration may indicate that another person is a more appropriate client or that other goals should be selected.

Interview Leads for Disadvantages

The helper can also use leads to have the client consider some risks or side effects that might accompany the desired change or might be the result of giving up the current behavior. Some examples of leads that the helper might use to explore the risks or disadvantages of change are the following:

"How could this change make life difficult for you?"

"Will pursuing this change affect your life in any adverse ways?"

"What might be some possible risks of doing this?"

"How would your life be changed if this happened?"

"What are some possible disadvantages of going in this direction? How willing are you to pay this price?"

"Who might disapprove of this action? How will that affect you?"

"What are some not so good things this change might have for you—or for others?"

"How will this change limit or constrain you?"

"What new problems in living might pursuing this goal create for you?"

The helper is looking for some indication that the client has considered the possible costs associated with the goal. If the client discounts the risks or cannot identify any, the helper can use immediacy or summarization to point out some disadvantages. Remember to be careful not to persuade or coerce the client to pursue another alternative simply because you believe it is better. Also remember to avoid labels such as "negative" when exploring disadvantages of change.

Decision Point: To Treat or Not

At this point in the process, the primary issue for the practitioner is whether she or he can help this client. Most people agree that this is one of the biggest ethical and, to some extent, legal questions the practitioner faces during the helping process. As Beutler and Clarkin (1990) observe, "The therapist must be aware that there are instances in which a decision *not* to treat at all is the optimal decision" (p. 24). They point out that therapy may be overused and unnecessary for well-adjusted persons experiencing a current life stressor. They also observe that therapy is unlikely to have much effect with clients who do not or cannot invest in the process. Or perhaps the client is "stuck" on goals that are simply not feasible.

The helper and client will need to choose whether to continue with counseling and pursue the selected goals, to continue with counseling but reevaluate the client's initial goals, or to seek the services of another practitioner. The particular decision is always made on an individual basis and is based on two factors: *willingness* and *competence* to help the client pursue the selected goals. Willingness involves your interest in working with the client toward identified goals and issues, your values, and your acceptance of the goals as worthwhile and important, given the overall functioning of the client. Competence involves your skills and knowledge and whether you are familiar with alternative intervention strategies and multiple ways to work with particular problems.

Referral Issues and Steps

If you have a *major* reservation about pursuing selected goals, a referral might be more helpful to the client (Gottman & Leiblum, 1974, p. 43).

Referral may be appropriate in any of the following cases: if the client wants to pursue a goal that is incompatible with your value system, if you are unable to be objective about the client's concern, if you are unfamiliar with or unable to use a treatment requested by the client, if you would be exceeding your level of competence in working with the client, or if more than one person is involved, and because of your emotions or biases, you favor one person instead of another. Assessment of client problems and identification of client goals sometimes reveal that the client needs services or resources not only beyond your own competence but ones that are unavailable in the setting in which you work. In these situations, referral involves "linking clients to other resource systems"; this process is referred to as *brokering* (Kirst-Ashman & Hull, 2002, p. 499). All of the professional codes of ethics that we cited in Chapter 2 discuss reasons for client referral.

In deciding to refer a client, the helper does have certain responsibilities. From the initial helping contacts, the helper and client have entered into at least an unwritten contract. Once the helper agrees to work with a client, he or she assumes responsibility for the client (Welfel, 2002). In deciding to terminate this "contract" by a referral, the referring practitioner can be considered legally liable if the referral is not handled with due care—that is, ensuring that clients have choices of referral therapists (when available) and ensuring that referred therapists are considered competent and do not have a reputation for poor service or unethical practices (Welfel, 2002). Providing referral choices is not only an ethical issue; in the case of reluctant clients, having referral choices may help these clients accept the referral. In addition, helpers have certain responsibilities to clients during the referral process. Hepworth and associates (1997) and Hackney and Cormier (2001) summarize some of these.

First, it is important to explore the client's readiness for a referral and to recognize that the client may already feel attached to you and be reluctant to pursue or accept a referral. This sort of resistance to referral may be especially true for clients who have been mandated for services such as substance abuse treatment (Hepworth et al., 1997, p. 38). As Hackney and Cormier (2001, p. 277), note, in these instances, "if you provide explanations that are complete and answer the client's questions clearly and thoroughly, and support the client's ambivalence, this resistance will ease." Hepworth and associates (1977, p. 38) add to this suggestion by noting that "client choice should be emphasized including options such as not pursuing the referral and accepting consequences, pursuing the referral for one's own reasons, or deciding to do it for the reasons suggested by others."

Once the client accepts the referral, it is important to be optimistic about the benefits of the referral but not to make unrealistic claims about the referral source (Hepworth et al., 1997). It is important to discuss any client anxieties about the new referral source and also to provide the client with sufficient information about the referral source. This process is also eased if you have first determined the availability of the new referral sources you recommend to the client. Once the client accepts a particular referral source, it is often useful to provide the new source with some information about the client, but remember that to do this you must first obtain a signed written consent from the client before releasing any information (Hackney & Cormier, 2001, p. 279). Finally, as Hepworth and associates (1977) point out, "after following the preceding steps, your responsibility to facilitate the referral does not end. You may ask the client to report back after making the contact or may personally initiate a contact to secure a progress report. Your continued interest and efforts may make the difference between a successful and unsuccessful referral" (p. 39). (See Learning Activity 10.2.)

MODEL DIALOGUE: THE CASE OF JOAN

To help you see how the leads for identifying goals are used with a client, the case of Joan, introduced in Chapter 8, is continued here as a dialogue in an interviewing session directed toward goal selection. Helper responses are prefaced by an explanation.

LEARNING ACTIVITY 10.2 Decision Point

For practice in thinking through the kinds of decisions you may face in the goal-setting process, try this learning activity. The exercise consists of three hypothetical situations. In each case, assume that you are the helper. Read through the case. Then sit back, close your eyes, and try to imagine being in the room with the client and being faced with this dilemma. How would you feel? What would you say? What would you decide to do? Why? Apply some of the critical thinking questions we described in the practice nexus from Chapter 1 to support your decision, such as the problem you are trying to solve, the perspective you are taking, the assumptions you are making, and the information you are using to arrive at your decision.

There are no right or wrong answers to these cases. You may wish to discuss your responses with another classmate, a co-worker, or your instructor.

Case 1

You are working with a family with two teenage daughters. The parents and the younger daughter seem closely aligned; the elder daughter is on the periphery of the family. The parents and the younger daughter report that the older daughter's recent behavior is upsetting and embarrassing to them because she recently "came out of the closet" to disclose that she is a lesbian. She has begun to hang out with a few other lesbian young women in their local high school. The parents and younger daughter indicate that they think she is just going through a "phase." They state that they want you to help them get this girl "back in line" with the rest of the family and get her to adopt their values and socially acceptable behavior. Based on the critical thinking questions above, what do you decide to do, and what are the implications of your decision?

Case 2

You are counseling a fourth-grader. You are the only counselor in this school. One day you notice that this boy seems to be all bruised. You ask him about this. After much hesitation, the child blurts out that he is often singled out on his way home by two big sixth-grade bullies who pick a fight, beat him up for a while, and then leave him alone until another time. Your client asks you to forget this information. He begs you not to say or do anything for fear of reprisal from these two bullies. He states he doesn't want to deal with this in counseling as he has come to see you about something else. Based on the critical thinking questions described above, what do you decide to do, and what are the implications of your decision?

Case 3

You are working with an elderly man whose relatives are dead. After his wife died six months ago, he moved from their family home to a retirement home. Although the client is relatively young (70) and is in good health and alert, the staff has requested your help because he seems to have become increasingly morbid and discouraged. In talking with you, he indicates that he has sort of given up on everything, including himself, because he doesn't feel he has anything to live for. Consequently, he has stopped going to activities, isolates himself in his room, and has even stopped engaging in personal hygiene and grooming, leaving such things up to the staff. He indicates that he doesn't care to talk with you if these are the kinds of things you want to talk about. Based on the critical thinking questions described above, what do you decide to do, and what are the implications of your decision?

In response 1, the helper starts out with a *review* of the last session.

1. **Helper:** Joan, last week we talked about some of the things that are going on with you right now that you're concerned about. What do you remember that we talked about?

Client: Well, we talked a lot about my problems in school—like my trouble in my math class. Also about the fact that I can't decide whether or not to switch over to a vocational curriculum—and if I did, my parents would be upset.

2. **Helper:** Yes, that's a good summary. We did talk about a lot of things—such as the pressure and anxiety you feel in competitive situations like your math class and your difficulty in making decisions. I believe we also mentioned that you tend to go out of your way to please others, like your parents, or to avoid making a decision they might not like.

Client: Mm-hmm. I tend to not want to create a hassle. I also just have never made many decisions by myself.

In response 3, the helper will move from problem definition to goal selection. Response 3 will consist of an *explanation* about goals and their *purpose*.

3. **Helper:** Yes, I remember you said that last week. I've been thinking that since we've kind of got a handle on the main issues you're concerned about, today it might be helpful to talk about things you might want to happen—or how you'd like things to be different. This way, we know exactly what we can be talking about and working on that will be most helpful to you. How does that sound?

Client: That's OK with me. I mean, do you really think there are some things I can do about these problems?

The client has indicated some uncertainty about possible change. The helper will pursue this in response 4 and indicate more about the *purpose* of goals and possible effects of counseling for this person.

4. **Helper:** You seem a little uncertain about how much things can be different. To the extent that you have some control over a situation, it is possible to make some changes. Depending on what kind of changes you want to make, there are some ways we can work together on this. It will take some work on your part, too. How do you feel about this?

Client: OK. I'd like to get out of the rut I'm in.

In response 5, the helper will explore the ways in which the client would like to change. The helper will use a lead to *identify client goals*.

5. **Helper:** So you're saying that you don't want to continue to feel stuck. Exactly how would you like things to be different—say, in three months from now—from the way things are now?

Client: I'd like to feel less pressured in school, especially in my math class.

The client has identified one possible goal, although it is stated in negative terms. In response 6, the helper will help the client identify the goal in *positive terms*.

6. **Helper:** OK, that's something you *don't* want to do. Can you think of another way to say it that would describe what you *do* want to do?

Client: I guess I'd like to feel confident about my ability to handle tough situations like math class.

In the next response, the helper *paraphrases* Joan's goal and checks it out to see whether she has restated it accurately.

7. **Helper:** So you're saying you'd like to feel more positively about yourself in different situations—is that it?

Client: Yeah, I don't know if that is possible, but that's what I would like to have happen.

In responses 8–14, the helper continues to help Joan *explore and identify desired outcomes*.

8. **Helper:** In a little while we'll take some time to explore just how feasible that might be. Before we do that, let's make sure we don't overlook anything else you'd like to work on—in what other areas is it important to you to make a change or to turn things around for yourself?

Client: I'd like to start making some decisions for myself for a change, but I don't know exactly how to start.

9. **Helper:** OK, that's part of what we'll do together—we'll look at how you can get started on some of these things. So far, then, you've mentioned two things you'd like to work toward—increasing your confidence in your ability to handle tough situations like math and starting to make some decisions by yourself without relying on help from someone else. Is that about it, or can you think of any other things you'd like to work on?

Client: I guess it's related to making my own decisions, but I'd like to decide whether to stay in this curriculum or switch to the vocational one.

10. **Helper:** So you're concerned also about making a special type of decision about school that affects you now.

Client: That's right. But I'm sort of afraid to, because I know if I decided to switch, my parents would have a terrible reaction when they found out about it.

11. **Helper:** It seems that you're mentioning another situation that we might need to try to get a different handle on. As you mentioned last week, in certain situations, like math class or with your parents, you tend to back off and let other people take over for you.

Client: That's true, and I guess this curriculum thing is an example of it. It's like a lot of things where I do know what I want to do or say, but I just don't follow through. Like not telling my folks about my opinion about this college prep curriculum. Or not telling them how their harping at me about grades makes me feel. Or even in math class, just sitting there and sort of letting the teacher do a lot of the work for me when I really do probably know the answer or could go to the board.

12. **Helper:** So what you're saying is that in certain situations with your folks or in math class, you may have an idea or an opinion or a feeling, yet you usually don't express it.

Client: Mm-hmm. Usually I don't because sometimes I'm afraid it might be wrong or I'm afraid my folks would get upset.

13. **Helper:** So the anticipation that you might make a mistake or that your folks might not like it keeps you from expressing yourself in these situations?

Client: I believe so.

14. **Helper:** Then is this another thing that you would like to work on?

Client: Yes, because I realize I can't go on withdrawing forever.

Because Joan has again stated the outcome in negative terms, in the next four responses (15–18), the helper helps Joan *restate the goal in positive terms.*

15. **Helper:** OK, now again you're sort of suggesting a way that you don't want to handle the situation. You don't want to withdraw. Can you describe something you *do* want to do in these situations in a way that you could see, hear, or grasp yourself doing it each time the situation occurs?

Client: I'm not exactly sure what you mean.

16. **Helper:** Well, for instance, suppose I need to lose weight to improve my health. I could say "I don't want to eat so much, and I don't want to be fat." But that just describes not doing what I've been doing. So it would be more helpful to describe something I'm going to do instead, like "Instead of eating between meals, I'm going to go out for a walk, or talk on the phone, or create a picture of myself in my head as a healthier person."

Client: Oh, yeah, I do see what you mean. So I guess instead of withdrawing, I—well, what is the opposite of that? I guess I think it would be more helpful if I volunteered the answers or gave my ideas or opinions—things like that.

17. **Helper:** OK, so you're saying that you want to express yourself instead of holding back. Things like expressing opinions, feelings, things like that.

Client: Yeah.

18. **Helper:** OK, now we've mentioned three things you want to work on—anything else?

Client: No, I can't think of anything.

In the next response, the helper asks Joan to *select one of the goals* to work on initially. Tackling all three outcomes simultaneously could be overwhelming to a client.

19. **Helper:** OK, as time goes on and we start working on some of these things, you may think of something else—or something we've talked about today may change. What might be helpful now is to decide which of these three things you'd like to work on first.

Client: Gee, that's a hard decision.

In the previous response, Joan demonstrated *in vivo* one of her problems—difficulty in making decisions. In the next response, the helper *provides* guidelines to help Joan make a choice but is careful not to make the decision for her.

20. **Helper:** Well, it's one decision I don't want to make for you. I'd encourage you to start with the area you think is most important to you now—and also maybe one that you feel you could work with successfully.

Client: [Long pause] Can this change, too?

21. **Helper:** Sure—we'll start with one thing, and if later on it doesn't feel right, we'll move on.

Client: OK, well, I guess it would be the last thing we talked about—starting to express myself in situations where I usually don't.

In the next response, the helper will discuss the degree to which Joan believes the *change represents something she will do* rather than something someone else will do.

22. **Helper:** OK, sticking with this one area, it seems like these are things that you could make happen without the help of anyone else or without requiring anyone else to change too. Can you think about that for a minute and see whether that's the way it feels to you?

Client: [Pause] I guess so. You're saying that I don't need to depend on someone else; it's something I can start doing.

In the next response, the helper shifts to exploring *possible advantages* of goal achievement. Note that the helper asks the client first to express her opinion about advantages; the helper is giving her *in vivo* practice in one of the skills related to her goal.

23. **Helper:** One thing I'm wondering about—and this will probably sound silly because in a way it's obvious—but exactly how will making this change help you or benefit you?

Client: Mm [Pause]. I'm thinking—well, what do you think?

In the previous response, the client shifted responsibility to the helper and "withdrew," as she does in other anxiety-producing situations, such as math class and interactions with her parents. In the next response, the helper *summarizes* this behavior pattern.

24. **Helper:** You know, it's interesting; I just asked you for your opinion about something, and instead of sharing it, you asked me to sort of handle it instead. Are you aware of this?

Client: Now that you mention it, I am. But I guess that's what I do so often that it's sort of automatic.

In the next three responses (25–27), the helper does some *in vivo* assessment of Joan's problems, which results in information that can be used later for *planning of subgoals and action steps.*

25. **Helper:** Can you run through exactly what you were thinking and feeling just then?

Client: Just that I had a couple of ideas, but then I didn't think they were important enough to mention.

26. **Helper:** I'm wondering if you also may have felt a little concerned about what I would think of your ideas.

Client: [Face flushes] Well, yeah. I guess it's silly, but yeah.

27. **Helper:** So is this sort of the same thing that happens to you in math class or around your parents?

Client: Yeah—only in those two situations I feel much more uptight than I do here.

In the next four responses, the helper continues to explore *potential advantages* for Joan of attaining this goal.

28. **Helper:** OK, that's really helpful because that information gives us some clues on what we'll need to do first in order to help you reach this result. Before we explore that, let's go back and see whether you can think of any ways in which making this change will help you.

Client: I think sometimes I'm like a doormat. I just sit there and let people impose on me. Sometimes I get taken advantage of.

29. **Helper:** So you're saying that at times you feel used as a result?

Client: Yeah. That's a good way to put it. Like with my girlfriends I told you about, usually we do what they want to on weekends, not necessarily what I want to do, because even with them I withdraw in this way and don't express myself.

30. **Helper:** So you are noticing some patterns here. OK, other advantages or benefits to you?

Client: I'd become less dependent and more self-reliant. If I do decide to go to college, that's only two years away, and I will need to be a whole lot more independent then.

31. **Helper:** OK, that's a good thought. Any other ways that this change would be worthwhile for you, Joan?

Client: Mm—I can't think of any. That's honest. But if I do, I'll mention them.

In the next responses (32–35), the helper initiates exploration of *possible disadvantages* of this goal.

32. **Helper:** OK, great! And the ones you've mentioned I think are really important ones. Now, I'd like you to flip the coin, so to speak, and see whether you can think of any disadvantages that could result from moving in this direction.

Client: I can't think of any in math. Well, no, in a way I can. I guess it's sort of the thing to do there. If I start expressing myself more, people might wonder what is going on.

33. **Helper:** So you're concerned about the reaction from some of the other students?

Client: Yeah, in a way. But there are a couple of girls in there who are pretty popular and also made the honor roll. So I don't think it's like I'd be a "geek" or anything. And actually with my girlfriends, I don't think they would mind if I spoke up; it just hasn't been my pattern with them. So they might be surprised, but I think that would be OK with them.

34. **Helper:** It sounds, then, like you believe that is one disadvantage you could live with. Any other ways in which doing this could affect your life in a less good way—or could create another problem for you?

Client: I think a real issue there is how my parents would react if I started to do some of these things. I don't know. Maybe they would welcome it. But I sort of think they would consider it a revolt or something on my part and would want to squelch it right away.

35. **Helper:** Are you saying you believe your parents have a stake in keeping you somewhat dependent on them?

Client: Yeah, I do.

This is a difficult issue. Without observing her family, it would be impossible to say whether this is Joan's perception (and a distorted one) or whether the parents do play a role in this problem—and, indeed, from a diagnostic standpoint, family members are often significantly involved when one family member has a dependent personality. The helper will thus *reflect both possibilities* in the next response.

36. **Helper:** That may or may not be true. It could be that you see the situation that way and an outsider like myself might not see it the same way. On the other hand, it is possible your parents might subtly wish to keep you from growing up too quickly. This might be a potentially serious enough disadvantage for us to consider whether it would be useful for all four of us to sit down and talk together.

Client: Do you think that would help?

In the next two responses, the helper and Joan continue to discuss potential *disadvantages* related to this goal. Note that in the next response, instead of answering the client's previous question directly, the helper shifts the responsibility to Joan and solicits her opinion, again giving her *in vivo* opportunities to demonstrate one skill related to the goal.

37. **Helper:** What do you think?

Client: I'm not sure. They are sometimes hard to talk to.

38. **Helper:** How would you feel about having a joint session—assuming they were agreeable?

Client: Right now it seems OK. How could it help exactly?

In the following response, the helper changes from an *individual* to a *systemic focus,* since the parents may have an investment in keeping Joan dependent on them or may have given Joan an injunction: "Don't grow up." The systemic focus avoids blaming any one person.

39. **Helper:** I think you mentioned it earlier. Sometimes when one person in a family changes the way she or he reacts to the rest of the family, it has a boomerang effect, causing ripples throughout the rest of the family. If that's going to happen in your case, it might be helpful to sit down and talk about it and anticipate the effects, rather than letting you get in the middle of a situation that starts to feel too hard to handle. It could be helpful to your parents, too, to explore their role in this whole issue.

Client: I see. Well, where do we go from here?

40. **Helper:** Our time is about up today. Let's get together in a week and map out a plan of action.

(*Note:* The same process of goal identification would also be carried out in subsequent sessions for the other two outcome goals that Joan identified earlier in this session.)

INTERVIEW LEADS FOR DEFINING GOALS

Most clients will select more than one goal. Ultimately, it may be more realistic for the client to work toward several outcomes. For example, in our model case, Joan selected three terminal outcome goals: acquiring and demonstrating at least four initiating skills, increasing positive self-talk about her ability to function adequately in competitive situations, and acquiring and using five decision-making skills (see Joan's goal chart on p. 296). These three outcomes reflect the three core issues revealed by the assessment interview (see Chapter 9). Selection of one goal may also imply the existence of other goals. For example, if a client states "I want to get involved in a relationship with a man that is emotionally and sexually satisfying," the client may also need to work on meeting men and her or his approach behaviors, developing communications skills designed to foster intimacy, and learning about what responses might be sexually satisfying for her or him.

At first, it is useful to have the client specify one or more desired goals for each separate concern. However, to tackle several outcome goals at one time would be unrealistic. The helper should ask the client to choose one of the outcome goals to pursue first. After identifying an initial outcome goal to work toward, the helper and client can define the three parts of the goal and identify subgoals. The next section of this chapter will introduce some interviewing leads used to help the client define the outcome goals of treatment and will present some probable responses that indicate client responsiveness to the leads. These leads are particularly useful for clients moving from the preparation phase to the action phase of the change model developed by Prochaska and associates (1992).

Defining Behaviors Related to Goals

Defining goals involves specifying in operational or behavioral terms what the client (whether an individual, group member, or organization) is to *do* as a result of counseling. This part of an outcome goal defines the particular behavior the client is to perform and answers the question "*What* will the client do, think, or feel differently?" Examples of behavior outcome goals include exercising more frequently, asking for help from a teacher, verbal sharing of positive feelings about oneself, and thinking about oneself in positive ways. As you can see, both overt and covert behaviors, including thoughts and feelings, can be included in this part of the outcome goal as long as the behavior is defined by what it means for each client. Defining goals behaviorally makes the goal-setting process specific, and specifically defined goals are more likely to create incentives and guide performance than vaguely stated intentions (Gollwitzer, 1999). When goals are behaviorally or operationally defined, it is easier to evaluate the effects of your intervention strategy.

Interview Leads for Defining Goal Behavior

The following are some leads a helper can use to identify the behavior part of a goal:

"When you say you want to, what do you see yourself doing?"

"What could I see you doing, thinking, or feeling as a result of this change?"

"You say you want to be more self-confident. What things would you be thinking and doing as a self-confident person?"

"Describe a good (and a poor) example of this goal."

"When you are no longer ____, what will you be doing instead?"

"What will it look like when you are doing this?"

It is important for the helper to continue to pursue these leads until the client can define the overt and covert behaviors associated with the goal. This is not an easy task, for most clients talk about changes in vague or abstract terms. If the client has trouble specifying behaviors, the practitioner can help with further instructions, information giving, or self-disclosing a personal goal. The practitioner can also help with behavioral definitions of the goal by encouraging the client to use action verbs to describe what will be happening when the goal is attained (Dixon & Glover, 1984). As we mentioned earlier, it is important to get clients to specify what they *want* to do, not what they don't want or what they want to stop. The goal is usually defined sufficiently when the helper can accurately repeat and paraphrase the client's definition.

Defining the Conditions of an Outcome Goal

The second part of an outcome goal specifies the conditions—that is, the *context* or *circumstances*—where the behavior will occur. This is an important element of an outcome goal for both the client and the helper. The conditions suggest a particular *person* with whom the client may perform the desired behaviors or a particular *setting,* and answers the question "*Where, when,* and *with whom* is the behavior to occur?" Specifying the conditions of a behavior sets boundaries and helps ensure that the behavior will occur only in desired settings or with desired people and will not generalize to undesired settings. This idea can be illustrated vividly. For example, a woman may wish to increase the number of positive verbal and nonverbal responses she makes toward her partner. In this case, time spent with her partner would be the condition or circumstances in which the behavior occurs. However, if this behavior generalized to include all persons, it might have negative effects on the very relationship that she is trying to improve.

Interview Leads for the Conditions of a Goal

Leads used to determine the conditions of the outcome goal include these:

"Where would you like to do this?"

"In what situations do you want to be able to do this?"

"When do you want to do this?"

"Whom would you be with when you do this?"

"In what situations is what you're doing now not meeting your expectations?"

The helper is looking for a response that indicates where or with whom the client will make the change or perform the desired behavior. If the client gives a noncommittal response, the helper may suggest client self-monitoring to obtain these data. The helper can also use self-disclosure and personal examples to demonstrate that a desired behavior may not be appropriate in all situations or with all people.

Defining a Level of Change

The third element of an outcome goal specifies the level or *amount* of the behavioral change. In other words, this part answers "*How much* is the client to do or to complete in order to reach the desired goal?" The level of an outcome goal serves as a barometer that measures the extent to which the client will be able to perform the desired behavior. For example, a man may state that he wishes to decrease cigarette smoking. The following week, he may report that he did a better job of cutting down on cigarettes. However, unless he can specify how much he actually decreased smoking, both he and the helper will have difficulty in determining how much the client really completed toward the goal. In this case, the client's level of performance is ambiguous. In contrast, if he had reported that he reduced cigarette smoking by two cigarettes per day in one week, his level of performance could be determined easily. If his goal were to decrease cigarette smoking by eight cigarettes per day, this information would help to determine progress toward the goal.

Like the behavior and condition parts of an outcome goal, the level of change should always be established individually for each client, whether the client is an individual, couple, group, or organization. The amount of satisfaction derived from goal attainment often depends on the level of performance established (Bandura & Simon, 1977, p. 178). A suitable level of change will depend on such factors as the present level of the undesired behavior, the present level of the desired behavior, the resources available for change, the client's readiness to change, and the degree to which other conditions or people are maintaining the present level of undesired behavior.

As an example, suppose that a client wants to increase the number of assertive opinions she expresses orally with her husband. If she now withholds all her opinions, her level of change might be stated at a lower level than that defined for another client who already expresses some opinions. And if the client's husband is accustomed to her refraining from giving opinions, this might affect the degree of change made, at least initially. The helper's and client's primary concern is to establish a level that is manageable—that the client can attain with some success. Occasionally, the helper may encounter a client who always wants to achieve more change than is desirable or even possible. If the level is set too high, the desired behavior may not occur, thus ruling out chances for success and subsequent progress and rewards. Generally, it is better to err by moving too slowly and thus setting the level too low rather than too high.

One way to avoid setting the level of a goal too high or making it too restrictive is to use a scale that identifies a series of *increasingly desired* outcomes for each given area. This concept, introduced by Kiresuk and Sherman (1968), is called "goal-attainment scaling" (GAS) and has been used increasingly in agencies that must demonstrate certain levels of client goal achievement in order to receive or maintain funding and third-party reimbursement. In goal-attainment scaling, the helper and client devise five outcomes for a given issue and arrange these by level or extent of change on a scale in the following order (each outcome is assigned a numerical value): most unfavorable outcome (-2), less than likely expected outcome (-1), most likely or expected outcome (0), more than likely expected outcome ($+1$), most favorable outcome ($+2$). Table 10.3 shows an example of the use of GAS for a client with ulcerative colitis. A review of this GAS model and similar models is presented by Ogles, Lambert, and Masters (1996). The GAS model can also be used to assess change at the systemic and organizational level as well as with individual clients. (See Learning Activity 10.3)

Leads to Identify the Level of Change

Here are some leads you can use to help identify the client's desired extent or level of change:

"How much would you like to be able to do this, compared with how much you're doing it now?"

"How often do you want to do this?"

"From the information you obtained during self-monitoring, you seem to be studying only about an hour a week now. What is a reasonable amount for you to increase this without getting bogged down?"

"You say you'd like to lose 40 pounds. Let's talk about a reasonable amount of time this might take and, to start with, what amount would be easy for you to lose just in the next 3 weeks."

TABLE 10.3	Goal-Attainment Scale for a Client with Ulcerative Colitis	
Date: 10/24/02		**Frequency of colitis attacks**
(−2)	Most unfavorable outcome thought likely	One per day
(−1)	Less than expected success with treatment	One every other day
(0)	Expected level of treatment success	One per week
(+1)	More than expected success with treatment	One every two weeks
(+2)	Best expected success with treatment	None per month

Source: Adapted from "Behavioral Treatment of Mucous Colitis," by K. J. Youell and J. P. McCullough, *Journal of Consulting and Clinical Psychology, 43,* pp. 740–745. Copyright © 1975 by the American Psychological Associaton. Adapted with permission.

"What amount of change is realistic, considering where you are right now?"

The helper is looking for some indication of the present and future levels of the desired behavior. This level can be expressed by either the number of times or the amount the client wants to be able to do something. In some cases, an appropriate level may be only one, as when a client's outcome goal is to make one decision about a job change. The practitioner can help the client establish an appropriate level of change by referring to the self-monitoring data collected during assessment. If the client has not engaged in monitoring, this is another point where it is almost imperative to have the client observe and record the present amounts of the undesired behavior and the goal behavior. This information will give some idea of the present level of behavior, referred to as the base rate or baseline level. This information is important because in setting the desired level, it should be contrasted with the present level of the overt or covert behaviors. As you may recall from Chapter 9, a client's data gathering is very useful for defining issues and goals and for monitoring progress toward the goals.

Level as an Indicator of Direction and Type of Change

The level reflected in an outcome goal specifies both the direction and the type of change desired. In the example of the client who wants to be more assertive, if the client's present level of a specified assertive response is zero, then the goal would be to acquire the assertive skill. When the base rate of a behavior is zero, or when the client does not seem to have certain skills in her or his repertoire, the goal is stated as acquiring a behavior. If, however, the client wants to improve or increase something that she or he can already do (but at a low level), the goal is stated as increasing a behavior. Increasing or acquiring overt and/or covert behaviors is a goal when the client's concern is a *response deficit,* meaning that the desired response occurs with insufficient intensity or frequency or in inappropriate form (Gambrill, 1977). Sometimes, a client has an overt behavioral response in his or her repertoire, but it is masked or inhibited by the presence of certain feelings—in which case the goal would be directed toward the feelings rather than the overt behavior. In this instance, the concern stems from *response inhibition,* and the resulting goal is a disinhibition of the response, usually by the working through of the emotional reactions standing in the way.

In contrast, if the client is doing too much of something and wants to lower the present level, the goal is stated as decreasing a behavior. Decreasing overt and/or covert behaviors is a goal when the client's concern is a *response excess,* meaning that a response occurs so often, so long, with such excessive intensity, or in socially inappropriate contexts that it is often annoying to the client and to others (Gambrill, 1977). In situations of response excesses, it is usually the frequency or amount of the response, rather than its form, that is problematic. It is almost always easier to work on developing or increasing a behavior (response increment or acquisition) than on decreasing a response (response decrement). This is another reason to encourage clients to state their goals in positive terms, working toward doing something or doing it more, rather than stopping something or doing it less.

Sometimes, the level of change may reflect a *restructuring.* For instance, a client trying to improve grades may desire to replace studying in a crowded room with the TV on with a quiet room free of distractions. This client's goal is stated in terms of restructuring something about her or his environment—in this case, the location of studying. Although this is an example of restructuring an overt behavior, restructuring can be cognitive as well. For example, a client may want to eliminate negative, self-defeating thoughts about difficulty when taking tests and replace these with positive, self-enhancing thoughts about the capacity to perform adequately in test-taking situations. Restructuring also often takes place during family therapy when boundaries and alliances between and among family members are shifted so that, for instance, a member on the periphery is pulled into the family, triangles are broken up, or overinvolved alliances between two persons are rearranged. Restructuring overt or covert behaviors is a goal when the concern is *inadequate, inappropriate, or defective stimulus control,* meaning that the necessary supporting environmental conditions either are missing or are arranged in such a way as to make it impossible or difficult for the desired behavior to occur.

In some instances, the level of a goal reflects maintenance of a particular overt or covert response at the current rate or frequency or under existing conditions. As you recall from our earlier discussion of client change in this chapter, not all goals will reflect a discrepancy between the client's present and future behavior. Some goals may be directed toward maintaining a desired or satisfying situation or response (stage 5 of the Prochaska change model). Such goals may be stated as, for example, "to maintain my present amount (three hours daily) of studying," "to maintain the present balance in my life between work on weekdays and play on weekends," "to maintain the positive communication I have with my partner in our daily talks," or "to maintain my present level (two a day) of engaging in relaxation sessions." A maintenance goal suggests that the client's present level of behavior is satisfying and sufficient, at least at this time. A maintenance goal may help to put things in perspective by acknowledging the areas of the client's life that are going well. Maintenance goals are also useful and necessary when one of the change goals has been achieved. For example, if a client wanted to improve grades and has done so successfully, then the helper and client need to be concerned about how the client can maintain the improvement. As we mentioned earlier, maintenance goals and programs are often harder to achieve and take greater effort and planning than initial change attempts.

To summarize, the level stated by the outcome goal will usually reflect one of the categories of responses and goals summarized in Table 10.4. Because most clients have more than one outcome goal, a client's objectives may reflect more than one of these directions of change. Knowledge of the direction and level of change defined in the client's goals is important in selecting intervention strategies. For example, self-monitoring (see Chapter 18) is used differently depending on whether it is applied to increase or to decrease a response. One change strategy might be used appropriately to help a client acquire responses; yet another strategy may be needed to help a client restructure some responses.

TABLE 10.4	Categories of Client Goals
A. Response deficit	Response increment
	Response acquisition
B. Response inhibition	Disinhibition of response
	Working through of emotional reactions
C. Response excess	Response decrement
D. Inadequate or inappropriate stimulus control	Response restructuring
E. Maintenance	Response maintenance at current frequency or amount or in current context

It is very important for the helper and client to spend sufficient time on specifying the level of the goal, even if this process seems elusive and difficult. Although our focus in this chapter is on defining goals with individual clients, Bloom, Fischer, and Orme (1999) provide an excellent example of outcome goals defined for a dyad and an agency in Table 10.5.

Identifying and Sequencing Subgoals or Action Steps

All of us can probably recall times when we were expected to learn something so fast that the learning experience was overwhelming and produced feelings of frustration, irritation, and discouragement. The change represented by outcome goals can be achieved best if the process is gradual. Any change program should be organized into a sequence that guides the client through small steps toward the ultimate desired behaviors (Bandura, 1969, p. 74). In defining goals, this gradual learning sequence is achieved by breaking down the ultimate goal into a series of smaller goals called *subgoals* or *action steps*. Subgoals help clients move toward the solution of problems in a planned way (Dixon & Glover, 1984, p. 136). The subgoals are usually arranged in a hierarchy, so the client completes subgoals at the bottom of the ranked list before the ones near the top. Although an overall outcome goal can provide a "general directive" for change, the specific subgoals may determine a person's immediate activities and degree of effort in making changes (Bandura & Simon, 1977, p. 178).

Sequencing goals into smaller subgoals is more likely to produce the desired results for two reasons. First, completion of subgoals may keep failure experiences to a minimum. Completing subgoals will encourage the client and will help maintain the client's motivation to change (Bandura, 1969, p. 75). Second, arranging the ultimate goal into subgoals indicates that immediate, daily subgoals may be more potent than distant, weekly subgoals (Reid & Misener, 2000).

Subgoals identified may represent covert as well as overt behavior, since a comprehensive change program usually in-

TABLE 10.5 Examples of Outcome Goals for a Dyod and Agency

Client Concerns	The Problem/Goals Operationally Defined	Verifying Source	The Goal of the Intervention
1a. Mary feels depressed.	a. Mary's score on a standardized depression test.	a. The practitioner scores the test.	a. Mary's scores should decrease to below the clinical cutoff.
1b. Mary and her mother get into a lot of arguments about her rights and responsibilities.	b. The number of times Mary and her mother argue each week.	b. They bring in a score sheet to the weekly appointment.	b. Mary and her mother will try to reduce the number of arguments per week by half, to the point of no arguments.
2a. A family agency has gradually had a reduction in numbers of clients which threatens the continuation of the agency.	2a. The number of active cases per month, as compared with the previous 5 years client census.	2a. Agency statistics.	2a(1). Increase the number of referrals from other agencies by 50% per month. 2a(2). Increase agency visibility through a community health fair. 2a(3). Initiate new program where there is an identified need for which staff has qualifications.

Source: Evaluating Practice (3rd ed.), by M. Bloom, J. Fischer, & J. Orme (pp. 90–91). Copyright © 1999 by Allyn & Bacon. Reprinted by permission.

LEARNING ACTIVITY 10.3 Defining Outcome Goals

We have found that the most difficult part of developing goals with a client is specifying the three parts of the outcome goal. We believe the reason is that the concept is foreign to most of us and difficult to internalize. This is probably because, in our own lives, we think about small, very mundane goals. With more-complex goals, we still don't assess the individual overt and covert behaviors to be changed, where and with whom change will occur, and the extent of the change. In this activity, role-play one of the cases in Learning Activity 10.2 in a triad or with a partner. The client will assume the identity of the person described in case 1, 2, or 3 in Learning Activity 10.2. As the helper, your task is to help the client identify an outcome goal that she or he feels comfortable with and committed to pursue. Your second task is to help the client define this outcome goal with the three parts we have described—the behavior, conditions, and level of the goal. Finally, collaborating with the role-play client, construct a Goal Attainment Scale for the client's goal. You may wish to refer to Table 10.3. The observer can help if you get stuck and can give you feedback.

---

volves changes in the client's thoughts and feelings as well as in overt behaviors and environmental situations. Subgoals may arise out of treatment approaches or recommended ways to resolve a particular concern or, when formal procedures are not available, from more informal and commonsense ideas. In any event, they are always actions that move the client in the direction of the desired outcome goal (Carkhuff, 1993).

After subgoals are identified and selected, they are ordered in a series of tasks—a hierarchy—according to *complexity* and *degree of difficulty and immediacy*. Because some clients are put off by the word *hierarchy*, we use the term *goal pyramid* instead and pull out an 8" × 11" sheet of paper that has a drawing of a blank pyramid on it, such as the one in Figure 10.2. A series of subgoal tasks may represent either increasing requirements of the same (overt or covert) behavior or demonstrations of different behaviors, with simpler and easier responses sequenced before more complex and difficult ones. The second criterion for ranking is immediacy. For this criterion, subgoals are ranked according to prerequisite tasks—that is, what tasks must be done before others can be achieved.

The sequencing of subgoals in order of complexity is based on learning principles called *shaping* and *successive approximations*. Shaping helps someone learn a small amount at a time, with reinforcement or encouragement for each task completed successfully. Gradually, the person learns the entire amount or achieves the overall result through these

Increase amount of daily exercise by walking at least one mile per day at a fast pace.
Increase physical feelings of relaxation while at home and at work by engaging in one 20-minute period of relaxation per day.
Increase time spent in eating first helpings at dinner by 10 minutes by chewing food slowly, putting fork down between bites, and carrying on a conversation.
Decrease second helpings at dinner by refusing them and by getting up from the table when finished with first helpings.
Increase positive thoughts about myself as a healthy person (think like a healthy person) by engaging in three positive visualizations per day.
Acquire verbal and nonverbal conversational skills and use them to become acquainted with at least one new person a week.
Maintain the previous six subgoals over the 12-month period.

Terminal goal: To think, feel, and look like a healthy person by losing 40 pounds over a 12-month period

Weekly goal: To think, feel, and look like a healthy person by losing 1 pound per week

Figure 10.2 Goal Pyramid

day-to-day learning experiences that successively approximate the overall outcome. Subgoals are important because "change itself is most typically a small, step by step, back and forth effort at trying new things out, changing, trying new things out and so on. . ." (Tallman & Bohart, 1999, p. 112).

Steps in Identifying and Sequencing Subgoals

Identification and arrangement of subgoals are critical to the client's success with the outcome goal. The following steps are involved in this process.

First, the client identifies the *initial* step he or she must take—that is, the first things that need to be done to move in the desired direction. The first step will be some action that is both comfortable and achievable (Gambrill, 1977). The first step is important because "getting started" is often one of the most critical and difficult parts of achieving a goal (Gollwitzer, 1999).

Second, if the client progresses satisfactorily on the first step, additional intermediate steps that bridge the gap between the first step and the terminal goal are identified and ranked. (If the client does not progress on the first step, discuss this issue and consider revising the initial step.) Effective intermediate steps are ones that build on existing client assets and resources, do not conflict with the client's value system, are decided on and owned by the client, and represent immediate, daily, or short-term actions rather than weekly, distant, or long-term actions (see also Bandura & Simon, 1977; Carkhuff, 1993; Reid & Misener, 2000).

There is no hard and fast rule concerning the number of intermediate steps identified, other than ensuring that the gap between adjacent steps is not too great. Each successive step gradually begins where the last step left off. The helper also needs to make sure that each intermediate step requires only one basic action or activity by the client; if two or more activities are involved, it is usually better to use two separate steps (Carkhuff, 1993).

As we mentioned earlier, intermediate steps are ranked on two aspects:

1. *Degree of difficulty and complexity.* "Which is easier; which is harder?" Less complex and demanding tasks are ranked ahead of others.
2. *Immediacy.* "What do I need to do before I can do this?" Prerequisite tasks are ranked before others.

Ranked steps are then filled in on the goal pyramid—usually in pencil, because in the process of moving through the hierarchy, the subgoals may need to be modified or rearranged.

Third, after all the steps have been identified and sequenced, the client starts to carry out the actions represented by the subgoals, beginning with the initial step and moving on. Usually, it is wise not to attempt a new subgoal until the client has successfully completed the previous one on the pyramid. Progress made on initial and subsequent steps provides useful information about whether the gaps between steps are too large or just right and whether the sequencing of steps is appropriate. As the subgoals are met, they become part of the client's current repertoire that can be used in additional change efforts toward the terminal goals. Gollwitzer (1999) refers to this process as "implementation intentions"—specifying the when, where, and how of behaviors leading to goal attainment (p. 494). These specific intentions help clients not only to initiate action toward goals but also to take action in difficult circumstances or in chronic, long-standing issues such as addictions (Gollwitzer, 1999).

An example may clarify the process of identifying and sequencing subgoals for a client. Suppose that you are working with a person who has just been diagnosed with adult-onset diabetes and advised to lose 40 pounds. Losing 40 pounds is not a goal that anyone can accomplish overnight or without small requisite changes along the way. First, the person will need to determine a reasonable weekly level of weight loss, such as 1 to 2 pounds. Next, you and the client will have to determine the tasks the client will need to complete to lose weight. These tasks can be stated as subgoals that the client can strive to carry out each day, starting with the initial subgoal, the one that feels most comfortable and easy to achieve, and working the way up the pyramid as each previous step is successfully completed and maintained in the client's repertoire.

Although weight loss may include action steps such as alteration of eating levels, increase in physical activity, restructuring of cognitions and belief systems, and development of additional social skills, the exact tasks chosen by two or more clients who want to lose weight may be quite different. The helper should be sensitive to such differences and not impose his or her method for solving the issue (such as weight loss) on the client. Similarly, each client will have a different idea of how subgoals will be best sequenced. In Figure 10.2 we illustrate how one particular client sequenced her identified subgoals on the goal pyramid. This client's rationale was that if she increased exercise and relaxation *first*, it would be easier to alter eating habits. For her, more difficult and also less immediate goals included restructuring her thoughts about herself as a healthier person and developing social skills necessary to initiate new relationships. This last subgoal she viewed as the most difficult one because her weight served partly to protect her from social distress situations. After all six subgoals are achieved, the final subgoal is simply to keep these actions going for at least a 12-month period. At the bottom of the pyramid, it would be important to discuss with her some ways in which she can maintain the subgoals over an extended period of time. Note, too, in this example that her terminal goal is stated in positive terms—not "I don't want to be overweight and unhealthy" but "I do want to feel, think, and look like a healthy person." The subgoals represent actions that she will take to support this desired outcome. Also note that all the subgoals are stated in the same way as the terminal outcome goal—with the definition of the behaviors to be changed, the level of change, and the conditions or circumstances of change so that the client knows what to do, where, when, with whom, and how much or how often. (See Learning Activity 10.4)

Interview Leads for Identifying Subgoals

In identifying subgoals, the helper uses leads similar to the following to help the client determine appropriate subgoals or action steps:

"How will you go about doing [or thinking, feeling] this?"

"What exactly do you need to do to make this happen?"

"Let's brainstorm some actions you'll need to take to make your goal work for you."

"What have you done in the past to work toward this goal? How did it help?"

"Let's think of the steps you need to take to get from where you are now to where you want to be."

The helper is always trying to encourage and support client participation and responsibility in goal setting, remembering that clients are more likely to carry out changes that they originate. Occasionally, however, after hearing leads like the ones above, some clients are unable to specify any desirable or necessary action steps or subgoals. The helper may then have to use prompts, either asking the client to think of other people who have similar concerns and to identify their strategies for action or providing a statement illustrating an example or model of an action step or subgoal (Dixon & Glover, 1984).

Interview Leads for Sequencing Subgoals

General leads to use to sequence and rank subgoals include the following:

"What is your first step?"

"What would you be able to do most easily?"

"What would be most difficult?"

"What is most important for you to do now? Least important?"

"How could we order these steps to maximize your success in reaching your goal?"

"Let's think of steps you need to take to get from where you are now to where you want to be, and arrange them in an order from what seems easiest to you to what seems hardest to you."

"Can you think of some things you need to do before some other things as you make progress toward your goal?"

Identifying Obstacles

To ensure that the client can complete each subgoal step successfully, it is helpful to identify any *obstacles* that could interfere. Obstacles may include overt and/or covert behavior. *Potential* obstacles to check out with the client include the presence or absence of certain feelings or mood states, thoughts, beliefs and perceptions, other people, and situations or events. Another obstacle could be lack of knowledge or skill. Mitchell, Levin, and Krumboltz (1999) note that deeply held beliefs that see problems as overwhelming or having fears about the reactions of others often pose obstacles that block client action steps. Identification of lack of knowledge or skill is important if the client needs information or training before the subgoal action can be attempted (Gambrill, 1977).

Interview Leads to Identify Obstacles

Clients are often not very aware of any factors that might interfere with completing a subgoal and may need prompts from the helper, such as the following ones, to identify obstacles:

"What are some obstacles you may encounter in trying to take this action?"

"What people [feelings, ideas, situations] might get in the way of getting this done?"

"What or who might prevent you from working on this activity?"

"In what ways might you have difficulty completing this task successfully?"

"What information or skills do you need in order to complete this action effectively?"

Four additional interviewing leads to explore obstacles have been identified by Mitchell and colleagues (1999, p. 122):

"How have you been blocked from doing what you want to do?"
"How could you find out how permanent that block is?"
"How have other people overcome blocks like that?"
"How would you begin overcoming that block?"

Occasionally, the helper may need to point out apparent obstacles that the client overlooks. If significant obstacles are identified, a plan to deal with or counteract the effects of these factors needs to be developed. Often this is similar to an "antisabotage plan," in which the helper and client try to predict ways in which the client might not do the desired activity and then work around the possible barriers. For example, suppose

---

LEARNING ACTIVITY 10.4 — Identifying and Sequencing Subgoals

This learning activity is an extension of Learning Activity 10.3. Continue to work with the same client on the same goal selected and defined in that activity. Continuing with the role play, your task as the helper in this activity is to work with the client to generate and sequence subgoals using the goal pyramid in Figure 10.2 as a guide. Again, the client continues to assume the same role as in the previous activity, and the observer provides feedback on this process of identifying and sequencing subgoals.

that you explore obstacles with the client we described in the earlier section, who wants to lose weight because she has been recently diagnosed with diabetes and wants to improve her health. Perhaps in exploring the first subgoal, walking at least one mile a day, she identifies two things that might keep her from doing this: rain and being alone. Ways to prevent these two factors from interfering with her walking might be to use an indoor facility and to walk with an exercise partner.

Identifying Resources

The next step is to identify *resources*—factors that will help the client complete the subgoal task effectively. Like obstacles, resources include overt and covert behaviors as well as environmental sources. *Potential* resources to explore include feelings, thoughts and belief systems, people, situations, information, and skills. In this step, the practitioner tries to help clients identify already present or developed resources that, if used, can make completion of the subgoal tasks more likely and more successful.

A specific resource involved in attaining desired outcomes is referred to by Bandura (1977, 1989) and others as *self-efficacy*. Self-efficacy has been the focus of a great deal of research in the last 15 years (Maddux, 1995). It involves two types of personal expectations that affect goal achievement; one is an *outcome* expectation, and the other is an *efficacy* expectation. The outcome expectation has to do with whether and how much a client believes that engaging in particular behaviors will in fact produce the desired results. For example, in the example given in Figure 10.2, the outcome expectation would be the extent to which this client believes that the actions represented by these subgoals will help her lose 40 pounds and become a healthier person. The efficacy expectation involves the client's level of confidence regarding how well she can complete the behaviors necessary to reach the desired results. Again, in our example of this client, the efficacy expectation is related to the degree of confidence with which the client approaches the subgoals and her accompanying actions and behaviors. Of these two types of personal expectations, the *efficacy* ones seem to be the most important, thus strengthening the client's overall sense of perceived efficacy. (We discuss self-efficacy further in Chapter 18, on self-management interventions.)

People in the client's environment, especially those who observe and lend support to the client's goals, are potent resources. Resources may also be found in the client's cultural community—these can be in the form of people, situations, events, and so on. For example, a young Latina identifies with Esmeralda, a character in a book that reflects aspects of her cultural community, *The House on Mango Street* (Cisneros, 1984). Like Esmeralda in the book, the client finds a resource in her connection with four skinny trees that grow despite the surrounding concrete. Much like herself, they "do not belong here but are here" (p. 74). She understands that their strength is secret, much like her own, supported by "ferocious roots beneath the ground" (p. 74). This cultural resource helps the client feel empowered enough to take action (Iglesias and Cormier, in press). Skills of the client or of others in the client's environment can also be used as resources. Mitchell and colleagues (1999) identify a series of skills that are especially helpful: curiosity, persistence, flexibility, optimism, and risk taking (p. 122).

Interview Leads for Identifying Resources

Possible leads include the following:

"Which resources do you have available to help you as you go through this activity [or action]?"

"What specific feelings [or thoughts] are you aware of that might make it easier for you to _____ ?"

"What kind of support system do you have from others that you can use to make it easier to _____ ?"

"What skills [or information] do you possess that will help you do _____ more successfully?"

"How much confidence do you have that you can do what it will take for you to _____ ?"

"To what extent do you believe that these actions will help you do _____ ?"

"What resources are available to you in your environment and culture that can help you take this action?"

For example, the client with diabetes might identify a friend as a resource she could use for daily exercise, as well as her belief that exercise promotes wellness and good feelings. She might also identify a diabetes support group and her own persistence as additional resources, as well as her weekly prayer or meditative group.

EVALUATION OF OUTCOME GOALS

Increasingly, helpers are under pressure to measure results with their clients. Mental-health-care providers who want to be chosen to be on the panels of managed care companies are also under increasing pressure to provide data about their effectiveness. By some estimates, up to 88 percent of managed care companies are using outcome measurements to determine which providers serve on their panels (Hutchins,

1995). Practitioners who fail to measure outcomes will more than likely not be included. Also, and more important, there are ethical reasons to evaluate client outcomes. The professional codes of ethics we cited in Chapter 2 specify that practitioners have a responsibility to provide the best and most effective treatments to their clients (Blythe & Reithoffer, 2000). Evaluating practice is not just about accounting, but also about improving services to clients.

Doing outcome evaluations also guides treatment planning. As Resnick (1995) notes, "Outcomes measurements should be viewed as a mechanism to enhance and expand psychotherapeutic and psychological treatment. Using research-based measures to guide treatment, we can develop treatment paradigms, inform patients of likely outcome, and even suggest alternative courses of treatment" (p. 2). In the following chapter, on treatment planning and selection, we describe practice guidelines for research-informed treatment. Many practitioners resist making outcome evaluations because of the time and complexity involved. As practitioners ourselves, we understand this concern, yet we hold fast to the premise that most of us cannot avoid putting off outcome evaluations too much longer. However, with the necessary monitoring and paperwork required by many insurance companies and also by government regulations, we have attempted to suggest ways to accomplish this that are brief, simple, and inexpensive. At the outset, we wish to note that doing evaluations of client outcomes is not synonymous with empirical research and is subject to less rigor, less control, and more bias. Abell and Hudson (2000) further elaborate on this distinction, noting that *research* is used to develop a science of groups or populations, whereas *practice evaluation* is used to develop a science of one person. Moreover, there are research designs such as single-case design (Hayes, Barlow, & Nelson-Gray, 1999; Jones, 1993; Lundervold & Belwood, 2000) and case study designs (Moras, Telfer, & Barlow, 1993) that lend themselves particularly well to practice evaluations. Even so, objections and myths will always be raised about practice evaluations. Among these, Kazdin (1993) has noted the following:

1. Evaluating outcomes is unnecessary because change can be seen when it occurs.
2. Evaluation is an interference with effective treatment.
3. Clients are individuals, and evaluation obscures individuality.
4. Evaluation minimizes or trivializes clients' concerns.
5. Client issues change, so a systematic evaluation cannot be done.

Kazdin (1993) does an excellent job of refuting these myths and also points out that a data-based evaluation of outcomes is an important way to overcome inherent limitations and biases of human judgment (p. 40). In addition, our accountability as practitioners depends on "responsive evaluation" (p. 42). In conclusion, Lambert and associates (1998) point out that outcome evaluation is now a worldwide phenomenon and that psychotherapists across continents are involved in evaluating outcomes either by choice or by requirement.

RESPONSE DIMENSIONS OF OUTCOMES: WHAT TO EVALUATE

The goal behaviors are evaluated by measuring the amount or level of the defined behaviors. Four dimensions commonly used to measure the direction and level of change in goal behaviors are frequency, duration, magnitude (intensity), and occurrence. One or a combination of these response dimensions may be measured depending on the nature of the goal, the method of assessment, and the feasibility of obtaining particular data. It is important to select targets to measure that are the focus of intervention or change strategies. This is because "targets that aren't the focus of an intervention will not be valid indicators of the effectiveness of that intervention" (Bloom, Fischer, & Orme, 1999, p. 79). The response dimensions should be individualized, particularly because they vary in the time and effort that they cost the client.

Frequency

Frequency reflects the number (how many, how often) of overt or covert behaviors and is determined by obtaining measures of each occurrence of the goal behavior. Frequency counts are typically used when the goal behavior is discrete and of short duration. Panic episodes and headaches are examples of behaviors that can be monitored with frequency counts. Frequency data can also be obtained from comments written in a diary. For example, the number of positive (or negative) self-statements before and after each snack or bingeing episode, reported in a daily diary, can be tabulated.

Sometimes, frequency counts should be obtained as percentage data. For example, knowing the number of times a behavior occurred may not be meaningful unless data are also available on the number of *possible* occurrences of the behavior. Use percentage measures when it is important to determine the number of opportunities the client has to perform the target behavior as well as the number of times the behavior actually occurs. For example, data about the number of times an overweight client consumes snacks might be more informative if expressed as a percentage. In this example, the denominator would reflect the number of opportunities the person had to eat snacks; the numerator would indicate the number of times the person actually did snack. The advantage of percentage scores is that they indicate whether the change is a function of an actual increase or decrease in the number of times the response occurs or merely a function of an increase or decrease in the number of opportunities to perform the behavior. Thus, a percentage score may give more accurate and more complete information than a simple frequency count. However, when it is hard to detect the available opportunities or when it is difficult for the client to collect data, percentage scores may not be useful.

Duration

Duration reflects the length of time a particular response or collection of responses occurs. Duration measurement is appropriate whenever the goal behavior is not discrete and lasts for varying periods (Ciminero, Nelson, & Lipinski, 1977, p. 198). Thinking about one's strengths for a certain period of time, the amount of time spent on a task or with another person, the period of time for depressive thoughts, and the amount of time that anxious feelings lasted are examples of behaviors that can be measured with duration counts. Duration may also involve time *between* an urge and an undesired response, such as the time one holds off before lighting up a cigarette or eating an unhealthy snack. It also can involve *elapsed* time between a covert behavior such as a thought or intention and an actual response, such as the amount of time before a shy person speaks up in a discussion (sometimes this is referred to as *latency*).

Frequency counts, percentage scores, and duration can be obtained in one of two ways: continuous recording or time sampling. If the client can obtain data *each time* he or she engages in the goal behavior, then the client is collecting data continuously. Continuous recording is sometimes impossible, particularly when the goal behavior occurs very often or when its onset and termination are hard to detect. In such cases, a time-sampling procedure may be more practical. In time sampling, a day is divided into equal time intervals—90 minutes, 2 hours, or 3 hours, for example. The client keeps track of the frequency or duration of the goal behavior only during randomly selected intervals. In using time sampling, data should be collected during at least three time intervals each day and during *different* time intervals each day so that representative and unbiased data are recorded. One variation of time sampling is to divide time into intervals and indicate the presence or absence of the target behavior for each interval in an "all or none" manner (Mahoney & Thoresen, 1974, p. 31). If the behavior occurred during the interval, a *yes* would be recorded; if it did not occur, a *no* would be noted. Time sampling is less precise than continuous recordings of frequency or duration of a behavior. Yet it does provide an estimate of the behavior and may be a useful substitute in monitoring high-frequency or nondiscrete target responses (Mahoney & Thoresen, 1974).

Intensity

The intensity or degree of the goal behavior can be assessed with a rating scale. For example, intensity of anxious feelings can be measured with ratings of 1 (not anxious) to 5 (panic) on a self-anchored scale. Cronbach (1990) suggests three ways of decreasing sources of error frequently associated with rating scales. First, the helper should be certain that what is to be rated is well defined and specified in the client's language. For example, if a client is to rate depressed thoughts, the helper and client specify, with examples, what constitutes depressed thoughts (such as "Nothing is going right for me," "I can't do anything right"). These definitions should be tailored to each client, on the basis of an analysis of the client's target behavior and contributing conditions. Second, rating scales should be designed that include a description for each point on the scale. For example, episodes of anxious feelings in a particular setting can be rated on a 5-point scale, with 1 representing little or no anxiety, 2 equal to some anxiety, 3 being moderately anxious, 4 representing strong anxious feelings, and 5 indicating very intense anxiety. Third, rating scales should be unidirectional, starting with 0 or 1. Negative points (points below 0) should not be included. In addition, the helper should consider the range of points in constructing the scale. There should be at least 4 points and no more than 7, with higher scores representing more of whatever is being measured. A scale of less than 4 points may limit a person's ability to discriminate, whereas a scale that includes more than 7 points may not produce reliable ratings by the client because too many discriminations are required. In using these self-anchored scales, it is also important to tell clients that there are equal intervals on the scale so that the difference between 1 and 2, for example, is the same as the difference between 3 and 4 or 5 and 6 (Corcoran & Fischer, 2000). One advantage of these sorts of individualized or self-anchored scales is that they can be used at multiple times during a day and then averaged to get a daily single score that can be plotted on a chart or graph for visual examination of progress (Bloom et al., 1999).

Occurrence

Occurrence refers to the presence or absence of target behaviors. Checklists can be used to rate the occurrence of behaviors. They are similar to rating scales. The basic difference is the type of judgment one makes. On a rating scale, a person can indicate the degree to which a behavior is present; a checklist simply measures the presence or absence of a behavior. Checklists describe a cluster or collection of behaviors that a client may demonstrate.

Characteristics measuring occurrence of behaviors are very useful in providing the sort of outcome evaluations required by third-party payers who not only want to see data regarding symptoms/distress relief but also evidence of back-to-work functioning and productivity. For example, one checklist may measure the presence or absence of certain classroom behaviors of a teacher who has been treated for stress. Another may measure the presence or absence of behaviors at work for a person treated for substance abuse. A checklist can also be used in conjunction with frequency and duration counts and rating scales. As evaluative tools, checklists may be very useful, particularly when the reference points on the list are clearly defined and are representative of the particular performance domain being assessed. If two people are available to do the frequency, duration, intensity, or occurrence measurements—such as the client and helper, or the client and another person in the client's environment—they can compare their observations to see if there is agreement (Cone, 2001).

CHOOSING OUTCOME MEASURES: HOW TO EVALUATE OUTCOMES

A major factor facing the typical practitioner in evaluating outcomes is how to choose the most useful measures of outcome, which are (1) psychometrically sound (accurate, reliable, and valid), (2) pragmatic and easy to use, (3) relevant to the client's stated goals, (4) relevant to the client's level of functioning, (5) related to client's resources and constraints, and (6) relevant to the client's gender and culture. From a recent survey of the literature, we have concluded that three pressing areas should be considered in evaluation of outcomes. One is *client satisfaction*—that is, how satisfied the client is with you, the helper, and with the overall results of therapy. A second is *clinical outcomes significance*—that is, whether there has been enough improvement toward the specified goals and in the overall functioning of the client to move the client from a dysfunctional to a functional level. (One study [Ankuta & Abeles, 1993] produced the interesting finding that a group of clients who showed such clinically significant symptom changes reported greater satisfaction and benefit from therapy than clients who changed only moderately or not at all.) The third variable is *cost effectiveness*—that is, whether the benefits of a particular change procedure outweigh the costs and, if there are several available treatment procedures for a particular problem, which one is most time efficient. We discuss cost effectiveness in greater detail in the following chapter, on treatment planning and selection. Lambert and colleagues (1998) argue that using a combination of these three measures to evaluate client outcomes may reduce or eliminate the outpatient case review required by managed care organizations.

In addition to examining these three areas of outcome, helpers should also evaluate outcomes at several different times:

1. At *intake* or the beginning of the helping process; before a change strategy
2. *During* the use of a change intervention strategy
3. After a change strategy and/or at *termination* of the helping process
4. At *follow-up*—one month to one year after termination of the helping process

Client Satisfaction Measures

Several brief and easy-to-use measures of client satisfaction are available (see Box 10.1). An additional source of client satisfaction measures can be found in Corcoran and Fischer's (2000) excellent two-volume compendium, *Measures for Clinical Practice*.

A measure of client satisfaction is considered a minimum part of an overall outcome evaluation; that is, it is better to have an indicator of client satisfaction than nothing at all. However, we believe this sort of measure needs to be supplemented with additional ones because some mental health consumers will not accurately judge the quality of service. A social desirability or self-presentation bias in measures of client satisfaction tends to result in scores that are skewed in a positive direction (Cone, 2001; Pekarik & Guidry, 1999). To counteract this potential bias, Blythe and Reithoffer (2000) recommend being "up front" with clients about this possibility by pointing out to clients there is a tendency to complete the satisfaction measure in a more positive way, perhaps to please the helper. Organizations may misinterpret client satisfaction data as indicative of superior treatment and equate client satisfaction with treatment efficacy (Pekarik & Guidry, 1999).

Another limitation of client satisfaction is that these measures do not assess the particular outcomes specified by the helper and client in the goal-setting process. At the same time, data from client satisfaction measures may be important for the economic viability of some agencies or treatment

> **BOX 10.1 MEASURES OF CLIENT SATISFACTION AND CLINICAL OUTCOMES**
>
> **CSQ8 Client Satisfaction Questionnaire**
>
> Copyright 1979, 1989, and 1990. Used with written permission of Clifford Attkisson, Ph.D. This instrument is copyrighted, and there is a fee for use. Contact Clifford Attkisson, Ph.D., Professor of Medical Psychology, University of California at San Francisco, Milberry Union, 200 West, San Francisco, CA 94143.
>
> **Session Evaluation Questionnaire**
>
> (Stiles & Snow, 1984). Contact W. B. Stiles, Dept. of Psychology, Miami University, Oxford, OH 45056, and the American Psychological Association for permission to use.
>
> **BASIS-32 (Behavior and Symptom Identification Scale)**
>
> Also includes a depression scale. Available as a self-report or a clinician report form. Information kit costs $20. Offers permission for individual providers and groups to copy free of charge. Licensing fee for software developers or consultants. Scoring available for a charge through the software company. Contact Evaluation Service Unit, McLean Hospital, 115 Mill St., Belmont, MA 02178-9106. (617) 855-2425, http://www.basis-32.org.
>
> **SF-36**
>
> A health status questionnaire (also available in a 12-question format, SF-12). Cost: $25, which includes copyrighting instructions. Contact Medical Outcomes Trust, P.O. Box 1917, Boston, MA 02205-8516. Attn: Linda Birdsong. (617) 636-8098, http://www.sf-36.com.
>
> **SCL-90-R**
>
> Symptom checklist. Cost: $78 for a hand-scoring starter kit for 50 patients. Contact National Computer Systems, NCS Assessments, P.O. Box 1416, Minneapolis, MN 55440. (612) 939-5000, http://assessments.ncs.com/assessments/tests/scl90r.htm.
>
> **Addiction Severity Index**
>
> Free. Contact Treatment Research Institute, One Commerce Square, Suite 1020, 2005 Market Street, Philadelphia, PA 19103. (800) 335-9874, http://www.tresearch.org/Employment/employ.html.
>
> **SUDDS (Substance Use Disorder Diagnosis Schedule)**
>
> Cost: $48.75, including 25 schedules with hand-scoring kit. New version based on *DSM-IV* coming soon. Contact New Standards, Inc., 1080 Montreal Ave., Suite 300, St. Paul, MN 55116. (800) 755-6299.
>
> **Beck Depression Inventory-II**
>
> The Psychological Corporation, 555 Academic Court, San Antonio, TX 78204-2498. (210) 299-1061, 1-800-228-0752, http://www.beckinstitute.org.
>
> **Katz Activities of Daily Living**
>
> Martin M. Katz, Clinical Research Branch, Resource Guild, National Institute of Mental Health, Chevy Chase, MD 20203.
>
> **FACES III**
>
> David H. Olson. Family Social Science Department, University of Minnesota, 290 McNeal Hall, 1985 Beuford Avenue, St. Paul, MN 55108. (612) 625-7250, http://www.lifeinnovations.com (look under Research section).
>
> **Child Behavior Checklist and Youth Self-Report**
>
> T. M. Achenbach, University Associates in Psychiatry, c/o Child Behavior Checklist, 1 South Prospect St., Burlington, VT 05401. (802) 656-8313, FAX: (802) 656-2602, http://www.ASEBA.org.
>
> **Outcome Questionnaire (OQ45)**
>
> A 45-item questionnaire. Manual includes patient progress profile and indices of clinical significance. Software available. For fee and permission to use, contact Center for Behavioral Health Care Efficacy, 36 So. State, Suite 2100, Salt Lake City, UT 84111, or M. J. Lambert, Dept. of Psychology, 272 TLRB, Brigham Young University, Provo, Utah, 84602.
>
> *Note:* Most of these instruments are copyrighted and require permission and a fee to use.
> *Source:* Adapted from "Readers Meet, Set Agenda," by J. Hutchins. Copyright ©1995 by the American Association of Marriage and Family Therapy. Reprinted with permission from the American Association of Marriage and Family Therapy.

centers. In these cases, client satisfaction measures are acceptable if used just for the purpose of a general assessment of services and when combined with other, more-specific measures of clinical outcome (Eckert 1994; Pekarik & Guidry, 1999). In the next section, we discuss ways to evaluate specific therapeutic goals and outcomes.

Goal-Related Outcome Measures

For the *researcher*, pragmatics is usually the least important criterion in choosing outcome measures. For the practitioner, who is faced with numbers of treatment plans to write and who may be paid according to the number of clients seen, pragmatics is usually the *most* important out-

> **BOX 10.2** **FORTY-SEVEN PROBLEM AREAS ADDRESSED IN *MEASURES FOR CLINICAL PRACTICE* (CORCORAN & FISCHER, 2000)**
>
> | | | |
> |---|---|---|
> | abuse | guilt | procrastination |
> | acculturation | health issues | psychopathology and psychiatric symptoms |
> | addiction and alcoholism | identity | rape |
> | anger and hostility | interpersonal behavior | satisfaction with life |
> | anxiety and fear | locus of control | schizotypal symptoms |
> | assertiveness | loneliness | self-concept and esteem |
> | beliefs | love | self-control |
> | children's behaviors/problems | marital/couple relationship | self-efficacy |
> | client motivation | mood | sexuality |
> | coping | narcissism | smoking |
> | couple relationship | obsessive-compulsive | social functioning |
> | death concerns | parent–child relationship | social support |
> | depression and grief | perfectionism | stress |
> | eating problems | phobias | substance abuse |
> | family functioning | problem-solving | suicide |
> | geriatric | | treatment satisfaction |

come. Given this consideration, we suggest two ways to proceed that are especially suitable to the demands of the typical practitioner's work environment. First, consider using the goal-attainment scaling system (Kiresuk & Sherman, 1968) (or some variation thereof) that we discussed in the section on defining goals. This system is especially useful for evaluating individual client change or "target complaints that focus on behaviors that are not necessarily specific to symptoms of diagnosable disorders" (Callaghan, 2001, p. 292). The GAS, which has been used extensively with a number of different client populations, simply requires you to take an outcome goal for any given client and construct a weighted scale of descriptions ranging from the most favorable result ($+2$) to the least favorable result (-2), with a sum of 0 representing the expected level of improvement. (You may wish to refer to Table 10.3 for a review of this process.) Using these numerical scores, you can then quantify levels of change in outcome goals by transforming these scores to standardized T scores (see also Kiresuk & Sherman, 1968). As Marten and Heimberg (1995) observe, the advantage of the GAS system lies in "its ability to allow practitioners a means of evaluating treatment outcome in an idiographic manner by examining client changes within specific problem areas in a concrete and systematized way" (p. 49). The GAS is also relatively free of bias about client "impairment." The GAS is constructed while the helper and client are developing outcome goals and prior to the beginning of any treatment protocol or change intervention. A particular advantage of this method is that the GAS can be constructed within, rather than outside, the helping situation and with the client's participation and assistance. Therefore, it requires almost no extra time from the helper, reinforces the client's role in the change process, and also provides a quantifiable method of assessing outcome. Note that while the GAS example we present in Table 10.3 uses *frequency* as the level of change, you can also construct a GAS using duration and intensity as indicators of change. The GAS rating system is useful because it describes each point on the rating scale in a quantifiable way, eliminating ambiguity. Another advantage of the GAS is its applicability to assess change in couples, families, and organizations, as well as individual clients (Ogles, Lambert, & Masters, 1996).

In addition to a numerical system of rating results, such as the GAS, the helper should consider giving clients some sort of paper-and-pencil rapid-assessment instrument (RAI) they can complete to provide self-report data about symptom reduction and level of improvement. The most comprehensive compendium of such measures we have found is in two volumes of Corcoran and Fischer's work (2000). These authors provide descriptions of several hundred RAIs for 47 problem areas (see Box 10.2), including a profile of the instrument and information regarding norms, scoring, reliability, validity, and availability. Another source of RAIs is a Web site (http://ericae.net/testcol.htm). Callaghan (2001) describes ways to use RAIs to aggregate and track data across different clients, across therapists, and also across varying treatment interventions.

In selecting an RAI, it is important to choose one that has good psychometric properties; is easy to read, use, and score; and relates directly to the client's identified problems and symptoms at intake and stated outcome goals of counseling. For example, the Beck Depression Inventory–II (BDI–II) (Beck, Steer, & Brown, 1996) is frequently used with clients who are depressed at intake and want to become less depressed. However, it would not be a suitable choice for someone who presents with a different problem such as anxiety, anger control, or marital dissatisfaction. Also, many of the psychometric properties of these RAIs have been normed on Caucasian clients, often middle-class college students. Caution must be applied when using some of these instruments with clients of color. If you cannot find a culturally relevant RAI, perhaps you should use the goal attainment scaling system instead. Helpers should use RAIs that are as relevant as possible to the client's culture and gender. For example, if you are measuring the stress level of an African American woman, it is better to use the African-American Women's Stress Scale (Watts-Jones, 1990) than some other stress measure. Cone (2001) points out that most rapid-assessment instruments can be used to assess outcomes at the beginning, midpoints, termination, and follow-up of treatment but not as repeated daily or weekly measures because they are not appropriately sensitive enough to change over short time intervals (p. 49). One outcome assessment system with good psychometric properties that is designed to measure outcomes and the quality of the helping relationship over short, repeated intervals is called the COMPASS (Howard et al., 1995).

In addition to RAIs such as the Beck or the Lehrer and Woolfolk (1982) anxiety inventory, there are also RAIs that tap into general levels of client functioning and a range of symptoms. For example, recall from our discussion of the *DSM-IV* in Chapter 8 that there is a global assessment of functioning (GAF) scale used to report on Axis V. This scale can help to measure the effect of treatment and to track the progress of clients in global terms with the use of a single measure. It is rated on a 0 to 100 scale regarding the client's psychological, social, and occupational functioning but not physical or environmental limitations. It can be used for ratings at both intake and termination although little psychometric data are available on the GAF, and like client satisfaction ratings, it is a very transparent measure (Davis & Meier, 2001). (Refer to Chapter 8 for a visual display of this scale.) RAIs that cover a wide range of symptoms include such measures as the Derogatis (1983) Symptom Checklist SCL-90-R and the Behavior and Symptom Identification Scale (Basis-32). An outcome measure suitable for evaluating the goals of child and adolescent clients is one we described in Chapter 9—the Child and Adolescent Functional Assessment Scale (CAFAS) (Hodges, 1997). The more-general RAIs are limited in that they do not directly measure the behaviors specified in the client's outcome goals. However, an advantage of a broader multifaceted RAI has to do with *clinical significance.* Within the last 10 years, there has been a major movement in the evaluation of mental health services toward criteria that reflect *clinically* significant outcomes (Goldfried, Greenberg, & Marmer, 1990; Jacobson, Follette, & Revenstorf, 1984; Jacobson & Truax, 1991).

Clinical significance refers to the effect of a treatment intervention on a single client and denotes improvement in client symptoms and functioning at a level comparable to that of the client's healthy peers (Jacobson et al., 1984). According to Cone (2001), the "simplest way to define clinically significant improvement is to consider a person to have improved when the score on a formal measure, such as the BDI, moves from the clinical to the nonclinical or 'normal' range" (p. 43). So for a client with an initial BDI score of 33 who drops to below a 9, this drop is indicative of clinically significant improvement. There are also statistical ways to define clinical significance (Jacobson et al., 1999; Kendall et al., 1999). Statistically reliable change refers to change that is greater than would be expected to occur due to behavioral variabililty and measurement error (Lundervold & Belwood, 2000, p. 96). Clinically significant criteria are applied to each psychotherapy case and not only answer the question of the degree to which the client makes the specified changes but also address the *relevance* of those changes to the client's overall functioning and lifestyle. In so doing, these criteria are considered to have a high degree of social validity (Kazdin, 1977). Increasingly, third-party payers are asking for outcome documentation from practitioners that not only includes symptom reduction but also the client's level of functioning in settings such as work, school, and home (Cavaliere, 1995). One brief outcome measure that appears to be reliable, valid, and suitable for repeated measurements, has available software, and provides statistically derived indices of clinical significance is the Outcome Questionnaire (OQ 45) (Lambert et al., 1998).

A new development in RAIs is computer-assisted practice evaluation (Nurius & Hudson, 1993). One such package is the Computer Assisted Assessment Package (CAAP) developed by Hudson (1996a). This package, along with an accompanying one called the CASS (Computer Assisted Social Services system) (Hudson, 1996b), stores and administers RAIs directly to clients, scores, interprets scores, prepares graphs of data, and automatically updates a client's file each time a scale is completed. In this system, information is stored so that only the helper or someone you designate can access the program and a client's information. These two systems also require minimal knowledge of computers. They are explained and presented as a software program in Bloom and associates (1999); see also their Web site (http://www.walmyr.com/scales.exe). Other database options are described by Cone (2001), Callaghan (2001), and Nugent, Sieppert, and Hudson (2001).

It is important to balance data obtained from more-general outcome measures with specific ones tailored to individual clients and their goals. This is because some clients may improve on a general outcome measure but don't reach their goals, whereas other clients, especially in outpatient or EAP settings, may score in the normal range of a general outcome measure (Lambert et al., 1998). An outcome measure that can be used in a very idiographic way to evaluate goal-related client outcomes is self-monitoring. Self-monitoring is a process of observing and recording aspects of one's own covert or overt behavior. In evaluating goal behaviors, a client uses self-monitoring to collect data about the number and amount (frequency, duration, intensity) of the goal behaviors. Self-monitoring is an excellent way to obtain a daily within-person measure of the behavior over days or weeks. This provides an indication of the "temporal patterning" of the behavior as well as of the level of change (Petry, Tennen, & Affleck, 2000, p. 100). Self-monitoring is also an especially good way to collect data about the target behaviors and the environmental and social influences or contributing conditions. The monitoring involves not only noticing occurrences of the goal behavior but also recording them with paper and pencil, mechanical counters, timers, or electronic devices. (In Chapter 18, we discuss the use of self-monitoring as a change/intervention strategy.) Self-monitoring is often necessary to collect information about frequency, duration, or intensity of target behaviors specified in a GAS. For example, in the GAS in Table 10.3, the client would need to self-monitor the frequency of colitis attacks during the day.

Self-monitoring has a number of advantages as a way to collect data about client progress toward goal behaviors. Self-monitoring, or an ongoing account of what happens in a person's daily environment, can have more concurrent validity than some other data-collection procedures. In other words, self-monitoring may produce data that more closely approximate the outcome goals than such measures as the rapid-assessment inventories we discussed earlier. Moreover, the predictive validity of self-monitoring may be superior to that of other measurement methods, with the exception of direct observation. Self-monitoring can also provide a thorough and representative sample of the ongoing behaviors in the client's environment. And self-monitoring is relatively objective. Finally, self-monitoring is flexible. It can be used to collect data on covert and physiological indices of change as well as more-observable behaviors. However, self-monitoring should not be used by clients who cannot engage in observation because of the intensity or diagnostic nature of their problems or because of medication. Also, self-monitoring may have a high cost for the client in the time and effort required to make such frequent records of the goal behavior.

Another consideration is that some clients may not monitor as accurately as others. To increase the accuracy of a client's self-monitoring, consider these guidelines:

1. The behaviors to be observed should be defined clearly so there is no ambiguity about what is to be observed and reported. The helper should spell out clearly the procedures for *what, where, when, how,* and *how long* to report the behaviors.
2. Any definition of the target behavior should be accompanied by examples so the client can discriminate instances of the observed behavior from instances of other behaviors. For example, a client should be instructed to observe particular responses associated with aggressiveness instead of just recording "aggressive behavior." In this case, the client might observe and record instances of raising his or her voice above a conversational tone, hitting another person, or using verbal expressions of hostility.
3. If possible, clients should be instructed to self-monitor *in vivo* when the behavior occurs, rather than self-recording at the end of the day, when the client is dependent on retrospective recall. The accuracy of client reports may be increased by having the client record the target behaviors immediately rather than after a delay. Using devices such as pagers, palmtop computers, voice mail, and e-mail to cue the client to self-record may enhance the accuracy of the data (Cone, 2001).

WHEN TO EVALUATE OUTCOMES

There are several times during which a helper and client can measure progress toward the goal behaviors. Generally, the client's performance should be evaluated before counseling, during counseling or during application of a change strategy, immediately after counseling, and some time after counseling at a follow-up. Repeated measurements of client change may provide more precise data than only two measurement times, such as before and after a change strategy. Moreover, third-party payers are increasingly requiring that practitioners track outcomes for clients over a longer period of time, including and up to a one-year follow-up contact (Cavaliere, 1995). In some states, Medicaid now requires 5 outcome measures to be collected every 90 days.

This form of practice evaluation is based on a single-subject, single-case, or single-system design. Its essential components include "a client, and a repeated administration of the measure over periods of time during which the intervention is absent or present" (Cone, 2001, p. 206). Comparisons and date collected are plotted on graphs for visual observation. While there are more sophisticated single-subject designs than what we present (see Bloom et al., 1999; Cone, 2001; Hayes et al., 1999; Nugent et al., 2001), the simplest way to do a planned comparison is between two key elements of the evaluation—nonintervention and intervention (Bloom et al., 1999, p. 382). This design is useful for busy practitioners with most clients in most settings and with any theoretical perspective. Bloom and colleagues (1999, p. 381) refer to it as the "workhorse" of practice evaluation. They assert that while it is not a perfect method, it is a "quantum leap from the subjective or intuitive approaches to evaluating practice commonly used" (p. 486). When it is used with reliable and valid measures, helpers can monitor client progress over time, capture changes in identified goal-related behaviors, and assess the correlation between the timing of the intervention and the onset of any measured change (Bloom et al., 1999, p. 539). This sort of evaluation gives clients and helpers feedback to evaluate the goals and make changes in the intervention if sufficient progress is not being made (Corcoran & Fischer, 2000). A good clinical description of this single-subject evaluation is provided by Callaghan (2001).

Measurement Before Treatment Strategies: Baseline

A pretreatment measurement evaluates the goal behaviors before treatment. This period is a reference point against which therapeutic change in the client's goal behavior can be compared during and after treatment. The length of the pretreatment period can be three days, a week, two weeks, or longer. One criterion for the length of this period is that it should be long enough to contain sufficient data points to serve as a *representative sample* of the client's behavior. For example, with a depressed client, the helper may ask the client to complete self-ratings on mood intensity at several different times during the next week or two. The helper may also ask the client to self-monitor instances or periods of depression that occur during this time. This situation is graphed in Figure 10.3. Note that several data points are gathered to provide information about the stability of the client's behavior. Usually, a minimum of three observations is necessary to "provide a reasonably accurate estimate of the pattern of the behavior" (Lundervold & Belwood, 2000, p. 94). If the helper does not collect any pretreatment data at all, determining the magnitude or amount of change that has occurred will be difficult because there are no precounseling data for comparison. The pretreatment period serves as a baseline of reference points showing where the client is before any treatment or intervention. In Figure 10.3, for example, you can see the number of depressed thoughts that occur for this client in the first two weeks of counseling but before any treatment plan or change intervention is used. In the third week, when the helper introduces and the client works with an intervention such as cognitive restructuring, the client continues to record the number of depressed thoughts. These records, as well as any taken after counseling, can be compared to the baseline data.

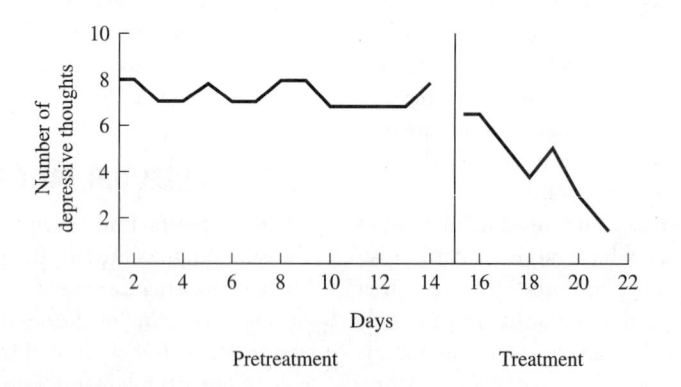

Figure 10.3 Graph of depessive thoughts: Pretreatment

Baseline measurement may not be possible with all clients, however. The client's concern may be too urgent or intense to allow you to take the time for gathering baseline data. Baseline measurement is often omitted in crisis situations. In a less urgent type of example, if a client reports "exam panic" and is faced with an immediate and very important test, the helper and client will need to start working to reduce the test anxiety at once. In such cases, the treatment or change strategy must be applied immediately. In these instances, a "retrospective" baseline may be better than nothing—retrospective meaning that the helper and the client establish a picture of what life was like during a relevant window prior to the intake (Abell & Hudson, 2000, p. 542).

Measurement During Treatment Strategies

During the helping process, the helper and client monitor the effects of a designated treatment on the goal behaviors after collecting pretreatment data and selecting an intervention or treatment strategy. The monitoring during the treatment phase is conducted by the continued collection of data on the same behaviors and using the same measures as during the pretreatment period. For example, if the client self-monitored the frequency and duration of self-critical thoughts during the pretreatment period, this self-monitoring would continue during the application of a helping strategy. Or if self-report inventories of the client's social skills were used during the pretreatment period, these same methods would be used to collect data during treatment. Data collection during treatment is a feedback loop that gives both the helper and the client important information about the usefulness of the selected treatment strategy and the client's demonstration of the goal behavior. Figure 10.4 shows the data of a client who self-monitored the number of depressed thoughts experienced during the application of two intervention or change strategies: cognitive restructuring and stimulus control. During this phase of data collection, it is important to specify the intervention as clearly as possible (Bloom et al., 1999).

If, as the helper, you can't do anything else in the way of data collection, you can be an accountable professional by at least measuring client goal-related outcomes during these two periods—before and during treatment—as we have just described. These two measurement periods can detect change in client goal behaviors although there is not enough information from these two data periods to tell much about causality. For example, it is hard to know if the change that occurred in the client's goal behaviors was a function of the specific intervention you used or if another event accounted for the observed results. While you cannot attribute client change directly to your intervention, this concern has more to do with the conducting of research

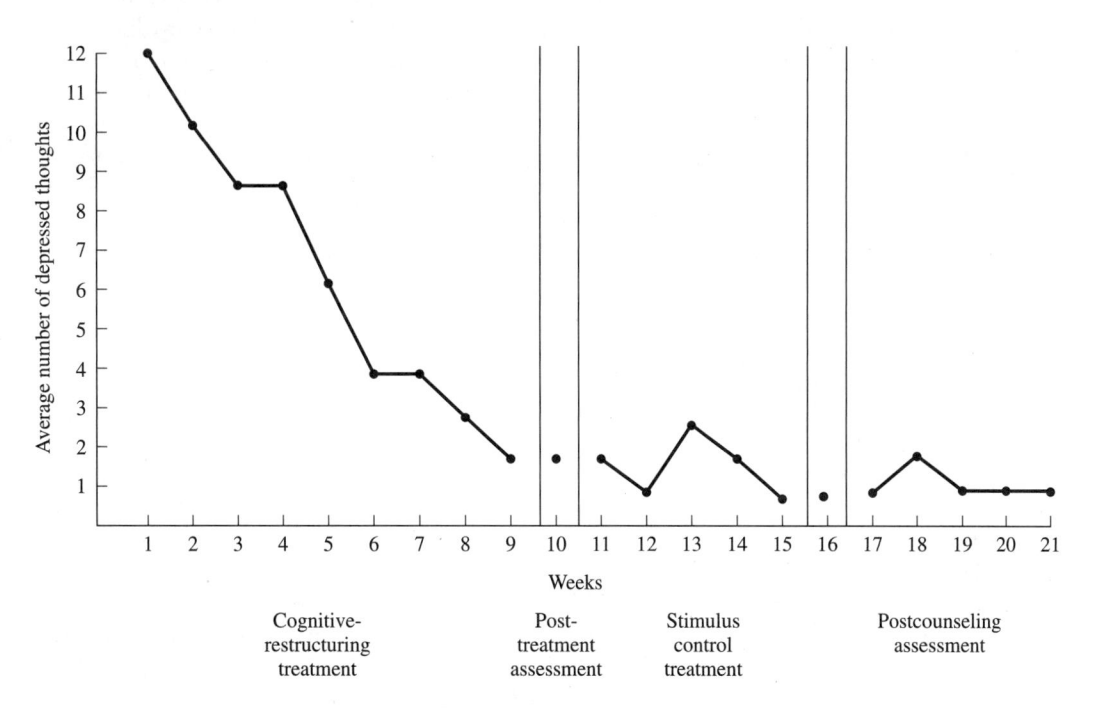

Figure 10.4 Graph of depressive thoughts: Posttreatment

than of practice evaluation (Bloom et al., 1999, p. 539). As Nugent and associates (2001) conclude, "given the conflicting demands of science and practice, this may be, except in the most unusual cases, the strongest evidence that can be provided in the practice context" (p. 88). If possible, it is even better to extend data collection to include measurements immediately after a treatment strategy and also when counseling has terminated, as well as at some time after counseling is over—called a follow-up. These added periods of evaluation of the client's goal behaviors help to determine if the changes noted maintain over time (Bloom et al., 1999). They also give us more information about whether the client's changes were achieved at least in part because of the treatment intervention used (although the most conclusive evidence of causality is found with the multiple baseline designs described in the books we noted above).

Posttreatment: Measurement After Intervention and After Counseling

At the conclusion of a treatment strategy and/or at the conclusion of counseling, the helper and client should conduct a posttreatment measurement to indicate how much the client has achieved the desired results (see also Figure 10.4). Specifically, the data collected during a posttreatment evaluation are used to compare the client's demonstration and level of the goal behavior after treatment with the data collected during the pretreatment period and during treatment.

The posttreatment assessment may occur at the conclusion of a change strategy or at the point when counseling is terminated—or both. For instance, if a helper is using cognitive restructuring (see Chapter 14) to help a client reduce depressed thoughts, the helper and client could collect data on the client's level of depressed thoughts after having finished working with the cognitive restructuring strategy. This assessment may or may not coincide with counseling termination. If the helper plans to use a second treatment strategy, then data would be collected at the conclusion of the cognitive restructuring strategy and prior to the use of another strategy. This example is depicted in Figure 10.4. Note that the client continued to self-monitor the number of depressed thoughts both between the cognitive restructuring and stimulus control treatments and after stimulus control, when counseling was terminated.

Ideally, the same types of measures used to collect data before and during counseling should be employed in the posttreatment evaluation. For instance, if the client self-monitored depressed thoughts before and during treatment, then, as Figure 10.4 illustrates, self-monitoring data would also be collected during posttreatment assessment. If the helper had also employed questionnaires such as the Beck Depression Inventory-II during the pretreatment period and treatment, these measures would be used during posttreatment data collection as well.

Follow-up Assessment

After the helping relationship has terminated, some type of follow-up assessment should be conducted. A helper can conduct both a short-term and a long-term follow-up. A short-term follow-up can occur three to six months after therapy. A long-term follow-up would occur one month to a year (or more) after counseling has been terminated. Generally, the helper should allow sufficient time to elapse before conducting a follow-up to determine the extent to which the client is maintaining desired changes without the helper's assistance.

There are several reasons for conducting follow-up assessments. First, a follow-up can indicate the helper's continued interest in the client's welfare. Second, a follow-up provides information that can be used to compare the client's performance of the goal behavior before and after counseling. Another important reason for conducting a follow-up is to determine how well the client is able to perform the goal behaviors in his or her environment without relying on the support and assistance of the helper. This reflects one of the most important evaluative questions: Has counseling helped the client to maintain desired behaviors and to prevent the occurrence of undesired ones in some self-directed fashion? As we have indicated, more and more third-party payers are expecting practitioners to provide some follow-up data on client outcomes.

Both short-term and long-term follow-ups can take several forms. The kind of follow-up that a practitioner conducts often depends on the client's availability to participate in a follow-up and the time demands of each situation. Here are some ways that a follow-up can be conducted:

1. Invite the client in for a follow-up interview. The purpose of the interview is to evaluate how the client is coping with respect to his or her "former" concern or issue. The interview may also involve client demonstrations of the goal behavior in simulated role plays.
2. Mail an inventory or questionnaire to the client, seeking information about her or his current status in relation to the original problem or concern.
3. Send a letter to the client asking about the current status of the problem. Be sure to include a stamped, self-addressed envelope.

4. Telephone the client for an oral report. The letter and telephone report could also incorporate the goal-attainment scale rating if that was used earlier.

These examples represent one-shot follow-up procedures that take the form of a single interview, letter, or telephone call. A more extensive (and sometimes more difficult to obtain) kind of follow-up involves the client's engaging in self-monitoring or self-rating of the goal behavior for a designated time period, such as two or three weeks. Figure 10.5 shows the level of depressed thoughts of a client at a six-month follow-up.

As you can see from the figures, data collected in an outcome evaluation are usually plotted on graphs for visual inspection, giving approximate information and rapid feedback about client goal-related changes. Assessment of changes from graphs is difficult, however, if the patterns are unclear or too variable to offer much meaning. (See Bloom et al., 1999, and Cone, 2001, for additional information about the meanings of graphed data.)

It is also important for helpers to think about introducing and including clients in practice evaluations, stressing that clients can help in monitoring progress, which is used to select and modify workable plans of action. However, challenges to this process occur with clients who are psychotic, cognitively impaired, or literate in languages other than English, as few RAIs have been translated (Callaghan, 2001, p. 296). In these instances, or with clients who may have severe clinical disorders, evaluation strategies often need to be tailored to the individual client. When possible, inform clients that you need to gather facts and that some portion of fact gathering or data collection will continue throughout your contacts together—even during intervention—in order to have "a continuing record of the pulse of the situation" (Bloom et al., 1999, p. 393). We illustrate this process in the following model example and dialogue with our client Joan.

MODEL EXAMPLE: THE CASE OF JOAN

Joan's first outcome goal was defined as to acquire and demonstrate a minimum of four initiating skills, including four of the following: (1) asking questions and making reasonable requests, (2) expressing differences of opinion, (3) expressing positive feelings, (4) expressing negative feelings, and (5) volunteering answers or opinions in at least four situations a week with her parents and in math class. This overall goal can be assessed by a GAS (see the model dialogue that follows). We would also give Joan a client satisfaction questionnaire at the end of counseling and at a six-month follow-up. Four subgoals are associated with the first goal:

1. To decrease anxiety associated with anticipation of failure in math class and rejection by parents from self-ratings of intensity of 70 to 50 on a 100-point scale during the next two weeks of treatment.
2. To increase positive self-talk and thoughts that "girls are capable" in math class and other competitive situations from zero or two times a week to four or five times a week over the next two weeks during treatment.
3. To increase attendance in math class from two or three times a week to four or five times a week during treatment.
4. To increase verbal participation and initiation in math class and with her parents from none or once a week to three or four times a week over the next two weeks during treatment. Verbal participation is defined as asking and answering questions with teacher or parents, volunteering answers or offering opinions, or going to the chalkboard. (For a summary of these goals and subgoals, see Joan's goal chart on p. 296.)

The helper and Joan need to establish the method of evaluating progress on each of the four subgoals and to determine the response dimension for each subgoal. We would recommend that a global self-report assessment inventory of anxiety (Lehrer & Woolfolk, 1982) be used to measure reductions in anxiety (subgoal 1). This RAI would be given before and during treatment and at follow-up times. For subgoal 1, Joan could also self-monitor intensity of anxiety associated with anticipated failure in math class and rejection from parents, on a scale ranging from 0 to 100. For subgoal 2, we recommend that Joan self-monitor her self-talk during math class and other competitive situations. She could be instructed to write (*in vivo*) her self-talk on notecards

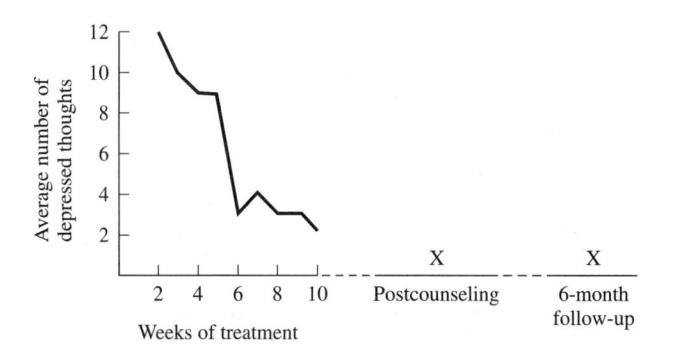

Figure 10.5 Graph of follow-up data

during baseline and treatment. Subgoal 3 is to increase her attendance in math class. Joan could keep a record of the days she attended class, and these data could be verified from the teacher's attendance records, with Joan's permission. For subgoal 4, verbal participation and initiation in math class and with her parents could be self-monitored (*in vivo*) by recording each time Joan performed these verbal responses. Again, the same data would be collected before, during, and after an intervention. We illustrate this evaluation process in the following continuation of our model dialogue.

MODEL DIALOGUE: THE CASE OF JOAN

The helper will start by *summarizing* the previous session and by checking out whether Joan's goals have changed in any way. Goal setting is a flexible process, subject to revisions along the way.

1. **Helper:** OK, Joan, last week when we talked, just to recap, you mentioned three areas you'd like to work on. Is this still accurate, or have you added anything or modified your thinking in any way about these since we last met?

Client: No, that's still where I want to go right now. And I still want to start with this whole issue of expressing myself and not worrying so much about what other people think. I've been doing a lot of thinking about that this week, and I think I'm really starting to see how much I let other people use me as a doormat and also control my reactions in a lot of ways.

2. **Helper:** Yes, you mentioned some of those things last week. They seem to be giving you some incentive to work on this.

Client: Yeah. I guess I'm finally waking up and starting to feel a little fed up about it.

In the next response, the helper explains the *purpose* of the session and solicits Joan's opinion, again giving her another opportunity to express her opinions.

3. **Helper:** Last week I mentioned it might be helpful to map out a plan of action. How does that sound to you? If it isn't where you want to start, let me know.

Client: No, I do. I've been kind of gearing up for this all week.

In the next two responses, the helper helps Joan define the *behaviors* associated with the goal—what she will be doing, thinking, and feeling.

4. **Helper:** OK, last week when we talked about this area of change, you described it as wanting to express yourself more without worrying so much about the reactions of other people. Could you tell me what you mean by expressing yourself—to make sure we're on the same wavelength?

Client: Well, like in math class, I need to volunteer the answers when I know them, and volunteer to go to the board. Also, I hesitate to ask questions. I need to be able to ask a question without worrying if it sounds foolish.

5. **Helper:** You've mentioned three specific ways in math class you want to express yourself [makes a note]. I'm going to jot these down on this paper in case we want to refer to these later. Anything else you can think of about math class?

Client: No, not really. The other situation I have trouble with is with my folks.

"Trouble" is not very specific. Again, a *behavioral definition* of the goal is sought in the next two responses.

6. **Helper:** OK, "trouble." Again, can you describe exactly how you'd like to express yourself when interacting with them?

Client: Kind of the same stuff. Sometimes I would like to ask them a question. Or ask for help or something. But I don't. I almost never express my ideas or opinions to them, especially if I don't agree with their ideas. I just keep things to myself.

7. **Helper:** So you'd like to be able to make a request, ask a question, talk about your ideas with them, and express disagreement.

Client: Yeah. Wow—sounds hard.

In the following response, the helper prepares Joan for the idea of working in *small steps* and also explores *conditions (situations, people)* associated with the goal.

8. **Helper:** It will take some time, and we won't try to do everything at once. Just one step at a time. Now, you've mentioned two different situations where these things are important to you—math class and with your parents. I noticed last week there was one time when you were reluctant to express your opinion to me. Is this something you want to do in any other situations or with any other people?

Client: Well, sure—it does crop up occasionally at different times or with different people, even friends. But it's worse in math and at home. I think if I could do it there, I could do it anywhere.

In the next response, the helper starts to explore the *level* or *desired extent of change*. The helper is attempting to establish a *current base rate* in order to know how much the client is doing now.

9. **Helper:** I'm making a note of this, too. Now could you estimate how often you express yourself in the ways you've described above *right now*, either in math class or with your folks, during the course of an average week?

Client: You mean how many times do I do these things during the week?

10. **Helper:** Yes.

Client: Probably almost never—at least not in math class or at home. Maybe once or twice at the most.

The helper continues to help Joan identify a *practical* and *realistic level of change*.

11. **Helper:** If you express yourself in one of these ways once or twice a week now, how often would you like to be doing this? Think of something that is also practical or realistic.

Client: Mm. Well, I don't really know. Offhand, I'd guess about four or five times a week—that's about once a day, and that would take a lot of energy for me to be able to do that in these situations.

At this point, the *behavior, conditions, and level of change* for this terminal goal are defined. The helper asks Joan whether this definition is the way she wants it.

12. **Helper:** I'll make a note of this. Check what I have written down—does it seem accurate? [Joan reads what is listed as the first terminal goal on her goal chart at the end of this dialogue.—see p. 296.]

Client: Yeah. Gosh, that sort of makes it official, doesn't it?

This is the second time Joan has expressed a little hesitation. So the helper will check out *her feelings* about the process in the next response.

13. **Helper:** Yes. What kinds of feelings are you having about what we're doing now?

Client: Kind of good and a little scared too. Like do I really have what it takes to do this?

In the next response, the helper responds to Joan's concern. Joan has already selected this goal, yet if she has difficulty later on moving toward it, they will need to explore *what her present behavior is trying to protect*.

14. **Helper:** One thing I am sure of is that you do have the resources inside you to move in this direction as long as this is a direction that is important to you and one that is not necessary to protect any parts of you. If we move along and you feel stuck, we'll come back to this and see how you keep getting stuck at this point.

Client: OK.

Next the helper introduces and *develops a goal attainment* scale for this particular goal (responses 15–20).

15. **Helper:** Let's spend a little time talking about this particular goal we've just nailed down. I'd like to set up some sort of a system with you in which we rank what you expect or would like to happen, but also the best possible and the least possible success we could have with this goal. This gives us both a concrete target to work toward. How does that sound?

Client: OK. What exactly do we do?

16. **Helper:** Well, let's start with a range of numbers from -2 to $+2$. It will look like this [draws the following numbers on a sheet of paper]:

-2
-1
0
$+1$
$+2$

Zero represents an acceptable and expected level, one you could live with. What do you think it would be in this case?

Client: I guess maybe doing this at least twice a week—at least once in math and once at home. That would be better than nothing.

17. **Helper:** We'll put that down opposite "0." If that's acceptable, would you say that the four per week you mentioned earlier is more than expected?

Client: Yes.

18. **Helper:** OK, let's put that down for +1 and how about eight per week for +2—that's sort of in your wildest dreams. How is that?

Client: Let's go for it.

19. **Helper:** Now, if two per week is acceptable for you, what would be less than acceptable—one or zero?

Client: One is better than nothing—zero is just where I am now.

20. **Helper:** So let's put one per week with −1 and none per week with −2. Now we have a way to keep track of your overall progress on this goal. Do you have any questions about this?

Client: No, it seems pretty clear.*

In the next response, the helper introduces the idea of *subgoals*, which represent small action steps toward the terminal goal, and asks Joan to identify the *initial step*.

21. **Helper:** Another thing that I think might help with your apprehension is to map out a plan of action. What we've just done is to identify exactly where you want to get to—maybe over the course of the next few months. Instead of trying to get there all at once, let's look at different steps you could take to get there, with the idea of taking just one step at a time, just like climbing a staircase. For instance, what do you think would be your first step—the first thing you would need to do to get started in a direction that moves directly to this result?

Client: Well, the first thing that comes to my mind is needing to be less uptight. I worry about what other people's reactions will be when I do say something.

In the next two responses, the helper helps Joan define the *behavior and conditions associated with this initial subgoal*, just as she did previously for the terminal goal.

22. **Helper:** So you want to be less uptight and worry less about what other people might think. When you say other people, do you have any particular persons in mind?

Client: My folks, of course, and to some degree almost anyone that I don't know too well or anyone like my math teacher, who is in a position to evaluate me.

23. **Helper:** So you're talking mainly about lessening these feelings when you're around your folks, your math teacher, or other people who you think are evaluating you.

Client: Yes, I think that's it.

---
*For a visual diagram of this GAS, see Table 10.6.

In response 24, the helper is trying to establish the *current level of intensity* associated with Joan's feelings of being uptight. She does this by using an *imagery assessment* in the interview. *Self-reported ratings of intensity* are used in conjunction with the imagery.

24. **Helper:** Now I'm going to ask you to close your eyes and imagine a couple of situations that I'll describe to you. Try to really get involved in the situation—put yourself there. If you feel any nervousness, signal by raising this finger. [The helper shows Joan the index finger of her right hand and describes three situations—one related to parents, one related to math class, and one related to a job interview with a prospective employer. In all three situations, Joan raises her finger. After each situation, the helper stops and asks Joan to rate the intensity of her anxiety on a 100-point scale, 0 being complete calm and relaxation and 100 being total panic.]

After the imagery assessment for base rate, the helper asks Joan to *specify a desired level of change for this subgoal*.

25. **Helper:** Now, just taking a look at what happened here in terms of the intensity of your feelings, you rated the situation with your folks about 75, the one in math class 70, and the one with the employer 65. Where would you like to see this drop down to during the next couple of weeks?

Client: Oh, I guess about a 10.

It is understandable that someone with fairly intense anxiety wants to get rid of it, and it is possible to achieve that within the next few months. However, such goals are more effective when they are *immediate rather than distant*. In the next two responses, the helper asks Joan to *specify a realistic level of change* for the immediate future.

26. **Helper:** That may be a number to shoot for in the next few months, but I'm thinking that in the next three or four weeks the jump from, say, 70 to 10 is pretty big. Does that gap feel realistic or feasible?

Client: Mm. I guess I was getting ahead of myself.

27. **Helper:** It's important to think about where you want to be in the long run. I'm suggesting three or four weeks mainly so you can start to see some progress and lessening of intensity of these feelings in a fairly short time. What number seems reasonable to you to shoot for in the short run?

TABLE 10.6	Goal-Attainment Scale for Joan's First Outcome Goal	
Date: 2/5/02		**Frequency of verbal initiating skills**
(−2)	Most unfavorable outcome	Zero per week
(−1)	Less than expected success	One per week—either with parents or in math class
(0)	Expected level	Two per week—at least one with parents and at least one in math class
(+1)	More than expected success	Four per week—at least two with parents and two in math class
(+2)	Best expected success	Eight or more per week—at least four with parents and four in math class

Client: Well, maybe a 45 or 50.

At this point, the helper and Joan continue to *identify other subgoals or intermediate steps* between the initial goal and the terminal outcome.

28. **Helper:** That seems real workable. Now, we've sort of mapped out the first step. Let's think of other steps between this first one and this result we've written down here. [Helper and client continue to generate possible action steps. Eventually they select and define the remaining three shown on Joan's goal chart.]

Assuming the remaining subgoals are selected and defined, the next step is to *rank-order* or *sequence* the subgoals and *list them in order on the goal pyramid*.

29. **Helper:** We've got the first step, and now we've mapped out three more. Consider where you will be after this first step is completed—which one of these remaining steps comes next? Let's discuss it, and then we'll fill it in, along with this first step, on this goal pyramid, which you can keep so you know exactly what part of the pyramid you're on and when. [Helper and Joan continue to rank-order subgoals, and Joan lists them in sequenced order on a goal pyramid.]

In response 30, the helper points out that *subgoals may change in type or sequence*. The helper then shifts the focus to exploration of potential *obstacles for the initial subgoal*.

30. **Helper:** Now we've got our overall plan mapped out. This can change, too. You might find later on you may want to add a step or reorder the steps. Let's go back to your first step—decreasing these feelings of nervousness and worrying less about the reactions of other people. Since this is what you want to start working on this week, can you think of anything or anybody who might get in your way or would make it difficult to work on this?

Client: Not really, because it is mostly something inside me. In this instance, I guess I am my own worst enemy.

31. **Helper:** So you're saying there don't seem to be any people or situations outside yourself that may be obstacles. If anyone sets up an obstacle course, it will be you.

Client: Yeah. Mostly because I feel I have so little control of those feelings.

The client has identified herself and her perceived lack of control over her feelings as *obstacles*. Later on, the helper will need to help Joan select and work with one or two *intervention strategies*.

32. **Helper:** So one thing we need to do is to look at ways you can develop skills and know-how to manage these feelings so they don't get the best of you.

Client: I think that would help.

In the next response, the helper explores *existing resources and support systems* that Joan might use to help her work effectively with the subgoal.

33. **Helper:** That's where I'd like to start in just a minute. Before we do, can you identify any people who could help you with these feelings—or anything else you could think of that might help instead of hinder you?

Client: Well, coming to see you. It helps to know I can count on that. And I have a real good friend who is sort of the opposite of me, and she's real encouraging.

"Social allies" are an important factor in effecting change, and the helper uses this word in response 34 to underscore this point.

34. **Helper:** OK, so you've got at least two allies.

Client: Yeah.

In response 35, the helper helps Joan develop a way to continue the *self-ratings of the intensity* of her nervous feelings. This gives both of them a *benchmark to use in assessing progress and reviewing* the adequacy of the first subgoal selected.

35. **Helper:** The other thing I'd like to mention is a way for you to keep track of any progress you're making. You know how you related these situations I described today? You could continue to do this by keeping track of situations in which you feel uptight and worry about the reactions of others—jot down a brief note about what happened and then a number on this 0 to 100 scale that best represents how intense your feelings are at that time. As you do this and bring it back, it will help both of us see exactly what's happening for you on this first step. This will also help us develop a plan of action and modify it if we need to. Does that sound like something you would find agreeable?

Joan's Goal Chart

Terminal goal	Related subgoals

Goal 1
(B) to acquire and demonstrate a minimum of four different initiating skills (asking a question or making a reasonable request, expressing differences of opinion, expressing positive feelings, expressing negative feelings, volunteering answers or opinions, going to the board in class)
(C) in her math class and with her parents
(L) in at least 4 situations a week
	1. (B) to decrease anxiety associated with anticipation of failure
	   (C) in math class or rejection by parents
	   (L) from a self-rated intensity of 70 to 50 on a 100-point scale during the next 2 weeks
	2. (B) to restructure thoughts or self-talk by replacing thoughts that "girls are dumb" with "girls are capable"
	   (C) in math class and in other threatening or competitive situations
	   (L) from 0–2 per day to 4–5 per day
	3. (B) to increase attendance
	   (C) at math class
	   (L) from 2–3 times per week to 4–5 times per week
	4. (B) to increase verbal participation skills (asking and answering questions, volunteering answers or offering opinions)
	   (C) in math class and with her parents
	   (L) from 0–1 times per day to 3–4 times per day

Goal 2
(B) to increase positive perceptions about herself and her ability to function effectively
(C) in competitive situations such as math class
(L) by 50% over the next 3 months
	1. (B) to eliminate conversations
	   (C) with others in which she discusses her lack of ability
	   (L) from 2–3 per week to 0 per week
	2. (B) to increase self-visualizations in which she sees herself as competent and adequate to function independently
	   (C) in competitive situations or with persons in authority
	   (L) from 0 per day to 1–2 per day
	3. (B) to identify negative thoughts and increase positive thoughts
	   (C) about herself
	   (L) by 25% in the next 2 weeks

Goal 3
(B) to acquire and use five different decision-making skills (identifying an issue, generating alternatives, evaluating alternatives, selecting the best alternative, and implementing action)
(C) at least one of which represents a situation in which significant others have given her their opinion or advice on how to handle it
(L) in at least two different situations during a month
	1. (B) to decrease thoughts and worry about making a bad choice or poor decision
	   (C) in any decision-making situation
	   (L) by 25% in the next 2 weeks
	2. (B) to choose a course of action and implement it
	   (C) in any decision-making situation
	   (L) at least once during the next 2 weeks

Key: B = behavior; C = condition; L = level.

Client: Yeah—do I need to do it during the situation or after?

Clients are more likely to do *self-ratings or self-monitoring if it falls into their daily routine,* so this is explored in the next response.

36. **Helper:** What would be most practical for you?

Client: Probably after, because it's hard to write in the middle of it.

The helper encourages Joan to make her notes soon after the situation is over. *The longer the gap, the less accurate* the data might be.

37. **Helper:** That's fine; try to write it down as soon as it ends or shortly thereafter, because the longer you wait, the harder it will be to remember. Also, to get an idea of your current level of anxiety, I'd like you to take a few minutes at the end of our session today to fill out a paper-and-pencil form that asks you some questions about what you may be feeling. There are no right or wrong answers on this, so it's not like a test! I'll be asking you to do this again several times during our work together. Would you feel comfortable doing this?

Before the session ends, they have to work on the *obstacle* Joan identified earlier—that she is her own worst enemy because her feelings are in control of her. At this point, some of the real nuts and bolts of the process begin. The helper will need to select an intervention strategy to use with Joan in this instance. (One such option, cognitive restructuring, is described and modeled in Chapter 14.)

38. **Helper:** Now, let's go back to that obstacle you mentioned earlier—that your feelings are in control of you. . . .

Upon exploring this issue, the helper will select treatment interventions to use with Joan. The process of treatment planning is described in the following chapter.

SUMMARY

The primary purpose of identifying goals is to convey to the client the responsibility and participation she or he has in contributing to the results of the helping process. Without active client participation, counseling may be doomed to failure. The selection of goals should reflect *client* choices. Effective goals are consistent with the client's cultural identity and belief systems. The helper's role is mainly to use leads that help with the client's goal selection. Together, the helper and client explore whether the goal is owned by the client, whether it is realistic, and what advantages and disadvantages are associated with it. However, some value judgments by both helper and client may be inevitable during this process. If the client selects goals that severely conflict with the helper's values or exceed the helper's level of competence, the helper may decide to refer the client or to renegotiate this goal. If helper and client agree to pursue the identified goals, these goals must be defined clearly and specifically. Throughout this process the client moves along a change continuum, ranging from contemplation to preparation and finally to action. Involuntary clients are often in a precontemplation stage of change and may get stuck there. One approach to help involuntary clients who resist change is motivational interviewing, a client-centered brief approach relying on helper empathy and reflective listening.

Well-defined goals make it easier to note and assess progress and also aid in guiding the client toward the desired goal(s). Goals are defined when you are able to specify the overt and covert behaviors associated with the goal, the conditions or context in which the goal is to be carried out or achieved, and the level of change. After the outcome goal is defined, the helper and the client work jointly to identify and sequence subgoals that represent intermediate action steps and lead directly to the goal. Obstacles that might hinder goal attainment and resources that may aid in goal attainment are also explored.

As you go through the process of helping clients develop goals, remember that goal setting is a dynamic and flexible process (Bandura, 1969). Goals may change or may be redefined substantially as counseling progresses.

For these reasons, the outcome goals should always be viewed as temporary and subject to change. Client resistance at later stages of helping may be the client's way of saying that the original goals need to be modified or redefined. The helper who is committed to meet the client's needs will remember that, at any stage, the client always has the prerogative of changing or modifying directions.

As outcome goals are defined, ways to evaluate progress toward these goals are also incorporated into the helping process. Practice evaluation is an important component of the helping process. Without it, practitioners have no knowledge of how their interventions are working to help clients achieve their outcome goals. Data related to client outcome goals are collected before, during, and after treatment. In addition to specific measures of goal-related outcomes, general outcome measures, clinical significance, and client satisfaction are also often used in practice evaluations as outcome indicators. A comprehensive practice evaluation uses multiple measures so that it is multidimensional in scope.

INFOTRAC® EXPLORATIONS

1. Search for *motivational interviewing*. What do your findings tell you?
2. Search for *single-subject research*. What do you find that is most useful for conducting a practice evaluation of client outcomes?

SUGGESTED RESOURCES

Readings

Abell, N., & Hudson, W. (2000). Pragmatic applications of single-case and group designs in social work practice evaluation and research. In P. Allen-Meares & C. Garvin (Eds.), *Handbook of social work direct practice* (pp. 535–550). Thousand Oaks, CA: Sage.

Baer, J., Kivlahan, D., & Donovan, D. (1999). Integrating skills training and motivational therapies. *Journal of Substance Abuse Treatment, 17,* 15–23.

Bloom, M., Fischer, J., & Orme, J. (1999). *Evaluating practice: Guidelines for the accountable professional* (3rd ed.). Boston, MA: Allyn & Bacon.

Callaghan, G. (2001). Demonstrating clinical effectiveness for individual practitioners and clinics. *Professional Psychology, 32,* 289–297.

Cone, J. D. (2000). *Evaluating outcomes: Empirical tools for effective practice.* Washington, DC: American Psychological Association.

Corcoran, K., & Fischer, J. (2000). *Measures for clinical practice* (3rd ed.). New York: Free Press.

Gollwitzer, P. (1999). Implementation intentions. *American Psychologist, 54,* 493–503.

Hayes, S., Barlow, D., & Nelson-Gray, R. (1999). *The scientist practitioner: Research and accountablity in the age of managed care* (2nd ed.). Boston: Allyn & Bacon.

Hohmann, M. (1998). Motivational interviewing: An intervention tool for child welfare case workers working with substance-abusing parents. *Child Welfare, 77,* 275–289.

Hubble, M., Duncan, B., & Miller, S. (Eds.). (1999). *The heart and soul of change.* Washington, DC: American Psychological Association.

Irvin, J., Bowers, C., Dunn, M., & Wang, M. (1999). Efficacy of relapse prevention: A meta-analytic review. *Journal of Consulting and Clinical Psychology, 67,* 563–570.

Jacobson, N., Roberts, L., Berns, S., & McGlinchey, J. (1999). Methods for defining and determining clinical significance of treatment effects: Description, application, and alternatives. *Journal of Consulting and Clinical Psychology, 67,* 300–307.

Kazdin, A. E. (1993). Evaluation in clinical practice: Clinically sensitive and systematic methods of treatment delivery. *Behavior Therapy, 24,* 11–45.

Killick, S., & Allen, C. (1997). Shifting the balance—motivational interviewing to help behavior change in people with bulimia nervosa. *European Eating Disorders Review, 5,* 33–41.

Lambert, M., Okiishi, J., Finch, A., & Johnson, L. (1998). Outcome assessment: From conceptualization to implementation. *Professional Psychology, 29,* 63–70.

Lawendowski, L. (1998). A motivational intervention for adolescent smokers. *Preventive Medicine, 27,* A39–A46.

Lundervold, D., & Belwood, M. (2000). The best kept secret in counseling: Single-case (N=1) experimental designs. *Journal of Counseling & Development, 79,* 92–102.

Mahoney, M. (2000). A changing history of efforts to understand and control change: The case of psychotherapy. In C. Snyder & R. Ingram (Eds.), *Handbook of psychological change* (pp. 3–12). New York: Wiley.

Miller, W. R. (1996). Motivational interviewing: Research, practice and puzzles. *Addictive Behaviors, 21,* 835–842.

Miller, W. R. (2000). Rediscovering fire: Small interventions, large effects. *Psychology of Addictive Behaviors, 14,* 6–18.

Mitchell, K., Levin, A., & Krumboltz, J. (1999). Planned happenstance: Constructing unexpected career opportunities. *Journal of Counseling & Development, 77,* 115–124.

Morgan, D., & Morgan, R. (2001). Single-participant research design. *American Psychologist, 56,* 119–127.

Nugent, W., Sieppert, J., and Hudson, W. (2001). *Practice evaluation for the 21st century.* Pacific Grove, CA: Brooks Cole and Wadsworth.

Pekarik, G., & Guidry, L. (1999). Relationship of satisfaction to symptom change, follow-up adjustment, and clinical significance in private practice. *Professional Psychology, 30,* 474–478.

Prochaska, J. (1999). How do people change, and how can we change to help many more people? In M. Hubble, B.

Duncan, & S. Miller (Eds.), *The heart and soul of change* (pp. 227–258). Washington, DC: American Psychological Association.

Prochaska, J. (2000). Change at differing stages. In C. Snyder & R. Ingram (Eds.), *Handbook of psychological change* (pp. 109–127). New York: Wiley.

Project MATCH Research Group (1997). Matching alcoholism treatment to client heterogeneity: Project MATCH post-treatment drinking outcomes. *Journal of Studies in Alcohol, 58,* 7–29.

Reid, W., & Misener, E. (2000). Adult change. In P. Allen-Meares & C. Garvin (Eds.), *Handbook of social work direct practice* (pp. 241–259). Thousand Oaks, CA: Sage.

Rollnick, S., Mason, P., & Butler, C. (1999). *Health behavior change: A guide for practitioners.* Philadelphia: Churchill Livingstone.

Treasure, J., & Ward, A. (1997). A practical guide to the use of motivational interviewing in anorexia nervosa. *European Eating Disorders Review, 5,* 102–114.

VandenBos, G. R. (Ed.). (1996). Outcome assessment of psychotherapy (Special Issue). *American Psychologist, 51* (10).

Web Sites

Abstracts of Empirical Studies (motivational interviewing)
http://www.motivationalinterview.org/library/abstractsemp.html

ERIC/AE Test Locator (outcome measures)
http://www.cricac.nct/tcstcol.htm

Walmyr assessment scales
http://www.walmyr.com/scales.exe

POST EVALUATION

Part One

Objective One asks you to identify a problem for which you identify, define, and evaluate an outcome goal. Use the Goal-Setting Worksheet below for this process. You can obtain feedback by sharing your worksheet with a colleague, supervisor, or instructor.

Goal-Setting Worksheet

1. Identify a concern.
2. State the desired outcome of the concern.
3. Assess the desired outcome (#2 above):
   a. Does it specify what you want to do? (If not, reword it so that you state what you want to do instead of what you don't want to do.)
   b. Is this something you can see (hear, grasp) yourself doing every time?
4. In what ways is achievement of this goal important to you? To others?
5. What will achieving this goal require of you? Of others?
6. To what extent is this goal something you want to do? Something you feel you should do or are expected to do?
7. Is this goal based on
   — rational, logical ideas?
   — realistic expectations and ideas?
   — irrational ideas and beliefs?
   — logical thinking?
   — perfectionistic standards (for self or others)?
8. How will achieving this goal help *you*? Help significant others in your life?
9. What problems could achieving this goal create for you? For others?
10. If the goal requires someone else to change, is not realistic or feasible, is not worthwhile, or poses more disadvantages than advantages, rework the goal. Then move on to #11.
11. Specify exactly *what* you will be
    a. doing _____
    b. thinking _____
    c. feeling _____
    as a result of goal achievement. Be specific.
12. Specify your goal definition in #11 by indicating:
    a. *where* this will occur: _____
    b. *when* this will occur: _____
    c. *with whom* this will occur: _____
    d. *how much or how often* this will occur: _____
13. Develop a plan that specifies *how* you will attain your goal by identifying action steps included in the plan.
    a. _____
    b. _____
    c. _____
    d. _____
    e. _____
    f. _____
    g. _____
    h. _____
    i. _____
    j. _____
    k. _____
    l. _____
14. Check your list of action steps:
    a. Are the gaps between steps small? If not, add a step or two.
    b. Does each step represent only one major activity? If not, separate this one step into two or more steps.
    c. Does each step specify what, where, when, with whom, and how much or how often? If not, go back and define your action steps more concretely.
15. Use the goal pyramid on the next page to sequence your list of action steps, starting with the easiest, most immediate step on the top and proceeding to the bottom of the pyramid by degree of difficulty and immediacy or proximity to the goal.
16. For each action step (starting with the first), brainstorm what could make it difficult to carry out or could interfere with doing it successfully. Consider feelings, thoughts, places, people, and lack of knowledge or skills. Write down the obstacles in the space provided on page 301.
17. For each action step (starting with the first), identify existing resources such as feelings, thoughts, situations, people and support systems, information, skills, beliefs, and self-confidence that would make it more likely for you to carry out the action or complete it more successfully. Write down the resources in the space provided on page 301.
18. Identify a way to monitor your progress for completion of each action step.

IDENTIFYING, DEFINING, AND EVALUATING OUTCOME GOALS **301**

10 POSTEVALUATION

19. Develop a plan to help yourself maintain the action steps once you have attained them.

Goal pyramid

| Obstacles | Action Steps | Resources |

_____
_____
_____
_____
_____
_____
_____
_____
_____
_____
_____
_____
_____

(continued)

10 POSTEVALUATION

(continued)

Part Two

In this part of the postevaluation, we describe a client case, the case of Manuel. Assuming that Manuel is your client, describe the steps you would go through to help him identify, define, and evaluate desired actions, given his stated problem (Chapter Objective Two). Try to include at least 11 of the 14 steps or categories we described in this chapter for identifying, defining, and evaluating outcome goals. You can do this orally with a partner, in small groups, or by yourself. If you do it by yourself, you may want to jot down your ideas in writing for someone else to look at. Feedback follows the postevaluation.

The Case of Manuel

Manuel Tréjos is a 52-year-old Latino who is the manager of an advertising firm. He has been with the firm for 17 years and has another 12 years to go before drawing a rather lucrative retirement package. Over the last 3 years, however, Manuel has become increasingly dissatisfied with his job specifically and with work in general. He says he feels as if he would want nothing better than to quit, but he and his wife want to build up a nest egg for their son's two young children, as their grandchildren are very important to them. He realizes that if he left the firm now, he would lose many of his retirement benefits. Manuel defines his problem as feeling burned out with the nine-to-five job routine. He wishes to have more free time, but as the head of his family he also feels a sense of great responsibility to provide financial security.

Part Three

According to Objective Three, you will be able to demonstrate, in an interview setting, at least 11 of the 14 categories for identifying, defining, and evaluating client outcome goals. We suggest that you complete this part of the postevaluation in triads. One person assumes the role of the helper and demonstrates helping the client with the goal-setting process in a 20- or 30-minute interview. The second person takes the role of the client. You may wish to portray the role and problem described for Manuel Tréjos in Part Two (if you choose to present something unfamiliar to the helper, be sure to inform the helper of your identified problem or concern before you begin). The third person assumes the role of the observer. The observer may act as the helper's alter ego and cue the helper during the role play, if necessary. The observer also provides feedback to the helper after the interview, using as a guide the Interview Checklist for Identifying, Defining, and Evaluating Goals that follows. If you do not have access to an observer, tape-record your interview so you can assess it yourself.

Interview Checklist for Identifying, Defining, and Evaluating Goals

Directions: Determine which of the following leads or questions the helper demonstrated. Check each helper question or lead demonstrated. Also check whether the client answered the content of the helper's question. Example leads and questions are provided next to each item of the checklist. These are only suggestions; be alert to other responses used by the helper.

Scoring	Category of information	Examples of helper leads or responses	Client response
___Yes ___No	1. Explain the purpose and importance of having goals or positive outcomes to the client.	"Let's talk about some areas you would like to work on during counseling. This will help us to do things that are related to what you want to accomplish."	___indicates understanding
___Yes ___No	2. Determine *positive* changes desired by client ("I would like" versus "I can't").	"What would you like to be doing [thinking, feeling] differently?" "Suppose some distant relative you haven't seen for a while comes here in several months. What would be different then from the way things are now?" "Assuming we are successful, what do you want to be doing, or how would this change for you?" "In what ways do you want to benefit from counseling?"	___identifies goal in positive terms

10 POSTEVALUATION

___Yes ___No	3. Determine whether the goal selected represents changes owned by the client rather than someone else ("I want to talk to my mom without yelling at her" rather than "I want my mom to stop yelling at me").	"How much control do you have to make this happen?" "What changes will this require of you?" "What changes will this require someone else to make?" "Can this be achieved without the help of anyone else?" "To whom is this change most important?"	___identifies who owns the goal
___Yes ___No	4. Identify advantages (positive consequences) to client and others of goal achievement.	"In what ways is it worthwhile to you and others to achieve this?" "How will achieving this goal help you?" "What problems will continue for you if you don't pursue this goal?" "What are the advantages of achieving this change—for you? Others?" "Who will benefit from this change—and how?"	___identifies advantages
___Yes ___No	5. Identify disadvantages (negative consequences) of goal achievement to client and others.	"What new problems in living might achieving this goal pose for you?" "Are there any disadvantages to going in this direction?" "How will achieving this change affect your life in adverse ways?" "How might this change limit or constrain you?"	___identifies disadvantages
___Yes ___No	6. Identify whether, as the helper, you can pursue counseling with this particular client.	"These are things I am able to help you work with." "I feel uncomfortable working with you on this issue because of my own personal values [or lack of knowledge]. I'd like to give you the names of several other helpers. . . ." "This would be hard for me to help you with because it seems as if you're choosing something that will restrict you and not give you any options. Let's talk more about this."	___responds to helper's decision
___Yes ___No	7. Identify what the client will be doing, thinking, or feeling in a concrete, observable way as a result of goal achievement ("I want to be able to talk to my mom without yelling at her," rather than "I want to get along with my mom").	"What do you want to be able to do [think, feel] differently?" "What would I see you doing [thinking, feeling] after this change?" "Describe a good and a poor example of this goal."	___specifies overt and covert behaviors
___Yes ___No	8. Specify under what conditions and what situations goals will be achieved: when, where, and with whom ("I want to be able to talk to my mom at home during the next month without yelling at her").	"When do you want to accomplish this goal?" "Where do you want to do this?" "With whom?" "In what situations?"	___specifies people and places

(continued)

POST EVALUATION

(continued)

____Yes ____No	9. Specify how often or how much client will do something to achieve goal ("I want to be able to talk to my mom at home during the next month without yelling at her at least once a day").	"How much [or how often] are you doing this [or feeling this way] now?" "What is a realistic increase or decrease?" "How much [or how often] do you want to be doing this to be successful at your goal?" "What amount of change is realistic, considering where you are right now?"	____specifies amount
____Yes ____No	10. Identify and list small action steps the client will need to take to reach the goal (that is, break the big goal down into little subgoals). *List of Action Steps* 1. 2. 3. 4. 5. 6. 7. 8. 9. 10.	"How will you go about doing [thinking, feeling] this?" "What exactly do you need to do to make this happen?" "Let's brainstorm some actions you'll need to take to make your goal work for you." "What have you done in the past to work toward this goal?" "How did it help?" "Let's think of the steps you need to take to get from where you are now to where you want to be."	____lists possible action steps
____Yes ____No	11. Sequence the action steps on the goal pyramid (a hierarchy) in terms of a. degree of difficulty (least to most) b. immediacy (most to least immediate)	"What is your first step?" "What would you be able to do most easily?" "What would be most difficult?" "What is your foremost priority?" "What is most important for you to do soon? least important?" "How could we order these steps to maximize your success in reaching your goal?" "Let's think of the steps you need to take to get from where you are now to where you want to be and arrange them in an order from what seems easiest to you to the ones that seem hardest." "Can you think of some things you need to do before some other things as you make progress toward this outcome?"	____assists in rank-ordering

Goal Pyramid (levels 1–10):
- 1: Least difficult, most immediate
- 10: Most difficult, least immediate

10 POSTEVALUATION

___Yes ___No	12. Identify any people, feelings, or situations that could prevent the client from taking action to reach the goal.	"What are some obstacles you may encounter in trying to take this action?" "What people [feelings, ideas, situations] might get in the way of getting this done?" "In what ways could you have difficulty completing this task successfully?" "What do you need to know to take this action?" or "What skills do you need to have?"		___identifies possible obstacles
___Yes ___No	13. Identify any resources (skill, knowledge, support) that client needs to take action to meet the goal.	"What resources do you have available to help you as you complete this activity?" "What particular thoughts or feelings are you aware of that might make it easier for you to ____?" "What kind of support system do you have from others that you can use to make it easier to ____?" "What skills [or information] do you possess that will help you do this more successfully?"		___identifies existing resources and supports
___Yes ___No	14. Develop a plan to evaluate progress toward the goal.	"Would it be practical for you to rate these feelings [count the times you do this] during the next two weeks? This information will help us determine the progress you are making." "Let's discuss a way you can keep track of how easy or hard it is for you to take these steps this week."		___agrees to monitor in some fashion

Part Four

Objective Four asks you to conduct an outcome evaluation with yourself, another person, or a client, specifying *what* will be measured, *when* it will be measured, and *how*. Use the following guidelines:

1. Define and give examples of a desired goal behavior.
2. Specify what type of data you or the other person will collect (for example, verbal reports, frequency, duration, ratings, or occurrence of the behavior).
3. a. Identify the methods to be used to collect these data (such as self-monitoring, inventories, and self-rating).
   b. For *each* method to be used, describe very specifically the instructions you or the client would need to use this method.
4. Collect data on the goal behaviors at least several times before implementing any treatment (change) strategy (pretreatment).
5. Following pretreatment data collection, implement some treatment strategy for a designated time period. Continue to collect data during the implementation of this treatment strategy.
6. Collect data after treatment. Graph all of your data, or visually inspect them. What do your data suggest about changes in the goal behavior and the effectiveness of your treatment? Share your results with a partner, a colleague, or your instructor.

POSTEVALUATION FEEDBACK

PART TWO

1. First, explain to Manuel the *purpose and importance* of developing goals.
2. Help Manuel state the goal or desired change in *positive terms*.
3. Help Manuel determine whether the goal he is moving toward represents *changes owned by him* and whether such factors are under his control. Probably, deciding to give up his job and/or take a leave of absence would be changes under his control.
4. Help Manuel identify *advantages* or *benefits* to be realized by achieving his goal. He seems to be thinking about increased leisure time as a major benefit. Are there others?
5. Help Manuel identify *disadvantages* or *possible costs* of making the desired change. He has mentioned loss of retirement benefits as one cost and subsequent loss of a nest egg for his grandchildren as another. Do the perceived benefits outweigh the costs? What effect would leaving his job have on his wife and family? Is this consistent with his cultural identity and his beliefs?
6. If Manuel's goal looks as if it will have too many costs, explore other options with him, leaving the final decision about goals up to him. At this point, you will need to *decide whether you are able to help* him pursue his goal.
7. Assuming you will continue to work with Manuel, help him *define his goal behaviorally* by specifying exactly what he will be doing, thinking, and feeling as a result of goal achievement.
8. Further specification of the goal includes *where, when,* and *with whom* this will occur.
9. It will also include *how much* or *how often* the goal will occur. An option that might be useful for Manuel is to develop and scale five possible outcomes, ranging from the most unfavorable one to the most expected one to the best possible one (goal-attainment scaling).
10. Help Manuel explore and *identify action steps or subgoals* that represent small approximations toward the overall goal. Help him choose action steps that are practical, are based on his resources, and support his values and culture.
11. Help Manuel sequence the action steps according to *immediacy and difficulty* so he knows what step he will take first and what step will be his last one.
12. Explore any *obstacles* that could impede progress toward the goal, such as the presence or absence of certain feelings, ideas, thoughts, situations, responses, people, knowledge, and skills.
13. Explore existing *resources* that could help Manuel complete the action steps more successfully. Like examination of obstacles, exploration of resources also includes assessing the presence or absence of certain feelings, ideas, thoughts, situations, responses, people, knowledge, skills, beliefs, and confidence in pursuing desired outcomes.
14. Help Manuel develop a *plan to review completion of the action steps* and *evaluate progress toward the goal*, including a way to monitor and reward himself for progress and a plan to help him maintain changes.

CHAPTER 11

TREATMENT PLANNING AND SELECTION

An increasingly important part of therapeutic activity involves treatment planning. Treatment planning includes case conceptualization and formulation and selection of the best possible approaches for helping clients. It is initiated after the issues are assessed and after the outcome goals and means for evaluating outcomes are defined. A treatment plan specifies which kinds of counseling interventions will help the client reach his or her stated goals (type of treatment), how long this process will take (duration of treatment), and the specific format or way in which the intervention will be delivered to the client (mode of treatment).

Treatment planning is not just a discrete activity that occurs at one point in time. It is a continuous process, and often the initial plan is readjusted whenever there is new information or the client or therapist becomes "stuck" (Caspar, 1995). Treatment planning has always been an important part of the helping process, and in the last decade its importance has at least doubled because it is required for third-party reimbursement from many managed care systems. We advocate the use of treatment plans for several more reasons. First, the plan is to be developed conjointly with the client as a collaborator. This process often increases the client's emotional investment in the helping process. Second, the use of treatment planning helps to ensure the likelihood that the best combination of interventions for a given client with particular outcome goals will be used. Third, treatment planning helps to keep the process on track; that is, it promotes a structure which ensures that the client's needs are being considered and met as well as possible. This is an important consideration reflected in the ethical codes of conduct for helpers that we described in Chapter 2.

OBJECTIVES

After completing this chapter, the student should be able to
1. For a given client case description and corresponding treatment plan, identify the following:
   a. Ways in which the selected treatment interventions used by the helper conflict with the client's cultural values and world view.
   b. Recommended type, duration, and mode of treatment you would use as the helper.
2. For a given client case, using a sample treatment planning form, develop in writing a treatment plan that specifies the type, duration, and mode of treatment.

TREATMENT PLANNING: COMMON FACTORS AND SPECIFIC INGREDIENTS OF TREATMENT

A central question underlying treatment planning is what treatments or change intervention strategies are likely to be useful for a particular client. This question reflects a deeper one, of what produces change in clients and in helping outcomes. Prior research informs us that client characteristics account for most of the outcome variance, followed by relationship characteristics, and then the specific type of change or treatment intervention (Lambert & Hill, 1994). This means that client characteristics play a pivotal role in the outcomes of any change intervention strategy used, regardless of its theoretical base. The quality of the helping relationship—which we discussed in Chapters 4 and 6—is also tremendously important in producing effective outcomes. These are called common factors in producing change. Specific interventions are useful for producing change perhaps not so much because specific ingredients of a change intervention strategy are superior to the other two factors, but because strategic and grounded interventions inform the client and form the working alliance (Wampold, 2000, p. 735). Further, while a specific change intervention or treatment strategy is not as responsible for producing therapeutic change as client characteristics or the relationship, "nevertheless, to the degree that these specific ingredients are necessary to construct a coherent treatment, in which therapists have faith and which provides a convincing rationale to clients, they are absolutely necessary in therapy" (Wampold, 2000, p. 735).

FACTORS AFFECTING TREATMENT SELECTION

Treatment planning is based on a number of important factors. According to Beutler and Clarkin (1990), "Effective treatment is a consequence of a sequence of fine-grained decisions" about a number of treatment variables that are linked together and contribute "synergistically" to effective client change (pp. 20–21). These factors include client characteristics, helper characteristics, and documentation and practice guidelines. (See Learning Activity 11.1)

Client Characteristics: Impairment, Coping Style, and Resistance

According to Beutler and Clarkin, "The characteristics that the patient brings to the treatment experience are the single most powerful sources of influence in the benefit to be achieved by treatment" (1990, p. 31). In subsequent research, Beutler and colleagues (Beutler, Clarkin, & Bongar, 2000; Beutler & Harwood, 2000) have identified three client characteristics or variables that affect the selection and implementation of treatment strategies (see also Petry et al., 2000): (1) functional impairment, (2) coping style, and (3) resistance level. It is important for helpers to recognize levels of these three client variables in order to select appropriate change or treatment intervention strategies. Also, these three client characteristics have been found to be effective ways to customize the helping relationship to individual clients (Norcross, in press).

Functional Impairment

The client's level of impairment is determined by the level of social support available to and used by the client and also by specific areas of functioning that are adversely affected by the client's problems. Note that these are both areas that we recommend assessing for in the assessment models described in Chapter 8. The assessment of client impairment is important because, according to Beutler and Harwood (2000), it in turn determines the frequency and intensity of treatment provided, since benefit of treatment directly corresponds with treatment intensity among functionally impaired clients (p. 74). Beutler and colleagues (2000) found that client level of impairment is a function of three indices:
1. presence of family problems, in the family of origin, the current family, or both
2. presence of social isolation and withdrawal
3. presence of nonsupportive relationships

In other words, the more family problems, social isolation, and nonsupportive relationships, the greater the degree of client impairment and the greater the need for more intense treatment (Beutler & Harwood, 2000). In addition to assessing for these three specific areas of client functioning, helpers can also get a "read" on the client's level of impairment by using the global assessment of functioning scale from the *DSM-IV* that we described in Chapters 8 and 10.

Coping Style

Beutler and Harwood (2000) identify two approaches that are used by clients to "reduce uncomfortable experiences" and are called externalized and internalized coping styles (p. 80). Beutler and Harwood further explain this concept: "People cope by activating behaviors that range from and combine those that allow direct escape or avoidance of the feared environment (externalizing) and those that allow one to passively and indirectly control internal experiences such as anxiety" (internalizing) (p. 80). It is important for helpers to recognize and differentiate between these two coping styles in order to select treatments that provide safe exposure for the client to the experiences that are being avoided (Beutler & Harwood, 2000; Ingram, Hayes, & Scott, 2000). Problems associated with externalized coping styles result from "excessive and disruptive behaviors." These clients are likely to anger, annoy, or irritate others and display behaviors seen as "too much" (Beutler & Harwood, 2000, p. 81). For example, a child who is always mouthing off and getting into fights or an adult who is continually verbally berating his or her children would be a client with these kinds of behaviors.

Problems associated with internalized coping styles are characterized by the absence of certain activities or insufficiency of certain behaviors (p. 81). Another description of this coping style is that these clients have "difficulty doing something" (p. 81). They often "tend to inhibit impulses and feelings, have a relatively low need to seek stimulation in their environments, and often are dominated by self-reflective, fearful ruminations and contemplations" (Beutler & Harwood, 2000, p. 81). The "chronic contemplator" that we described in Chapter 10 in the Prochaska and DiClemente

(1982) stages of change model is an example of someone like this, as is someone who suffers a stress-linked illness from worrying.

Another way to view these two coping styles is with the concept of containment and holding. Clients with externalized coping styles are usually undercontained or undercontrolled and have trouble holding or containing feelings, thoughts, and behaviors. These clients feel constant urges to express themselves in all kinds of situations and with all kinds of people. Obviously, expression in some of these situations would be inappropriate. Clients with internalizing coping styles are usually overcontrolled, overcontained, and underexpressive of their feelings, thoughts, and behaviors. Often a client exhibits both of these coping patterns at different times or with different conflicts, although "most people tend to favor one or the other coping style in treatment-relevant events" (Beutler & Harwood, 2000, p. 82). It is important for helpers to "get a handle" on the predominant coping style clients use, for this "establishes the nature of the treatment focus" (p. 82). Clients with internalized coping styles are usually more capable of insight than those with externalized coping styles (p. 82). Generally, treatments based on exposure and skill building are selected for clients with externalized coping styles whereas insight and emotional awareness interventions are selected for clients with internalized coping styles (Beutler & Harwood, 2000, pp. 86–87).

Resistance Level

A third dimension of client characteristics that affects treatment selection and planning is the client's resistance level. Beutler and Harwood observe that resistance occurs when a client's "sense of freedom, image of self, safety, psychological integrity or power is threatened" (p. 115). In an interpersonal relationship such as the helping one, resistance suggests the client "is trying to prevent or restore these threatened losses" (p. 115). In this model, client resistance may be both an enduring aspect of the client's personality or character (a trait) and/or a situational reaction to feeling threatened (a state) (Beutler & Harwood, 2000). When resistance is an enduring client trait, it is apt to be seen by the helper at the outset of the helping process and throughout all phases of the helping process. It can also be identified in the way the client describes and relates to other events and people in her or his life. If the resistance is temporary, it usually occurs in the helping process as a *change* in the client's typical behavior—for example, a client who has normally been punctual starts showing up late for your sessions (p. 119). In these instances, it is likely that the emerging resistance represents something about the interaction between the client and helper and may be "an understandable response" to the helper's behaviors or attitudes (Safran & Muran, 2000, p. 50).

Assessing client levels of resistance is important because with clients who have high or recurring levels of resistance, the treatments selected and used need to have low levels of helper directiveness provided in the context of safety (Beutler & Harwood, 2000, p. 119). Clients who are not resistance-prone or who have situational and short-term resistance are likely to benefit from more-directive interventions such as information giving, interpretations, and structured homework assignments. One way to tap into the client's overall level of resistance is to assess the client's "reactance level" (J. W. Brehm, 1966; S. S. Brehm, 1976). Psychological reactance is the need to preserve one's freedom. Clients who are high in reactance are typically oppositional and often find ways to try to defeat or diffuse the helper, usually by saying or doing the opposite of whatever the helper says. Clients who are low on reactance potential are typically cooperative and comply with the helper's ideas. Helpers can assess this dimension early on in the process by noticing whether the client consistently takes positions opposite or complementary to the helper's views and/or by assigning a straightforward task and noticing whether the client carries out or forgets the task.

With clients who are high in reactance, paradoxical treatment interventions have been found to be useful—especially ones called *restraining* (Petry et al., 2000; Shoham et al., 1996). Restraining interventions are those in which the helper discourages or inhibits change. The underlying message in a restraining paradox is in order to change, stay the same or give up (Rohrbaugh et al., 1981). Restraining interventions are used mainly when the helper expects the client to defy the directive by instructing the client to delay change. In delaying change, the helper moves more slowly than the client expects. Messages that encourage delayed compliance reduce resistance by decreasing threat. Fisch and colleagues (1982, p. 159) refer to this intervention as the injunction to "go slow." For example, "the client is not instructed to do anything, certainly nothing specific" (p. 159). The rationale offered is that "change occurring slowly and step by step makes for a more solid change than change which occurs too suddenly" (p. 159). This "go slow" injunction appears to work either directly by reassuring the client, or paradoxically by enhancing the client's sense of control.

The strategy of delaying change is especially useful for clients who deny problems and for clients who press the helper for urgent solutions while remaining passive and inactive themselves (Anderson & Stewart, 1983). Beutler and

Harwood (2000, p. 128) explain the usefulness of paradoxical interventions with clients who have high reactance and persistent resistance levels: "Although the usual efforts of helpers tend to drive resistant patients to defend their autonomy by being stridently against any changes, the imposition of a suggestion that they are unable to change, or should not change, directs their efforts to assert autonomy in the act of changing."

Paradoxical interventions are usually reserved for clients who have persistent levels of resistance that are linked to their personality or character and who don't respond first to nondirective interventions. Another treatment approach for these clients has been developed by Benjamin (2000) and is called reconstructive learning theory (RLT). Later in the chapter we present an alternative view of client resistance developed by multicultural and feminist approaches to helping.

Helper Characteristics and Preferences

Beutler and Clarkin (1990) observe that the helper's capacity to be flexible and adaptive to the idiosyncratic needs of each client is more powerful in treatment selection than the right match between helper and client. As Caspar (1995) states, the more possible ways of proceeding that a helper can choose from, the higher the probability that he or she can achieve a favorable effect with a maximum of benefits and a minimum of costs (p. 215).

This sort of flexibility requires helpers to have a high level of awareness of themselves, of each client, and of the interactional pattern between the two. Some of this awareness is developed by intuition or instinct, but some of it requires analysis, planning, and consultation with another therapist or supervisor.

Helper preferences for particular theories and interventions also play a role in treatment selection. Often, helpers select interventions on the basis of how they have been trained, what they feel most comfortable with, and which strategies they feel competent to carry out. Sometimes, too, helpers are encouraged to "stretch" a bit in their plans and interventions by their supervisors! From an ethical standpoint, it is important to practice within your limits of training and experience. If you have been trained only in cognitive change approaches, it is unlikely that you would be able to implement a Gestalt intervention without additional training and experience. All too often, however, treatment decisions are made on the basis of the helper's allegiance to a favorite counseling treatment orientation (refer to Chapter 1 for a synopsis of these) rather than on the kinds of problems presented and outcomes desired by the client. You know this is happening when a helper treats all clients with the same theoretical orientation. The importance of having multitheoretical perspectives in effective treatment planning cannot be overemphasized. To use a golf analogy, if you have only one club in your golf bag to use in various situations, you are much more limited in your game. If you feel hampered in this way by your own training and/or experience, you have the option of referring a client who needs a particular kind of treatment outside the realm of your own competence or of expanding your own training and supervised experience to include more-diverse perspectives.

Helpers also select treatment approaches based on the settings in which we work. For example, a helper working as a school or agency worker or counselor or as a mental health agency psychologist may focus on individual modes of helping. And, due to time and funding pressures, these helpers also may work with groups within the school or agency as well. Other helpers who work in family treatment centers are less likely to use individual modes of helping and much more likely to work with couple and family systems. Helpers employed as human service and social workers may be more interested in providing treatment in groups and working with environmental systems. Recall from our practice nexus in Chapter 1 that helpers of all disciplines are being trained to work with groups and with ecological or environmental issues as well as with individuals (see also the person-in-environment model in Chapter 8). Beutler and Harwood (2000, p. 12) found that empirical evidence supports the contention that some treatment procedures are relatively effective across clients "but arise from different levels of training, skill, perspectives, and knowledge" of helpers. Also, irrespective of the procedure or intervention strategy, the helper's capacity to form a safe and trusting relationship or working alliance with clients is paramount.

In addition to your work setting and training and the client's characteristics, it is also important to consider the available literature supporting the use of particular kinds of interventions for particular client problems.

Documentation and Practice Guidelines: Research-Informed Treatment

Varying amounts of data exist for different treatment procedures. These data can help you determine for your treatment plan the ways in which the strategy has been used successfully and with what types of client problems. All the strategies presented in the remainder of this book have some empirical support. And as we noted in the practice nexus of Chapter 1, evidence-based treatments play an increasingly important role in practice.

Documentation about therapeutic interventions is being used as a basis for emerging *practice guidelines* (see Nathan, 1998). Practice guidelines discuss ways to implement given therapeutic procedures. Practice guidelines are defined as "systematically developed statements to assist practitioner and patient decisions about appropriate health care for specific clinical circumstances" (AHCPR, 1990, p. 3). Practice guidelines are currently available for panic disorder and suicide management (Fishelman, 1991; Gottleib, 1991) and also depression (AHCPR, 1993; Antonuccio, Danton, & DeNelsky, 1995; Jacobson & Hollon, 1996; Karasu, Docherty, Gelenberg, Kupfer, Merriam, & Shadoan, 1993); guidelines are in progress for various other problems. AHCPR guidelines were developed by a multidisciplinary process that included representatives of affected provider groups, although some critics contend that AHCPR guidelines have favored medication treatments over psychotherapeutic ones (Nathan, 1998). Practice guidelines for other *DSM-IV* clinical disorders have also been developed by the American Psychiatric Association. More recently, practice guidelines for psychological therapies have been developed by the Clinical Psychology Division (Division 12) of the APA. Their first report, published in 1995, listed 22 well-established treatments as empirically validated treatments (EVTs). In their extensive review of empirical data on treatments, they proposed three levels of treatment efficacy: well established, established, and probably efficacious and experimental treatments. An updated report appeared in 1996. Standardized treatment manuals and training opportunities in the treatments were also published (available at the Web site below). Currently, the Division 12 former task force is now simply called the Committee on Science and Practice, and instead of referring to research-based treatments as EVTs or a subsequent term of empirically supported treatments (ESTs), the current term is evidence-based treatments (EBTs) (W. Sanderson, personal communication, March 19, 2001). The committee expects to issue a new report in 2002; again in this report we can expect to see new guidelines, criteria, and treatments (W. Sanderson, personal communication, March 21, 2001). The new report will be available on the Web site (http://www.apa.org/divisions/div12/est). Currently, there is also an APA Division 17 (Counseling Psychology) special task force at work that has developed a set of principles for establishing empirical support for treatments in counseling psychology (Waehler and associates, 2000; Wampold, Lichtenberg, & Waehler, 2002).

In spite of six caveats noted in the Division 12 task force 1996 report, these practice guidelines have provoked great controversy and debate. Indeed, even writing about these seems akin to opening up "Pandora's box"! Criticisms of the EVT movement include the following:

1. Definitions used and confusion about terminology. Although the original task force took great pains to avoid any connotation that an EVT was the equivalent to completed research on a treatment, some have objected to that term. Other literature (Chambless & Hollon, 1998) has used the term empirically supported treatments (ESTs). Some have used the terms EVTs and ESTs as though the two are interchangeable. However, as Patton (2000) points out, EVT is used to denote the criteria used to establish comparative treatment efficacy while EST has a broader, more inclusive meaning. We suspect that the use of the new term, EBTs, will alleviate some current confusion over the terminology of these practice guidelines. We support the definition of evidence-based practice offered by Gibbs (in press): a process of lifelong learning that involves continually posing specific questions of direct practical importance to clients, searching objectively and efficiently for the current best evidence relative to each question, and taking appropriate action guided by that evidence.

2. Feasibility of EVTs and applicability to real-life settings. A second criticism is that the list of effective treatments may not be feasible to use in real-world settings. The studies used by Division 12 to establish empirical validity are called *efficacy* studies. As Ingram and colleagues (2000) note, "the term efficacy refers to the internal validity of outcome research, and it is best demonstrated when a therapy is shown to work in a well-controlled study. . . ." However, the criteria for efficacy studies do not evaluate treatment *effectiveness,* "which refers to the external validity of a therapy or to evidence that a therapy works outside of the controlled experimental context" (p. 42). Effectiveness studies are large field studies of actual clients with a variety of coexisting disorders. Establishing treatment effectiveness is important since the primary goal of these practice guidelines is to discover treatment interventions that can be used effectively in applied settings. An example of a large-scale effectiveness study on psychotherapeutic treatments was reported by *Consumer Reports* (1995, November). (See VandenBos, 1996, for a review, a summary, and a critique of this effectiveness study.) As Nathan (1998) observes, both efficacy and effectiveness studies will ultimately need to be used to establish treatment practice guidelines.

3. Diversity issues. A third criticism of the EVTs has to do with diversity issues. In considering practice guidelines, evidence-based treatments, and standardized treatment manuals, it is critical to note that all this documentation is in the infancy stage with respect to significant client demographic variables, particularly for clients of color (Quintana & Atkinson, 2002). So far, the efficacy of these

treatments has not been established with ethnic minority clients (or with other cultural dimensions of diversity as well). This area needs to develop in the future. Many of the treatment manuals have very little information available with respect to ethnocultural aspects of problems and of treatment procedures. Fortunately, other sources are now beginning to compile more ethnocultural data. For example, Marsella, Friedman, Gerrity, and Scarsfield (1996) have published a book on ethnocultural aspects of post-traumatic stress syndrome. Still, attention to ethnocultural factors in practice guidelines is relatively sparse. (For general guidelines on race and ethnicity in outcome research, refer to Gray-Little and Kaplan's review [2000].)

A comprehensive review of psychotherapy and medication for the treatment of bipolar depression (Antonuccio et al., 1995) pointed out that issues of ethnicity and gender in almost all the studies were "sorely neglected" (1995, p. 380). This omission is problematic. Because most of the samples used are typically 90 percent Caucasian, it is difficult to specify how the results apply to clients of color. Also, in the studies of depression, because 65 percent to 80 percent of all subjects are women, it is unclear how the results will generalize to men.

4. Overemphasis of specific ingredients and underemphasis of common factors. A final criticism is that the emphasis on efficacy of treatments overemphasizes the contributions of the specific treatments and underemphasizes the common contributions to effective outcomes—namely, the client's characteristics, the helper's skills, and the quality of the working alliance (Waehler et al., 2000). In the worst-case scenarios, helpers are reduced to technicians trained and monitored to produce prescribed treatments in situations in which the helper's clinical judgment is often overruled (Cushman & Gilford, 2000). Waehler and associates (2000) recommend that we recognize practice guidelines and evidence-based treatments for just what they are—*guidelines* to be used as "judgments for which there are still alternative perspectives"—rather than *standards* for which "there is virtually unanimous endorsement by practitioners so that their implementation should be considered mandatory" (p. 667). Still, the concerns about the overuse of practice guidelines for reimbursed practice by managed care organizations abound. An impassioned plea has been offered by Cushman and Gilford (2000), who assert that in managed care, "the art of complying with rules, procedures, and cultural prescriptions comes dangerously close to *constituting* successful treatment" (p. 994). They, like others, are concerned that practitioners' flexibility, creativity, and professional judgment are being discarded in favor of standardized treatment regimens in order to receive insurance reimbursement. We propose that one way to address these criticisms and ethical implications is to practice research-informed treatment in which practitioners find sources of relevant research results that are feasible to use in a variety of practice settings with a wide range of clients with multiple problems. We have provided a list of example sources in Box 11.1. It is also important to be able to evaluate critically the results of literature and research that we use to select treatments. Kazdin (1993) suggests the following evaluative questions:

1. What is the outcome of treatment versus receiving no treatment?
2. What are the components of the intervention contributing to any change?
3. What are the parameters of the intervention that can be changed by the therapist in order to improve the outcome?
4. What therapy approaches can be combined in order to improve treatment outcome?
5. What is the impact of differing characteristics of client, family, or therapist singly or in combination with various treatment approaches? (pp. 504–505)

When evaluating the results and recommendations of research about practice, also consider asking the following questions recommended by Brown (1994):

What are the writer's assumptions about norms, values, and appropriate behaviors?

Is the researcher measuring a way of being that is usual and normative within a culture or a response to the researcher's own dominant status?

Is the meaning ascribed to the behaviors centered in the culture, or does it evolve from a biased perspective?

These questions are even more critical when the researchers are members of the mainstream culture.

Once relevant research sources to inform practice are identified, the next step involves the application of critical thinking that we described in Chapter 1's practice nexus. Ingram and colleagues (2000) refer to this as principle-based rather than technique-based thinking. For example, "a principle emerging from anxiety disorders and trauma literature is that exposure to corrective information without avoidance is a potent way to facilitate change" (Ingram et al., 2000, p. 52). The principles of exposure treatment (see Chapter 17) "can be applied and tailored to other problems of avoidance that are conceptually similar to the anxiety disorders, such as substance abuse, eating disorders, and the somatoform and dissociative disorders"

> **BOX 11.1 EXAMPLE SOURCES OF EVIDENCE-BASED TREATMENTS**
>
> Books
>
> Allen-Meares, P., & Garvin, C. (Eds.). (2000). *Handbook of social work direct practice*. Thousand Oaks, CA: Sage.
>
> Barlow, D. H. (Ed.). (2001). *Clinical handbook of psychological disorders* (3rd ed.). New York: Guilford.
>
> Geyman, J. P., Deyo, R. A., & Ramsey, S. D. (2000). *Evidence-based clinical practice: Concepts and approaches*. Boston: Butterworths/Heinemann.
>
> Nathan, P., & Gorman, J. (Eds.). (2002). *A guide to treatments that work*. New York: Oxford University Press.
>
> Articles
>
> *Anger Management*
> Deffenbacher, J. L., Oetting, E. R., and DiGiuseppe, R. A. (2002). Principles of empirically supported interventions applied to anger management. *The Counseling Psychologist, 30*, 262–280.
>
> *Career Counseling*
> Whiston, S. C. (2002). Application of the principles: Career counseling and interventions. *The Counseling Psychologist, 30*, 218–237.
>
> *Children and Adolescents*
> Kazdin, A., & Weisz, J. (1998). Identifying and developing empirically supported child and adolescent treatments. *Journal of Consulting & Clinical Psychology, 66*, 19–36.
>
> Ollendick, T., & King, N. (2000). Empirically supported treatments for children and adolescents. In P. Kendall (Ed.), *Child and adolescent therapy: Cognitive–behavioral procedures* (pp. 386–425). New York: Guilford.
>
> Roberts, M., Vernberg, E., & Jackson, Y. (2000). Psychotherapy with children and families. In C. Snyder & R. Ingram (Eds.), *Handbook of psychological change* (pp. 501–519). New York: Wiley.
>
> *School Counseling*
> Whiston, S., & Sexton, T. (1998). A review of school counseling outcome research: Implications for practice. *Journal of Counseling & Development, 76*, 412–426.
>
> *Health Psychology*
> Compas, B., Haaga, D., Keefe, F., Leitenberg, H., & Williams, D. (1998). Sampling of empirically supported psychological treatments from health psychology: Smoking, chronic pain, cancer, and bulimia nervosa. *Journal of Consulting & Clinical Psychology, 66*, 89–112.
>
> Smith, T., Nealey, J., & Hamann, H. (2000). Health psychology. In C. Snyder & R. Ingram (Eds.), *Handbook of psychological change* (pp. 563–590). New York: Wiley.
>
> *Race and Ethnic Variables*
> Gray-Little, B., & Kaplan, D. (2000). Race and ethnicity in psychotherapy research. In C. Snyder & R. Ingram (Eds.), *Handbook of psychological change* (pp. 591–613). New York: Wiley.
>
> Quintana, S. and Atkinson, D. R. (2002). A multicultural perspective on principles of empirically supported interventions. *The Counseling Psychologist, 30*, 281–290.
>
> *Adult Mental Disorders*
> DeRubeis, R., & Crits-Cristoph, P. (1998). Empirically supported individual and group psychological treatments for adult mental disorders. *Journal of Consulting & Clinical Psychology, 66*, 37–52.
>
> *Couples, Marriages, and Families*
> Baucom, D., Epstein, N., & Coop Gordon, R. (2000). Marital therapy: Theory, practice and empirical status. In C. Snyder & R. Ingram (Eds.), *Handbook of psychological change* (pp. 281–307). New York: Wiley.
>
> Baucom, D., Shoham, V., Mueser, K., Daivto, A., & Stickle, T. (1998). Empirically supported couple and family interventions for marital distress and adult mental health problems. *Journal of Consulting & Clinical Psychology, 66*, 53–88.
>
> Friedlander, M., & Tuason, T. (2000). Processes and outcomes in couples and family therapy. In S. Brown & R. Lent (Eds.), *Handbook of counseling psychology* (3rd ed.) (pp. 797–824). New York: Wiley.
>
> Sexton, T. L. and Alexander, J. F. (2002). Family-based empirically supported interventions. *The Counseling Psychologist, 30*, 238–261.
>
> *Community Treatment Approaches*
> Goromy, T. (1999). Programs of assertive community treatment (PACT): A critical review. *Ethical Human Sciences and Services, 1*, 147–163.

(p. 52). Another example of principle-based critical thinking is in the treatment proposed by Salkovskis and Clark (1993) for hypochondriasis—currently, there is no empirically supported treatment for this problem. They see hypochondriasis as "conceptually similar to panic disorder in that both are based on misinterpretations of somatic functioning," and they are "tailoring the treatment for panic to a different but conceptually similar problem" (Ingram et al., 2000, p. 52).

In the following section, we provide another example of principle-based, research-informed treatment selection in a model we describe that was developed and researched by Beutler and associates (Beutler, 2000). New information about treatments is being generated faster than any of us can write about it! However, what is as important as learning about specific treatment interventions (such as those that follow in Chapters 12–18) is learning how to think critically and creatively, how to continue to learn, and how to generate new information (Ingram et al., 2000, p. 54). It is worth recapping the critical thinking questions we cited in Chapter 2, since they are highly relevant to treatment planning decisions:

LEARNING ACTIVITY 11.1 Factors Affecting Treatment Selection

Using the case of Jane Wiggins described below, respond to the following questions. You may wish to do this with a partner or in a small group. What client characteristics do you see in Jane Wiggins that would affect your choice of treatment intervention strategies and also the overall therapeutic outcomes? How would your training, theoretical orientation to helping, and your practice setting affect your choice of change intervention strategies? How aware are you of any evidence-based treatments that would be useful here? What questions would you ask about these treatments? If you are not aware of any, how could you find these?

The Case of Jane Wiggins

Jane Wiggins is a 34-year-old Euro-American woman living in an isolated rural area. She has been referred to the nearest mental health center because she sought treatment at the local health care clinic following a rape.

She is very suspicious of the helper, who is a Caucasian man, and she talks reluctantly and without much eye contact. Gradually, she reveals that she is married, unemployed, has no children, and lives with her husband, who receives Social Security disability payments because of his very poor health. She has lived in this area all her life. She indicates that she has been followed for the last year by a white man who also grew up in the area. She knows him by name and sight only. In addition to following her, he has also sent her numerous letters and has made phone calls containing lewd and suggestive remarks. She indicates that she and her husband went to the sheriff's office several times to complain, but the complaints were never followed up. It appears that this man may be related to a deputy in the sheriff's office.

Several weeks ago her husband had gone over the hill to a neighbor's house to visit and, unknown to her, had left the door unlocked. The man who has been following her apparently was around, noticed the husband's departure, and came into her house and raped her. She said she had told no one other than the neighbor and her husband because she feels so ashamed. She indicates she is a very religious person and has been reluctant to go to church or to confide in her minister for fear of what the church people may say. She has also been reluctant to tell her parents and sister, who live nearby, for the same reason. She sees no point in reporting the rape to the authorities because they dismissed her earlier reports.

She feels a lot of guilt about the rape because she thinks she should have been able to prevent it. She has been doing a lot of praying about this. As a few sessions go by, she gradually becomes more open with the helper and indicates she is willing to come back for a few more sessions to deal with her guilt and sadness; she would like to be able to feel happy again and not be so consumed by guilt. She finally discloses she would feel more comfortable talking these things out with another woman, as this is really a "female problem."

What is the purpose of my thinking?

What is the question about treatment I am trying to answer?

Within what point of view or perspective am I thinking?

What concepts or ideas are central to my thinking?

What assumptions am I making?

What information am I using?

How am I interpreting that information?

What conclusions am I coming to?

If I accept the conclusions, what are the treatment implications?

(adapted from Paul, 1993, cited in Gibbs and Gambrill, 1999.)

Another useful critical thinking model for evidence-based practice has been developed by Gibbs (in press), who describes different types of treatment questions to assess the type of client and problem, the practitioner's goals, and the practitioner's alternative course of intervention.

DECISION RULES IN PLANNING FOR TYPE, DURATION, AND MODE OF TREATMENT

A decision rule is a series of mental questions or heuristics that the helper constantly asks himself or herself during interviews in order to match techniques to clients and their identified concerns. More-recent formulations of this sort of helper–client matching have been discussed by Beutler and Clarkin (1990), Beutler and Harwood (2000), Beutler and colleagues (2000), Santiago-Rivera (1995), Hackney and Cormier (2001), and Seligman (1998).

The Seligman (1998) model is anchored in the *DSM-IV*. This model describes various diagnoses, links these diagnoses with specific assessment data, and then describes recommended treatment procedures for each diagnostic category. For each clinical disorder, she describes associated client characteristics of the disorder, preferred helper characteristics, suggested intervention strategies, and prognosis. She also provides a general summary of the disorders called a client map that concisely summarizes the treatment recommendations. For an example, we provide her client map for the anxiety disorders of adulthood in Box 11.2. A strength of this model is its comprehensiveness of treatment planning for specific *DSM-IV* disorders. Limited cultural characteristics of clients are provided.

The Santiago-Rivera (1995) model is one that integrates various dimensions of culture. We discuss this model later in this chapter in the section on multicultural and gender issues in treatment planning.

The Hackney and Cormier (2001) model matches types of problems in five categories—affective, cognitive, behavioral, systemic, and cultural, and particular manifestations of these problems—to corresponding types of interventions and theoretical orientations. Their model is depicted in Box 11.3. A strength of this model is that it suggests treatment modalities that cut across multiple domains, therefore integrating interventions from a variety of theoretical approaches. This often helps students and practitioners see how their training and theoretical orientations affect treatment interventions.

The Beutler and Clarkin (1990) model is an integrated one that considers client characteristics, the nature of the client's problem, and the treatment objectives, although consideration of cultural variables is very limited. This original model has been expanded more recently by an empirically guided model that provides treatment guidelines for depressed clients (Beutler, Clarkin, & Bongar, 2000) and by one that links treatment selection to the three client variables that we described earlier: level of impairment, type of coping style, and level of resistance (Beutler & Harwood, 2000). Recall that these three variables have been found to be effective ways to customize the helping relationship (Norcross, in press). These three client variables have moderating effects on treatments (Beutler & Harwood, 2000). Their model is summarized in Box 11.4. (For the full complexity of their model, we refer you to their books.)

Type of Treatment

To summarize the Beutler and Clarkin (1990) model, client issues can be characterized in one of two ways: those issues involving symptom distress and those issues involving symbolic conflicts. The easiest way to distinguish between the two is to consider this question: "Are these problems simple habits maintained by the environment or are they symbolized expressions of unresolved conflictual experiences?" (Beutler & Clarkin, 1990, p. 226). Problems that are specific to environment and clearly related to antecedents and consequences are symptom problems. For example, a teenage girl is referred to you by her parents, who are convinced that during the last few months she has become more "distant and withdrawn" from them; specifically, they have noticed this behavior since she developed a relationship with an older boy.

On the other hand, recurrent symptom patterns that do not seem to be functionally related to specific environmental antecedents and consequences, and continue to be evoked in situations that have little resemblance to the originally evolving situation are indicative of underlying conflict (Beutler & Clarkin, 1990, p. 226). For example, another teenage girl is referred to you and comes to see you with her parents, who are concerned with their daughter's "distance and withdrawal" not only from them but also from her younger brother. However, they note that this behavior is nothing new; it has been a pattern since they adopted her at age two along with her infant brother. Prior to age two, she was left alone for several days in an abandoned house by her biological mother. She describes herself as a loner and doesn't have any real friends. In symptom-based client problems, the targets of change are observed behavioral excesses or deficits and dysfunctional cognitions. In conflict-based client problems, the targets of change are feelings that are masked by the symptoms and underlying unconscious conflicts.

For issues that are primarily symptom based and involve changes in altering behaviors and cognitions, recommended treatment strategies involve behavioral and cognitive interventions such as modeling, exposure and graded practice, cognitive restructuring, and self-monitoring (see Box 11.4), depending on the degree to which symptoms are overt or covert. Overt, external symptoms are more responsive to behavioral strategies; covert symptoms are more responsive to cognitive therapies (Beutler & Clarkin, 1990). Note that symptom distress or a behavioral type of treatment package works best with clients who have predominantly externalized coping styles (Beutler & Harwood, 2000). For problems that are primarily conflict based and involve changes in

BOX 11.2 TREATMENT RECOMMENDATIONS: CLIENT MAP

Treatment recommendations for the Anxiety Disorders discussed in this chapter are summarized here according to the framework of the Client Map.

Client Map

Diagnoses

Anxiety Disorders (Panic Disorder, Agoraphobia, Specific Phobia, Social Phobia, Obsessive–Compulsive Disorder, Acute Stress Disorder, Post-Traumatic Stress Disorder, and Generalized Anxiety Disorder)

Objectives of Treatment

Reduce anxiety and related behavioral and somatic symptoms of the disorder

Improve stress management, social and occupational functioning, sense of mastery

Assessments

Often will include physical examination to rule out medical disorder

Measures of anxiety or fear

Clinician Characteristics

Patient

Encouraging

Supportive yet firm and flexible

Concerned but not controlling

Calming and reassuring

Comfortable with a broad range of behavioral and cognitive interventions

Location of Treatment

Generally outpatient, sometimes contextual

Interventions to Be Used

Cognitive–behavioral and behavior therapy, especially in vivo and imaginal desensitization, exposure, and response prevention

Training in anxiety management

Stress inoculation

Problem solving

Relaxation

Assertiveness training

Self-monitoring of progress

Homework assignments

Emphasis of Treatment

Usually present-oriented

Moderately directive

Supportive

Cognitive and behavioral

Numbers

Individual or group therapy, according to the nature of the disorder

Ancillary family therapy as needed, particularly for heritable disorders

Timing

Usually weekly treatment of brief to moderate duration (eight to twenty sessions)

Moderate pacing

Possibly flexible scheduling, as necessitated by contextual treatment

Medications Needed

Usually not needed unless anxiety is disabling

May supplement treatment in some forms of Anxiety Disorders, especially Obsessive–Compulsive Disorder

Adjunct Services

Hypnotherapy

Biofeedback

Meditation

Exercise

Other approaches to stress management

Planned pleasurable activities

Prognosis

Variable according to the specific disorder

Generally good for amelioration of symptoms

Fair for complete elimination of signs of the disorder

Source: From *Selecting Effective Treatments,* by L. Seligman, pp. 233–234. Copyright © 1998 by Jossey-Bass. Reprinted by permission of John Wiley & Sons, Inc.

BOX 11.3 TREATMENT STRATEGIES AND CORRESPONDING MANIFESTATIONS OF CLIENT PROBLEMS

Affective	Cognitive	Behavioral	Systemic	Cultural
Person-centered therapy; Gestalt therapy; body awareness therapies; psychodynamic therapies; experiential therapies: Active listening; empathy; positive regard; genuineness; awareness techniques; empty chair; fantasy; dreamwork; bioenergetics; biofeedback; core energetics; radix therapy; free association; transference analysis; dream analysis; focusing techniques.	**Rational-emotive therapy; Beck's cognitive therapy; transactional analysis; reality therapy:** A-B-C-D-E analysis; homework assignments; counter-conditioning; bibliotherapy; media-tapes; brainstorming; identifying alternatives; reframing; egograms; script analysis; problem definition; clarifying interactional sequences; coaching; defining boundaries; shifting triangulation patterns; prescribing the problem (paradox).	**Skinner's operant conditioning; Wolpe's counter-conditioning; Bandura's social learning; Lazarus's multimodal therapy:** Guided imagery; role-playing; self-monitoring; physiological recording; behavioral contracting; assertiveness training; social skills training; systematic desensitization; contingency contracting; action planning; counter-conditioning.	**Structural therapy; strategic family therapy; intergenerational systems:** Instructing about subsystems; enmeshment and differentiation; addressing triangulation, alliances, and coalitions; role restructuring; clarifying interactional systems; reframing; prescribing the problem (paradox); altering interactional sequences; genogram analysis; coaching; defining boundaries; shifting triangulation patterns.	**Multicultural counseling; cross-cultural counseling:** meta-theoretical, multimodal, culturally based interventions; focus on world views, cultural orientation, cultural identity; liberation and empowerment perspectives; culturally sensitive language, metaphors, rituals, practices, and resources; collaboration; networking; consciousness raising; advocacy.
Manifestations Emotional expressiveness and impulsivity; instability of emotions; use of emotions in problem solving and decision making; sensitivity to self and others; receptive to feelings of others.	*Manifestations* Intellectualizing; logical rational, systematic behavior; reasoned; computer-like approach to problem solving and decision making; receptive to logic, ideas, theories, concepts, analysis, and synthesis.	*Manifestations* Involvement in activities; strong goal orientation; need to be constantly doing something; receptive to activity, action, getting something done; perhaps at expense of others.	*Manifestations* Enmeshed or disengaged relationships; rigid relationship boundaries and rules; dysfunctional interaction patterns.	*Manifestations* Level of acculturation; type of world view; level of cultural identity; bi- or trilingual; presenting problems are, to some degree, culturally based.

Source: From *The Professional Counselor* (4th ed.), by H. Hackney and L. S. Cormier, pp. 128–129. Copyright © 2001 by Allyn & Bacon. Reprinted by permission.

altering feelings, recommended treatment strategies include interventions for enhancing emotional and sensory outcomes (Greenberg & Goldman, 1988), such as reflection of feelings, Gestalt two-chair work and dream work, imagery, and body expression and related activities (see Box 11.4). Recommended treatment strategies for resolving unconscious conflict include interventions for addressing unconscious experience and recurrent interpersonal patterns as well as hidden motives (Luborsky, 1984; Strupp & Binder, 1984), such as interpretation, confrontation, early recollections, genograms, and two-chair work (see Box 11.4). Note that these insight-focused treatments work best with clients who have predominantly internalized coping styles (Beutler & Harwood, 2000).

In general, with respect to type of treatment, Beutler and Harwood (2000) offer three guiding principles for selecting type of treatment:

1. "Efforts to directly modify symptomatic problems should be initiated early in treatment, preceding the application of

BOX 11.4 — BEUTLER AND CLARKIN'S (1990) MODEL OF SYSTEMATIC TREATMENT SELECTION

Nature of problem	Targets of change	Corresponding treatments	Coping style
Symptom Distress	Behaviors (1st order change)	1. Social skills training 2. *In vivo* or *in vitro* exposure to avoided events 3. Graded practice 4. Reinforcement (Beutler & Clarkin, 1990, p. 244)	Externalized
	Cognitions (1st order change)	1. Identification of cognitive errors 2. Evaluation of risk or degree of distortion 3. Questioning of dysfunctional assumptions and beliefs 4. Self-monitoring 5. Self-instruction 6. Practice alternative thinking 7. Testing of new assumptions (Beutler & Clarkin, 1990, pp. 244–245)	
Symbolic Conflicts	Feelings (2nd order change)	1. Focus on sensory states 2. Reflection of feelings 3. Two-chair work on emotional "splits" 4. One- and two-chair work related to unfinished business 5. Structured imagery 6. Gestalt dream work 7. Reflective mirroring of the hidden self 8. Enacting emotional opposites 9. Free association to sensory cues 10. Physical expression and release exercises (Beutler & Clarkin, 1990, p. 248)	Internalized
	Unconscious Conflicts (2nd order change)	1. Free association 2. Dream interpretation 3. Encouragement of transferential projections 4. Interpretation of resistance and defense 5. Analysis of hidden motives through assessment of common mistakes or slips 6. Free fantasy explorations 7. Discussion of early memories 8. The construction and analysis of genograms 9. Two-chair work on intrapersonal "splits" (Beutler & Clarkin, 1990, p. 249)	

Source: Abridged from *Systematic Treatment Selection*, by L. Beutler and J. Clarkin, p. 226, Copyright © 1990 by Larry Beutler & J. Clarkin. Reprinted by permission of Dr. Beutler.

procedures that seek to indirectly influence symptoms, through insight and understanding" (p. 85).

2. If a client's "most typical method of coping is characterized by active avoidance of blame or responsibility, impulsivity, aggression, or other externally derived symptoms, the preferred treatment strategy is to inform the client of the feared consequences of failing to engage in these avoided acts and instituting skill development to facilitate alternative behaviors" (pp. 85–86).

3. If the client's most typical coping method "emphasizes self-reflection and criticism, social withdrawal, emotional avoidance, and control of internal reactions, the preferred

> **BOX 11.5**
>
> **Directive Interventions**
> 1. Asking closed questions during the session
> 2. Making interpretations during the session
> 3. Being confrontational during the session
> 4. Interrupting client's speech or behavior during the session
> 5. Giving information or instructions to the client
> 6. Assigning structured homework
> 7. Analyzing A-B-C relationships
> 8. Evidence gathering and analysis
> 9. Monitoring and recordkeeping
> 10. Activity scheduling
> 11. Interpersonal analysis
> 12. Directed experiential techniques
> 13. Voice work
>
> **Non-Directive Interventions**
> 1. Asking open-ended questions during the session
> 2. Passive acceptance of the client's feelings and thoughts
> 3. Reflecting the client's emotional states during the session
> 4. High percentage of time following the client's lead
> 5. Low percentage of incidences in which the therapist introduced topics
> 6. High percentage of incidences in which patient introduced topics
> 7. Self-monitored homework
> 8. Self-directed therapy work
> 9. Nondirective and paradoxical work
> 10. Evocative, narrative work
>
> *Source:* From Prescriptive Psychotherapy, by L. Beutler, Copyright © 2000 by Oxford University Press, Inc. Used by permission of Oxford University Press, Inc.

treatment strategy is to facilitate awareness of how these events have and do affect" the client (p. 86).

Directiveness of Treatment

The level of directiveness in treatments is a function of the client's resistance and reactance levels. With clients who have high resistance and reactance levels, nondirective treatments are more useful whereas directive interventions can be used more easily with clients with low levels of resistance (Beutler & Harwood, 2000). Beutler and Harwood (2000) summarize this treatment principle as follows: Helpers should avoid disagreement with resistant clients and offer treatments that increase their levels of perceived freedom and capacity for self-direction—for example, motivational interviewing (Chapter 10) and paradoxical interventions are very useful with these clients. Helpers should reserve the use of direction and guidance for clients who are generally nonresistant (p. 120). Sample directive and nondirective treatment interventions are given in Box 11.5.

Duration of Treatment

Beutler and Clarkin (1990) argue that beginning a treatment plan with a symptom-focused treatment is useful because there is no evidence that using a narrow band of treatment to deal with a complex issue yields negative results, but using a broad base of treatment (such as conflict focused) to treat a more simple concern is overkill. They acknowledge that although "symptom patterns may recur when more narrowly focused treatments are applied alone to complex problems, . . . mixing treatments of varying breadths actually may allay this recurrence" (Beutler & Clarkin, 1990, p. 234). They point out that as the targets of change increase and the client's strengths and resources decline, a longer duration of treatment does become important. According to Beutler and Harwood (2000), duration of treatment is affected by the level of the client's functional impairment: "Therapeutic change is likely and maximal when the intensity of treatment is consistent with the client level of psychological and functional impairment" (p. 168). Clients with high levels of impairment are offered more-frequent sessions that are often spaced closer together than clients with low levels of impairment. However, some settings and some managed care companies have policies that limit the duration of therapy to a few sessions, depending on the client's diagnosis. Clients who present with transient situational concerns are good candidates for crisis intervention, but we cannot assume that all clients are automatically good candidates for brief or time-limited therapy. Brief therapy seems to work better with clients who may drop out of therapy early, such as clients who are at the precontemplation stage of the transtheoretical model of change and who have unidimensional symptoms or conflictual issues. Also, briefer therapy may better fit the preferences and belief systems of some clients of color. Duration of treatment should be a clinical rather than an economic decision. There are ethical issues in providing too little care due to cost containment and too much care under fee-for-service models of reimbursement.

Mode of Treatment

Mode of treatment refers to the specific way the interventions are delivered to the client:
1. Individual treatment
2. Couple and/or family treatment

3. Group treatment
4. Medication

All these modes have certain advantages. Individual therapy promotes greater privacy, self-disclosure, sharing, individualized attention, and identification with the helper than the other modes (Beutler & Clarkin, 1990, p. 123). Couples therapy allows for the direct observation of interaction between the partners; deals with both parties, including both "sides" of conflict; and allows for the development of mutual support, communication, and conflict-resolution sources (Beutler & Clarkin, 1990, p. 123). These same advantages are extended to family therapy. A group mode allows for extensive modeling, support, and feedback from others. Couples, group, and family interventions are good settings for providing education and skills training. Individual, couple/family, and group modes of treatment do not typically involve adverse side effects although it goes without saying that not all clients improve with treatment. Medication management involves the use of psychotropic drugs to help alleviate and/or manage psychological disorders for which there is a clear biochemical imbalance. Generally, these disorders include psychotic conditions and endogenous or major depression and bipolar disorders (Thase, 2000). If medication management seems warranted, the client will also need to be evaluated and followed by a physician. Clients rarely learn new ways of problem solving and coping with *just* medication, so some mode of psychotherapy in addition is often warranted. Also, medications pose greater risks and adverse side effects to clients than do the other modes of treatment.

The mode of treatment is often indicated by the nature of the client's issue. As Beutler and Clarkin (1990) observe,

> In general, if the symptom of conflict reflects a transient or uncomplicated pattern that is under the control or direction of the individual patient, with little confounding from the current family environment, then it can be dealt with in either individual or group therapy. If, however, the symptom or conflict is significantly confounded by the current marital/family interpersonal environment, then family/marital therapy format may be the format of choice. Likewise, if the symptom or conflict is interpersonal in nature, extends beyond the home environment, is easily observed to be destructive in group interactions, group therapy may be the format of choice. (pp. 119–120)

Specific descriptions of clients and client problems suitable for various modes of treatment are presented in Table 11.1. Although the guidelines in this table are not necessarily inclusive of all the conditions leading to specific modes of treatment, one advantage of having guidelines such as these (and indeed an advantage of even doing treatment planning) is that such guides may counteract the tendencies of some helpers to develop plans and select and use interventions on the basis of how they have been trained rather than on the basis of the client's identified concerns and goals. This unidimensional focus leads to unidimensional treatment. So, for example, someone who received training primarily in couples and family- or system-based approaches may view all presenting issues and corresponding interventions as family oriented, whereas someone else who has been trained solely in individual interventions may miss or overlook important group and systemic parts of the issue as well as other nonindividual interventions. The importance of having a multidimensional treatment perspective cannot be overemphasized! For example, in the area of marriage and family therapy, the more severe and pervasive the issue, the more critical the use of multiple modes of treatment (Pinsof & Wynne, 1995).

Another consideration in choosing mode of treatment has to do with cost effectiveness. Although we discuss this in the following section in greater detail, the individual mode requires the most time from the helper and client, the group mode requires the least, and couples and family therapy follow somewhere between as two or more clients are seen by a helper in a single session. Couples treatment and family treatment have also been found to be more cost effective for standard inpatient and/or residential treatment for schizophrenia, delinquency, severe adolescent conduct disorders, and adolescent and adult substance abuse (Pinsof & Wynne, 1995).

COST EFFECTIVENESS OF TREATMENT

As mentioned in the previous section, an increasingly important factor in selecting types, duration, and modes of treatment is cost effectiveness. According to Herron, Javier, Primavera, and Schultz (1994), the cost "reflects specific conceptions of mental health involving a range of available goals . . . the current controversy is the latest development in society's historical uncertainty about the value and, therefore, the cost of different levels of mental health" (p. 106). As these authors point out, current funding policies tend to take the view that the amount of psychotherapy to be covered by insurance is whatever is deemed enough to restore or maintain a client's mental health "at the level of necessity"—that is, "the absence of symptoms that prevent individuals from carrying out the tasks necessary for maintaining their life" (p. 106). One of the implications of this "standard of care" from a *cost* viewpoint is that there is little concern with either *improvement* or *prevention*. As Herron and colleagues (1994) note, "Levels of functioning below the acceptable range are considered

TABLE 11.1	Relationship of Client Problems and Mode of Therapy Treatment
Mode	**Client characteristics and problems**
Individual	1. The client's symptoms or problematic ways of relating interpersonally are based on internal conflict and a coping style that manifests itself in repetitive life patterns that transcend the particulars of the current interpersonal environment. 2. The client is an adolescent or young adult who is striving for autonomy from family of origin. 3. Problems or difficulties are of such an embarrassing nature that the privacy of individual treatment is required for the clients to feel safe.
Couple	1. The partners are committed to each other and present with symptoms/conflicts that occur almost exclusively within the coupleship. 2. One partner has an individual symptom—for example, agoraphobia or depression—that is maintained or exacerbated by the couple's interaction patterns. 3. There is a need to involve one partner in an effective treatment program for the other (e.g., one person suffers from anorexia or obesity, or from phobias, and the partner is needed to assist in behavioral treatment, increase treatment compliance, and provide general support). 4. The couple's relationship suggests the presence of some role inflexibility.
Family	1. Family problems are presented as such without any one family member designated as the identified client; problems are predominantly within the relationship patterns. 2. Family presents with current structured difficulties in intrafamilial relationships, with each person contributing collusively or openly to the reciprocal interaction problems. 3. Acting-out behavior is exhibited by an adolescent member. 4. Improvement of one family member has led to symptoms or signs of deterioration in another. 5. Chronic mental disorder (e.g., schizophrenia) is present in one family member; there is a need for the family to cope with the condition.

Group	A. Heterogeneous Groups (clients in group have different problems)
	  1. Client's most pressing problems occur in current interpersonal relationships, both outside and inside family situations. Examples could include these:
	    (a) client is lonely and wishes to get closer to others; has social and work inhibitions, excessive shyness
	    (b) client has an inability to share; manifests selfishness and exhibitionism; needs excessive admiration; has difficulty perceiving and responding to the needs of others
	    (c) client is excessively argumentative; oppositional toward authority; shows passive–aggressive traits
	    (d) client is excessively dependent; relatively unable to individuate from family of origin; has difficulties with self-assertion
	    (e) client has an externalizing coping style in interpersonal situations; tends to act immediately on feelings
	  2. The client may not have predominant interpersonal problems, but there may be other reasons to refer to heterogeneous group, such as these:
	    (a) becomes intensely involved with individual therapist and cannot maintain self-observation
	    (b) is extremely intellectualized and may benefit by being confronted about this defensive style
	B. Homogeneous Groups (clients in group share a specific and common problem)
	  1. specific impulse problems such as obesity, alcoholism, addictions, gambling, violence
	  2. problems adapting to and coping with acute, environmental stressors such as cardiac ailments, divorce, terminal illness
	  3. problems associated with a specific but transient developmental phase of life such as child rearing, geriatrics
	  4. specific symptom constellations such as phobias, schizophrenia, bipolar disorder

Source: From *Systematic Treatment Selection,* by L. Beutler and J. Clarkin, pp. 126–131. Copyright © 1990 by Larry Beutler & J. Clarkin. Reprinted with permission of Dr. Beutler.

grounds for psychotherapy but the need for a higher level is considered unnecessary," at least from the point of view of managed mental health care (p. 106). Cushman and Gilford (2000) argue that the emphasis on managed care cost containment has changed the nature of our conversation about the helping process and what it means to be a helper and also a client: "there appears to be little time in managed care's arrangement of psychotherapy for an examination of the therapist–patient relationship, disagreements, complaints, arguments, the voicing of hurt or angry feelings, the exploration of misunderstandings or puzzlements, or the challenge of monetary arrangements, roles, and power distributions within the hour" (p. 990). Further, there is no attention given to the consideration that "material or cultural conditions of one's life might be partly the sources of one's psychological problems" (p. 988).

Herron and colleagues (1994) identified an area that all of us must be concerned with in considering the costs and benefits of helping: the incorrect but frequent assumption that equates usage with effectiveness. Managed care companies have relied on utilization review to limit both the number of treatment sessions and the kind of provider. As a result, some providers who charge higher fees or use more treatment sessions have been excluded from provider panels;

worse yet, some clients have been pushed out of therapy too soon. Cushman and Gilford (2000) observe that implicit in this process is the idea that clients "should accept the therapist's evaluations, use the therapist's opinions, guidance, or behavioral directives and carry them out as instructed" (p. 988). Clients who do not comply may be threatened with loss of benefits or with an Axis II *DSM-IV* diagnosis that is not likely to be covered for reimbursement.

Many health maintenance organizations limit mental health coverage to 20 sessions or fewer per year and assume that this number of visits represents a "safe harbor" for even those people needing more than the average amount of therapy. Yet as Herron and colleagues (1994) point out, data exist that dispute this assumption. One very comprehensive study suggested that 52 sessions per year was the best number for maximum effectiveness for the largest number of people (Howard, Kopta, Krause, & Orlinsky, 1986). On the other side of the coin, Cummings and his colleagues have reported over 20 years of research showing that when practitioners are trained in both short- and long-term helping methods, 85 percent of clients "responded" in under 15 sessions (Cummings, Budman, & Thomas, 1998, p. 462). At the same time, other clients who had especially difficult issues needed to be seen throughout their life cycle, and some of these clients received 150–300 sessions per therapeutic "episode" (Cummings et al., 1998, p. 462). Cummings and associates recommend that practitioners choose a treatment that is based on client need rather than on the inability of the helper to conduct either short- or long-term therapy. Obviously, there will be clients who need more sessions and, lacking in either their own resources or in access to insurance coverage, will be deprived of needed treatment. Indigent clients and some clients of color are at greater risk of not having access to mental health services than are those in more-favorable circumstances. It is difficult to make sweeping generalizations about an effective duration for *all* clients; indeed, this is why treatment plans are developed for each individual client.

An assessment of cost effectiveness of therapy treatment addresses such questions as these:
1. With this particular client, who has this set of identified concerns and goals, is treatment A more cost effective than treatment B?
2. Do the benefits of this particular treatment outweigh the costs?
3. How I can achieve the best possible outcomes with this client in the least amount of time?

Since combined modes of treatments are usually more costly than a single treatment mode, it is important to know when and when not to use combined modalities (Thase, 2000). For the typical practitioner, cost effectiveness means the following:
1. Describe alternative treatments, interventions, or modalities available for each client's stated goal.
2. Generate a list of both costs and benefits for each treatment modality. Costs include such things as the helper's or clinic's fee for provision of the service; costs borne by the client, including any lost time from work; and also any overhead costs associated with the helper's practice or work setting. Costs also involve an estimate of the number of sessions that would be required to use treatment A and/or treatment B. Benefits include such things as changes in the client's overall level of functioning, level of improvement in symptom reduction, and any changes in the client's overall quality of life. Benefits also include an assessment of the effect of treatment on significant others and an assessment of significant settings in the client's life, family, school, and work. Obviously, time spent on any given treatment modality that takes less time to achieve the desired results is also a benefit. Another benefit is when providing psychological services reduces a client's use of other, more expensive medical services; this is called medical cost offset. Roberts, Vernberg, and Jackson (2000) report some preliminary evidence to support this benefit for some child and adult psychological treatments.
3. Select and use the treatment modality that is the most cost and clinically effective and where the likelihood of helping clients reach their goals is greatest; that is where the benefits outweigh the costs.

MULTICULTURAL AND GENDER ISSUES IN TREATMENT PLANNING AND SELECTION

At the outset, practitioners need to realize the origins of psychotherapeutic treatment strategies and interventions and the implications of these origins for treatment planning with clients who feel "marginalized" or out of the mainstream. Most of the strategies we describe in the second half of this book are drawn from theoretical positions developed by a founding father or fathers. As a result, the most widely used therapeutic strategies often reflect the dominant values of the mainstream culture, defined by "whiteness, middle-class position, youth, able-bodiedness, heterosexuality and maleness" (Brown, 1994,

LEARNING ACTIVITY 11.2 — Decision Rules in Treatment Planning

Use the following two case descriptions to identify some decision rules about treatment selection and planning. Respond either orally or in writing to the following five questions, which represent decision rules about treatment selection. You may want to do this with a partner or in a small group. Feedback follows below.

1. What is this client's level of functional impairment? Give data to support your decision. Based on this, what would you recommend about treatment duration for this client?
2. What is this client's predominant coping style (externalized or internalized)? Give data to support your decision. Based on this, what type of treatment would you select for this client—behavioral focus or insight–reflective focus?
3. What mode of treatment might work best for this client? Give data to support your choice.
4. How would you assess the client's level of resistance, low or high? Give data to support your choice. Based on this, would you use directive or nondirective intervention strategies?
5. Consider how your training, practice setting, and theoretical orientation(s) to helping might affect your decision about treatment selection.

The Case of Antonio

Antonio is a 15-year-old boy who lives with his dad after his mother kicked him out because he stopped going to school and got in trouble with the law for stealing. His parents are divorced. His dad owns a bar, and Antonio is now staying with his dad but says he doesn't see him much. He says he quit going to school because he didn't have any friends there, it was too lonely, and he got into trouble all the time for fighting. He spends his time now on video games although arrangements have been made for him to be home schooled for the rest of the year. He denies any substance use. He doesn't understand why he has to see you.

The Case of Mr. Sharn

Mr. Sharn is a 72-year-old man who has come to see you because he has had trouble sleeping and has noticed some problems with his memory, a problem that he says is unusual. Also, his appetite is low. He has been retired for seven years and has really enjoyed himself until lately. He and his wife recently returned from visiting their son and grandchildren, who live in a town a few hours away. His other son lives in the same town as Mr. Sharn. He says he has lots of friends, especially golfing buddies. He reports being close to both sons. He says they had a good visit, but ever since he has been back he has noticed some things about his sleep, memory, and appetite. He does report feeling kind of blue but not overwhelmed by it, and he denies any suicidal thoughts. He is hoping you can help him. Although he has never been to see a professional helper before, he doesn't want to burden his wife or his sons with too many problems.

FEEDBACK 11.2 — Decision Rules in Treatment Planning

The Case of Antonio

1. His functional impairment seems high, due to his family problems, his lack of social support, and his social isolation and withdrawal. As a result, treatment intensity would be increased, with more-frequent sessions spaced closer together.
2. His coping style seems to be externalized. He has been in trouble with the law for stealing and has been in trouble at school for fighting. As a result, your treatment focus would be behavioral.
3. Due to his family issues, social isolation, and lack of social support, family and group modes of treatment may be better than individual.
4. His level of resistance appears to be high (he doesn't know why he has to see you). Nondirective interventions would be more useful.

The Case of Mr. Sharn

1. His degree of impairment seems relatively low in that he has a supportive and functional family, lots of friends, and

(continued)

> **11.2 FEEDBACK**
> **Decision Rules in Treatment Planning** *(continued)*
>
> seems to have a good overall support system. So treatment intensity and duration would probably remain at once weekly. Of course, his level of depression would need to be carefully monitored to ensure he is not a danger to himself.
>
> 2. He seems to have a more internalized coping style, as he views himself as the cause of the problems, and he internalizes feelings of distress and sadness.
>
> 3. It would be useful to use individual sessions with him; also, a possible evaluation with a physician may be necessary due to his sleep, appetite, and memory problems.
>
> 4. His level of resistance is low. He appears to be eager to accept your help, so you can use more-directive interventions.

p. 63). Clients who do not have these characteristics are more likely to feel marginalized. Another important point is to recognize that some traditional psychotherapeutic techniques found to be successful with Euro-American clients may be culturally contraindicated for clients who fall outside these descriptions. Typically, traditional treatment planning and selection have not addressed issues of race, gender, and social class—particularly poverty and international perspectives (Brown, 1994). Two important questions for practitioners to address in overall treatment planning are these:

1. Do the usual or recommended treatment approaches oppress a client even more?
2. What should the helping process look like and offer when treating "multiply oppressed" clients? (Brown, 1994)

If such questions are not addressed, practitioners run a greater risk of having Eurocentric and androcentric ideas reflected in their treatment plans.

A Multicultural Perspective of Resistance

Even the concept of resistance to treatment has Eurocentric roots, particularly the perspective we offered earlier in the chapter. However, in multicultural treatment planning and implementation, "understanding and coping with client resistance calls for an alternative perspective," for people of color and other clients from varied cultural groups often "are reluctant to approach human service agencies that are controlled and dominated" by white people (Lum, 2000, p. 143). Also, seeking help from an outsider may represent a "last resort" strategy by the client that is used only after "families, friends, and the community and natural resources" have been approached first (Lum, 2000, p. 142).

In the multicultural treatment planning models we discuss, you will note a different view of resistance, a view in which resistance is cultivated rather than discouraged or deflected. This is because in multicultural and feminist views, resistance "refers to the development of a resilient capacity to refuse to merge with the dominant cultural norms and to attend in some manner to one's own voice and integrity" (L. Brown, 2000, p. 366). In these models, resistance is actually promoted by fostering of "skillful, self-protective, and self-respectful strategies" to do so (L. Brown, 2000, p. 367). For example, rather than fostering shame and the lack of self-esteem that clients may feel from not trying harder, promoting resistance uncovers the assumptions underlying these perceptions: "It replaces the illusions of level playing fields and the denial of power differences . . . and clarifies the client's position in the social context, where power is unevenly distributed and value parceled out according to arbitrary characteristics rather than effort or talent" (L. Brown, 2000, p. 367). Further, resistance is reframed as success at engaging in individual or collective acts of courage and strength in response to harm and deception (p. 367—see also Chapter 13).

As a result, clients credit themselves for participating in such "acts of resistance" (L. Brown, 2000, p. 367). This process of promoting resistance requires helpers who are "capable of seeing beyond the options presented by the dominant culture" and who are able to identify and support paths of resistance and subversion that may not be authorized by mainstream values (p. 367). For example, at an individual level, this may mean helping the client resist an inequitable contract or work-load agreement in her job that has been created without divergent voices and imposed by people who hold the power. Treatment strategies would be selected and implemented toward this act of resistance. At a systems level, both the helper and client may need to resist system-wide practices that substitute compliance for difference and agreement for disagreement. Cushman and

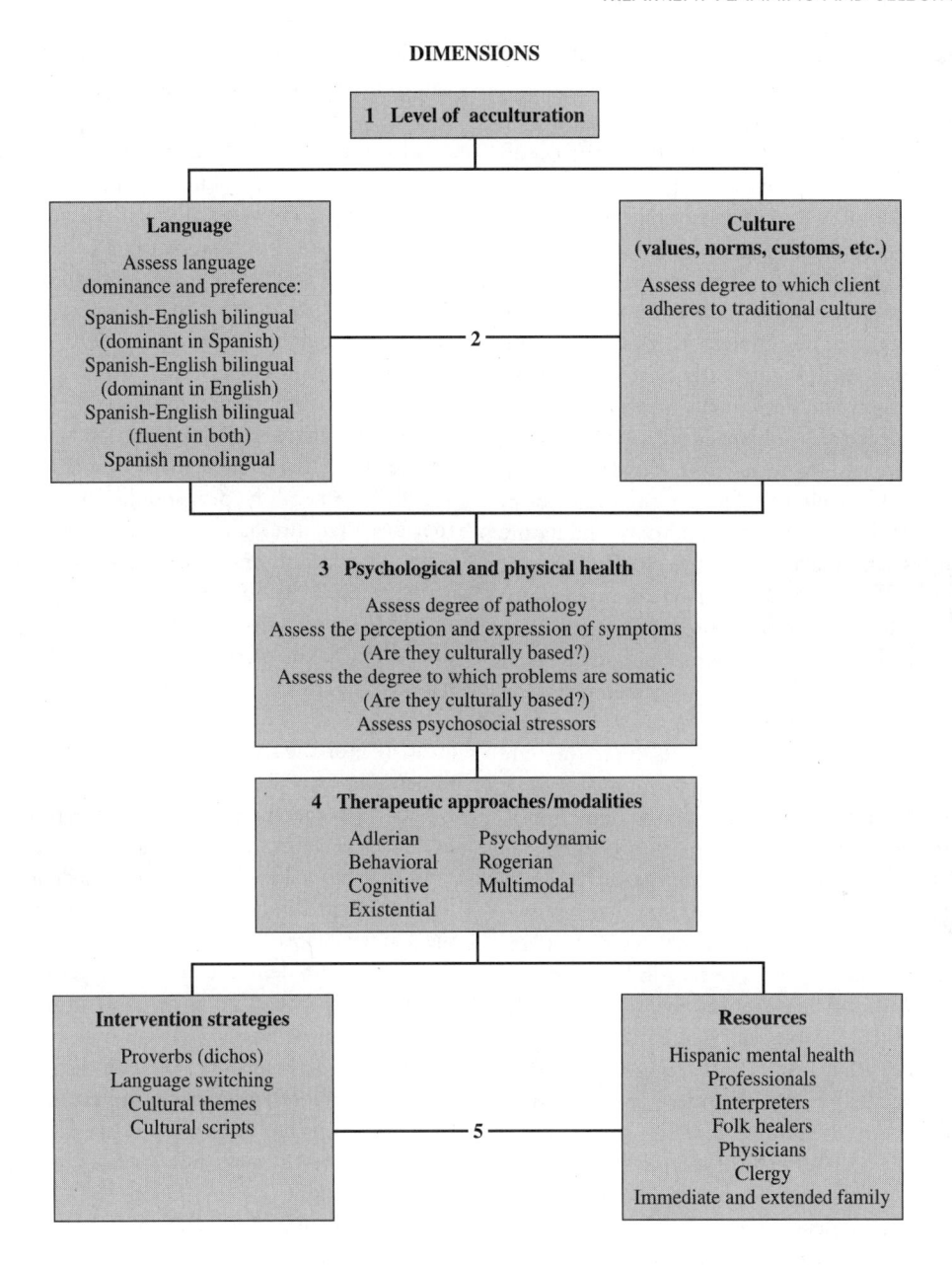

DIMENSIONS

```
                    ┌─────────────────────────┐
                    │  1  Level of acculturation │
                    └─────────────────────────┘
                         /              \
        ┌────────────────┐              ┌────────────────────────┐
        │   Language     │              │   Culture              │
        │                │              │ (values, norms,        │
        │ Assess language│              │  customs, etc.)        │
        │ dominance and  │      2       │ Assess degree to which │
        │ preference:    │              │ client adheres to      │
        │ Spanish-English│              │ traditional culture    │
        │ bilingual      │              │                        │
        │ (dominant in   │              │                        │
        │  Spanish)      │              │                        │
        │ Spanish-English│              │                        │
        │ bilingual      │              │                        │
        │ (dominant in   │              │                        │
        │  English)      │              │                        │
        │ Spanish-English│              │                        │
        │ bilingual      │              │                        │
        │ (fluent in     │              │                        │
        │  both)         │              │                        │
        │ Spanish        │              │                        │
        │ monolingual    │              │                        │
        └────────────────┘              └────────────────────────┘
                         \              /
                ┌──────────────────────────────────────┐
                │ 3  Psychological and physical health │
                │                                      │
                │      Assess degree of pathology      │
                │ Assess the perception and expression │
                │  of symptoms (Are they culturally    │
                │              based?)                 │
                │ Assess the degree to which problems  │
                │  are somatic (Are they culturally    │
                │              based?)                 │
                │    Assess psychosocial stressors     │
                └──────────────────────────────────────┘
                                 │
                ┌──────────────────────────────────────┐
                │ 4  Therapeutic approaches/modalities │
                │                                      │
                │   Adlerian       Psychodynamic       │
                │   Behavioral     Rogerian            │
                │   Cognitive      Multimodal          │
                │   Existential                        │
                └──────────────────────────────────────┘
                         /              \
    ┌────────────────────┐              ┌─────────────────────────┐
    │ Intervention       │              │     Resources           │
    │ strategies         │              │                         │
    │                    │              │ Hispanic mental health  │
    │ Proverbs (dichos)  │      5       │ Professionals           │
    │ Language switching │              │ Interpreters            │
    │ Cultural themes    │              │ Folk healers            │
    │ Cultural scripts   │              │ Physicians              │
    │                    │              │ Clergy                  │
    │                    │              │ Immediate and extended  │
    │                    │              │ family                  │
    └────────────────────┘              └─────────────────────────┘
```

Figure 11.1
Source: From "Developing a culturally sensitive Treatment Modality for Bilingual Spanish-Speaking Clients," by A.L. Santiago-Rivera, *Journal of Counseling and Development*, 74, p. 14. Copyright © 1995 ACA. Reprinted with permission. No further reproduction authorized without written permission of the American Counseling Association.

Gilford (2000) provide an example of how some managed care practices have the effect of subtly influencing clients to renounce difference and to conform to the status quo. Clients are not helped to "question or resist the sociohistorical, material conditions" from which they may suffer (p. 994). From a multicultural perspective, clients' acts of resistance help them feel empowered due to "naming, validating, resisting and subverting external events and influences that are problematic and often oppressive" (L. Brown, 2000, p. 366).

World View in Multicultural Treatment Planning Models

A comprehensive treatment planning model that is *not* based on Eurocentric notions and is culturally sensitive is offered by Santiago-Rivera. Her model integrates various cultural dimensions, including level of acculturation, culturally sensitive types of treatment, and availability of culturally relevant resources (see Figure 11.1). This model is especially useful in that it has the greatest focus on cultural variables of any of the treatment planning models we describe in this chapter. One thing that distinguishes her model from the models previously discussed is differences in world view.

"World view" is defined as our basic perceptions and understanding of the world (Treviño 1996). World view is important because it "affects how we perceive and evaluate appropriate outcomes based upon our appraisal—the nature of clinical reality is very much linked to worldview" (Sue & Sue, 1999, p. 165). World view has important implications for treatment. Recall from our discussion of the person-in-environment model in Chapter 8 that the individual client is in a social, political, and cultural environment or system. At times, "systemic forces may be so overpowering and stacked against culturally different clients, that they are truly not responsible for their fate and cannot exercise enough systemic control to change or alter the outcome . . . from this perspective the therapeutic solution is to change the system rather than the person (acculturate)" (Sue & Sue, 1999, p. 166). Sue and Sue propose that there are two major dimensions of world view that affect treatment planning: locus of control and locus of responsibility. Locus of control (Rotter, 1966) can be either internal or external. In internal locus of control, people believe that they can shape their own destiny by their beliefs and actions. In external locus of control, they believe that their destiny is shaped by "fate, beliefs about social–political matters, beliefs about powerful others, beliefs about luck or chance, beliefs about potential for control, or beliefs about cultural or family values" and that it occurs independently of their own actions (Marks, 1998, p. 256). Locus of responsibility, derived from attribution theory (Jones et al., 1972), also can be internal or external. If it is internal, people feel that they are responsible for their success or failure. If it is external, they feel that the system is responsible for both their problems and their successes. Sue and Sue (1999) point out that the trait of internality and externality is not unidimensional. The locus of control concept reflects a continuum, and more distinction is needed, especially around the external end of the continuum. As they illustrate, externality attributed to chance and luck is different than externality that is ascribed to cultural forces and powerful others. This is because chance and luck exist equally for all people across situations whereas cultural forces and power do not. For example, powerlessness is the expectation that one's behavior cannot determine the outcomes or reinforcement that one seeks (p. 170). However, if one is not given equal opportunities, powerlessness is an accurate perception of a discrepancy between one's ability and the attainment of one's goals. This is the situation that in reality exists for many culturally different clients (Sue & Sue, 1999, p. 170). In this situation, externality is seen as a "malevolent force" (p. 170). At the same time, some cultural groups across countries simply have an external orientation that is valued, accepted, and seen as a benevolent force (Marks, 1998; Sue & Sue, 1999). In general, helpers should avoid "globally applying the idea that internality is always the most beneficial by weighing ethnicity and other demographic factors" (Marks, 1998, p. 257). As Sue and Sue (1999) point out, externality can be "motivationally healthy if it results from assessing one's chances for success against systematic and real external obstacles rather than unpredictable fate" (p. 170).

Figure 11.2 is derived from transactional analysis and shows an analysis of Sue and Sue's (1999) quadrants of four possible dimensions of locus of control and locus of responsibility. The type of client that we described earlier in this chapter—white, middle class, young, able-bodied, heterosexual, and male—is most likely to fall in the upper left quadrant, IC–IR, reflecting the "rugged individualism" of the mainstream culture in the United States. Treatment approaches such as cognitive therapy and problem solving that are person centered, reflect an individual focus, and are rational in orientation fall into this quadrant, as do self-help groups. These treatment approaches are likely to work best with clients who subscribe to dimensions of both internal control and internal responsibility. However, it has become increasingly clear that minority persons hold world views different from members of the dominant culture (Sue & Sue, 1999, p. 166). Sue and Sue explain that for many minority clients in the United States, "a strong determinant of worldviews is very much related to racism and the subordinate position assigned to them in society" (Sue & Sue, 1999, p. 166). In addition to race and ethnicity, religion, sexual orientation, gender, age, and economic and social class also affect world views.

Clients who feel in some way marginalized and encounter a number of specific problem situations in their relationships with the mainstream society are more likely to hold world views falling in the other three quadrants shown in Figure 11.2. Lum (2000, pp. 138–139) has described five specific treatment strategies relevant to clients with the kinds of world

IC–IR I. I'm OK and have control over myself. Society is OK, and I can make it in the system.	IC–ER III. I'm OK and have control, but need a chance. Society is not OK, and I know what's wrong and seek to change it.
EC–IR II. I'm OK, but my control comes best when I define myself according to the definition of the dominant culture. Society is OK the way it is; it's up to me.	EC–ER IV. I'm not OK and don't have much control; I might as well give up or please everyone. Society is not OK and is the reason for my plight; the bad system is all to blame.

Figure 11.2 Sue's cultural identity quadrants
Source: From *Counseling and Development in a Multicultural Society* (5th ed.), by J. A. Axelson, p. 414. Copyright 1999 by Brooks/Cole, an imprint of the Wadsworth Group, a division of Thomson Learning. Reprinted with permission.

Liberation (vs. oppression) is the client's experience of release or freedom from oppressive barriers and control when change occurs. For some, it accompanies personal growth and decision-making: The client has decided no longer to submit to oppression. In other cases, liberation occurs under the influence of environmental change—for example, the introduction of a job-training program or the election of an ethnic mayor who makes policy, legislative, and program changes on behalf of people of color.

Empowerment (vs. powerlessness) is a process in which persons who belong to a stigmatized social category can be assisted to develop and increase skills in the exercise of interpersonal influence. Claiming the human right to resources and well-being in society, individuals experience power by rising up and changing their situational predicament. The first step to empowerment is to obtain information about resources and rights. Then, choosing an appropriate path of action, the client participates in a situation in which his or her exercise of power confers palpable benefits. Practical avenues of empowerment include voting, influencing policy, or initiating legislation on the local level.

Parity (vs. exploitation) relates to a sense of equality. For people of color, parity entails being of equal power, value, and rank with others in society and being treated accordingly. Its focal theme is fairness and the entitlement to certain rights. Parity is expressed in terms of resources that guarantee an adequate standard of living, such as entitlement programs (Social Security, Medicare), income maintenance, and medical care.

Maintenance of culture (vs. acculturation) asserts the importance of the ideas, customs, skills, arts, and language of a people. By tracing the history of an ethnic group, counselor and client can identify moments of crisis and challenge through which it survived and triumphed. Applying such lessons of history to the present inspires the client to overcome obstacles and provides a source of strength on which the client may draw. Maintenance of culture secures the client's identity as an ethnic individual.

Unique personhood (vs. stereotyping) is an intervention strategy by which stereotypes are transcended. Functional casework asserts the view that each person is unique in the helping relationship and that there is something extraordinary in each individual. When people of color act to gain freedom from social stereotypes, they assert their unique personhood and discover their humanity.

Source: From *Social Work Practice and People of Color: A Process-stage approach*, (5th ed.), by D. Lum, pp. 138–139. Copyright © 2000. Reprinted with permission of the Wadsworth Group, a division of Thomas Learning.

---

view depicted in these three categories. These five kinds of interventions are described in the above box.

Coupled with these treatment interventions are descriptions of *roles* of helpers that may be more useful for working with clients who hold varied world views. These roles are alternatives to the more conventional role in which many practitioners are trained, and, in general, these alternative roles involve helpers more actively in the client's life experiences (Atkinson, Thompson, & Grant, 1993). (See Box 11.6.) The treatment processes described by Lum (2000) and the roles

> **BOX 11.6 HELPER ROLES**
>
> 1. Adviser
> 2. Advocate
> 3. Facilitator of Indigenous Support Systems
> 4. Facilitator of Indigenous Healing Systems
> 5. Consultant
> 6. Change Agent
>
> *Source:* Atkinson, Thompson, and Grant, 1993.

described by Atkinson and colleagues (1993) have important implications for clients who have different world views. In the bottom left quadrant, EC–IR, we find clients who reflect the U.S. mainstream culture's definition of self-responsibility (IR) but have very little real control in their lives (EC). These are likely to be clients who feel caught between the mainstream culture and some other cultural affiliation of their own that affects their destiny, such as being a woman; having a mental or physical challenge; being elderly, poor, or gay/lesbian or bisexual; and/or being of a different racial/ethnic origin than Euro-American. Although they share aspects of two or more cultures, these individuals have become more acculturated to aspects of the mainstream culture than to their original culture and tend to deny the impact of their other cultural affiliations. This situation may be perpetuated by a "culturally encapsulated" white practitioner who does "not understand the sociopolitical dynamics of the client's concerns" (Sue & Sue, 1999, p. 177). They are likely to be at the conformity stage of the racial and cultural identity model we discussed in Chapter 2. They are likely to be in subordinate positions of a dominant–subordinate power structure yet either do not realize this or believe it to be their fault. Women who are battered by their male partners are an example. Non-Euro-American clients who hold this world view often prefer a Euro-American helper because of their rejection of their own race and culture (Sue & Sue, 1999).

Treatment approaches that are likely to be helpful with clients with this world view are ones that are more intuitive and subjective rather than rational and objective, help clients recognize the effects of their acculturation to the mainstream culture, help them recognize the effects of a dominant–submissive hierarchy, and also help them develop a voice, agency, and resources about themselves—specifically about reclaiming their strengths and achievements, about their own needs and desires, and about their own experiences and expressions of personal authority and self-worth (Young-Eisendrath, 1984). The practitioner also needs to help these clients identify the difference between positive attempts to acculturate and negative rejection of their own cultural values (Sue & Sue, 1999, p. 177). Using Atkinson and colleagues' model of helper roles, the roles most frequently used with these clients are *adviser* and *consultant*. In these roles, helpers are providing information, working in an alliance based on collaboration and mutual respect, and embracing a position of antidenomination. Using Lum's (2000) model, *maintenance of culture* and *liberation* are especially useful with clients of this world view. Reframing the issues presented by these clients as social–contextual problems and helping clients separate their identities from these issues can also be helpful (Young-Eisendrath, 1984). The relationship and communication skills that we describe in Chapters 2 through 6 are especially useful for EC–IR clients, particularly the use of empathy and listening responses as ways of consciously validating the client's voice and experiences. As Young-Eisendrath (1984) notes, "Consensual validation is the foundation of human sanity in that it is the means by which we know the truthfulness of an experience and by which we replenish our self-esteem" (p. 60). Thinking of this another way, it does little good to give the client a *voice* if the therapist does not have an *ear* or a way to understand the newly emerging perspectives that a client in the EC–IR mode may be trying to articulate (Young-Eisendrath, 1984).

At the upper right of the quadrant are clients who hold the opposite world view—IC–ER—in the sense that they believe in their personal ability to shape their lives if given the opportunities (IC). They also realistically perceive that the "system" blocks opportunities because of oppression, stereotyping, and exploitation (Sue & Sue, 1999). As Sue and Sue (1999, p. 178) note, "there is a considerable body of evidence to support this." In contrast to the EC–IR clients, IC–ER clients typically identify with and take pride in aspects of their own cultural identity, even if it is different from what is espoused by the mainstream. These are clients who have sufficiently worked through levels of their racial, sexual, or gender identity (as we described earlier in Chapter 2) to now reclaim and honor the characteristics of their cultural affiliations and gender. Sue and Sue (1999) predict that as clients who vary from the nondominant culture become increasingly conscious of aspects of their cultural identity, there will be more and more clients with this IC–ER world view. The authors contend that clients with this world view will be the least trusting and most difficult for typical Euro-American practitioners, who hold the IC–IR views of the dominant culture. These clients are likely to terminate helping even before the treatment planning stage occurs because of their dissatisfaction with the helper and the ways in which helping is conducted that does not "fit" for them. These clients are also more likely to challenge helper statements or actions that appear to be oppressive or stereotypical. In working with clients who hold an IC–ER view, helpers can expect to deal with more of the "tests of trust" described in Chapter 6. These clients may also be more reluctant to be open, particularly with a helper who holds an IC–IR world view.

Clients with an IC–ER belief are also more likely to view the problems as being outside themselves and as the product of "the Establishment"; they will be less likely to establish an alliance with a helper who holds an IR world view and sees problems as residing within the client. These clients are much more likely to expect and use treatment approaches that are directive in style, action oriented in technique, and systems oriented in focus. As Sue and Sue (1999) note, with IC–ER clients, "demands for the counselor to take external action on the part of the client will be strong . . . while most of us have been taught not to intervene externally on behalf of the client, all of us must look seriously at the value base of this dictate" (p. 182). In line with this, using the Atkinson and colleagues model of helper roles, the change agent role and the facilitator of indigenous support and healing systems roles will work well with many of these IC–ER clients. Also, the action-oriented influencing skills we described in Chapter 7 and many behavioral interventions are quite useful. Using Lum's (2000) model, *parity, unique personhood,* and *liberation* are also especially useful interventions for these clients.

In the fourth quadrant, in the lower right, are clients who hold an EC–ER world view. These clients are the ones most likely to feel hopeless, discouraged, and disempowered as they are high in both external control and feeling powerless over the system that has been oppressive, believing there is little they can do to overcome severe external obstacles such as discrimination and exploitation (Sue & Sue, 1999). Their high EC response may indicate that they have truly given up and have developed what Seligman (1982) refers to as "learned helplessness," the idea that people "exposed to prolonged noncontrol in their lives develop expectation of helplessness in later situations" (p. 151). The high EC response can also indicate that these clients have simply learned that the best way to deal with their disempowerment is to placate the powerful: "Passivity in the face of oppression is the primary reaction of the placater" (Sue & Sue, 1999, p. 178).

Both learned helplessness and placating behaviors represent survival strategies by the people who adopt them; direct expression of anger or healthy assertiveness is viewed as too risky because of the potential for punishing consequences from some aspect of the environment (Taylor, Gilligan, & Sullivan, 1995). When slavery existed, if African Americans did not show deferential behavior to their white "masters," they were severely punished. Unfortunately, "holdover" aspects of this demeaning and objectionable social phenomenon still exist at a conscious level in many current interactions between Euro-American and non-Euro-American races. At some level we are all constantly influenced as well by *unconscious* stereotyping and bias about race, ethnicity, sex roles, sexual orientation, and so on. Women have also learned the risks of direct expression of anger in a society in which power is held largely by men. As Young-Eisendrath (1984) notes, "When a woman, in any social context, is insistent, angry, or convinced of her authority, she is often interpreted as domineering, overwhelming, or overcontrolling. Rarely is she simply understood to be angry or authoritative" (p. 72).

EC–ER clients may be overly polite and deferential with helpers and, unlike IC–ER clients, may not challenge or confront aspects of a helper's bias because they perceive such behavior as either too risky or as not worth the effort. They are also unlikely to become directly and openly angry with you, even when you have said or done something that in some way violates them. They may act as though they believe your ideas are of value, but once outside the session, they may discard your ideas as unworkable or untenable for them in their particular life space. In planning treatment approaches with EC–ER clients, first you must recognize the survival values of their behaviors so you do not perceive these clients as "lacking in courage and ego strength" (Sue & Sue, 1999, p. 178). As with EC–IR clients, validation and respect form the foundation for all treatment approaches. Validation of their anger and resentment and also of their strengths and successes is very useful. Unlike EC–IR clients, EC–ER clients "do understand the political forces that have subjugated their existence" (Sue & Sue, 1999, p. 178). In addition, the use of EC interventions that teach these clients new coping strategies is very helpful (Sue & Sue, 1999). In Lum's (2000) model, *empowerment* interventions are particularly useful with these clients as well. In the Atkinson and colleagues model of helper roles, the role of advocate is very useful with these clients.

Often, clients who hold an EC–ER world view are victims of trauma. A primary feature of trauma is the individual's feelings of helplessness about not being able to do anything to ward off the trauma and the perpetrator(s). There are many kinds of trauma—physical, sexual, and emotional abuse are perhaps the more well-known kinds of trauma, and various treatment strategies exist (Courtois, 1996; 1999; Meichenbaum, 1994; Foa, Keane, & Friedman, 2000). Another kind of trauma that unfortunately seems to be increasing around the world is trauma resulting from hate due to difference. Hate crimes may include assault, homicide, harassment, and property damage, and may be directed toward an individual, a family, a group of people, a community, or, as we saw on September 11, 2001, a country.

Dunbar (2001) has provided an important contribution to our understanding of comprehensive treatment planning and practices with this kind of trauma. Often, acute stress disorders or posttraumatic stress disorders as well as anxiety and depression develop as a result of hate trauma. Dunbar's five-phase model includes "the reduction of trauma symptoms of intrusive ideation, physiological arousal, numbing, and avoidance behavior" (2001, p. 285). Multimodal interventions using many of the strategies we describe in Chapters 12–18 are also employed. (We describe some related Web sites at the end of this chapter.)

In applying this cultural identity model to treatment planning, remember several caveats, as noted by Sue and Sue (1999, pp. 181–183). First, each world view has something to offer that is useful and positive; for example, "the individual responsibility and achievement orientation of quadrant I, biculturalism and cultural flexibility of quadrant II, ability to compromise and adapt to life conditions of quadrant III, and collective action and social concern of quadrant IV need not be at odds with one another" (Sue & Sue, 1999, p. 183). The helper's task is to plan treatment approaches that help clients to integrate aspects of the world view that will increase their effectiveness and well-being. Second, research on this model is in a developing stage, so some of the observations we have made are tentative (Treviño, 1996). Third, the four styles described are conceptual, and in reality, "most people represent mixes of each rather than a pure standard" (Sue & Sue, 1999, p. 183). Thus, in practice, helpers will provide treatment planning to clients who hold both primary and secondary views about control and responsibility.

In general, we offer the following guidelines for developing multicultural treatment plans. We have developed these guidelines from the literature. Note that these guidelines are *not* extensions of the evidence-based practice guidelines we discussed earlier in the chapter.

1. Make sure that your treatment plan is culturally as well as clinically *literate* and relevant. Consider the cultural illiteracy of the suggestion that an Asian parent discipline his or her child by the American parenting technique of "grounding" or "time out": "For Asian families, being excluded from the family is the worst possible punishment one can endure; exclusion is extremely rare. Therefore, when children misbehave, they are threatened with banishment from the family and told to get out. Of course, the children have to fight to stay in the family. Once in, they never leave; sons bring their wives in and expect the parents to help raise the grandchildren" (Berg & Jaya, 1993, p. 32). In other words, make sure the plan reflects the values and world views of the *client's* cultural identity, not your own.

2. Make sure that your treatment plan addresses the needs and impact of the client's *social system* as well as the individual client, including (but not limited to) oppressive conditions within the system. For example, consider the case of a Native American youth you are working with for substance use. Whereas some cognitive–behavioral interventions may be useful, they are not sufficient unless accompanied by an exploration of the client's cultural context and what and how oppressive acts may contribute to the use of substances. Freire (1972), in the classic book *The Pedagogy of the Oppressed,* states that an important purpose of counseling is *conscientizacào,* the development of "critical consciousness"—specifically, the development of awareness of oneself in a social context. Reid and Misener (2000) note that the changes made by individual clients will reverberate throughout the systems with which they interact. As a result, they suggest "utilizing treatment interventions related to a multisystemic range of change activities" (p. 243).

3. Make sure that your treatment plan addresses the relevant *indigenous* practices and *supports* of your client. In other words, make sure that your treatment plan considers the role of important *subsystems* and *resources* in the client's life, such as the family structure and external support systems. Networking with these resources of extended family, local community, and spiritual practices is useful, as numerous studies have shown collaboration between the helper and local support systems helps the practitioner develop a treatment plan that is more "culturally syntonic" (Rosado & Elias, 1993, p. 454).

4. Make sure that your treatment plan addresses the client's view of *health* and *recovery* and *ways of solving problems.* The client's spirituality may play an important role in this regard; folk beliefs, mythology, and supernatural forces may all be significant factors.

5. Assess for and consider the client's level of acculturation and language dominance and preference in planning treatment. Incorporate the use of culturally relevant themes, scripts, folk tales, proverbs, metaphors, and also the possibility of "language switching" as culture-specific treatment interventions into your overall treatment plan (Santiago-Rivera, 1995).

6. Make sure that the length of your proposed treatment matches the needs and *time perspective* held by the client. As Rosado and Elias (1993) note, clients must survive before they can thrive (p. 452). Pragmatic strategies, tangible coping skills, and short-term treatments may be fa-

vored by some clients. Rosado and Elias (1993) recommend tailoring treatment plans to the ecological needs of the client even if this means that treatment is of shorter duration: "It is more desirable to have the client return several times a year for specific issues than to drop out and never to return for much-needed mental health issues" (Rosado & Elias, 1993, p. 454).

In the work of Cheatham, Ivey, Ivey, and Simek-Morgan (1993), we have found a very useful case illustration describing the design of helping interventions from a multicultural framework. The case involves work with a low-income Puerto Rican woman who suffers from *ataques de nervios* (physiological reactions that may be typically related to trauma and grief in the Puerto Rican culture). Notice when you read this case how skillfully the helper weaves aspects of treatment planning into and with the client's cultural identity. We provide you with an opportunity to do this on your own—see Box 11.7 on pp. 332–333.

THE PROCESS OF TREATMENT PLANNING AND EMPOWERED CONSENT

In our opinion, the choice of appropriate helping strategies is a joint decision in which both client and helper are actively involved. We believe it is a misuse of the inherent influence of the helping process for the helper to select a strategy or to implement a treatment plan independent of the client's input.

During the last decade, we have also witnessed an increasing consumerism movement in practice, which has led to the following changes:

1. The client needs to be an active, rather than passive, participant in treatment planning.
2. The client's rights need to be made explicit.
3. The treatment planning process needs to be demystified. This demystification can occur by having the helper develop the treatment plan jointly with the client.
4. The client must consent to treatment. This step is important for all clients, regardless of the setting in which they are helped. Helpers must also take special precautions with clients of "low power," such as minors and institutionalized persons, to ensure that their rights are not violated and that treatment programs are not implemented without their participation and consent. Occasionally, some practitioners argue that they are withholding information about treatment in order to base a therapeutic strategy on "confusion." However, limited data, as well as ethical and legal principles, suggest that each client has the right to choose services and strategies appropriate to his or her needs.

We believe that the helper is acting in good faith to protect clients' rights and welfare by providing the following kinds of information to clients about treatment strategies:
1. A description of *all* relevant and potentially useful treatment approaches for this particular client with this particular problem
2. A rationale for each procedure
3. A description of the helper's role in each procedure
4. A description of the client's role in each procedure
5. Discomforts or risks that may occur as a result of the procedure
6. Benefits expected to result from the procedure
7. The estimated time and cost of each procedure

Licensing boards in some states now require professional disclosure statements to be made available to clients. According to Keel and Brown (1999), "a professional disclosure statement will reflect the distinctive qualities and characteristics of the individual helper as well as the purpose, goals, techniques, procedures, limitations, risks, and benefits of services to be provided" (p. 14). As these authors note, the advantages of a written disclosure statement are many; it is a useful self-assessment tool for helpers, and it "contributes to ownership, accountability, and being in alignment with who you are and what you do in your work" (Keel & Brown, 1999, p. 15).

The practitioner also needs to state that he or she will try to answer any questions the client has now or later about the procedure and that the client is always free to discontinue participation in the procedure at any time. If the client is a minor, consent must be obtained from a parent or legal guardian, just as consent must be obtained from a guardian or legal representative if the client has been declared mentally incompetent to give consent. Sometimes, helpers experience an ethical conflict between their responsibility to provide a disclosure statement and empowered consent, and what is known in some managed care companies as a "gag clause." A gag clause refers to a portion of a contract with the helper who serves on a provider list or panel of a managed care company that prevents the helper from discussing treatment possibilities with the client not covered by the insurance plan (Davis & Meier, 2001, p. 85). This raises the question of who really benefits from empowered consent.

Informed consent was initially proposed in the 1970s by feminist therapists as a way to help clients by giving them active roles as consumers of mental health services. By the 1990s, informed consent had become part of mainstream practice.

But as Brown (1994) points out, the impetus for providing informed consent has shifted from empowering the

BOX 11.7   CASE STUDY: A PUERTO RICAN WOMAN SUFFERING FROM *ATAQUES DE NERVIOS*

The client colleague is a single parent, twenty-five years of age with two children. [As once was common in Puerto Rico,] she has been sterilized with only minimal information given to her before she gave consent. She has suffered physical abuse both as a child and in more recent relationships. The following is an example of how multicultural counseling and therapy might use cultural identity development theory to facilitate *conscientizacão*, the generation of critical consciousness and effective treatment planning.

Acceptance—diagnostic signs. The client enters counseling hesitatingly as her *ataques de nervios* are increasing in frequency. A physician has referred the client to you believing that the fainting spells are psychological in origin as no physical reasons can be found. As you talk with the client, you discover that she blames herself for the failures in her life. She comments that she is "always choosing the wrong man," and she states she should have been sterilized sooner and thus fewer children would be born.

Acceptance—helping interventions and producing dissonance. Your intervention at this stage is to listen, but following Freire (1972, pp. 114–116), you can seek to help her codify or make sense of her present experience. You use guided imagery [see Chapter 12] as you help her review critical life events—the scenes around sterilization, the difficulties of economic survival when surrounded by others who have wealth, and actual discrimination against Puerto Ricans in nearby factories. . . . Through listening, the move to a more critical consciousness is begun. But, at the same time, your client colleague needs help. You may see that she has sufficient food and shelter; you may help her find a job. You may teach her basic stress management and relaxation [see Chapters 15 and 16], but especially you listen and learn [see Chapter 5].

Naming and resistance—diagnostic signs. At this point, your client is likely to become very angry, for the responsibility or "fault" which she believed was hers is now seen as almost totally in the oppressive environment. Her eyes may flash as she talks about "them." An emotional release may occur as she becomes aware that the decision for sterilization was not truly hers, but imposed by an authoritarian physician. The woman is likely to seek to strike back wherever possible against those who she feels have oppressed her. In the early stages of naming, she may fail to separate people who have truly victimized her from those who have merely stood by and said nothing.

Naming and resistance—interventions to help and to produce dissonance. Early in this stage, you are very likely to do a lot of listening. You may find it helpful to teach the client culturally-appropriate assertiveness training and anger management. There may be a delayed anger reaction to traditional sex roles. Later, this client may profit from reality therapy. However, the therapy must be adapted to her relational Puerto Rican heritage. You may support constructive action on her part to change oppressive situations. In the later stages of work with her, you may want to help her see that much of her consciousness and being depends on her *opposition* to the status quo and that she has given little attention to her own real needs and wishes. (At this point, identifying and naming contradictions between self and society may be especially important.)

Reflection and redefinition—diagnostic signs. It gets very tiring to spend one's life in total anger toward society and others. The consciousness-raising theories find that at this stage that clients often retreat to their own gender and/or cultural community to reflect on what has happened to them and to others. Responsibility is now seen as more internal in nature, but keen awareness of external issues remains. You may note that the client colleague at this stage is less interested in action and more interested in understanding self and culture. There may be a great interest in understanding and appreciating her Puerto Rican heritage and how it plays itself out in North America.

Reflection and redefinition—interventions to help and produce dissonance. Teaching clients the cultural identity development theories can be useful for them at this stage in that they help explain issues of development in culture. In addition, culturally appropriate theories such as . . . feminist theory may be especially helpful, although they are useful at all consciousness levels. Cognitive–behavioral, psychodynamic, and person-centered theories may be used if adapted to the culture and needs of the person. (The reflective consciousness is still considered a form of naive consciousness by Freire, as much of the emphasis is on the individual with insufficient attention given to systemic roots of difficulties.)

Multiperspective integration—diagnostic signs. The client draws from all previous stages as appropriate to the situation. At times, she may accept situations; at other times, be appropriately aggressive and angry, and later withdraw and reflect on herself and her relationships to others and society. She is likely to be aware of how her physical symptoms of *ataques de nervios* were a logical result of the position of women in her culture. She is able to balance responsibility between herself and society. At the same time, she does not see her level of *conscientizacão* as "higher" than others. She respects alternative frames of reference.

> **BOX 11.7   CASE STUDY: A PUERTO RICAN WOMAN SUFFERING FROM ATAQUES DE NERVIOS** CONTINUED
>
> *Multiperspective integration—interventions to help and produce dissonance.* You as helper may ask the client to join with you and your group to attack some of the issues that "cause" emotional, personal, and financial difficulty. The Puerto Rican woman may establish a family planning clinic with accurate information on the long-term effects of sterilization or she may establish a day-care center. The woman is clearly aware of how her difficulties developed in a system of relationships, and she balances internal and external responsibility for action. In terms of introducing dissonance, your task may require helping her with time management, stress management, and balancing the many possible actions she encounters. You may also arrange to see that she has accurate feedback from others about her own life and work. (You do not merely encourage her to work to transform the system. You also work with her to facilitate the process. You and your client colleague are now working together to produce cultural change in oppressive conditions.)
>
> Source: From "Multicultural Counseling and Therapy," by H. Cheatham, A. Ivey, M. B. Ivey, and L. Simek-Morgan. In *Counseling and Psychotherapy: A Multicultural Perspective,* (3rd ed.), by A. Ivey, M. B. Ivey, and L. Simek-Morgan, pp. 114–115. Copyright © 1993 by Allyn & Bacon. Reprinted by permission.

> **LEARNING ACTIVITY 11.3   Gender and Multicultural Factors in Treatment Planning and Selection**
>
> In this activity, refer back to page 314 for the case of Jane Wiggins, a low-income woman living in a rural area. Your task is to read the case carefully and identify the potential multicultural factors that are present in working with this woman, using the six guidelines we discuss on p. 330. After this, with a partner or in a small group, identify a treatment plan implementing various interventions that address the multicultural factors you have identified above. Consider the type, duration, and mode of treatment based on the client's identified concerns and stated goals. Also in your treatment plan, consider what oppressive events that Ms. Wiggins needs to be able to name, validate, and resist. Feedback follows on p. 334.

client to protecting the helper and/or the insurance company from litigation. As a result, the primary reasons for even providing consent information to clients—"respect, relationality and empowerment"—have come to be disregarded and amended in contemporary practice (Brown, 1994, p. 182). We like Brown's use of the term *empowered* consent rather than *informed* consent because, as she points out, the word *informed* raises such questions as "Who is being informed? How? By and about what or whom? Under what conditions of freedom of choice or 'friendly' coercion is consent being given?" (p. 180). Empowered consent is designed to provide complete and meaningful disclosure in a way that supports the client's freedom of choice (Brown, 1994). Moreover, as Brown (1994) notes, providing information and consent is not a one-step activity but an ongoing process throughout the therapeutic relationship.

In Chapter 9 and in Figure 11.3 we provide an illustration of a sample outpatient treatment form. This form is representative of many that are currently used by practitioners in various human services settings. Section A, "Assessment," incorporates the various assessment information that we described in Chapters 8 and 9. Section B, "Treatment Plan," incorporates the material on defining and evaluating outcome goals and planning treatments that we have described in this chapter and in Chapter 10. Section C contains three treatment update reports in which progress on outcome goals is noted, based on evaluation of these goals, as well as changes, obstacles, and request for some type of continued services. Section D, "Discharge Report," occurs at termination and indicates the degree to which the outcome goals for counseling have been met. We believe that the process of treatment planning is most effective when the helper actively uses such a form such as the one depicted in Figure 11.3 during the assessment, goal-setting, evaluation, and treatment selection sessions. Having the client participate in the completion of this form and including a place on the form for client comments helps ensure that the client plays an active role in the helping process.

11.3 FEEDBACK
Gender and Multicultural Factors in Treatment Planning and Selection

Consider these guidelines about your plan for Ms. Wiggins:

1. To what extent is your treatment plan "*culturally literate*"—that is, does it match the *client's* values and world view? In this case, have you considered that Ms. Wiggins is a low-income Euro-American woman who has lived in the same rural community all her life surrounded by family and friends from church? She holds herself responsible for the rape and also feels powerless to get help from local authorities, who in fact have been unresponsive to her requests for assistance.

2. How has your plan addressed the impact of the client's *social system,* including oppressive conditions within that system? In this case, have you noted that Ms. Wiggins is a poor, white woman living with a husband on disability due to poor health in a rural area near a small town and that their complaints to local authorities have not been taken seriously, compounded by the fact that the man who raped her is related to a deputy in the sheriff's office? In essence, she feels disempowered and silenced by the system. Also, Ms. Wiggins views the rape at this time as a "female" problem and does not yet really see it as an act of social violence and misuse of power.

3. In what ways has your plan addressed any relevant *indigenous practices, supports,* and *resources*? In this case, Ms. Wiggins reports herself to be a very spiritual person who relies on the power of prayer to help her through tough times. (Are you familiar with the book *Healing Words* by Dossey, 1993?) How has your plan considered the role of important *subsystems* in the client's life? For this client, the most important subsystems are her family and her church. However, with the exception of her husband, who supports her, she feels cut off from both these subsystems because of the nature of the issue, her own views about it, and her fears of her friends' and family's reactions.

4. Does your plan reflect the client's view of *health, recovery,* and *ways of solving problems*? For example, with Ms. Wiggins, spirituality seems to play an important role in the way she solves problems. Gender also appears to be an issue: She seems to feel that a female helper would be better equipped to help her with this issue (consider a referral to a woman helper and/or to a women's support group).

5. Have you considered the *level of acculturation* and any *language preferences* she has? (Also the use of culturally relevant themes, scripts, proverbs, and metaphors.)

   Implied in this framework is considering the role of the general history of Ms. Wiggins; the geographic location in which she lives and how long she has lived there; the type of setting; her socioeconomic status, age, gender, and role; and the specific effects of all of this on her language use and comprehension.

   In the case of Ms. Wiggins, she is a relatively young white woman on a limited and fixed income and has lived all her life in the same area—an isolated rural area near a small town. These demographics make for some interesting contradictions: She feels safe living in this region, enough to keep doors unlocked, yet she has been raped. The area is small enough to know who lives in it and who is a stranger, yet she has no support from the local sheriff's office because the assailant in this case (rather than the victim) is a relative of a deputy.

   Influenced by the societal and cultural norms of the area, she feels ashamed about what has happened to her. All these things are likely to affect your plan—for example, she may be mistrustful of you because you are a male and an outsider. She may also view you as part of a social system that, in her eyes, is similar to the sheriff's office.

   The themes of cultural mistrust and gender-linked shame can be addressed in the types of treatment you use with Ms. Wiggins.

6. How does the proposed *length* of your plan meet the needs and the perspective of Ms. Wiggins? To what extent does her willingness to return for additional sessions depend on the gender of the helper? How will her income and her husband's disability status affect her ability to come in for more sessions? Does your agency offer free services or a sliding scale for low-income clients? If not, how can you be her advocate so she can receive the number of sessions she needs?

7. Did you list some or any of the following *oppressive forces* that Ms. Wiggins needs to name, validate, and resist: local authorities and people in her church and family who would shame her or make her feel guilty about being raped or who would not believe her?

Of course, there are many other available forms for treatment planning, but almost all share the following elements, as described by Davis and Meier (2001, p. 32):

a clinical formulation of client's presenting issues and current concerns;
a diagnosis;
a description of how the helper plans to intervene; and
an expected outcome(s).

Many clients belong to insurance plans that will not pay for mental health services until the treatment plan is reviewed by the insurance company (this is usually called a utilization review). Helpers completing the treatment planning forms need knowledge of the company's diagnoses and treatment requirements, which may vary by month or reviewer (Davis & Meier, 2001, p. 32). When a treatment plan is reviewed, two questions are typically asked:

1. Does the level of care match the severity of the client's symptoms and issues?
2. Is the proposed treatment approach appropriate given the client's symptoms and issues? (Leahy & Holland, 2000, p. 3)

For example, medication may not be suggested as a treatment mode if the client's symptoms are mild to moderate, but if the client either does not show improvement or has more severe presenting symptoms, the reviewers are likely to request a medication evaluation. There are several other things that are usually assessed in a utilization review. First, when specifying a treatment approach, it is not specific enough to say you are going to be using a cognitive–behavioral approach. It is important to identify specific change intervention strategies that you will be using with your client such as stress-inoculation training or problem-solving training. Also, when reporting goals and improvement, although most helpers think in terms of feelings, it is often insufficient to say that the client will be less depressed or more satisfied with life. Although these may be included in the outcomes and improvements, it is also important to note specific ways in which the client's level of functioning has improved as well across all of the client's life settings.

Many insurance companies do not automatically authorize 20 mental health sessions. Usually, they authorize a few at a time and ask the practitioner to provide progress reports and updates. (Similarly, for inpatient treatments, usually the least amount of time is authorized first.) In these updates, you are usually asked to provide evidence that the client is making progress and evidence of continued client symptoms and problems that warrant additional treatment. (See Figure 11.3.) If there have been obstacles to client progress, it is important to note these as well. Also, if any additional diagnoses become apparent, these are also noted in updates. The updates are provided either in writing or on the telephone (Leahy & Holland, 2000, p. 9). This situation calls for an understanding of termination issues in the helping process, which we discuss in the following section.

TERMINATION ISSUES IN HELPING

Termination of helping involves ethical, practice, and cultural considerations. Termination can be initiated by clients, by helpers, and by insurance companies. Clients may terminate helping because they feel that their goals have been accomplished, because they lack resources to continue, or because they are dissatisfied with the helper or the helping process (Hackney & Cormier, 2001, p. 272). Helpers may initiate termination because their evaluation of the helping goals indicates that the client is ready to terminate or because, as we mentioned in Chapter 10, they need to refer the client. Helpers can also terminate because of some external constraint, such as moving out of town or ending a semester of training at a site. Insurance companies often terminate when they refuse to authorize additional benefits for a client. As you can see, in some of these instances termination seems to occur prematurely, although bear in mind that clients from some cultural groups may have different notions about time and termination than their helpers.

When termination does occur, both clients and helpers are likely to have feelings aroused by the termination process. Some clients may feel abandoned by the helper. This is especially true for those clients who either have formed a strong attachment to the helper or have been encouraged to become dependent on the helper (Hepworth et al., 1997, p. 42). Reluctant clients may feel relief upon termination (Hepworth et al., 1997). When helpers terminate, especially because of external constraints, they may feel guilt. When clients terminate prematurely, helpers may feel disappointed and incompetent. Often, there is a sense of loss for both helpers and clients.

For these reasons, there are steps to take during the termination process to promote effective and ethical practice. First, recognize that termination is usually a process. In situations where there is a known terminal date, perhaps due to limits of insurance reimbursement, limits of sessions offered by an agency, or limits of the helper such as ending a semester, "ethical practice dictates that the client be informed in the first session that a terminal date already exists"

MENTAL HEALTH NETWORK: OUTPATIENT TREATMENT REPORT (OTR)   Provider: _____

Client Name: _____ Birthdate: _____ Age: ____ Sex: M   F

A. ASSESSMENT

1. Presenting Problem (Client's Perspective): _____
   _____

2. Precipitating Event(s) (Why Help-seeking Now?): _____
   _____

3. Relevant Medical History (Medications, Drug/ETOH use, Illness, Injury, Surgery, etc.): _____
   _____

4. Prior Psychiatric/Psychological Conditions & Treatments: _____
   _____

5. Other Relevant History (Vocational/School, Relationship/Sexual, Social/Legal): _____

6. Brief Mental Status Evaluation: (Check as necessary)

APPEARANCE/DRESS	INTELLIGENCE	JUDGMENT/INSIGHT	DELUS./HALLUCIN.	THOUGHT DISORDER	RECENT MEMORY	REMOTE MEMORY
__ appropriate	__ high	__ intact	__ absent	__ absent	__ intact	__ intact
__ inappropriate	__ average	__ impaired	__ present	__ present	__ impaired	__ impaired
__ not assessed	__ low	__ not assessed	__ not assessed	__ not assessed	__ not assessed	__ not assessed

7. Mood/Affect: (Describe) _____

8. Suicide Assessment: (Risk, priors, plan) _____ Homicide Assessment: (Victim, violence, plan) _____

9. Clinical Formulation (Explanation of symptoms; include strengths/resources, obstacles to treatment/hidden agendas): Please be specific yet brief and clear ___
   _____

10. Code Nos. & Names DSM-4 Axis II: _____ Diagnostic Impressions: DSM-4 Axis I: _____

B. TREATMENT PLAN:

1. Focused, Targeted, Behavior & Measurable GOALS (Prioritize) Specifically Addressing Presenting Problems(s): Use as many rows as needed.

2. TYPE OF TREATMENT: Cognitive/Behavioral Interpersonal/Insight/Emotional Awareness Other: _____

3. DURATION: Service dates this OTR: _____ \# Sessions expected for DISCHARGE: _____ \# Discharge by (DATE): _____

4. MODE: Individual   Couple   Family   Individual/Family combination   Medication management   Group (if available)   Other (____)
              (90806)   (90847)   (90862)   (90853)   CPT Code____

PROBLEM(S)	GOALS	MEASURABLE SUCCESS CRITERION	SELECTED INTERVENTIONS
1. _____	_____	_____	_____
2. _____	_____	_____	_____
3. _____	_____	_____	_____

Therapist Signature & Phone: _____ Lic.No.: _____ Date: _____

Client Comments:

Figure 11.3 Sample treatment planning form
Source: Adapted from the Treatment Planning Form, by Mental Health Network, Inc., 771 Corporate Drive, Suite 410, Lexington, KY. Reprinted by permission.

Treatment Update Report #1. Service Dates since Intake OTR: _____ Pt. Name: _____

C. Goals (As indicated on reverse)   Progress On Criterion   Comments

                                          Yes   Some   No

1. _____   ____   ____   ____   _____
2. _____   ____   ____   ____   _____
3. _____   ____   ____   ____   _____

Significant changes or interferences: _____

_____

Requested treatment services: _____

Therapist Signature: _____ Lic. No. _____ Date: _____

Update 1 Therapist Phone: _____ C.M. Signature: _____ Cert. Vst. _____ Den. _____ Date: _____

Treatment Update Report #2. Service Dates since Update #1: _____ No. Sessions to date: _____

Goals (As indicated on reverse)   Progress on Criterion   Comments

                                          Yes   Some   No

1. _____   ____   ____   ____   _____
2. _____   ____   ____   ____   _____
3. _____   ____   ____   ____   _____

Significant changes or interferences: _____

_____

Requested treatment services: _____

Therapist Signature: _____ Lic. No. _____ Date: _____

Update 2 Therapist Phone: _____ C.M. Signature: _____ Cert. Vst. _____ Den. _____ Date: _____

Treatment Update Report #3. Service Dates since Update #2: _____ No. Sessions to date: _____

Goals (As indicated on reverse)   Progress on Criterion   Comments

                                          Yes   Some   No

1. _____   ____   ____   ____   _____
2. _____   ____   ____   ____   _____
3. _____   ____   ____   ____   _____

Significant changes or interferences: _____

_____

Requested treatment services: _____

Therapist Signature: _____ Lic. No. _____ Date: _____

Update 3 Therapist Phone: _____ C.M. Signature: _____ Cert. Vst. _____ Den. _____ Date: _____

D. Discharge Report: Service Dates since Update #3: Final Session Date: _____ Total Sessions: _____

Goals (As indicated on reverse/above)   Success Criterion Met   *Discharge Reason*

                                              Yes   Some   No   Comments   __Goals met

1. _____   ____   ____   ____   _____   __Ineffective (pt.)
2. _____   ____   ____   ____   _____   __Ineffective (tx.)
3. _____   ____   ____   ____   _____   __Patient moved
                                                                                                                                 __Ineligibility
                                                                                                                                 __Patient dropped

Therapist Signature & Phone: _____ Lic. No.: _____ Date: _____

(Hackney & Cormier, 2001, p. 273). Also, in cross-cultural helping situations, "the time element of termination needs to be discussed, negotiated, and understood from the client's perspective, as well" (Cormier & Hackney, 1999, p. 74).

When termination does approach, either because of constraints or because the evaluation of helping goals suggests client readiness, initiate a discussion of termination at least several weeks ahead of time. Be sure to address the client's feelings as termination approaches or ensues. It is the responsibility of the helper to initiate discussion of these feelings. Also, as a helper, be open to your own feelings during termination and if these feelings are persistent, discuss them with a supervisor or colleague. Remember to address the changes the client has made. This can be done with a summarization response (Chapter 5) that lists the changes made and gives the client credit for the hard work of change. Fourth, note what changes will need to be maintained by the client and how the client will do that in his or her world—this discussion may include planning about things that could sabotage the client's gains (Hackney & Cormier, 2001).

Fifth, plan for follow-up, "the nature and amount of professional contact that occurs between the helper and client after termination has occurred" (Hackney & Cormier, 2001, p. 275). Good ethical practice recommends that helpers provide clients with a way to initiate a professional contact in the future. Sometimes a future session is even scheduled at termination. If the client has a great deal of anxiety aroused during the termination process, it may be useful to terminate gradually by spacing the time between the last few sessions (Cormier & Hackney, 1999). When, as the helper, you have to terminate due to your own circumstances such as moving out of town or ending a field placement, it is also imperative to provide the client with a referral to another helper, following the guidelines we discussed in Chapter 10 on the referral process. During any kind of termination, it is always important to remember that the ultimate "goal at termination is to empower the client" (Kirst-Ashman & Hull, 2002, p. 283). As you probably can see, termination affects the treatment planning process in important ways. If you have the possibility of working with the client over a longer period of time and this is consistent with the client's wishes, you and the client can select treatment interventions that take a longer time to use and also probably target different subgoals and deeper levels of change. However, if your time is more limited, perhaps because of client constraints or wishes, or agency or insurance constraints, it is important to select treatment approaches and target subgoals that can be used realistically within the shorter time frame. We illustrate the process of treatment planning with our client Joan in the following dialogue.

MODEL DIALOGUE: THE CASE OF JOAN

In this dialogue, the helper will explore and help Joan plan some of the treatment strategies they could use to work with the first subgoal on Joan's goal chart (Chapter 10) for Terminal Outcome Goal 1. This dialogue is a continuation of the ones described in Chapters 9 and 10. In this session, Joan and the helper will explore strategies that could help Joan decrease her nervousness about math class and anticipation of rejection from her parents. Note that all three strategies suggested are based on Joan's diagnostic pattern of specific (focal) anxiety, as opposed to generalized anxiety.

In the initial part of the interview, the helper will summarize the previous session and will introduce Joan to the idea of *exploring treatment strategies*.

1. **Helper:** Last week, Joan, we talked about some of the things you would like to see happen as a result of counseling. One of the things you indicated was pretty important to you was being able to do more initiating. You had mentioned things like wanting to be able to ask questions or make responses, express your opinions, and express your feelings. We had identified the fact that one thing that keeps you from doing these things more often is the apprehension you feel in certain situations with your parents or in math class. There are several ways we might deal with your apprehension. I thought today we might explore some of the procedures that may help. These procedures are things we can do together to help you get where you want to be. How does that sound?

Client: It's OK. So we'll find a way, maybe, that I could be less nervous and more comfortable at these times.

In the second response, the helper tries to explain to Joan what treatment planning involves and the importance of *Joan's input*.

2. **Helper:** Yes. One thing to keep in mind is that there are no easy answers and there is not necessarily one right way. What we can do today is explore some ways that are typically used to help people be less nervous in specific situations and try to come up with a way that *you* think is most workable for you. I'll be giving you some

information about these procedures for your input in this decision.

Client: OK.

In responses 3 and 4, the helper suggests possible strategies for Joan to consider. The helper also explains how one intervention strategy, relaxation, *is related to Joan's concerns and can help her achieve her goal.* Since Joan's level of resistance is low, note throughout this process the helper will be more directive and will offer guidance and suggestions.

3. **Helper:** From my experience, I believe that there are a couple of things that might help you manage your nervousness to the point where you don't feel as if you have to avoid the situation. First of all, when you're nervous, you're tense. Sometimes when you're tense, you feel bad or sick or just out of control. One thing we could do is to teach you some relaxation methods [see Chapter 16]. The relaxation can help you learn to identify when you're starting to feel nervous, and it can help you manage this before it gets so strong you just skip class or refuse to speak up. Does this make sense?

Client: Yes, because when I really let myself get nervous, I don't want to say anything. Sometimes I force myself to, but I'm still nervous, and I don't feel like it.

4. **Helper:** That's a good point. You don't have the energy or desire to do something you're apprehensive about. Sometimes, for some people, just learning to relax and control your nervousness might be enough. If you want to try this first and it helps you be less nervous to the point where you can be more initiating, then that's fine. However, there are some other things we might do also, so I'd like you to know about these action plans, too.

Client: Like what?

The helper proposes an additional intervention strategy in response 5 and indicates how this procedure can help Joan decrease her nervousness by *describing how it is also related to Joan's concern and goal.*

5. **Helper:** Well, one procedure has a very interesting name—it's called "stress inoculation" [see Chapter 15]. You know when you get a shot like a tetanus inoculation, the shot helps to prevent you from getting tetanus. Well, this procedure helps you to prevent yourself from getting so overwhelmed in a stressful situation, such as your math class or with your folks, that you want to avoid the situation or don't want to say anything.

Client: Is it painful like a shot?

The helper provides more information about what stress inoculation would involve from Joan in terms of the *time, advantages, and risks of the procedure;* this information should help Joan assess her preferences.

6. **Helper:** No, not like that, although it would involve some work on your part. In addition to learning the relaxation training I mentioned earlier, you would learn how to cope with stressful situations—through relaxing your body and thinking some thoughts that would help you handle these difficult or competitive situations. When you are able to do this successfully with me, you would start to do it in your math class and with your folks. Once you learned the relaxation, it would take several sessions to learn the other parts. The advantage of stress inoculation is that it helps you learn how to cope with rather than avoid a stressful situation. Of course, it does require you to practice the relaxation and the coping thoughts on your own, and this takes some time each day. Without this sort of daily practice, this procedure may not be that helpful.

Client: It does sound interesting. Have you used it a lot?

The helper indicates some *information and advantages* about the strategy based on the helper's *experience,* training, and use of it with others in this setting.

7. **Helper:** I believe I tend to use it, or portions of it, whenever I think people could benefit from learning to manage nervousness and not let stressful situations control them. I know other counselors have used it and found that people with different stresses can benefit from it. It has a lot of potential if you're in a situation where your nervousness is getting the best of you and where you can learn to cope with the stress. Another advantage of this procedure is that it is pretty comprehensive. By that, I mean it deals with different parts of a nervous reaction—like the part of you that gets sweaty palms and butterflies in your stomach, the part of you that thinks girls are dumb in math or girls don't have much to say, and then the part of you that goes out of your way to avoid these sticky situations. It's kind of like going shopping and getting a whole outfit—jeans, shirt, and shoes—rather than just the shoes or just the shirt.

Client: Well, it sounds OK to me. I also like the idea of the relaxation that you mentioned earlier.

The helper moves on in response 8 to describe another possible treatment strategy, explaining what this involves and how it might help Joan manage her nervousness, and *relates the use of the procedure to her concern and goal*.

8. **Helper:** There's also another procedure called "desensitization" that is a pretty standard one to help a person decrease anxiety about situations [see Chapter 17]. It is a way to help you desensitize yourself to the stress of your math class.

Client: How exactly does that work—to desensitize yourself to something?

The helper explains how this strategy can help Joan decrease her nervousness and explains *elements, advantages, and risks of this strategy*.

9. **Helper:** It works on the principle that you can't be relaxed and nervous at the same time. So, after teaching you how to relax, then you imagine situations involving your math class—or with your folks. However, you imagine a situation only when you're relaxed. You practice this way to the point where you can speak up in class or with your folks without feeling all the nervousness you do now. In other words, you become desensitized. Most of this process is something we would do together in these sessions and is an advantage over something requiring a lot of outside work on your part.

Client: Does that take a long time?

The helper gives Joan some information about the *time* or *duration* involved.

10. **Helper:** This may take a little longer than the other two procedures. This procedure has helped a great many people decrease their nervousness about specific situations—like taking a test or flying. Of course, keep in mind that any change plan takes some time.

Client: It sounds helpful.

The helper points out more of the *time factors* and the *mode (individual)* involved in these procedures.

11. **Helper:** We would be working together in these individual sessions for several months.

Client: That's OK. I have study hall during this period, and I usually just talk to my friends then anyway.

In response 12, the helper indicates *his or her preferences* and provides information about *documentation*.

12. **Helper:** I'd like us to make the decision together. I feel comfortable with all of these things I've mentioned. Also, all three of these procedures have been found to be pretty effective in dealing with many people who are concerned about working on their nervousness in situations so that it isn't a handicap. In fact, for some of these procedures there are even guidelines I can give you so you can practice on your own.

Client: I'm wondering exactly how to decide where to go from here.

In response 13, the helper elicits information about *client preferences*.

13. **Helper:** Perhaps if we reviewed the action plans I've mentioned and go over them, you can see which one you feel might work best for you, at least for now. We can always change something at a later point. How does that sound?

Client: Good. There's a lot of information, and I don't know if I remember everything you mentioned.

In response 14, the helper summarizes the possible change strategies; note that *these are directed toward Joan's predominant coping style (internalizing)*.

14. **Helper:** OK. We talked first about relaxation as something you could learn here and then do on your own to help you control the feelings and physical sensations of nervousness. Then we discussed stress inoculation, which involves giving you a lot of different skills to use to cope with the stressful situations in your math class. The third plan, desensitization, involves using relaxation first but also involves having you imagine the scenes related to your math class and to interactions with your parents. This procedure is something we would work on together, although the relaxation requires daily practice from you. What do you think would be most helpful to you at this point?

Client: I think maybe the relaxation might help, since I can practice with it on my own. It also sounds like the simplest to do, not so much in time but just in what is involved.

In the last response, the helper pursues the option that Joan has been leaning toward during the session, thus building on *client preferences*. Since Joan's level of impairment is low, the helper will suggest *weekly sessions*.

15. **Helper:** That's a good point. Of the three procedures I mentioned, relaxation training is probably the easiest

and simplest to learn to use. You have also mentioned once or twice before in our session that you were intrigued with this idea, so it looks as if you've been mulling it over for a little while and it still sounds appealing and workable to you. If so, we can start working with it today. Then I would like to see you once every week during this time if that is possible for you.

SUMMARY AND INTRODUCTION TO THE TREATMENT CHANGE STRATEGY CHAPTERS

Most clients will present complex problems with a diverse set of outcome goals. Addressing these will require a set of interventions and combinations of strategies designed to work with all the major target areas of a person's functioning. Both helper and client should be active participants in developing a treatment plan and selecting treatment strategies that are appropriate for the client's concerns and desired outcomes. The strategies reflected by the overall treatment plan should be relevant to the client's gender and culture, sufficient to deal with all the important target areas of change, and matched, as well as possible, to the response components of the defined issue as well as to the client's level of impairment, resistance, and coping style. After the strategies have been selected, the helper and client will continue to work together to implement the procedures, to evaluate the results, and to work toward a planned termination process once the client's goals are achieved.

In the following chapters (12–18), we describe a number of treatment strategies that are primarily (though not exclusively) cognitive–behavioral. We do so because we agree with Beutler and Clarkin (1990) that initial treatment choice is usually symptom focused rather than conflict focused and also because many of these strategies are evidence based. However, we would be remiss if we did not point out that cognitive–behavior therapy has only recently begun to address issues of complex cultural and gender influences and the identities of clients served by these strategies. In the following chapters, we include a section on the use of the change strategy with diverse populations. However, Hays (1995) concluded that this list is quite small because of a "dearth of cognitive–behavior therapy research with minority groups" (p. 313). Lum (2000) has also concluded that until recently, culturally diverse social work practice has also been too sparse.

The questions addressed by Brown (1994) about treatment planning for clients who fall outside the mainstream have also been raised in critiques about the multicultural application of cognitive–behavioral strategies. Kantrowitz and Ballou (1992) note that there is nothing *inherent* in cognitive–behavioral therapy approaches that enhances sensitivity to gender, role, and class issues. In a similar vein, Hays (1995) has noted that "cognitive–behavior therapy does not exclude the consideration of socio-cultural influences, but because it has not been explicit about the impact of racism and other forms of oppression in clients, these forces are easily overlooked, particularly by therapists of dominant cultural groups" (p. 311). As an example of this, there is often a lack of attention to cultural differences, including aspects of oppression and aspects of strengths in a cognitive–behavioral assessment. We have attempted to incorporate this in the model we present in Chapters 8 and 9, and we exhort each of you to make explicit attempts to consider such factors in all phases of the helping process—from the working alliance, to assessment, to selecting and evaluating goals, to planning, implementing, and evaluating treatment strategies, and to ethical and effective termination.

Still, cognitive–behavioral approaches have potential strengths for use with culturally diverse clients (Hays, 1995). These include the emphasis on the uniqueness of the individual and the adaptation of the helping process to meet this uniqueness, a focus on client empowerment, commitment to helper–client collaboration, use of direct and pragmatic treatment focus, and emphasis on conscious (versus unconscious) processes and specific (versus abstract) behaviors and treatment protocols (Hays, 1995; Kantrowitz & Ballou, 1992). In conclusion, recent changes in the delivery of health care and mental health services have posed a number of challenges to practitioners, who are now faced with often having to justify their treatment plans to nonpractitioners for insurance reimbursement. As Cushman and Gilford (2000, p. 994) point out, current therapeutic practices valued by insurance companies seem to be mirroring life itself, which has become "faster and shallower," where "action is preferable to critical reflection, parsimony better than generosity, superficiality valued over complexity, image preferable to substance, and solutions prized above questions." In your own model of treatment planning, we urge you to continue asking the questions!

INFOTRAC® EXPLORATIONS

1. Search for *evidence-based medicine*. See what articles you can find that discuss the general advantages and disadvantages of *any* evidence-based practice. Share your results with your colleagues or classmates.

2. Search for *internalizing and externalizing,* and see what you can find that may affect treatment selection with child and adolescent clients.

SUGGESTED RESOURCES

Readings

Beutler, L., Clarkin, J., & Bongar, B. (2000). *Guidelines for the systematic treatment of the depressed patient.* New York: Oxford University Press.

Beutler, L., & Harwood, T. (2000). *Prescriptive psychotherapy: A practical guide to systematic treatment selection.* New York: Oxford University Press.

Brown, L. (2000). Feminist therapy. In C. Snyder & R. Ingram (Eds.), *Handbook of psychological change* (pp. 358–379). New York: Wiley.

Courtois, C. (1999). *Recollections of sexual abuse: Treatment principles and guidelines.* New York: Norton.

Cushman, P., & Gilford, P. (2000). Will managed care change our way of being? *American Psychologist, 55,* 985–996.

Dunbar, E. (2001). Counseling practices to ameliorate the effects of discrimination and hate events: Toward a systematic approach to assessment and intervention. *The Counseling Psychologist, 29,* 276–307.

Foa, E., Keane, T., and Friedman, M. (Eds.). (2000). *Effective treatments for PTSD.* New York: Guilford.

Gambrill, E. (1999). Evidence based practice: An alternative to authority based practice. *Families in Society, 80,* 342–350.

Geyman, J. P., Deyo, R. A., & Ramsey, S. D. (2000). *Evidence-based clinical practice: Concepts and approaches.* Boston: Butterworths/Heinemann.

Gibbs, L. (in press). *Evidence-based practice for social workers.* Pacific Grove, CA: Brooks/Cole.

Gomory, T. (1999). Programs of assertive community treatment (PACT): A critical review. *Ethical Human Sciences and Services, 1,* 147–163.

Hackney, H., & Cormier, S. (2001). *The professional counselor* (4th ed.). Needham Heights, MA: Allyn & Bacon.

Ingram, R., Hayes, A., & Scott, W. (2000). Empirically supported treatments: A critical analysis. In C. Snyder & R. Ingram (Eds.), *Handbook of psychological change* (pp. 40–60). New York: Wiley.

Kendall, P., & Chambless, D. (Eds.). (1998). Empirically supported psychological therapies (special issue). *Journal of Consulting & Clinical Psychology, 66,* (1).

Kirst-Ashman, K., and Hull, G. (2002). *Understanding generalist practice* (3rd ed.). Pacific Grove, CA: Brooks/Cole/Wadsworth Group.

Lum, D. (2000). *Social work practice and people of color* (4th ed.). Belmont, CA: Wadsworth.

Nathan, P. (1998). Practice guidelines: Not yet ideal. *American Psychologist, 53,* 250–299.

Quintana, S. and Atkinson, D.R. (2002). A multicultural perspective on principles of empirically supported interventions. *The Counseling Psychologist, 30,* 281–290.

Santiago-Rivera, A. (1995). Developing a culturally sensitive treatment modality for Spanish-speaking clients. *Journal of Counseling & Development, 74,* 12–17.

Seligman, L. (1998). *Selecting effective treatments.* San Francisco: Jossey-Bass.

Sue, D. W., & Sue, D. (1999). *Counseling the culturally different* (3rd ed.). New York: Wiley.

Waehler, C., Kalodner, C., Wampold, B., & Lichtenberg, J. (2000). Empirically supported treatments (ESTS) in perspective. *The Counseling Psychologist, 28,* 657–671.

Wampold, B. (2000). Outcomes of individual counseling and psychotherapy: Empirical evidence addressing two fundamental questions. In S. D. Brown & R. W. Lent (Eds.), *Handbook of Counseling Psychology* (pp. 711–739). New York: Wiley.

Wampold, B., Lichtenberg, J., & Waehler, C. (2002). Principles of empirically supported interventions in counseling psychology. *The Counseling Psychologist, 30,* 197–217.

Note: Also consider those sources listed in Box 11.1.

Web Sites

APA Division 12 committee report on evidence based treatments
http://www.apa.org/divisions/div12/est

Center for Evidence-Based Social Services
S.E.Bosley@exeter.ac.uk

CenterWatch Clinical Trials Listing Service
http://www.centerwatch.com

Internet Mental Health
http://www.mentalhealth.com

Manuals for Empirically Supported Treatment: 1998 Update
http://www.apa.org/divisions/div12/est/manual60.html

Mental Health Policy Information Exchange
http://www.pie.org

National Center for PTSD Treatment
http://www.ncptsd.org

The Center for Patient Advocacy
http://www.patientadvocacy.org

The Child Survivor of Traumatic Stress
http://users.umassmed.edu/Kenneth.Fletcher/kidsurv.html

What happens after the trauma
http://www.wright.edu/~scott.williams/forum/trauma.htm

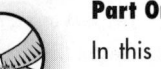

11 POST EVALUATION

Part One

In this section, we describe the case and treatment plan of David Chan (Sue & Sue, 1990, p. 259). After you read the case, identify (1) ways in which the selected treatment interventions used by the helper conflicted with the client's cultural values and world view, and (2) the recommended type, duration, and mode of treatment you would follow as David's helper (Chapter Objective One). Feedback follows.

David Chan is a 21-year-old student majoring in electrical engineering. He first sought counseling because he was having increasing study problems and was receiving failing grades. These academic difficulties became apparent during the first quarter of his senior year and were accompanied by headaches, indigestion, and insomnia. Since he had been an excellent student in the past, David felt that his lowered academic performance was caused by illness. However, a medical examination failed to reveal any organic disorder.

During the initial interview, David seemed depressed and anxious. He responded to inquiries with short, polite statements and would seldom volunteer information about himself. He avoided any statements that involved feelings and presented his problem as strictly an education one. Although he never expressed it directly, David seemed to doubt the value of counseling and needed much reassurance and feedback about his performance in the interview.

After several sessions, the helper was able to discern one of David's major concerns. David did not like engineering and felt pressured by his parents to go into this field. Yet he was afraid to take responsibility for changing this decision without their approval; felt dependent on his parents, especially for bringing honor to them; and was afraid to express the anger he felt toward them. Using the Gestalt "empty chair" technique, the helper had David pretend that his parents were seated in empty chairs opposite him. The helper encouraged him to express his true feelings toward them. Initially, David found this very difficult to do, but he was able to ventilate some of his true feelings under constant encouragement by the helper. Unfortunately, the following sessions with David proved unproductive in that he seemed more withdrawn and guilt-ridden than ever.

Questions

1. How did the treatment intervention used by this helper (Gestalt empty chair) conflict with this client's traditional Asian culture values and world view?

2. If you were David's helper, what type, duration, and mode of treatment would you use? Provide information to support your choices.

Part Two

Chapter Objective Two asks you to develop in writing a treatment plan for a given client case using the Sample Treatment Planning Form (Figure 11.3), specifying the type, duration, and mode of treatment. If you currently have a client caseload of your own, we suggest you do this for one of your actual clients and consult with your supervisor, a colleague, or your instructor after you and your client have completed the treatment planning form. If you are a student and do not yet have clients, we suggest you use the case of Joan described in Chapter 8. Complete Part A, "Assessment," based on the model dialogue information in Chapter 9. Complete Part B, "Treatment Planning," based on the model dialogue information in Chapter 10 and in this chapter. Do Part B for Joan's first problem and goal listed on her goal chart in Chapter 10 on p. 296 so that you have a description for #1 only of the problem, goal, measurable outcome, and selected intervention on 2–B of the treatment planning form. Feedback for the case of Joan follows.

POST EVALUATION FEEDBACK

PART ONE

1. The helper used a Gestalt empty chair treatment intervention. This intervention, which encouraged David to express feelings toward his parents, clashes with the traditional Asian value of respecting your elders (parents) and refraining from arguing with them even when you don't agree with their views.

2. As David's helper, it is important first to clarify *David's* expectations for the helping process because they may be different from your own. It is also important to select a type of treatment that honors and respects David's traditional Asian cultural values—restraint of feelings, restraint of open discussion of problems with a stranger, and collective/family responsibility. Interventions that focus on behaviors and cognitions rather than feelings are going to be more consistent with David's cultural beliefs. However, interventions that require individual self-assertion and expression of feelings are not useful because these clash with his world view. It is also important to honor and validate the bicultural conflict that David is experiencing between obeying his parents' wishes for an engineering career and his own values and preferences. Because of this focus, the *duration* of treatment is likely to be short term. Due to the nature of the conflict and also the Asian value of belonging to a family, family consultation as a *mode* of treatment rather than individual counseling may be helpful. However, in working with David and his parents, it would be important not to force self-disclosure, to respect the family's hierarchy, and to try to arrive at a resolution that is mutually acceptable to all parties.

PART TWO

If you used the case of Joan, check your responses with the ones on the form on page 345.

MENTAL HEALTH NETWORK: OUTPATIENT TREATMENT REPORT (OTR)   Provider: _____

Name: _Joan_ Birthdate: ____ Age: _16_ Sex: M (F)

A. ASSESSMENT

1. **Presenting Problem (Client's Perspective):** _Unhappy with school, especially math. Feels anxious about "competition." She withdraws socially. Dropping grades. Cuts class. Feels pressure from parents about grades and college. Feels afraid to speak up. Describes herself as indecisive._

2. **Precipitating Event(s) (Why Help-seeking Now?):** _She is doing poorly in school, especially math and is getting "flak" from parents._

3. **Relevant Medical History (Medications, Drug/ETOH use, Illness, Injury, Surgery, etc.):** _None—no medication, illness, surgery, etc. No report of drug use, no prescription meds._

4. **Prior Psychiatric/Psychological Conditions & Treatments:** _None_

5. **Other Relevant History (Vocational/School, Relationship/Sexual, Social/Legal):** _School homework ok until this year. An only child. Parents have made decisions for her. She has a number of good friends._

6. **Brief Mental Status Evaluation: (Check as necessary)**

APPEARANCE/DRESS	INTELLIGENCE	JUDGMENT/INSIGHT	DELUS./HALLUCIN.	THOUGHT DISORDER	RECENT MEMORY	REMOTE MEMORY
X appropriate	X high	X intact	__ absent	__ absent	__ intact	__ intact
__ inappropriate	__ average	__ impaired	__ present	__ present	__ impaired	__ impaired
__ not assessed	__ low	__ not assessed	X not assessed	X not assessed	X not assessed	X not assessed

7. **Mood/Affect: (Describe)** _Anxious, somewhat reticent to speak up_

8. **Suicide Assessment:** (Risk, priors, plan) _____ **Homicide Assessment:** (Victim, violence, plan) _____

9. **Clinical Formulation** (Explanation of symptoms; include strengths/resources, obstacles to treatment/hidden agendas): Please be specific yet brief and clear ___
   Recent problems in school appear to provide her with a way to be more assertive with parents and to resolve "crisis" with them in terms of her own identity and autonomy.

10. **Code (Nos. & Names) DSM-IV Axis II:** _V71.09_   **Diagnostic Impressions:** DSM-IV Axis I: _V62.3 313.82_

B. TREATMENT PLAN:

1. **Focused, Targeted, Behavior & Measurable GOALS (Prioritize) Specifically Addressing Presenting Problems(s):** Use as many rows as needed.

2. **TYPE OF TREATMENT:** (Cognitive/Behavioral) Interpersonal/Insight/Emotional Awareness Other: _____

3. **DURATION:** Service dates this OTR: _Feb. 21, 2002_ # Sessions expected for DISCHARGE: _13 sessions_ Discharge by (DATE): _June 8, 2002_

4. **MODE:** (Individual (90806)) Couple Family Individual/Family combination Medication management Group (if available) Other (___)
       (90847)   (90862)   (90853)   CPT Code___

PROBLEM(S)	GOALS	MEASURABLE SUCCESS CRITERION	SELECTED INTERVENTIONS
1. _anxiety over self assertion_	_Use of four initiating skills at least four times a week_	_A plus one or above rating on a 5-point goal attainment scale._	_Relaxation_
2. _____	_____	_Reduction of anxiety from 70 to 50 on a 100 pt. SUDS scale._	_Stress inoculation_
3. _____	_____		_Systematic desensitizaton_

Therapist Signature & Phone: _____   Lic.No.: _____   Date: _____

Client Comments: _____

Source: Adapted from the Treatment Planning Form, by Mental Health Network, Inc., 771 Corporate Drive, Suite 410, Lexington, KY. Reprinted by permission.

CHAPTER 12

IMAGERY AND MODELING STRATEGIES

OBJECTIVES

After completing this chapter, the student should be able to

1. Develop and try out a script for a modeling intervention with a role play or actual client. After completing the script, evaluate it on the Checklist for Developing Model Scripts at the end of the chapter.
2. Describe how you would apply the four components of participant modeling in a simulated client case.
3. Demonstrate at least 14 out of 17 steps associated with participant modeling in a role play.
4. Given seven examples of helper leads, identify which of the five steps of the guided imagery procedure are presented in each helper lead. You should be able to identify accurately at least six out of seven examples.
5. Demonstrate 10 out of 13 steps of guided imagery in a role play, using the Interview Checklist for Guided Imagery at the end of the chapter to assess your performance.
6. Describe how you would apply the five components of covert modeling, given a simulated client case.
7. Demonstrate at least 22 out of 28 steps associated with covert modeling in a role play, using the Interview Checklist for Covert Modeling at the end of the chapter to assess your use of this strategy.

Picture the following series of events. A young girl is asked what she wants to be when she grows up. Her reply: "A doctor, just like my mom." Think of a child who points a toy gun and says "Bang, bang, you're dead" after watching gunfire in an action program. Think of people flocking to stores to buy clothes that reflect the "outdoor," "sophisticated hipster," or "sleek spandex" look featured in some magazines. Imagine a television news program showing pictures of teenagers breaking glass doors and windows of stores, and entering and stealing whatever they can carry in 30 seconds or less. Several days later, after the story is shown on television, there is an increase in the number of teenager robberies similar to the ones reported on the news. Consider a person reporting dysfunctional patterns of behaving similar to his or her own that were displayed by a parent when he or she was a child. All these events are examples of a process called imitation, copying, mimicry, vicarious learning, identification, observational learning, or modeling. Rosenthal and Steffek (1991, p. 70) define modeling as "the processes by which information guides an observer (often without messages conveyed through language), so that conduct is narrowed from 'random' trial-and-error toward an intended response. By intended response, we mean that much of the practice takes place covertly, through information-processing, decision-making, and evaluative events *in advance* of visible or audible overt performance."

There are several ways people can learn through modeling. A person can acquire new behaviors from live or symbolic modeling. Modeling can help a person perform an already acquired behavior in more appropriate ways or at more desirable times. Modeling can also extinguish client fears. Modeling procedures have been used to help clients acquire parent and caregiver behaviors, change misbehavior, reduce fears, reduce anxiety disorders, decrease stress, reduce weight and smoking, and change their perspective about themselves. Modeling strategies have also been used in preventive and behavioral medicine (Rosenthal & Steffek, 1991).

Matson (1985) differentiates modeling, imitation, and observational learning. Modeling encompasses the other two. Imitation is observing and then displaying a series of behaviors or responses. Observational learning occurs by observing others but not necessarily imitating the behaviors exactly (Matson, 1985, p. 150). Modeling is a process of observing an individual or group (observation learning) and imitating similar behaviors. The model acts as a stimulus for thoughts, beliefs, feelings, and actions of the observer.

> **BOX 12.1 PARTICIPANT MODELING RESEARCH**
>
> *AIDS prevention*
> Maibach, E., & Flora, J. A. (1993). Symbolic modeling and cognitive rehearsal: Using video to promote AIDS prevention self-efficacy. Special issue: The role of communication in health promotion. *Communication Research, 20,* 517–545.
>
> *Anger and aggression*
> Larson, J. D. (1992). Anger and aggression management techniques through the Think First curriculum. *Journal of Offender Rehabilitation, 18,* 101–117.
>
> *Anxiety*
> Hughes, D. (1990). Participant modeling as a classroom activity. *Teaching of Psychology, 17,* 238–240.
>
> *Fear*
> Samson, D., & Rachman, S. (1989). The effect of induced mood on fear reduction. *British Journal of Clinical Psychology, 28,* 227–238.
>
> *Gender stereotyping modification*
> Katz, P. A., & Walsh, P. V. (1991). Modification of children's gender-stereotyped behavior. *Child Development, 62,* 338–351.
>
> *Participation*
> Hartley, E. T., Bray, M. A., & Kehle, T. J. (1998). Self-modeling as an intervention to increase student classroom participation. *Psychology in the Schools, 35,* 363–372.
>
> *Peer counseling training*
> Romi, S., & Teichman, M. (1995). Participant and symbolic modelling training programmes. *British Journal of Guidance and Counselling, 23,* 83–94.
>
> *Phobias*
> Ritchie, E. C. (1992). Treatment of gas mask phobia. *Military Medicine, 157,* 104–106.
> Sanders, M. R., & Jones, L. (1990). Behavioural treatment of injection, dental, and medical phobias in adolescents: A case study. *Behavioral Psychotherapy, 18,* 311–316.
>
> *Self-injections*
> Erasmus, U. (1992). Behavioral treatment of needle phobia. *Tijdschrift voor Psychotherapie, 18,* 335–347.
>
> *Self-efficacy*
> Newman, E. J., & Tuckman, B. W. (1997). The effects of participant modeling on self-efficacy, incentive, productivity, and performance. *Journal of Research & Development in Education, 31,* 38–45.
>
> *Sexual abuse of children*
> Wurtele, S. K., Marrs, S. R., & Miller-Perrin, C. L. (1987). Practice makes perfect? The role of participant modeling in sexual abuse prevention programs. *Journal of Consulting and Clinical Psychology, 55,* 599–602.
>
> *Stress*
> Romi, S., & Teichman, M. (1998). Participant modelling training programme: Tutoring the paraprofessional. *British Journal of Guidance & Counseling, 26*(2), 297–301.
>
> *Stuttering*
> Bhargava, S. C. (1988). Participant modeling in stuttering. *Indian Journal of Psychiatry, 30,* 91–93.
>
> *Surgery*
> Faust, J., Olson, R., & Rodriguez, H. (1991). Same-day surgery preparation: Reduction of pediatric patient arousal and distress through participating modeling. *Journal of Consulting and Clinical Psychology, 59,* 475–478.
>
> *Verbally aggressive behavior*
> Vaccaro, F. J. (1990). Application of social skills training in a group of institutionalized aggressive elderly subjects. *Psychology and Aging, 5,* 369–378.
>
> *Women's self-defense skills*
> Ozer, E. M., & Bandura, A. (1990). Mechanisms governing empowerment effects: A self-efficacy analysis. *Journal of Personality and Social Psychology, 58,* 472–486.

Rosenthal and Steffek (1991) advise that "it is not enough to acquire the skills to earn desired outcomes. People must also gain enough self-efficacy (confidence) that they can perform the needed acts despite stresses, dangers, moments of doubts, and can persevere in the face of setbacks" (p. 75). (Refer to Chapter 18 for a discussion of the importance of self-efficacy for implementing any treatment strategy.) Rosenthal and Steffek (1991) also emphasize the importance of restructuring vulnerable thoughts with positive coping statements (see Chapter 14) and other cognitive aids to support the perseverance of the desired behavior. Higher self-efficacy is achieved by enhancing confidence for each component of the series or graduated hierarchy of behaviors to be acquired. Also, self-efficacy enhancement serves as an inducement and a support for prompting behavioral changes.

We present participant modeling, imagery, and covert modeling in this chapter. Box 12.1 is a sample of the recent research on symbolic and participant modeling. With some client concerns, a helper may find that it is impossible or unrealistic to provide live or symbolic (e.g., media depiction) models or to have the client engage in overt practice of the goal behaviors. In symbolic modeling, the model is derived from media formats, such as stories, cartoons, films, advertisements, and information technology. In these cases, it may be more practical to employ strategies that use the client's imagination for the modeling or rehearsal. This chapter describes two therapeutic procedures that make good use of client imagery: guided imagery and covert modeling. In both these strategies, scenes are developed that the client visualizes or rehearses by imagination. Initially, some people have trouble generating strong, vivid images or have reservations about doing so. We have found that most clients have the capacity to evoke vivid images and that with help from the helper they can elicit their visualization potential, but comfort and appropriateness must be assessed.

Often people use the terms *emotive imagery, visualization,* and *guided imagery* interchangeably. The tenth edition (1993) of Merriam-Webster's Collegiate Dictionary defines visualization as the "formation of mental images; the act or process of interpreting in visual terms or of putting into visible form" (p. 1321). Visualization of mental images or pictures can be spontaneous or guided. Visualizations or mental simulations that have emotive, emotional, or mental connections are increasingly being found fruitful in self-change and the ability to self-regulate (Taylor, Pham, Rivkin, & Armor, 1998). Building upon visualization (e.g., of a change in oneself or in one's circumstances), cognitive modeling (Chapter 13) provides a narrative of the task (e.g., talking a client through the steps necessary to make the change), which can then be followed by self-instructional training in which the client talks (aloud or mentally) herself or himself through the steps.

Collectively, these strategies have an extremely broad applicability and have achieved empirical support with a range of social problems and populations. Used appropriately, they can be important tools for collaborative, empowerment-oriented practice—for example, toward envisioning changed possibilities, gaining skills and insights for how to achieve desired change, and gaining independence from the practitioner in one's ability to undertake such imaging, rehearsal, and self-instruction alone or with supportive others in a client's social network.

PARTICIPANT MODELING

Participant modeling consists of modeled demonstration, guided practice, and successful experiences (Bandura, 1977, 1986). Participant modeling assumes that a person's successful performance is an effective means of producing change. By successfully performing a formerly difficult or fearful response, a person can achieve potentially enduring changes in behavior. Participant modeling has been used to reduce avoidance behavior and the person's associated feelings about fearful activities or situations. For example, imagine an outside house painter who develops acrophobia. Participant modeling could be used to help the painter gradually climb "scary" heights by dealing directly with the anxiety associated with being in high places. In participant modeling with phobic clients, successful performance in fearful activities or situations helps the person learn to cope with the feared situation.

Another application of participant modeling is with people who have behavioral deficits or who lack such skills as social communication, assertiveness, child management, or physical fitness. Some of these skills might be taught as preventive measures in schools or community agencies. For example, parents can be taught child-management skills by modeling and practicing effective ways of dealing with and communicating with their children.

There are four major components of participant modeling: rationale, modeling, guided participation, and successful experiences (homework). These components are essentially the same whether participant modeling is used to reduce fearful avoidance behavior or to increase some behavior or skill. As you can see from the Interview Checklist for Participant Modeling at the end of the chapter, each component includes several parts. For each component, we present a description, a hypothetical helper/client dialogue illustrating the implementation and use of the participant modeling strategy, and a learning activity.

Treatment Rationale

Here is an example of a rationale that the helper might give for participant modeling:

> This procedure has been used to help other people overcome fears or acquire new behaviors [rationale]. There are three primary things we will do. First, you will see some people demonstrating. Next, you will practice this with my assistance in the interview. Then we'll arrange for you to do this outside the interview in situations likely to be successful for you. This type of practice will help you perform what is now difficult for you to do [overview]. Are you willing to try this now [client's willingness]?

Modeling

The modeling component of participant modeling consists of five parts:

1. The goal behaviors, if complex, are divided into a series of subtasks or subskills.
2. The series of subskills is arranged in a hierarchy.
3. Models are selected.
4. Instructions are given to the client before the modeled demonstration.
5. The model demonstrates each successive subtask with as many repetitions as necessary.

Dividing the Goal Behaviors

Before you (the helper) or someone else models the behavior to be acquired by the client, determine whether the behavior should be divided. Complex patterns of behavior should be divided into subskills or tasks and arranged by small steps or by a graduated series of tasks in a hierarchy. Dividing patterns of behavior and arranging them in order of difficulty may ensure that the client can perform initial behaviors or tasks. This is a very important step in the participant modeling strategy because you want the client to experience success in performing what is modeled. Start with a response or a behavior that the client can perform.

For our house painter who fears heights, the target behavior might be engaging in house painting at a height of 30 feet off the ground. This response could be divided into subtasks of painting at varying heights. Each task might be elevated by several feet at a time.

Arranging the Subskills or Tasks in a Hierarchy

The practitioner and client then arrange the subskills or subtasks in a hierarchy. The first situation in the hierarchy is the least difficult or threatening; other skills or situations of greater complexity or threat follow. Usually, the first behavior or response in the hierarchy is worked with first. After each of the subtasks has been successfully practiced one at a time, the client can practice all the subskills or tasks. With a nonassertive client, the practitioner and client may decide that it would be most helpful to work on eye contact first, then speech errors, then response latency, and finally all these behaviors at once.

In phobic cases, the content and arrangement of each session can be a hierarchical list of feared activities or objects. First, work with the situation that poses the least threat or provokes the least fear for the client. For our acrophobic house painter, we would begin with a situation involving little height and gradually progress to painting at greater heights.

Selecting a Model

Before implementing the modeling component, an appropriate model should be selected. At times, it may be most efficient, if appropriate, to use the helper as the model. However, therapeutic gains may be greater when multiple models are used who are somewhat similar to the client. For example, phobia clinics have successfully employed participant modeling to extinguish phobias by using several formerly phobic clients as the multiple models. Learning Activity 12.1 provides an exercise with feedback in selecting or constructing a model.

Prior Instructions to the Client

Immediately before the modeled demonstration, the practitioner should instruct the client about what will be modeled in order to draw the client's attention to the model. The client should be told to note that the model (the person providing the modeling) will be engaging in certain responses without experiencing any adverse consequences. With a nonassertive client, this might be something like "Notice the way this person looks at you directly when refusing to type your paper." With the house painter, one might say "Look to see how the model moves about the scaffolding easily at a height of five feet."

Modeled Demonstrations

In participant modeling, a live model demonstrates one subskill at a time. Often, repeated demonstrations of the same response are necessary. Multiple demonstrations can be arranged by having a single model repeat the demonstration or by having several models demonstrate the same activity or response. For example, one model could show moving about on the scaffolding without falling several times, or several models could demonstrate this same activity. When it is feasible to use several models or ones carefully selected with specific clients in mind, you should do so. Multiple models lend variety to the way the activity is performed and believability to the idea that adverse consequences will not occur. With diversity in mind (e.g., sex, sexual orientation, disability status, race/ethnicity), multiple models or models similar to the client may be particularly important, depending on the nature of the concern and goal.

Guided Participation

After the demonstration of the behavior or activity, the client is given opportunities and the necessary guidance to perform the modeled behaviors. Guided participation or performance is one of the most important components of learning to cope, to reduce avoidance of fearful situations, and to acquire new behaviors. People must experience success in using what has been modeled. The client's participation in the helping session should be structured in a nonthreatening manner.

Guided participation consists of the following five steps (Bandura, 1976, p. 262):

1. Client practice of the response or activity with helper assistance
2. Helper feedback
3. Use of various induction aids for initial practice attempts
4. Fading of induction aids
5. Client self-directed practice

Each of these steps is described and illustrated.

Client Practice

After the model has demonstrated the activity or behavior, the client is asked to do what has been modeled. The helper has the client perform each activity or behavior in the hierarchy. The client performs each activity or behavior, starting with the first one in the hierarchy, until he or she can do this skillfully and confidently. It is quite possible that for an occasional client, there does not need to be a breakdown of the behaviors or activities. For these clients, guided practice of the entire ultimate goal behavior may be sufficient without a series of graduated tasks.

Our house painter would practice moving about on a ladder or scaffolding at a low height. Practices would continue at this height until the painter could move about easily and comfortably; then practices at the next height would ensue.

Practitioner Feedback

After each client practice attempt, the practitioner provides verbal feedback to the client about his or her performance. There are two parts to the feedback: (1) praise or encouragement for successful practice and (2) suggestions for correcting or modifying errors. With the house painter, the practitioner might say "You seem comfortable at this height. You were able to go up and down the ladder very easily. Even looking down didn't seem to bother you. That's really terrific."

Use of Induction Aids

Induction aids are aids arranged by the helper to assist a client in performing a feared or difficult response. Many people consider successful performance a good way to reduce anxiety. However, most people are just not going to participate in something they dread simply because they are told to do so. For instance, can you think of something you really fear, such as holding a snake, riding in an airplane or a boat, formal public speaking, or getting in a car after a severe accident? If so, you probably realize you would be very reluctant to engage in this activity just because at this moment you read the words *do it*. However, suppose that we were to be there and hold the snake first, then hold the snake while you touch it, then hold its head and tail while you hold the middle, then hold its head while you hold the tail, and so on. You might be more willing to do this or something else you fear under conditions that incorporate some induction aids.

To help our acrophobic painter reduce fear of heights, an initial induction aid might be joint practice. If actual practice with a ladder or scaffold is possible, nothing may be more supportive than having the model up on the scaffold with the painter or standing directly behind or in front of the painter on a ladder. This also functions as a type of protective aid. Of course, this scenario requires a model who is not afraid of heights. In the experience of one couple, the one who is nonacrophobic induces the other to climb lighthouses, landmarks, hills, and other such "scenic views" by going first and extending a hand. This type of induction aid enables both of them to enjoy the experience together. As a result, the fears of one person have never interfered with the pleasures of the other, because continued practice efforts with some support have reduced the fear level substantially.

Induction aids can be used in the counseling session, but they should also be applied in settings that closely approximate the natural setting. If at all possible, the helper or a model should accompany the client into the "field," where the client can witness further demonstrations and can participate in the desired settings. For example, teaching assertive behavior to a client in the interview must be supplemented with modeling and guided participation in the natural setting in which the final goal behavior is to occur. It is doubtful that a helper would be equipped with scaffolds so that our acrophobic house painter could practice the modeled activities at different heights. The helper could use covert rehearsal instead of overt practice. Our point is that the helper who uses live participant modeling procedures must be prepared to provide supports that help the client practice as closely as possible the desired goal behavior. If this cannot be done, the next best alternative is to simulate those activities as closely as possible in the client's real situation.

Fading of Induction Aids

Induction aids can be withdrawn gradually. With a nonassertive client, the initial use of four induction aids might be gradually reduced to three, two, and one. Or, with the painter, a very supportive aid, such as joint practice, could be replaced by a less supportive aid, such as verbal coaching. The gradual withdrawal of induction aids bridges the gap between helper-assisted and client-directed practice.

Client Self-Directed Practice

At some point, the client should be able to perform the desired activities or responses without any induction aids or assistance. A period of client self-directed practice may reinforce changes in the client's beliefs and self-evaluation and may lead to improved behavioral functioning. Therefore, the helper should arrange for the client to engage in successful performance of the desired responses independently unassisted. Ideally, client self-directed practice would occur both within the interview and in the client's natural setting.

For example, the house painter would practice moving on the ladder or scaffold alone. Client self-directed practice is likely to be superior to practitioner-directed practice.

In addition to application of the participant modeling procedures in the counseling sessions, aiding the transfer of behavior from the training session to the natural environment should be an integral part of counseling. Generalization of desired changes can be achieved by success or by reinforcing experiences that occur as part of a transfer-of-training program.

Success, or Reinforcing, Experiences

The last component of the participant modeling procedure is success (reinforcing) experiences. Clients must experience success in using what they are learning. Further, as Bandura points out, psychological changes "are unlikely to endure unless they prove effective when put into practice in everyday life" (1976, p. 248). Success experiences are arranged by tailoring a transfer-of-training program for each client. In an adequate transfer-of-training program, the client's new skills are used first in low-risk situations in the client's natural environment or in any situation in which the client will probably experience success or favorable outcomes. Gradually, the client extends the application of the skills to natural situations that are more unpredictable and involve a greater threat.

To summarize, success experiences are arranged through a program that transfers skill acquisition from the interview to the natural setting. This transfer-of-training program involves the following steps:

1. The practitioner and client identify situations in the client's environment in which the client desires to perform the target responses.
2. These situations are arranged in a hierarchy, starting with easy, safe situations in which the client is likely to be successful and ending with more unpredictable and risky situations.
3. The practitioner accompanies the client into the environment and works with each situation on the list by modeling and guided participation. Gradually, the practitioner's level of participation is decreased.
4. The client is given a series of tasks to perform in a self-directed manner.

Bandura (1976) concludes that participant modeling achieves results, given adequate demonstration, guided practice, and positive experiences. One advantage of participant modeling is that "a broad range of resource persons," such as peers or former clients, can serve as therapeutic models (p. 249). Bandura also points out that participant modeling helps clients to learn new responses under "lifelike conditions."

As a result, the problems of transfer of learning from the interview to the client's real-life environment are minimized.

MULTICULTURAL APPLICATIONS OF MODELING

The primary areas in which we have seen applications of modeling with diverse populations have been substance use and prevention and parenting/family/child behavior issues (see Box 12.2). Testing a longitudinal model of smoking initiation and maintenance of 233 black seventh-grade students, Botvin, Baker, Botvin, and Dusenbury (1993) found that social modeling—in the form of friends' smoking—was the most important early factor in the smoking *initiation* process, although perceived smoking norms and intrapersonal factors were more important in smoking *maintenance.*

Modeling is also a strong predictor in beginning the use of smokeless tobacco among three groups of adolescent females and males: African Americans, Caucasians, and Native Americans (Riley et al., 1990, 1991). Mail (1995) has suggested that substance use prevention programs include modeling as a major component but that all prevention programs be culturally adapted.

The use of culturally sensitive helpers as models in both HIV/AIDS prevention and in group treatment for lesbian and gay males in chemical dependency recovery has also been noted by Rhodes and Humfleet (1993) and Picucci (1992), as well as in group work with African American men and family violence (Williams, 1994). Helpers who are culturally similar to clients are likely to be of greatest support and value. In a recent ethnographic study of poor African American, Caucasian, and Latina adolescent girls, Taylor, Gilligan, and Sullivan (1995) found that the most important connections with adults reported by these girls were with adults from cultural backgrounds that were similar to or the same as their own. Anderson and McMillion (1995) used similar models with African American women to increase their confidence and intentions to perform breast self-examinations.

Parental modeling is also an important factor in a variety of ways. In an excellent article, Hurd, Moore, and Rogers (1995) examined strengths among 53 African American parents. In describing the values and behaviors that they imparted to their children, a high frequency of positive role modeling emerged as a significant factor as well as parental involvement and support from other adults. Parental modeling has also emerged as a critical factor in the way African American children and adolescents with sickle cell disease cope with their illness (Kliewer & Lewis, 1995). Reyes,

> **BOX 12.2 MULTICULTURAL RESEARCH ON MODELING**
>
> *Altering smokeless tobacco use*
> Riley, W., Barenie, J., Mabe, P., & Myers, D. (1990). Smokeless tobacco use in adolescent females: Prevalence and psychosocial factors among racial/ethnic groups. *Journal of Behavioral Medicine, 13,* 207–220.
> Riley, W., Barenie, J., Mabe, P., & Myers, D. (1991). The role of race and ethnic status on the psychosocial correlates of smokeless tobacco use in adolescent males. *Journal of Adolescent Health, 12,* 15–21.
>
> *Anxiety reduction*
> Malgady, R., Rogler, T., & Costantino, G. (1990). Culturally sensitive psychotherapy for Puerto Rican children and adolescents: A program of treatment outcome research. *Journal of Consulting and Clinical Psychology, 58,* 704–712.
>
> *Breast self-examination*
> Anderson, R., & McMillion, P. (1995). Effects of similar and diversified modeling on African American women's efficacy expectations and intentions to perform breast self-examination. *Health Communication, 7,* 327–343.
>
> *Child safety*
> Alvarez, J., & Jason, L. (1993). The effectiveness of legislation, education, and loaners for child safety in automobiles. *Journal of Community Psychology, 21,* 280–284.
>
> *Family violence*
> Williams, O. (1994). Group work with African American men who batter: Toward more ethnically sensitive practice. *Journal of Comparative Family Studies, 25,* 91–103.
>
> *HIV/AIDS risk/chemical dependence*
> Picucci, M. (1992). Planning an experiential weekend workshop for lesbians and gay males in recovery. *Journal of Chemical Dependency Treatment, 5,* 119–139.
> Rhodes, F., & Humfleet, G. (1993). Using goal-oriented counseling and peer support to reduce HIV/AIDS risk among drug users not in treatment. *Drugs and Society, 7,* 185–204.
>
> *Pain*
> Neill, K. (1993). Ethnic pain styles in acute myocardial infarction. *Western Journal of Nursing Research, 15,* 531–543.
>
> *Parenting*
> Hurd, E., Moore, C., & Rogers, R. (1995). Quiet success: Parenting strengths among African Americans. *Families in Society, 76,* 434–443.
> Kliewer, W., & Lewis, H. (1995). Family influences on coping processes in children and adolescents with sickle cell disease. *Journal of Pediatric Psychology, 20,* 511–525.
> Middleton, M., & Cartledge, G. (1995). The effects of social skills instruction and parental involvement on the aggressive behavior of African American males. *Behavior Modification, 19,* 192–210.
> Reyes, M., Routh, D., Jean-Gilles, M., & Sanfilippo, M. (1991). Ethnic differences in parenting children in fearful situations. *Journal of Pediatric Psychology, 16,* 717–726.
>
> *Prosocial behavior in children*
> Reichelova, E., & Baranova, E. (1994). Training program for the development of prosocial behavior in children. *Psycholigia a Patopsychologia Dietata, 29,* 41–50.
>
> *Skill training in children*
> Dowrick, P., & Raeburn, J. (1995). Self-modeling: Rapid skill training for children with physical disabilities. *Journal of Developmental and Physical Disabilities, 7,* 25–37.
>
> *Substance use/substance prevention*
> Botvin, G., Baker, E., Botvin, E., & Dusenbury, L. (1993). Factors promoting cigarette smoking among black youth: A causal modeling approach. *Addictive Behaviors, 18,* 397–405.
> Mail, P. (1995). Early modeling of drinking behavior by Native American elementary school children playing drunk. *International Journal of the Addictions, 30,* 1187–1197.

Routh, Jean-Gilles, and Sanfilippo (1991) have noted several differences among various ethnic groups in the use of parental modeling and have urged practitioners to be alert to both historical and cultural trends when using modeling approaches with a diverse group of parents.

As a treatment/intervention strategy, modeling has been an important component of child safety educational programs for African American, Asian American, Caucasian, and Hispanic parents (Alvarez & Jason, 1993) and in prosocial behavior training for Slovak school-age children (Reichelova & Baranova, 1994). An excellent example of multicultural symbolic modeling with young Puerto Rican children involves the use of Puerto Rican *cuentos* (folk tales). The characters in these tales are used as therapeutic peer models depicting beliefs, values, and target behaviors that children can first attend to and then identify with and imitate (Malgady, Rogler, & Costantino, 1990). For bicultural children, stories can be developed that bridge two or more different cultures, such as Puerto Rican and American. With Puerto Rican adolescents, biographical stories of heroic Puerto Ricans have been used to expose the teenagers to successful adult models in their own culture (Malgady et al., 1990).

Guidelines for Using Modeling with Diverse Groups of Clients

When you are developing a social modeling intervention for culturally diverse clients, consider the following guidelines:

1. Make sure that your live or symbolic (e.g., from television, movies, books, or computer games) model is cultur-

> **LEARNING ACTIVITY 12.1** — Modeling Selection
>
> Your client is a young, biracial woman whose mother is Filipino and whose father is Mexican. Both her parents are émigrés to the United States. Your client is the only child of these parents. She is applying for a job at a local child-care center and is interested in learning some child-care skills because she has never had siblings or baby-sitting experience.
>
> 1. Describe the type of model you would select, including age, gender, race, a coping or mastery model, and skills.
>
> 2. Develop an outline for a script you would use for the audiotaped model. Include in the script instructions to the client, a description of the model, a brief example of one modeled scenario, an example of a practice opportunity, feedback about the practice, and a summarization of the script. Feedback follows.

ally compatible with the client's background. For example, if you are developing a modeling program for African American youth with substance use issues, a model who is also African American, relatively young, and familiar with substance use issues will be more effective than an older, Caucasian model who knows little about or has had scant experience with substance use issues.

2. Make sure that the *content* of your modeled presentation is culturally relevant to the client and not simply a reflection of what may be your or your society's Eurocentric values. For example, the concept of social skills training is more relevant to many middle-class clients than to poorer clients and some clients of color. Similarly, a model of assertion training is more relevant to many Caucasian clients and less applicable to many Asian American clients. Modeling of boundary work is more relevant to some Caucasian clients and less relevant to some Native American clients.

3. Keep in mind the cultural differences in the way people attend to, learn from, and use modeling approaches. Determine whether your particular client or group of clients will find value in even having or seeing a model.

Malgady and colleagues (1990) found complex treatment effects when using culturally sensitive models with Puerto Rican children and adolescents. They noted that client process variables such as the client's cognitive responses and the client's familial context can affect treatment outcomes. (See Learning Activity 12.1)

MODEL DIALOGUE: PARTICIPANT MODELING

Here is an example of the use of participant modeling with our client Joan. The participant modeling will be used to help Joan perform the four behaviors in math class that she

> **FEEDBACK 12.1** — Modeling Selection
>
> Keep in mind that your client is both biracial and bicultural. You would want to select other young female models—ideally one who is Filipino, or at least Asian American, and one who is a Mexican or Latina (bearing in mind the value of client input to selection). In developing the script, consider that a mastery model may be too discouraging; initial modeling by coping models is preferred. The script and skills presented by the models would be similar to what your client wants to acquire—child-care skills. Using models who have already had some child-care experience would be useful.

typically avoids. The rationale for the helper responses is set off by the comments that precede the responses.

Session 1

In the first response, the helper will provide a *rationale* about the strategy and a brief *overview* of the procedure.

1. **Helper:** This procedure has been of help to other people who have trouble in classroom participation. We'll take each of the ways you would like to participate, and either I myself or maybe one of your classmates will show you a way to do this, then help you practice it. At first we'll just practice here. Then gradually you'll try this out in your other classes and, of course, finally in your math class. What do you think about this?

Client: It's OK with me. It's just something I know I can do but I don't because I'm a little nervous.

The helper will pick up on Joan's previous response and use it to provide an *additional rationale* for the participant modeling strategy.

2. **Helper:** And nervousness can keep you from doing something you want. This procedure helps you to learn to do something in small steps. As you accomplish each step, your confidence in yourself will increase and your nervousness will decrease.

Client: I think that will definitely help. Sometimes I just don't believe in myself.

In response 3, the helper ignores Joan's previous self-effacing comment. The helper instead begins with the *modeling component* by reviewing the ways that Joan wanted to increase selected initiating skills in math class.

3. **Helper:** You know, last week I believe we found some ways that you would like to increase your participation in math class. And I think we arranged these in an order, starting with the one that you thought was easiest for you now, to the one that was hardest for you. Can you recall these things and this order?

Client: Yes, I believe it was like this: answering questions, going to the board, volunteering answers, and then volunteering opinions or ideas.

The helper asks the client *whether additional activities* need to be added or *whether the hierarchy order* needs to be rearranged.

4. **Helper:** After thinking about it for a week, have you thought of any other ways you'd like to participate—or do you think this order needs to be rearranged at all?

Client: Well, one more thing—I would like to be able to work the problems on my own after I ask Mr. Lamborne for help. That's where I want to begin. He usually takes over and works the problems for me.

In response 5, the helper will explore a *potential model* for Joan and obtain Joan's input about this decision.

5. **Helper:** One thing we need to do now is to consider who might model and help you with these activities. I can do it, although if you can think of a classmate in math who participates the way you want to, this person could assist you when you try this out in your class. What do you think?

Client: Is it necessary to have someone in the class with me? If so, I think it would be less obvious if it were someone already in the class.

The helper picks up on Joan's discomfort about the helper's presence in her class and *suggests a classmate* as the model.

6. **Helper:** Well, there are ways to get around it, but it would be more helpful if someone could be there in your class, at least initially. I think you would feel more comfortable if this person were a classmate rather than me. If there is someone you could pick who already does a good job of participating, I'd like to talk to this person and have him or her help during our next sessions. So try to think of someone you like and respect and feel comfortable around.

Client: Well, there's Debbie. She's a friend of mine, and she hardly ever gets bothered by answering Mr. Lamborne's questions or going to the board. I could ask her. She'd probably like to do something like this. She works independently, too, on her math problems.

The helper provides *a rationale* for how Joan's friend will be used as the model so that Joan understands how her friend will be involved. Note that Joan's reaction to this is solicited. If Joan were uncomfortable with this, another option would be explored.

7. **Helper:** If you ask her and she agrees, ask her to drop by my office. If that doesn't work out, stop back and we'll think of something else. If Debbie wants to do this, I'll train her to help demonstrate the ways you'd like to participate. At our session next week, she can start modeling these things for you. How does that sound?

Client: OK. It might be kind of fun. I've helped her with her English themes before, so now maybe she can help with this.

The helper encourages the idea of these two friends' providing *mutual help* in the next response.

8. **Helper:** That's a good idea. Good friends help each other. Let me know what happens after you talk to Debbie.

After session 1, Joan stopped in to verify that Debbie would be glad to work with them. The helper then arranged a meeting with Debbie to explain her role in the participant modeling strategy. Specifically, Debbie practiced modeling the other four participation goals Joan had identified. The helper gave Debbie instructions and feedback so that each behavior was modeled clearly and in a coping manner. The helper also trained Debbie in ways to assist Joan during the guided-participation phase. Debbie practiced this, with the helper taking the role of Joan. In these practice attempts, Debbie also practiced using various induction aids that she might use with Joan, such as joint practice, verbal coaching, and graduated time intervals and difficulty of task. Debbie also practiced having the helper (as Joan) engage in self-directed practice. Classroom simulations of success experiences were also rehearsed so Debbie could learn her role in arranging for actual success experiences with Joan. When Debbie felt comfortable with her part in the strategy, the next session with Joan was scheduled.

Session 2

In response 1, the helper gives *instructions to Joan about what to look for* during the modeled demonstration. Note that the helper also points out the *lack of adverse consequences* in the modeling situation.

1. **Helper:** It's good to see you today, Joan. I have been working with Debbie, and she is here today to do some modeling for you. What we'll do first is to work with one thing you mentioned last week, telling Mr. Lamborne you want to work the problems yourself after you ask him for an explanation. Debbie will demonstrate this first. So I'll play the part of Mr. Lamborne, and Debbie will come up to me and ask me for help. Note that she tells me what she needs explained, then firmly tells Mr. Lamborne she wants to try to finish it herself. Notice that this works out well for Debbie—Mr. Lamborne doesn't jump at her or anything like that. Do you have any questions?

Client: No, I'm ready to begin. [Modeling ensues.]

Debbie (as model): Mr. Lamborne, I would like some explanation about this problem. I need you to explain it again so I can work it out all right.

Helper (as Mr. Lamborne): Well, here is the answer. . . .

Debbie (as model, interrupts): I'd like to find the answer myself, but I'd like you to explain this formula again.

Helper (as Mr. Lamborne): Here's how you do this formula. . . .

Debbie (as model): That really helps. Thanks a lot. I can take it from here. [Debbie goes back to her seat.]

After the modeling, the helper *asks Joan to react* to what she saw.

2. **Helper:** What reactions did you have to that, Joan?

Client: Well, it looked fairly easy. I guess when I do ask him for help, I have a tendency just to let him take over. I am not really firm about telling him to let me finish the problem myself.

The helper picks up on Joan's concern and *initiates a second modeled demonstration*.

3. **Helper:** That's an important part of it—first being able to ask for an additional explanation and then being able to let him know you want to apply the information and go back to your seat and try that out. It might be a good idea to have Debbie do this again—see how she initiates finishing the problem so Mr. Lamborne doesn't take over.

Client: OK. [Second modeled demonstration ensues.]

In response 4, the helper asks Joan for her opinion *about engaging in a practice*.

4. **Helper:** How ready do you feel now to try this out yourself in a practice here?

Client: I believe I could.

Before the first practice attempt, the helper will introduce *one induction aid, verbal coaching,* from Debbie.

5. **Helper:** Now I believe one thing that might help you is to have Debbie sort of coach you. For instance, if you get stuck or start to back down, Debbie can step in and give you a cue or a reminder about something you can do. How does that sound?

Client: Fine. That makes it a little easier. [The first practice attempt begins.]

6. **Helper:** Let's begin. Now I'll be Mr. Lamborne, and you get up out of your seat with the problem.

Client: Mr. Lamborne, I don't quite understand this problem.

Helper (as Mr. Lamborne): Let me just give you the answer; you'll have one less problem to do then.

Client: Uh, I'm not sure the answer is what I need.

Helper (as Mr. Lamborne): What do you mean?

Debbie (intervenes to prompt): Joan, you might want to indicate you would prefer to work out the answer yourself, but you do need another explanation of the formula.

Client: I'd like to find the answer myself. I do need another explanation of the formula.

Helper (as Mr. Lamborne): Well, it goes like this . . .

Client: OK, thanks.

Debbie: Now be sure you end the conversation there and go back to your seat.

The helper will *assess Joan's reactions* to the practice.

7. **Helper:** What did you think about that, Joan?

Client: It went pretty well. It was a help to have Debbie here. This is a good idea.

In the next response, the helper *provides positive feedback* to Debbie and to Joan. *Another practice is initiated;* this also serves as an *induction aid.*

8. **Helper:** I think she helps, too. You seemed to be able to start the conversation very well. You did need a little help in explaining to him what you wanted and didn't want. Once Debbie cued you, you were able to use her cue very effectively. Perhaps it would be a good idea to try this again. Debbie will prompt this time only if she really needs to. [Second practice ensues; Debbie's amount of prompting is decreased.]

The helper explores the idea of a *self-directed practice.*

9. **Helper:** That seemed to go very smoothly. I think you are ready to do this again without any assistance. How does that sound?

Client: I think so, too.

After obtaining an affirmative response from Joan, the helper asks Debbie to leave the room. Just Debbie's physical presence could be a protective condition for Joan, which is another induction aid, so Debbie leaves to make sure that the *self-directed practice occurs.*

10. **Helper:** I'm going to ask Debbie to leave the room so you'll be completely on your own this time. [Self-directed practice ensues.]

Next the helper cues Joan to provide herself with *feedback* about her self-directed practice.

11. **Helper:** How did you feel about that practice, Joan?

Client: I realized I was relying a little on Debbie. So I think it was good to do it by myself.

The helper notes the link between self-directed performance and confidence, and starts to work on *success experiences* outside counseling.

12. **Helper:** Right. At first it does help to have someone there. Then it builds your confidence to do it by yourself. At this point, I think we're ready to discuss ways you might actually use this in your class. How does that sound?

Client: Fine. A little scary, but fine.

The helper introduces the idea of *Debbie's assistance as an initial aid in Joan's practice outside the session.*

13. **Helper:** It's natural to feel a little apprehensive at first, but one thing we will do to help you get started on the right foot is to use Debbie again at first.

Client: Oh, good. How will that work?

The helper *identifies a hierarchy of situations* in Joan's math class. Joan's first attempts will be assisted by Debbie to ensure success at each step.

14. **Helper:** Apparently, math is the only class where you have difficulty doing this, so we want to work on your using this in math class successfully. Since Debbie is in the class with you, instead of going up to Mr. Lamborne initially by yourself, first you can go with her. In fact, she could initiate the request for help the first time. The next time you could both go up, and you could initiate it. She could prompt you or fill in. Gradually, you would get to the point where you would go up by yourself. But we will take one step at a time.

Client: That really does help. I know the first time it would turn out better if she was there, too.

15. **Helper:** Right. Usually in doing anything new, it helps to start slowly and feel good each step of the way. So maybe Debbie can come in now, and we can plan the first step.

Debbie will model and guide Joan in using these responses in their math class. Next, the entire procedure will be repeated to work with the other initiating skills that Joan wants to work on. This is a good time to try an exercise of your own in participant modeling (see Learning Activity 12.2).

CLIENT IMAGERY: ASSESSMENT AND TRAINING

In both guided imagery and covert modeling, assessing the client's potential for engaging in imagery or mental simulation is essential. To some extent, the success of these two strategies may depend on the client's capacity to generate vivid images. Some clients may be turned off by imagery or be reluctant to use imagery (for example, on the basis of personal beliefs); others may have difficulty picturing vivid scenes in

> ### LEARNING ACTIVITY 12.2 Participant Modeling
>
> This activity is designed to be completed so that you can acquire a new skill. You will need a partner to complete this activity.
>
> 1. Select a skill that you wish to acquire.
> 2. Define the skill by describing what you would be doing, thinking, and/or feeling differently. Decide whether the skill is so broad that it needs to be divided into a series of subskills. If so, identify these, and arrange them on a hierarchy in order of difficulty.
> 3. Ask your partner to model or demonstrate the skill for you. (You can also arrange to observe other people you know and respect who might be likely to use similar skills in naturally occurring circumstances.)
> 4. With the help of your partner, prepare for your own initial practice of the skill or of the first subskill on the hierarchy. Your partner should aid your initial practice attempts with at least one or two induction aids, such as joint practice or verbal coaching. With successive practice attempts, these induction aids will gradually be removed. Your partner also needs to provide feedback after each practice.
> 5. With your partner, identify actual situations in which you want to apply your newly acquired skill. Rehearse such attempts, and identify any induction aids that may be necessary in your initial efforts at skill application in these situations.
> 6. Call or see your partner to report on how you handled your rehearsal efforts in step 5. Identify whether you need additional modeling, practice, or induction aids.

their minds or envisioning themselves or their situations as significantly different than they currently perceive them to be.

Here is a way to assess the intensity and clarity of client images. First, before using guided imagery or covert modeling, you can ask clients to recall some recent event that they enjoyed or an event that made them feel relaxed and pleasant. Tell clients to close their eyes, take a couple of deep breaths to relax, and describe the enjoyable event to you. After the clients describe the event, ask them to rate its vividness, using 4 for a very clear image, 3 for a moderately clear image, 2 for a fairly clear image, 1 for an unclear image, and 0 for an indiscernible image. You can assess the vividness of clients' imagery using the rating scale displayed in Box 12.3. A score of 60 or more means that clients probably can evoke vivid images very easily. A total score lower than 30 might suggest that they need more training to evoke more vivid images. The vividness scale may be self-administered, or the practitioner may read the instructions and items to the client and obtain a rating for each item. We have found that reading the instructions and items to clients is less disruptive because they do not have to open their eyes to read each item of the scale.

To train clients to add more vividness to imagery or mental scenes, the practitioner and the clients may also develop practice scenes that clients can use to generate images. For example, the practitioner might instruct a client to "visualize a scene or an enjoyable event that makes you feel relaxed and pleasant. Select an event that you enjoy and feel good about—relax your body and mind, and try to be aware of all your sensations while visualizing the image of the event." We have found that instructing clients about sensations associated with the scene is a powerful induction aid for enhancing the scene's vividness. The practitioner can provide sensory cues by asking "What objects are pictured in the scene? "What colors do you see?" "How is the light in the scene—is it dark or light?" "What is the degree of temperature that you feel in the scene?" "What odors do you experience?" "What sounds do you hear?" "What sensation of taste do you experience in your mouth?" "What sensations do you experience in your body?" When clients have input in selecting and developing the details of a practice scene, they develop more self-efficacy or confidence in using imagery. As practitioners assess clients' ability to visualize or when they train clients to have vivid images, they should suggest selecting a scene or an event that was very enjoyable and pleasurable. We are much more aware of the sensations we experience in pleasurable events or situations. Table 12.1 illustrates dimensions of the senses and some examples of sensory experiences.

If clients have difficulty imagining specific details, the practitioner can train them to engage in more detailed imagery. If this seems too time-consuming or if clients are reluctant to use or are uninterested in using imagery, a strategy

> **BOX 12.3** **EXAMPLE OF A VIVIDNESS IMAGERY SCALE**
>
> Let's try a simple test. You will be asked to picture certain images. If your image is "very clear," give it a rating of 4; if it is "moderately clear," give it a 3. A "fairly clear" image rates a 2, and an "unclear" image rates a 1. If you cannot form an image or if it is "very unclear" or "indiscernible," give it 0. After reading each item, close your eyes, picture it as clearly as you can, and then record your own rating. *Authors' addition:* Then add the ratings together. If your score is 60 or greater, you can form images quite easily and vividly. If your score is 30 or lower, more training in imagery may be needed before using this guided imagery intervention.
>
> Think about a very close relative or friend:
>
>   *Rating*
>
> 1. See him/her standing in front of you. ( )
> 2. Imagine him/her laughing. ( )
> 3. Picture his/her eyes. ( )
> 4. Picture of bowl of fruit. ( )
> 5. Imagine driving down a dry, dusty road. ( )
> 6. See yourself throwing a ball. ( )
> 7. Picture your childhood home. ( )
> 8. See a white, sandy beach. ( )
> 9. Imagine looking into a shop window. ( )
> 10. See a blank television screen. ( )
> 11. Imagine the sound of a barking dog. ( )
> 12. Imagine the sound of an exploding firecracker. ( )
> 13. Feel the warmth of a hot shower. ( )
> 14. Imagine feeling the texture of rough sandpaper. ( )
> 15. Picture yourself lifting a heavy object. ( )
> 16. Imagine yourself walking up a steep stairway. ( )
> 17. Imagine the taste of lemon juice. ( )
> 18. Think of eating ice cream. ( )
> 19. Imagine the smell of cooking cabbage. ( )
> 20. Imagine yourself smelling a rose. ( )
>
> *Source: In the Mind's Eye: The Power of Imagery for Personal Enrichment*, by A. Lazarus, pp. 9–11. Copyright © 1984 by The Guilford Press. Reprinted by permission.

techniques. That is, when adults vividly imagine the occurrence of fictional events (events assigned to them in experimental research) that took place in their childhood, their confidence that these events actually happened to them increases (Paddock et al., 1999). Notably, this effect is considerably more evident with young adult students than with middle-aged community samples (Clancy, McNally, & Schacter, 1999; Paddock et al., 1998). Reviews are somewhat mixed with respect to the level of concern and recommendations. Brown, Sheflin, and Hammond (1998) conclude that memory confusion or distortion associated with guided imagery is likely more a function of how the interviewing is conducted than use of guided imagery per se. Arbuthnott, Arbuthnott, and Rossiter (2001a), reviewing a different set of findings, express more caution about the use of guided imagery as a memory-recovery technique, as contrasted to uses such as assisting exploration and problem solving of current issues, especially clarifying emotional and interpersonal themes and responses. They also suggest use of metaphorical imagery rather than realistic imagery in some cases to lessen the client's risk of confusing imagined and experienced events. An example of the latter is adding clearly fabricated but nonclinically significant detail, such as pink trees, to an imagery session to help the client maintain separation between the imagined and actual experienced events (Arbuthnott, Arbuthnott, & Rossiter, 2001b).

Courtois (2001) and Enns (2001) underscore cautions that memory recall or retrieval conditions should be carefully structured and monitored in treatment and that practitioners should be well versed in the issues and prepared for ethical use of techniques. Suggestions include assessing clients' susceptibility to dissociate, to have a strong sense of external control, or to be particularly oriented to pleasing the helper, being particularly cautious with those higher on these factors. The practitioner should make conditions as neutral or open-ended as possible, with no preconceived expectations on the part of the practitioner; should use a term like *images* rather than *memories* when discussing the content of imagined events; should use a variety of therapeutic and assessment tools; and should initiate forthright discussion about the issues of memory distortion and the importance of appropriate expectations. In summary, recent contributions have reinforced the robust potential of imagery techniques and the strong empirical base, with caveats about ethical, constructive use.

MULTICULTURAL APPLICATIONS OF IMAGERY

To date, imagery has been used in fairly limited ways with diverse groups of clients. Herring and Meggert (1994) used imagery processes as a counseling strategy with Native

that does not involve imagery may be more appropriate. If a client has good feelings about imagery and can adapt to practicing it, then the practitioner and client may decide to continue with either guided imagery or covert modeling, depending on the client's concern and goal behavior.

Some recent research has raised concern about the risk of imagination inflation in use of guided imagery or visualization

TABLE 12.1	Sensations to Enhance Vividness of Imagery	
Senses	**Dimensions**	**Experiences**
Seeing	Colors, lightness, darkness, depth of field	Perception of proximity, distance, movement, stillness, physical objects, events, animals, people, nature
Hearing	Noise, sound, direction, pitch, loudness	Perception of sound: euphonious, unpleasant, from people, music, objects, nature
Smelling	Molecules of substances—odors, scent, or aroma	Airborne molecules drawn into the nose from substances, such as plants, animals, people, objects, nature, traffic, cooking, perfume, cologne, smoke, smog, moisture, pollution, fragrance of flowers, air
Tasting	Sour, bitter, sweet, salty	"Gruesome scene left bad taste in my mouth" or "the ocean breeze left a pleasant taste." Taste and smell provide experience of flavor.
Touching	Pressure, pain, temperature	Perception of touch: moisture and feelings of warmth or coolness, usually experienced as skin sensations
Moving and positioning of head and body	Motion, body's position in space	Which end is up? Different movements provide feedback on body's position.

American children. Andrada and Korte (1993) used imagery scenes with auditory, tactile, verbal, visual, and taste stimuli to enhance reminiscing among elderly Hispanic men and women living in a nursing home. Omizo, Omizo, and Kitaoka (1998) reported the effectiveness of a 10-session group intervention among children of Hawaiian ancestry in elevating self-esteem. Brigham (1994) describes specific imagery scenes for use with clients who are HIV positive, and Eller (1999) found differential effects for guided imagery across the HIV disease cycle, with larger effects for those at mid-stage disease.

There are several guidelines to consider in using imagery with diverse groups of clients. First, the models of imagery used across cultures are likely to be different. Gaines and Price-Williams (1990) and Brigham (1994) have noted that the imaginative model of Euro-Americans is individualistic whereas the imaginative model for some other cultural groups is collective.

Specific mode and content of imagery scenes appear to be correlated with a person's philosophical and cultural settings (Gaines & Price-Williams, 1990). Therefore, imagery must be viewed within the context of the client's notion of both self and culture. Also, the imagery used must be culturally relevant to the client. For example, a Native American client may choose to visualize the use of a "power shield" to ward off bad spirits and to enter into harmony with nature. Other clients may choose to visualize themselves as "peace warriors."

If healing symbols are used in imagery, they need to be culturally specific or at least universally recognized. One such symbol is the mandala, a circle of wholeness and sacred space (Brigham, 1994). Myths, folk tales, and legends indigenous to a client's culture can also be used in imagery. For example, Brigham (1994) uses the compact disc *Skeleton Woman,* in which the group Flesh and Bone has set music to the legend made so well-known in *Women Who Run with the Wolves* (Estes, 1992). The Skeleton Woman tale can be read, and then the client can imagine some aspect of this legend.

GUIDED IMAGERY

In using the guided imagery procedure, a person focuses on positive thoughts or images while imagining a discomforting or anxiety-arousing activity or situation. By focusing on positive and pleasant images, the person is able to "block" the painful, fearful, or anxiety-provoking situation. One can think of blocking in emotive imagery as a process that takes advantage of the difficulty of focusing on pleasant thoughts and on anxiety, pain, or tension at the same time. This is difficult because these emotions are incompatible.

Self-initiated imagery has been used to help a variety of different types of concerns. Box 12.4 presents a sample of research illustrating the variety of uses for guided imagery. As you see, the uses of guided imagery are very diverse, ranging from helping people control allergic responses to ragweed, to helping individuals cope with loss and grief, to strengthening the immune function, to reducing migraine headaches, to improving a person's problem-solving ability. In recent years, guided imagery has become a very important part of sports psychology (Martin & Hall, 1995; Suinn, 1986). Also, like many other strategies presented in this text, guided imagery has been used to complement other treatment strategies, such as muscle relaxation, desensitization, eye movement desensitization and reprocessing, goal setting, and problem solving. The use of visualization in muscle relaxation training

BOX 12.4 GUIDED IMAGERY RESEARCH

Abuse memory
Clancy, S., McNally, R. J., & Schacter, D. L. (1999). Effects of guided imagery on memory distortion in women reporting recovered memories of childhood sexual abuse. *Journal of Traumatic Stress, 12,* 559–569.

Allergies
Cohen, R. E., Creticso, P. S., & Norman, P. S. (1993/1994). The effects of guided imagery (GI) on allergic subjects' responses to ragweed-pollen nasal challenge: An exploratory investigation. *Imagination, Cognition and Personality, 13,* 259–269.

Breast cancer
Gruber, B. L., Hersh, S. P., Hall, N. R., & Waletsky, L. R. (1993). Immunological responses of breast cancer patients to behavioral interventions. *Biofeedback and Self-Regulation, 18,* 1–22.

Cancer
Baider, L., Uziely, B., & Kaplan-DeNour, A. (1994). Progressive muscle relaxation and guided imagery in cancer patients. *General Hospital Psychiatry, 16,* 340–347.
Gawler, I. (1998). The creative power of imagery: Specific techniques for people affected by cancer. *Australian Journal of Clinical Hypnotherapy & Hypnosis, 19,* 17–30.

Chemical dependency
Avants, S. K., Margolin, A., & Singer, J. L. (1994). Self-reevaluation therapy: A cognitive intervention for the chemically dependent patient. *Psychology of Addictive Behaviors, 8,* 214–222.
Cassel, R. N., Hoey, D., & Riley, A. D. (1991). Guided imagery with subliminal stimulus in a mind-body-health program for chemical dependency rehabilitation (New Beginnings basic program). Special issue: Special recognition to Dr. Russell N. Cassel. *Psychology: A Journal of Human Behavior, 27,* 3–9.

Children
Myrick, R. D., & Myrick, L. S. (1993). Guided imagery: From mystical to practical. Special issue: Counseling and children's play. *Elementary School Guidance and Counseling, 28,* 62–70.

Complementary role of imagery
Overholser, J. C. (1991). The use of guided imagery in psychotherapy: Modules for use with passive relaxation training. *Journal of Contemporary Psychotherapy, 21,* 159–172.

Eating disorder
Esplen, M. J., Gallop, R., & Garfinkel, P. E. (1999). Using guided imagery to enhance self-soothing in women with bulimia nervosa. *Bulletin of the Menninger Clinic, 63,* 174–190.
Esplen, M. J., Garfinkel, P. E., Olmsted, M., Gallop, R. M., & Kennedy, S. (1998). A randomized controlled trial of guided imagery in bulimia nervosa. *Psychological Medicine, 28,* 1347–1357.

Emotionally charged memories and states
Edwards, D. J. (1990). Cognitive therapy and the restructuring of early memories through guided imagery. *Journal of Cognitive Psychotherapy, 4,* 33–50.
Rosenthal, T. L. (1993). To soothe the savage beast. *Behaviour Research and Therapy, 31,* 439–462.

Grief
Brown, J. C. (1990). Loss and grief: An overview and guided imagery intervention model. *Journal of Mental Health Counseling, 12,* 434–445.

HIV
Auerbach, J. E., Olsen, T. D., & Solomon, G. F. (1992). A behavioral medicine intervention as an adjunctive treatment for HIV-related illness. Special issue: Biopsychosocial aspects of HIV infection. *Psychology and Health, 6,* 325–334.

Immune function
Zachariae, R., Kristensen, J. S., Hokland, P., & Ellegaard, J. (1990). Effect of psychological intervention in the form of relaxation and guided imagery on cellular immune function in normal healthy subjects: An overview. *Psychotherapy and Psychosomatics, 54,* 32–39.
Zachariae, R., Hansen, J. B., Andersen, M., & Jinquan, T. (1994). Changes in cellular immune function after immune specific guided imagery and relaxation in high and low hypnotizable healthy subjects. *Psychotherapy and Psychosomatics, 61,* 74–92.

Information processing
Huder, J. A., Hudetz, A. G., & Klaymann, J. (2000). Relationship between relaxation by guided imagery and performance of working memory. *Psychological Reports, 28,* 15–20.

Learned helplessness
Weisenberg, M., Gerby, Y., & Mikulincer, M. (1993). Aerobic exercise and chocolate as means for reducing learned helplessness. *Cognitive Therapy and Research, 17,* 579–592.

Migraine headache
Ilacqua, G. E. (1994). Migraine headaches: Coping efficacy of guided imagery training. *Headache, 34,* 99–102.

Music with imagery
Maack, C., & Nolan, P. (1999). The effects of guided imagery and music therapy on reported change in normal adults. *Journal of Music Therapy, 36,* 39–55.

Pain
Dunne, P. W., Sanders, M. R., Rowell, J. A., & McWhirter, W. R. (1991). An evaluation of cognitive–behavioural techniques in the management of chronic arthritic pain in men with hemophilia. *Behaviour Change, 8,* 70–78.
Kwekkeboom, K., Huseby-Moore, K., & Ward, S. (1998). Imaging ability and effective use of guided imagery. *Research in Nursing & Health, 21,* 189–198.

Panic attacks
Der, D. F., & Lewington, P. (1990). Rational self-directed hypnotherapy: A treatment for panic attacks. *American Journal of Clinical Hypnosis, 32,* 160–167.

Personal meaning
Rancour, P. (1991). Guided imagery: Healing when curing is out of the question. *Perspectives in Psychiatric Care, 27,* 30–33.

Physically challenged
Short, A. E. (1992). Music and imagery with physically disabled elderly residents: A GIM adaptation. *Music Therapy, 11,* 65–98.

> **BOX 12.4   GUIDED IMAGERY RESEARCH**
>
> *Problem solving*
> Koziey, P. W. (1990). Patterning language usage and themes of problem formation/resolution. *Canadian Journal of Counselling, 24,* 230–239.
>
> *Psychodynamic therapy*
> Feinberg, M., Beverly, B., & Oatley, K. (1990). Guided imagery in brief psychodynamic therapy: Outcome and process. *British Journal of Medical Psychology, 63,* 117–129.
>
> *Respiratory problems*
> Connolly, M. J. (1993). Respiratory rehabilitation in the elderly patient. *Reviews in Clinical Gerontology, 3,* 281–294.
>
> *Smoking cessation*
> Wynd, C. A. (1992). Personal power imagery and relaxation techniques used in smoking cessation programs. *American Journal of Health Promotion, 6,* 184–189, 196.
>
> *Sports psychology*
> Martin, K., & Hall, C. (1995). Using mental imagery to enhance intrinsic motivation. *Journal of Sports and Exercise Psychology, 17,* 54–65.
>
> Suinn, R. (1986). *Seven steps to peak performance: The mental training manual for athletes.* Lewiston, NY: Huber.
>
> *Stress/tension reduction*
> Mannix, L. K., Chandurkar, R. S., Rybicki, L. A., Tusek, D. L., & Solomon, G. D. (1999). Effect of guided imagery on quality of life for patients with chronic tension-type headache. *Headache, 39,* 326–334.
> Prerost, F. J. (1993). A strategy to enhance humor production among elderly persons: Assisting in the management of stress. *Activities, Adaptation and Aging, 17,* 17–24.
> Weinburger, R. (1991). Teaching elderly stress reduction. *Journal of Gerontological Nursing, 17,* 23–27.
>
> *Vomiting*
> Torem, M. S. (1994). Hypnotherapeutic techniques in the treatment of hyperemesis gravidarum. *American Journal of Clinical Hypnosis, 37,* 1–11.
> Watson, M., & Marvell, C. (1992). Anticipatory nausea and vomiting among cancer patients: A review. *Psychology and Health, 6,* 97–106.

can create as great a physiological response as the actual experience of tightening and relaxing the muscles (Overholser, 1990, 1991).

Many people experience thoughts and emotions in the form of images or mental pictures. Judith Beck (1995) teaches clients to access their distressing images as a technique in assessment. She might say to the client "When you had that thought or emotion, what image or picture did you have in your head?" (p. 230). If the practitioner and client can identify the distressing image, they can create a new image and later restructure the thought or emotions associated with the distressing image. Guided imagery has become very popular as a complementary strategy in medicine. Jeanne Achterberg in her *Imagery in Healing* (1985) describes the many uses of imagery in medicine. Finally, there are commercial audiotapes that offer ways for effective visualization, techniques for improving vividness of mental imagery, visualization and achieving goals, using one's inner adviser, and imagery exercises that contribute to alertness and mindfulness (L. Pulos, 1996).

Guided imagery involves five steps: a rationale, assessment of the client's imagery potential, development of imagery scenes, practice of scenes, and homework. See the Interview Checklist for Guided Imagery at the end of the chapter for some examples of practitioner leads associated with these steps. (See Learning Activity 12.3)

Treatment Rationale

The following illustration of the purpose and overview of guided imagery can be used with people who have anxiety about a medical procedure and for relieving discomfort of such a procedure:

> Here is how guided imagery works while you are having the procedure. Often people have a lot of anxiety about the procedure just before they go to the hospital. This is normal and natural. It is often very difficult to shake this belief. Usually the belief intensifies anxiety about the procedure. When some discomfort occurs, the result is even more anxiety.
>
> Now, since the anxiety magnifies the effect of the medical procedure, the more anxious you become, the more actual pain you will probably experience. You can say the anxiety you experience escalates or intensifies the pain. This vicious circle happens often with patients undergoing this procedure. You can reverse the anxiety-pain cycle by using a technique called guided imagery. It works like this: You visualize a scene or an event that is pleasant for you and makes you feel relaxed while the procedure is occurring. You cannot feel calm, relaxed, secure—or whatever other emotion the scene

evokes—and anxious at the same time. You cannot experience feelings of anxiety and relaxation or calmness at the same time. These two different emotions are incompatible with each other.

So you select a scene that you can get into and that makes you feel relaxed, calm, and pleasant. You visualize the image or scene you have selected while the medical procedure is being performed. The imagery blocks the anxiety that can lead to increased discomfort while the procedure is being performed. People who have used guided imagery have reported that visualizing and holding a pleasant scene or image raises their threshold of pain. Using imagery while the medical procedure is performed on you eliminates anxiety-related discomfort and also has a dulling effect on what might be experienced as pain.

The rationale ends with a request for the client's willingness to try the strategy.

Assessment of Client's Imagery Potential

Because the success of the guided imagery procedure may depend on the amount of positive feeling and calmness that a client can derive from visualizing a particular scene, it is important for the practitioner to get a feeling for the client's potential for engaging in imagery. The practitioner can assess the client's imagery potential by the methods discussed at the beginning of this chapter: a self-report questionnaire, a practice scene with client narration, or practitioner "probes" for details.

Development of Imagery Scenes

If the decision is made to continue with the guided imagery procedure, the client and practitioner will then develop imagery scenes. They should develop at least two scenes, although one might be satisfactory for some clients. The exact number and type of scenes developed will depend on the nature of the concern and the individual client.

Two basic ingredients should be included in the selection and development of the scene. First, the scenario should promote calmness, tranquility, or enjoyment for the client. Examples of such client scenes might include skiing on a beautiful slope, hiking on a trail in a large forest, sailing on a sunny lake, walking on a secluded beach, listening to and watching a symphony orchestra perform a favorite composition, or watching an athletic event. The scenes can involve the client as an active participant or as a participant observer or spectator. For some clients, the more active they are in the scene, the greater the degree of their involvement.

The second ingredient of the scene should be as much sensory detail as possible, such as sounds, colors, temperature, smell, touch, and motion. There may be a high positive correlation between the degree and number of sensations a scene elicits for the client and the number or intensity of pleasant and enjoyable sensations the client experiences in a particular imagery scene. The helper and client should decide on the particular senses that will be incorporated into the imagery scenes. Remember that the scene needs to be culturally relevant for the client.

As an example, the following imagery scene can be used with a client who experiences discomfort about a medical procedure. Note the sensations described in the scene instructions:

> Close your eyes, sit back, take a couple of deep breaths [pause], and relax. With your eyes closed, sitting back in the chair and feeling relaxed, visualize yourself on a beautiful ocean beach. Visualize a few puffy clouds scattered throughout a dazzling blue sky. Notice the blue-green ocean water with the white caps of the surf rolling in toward the beach. See yourself wearing a bathing suit, and feel bright, warm rays of sun on your body. Take a deep breath, and experience the fresh and clean air. Hear the waves gently rolling in onto the beach and the water receding to catch the next wave. Smell the salt and moisture in the air. Experience the touch of a gentle breeze against your body. See yourself unfolding a beach towel, and feel the texture of the terry cloth material as you spread it on the sandy beach. Notice the sand on your feet; experience the warmth of the sand and feel the relaxing and soothing sensations the sand provides. Now visualize yourself walking toward the surf and standing in ankle-deep water, experiencing the wetness of the ocean. You experience the water as warm and comfortable. You are all alone, and you walk out in the surf up to your waist, then up to your chest. You hear the waves and see the sun glistening off the blue-green water. Smell the salt in the air as you surface dive into the oncoming surf. Experience the warmth of the water on your body as you swim out just beyond where the surf is breaking. See yourself treading water, and experience the gentle movement of going up and down on the surface of the water. Notice how warm the sun and water feel, and how relaxing it is just to linger there in the water. Experience the gentle motions of your arms and legs moving beneath the surface. Picture yourself slowly swimming

back to the beach, catching a wave, and riding it in. Visualize yourself standing up and walking slowly toward your beach towel. Feel the warm sun and the air temperature of about 90 degrees on your wet body. You reach the beach towel, and you stretch out and lie down. You are alone; there is no else in the water or on the beach. You feel the warmth of the sun on the front of your body. Every muscle in your body feels totally relaxed. You look up at the sky, watching the large billowy clouds drifting by.

Practice of Imagery Scenes

After the imagery scenes have been developed, the client is instructed to practice using them. There are two types of practice. In the first type, the client is instructed to focus on one of the scenes for about 30 seconds and to picture as much detail as was developed for that scene and to feel all the sensations associated with it. The helper cues the client after the time has elapsed. After the client uses the scene, the practitioner obtains an impression of the imagery experience—the client's feelings and sensory details of the scene. If other scenes are developed, the client can be instructed to practice imagining them. Variations on this type of practice might be to have the client use or hold a scene for varying lengths of time.

The second type of practice is to have the client use the scenes in simulated anxious, tense, fearful, or painful situations. The helper and client should simulate the target situations while using the imagery scenes. Practice under simulated conditions permits the practitioner and client to assess the effectiveness of the scenes for blocking out the discomfort or for reducing the anxiety or phobic reaction. Simulated situations can be created by describing vividly the details of an anxiety-provoking situation while the client uses a scene. For example, the practitioner can describe the pleasant scene while interweaving a description of the discomforting situation. The helper can simulate painful situations by squeezing the client's arm while the client focuses on one of the scenes. Or, to simulate labor contractions, the labor coach squeezes the woman's thigh while she focuses on a pleasant image. Another simulation technique is to have clients hold their hands in ice water for a certain length of time. Simulated practice may aid in generalization of the scene application to the actual life situation. After the simulated practices, the practitioner should assess the client's reactions to using the scene in conjunction with the simulated discomfort or anxiety.

Homework and Follow-Up

The client is instructed to apply the guided imagery *in vivo*—that is, to use the scenes in the fearful, painful, tense, or anxious situation. The client can use a homework log to record the day, time, and situation in which guided imagery was used. The client can also note reactions before and after using guided imagery with a 5-point scale, 1 representing minimum discomfort and 5 indicating maximum discomfort. The client should be told to bring the homework log to the next session or to a follow-up session.

MODEL EXAMPLE: GUIDED IMAGERY

In this model example, we deviate from a clinical illustration to a normative life experience—specifically, the use of guided imagery before and during labor for childbirth. Part of the intent here is to illustrate ways that clients can be assisted to apply intervention techniques in their lives outside of formal sessions, on their own or in cooperation with supportive others. This involves a heterosexual couple, Jayne and Bob.

1. Rationale: First, include a rationale for using guided imagery during labor in conjunction with the breathing and relaxation techniques (see Chapters 15 and 16) that are commonly part of prepared-childbirth classes. Consider how and when the component of guided imagery may be needed; in this case, that might be at a point during labor when the breathing needs to be supplemented with something else. In conditions such as this, when verbal communication is likely to be constrained, consider working out in advance something both will recognize, such as a finger-signaling system to use during contractions so that Jayne could inform Bob whether to continue or stop with the imagery scenes, depending on their effectiveness.

2. Assessment of imagery potential: Discuss what is likely to be realistic under circumstances of stress: in this case, the physical strain and intense emotionality associated with childbirth. Here, Jayne and Bob discussed whether Jayne would be able to use fantasy effectively enough to concentrate during a labor contraction. They tested this out by having Bob describe imagery stimuli and having Jayne imagine these and try to increase use of all sensations to make the imagery scenes as vivid as possible.

3. Development of imagery scenes: Together, the partners select scenes to practice with before labor and to use during labor. One scene involved being on a sailboat on a sunny, warm day and sailing quite fast with a good breeze. This was selected because it evoked happy, relaxing memories for Jayne, had a lot of detailed sensory experience for her, and was one she felt from practice

---

LEARNING ACTIVITY 12.3 — Guided Imagery

This learning activity is designed to help you learn the process of guided imagery. It will be easier to do this with a partner, although you can do it alone if a partner is not available. You may wish to try it with a partner first and then by yourself.

Instructions for Dyadic Activity

1. In dyads, one of you can take the helper role; the other takes the part of the one helped. Switch roles after the first practice with the strategy.
2. The helper should give an explanation about the guided imagery procedure.
3. The helper should determine the potential for imagination of the one being helped by asking the person to imagine several pleasant scenes and then probe for details.
4. The two together should develop two imagery scenes that the one being helped can vividly imagine. Imagination of these scenes should produce pleasant, positive feelings and should be culturally relevant to the one being helped.
5. The person should practice imagining these scenes—as vividly and as intensely as possible.
6. He or she should practice imagining a scene while the helper simulates a problem situation. For example, the helper can simulate an anxiety-provoking situation by describing it while the other engages in imagery, or the helper can simulate pain by squeezing the other person's arm during the imagination.

Instructions for Self-Activity

1. Think of two scenes you can imagine very vividly. These scenes should produce positive or pleasant feelings for you and be culturally relevant for you. Supply as many details for these scenes as you can.
2. Practice imagining these scenes as intensely as you can.
3. Next, practice imagining one of these scenes while simulating a problem (discomforting) situation such as grasping a piece of ice in your hands or holding your hands under cold water. Concentrate very hard on the imagery as you do so.
4. Practice this twice daily for the next three days. See how much you can increase your tolerance for the cold temperature with daily practice of the imagery scene.

---

helped her feel calmer. The second scene involved being anchored at night on the boat on a warm night with a soft breeze. Because both these scenes represented actual experiences, the couple felt these might work better than sheer fantasy.

4. Practice of imagery scenes: As with most techniques used during situations of stress, the success of using guided imagery during labor would depend on the degree to which the couple worked with it before labor. Thus, they practiced with the imagery scenes in two ways. First, Jayne imagined these scenes on her own, sometimes in conjunction with her self-directed practice in breathing and relaxation, and sometimes just as something to do—for instance, in a boring situation. Second, Jayne evoked the scenes deliberately while Bob simulated a contraction by tightly squeezing her upper arm.
5. Homework—In vivo: There was, naturally, the time to put the preparation fully into service during labor itself. During the active phase of labor, the couple started to use the guided imagery procedures they had practiced—about midway through the time of labor, when the contractions were coming about every two minutes. In looking back, they felt it was a useful supplement to the breathing and relaxation typically taught in the Lamaze childbirth method. Jayne felt that a lot of the effectiveness had to do with the soothing effect of hearing Bob's vocal descriptions of the scenes—in addition to the images she produced during the scene descriptions.

Before moving on to covert modeling, review the self and dyadic exercises in Learning Activity 12.3 for implementing guided imagery.

COVERT MODELING

Covert modeling is a procedure in which the client imagines a model performing behaviors by means of instructions. A live or symbolic performance by a model is not necessary. Instead, the client is directed to imagine someone demonstrating the desired behavior. Covert modeling involves mental simulation of situations, either potential future ones or reconstructed past ones. Properly undertaken, the mental simulations within covert modeling are more than passing fantasy, and they have considerable research support for making envisioned situations seem real and helping people translate thought into action (e.g., develop plans for how to undertake desired changes, gain insight and rehearsal experience in how to go about it, and manage difficult emotions likely to arise in the situations [Taylor & Pham, 1996]).

Covert modeling has several advantages. The procedure does not require elaborate therapeutic or induction aids, scenes can be developed to deal with a variety of problems, the scenes can be individualized to fit the unique concerns of the client, the client can practice the imagery scenes alone, the client can use the imagery scenes as a self-control procedure in troubling situations, and covert modeling may be a good alternative when live or filmed models cannot be used or when it is difficult to use overt rehearsal in the interview.

Some questions about certain aspects of covert modeling remain unanswered, such as the importance of the identity of the model, the role of reinforcing consequences, and the type and duration of imagery scenes best used in the procedure. We have tried to point out the possible alternatives in our description of the components of the covert modeling strategy. The five major components of covert modeling are rationale about the strategy, practice scenes, developing treatment scenes, applying treatment scenes, and homework. Within each of these five components are several substeps. If you would like an overview of the procedure, see the Interview Checklist for Covert Modeling at the end of the chapter.

Treatment Rationale

After the practitioner and client have reviewed the targets of change and the goal behaviors, the practitioner presents the rationale for covert modeling. Here is an example of an explanation for using covert modeling, in this case with someone seeking to complete school and successfully transition to steady working following incarceration:

> We have discussed your goals and some of the concerns you have about achieving them. We have chosen covert modeling as a tool to mentally envision and "walk through" the steps you will need to be taking toward your goals. This is a kind of mental simulation in which we can help you rehearse scenes that you will be encountering. We will start this in session, and then you can practice it on your own. In this way, we can include difficulties you are likely to encounter and better prepare you to deal with them. You will likely experience the same kinds of thoughts and feelings (like anxiety and pride) in the imagined situations that you will as you actually encounter them. We can discuss these to help give you insight and preparation.

The following provides an illustration of detailing the steps involved in covert modeling.

> As we go through each situation, I'll ask you to close your eyes and try to imagine, as clearly as possible, that you are observing yourself in that situation. Try to use your senses in your visualization of each situation, including your emotions. I will give you prompts to focus and to experience the senses as you visualize going into each situation. After we complete visualizing a situation, I will ask you some questions concerning your thoughts and feelings about the sequence and any difficulties, insights, or questions you have. We will progressively work through a range of situations tied to your goals, adjusting them as needed.

Practice Scenes

After providing a rationale to the client, the practitioner may decide to try out the imagery process with several practice scenes. For most clients, imagining a scene may be a new experience and may seem foreign. Kazdin (1976, p. 478) suggests that practice scenes may help to familiarize clients with the procedure and sensitize them to focus on specific details of the imagery. Use of practice scenes also helps the practitioner assess the client's potential for carrying out instructions in the imagination.

The practice scenes usually consist of simple, straightforward situations that are unrelated to the goal behaviors. For example, if you are using covert modeling to help a client acquire job-interview skills, the practice scenes would be unrelated to job-seeking responses. You might use some of the following as practice scenes:

1. Imagine watching a person at a golf match on the eighteenth hole of a beautiful golf course on a gorgeous day.
2. Imagine someone hiking to the top of a mountain with a panoramic view.
3. Imagine watching a comedian at a comedy club.
4. Imagine someone taking a walk on a beautiful day.

In using practice scenes with a client, the helper usually follows six steps.

1. The helper instructs the client to close his or her eyes and to sit back and relax. The client is instructed to tell the helper when he or she feels relaxed. If the client does not feel relaxed, the helper may need to decide whether relaxation

procedures (see Chapter 16) should be introduced. The effect of relaxation on the quality of imagery in covert modeling has not been evaluated. However, live and symbolic modeling may be aided when the client is relaxed.

2. The helper describes a practice scene and instructs the client to imagine the scene and to raise an index finger when the scene has been imagined vividly. The practice scenes are similar to the four previous examples. The helper reads the scene or instructs the client about what to imagine.

3. The helper asks the client to open his or her eyes after the scene is vividly imagined (signal of index finger) and to describe the scene or to narrate the imagined events.

4. The helper probes for greater details about the scene—the clothes or physical features of a person in the imagery, the physical setting of the situation, the amount of light, colors of the furniture, decorative features, noises, or smells. This probing may encourage the client to focus on details of the imagery scene.

5. The helper may suggest additional details for the client to imagine during a subsequent practice. Working with practice scenes first can help with the development of the details in the actual treatment scenes.

6. Usually, each practice scene is presented several times. The number of practice scenes used before moving on to developing and applying treatment scenes will depend on several factors. If the client feels comfortable with the novelty of the imagined scenes after several presentations, the helper might consider this a cue to stop using the practice scenes. Additionally, if the client can provide a fairly detailed description of the imagery after several practice scenes, this may be a good time to start developing treatment scenes. If a client reports difficulty in relaxing, the helper may need to introduce relaxation training before continuing. For a client who cannot generate images during the practice scenes, another modeling strategy may be needed in lieu of covert modeling.

Developing Treatment Scenes

The treatment scenes used in covert modeling are developed in conjunction with the client and grow out of the desired client outcomes or goals. The scenes consist of a variety of situations in which the client wants to perform the target response in the real-life environment. If a client wants to acquire effective job-interview skills, the treatment scenes are developed around job-interview situations.

Five things should be considered in the development of treatment scenes: the model characteristics, whether to use individualized or standardized scenes, whether to use vague or specific scenes, the ingredients of the scenes, and the number of scenes. It is important for the client to help in the development of treatment scenes because client participation can provide many specifics about situations in which the goal behavior is to be performed.

Model Characteristics

Similarity between the model and the client contributes to client change. Models of the same sex and age as the client may be more effective. Also, clients who imagine several models may show more change than clients who imagine only one model. Recall that clients are more likely to learn from a model who is similar to them in gender, race, and ethnicity. Coping models may also be generally more effective in covert modeling than mastery models. A coping model who self-verbalizes his or her anxiety and uses covert self-talk for dealing with fear may enhance the behaviors to be acquired.

One of the most interesting questions about the covert model is the identity of the model: clients who imagine *themselves* as the model and clients who imagine *another person* as the model. We believe that for most people, imagining themselves may be more powerful. However, there are not sufficient data to indicate who the model should be in the covert modeling procedure. We suspect that the answer varies with clients, and we suggest that you give clients the option of deciding whether to imagine themselves or another person as the model. For multi- or bicultural clients, this may mean asking them which part of their culture they identify with the most or if the multiple identities are important to include. One key factor for any individual may involve the particular identity that the client can imagine most easily or feels is most relevant (e.g., factors such as gender, culture, or sexuality may or may not be key; other factors such as shyness or lack of confidence may be more salient for a given concern or goal). For clients who feel some stress at first in imagining themselves as models, imagining someone else might be introduced first and later replaced with self-modeling. Using yourself as the model is a good option when culturally similar models are not readily available.

Individualized Versus Standardized Scenes

The treatment scenes used in covert modeling can be either standardized or individualized. Standardized scenes cover different situations in everyday life and are presented to a group of clients or to all clients with the same target responses. For example, a practitioner can use a series of standardized scenes describing situations of job-interviewing behavior. Individualized scenes represent situations specifically tailored to suit an individual client. For example, one nonassertive client may need scenes developed around situations with strangers; another may need scenes that involve close friends. Generally, treatment scenes should be individualized for those who have unique concerns and who are helped individually, as some standardized scenes may not be relevant for a particular client.

Specificity of Scenes

Another consideration in developing treatment scenes is the degree of specificity of instruction that should be included. Some clients may benefit from very explicit instructions about the details of what to imagine. Other clients may derive more gains from covert modeling if the treatment scenes are more general, allowing the client to supply the specific features. A risk of not having detailed instructions is that some clients will introduce scene material that is irrelevant or detracts from the desired outcomes. We suggest this decision should consider the client's preferences. Here is an example of a fairly general treatment scene for a prison inmate about to be released on parole who is seeking employment:

> Picture yourself (or someone else like you) in a job interview. The employer asks why you didn't complete high school. You tell the employer you got in some trouble, and the employer asks what kind of trouble. You feel a little uptight but tell her you have a prison record. The employer asks why you were in prison and for how long. The employer then asks what makes you think you can stay out of trouble and what you have been doing while on parole. Imagine yourself saying that you have been looking for work while on parole and have been thinking about your life and what you want to do with it.

The generality of the treatment scene in this example assumes that the client knows what type of response to make and what details to supply in the scene.

A more detailed treatment scene would specify more of the actual responses:

> Picture yourself (or someone else) in a job interview and imagine the following dialogue. The employer says, "I see that you have only finished three years of high school. You don't intend to graduate?" Picture yourself saying (showing some anxiety): "Well, no, I want to go to vocational school while I'm working." The employer asks: "What happened? How did you get so far behind in school?" Imagine yourself (or someone else) replying: "I've been out of school for a while because I've been in some trouble." Now imagine the employer is showing some alarm and asks: "What kind of trouble?" You decide to be up front as you imagine yourself saying: "I want you to know that I have a prison record." As the employer asks: "Why were you in prison?" imagine yourself feeling a little nervous but staying calm and saying something like "I guess I was pretty immature. Some friends and I got involved with drugs. I'm on parole now. I'm staying away from drugs, and I'm looking hard for a job. I really want to work."

Remember, the degree of specificity of each scene will depend largely on the client, the concern, and the goals for counseling.

Ingredients of the Scene

Three ingredients are required for a treatment scene in the covert modeling procedure: a description of the situation or context in which the behavior is to occur, a description of the model demonstrating the behavior to be acquired, and a depiction of some favorable outcome of the goal behavior.

Situation Imagine yourself playing tennis on a bright, sunny day. You are playing in a tournament. Your opponent hits the ball to your forehand, and you return it. On your opponent's return, the ball is hit low to your backhand.

Demonstrating the desired behavior You see yourself put both hands on the racket and pull your arms back ready to hit the low ball. You see yourself hit the ball across the net and inside the line. Notice the bodily sensation you experience while hitting the ball across the net.

Below is a covert modeling scene that includes a favorable outcome for an adult who wants to stop smoking:

> Imagine yourself in a restaurant having a drink with some friends before your reservation to be seated for dinner. All your friends in the group are smoking, and the smell of the smoke makes you want a cigarette. You have been drinking with them for about ten minutes, and one of them offers you a cigarette. In the past, you would have taken a cigarette if you did not have any of your own. Now cope with the situation in your imagination. Imagine yourself feeling the urge to smoke, but see yourself refuse and focus on what the group is discussing.

Inclusion of a favorable consequence as a scene ingredient is based on research indicating that if a client sees a model rewarded for the behavior or feels good about the outcome of the behavior, the client is more likely to perform the response. Moreover, specifying a possible favorable outcome to imagine may prevent a client from inadvertently imagining an unfavorable one. Clients who receive covert modeling treatment scenes that are resolved favorably are more likely to engage in the desired goal behaviors than clients who imagine scenes without any positive consequences.

We believe that the favorable outcome in the scene should take the form of some action initiated by the client or of covert self-reinforcement or praise. For example, the favorable outcome illustrated in the scene for the "stop smoking" client was the client's self-initiated action of refusing to take a cigarette. We prefer that the action be initiated by the client or model instead of someone else in the scene because, in a real situation, it may be too risky to have the client rely on someone else to deliver a favorable outcome in the form of a certain response. We cannot guarantee that clients will always receive favorable responses from someone else in the actual situation.

Another way to incorporate a favorable outcome into a treatment scene is to include an example of client (or model) self-reinforcement or praise. For instance, models might congratulate themselves by saying "That is terrific. I am proud of myself for what I said to the hotel clerk." A favorable consequence in the form of model or client self-praise is self-administered. Again, in a real-life situation it may be better for clients to learn to reward themselves than to expect external encouragement, which might not be forthcoming.

The person who experiences the favorable outcomes will be the same person the client imagines as the model. If the client imagines someone else as the model, then the client would also imagine that person initiating a favorable outcome or reinforcing himself or herself. Clients who imagine themselves as the models would imagine themselves receiving the positive consequences. There is very little actual evidence on the role of reinforcement in covert modeling. Some of the effectiveness of adding favorable consequences to the treatment scene may depend on the identity of the covert model and the particular value of the consequences for the client, all of which may vary depending on the client's gender, age, and culture.

Number of Scenes

The practitioner and client can develop different scenes that portray the situation in which the client experiences difficulty or wants to use the newly acquired behavior. Multiple scenes can depict different situations in which the desired behavior is generally appropriate. The number of scenes that the practitioner and client develop will depend on the client and his or her concerns. Although there is no set number of scenes that should be developed, certainly several scenes provide more variety than only one or two.

Applying Treatment Scenes

After all the scenes have been developed, the helper can apply the treatment scenes by having the client imagine each one. The basic steps in applying the treatment scenes are these:
1. Arranging the scenes in a hierarchy
2. Instructing the client before scene presentation
3. Presenting one scene at a time from the hierarchy
4. Presenting a scene for a specified duration
5. Obtaining the client's reactions to the imagined scene
6. Instructing the client to develop verbal summary codes and/or to personalize each treatment scene
7. Presenting each scene at least twice with the aid of the helper or tape recorder
8. Having the client imagine each scene at least twice while directing himself or herself
9. Selecting and presenting scenes from the hierarchy in a random order

Hierarchy

The scenes developed by the practitioner and client should be arranged in a hierarchy for scene presentation. The hierarchy is an order of scenes beginning with one that is relatively easy for the client to imagine with little stress. More difficult or stressful scenes would be ranked by the client.

Instructions

It may be necessary to repeat instructions about imagery to the client if a great amount of time has elapsed since using the practice scenes. With the adult who wants to stop smoking, for instance, the practitioner might say this:

> Close your eyes, take a couple of deep breaths, and relax. I want you to imagine as vividly and clearly as possible that you are observing yourself having drinks with friends when you are offered a cigarette. Tune in and use all your senses. For example, try to envision the restaurant, who is there, the sounds around you. What odors or smells do you experience? What is the taste in your mouth? Notice the sensations you experience in your body. Notice your thoughts. In a moment, I will ask you some questions concerning your feelings about the entire sequence of the scene and how clearly you imagined it.

If a person other than the client is the model, the client is instructed to picture someone of his or her own age, gender, and culture whom he or she knows. The client is told that the person who is pictured as the model will be used in all the treatment scenes. The practitioner also instructs the client to signal by raising an index finger as soon as the scene is pictured clearly and to hold the scene in imagery until the practitioner signals to stop.

Sequence of Scene Presentation

Initially, the first scene in the hierarchy is presented to the client. Each scene is presented alone. When one scene has been covered sufficiently, the next scene in the hierarchy is presented. This process continues until all scenes in the hierarchy have been covered.

Duration of Scenes

There are no general ground rules for the amount of time to hold the scene in imagery once the client signals. For some clients, a longer duration may be more beneficial; for others, a shorter duration may be. We feel that the choice will depend on the practitioner's assessment of any given client, the practitioner's experience with the covert modeling procedure, the nature of the client's concerns, the goal behavior for counseling, and—perhaps most important—the client's input about the scene duration. After one or two scenes have been presented, the practitioner can query the client about the suitability of the scene duration. Generally, a scene should be held long enough for the client to imagine the three scene ingredients vividly without rushing. We have found that visualizing a scene is perceived as much longer in time than it is in "real" time.

Client Reactions to the Scene

After the client has imagined a particular scene, the practitioner queries the client about how clearly it was imagined. The client is asked to describe feelings during particular parts of the scene. The practitioner should also ask whether the scene was described too rapidly or the duration of the scene was adequate for the client to imagine the scene ingredients clearly. These questions enable the practitioner and client to modify aspects of a scene before it is presented the second time. Client input about possible scene revision can be very helpful. If particular episodes of the scene elicit intense feelings of anxiety, the content of the scene or the manner of presentation can be revised. Perhaps the order of the scenes in the hierarchy needs rearrangement.

Another way to deal with the client's unpleasant feelings or discomfort with a scene is to talk it over. If the client feels stressful when the model (or the self) is engaging in the behavior or activity in the scene, examine with the client what episode in the scene is producing the discomfort. In addition, if the client is the model and has difficulty performing the behavior or activity, discuss and examine the block. Focus on the adaptive behavior or the coping with the situational ingredient of the scene rather than on the anxiety or discomfort.

After each scene presentation, the practitioner should assess the rate of delivery for the scene description, the clarity of the imagery, and the degree of unpleasantness of the scene for the client. Perhaps if the client has a great deal of input in developing the scene, the level of discomfort produced will be minimized. In addition, the intensity of the imagined scene can be enhanced by using verbal summary codes or by personalizing the scene.

Verbal Summary Codes and Personalization

Verbal summary codes are brief descriptions about the behavior to be acquired and the context in which the behavior is to occur *in the client's own words*. Verbal coding of the modeling cues can help with acquisition and retention of the behaviors to be modeled and may maintain client performance during and after treatment by helping clients encode desired responses in their working memory. The verbalizations (or verbal summary codes) of the scene provide an alternative representational process to imagery or covert modeling. The practitioner instructs the client to use his or her descriptions of the behavior and the situation. We recommend that clients rehearse using verbal summary codes with *practice* scenes and receive feedback from the helper about the descriptions of the practice scenes. The practice should occur before presentation of the *treatment* scenes. Then the treatment scenes are presented, and the client is instructed to develop his or her own verbal summary codes (descriptions of behavior and situation) for the scene. Have the client "try out" the treatment scene on the first presentation *without* the use of the summary code. On the second presentation of the scene, instruct the client to use the summary code and to say aloud exactly what it is.

Personalization of treatment scenes is another technique that can enhance covert modeling. After the scene has been presented once as developed, then the client is instructed *to change the treatment scene in any way as long as the model responses to be acquired are represented in the scene*. As with verbal summary codes, the client is asked to rehearse personalizing (individualizing) or elaborating a scene using a practice scene, and he or she then receives feedback about the elaboration. The practitioner should encourage the client to use variations within the context of the situation presented by the scene. Variations include more details about the model responses and the situation in which the responses are to occur. The client is asked to elaborate the scene the second time the treatment scene is presented. Elaboration may lead to more client involvement because the scenes are individualized.

Remember to have the client experience imagining a scene first without instructions to use verbal summary codes or to personalize the scene. Then, on the second presentation of the treatment scene, the client is instructed to use one of these techniques. To verify that the client is complying with the instructions, the helper can instruct the client to say aloud the verbal summary code or elaboration being used.

Helper-Directed Scene Repetition

After presenting the first scene and making any necessary revisions, the helper may want to repeat the scene a couple of times. The number of scene repetitions may be dictated by the degree of comfort the client experiences while imagining the scene and the complexity of the activities or behaviors the client imagines. For example, a complex series of motor skills may require more repetitions, and engaging in some situations may require repetition until the client feels reasonably comfortable. Again, make the decision about the number of scene repetitions on the basis of client input: Ask the client. If you use the verbal summary codes or personalization of the scene, remember to instruct the client to use the technique during later repetitions of each scene.

Client-Directed Scene Repetition

In addition to helper-directed scene practice, the client should engage in self-directed scene practice. Again, the number of client practices is somewhat arbitrary, although perhaps two is a minimum. Generally, the client can repeat imagining the scenes alone until he or she feels comfortable in doing so. The client can either use the verbal summary codes without saying the codes aloud or can personalize the scenes. Overt rehearsal of the scene can help with acquisition and retention of the imagined behaviors. The client should be instructed to overtly enact (rehearse) the scene with the helper after the second or third time that each scene is presented.

Random Presentation of Scenes

After all the scenes in the hierarchy have been presented adequately, the practitioner can check out the client's readiness for self-directed homework practice by presenting some of the scenes in random order. This random presentation guards against any "ordering" effect that the hierarchy arrangement may have had in the scene presentation.

Homework and Follow-Up

Self-directed practice in the form of homework is perhaps the most important therapeutic ingredient for generalization. If a person can apply or practice the procedure outside the counseling session, the probability of using the "new" behavior or of coping in the actual situation is greatly enhanced. Homework can consist of having clients identify several situations in their everyday lives in which they could use the desired responses.

In arranging the homework tasks, the helper and client should specify how often, how long, what times during the day, and where practice should occur. The helper should also instruct the client to record the daily use of the modeling scenes on log sheets. The helper should verify whether the client understands the homework and should arrange for a follow-up after some portion of the homework is completed.

MODEL DIALOGUE: COVERT MODELING

Here is an example of a covert modeling dialogue with our client Joan to help her increase initiating skills in her math class. (See also Learning Activity 12.4.)

In response 1, the helper briefly describes the *rationale* and gives an *overview* of the strategy.

1. **Helper:** Joan, one way we can help you work on your initiating skills in math class is to help you learn the skills you want through practice. In this procedure, you will practice using your imagination. I will describe situations to you and ask you to imagine yourself or someone else participating in the way described in a situation. How does that sound?

Client: OK. You mean I imagine things like daydreaming?

Further *instructions* about the strategy are provided in helper response 2.

2. **Helper:** It has some similarities. Only instead of just letting your mind wander, you will imagine some of the skills you want to use to improve your participation in your math class.

Client: Well, I'm a pretty good daydreamer, so if this is similar, I will probably learn from it.

In response 3, the helper initiates the idea of using *practice scenes* to determine Joan's level and style of imagery.

3. **Helper:** Let's see. I think it might help to see how easy or hard it is for you to actually imagine a specific situation as I describe it to you. So maybe we could do this on a try-out basis to see what it feels like for you.

Client: OK, what happens?

In response 4, the helper instructs Joan to *sit back and relax before imagining the practice scene.*

4. **Helper:** First of all, just sit back, close your eyes, and relax [gives Joan a few minutes to do this]. You look pretty comfortable. How do you feel?

Client: Fine. It's never too hard for me to relax.

In response 5, the helper instructs Joan *to imagine the scene vividly and to indicate this by raising her finger.*

LEARNING ACTIVITY 12.4 — Covert Modeling

As you may recall from reading the goals and subgoals of Ms. Weare (Chapter 10), one of her subgoals was to arrange a school conference with Freddie's teacher. Ms. Weare was going to use the conference to explain her new strategy in dealing with Freddie and request help and cooperation from the school. Specifically, Ms. Weare would point out that one thing that may happen initially might be an increase in Freddie's tardiness at school. Assume that Ms. Weare is hesitant to initiate the conference because she is unsure about what to say during the meeting. Describe how you would use covert modeling to help Ms. Weare achieve this subgoal. Describe specifically how you would use (1) a rationale, (2) practice scenes, (3) development of treatment scenes, (4) application of treatment scenes, and (5) homework to help Ms. Weare in this objective. Feedback follows; see whether some of your ideas are similar.

FEEDBACK 12.4 — Covert Modeling

1. Rationale. First, you would explain that covert modeling could help Ms. Weare find ways to express herself and could help her practice expressing herself before having the actual conference. Second, you would briefly describe the strategy, emphasizing that she will be practicing her role and responses in the school conference, using her imagination.

2. Practice Scenes. You would explain that it is helpful to see how she feels about practicing through her imagination. You would select several unrelated scenes, such as imagining someone coming to her home, imagining an old friend calling her, or imagining a new television show about a policewoman. You would present one practice scene and instruct Ms. Weare first to close her eyes, imagine the scene intensely, and signal to you with her finger when she has a strong picture in her mind. After this point, you could tell her to open her eyes and to describe the details of what she imagined. You might suggest additional details and present the same scene again or present a different scene. If Ms. Weare is able to use imagery easily and comfortably, you could move on to developing the actual treatment scenes.

3. Developing Treatment Scenes. At this point, you would seek Ms. Weare's input about certain aspects of the scenes to be used as treatment scenes. Specifically, you would decide who would be used as the model, whether individualized or standardized scenes would be used, and whether Ms. Weare felt she could benefit from general or specific scenes. Our preference would be to use fairly specific, individualized scenes in which Ms. Weare imagines herself as the model, as she will ultimately be carrying out the action. Next, you should specify the three ingredients of the scenes: (1) the situation in which the behaviors should occur, (2) the behaviors to be demonstrated, and (3) a favorable outcome. For example, the scenes could include Ms. Weare calling the teacher to set up the conference, beginning the conference, explaining her strategy in the conference, and ending the conference. Specific examples of things she could say would be included in each scene. Favorable outcomes might take the form of covert self-praise or of relief from stressful, anxious feelings.

4. Applying Treatment Scenes. After all the treatment scenes have been developed, Ms. Weare would arrange them in a hierarchy from least to most difficult. Starting with the first scene in the hierarchy, you would again instruct Ms. Weare about how to imagine. After the first scene presentation, you would obtain Ms. Weare's reactions to the clearness of her imagery, the duration of the scene, and so on. Any needed revisions could be incorporated before a second presentation of the same scene. You would also encourage Ms. Weare to develop a verbal summary code for each scene after the initial presentation of that scene. You would present each scene to Ms. Weare several times, then have her self-direct her own scene imagining several times. After all the scenes in the hierarchy had been covered adequately, Ms. Weare would be ready for homework.

(continued)

FEEDBACK
12.4 Covert Modeling (continued)

5. Homework. You would instruct Ms. Weare to continue to practice the scenes in her imagination outside the session. A follow-up should be arranged. You should be sure that Ms. Weare understands how many times to practice and how such practice can benefit her. Ms. Weare might record her practice sessions on log sheets. She could also call in and verbalize the scenes, using a phone mate.

---

5. **Helper:** OK, now, Joan, I'm going to describe a scene to you. As I do so, I want you to imagine the scene as vividly as possible. When you feel you have a very strong picture, then raise your index finger. Does that seem clear?

Client: Yes.

The helper will offer a practice scene next. Note that the *practice scene* is simple and relatively mundane. It asks Joan only to imagine another person.

6. **Helper:** Imagine that someone is about to offer you a summer job. Just picture a person who might offer you a job like this [gives Joan time until Joan raises her index finger].

In response 7, the helper asks Joan *to describe what she imagined.*

7. **Helper:** Joan, now open your eyes. Can you tell me what you just imagined?

Client: I pictured myself with a middle-aged man who asked me if I wanted to lifeguard this summer. Naturally I told him yes.

Joan's imagery report was specific in terms of the actions and dialogue, but she didn't describe much about the man, so the helper *will probe for more details.*

8. **Helper:** Fine. What else did you imagine about the man? You mentioned his age. What was he wearing? Any physical characteristics you can recall?

Client: Well, he was about 35 [a 16-year-old's impression of "middle age" is different from a 30-, 40-, or 50-year-old person's definition], and he was wearing shorts and a golf shirt—you see, we were by the pool. That's about it.

Joan was able to describe the setting and the man's dress but no other physical characteristics, so the helper *will suggest that Joan add this to the next practice attempt.*

9. **Helper:** So you were able to see what he was wearing and also the setting where he was talking to you. I'd like to try another practice with this same scene. Just imagine everything you did before, only this time try to imagine even more details about how this man actually looks. [Helper presents the same scene, which goes on until Joan raises her finger.]

In response 10, the helper will again *query Joan about the details of her imagery.*

10. **Helper:** OK, let's stop. What else did you imagine this time about this person or the situation?

Client: He was wearing white shorts and a blue shirt. He was a tall man and very tanned. He had dark hair, blue eyes, and had sunglasses on. He was also barefoot. We were standing on the pool edge. The water was blue, and the sun was out and it felt hot.

In response 11, the helper *will try to determine how comfortable Joan is with imagery* and whether more practice scenes are necessary.

11. **Helper:** That's great. Looks like you were able to imagine colors and temperature—like the sun feeling hot. How comfortable do you feel now with this process?

Client: Oh, I like it. It was easier the second time you described the scene. I put more into it. I like to imagine this anyway.

In response 12, the helper decides Joan can move ahead and *initiates development of treatment scenes.*

12. **Helper:** I believe we can go on now. Our next step is to come up with some scenes that describe the situations you find yourself in now with respect to participation in math class.

Client: And then I'll imagine them in the same way?

The helper sets the stage to *obtain all the necessary information to develop treatment scenes*. Note the emphasis in response 13 on Joan's *participation* in this process.

13. **Helper:** That's right. Once we work out the details of these scenes, you'll imagine each scene as you just did. Now we have sort of a series of things we need to discuss in setting up the scenes in a way that makes it easiest for you to imagine, so I'll be asking you some questions. Your input is very valuable here to both of us.

Client: OK, shoot.

In response 14, the helper *asks Joan whether she would rather imagine herself or someone else* as the model.

14. **Helper:** First of all, in that practice scene I asked you to imagine someone else. Now, you did that, but you were also able to picture yourself from the report you gave me. In using your class scenes, which do you feel would be easiest and least stressful for you to imagine—yourself going through the scene or someone else, maybe someone similar to you, but another person? [Gives Joan time to think.]

Client (pauses): Well, that's hard to say. I think it would be easier for me to imagine myself, but it might be a little less stressful to imagine someone else . . . [pauses again]. I think I'd like to try using myself.

In the next response, the helper *reinforces Joan's choice and also points out the flexibility of implementing the procedure*.

15. **Helper:** That's fine. And besides, as you know, nothing is that fixed. If we get into this and that doesn't feel right and you want to imagine someone else, we'll change.

Client: Okey-dokey.

In response 16, the helper *introduces the idea of a coping model*.

16. **Helper:** Also, sometimes it's hard to imagine yourself doing something perfectly to start with, so when we get into this, I might describe a situation where you might have a little trouble but not much. That may seem more realistic to you. What do you think?

Client: That seems reasonable. I know what you mean. It's like learning to drive a car. In Driver's Ed, we take one step at a time.

In response 17, the helper *will pose the option of individualizing the scenes* or using *standardized scenes*.

17. **Helper:** You've got the idea. Now we have another choice also in the scenes we use. We can work out scenes just for you that are tailored to your situation, or we can use scenes on a cassette tape I have that have been standardized for many students who want to improve their class-participation skills. Which sounds like the best option to you?

Client: I really don't know. Does it really make a difference?

It is not that uncommon for a client not to know which route to pursue. In the next response, the helper will *indicate a preference* and check it out with Joan.

18. **Helper:** Probably not, Joan. If you don't have a choice at this point, you might later. My preference would be to tailor-make the scenes we use here in the session. Then, if you like, you could use the taped scenes to practice with at home later on. How does that sound to you?

Client: It sounds good, like maybe we could use both.

In responses 19 and 20, the helper asks Joan to *identify situations in which Joan desires to increase these skills*. This is somewhat a review of goal behavior, described in Chapter 10.

19. **Helper:** Yes, I think we can. Now let's concentrate on getting some of the details we need to make up the scenes we'll use in our sessions. First of all, let's go over the situations in math class in which you want to work on these skills.

Client: It's some of those things we talked about earlier, like being called on, going to the board, and so on.

Next, the helper *explores whether Joan prefers a very general description or a very specific one*. Sometimes this makes a difference in how the person imagines.

20. **Helper:** OK, Joan, how much detail would you like me to give you when I describe a scene—a little detail, to let you fill in the rest, or do you want me to describe pretty completely what you should imagine?

Client: Maybe somewhere in between. I can fill in a lot, but I need to know what to fill in.

In response 21, the helper is *asking about the specific situations* in which Joan has trouble participating in her math class.

21. **Helper:** Let's fill out our description a little more. We're talking about situations you confront in your math class. I remember four situations in which you wanted to increase these skills—you want to answer more when

Mr. Lamborne calls on you, volunteer more answers, go to the board, and tell Mr. Lamborne you want to work the problems yourself after you ask for an explanation. Any others, Joan?

Client: I can't think of any offhand.

In responses 22–27, the helper asks Joan to *identify the desired behaviors for these situations*. Again, much of this is a review of identifying outcome goals (see Chapter 10).

22. **Helper:** So we've got about four different situations. Let's take each of these separately. For each situation, can we think of what you would like to do in the situation—like when Mr. Lamborne calls on you, for instance?

Client: I'd like to give him the answer instead of saying nothing or saying "I don't know."

23. **Helper:** Good. And if you did give him the answer—especially when you do know it—how would you feel?

Client: Good, probably relieved.

24. **Helper:** OK. Now what about volunteering answers?

Client: Well, Mr. Lamborne usually asks who has the answer to this; then he calls on people who raise their hand. I usually never raise my hand even when I do know the answer, so I need to just raise my hand and, when he calls on me, give the answer. I need to speak clearly, too. I think sometimes my voice is too soft to hear.

25. **Helper:** Now, how could you tell Mr. Lamborne to let you work out the problems yourself?

Client: Just go up to him when we have a work period and tell him the part I'm having trouble with and ask him to explain it.

26. **Helper:** So you need to ask him for just an explanation and let him know you want to do the work.

Client: Yup.

27. **Helper:** Now, what about going to the board?

Client: Well, I do go up. But I always feel like a fool. I get distracted by the rest of the class, so I hardly ever finish the problem. Then he lets me go back to my seat even though I didn't finish it. I need to concentrate more so I can get through the entire problem on the board.

Now that the content of the scenes has been developed, the helper asks Joan to *arrange the four scenes in a hierarchy*.

28. **Helper:** So we've got four different situations in your math class where you want to improve your participation in some way. Let's take these four situations and arrange them in an order. Could you select the situation that right now is easiest for you and least stressful to you, and rank the rest in terms of difficulty and degree of stress?

Client: Sure, let me think. . . . Well, the easiest thing to do out of all of these would be to tell Mr. Lamborne I want to work out the problems myself. Then I guess it would be answering when he calls on me and then going to the board. I have a lot of trouble with volunteering answers, so that would be hardest for me.

The helper emphasizes the *flexibility of the hierarchy* and provides *general instructions to Joan about how they will work with these scenes*.

29. **Helper:** OK. Now, this order can change. At any point if you feel it isn't right, we can reorder these situations. What we will do is to take one situation at a time, starting with the easiest one, and I'll describe it to you in terms of the way you want to handle it and ask you to imagine it. So the first scene will involve your telling Mr. Lamborne what you need explained in order to work the problems yourself.

Client: So we do this just like we did at the beginning?

The helper will *precede the scene presentation with very specific instructions* to Joan.

30. **Helper:** Right. Just sit back, close your eyes, and relax . . . [gives Joan a few minutes to do so]. Now remember, as I describe the scene, you are going to imagine yourself in the situation. Try to use all your senses in your imagination—in other words, get into it. When you have a very vivid picture, raise your index finger. Keep imagining the scene until I give a signal to stop. OK?

Client: Yeah.

The helper *presents the first scene in Joan's hierarchy slowly* and with ample pauses to give Joan time to generate the images.

31. **Helper:** Joan, picture yourself in math class . . . [pause]. Mr. Lamborne has just finished explaining how to solve for x and y. . . . Now he has assigned problems to you and has given you a work period. . . . You are starting to do the problems, and you realize there is some part of the equation you can't figure out. You take your worksheet and get up out of your seat and go to Mr. Lamborne's desk. You are telling Mr. Lamborne what part of the equation you're

having trouble with. You explain to him you don't want him to solve the problem, just to explain the missing part. Now you're feeling good that you were able to go up and ask him for an explanation. [The helper waits for about 10 seconds after Joan signals with her finger.]

The helper *signals Joan to stop* and in responses 32–35 *solicits Joan's reactions* about the imagery.

32. **Helper:** OK, Joan, open your eyes now. What did you imagine?

Client: It was pretty easy. I just imagined myself going up to Mr. Lamborne and telling him I needed more explanation but that I wanted to find the answers myself.

33. **Helper:** So you were able to get a pretty vivid picture?

Client: Yes, very much so.

34. **Helper:** What were your feelings during this—particularly as you imagined yourself?

Client: I felt pretty calm. It didn't really bother me.

35. **Helper:** So imagining yourself wasn't too stressful. Did I give you enough time before I signaled to stop?

Client: Well, probably. Although I think I could have gone on a little longer.

On the basis of Joan's response about the length of the first scene, the helper will *modify the length during the next presentation*.

36. **Helper:** OK, I'll give you a little more time the next time.

Before the helper presents the treatment scenes the second time, the helper explores whether the client would like to use *verbal summary codes* or to *personalize the treatment scenes*.

37. **Helper:** Joan, there are two techniques that you can use to enhance your imagery scene of Mr. Lamborne's math class. One technique is to describe briefly the behavior you want to do and the situation in Mr. Lamborne's class when you will perform the behavior. All that you are doing is just describing the scene in your own words. This process can help you remember what to do. With the other technique, you can change the scene or elaborate on the scene in any way as long as you still imagine engaging in the behaviors you want to do. Do you have any questions about these two techniques?

Client: You think these techniques might help me imagine the scene better?

38. **Helper:** That's right. Is there one technique you think might be more helpful to you?

Client: Yes, I think that for me to describe the scene in my own words might work better for me. It might help me to remember better what to do.

39. **Helper:** OK, for the first scene, what verbal summary or description would you use?

Client: Well—after Mr. Lamborne explains how to solve for x and y and assigns problems, I might find something I can't figure out. I get out of my seat and go up to Mr. Lamborne and tell him I need more explanation but I want to find the answer myself.

40. **Helper:** That's great, Joan!

The helper *presents the same scene again*. Usually each scene is presented *a minimum of two times* by the helper or on a tape recorder. If the client has chosen one or both treatment-scene enhancement techniques, instruct the client on the technique with each scene.

41. **Helper:** Let's try it again. I'll present the same scene, and I'll give you more time after you signal to me that you have a strong picture [presents the same scene again and checks out Joan's reactions after the second presentation].

After the helper-presented scenes, the helper *asks Joan to self-direct her own practice*. This also occurs a minimum of two times for each scene.

42. **Helper:** You seem pretty comfortable now in carrying out this situation the way you want to. This time, instead of my describing the scene orally to you, I'd like you just to go through the scene on your own—sort of a mental practice without my assistance.

Client: OK [pauses to do this for several minutes].

43. **Helper:** How did that feel?

Client: It was pretty easy even without your instructions, and I think I can see where I can actually do this now with Mr. Lamborne.

The other scenes in the hierarchy are worked through in the same manner.

44. **Helper:** Good. Now we will work through the other three scenes in the same manner, sticking with each one until you can perform your desired behaviors in your imagination pretty easily. [The other three situations in the hierarchy are worked through.]

45. **Helper:** Well, how do you feel now that we've gone over every scene?

Client: Pretty good. I never thought that my imagination would help me in math class!

After the hierarchy has been completed, the helper *picks scenes to practice at random*. This is a way to see how easily the client can perform the scene when it is not presented in the order of the hierarchy.

46. **Helper:** Sometimes imagining yourself doing something helps you learn how to do it in the actual situation. Now I'd like to just pick a scene here at random and present it to you and have you imagine it again [selects a scene from the hierarchy at random and describes it].

Client: That was pretty easy, too.

The helper *initiates homework practice* for Joan.

47. **Helper:** I just wanted to give you a chance to imagine a scene when I took something out of the order we worked with today. I believe you are ready to carry out this imagination practice on your own during the week.

Client: Is this where I use the tapes?

The *purpose of homework* is explained to Joan.

48. **Helper:** Sure. This tape has a series of scenes dealing with verbal class participation. So instead of needing me to describe a scene, the tape can do this. I'd like you to practice with this daily, because daily practice will help you learn to participate more quickly and easily.

Client: So I just go over a scene the way we did today?

The helper instructs Joan on *how to complete the homework practice*.

49. **Helper:** Go over the scenes one at a time—maybe about four times for each scene. Make your imagination as vivid as possible. Also, each time you go over a scene, make a check on your log sheets. Indicate the time of day and place where you use this—also, the length of each practice. And after each practice session, rate the vividness of your imagery on this scale: 1 is not vivid, and 5 is very vivid. How about summarizing what you will do for your homework?

Client: Yes. I just do what we did today and check the number of times I practice each scene and assign a number to the practice according to how strongly I imagined the scene.

At the termination of the session, the helper *indicates that a follow-up on the homework* will occur at their next meeting.

50. **Helper:** Right. And bring your log sheets in at our next meeting, and we'll go over this homework then. OK? We had a really good session today. You worked hard. I'll see you next Tuesday.

SUMMARY

The modeling strategies presented in this chapter can be used to help clients acquire new responses or extinguish fears or other barriers. The modeling procedures differ slightly. Participant modeling usually employs a live modeling demonstration designed to promote learning by providing a model of goal behaviors for the client. Guided imagery and covert modeling may be useful when live modeling is not feasible. These strategies can be used without elaborate therapeutic aids or expensive equipment. Both strategies involve imagery, which makes the procedures quite easy for a client to practice in a self-directed manner. The capacity of clients to generate vivid images may be important for the overall effectiveness of guided imagery and covert modeling. Assessing client potential to engage in imagery is a necessary prerequisite before using either of these procedures. Assuming that clients can produce clear images, helpers may use guided imagery to help them deal with fears or discomfort or to teach them covert modeling to promote desired responses.

Modeling appears to have applicability across diverse client groups and subgroups, although the research base is not yet highly developed. When modeling has been found to be an effective and appropriate intervention for a diverse group of clients—including but not limited to age and cognitive ability—the type of model should be culturally and/or contextually similar to the client, and the content of the modeled presentation should be culturally relevant. Although imagery has been used in limited ways with diverse clients, it is an intervention that can be helpful if the imagery is adapted to and relevant to the client's context and sense of self. Modeling and self-instructional techniques are quite amenable to educational and collaborative work style between client and helper, yielding self-help tools that clients can use outside and beyond formal work with the practitioner.

INFOTRAC® EXPLORATIONS

1. Search for the term *guided imagery*. Select three articles, and compare the types of issues they target and the outcomes they aim to effect (e.g., development of new cognitive schemas, greater relaxation, relieving pain).

2. InfoTrac® does not presently organize under terms related to *modeling*. An alternative is to use a database such as PsychInfo, search for *modeling*, and contrast the types of issues for which varying forms of modeling (participant, covert, symbolic) are applied.

SUGGESTED RESOURCES

Readings

Achterberg, J. (1985). *Imagery in healing: Shamanism and modern medicine*. Boston: Shambhala.

Arbuthnott, K. D., Arbuthnott, D. W., & Rossiter, L. (2001a). Guided imagery and memory: Implications for psychotherapists. *Journal of Counseling Psychology, 48,* 123–132.

Baider, L., Uziely, B., & Kaplan-DeNour, A. (1994). Progressive muscle relaxation and guided imagery in cancer patients. *General Hospital Psychiatry, 16,* 340–347.

Beck, J. S. (1995). *Cognitive therapy: Basics and beyond*. New York: Guilford.

Botvin, G., Baker, E., Botvin, E., & Dusenbury, L. (1993). Factors promoting cigarette smoking among black youth: A causal modeling approach. *Addictive Behaviors, 18,* 397–405.

Brigham, D. (1994). *Imagery for getting well*. New York: Norton.

Clancy, S. M., McNally, R. J., & Schacter, D. L. (1999). Effects of guided imagery on memory distortion in women reporting recovered memories of childhood sexual abuse. *Journal of Traumatic Stress, 12,* 559–569.

Faust, J., Olson, R., & Rodriguez, H. (1991). Same-day surgery preparation: Reduction of pediatric patient arousal and distress through participating modeling. *Journal of Consulting and Clinical Psychology, 59,* 475–478.

Hughes, D. (1990). Participant modeling as a classroom activity. *Teaching of Psychology, 17,* 238–240.

Ilacqua, G. E. (1994). Migraine headaches: Coping efficacy of guided imagery training. *Headache, 34,* 99–102.

Lazarus, A. (1984). *In the mind's eye: The power of imagery for personal enrichment*. New York: Guilford.

Maibach, E., & Flora, J. A. (1993). Symbolic modeling and cognitive rehearsal: Using video to promote AIDS prevention self-efficacy. Special Issue: The role of communication in health promotion. *Communication Research, 20,* 517–545.

Mail, P. (1995). Early modeling of drinking behavior by Native American elementary school children playing drunk. *International Journal of Addictions, 30,* 1187–1197.

Matson, J. (1985). Modeling. In A. S. Bellack & M. Hersen (Eds.), *Dictionary of behavior therapy techniques* (pp. 150–151). New York: Pergamon.

Myrick, R. D., & Myrick, L. S. (1993). Guided imagery: From mystical to practical. Special Issue: Counseling and children's play. *Elementary School Guidance and Counseling, 28,* 62–70.

Overholser, J. C. (1991). The use of guided imagery in psychotherapy: Modules for use with passive relaxation training. *Journal of Contemporary Psychotherapy, 21,* 159–172.

Reyes, M., Routh, D., Jean-Gilles, M., & Sanfilippo, M. (1991). Ethnic differences in parenting children in fearful situations. *Journal of Pediatric Psychology, 16,* 717–726.

Romi, S., & Teichman, M. (1995). Participant and symbolic modelling training programmes. *British Journal of Guidance and Counseling, 23,* 83–94.

Rosenthal, T. (1993). To soothe the savage beast. *Behaviour Research and Therapy, 31,* 439–462.

Rosenthal, T. L., & Steffek, B. D. (1991). Modeling methods. In F. H. Kanfer & A. P. Goldstein (Eds.), *Helping people change* (4th ed., pp. 70–121). New York: Pergamon.

Suinn, R. (1986). *Seven steps to peak performance: The mental training manual for athletes*. Lewiston, NY: Huber.

Wurtele, S. K., Marrs, S. R., & Miller-Perrin, C. L. (1987). Practice makes perfect? The role of participant modeling in sexual abuse prevention programs. *Journal of Consulting and Clinical Psychology, 55,* 599–602.

Wynd, C. A. (1992). Personal power imagery and relaxation techniques used in smoking cessation programs. *American Journal of Health Promotion, 6,* 184–189, 196.

Web Sites*

Guided Imagery
Academy for Guided Imagery Online
http://www.healthy.net/agi/index_explorer.html

*Video and CD resources are available through these and other Web sites.

Guided Imagery, Hypnosis, Eriksonian Therapy
http://www.e-help.com/hypnosis_guided_imagery_ericksonian_therapy.htm

Joint Commission on Accreditation of Healthcare Organizations (JCAHO), guidelines for use of strategies in pain management (e.g., imagery, massage, self-statements, and relaxation)
http://www.jcaho.org/

What Is Guided Imagery?
http://www.guidedimageryinc.com/guided.html

Interventions:
CMHC Systems
http://www.cmhc.com

Internet Mental Health
http://www.mentalhealth.com

Merlin Cap College Therapy Web Links
http://merlin.capcollege.bc.ca/psych/chapter%20links/15.htm

Online Dictionary of Mental Health
http://www.shef.ac.uk/~psysc/psychotherapy

Psych Central: Dr. John Grohol's Mental Health Page
http://www.grohol.com

12 POSTEVALUATION

Part One

Objective One asks you to develop a script for a symbolic model. Your script should contain the following:

1. Examples of the modeled dialogue
2. Opportunities for practice
3. Feedback
4. Summarization

Use the Checklist for Developing Model Scripts as a guide.

Part Two

Objective Two asks you to describe how you would apply the four components of participant modeling with a hypothetical client case. Describe how you would use the four components (rationale, modeling, guided practice, and success experiences) to help a client acquire verbal and nonverbal skills necessary to initiate social contacts with someone he or she wants to ask out.

Part Three

Objective Three asks you to demonstrate 14 out of 17 steps of participant modeling with a role-play client. The client might take the role of someone who is afraid to perform certain responses or activities in certain situations. You can assess yourself, using the Interview Checklist for Participant Modeling below. Feedback for the postevaluation follows.

Checklist for Developing Model Scripts

Instructions: Determine whether the following guidelines have been incorporated into the construction of your model script. Check if completed:

_____ 1. Determine what clients will use the symbolic modeling procedure and identify their characteristics.
  _____ Age
  _____ Gender
  _____ Ethnic origin, cultural practices, and race
  _____ Coping or mastery model portrayed
  _____ Possesses similar concern to that of client group or population

_____ 2. Goal behaviors to be modeled by client have been enumerated.

_____ 3. Medium is selected (for example, written script, imaginary character from film or other source, someone the client knows and can either envision or interact with, self).

_____ 4. Script includes the following ingredients:
  _____ Instructions
  _____ Modeled dialogue
  _____ Practice
  _____ Written feedback
  _____ Written summarization of what has been modeled, with its importance for client

_____ 5. Written script has been field-tested.

Interview Checklist for Participant Modeling

Instructions: Determine which of the following leads the counselor used in the interview. Check the leads used.

Item	Examples of helper leads
I. Rationale about Strategy	
_____ A. Helper provides rationale about participant modeling strategy.	"This procedure has been used with other people who have concerns similar to yours. It is a way to help you overcome your fear of or to help you acquire these skills."
_____ B. Helper provides brief description of components of participant modeling.	"It involves three things. I'll model what you want to do, you'll practice this with my assistance, and then you'll try this out in situations that at first will be pretty easy for you so you can be successful."
_____ C. Helper asks for client's willingness to use strategy.	"Would you be willing to try this now?"

(continued)

12 POST EVALUATION

(continued)

II. Modeling

_____ 4. Helper and client decide whether to divide goal behaviors into a series of subtasks or skills.

"Well, let's see . . . Right now you hardly ever go out of the house. You say it bothers you even to go out in the yard. Let's see whether we can identify different activities in which you would gradually increase the distance away from the house, like going to the front door, going out on the porch, out in the yard, out to the sidewalk, to the neighbor's house, and so on."

_____ 5. If goal behaviors are divided (step 4), these subskills are arranged by helper and client in a hierarchy according to order of difficulty.

"Perhaps we can take our list and arrange it in an order. Start with the activity that is easiest for you now, such as going to the door. Arrange each activity in order of increasing difficulty."

_____ 6. Helper and client determine and select appropriate model.

"I could help you learn to do this, or we could pick someone whom you know or someone similar to yourself to guide you through this. What are your preferences?"

_____ 7. Helper provides instructions to client before demonstration of what to look for.

"Notice that when the doorbell rings, I will go to the door calmly and quickly and open it without hesitation. Also notice that after I go to the door, I'm still calm; nothing has happened to me."

_____ 8. Model demonstrates target response at least once; more demonstrations are repeated if necessary. If hierarchy is used, first skill is modeled, followed successively by all others, concluding with demonstration combining all subskills.

"OK, let me show this to you again."
"Now that I've done the first scene, next I'll show you stepping out on the porch. Then we'll combine these two scenes."

III. Guided Participation

_____ 9. Client is asked to perform target response. If a hierarchy is used, first skill in hierarchy is practiced first, successfully followed by second, third, and so on.

"This time you try going to the door when the doorbell rings. I will assist you as you need help."

_____ 10. After each practice, model or helper provides feedback consisting of positive feedback and error corrections.

"That was quite smooth. You were able to go to the door quickly. You still hesitated a little once you got there. Try to open the door as soon as you see who is there."

_____ 11. Initial practice attempts of each skill by client include a number of induction aids, such as

"I'm going to assist you in your first few practices."

_____ a. Joint practice with model or helper.

"Let's do it together. I will walk with you to the door."

_____ b. Verbal and/or physical coaching or guiding by model or helper.

"Let me give you a suggestion here. When you open the door, greet the person there. Find out what the person wants."

_____ c. Repeated practice of one subtask until client is ready to move on to another.

"Let's work on this a few more times until you feel really comfortable."

_____ d. Graduated time intervals for practice (short to long duration).

"This time we'll increase the distance you have to walk to the door. Let's start back in the kitchen."

12 POSTEVALUATION

	e. Arrangement of protective conditions for practice to reduce likelihood of feared or undesired consequences.	"We'll make sure someone else is in the house with you."
	f. Graduated levels of severity of threat or complexity of situation.	"OK, now we've worked with opening the door when a good friend is there. This time let's pretend it's someone you are used to seeing but don't know as a friend, like the person who delivers your mail."
____	12. In later practice attempts, number of induction aids is gradually reduced.	"I believe now that you can do this without my giving you so many prompts."
____	13. Before moving on, client is able to engage in self-directed practice of all desired responses.	"This time I'm going to leave. I want you to do this by yourself."

IV. Success Experiences (Homework)

____	14. Helper and client identify situations in client's environment in which client desires to perform target responses.	"Let's list all the actual times and places where you want to do this."
____	15. Situations are arranged in hierarchy from easy with least risk to difficult with greater risk.	"We can arrange these in an order. Put the easiest one first, and follow it by ones that are successively harder or more threatening for you."
____	16. Starting with easiest and least risky situation, helper (or model) and client use live or symbolic modeling and guided practice in client's real-life environment. Steps 4–11 are repeated outside session until gradually helper (or model) reduces level of assistance.	"Starting with the first situation, we're going to work with this when it actually occurs. At first I'll assist you until you can do it on your own."
____	17. Client is assigned a series of related tasks to carry out in a self-directed manner.	"Now you're ready to tackle this situation without my help. You have shown both of us you are ready to do this on your own."

Part Four

According to Objective Four, you should be able to identify accurately six out of seven examples of guided imagery steps represented in written examples of helper leads. For each of the following seven helper leads, write down which part of guided imagery the helper is implementing. More than one helper lead may be associated with any part of the procedure, and the leads given here are not in any particular order. The five major parts of emotive imagery are as follows:

1. Rationale
2. Determining the client's potential to use imagery
3. Developing imagery scenes
4. Imagery-scene practice training
5. Homework and follow-up

Feedback follows the Postevaluation on page 389.

1. "Can you think of several scenes you could imagine that give you calm and positive feelings? Supply as many details as you can. You can use these scenes later to focus on instead of the anxiety."
2. "It's important that you practice with this. Try to imagine these scenes at least several times each day."
3. "This procedure can help you control your anxiety. By imagining very pleasurable scenes, you can block out some of the fear."
4. "Let's see whether you feel that it's easy to imagine something. Close your eyes, sit back, and visualize anything that makes you feel relaxed."
5. "Now, select one of these scenes you've practiced. Imagine this very intensely. I'm going to apply pressure to your arm, but just focus on your imaginary scene."

(continued)

12 POSTEVALUATION

(continued)

6. "What we will do, if you feel that imagination is easy for you, is to develop some scenes that are easy for you to visualize and that make you feel relaxed. Then we'll practice having you focus on these scenes while also trying to block out fear."

7. "Now I'd like you just to practice these scenes we've developed. Take one scene at a time, sit back, and relax. Practice imagining this scene for about 30 seconds. I will tell you when the time is up."

Part Five

Objective Five asks you to demonstrate 10 out of 13 steps of guided imagery with a role-play client. You or an observer can rate your performance, assisted by the Interview Checklist for Guided Imagery below.

Part Six

Objective Six asks you to describe how you would use the five components of covert modeling with a simulated client case. Use the case of Mr. Huang (Chapter 8) and his stated goal of wanting to decrease his worrying about retirement and increase his positive thoughts about retiring, particularly in his work setting. Describe how you would use a rationale, practice scenes, developing treatment scenes, applying treatment scenes, and homework to help Mr. Huang do this. Feedback follows the Postevaluation.

Part Seven

Objective Seven asks you to demonstrate at least 22 out of 28 steps associated with covert modeling with a role-play client. The client might take the part of someone who wants to acquire certain skills or to perform certain activities. Use the Interview Checklist for Covert Modeling on pages 384–388 to help you assess your interview.

Interview Checklist for Guided Imagery

Instructions: In a role-play helper/client interview, determine which of the following helper leads or questions were demonstrated. Indicate by a check the leads used by the helper. A few examples of helper leads are presented in the right column.

Item	Examples of helper leads
I. Rationale	
_____ A. Helper describes purpose of guided imagery.	"The procedure is called guided imagery because you can emote pleasant thoughts or images in situations that evoke fear, pain, tension, anxiety, or routine boredom. The procedure helps you block your discomfort or reduce the anxiety that you experience in the difficult situation. The technique involves focusing on imaginary scenes that please you and make you feel relaxed while in the uncomfortable situation. This procedure works because it is extremely difficult for you to feel pleasant, calm, happy, secure, or whatever other emotion is involved in the scene and anxious (tense, fearful, stressed) at the same time. These emotions are incompatible."
_____ B. Helper gives an overview of procedure.	"What we will do first is to see how you feel about engaging in imagery and look at the details of the scene you used. Then we will decide whether guided imagery is a procedure we want to use. If we decide to use it, we will develop scenes that make you feel calm and good and generate positive feelings for you. We will practice using the

12 POSTEVALUATION

scenes we have developed and try to rehearse using those scenes in a simulated fashion. Later, you will apply and practice using the scene in the real situation. Do you have any questions about my explanation?"

_____ C. Helper assesses client's willingness to try strategy.

"Would you like to go ahead and give this a try now?"

II. Assessment of Client's Imagery Potential

_____ A. Helper instructs client to engage in imagery that elicits good feelings and calmness.

"Close your eyes, sit back, and relax. Visualize a scene or event that makes you feel relaxed and pleasant. Select something you really enjoy and feel good about. Try to be aware of all your sensations in the scene."

_____ B. After 30 seconds to a minute, the helper probes to ascertain the sensory vividness of the client's imagined scene (colors, sounds, movement, temperature, smell). Helper asks client's feelings about imagery and about "getting into" the scene (feeling good with imaginal process).

"Describe the scene to me."
"What sensations did you experience while picturing the scene?"
"What temperature, colors, sounds, smells, and motions did you experience in the scene?"
"How do you feel about the imagery?"
"How involved could you get with the scene?"

_____ C. Helper discusses with client the decision to continue or discontinue guided imagery. Decision is based on client's attitude (feelings about imagery) and imaginal vividness.

"You seem to feel good with the imagery and are able to picture a scene vividly. We can go ahead now and develop some scenes just for you."
"Perhaps another strategy that would reduce tension without imagery would be better as it is hard for you to 'get into' a scene."

III. Development of Imagery Scenes

_____ A. Helper and client develop at least two scenes that promote positive feelings for client, involve many sensations (sound, color, temperature, motion, and smell), and are culturally relevant.

"Now I would like to develop an inventory of scenes or situations that promote calmness, tranquility, and enjoyment for you. We want to have scenes that will have as much sensory detail as possible for you so that you can experience color, smell, temperature, touch, sound, and motion. Later, we will use the scenes to focus on instead of anxiety, so we want to find scenes for you that are also consistent with and meaningful to you culturally. What sort of scenes can you really get into?"

IV. Practice of Imagery Scene

_____ A. Helper instructs client to practice focusing on the scene for about 30 seconds.

"Take one of the scenes, close your eyes, sit back, and relax. Practice or hold this scene for about 30 seconds, picturing as much sensory detail as possible. I will cue you when the time is up."

_____ B. Helper instructs client to practice focusing on scene with simulated discomfort or anxiety.

"Let us attempt to simulate or create the difficult situation and to use the scenes. While I squeeze your arm to have you feel pain, focus on one of the imagery scenes we have developed."
"While I describe the feared situation or scene to you, focus on the scene."

(continued)

POST EVALUATION

(continued)

_____ C. Helper assesses client's reaction after simulated practice.	"How did that feel?" "What effects did my describing the discomforting situation [my application of pain] have on your relaxation?" "Rate your ability to focus on the scene with the discomfort." "How comfortable did you feel when you imagined this fearful situation then?"
V. Homework and Follow-Up	
_____ A. Helper instructs client to apply guided imagery *in vivo*.	"For homework, apply the guided imagery scenes to the discomforting situation. Focus on the scene as vividly as possible while you are experiencing the activity or situation."
_____ B. Helper instructs client to record use of guided imagery and to record level of discomfort or anxiety on log sheets.	"After each time you use guided imagery, record the situation, the day, the time, and your general reaction on this log. For each occasion that you use imagery, record also your level of discomfort or anxiety, using a 5-point scale, with 5 equal to maximum discomfort and 1 equal to minimum discomfort."
_____ C. Helper arranges a follow-up session.	"Let's get together again in two weeks to see how your practice is going and to go over your homework log."

Observer comments: _____

Interview Checklist for Covert Modeling

Instructions: Determine which of the following leads the helper used in the interview. Check the leads used.

Item	Examples of helper leads
I. Rationale	
_____ A. Helper describes purpose of strategy.	"This strategy can help you learn how to discuss your prison record in a job interview. I will coach you on some things you could say. As we go over this, gradually you will feel as if you can handle this situation when it comes up in an actual interview."
_____ B. Helper provides overview of strategy.	"We will be relying on your imagination a lot in this process. I'll be describing certain scenes and asking you to close your eyes and imagine that you are observing the situation I describe to you as vividly as you can."
_____ C. Helper confirms client's willingness to use strategy.	"Would you like to give this a try now?"
II. Practice Scenes	
_____ A. Helper instructs client to sit back, close eyes, and relax in preparation for imagining practice scenes.	"Just sit back, relax, and close your eyes."
_____ B. Helper describes a practice scene unrelated to goal and instructs client to imagine scene as	"As I describe this scene, try to imagine it very intensely. Imagine the situation as vividly as possible. When you feel

12 POSTEVALUATION

        helper describes it and to raise index finger when scene is vividly imagined.

_____ C. After client indicates vivid imagery, helper instructs client to open eyes and describe what was imagined during scene.

_____ D. Helper probes for additional details about scene to obtain a very specific description from client.

_____ E. Helper suggests ways for client to attend to additional details during subsequent practice.

_____ F. Helper initiates additional practices of one scene or introduces practice of new scene until client is comfortable with the novelty and is able to provide a detailed description of imagery.

_____ G. After practice scenes, helper does one of the following:
    a. Decides to move on to developing treatment scenes.
    b. Decides that relaxation or additional imagery training is necessary.

    c. Decides to terminate covert modeling because of inadequate client imagery.

III. Developing Treatment Scenes

_____ H. Helper and client decide on appropriate characteristics of model to be used in treatment scenes, including
    _____ a. Identity of model (client or someone else)

    _____ b. Coping or mastery model

    _____ c. Single or multiple models

    _____ d. Specific characteristics of model to maximize client/model similarity

_____ I. Helper and client specify
    _____ a. Individualized scenes
    _____ b. Standardized scenes

_____ J. Helper and client decide to use either
    a. General descriptions of scenes
    b. Specific, detailed descriptions of scenes

you have a vivid picture, raise your index finger."

"OK, now let's stop—you can open your eyes. Tell me as much as you can about what you just imagined."

"Did you imagine the color of the room? What did the people look like? Were there any noticeable odors around you? How were you feeling?"

"Let's do another scene. This time try to imagine not only what you see but what you hear, smell, feel, and touch."

"Let's go over another scene. We'll do this for a while until you feel pretty comfortable with this."

"OK, this seems to be going pretty easily for you, so we will go on now."

"I believe before we go on it might be useful to try to help you relax a little more. We can use muscle relaxation for this purpose."

"Judging from this practice, I believe another approach would be more helpful where you can actually see someone do this."

"As you imagine this scene, you can imagine either yourself or someone else in this situation. Which would be easier for you to imagine?"

"Sometimes it's easier to imagine someone who doesn't do this perfectly. What do you think?"

"We can have you imagine just one other person—someone like you—or several other people."

"Let's talk over the specific type of person you will imagine, someone similar to you."

"We have two options in developing the scenes you will imagine. We can discuss different situations and develop the scenes just to fit you, or we can use some standardized scenes that might apply to anyone with a prison record going through a job interview. What is your preference?"

"On the basis of these situations you've just described, I can present them to you in one of two ways. One way is to

(continued)

POSTEVALUATION

(continued)

_____ K. Helper and client develop specific ingredients to be used in scenes. Ingredients include
    _____ a. Situations or context in which behaviors should occur

    _____ b. Behaviors and coping methods to be demonstrated by model

    _____ c. Favorable outcome of scene, such as
        _____ 1. Favorable client self-initiated action
        _____ 2. Client self-reinforcement

_____ L. Helper and client generate descriptions of multiple scenes.

IV. Applying Treatment Scenes
_____ A. Helper and client arrange multiple scenes in a hierarchy for scene presentation according to
    _____ a. Client degree of discomfort in situation
    _____ b. Degree of difficulty or complexity of situation

_____ B. Helper precedes scene presentation with instructions to client, including
    _____ a. Instructions to sit back, relax, close eyes
    _____ b. Instructions on whom to imagine
    _____ c. Instructions to imagine intensely, using as many senses as possible
    _____ d. Instructions to raise index finger when vivid imagery occurs
    _____ e. Instructions to hold imagery until helper signals to stop

_____ C. Helper presents one scene at a time, by describing the scene orally to client or with

give you a general description and leave it up to you to fill in the details. Or I can be very detailed and tell you specifically what to imagine. Which approach do you think would be best for you?"

"Let's decide the kinds of things that will go in each scene."

"In the scene in which you are interviewing for a job, go over the type of job you might seek and the kind of employer who would be hard to talk to."

"Now, what you want to do in this situation is to discuss your record calmly, explaining what happened and emphasizing that your record won't interfere with your job performance."

"At the end of the scene you might want to imagine you have discussed your record calmly without getting defensive."

"At the end of the scene, congratulate yourself or encourage yourself for being able to discuss your record."

"OK, now the job interview is one scene. Let's develop other scenes where you feel it's important to be able to discuss your record—for example, in establishing a closer relationship with a friend."

"Now I'd like you to take these six scenes we've developed and arrange them in an order. Start with the situation that you feel most comfortable with and that is easiest for you to discuss your record in now. End with the situation that is most difficult and gives you the most discomfort or tension."

"I'm going to tell you now what to do when the scene is presented."

"First, just sit back, close your eyes, and relax."

"Now come up with an image of the person you're going to imagine, someone similar to you."

"As I describe the scene, imagine it as vividly as possible. Use all your senses—sight, smell, touch, and so on."

"When you start to imagine very vividly, raise your finger."

"And hold that vivid image until I tell you when to stop."

"Here is the first scene. . . . Imagine the employer is now asking you why you got so far behind in school. Imagine

12 POSTEVALUATION

	a tape recorder.	that you are explaining what happened in a calm voice." "You should be able to imagine yourself saying all you want to about your record before I stop you."
____ D.	Duration of each scene is determined individually for client and is held until client imagines model performing desired behavior as completely as possible (perhaps 20–30 seconds).	
____ E.	After first scene presentation, helper solicits client reactions about	
	____ a. Rate of delivery and duration of scene	"How did the length of the scene seem to you?"
	____ b. Clearness and vividness of client imagery	"How intense were your images? What did you imagine?"
	____ c. Degree of discomfort or pleasantness of scene	"How did you feel while doing this?"
____ F.	On basis of client reactions to first scene presentation, helper does one of the following:	
	____ a. Presents scene again as is	"I'm going to present this same scene again."
	____ b. Revises scene or manner of presentation before second presentation	"Based on what you've said, let's change the type of employer. Also, I'll give you more time to imagine this the next time."
	____ c. Changes scene order in hierarchy and presents another scene next	"Perhaps we need to switch the order of this scene and use this other one first."
	____ d. Precedes another presentation of scene with relaxation or discussion of client discomfort	"Let's talk about your discomfort."
____ G.	Imagery enhancement techniques explained to client:	
	____ a. Verbal summary codes	"You can briefly describe the scene in your own words, which can help you remember the behaviors to perform in the situation."
	____ b. Personalization or elaboration of treatment scene	"You can change or elaborate on the scene in any way as long as you still imagine the behavior you want to do."
____ H.	Each scene is presented a minimum of two times by helper or on tape recorder.	"OK, now I'm going to present the same scene one or two more times."
____ I.	Following helper presentations of scene, client repeats scene at least twice in a self-directed manner.	"This time I'd like you to present the scene to yourself while imagining it, without relying on me to describe it."
____ J.	After each scene in hierarchy is presented and imagined satisfactorily, helper presents some scenes to client in a random order, following steps IV C, D, and E.	"Now I'm just going to pick a scene at random and describe it while you imagine it."

V. Homework

____ A.	Helper instructs client to practice scenes daily outside session and explains purpose of daily practice.	"During the week, I'd like you to take these cards where we've made a written description of these scenes and practice the scenes on your own. This will help you acquire this behavior more easily and quickly."
____ B.	Instructions for homework include	

(continued)

POSTEVALUATION

(continued)

     _____ a. What to do

     _____ b. How often to do it

     _____ c. When and where to do it

     _____ d. A method for self-observation of homework completion

_____ C. Helper arranges for a follow-up after completion of some amount of homework.

"Just go over one scene at a time—make your imagination as vivid as possible."
"Go over this five times daily."
"Go over this two times at home and three times at school."
"Each time you go over the scene, make a tally on your log sheet. Also, after each practice session, rate the intensity of your imagery on this scale."
"Bring these sheets next week so we can discuss your practices and see what we need to do as the next step."

Observer comments: _____
_____
_____

POSTEVALUATION FEEDBACK

PART ONE

Check the contents of your script outline with item 4 on the Checklist for Developing Model Scripts on page 379.

PART TWO

Here is a brief description of how you might use participant modeling to help your client:

Rationale First, you would explain to your client that the procedure can help him or her acquire the kinds of skills he or she will need to initiate social contacts with someone to ask out. You would also tell him or her that the procedure involves modeling, guided practice, and success experiences. You might emphasize that the procedure is based on the idea that change can occur when the desired activities are learned in small steps with successful performance emphasized at each step.

Modeling You and your client would explore the verbal and nonverbal responses that might be involved in approaching people and asking them to lunch, for a drink, and so on. For example, these skills might be divided into making a verbal request, speaking without hesitation or errors, and speaking in a firm, strong voice. After specifying all the components of the desired response, you and your client would arrange them in a hierarchy according to order of difficulty.

You and your client would select a culturally appropriate model—yourself or an aide. The model selected would demonstrate to the client the first response in the hierarchy (followed by all the others). Repeated demonstrations of any response might be necessary.

Guided Participation After the modeled demonstration of a response, you would ask your client to perform it. The first attempts would be assisted with induction aids administered by you or the model. For example, you might verbally coach the client to start with a short message and gradually increase it. After each practice, you would give your client feedback, being sure to encourage his or her positive performance and to make suggestions for improvement. Generally, your client would practice each response several times, and the number of induction aids would be reduced gradually. Before moving on to practice a different response, your client should be able to perform the response in a self-directed manner without your presence or support.

Success Experiences You and your client would identify situations in his or her environment in which the client would like to use the learned skills. In this case, most of the applications would be in social situations. Some of these situations

12 POSTEVALUATION FEEDBACK

involve more risk than others. The situations should be arranged in order, from the least to the most risky. The client would work on the least risky situation until he or she was able to do that easily and successfully before going on. Ideally, it would help to have the helper or model go along with the client to model and guide. If the model was one of the client's colleagues, this would be possible. If this was not possible, the client could telephone the helper just before the "contact" to rehearse and to receive coaching and encouragement.

PART THREE

Use the Interview Checklist for Participant Modeling to assess your performance or to have someone else rate you.

PART FOUR

1. *Instructing the client to develop imagery scenes*—used to focus on to block the unpleasant sensation.
2. Part of *homework*—*in vivo* application of imagery.
3. *Rationale*—giving the client a reason for guided imagery.
4. *The client's potential to use imagery*—determining the level.
5. *Imagery-scene practice*—with a pain-provoking situation.
6. *Rationale*—giving an overview of the procedure.
7. *Imagery-scene practice*—training the client to imagine the scenes very vividly before using them in simulation of anxiety-provoking situations.

PART FIVE

Rate your performance with the Interview Checklist for Guided Imagery, found in the Postevaluation.

PART SIX

Rationale First you would give Mr. Huang an explanation of covert modeling. You would briefly describe the process to him and explain how using his imagination to "see" someone doing something could help him perform his desired responses.

Practice Scenes Next you would present a couple of unrelated practice scenes. You would instruct Mr. Huang to close his eyes, relax, and imagine the scene as you describe it. When Mr. Huang signals that he is imagining the scene, you would stop and query him about what he imagined. You might suggest additional details for him to imagine during another practice scene. Assuming that Mr. Huang feels relaxed and can generate vivid images, you would go on to develop treatment scenes.

Developing Treatment Scenes You and Mr. Huang would specify certain components to be included in the treatment scenes, including the identity of the model (Mr. Huang or someone else), type of model (coping or mastery), single or multiple models, and specific characteristics of the model to maximize client/model similarity. Next you would decide whether to use individualized or standardized scenes; perhaps in Mr. Huang's case, his own scenes might work best. You would also need to decide how detailed the scene should be. In Mr. Huang's case, a scene might include some examples of positive thoughts and allow room for him to add his own. You and Mr. Huang would generate a list of scenes to be used, specifying the following:

1. The situation (which, for him, would be at work when the negative thoughts crop up)
2. The behavior and coping methods he would acquire (stopping interfering thoughts, generating positive thoughts about retirement, and getting back to his project at work)
3. Favorable outcomes (for Mr. Huang, this might be being able to get his work done on time, which would help him avoid shame and maintain pride in his work)

Applying Treatment Scenes You and Mr. Huang would arrange the scenes in order—starting with a work situation in which his thoughts are not as interfering and proceeding to situations in which they are most interfering. Starting with the first scene, you would give Mr. Huang specific instructions on imagining. Then you would present the scene to him and have him hold the scene in imagination for a few seconds after he signals a strong image. After the scene presentation, you would get Mr. Huang's reactions to the scene and make any necessary revisions in duration, scene content, order in the hierarchy, and so on. At this time Mr. Huang could either develop a verbal summary code or personalize the scene by changing or elaborating on it in some way. The same scene would be presented to Mr. Huang at least one more time, followed by several practices in which he goes through the scene without your assistance. After you had worked through

(continued)

POSTEVALUATION FEEDBACK

(continued) all scenes in the hierarchy, you would present scenes to him in a random order.

Homework After each scene presentation in the session, you would instruct Mr. Huang to practice the scenes daily outside the session. A follow-up on this homework should be arranged.

PART SEVEN

Assess your interview or have someone else assess it, using the Interview Checklist for Covert Modeling on page 384–388.

CHAPTER 13

REFRAMING, COGNITIVE MODELING, AND PROBLEM-SOLVING STRATEGIES

OBJECTIVES

After completing this chapter, the student should be able to
1. Demonstrate 8 out of the 11 steps of reframing in a role-play interview.
2. Using a simulated client case, describe how you would apply the seven components of cognitive modeling and self-instructional training.
3. Demonstrate 16 out of 21 steps of cognitive self-instructional modeling in a role play, using the Interview Checklist for Cognitive Modeling at the end of the chapter to rate your performance.
4. Identify which step of the problem-solving strategy is reflected in each of 10 helper responses, accurately identifying at least eight of the ten examples.
5. Demonstrate 16 out of 19 steps of problem solving in a role-play interview, using the Interview Checklist for Problem Solving at the end of the chapter to assess your performance.

Most systems of therapy recognize the importance of overt behavior change *and* cognitive and affective (covert) behavior change. In recent years, increasing attention and effort have been directed toward developing and evaluating procedures aimed at modifying thoughts, moods, emotions, attitudes, and beliefs. These procedures come under the broad umbrella of cognitive therapy or cognitive behavior modification. Several assumptions are made about cognitive-change procedures. One of the basic assumptions is that a person's thoughts and beliefs can contribute to maladaptive behavior. Another is that maladaptive behaviors can be altered by dealing directly with the person's beliefs, attitudes, or thoughts. In many instances, a client's unreasonable self-standards and negative thoughts about self or circumstances can be problem areas in their own right or are diminishing the power of some other aspect of a treatment program. Attention to the client's beliefs and expectations may be necessary for other therapeutic strategies to be successful.

Three cognitive change procedures are presented in this chapter: reframing, cognitive modeling, and problem solving. More extensive attention to cognitive therapy and cognitive restructuring strategies are described in Chapter 14. You will quickly see that the term *cognitive* can be misleading if one presumes a wholly rationalistic, knowledge-based definition. In contrast, the intervention strategies that we present here attend to ways that cognition is "hot"—that is, deeply interwoven with our values, goals, emotions, and evaluations about ourselves, others, and the world as we understand it.

THE PROCESS OF REFRAMING

People who grow up in chaotic, abusive, rejecting, or disorganized attachment-style environments will generally display distorted attribution processes. These people often perceive problems in living in ways that appear to have no workable solution for emotional relief. For example, a man who has experienced rejection from his parents while growing up may say "I don't have the skills to work with people." From this man's frame of reference, he views "lack of interpersonal skills" as unchangeable, and he experiences a sense of hopelessness about working with people. It is his personal script, belief, or frame of reference about his interpersonal skills. This habitual schema leads to self-limiting patterns of feeling, thinking, and behaving with people. If the man in the example continues the cycle of self-indictment, he will experience a sense of despair and become regressive and withdrawn from social interactions. The man in the above example feels stuck in his schema, which was created at least in part by the state-dependent memory, learning, and behaving that he experienced in his family. The meaning and emotions that he experiences in social interactions lock him in a tenacious cycle which only limits his perceptions, beliefs, and options for alternative ways of behaving. Reframing might be one intervention that could help this man revise his way of perceiving and modifying his interpersonal skills.

Reframing means to explore how an incident or situation is typically perceived and to offer another view or frame for the situation. Reframing helps a client to change emotions, meaning, and perceived options. The reframe can change clients' everyday conscious sets and perceptions of their personal limitations, of situations, and of others' behavior that has become entrenched. As Gendlin (1996) argues, reframing "sometimes works, and sometimes not. To determine whether the reframing is effective, you must sense whether it has brought a *bodily* change or not. You must sense what actually comes in your body in response to a reframing. A real change is a shift in the concrete bodily way you have the problem, and not *only* a new way of thinking" (p. 9). We take this to mean that, at its best, reframing goes beyond an intellectual shift to stimulate a sensed effect such as a weight being lifting, a physical freeing, and renewed energy to move forward. Opening this window of hope about being able to realize changes that previously felt stymied or impossible is part of what makes reframing an effective tool when paired with subsequent change strategies that build further insights, skills, and changed circumstances.

Reframing (sometimes also called *relabeling*) is an approach that modifies or restructures a client's perceptions of a difficult situation or a behavior. Efforts to reframe are implicitly constructivistic in that, rather than a single truth, they reflect that a circumstance can have multiple meanings across individuals and from the perspective of any one person. The aim is not self-deception but rather the search for *useful* ways to understand a circumstance, relative to clients' goals and/or perspectives that may be impeding their efforts to achieve those goals. Reframing is used frequently in family therapy as a way to redefine presenting problems so as to shift the focus away from an "identified patient" or "scapegoat" and onto the family as a whole, as a system in which each member is an interdependent part. When used in this way, reframing changes the way that a family encodes an issue or a conflict.

With individual clients, reframing has a number of uses as well. By changing or restructuring what clients encode and perceive, reframing can reduce defensiveness and mobilize the client's resources and forces for change. Second, it can shift the focus from overly simplistic trait attributions of behavior that clients are inclined to make ("I am lazy" or "I am not assertive") to analyses of important contextual and situational cues associated with the behavior. Finally, reframing can be a useful strategy for helping with a client's self-efficacy (see Chapter 18).

Wachtel (1993) illustrates that reframing is often used as one part of a larger intervention to help clients come to grips with conflicts such as contradictions of vicious circles that are at the root of their issues. In one case example, Wachtel is working with a man who is confused by some of his interpersonal dynamics, juggling strong needs to please and be valued by others with an equally strong desire to have a clearer sense of what *he* values and who he sees his true self to be. The helper offers a reframe showing that the confusion the client is experiencing is, at that moment, a real part of the real person and thus, rather than shameful and something to hide, a genuine expression of who he is and a valuable resource to explore further. Reframing the confusion in terms of authentic self offers a foothold onto ground consistent with what the client wants to better understand and thus to pursue rather than to evade.

In another example, Wachtel (1993) illustrates how reframing can help one understand another person's experience, which may, in turn, make it easier for the client to behave differently toward the other and thus disrupt the negative cycles the two people are caught within. This involved a woman who felt hurt by a perception that her husband was not interested in her and did not want to spend time with her. After inquiring about recent fights between the couple, the practitioner offered a reframe of the husband's behavior in the following way: "I wonder if we might take his withdrawal here not as a sign of his not caring but as a sign that he felt hurt. . . . He seems to deal with feeling hurt in much the same way you do; he withdraws and feels he has to hide how hurt and vulnerable he feels. I think his withdrawal could be a sign that he feels hurt rather than that he's not interested" (pp. 194, 195). With the aid of the reframing, the woman was better positioned to see both sets of feelings and needs, to try out different interpretations she had not previously considered regarding how her husband may be interpreting her behavior, and to consider new ways of communicating.

Uses of Reframing

Box 13.1 presents a sample of reframing research. A quick glance at the listing in the table reveals that reframing has been used for a number of purposes, such as to change the message about AIDS, to reduce social and test anxiety, to deal with difficult children, to effect cognitive change, and to help clients cope with depression, illness, pain, and panic.

BOX 13.1 RESEARCH ON REFRAMING

AIDS prevention
Citizens Commission on AIDS for New York City and Northern New Jersey. (1991). AIDS prevention and education: Reframing the message. *AIDS Education and Prevention, 3,* 147–163.

Anxiety
Ishiyama, F. I. (1991). A Japanese reframing technique for brief social anxiety treatment: An exploratory study of cognitive and therapeutic effects of Morita therapy. *Journal of Cognitive Psychotherapy, 5,* 55–70.
Kass, R. G., & Fish, J. M. (1991). Positive reframing and the test performance of test anxious children. *Psychology in the Schools, 28,* 43–52.

Children and adolescents
Komori, Y., Miyazato, M., & Orii, T. (1991). The Family Journal Technique: A simple, positive-reframing technique in Japanese pediatrics. *Family Systems Medicine, 9,* 19–24.
Ritchie, M. H. (1994). Counseling difficult children. Special Issue: Perspective on working with difficult clients. *Canadian Journal of Counseling, 28,* 58–68.
Rodriguez, C., & Moore, N. (1995). Perceptions of pregnant/parenting teens: Reframing issues for an integrated approach to pregnancy problems. *Adolescence, 30,* 685–706.

Couples
Davidson, G. N. S., & Horvath, A. O. (1997). Three sessions of brief couples therapy: A clinical trial. *Journal of Family Psychology, 11,* 422–435.

Depression
Boer, C. (1992). Reframing depression: A systems perspective. *Family Systems Medicine, 10,* 405–411.
Brack, G., LaClave, L., & Wyatt, A. S. (1992). The relationship of problem solving and reframing to stress and depression in female college students. *Journal of College Student Development, 33,* 124–131.
Swoboda, J. S., Dowd, E. T., & Wise, S. L. (1990). Reframing and restraining directives in the treatment of clinical depression. *Journal of Counseling Psychology, 37,* 254–260.

Disability
Larson, E. (1998). Reframing the meaning of disability to families: The embrace of paradox. *Social Science & Medicine, 47,* 865–675.

Failure of reframe
Brack, G., Brack, C. J., & Hartson, D. (1991). When a reframe fails: Explorations into students' ecosystems. *Journal of College Student Development, 6,* 103–118.

Family therapy
Lawson, D. M. (1991). Reframing family change rate. *Journal of Family Psychotherapy, 2,* 75–87.
Prinz, R. J. (1992). Overview of behavioural family interventions with children: Achievements, limitations, and challenges. *Behaviour Change, 9,* 120–125.

Group counseling
Clark, A. J. (1998). Reframing: A therapeutic technique in group counseling. *Journal of Specialists in Group Work, 23,* 66–73.

Illness
Kleinman, A. (1992). Local worlds of suffering: An interpersonal focus for ethnographies of illness experience. *Qualitative Health Research, 2,* 127–134.

Mental health
Johnson, G. B., & Werstlein, P. O. (1990). Reframing: A strategy to improve care of manipulative patients. *Issues in Mental Health Nursing, 11,* 237–241.
Pesut, D. J. (1991). The art, science, and techniques of reframing in psychiatric mental health nursing. Special Issue: Psychiatric nursing for the 1990s: New concepts, new therapies. *Issues in Mental Health Nursing, 12,* 9–18.

Multicultural consultation
Soo-Hoo, T. (1998). Applying frame of reference and reframing techniques to improve school consultation in multicultural settings. *Journal of Educational & Psychological Consultation, 9,* 325–245.

Older adults
Dressel, P. L., & Barnhill, S. K. (1994). Reframing gerontological thought and practice: The case of grandmothers with daughters in prison. *Gerontologist, 34,* 685–691.
Motenko, A. K., & Greenberg, S. (1995). Reframing dependence in old age. *Social Work, 40,* 382–390.

Pain
Shutty, M. S., & Sheras, P. (1991). Brief strategic psychotherapy with chronic pain patients: Reframing and problem resolution. *Psychotherapy, 28,* 636–642.

Panic
Neeleman, J. (1992). The therapeutic potential of positive reframing in panic. *European Psychiatry, 7,* 135–139.

Parenting
Lam, J. A., Rifkin, J., & Townley, A. (1989). Reframing conflict: Implications for fairness in parent–adolescent mediation. *Mediation Quarterly, 7,* 15–31.

Pastoral counseling
Slok, C. (1997). Short-term counseling and the use of reframing. *Pastoral Counseling, 46,* 119–129.

Perimenstrual impairment
Morse, G. G. (1997). Effect of positive reframing and social support on perception of perimenstrual changes among women with premenstrual syndrome. *Health Care for Women International, 18,* 175–193.

Resistance
Robinson, T., & Ward, J. V. (1991). "A belief in self far greater than anyone's disbelief": Cultivating resistance among African American female adolescents, Special Issue: Women, girls and psychotherapy: Reframing resistance. *Women and Therapy, 11* (3–4), 87–103.
Stern, L. (1991). Disavowing the self in female adolescence. Special issue: Women, girls and psychotherapy: Reframing resistance. *Women and Therapy, 11* (3/4), 105–117.

(continued)

> **BOX 13.1   RESEARCH ON REFRAMING** *CONTINUED*
>
> *Smoking relapse*
> Haaga, D. A. F., & Allison, M. L. (1994). Thought suppression and smoking relapse: A secondary analysis of Haaga (1989). *British Journal of Clinical Psychology, 33,* 327–331.
>
> *Supervision*
> Masters, M. A. (1992). The use of positive reframing in the context of supervision. *Journal of Counseling and Development, 70,* 387–390.
>
> *Terminally ill*
> Baack, C. M. (1993). Nursing's role in the nutritional care of the terminally ill: Weathering the storm. Special issue: Nutrition and hydration in hospice care: Needs, strategies, ethics. *Hospice Journal, 9,* 1–13.
>
> *Trauma*
> Malon, D., & Hurley, W. (1994). Ericksonian utilization of depressive self-blame in a traumatized patient. *Journal of Systemic Therapies, 13,* 38–46.

Reframing Meaning

Helpers reframe whenever they ask or encourage clients to see an issue from a different perspective. In this chapter, we propose a more systematic way for helpers to help clients reframe an issue. The most common method of reframing—and the one that we illustrate in this chapter—is to reframe the *meaning* of a problematic situation or behavior. When you reframe meaning, you are challenging the meaning that the client (or someone else) has assigned. Usually, the longer a particular meaning (or label) is attached to a behavior, or situation the more necessary the behavior or situation itself becomes in maintaining predictability and equilibrium in the client's functioning. Also, when meanings are attached to something over a long period of time, clients are more likely to develop "functional fixity"—that is, seeing things from only one perspective or being fixated on the idea that this particular situation, behavior pattern, or attribute is *the* issue. Reframing helps clients by providing alternative ways to view the issue in question without directly challenging the behavior or situation itself and by loosening a client's perceptual frame, thus setting the stage for other kinds of interventive work. Once the *meaning* of a behavior or a situation changes, the person's response to it usually also changes, providing the reframe is valid and acceptable to the client. The essence of a meaning reframe is to give a situation, a behavior, or other issue of concern a new label or a new name that has a different meaning. This new meaning has a different connotation, and usually it is positive or at least less troubling to the client. For example, "stubbornness" might be reframed as "independence," or "greediness" might be reframed as "ambition." Reframing involves six steps:

1. Rationale: purpose and overview of the procedure
2. Identification of client perceptions and feelings in situations of concern
3. Deliberate enactment of selected perceptual features
4. Identification of alternative perceptions
5. Modification of perceptions in situations of concern
6. Homework and follow-up

A detailed description of the steps associated with these components is included in the Interview Checklist for Reframing at the end of this chapter and Learning Activity 13.1.

Treatment Rationale

The rationale for reframing attempts to strengthen the client's belief that perceptions or attributions about the situation can cause emotional distress. Here is a rationale that can be used to introduce reframing:

> When we think about or when we are in a difficult situation, we automatically attend to selected features of the situation. As time goes on, we tend to get fixated on these same features of the situation and ignore other aspects of it. This can lead to some uncomfortable emotions, such as the ones you're feeling now. In this procedure, I will help you identify what you are usually aware of during these situations. Then we'll work on increasing your awareness of other aspects of the situation that you usually don't notice. As this happens, you will notice that your feelings about and responses to this issue will start to change. Do you have any questions?

Identification of Client Perceptions and Feelings

Assuming that the client accepts the rationale the helper provides, the next step is to help clients become aware of what they automatically attend to in these situations. Clients are often unaware of what features or details they attend to in a situation and what information about these situations they encode. For example, clients who have a fear of water may attend to how deep the water is because they cannot see the bottom and encode the perception that they might drown. Clients who experience test anxiety might attend to the large size of the room or how quickly the other people seem to be working. These features are encoded and lead to the clients' feeling overwhelmed, anxious, and lacking in confidence. In turn, these feelings can lead to impaired performance in or avoidance of the situation.

Within the interview, the helper helps clients discover what they typically attend to in problem situations. The helper can use imagery or role play to help clients reenact the situation(s) in order to become aware of what they notice and encode. While engaging in role play or in imagining the situation, the helper can help the client become more aware of typical encoding patterns by asking questions like these:

"What are you attending to now?"

"What are you aware of now?"

"What are you noticing about the situation?"

In order to link feelings to individual perceptions, these questions can be followed with further inquiries, such as these:

"What are you feeling at this moment?"

"What do you feel in your body?"

The helper may need to assist clients engage in role play or imagery several times so that they can reconstruct the situation and become more aware of salient encoded features. The helper may also suggest what the client might have felt and what the experience appears to mean to the client in order to bring these automatic perceptions into awareness. The practitioner also helps clients notice "marginal impressions"—fleeting images, sounds, feelings, and sensations that were passively rather than deliberately processed by the client yet affect the client's reaction to the situation.

Deliberate Enactment of Selected Perceptual Features

After clients become aware of their rather automatic attending, they are asked to reenact the situation and intentionally attend to the selected features that they have been processing automatically. For example, the water-phobic client reenacts (through role play or imagery) approach situations with the water and deliberately attends to the salient features such as the depth of the water and his or her inability to see the bottom of the pool. By deliberately attending to these encoded features, a client is able to bring these habitual attentional processes fully into awareness and under direct control. This sort of "dramatization" seems to sharpen the client's awareness of existing perceptions. When these perceptions are uncovered and made more visible through this deliberate reenactment, it is harder for the client to maintain prior response habits. This step may need to be repeated several times during the session or assigned as a homework task.

Identification of Alternative Perceptions

The helper can help the client change his or her attentional focus by selecting other features of the target situation to attend to rather than ignore. For example, the water-phobic client who focuses on the depth of the water might be instructed to focus on how clear, clean, and wet the water appears. For the test-anxious client who attends to the size of the room, the helper can redirect the client's attention to how roomy (nonconstricting) the testing place is or how comfortable the seats are. Both clients and practitioners can suggest other features of the situation or person to use that have a positive or at least a neutral connotation. The practitioner can ask the client what features provide a felt sense of relief.

For reframing to be effective, the alternative perceptions must be acceptable to the client. The best reframes are the ones that are linked to difficulties that the client is having in moving forward and are as valid a way of looking at the world as the way the person sees things now. All reframes or alternative perceptions have to be tailored to the client's values, style, and sociocultural context, and they have to fit the client's experience and model of his or her world. The alternative perceptions or reframes that you suggest also need to match the external reality of the situation closely enough to be plausible. If, for example, a husband is feeling very angry with his wife because of her extramarital affair, reframing his anger as "loving concern" is probably not representative enough of the external situation to be plausible to the client. A more plausible reframe might be something like "frustration from not being able to protect the (marital) relationship."

The delivery of a reframe is also important. When suggesting alternative perceptions to clients, it is essential that the practitioner's nonverbal behavior be congruent with the tone and content of the reframe. It is also important to use your voice effectively in delivering the reframe by emphasizing key words or phrases.

Modification of Perceptions in Situations of Concern

Modifying what clients attend to can be helped with role play or imagery. The helper instructs the client to attend to other features of the situations during the role play or imagery enactment. This step may need to be repeated several times. Repetition is designed to embody new perceptual responses so that the client gradually experiences a felt sense of relief, strength, or optimism (Gendlin, 1996).

Homework and Follow-Up

The helper can suggest to the client that during *in vivo* situations, the client follow the same format used in their sessions. The client is instructed to become more aware of salient encoded features of a stressful or arousing situation, to link these to uncomfortable feelings, to engage in deliberate enactments or practice activities, and to try to make "perceptual shifts" during these situations to other features of the situation previously ignored.

As the client becomes more adept at this process, the helper will need to be alert to slight perceptual shifts and point these out to clients. Typically, clients are unskilled at detecting these shifts in encoding. Helping the client discriminate between old and new encodings of target situations can be very useful in promoting the overall goal of the reframing strategy—to alleviate and modify encoding or perceptual errors and biases.

Reframing Context

Although the steps we propose for reframing involve reframing meaning, another way you can reframe is to reframe the *context* of a concern. Reframing the context helps a client to explore and decide *when, where,* and *with whom* a given behavior, for example, is useful or appropriate. Context reframing is based on the assumption that many behaviors are useful in *some* but not all contexts or conditions. Thus, when a client states "I'm too lazy," a context reframe would be "In what situations (or with what people) is it useful or even helpful to be lazy?" The client may respond by noting that it is useful to be lazy whenever she wants to play with the children. At this point, the practitioner can help the client sort out and contextualize a given behavior so that clients can see where and when they do and do not want the behavior to occur. Context reframes are most useful when dealing with client generalizations—for example, "I'm *never* assertive" or "I'm *always* late."

MULTICULTURAL APPLICATIONS OF REFRAMING

As we mentioned earlier, for a reframe to be effective, it must be plausible and acceptable to the client. Client demographic factors such as age, gender, race or ethnicity, sexuality, and disability are very important components to consider in developing reframes with diverse groups of clients. An excellent example of a culturally relevant meaning reframe is given by Oppenheimer (1992) in working with a severely depressed 67-year-old Latina. The woman was able to improve only after she could reframe her depression within the context of her Latino spiritualist beliefs. Her helper, also a Latina, not only refrained from labeling as pathological the client's belief in the supernatural, but she used these beliefs to create a valid meaning reframe by taking the client's references to "intranquil spirits or ghosts" to reframe her pain surrounding a loss. Similar examples of culturally sensitive reframes have been used with Asian American adolescents to negotiate conflicting cultural values (Huang, 1994), with HIV-positive men to reframe stress around the threat of AIDS (Leserman, Perkins, & Evans, 1992), and with elderly people to reframe dependence (Motenko & Greenberg, 1995).

A good example of a multiculturally useful reframe is the feminist notion of the meaning of *resistance.* Recall from prior chapters that, rather than referring to resistance as the client's conscious and unconscious attempts "to avoid the truth and evade change," it means "the refusal to merge with dominant cultural norms and to attend to one's own voice and integrity" (Brown, 1994, p. 15). The meaning of resistance shifts from something that is pathological to something that is healthy and desirable. In this sense, resistance means "learning the ways in which each of us is damaged by our witting or unwitting participation in dominant norms or by the ways in which such norms have been thrust upon us" (Brown, 1994, p. 25). An example might be what we do when our competent, conscientious, and loyal office manager is in danger of losing her or his job because of organizational restructuring and "downsizing." Do we look the other way, do we ignore it, or do we speak on her or his behalf to persons holding the power in the dominant social structure of the organization? And as the office manager's helper, do we attempt to soothe the manager and have her or him adjust, or do we attempt to help the person to give voice to his or her anger and outrage?

In this sense, to resist means to tell the truth as we see it about what is actually happening and what is possible and available to each client as "avenues for change" (Brown, 1994, p. 26). Gay, lesbian, and bisexual clients are confronted with this sort of resistance daily in the "coming out" process. Smith (1992) notes that as an African American girl she was brought up to be a "resister": to be honest and self-reliant, and to stand up for herself, an experience echoed in research that many African American adolescent girls have a strong sense of healthy resistance (Taylor, Gilligan, & Sullivan, 1995). Robinson and Ward (1992) have made an important contribution to the notion of healthy resistance by distinguishing between resistance strategies for *survival* versus resistance strategies for *liberation.* They differentiate resistance strategies for survival as being crisis-oriented, short-term methods that include self-denigration, *excessive* autonomy at the expense of connectedness to one's collective culture, and "quick fixes" such as early and unplanned pregnancies, substance use, and school failure and/or dropping out. Resistance strategies for liberation include strategies in which problems of oppression are acknowledged, collectivity is valued, and demands for change are empowered. Robinson and Ward (1991) base their strategies for liberation on an African-centered Nguzo Saba value system (Karenga, 1980), as summarized in Table 13.1, although parallels to other groups and histories are evident.

Reframing within a framework of diversity and critical consciousness helps us see that "frame of reference" can involve multiple levels of analysis and contextualizing. For example, Soo-Hoo (1998) describes ways that understanding differences in the frame of reference of people from varying cultural backgrounds and participatory roles is important to providing effective, efficient, and innovative solutions for school consultation in multicultural settings. Larson (1998) provides a compelling portrayal of how internal tensions in one's perspective and emotions surrounding issues need to be understood for reframing to be meaningful. This involved use of a life metaphor, the embrace of paradox, to help manage the internal conflicts of mothers parenting children with disabilities (e.g., loving one's children as they are versus wanting to erase the disability, dealing with incurability while seeking solutions, maintaining hope in the face of negative information and fear). In this case, reframing needed to incorporate both the internal sense of opposing forces as well as contextual factors associated with culture and socioeconomics (the mothers were of Mexican origin living at or near poverty-level conditions).

MODEL CASE: REFRAMING

The model case on page 398 illustrates the process of the reframing intervention. In it, the helper reframes the respective roles of a mother and her son in relationship contexts. Note how the reframes are grounded in the family's cultural values. The helper considers Asian American family ties in reframing Mrs. Kim's responsibilities as a mother and her son's duties as a son and a parent.

COGNITIVE MODELING WITH COGNITIVE SELF-INSTRUCTIONAL TRAINING

Cognitive modeling is a procedure in which practitioners show people what to say to themselves while performing a task. Cognitive modeling and self-instructional training have been applied to a variety of client concerns. Box 13.2 on page 400 presents a list of research studies about cognitive

TABLE 13.1	Resistance Strategies
Survival/Oppression	**Liberation/Empowerment**
Isolation and disconnectedness from the larger African American community	Unity with African people that transcends age, socioeconomic status, geographic origin, and sexual orientation (Umoja)
Self defined by others (the media, educational system) in a manner that oppresses and devalues blackness	Self-determination through confrontation and repudiation of oppressive attempts to demean self. New models used to make active decisions that empower and affirm self and racial identity (Kujichagulia)
Excessive individualism and autonomy; racelessness	Collective work and responsibility; the self seen in connection with the larger body of African people, sharing a common destiny (Ujima)
"I've got mine, you get yours" attitude	Cooperative economics advocating a sharing of resources through the convergence of the "I" and the "we" (Ujaama)
Meaninglessness in life, immediate gratification to escape life's harsh realities; the use of "quick fixes"	Purpose in life that benefits the self and the collective, endorses delaying gratification as a tool in resistance (Nia)
Maintaining status quo, replicating existing models, although they may be irrelevant	Creativity through building new paradigms for the community through dialogue with other resisters (Kuumba)
Emphasis on the here and now, not looking back and not looking forward; myopic vision	Faith through an intergenerational perspective where knowledge of the history of Africa and other resisters and care for future generations gives meaning to struggle and continued resistance (Imani)

Source: From "A Belief in Self Far Greater than Anyone's Belief: Cultivating Resistance among African American Female Adolescents," by T. Robinson and J. Ward. In *Women, Girls, and Psychotherapy: Reframing Resistance,* by C. Gilligan, A. Rogers, and D. Tolman (Eds.), p. 99, Table 1. Copyright © 1992 by the Haworth Press, Inc., Binghamton, NY. Reprinted by permission.

MODEL EXAMPLE: THE KIM FAMILY *CONTINUED*

Some months ago the local hospital asked the author to help with an elderly Korean lady who was about to be discharged. It appeared that the lady was very likeable and a good patient. She loved to be pampered by the staff, which concerned them because she appeared to be settling in for a long hospital stay. She was generally reluctant to use her weekend pass to go home, preferring to stay at the hospital and acting as if she were going to be there forever. She was becoming dependent on the staff and asking for more medication and care than she needed.

The hospitalization of 67-year-old Mrs. Kim had been precipitated by her attempted suicide (by cutting her throat with a butcher knife). She had been in the hospital for about a month, and her wound was healing nicely, a fact which the patient tended to minimize. The initially positive relationship between the patient and the staff appeared to be souring. Puzzled and frustrated by the lack of progress, the staff called the author, saying that there seemed to be a "family problem."

The staff had been encouraging Mrs. Kim to be independent and not to lean on her oldest son but to rely more on her husband. To their dismay, the husband seldom visited, but the oldest son came to see her every day even though he had a grueling schedule going to school, working full time, and raising two children as a single parent. They said they had talked to both mother and son to no avail and were getting somewhat frustrated with the dependent posture she was taking with her son.

The author decided that a joint session would be unproductive since mediated negotiation is more productive than confrontation in working with Asian-American families. The therapeutic task for this family was two-fold: to find a way to help Mrs. Kim get back to live with her husband without losing face and to help her son find a way to get back to being a responsible father and a loyal son without "killing himself" in the process.

The separate interviews with the mother and son revealed the following. The son, the oldest of three sons, had come to this country about 12 years ago to seek honor for the family by earning a college degree and getting an important job. Instead, he fell in love with an American woman, married, had two children, and had to drop out of school in order to support the family. Only recently had he resumed his pursuit of his education part-time. The marriage had ended in divorce, and he had custody of the children. In order to show responsibility to his family, he had managed to bring his two younger brothers and his aging parents to the U.S. However unhappy and difficult their lives were here, none of the Kim family was in a position to return to Korea since the shame of failure in this country would be intolerable to face.

When the parents first came to this country a couple of years ago, they had moved in with the son and his children. It appears that the grandchildren were not properly respectful to their grandparents; they were noisy, expressed their opinions freely, and did not appreciate the cultural heritage or customs, at times making rude remarks about the "old world" ways of the grandparents. They complained loudly to their father about their grandparents' "unreasonable" expectations, strange food, and strange way of doing things. In order to make things easier for everyone, the son made arrangements for his parents to move into a housing project for the elderly.

In order to pay deference to her status and age, the author met with Mrs. Kim alone first. Using the authority and status of a consultant brought in by the hospital, the author talked to her about how impressed she was with her dutiful son and what a fine job she had done raising such a bright, responsible son. The therapist and Mrs. Kim talked about her family and how much she must be suffering in a strange land so far away from home. The therapist commiserated with her about the young people nowadays, particularly those children who were born and raised in American ways, about how selfish they were and so on. This was designed to align the author with Mrs. Kim and to lay the groundwork for reframing her suicide attempt as a selfless sacrifice. In order to do so, the author joined with Mrs. Kim in her view of the situation she had tried to leave.

Mrs. Kim was reluctant to talk at first, but she gradually warmed up. By the second visit with her in the hospital, she was more willing to open up and talk about her sense of failure as a mother and humiliation at being pushed out of her son's home by the grandchildren. Seizing on this opportunity of her willingness to talk about the circumstances, the author reframed the son's behavior as an expression of his misguided but well-intentioned sense of responsibility toward his own children, which the author was sure that the mother had instilled in him. It was pointed out that no mother would want to see her son fail as a parent since that would surely mean that she had failed as a mother. Besides, had she succeeded in her suicide attempt, she would have left her son to fail permanently in his children's eyes, and she certainly cared about her son more than that. On the other hand, the author told

(continued)

THE KIM FAMILY

her how impressed she was that she took her duty as a mother seriously enough to want to end her life.

The therapist reminded her that—as she well knew already—young people not only have a responsibility toward parents but we, as the older generation, have a duty to protect and encourage our children to succeed. The therapist added that this duty included being happy with our spouse so that we free our children from worrying about us. It is our responsibility to give our children all the chances they need to succeed. Mrs. Kim agreed and thanked me for coming.

Mrs. Kim's view was supported and reframed as her attempt to fulfill her cultural role as an elder of the family. Moreover, her return to her husband was depicted as important and vital—a necessity for her son as he carried out the family honor in raising his children.

When talking with the son, the author complimented him on being a dutiful son and doing so much for his parents and his younger brothers. The author suggested that he must have been taught well by his mother since he was not only dutiful to his parents and to his brothers but also responsible to his children. Since a failure to take care of his children would indeed be a dishonor to his parents, he was urged to continue to work hard in order to help his own children to succeed. His world view was supported by the therapist and viewed as necessary.

Mrs. Kim was discharged to her husband's care soon after this session. A 1-year follow-up indicated that she was doing well and that there had been no recurrence of the depression.

The two interventions are interwoven and clearly address the norm of close-knit family ties often found in Asian-American families. Techniques of reframing in relationship contexts were used to respect the world view presented by each client. The tasks implied and suggested were designed to respect the client's view and failed attempts to solve the problem.

Source: From "Different and Same: Family Therapy with Asian-American Families," by I. K. Berg and A. Jaya. Reprinted from Volume 19, pp. 36–38, of the *Journal of Marital and Family Therapy.* Copyright © 1993 by the American Association for Marriage and Family Therapy. Reprinted with permission.

LEARNING ACTIVITY 13.1 Reframing

This activity is designed to help you use the reframing procedure with yourself.

1. Identify a situation that typically produces uncomfortable or distressing feelings for you. Examples:
   a. You are about to initiate a new relationship with someone.
   b. You are presenting a speech in front of a large audience.
2. Try to become aware of what you rather automatically attend to or focus on during this situation. Role play it with another person, or pretend you're sitting in a movie theater and project the situation onto the screen in front of you. As you do so, ask yourself:
   "What am I aware of now?"
   "What am I focusing on now?"
   Be sure to notice fleeting sounds, feelings, images, and sensations.
3. Establish a link between these encoded features of the situation and your resulting feelings. As you reenact the situation, ask yourself: "What am I feeling at this moment?" "What am I experiencing now?"
4. After you have become aware of the most salient features of this situation, reenact it either in a role play or in your imagination. This time, deliberately attend to these selected features during the reenactment. Repeat this process until you feel that you have awareness and control of the perceptual process you engage in during this situation.
5. Next, select other features of the session (previously ignored) that you could focus on or attend to during this situation that would allow you to view and handle the situation differently. Consider images, sounds, and feelings as well as people and objects. Ask yourself questions such as "What other aspects of this same situation aren't readily apparent to me that would provide me with a different way to view the situation?" You may wish to query another person for ideas. After you have identified alternative features, again reenact the situation in a role play or your imagination—several times if necessary—in order to break old encoding patterns.
6. Construct a homework assignment for yourself that encourages you to apply this process as needed for use during actual situations.

> **BOX 13.2 COGNITIVE MODELING AND SELF-INSTRUCTIONAL TRAINING RESEARCH**
>
> *Anger and hostility*
> Normand, D., & Robert, M. (1990). Modeling of anger/hostility control with preadolescent Type A girls. *Child Study Journal, 20,* 237–262.
>
> *Attention deficit hyperactivity disorder*
> Westby, C. E., & Cutler, S. K. (1994). Language and ADHD: Understanding the bases and treatment of self-regulatory deficits. Special Issue: ADD and its relationship to spoken and written language. *Topics in Language Disorders, 14,* 58–76.
>
> *Consultation*
> Gutkin, T. B. (1993). Cognitive modeling: A means for achieving prevention in school-based consultation. *Journal of Educational and Psychological Consultation, 4,* 179–183.
>
> *Learning disability*
> Johnson, L. A., Graham, S., & Harris, K. R. (1997). The effects of goal setting and self-instruction on learning a reading comprehension strategy: A study of students with learning disabilities. *Journal of Learning Disabilities, 30,* 80–91.
> Simmonds, E. P. (1990). The effectiveness of two methods for teaching a constraint-seeking questioning strategy to students with learning disabilities. *Journal of Learning Disabilities, 23,* 229–232.
> Taylor, I., & O'Reilly, M. F. (1997). Toward a functional analysis of private verbal self-regulation. *Journal of Applied Behavior Analysis, 30,* 43–58.
> Van Reusen, A. K., & Head, D. N. (1994). Cognitive and metacognitive interventions: Important trends for teachers of students who are visually impaired. *REiview, 25,* 153–162.
>
> *Problem solving*
> Gorrell, J. (1993). Cognitive modeling and implicit rules: Effects on problem-solving performance. *American Journal of Psychology, 106,* 51–65.
>
> *Self-efficacy*
> Schwartz, L. S., & Gredler, M. E. (1998). The effects of self-instructional materials on goal-setting and self-efficacy. *Journal of Research & Development in Education, 31*(2), 83–89.
>
> *Shyness*
> Nagae, N., Nadate, L., & Sekiguchi, Y. (1999). Self-instructional training for shyness: Differences in improvements produced by different types of coping self-statements. *Japanese Journal of Counseling Science, 32,* 32–42.
>
> *Stress*
> Cary, M., & Dua, J. (1999). Cognitive–behavioral and systematic desensitization procedures in reducing stress and anger in caregivers for the disabled. *International Journal of Stress Management, 6*(2), 75–87.
>
> *Teaching*
> Hazaressingh, N. A., & Bielawski, L. L. (1991). The effects of cognitive self-instruction on student teachers' perceptions of control. *Teaching and Teacher Education, 7,* 383–393.
> Payne, B. D., & Manning, B. H. (1990). The effect of cognitive self-instructions on preservice teachers' anxiety about teaching. *Contemporary Educational Psychology, 15,* 261–267.
> Tao, X., Chongde, L., & Jiliang, S. (1999). Effect of cognitive self-instruction training on the improvement of teachers' teaching-regulated ability. *Psychological Science, 22,* 5–9.
>
> *Test anxiety*
> Sud, A. (1993). Efficacy of two short term cognitive therapies for test anxiety. *Journal of Personality and Clinical Studies, 9,* 39–46.
>
> *Training and supervision*
> Morran, D. K., Kurpius, D. J., Brack, C. J., & Brack, G. (1995). A cognitive-skills model for counselor training and supervision. *Journal of Counseling & Development, 73,* 384–389.
> Nutt-Williams, E., & Hill, C. E. (1996). The relationship between self-talk and therapy process variables for novice therapists. *Journal of Counseling Psychology, 43,* 170–177.

modeling and self-instructional training. These procedures have been used in very diverse populations—for example, with children who have attention deficit and hyperactivity disorder, for controlling anger and hostility, as preparation for cardiac catheterization, for school-based consultation, in helping students with learning disabilities, for helping with problem solving, in enhancing self-efficacy, in skill building with parents with intellectual disabilities, with preservice and active teachers to reduce anxiety and increase perception of control, in decreasing test anxiety and worry for ninth-grade girls, and for training and supervision.

Although there is racial or cultural diversity in some study samples, we have found limited research explicitly attentive to cultural groups. Hains (1989), for example, used cognitive modeling with self-guiding verbalizations to teach anger-control skills to African American, European American, and Hispanic male juvenile offenders. After training, 75 percent of the participants had an increased use of self-instruction and thinking-ahead statements during both provoking incidents and interpersonal conflicts. Rath (1998), Nagae, Nedate, and Sekiguchi (1999), and Taylor and O'Reilly (1997) provide international perspectives from research in India, Japan, and Ireland on the utility of self-instructional training with reading-disabled children, for shyness, and acquiring shopping skills among persons with mild intellectual disabilities.

Cognitive modeling with a self-instructional training strategy consists of five steps:
1. The helper serves as the model (or a symbolic model can be used) and first performs the task while talking aloud to himself or herself.
2. The client performs the same task (as modeled by the helper) while the helper instructs the client aloud.
3. The client is instructed to perform the same task again while instructing himself or herself aloud.
4. The client whispers the instructions while performing the task.
5. Finally, the client performs the task while instructing himself or herself covertly.

Note that cognitive modeling is reflected in step 1, whereas in steps 2–5, the client practices self-verbalizations while performing a task or behavior. The client's verbalizations are faded from an overt to a covert level.

We propose that cognitive modeling and self-instructional training should be implemented with seven steps as guidelines:
1. A rationale about the procedure
2. Cognitive modeling of the task and of the self-verbalizations

Client practice in the following form:
3. Overt external guidance
4. Overt self-guidance
5. Faded overt self-guidance
6. Covert self-guidance
7. Homework and follow-up

Each of these steps is explained in the following section. Illustrations are also provided in the Interview Checklist for Cognitive Modeling at the end of the chapter.

Treatment Rationale

Here is an example of the practitioner's rationale for cognitive modeling:

> It has been found that some people have difficulty in performing certain kinds of tasks. Often the difficulty is not because they don't have the ability to do it but because of what they say or think to themselves while doing it. In other words, a person's "self-talk" can get in the way or interfere with performance. For instance, if you get up to give a speech and you're thinking "What a flop I'll be," this sort of thought may affect how you deliver your talk. This procedure can help you perform something the way you want to by examining and coming up with some helpful planning or self-talk to use while performing [rationale]. I'll show what I am saying to myself while performing the task. Then I'll ask you to do the task while I guide or direct you through it. Next, you will do the task again and guide yourself aloud while doing it. The end result should be your performing the task while thinking and planning about the task to yourself [overview]. How does this sound to you [client willingness]?

After the rationale has been presented and any questions have been clarified, the helper begins by presenting the cognitive model.

Model of Task and Self-Guidance

First, the helper instructs the client to listen to what the helper says to herself or himself while performing the task. Next, the helper models performing a task while talking aloud.

Questions
1. What has to be done?
2. Answers question in form of planning what to do.
3. Self-guidance and focused attention.
4. Self-reinforcement.
5. Coping self-evaluative statements with error correction options.

Dialogue
1. "OK, what is it I have to do?"
2. "You want me to copy the picture with different lines."
3. "I have to go slow and be careful. OK, draw the line down, down, good; then to the right, that's it; now down some more and to the left."
4. "Good. Even if I make an error I can go on slowly and carefully. OK, I have to go down now." "Finished. I did it."
5. "Now back up again. No, I was supposed to go down. That's OK. Just erase the line carefully."

As this example indicates, the helper's modeled self-guidance should include five parts. The first part of the verbalization asks a question about the nature and demands of the task to be performed. The purposes of the question are to compensate for a possible deficiency in comprehending what to do, to provide a general orientation, and to create a cognitive set. The second part of the modeled verbalization answers the question about what to do. The answer is designed to model cognitive rehearsal and planning to focus the client's attention on relevant task requirements. Self-instruction in the form of self-guidance while performing the task is the third part of the modeled verbalization. The purpose of self-guidance is to concentrate attention on the task and to inhibit any possible overt or covert distractions or task irrelevancies. In the

LEARNING ACTIVITY 13.2 — Modeled Self-Guidance

The following helper verbalization is a cognitive model for a rehabilitation client with a physical challenge who is learning how to use a wheelchair. Identify the five parts of the message: (1) questions of what to do, (2) answers to the question in the form of planning, (3) self-guidance and focused attention, (4) coping self-evaluative statements, and (5) self-reinforcement. Feedback for this activity follows.

"What do I have to do to get from the parking lot over the curb onto the sidewalk and then to the building? I have to wheel my chair from the car to the curb, get over the curb and onto the sidewalk, and then wheel over to the building entrance. OK, wheeling the chair over to the curb is no problem. I have to be careful now that I am at the curb. OK, now I've just got to get my front wheels up first. They're up now. So now I'll pull up hard to get my back wheels up. Whoops, didn't quite make it. No big deal—I'll just pull up very hard again. Good. That's better, I've got my chair on the sidewalk now. I did it! I've got it made now."

---

example, modeled self-reinforcement is the fourth part and is designed to maintain task perseverance and to reinforce success. The last part in the modeled verbalization contains coping self-statements to handle errors and frustration, with an option for correcting errors. The example of the modeled verbalization used by Meichenbaum and Goodman (1971) depicts a coping model. In other words, the model does make an error in performance but corrects it and does not give up at that point. See whether you can identify these five parts of modeled self-guidance in Learning Activity 13.2.

Overt External Guidance

After the helper models the verbalizations, the client is instructed to perform the task (as modeled by the helper) while the helper instructs or coaches. The helper coaches the client through the task or activity, substituting the personal pronoun *you* for *I* (for example, "What is it that *you* . . .; *you* have to wheel your chair . . .; *you* have to be careful"). The helper should make sure that the coaching contains the same five parts of self-guidance that were previously modeled: question, planning, focused attention, coping self-evaluation, and self-reinforcement. Sometimes in the client's real-life situation, other people may be watching when the client performs the task—as could be the case whenever the client in a wheelchair appears in public. If the presence of other people appears to interfere with the client's performance, the helper might say, "Those people may be distracting you. Just pay attention to what you are doing." This type of coping statement can be included in the helper's verbalizations when using overt external guidance in order to make this part of the procedure resemble what the client will actually encounter.

FEEDBACK 13.2 — Modeled Self-Guidance

Question
"What do I have to do to get from the parking lot over the curb onto the sidewalk and then to the building?"

Answers with planning
"I have to wheel my chair from the car to the curb, get onto the curb and onto the sidewalk, and then wheel over to the building entrance."

Self-guidance and focused attention
"OK, wheeling the chair over to the curb is no problem. I have to be careful now that I am at the curb. OK, now I've just got to get my front wheels up first. They're up now. So now I'll pull up hard to get my back wheels up."

Coping self-evaluation and error-correction option
"Whoops, didn't quite make it. No big deal—I'll just pull up very hard again."

Self-reinforcement
"Good. That's better; I've got my chair on the sidewalk now. I did it! I've got it made now."

Overt Self-Guidance

The practitioner next instructs the client to perform the task while instructing or guiding himself or herself aloud. The purpose of this step is to have the client practice the kind of self-talk that will strengthen attention to the demands of the task and will minimize outside distractions. The practitioner should attend carefully to the content of the client's self-verbalizations. Again, as in the two preceding steps, these verbalizations should include the five component parts, and the client should be encouraged to use his or her own words. If the client's self-guidance is incomplete or if the client gets stuck, the practitioner can intervene and coach. If necessary, the practitioner can return to the previous steps—either modeling again or coaching the client while the client performs the task (overt external guidance). After the client completes this step, the practitioner should provide feedback about parts of the practice that the client completed adequately and about any errors or omissions. Another practice might be necessary before moving on to the next step: faded overt self-guidance.

Faded Overt Self-Guidance

The client next performs the task while whispering (lip movements). This part of cognitive modeling serves as an intermediate step between having the client verbalize aloud, as in overt self-guidance, and having the client verbalize silently, as in the next step, covert self-guidance. In other words, whispering the self-guidance is a way for the client to approximate successively the result of the procedure: thinking the self-guidance steps while performing them. In our own experience with this step, we have found that it is necessary to explain this to an occasional client who seems hesitant or concerned about whispering. If a client finds the whispering to be too awkward, he or she might prefer to repeat overt self-guidance several times and finally move directly to covert self-guidance. If the client has difficulty performing this step or leaves out any of the five parts, an additional practice may be required before moving on.

Covert Self-Guidance

Finally, clients perform the task while guiding or instructing covertly, or "in their heads." It is very important for clients to instruct themselves covertly after practicing the self-instructions overtly. After the client does this, the practitioner might ask for a description of the covert self-instructions. If distracting or inhibiting self-talk has occurred, the helper can offer suggestions for more appropriate verbalizations or self-talk and can initiate additional practice. Otherwise, the client is ready to use the procedure outside the session.

Homework and Follow-Up

Assigning the client homework is essential for generalization to occur from the interview to the client's environment. The helper should instruct the client to use the covert verbalizations while performing the desired behaviors alone, outside the helping session. The homework assignment should specify what the client will do, how much or how often, and when and where. The helper should also provide a way for the client to monitor and reward himself or herself for completion of homework. The helper should also schedule follow-up on the homework task.

These seven components of cognitive modeling are modeled for you in the following dialogue with our client Joan. Again, this strategy is used as one way to help Joan achieve her goal of increasing her verbal participation in math class. (See Learning Activity 13.3)

MODEL DIALOGUE: COGNITIVE MODELING WITH COGNITIVE SELF-INSTRUCTIONAL TRAINING

In response 1, the helper introduces the possible use of cognitive modeling to help Joan achieve the goal of increasing initiating skills in her math class. The helper is giving a *rationale* about the strategy.

1. **Helper:** One of the goals we developed was to help you increase your participation level in your math class. One of the ways we might help you do that is to use a procedure in which I demonstrate the kinds of things you want to do—and also I will demonstrate a way to think or talk to yourself about these tasks. So this procedure will help you develop a plan for carrying out these tasks, as well as showing you a way to participate. How does that sound?

Client: OK. Is it hard to do?

In response 2, the helper provides an *overview* of the procedure, which is also a part of the rationale.

2. **Helper:** No, not really, because I'll go through it before you do. And I'll sort of guide you along. The procedure involves my showing you a participation method, and while I'm doing that, I'm going to talk out loud to myself to sort of guide myself. Then you'll do that. Gradually, we'll go over the same participation method until you do it on your own and can think to yourself how to do it. We'll take one step at a time. Does that seem clear to you?

Client: Pretty much. I've never done anything like this, though.

In response 3, the helper determines *Joan's willingness* to try out the procedure.

3. **Helper:** Would you like to give it a try?

Client: Sure.

In responses 4 and 5, the helper sets the stage for modeling of the task and accompanying self-guidance and instructs the client in what will be done and what to look for in this step.

4. **Helper:** We mentioned there were at least four things you could do to increase your initiating skills—asking Mr. Lamborne for an explanation only, answering more of Mr. Lamborne's questions, going to the board to do problems, and volunteering answers. Let's just pick one of these to start with. Which one would you like to work with first?

Client: Going to the board to work algebra problems. If I make a mistake there, it's visible to all the class.

5. **Helper:** Probably you're a little nervous when you do go to the board. This procedure will help you concentrate more on the task than on yourself. Now, in the first step, I'm going to pretend I'm going to the board. As I move out of my chair and up to the board, I'm going to tell you what I'm thinking that might help me do the problems. Just listen carefully to what I say, because I'm going to ask you to do the same type of thing afterward. Any questions?

Client: No, I'm just waiting to see how you handle this. I'll look like Mr. Lamborne. His glasses are always down on his nose, and he stares right at you. It's unnerving.

In responses 6 and 7, the helper *initiates and demonstrates* the task with accompanying *self-guidance*. Note, in the modeled part of response 7, the *five components of the self-guidance process*. Also note that a simple problem has been chosen for illustration.

6. **Helper:** You do that. That will help set the scene. Why don't you start by calling on me to go to the board?

Client (as teacher): Joan, go to the board now and work this problem.

7. **Helper** (gets out of seat, moves to imaginary board on the wall, picks up the chalk, verbalizing aloud):

What is it I need to do? He wants me to find y. OK, I need to just go slowly, be careful, and take my time. The problem here reads $4x + y = 10$, and x is 2.8. I can use x to find y. [Helper asks *question* about task.] I'm doing fine so far. Just remember to go slowly. OK, y has to be $10 - 4x$. If x is 2.8, then y will be $10 - 4$ multiplied by 2.8. [Helper focuses *attention* and uses *self-guidance*.] Let's see, 4×2.8 is 10.2. Oops, is this right? I hear someone laughing. Just keep on going. Let me refigure it. No, it's 11.2. Just erase 10.2 and put in $y = 10 - 11.2$. OK, good. If I keep on going slowly, I can catch any error and redo it. [Helper uses *coping self-evaluation* and makes *error correction*.] Now it's simple. $10 - 11.2$ is -1.2, and y is -1.2. Good, I did it, I'm done now, and I can go back to my seat. [Helper *reinforces self*.]

In responses 8 and 9, the helper initiates *overt external guidance:* The client performs the task while the helper continues to verbalize aloud the self-guidance, substituting *you* for I as used in the previous sequence.

8. **Helper:** That's it. Now let's reverse roles. This time I'd like you to get up out of your seat, go to the board, and work through the problem. I will coach you about what to plan during the process. OK?

Client: Do I say anything?

9. **Helper:** Not this time. You just concentrate on carrying out the task and thinking about the planning I give you. In other words, I'm just going to talk you through this the first time.

Client: OK, I see.

In response 10, the helper *verbalizes self-guidance while the client performs the problem.*

10. **Helper:** I'll be Mr. Lamborne. I'll ask you to go to the board, and then you go and I'll start coaching you (as teacher): Joan, I want you to go to the board now and work out this problem: If $2x + y = 8$ and $x = 2$, what does y equal? [Joan gets up from chair, walks to imaginary board, and picks up chalk.] OK, first you write the problem on the board. $2x + y = 8$, and $x = 2$. Now ask yourself "What do I have to do with this problem?" Now answer yourself [question].

You need to find the value of y [answer to question]. Just go slowly, be careful, and concentrate on what you're doing. You know $x = 2$, so you can use x to find y. Your first step is to subtract $8 - 2x$. You've got that up there. You're doing fine—just keep going slowly [focuses attention and uses self-guidance].

$8 - (2$ multiplied by $2)$, you know, is $8 - 4$. Someone is laughing at you. But you're doing fine; just keep thinking about what you're doing. $8 - 4$ is 4, so $y = 4$ [coping self-evaluation]. Now you've got y. That's great. You did it. Now you can go back to your seat [self-reinforcement].

In response 11, the helper *assesses the client's reaction* before moving on to the next step.

11. **Helper:** Let's stop. How did you feel about that?

Client: Well, it's such a new thing for me. I can see how it can help. See, usually when I go up to the board I don't think about the problem. I'm usually thinking about feeling nervous or about Mr. Lamborne or the other kids watching me.

In response 12, the helper reiterates the *rationale* for the cognitive modeling procedure.

12. **Helper:** Yes, those kinds of thoughts distract you from concentrating on your math problems. That's why this kind of practice may help. It gives you a chance to work on concentrating on what you want to do.

Client: I can see that.

In responses 13 and 14, the helper instructs the client to perform the task while verbalizing to herself *(overt self-guidance)*.

13. **Helper:** This time I'd like you to go through what we just did—only on your own. In other words, you should get up, go to the board, work out the math problem, and as you're doing that, plan what you're going to do and how you're going to do it. Tell yourself to take your time, concentrate on seeing what you're doing, and give yourself a pat on the back when you're done. How does that sound?

Client: I'm just going to say something similar to what you said the last time—is that it?

14. **Helper:** That's it. You don't have to use the same words. Just try to plan what you're doing. If you get stuck, I'll step in and give you a cue. Remember, you start by asking yourself what you're going to do in this situation and then answering yourself. This time let's take the problem $5x + y = 10$; with $x = 2.5$, solve for y.

Client (gets out of seat, goes to board, writes problem):

What do I need to do? I need to solve for y. I know $x = 2.5$. Just think about this problem. My first step is to subtract 10 − $5x$. 5 multiplied by 2.5 is 12.5. So I'll subtract 10 − 12.5. [Helper laughs; Joan turns around.] Is that wrong?

Helper: Check yourself but stay focused on the problem, not on my laughter.

Client: Well, 10 − 12.5 is −2.5, so $y = -2.5$. Let's see if that's right. $5 \times 2.5 = 12.5 - 2.5 = 10$. I've got it. Yeah.

In response 15, the helper *gives feedback* to Joan about her practice.

15. **Helper:** That was really great. You only stumbled one time—when I laughed. I did that to see whether you would still concentrate. But after that, you went right back to your work and finished the problem. It seemed pretty easy for you to do this. How did you feel?

Client: It really was easier than I thought. I was surprised when you laughed. But then, like you said, I just tried to keep going.

In responses 16–18, the helper instructs Joan on how to *perform the problem while whispering instructions* to herself *(faded overt self-guidance)*.

16. **Helper:** This time we'll do another practice. It will be just like you did the last time, with one change. Instead of talking out your plan aloud, I just want you to whisper it. Now you probably aren't used to whispering to yourself, so it might be a little awkward at first.

Client (laughs): Whispering to myself? That seems sort of funny.

17. **Helper:** I can see how it does. But it is just another step in helping you practice this to the point where it becomes a part of you—something you can do naturally and easily.

Client: Well, I guess I can see that.

18. **Helper:** Let's try it. This time let's take a problem with more decimals, since you get those, too. If it seems harder, just take more time to think and go slowly. Let's take $10.5x + y = 25$, with $x = 5.5$.

Client (gets out of seat, goes to board, writes on board, whispers):

What do I need to do with this problem? I need to find y. This has more decimals, so I'm just going to go slowly. Let's see, $25 - 10.5x$ is what I do first. I need to multiply 10.5 by 5.5. I think it's 52.75. [Helper laughs.] Let's see, just think about what I'm doing. I'll redo it. No, it's 57.75. Is that right? I'd better check it again. Yes, it's OK. Keep going. 25 − 57.75 is equal to −32.75, so $y = -32.75$. I can check it—yes, 10.5×5.5 is $57.75 - 32.75 = 25$. I got it!

Helper *gives feedback* in response 19.

19. **Helper:** That was great, Joan—very smooth. When I laughed, you just redid your arithmetic rather than turning around or letting your thoughts wander off the problem.

Client: It seems like it gets a little easier each time. Actually, this is a good way to practice math, too.

In responses 20 and 21, the helper gives Joan instructions on how to *perform the problem while instructing herself covertly (covert self-guidance)*.

20. **Helper:** That's right—not only for what we do in here, but even when you do your math homework. Now, let's just go through one more practice today. You're really doing this very well. This time I'd like you to do the same thing as before—only this time I'd like you to just think about the problem. In other words, instead of talking out these instructions, just go over them mentally. Is that clear?

Client: You just want me to think to myself what I've been saying?

21. **Helper:** Yes—just instruct yourself in your head. Let's take the problem $12x - y = 36$, with $x = 4$. Solve for y. [Joan gets up, goes to the board, and takes several minutes to work through this.]

In response 22, the helper *asks the client to describe what happened during covert self-guidance practice*.

22. **Helper:** Can you tell me what you thought about while you did that?

Client: I thought about what I had to do, then what my first step in solving the problem would be. Then I just went through each step of the problem, and after I checked it, I thought I was right.

In response 23, the helper *checks to see whether another practice is needed* or whether they can move on to homework.

23. **Helper:** So it seemed pretty easy. That is what we want you to be able to do in class—to instruct yourself mentally like this while you're working at the board. Would you like to go through this type of practice one more time, or would you rather do this on your own during the week?

Client: I think on my own would help right now.

In response 24, the helper sets up Joan's *homework assignment* for the following week.

24. **Helper:** I think it would be helpful if you could do this type of practice on your own this week—where you instruct yourself as you work through math problems.

Client: You mean my math homework?

In response 25, the helper instructs Joan on how to do homework, including what to do, where, and how much.

25. **Helper:** That would be a good way to start. Perhaps you could take seven problems a day. As you work through each problem, go through these self-instructions mentally. (Do this at home.) Does that seem clear?

Client: Yes, I'll just work out seven problems a day the way we did here for the last practice.

In response 26, the helper instructs Joan *to observe her homework completion* on log sheets and *arranges for a follow-up* of homework at their next session.

26. **Helper:** Right. One more thing. On these blank log sheets, keep a tally of the number of times you actually do this type of practice on math problems during the day. This will help you keep track of your practice. And then next week bring your log sheets with you, and we can go over your homework.

Now that you've seen an example, try the exercise in Learning Activity 13.3 applying cognitive modeling.

PROBLEM-SOLVING THERAPY

Problem-solving therapy or problem-solving training emerged in the late 1960s and early 1970s as a trend in the development of intervention and prevention strategies for enhancing competence in specific situations. D'Zurilla (1988) defines problem solving as a "cognitive–affective-behavioral process through which an individual (or group) attempts to identify, discover, or invent effective means of coping with problems encountered in every day living" (p. 86). Rose and LeCroy (1991) describe problem solving as a strategy whereby "the client learns to systematically work through a set of steps for analyzing a problem, discovering new approaches, evaluating those approaches, and developing strategies for implementing those approaches in the real world" (p. 439). Problem-solving therapy or training has been used with children, adolescents, adults, and elders as a treatment strategy, a treatment-maintenance strategy, or a prevention strategy. As a treatment strategy, problem solving has been used alone or in conjunction with other treatment strategies presented in this book.

The list in Box 13.3 shows that problem-solving therapy has been used effectively for a wide range of purposes. It has helped in treatment of anger and aggression, coping with cancer and other serious medical conditions, managing smoking and other substance use, working with children who have learning and behavior difficulties, and a variety of relationship and

| LEARNING ACTIVITY | 13.3 | Cognitive Modeling with Cognitive Self-Instructional Training |

You may recall from the case of Ms. Weare and Freddie (Chapter 8) that Ms. Weare wanted to eliminate the assistance she gave Freddie in getting ready for school in the morning. One of Ms. Weare's concerns is to find a successful way to instruct Freddie about the new ground rules—mainly that she will not help him get dressed and will not remind him when the bus is five minutes away. Ms. Weare is afraid that after she tells Freddie, he will either pout or talk back to her. She is concerned that she will not be able to follow through with her plan or will not be firm in the way she delivers the rules to him. (1) Describe how you would use the seven major components of cognitive modeling and self-instructional training to help Ms. Weare to do this, and (2) write out an example of a cognitive modeling dialogue that Ms. Weare could use to accomplish this task. Make sure that this dialogue contains the five necessary parts of the self-guidance process: question, answer, focused attention, self-evaluation, and self-reinforcement. Feedback follows.

FEEDBACK

13.3 Cognitive Modeling with Cognitive Self-Instructional Training

1. Description of the seven components:
   a. *Rationale.* First, you would explain to Ms. Weare how cognitive modeling could help her in instructing Freddie and what the procedure would involve. You might emphasize that the procedure would be helpful to her in both prior planning and practice.
   b. *Model of task and self-guidance.* In this step, you would model a way that Ms. Weare could talk to Freddie. You need to make sure that you use language that is relevant and acceptable to Ms. Weare. Your modeling would include both the task (what Ms. Weare could say to Freddie) and the five parts of the self-guidance process.
   c. *Overt external guidance.* Ms. Weare would practice giving her instructions to Freddie while you coach her on the self-guidance process.
   d. *Overt self-guidance.* Ms. Weare would perform the instructions while verbalizing aloud the five parts of the self-guidance process. If she gets stuck or if she leaves out any of the five parts, you can cue her. This step also may need to be repeated before moving on.
   e. *Faded overt self-guidance.* Assuming that Ms. Weare is willing to complete this step, she would perform the instructions to give Freddie while whispering the self-guidance to herself.
   f. *Covert self-guidance.* Ms. Weare would practice giving the instructions to Freddie while covertly guiding herself. When she is able to do this comfortably, you would assign homework.
   g. *Homework.* You would assign homework by asking Ms. Weare to practice the covert self-guidance daily and arranging for a follow-up after some portion had been completed.
2. Example of a model dialogue:

"OK, what is it I want to do in this situation [question]? I want to tell Freddie that he is to get up and dress himself without my help, that I will no longer come up and help him even when it's time for the bus to come [answer]. OK, just remember to take a deep breath and talk firmly and slowly. Look at Freddie. Say, "Freddie, I am not going to help you in the morning. I've got my own work to do. If you want to get to school on time, you'll need to decide to get yourself ready" [focused attention and self-guidance]. Now, if he gives me flak, just stay calm and firm. I won't back down [coping self-evaluation]. That should be fine. I can handle it [self-reinforcement]."

BOX 13.3 PROBLEM-SOLVING RESEARCH

Aggression and anger
Guervremont, D. C., & Foster, S. L. (1993). Impact of social problem-solving training on aggressive boys: Skill acquisition, behavior change, and generalization. *Journal of Abnormal Child Psychology, 21,* 13–27.
Stern, S. B. (1999). Anger management in parent–adolescent conflict. *American Journal of Family Therapy, 27,* 181–193.

Behavior problems
Hains, A. A., & Fouad, N. A. (1994). The best laid plans . . .: Assessment in an inner-city high school. Special issue: Multicultural assessment. *Measurement and Evaluation in Counseling and Development, 27,* 116–124.

Cancer
Fawzy-Fawzy, I., Cousins, N., Fawzy, N. W., & Kemeny, M. E. (1990). A structured psychiatric intervention for cancer patients: I. Changes over time in methods of coping and affective disturbance. *Archives of General Psychiatry, 47,* 720–725.
Nezu, A. M., Nezu, C. M., Houts, P. S., Friedman, S. H., & Faddis, S. (1999). Relevance of problem-solving therapy to psychosocial oncology. *Journal of Psychosocial Oncology, 16*(3/4), 5–6.
Schwartz, M. D., Lerman, C., Audrain, J., Cella, D., Rimer, B., Stefanek, M., Garber, J., Lin, R. H., & Vogel, V. (1998). The impact of a brief problem-solving training intervention for relatives of recently diagnosed breast cancer patients. *Annals of Behavioral Medicine, 20,* 1–7.
Varni, J. W., Sahler, O. J., Katz, E. R., Mulhern, R. K., Copeland, D. R., Noll, R. B., Phipps, S., Dolgin, M. J., & Roghmann, K. (1999). Maternal problem-solving therapy in pediatric cancer. *Journal of Psychosocial Oncology, 16*(3/4), 41–71.

Children
Erwin, P. G., & Ruane, G. E. (1993). The effects of a short-term social problem solving programme with children. *Counselling Psychology Quarterly, 6,* 317–323.
Flanagan, R., Povall, L., Delino, M. J., & Byrne, L. (1998). A comparison of problem solving with and without rational emotive behavior therapy to improve children's social skills. *Journal of Rational–Emotive & Cognitive Behavior Therapy, 16,* 125–134.
Shure, M. B. (1993). I can problem solve (ICPS): Interpersonal cognitive problem solving for young children. Special issue: Enhancing young children's lives. *Early Child Development and Care, 96,* 49–64.

Depression
Barrett, J. E., Williams, J. W., Jr., Oxman, T. E., Katon, W., Frank, W., Hegel, M. T., Syllivan, M., & Schulberg, H. C. (1999). The treatment effectiveness project. A comparison of the effectiveness of paroxetine, problem-solving therapy, and placebo in the treatment of minor depression and dysthymia in primary care patients: Background and research plan. *General Hospital Psychiatry, 21,* 260–273.
Nezu, A. M., Nezu, C. M., & Perri, M. G. (1990). Psychotherapy for adults within a problem-solving framework: Focus on depression. *Journal of Cognitive Psychotherapy, 4,* 247–256.
Wood, B. C., & Mynors-Wallis, L. M. (1997). Problem-solving therapy in palliative care. *Palliative Medicine, 11,* 49–54.

Dietary self-management
Goodall, T. A., Halford, W. K., & Mortimer, R. (1993). Problem solving training to enhance dietary self-management in a diabetic patient. *Behavioural Psychotherapy, 21,* 147–155.

Families
Bentley, K. J., Rosenson, M. K., & Zito, J. M. (1990). Promoting medication compliance: Strategies for working with families of mentally ill people. *Social Work, 35,* 274–277.
Nangle, D. W., Carr-Nangle, R. E., & Hansen, D. J. (1994). Enhancing generalization of a contingency-management intervention through the use of family problem-solving training: Evaluation with a severely conduct-disordered adolescent. *Child and Family Behavior Therapy, 16,* 65–76.

Health
Audrain, J., Rimer, B., Cella, D., Stefanek, M., Garber, J., Pennanen, M., Helzsouer, K., Vogel, V., Lin, T. H., & Lerman, C. (1999). The impact of a brief coping skills intervention on adherence to breast self-examination among first-degree relatives of newly diagnosed breast cancer patients. *Psycho-Oncology, 8,* 220–229.
Elliott, T. R., & Marmarosh, C. L. (1994). Problem-solving appraisal, health complaints, and health-related expectancies. *Journal of Counseling & Development, 72,* 531–537.

Learning and behavior problems
Coleman, M., Wheeler, L., & Webber, J. (1993). Research on interpersonal problem-solving training: A review. *RASE Remedial and Special Education, 14,* 25–37.

Marital therapy
Bodenmann, G. (1997). Can divorce be prevented by enhancing the coping skills of couples? *Journal of Divorce & Remarriage, 27*(3/4), 177–194.
Upton, L. R., & Jensen, B. J. (1991). The acceptability of behavioral treatment for marital problems: A comparison of behavioral exchange and communication skills training procedures. *Behavior Modification, 15,* 51–63.

Mental illness and disability
Leclerc, C., Lesage, A. D., Ricard, N., Lecomte, T., & Cyr, M. (2000). Assessment of a new rehabilitative coping skills module for persons with schizophrenia. *American Journal of Orthopsychiatry, 70,* 380–388.
Nezu, C. M., Nezu, A. M., & Arean, P. (1991). Assertiveness and problem-solving training for mildly mentally retarded persons with dual diagnoses. *Research in Developmental Disabilities, 12,* 371–386.
O'Reilly, M. F., & Chadsey-Rusch, J. (1992). Teaching a social skills problem-solving approach to workers with mental retardation: An analysis of generalization. *Education and Training in Mental Retardation, 27,* 324–334.

Older adults
Collins, K., Luszcz, M., Lawson, M. & Keeves, J. (1997). Everyday problem-solving in elderly women: Contributions of residence, perceived control, and age. *Gerontologist, 37,* 293–302.

> **BOX 13.3 PROBLEM-SOLVING RESEARCH**
>
> Kant, G. L., D'Zurilla, T. J., & Maydeu-Olivares, A. (1997). Social problem solving as a mediator of stress-related depression and anxiety in middle-aged and elderly community residents. *Cognitive Therapy & Research, 21,* 73–96.
>
> Zarit, J. M. (1999). Caring for the caregivers of the elderly: Having fun while doing good. *Family Relations: Interdisciplinary Journal of Applied Family Studies, 48,* 429–431.
>
> *Parenting skills*
> Cunningham, C. E., Davis, J. R., Bremner, R., & Dunn, K. W. (1993). Coping modeling problem solving versus mastery modeling: Effects on adherence, in-session process, and skill acquisition in a residential parent-training problem. *Journal of Consulting and Clinical Psychology, 61,* 871–877.
>
> Doll, B., & Kratochwill, T. R. (1992). Treatment of parent–adolescent conflict through behavioral technology training: A case study. *Journal of Educational and Psychological Consultation, 3,* 281–300.
>
> Gammon, E. A., & Rose, S. D. (1991). The Coping Skills Training Program for parents of children with developmental disabilities: An experimental evaluation. *Research on Social Work Practice, 1,* 244–256.
>
> Kazdin, A. E., Siegel, T. C., & Bass, D. (1992). Cognitive problem-solving skills training and parent management training in the treatment of antisocial behavior in children. *Journal of Consulting and Clinical Psychology, 60,* 733–747.
>
> Spaccarelli, S., Cotler, S., & Penman, D. (1992). Problem-solving skills training as a supplement to behavioral parent training. *Cognitive Therapy and Research, 16,* 1–17.
>
> *Single parenting*
> Pfiffner, L. J., Jouriles, E. N., Brown, M. M., & Etscheidt, M. A. (1990). Effects of problem-solving therapy on outcomes of parent training for single-parent families. *Child and Family Behavior Therapy, 12,* 1–11.
>
> *Smoking*
> Tsoh, J. Y., McClure, J. B., Skaar, K. L., Wettner, D. W., et al. (1997). Smoking cessation: 2. Components of effective intervention. *Behavioral Medicine, 23,* 15–27.
>
> *Solution effectiveness*
> Yoman, J., & Edelstein, B. A. (1993). Relationship between solution effectiveness ratings and actual solution impact in social problem solving. *Behavior Therapy, 24,* 409–430.
>
> *Stress management*
> D'Zurilla, T. J. (1990). Problem-solving training for effective stress management and prevention. *Journal of Cognitive Psychotherapy, 4,* 327–354.
>
> *Worry*
> Dugas, M. J., Letarte, H., Rheaume, J., & Freeston, M. H. (1995). Worry and problem solving: Evidence of a specific relationship. *Cognitive Therapy and Research, 19,* 109–120.

family conflict issues. It has been used successfully to improve clients' communication skills, dietary and medication management, conflict resolution, parenting skills, stress management, and effectiveness in applying solutions. Using problem-solving therapy, clients have reduced their depression, health complaints and expectancies, HIV/AIDS risk, and worry. A literature review of promising treatments for conduct disorders in children and adolescents provides an overview of findings for problem-solving skills training (Kazdin, 1997).

Problem-solving therapy or training is emblematic of the practice nexus in several respects. It has been used with a wide range of issues across multiple disciplines. It has been found useful across diverse groups and is explicitly collaborative in nature. Although the emphasis is on individuals (or groups or families), we see problem-solving training as a potentially valuable tool for supporting critical thinking and locating persons within their environments. The stresses of a problematic situation may stem to a greater or lesser degree from the environment (e.g., requirements, resource insufficiency, oppression) or the person (e.g., personal goals, patterns, limitations)—refer to Chapter 8 for discussion of environmental factors as part of conceptualizing and assessing client concerns. Problem-solving treatment tends to adopt a transactional view of problems in living as stemming from the nature of the person–environment relationship (e.g., imbalances and discrepancies). The same conditions are not inherently or automatically problematic for all people, or problems of the same type or level. "Solutions," then, must be situation- or context-specific if they are to be a realistic match for that person in that set of environmental conditions.

Heppner (1988) has developed a problem-solving inventory (PSI): The scales of the inventory include problem-solving confidence (or self-assurance while engaging in targeted activities), the tendency to approach or avoid problem-solving activities, and the extent to which individuals believe they are in control of their behaviors and emotions while solving difficulties. D'Zurilla and Nezu (1990) developed an inventory that focuses on social problem solving. More recently, D'Zurilla and Nezu (1999) provided a Problem-Solving Self-Monitoring (PSSM) form that assesses the problem, emotions, solution, and outcome as well as a scoring format, and Moorey and colleagues (2000) presented a Problem Solving Scale that measures the problem-solving component of self-control.

Perceptions and attitudes about problem solving can play either a helpful or a disruptive role. If perceptions and attitudes have a helpful role, the client is motivated to learn and engage in problem-solving behaviors. Clients who are unmotivated or avoid dealing with issues because of their perception about them may well not want to learn the problem-solving strategy. In these cases, the helper will have to first help the client deal with these perceptions and attitudes. The helper can also help the client engage in some effective coping activities or behaviors that can contribute to the problem-solving process. If the perceptual, attitudinal, and emotional components of behavior are dealt with, problem-solving training will be more than an intellectual exercise (D'Zurilla, 1988, pp. 116–117). It may be that intervention to change clients' self-appraisals about the value of problem solving and their ability to undertake problem solving will have benefits complementary to the problem-solving activities themselves. Dixon (2000), for example, found that appraisal of oneself to be an effective problem solver significantly corresponded with recovery from depression.

Many clients prefer to ignore or to avoid a significant issue because they believe it will probably go away by itself. Although some issues may simply disappear, others will not vanish if ignored or avoided. In fact, some may get worse and can become antecedents to greater issues if the client does not solve the initial difficulty. The role of the helper is to help the client take responsibility for solving problems within their means and commit to spending the time and energy needed to solve them by changing the client's attitudes and perceptions about these issues.

MULTICULTURAL APPLICATIONS OF PROBLEM SOLVING

Of all of the intervention strategies we describe in this book, problem solving has been the one most widely used with diverse groups of clients. We suspect this is true in part because problem solving is a strategy that focuses on direct action and observable, attainable results. Problem solving has been used with diverse groups of clients in several areas, including the development of educational and academic achievement skills and the development of coping skills and conflict management skills; it has also been incorporated as a component of various prevention programs, including HIV prevention, tobacco use prevention, and violence prevention (see Box 13.4).

Armour-Thomas, Bruno, and Allen (1992) examined the nature of higher-order thinking in academic problem-solving situations involving African American and Latino high school students. They found that both planning and monitoring were important components of solving academic problems for these students, especially in the area of mathematics. In a study conducted by Pollard (1993), African American male and female students who were successful achievers in school used more problem-solving strategies than did their less successful peers.

Two studies have been conducted that specifically focused on culturally relevant educational processes and problem solving. In one of these, Bell, Brown, and Bryant (1993) compared the performance of African American college students on a problem-solving task. Students were given both a traditional, analytic presentation of the task and a culturally relevant, holistic presentation. The students who received the culturally relevant presentation did better on the task than those given the traditional presentation. These authors note the impact of cultural factors on problem solving and also stress the importance for African American students of exposure to models of education that are Afrocentric rather than Eurocentric in nature.

In another culturally relevant study of problem solving, Mehan, Hubbard, and Villaneuva (1994) describe a program implemented in the San Diego high schools. In this program, African American and Latino students who took college preparatory classes were also offered a special elective class emphasizing collaborative instruction, writing, and problem solving. The program is called AVID—Advancement Via Individual Determination. The students who went through the AVID program enrolled in four-year colleges at a level well above the national average. An interesting result of the AVID program is students in the program reported that they were able to achieve at these schools without compromising their ethnic identity. They did this in a way that is reported frequently by students of color involved in mainstream schools: they supported one another and bypassed teachers and counselor who were not prepared to assist racially sensitive skill building.

Other studies have explored nonacademic uses of problem solving. In one of these, Rao and Kramer (1993) interviewed African American mothers of infants with sickle cell anemia and infants with sickle cell trait to explore the coping skills that the mothers used to care for their children. Mothers of both groups reported using social support, positive reappraisal, and planned problem solving most frequently to cope with stressors related to parenting their chil-

> **BOX 13.4 MULTICULTURAL PROBLEM-SOLVING RESEARCH**
>
> *Developing educational and academic achievement skills*
> Armour-Thomas, E., Bruno, K., & Allen, B. (1992). Toward an understanding of higher-order thinking among minority students. *Psychology in the Schools, 29,* 273–280.
> Bell, Y., Brown, R., & Bryant, A. (1993). Traditional and culturally relevant presentations of a logical reasoning task and performance among African-American students. *Western Journal of Black Studies, 17,* 173–178.
> Mehan, H., Hubbard, L., & Villanueva, I. (1994). Forming academic identities: Accommodations without assimilation among involuntary minorities. *Anthropology and Education Quarterly, 25,* 91–117.
> Malloy, Carol E., & Jones, M. G. (1998). An investigation of African American students' mathematical problem solving. *Journal for Research in Mathematics Education, 29,* 143–163.
> Pollard, D. (1993). Gender, achievement, and African-American students' perceptions of their school experience. *Educational Psychologist, 28,* 341–356.
>
> *Developing problem-solving and coping skills*
> Chang, E. C. (1998). Cultural differences, perfectionism, and suicidal risk in a college population: Does social problem solving still matter? *Cognitive Therapy & Research, 22,* 237–254.
> Rao, R., & Kramer, L. (1993). Stress and coping among mothers of infants with sickle cell condition. *Children's Health Care, 22,* 169–188.
> Rixon, R., & Erwin, P. G. (1999). Measures of effectiveness in a short-term interpersonal cognitive problem solving programme. *Counselling Psychology Quarterly, 12,* 87–93.
> Whitfield, K. E., Baker-Thomas, T., Heyward, K., Gatto, M., & Williams, Y. (1999). Evaluating a measure of everyday problem solving for use in African Americans. *Experimental Aging Research, 25,* 209–221.
>
> Yang, B., & Clum, G. (1994). Life stress, social support, and problem-solving skills predictive of depression symptoms, hopelessness, and suicide ideation in an Asian student population: A test of a model. *Suicide and Life Threatening Behavior, 24,* 127–139.
>
> *Promoting conflict management skills*
> Watson, D., Bell, P., & Chavez, E. (1994). Conflict handling skills used by Mexican American and white non-Hispanic students in the educational system. *High School Journal, 78,* 35–39.
>
> *As a component of prevention programs*
> HIV prevention
> Bracho-de-Carpio, A., Carpio-Cedraro, F., & Anderson, L. (1990). Hispanic families and teaching about AIDS: A participatory approach at the community level. *Hispanic Journal of Behavioral Sciences, 12,* 165–176.
> Kelly, J., & St. Lawrence, J. (1990). The impact of community-based groups to help persons reduce HIV infection risk behaviors. *AIDS Care, 2,* 25–36.
> St. Lawrence, J., Brasfield, T., Jefferson, K., Alleyne, E., O'Bannon, R., & Shirley, A. (1995). Cognitive–behavioral intervention to reduce African American adolescents' risk for HIV infection. *Journal of Consulting and Clinical Psychology, 63,* 221–237.
> Tobacco use prevention
> Moncher, M., & Schinke, S. (1994). Group intervention to prevent tobacco use among Native American youth. *Research on Social Work Practice, 4,* 160–171.
> Violence prevention
> Hammond, R., & Yung, B. (1991). Preventing violence in at-risk African American youth. *Journal of Health Care for the Poor and Underserved, 2,* 359–373.

dren. Whitfield and associates (1999) examined a measure of everyday problem solving with a community sample of African Americans and found that the measure achieved good psychometric support for use. We can also get some initial insights into cultural relevance through research with people of cultures outside the United States, such as Jiang, Sun, and Wu's (1999) findings of reduced problem-solving ability among elderly diabetics in China relative to matched healthy elders. A qualitative study with young African developmental activists in South Africa (Van Vlaenderen, 1999) showed both the importance of cultural philosophy—in this case, Ubuntu notions of social harmony, holism, pursuit of practice purpose, and primacy of collective reality—in shaping perceptions of concepts of problems and problem solving, but also evidence of emerging assumptions that suggest shifts from traditional African philosophy towards a more Western philosophy.

Yang and Clum (1994) explored the relationship between a problem-solving model and a social-support model and stress, depression, hopelessness, and suicidal ideation among Asian international students (aged 18–40 years) living in the United States. The problem-solving model was related to stress, depression, hopelessness, and suicidal ideation. Specifically, students who were depressed and hopeless had deficits in problem-solving skills, suggesting that training in these skills for the international students could help them cope with stress and depression.

Watson, Bell, and Chavez (1994) explored differences in problem solving in the area of conflict-handling skills among Mexican American and white non-Hispanic high school students and dropouts. The white students generally used a competitive problem-solving approach to conflict management whereas the Mexican American students and dropouts used a more cooperative problem-solving approach. These authors recommend that school systems provide opportunities for collaborative problem solving for all students, including students of various racial and ethnic groups.

In another area, a major thrust in the use of problem-solving training with diverse clients has been in HIV prevention. Bracho-de-Carpio, Carpio-Cedraro, and Anderson (1990) reported the use of an HIV prevention program based on problem solving with Hispanic families. Kelly and St. Lawrence (1990) described the usefulness of a problem-solving training model for HIV prevention with gay men. Schinke, Botvin, Orlandi, and Schilling (1990) developed a culturally sensitive HIV prevention program incorporating problem solving with HIV facts and elements of ethnic pride. Their program is designed for African American and Hispanic American adolescents, and it can be used in both school and nonschool settings. An interactive microcomputer-based training approach using their model is also available (Schinke, Orlandi, Gordon, & Weston, 1989).

In an excellent empirical study of HIV prevention programs, African American adolescents (28% male and 72% female) were given either education (EC) training only or behavioral skills training (BST) that involved correct condom use, sexual assertion, refusal, information, self-management, risk recognition, and problem solving (St. Lawrence et al., 1995). For example, participants identified difficult situations they had encountered in the past as well as ones they anticipated in the future, then practiced problem-solving skills to deal with these situations. The outcomes in lowering the participants' risk for HIV infection were evaluated on multiple measures at both post-intervention and at a one-year follow-up. These evaluations indicated significantly greater benefit for the youths in the skills-training program than in the information-only intervention. Although these results held for both female and male participants, some gender differences emerged. These authors conclude that because HIV risk behavior is influenced by a variety of "cognitive, interpersonal and situational determinants, multifaceted intervention approaches" are needed (p. 236). Also, for such training to be most effective with diverse groups of clients, they must be "developmentally appropriate and culturally relevant" (p. 235).

Moncher and Schinke (1994) developed a group intervention for tobacco use prevention for Native American youth. The intervention included information on bicultural competence, coping skills, and problem-solving skills. Hammond and Yung (1991) developed a violence prevention program called PACT (Positive Adolescents Choices Training) targeted specifically at black adolescents. In a pilot study of the PACT program, the participants' communication, problem-solving, and negotiation skills were improved.

Guidelines for Using Problem Solving with Diverse Groups of Clients

Problem solving has been shown to be an effective intervention strategy with diverse groups of clients in different ways, but there are some guidelines to consider in enhancing its effectiveness. First, there is evidence that the specific nature of problem-solving skills varies according to gender, race, and ethnic group. It is unwise to assume that diverse groups of clients will solve issues in the same way. The traditional, individualistic Eurocentric and androcentric model of problem solving is used widely by some male and Caucasian clients whereas many females and clients of color prefer a more collaborative and cooperative approach. As a result, both intervention and prevention programs that incorporate problem-solving training must be adapted for client characteristics such as age, gender, race, and ethnic affiliation to make problem solving both developmentally appropriate and culturally relevant.

Second, problem-solving training for clients from diverse cultures will be more effective for these clients when the training is conducted in a culturally sensitive manner—that is, in a way that respects the rituals and traditions of the client's culture, that promotes relevant cultural identity such as sexual and/or racial identity and also ethnic pride, that develops biracial and/or bicultural competence, and that helps these clients to acquire problem-solving skills without having to assimilate the norms of the mainstream culture.

As always, it is important with problem-solving intervention to be aware of intersections among factors such as culture, socioeconomic status, and other issues that may marginalize some people from supportive services. Gammon's (2000) study of rural caregivers of adults with severe developmental disabilities emphasized that to "empower caregiving families, particularly minorities, service providers must continually involve consumers in the assessment of needs and the design and delivery of programs" (p. 183). Noting significantly higher use of "passive" problem-solving strategies by non-Caucasian (predominantly African American) families, this study illustrates the value of considering the broader context within which families are striving to cope and their experience to date with seeking services; for example, relative inaccessibility or nonresponsiveness to needs fosters passive appraisals. In addition to engaging family members as collaborators in developing programs most needed by their children, Gammon (2000) argues that rural providers in particular need to be inventive in pulling together problem-solving supports, such as partnering with churches to help provide respite care, transportation, and socialization; coordinating caregiving exchanges among rural families; and encouraging use of the Internet to access self-advocacy groups and legal information.

STAGES OF PROBLEM SOLVING

We propose the following stages enumerated by D'Zurilla (1986):

1. Treatment rationale (initial structuring): to discuss the goals, rationale, and general format of the training; to begin training in recognizing and labeling concerns, including use of problem-solving self-monitoring; to discuss the limited capacity of the conscious mind during problem solving.
2. Problem orientation: to assess the client's problem-solving coping style; to educate clients about maladaptive and facilitative problem-solving coping skills; to determine cognitive and emotional obstacles to problem solving, and then to train the client to overcome these, attacking the concern from many different vantage points and assessing the time, energy, and commitment needed to resolve the difficulty.
3. Problem definition and formulation: to help the client gather relevant and factual information for understanding the issues, to identify problem-focused and/or emotion-focused components of the issues, and to identify problem-solving goals for each one.
4. Generation of alternative solutions: to instruct the client to think about different ways to handle each goal and to use the deferment of judgment, quantity, and variety principles.
5. Decision making: to instruct the client to screen the list of alternative solutions, to evaluate (judge and compare) solution outcomes for each goal, and to select solution plans.
6. Solution implementation and verification: to encourage the client to carry out several alternative solutions simultaneously; to have the client self-monitor, evaluate, and reinforce the implementation of the solutions; and to help the client troubleshoot and recycle the problem-solving strategy if the solutions do not work.

Each of these stages is described in this section. A detailed description of these six components is included in the Interview Checklist for Problem Solving at the end of the chapter. D'Zurilla and Nezu (1999) have been inclined to separate and amplify the use and control of emotions in problem solving as a discrete stage. Here the goals are to discuss the roles of emotions, including ways emotion can be used to aid in problem-solving effectiveness, and to provide instruction in the use of coping methods to manage disruptive emotions. D'Zurilla and Nezu (1999) also recommend adding content to support maintenance and generalization of effective problem-solving performance.

Treatment Rationale

The rationale used in problem-solving therapy is that it attempts to strengthen the client's belief that problem solving can be an important coping skill for dealing with a variety of concerns requiring effective functioning. The overall goal is to help individuals increase their ability to apply problem-solving strategies designed to help cope effectively with problematic situations that create stress for them. The following is an example of the rationale for problem-solving treatment:

> Each of us is faced with both minor and important challenges. Some challenges are routine, such as trying to decide what to wear to a meeting or how to get the family out of the house more efficiently in the morning. Other challenges are more stressful, such as dealing with a difficult relationship. One way to enhance responsibility and self-control is to learn techniques for solving our difficulties. To take the time, energy, and commitment necessary to solve or deal with problems immediately may relieve future frustration and pain created by a concern.

Here is an example of an overview of the procedure. Keep in mind that this is a very general statement. The rationale and treatment overview must be relevant for the client's culture, beliefs, and life circumstances.

> You will learn how to become aware of how you see an issue. You will look at how much control, time and effort, and commitment you feel you have for solving the issue. We will need to gather information to understand and define the key problem. Also, we'll need to look at what might prevent you from solving the problem. It is important that we explore a variety of solutions for solving the problem. After obtaining several solutions, you will decide which solutions feel most reasonable to implement simultaneously. Finally, you will implement the solution plans. I'm wondering what your thoughts and feelings are regarding what I have described. Do you have any questions?

Problem Orientation

After giving a rationale to the client, the helper asks the client to describe how she or he typically solves problems. The helper determines whether the client has a maladaptive or helpful problem-solving style and then helps the client distinguish between these two coping styles. People with maladaptive coping styles blame themselves or others for the issue or situation. These people often believe that something is wrong with them and may feel abnormal, hopeless, depressed, stupid, or unlucky (D'Zurilla, 1988). Maladaptive coping styles are often exhibited in persons who either minimize the benefits of problem solving or who maximize or exaggerate the losses that may occur from failure to solve the issue successfully. Individuals with poor problem-solving skills often perceive the problem as hopeless and so avoid dealing with it. Also, poor problem solvers may feel inadequate or incompetent, and they prefer having someone else produce a solution (D'Zurilla, 1988). Some people have difficulty solving problems because they either never learned how or feel that the difficulty is too overwhelming.

The role of the helper is to help the client engaging in a maladaptive problem-solving style to change his or her perception about problem solving. However, the helper must do this in a culturally sensitive way, for there are differences in problem-solving styles across gender, age, race, ethnicity, and religious affiliation. It is critical not to equate maladaptive problem solving with non-Eurocentric world views. Instead of viewing difficulties as a threat or a personal inadequacy, the helper assists the client to see them as an opportunity for personal growth and self-improvement (D'Zurilla, 1988). Clients may feel that it is easier not to solve the problem and just wait for things to get better. Helpers need to get these clients to realize that if a problem is not solved, it may very well come back to haunt them later (Peck, 1978). Clients need to believe that there is a solution and that they have the capacity and self-control to find the solution independently and successfully (D'Zurilla, 1988). An expectation that one can cope with and solve a problem successfully will produce the ability to do so.

Problem solving takes time and energy. It is sometimes easier to avoid dealing with issues when they are influenced more by a person's feelings than by his or her reason. People often respond to issues impulsively and do not take time and effort to think about viable solutions. Problem solving requires time, energy, and commitment—a delay of gratification. The helper needs to assess the client's willingness to spend time and energy, to be committed, and to delay gratification, and the helper may have to motivate the client to make the necessary commitment to solve the problem.

Another component of problem orientation is discussing how the client's cognitions and emotions affect problem solving. Clients may be unmotivated to work on the problem because of how they think about it. Also, poor cognitions or self-talk, such as "it is their fault," "it will go away," or "I can't work on it," inhibits the motivation to work on an issue. The purpose of this change intervention is to instruct and to train the client in positive coping methods, with the intent to overcome cognitive and/or emotional obstacles to problem solving (D'Zurilla, 1986, 1988). Strategies such as cognitive restructuring, reframing, stress inoculation, meditation, muscle relaxation, exposure or systematic desensitization, breathing exercises, and self-management (see Chapters 13–18) as well as environmental interventions may help a client deal with cognitive and/or emotional barriers to problem solving. Once significant barriers have been minimized, the client is ready for the next phase of the problem-solving strategy.

Problem Definition and Formulation

The purpose of the defining and formulating step in problem solving is for the helper to help the client gather as much objective information about the problem as possible. In cases where a client has a distorted cognitive view or perception of the problem, the helper may have to use rational–emotive therapy or cognitive restructuring (see Chapter 14). The helper explains that problem solving is a skill and a practical approach whereby a person attempts to identify, explore, or create effective and adaptive ways of coping with everyday challenges (D'Zurilla, 1986). A problem can be viewed as a discrepancy between how a present situation is being experienced and how that situation should or could be experienced (D'Zurilla, 1988). In a shorthand version, this can be thought of as questions that provide the client's view of

1. "What is"—what present conditions are unacceptable and to whom?
2. "What should be"—what conditions are demanded or desired and by whom?
3. What obstacles are influencing the availability of an effective response for reducing this discrepancy? (D'Zurilla & Nezu, 1999)

The client needs to obtain relevant information about the problem by identifying the obstacles that are creating the discrepancy or are preventing effective responses for reducing the discrepancy. It is also important to examine antecedent conditions or unresolved issues that may be contributing to or causing the present concern. Helpers may want to use the techniques presented in Chapter 9 for this step of defining client concerns. These questions are then followed by goal-oriented "How can I . . ." or "What can I do to . . ." questions. These goals, as with any change goals, need to be realistic and stated in specific, concrete terms. In some cases, however, being too specific may miss the mark by being too narrowly defined. For example, D'Zurilla and Nezu (1999) cite the example of a small church with limited finances that hired a painter to repaint the church in time for an important event. It soon became apparent that the painter was very slow and that the quality of the work was very poor. The church committee initially framed their goal question as "How can we get the painter to improve the quality and efficiency of his work so that the church will be painted adequately in time for the celebration?" A way to frame this question to make available a greater range of alternative solutions might look something like "How can we get the church painted adequately in time for the celebration at the lowest possible cost?" (p. 127).

Some practitioners make an important distinction between problem-focused and emotion-focused problem definition (D'Zurilla, 1988). Problems that have problem-focused definitions center on problem-solving goals, with the purpose of changing the problem situation for the better. Problems with an emotion-focused definition concentrate on changing the client's personal reactions to the problem (D'Zurilla, 1988). Alternatively, D'Zurilla (1988) suggests that if the problem situation is assessed as *changeable,* the problem-focused definition should be emphasized in therapy. If problem-focused problems are *unchangeable,* the helper helps the client deal with the client's reaction to the problem (D'Zurilla, 1988). In some cases, the client's problem may be first assessed as problem focused but later the helper and client discover the problem is unchangeable, and the therapeutic focus then becomes changing the personal reaction. It has been our experience that it is best to include both problem-focused and emotion-focused goals in defining the client's problem. Again, problem-focused and emotion-focused definitions of a problem and corresponding goals seem to have some gender and cultural variation.

After the concern has been identified and defined (see Chapter 9), the practitioner and the client set realistic emotion-focused and/or problem-focused goals (see Chapter 10). A goal is defined as what the client would like to have happen as a consequence of solving the problem. The goals should be realistic and attainable, and they should specify the type of behavior, level of behavior, and conditions under which the goal will aid in solving the problem. The practitioner should help the client identify obstacles that might interfere with problem-solving goals. Finally, the practitioner should help the client understand that the complexities involved in most problem situations usually require attacking the problem from many different vantage points (Nezu & Nezu, 1989). Establishing problem-solving goals will help the client with the next step in the therapy: creating alternative solutions.

Generation of Alternative Solutions

The purpose of the next stage of problem solving is to have the client generate as many alternative solutions as possible. The helper instructs the client to think of *what* she or he could do, or *ways* to handle the situation. The helper also instructs the client not to worry about *how* to go about making a plan work or how to put the solution into effect; that will come later. The client is instructed to imagine a great variety of new and original solutions, no matter how ridiculous any given solution may seem. According to D'Zurilla (1986, 1988), the greater the quantity of alternative solutions that the client produces, the greater the quality of the solutions available for the client to choose. Similarly, when the client defers judgment or critical evaluation of the solutions, greater-quality solutions will be produced by the client.

After generating this list of alternative solutions, the client is asked to identify the number of different strategies represented. If too few strategies are represented, the client is instructed to generate more strategy solutions or more solutions for a specific strategy. This "freewheeling" or brainstorming process is intended to filter out functional fixity, practicality, and feasibility in generating solutions. If there are several goals the helper encourages the client to generate several alternative solutions for each problem goal, the rationale being that most issues are complicated and a simple alternative is often inadequate.

Decision Making

The purpose of the decision-making step is to help the client decide on the best solution by judging and comparing all the alternatives. The client is first instructed to screen the list of available alternatives and to eliminate any solution that may be a risk or not feasible (D'Zurilla, 1988). The best solutions maximize benefits and minimize costs for the client's personal, immediate, and long-term welfare. The client is instructed to anticipate outcomes for each alternative

(D'Zurilla, 1988) and then is asked to evaluate each solution using the following four criteria: (1) Will the problem be solved? (2) What will be the status of the client's emotional well-being? (3) How much time and effort will be needed to solve the problem? (4) What effect will the solution have on the client's overall personal and social well-being? (D'Zurilla, 1988). When working with diverse groups of clients, it is important not to impose your own values and culture on this process.

After the client selects and evaluates all the alternative solutions, D'Zurilla (1988) recommends that the client be instructed to answer the following three questions: (1) Can the problem be solved? (2) Is more information needed before a solution can be selected and implemented? (3) What solution or combination of solutions should be used to solve the problem? If the concern cannot be solved with one of the existing solutions, the helper may have to help the client redefine the issue and/or gather more information about the problem. If the previous three questions have been satisfactorily answered, the client is ready to implement the solution, as long as the chosen solution is consistent with the goal for solving the concern as fully as possible.

During the first five stages of the problem-solving strategy, the helper assumes a directive role with the client to ensure a thorough application of the following steps: problem orientation, problem definition, generation of alternatives, and decision making. The helper assumes a less directive role with the client during the solution implementation stage. The therapeutic goal during the last stage of the strategy is to have the client become more responsible.

Solution Implementation and Verification

The purpose of solution implementation and verification in problem solving is to test the chosen solutions to the problem-solving goals and to verify whether these solutions solve the problem. The client simultaneously implements as many solutions as possible. According to D'Zurilla (1988), there are four parts in verifying whether the solution plan is working. The first part is to implement the chosen solution. If there are obstacles (behavioral deficits, emotional concerns, or dysfunctional cognitions) to implementing the solution, the client can acquire performance skills, defuse affective concerns, and restructure cognition to remove the obstacles.

Second, the client can use self-monitoring techniques (see Chapter 18) to assess the effects of the chosen solutions for solving the problem: The helper instructs the client to keep a daily log or journal of the self-talk or emotional reactions to the chosen solutions. The self-talk or statements recorded in the journal can be rated on a scale where 5 = extremely negative, 0 = neutral, and −5 = extremely positive. The accompanying affect state also can be recorded, such as loved, depressed, frustrated, guilty, happy, or neutral. This step can increase the level of emotional awareness.

Third, the client assesses whether the chosen solution achieves the desired goals. This self-evaluation process is assessed in relationship to the solution in the following areas: (1) problem resolution, (2) emotional well-being, (3) time and effort exerted, and (4) the ratio of total benefit to cost (D'Zurilla, 1988).

Finally, if the chosen solution meets all the criteria, the client engages in some form of self-reward (see Chapter 18) for having successfully solved the problem. However, if the chosen solutions do not solve the concern, the helper and client try to pinpoint trouble areas and retrace the problem-solving steps. Some common trouble areas that clients have are emotional reaction to the problem, inadequate definition of the problem, unresolved antecedent issues to the problem, problem-focused instead of emotion-focused definition, and unsatisfactory solution choices.

Use and Control of Emotions in Problem Solving

Problematic situations are often stressful because they involve some difficulty, loss, conflict, or potential pain or harm. Emotions, positive or negative, inevitably are a part of problem solving and can either impede or aid problem-solving performance. Emotions can arise from (a) the problem situation itself; (b) clients' beliefs, appraisals, and expectancies about the problem and their ability to deal with it successfully; and/or (c) the problem-solving tasks used in attempting to solve the problem (D'Zurilla & Nezu, 1999). Although low or moderate levels of emotional arousal can be helpful to motivate problem-solving efforts, sustained high levels of emotional stress are likely to impair problem solving and can result in negative outcomes of their own, such as fatigue, depression, and inertia. In addition, unchecked emotional experience can influence problem solving in ways not readily evident—for example, by narrowing or distorting how problems are labeled, how goals are set, and evaluations made along the way.

With these issues in mind, D'Zurilla and Nezu (1999) identify ways to increase problem-solving effectiveness by using one's emotional responses as

1. a cue for problem recognition, such as using negative emotional feelings as a trigger to look for what may be eliciting it

2. motivation to galvanize problem solving, such as purposefully using reframing to view the problem as a challenge rather than a threat
3. a problem-solving goal in its own right—if negative states such as anger or anxiety seem counterproductive, it is reasonable to set problem-solving goals to minimize these emotional responses and perhaps stimulate counterbalancing ones
4. a possible consequence of some parts of problem solving—for example, when evaluating solution alternatives, the emotions likely to be associated with various alternatives may be important to consider in decision making
5. a criterion for evaluating the solution outcome—expanding the point above, evaluating the effectiveness of a solution relative to a problem and goal may benefit from considering the emotional response to the outcome (e.g., sometimes a solution to one problem creates a new emotional outcome problem)
6. a reinforcer of effective problem solving behavior—the counterpoint to point 5, achieving emotions such as hope, relief, and pride can be powerful outcomes of their own and reinforce subsequent problem-solving behavior.

In terms of controlling disruptive emotions, an assessment can determine what kinds of resources clients have for reducing and controlling emotional effects of stressful issues, such as social support, adaptive avenues for distraction, exercise, and informational or tangible resources. Some individuals may need specialized emotion-focused coping techniques (see Chapter 15 for elaboration on stress management and coping) whereas others may need more limited training in how to (a) recognize potentially disruptive feelings and thoughts, (b) identify various resources they have for coping with these negative effects, and (c) use these resources when needed to reduce, manage, or prevent these effects (D'Zurilla & Nezu, 1999).

Maintenance and Generalization

Supporting clients' ability to take training out of the context of formal helping into their lives and futures is consistent with an empowering, collaborative approach to helping. D'Zurilla and Nezu (1999) suggest helping to consolidate maintenance and generalization of problem-solving training by (a) continuing positive reinforcement and corrective feedback (identifying how and by whom this could be undertaken is one strategy), (b) reviewing positive problem-orientation cognitions and strengthening them (for example, explicitly detailing significant gains made in learning how to generate these and in coping more effectively over the course of treatment), (c) directing attention to types of real-life issues that clients may well encounter for which their problem-solving skills can be applied, and (d) anticipating and preparing for obstacles to implementing clients' problem-solving agenda in ways consistent with the problem-solving approach.

Practice followed by reflection and feedback is one strategy to develop skills and help generalize their use across different types of problems. D'Zurilla and Nezu (1999) suggest use of a rapid problem-solving framework in the final session(s) of training to foster maintenance and generalization. Learning Activity 13.4 presents an example of how to consolidate problem-solving training into a rapid problem-solving format. We suggest spending time with these exercises to achieve a working feel for applying the method. It's not that all problems can be handled in a 1–5-minute span—not at all! Rather, repetitions of problem-solving steps with tricky but delimited problems can help make them easier to recall and use with more-cumbersome problems. For a more thorough overview of problem-solving intervention and learning exercises, see Learning Activity 13.5 and the Interview Checklist for Problem Solving in the Postevaluation.

Some Cautions and Treatment Do's and Don'ts

D'Zurilla (1988) offers three cautions about the problem-solving strategy. One concern is the possible failure of the practitioner to recognize when other strategies are more appropriate. A client with a serious concern or severe maladaptive behavior will require other strategies. For example, a depressed person may require intensive cognitive restructuring (see Chapter 14) before problem-solving therapy could be considered an appropriate strategy (D'Zurilla, 1988). The second caution is the danger of viewing problem-solving therapy as a "rational," "intellectual," or "head-trip therapy or exercise" rather than as a coping strategy that involves all three components of behavior, cognition, and affect (D'Zurilla, 1988). The problem-solving strategy should be viewed as an overall or general system for personal change that must include the emotional, behavioral, and cognitive modes of a person and be culturally relevant as well. The third caution is the potential failure of practitioners to recognize that rapport with the client or a positive therapeutic relationship is a necessary condition for successful therapy (D'Zurilla, 1988). The ingredients of ethical and sensitive therapy (see Chapters 1 and 2) and the variables that enhance the therapeutic relationship (see Chapter 4) are important for successful application of any strategy; the problem-solving strategy is no exception. Problem solving can sometimes be difficult for clients who are not accustomed to

LEARNING ACTIVITY 13.4 Rapid Problem Solving

After initial problem-solving training, ongoing rapid practice can help form quick-response habits and one's ability to problem solve in different kinds of situations. Give yourself very brief time limits for the following, literally two or three minutes. Think about a couple of relatively small dilemmas from your own life or something you can imagine (e.g., forgetting something important, an awkward situation, conflict about how to respond in a moment). Then walk through the steps of rapid problem solving either alone or with a student colleague, trying to stay within the time limits. Debrief afterwards—for example, did you draw a blank or get stuck at any step? It may help to write out some of your responses and review what might help to be effective. Repeat the exercise with one or more training exercises until you have a good sense of the progression of steps and activities.

Step 1. Make the following self-statements:

"Take a deep breath and calm down."
"There is no immediate catastrophe."
"Think of this problem as a challenge."
"I can handle it."
"Stop and think."

Step 2. Ask yourself the following questions:

"What's the problem?" (State the discrepancy between "what is" and "what should be.")
"What do I want to accomplish?" (State a goal.)
"Why do I want to achieve this goal?" (Broaden the goal, if appropriate.)

Step 3. Think of a solution. Now think of several other alternative solutions (at least two or three).

Step 4. Think of the most important criteria for evaluating your solution ideas (at least two or three, such as "Will it achieve my goals?" "What effect will it have on others?" "How much time and effort will it take?" or some other important criterion). Decide quickly on the solution alternative that seems best. Think of one or two quick ways to improve the solution.

Step 5. Implement the solution. Are you satisfied with the outcome? If not, try out your second choice if you still have time (D'Zurilla & Nezu, 1999, p. 147)

LEARNING ACTIVITY 13.5 Problem Solving

This learning activity provides an opportunity to try out problem solving. Think of a problem that you have, and apply the steps to problem solving to your problem. Do this in a quiet place when you will not be interrupted.

1. Determine how you solve problems. How is your approach affected by your gender and culture?
2. Assess your problem-solving style. How does it reflect your world view(s)?
3. Use the following questions to define the underlying discrepancy and your goals: What is? What should be? What obstacle(s) might be barriers to solving problems? How can I. . .?
4. How much time, energy, and commitment do you have for solving the problem?
5. Define your problem, and determine whether your problem is problem focused, emotion focused, or both.
6. Generate solutions for solving the problem. Be sure to think of a variety of solutions that fit your culture.
7. Select the best solutions, using the criteria in item 13 of the Interview Checklist for Problem Solving on p. 430.
8. Implement your solutions to the problem, or at least think about how to implement the solutions. Choose a method for verifying the effectiveness of each solution.

thinking of long-range effects, such as many adolescents and some clients with severe trauma histories who don't allow themselves to think much into the future. Bly (1996) contends that many Euro-Americans in the United States are shortsighted in problem solving and lack the *vertical gaze*—that is, the Native American custom of looking ahead to the possible effects of a given solution for the next seven generations. We add the reminder that many problems in living stem from environmental factors. Careful assessment must guide how much it is the environment rather that the person that needs to change whether through problem solving or other change strategies.

Finally, Nezu, Nezu, and Perri (1989, pp. 133–136) offer some guidelines for implementing the problem-solving strategy, summarized also in D'Zurilla and Nezu (1999):

1. Training in problem solving should *not* be presented in a mechanistic manner. Training is best accomplished through interactive, engaging methods.
2. The helper should attempt to individualize the training and make it relevant to the specific needs of a client or group.
3. Homework and *in vivo* practice of the problem-solving components are crucial. Encourage as much between session practice as possible. Handouts can be useful during and beyond formal intervention, for they remind clients of homework.
4. The helper should be caring and sensitive to the client's concerns and feelings. Correct implementation of the intervention is important to effectiveness, but the client's needs and responses must be of primary focus.
5. For the intervention to be most useful, the problems being targeted should not be only superficial but also include those most crucial for a given client.
6. The helper always needs to ensure that an accurate assessment of the problem has been obtained.
7. The helper should encourage the client to implement as many solutions as possible during training in order to obtain feedback about resolution or progress.
8. The helper must make a thorough evaluation of the patient's abilities and limitations in order to implement a solution alternative. The evaluation would also include how much control that the client has over the problem situation.
9. Generally, both problem-focused coping and emotion-focused coping will be components of problem-solving coping. The helper must determine the forms or combination needed in the client's situation.

One role of the helper throughout the problem-solving process is to educate the client about the problem-solving strategy and to guide the client through the problem-solving steps. As we mentioned before, the helper is less directive with the client during the last stage of the problem-solving process in order to help the client become more independent and take responsibility for applying the chosen problem solutions and verifying their effectiveness. The helper can help the client to maintain these problem-solving skills and to generalize them to other concerns. The helper also can assist the client in anticipating obstacles to solving strategies and prepare the client for coping with them. The client should be able to cope fairly well if he or she takes the time to *examine critically and carefully* her or his orientation to the problem, to carefully define the concern, to generate a variety of alternative solutions, and to make a decision about solution alternatives that are compatible with goals or desired outcomes. Solution implementation may be easier if the first four stages of the problem-solving process have been thoroughly processed. (See also Learning Activity 13.5.)

MODEL EXAMPLE: PROBLEM-SOLVING THERAPY

In this model example, we present a narrative account of how problem-solving therapy might be used with a 49-year-old male client. Yoshi, an air traffic controller, has reported that he would like to decrease the stress he experiences in his job. He believes that decreasing this stress will help his ulcer and help him cope better with his job. In addition to the physical signs of stress (insomnia), Yoshi also reports that he worries constantly about making mistakes in his job. He has also thought about taking early retirement, which would relieve him of the stress and worry.

Rationale

First, we explain to Yoshi that all of us face concerns and that sometimes we feel stuck because we don't know how to handle an issue. We tell Yoshi that solving problems as they occur can prevent future discomfort. We provide Yoshi with an overview of problem-solving therapy, telling him that we'll need to look at how he sees the problem and what obstacles there are to solving the problem. We tell him that we will need to define the concern, think of many different solutions, select several solutions, and try out the solutions and see how well the solutions solve the central concern. We emphasize that problem solving is a collaborative, cooperative process. Finally, we confirm Yoshi's willingness to use problem-solving strategy and answer any questions he may have about the procedure.

Problem Orientation

We determine how Yoshi typically solves problems. We ask him to give an example of a concern he has had in the past and how and what he did to solve it. Then we describe for Yoshi the difference between maladaptive and helpful problem solving. We explain to him that most people inherently have problem-solving ability but something blocks the use of it. We tell him that problem-solving therapy removes the blocks or obstacles that are maladaptive for good problem solving. We explain that healthy problem solving is the capacity to view issues as an opportunity. If Yoshi is encountering cognitive or emotional obstacles in his problem-solving attempts, we would introduce appropriate strategies to help remove them. Finally, we assess how much time, energy, and commitment Yoshi has for solving the issue.

Problem Definition and Formulation

We briefly describe the problem-solving strategy for Yoshi. We explain to him that we need to gather information about the concern, such as his thoughts and feelings on the matter, what unresolved issues are contributing, how intense the issue is, what has been done to solve the issue, and when and where the issue occurs. We ask Yoshi what other information is needed to define the problem. If he has distorted views or perceptions of the issue, we would have to help him reframe his perception. We have to determine whether Yoshi's problem is problem focused, emotion focused, or both. For example, we can probably change his emotional and cognitive reaction to the work situation and help him reduce the stress, but he cannot change the job requirements unless he leaves or retires. We can help Yoshi identify problem-solving goals or what he would like to have happen so that the problem would be solved. For Yoshi, one of the most attainable and realistic goals might be to reduce job stress.

Generation of Alternative Solutions

Yoshi is instructed to generate as many alternative solutions as possible for solving the problem. We inform him not to worry about how to go about making the alternatives work or how to put the solution into effect. Also, he is instructed to defer judgment about how good or feasible his ideas or solutions are until later, to generate as many alternatives as he can think of (because quantity produces quality), and to be creative and to think of nontraditional and unconventional solutions as well.

Decision Making

We instruct Yoshi to screen the list of alternatives and to use the following criteria for evaluating each solution: Will the concern be solved with this solution? What will be the status of his emotional well-being? How much time and effort will be needed to use the alternative solutions? What will be his overall personal and social well-being using each of these alternative solutions? Yoshi is reminded that it is important to evaluate each solution by answering these four criteria questions. Finally, he is instructed to select the best solutions that are compatible with the problem-solving goals and that fit best with his own culture.

Solution Implementation and Verification

We instruct Yoshi to try his chosen solutions for solving the concern. We also instruct him to self-monitor the alternative solutions he chose to solve the problem in order to determine their effectiveness. Suppose that he chooses to reduce his stress in the workplace by using meditation as one solution. We instruct Yoshi to self-monitor by keeping a written log or journal of the effectiveness of meditation using the following criteria questions: How effective is meditation in reducing job stress? How well does he feel emotionally about the meditative experience? Are the time and effort spent with daily meditations worth it? Are there more benefits for using meditation than costs, and what are his thoughts, feelings, and behavior in relationship to the solution implementation? Yoshi is instructed to complete the self-monitoring or journal each day just before bedtime. He is instructed to rate each of the criteria questions on a five-point scale, with descriptive words for each point on the scale. We tell him that he needs to reward himself after successfully solving the problem (reducing the stress) by selecting rewarding things or activities. Also, we tell him to determine the best time to receive something or to engage in rewarding activity. If, for example, the meditation did not contribute to solving the issue, we instruct Yoshi to look at trouble areas that might be obstacles to solving the problem, such as his emotional reactions, the fact that the issue may not be well defined, or unresolved issues that may be contributing.

SUMMARY

Reframing is a useful way to help the client develop alternative ways to view a concern. To be effective, the reframe must be plausible, acceptable, and culturally meaningful to the client. An example of a meaning reframe is the newer notion of "healthy resistance," meaning clients' empowerment to resist oppression and to stand up for themselves and their beliefs. Reframing can serve as an important complement to other intervention strategies—for example, new ways to view an issue or goal can foster motivation to undertake subsequent change efforts such as cognitive modeling or problem solving. Cognitive modeling and self-instruction go a step further than the modeling strategies we reviewed in Chapter 12: aiming to help people learn how to use self-talk to enhance performance. In this strategy, implicit or covert responses as well as overt responses are modeled. Self-instructional training can be paired with a great many interventions and can be very useful toward supporting collaborative and person-in-environment helping approaches. For example, envisioning oneself undertaking the desired actions within one's social context can help illuminate potential difficulties that can be addressed before the client works toward enacting these steps in their actual circumstances.

Problem-solving therapy or training provides clients with a formalized system for viewing issues more constructively. As a treatment strategy, problem solving can be used alone or in conjunction with other treatment strategies presented in this book. Problem solving has been used in a number of ways with diverse groups of clients. Some differences in problem-solving styles are apparent in client characteristics such as age, gender, race, and ethnicity. Culturally sensitive problem-solving training also includes elements of ethnic identity, critical consciousness, and multicultural competence. Problem solving is often about changing aspects of one's environment—whether in terms of tangible, relational, power, sociocultural, or other dimensions—that are the root or at least a considerable part of the client's problem. At its best, the breadth of applicability, environmental sensitivity, empirical support, collaborative nature, and nurturance of creative critical thinking situate problem solving firmly within the practice nexus.

In the next chapter we see how clients can be taught to alter self-defeating thoughts by learning to replace these with incompatible coping thoughts and skills. The strategy of cognitive restructuring, presented in Chapter 14, is directed toward replacing or reformating self-defeating thoughts and schemata.

INFOTRAC® EXPLORATIONS

1. Search for *reframing*, and select three or four articles on counseling-related interventions. Do the articles provide sufficient detail to determine if meaning reframes or context reframes were more prominent? What specific steps were undertaken to help the client establish the reframe or to determine if the reframe seemed consistent with the client's values and culture?

2. Search for the term *problem-solving therapy*. Because this term is used in common language for many different things, it is important to determine whether a practice application is consistent with the tenets of problem solving and the training components supported by clinical and research findings. Assess three to five articles in this regard.

SUGGESTED RESOURCES

Readings

Clark, A. J. (1998). Reframing: A therapeutic technique in group counseling. *Journal for Specialists in Group Work, 23*, 66–73.

Dixon, W. A. (2000). Problem-solving appraisal and depression: Evidence for a recovery model. *Journal of Counseling & Development, 78*, 87–91.

D'Zurilla, T. J. (1988). Problem-solving therapies. In K. S. Dobson (Ed.), *Handbook of cognitive–behavioral therapies* (pp. 85–135). New York: Guilford.

D'Zurilla, T. J., & Nezu, A. M. (1999). *Problem-solving therapy: A social competence approach to clinical intervention* (2nd ed.). New York: Springer.

Gendlin, E. T. (1996). *Focusing-oriented psychotherapy: A manual of the experiential method.* New York: Guilford.

Goldstein, A. P. (1999). *The Prepare Curriculum: Teaching prosocial competencies.* Champaign, IL: Research Press.

Huang, L. N. (1994). An integrative approach to clinical assessment and intervention with Asian-American adolescents. *Journal of Clinical Child Psychology, 23*, 21–31.

Joiner, T. E., Jr., Voelz, Z. R., & Rudd, M. D. (2001). For suicidal young adults with comorbid depressive and anxiety disorders, problem-solving treatment may be better than treatment as usual. *Professional Psychology, 32*, 278–282.

Kazdin, A. E. (1997). Practitioner review: Psychosocial treatments for conduct disorder in children. *Journal of Child Psychology & Psychiatry & Allied Disciplines, 38*, 161–178.

Motenko, A. K., & Greenberg, S. (1995). Reframing dependence in old age. *Social Work, 40*, 382–390.

Needleman, L. D. (1999). *Cognitive case conceptualization.* New York: Erlbaum Associates.

Nezu, A. M., Nezu, C. M., Friedman, S. H., Faddis, S., & Houts, P. S. (1998). *Helping cancer patients cope: A problem-solving approach.* Washington, DC. American Psychological Association.

Rath, S. (1998). Verbal self-instructional training: An examination of its efficacy, maintenance, and generalization. *European Journal of Psychology of Education, 13,* 399–409.

Shure, M. B. (1992). *I can problem solve: An interpersonal cognitive problem-solving program: Intermediate elementary grades.* Champaign, IL: Research Press.

Soo-Hoo, T. (1998). Applying frame of reference and reframing techniques to improve school consultation in multicultural settings. *Journal of Educational & Psychological Consultation, 9,* 325–345.

St. Lawrence, J., Brasfield, T., Jefferson, K., Alleyne, E., O'Bannon, R., & Shirley, A. (1995). Cognitive-behavioral interventions to reduce African American adolescents' risk for HIV infection. *Journal of Consulting and Clinical Psychology, 63,* 221–237.

Watson, D., Bell, P., & Chavez, E. (1994). Conflict handling skills used by Mexican American and white non-Hispanic students in the educational system. *High School Journal, 78,* 35–39.

Yang, B., & Clum, G. (1994). Life stress, social support, and problem-solving skills predictive of depression symptoms, hopelessness, and suicide ideation in an Asian student population: A test of a model. *Suicide and Life Threatening Behavior, 24,* 127–139.

Web Sites

Conflict Resolution Programs in Schools
http://www.ed.gov/databases/ERIC_Digests/ed338791.html

Program to Encourage Active, Rewarding Lives for Seniors
http://depts.washington.edu/nwpec/pearls.htm

Self-Therapy
www.helpyourselftherapy.com

VRCbd (therapy applications with children)
http://www.coe.missouri.edu/vrcbd/projres1.shtml

13 POST EVALUATION

Part One

Objective One asks you to demonstrate at least 8 out of 11 steps of the reframing procedure with a role-play client. Assess this activity using the Interview Checklist for Reframing.

Interview Checklist for Reframing

Instructions to observer: Determine whether the helper demonstrated the lead listed in the checklist. Check which leads were used.

Item	Examples of helper leads
I. Rationale for Reframing	
____ 1. Helper explains purpose of reframing.	"Often when we think about a problem situation, our initial or intuitive reaction can lead to emotional distress. For example, we focus only on the negative features of the situation and overlook other details. By focusing only on the selected negative features of a situation, we can become nervous or anxious about the situation."
____ 2. Helper provides overview of reframing.	"We'll identify what features you attend to when you think of the situation. Once you become aware of these features, we will look for other neutral or positive aspects of the situation that you may ignore or overlook. Then we will work on incorporating these other things into your perceptions of the problem situation."
____ 3. Helper confirms client's willingness to use the strategy.	"How does this all sound? Are you ready to try this?"
II. Identification of Client Perceptions and Feelings in Problem Situations	
____ 4. Helper has client identify features typically attended to during situation (may have to use imagery with some clients).	"When you think of the situation or one like it, what features do you notice or attend to? What is the first thing that pops into your head?"
____ 5. Helper has client identify typical feelings during situation.	"How do you usually feel?" "What do you experience [or are you experiencing] during this situation?"
III. Deliberate Enactment of Selected Perceptual Features	
____ 6. Helper asks client to reenact situation (by role play or imagery) and to deliberately attend to selected features. (This step may need to be repeated several times.)	"Let's set up a role play [or imagery] in which we act out this situation. This time I want you to deliberately focus on these aspects of the situation we just identified. Notice how you attend to ____."
IV. Identification of Alternative Perceptions	
____ 7. Helper instructs client to identify positive or neutral features of situation. The new reframes are plausible and acceptable to the client, and fit the client's values and age, gender, race, and ethnicity.	"Now, I want us to identify other features of the situation that are neutral or positive. These are things you have forgotten about or ignored. Think of other features." "What other aspects of this situation that aren't readily apparent to you could provide a different way to view the situation?"

(continued)

13 POSTEVALUATION

(continued)

V. Modification of Perceptions in Situations

_____ 8. Helper instructs client to modify perceptions of situation by focusing on or attending to the neutral or positive features. (Use of role play or imagery can help with this process for some clients.) (This step may need to be repeated several times.)

"When we act out the situation, I want you to change what you attend to in the situation by thinking of the neutral or positive features we just identified. Just focus on these features."

VI. Homework and Follow-Up

_____ 9. Helper encourages client to practice modifying perceptions during *in vivo* situations.

"Practice is very important for modifying your perceptions. Every time you think about or encounter the situation, focus on the neutral or positive features of the situation."

_____ 10. Helper instructs client to monitor aspects of the strategy on homework log sheet.

"I'd like you to use this log to keep track of the number of times you practice or use this. Also record your initial and resulting feelings before and after these kinds of situations."

_____ 11. Helper arranges for a follow-up. (During follow-up, helper comments on client's log and points out small perceptual shifts.)

"Let's get together in two weeks. Bring your log sheet with you. Then we can see how this is working for you."

Observer comments: _____

Part Two

Describe how you would use the seven components of cognitive modeling and self-instructional training to help Mr. Huang (from Chapter 8) initiate social contacts with his boss (Objective Two). These are the seven components:

1. Rationale
2. Model of task and self-guidance
3. Overt external guidance
4. Overt self-guidance
5. Faded overt self-guidance
6. Covert self-guidance
7. Homework and follow-up

Feedback follows the evaluation.

Part Three

Objective Three asks you to demonstrate at least 16 out of 21 steps of the cognitive self-instructional modeling procedure with a role-play client. You can audiotape your interview or have an observer assess your performance, using the Interview Checklist for Cognitive Modeling on page 425.

Part Four

Objective Four asks you to identify accurately the steps of the problem-solving therapy represented by at least 8 out of 10 examples of helper interview responses. For each of the following helper responses, identify on paper which step of the problem-solving procedure is being used. There may be more than one helper response associated with a step. The six major steps of problem solving are as follows:

1. Rationale for problem solving
2. Problem orientation
3. Problem definition and formulation
4. Generation of alternative solutions
5. Decision making
6. Solution implementation and verification

Feedback for the Postevaluation follows on page 432.

1. "Self-monitoring involves keeping a diary or log about your thoughts, feelings, and behaviors."

2. "To help you assess each solution, you can answer several questions about how effective the solution will be in solving the problem."

13 POST EVALUATION

3. "Be creative and freewheeling. Let your imagination go. Write down whatever comes into your mind."
4. "What goals do you want to set for your emotional or personal reaction to the issue?"
5. "When you have concerns, give me an example of the concern and describe how you typically solve it."
6. "Solving problems as they occur can prevent future discomfort."
7. "Most people have an ability to solve problems, but often they block the use of it and become poor problem solvers."
8. "What unresolved issues may be contributing to the problem? When does the problem occur? Where does it occur?"
9. "Look over your list of solutions to see how much variety is on your list; think of new and original ones."
10. "You need to think about what you can reward yourself with after you complete this step."

Part Five

Objective Five asks you to demonstrate 16 out of 19 steps associated with the problem-solving strategy in a role-play interview. You can audiotape your interview or have an observer rate it, using the Interview Checklist for Problem Solving on page 427.

Interview Checklist for Cognitive Modeling

Instructions: Determine which of the following leads the helper used in the interview. Check each of the leads used. Some examples of helper leads are provided in the right column; however, these are only suggestions.

Item	Examples of helper leads
I. Rationale About Strategy	
___ 1. Helper provides a rationale for the strategy.	"This strategy is a way to help you do this task and also plan how to do it. The planning will help you perform better and more easily."
___ 2. Helper provides overview of strategy.	"We will take it step by step. First, I'll show you how to do it, and I'll talk to myself aloud while I'm doing it so you can hear my planning. Then you'll do that. Gradually, you'll be able to perform the task while thinking through the planning to yourself at the same time."
___ 3. Helper checks client's willingness to use strategy.	"Would you like to go ahead with this now?"
II. Model of Task and Self-Guidance	
___ 4. Helper instructs client in what to listen and look for during modeling.	"While I do this, I'm going to tell you orally my plans for doing it. Just listen closely to what I say as I go through this."
___ 5. Helper engages in modeling of task, verbalizing self-guidance aloud, using language relevant to the client.	"OK, I'm walking in for the interview. [Helper walks in.] I'm getting ready to greet the interviewer and then wait for his cue to sit down" [sits down].
___ 6. Self-guidance demonstrated by helper includes five components:	
___ a. *Question* about demands of task	"Now what is it I should be doing in this situation?"
___ b. *Answers* question by planning what to do	"I just need to greet the person, sit down on cue, and answer the questions. I need to be sure to point out why they should take me."

(continued)

POST EVALUATION

(continued)

    ____ c. *Focused attention* to task and *self-guidance* during task

"OK, just remember to take a deep breath, relax, and concentrate on the interview. Just remember to discuss my particular qualifications and experiences and try to answer questions completely and directly."

    ____ d. *Coping self-evaluation* and, if necessary, *error correction*

"OK, now, if I get a little nervous, just take a deep breath. Stay focused on the interview. If I don't respond too well to one question, I can always come back to it."

    ____ e. *Self-reinforcement* for completion of task

"OK, doing fine. Things are going pretty smoothly."

III. Overt External Guidance

____ 7. Helper instructs client to perform task while helper coaches.

"This time you go through the interview yourself. I'll be coaching you on what to do and on your planning."

____ 8. Client performs task while helper coaches by verbalizing self-guidance, changing *I* to *you*. Helper's verbalization includes the five components of self-guidance:

"Now just remember you're going to walk in for the interview. When the interview begins, I'll coach you through it."

    ____ a. Question about task

"OK, you're walking into the interview room. Now ask yourself what it is you're going to do."

    ____ b. Answer to question

"OK, you're going to greet the interviewer. [Client does so.] Now he's cuing you to sit down." [Client sits.]

    ____ c. Focused attention to task and self-guidance during task

"Just concentrate on how you want to handle this situation. He's asking you about your background. You're going to respond directly and completely."

    ____ d. Coping self-evaluation and error correction

"If you feel a little nervous while you're being questioned, just take a deep breath. If you don't respond to a question completely, you can initiate a second response. Try that now."

    ____ e. Self-reinforcement

"That's good. Now remember you want to convey why you should be chosen. Take your time to do that. [Client does so.] Great. Very thorough job."

IV. Overt Self-Guidance

____ 9. Helper instructs client to perform task and instruct self aloud.

"This time I'd like you to do both things. Talk to yourself as you go through the interview in the same way we have done before. Remember, there are five parts to your planning. If you get stuck, I'll help you."

____ 10. Client performs task while simultaneously verbalizing aloud self-guidance process. Client's verbalization includes five components of self-guidance:

    ____ a. Question about task

"Now what is it I need to do?"

    ____ b. Answer to question

"I'm going to greet the interviewer, wait for the cue to sit down, then answer the questions directly and as completely as possible."

    ____ c. Focused attention and self-guidance

"Just concentrate on how I'm going to handle this situation. I'm going to describe why I should be chosen."

13 POST EVALUATION

____	d. Coping self-evaluation and error correction	"If I get a little nervous, just take a deep breath. If I have trouble with one question, I can always come back to it."
____	e. Self-reinforcement	"OK, things are going smoothly. I'm doing fine."
____ 11.	If client's self-guidance is incomplete or if client gets stuck, helper either	
____	a. Intervenes and cues client or	"Let's stop here for a minute. You seem to be having trouble. Let's start again and try to. . . ."
____	b. Recycles client back through step 10	"That seemed pretty hard, so let's try it again. This time you go through the interview, and I'll coach you through it."
____ 12.	Helper gives feedback to client about overt practice.	"That seemed pretty easy for you. You were able to go through the interview and coach yourself. The one place you seemed a little stuck was in the middle, when you had trouble describing yourself. But overall, it was something you handled well. What do you think?"

Interview Checklist for Problem Solving

Instructions: Determine whether the helper demonstrated each of the leads listed in the checklist. Check which leads were used.

Item	Examples of helper leads
I. Rationale for Problem Solving	
____ 1. Helper explains purpose of problem-solving therapy in a way that is consistent with the client's culture.	"All of us are faced with little and big concerns. Sometimes we feel stuck because we don't know how to handle a concern. This procedure can help you identify and define a difficulty and examine ways of solving it. You can be in charge of the issue instead of the issue being in charge of you. Solving difficulties as they occur can prevent future discomfort."
____ 2. Helper provides brief overview of procedure in a way that is consistent with the client's culture.	"There are five steps we'll do in using this procedure. Most problems in living are complex, and achieving changes often requires many different perspectives. First, we'll need to look at how you see the problem. We'll examine what are unhelpful and helpful problem-solving skills. Another part of this step is to explore how to overcome thoughts and feelings that could be obstacles to achieving your goals. We'll also need to see how much time and energy you are willing to use to solve the problem. Second, we will define the problem by gathering information about it. Third, we'll want to see how many different solutions we can come up with for solving the problem. Next, we'll examine the solutions and decide which one to use. Finally, you will try out the chosen solutions and see how well they solve the problem. What are your thoughts about what I have described? Do you have any questions?"

(continued)

13 POST EVALUATION

(continued)

II. Problem Orientation

_____ 3. Helper determines how the client solves problems.

"When you have concerns or problems, give me an example of the problem and describe how you typically solve it."

_____ 4. Helper describes the difference between maladaptive and helpful problem solving, recognizing variations across gender, age, and culture and world views.

"Most people have the ability to solve problems, but often they block the use of it. Problem-solving therapy helps to remove blocks or obstacles and helps bring important issues into focus. Problem-solving therapy provides a formalized system for viewing problems differently. People who don't solve problems very well may feel inadequate or incompetent to solve their problem. Often these people want to avoid the problem or want someone else to solve it. People sometimes feel it is easier not to solve the problem, and things will get better. At times, poor problem solvers feel hopeless, depressed, or unlucky. If you feel like a poor problem solver, we'll have to consider ways that make you feel like you are in charge. You can solve problems; they are a part of daily living. There are usually a variety of solutions to every problem, and you have the capacity to find the solution. It can be helpful to think of problems as an opportunity."

_____ 5. Helper determines what cognitive and emotional obstacles the client might have as barriers to solving the problem.

"When you think about your problem, what thoughts do you have concerning the problem? What are you usually thinking about during this problem? Do you have any 'shoulds' or beliefs concerning the problem? What feelings do you experience when thinking about the problem? Are there any holdover or unfinished feelings from past events in your life that still affect the problem? How do your thoughts and feelings affect the problem and your ability to solve it? You may not be aware of it, but think about some past issues or unfinished business you may have as we do problem solving." (If there are any obstacles, the helper introduces a strategy or strategies [for example, rational emotive therapy, cognitive restructuring, reframing, meditation, muscle relaxation] to help the client remove cognitive or emotional obstacles to problem solving.)

_____ 6. Helper assesses the client's time, energy, and commitment to solving the problem.

"Any problem usually takes time, effort, and commitment to solve. But it is often important to solve the problem now rather than wait and solve it later—or not at all. It is important to know how committed you are to solving the problem. (Wait for the answer.) Also, solving a problem takes time; do you feel you have enough time to work on the problem? (Pause, wait for answer.) Thinking about and working on a problem can take a lot of energy. How energized do you feel about working on this problem?" (Pause for answer.)

13 POST EVALUATION

III. Problem Definition and Formulation

_____ 7. Helper describes the problem-solving strategy for the client in a culturally relevant way.

"People have problems or concerns. Some concerns are minor, and some are major. Problem solving is a skill and a practical approach. People use problem solving to identify, explore, or create effective ways of dealing with everyday concerns or difficult situations."

_____ 8. Helper helps the client gather information about the problem. (The steps in assessing client concerns presented in Chapter 9 can be used for problem solving.)

"We want to gather as much information about the concern as we can. What type of issue or situation is it? What thoughts do you have when the difficulty occurs? What feelings do you experience? How often does the difficulty occur, or is it ongoing? What unresolved issues may be contributing? Who or what other people are involved? When does the problem occur? Where does it occur? How long has this been going on? How intense is the problem? What have you done to solve the problem? What obstacles can you identify that prevent you from making desired changes? Tell me, how do you see the issue or troubling situation?" "What other information do we need to define the problem? What is your definition of the problem?"

_____ 9. Helper determines whether the client's problem is problem focused, emotion focused, or both.

"From the way you have defined the problem, how can the problem be changed? What aspects of the problem can be changed? What emotional reactions do you have about the problem? How would you like to change your personal/emotional reaction to the problem? There may be some things about the problem you cannot change. Some problem situations are unchangeable. If there are aspects of the problem that are changeable, we will work on those things that can be changed. One thing we can change is your emotional or personal reaction to the problem."

_____ 10. Helper helps the client identify culturally relevant problem-solving goals. (The steps in goal setting presented in Chapter 10 can be used for this step.)

"Now that we have identified and defined the problem, we need to set some goals. A goal is what you would like to have happen so that the problem would be solved. The goals should be things you can do or things that are attainable and realistic."

"How many obstacles are there that prevent you from setting problem-solving goals? How can you remove these obstacles? What goals do you want to set for your emotional or personal reaction to the problem? What behaviors do you want to change? How much or what level of behavior is going to change? Under what condition or circumstance will the behavior change occur? What goals do you want to set for things that are changeable in the problem situation? What behaviors or goals do you want to set for yourself, the frequency of these behaviors, and in what problem conditions? These goals will help us in the next step of problem solving."

(continued)

13 POST EVALUATION

(continued)

IV. Generation of Alternative Solutions

____ 11. Helper presents the guidelines for generating alternative solutions.

"We want to generate as many alternative solutions for solving the problem as possible. We do this because problems are often complicated and a single alternative is often inadequate. We need to generate several alternative solutions for each problem-solving goal."

____ a. What options

"Think of what you could do or ways to handle the problem. Don't worry about how to go about making your plan work or how to put the solution into effect—you'll do that later."

____ b. Defer judgment

"Defer judgment about your ideas or solutions until later. Be loose and open to any idea or solution. You can evaluate and criticize your solutions later."

____ c. Quantity

"Quantity breeds quality. The more alternative solutions or ideas you can think of, the better. The more alternatives you produce, the more quality solutions you'll discover."

____ d. Variety

"Be creative and freewheeling. Let your imagination go. Write down whatever comes into your mind. Allow yourself to think of a variety of unusual or unconventional solutions as well as more traditional or typical ones. Look over your list of solutions, and see how much variety there is. If there is little variety on your list, generate more and think of new and original solutions."

V. Decision Making

____ 12. Helper instructs the client to screen the list of alternative solutions.

"Now you need to screen and look over your list of alternative solutions for solving the problem. You want to look for the *best* solutions. The best solutions are the ones that maximize benefits and minimize costs for your personal, social, immediate, and long-term welfare."

____ 13. Helper provides criteria evaluating each solution.

"To help you assess *each* solution, you answer the following four questions:

____ a. Will the problem be solved with this particular solution?

____ b. By using this solution, what will be the status of my emotional well-being?

____ c. If I use this solution, how much time and effort will be needed to solve the problem?

____ d. What will be my overall personal and social well-being if I use this solution?

Remember that it is important to evaluate *each* solution by answering these four questions."

____ 14. Helper instructs the client to make a decision and select the best solutions compatible with problem-solving goals and the client's culture.

"Select as many solutions that you think will work or solve the problem. Answer these questions:

____ a. Can the problem be solved reasonably well with these solutions?

13 POST EVALUATION

_____ b. Is more information about the problem needed before these solutions can be selected and implemented?

Decide whether the solutions fit with the problem-solving goals." (If the answer to questions one and two are yes and no, respectively, move on to the next step. Answers of no to question one and yes to question two may require recycling by redefining the problem, gathering more information, and determining problem obstacles.)

VI. Solution Implementation and Verification

_____ 15. Helper instructs the client to carry out chosen solutions.

"For the last stage of problem solving, try out the solutions you have chosen. If there are obstacles to trying out the solutions, we'll have to remove them. You can use several alternative solutions at the same time. Use as many solutions as you can."

_____ 16. Helper informs client about self-monitoring strategy (described in Chapter 18).

"We'll need to develop a technique for you to see whether the solution solves the problem. Self-monitoring involves keeping a diary or log about your thoughts, feelings, and behavior. You can record these behaviors as you implement your chosen solutions. We'll need to discuss what responses you'll record, when you'll record, and method of recording."

_____ 17. Helper instructs the client to use these criteria to assess whether the solution achieves the desired goal for solving the problem.

"You'll need to determine whether your solution solves the problem. One way to do this is to ask yourself the following:

_____ a. Problem resolved
_____ b. Emotional well-being

"Did the solutions solve the problem?"
"How is your emotional well-being after you used the solutions?"

_____ c. Time and effort exerted
_____ d. Ratio of total benefits to total costs

"Was the time and effort you exerted worth it?"
"Were there more benefits for using the solutions than costs?"

_____ 18. Helper instructs the client about self-reward (see Chapter 18 for a description of the self-reward strategy).

"You need to think about how you can reward yourself after successfully solving the problem. What types of things or activities are rewarding to you? When would be the best time to receive something or to engage in a rewarding activity?"

_____ 19. Helper instructs the client on what to do if solutions do not solve the problem.

"When the solutions do not solve the problem, we need to look at some trouble areas that might be obstacles to solving the problem. What is your emotional reaction to the problem? The problem may not be defined well. There may be old unresolved problems contributing to the present problem."

POSTEVALUATION FEEDBACK

PART ONE

Use the Interview Checklist for Reframing to assess your interview.

PART TWO

1. *Rationale* First, you would explain the steps of cognitive modeling and self-instructional training to Mr. Huang. Then you would explain how this procedure could help him practice and plan the way he might approach his boss.
2. *Model of task and self-guidance* You would model for Mr. Huang a way he could approach his boss to request a social contact. You would model the five parts of the self-guidance process: (1) the question about what he wants to do, (2) the answer to the question in the form of planning, (3) focused attention on the task and guiding himself through it, (4) evaluating himself and correcting errors or making adjustments in his behavior in a coping manner, and (5) reinforcing himself for adequate performance. In your modeling, it is important to use language that is relevant to Mr. Huang.
3. *Overt external guidance* Mr. Huang would practice making an approach or contact while you coach him through the five parts of self-guidance as just described.
4. *Overt self-guidance* Mr. Huang would practice making a social contact while verbalizing aloud the five parts of the self-guidance process. If he got stuck, you could prompt him, or you could have him repeat this step or recycle step 3.
5. *Faded overt self-guidance* Mr. Huang would engage in another practice attempt, but this time he would whisper the five parts of the self-guidance process.
6. *Covert self-guidance* Mr. Huang would make another practice attempt while using the five parts of the self-guidance process covertly. You would ask him afterward to describe what happened. Additional practice with covert self-guidance or recycling to step 4 or 5 might be necessary.
7. *Homework* You would instruct Mr. Huang to practice the self-guidance process daily before actually making a social contact with his boss.

PART THREE

Rate an audiotape of your interview or have an observer rate you, using the Interview Checklist for Cognitive Modeling on page 425.

PART FOUR

1. Solution Implementation and Verification
2. Decision Making
3. Generation of Alternative Solutions
4. Problem Definition and Formulation
5. Problem Orientation
6. Rationale for Problem Solving
7. Problem Orientation
8. Problem Definition and Formulation
9. Generation of Alternative Solutions
10. Solution Implementation and Verification

PART FIVE

Rate an audiotape of your interview or have someone else rate it, using the Interview Checklist for Problem Solving on page 427.

CHAPTER 14

COGNITIVE CHANGE AND COGNITIVE RESTRUCTURING STRATEGIES

OBJECTIVES

After completing this chapter, the student should be able to

1. Identify and describe the six components of cognitive restructuring from a written case description.
2. Teach the six major components of cognitive restructuring to another person, or demonstrate these components in a role-play interview.
3. Describe ways that schemas are involved in cognitive functioning.

Since the first edition of this book, almost 25 years ago, considerable changes have emerged in the concept and practice of cognitive therapy. Cognitive therapy includes a variety of techniques and approaches that assume problematic emotions and behaviors to be the result of how clients perceive and interpret events. Three levels of cognition appear to play a significant role in producing emotional and behavioral difficulties: (1) automatic thoughts, (2) schemas or underlying assumptions, and (3) cognitive distortions (Beck, 1967). Clinical improvement depends on changes in these three levels of cognition, or *cognitive restructuring*.

Building on the covert and cognitive strategies presented in Chapters 12 and 13, this chapter focuses on cognitive therapy and cognitive restructuring strategies. Cognitive therapies constitute quite a large umbrella. As Prochaska and Norcross (1999) note, cognitive therapies are often blended with other therapies, such as cognitive analytic therapy (integrating with psychoanalytic therapy), increasingly popular in Europe, and with therapies focused on affective and emotional patterns. Computer-administered cognitive treatments are on the rise as are cognitive therapies in self-help and Web-accessed formats. The breadth of applicability of cognitive therapies and their demonstrated effectiveness for wide-ranging problems and populations are part of why we have chosen to include cognitive interventions within the practice nexus. Cognitive therapies tend to be approached in psychoeducationally oriented ways that can be consistent with collaborative practice. In addition to a collaborative relationship, the client and therapeutic helper work together as an investigative team—for example, treating problematic automatic thoughts and schemas as hypotheses to be assessed relative to evidence that seems to be consistent or inconsistent. Some developers strive for "deepening" cognitively oriented therapies through approaches to tap less easily accessed core aspects of personal knowledge, the complexity of personal meaning systems, and the social embeddedness of people, problems, and meaning (see Neimeyer and Raskin, 2001, for a review of constructivisms in psychotherapy).

In short, cognitive therapies are among the most widely used tools in the clinical practitioner's tool belt, and this trend promises to continue in the anticipated future. However, we encourage you to keep in mind that there are no one-size-fits-all or "silver bullet" change strategies. Cognitively oriented interventions have their share of limitations. For example, although one can well use cognitive therapies in a contextualized manner, consistent with assessing and helping people within their real-world circumstances, the emphasis is inwardly directed—focusing on distorted, irrational, or otherwise maladaptive thinking (Prochaska & Norcross, 1999). We urge you to maintain your own critical consciousness in applying these or other interventions and to balance attention to environmental contributors, including sociopolitical and cultural factors that can easily be devalued or overlooked.

A word about terminology: The definitional boundaries can be unclear—between cognitive and cognitive behavioral interventions, for example. By and large, we see the interventions presented in this book as being consistent with three propositions considered fundamental to cognitive behavioral therapy: (1) cognitive activity affects behavior, (2) cognitive activity may be monitored and altered, and (3) desired behavior change may be affected through cognitive change (Dobson & Dozois, 2001). In this chapter, we use the term *cognitive therapy* not so much to distinguish these interventions from cognitive behavioral as to focus more attention on the underpinnings of human cognition and how it works (in normative and problematic ways) and on strategies targeting cognitive change.

DEVELOPMENTS IN COGNITIVE THERAPY

Mahoney (1995) suggests that "the major conceptual developments in the cognitive psychotherapies over the past three decades have been (a) the differentiation of rationalist and constructivist approaches to cognition; (b) the recognition of social, biological, and embodiment issues; (c) the reappraisal of unconscious processes; (d) an increasing focus on self and social systems; (e) the reappraisal of emotional and experiential processes; and (f) the contribution of the cognitive psychotherapies to the psychotherapy integration movement" (p. 6). Some of the contributors to these developments are listed in Table 14.1. This table gives a historical context for the development of cognitive therapy.

Albert Ellis (1962) founded a form of cognitive therapy based on the cognitive control of irrational thinking. Some of the additional foundation for the therapeutic application of cognitive behavior modification started with the covert conditioning described by Homme (1965) and in Cautela's (1966) covert sensitization. The work of Homme and Cautela laid the base from which others developed the cognitive strategies described in Chapter 12 (about guided imagery) and the desensitization procedure presented in Chapter 17. Meichenbaum and Goodman's (1971) self-instructional training demonstrated the influence between verbal self-instruction and behavior described in the cognitive modeling section of Chapter 13. In 1967, Beck presented his thesis that emotional disorders are the consequence of distorted thinking or an unrealistic cognitive appraisal of life events. This chapter presents a description of cognitive restructuring similar to the ideas of A. T. Beck (1967, 1976) and J. Beck (1995). The anxiety management training developed by Suinn and Richardson (1971) is based on the process of reciprocal inhibition. Clients are taught to use relaxation (Chapter 15, stress management) to control their anxious feelings. The problem-solving therapy we described in Chapter 13 (D'Zurilla & Goldfried, 1971) is a cognitive form of self-control in which the client explores response alternatives for coping with problem sit-

TABLE 14.1	Contributors to the Development of Cognitive Therapies
Therapy	**Author and work**
Rational–Emotive Therapy	Ellis, A. (1962). *Reason and emotion in psychotherapy.* New York: Stuart.
Covert Conditioning	Homme, L. (1965). Perspectives in psychology: XXIV. Control of coverants, the operants of the mind. *Psychological Record, 15,* 501–511.
Covert Sensitization	Cautela, J. R. (1966). The treatment of compulsive behavior by covert sensitization. *Psychological Record, 16,* 33–41.
Self-Instructional Training	Meichenbaum, D. H., & Goodman, J. (1971). Training impulsive children to talk to themselves. *Journal of Abnormal Psychology, 77,* 127–132.
Cognitive Therapy	Beck, A. T. (1967). *Depression: Causes and treatment.* Philadelphia: University of Pennsylvania Press.
Anxiety Management Training	Suinn, R. M., & Richardson, F. (1971). Anxiety management training: A nonspecific behavior therapy program for anxiety control. *Behavior Therapy, 2,* 498–510.
Problem-Solving Therapy	D'Zurilla, T. J., & Goldfried, M. R. (1971). Problem-solving and behavior modification. *Journal of Abnormal Psychology, 78,* 107–126.
	Spivack, G., Platt, J. J., & Shure, M. B. (1976). *The problem-solving approach to adjustment.* San Francisco: Jossey-Bass.
Self-Control	Mahoney, M. J., & Thoresen, C. E. (1974). *Self-control: Power to the person.* Monterey, CA: Brooks/Cole.
Stress Inoculation Training	Meichenbaum, D., Turk, D., & Burstein, S. (1975). The nature of coping with stress. In I. G. Sarason & C. D. Spielberger (Eds.), *Stress and anxiety: Vol. II.* New York: Wiley.
Social Learning	Bandura, A. (1985). *Social foundations of thought and actions: A social cognitive theory.* Englewood Cliffs, NJ: Prentice Hall.

uations. Spivack, Platt, and Shure (1976) developed an interpersonal cognitive problem-solving treatment approach based on the same skills first identified by D'Zurilla and Goldfried. Mahoney and Thoresen (1974) contributed self-control to the literature of cognitive therapies in general and specifically to self-management, presented in Chapter 18. Finally, the participant modeling approaches discussed in Chapter 12 and self-efficacy, described in the last section of Chapter 18, are based on the social learning theory of Bandura (1986).

This chapter describes an intervention considered the cornerstone of cognitive–behavioral approaches: *cognitive restructuring.* You may also see it referred to as *cognitive replacement,* or the shift from old mental pictures and rules to new ones. There are also cognitive restructuring underpinnings in some of the constructivistic practice that aims to understand people's personal meanings and to modify their narratives, interpretations, and patterns in line with their change goals. Cognitively oriented therapies have also been "heating up" over the years, with growing inclusion of "hot" factors such as emotion, motivation, goals, and values, reflecting the integration of findings from arenas such as physiology, neuroanatomy, linguistics, computer science, and cultural anthropology. Recent work has advanced our understanding of the profound interdependence of mind and culture. Markus, Kitayama, and Heiman (1996), for example, provide a detailed review of the multiple ways that culture influences structures, systems, and transactional dynamics of cognition and meaning making. They emphasize that

> Cultural, societal, or collective contexts provide the very frames within which psychological systems can develop, and the psychological systems of the person develop in ways that are culturally resonant and that help establish the person as a member in good standing in any given group or social context. Understanding culturally mediated psychological processes necessarily involves an analysis of the meanings (the metaphors, the values, the beliefs, the goals, the schemas) and the practices (the tacit patterns of living) within which any given event or act can be made meaningful. (p. 903)

Consistent with the practice nexus, we emphasize a contextualized and culturally sensitive approach to understanding variation not only in cognitive content (e.g., schemas, beliefs, and goals as well as whether we would evaluate these as "distorted" or "maladaptive") but also in the circumstances, norms, and power dynamics that constitute the surrounding environment and conventions of daily life. Keep in mind also that the notion of culture may usefully be applied to many collectives beyond those defined by national or racial heritage—for example, cultural dimensions related to disability, older age, sexual orientation, religion, and small town or rural life. More-recent discussions of the practice of cognitive therapy are provided by Beck (1995), Berlin (2001), Dobson (2001), Goldfried (1995), Leahy and Holland (2000), Mahoney (1995), and Salkovskis (1996).

USES OF COGNITIVE RESTRUCTURING

Cognitive restructuring (CR) has its roots in the elimination of distorted or invalid inferences (Beck, Rush, Shaw, & Emery, 1979), disputing irrational thoughts or beliefs (Ellis & Harper, 1975), and promoting rule-governed behavior (described by Meichenbaum, 1977). In many ways, cognitive restructuring is considered an essential component of almost every cognitive–behavioral procedure. A sample of the cognitive restructuring research is listed in Box 14.1. Inspection of this list of research reveals a variety of concerns to which cognitive restructuring has been applied. We have listed several studies using CR to help control generalized and domain-specific anxiety, panic, phobias, and test and math anxiety. CR has also been used in a wide range of situations involving, among others, anger, depression, marital and family therapy, pain, stress, trauma, substance use, gambling, relapse prevention, memory and belief issues, self-esteem, coping, and obsessive–compulsive disorder (see Box 14.1).

Although we cannot fully address in this book the spectrum of interventions across the lifespan, we present in Table 14.2 a summary of the empirical support base regarding efficacious interventions for child behavior disorders. You will find guidance for many of these interventions in this book, although we refer you to sources such as Ollendick and King (2000) and Kendall (2000) for instruction specific to children and adolescents. We note also that any list such as this should be regarded as tentative. The empirical base is simply limited at present regarding the types of interventions that have been evaluated with differing presenting problems as well as the generalizability of findings. We also point you to encouraging intervention development and testing applicable to children with disabilities that incorporate processes of social cognition and emotional regulation with developmentally appropriate practices (Guralnick, 1993; Guralnick & Neville, 1997).

BOX 14.1 COGNITIVE RESTRUCTURING RESEARCH

Anger
Dahlen, E. R., & Deffenbacher, J. L. (2000). A partial component analysis of Beck's cognitive therapy for the treatment of general anger. *Journal of Cognitive Psychotherapy, 14,* 77–95.
Deffenbacher, J. L., Oetting, E. R., Huff, M. E., & Thwaites, G. A. (1995). Fifteen-month follow-up of social skills and cognitive-relaxation approaches to anger reduction. *Journal of Counseling Psychology, 42,* 400–405.
Deffenbacher, J. L., Thwaites, G. A., Wallance, T. L., & Oetting, E. R. (1994). Social skills and cognitive-relaxation approaches to general anger reduction. *Journal of Counseling Psychology, 41,* 386–396.

Anxiety
Carter, M. M., Marin, N. W., & Murrell, K. L. (1999). The efficacy of habituation in decreasing subjective distress among high anxiety-sensitivity college students. *Journal of Anxiety Disorders, 13,* 575–589.
Strumpf, J. A., & Fodor, I. (1993). The treatment of test anxiety in elementary school-age children: Review and recommendations. *Child and Family Behavior Therapy, 15,* 19–42.
Sud, A. (1993). Efficacy of two short-term cognitive therapies for test anxiety. *Journal of Personality and Clinical Studies, 9,* 39–46.
Vance, W. R., & Watson, T. S. (1994). Comparing anxiety management training and systematic rational restructuring for reducing mathematics anxiety in college students. *Journal of College Student Development, 35,* 261–266.

Cultural differences
Giannini, A. J., Quinones-Delvalle, R. M., & Blackshear, G. The use of cognitive restructuring in cross-cultural therapy. *Psychiatric Forum, 15,* 30–32.

Depression
Emerson, P., West, J. D., & Gintner, G. G. (1991). An Adlerian perspective on cognitive restructuring and treating depression. *Journal of Cognitive Psychotherapy, 5,* 41–53.
Pace, T. M., & Dixon, D. N. (1993). Changes in depressive self-schemata and depressive symptoms following cognitive therapy. *Journal of Counseling Psychology, 40,* 288–294.

Epilepsy
Upton, D., & Thompson, P. J. (1992). Effectiveness of coping strategies employed by people with chronic epilepsy. *Journal of Epilepsy, 5,* 119–127.

Gambling
Sharpe, L., & Tarrier, M. (1992). A cognitive–behavioral treatment approach for problem gambling. *Journal of Cognitive Psychotherapy, 6,* 193–203.
Sylvain, C., & Ladouceur, R. (1992). Corrective cognition and gambling habits in players of video poker. *Canadian Journal of Behavioural Science, 24,* 479–489.

Internet intervention
Kovalski, T. M., & Horan, J. J. (1999). The effects of Internet-based cognitive restructuring on the irrational career beliefs of adolescent girls. *Journal of Cognitive Psychotherapy, 13,* 145–152.

Marital therapy
Halford, W. K., Sanders, M. R., & Behrens, B. C. (1993). A comparison of the generalization of behavioral marital therapy and enhanced behavioral marital therapy. Special section: Couples and couple therapy. *Journal of Consulting and Clinical Psychology, 61,* 51–60.

Memory and belief
Lachman, M. E., Weaver, S. L., Bandura, M., & Elliott, E. (1992). Improving memory and control beliefs through cognitive restructuring and self-generating strategies. *Journal of Gerontology, 47,* P293–P299.
Claridge, K. E. (1992). Restructuring memories of abuse: A theory-based approach. *Psychotherapy, 29,* 243–252.

Obsessive–compulsive disorder
Jones, M., & Menzies, R. G. (1997). Danger ideation reduction therapy (DIRT): Preliminary findings with three obsessive–compulsive washers. *Behavior Research & Therapy, 35,* 955–960.
Sookman, D., Pinard, G., & Beauchemin, N. (1994). Multidimensional schematic restructuring treatment for obsessions: Theory and practice. *Journal of Cognitive Psychotherapy, 8,* 175–194.

Pain
Basler, H. D. (1993). Group treatment for pain and discomfort. Special issue: Psychosocial aspects of rheumatic diseases. *Patient Education and Counseling, 20,* 167–175.
Grant, L. D., & Haverkamp, B. E. (1995). A cognitive–behavioral approach to chronic pain management. *Journal of Counseling & Development, 74,* 25–31.
Subramanian, K. (1994). Long-term follow-up of a structured group treatment for the management of chronic pain. Special issue: Empirical research on the outcomes of social work with groups. *Research on Social Work Practice, 4,* 208–223.

Panic
Craske, M. G., Rowe, M., Lewin, M., & Noriega-Dimitri, R. (1997). Interoceptive exposure versus breathing retraining within cognitive–behavioral therapy for panic disorder with agoraphobia. *British Journal of Clinical Psychology, 36,* 85–99.
DiFilippo, J. M., & Overholser, J. C. (1999). Cognitive–behavioral treatment of panic disorder: Confronting situational precipitants. *Journal of Contemporary Psychotherapy, 29*(2), 99–113.
Hecker, J. E., Finnk, C. M., Vogeltanz, N. D., Thorpe, G. L., & Sigmon, S. T. (1998). Cognitive restructuring and interoceptive exposure in the treatment of panic disorder: A crossover study. *Behavioural & Cognitive Psychotherapy, 26,* 115–121.

Parenting
Gammon, E. A., & Rose, S. D. (1991). The Coping Skills Training Program for parents of children with developmental disabilities: An experimental evaluation. *Research on Social Work Practice, 1,* 244–256.
Morgan, B., & Hensley, L. (1998). Supporting working mothers through group work: A multilevel psychoeducational approach. *Journal for Specialists in Group Work, 23,* 298–311.

> **BOX 14.1 COGNITIVE RESTRUCTURING RESEARCH**
>
> *Phobia*
> Ball, S. G., & Otto, M. W. (1994). Cognitive–behavioral treatment of choking phobia: 3 case studies. *Psychotherapy and Psychosomatics, 62,* 207–211.
> Heard, P. M., Dadds, M. R., & Conrad, P. (1992). Assessment and treatment of simple phobias in children: Effects on family and marital relationships. *Behaviour Change, 9,* 73–82.
> Oest, L. G., Brandennburg, M., & Alm, T. (1997). One versus five sessions of exposure in the treatment of flying phobia. *Behavior Research & Therapy, 35,* 987–996.
> Taylor, S., Woody, S., Koch, W. J., McLean, P., Paterson, R. J., & Anderson, K. W. (1997). Cognitive restructuring in the treatment of social phobia. *Behavior Modification, 21,* 487–511.
>
> *Relapse prevention*
> Bakker, L., Ward, T., Cryer, M., & Hudson, S. M. (1997). Out of the rut: A cognitive–behavioral treatment program for driving-while-disqualified offenders. *Behaviour Change, 14,* 29–38.
>
> *Self-esteem*
> Horan, J. (1996). Effects of computer-based cognitive restructuring on rationally mediated self-esteem. *Journal of Counseling Psychology, 43,* 371–375.
>
> *Smoking*
> Haaga, D. A. F., & Allison, M. L. (1994). Thought suppression and smoking relapse: A secondary analysis of Haaga (1989). *British Journal of Clinical Psychology, 33,* 327–331.
>
> *Stress*
> Hains, A. A. (1992). Comparison of cognitive–behavioral stress management techniques with adolescent boys. *Journal of Counseling and Development, 70,* 600–605.
>
> *Substance abuse*
> Steigerwald, F., & Stone, D. (1999). Cognitive restructuring and the 12-step program of Alcoholics Anonymous. *Journal of Substance Abuse Treatment, 16,* 321–327.
> Wolberg, J. M., Hovland, R., & Hopson, R. E. (1999). Cognitive restructuring as a relapse prevention strategy: Teaching alcoholics to talk back to beer ads. *Alcoholism Treatment Quarterly, 17*(4), 29–51.
>
> *Trauma*
> Echeburua, E., de Corral, P., Zubizarreta, I., & Sarasua, B. (1997). Psychological treatment of chronic posttraumatic stress disorder in victims of sexual aggression. *Behavior Modification, 21,* 433–456.
> Marks, I., Lovell, K., Noshirvani, H., Livanou, M., & Thrasher, S. (1998). Treatment of posttraumatic stress disorder by exposure and/or cognitive restructuring: A controlled study. *Archives of General Psychiatry, 55,* 317–325.
>
> *Writing*
> Nedate, Y., & Tagami, F. (1994). Effects of instruction through writing on subjective well-being modification: When adopting a cognitive restructuring approach. *Japanese Journal of Counseling Science, 27,* 21–26.

MULTICULTURAL APPLICATIONS OF COGNITIVE THERAPY AND COGNITIVE RESTRUCTURING

In recent years, the use of cognitive therapy with diverse groups of clients has received increased attention, although as Hays (1995) notes, such multicultural applications are still too few. Critiquing cognitive therapy from a multicultural viewpoint, Hays (1995) observed that the values embraced in this approach are those supported by the status quo of the mainstream culture. As an example, the emphasis on self-control that fits with the Euro-American value of personal autonomy may be empowering for some clients but may also "imply placing blame on the individual for problems that are previously a result of unjust social conditions" (Hays, 1995, p. 311; Ivey, Ivey, & Simek-Morgan, 1997).

Cognitive therapy and cognitive restructuring have also been critiqued by feminist therapists (Brown, 1994; Kantrowitz & Ballou, 1992). In the early days of feminism, cognitive–behavioral therapy was seen as admirable "for teaching women new ways of behaving" (Brown, 1994, p. 55). This was in the era when individual change was viewed as the primary solution to societal problems. Current models of feminist therapy, multicultural therapy, and ecological therapy do not agree with the assertion that if you change an oppressed individual's way of thinking, the presenting problems will automatically be resolved. Further, as Kantrowitz and Ballou (1992) suggest, the "rational thinking" orientation of cognitive therapy and cognitive restructuring reinforces world views and cognitive processes that are stereotypically both Euro-American and masculine; other world views and cognitive processes are at the least overlooked and at the worst devalued. Thus, the cognitive processing styles of some women and some persons of color may be rejected. In addition, as Brown (1994) observes, a useful response to the cognitive therapy notion of "irrational thinking" is the suggestion "that for some people, in some places and at some times, these supposedly universally pathological conditions might be reasonable, or even life saving" (p. 61). Moreover, cognitive therapy and cognitive restructuring, as a cornerstone of the procedure, challenge one's beliefs and thoughts. As Kantrowitz and Ballou (1992) suggest, this challenging may not fit with some culture and gender socialization patterns (p. 81). For example,

TABLE 14.2 Well-Established and Probably Efficacious Psychosocial Treatments for Children		
	Treatments	
Problem/disorder	**Well-established**	**Probably efficacious**
Autism	None	None
Depression	None	Behavioral self-control therapy
		Cognitive–behavioral coping skills
Anxiety	None	Cognitive–behavioral therapy
		Cognitive–behavioral therapy plus family anxiety management
Phobias	Participant modeling	Imaginal desensitization
	Reinforced practice	*In vivo* desensitization
		Live modeling
		Filmed modeling
		Cognitive–behavioral therapy
ADHD	Behavioral parent training	Cognitive–behavioral therapy
	Operant classroom management	
ODD/CD	Behavioral parent training	Anger control training with stress inoculation
	Videotape modeling	Anger coping therapy
	Parent training	Assertiveness training
		Delinquency prevention program
		Multisystemic therapy
		Parent–child interaction therapy
		Parent training program
		Problem-solving skills training
		Rational–emotive therapy
		Time out plus signal seat treatment

Note: ADHD, attention-deficit/hyperactivity disorder; ODD, oppositional defiant disorder; CD, conduct disorder.
Source: "Empirically Supported Treatments for Children and Adolescents," by T. H. Ollendick and W. H. King. In P. C. Kendall (Ed.), *Child and Adolescent Therapy: Cognitive Behavioral Procedures,* (2nd ed.), pp. 386–425. Copyright ©2000 The Guilford Press. Reprinted with permission.

Asians "have been taught to create emotional harmony and avoid conflict in accordance with their cultural norms" (Kantrowitz & Ballou, 1992, p. 81).

In light of all this, Hays (1995) does assert that cognitive therapy can be useful with diverse groups of clients if cultural adaptations in the intervention are made. We have found useful adaptations of cognitive restructuring with diverse groups of clients. Several of these are listed in Box 14.2. Ahijevych and Wewers (1993) have suggested the use of cognitive restructuring as an intervention for nicotine-dependent African American women who want to stop smoking. Addressing a different problem, Hatch and Paradis (1993) have developed a 12-week group treatment incorporating cognitive restructuring, breathing, and relaxation for African American women with panic disorder. They found that the women in the group particularly valued audiovisual aids and self-help material but noted the small number of African Americans represented in television programs as well as among the group facilitators who were the role models. An African American woman who had completed successful treatment for panic attacks was invited to speak to the group. Addressing racial issues and providing access to other African Americans for both education and support seem to be critical parts of this cognitive intervention.

Earlier, we addressed the relevance of cognitive restructuring for Asians. Iwamasa (1993) contends that cognitive restructuring can be culturally compatible for some Asian American clients, especially those who are well educated and achievement oriented. He notes that part of the appeal of this intervention is that it is structured (versus unstructured), emphasizes thoughts and behaviors, and does not require the Asian American client to oppose the traditional Asian value of not revealing very personal and/or familial difficulties to strangers.

Johnson and Ridley (1992) have described an adaptation of cognitive restructuring for clients who sought "Christian counseling." The clients were encouraged to challenge problematic beliefs by using Biblical scriptures as the basis for the

> **BOX 14.2 MULTICULTURAL COGNITIVE THERAPY RESEARCH**
>
> *African American clients*
> Ahijevych, K., & Wewers, M. (1993). Factors associated with nicotine dependence among African American women cigarette smokers. *Research in Nursing and Health, 16,* 283–292.
> Haley, W., Roth, D., Coleton, M., & Ford, G. (1996). Appraisal, coping and social support as mediators of well-being in black and white family caregivers of patients with Alzheimer's disease. *Journal of Consulting and Clinical Psychology, 64,* 121–129.
> Hatch, M., & Paradis, C. (1993). Panic disorder with agoraphobia. A focus on group treatment with African Americans. *The Behavior Therapist, 16,* 240–242.
>
> *Asian American clients*
> Iwamasa, G. Y. (1993). Asian Americans and cognitive behavioral therapy. *The Behavior Therapist, 16,* 233–235.
>
> *Christian clients*
> Johnson, W. B., & Ridley, C. R. (1992). Brief Christian and non-Christian rational–emotive therapy with depressed Christian clients: An exploratory study. *Counseling and Values, 36,* 220–229.
>
> *Clients with physical challenges*
> Ellis, A. (1997). Using rational emotive behavior therapy techniques to cope with disability. *Professional Psychology, 28,* 17–22.
>
> *Elderly clients*
> Arean, P. A. (1993). Cognitive behavioral therapy with older adults. *The Behavior Therapist, 16,* 236–239.
> Dick, L. P., & Gallagher-Thompson, D. (1995). Cognitive therapy with the core beliefs of a distressed, lonely caregiver. *Journal of Cognitive Psychotherapy, 9,* 215–227.
> Lopez, M., & Mermelstein, R. (1995). A cognitive–behavioral program to improve geriatric rehabilitation outcome. *Gerontologist, 35,* 696–700.
> Thompson, L. W. (1996). Cognitive–behavioral therapy and treatment for late-life depression. *Journal of Clinical Psychiatry, 57,* 29–37.
> Weiss, J. (1995). Cognitive therapy and life-review therapy. *Journal of Mental Health Helpers, 17,* 157–172.
>
> *Gay clients*
> Kuehlwein, K. T. (1992). Working with gay men. In A. Freemen & F. M. Dattillio (Eds.), *Comprehensive casebook of cognitive therapy* (pp. 249–255). New York: Plenum.
> Ussher, J. (1990). Cognitive behavioral couples therapy with gay men referred for counseling in an AIDS setting: A pilot study. *AIDS-Care, 2,* 43–51.
>
> *Latino clients*
> Organista, K., Dwyer, E. V., & Azocar, F. (1993). Cognitive behavioral therapy with Latino outpatients. *The Behavior Therapist, 16,* 229–232.
>
> *Lesbian clients*
> Wolfe, J. L. (1992). Working with gay women. In A. Freeman & F. M. Dattillio (Eds.), *Comprehensive casebook of cognitive therapy* (pp. 249–255). New York: Plenum.
>
> *Low-income clients*
> Miranda, J., & Dwyer, E. V. (1993). Cognitive behavioral therapy for disadvantaged medical patients. *The Behavior Therapist, 16,* 226–228.
>
> *Native American clients*
> Renfrey, G. S. (1992). Cognitive–behavior therapy and the Native American client. *Behavior Therapy, 23,* 321–340.
>
> *Religion*
> Tix, A. P., & Frazier, P. A. (1998). The use of religious coping during stressful life-events: Main effects, moderation, and mediation. *Journal of Consulting & Clinical Psychology, 66,* 411–422.

disputation. These authors contended that cognitive restructuring can be adapted to culture-specific values of some Christian clients. In examining the role of religious coping during stressful life events, Tix and Frazier (1998) discuss the varied forms this can take and the importance in targeting both social support as well as cognitive restructuring and perceived control to help people make needed adjustments over time.

Increasingly, cognitive restructuring is being used with the elderly, especially those with major depressive disorders (Thompson, 1996). This use of the technique is especially important because many older people have serious side effects with some antidepressant medications. The best attempts at using cognitive restructuring with older persons have presented the intervention as an educational rather than a therapeutic experience (Freiberg, 1995), with sensitivity to the older clients' fears and biases about disclosing concerns and dealing with their beliefs about being old (Arean, 1993). Group modes of cognitive therapies are especially useful because they provide greater social involvement and support (Arean, 1993; Freiberg, 1995). Also, the delivery of the intervention may need to be modified depending on the client's hearing and seeing abilities and other special needs (Thompson, 1996). Cognitive therapy has also been used to improve rehabilitation outcomes in elderly persons (Lopez & Mermelstein, 1995) and to aid with life-review work of the elderly (Weiss, 1995).

Cognitive restructuring has also been used with gay men and lesbian women. Ussher (1990) and Kuehlwein (1992) have used cognitive restructuring to help gay male clients examine and correct internalized heterosexist beliefs and thoughts. Wolfe (1992) has described the use of cognitive restructuring with a lesbian client who was dealing with both parental and social discrimination as a result of her sexual orientation.

Organista, Dwyer, and Azocar (1993) describe some very specific modifications of cognitive restructuring for Latino clients. First, it is important to have a linguistic match between predominantly Spanish-speaking clients and their helpers. Second, Organista and colleagues have found consistent issues and theories for Latino clients related to marriage and family and acculturation stress. Culture and gender-related issues are common with Latinas and often produce depression, partly because of the culture's emphasis on *marianismo*—a cultural trait that values a Latina's role in the family as one who is self-sacrificing and willing to endure suffering—and also because of the concept of *guadar*—holding in rather than expressing anger. These authors do use cognitive restructuring, but with Latino clients, they recommend a one-step rather than a multistep disputational process to challenge errors in thinking such as "yes, but."

Miranda and Dwyer (1993) discuss the use of cognitive therapy with low-income medical patients. They also note the importance of having bilingual and multicultural treatment staff available. They use treatment manuals to teach cognitive restructuring and recommend that the content and reading level be adapted to the client. For example, rather than using the term *generalization,* they use the phrase "thinking all bad things means everything will be bad" (Miranda & Dwyer, 1993, p. 227). They also note the importance of dealing with psychosocial stressors as well as with cognitions. They find that group rather than individual cognitive treatment is more effective for most of their clients.

Renfrey (1992) discusses the use of cognitive therapy with Native American clients. Renfrey (1992) notes that current mental health needs of many Native Americans are great, largely because of acculturation and deculturation stressors brought on by the European American culture. Native Americans' mental health needs are also underserved. Renfrey (1992) recommends that a helper collaborate with traditional healers in the Native American community. He believes that culturally sensitive cognitive therapy can be useful because it is specific and direct, involves homework, and focuses on altering present actions rather than emotional states. He recommends making an initial assessment of the client's acculturation status prior to any intervention because this variable will affect treatment process and outcomes. At the very least, cognitive restructuring must be offered in a way that promotes bicultural competence so that treatment begins with enhancement of the Native American's traditional identity and focuses on skills to help the client meet the demands of the indigenous culture, the mainstream culture, and the transculture (Renfrey, 1992, p. 330).

Guidelines for Using Cognitive Restructuring with Diverse Groups of Clients

As Hays (1995) has noted, cognitive therapy and cognitive restructuring are potentially quite applicable to diverse groups of clients, depending on the way the procedure is implemented and on the "therapist's sensitivity to diverse perspectives" (p. 312). We offer the following guidelines for using cognitive restructuring in a culturally sensitive way.

First, be very careful about the language you use when describing client cognitions. Although we don't recommend the use of the terms *rational* and *irrational* with any client, we consider these terms—and even others like *maladaptive* or *dysfunctional*—to be particularly inappropriate for women, gays, lesbians, clients of color, and all others who feel marginalized by the mainstream culture. These terms can further diminish a sense of self-efficacy and increase a sense of marginalization.

Second, present a rationale for cognitive restructuring that is educational rather than therapeutic to help remove the stigma that some clients of some cultural groups may have learned about mental health treatment. A didactic approach that includes specific and direct homework assignments is useful.

Third, adapt the language presented in cognitive restructuring to the client's primary language, age, educational level, and hearing, seeing, and reading abilities. Avoid jargon. Consider streamlining the procedure, focusing on one or two steps rather than multistep processes such as challenging self-defeating thoughts. Provide examples of skills and coping thoughts that are bicultural and transcultural as appropriate.

Fourth, use and/or collaborate with bilingual, ethnically similar helpers and/or traditional healers who can help you address issues of psychosocial stressors, race, and discrimination. Remember that for clients who feel marginalized, addressing these issues is as important as addressing issues of internal cognition. Also consider the usefulness for some of these clients of cognitive restructuring offered in a group rather than an individual setting.

SIX COMPONENTS OF COGNITIVE RESTRUCTURING

Our presentation of cognitive restructuring reflects the research presented in Box 14.1, Box 14.2, and the suggested readings at the end of this chapter as well as our own adaptations of cognitive restructuring based on clinical usage. We present cognitive restructuring in six major parts:

1. Rationale: purpose and overview of the procedure
2. Identification of client thoughts and schemas during problem situations
3. Introduction and practice of coping thoughts
4. Shifting from self-defeating to coping thoughts
5. Introduction and practice of positive or reinforcing self-statements
6. Homework and follow-up

Each of these parts is described in this section. A detailed description of these six components can be found in the Interview Checklist for Cognitive Restructuring at the end of the chapter and in Learning Activity 14.3.

Treatment Rationale

The rationale used in cognitive restructuring attempts to strengthen the client's belief that "self-talk" can influence performance and particularly that self-defeating thoughts or negative self-statements can cause emotional distress and interfere with performance. The examples used should be relevant to the client's gender and culture.

Rationale

The following general performance anxiety rationale can be used with clients with different concerns. You can fashion the rationale based on the specific client concern.

> One of our goals is for you to become aware of your thoughts or what you say to yourself that seems to maintain your anxiety when you are doing this activity (or while you are performing). Once we have identified these automatic thoughts, we can replace or change them. The thoughts about your performance are probably contributing to your anxiety. The performance situation may create these automatic thoughts, or perhaps the feelings you have about the situation create these thoughts. In either case, the thoughts or the feelings create physiological responses in your body, and these responses as well as your feelings and thoughts influence your performance. When we become aware of these automatic thoughts, we can deal with them by changing what you think about.

Overview

Here is an example of an overview of the procedure:

> We will learn how to deal with your automatic thoughts by becoming aware of when the thoughts occur or discovering what you say to yourself and what these internal self-statements are. Awareness of self-defeating automatic thoughts is one of the first steps in changing and decreasing the anxiety while performing. Once we know what the self-defeating statements are, they can act as a red flag for you to shift your self-talk to more self-enhancing performance statements. In other words, we will generate self-enhancing thoughts to shift to when you become aware of the automatic self-defeating thoughts. By shifting to the self-enhancing statements, your physiological and emotional responses will also become self-enhancing, and this will help you perform with less self-defeating anxiety. We will learn how to shift to self-enhancing statements while you are performing, and before and after your performances.

The Difference Between Self-Defeating and Self-Enhancing Thoughts

In addition to providing a standard rationale such as the one just illustrated, the cognitive restructuring procedure should be prefaced by some contrast between self-enhancing thoughts and self-defeating thoughts. In some literature, this is characterized in terms of rational versus irrational thinking. Our reading of cognitive behavioral principles is to help focus clients on both the (1) available evidence for the automatic thoughts (e.g., noting contradictions between thoughts such as "I'm hopelessly incompetent" with evidence of achievement and effectiveness in various life roles) and (2) distinguishing self-enhancing and self-defeating thoughts in terms of how helpful or hurtful that any given thoughts are to the client and his or her goals. This explanation may help clients discriminate between their own self-enhancing and self-defeating thoughts during treatment. Many clients who could benefit from cognitive restructuring are all too aware of their self-defeating thoughts but are unaware of or unable to generate self-enhancing thoughts. Providing a contrast may help them see that they can develop more realistic thinking styles.

One way to contrast these two types of thinking is to model some examples of both positive, enhancing self-talk and negative, defeating self-talk. These examples can come out of your personal experiences or can relate to the client's problem situations. Again, providing culturally relevant examples is important. The examples might occur *before, during,* or *after* a problem situation. For instance, you might say to the client that in a situation that makes you a little uptight, such as meeting a person for the first time, you could get caught up in very negative thoughts:

Before meeting:

"What if I don't come across very well?"

"What if this person doesn't like me?"

"I'll just blow this chance to establish a good relationship."

During meeting:

"I'm not making a good impression on this person."

"This person is probably wishing our meeting were over."

"I'd just like to leave and get this over with."

"I'm sure this person won't want to see me after this."

After meeting:

"Well, that's a lost cause."

"I can never talk intelligently to a stranger."

"I might as well never bother to set up this kind of meeting again."

"How stupid I must have sounded!"

In contrast, you might demonstrate some examples of positive, self-enhancing thoughts about the same situation:

Before meeting:

"I'm just going to try to get to know this person."

"I'm just going to be myself when I meet this person."

"I'll find something to talk about that I enjoy."

"This is only an initial meeting. We'll have to get together more to see how the relationship develops."

During meeting:

"I'm going to try to get something out of this conversation."

"This is a subject I know something about."

"This meeting is giving me a chance to talk about."

"It will take some time for me to get to know this person, and vice versa."

After meeting:

"That went OK; it certainly wasn't a flop."

"I can remember how easy it was for me to discuss topics of interest to me."

"Each meeting with a new person gives me a chance to see someone else and explore new interests."

"I was able just to be myself then."

The Influence of Self-Defeating Thoughts on Performance

The last part of the rationale for cognitive restructuring should be an *explicit* attempt to point out how self-defeating thoughts or negative self-statements are unproductive and can influence emotions and behavior. You are trying to convey to the client that we are likely to believe and to act on whatever we tell ourselves. However, it is also useful to point out that in some situations, people don't *literally* tell themselves something. In many situations, our thoughts are so well learned that they reflect our core beliefs or schemas. For this reason, you might indicate that you will often ask the client to monitor or log what happens during actual situations between sessions.

The importance of providing an adequate rationale for cognitive restructuring cannot be overemphasized. If one begins implementing the procedure too quickly, or without the client's agreement, the process can backfire. One way to prevent difficulty in implementing the procedure is to enhance the client's self-efficacy. The helper can do this by practicing with the client in the session so that the client is comfortable with the shifting facets of the procedure. With repeated practice, the client can gain enough experience that the self-enhancing thoughts become almost as automatic as the self-defeating ones. Practice helps loosen the grip on self-defeating thoughts and enables the client to formulate experiences more realistically (Beck, 1993). Also, repeated practice can enhance the client's self-efficacy with the procedure. The helper should not move ahead until the client's commitment to work with the strategy is obtained.

Identifying Client Thoughts in Problem Situations

Assuming that the client accepts the rationale provided about cognitive restructuring, the next step involves an analysis of the client's thoughts in anxiety-provoking or distressing situations. Both the range of situations and the content of the client's thoughts in these situations should be explored.

Description of Thoughts in Problem Situations

Within the interview, the practitioner should query the client about the particular distressing situations encountered and the things the client thinks about before, during, and after these situations. The practitioner might say something like "Sit back and think about the situations that are really upsetting to you. What are they?" Then "Can you identify exactly what you are thinking about or telling yourself before you go to _____? What are you thinking during the situation? And afterward?"

In identifying negative or self-defeating thoughts, the client might be aided by a description of possible cues that compose a self-defeating thought. The practitioner can point out that a negative thought may have a "worry quality" such as "I'm afraid . . ." or a "self-oriented quality" such as "I won't do well." Negative thoughts may also include elements of catastrophizing ("If I fail, it will be awful") or exaggerating ("I *never* do well" or "I *always* blow it"). Box 14.3 identifies several types of thoughts that may become habitual or automatic for clients, particularly in problem situations, and contribute to their difficulties. Each category is followed by a general description of the type of thought and an example.

It may be useful to see if clients recognize their own thought patterns among these. Examine with the client what evidence may or may not be available to support such a thought and how helpful this type of thought pattern is or isn't, based on how it affects coping and distress. Clients can identify the extent to which such thoughts contribute to situational anxiety by asking themselves "Do I (1) make unreasonable demands of myself, (2) feel that others are evaluating my performance or actions, and (3) forget that this is only one small part of my life?"

Modeling of Links Between Events and Emotions

If clients have trouble identifying negative thoughts, Guidano (1995) suggests that they engage in what he calls the "movieola" technique. Clients are instructed to run scenes of the situation in their heads: "Then, as if [he or she] were in an editing room, the client is instructed to 'pan' the scenes, going back and forth in slow motion, thereby allowing the client to 'zoom in' on a single scene, to focus on particular aspects" of the scene (p. 157). The therapist may need to point out that the thoughts are the link between the situation and the resulting emotion, and ask the client to notice explicitly what this link seems to be. If the client is still unable to identify thoughts, the practitioner can model this link, using either the client's situations or situations from the practitioner's life. For example, the practitioner might say this:

> Here is one example that happened to me. I was a music major in college, and several times a year I had to present piano recitals that were graded by several faculty members and attended by faculty, friends, and strangers. Each approaching recital got worse—I got more nervous and more preoccupied with failure. Although I didn't realize it at the time, the link between the event of the recital and my resulting feelings of nervousness was things I was thinking that I can remember now—like "What if I get out there and blank out?" or "What if my arms get so stiff I can't perform the piece?" or "What if my shaking knees are visible?" Now can you try to recall the specific thoughts you had when you felt so upset about _____?

In working with the client to identify and even elicit automatic thoughts in problem situations, the practitioner can note and bring to the client's attention any emotional responses or changes during the session, such as increases in anxiety, anger, or sadness. Getting a working sense of the paired nature of certain types of activating events, thoughts, emotions, and behaviors can be a significant step toward self-observation and change efforts outside the helping session.

Identifying Client Schemas Underlying Distorted Thoughts

Developments in cognitive therapy note layers of cognitive content and process important for treatment. Underlying automatic thoughts, for example, are assumptions and, fundamentally, our schemas. Assumptions are the if-then understandings of how things work, the conclusions, the "shoulds" that we all carry with us but that can become maladaptive in their effects. For example, a heterosexual woman who finds social situations stressful may experience an automatic thought ("He'll reject me") based on a maladaptive assumption ("I need the approval of men to like myself") fueled by schemas of self and others ("I'm unlovable. Men are rejecting.") (Leahy & Holland, 2000).

Our *schemas,* defined by Goldfried (1995) as a "cognitive representation of one's past experiences with situations or people" (p. 55), are thought to provide a way of understanding the distortions in automatic thoughts and beliefs that clients make in processing information about themselves, other persons, and their environments. For example, if a client has a schema of being inferior and abandoned, she or he will use selective attention to focus on information related to failure, isolation, and rejection, and will overlook or dismiss information related to success, relational connection, and acceptance (Leahy, 1996). Thus, it is not enough to assess the cognitive content of problematic schemas but also necessary to identify the perceptual and interpretive habits the client may unwittingly be engaging in that are consistent with the schema and tend to reinforce the schema's depiction of self, others, and what can be expected in the world.

> **BOX 14.3   CATEGORIES OF DISTORTED AUTOMATIC THOUGHTS: A GUIDE FOR PATIENTS**
>
> 1. *Mind reading:* You assume that you know what people think without having sufficient evidence of their thoughts. "He thinks I'm a loser."
>
> 2. *Fortunetelling:* You predict the future negatively: Things will get worse, or there is danger ahead. "I'll fail that exam," or "I won't get the job."
>
> 3. *Catastrophizing:* You believe that what has happened or will happen will be so awful and unbearable that you won't be able to stand it. "It would be terrible if I failed."
>
> 4. *Labeling:* You assign global negative traits to yourself and others. "I'm undesirable," or "He's a rotten person."
>
> 5. *Discounting positives:* You claim that the positive things you or others do are trivial. "That's what wives are supposed to do—so it doesn't count when she's nice to me," or "Those successes were easy, so they don't matter."
>
> 6. *Negative filtering:* You focus almost exclusively on the negatives and seldom notice the positives. "Look at all of the people who don't like me."
>
> 7. *Overgeneralizing:* You perceive a global pattern of negatives on the basis of a single incident. "This generally happens to me. I seem to fail at a lot of things."
>
> 8. *Dichotomous thinking:* You view events or people in all-or-nothing terms. "I get rejected by everyone," or "It was a complete waste of time."
>
> 9. *Shoulds:* You interpret events in terms of how things should be, rather than simply focusing on what is. "I should do well. If I don't, then I'm a failure."
>
> 10. *Personalizing:* You attribute a disproportionate amount of the blame to yourself for negative events, and you fail to see that certain events are also caused by others. "The marriage ended because I failed."
>
> 11. *Blaming:* You focus on the other person as the *source of* your negative feelings, and you refuse to take responsibility for changing yourself. "She's to blame for the way I feel now," or "My parents caused all my problems."
>
> 12. *Unfair comparisons:* You interpret events in terms of standards that are unrealistic—for example, you focus primarily on others who do better than you and find yourself inferior in the comparison. "She's more successful than I am," or "Others did better than I did on the test."
>
> 13. *Regret orientation:* You focus on the idea that you could have done better in the past, rather on what you can do better now. "I could have had a better job if I had tried," or "I shouldn't have said that."
>
> 14. *What if?:* You keep asking a series of questions about "what if" something happens, and you fail to be satisfied with any of the answers. "Yeah, but what if I get anxious?" or "What if I can't catch my breath?"
>
> 15. *Emotional reasoning:* You let your feelings guide your interpretation of reality. "I feel depressed; therefore, my marriage is not working out."
>
> 16. *Inability to disconfirm:* You reject any evidence or arguments that might contradict your negative thoughts. For example, when you have the thought "I'm unlovable," you reject as *irrelevant* any evidence that people like you. Consequently, your thought cannot be refuted. "That's not the real issue. There are deeper problems. There are other factors."
>
> 17. *Judgment focus:* You view yourself, others, and events in terms of evaluations as good–bad or superior–inferior, rather than simply describing, accepting, or understanding. You are continually measuring yourself and others according to arbitrary standards, and finding that you and others fall short. You are focused on the judgments of others as well as your own judgments of yourself. "I didn't perform well in college," or "If I take up tennis, I won't do well," or "Look how successful she is. I'm not successful."
>
> *Source: Treatment Plans and Interventions for Depression and Anxiety Disorders*, by R. H. Leahy and S. J. Holland, p.299. Copyright ©2000 The Guilford Press. Reprinted with permission.

Figure 14.1 illustrates ways that schemas can function (Persons & Davidson, 2001, p. 98). Situational events that are either external, such as the behavior of others, or internal, such as our own thoughts or bodily sensations, activate schemas, drawing them into an active state influencing our information processing and behavior at that point in time. This process works the same for adaptive and maladaptive schemas, but the outcomes will obviously be different for the two types. Thus, we can see the importance of assessing what types of situations tend to be problematic in that they trigger maladaptive schemas (e.g., "I'm incapable, undeserving"). These schemas carry with them emotional valences (e.g., depressed, discouraged feeling) from prior experiences that influence how the person is feeling in the moment. Schemas contain understandings or assumptions of oneself, others, the world ("If I take action I will fail; others will be critical or disappoint me") that influence observations, expectations, and interpretations in the moment. Collectively, these activated schemas and their content-consistent thoughts and mood bias the behaviors that the person will take in this moment and situation (e.g., passivity, withdrawal). The experience itself and its outcomes (e.g., failure to achieve goals) serve to confirm the felt "reality" represented by the schema and, thus, its strength and likelihood of future activation under similar circumstances.

Schemas can be tenaciously resistant to challenge and change. By and large, this is a strength. This stability is part of what helps us all to retain a sense of coherence, understandability, and predictability of ourselves, others, and the world. However, it means that a client and helper are working against the grain of cognitive functioning in their collaborative work to selectively target and reconstruct or replace long-standing schemas and habits of thinking and feeling that may have become central to a client's identity or world view.

It is believed that some schemas about self and others grow out of object representations and experiences in early childhood, including the early attachment styles, which are then carried forward as internal working models of relationships (Bowlby, 1988). These schemas then serve as building blocks upon which subsequent learning and representation take cognitive form, rendering those early schemas more and more elaborated and networked with other schemas, sensory states (e.g., moods, sights, smells, bodily sensations), and complex understandings. We are continuously developing and accessing schemas, and all problematic schemas are not

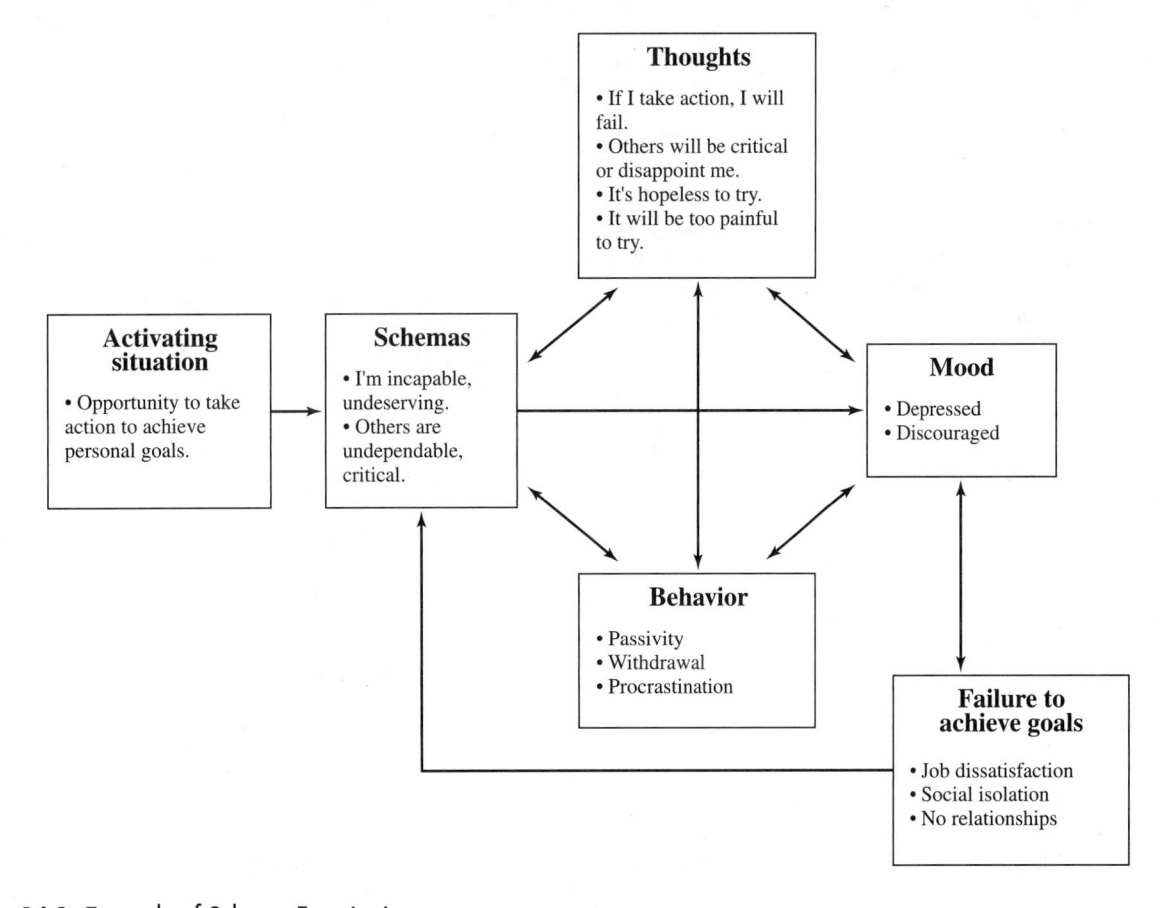

Figure 14.1 Example of Schema Functioning
Source: "Cognitive–Behavioral Case Formulation," by J. B. Persons and J. Davidson. In K. S. Dobson (Ed.), *Handbook of Cognitive-Behavioral Therapies*, (2nd ed.), pp. 86–110. Copyright ©2001 by the Guilford Press. Reprinted with permisson.

necessarily rooted in childhood. However, those that have become broad-based in their negative impact are generally those that the client has been living with and through for some time and that have become deeply integrated with multiple understandings, aspects of self, and a range of life situations.

The cultural context and the sociopolitical context of a person's life are other examples of powerful environmental forces that can influence developing schemas. (Consider this in reference to the various world views discussed in Chapter 11.) These may take many normative forms due to exposure to different languages, traditions, norms for interaction, codes of behavior, priorities, and so forth. These differences may also offer a better understanding of difficulties; for example, children who experience or witness instances of discrimination and oppression or traumatic events probably develop different schemas than children who are not affected in those ways. In a longitudinal study, Nolen-Hoeksema, Girgus, and Seligman (1992) found that stressful life events caused children to develop a negative cognitive style that was predictive of later depression if additional stressors occurred. Differing developmental histories may also hold different sources of strength, resilience, or conceptualizations to build on. For example, identity research (Oyserman, Gant, & Ager, 1995) suggests that when social context is limiting and group memberships such as race, gender, and socioeconomic status shape the selves that one experiments with and develops, conceptualizing oneself as a group member, having awareness of stereotypes and limitations, and developing a schema-based vision of oneself succeeding *as a group member* contribute toward academic achievement among youth.

Leahy (1996) notes the difficulty in challenging schemas that were established when the client was operating at a preoperational level of processing, such as childhood, "marked by egocentrism, centration, magical thinking and moral realism" (p. 192). Nonetheless, understanding how schema development and processing works is an important part of cognitive therapy. This understanding can help normalize in clients' eyes how they arrived at their current struggle as well as help guide their cognitive reconstruction efforts. An "investigative" approach is fundamental to cognitive therapy, whereby the practitioner helps the client to systematically gather data, evaluate evidence, draw conclusions, and generate alternatives. These steps are indeed constituent parts of the ongoing self-observation and cognitive–affective–behavioral change process that the client will need to continue after the end of formal helping. Consistent with this investigative aim, Leahy (1996) provides some sample questions to illustrate this identification process:

How did your parents (siblings, peers, teachers) teach you that you are _____? (Fill in the word that best describes the client's schema.)

When you learned the schema, you were 5 years old. Do you think it is wise to guide your life by what a 5-year-old thinks?

What evidence is there that you are not _____?

Or that you are _____? (Fill in the word that best describes the client's schema.)

What is the consequence of demanding this of yourself? Is it ever OK to be helpless? To fail? To depend on others? To be disapproved of?

How would you challenge your mother and father, now that you are an adult, if they were to describe you as _____? (Fill in the word that best describes the client's schema.) (Leahy, 1996, p. 194)

Schema-focused treatment has been referred to as relapse prevention. That is, even after clients began to feel better from depression, for example, they remain vulnerable to future similar difficulties due to maladaptive schemas that, unless identified and modified, could pull them back into negative patterns of information processing and social interaction. Young, Beck, and Weinberger (1998) describe schema assessment consisting of

1. a focused review of the client's history, with the aim of linking past experiences to current problems through the formation and reinforcement of maladaptive schemas
2. use of the Schema Questionnaire, designed to assess schemas
3. an experiential component to trigger schemas; that is, to activate them from long-term memory into active working memory.

Young and colleagues (1998) describe a case example with a woman (Michelle) whose problems included the inability to express herself and ask for things, especially with her husband, and recurrent thoughts that her husband had "one step out the door" of their marriage. The focused life review probed her childhood relative to the onset of her emotional difficulties and previous experiences with psychotherapy and depression. Part of the goal was to determine if a series of experiences contributed to development of schemas that were subsequently activated and reinforced, creating a vicious cycle. This review revealed themes of an "absentee" father, emotional isolation, anxiety about self-expression, and devaluation. The therapist hypothesized that these experiences generated schemas that fell in the Disconnection and Undesirability domain (Box 14.4).

The Schema Questionnaire (Young, 1999; Young et al. 1998) consists of 205 items and is used to formally assess the

18 underlying schemas listed in Box 14.4. This tool allows clients to indicate the extent to which they see statements operationalizing the schema as representing them. The practitioner can review responses carefully with the client for clarification, to gain additional information, and to ensure that the responses line up well with the issues of greatest concern to the client. Through the focused review and use of the schema questionnaire, the helper and client identified four schemas that seemed most salient to the problems of concern to the client.

Use of an experiential exercise can be useful by activating the schemas to help the client more directly experience the content and intensity of the schema, including a high degree of affect. As Beck and associates (1990) have noted, "The arousal of a strong feeling suggests not only that a core schema has been exposed, but also that the dysfunctional thinking is more accessible to modification" (quoted in Young, Beck, & Weinberger, 1998, p. 299). After providing a rationale for the exercise, strategies such as relaxation and guided imagery can be useful for these purposes. An excerpt from this case example provides an illustration (Young et al., 1998, p. 299). The practitioner and client were aiming to identify origins of the client's abandonment schema:

T: Michelle, why don't you close your eyes now and see if you can get a visual image of anything that comes into your mind.
M: Do I have to see it?
T: Yes, it's not thoughts but pictures that we want. It could be a picture of a person, of a place, anything at all; almost as if you were looking at a movie in your head.
M: What is the point of all this again?
T: Well the point is to try to discover feelings and themes, buttons if you like, that are getting pushed, but that you're not aware of right now, like, right now you told me you're feeling butterflies but you don't know why. We often find that when people close their eyes, they get pictures that tell them why they're feeling those butterflies, why they're nervous, so it's a way of sort of getting to the deeper issues without directly talking about them, but rather through picturing them . . .
M: I'm seeing something. I see my father leaving the house. He doesn't want to come in and be with me.
T: You're actually picturing him leaving the house?
M: Yeah, he's outside the house now leaving, and he knows I'm inside, he knows I want to be with him, but he just doesn't care to be with me. (cries)

The therapist continued use of guided imagery to assess whether there was a link between these childhood experiences and the client's current problems with her husband.

T: Now Michelle, please keep your eyes closed and see if you can get an image of Jim and tell me what you see.
M: Well, as you said that, what I saw Jim doing was just walking out the door and just slamming the door. He had his suitcase packed and with him, and he just walked out the door and there I was in the house all alone by myself.
T: Just like you were with your father, the same feeling that you had before?
M: Yeah, it feels exactly the same.

Putting together all the information, the practitioner develops a formulation of the schemas that appear to be centrally involved in the most troubling issues and situations. This formulation needs to be reviewed with the client to determine if it seems accurate and to be functioning in the manner that the practitioner believes. This assessment then informs subsequent schema content and activation change efforts. (See Learning Activity 14.1)

Client Monitoring of Thoughts

The practitioner can also have the client identify situations and thoughts by monitoring and recording events and thoughts outside the interview in the form of homework. An initial homework assignment might be to have the client observe and record for one week at least three self-defeating statements and emotions per day in the stressful situation. For each day of the week, the client could record on a daily log the self-defeating self-statements and emotions for each situation in which these statements were noted (see Figure 14.2).

Using the client's data, the practitioner and client can determine which of the thoughts were self-enhancing and productive and which were self-defeating and unproductive. The practitioner should try to have the *client* discriminate between the two types of statements and identify why the negative ones are unproductive. The identification serves several purposes. First, it is a way to determine whether the client's present repertory consists of both positive and negative self-statements or whether the client is generating or recalling only negative thoughts. These data may also provide information about the client's degree of distress in a particular

Date: _____ Week: _____

Situation	Emotions	Self-Defeating Statements
1.	1.	1.
2.	2.	2.
3.	3.	3.

Figure 14.2 Example of daily log

BOX 14.4 EARLY MALADAPTIVE SCHEMAS

Disconnection and Rejection
(Expectation that one's needs for security, safety, stability, nurturance, empathy, sharing of feelings, acceptance, and respect will not be met in a predictable manner. Typical family origin is detached, cold, rejecting, withholding, lonely, explosive, unpredictable, or abusive.)

1. *Abandonment/Instability (AB)* The perceived *instability* or *unreliability* of those available for support and connection. Involves the sense that significant others will not be able to continue providing emotional support, connection, strength, or practical protection because they are emotionally unstable and unpredictable (e.g., angry outbursts), unreliable, or erratically present; because they will die imminently; or because they will abandon the patient in favor of someone better.

2. *Mistrust/Abuse (MA)* The expectation that others will hurt, abuse, humiliate, cheat, lie, manipulate, or take advantage. Usually involves the perception that the harm is intentional or the result of unjustified and extreme negligence. May include the sense that one always ends up being cheated relative to others or "getting the short end of the stick."

3. *Emotional Deprivation (ED)* Expectation that one's desire for a normal degree of emotional support will not be adequately met by others. The three major forms of deprivation are

   A. Deprivation of Nurturance: Absence of attention, affection, warmth, or companionship.
   B. Deprivation of Empathy: Absence of understanding, listening, self-disclosure, or mutual sharing of feelings from others.
   C. Deprivation of Protection: Absence of strength, direction, or guidance from others.

4. *Defectiveness/Shame (DS)* The feeling that one is defective, bad, unwanted, inferior, or invalid in important respects; or that one would be unlovable to significant others if exposed. May involve hypersensitivity to criticism, rejection, and blame; self-consciousness, comparisons, and insecurity around others; or a sense of shame regarding one's perceived flaws. These flaws may be *private* (e.g., selfishness, angry impulses, unacceptable sexual desires) or *public* (e.g., undesirable physical appearance, social awkwardness).

5. *Social Isolation/Alienation (SI)* The feeling that one is isolated from the rest of the world, different from other people, and/or not part of any group or community.

Impaired Autonomy and Performance
(Expectations about oneself and the environment that interfere with one's perceived ability to separate, survive, function independently, or perform successfully. Typical family origin is enmeshed, undermining of child's confidence, overprotective, or failing to reinforce child for performing competently outside the family.)

6. *Dependence/Incompetence (DI)* Belief that one is unable to handle one's *everyday responsibilities* in a competent manner, without considerable help from others (e.g., take care of oneself, solve daily problems, exercise good judgment, tackle new tasks, make good decisions). Often presents as helplessness.

7. *Vulnerability to Harm or Illness (VH)* Exaggerated fear that *imminent* catastrophe will strike at any time and that one will be unable to prevent it. Fears focus on one or more of the following: (A) *medical catastrophes*: e.g., heart attacks, AIDS; (B) *emotional catastrophes*: e.g., going crazy; (C) *external catastrophes*: e.g., elevators collapsing, victimized by criminals, airplane crashes, earthquakes.

8. *Enmeshment/Undeveloped Self (EM)* Excessive emotional involvement and closeness with one or more significant others (often parents), at the expense of full individuation or normal social development. Often involves the belief that at least one of the enmeshed individuals cannot survive or be happy without the constant support of the other. May also include feelings of being smothered by, or fused with, others *or* insufficient individual identity. Often experienced as a feeling of emptiness and floundering, having no direction, or in extreme cases questioning one's existence.

9. *Failure (FA)* The belief that one has failed, will inevitably fail, or is fundamentally inadequate relative to one's peers, in areas of *achievement* (school, career, sports, etc.). Often involves beliefs that one is stupid, inept, untalented, ignorant, lower in status, less successful than others, etc.

Impaired Limits
(Deficiency in internal limits, responsibility to others, or long-term goal-orientation. Leads to difficulty respecting the rights of others, cooperating with others, making commitments, or setting and meeting realistic personal goals. Typical family origin is characterized by permissiveness, overindulgence, lack of direction, or a sense of superiority—rather than appropriate confrontation, discipline, and limits

BOX 14.4 EARLY MALADAPTIVE SCHEMAS

in relation to taking responsibility, cooperating in a reciprocal manner, and setting goals. In some cases, child may not have been pushed to tolerate normal levels of discomfort, or may not have been given adequate supervision, direction, or guidance.)

10. *Entitlement/Grandiosity (ET)* The belief that one is superior to other people; entitled to special rights and privileges; or not bound by the rules of reciprocity that guide normal social interaction. Often involves insistence that one should be able to do or have whatever one wants, regardless of what is realistic, what others consider reasonable, or the cost to others; *or* an exaggerated focus on superiority (e.g., being among the most successful, famous, wealthy)—in order to achieve *power* or *control* (not primarily for attention or approval). Sometimes includes excessive competitiveness toward, or domination of, others: asserting one's power, forcing one's point of view, or controlling the behavior of others in line with one's own desires—without empathy or concern for others' needs or feelings.

11. *Insufficient Self-Control/Self-Discipline (IS)* Pervasive difficulty or refusal to exercise sufficient self-control and frustration tolerance to achieve one's personal goals, or to restrain the excessive expression of one's emotions and impulses. In its milder form, patient presents with an exaggerated emphasis on *discomfort-avoidance*: avoiding pain, conflict, confrontation, responsibility, or overexertion—at the expense of personal fulfillment, commitment, or integrity.

Other-Directedness

(An excessive focus on the desires, feelings, and responses of others, at the expense of one's own needs—in order to gain love and approval, maintain one's sense of connection, or avoid retaliation. Usually involves suppression and lack of awareness regarding one's own anger and natural inclinations. Typical family origin is based on conditional acceptance; children must suppress important aspects of themselves in order to gain love, attention, and approval. In many such families, the parents' emotional needs and desires—or social acceptance and status—are valued more than the unique needs and feelings of each child.)

12. *Subjugation (SB)* Excessive surrendering of control to others because one feels *coerced*—usually to avoid anger, retaliation, or abandonment. The two major forms of subjugation are

   A. Subjugation of Needs: Suppression of one's preferences, decisions, and desires.

   B. Subjugation of Emotions: Suppression of emotional expression, especially anger.

Usually involves the perception that one's own desires, opinions, and feelings are not valid or important to others. Frequently presents as excessive compliance, combined with hypersensitivity to feeling trapped. Generally leads to a build-up of anger, manifested in maladaptive symptoms (e.g., passive–aggressive behavior, uncontrolled outbursts of temper, psychosomatic symptoms, withdrawal of affection, "acting out," substance abuse).

13. *Self-Sacrifice (SS)* Excessive focus on *voluntarily* meeting the needs of others in daily situations, at the expense of one's own gratification. The most common reasons are to prevent causing pain to others; to avoid guilt from feeling selfish; or to maintain the connection with others perceived as needy. Often results from an acute sensitivity to the pain of others. Sometimes leads to a sense that one's own needs are not being adequately met and to resentment of those who are taken care of. (Overlaps with concept of co-dependency.)

14. *Approval-Seeking/Recognition-Seeking (AS)* Excessive emphasis on gaining approval, recognition, or attention from other people, or fitting in, at the expense of developing a secure and true sense of self. One's sense of esteem is dependent primarily on the reactions of others rather than on one's own natural inclinations. Sometimes includes an overemphasis on status, appearance, social acceptance, money, or achievement—as means of gaining *approval, admiration,* or *attention* (not primarily for power or control). Frequently results in major life decisions that are inauthentic or unsatisfying; or in hypersensitivity to rejection.

Overvigilance and Inhibition

(Excessive emphasis on suppressing one's spontaneous feelings, impulses, and choices or on meeting rigid, internalized rules and expectations about performance and ethical behavior—often at the expense of happiness, self-expression, relaxation, close relationships, or health. Typical family origin is grim, demanding, and sometimes punitive: performance, duty, perfectionism, following rules, hiding emotions, and avoiding mistakes predominate over pleasure, joy, and relaxation. There is usually an undercurrent of pessimism and worry—that things could fall apart if one fails to be vigilant and careful at all times.)

15. *Negativity/Pessimism (NP)* A pervasive, lifelong focus on the negative aspects of life (pain, death, loss, disappointment, conflict, guilt, resentment, unsolved problems, potential

(continued)

BOX 14.4 EARLY MALADAPTIVE SCHEMAS

(continued)

mistakes, betrayal, things that could go wrong, etc.) while minimizing or neglecting the positive or optimistic aspects. Usually includes an exaggerated expectation—in a wide range of work, financial, or interpersonal situations—that things will eventually go seriously wrong, or that aspects of one's life that seem to be going well will ultimately fall apart. Usually involves an inordinate fear of making mistakes that might lead to financial collapse, loss, humiliation, or being trapped in a bad situation. Because potential negative outcomes are exaggerated, these patients are frequently characterized by chronic worry, vigilance, complaining, or indecision.

16. *Emotional Inhibition (EI)* The excessive inhibition of spontaneous action, feeling, or communication—usually to avoid disapproval by others, feelings of shame, or losing control of one's impulses. The most common areas of inhibition involve (a) inhibition of *anger* and aggression; (b) inhibition of *positive impulses* (e.g., joy, affection, sexual excitement, play); (c) difficulty expressing *vulnerability* or *communicating* freely about one's feelings, needs, etc.; or (d) excessive emphasis on *rationality* while disregarding emotions.

17. *Unrelenting Standards/Hypercriticalness (US)* The underlying belief that one must strive to meet very high *internalized standards* of behavior and performance, usually to avoid criticism. Typically results in feelings of pressure or difficulty slowing down; and in hypercriticalness toward oneself and others. Must involve significant impairment in pleasure, relaxation, health, self-esteem, sense of accomplishment, or satisfying relationships.

Unrelenting standards typically present as (a) *perfectionism,* inordinate attention to detail, or an underestimate of how good one's own performance is relative to the norm; (b) *rigid rules* and "shoulds" in many areas of life, including unrealistically high moral, ethical, cultural, or religious precepts; or (c) preoccupation with *time and efficiency,* so that more can be accomplished.

18. *Punitiveness (PU)* The belief that people should be harshly punished for making mistakes. Involves the tendency to be angry, intolerant, punitive, and impatient with those people (including oneself) who do not meet one's expectations or standards. Usually includes difficulty forgiving mistakes in oneself or others, because of a reluctance to consider extenuating circumstances, allow for human imperfection, or empathize with feelings.

Source: Copyright 1998, Jeffrey Young, Ph.D. Unauthorized reproduction without written consent of the author is prohibited. For more information, write: Cognitive Therapy Center of New York, 120 East 56th Street, Suite 530, New York, NY 10022.

LEARNING ACTIVITY 14.1 Schema Identification

Learning Activity 14.3 addresses the overall array of steps involved in cognitive restructuring, asking you to personalize and get familiar with these by applying them to yourself. We ask you to begin those steps, focusing here on the schema component. This is intended to give you a working understanding of schemas as critical building blocks in both adaptive and maladaptive perceptions and cognitive functioning.

First, for the statements you deem to be self-defeating in Section I of Learning Activity 14.3, how would you categorize these according to the five domains of maladaptive schemas listed in Box 14.4 (see p. 448).

Second, examine the self-defeating thoughts you record in your week log as part of Learning Activity 14.3. How would you categorize these relative to the five domains of maladaptive schemas? If you have difficulty with this, try a guided imagery exercise such as that depicted in the case example with Michelle. What feeling states are evoked? Do these emotional reactions aid you in identifying the schema that may cognitively represent self-defeating thoughts that trouble you?

situation. If some self-enhancing thoughts are identified, the client becomes aware that alternatives are already present in his or her thinking style. If no self-enhancing thoughts are reported, this is a cue that some specific attention may be needed in this area. The practitioner can demonstrate how the client's unproductive thoughts can be changed by showing how self-defeating thoughts can be restated more constructively.

Introduction and Practice of Coping Thoughts

At this point in the procedure, there is a shift in focus from the client's self-defeating thoughts to other kinds of thoughts that are incompatible with the self-defeating ones. These incompatible thoughts may be called coping thoughts, coping statements, or coping self-instructions. They are developed for each client. There is no attempt to have all clients accept a common core of rational beliefs, as is often done in rational–emotive therapy.

Introduction and practice of coping statements are, as far as we know, crucial to the overall success of the cognitive restructuring procedure. Rehearsal of coping statements, by itself, is almost as effective as the combination of identifying negative statements and replacing these with incompatible coping thoughts.

Explanation and Examples of Coping Thoughts

The purpose of coping thoughts should be explained clearly. The client should understand that it is difficult to think of failing at an experience (a self-defeating thought) while concentrating on just doing one's best, regardless of the outcome (a coping thought). Here's an example explaining the purpose and use of coping thoughts:

> So far we've worked at identifying some of the self-defeating things you think during _____. As long as you're thinking about those kinds of things, they can make you feel anxious. But as soon as you replace these with coping thoughts, then the coping thoughts take over, because it is almost impossible to concentrate on both failing at something and coping with the situation at the same time. The coping thoughts help you to manage the situation and to cope if you start to feel overwhelmed.

The helper should also model some examples of coping thoughts so that the client can clearly differentiate between a self-defeating and a coping thought. Some examples of coping thoughts to use *before* a situation might be these:

"I've done this before, and it is never as bad as I think."
"Stay calm in anticipating this."
"Do the best I can. I'm not going to worry how people will react."
"This is a situation that can be a challenge."
"It won't be bad—only a few people will be there."

Examples of coping thoughts to use *during* a situation include these:

"Focus on the task."
"Just think about what I want to do or say."
"What is it I want to accomplish now?"
"Relax so I can focus on the situation."
"Step back a minute, take a deep breath."
"Take one step at a time."
"Slow down, take my time, don't rush."
"OK, don't get out of control. It's a signal to cope."

If you go back and read over these lists of coping examples, you may note some subtle differences among them. There can be four types of coping statements. *Situational coping statements* help the client reduce the potential level of threat or severity of the anticipated situation. Examples of this first type are "It won't be too bad" or "Only a few people will be watching me." Other coping statements refer more to the plans, steps, or behaviors the person will need to demonstrate during the situation, such as "concentrate on what I want to say or do," "think about the task," or "what do I want to accomplish?" These are called *task-oriented coping statements Coping with being overwhelmed* is another type, such as "keep cool," "stay calm," or "relax, take a deep breath." A fourth type of coping statement, which we call *positive self-statements,* is used to have clients reinforce or encourage themselves for having coped. These include such self-instructions as "Great, I did it" or "I managed to get through that all right." Positive self-statements can be used during a stressful situation and especially after the situation. The use of positive self-statements in cognitive restructuring is described in more detail later in this chapter.

In explaining about and modeling potential coping thoughts, you may want to note the difference between *coping* and *mastery* thoughts. Coping thoughts are ones that help a client deal with or manage a situation, event, or person adequately. Mastery thoughts are ones that are directed toward helping a person "conquer" or master a situation in almost a flawless manner. For some clients, mastery self-instructions may function as perfectionistic standards that are, in reality, too difficult to attain. For these clients, use of mastery thoughts can make them feel more pressured rather than more relieved. For these reasons, we recommend that helpers avoid modeling mastery self-statements and also remain alert to clients who may spontaneously use mastery self-instructions in subsequent practice sessions during the cognitive restructuring procedure.

Client Examples of Coping Thoughts
After providing some examples, the practitioner should ask the client to think of additional coping statements. The client may come up with self-enhancing or positive statements that she or he has used in other situations. The client should be encouraged to select coping statements that feel most natural. Clients can identify coping thoughts by discovering convincing counterarguments for their unrealistic thoughts.

Client Practice
Using these client-selected coping statements, the practitioner should ask the client to practice verbalizing coping statements aloud. This is very important because most clients are not accustomed to using coping statements. Such practice may reduce some of the client's initial discomfort and can strengthen confidence in being able to produce different "self-talk." In addition, clients who are "formally" trained to practice coping statements systematically may use a greater variety of coping thoughts, may use more specific coping thoughts, and may report more consistent use of coping thoughts *in vivo*.

At first, the client can practice verbalizing the individual coping statements she or he selected to use before and during the situation. Gradually, as the client gets accustomed to coping statements, the coping thoughts should be practiced in the natural sequence in which they will be used. First, the client would anticipate the situation and practice coping statements before the situation to prepare for it, followed by practice of coping thoughts during the situation—focusing on the task and coping with feeling overwhelmed.

It is important for the client to become actively involved in these practice sessions. Try to ensure that the client does not simply rehearse the coping statements by rote. Instead, the client should use these practices to try to internalize the meaning of the coping statements. One way to encourage more client involvement and self-assertion in these practice attempts is to suggest that the client pretend he or she is talking to an audience or a group of persons and needs to talk in a persuasive, convincing manner to get his or her point across.

Shifting from Self-Defeating to Coping Thoughts
After the client has identified negative thoughts and has practiced alternative coping thoughts, the practitioner introduces the rehearsal of shifting from self-defeating to coping thoughts during stressful situations. Practice of this shift helps the client use a self-defeating thought as a cue for an immediate switch to coping thoughts. The importance of repeated and supported practice both within and outside of sessions, the latter being where most of the naturally occurring stressful situations will occur, cannot be overstated. New response patterns have to compete with older ones to gain their accessibility and salience at times most needed. Practice with support is essential to forming these new patterns.

Helper Demonstration of Shift
The helper should model this process before asking the client to try it. This gives the client an accurate idea of how to practice this shift. Here is an example of modeling for a high school student who constantly "freezes up" in competitive situations:

> OK, I'm sitting here waiting for my turn to try out for cheerleader. Ooh, I can feel myself getting very nervous. [*anxious feeling*] Now, wait, what am I so nervous about? I'm afraid I'm going to make a fool of myself. [*self-defeating thought*] Hey, that doesn't help. [*cue to cope*] It will take only a few minutes, and it will be over before I know it. Besides, only the faculty sponsors are watching. It's not like the whole school. [*situation-oriented coping thoughts*]
>
> Well, the person before me is just about finished. Oh, they're calling my name. Boy, do I feel tense. [*anxious feelings*] What if I don't execute my jumps? [*self-defeating thought*]. OK, don't think about what I'm not going to do. OK, start out; it's my turn. Just think about my routine—the way I want it to go. [*task-oriented coping thoughts*]

Client Practice of the Shift
After the demonstration, the client should practice identifying and stopping self-defeating thoughts and replacing them with coping thoughts. The practitioner can monitor the client's progress and coach if necessary. Rehearsal of this shift involves four steps:

1. The client imagines the stressful situation or carries out his or her part in the situation by means of a role play.

2. The client is instructed to recognize the onset of any self-defeating thoughts and to signal this by raising a hand or finger.
3. Next, the client is told to stop these thoughts or to reframe these thoughts.
4. After the self-defeating thought is stopped, the client immediately replaces it with the coping thoughts. The client should be given some time to concentrate on the coping thoughts. Initially, it may be helpful for the client to verbalize coping thoughts; later, this can occur covertly.

As the client seems able to identify, stop, and replace the self-defeating thoughts, the practitioner can gradually decrease the amount of assistance. Before homework is assigned, the client should be able to practice and carry out this shift in the interview setting in a completely self-directed manner. Social support, such as friends or family members, can also support the client in this self-directed goal—for example, by anticipating stressful situations and walking through them, reviewing situations, and reinforcing use of the coping thoughts identified with the helper. This kind of contextual support is best formulated with the helper and can be a powerful resource toward situating clients' change efforts within their support systems and working realistically with their social environments.

Introduction and Practice of Reinforcing Self-Statements

The last part of cognitive restructuring involves teaching clients how to reinforce themselves for having coped. This is accomplished by modeling by the practitioner and possibly by others, as relevant, and by client practice of positive, or reinforcing, self-statements. Many clients who could benefit from cognitive restructuring report not only frequent self-defeating thoughts but also few or no positive or rewarding self-evaluations. Some clients may learn to replace self-defeating thoughts with task-oriented coping ones and feel better, but not be satisfied with their progress. The purpose of including positive self-statements in cognitive restructuring is to help clients learn to praise or congratulate themselves for signs of progress. Although the helper can provide social reinforcement in the interview, as well as can others in the support network, the client cannot always be dependent on encouragement from someone else when confronted with a stressful situation.

Purpose and Examples of Positive Self-Statements

The helper should explain the purpose of reinforcing self-statements to the client and provide some examples. An explanation might sound like this:

You know, Joan, you've really done very well in handling these situations and learning to stop those self-defeating ideas and to use some coping thoughts. Now it's time to give yourself credit for your progress. I will help you learn to encourage yourself by using rewarding thoughts so that each time you're in this situation and you cope, you also give yourself a pat on the back for handling the situation and not getting overwhelmed by it. This kind of self-encouragement helps you to note your progress and prevents you from getting discouraged.

Then the helper can give some examples of reinforcing self-statements:

"Gee, I did it."

"Hey, I handled that OK."

"I didn't let my emotions get the best of me."

"I made some progress, and that feels good."

"See, it went pretty well after all."

Client Selection of Positive Self-Statements

After providing examples, the client should be asked for additional positive statements. The client should select those statements that feel suitable. This is particularly important in using reinforcing statements because the reinforcing value of a statement may be very idiosyncratic.

Helper Demonstration of Positive Self-Statements

The helper should demonstrate how the client can use a positive self-statement after coping with a situation. Here is an example of modeling the use of positive self-statements during and after a stressful situation. In this case, the client was an institutionalized adolescent who was confronting her parents in a face-to-face meeting:

OK, I can feel them putting pressure on me. They want me to talk. I don't want to talk. I just want to get the hell out of here [*self-defeating thought*]. Slow down; wait a minute. Don't pressure yourself. Stay cool [*coping with being overwhelmed*]. Good. That's better [*positive self-statement*].

Well, it's over. It wasn't too bad. I stuck it out. That's progress [*positive self-statement*].

Client Practice of Positive Self-Statements

The client should be instructed to practice using positive self-statements during and after the stressful situation. The practice occurs first within the interview and gradually outside the interview with *in vivo* assignments.

Homework and Follow-Up

Although homework is an integral part of every step of the cognitive restructuring procedure, the client should ultimately be able to use cognitive restructuring whenever it is needed in actual distressing situations. The client should be instructed to use cognitive restructuring *in vivo* but cautioned not to expect instant success. Clients can be reminded of the time they have spent playing the old tape over and over in their heads and of the need to make frequent and lengthy substitutions with the new tape. The client can monitor and record the instances in which cognitive restructuring was used over several weeks.

The practitioner can help with the written recording by providing a homework log sheet that might look something like Figure 14.3. The client's log data can be reviewed at a follow-up session to determine the number of times the client is using cognitive restructuring and the amount of progress that has occurred. The helper can also use the follow-up session to encourage the client to apply the procedure to stressful situations that could arise in the future. This may encourage the client to generalize the use of cognitive restructuring to situations other than those that are presently considered problematic.

Occasionally, a client's level of distress may not diminish even after repeated practice in restructuring self-defeating thoughts. In some cases, negative self-statements do not precede or contribute to the person's strong feelings. Some emotions may be classically conditioned and therefore may be better treated by a counterconditioning procedure, such as exposure or systematic desensitization (see Chapter 17). However, even in classically conditioned fears, cognitive processes may also play some role in maintaining or reducing strong emotions such as fear.

When cognitive restructuring does not reduce a client's level of distress, depression, or anxiety, the practitioner and client may need to redefine the concern and goals. Perhaps the focus of treatment may need to be more on external psychosocial stressors rather than on internal events. The helper should consider the possibility that his or her assessment has been inaccurate and that there are, in fact, no persistent thought patterns that are functionally tied to this particular client's issue. Remember that assessment of initial issues in living may not always turn out to be valid or accurate, that changes over the course of helping affect an intervention plan, and flexibility is needed to meet each client's unique needs.

Assuming that the original problem assessment is accurate, perhaps a change in parts of the cognitive restructuring procedure is necessary. Here are some possible revisions:

1. The amount of time the client uses to shift from self-defeating to coping thoughts and to imagine coping thoughts can be increased.
2. The coping statements selected by client may not be very helpful; you may need to help the client change the type of coping statements.
3. Cognitive restructuring should be supplemented either with additional coping skills, such as deep breathing or relaxation, or with skill training.

Another reason for failure of cognitive restructuring may be that the client's behaviors result from errors in encoding rather than errors in reasoning. A strategy described earlier—reframing, designed to alter encoding or perceptual errors—may be useful, as may be such strategies as reverse role plays, guided imagery, or individualized flash cards, all with prompts to attend to in order to "read" situational cues in different ways.

MODEL DIALOGUE: COGNITIVE RESTRUCTURING

We demonstrate with Joan, whom we met earlier and who is having problems in math class. The interview will be directed toward helping Joan replace self-defeating thoughts with coping thoughts. This is the nuts and bolts of cognitive restructuring.

1. **Helper:** Good to see you again, Joan. How did your week go?

Client: Pretty good. I did a lot of practice. I also tried to do this in math class. It helped some, but I still felt nervous. Here are my logs.

In response 2, the helper gives a *rationale* for cognitive restructuring, *explains the purpose of "coping" thoughts to Joan,* and gives an *overview* of the strategy.

2. **Helper:** Today we're going to work on having you learn to use some more constructive thoughts. I call these coping thoughts. You can replace the negative thoughts with coping thoughts that will help you when you're anticipating your class, in your class itself, and when things happen in your class that are especially hard for you—like taking a test or going to the board. What questions do you have about this?

Client: I don't think any—although I don't know if I know exactly what you mean by a coping thought.

The helper, in response 3, will *explain and give some examples of coping thoughts* and particular times or phases when Joan might need to use them.

Directions: When you notice your mood getting worse, ask yourself, "What's going through my mind right now?" and as soon as possible jot down the thought or mental image in the Automatic Thought column.

Date/time	Situation	Automatic thought(s)	Emotion(s)	Adaptive response	Outcome
	1. What actual event or stream of thoughts, or daydreams or recollection led to the unpleasant emotion? 2. What (if any) distressing physical sensations did you have?	1. What thought(s) and/or image(s) went through your mind? 2. How much did you believe each one at the time (0 to 100%)?	1. What emotion(s) (sad/anxious/angry/etc.) did you feel at the time? 2. How intense (0–100%) was the emotion?	1. (optional) What cognitive distortion did you make? 2. Use questions at bottom to compose a response to the automatic thought(s). 3. How much do you believe each response?	1. How much do you now believe each automatic thought? 2. What emotion(s) do you feel now? How intense (0–100%) is the emotion? 3. What will you do (or did you do)?
Friday 2/23 10 A.M. Tuesday 2/27 12 P.M. Thursday 2/29 5 P.M.	Talking on the phone with Donna. Studying for my exam. Thinking about my economics class tomorrow. Noticing my heart beating fast and my trouble concentrating.	She must not like me anymore. 90% I'll never learn this. 100% I might get called on and I won't give a good answer. 80% What's wrong with me?	Sad 80% Sad 95% Anxious 80% Anxious 80%		

Questions to help compose an alternative response: (1) What is the evidence that the automatic thought is true? Not true? (2) Is there an alternative explanation? (3) What's the worse that could happen? Could I live through it? What's the best that could happen? What's the most realistic outcome? (4) What's the effect of my believing the automatic thought? What could be the effect of my changing my thinking? (5) What should I do about it? (6) If ____[friend's name] was in the situation and had this thought, what would I tell him/her? (See also Learning Activity 14.2)

Figure 14.3 Example of homework log sheet
Source: *Cognitive Therapy: Basics and Beyond*, by J. S. Beck, p. 126. Copyright ©1995 by The Guilford Press. Reprinted by permission.

LEARNING ACTIVITY 14.2 — Creating Adaptive Responses

Here we combine the therapeutic tool in Figure 14.3 with the Learning Activity 14.3, in which you are working with all components of cognitive restructuring relative to problematic automatic thoughts of your own. As in Learning Activity 14.1, this learning activity focuses on one aspect of cognitive restructuring—specifically, to prepare you to help clients build on their self-observations of problematic patterns toward brainstorming and trying out alternative ones.

Figure 14.3 provides an example of a homework log sheet to use with a client. Review that example. Note that one part of the homework is to use questions at the bottom to compose an alternative response to a problematic automatic thought.

Use the six questions at the bottom of Figure 14.3 in your own cognitive restructuring exercise. Answer each question. Do these questions help you gain a new way of looking at yourself or the situation that was unpleasant or distressing? Develop one or more alternative responses to the distressing situation that would be more adaptive. How readily can you do this? If generating adaptive alternatives is something of a struggle, consider what might be helpful (e.g., having a professional helper generate examples, role playing in either the client or helper role, hearing examples from others who have made some gains with similar kinds of issues.)

---

3. **Helper:** Let me explain about these and give you some examples. Then perhaps you can think of your own examples. The first thing is that there are probably different times when you could use coping thoughts—like before math class, when you're anticipating it. Only, instead of worrying about it, you can use this time to prepare to handle it. For example, some coping thoughts you might use before math class are "No need to get nervous. Just think about doing OK" or "You can manage this situation" or "Don't worry so much—you've got the ability to do OK." Then, during math class, you can use coping thoughts to get through the class and to concentrate on what you're doing, such as "Just psych yourself up to get through this" or "Look at this class as a challenge, not a threat" or "Keep your cool; you can control your nervousness." Then, if there are certain times during math class that are especially hard for you, like taking a test or going to the board, there are coping thoughts you can use to help you deal with really hard things, like "Think about staying very calm now" or "Relax, take a deep breath" or "Stay as relaxed as possible. This will be over shortly." After math class, or after you cope with a hard situation, you can learn to encourage yourself for having coped by thinking things like "You did it" or "You were able to control your negative thoughts" or "You're making progress." Do you get the idea?

Client: Yes, I think so.

Next, in responses 4–7, the helper will instruct Joan *to select and practice coping thoughts at each critical phase*, starting with *preparing for class*.

4. **Helper:** Joan, let's take one thing at a time. Let's work just with what you might think before your math class. Can you come up with some coping thoughts you could use when you're anticipating your class?

Client: Well [pauses]. I could think about just working on my problems and not worrying about myself. I could think that when I work at it, I usually get it even if I'm slow.

5. **Helper:** OK, good. Now just to get the feel for these, practice using them. Perhaps you could imagine you are anticipating your class—just say these thoughts aloud as you do so.

Client: I'm thinking that I could look at my class as a challenge. I can think about just doing my work. When I concentrate on my work, I usually do get the answers.

6. **Helper:** Good! How did that feel?

Client: OK, I can see how this might help. Of course, I don't usually think these kinds of things.

7. **Helper:** I realize that, and later on today we'll practice actually having you use these thoughts. You'll get to the point where you can use your nervousness as a signal to cope. You can stop the self-defeating thoughts and use these coping thoughts instead. Let's practice this some more. [Additional practice ensues.]

In responses 8–10, the helper asks Joan *to select and practice verbalizing coping thoughts* she can use during class.

8. **Helper:** Joan, now you seem to have several kinds of coping thoughts that might help you when you're an-

LEARNING ACTIVITY 14.3 Cognitive Restructuring

Part One

Listed below are eight statements. Read each statement carefully, and decide whether it is a self-defeating or a self-enhancing statement. Remember, a self-defeating thought is a negative, unproductive way to view a situation; a self-enhancing thought is a realistic, productive interpretation of a situation or of oneself. Write down your answers. Feedback is given on page 458.

1. "Now that I've had this accident, I'll *never* be able to do anything I want to do again."
2. "How can I ever give a good speech when I don't know what I want to say?"
3. "Using a wheelchair is not as hard as it looks. I can get around wherever I want to go."
4. "I had to come to this country without my son and now that he is coming here too, I know he won't want to have anything to do with me."
5. "What I need to think about is what I want to say, not what I think I *should* say."
6. "If I just weren't a diabetic, a lot more opportunities would be available to me."
7. "Why bother? She probably wouldn't want to go out with me anyway."
8. "Of course I would prefer that my daughter marries a man, but if she chooses to be single or be with another woman, I'm OK with that too. It's her life, and I love her no matter what."

Part Two

This learning activity is designed to help you personalize cognitive restructuring in some way by using it yourself.

1. Identify a problem situation for yourself—a situation in which you don't do what you want to, not because you don't have the skills but because of your negative, self-defeating thoughts. Some examples:
   a. You need to approach your boss about a raise, promotion, or change in duties. You know what to say, but you are keeping yourself from doing it because you aren't sure it would have any effect and you aren't sure how the person might respond.
   b. You have the skills to be an effective helper, yet you constantly think that you aren't.
   c. You continue to get positive feedback about the way you handle a certain situation, yet you are constantly thinking you don't do this very well.
2. For about a week, every time this situation comes up, monitor all the thoughts you have *before, during,* and *after* the situation. Write these thoughts in a log. At the end of the week,
   a. Identify which of the thoughts are self-defeating.
   b. Identify which of the thoughts are self-enhancing.
   c. Determine whether the greatest number of self-defeating thoughts occur before, during, or after the situation.
3. In contrast to the self-defeating thoughts you have, identify some possible coping or self-enhancing thoughts you could use. On paper, list some you could use before, during, and after the situation, with particular attention to the time period when you tend to use almost all self-defeating thoughts. Make sure that you include in your list some positive or self-rewarding thoughts, too—for coping.
4. Imagine the situation—before, during, and after it. As you do this, stop any self-defeating thoughts and replace them with coping and self-rewarding thoughts. You can even practice this in a role play. This step should be practiced until you can feel your coping and self-rewarding thoughts taking hold.
5. Construct a homework assignment for yourself that encourages you to apply this as needed when the self-defeating thoughts occur.

ticipating math class. What about some coping thoughts you could use during the class? Perhaps some of these could help you concentrate on your work instead of your tenseness.

Client: Well, I could tell myself to think about what I need to do—like to get the problems. Or I could think—just take one situation at a time. Just psych myself up 'cause I know I really can do well in math if I believe that.

9. **Helper:** It sounds like you've already thought of several coping things to use during class. This time, why don't you pretend you're sitting in your class? Try out some of these coping thoughts. Just say them aloud.

Client: OK. I'm sitting at my desk; my work is in front of me. What steps do I need to take now? I could just think about one problem at a time, not worry about all of them. If I take it slowly, I can do OK.

14.3 FEEDBACK Cognitive Restructuring

PART ONE

1. *Self-defeating:* the word *never* indicates the person is not giving himself or herself any chance for the future.
2. *Self-defeating:* the person is doubting both his or her ability to give a good speech and his or her knowledge of the subject.
3. *Self-enhancing:* the person is *realistically* focusing on what she or he can do.
4. *Self-defeating:* the person is saying with certainty, as evidenced by the word *know*, that there is no chance to regain a relationship with his or her son. This is said without supporting evidence.
5. *Self-enhancing:* the client is realistically focusing on his or her own opinion, not on the assessment of others.
6. *Self-defeating:* the person is viewing the situation only from a negative perspective.
7. *Self-defeating:* the person predicts a negative reaction without supporting evidence.
8. *Self-enhancing:* the person recognizes a preference yet focuses on her love for her daughter.

---

10. **Helper:** That seemed pretty easy for you. Let's do some more practice like this just so these thoughts don't seem unfamiliar to you. As you practice, try hard to think about the meaning of what you're saying to yourself. [More practice occurs.]

Next, Joan *selects and practices coping thoughts* to help her deal with especially *stressful or critical situations* that come up in math class (responses 11–13).

11. **Helper:** This time, let's think of some particular coping statements that might help you if you come up against some touchy situations in your math class—things that are really hard for you to deal with, like taking a test, going to the board, or being called on. What might you think at these times that would keep the lid on your nervousness?

Client: I could think about just doing what is required of me—maybe, as you said earlier, taking a deep breath and just thinking about staying calm, not letting my anxiety get the best of me.

12. **Helper:** OK, great. Let's see—can you practice some of these aloud as if you were taking a test or had just been asked a question or were at the board in front of the class?

Client: Well, I'm at the board, I'm just going to think about doing this problem. If I start to get really nervous, I'm going to take a deep breath and just concentrate on being calm as I do this.

13. **Helper:** Let's practice this several times. Maybe this time you might use another tense moment, like being called on by your teacher. [Further practice goes on.]

Next, the helper *points out how Joan may discourage or punish herself after class* (responses 14 and 15). Joan selects and *practices encouraging or self-rewarding thoughts* (responses 16–18).

14. **Helper:** Joan, there's one more thing I'd like you to practice. After math class, what do you usually think?

Client: I feel relieved. I think about how glad I am it's over. Sometimes I think about the fact that I didn't do well.

15. **Helper:** Well, those thoughts are sort of discouraging, too. What I believe might help is if you could learn to encourage yourself as you start to use these coping thoughts. In other words, instead of thinking about not doing well, focus on your progress in coping. You can do this during class or after class is over. Can you find some more positive things you could think about to encourage yourself—like giving yourself a pat on the back?

Client: You mean like I didn't do as bad as I thought?

16. **Helper:** Yes, anything like that.

Client: Well, it's over, it didn't go too badly. Actually I handled things OK. I can do this if I believe it. I can see progress.

17. **Helper:** Now let's assume you've just been at the board. You're back at your seat. Practice saying what you might think in that situation that would be encouraging to you.

Client: I've just sat down. I might think that it went fast and I did concentrate on the problem, so that was good.

18. **Helper:** Now let's assume class is over. What would you say would be positive, self-encouraging thoughts after class?

Client: I've just gotten out. Class wasn't that bad. I got something out of it. If I put my mind to it, I can do it. [More practice of positive self-statements occurs.]

In response 19, the helper instructs Joan *to practice the entire sequence* of stopping a self-defeating thought and using a coping thought before, during, and after class. Usually the client practices this by *imagining the situation*.

19. **Helper:** So far we've been practicing these coping thoughts at the different times you might use them so you can get used to these. Now let's practice this in the sequence that it might actually occur—like before your class, during the class, coping with a tough situation, and encouraging yourself after class. If you imagine the situation and start to notice any self-defeating thoughts, you can practice stopping these. Then switch immediately to the types of coping thoughts that you believe will help you most at that time. Concentrate on the coping thoughts. How does this sound?

Client: OK, I think I know what you mean [looks a little confused].

Sometimes long instructions are confusing. Modeling may be better. In responses 20 and 21, the helper *demonstrates how Joan can apply coping thoughts in practice.*

20. **Helper:** Well, I just said a lot, and it might make more sense if I showed this to you. First, I'm going to imagine I'm in English class. It's almost time for the bell; then it's math class. Wish I could get out of it. It's embarrassing. Stop! That's a signal to use my coping thoughts. I need to think about math class as a challenge. Something I can do OK if I work at it [pauses]. Joan, do you get the idea?

Client: Yes, now I do.

21. **Helper:** OK, I'll go on and imagine now I'm actually in the class. He's given us a worksheet to do in 30 minutes. Whew! How will dumb me ever do that! Wait a minute. I know I can do it, but I need to go slowly and concentrate on the work, not on me. Just take one problem at a time. Well, now he wants us to read our answers. What if he calls on me? I can feel my heart pounding. Oh well, if I get called on, just take a deep breath and answer. If it turns out to be wrong, it's not the end of the world.
    Well, the bell rang. I am walking out. I'm glad it's over. Now, wait a minute—it didn't go that badly. Actually I handled it pretty well. Now, why don't you try this? [Joan practices the sequence of coping thoughts several times, first with the helper's assistance, gradually in a completely self-directed manner.]

Before terminating the session, the helper *assigns daily homework practice.*

22. **Helper:** This week I'd like you to practice this several times each day—just like you did now. Keep track of your practices on your log. And you can use this whenever you feel it would be helpful—such as before, during, or after math class. Jot these times down too, and we'll go over this next week.

SUMMARY

Various cognitive change procedures of cognitive modeling, problem solving, reframing, stress inoculation, and cognitive restructuring are being used more frequently in helping practice. An individual's construction of a particular situation is like a photograph. The individual's influence or bias can blur or distort the mental picture or the construction may in other ways not be serving the client well. Cognitive restructuring is like providing the client with other pictures or a different construction or mental picture of a situation. Cognitive structural change can be more than modifying habitual cognitions, rules, expectancies, assumptions, and imperatives; it can also provide emotional relief.

As with any intervention, adaptations need to be made depending on the client's gender and culture. For example, some clients may benefit if cognitive restructuring is offered in a group setting. Professional helpers using cognitive restructuring also need to be sensitive to the diverse perspectives reflected by the client's culture. We present related cognitive change procedures, focusing on stress management, in the next chapter.

INFOTRAC® EXPLORATIONS

1. Search for the term *cognitive therapy* and the subdivisions of *evaluation* and *research*. Select three to five articles that directly address intervention, and write a description about what you understand the interventions to include. Do the articles address schemas? How do the strategies compare to those outlined in this chapter? Do the intervention descriptions provide sufficient detail to allow a practitioner to replicate the intervention? See if you can find one article that is strong in this regard and one that is weak, and share this exercise with your classroom or field-based colleagues. At the end, see if you feel comfortable talking about cognitive therapy to clients.

2. Search for the term *cognitive therapy*, and select two to three articles published within the last three years and two to three published 15 years ago (you may need to get the earlier ones from another database, such as PsychInfo). Briefly, develop a list of points of descriptions that appear consistent between the two sets and descriptions that appear noticeably different (e.g., greater attention to how emotion is cognitively represented or how emotions interact with cognitions, different ways in talking about memory, more or less attention to environmental factors). Exchange your findings as part of a group exercise.
3. Search for the term *cognitive therapy* (InfoTrac does not presently organize published work using the term *cognitive restructuring*) and the subdivision *usage*. Select three to five articles across different populations or problem topics (e.g., elderly, children, disabled, women or phobia, depression, alcohol dependence). Look for ways that differential life beliefs or experiences of this group (e.g., contexts, oppression, vulnerability, values, history) are noted. Identify additional factors that you deem important.

SUGGESTED RESOURCES

Readings

Beck, J. S. (1995). *Cognitive therapy.* New York: Guilford.

Brower, A. M., & Nurius, P. S. (1993). *Social cognition and individual change.* Newbury Park, CA: Sage.

Clark, D. A., Beck, A. T., & Alford, B. A. (1999). *Scientific foundations of cognitive theory and therapy of depression.* Philadelphia: Wiley.

DeRubeis, R. J., Tang, T. Z., & Beck, A. T. (2001). Cognitive therapy. In K. S. Dobson (Ed.), *Handbook of cognitive–behavioral therapies* (2nd ed., pp. 349–392). New York: Guilford.

Dobson, K. S. (Ed.). (2001). *Handbook of cognitive–behavioral therapies* (2nd ed.). New York: Guilford.

Dobson, K. S., Backs-Dermott, B. J., & Dozois, D. (2000). Cognitive and cognitive–behavioral therapies. In C. R. Synder & R. E. Ingram (Eds.), *Handbook of psychological change: Psychotherapy processes and practices for the 21st century* (pp. 409–428). New York: Wiley.

Greenberger, D., & Padesky, C. (1995). *Mind over mood: A cognitive therapy treatment manual for clients.* New York: Guilford.

Hays, P. (1995). Multicultural applications of cognitive behavior therapy. *Professional Psychology, 26,* 309–315.

Horan, J. (1996). Effects of computer-based cognitive restructuring on rationally mediated self-esteem. *Journal of Counseling Psychology, 43,* 371–375.

Kendall, P. C. (Ed.). (2000). *Child and adolescent therapy: Cognitive behavioral procedures* (2nd ed.). New York: Guilford.

Leahy, R. (1996). *Cognitive therapy: Basic principles and implications.* Northvale, NJ: Aronson.

Leahy, R. L., & Holland, S. J. (2000). *Treatment plans and interventions for depression and anxiety disorders.* New York: Guilford.

Park, D. C., & Schwarz, N. (Eds.). (1999). *Cognitive aging: A primer.* New York: Psychology Press.

Wells, A. (2001). *Emotional disorders & metacognition: Innovative cognitive therapy.* New York: Wiley.

Young, J. E. (1999). *Cognitive therapy for personality disorders: A schema-focused approach* (3rd ed.). Sarasota, FL: Professional Resource Press.

Web Sites

American Institute for Cognitive Therapy
http://www.cognitivetherapynyc.com

Beck Institute for Cognitive Therapy and Research
http://www.beckinstitute.org

Behavioral Associates (What is Cognitive-Behavior-Therapy)
http://www.behavioralassociates.com

Habitsmart (Cognitive Therapy Pages)
http://www.habitsmart.com/cogtitle.html

Mindstreet
http://mindstreet.com

National Association of Cognitive–Behavioral Therapists
http://www.nacbt.org

14 POSTEVALUATION

Part One

Objective One asks you to identify and describe the six major components of cognitive restructuring in a client case. Using the case described here, explain briefly how you would use the steps and components of cognitive restructuring with *this* client. You can use the six questions following the client case to describe your use of this procedure. Feedback follows on page 466.

Description of client: Doreen is a junior in college, majoring in education and getting very good grades. She reports that she has an active social life and has some good close friendships with both males and females. Despite obvious "pluses," the client reports constant feelings of being worthless and inadequate. Her standards for herself seem to be unrealistically high: Although she has almost a straight-A average, she still chides herself that she does not have all A's. Although she is attractive and has an active social life, she thinks that she should be more attractive and more talented. At the end of the initial session, she adds that as an African American woman she always has felt as though she has to prove herself more than the average person.

1. How would you explain the rationale for cognitive restructuring to this client? How would you explain the schema component?
2. Give an example you might use with this client to point out the difference between a self-defeating and a self-enhancing thought. Try to base your example on the client's self-description.
3. How would you have the client identify her thoughts about herself—her grades, appearance, social life, and so on? How would you help her identify schemas underlying maladaptive ways of thinking?
4. What are some coping thoughts this client might use?
5. Explain how, in the session, you would help the client practice shifting from self-defeating to coping thoughts.
6. What kind of homework assignment would you use to help the client increase her use of coping thoughts about herself?

Part Two

Objective Two asks you to teach the six components of cognitive restructuring to someone else or to demonstrate these components with a role-play client. Use the Interview Checklist for Cognitive Restructuring below as a teaching and evaluation guide.

Interview Checklist for Cognitive Restructuring

Instructions to observer: Determine whether the helper demonstrated the lead listed in the checklist. Check which leads the helper used.

Item	Examples of helper leads
I. Rationale and Overview	
_____ 1. Helper explains purpose and rationale of cognitive restructuring.	"You've reported that you find yourself getting anxious and depressed during and after these conversations with the people who have to evaluate your work. This procedure can help you identify some things you might be thinking in this situation that are just beliefs, not facts, and are unproductive. You can learn more realistic ways to think about this situation that will help you cope with it in a way that you want to."
_____ 2. Helper provides brief overview of procedure.	"There are several things we'll do in using this procedure. *First,* this will help you identify the kinds of things you're thinking before, during, and after these situations that are self-defeating. *Second,* we'll work to determine ways that these self-defeating beliefs (schemas) developed over time

(continued)

(continued)

_____ 3. Helper explains difference between self-enhancing thoughts and self-defeating thoughts and provides culturally relevant examples of each.

_____ 4. Helper explains influence of irrational and self-defeating thoughts on emotions and performance.

_____ 5. Helper confirms client's willingness to use strategy.

II. Identifying Client Thoughts in Problem Situations

_____ 6. Helper asks client to describe problem situations and identify examples of self-enhancing thoughts and of self-defeating thoughts that client typically experiences in these situations.

_____ 7. If client is unable to complete step 6, helper models examples of thoughts or "links" between event and client's emotional response.

_____ 8. Helper instructs client to monitor and record content of thoughts *before, during,* and *after* stressful or upsetting situations before the next session.

_____ 9. Using client's monitoring, helper and client identify client's self-defeating thoughts.

and what conditions tend to activate them. *Third,* this will help us develop cues and strategies for you to catch a self-defeating thought and replace it with a coping thought. *Fourth,* this will help you see ways to break long-standing patterns of responding and learn how to give yourself credit for changing these self-defeating thoughts."

"A self-defeating thought is one way to interpret the situation, but it is usually negative and unproductive, like thinking that the other person doesn't value you or what you say. In contrast, a self-enhancing thought is a more constructive and realistic way to interpret the situation—like thinking that what you are talking about has value to you."

"When you're constantly preoccupied with yourself and worried about how the situation will turn out, this can affect your feelings and your behavior. Worrying about the situation can make you feel anxious and upset. Concentrating on the situation and not worrying about its outcome can help you feel more relaxed, which helps you handle the situation more easily."

"Are you ready to try this now?"

"Think of the last time you were in this situation. Describe for me what you think before you have a conversation with your evaluator. . . . What are you usually thinking during the conversation? . . . What thoughts go through your mind after the conversation is over? Now let's see which of those thoughts are actual facts about the situation or are constructive ways to interpret the situation. Which ones are your beliefs about the situation that are unproductive or self-defeating?"

"OK, think of the thoughts that you have while you're in this conversation as a link between this event and your feelings afterward of being upset and depressed. What is the middle part? For instance, it might be something like 'I'll never have a good evaluation, and I'll lose this position' or 'I always blow this conversation and never make a good impression.' Can you recall thinking anything like this?"

"One way to help you identify this link or your thoughts is to keep track of what you're thinking in these situations as they happen. This week I'd like you to use this log each day. Try to identify and write down at least three specific thoughts you have in these situations each day, and bring this in with you next week."

"Let's look at your log and go over the kinds of negative thoughts that seem to be predominant in these situations.

COGNITIVE CHANGE AND COGNITIVE RESTRUCTURING STRATEGIES   463

14 POSTEVALUATION

_____ 10. Helper assesses client's schemas.

We can explore how these thoughts affect your feelings and performance in this situation—and whether you feel there is any evidence or rational basis for these."

In some cases, more focal assessment of underlying schemas is needed. In-depth assessment of schemas (adaptive or maladaptive) can involve multiple tools such as a focused review of the client's history relative to the current problem, use of schema inventories, experiential exercises to trigger certain schemas, and client education about schemas (Young et al., 1998). As part of a case conceptualization, Leahy (1996, p. 194) suggests the following questions to get a better sense of how the client sees this. For each blank line, fill in the word that describes the schema in question.

"How did your (parents, other family members, peers, teachers, partner as relevant) teach you that you were ____? What evidence is there that you are not ____? How would you rate yourself on a continuum from ____ to (the opposite)? Does this depend on the situation or other factors? If so, how and why? What is the consequence of believing or demanding this of yourself? Is it ever OK to be ____? How would you challenge your (parent, teacher, as appropriate) now that you are an adult, if they were to describe you as ____?"

III. Introduction and Practice of Coping Thoughts
_____ 11. Helper explains purpose and potential use of "coping thoughts" and gives some examples of coping thoughts to be used:
    _____ a. Before the situation—preparing for it
    _____ b. During the situation
        _____ 1. Focusing on task
        _____ 2. Dealing with feeling overwhelmed

"Up to this point, we've talked about the negative or unproductive thoughts you have in these situations and how they contribute to your feeling uncomfortable, upset, and depressed. Now we're going to look at some alternative, more constructive ways to think about the situation—using coping thoughts. These thoughts can help you prepare for the situation, handle the situation, and deal with feeling upset or overwhelmed in the situation. As long as you're using some coping thoughts, you avoid giving up control and letting the old self-defeating thoughts take over. Here are some examples of coping thoughts."

_____ 12. Helper instructs client to think of additional coping thoughts that client could use or has used before.

"Try to think of your own coping thoughts—perhaps ones you can remember using successfully in other situations, ones that seem to work for you."

(continued)

14 POST EVALUATION

(continued)

____ 13. Helper instructs client to practice verbalizing selected coping statements.

"At first you will feel a little awkward using coping statements. It's like learning to drive a stick shift after you've been used to driving an automatic. So one way to help you get used to this is for you to practice these statements aloud."

____ a. Helper instructs client first to practice coping statements individually. Coping statements to use before a situation are practiced, then coping statements to use during a situation.

"First, just practice each coping statement separately. After you feel comfortable with saying these aloud, practice the ones you could use before this conversation. OK, now practice the ones you could use during this conversation with your evaluator."

____ b. Helper instructs client to practice sequence of coping statements as they would be used in actual situation.

"Now let's put it all together. Imagine it's an hour before your meeting. Practice the coping statements you could use then. We'll role-play the meeting. As you feel aroused or overwhelmed, stop and practice coping thoughts during the situation."

____ c. Helper instructs client to become actively involved and to internalize meaning of coping statements during practice.

"Try to really put yourself into this practice. As you say these new things to yourself, try to think of what these thoughts really mean."

IV. Shifting from Self-Defeating to Coping Thoughts

____ 14. Helper models shift from recognizing a self-defeating thought and stopping it to replacing it with a coping thought.

"Let me show you what we will practice today. First, I'm in this conversation. Everything is going OK. All of a sudden I can feel myself starting to tense up. I realize I'm starting to get overwhelmed about this whole evaluation process. I'm thinking that I'm going to blow it. No, I stop that thought at once. Now, I'm just going to concentrate on calming down, taking a deep breath, and thinking only about what I have to say."

____ 15. Helper helps client practice shift from self-defeating to coping thoughts. Practice consists of four steps:

"Now let's practice this. You will imagine the situation. As soon as you start to recognize the onset of a self-defeating thought, stop it. Verbalize the thought aloud, and tell yourself to stop. Then verbalize a coping thought in place of it and imagine carrying on with the situation."

____ a. Having client imagine situation or carry it out in a role play (behavior rehearsal).
____ b. Recognizing self-defeating thought (which could be signaled by a hand or finger).
____ c. Stopping self-defeating thought (which could be supplemented with a hand clap).
____ d. Replacing thought with coping thought (possibly supplemented with deep breathing).

____ 16. Helper helps client practice using shift for each problem situation until anxiety or stress felt by client while practicing the situation is decreased to a reasonable or negligible level and client can carry out practice and use coping thoughts in a self-directed manner.

"Let's keep working with this situation until you feel pretty comfortable with it and can shift from self-defeating to coping thoughts without my help."

14 POSTEVALUATION

V. Introduction and Practice of Positive, or Reinforcing, Self-Statements

_____ 17. Helper explains purpose and use of positive self-statements and gives some examples of these to client.

"You have really made a lot of progress in learning to use coping statements before and during these situations. Now it's time to learn to reward or encourage yourself. After you've coped with a situation, you can pat yourself on the back for having done so by thinking a positive or rewarding thought like 'I did it' or 'I really managed that pretty well.'"

_____ 18. Helper instructs client to think of additional positive self-statements and to select some to try out.

"Can you think of some things like this that you think of when you feel good about something or when you feel like you've accomplished something? Try to come up with some of these thoughts that seem to fit for you."

_____ 19. Helper models application of positive self-statements as self-reinforcement for shift from self-defeating to coping thoughts.

"OK, here is the way you reward yourself for having coped. You recognize the self-defeating thought. Now you're in the situation using coping thoughts, and you're thinking things like 'Take a deep breath' or 'Just concentrate on this task.' Now the conversation is finished. You know you were able to use coping thoughts, and you reward yourself by thinking 'Yes, I did it' or 'I really was able to manage that.'"

_____ 20. Helper instructs client to practice use of positive self-statements in interview following practice of shift from self-defeating to coping thoughts. This should be practiced in sequence (coping *before* and *during* situation and reinforcing oneself *after* situation).

"OK, let's try this out. As you imagine the conversation, you're using the coping thoughts you will verbalize.... Now, imagine the situation is over, and verbalize several reinforcing thoughts for having coped."

VI. Homework and Follow-Up

_____ 21. Helper instructs client to use cognitive restructuring procedure (identifying self-defeating thought, stopping it, shifting to coping thought, reinforcing with positive self-statement) in situations outside the interview.

"OK, now you're ready to use the entire procedure whenever you have these conversations in which you're being evaluated—or any other situation in which you recognize your negative interpretation of the event is affecting you. In these cases, you recognize and stop any self-defeating thoughts, use the coping thoughts before the situation to prepare for it, and use the coping thoughts during the situation to help focus on the task and deal with being overwhelmed. After the situation is over, use the positive self-thoughts to reward your efforts."

_____ 22. Helper instructs client to monitor and record on log sheet the number of times client uses cognitive restructuring outside the interview.

"I'd like you to use this log to keep track of the number of times you use this procedure and to jot down the situation in which you're using it. Also rate your tension level on a 1-to-5 scale before and after each time you use this."

_____ 23. Helper arranges for follow-up.

"Do this recording for the next two weeks. Then let's get together for a follow-up session."

Observer comments: _____
_____

POST EVALUATION FEEDBACK

PART ONE

1. One overall goal may be for Doreen to feel more empowered about herself and to feel less pressure to have to constantly prove herself as a black woman. You can explain that CR would help her identify some of her thoughts about herself that are beliefs, not inherent "facts," and are contestable—perhaps unrealistic thoughts, leading to feelings of depression and worthlessness. In addition, CR would help her learn to think about herself in more realistic, self-enhancing ways in line with her values. See the Interview Checklist for Cognitive Restructuring on pages 461–465 for another example of the CR rationale.

   You could explain that the word *schema* refers to how information gets organized and stored in memory. Schemas are built up over time and experience, from input we get from others as well as our own reflections and evaluations. Schemas are not just passive "file drawers" but rather are more like complex filters that screen, direct, and shape what we notice, how we interpret ourselves and our world, and how we respond. We have too many schemas for them all to be actively working at any one time. Rather, we tend to develop patterns and habits such that some schemas get punched much like buttons, and when these get punched, we are filled with the sense of them, and it is hard to get to schemas that may run counter to them. For example, when our schema of inadequacy is pushed, it brings with it related schemas like shame and worthlessness, which make it difficult to access schemas we may have about our talent, promise, and hope.

2. A core issue for Doreen to challenge is her belief system about her race and gender—that as an African American and as a woman she must constantly prove herself in order to be a worthy person. Thinking that she is not good enough is self-defeating. Self-enhancing or positive thoughts about herself are more realistic interpretations of her experiences—good grades, close friends, active social life, and so on. Recognition that she is intelligent and attractive is a self-enhancing thought.

3. You could ask the client to describe different situations and the thoughts she has about herself in them. She could also observe this during the week. You could model some possible thoughts she might be having. See leads 6–9 in the Interview Checklist for Cognitive Restructuring. For schema identification, several tools and sample questions are listed in lead 10.

4. There are many possible coping thoughts she could use. Here are some examples: "Hey, I'm doing pretty well as it is." "Don't be so hard on myself. I don't have to be perfect." "That worthless feeling is a sign to cope—recognize my assets." "What's more attractive anyway? I am attractive." "Don't let that one B get me down. It's not the end of the world." "I'm an African American woman, and I'm proud of it. I feel OK about myself the way I am. I don't have to prove my worth to anyone."

5. See leads 14–16 on the Interview Checklist for Cognitive Restructuring.

6. Many possible homework assignments might help. Here are a few examples:
   a. Every time Doreen uses a coping thought, she could record it on her log.
   b. She could cue herself to use a coping thought by writing these down on note cards and reading a note before doing something else, like getting a drink or making a phone call, or by using a phone-answering device to report and verbalize coping thoughts.
   c. She could enlist the aid of a close friend or roommate. If the roommate notices that the client starts to "put herself down," she could interrupt her. Doreen could then use a coping statement.

PART TWO

Use the Interview Checklist for Cognitive Restructuring on pages 461–465 to assess your teaching or counseling demonstration of this procedure.

CHAPTER 15
STRESS MANAGEMENT STRATEGIES

Feel anxious? Stressful? Wired?

Do you have tension headaches?

Do you abuse "soft" drugs—alcohol or tobacco?

Do you feel chronic fatigue?

Are you irritable, with low frustration tolerance?

Do you have high blood pressure in certain situations or at certain times?

Does your immune system seem not to be working well?

A great number of people would respond yes to one or more of these questions. Anxiety is one of the most common concerns reported by clients, and stress is related to physiological discomfort such as headaches and indigestion. Stress is also correlated with heart disease, cancer, and other serious diseases. Perhaps as a consequence of the "stress syndrome," the last several years have produced an explosion in procedures for management of stress or anxiety, originally introduced in 1929 as "progressive relaxation" (Jacobson, 1929). Many books related to stress management have appeared in book stores in the health and self-help sections (Benson, 1976; Benson & Stuart, 1992; Borysenko, 1988; Kabat-Zinn, 1990, 1994; Ornish, 1990). There has been a considerable amount of research exploring the relative strengths and weaknesses of stress management approaches and a number of current guides available applicable to children and adults (Clark, 1996; Crum, 2000; Fink, 2000; Greenberg, 1996; Humphrey, 1998; Johnson 1998; Lehrer & Woolfolk, 1993; McGuigan, 1999; Rice, 2000; Zalaquett & Wood, 1997).

This chapter addresses stress and its management. We will be looking at forms that stress takes, including cultural variations, and will examine both physiological and cognitive dimensions of stress management. This will include the physiology of breathing and techniques applicable in broad-based practice as well as stress inoculation therapy. As with other cognitive therapies (see Chapter 14), stress inoculation assumes that maladaptive emotions and thinking are influenced or mediated by one's core beliefs, schemas, perceptions, and cognitions. Stress inoculation has components of cognitive restructuring as well as coping skills. These two procedures help clients to access and to determine the relations among their perceptions, cognitions, emotions, and actions; to identify how clients interpret their situations and experiences; and to urge clients to substitute a new interpretive frame (Gendlin, 1996, p. 242). We will also attend to the growing recognition of spirituality as an important dimension of coping and stress management for many people. Chapter 16 provides complementary stress management content, focusing on meditation and forms of movement such as muscle relaxation and exercise.

OBJECTIVES

After completing this chapter, the student should be able to

1. Assess your breathing by using 4 of the 5 instructions for "breathing awareness."
2. Demonstrate 10 of the 12 steps for diaphragmatic breathing. You may wish to audiotape the instructions, which might enhance your focus on the exercise.
3. Using a simulated client case, describe how the 5 components of stress inoculation would be used with a client.
4. Demonstrate 17 out of 21 steps of stress inoculation in a role-play interview.

STRESS AND COPING

Stress has been widely studied in recent decades and has become a commonplace concept in our daily lives and language ("I am so stressed out!"). Stress essentially refers to conditions stemming from demands exceeding capacity.

This, of course, covers a lot of ground, such as roles, tasks, or expectations from one's environment, oneself, or others that exceed our abilities or conditions. Stress can stem from what we might regard in largely positive terms (e.g., a desired job promotion, marriage or partnering, parenthood, a holiday, a move) as well as what we would regard in negative terms (e.g., significant losses; injuries or illnesses; serious financial, relationship, or mental health threats). Stress has multiple levels of effects. For example, we are all aware of what being stressed feels like, such as elevated heart rate, muscle tension, effects on breathing, anxiety, rumination. There are layers of psychophysiological effects and processes engaged with stress as well, involving the brain, the endocrine, autonomic nervous, cardiovascular, gastrointestinal, and immunological systems as well as muscles, skin, and perceptual receptors (e.g., vision, hearing, touch) (Greenberg, 1996).

Although we will not be reviewing all these dimensions of the causes and effects of stress, it is useful to recognize that there is enormous variability in factors that may be fostering stress, how stress is experienced, what stress and the stressors mean to the people involved, underlying mind–body connections in stress and its management, and choices for how to handle the issue(s). As with self-management (Chapter 18), many of the interventions described in this book may be useful components in stress management, depending on the assessment and match of intervention plan to needs and conditions. Stress management may involve managing the symptoms or phenomenology of the stress itself (relaxation, exercise, biofeedback), affecting factors that are creating the stress (problem solving, advocacy, conflict resolution, changing environmental stressors), fostering factors that will help buffer or otherwise weather or transform the stress (social supports networking, spirituality, meditation), and a whole range of methods for decreasing one's own stressful behavior, lifestyle characteristics, or ways of perceiving and responding to targeted stressors.

As we reviewed in earlier chapters (e.g., reframing in Chapter 13 and cognitive restructuring in Chapter 14), one's cognitive interpretations or appraisals of a life situation and its implications are crucial components in the meaning that the situation holds for an individual, emotional reactions, physiological responding, attributions and perceptions of options and likely outcomes, and actions taken or not taken. Figure 15.1 illustrates the process of coping with stress. This depiction is rooted in a transactional, ecological view (Lazarus, 1990; Lazarus & Folkman, 1984) wherein both person and environment characteristics are considered as well as factors comparatively "objective" in nature (e.g., the mix of resources and demands in place, situational factors, one's own and others' behaviors) as well as how these factors are uniquely interpreted (perceived, appraised) and experienced by the people involved. All these boxes and arrows make for a complex picture, but an important one for showing that there are typically multiple points of helping that may make a significant difference in achieving improved outcomes or bolstering resiliency, *if* you understand the relationships among these person and environmental factors relative to coping. For example, focusing only on resources (including social currency, as illustrated, but possibly including many other types of resources) is unlikely to be sufficient if one does not take other coping, contextual, and sociocultural factors into account. Similarly, if one works only to change certain coping behaviors, this alone is likely insufficient, given factors influencing these behaviors as well as outcomes separate from coping behaviors. Although health outcomes are used in Figure 15.1, the problematic or desired outcomes could take many forms.

Briefly, we'll review some of the features of stress and coping relevant to assessment and intervention planning. What is the antecedent profile of person and environment strengths and vulnerabilities involved? What is the person's perceived social support relative to the stress and needs in question? Sense of self-efficacy? Primary appraisal refers to whether the stressor itself is perceived as a threat of harm or loss or more in positive challenge terms? Secondary appraisals involve questions like these: Who or what is responsible for this situation? Does the person have what is needed to handle this? What are the likely outcomes—positive and negative? The nature of one's emotions can make a huge difference (e.g., feeling angry versus feeling guilty positions one very differently for how one is likely to respond), and emotions stem in part from how the circumstances have been appraised and the meaning they hold for the individual (family, group, community) in question.

As we noted in earlier chapters, coping has often been distinguished between problem-focused and emotion-focused coping. Although an oversimplification, these can be thought of as actions to manage the stressor versus actions to manage emotions associated with the stressor and context. Coping is not a one-shot step but rather an ongoing, constantly changing process, which includes how people reappraise (naturally occurring or through helping interventions) the stress context, themselves, and their anticipated future. These appraisal, emotion, and behavioral components of grappling with stress mediate the effects of stressors on the person's outcomes and well-being. And this whole set of experiences does not stop there but rather positions the individual—positively or negatively—in a different place

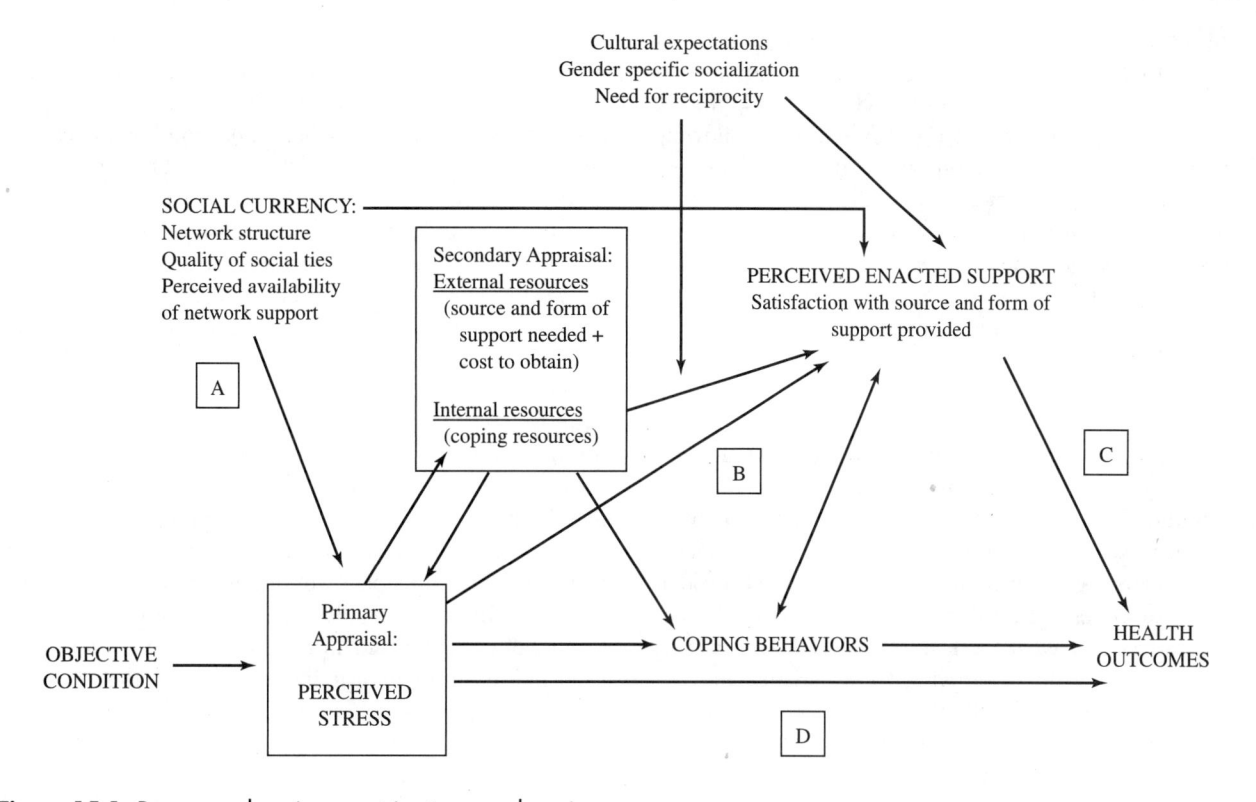

Figure 15.1 Person and environment in stress and coping
Source: From "Social Support: The Promise and the Reality," by P. W. Underwood. In V. H. Rice (Ed.), *Handbook of stress, coping, and Health: Implications for Nursing Research, Theory, and Practice*, pp. 367–391. Copyright © 2000 and is held by Patricia W. Underwood. Reprinted with permission of P. W. Underwood.

relative to encountering the next life stressor (Fink, 2000; Greenberg, 1996; Nurius, 2000; Rice, 2000; Zeidner & Endler, 1996 offer recent overviews of stress and coping).

Current views generally recognize that both stress and coping are dynamic, with individual uniqueness and environmental forces important at each step of the way and changing as they interact (Moos & Schaefer, 1993). Social support is a good example of this. Figure 15.1 shows a number of ways that social support is being examined relative to the different ways it may relate, positively or negatively, to perceived stress, secondary appraisals, coping behaviors, and outcomes (Underwood, 2000). For example, having social resources (the notion of "social currency") may buffer the effect of stress ("A" in the model); for example, as with informational and material resources, people high in helpful and available social support may experience lower stress from the same threatening circumstances than those low in social currency. How satisfied one is with the source and type of support will likely influence how much and in what ways that support affects outcomes ("C" in the model—for example, not all "support" is helpful and can actually exacerbate a problem or undermine adaptive coping as well as provide important benefits). Perceived social support may directly mediate perceived stress, independently or in relation to coping behaviors ("D" in the model). And, of course, there are many individual differences that people bring (personality, coping preferences, gender and cultural socialization, and beliefs or expectations) that can influence how social support is conceptualized and experienced ("B" in the model).

By the time clients seek professional help, their level of stress and the salience of avoiding or minimizing negative outcomes may understandably be running very high. In addition to focusing on reducing negative outcomes, stress management research is suggesting the value of looking also at potential positive outcomes that may follow or come from coping with adversity or traumatic events. Davis, Nolen-Hoeksema, and Larson (1998) distinguish between two forms of meaning making, both of which appear to be important to adjustment but are not correlated: (1) "making sense" of the event in terms of an explanation or deeper comprehension and (2) achieving an increased sense of meaning through finding some kind of positive outcome or benefit. Tedeschi and Calhoun's (1995; Calhoun & Tedeschi, 1998, 1999) work on perceived growth following trauma argues that intervention can build on the shattering and trauma-related disruption to help clients build new conceptions of self, meaning, and future. As Antoni and colleagues (2001) and others (Folkman, 1997) have pointed out, this trend reinforces the importance of carefully considering with clients the unique meaning that an adverse or traumatic experience holds for them as part of assessment, including perceived positive as well as negative possibilities or outcomes.

The point of these illustrations is not to cause you worry about understanding all that is involved in stress and coping! Rather, it is to underscore that individuals are continuously embedded in contexts, histories, and multi-layered environments. We may think of stress as something that happens to us, but we need to appreciate that how we approach stress and what we bring with us to the coping process can markedly affect what we experience and our outcomes. As Figure 15.1 illustrates, there are a number of points in and contributors to the stress process to consider for intervention, including external and internal factors that may have mediating effects of stressful life events on subsequent health and well-being outcomes. Recent years have seen growing attention to these potential mediators. Particularly within cognitive behavioral interventions there has been growing attention to both clients' cognitive appraisals of their stress-provoking life situations as well as appraisal-related habits or patterns that may have become part of the stress cycle and outcomes, such as triggered anxiety, anger, or sense of helplessness or hopelessness that are impeding desired actions. Stress inoculation training, presented later in this chapter, builds on the notion of a mediated process, combining coping skills training with an educational phase regarding stress and ways that one's appraisals, emotions, and supports (or lack thereof) influence how we experience and respond to stress.

CULTURAL AND LIFE COURSE VARIATIONS IN STRESS

The model of stress and the particular interventions that we present in this chapter derive, as does much of practice-related research, predominantly from Euro-American roots. Therefore, particular care is needed in how stress is assessed and what may and may not be appropriate or useful for various clients. The need to attend to cultural, historical, life course, and other forms of diversity is becoming increasingly apparent to understand the stress experience and how coping works. Leininger (1988) views culture as the "learned, shared, and transmitted values, beliefs, norms, and life practices of a particular group that guides thinking, decisions, and actions in patterned ways" (p. 156) and has developed a model of cultural care diversity and universality. Cultural care involves understanding beliefs, values, and patterned expressions that "assist, support, or enable another individual or group to maintain well-being, improve a human condition or lifeway, or face death and disabilities" (p. 156, cited in Cohen & Welch, 2000). The historical, cultural, and social contexts of people influence care expressions as well as patterns and practice of well-being and holistic health through ethnohistory, language, and environmental contexts. Folk or other culturally specific resources or systems may be important components of helping, alone or combined with professional systems such as those that many of you work in or anticipate working in. In short, this model helps us think about the ways that culture is infused throughout current and historical dimensions of people's lives. This infusion, in turn, shapes and colors the encounter and experience of stress, as well as helping interventions.

Cultural differences exist, both globally and within the United States, in the concept and management of stress and the values and ideologies involved in stress reactions, perceptions of control or influence, and coping mechanisms. Examples of presentations of anxiety and stress in other countries, as summarized by Castillo (1997), include the following:

1. The *dhat* syndrome in India, characterized by somatic symptoms and anxiety over a loss of semen (which is thought to result in loss of spiritual power).
2. *Nervios* in Latin American countries, characterized by generalized anxiety along with a range of principal symptoms.
3. *Hwa-byung* syndrome in Korea, characterized by anxiety and somatic symptoms often associated with the suppression of anger. (See Castillo's book for a complete discussion of these cultural variations.)

Among some cultural groups in India, for example, stress is not viewed as a major problem and certainly not a concern to bring to an "expert" (Laungani, 1993). Instead, stress is viewed as an integral part of life. Within this culture, one may see a widespread acceptance of a magical or more spiritually based explanation of stress and of coping, and persons particularly qualified to remove spells and exorcise evil spirits are often used. As in many cultures, people seeking relief from various concerns also make offerings to deities, make pilgrimages to shrines, or access what would be referred to in the United States as alternative resources such as faith healers, gurus, and homeopathic practitioners. Further, there is a greater reliance on self-healing forms of managing stress such as meditation and yoga. This illustration is intended to illustrate the importance of a cultural lens (including, but not limited to racial and national heritage) in understanding how stress is being experienced, what targets of change are likely to result in reduced stress, and what interventions and resources are likely to be most appropriate for clients' goals and contexts.

Lam and Palsane (1997) have reviewed contemporary research on stress and coping undertaken in Asian societies. They note both similarities and differences in the conceptualization and findings from research that applies Western findings in an Asian context (e.g., whether social support buffers effects of stress) and that which aims to identify indigenous patterns of stress and coping relative to culture-specific manifestations (e.g., exploring the nature and function of social support in specific cultures). They make the important point that cultural examinations of stress, coping, and implications for well-being need to be undertaken with structural and quality-of-life conditions in mind. For example, factors such as incidence of poverty, malnutrition, inaccessible or poor medical services, poor housing quality, and limited protection from injustices create contexts of adversity that may confound cultural dimensions. Differences among Asian and Western societies (e.g., differences in stress proneness and stress resistance, in how stress is experienced, in ways of coping) warrant further examination, but so too do differences among different Asian cultures and within each society. We see many of these points applying to practitioners within the United States. Our pluralistic society will become even more varied in years to come, including marked differentials in economic and political issues as well as in cultural factors.

There are also variations in the prevalence of stress and stressors among various cultural groups. For example, in the United States, a much higher number of women than men are diagnosed with anxiety and stress-related disorders (Barlow & Durand, 1995). Stress syndromes are also highly prevalent among refugee and veteran groups because of related traumas, including torture, which has lagged in empirical study yet holds potential for informing concepts of coping and adaptation (Basoglu, 1997). Post-traumatic stress syndromes (PTSDs) are also seen in non-Western civilian populations—for example, associated with natural disasters and with systems of social order involving widespread violence against women or other targeted hardships or injustices. Boehnlein and Kinzie (1997) point out complexities in cross-cultural analysis and treatment of PTSD. For example, although reconstructing meaning and purpose in lives affected by trauma is highly culturally determined (e.g., cultural symbols, communication patterns, identity and values, and healing approaches), the cognitive disruption and existential pain constitute a universal human response to severe traumatic events. Issues of diagnostic and measurement appropriateness across cultures also remain in question, signaling the importance of cultural consultation in rendering culturally sensitive assessment and intervention with highly stressed and trauma-related cases.

Diversity is, of course, layered, as illustrated by Sharma and Sud's (1990) findings of consistently higher test anxiety among girls, irrespective of culture (the United States and four Asian and four European nations), as well as differences in the levels and patterns of test anxiety both within and among the various Asian and European and American samples. Although understanding values, beliefs, or norms that appear to be generally patterned within a group can be helpful, stereotyped or overly generalized expectations can lead to error. For example, Alferi and colleagues (2001) report that Hispanic cultural norms of family serving as a key source of support were not reflected in their findings of support beyond spouses among low-income Hispanic women in early stages of breast cancer. The reasons for this outcome were not clear in the study, illustrating the importance of case-by-case assessment and the appreciation that coping and social support are dynamic phenomena that can change over the course of sustained stress and distress.

People who feel marginalized from the sociocultural and political mainstream, such as persons of color, gays and lesbians, the elderly, and the physically and mentally challenged, "are more likely to experience increased numbers of stressful events in the form of discrimination, poverty, humiliation, and harassment" (Castillo, 1997, p. 173). Broad-based exposure to prejudice and inequalities not only poses a threat to negative health outcomes such as elevated blood pressure, heart conditions, low birth weight, higher infant mortality, HIV/AIDS, other somatic health problems, and mental health (e.g., depression, distress); it can also include differential exposure, susceptibility, and responses—both social and biological—to factors such as these (Krieger, 1999, p. 332):

- *Economic and social deprivation:* at work, at home, in the neighborhood, and other relevant socioeconomic regions.
- *Toxic substances and hazardous conditions* (pertaining to physical, chemical, and biological agents): at work, at home, and in the neighborhood.

- *Socially inflicted trauma* (mental, physical, or sexual, ranging from verbal to violent): at work, at home, in the neighborhood, and in society at large.
- *Targeted marketing of legal and illegal psychoactive substances* (alcohol, tobacco, other drugs) and other commodities (e.g., junk food).
- *Inadequate health care*, by health care facilities and by specific providers (including access to care, diagnosis, and treatment).

Issues related to life course development and the various roles and circumstances we inhabit over a lifetime are also important considerations in understanding stress, its costs or effects, and how we attempt to manage stress. For example, Greenberg (1996) reviews a range of life domains and roles relative to some of the factors that can contribute to stress:

- *Stress and educational attainment:* pressure for grades, performance, or competition; combined pressure for many of work, school, and family life; lifestyle changes that often involve health risks; debt; self-doubt; loss of support relationships and the need to create new ones; developmental challenges that often correspond with the years one is in school; confrontation with challenges to one's beliefs, values, and expectations; additional stressors for minority students (e.g., people of color, those for whom English is not a first language, older students, students with disabilities).
- *Family stress:* the changing definition and form of family (e.g., nuclear, extended, blended, family of choice, multigenerational, dual-career, single parent); financial concerns; separation/divorce; family planning; parenting; relationship conflict; role overload or conflict.
- *Aging and stress:* loss and adjustment in later years—for example, loss of valued roles, independence, health and physical strength, and mobility; loss of others and grief; the need to accept caregiving, role reversals, death and dying; losses of dignity; stereotyping or condescending attitudes or behavior from others.
- *Occupational stress:* stressors directly related to work, such as work overload or conflict, time pressures, poor working conditions, exposure to dangers of various kinds, lack of job security, thwarted goals or advancement, constraints on decision making or options, poor relations with boss/subordinate/co-workers, office politics, etc.

However, occupational stress is often used to convey not just stress due to the job but also stress that workers bring to the job. Increasingly, employers are becoming attentive to the cumulative and dangerous effects of unchecked stress on workers. Stress research and interventions associated with work can be particularly informative in the overarching picture provided. Table 15.1 provides an illustration of this. Note the multiple levels and life domains that can carry stress and need to be considered for an inclusive assessment. This stress evaluation grid is by no means totally comprehensive but does provide a useful reminder that stress is best thought of in pluralistic ways and that interventions can, similarly, span a wide range of options that are well suited to the person(s) and circumstances. (See also Learning Activity 15.1)

THE PHYSIOLOGY OF BREATHING AND STRESS

An overview of the physiology of breathing is helpful in explaining what happens to the mind/body when breathing is disordered. The function of breathing is to supply the body with oxygen. Respiration (inspiration) oxygenates body cells, and ventilation (expiration) removes excess carbon dioxide. Inhalation or respiration brings air into the lungs. The heart and lungs work together. The heart takes the oxygen-rich blood from the lungs and pumps the blood through the aorta to all parts of the body. The oxygen-poor blood—carrying carbon dioxide—is pumped to the lungs for the exchange of gases. From the lungs, some of the oxygen moves from the air into the bloodstream. At the same time, carbon dioxide moves from the blood into air and is breathed out (ventilation).

Metabolic activity provides oxygenation to the body, a process achieved by blood circulation or by the oxygen transport system that adjusts the amount of oxygen delivery needed. When there is an increase in metabolic demand, a homeostatic (stable state of equilibrium or balance) adjustment can contribute "to physiological by-products favoring a compromise that may result in chronic graded hypoxia" (Fried, 1993, p. 302). Fried distinguishes between hypoxia (decreased oxygen availability) and anoxia (no oxygen) (p. 302). Hyperventilation can be viewed as evidence of hypoxia and as one extreme on a continuum of stress reactions. According to Fried (1993), hyperventilation does not describe behavior but rather its outcome: hypocapnia, or decreased alveolar carbon dioxide (p. 305): "Hypocapnia impairs all organ systems, including muscle, myocardial tissue, and nerves, but especially the blood and arteries. . . . Hypocapnia causes profound cerebral and peripheral arterial vasoconstriction, reducing blood flow to body extremities and to the brain" (Fried, 1993, p. 306). One of the most important symptoms of stress is hyperventilation, or disordered breathing and hypocapnia (Fried, 1993, p. 306). Box 15.1 lists the various symptoms reported by

TABLE 15.1 Occupational Stress Evaluation Grid (OSEG)

Levels	Stressors	Interventions Formal	Interventions Informal
Sociocultural	Racism; sexism Ecological shifts Economic downturns Political changes Military crises	Elections Lobbying/political action Public education Trade associations	Grass roots organizing Petitions Demonstrations Migration Spouse employment
Organizational	Hiring policies Plant closings Layoffs, relocation Automation, market shifts, retraining Organizational priorities	Corporate decision Reorganization New management model Management consultant (inservice/retraining)	Social activities Contests; incentives Manager involvement and ties with workers Continuing education Moonlighting
Work setting	Task (time, speed, autonomy, creativity) Supervision Coworkers Ergonomics Participation in decision making	Supervisor meetings Health/safety meetings Union grievance Employee involvement Quality circles Job redesign Inservice training	Slow down/speed up Redefine tasks Support of other workers Sabotage, theft Quit, change jobs
Interpersonal	Divorce, separation, marital discord Conflict, family/friend Death, illness in family Intergenerational conflict Legal/financial difficulties Early parenthood	Legal/financial services Leave of absence Counseling, psychotherapy Insurance plans Family therapy Loans/credit unions Day care	Seek social support/advice Seek legal/financial assistance Self-help groups Vacation/sick days Child care
Psychological	Neurosis, mental illness Disturbance of affect, cognition, or behavior Ineffective coping skills Poor self-image Poor communication Addictive behavior	Employee assistance (referral/in house) Counseling, psychotherapy Medication Supervisory training Stress management Workshop	Seek support from friends, family, church Self-help groups/books Self-medication Recreation, leisure Sexual activity "Mental health" days
Biological	Disease, disability Sleep, appetite disturbance Chemical dependency Biochemical imbalance Pregnancy	Preplacement screening Counseling Medical treatment Health education Employee assistance Maternity leave	Change sleep/wake habits Bag lunch Self-medication Cosmetics Diets, exercise Consult physician
Physical/environmental	Poor air, climate Noise exposure Toxic substance exposure Poor lighting Radiation exposure Poor equipment design Bad architecture	Protective clothing/equipment Climate control Health/safety committee Interior decoration Muzak Union grievance	Own equipment, decoration Walkman, radio Consult personal physician Letters of complaint

Source: From "A Review of NIOSH Psychological Stress Research–1997," by M. J. Smith, et al., March, 1978, *NIOSH Proceedings of Occupational Stress Conference* (Cincinnati, Ohio: National Institute of Occupational Stress and Health), pp. 27–28. Cited in *Comprehensive Stress Management* by J. S. Greenberg, p. 249, Brown & Berchmark, 1996.

LEARNING ACTIVITY 15.1 — Cultural and Life Course Variations of Stress

In this learning activity, we ask you to reflect alone and with colleagues on ways that differences in culture and life course development can affect what is experienced as stressful and subsequent implications for stress management relevant to these differences.

First, on your own, think of two personally stressful times of life that are separated by at least a few years. Consider environmental context, language, and ethnohistory factors (e.g., education, economics, political and legal, cultural values and lifestyle, kinship and social relations, religion and philosophy, technology) that you believe may have been shaping why and how that event or set of conditions was stressful. For example, were there values about responsibility, threats to something cherished, or external constraints that were prominent?

Repeat this exercise with the second stressful time of life. What are some differences you notice that may be partly due to the different points of life—for example, differences due to experience, personal power or resources, or changed roles from one's youth to adulthood? What are some implications for these contextual differences in stress and coping for directions you would see appropriate for stress management intervention?

In a group exercise, compare selected parts of your self-analysis with those of student colleagues. What differences do you notice in environmental, cultural, or life course development factors that may be related to how stress arose, was experienced, coping efforts, and what would be most useful?

---

stress sufferers that were identical to symptoms of the hyperventilation syndrome. As Box 15.1 reveals, disordered breathing influences emotions and can contribute to psychophysiological disorders.

The practice of diaphragmatic or abdominal breathing, in contrast to chest or shallow breathing, balances the sympathetic and parasympathetic nervous systems. These two systems govern the internal organs and blood vessels, affecting heart rate, blood pressure, unconscious breathing, and digestion. The sympathetic nervous system (SNS) activates the stress response and disordered breathing. The SNS is critically important for self-protection, and the altered breathing is a normal part of the stress response. The SNS responds to threatening situations. The parasympathetic nervous system (PNS) produces the relaxation response that can evoke deep, abdominal breathing. The PNS performs a homeostatic and balancing function.

The pattern of breathing influences the body and mind, as shown in a person's physical, emotional, psychological, and spiritual well-being (Patel, 1993, p. 119). Chest or shallow breathing created by stress or by learned breathing patterns causes psychological and/or physiological states of disequilibrium, or lack of homeostasis with the body and mind systems. Because there is a reciprocal relationship between breathing and the mind, diaphragmatic or abdominal breathing leads to mental relaxation.

BOX 15.1 — SYMPTOMS REPORTED BY STRESS SUFFERERS THAT ARE IDENTICAL TO THE HYPERVENTILATION SYNDROME

- Tension (a "feeling of tension," muscle ache)
- Irritability, low frustration tolerance
- Anxiety (apprehension, heightened vigilance)
- Dyspnea (inability to catch one's breath, choking sensation, feeling of suffocation, frequent sighing, chest heaving, lump in throat)
- Fatigue, tiredness, burnout
- Insomnia
- Heart palpitations (pounding in chest, seemingly accelerated pulse rate, sensation of heaviness or weight on the chest, diffuse chest pain)
- Depression, restlessness, nervousness
- Dizzy spells, shakiness, trembling
- Coldness of the hands and feet, occasional tingling sensations
- Inability to concentrate
- Bloating

Source: Adapted from "The Role of Respiration in Stress and Stress Control: Toward a Theory of Stress as a Hypoxic Phenomenon," by R. Fried. In *Principles and Practice of Stress Management*, (2nd ed.), by P. M. Lehrer and R. L. Woolfolk, pp. 310–311. Copyright © 1993 by The Guilford Press. Used by permission.

STEPS FOR BREATHING

Take a little time to answer the following questions:

Do you inflate your chest when you take a deep breath?

Do you experience queasy sensations in your chest or stomach?

Is your breath mostly up in your chest?

Is your breathing shallow?

Do you often feel that you are not getting a full breath?

Do you get mild or more severe headaches, often in the afternoon?

Do you sometimes have painful sensations in your rib cage or shooting pains that make you want to hold your breath?

Are your muscles often tense or sore to the touch?

Do you sigh often?

Do you feel breathless fairly often?

Do you tire easily or wake up tired?

When you are calm and restful, do you breathe more than 15 times a minute? (Hendricks 1995, p. IX)

With a yes answer to any of the above questions, a client may benefit from breathing exercises. We review diaphragmatic breathing here. Hendricks (1995) offers a more extensive review of additional breathing exercises. You can discuss with the client whether breathing exercises might help with his or her presenting concerns. Benefits of conscious breathing exercises can be one or a combination of the following: releases stress and tension, builds energy and endurance, contributes to emotional mastery, prevents and heals physical problems, manages pain, contributes to graceful aging, enhances mental concentration and physical performance, and promotes psychospiritual transformation (Hendricks, 1995, pp. 7–31).

When you are teaching awareness orientation to breathing or teaching breathing exercise, consider the client's age, gender, class, and ethnicity. Also, determine whether the client has any medical or physical condition that could make these breathing exercises inappropriate. If you or the client has any doubts, instruct the client to confer with his or her primary care physician and receive approval to engage in the exercise *before* you begin the instruction. Also, refer to the section on "Contraindications and Adverse Effects of Diaphragmatic Breathing" later in the chapter.

Awareness of Breathing

The awareness of breathing orientation is a technique used to help a person become aware and conscious of her or his breathing. The orientation process has five steps:

1. Ask client to get in a comfortable position (in a recliner chair or whatever is comfortable) with legs apart, the feet relaxed and off to the side; one arm is bent at the elbow and placed on the navel; the other arm and hand are relaxed and alongside the body.
2. Instruct the client to breathe slowly through the nose and to become aware and conscious; he or she is to feel the movement of the abdomen when inhaling and exhaling.
3. Instruct the client to keep breathing slowly and deeply, and to be relaxed.
4. After several minutes of the client's breathing while lying down, instruct the client to sit up straight with the spine erect; he or she is to place one hand below the navel and the other hand on the upper chest.
5. Ask the client to notice the movement of the hands during inhalation and exhalation, and to assess which hand moves more. If the hand on the upper chest moves more than the other hand, it probably means the client is breathing from the chest rather than the abdomen, in which case the breathing is shallow and not as deep as diaphragmatic or abdominal breathing.

For some clients, this exercise brings awareness or consciousness of breathing before the rationale for diaphragmatic breathing and training is presented. We have found that providing this awareness exercise will enhance diaphragmatic breathing training for some clients. For other clients, the practitioner can begin with the rationale and overview for breathing, and start the diaphragmatic breathing training without the awareness exercise, and in Learning Activity 15.2.

How to Work with Breath

Table 15.2 presents ways to work with breath, differentiating among dimensions of breath and type of problems in breathing. For example, the practitioner can (1) observe the location of the client's breath—chest for problem breathing, belly for relaxed breathing, (2) bring awareness to the client of the depth of breath—shallow for problem breathing, deep for relaxed breathing, (3) determine the rate of breathing—fast for problem breathing, slow for relaxed breathing, (4) observe whether the client holds or has a rapid exhalation of the breath, and (5) observe whether the client's inhalation is choppy and shallow. For any of these issues, the helping practitioner can teach one of the appropriate exercises in Table 15.2, and in Learning Activity 15.2.

Empowered Consent for Breathing Exercises

The helper needs to act in good faith to protect clients' rights and welfare by informing them adequately about the breathing exercises. The helper should obtain clients'

TABLE 15.2 How to Work with the Breath

Dimensions of the breath	Problems in breathing	Relaxed breathing	Levels of interaction
Location of breath	Chest	Belly	Observe only
Depth of breath	Shallow	Deep	Bring to awareness
Rate of breath	Fast	Slow	Teach or use one of the breath exercises to modify problems in breathing
Exhalation of breath	Holding or rapid	Released (often with sound) slowly	Teach or use one of the breath exercises to modify problems in breathing
Inhalation of breath	Choppy and shallow	Deep and smooth	Teach or use one of the breath exercises to modify problems in breathing

Note: All the above apply to both the helper and the client.

consent and willingness to use the exercise(s) prior to offering any instruction. As part of the consent process, the helper should give clients the following information:

1. Description of breathing exercises
2. Rationale, purpose, and potential benefits of the breathing exercises
3. Description of the helper's role
4. Description of the client's role
5. Description of possible risks or discomforts
6. Description of expected benefits
7. Estimated time needed for the exercise
8. Answers to client's questions about the breathing exercises
9. Explanation of client's right to discontinue the exercises at any time
10. Summary and clarification/exploration of client's reactions

You can use these items to construct a written consent form that clients will sign indicating that they have received this information. Also, refer to the contraindications on page 478 for use of diaphragmatic breathing. If you or any clients have doubts about performing these exercises, clients should consult with their primary care physician.

Rationale and Overview for Breathing Training

The rationale and overview for breathing training could be presented like this:

> A lot of people do not breathe deeply enough. Learning to breathe with greater use of your diaphragm or abdomen can increase your oxygen intake. This way of breathing uses the full capacity of the lungs and enables you to inhale about seven times more oxygen than with normal shallow breathing. Also, you can practice this any time during the day—while you are waiting in a line or in your car stuck in traffic. Increased oxygen capacity can have many mental and physical benefits. Breathing training stimulates the PNS or relaxation response, and calms the central nervous system. In the beginning you might experience a little discomfort or lightheadedness, but such discomfort is rare. The benefits you could derive are numerous and include the following: releases stress and tension, builds energy and endurance, contributes to emotional mastery, prevents and heals physical problems, helps with pain management, contributes to graceful aging, and enhances mental concentration and physical performance. There are no known risks in learning and practicing breathing exercises, although for some clients there may be contraindications. If you feel any pain or discomfort, which is very unlikely, we will stop immediately. The process will include training you in abdominal breathing, or breathing with your diaphragm. We can explore other breathing exercises that you might find helpful. You will practice the breathing exercises during the week. If you practice once a day, you will spend five or six minutes. The time is doubled if you practice twice a day. Also, you will learn to use deep breathing when you are in stressful situations, or when you need a break, or for a refreshing relief to reenergize yourself. You can be trained to use the breathing exercises in one session. You can practice during the week, and if you feel the need, we can check in by phone to see how you are doing. Practice helps you incorporate deep breathing in your everyday life and in stressful situations. How does that sound?

Diaphragmatic Breathing

It may be useful to start training either by describing how a diaphragm works or with a picture that illustrates the diaphragm as a wide, fan-shaped muscle below the lungs that contracts and relaxes, pulling air in or pushing it out, respectively. You can use the following steps as a guide in teaching this exercise. (Also see Learning Activity 15.2)

1. The helper provides the client with a rationale. You can say to the client, "Notice that at the start of each breath your stomach rises and the lower edge of your rib cage expands. If your breathing is too shallow, diaphragmatic breathing should help you acquire a deeper pattern of breathing." The helper explains to the client that when one inhales, the muscle fibers of the diaphragm contract and are drawn downward toward the abdomen. A picture may help the client to visualize the movement of the diaphragm at the beginning of diaphragmatic training. Diaphragmatic training includes six steps. This exercise is also called belly or abdominal breathing because the movement of the abdomen is out during inhalation and in during exhalation.

2. The helper instructs the client to get in a comfortable position and to breathe through the nose. Legs are comfortably apart, with feet relaxed and off to the side.

3. The client is told to bend the arms at the elbow and place the thumbs gently below the rib cage; the rest of the hand and fingers are pointing toward each other and perpendicular to the body. Then the client is asked to visualize the diaphragm upon inhaling to see its muscular fibers contract and draw downward. The helper tells the client upon exhalation to visualize the diaphragm being drawn upward as the air is pushed out of the lungs and forms a cone shape: "As you inhale, extend your abdomen outward, and as you exhale, allow your abdomen to come inward. You may wish to exaggerate this movement. Always breathe through your nostrils in an even and smooth manner. When you start, it is helpful to focus on the rise and fall of your hand as you inhale and exhale. Focus on each inhalation: Your hand goes up, and your belly comes out. On your exhalation, press in and back on your abdominal muscles (allowing the abdomen to draw inward toward the spine), and your hand goes down. Remember the diaphragm is a muscle, and like any muscle it can be trained and strengthened."

4. The client is instructed to simulate the movement of the diaphragm with the hands. The thumbs are just below the rib cage on the abdomen, and the fingers are slightly interlaced. As the client inhales, the interlaced fingers are flattened to simulate the diaphragm being drawn downward. On the exhalation, the client is instructed to curve the fingers so they are cone shaped, simulating the movement of the diaphragm being drawn upward as the air is being pushed out of the lungs. On the inhalation, the muscle fibers of the diaphragm contract and are drawn downward. The diaphragm becomes less cone shaped and almost flat. As the diaphragm descends, it presses on the stomach, liver, and other organs, and gently massages and stimulates them: "When you exhale, the muscles contract and the diaphragm becomes cone shaped and pushes upward toward the lungs. Visualize your diaphragm working and exercising the internal organs of digestion and elimination, massaging and kneading them for each inhalation and exhalation, forcing the blood into the organs and then squeezing the blood out. This way of breathing uses the full capacity of your lungs" (Birch, 1995, p. 45).

5. The client is instructed to sit up with the spine erect and eyes closed, to visualize the diaphragm's position while inhaling and exhaling, and to feel the abdomen rising and falling like the tide.

6. The helper instructs the client to practice diaphragmatic breathing for homework at least twice daily. The helper

---

LEARNING ACTIVITY 15.2 — Breathing Exercises

In this learning activity, you will use a breathing exercise so that your practice with conscious breathing will help with your teaching others.

1. Try the breathing awareness exercise and the diaphragmatic breathing exercise presented in the chapter. Do the exercise for several days so that you become familiar with it and experience its effects.

2. Try to use the diaphragmatic breathing in real, stressful situations: any time that you need to feel calmer, feel more in control, or become energized.

3. During the two-week period, keep a journal or log of each practice session, describing what you experienced in your practice. Record your overall energy and level of relaxation in what you perceive as a consequence of your practice with the breathing exercises.

reminds the client to find a time and place to practice that will be free of distractions and interruptions. The client is also instructed to use abdominal or diaphragmatic breathing when in a stressful situation or to reenergize the mind or body. This way of breathing uses the full capacity of the lungs. It enables one to inhale about seven times more oxygen than with normal shallow breathing. Instruct the client to use diaphragmatic breathing at any time during the day. Learning Activity 15.2 outlines activities for implementing breathing exercises.

CONTRAINDICATIONS AND ADVERSE EFFECTS OF DIAPHRAGMATIC BREATHING

Deep abdominal/diaphragmatic breathing may not be helpful for everyone. For example, some people doing these exercises may develop cramps. Fried (1993) offers clients the following instructions:

> If an exercise causes pain or discomfort, stop it immediately. Also, do not do any exercise if you have any physical or medical condition or any injury that would contraindicate its safety. Among such conditions are the following:
>
> 1. Muscle or other tissue or organ malformation or injury—for example, sprained or torn muscles, torticolis, fractures, or recent surgery.
> 2. Any condition causing metabolic acidosis, where hyperventilation may be compensatory such as diabetes, kidney disease, heart disease, severe hypoglycemia, etc. If you are in doubt, please bring your condition to my attention.
> 3. Low blood pressure or any related condition, such as syncope (fainting). Deep abdominal breathing may cause a significant decrease in blood pressure.
> 4. Insulin-dependent diabetes. If you are an insulin-dependent diabetic, you should not do this or any other deep relaxation exercise without the expressed approval by your physician and his or her close monitoring of your insulin needs. (Fried, 1993, p. 323)

Pregnancy may also affect the client's capacity to do some of the breathing. Smokers also have more trouble with breathing exercises, and Hendricks (1995) does not use breathing until after a person stops smoking.

MODEL EXAMPLE: DIAPHRAGMATIC BREATHING

In this model example, we present a narrative account of how two breathing exercises might be used with Yoshi, a 49-year-old male Japanese American air traffic controller.

1. *Rationale:* First, we explain to Yoshi that learning to breathe with his diaphragm or abdomen can increase his oxygen intake. We tell Yoshi that this way of breathing uses the full capacity of the lungs and enables him to inhale about seven times more oxygen than with normal shallow breathing. We tell him that the benefits of diaphragmatic breathing include releasing stress and tension and enhancing mental concentration. We provide an overview by telling him that the process will include training in diaphragmatic breathing. We tell Yoshi that he can practice during the week and use deep breathing in stressful situations. We confirm Yoshi's willingness to try diaphragmatic breathing and answer any questions he may have about the procedure. We provide all the elements of information illustrated in the example of a rationale previously described.

2. *Show Diagram of Diaphragm and Instructions About Position:* We show Yoshi a diagram of the position of the diaphragm for exhalation and inhalation. Yoshi is instructed to get into a comfortable position and to breathe through his nose. He is to place one hand on his navel and the other hand just below his rib cage. We request that he breathe through his nose, notice his breath (while breathing through his nose), and observe what happens to his hand as he exhales and inhales. We ask Yoshi what the movement is like for the hand on his navel and the hand below his rib cage. For example, is the movement of the hands the same, or does one hand move more than the other? If one hand moves more, is it the hand on the rib cage or the navel? We explain to him that if he is breathing diaphragmatically, the hand on the navel is moving more during the exhalation and inhalation than the hand below the rib cage. We ask Yoshi to relax and just notice his breathing.

3. *Visualize the Movement of the Diaphragm and Placement of the Hands:* We ask Yoshi to bend his arms and place his thumbs gently below his rib cage (we model the position of the hands for him). Yoshi is instructed to place the rest of his fingers on each hand perpendicular to his body. We ask him to visualize the diaphragm, and as he inhales, we remind him that the muscular fibers of the diaphragm contract and are drawn downward. We describe—as he exhales—the diaphragm being drawn upward and forming a cone shape as the air is pushed out of the lungs.

4. *Simulation of the Diaphragm with the Fingers:* Yoshi is instructed to simulate the movement of the diaphragm with his hands. We tell him, as he inhales, to straighten the fingers out flat. As he exhales, he is to curve the fin-

gers so that they become cone shaped. We ask him to do this for several breaths, simulating the movement of the diaphragm while his breathing is gentle and relaxed.

5. *Diaphragmatic Breathing While Sitting:* Yoshi is instructed to sit up with his spine erect, his eyes closed, and his hands on his lap, his knees, or wherever is comfortable for him. We ask him to visualize his abdomen expanding or rising and falling like the tide, and to breathe in this relaxed fashion for a couple of minutes.

6. *Homework Practice and in Vivo Use:* Yoshi is instructed to practice diaphragmatic breathing twice a day for five minutes, once after getting up in the morning and once in the late afternoon or early evening. We remind Yoshi to find a quiet place to practice that is free of distractions and interruptions. Yoshi is instructed to visualize the movement of his diaphragm while he is practicing and when he uses abdominal breathing in stressful situations.

STRESS INOCULATION: PROCESS AND USES

Stress management can, and typically does, involve change interventions that are integrated by the helper and the client into an integrated set that is appropriate to case-specific factors such as the nature of the stressors and goals. For example, Antoni and colleagues (2001) describe a stress management intervention for women diagnosed with breast cancer that includes 10 two-hour sessions with in-session didactic material, experiential components, and between-session assignments (e.g., practicing relaxation techniques and monitoring stress responses). This included both problem-focused (e.g., active coping and planning, replacement of doubt appraisals with a sense of confidence via cognitive restructuring) as well as emotion-focused (e.g., relaxation training, emotional expression, and use of social support) coping strategies. This was an intervention designed for a certain kind of life stress. The specific array for a different type of conditions or client(s) may be revised accordingly. For example, many forms of stress are due to more chronic and pervasive factors, such as poverty, oppression, trauma, and long-standing conditions of need. Understanding how stress is experienced and what is typically involved in the coping process (both the person and environmental factors)—content we reviewed earlier in this chapter—will guide your selection of change strategies.

Stress inoculation is an approach to teaching both physical and cognitive coping skills. As the name implies, the aim is to enhance resistance to stress by better preparing the client to respond more effectively when stressors are encountered. Meichenbaum (1993) states that stress inocula-tion training "helps clients acquire sufficient knowledge, self-understanding, and coping skills to facilitate better ways of handling expected stressful encounters. Stress inoculation training combines elements of Socratic and didactic teaching, client self-monitoring, cognitive restructuring, problem solving, self-instructional and relaxation training, behavioral and imagined rehearsal, and environmental change" (p. 381). Eliot and Eisdorfer (1982) and Meichenbaum (1993) classify stressful events as the following types:

1. One event that is time limited and not chronic, such as a medical biopsy, surgery, a dental procedure, an oral examination.
2. One event that triggers a series of stressful reactions, such as job loss, divorce, death of loved one, natural or man-made disaster, or sexual assault.
3. Chronic and intermittent events, such as musical performances, athletic competitions, military combat, recurrent headaches.
4. Chronic and continual events, such as chronic medical or mental illness, marital conflict, chronic physical–emotional or psychological abuse, some professions—nursing, teaching, or policework (Meichenbaum, 1993, p. 373).

Stress inoculation training varies with the type of stress involved in the case and the particular coping and stress management skills incorporated, but is consistent in having (1) an educational phase (helping the client better understand the nature of stress and stress effects), (2) a skill acquisition and rehearsal phase (developing and practicing a repertoire of coping skills), and (3) an application and generalization phase (using coping skills in conditions approximating problem situations as well as those with potential stress effects. In a meta-analytic review, Saunders, Driskell, Johnston, and Salas (1996) found stress inoculation training to be an effective means of reducing performance anxiety, reducing more generalized anxiety, and enhancing performance under stress, with no evidence among the studies reviewed of limitations on the application of stress inoculation to applied training environments. Box 15.2 presents a sample of stress inoculation research used with a variety of concerns. These include academic performance, anger management and reduction, anxiety associated with wide-ranging life experiences, child and family issues, athletic performance, exercise, pain management, stress burnout, dental treatment, use with older adults, hypertension, and trauma.

Although Saunders and colleagues (1996) specifically tested for differences in populations in terms of high and low anxiety, their review does not speak to other dimensions of client populations that could make a difference relative to

BOX 15.2 STRESS INOCULATION RESEARCH

Academic performance

Kiselica, M. S., Baker, S. B., Thomas, R. N., & Reedy, S. (1994). Effects of stress inoculation training on anxiety, stress, and academic performance among adolescents. *Journal of Counseling Psychology, 41,* 335–342.

Anger

Deffenbacher, J., McNamara K., Stark, R., & Sabadell, P. (1991). A combination of cognitive relaxation and behavioral coping skills in the reduction of anger. *Journal of College Student Development, 26,* 114–212.

Timmons, P. L., Oehlert, M. E., Sumerall, S. W., Timmons, C. W., et al. (1997). Stress inoculation training for maladaptive anger: Comparison of group counseling versus computer guidance. *Computers in Human Behavior, 13,* 51–64.

Wilcox, D., & Dowrick, P. W. (1992). Anger management with adolescents. *Residential Treatment for Children and Youth, 9,* 29–39.

Anxiety

Burnley, M. C., Cross, P. A., & Spanos, N. P. (1993). The effects of stress inoculation training and skills training on the treatment of speech anxiety. *Imagination, Cognition and Personality, 12,* 355–366.

Fontana, A. M., Hyra, D., Godfrey, L., & Cermak, L. (1999). Impact of a peer-led stress inoculation training intervention on state anxiety and heart rate in college students. *Journal of Applied Biobehavioral Research, 4,* 45–63.

Saunders, T., Driskell, J., Johnston, J. H., & Salas, E. (1996). The effect of stress inoculation training on anxiety and performance. *Journal of Occupational Health Psychology, 1,* 170–186.

Schneider, W. J., & Nevid, J. S. (1993). Overcoming math anxiety: A comparison of stress inoculation training and systematic desensitization. *Journal of College Student Development, 34,* 283–288.

Asthma

Benedito-Monleon, C., & Lopez-Andreu, J. A. (1994). Psychological factors in childhood asthma. *Behavioural and Cognitive Psychotherapy, 22,* 153–161.

Athletic performance

Kerr, G., & Leith, L. (1993). Stress management and athletic performance. *Sport Psychologist, 7,* 221–231.

Burnout among nurses

Freedy, J. R., & Hobfoll, S. E. (1994). Stress inoculation for reduction of burnout: A conservation of resources approach. *Anxiety, Stress and Coping: An International Journal, 6,* 311–325.

Cancer

Elsesser, K., Van Berkel, M., Sartory, G., & Biermann-Gocke, W. (1994). The effects of anxiety management training on psychological variables and immune parameters in cancer patients: A pilot study. *Behavioural and Cognitive Psychotherapy, 22,* 13–23.

Children and adolescents

Maag, J. W., & Kotlash, J. (1994). Review of stress inoculation training with children and adolescents: Issues and recommendations. *Behavior Modification, 18,* 443–469.

Dental treatment

Law, A., Logan, H., & Baron, R. S. (1994). Desire for control, felt control, and stress inoculation training during dental treatment. *Journal of Personality and Social Psychology, 67,* 926–936.

Exercise

Kerr, G., & Goss, J. (1996). The effects of a stress management program on injuries and stress levels. *Journal of Applied Sport Psychology, 8,* 109–117.

Long, B. C. (1993). Aerobic conditioning (jogging) and stress inoculation interventions. An exploratory study of coping. Special issue: Exercise and psychological well-being. *International Journal of Sport Psychology, 24,* 94–109.

Hypertension

Garcia-Vera, M. P., Labrador, F. J., & Sanz, J. (1997). Stress management training for essential hypertension: A controlled study. *Applied Psychophysiology & Biofeedback, 22*(4), 261–283.

Impulsive behavior

Aeschleman, S. R., & Imes, C. (1999). Stress inoculation training for impulsive behaviors in adults with traumatic brain injury. *Journal of Rational–Emotive & Cognitive Behavior Therapy, 17,* 51–65.

Military intense operations

Rosebush, P. A. (1998). Psychological intervention with military personnel in Rwanda. *Military Medicine, 163,* 559–563.

Older adults

Kelly, K., Hayslip, B., Hobdy, J., Servaty, H., Ennis, M., & Pavur, R. (1998). The relationship of cortisol to practice-related gains in intelligence among older persons. *Experimental Aging Research, 24,* 217–230.

Lopez, M. A., & Silber, A. (1991). Stress management for the elderly: A preventive approach. *Clinical Gerontologist, 10,* 73–76.

Pain

Ross, M., & Berger, R. (1996). Effects of stress inoculation training on athletes' postsurgical pain and rehabilitation after orthopedic injury. *Journal of Consulting and Clinical Psychology, 64,* 406–410.

Whitmarsh, B. G., & Alderman, R. B. (1993). Role of psychological skills training in increasing athletic pain tolerance. *Sport Psychologist, 7,* 388–399.

Parents

Jay, S. M., & Elliott, C. H. (1990). A stress inoculation program for parents whose children are undergoing painful medical procedures. *Journal of Consulting and Clinical Psychology, 58,* 799–804.

> **BOX 15.2 STRESS INOCULATION RESEARCH** *CONTINUED*
>
> *Prevention*
> Hains, A. A., & Ellmann, S. W. (1994). Stress inoculation training as a preventative intervention for high school youths. *Journal of Cognitive Psychotherapy, 8,* 219–232.
>
> *Stepcouples*
> Fausel, D. (1995). Stress inoculation training for stepcouples. *Marriage and Family Review, 21,* 137–155.
>
> *Trauma*
> Davidson, J. R., & Connor, K. M. (1999). Management of posttraumatic stress disorder: Diagnostic and therapeutic issues. *Journal of Clinical Psychiatry, 60* (Suppl. 18), 33–38.
>
> Falsetti, S. A. (1997). The decision-making process of choosing a treatment for patients with civilian trauma-related PTSD. *Cognitive & Behavioral Practice, 4,* 99–121.
> Foss, E. B. (1997). Trauma and women: Course, predictors, and treatment. *Journal of Clinical Psychiatry, 58* (Suppl. 9), 25–28.
> Nayak, M. B., Resnick, H., & Holmes, M. M. (1999). Treating health concerns within the context of childhood sexual assault: A case study. *Journal of Traumatic Stress, 12,* 101–109.
> Triffleman, E., Carroll, K., & Kellogg, S. (1999). Substance dependence posttraumatic stress disorder therapy: An integrated cognitive–behavioral approach. *Journal of Substance Abuse Treatment, 17*(½), 3–14.

good fit or effectiveness. In one of a limited number of culture-specific studies, Chiu (1997) concluded that the basic principles of stress inoculation, such as fostering realistic advance preparation for future stressors, will have cross-cultural applicability, although content and selection of training components should be reflective of individual differences and cultural characteristics. In her study of changes over time of newly arrived Asian students during their first year at a U.S. university, Chiu found outcome differences for students with low, moderate, and high levels of anticipatory fear. Implications of this research include tailoring interventions to clients with different needs (such as anticipatory fear) and different coping histories, as well as exploration of specific coping strategies likely to be more readily applied by people of different cultures.

SEVEN COMPONENTS OF STRESS INOCULATION

Stress inoculation* has seven major components:
1. Rationale
2. Information giving
3. Acquisition and practice of direct-action coping skills
4. Acquisition and practice of cognitive coping skills
5. Application of all coping skills to problem-related situations
6. Application of all coping skills to potential problem situations
7. Homework and follow-up

A detailed description of each step associated with these seven parts is presented in the Interview Checklist for Stress Inoculation at the end of this chapter and Learning Activity 15.3.

*We wish to acknowledge the work of Meichenbaum (1993, 1994) in our presentation of stress inoculation training.

Treatment Rationale
Here is an example of a rationale that a helping practitioner might use for stress inoculation.

Purpose
The helper might explain as follows the purpose of stress inoculation for a client having trouble with hostility:

> You find yourself confronted with situations in which your temper gets out of hand. You have trouble managing your anger, especially when you feel provoked. This procedure can help you learn to cope with provoking situations and can help you manage the intensity of your anger when you're in these situations so it doesn't control you.

Overview
Then the helper can give the client a brief overview of the procedure:

> First, we will try to help you understand the nature of your feelings and how certain situations may provoke your feelings and lead from anger to hostility. Next, you will learn some ways to manage this and to cope with situations in which you feel this way. After you learn these coping skills, we will set up situations where you can practice using these skills to help you control your anger. How does this sound to you?

Information Giving
Before learning and applying various coping strategies, the client should be given some information about the nature of a stress reaction and the possible coping strategies that might be used. It is helpful for the client to understand the nature

of a stress reaction and how various coping strategies can help manage the stress. The education phase of stress inoculation helps the client conceptualize reactions to stressful events and builds a foundation for the components.

Three issues should be explained to the client: a framework for the client's emotional reaction, information about the phases of reacting to stress, and examples of types of coping skills and strategies.

Framework for Client's Reaction
In setting a framework, the helper should first explain the nature of the client's reaction to a stressful situation. Although understanding one's reaction may not be sufficient for changing it, the conceptual framework lays some groundwork for beginning the change process. An explanation of some kind of stress (anxiety, hostility, pain) usually involves describing the stress as having two components: physiological arousal and covert self-statements or thoughts that provoke anxiety, hostility, or pain. This explanation may help the client realize that coping strategies must be directed toward the arousal behaviors *and* the cognitive processes. For example, to describe such a framework to a client who has trouble controlling hostility, the helper could say something like this:

> Perhaps you could think about what happens when you get very angry. You might notice that certain things happen to you physically—perhaps your body feels tight, your face may feel warm, you may experience more rapid breathing, or your heart may pound. This is the physical part of your anger. However, there is another thing that probably goes on while you're very angry—that is, what you're thinking. You might be thinking such things as "He had no right to attack me; I'll get back at him; boy, I'll show him who's boss; I'll teach her to keep her mouth shut." These kinds of thoughts only intensify your anger. So the way you interpret and think about an anger-provoking situation also contributes to arousing hostile feelings.

(Note that in the case of this and related examples, we are differentiating between appropriate, legitimate feelings of anger and hostility that leads to abuse or damage.)

Phases of Stress Reactions
After explaining a framework for emotional arousal, the helper should describe the kinds of times or phases when the client's arousal level may be heightened. For example, phobic clients may view their anxiety as one "massive panic reaction." Similarly, clients who are angry, depressed, or in pain may interpret their feelings as one large, continuous reaction that has a certain beginning and end. Clients who interpret their reactions this way may perceive the reaction as too difficult to change because it is so massive and overwhelming.

One way to help the client see the potential for coping with feelings is to describe the feelings by individual stages or phases of reacting to a situation. Meichenbaum (1993, 1994) used four stages to help the client conceptualize the various critical points of a reaction: (1) preparing for a stressful, painful, or provoking situation; (2) confronting and handling the situation or the provocation; (3) coping with critical moments or with feelings of being overwhelmed or agitated during the situation; and (4) rewarding oneself after the stress for using coping skills in the first three phases. Explanation of these stages in the preliminary part of stress inoculation helps the client understand the sequence of coping strategies to be learned. To explain the client's reaction as a series of phases, the helper might say something like this:

> When you think of being angry, you probably just think of being angry for a continuous period of time. However, you might find that your anger is probably not just one big reaction but comes and goes at different points during a provoking situation. The first critical point is when you anticipate the situation and start to get angry. At this point, you can learn to prepare yourself for handling the situation in a manageable way. The next point may come when you're in the middle of the situation and you're very angry. Here you can learn how to confront a provoking situation in a constructive way. There might also be times when your anger really gets intense and you can feel it starting to control you—and perhaps feel yourself losing control. At this time, you can learn how to cope with intense feelings of agitation. Then, after the situation is over, instead of getting angry with yourself for the way you handled it, you can learn to encourage yourself for trying to cope with it. In this procedure, we'll practice using the coping skills at these especially stressful or arousing times.

Information About Coping Skills and Strategies
Finally, the helper should provide some information about the kinds of coping skills and strategies that can be used at these critical points. The helper should emphasize that there is a *variety* of useful coping skills; clients' input in selecting and tailoring these for themselves is *most* important. Allow clients to choose coping strategies that reflect their own pref-

erences. In using stress inoculation, both "direct-action" and "cognitive" coping skills are taught (Meichenbaum, 1993). *Direct-action* coping strategies are designed to help the client use coping behaviors to handle the stress; *cognitive* coping skills are used to give the client coping thoughts (self-statements) to handle the stress. The client should understand that *both* kinds of coping skills are important and that the two serve different functions, although some clients may prefer to rely more on one type than another, depending on their gender and culture. To provide the client with information about the usefulness of these coping skills, the helper might explain them this way:

> In the next phase of this procedure, you'll be learning a lot of different ways to prepare for and handle a provoking situation. Some of these coping skills will help you learn to cope with provoking situations by your actions and behaviors; others will help you handle these situations by the way you interpret and think about the situation. Not all the strategies you learn may be useful or necessary for you, so your input in selecting the ones you prefer to use is important.

Acquisition and Practice of Direct-Action Coping Skills

In this phase of stress inoculation, the client acquires and practices some direct-action coping skills. The helper first discusses and models possible action strategies; the client selects some to use and practices them with the helper's encouragement and assistance. As you may recall, direct-action coping skills are designed to help the client acquire and apply coping behaviors in stressful situations. The most commonly used direct-action coping strategies are these:

1. Collecting objective or factual information about the stressful situation
2. Identifying short-circuit or escape routes or ways to decrease the stress
3. Palliative coping strategies
4. Mental relaxation methods
5. Physical relaxation methods

Information Collection

Collecting objective or factual information about a stressful situation may help the client evaluate the situation more realistically. The assessment process is very helpful in collecting information (see Chapter 9). Moreover, information about a situation may reduce the ambiguity for the client and indirectly reduce the level of threat. For example, for a client who may be confronted with physical pain, information about the source and expected timing of pain can reduce stress. This coping method is widely used in childbirth classes. The women and their "labor coaches" are taught and shown that the experienced pain is actually a uterine contraction. They are given information about the timing and stages of labor and the timing and intensity of contractions so that when labor occurs, their anxiety will not be increased by misunderstanding or a lack of information about what is happening in their bodies.

Collecting information about an anxiety- or anger-engendering situation serves the same purpose. For example, in using stress inoculation to help clients control anger, collecting information about the people who typically provoke them may help. Clients collect information that can help them view provocation as a *task* or a problem to be solved, rather than as a *threat* or a personal attack.

Identification of Escape Routes

Identifying escape routes is a way to help the client cope with stress before it gets out of hand. The idea of an escape route is to short-circuit the explosive or stressful situation or to deescalate the stress before the client behaves in a way that may "blow it." This coping strategy may help abusive clients learn to identify cues that elicit their physical or verbal abuse and to take some preventive action before striking out. This is similar to the stimulus-control self-management strategy discussed in Chapter 18. These escape or prevention routes can be very simple things that the client can *do* to prevent losing control or losing face in the situation. An abusive client could perhaps avoid striking out by counting to 60, leaving the room, or talking about something humorous.

Palliative Coping Strategies

Meichenbaum (1993, 1994) describes palliative coping strategies that may be particularly useful for aversive or stressful situations that cannot be substantially altered or avoided, such as chronic or life-threatening illnesses:

> Train emotionally focused palliative coping skills, especially when the client has to deal with unchangeable and uncontrollable stressors; e.g., perspective taking, selective attention diversion procedures, as in the case of chronic pain patients; adaptive modes of affective expression such as humor, relaxation, and reframing the situation. (Meichenbaum, 1993, p. 384)

Mental Relaxation

Mental relaxation can also help clients cope with stress. This technique may involve attention-diversion tactics: Angry clients can control their anger by concentrating on a problem to solve, counting floor tiles in the room, thinking about a funny or erotic joke, or thinking about something positive about themselves. Attention-diversion tactics are commonly used to help people control pain. Instead of focusing on the pain, the person may concentrate very hard on an object in the room or on the repetition of a word (a mantra) or a number. Again, in the Lamaze method of childbirth, women are taught to concentrate on a "focal point" such as an object in the room or, as the authors used, a picture of a sailboat. In this way, the woman's attention is directed to an object instead of to the tightening sensations in her lower abdomen.

Some people find that mental relaxation is more successful when they use imagery or fantasy. People who enjoy daydreaming or who report a vivid imagination may find imagery a particularly useful way to promote mental relaxation. Generally, imagery as a coping method helps the client go on a fantasy trip instead of focusing on the stress, the provocation, or the pain. For example, instead of thinking about how anxious or angry he feels, the client might learn to fantasize about lying on a warm beach, being on a sailboat, making love, or eating a favorite food (see "Guided Imagery" in Chapter 12). For pain control, the person can imagine different things about the pain. A woman in labor can picture the uterus contracting like a wave instead of thinking about pain. Or a person who experiences pain from a routine source, such as the extraction of a wisdom tooth, can use imagery to change the circumstances producing the pain. Instead of thinking about how terrible and painful it is to have a tooth pulled, the person can imagine that the pain is only the aftermath of intense training for a marathon race or comes from the person being the underdog who was hit in the jaw during a boxing match with the world champion.

Physical Relaxation
Physical relaxation methods are particularly useful for clients who report physiological components of anxiety and anger, such as sweaty palms, rapid breathing or heartbeat, or nausea. Physical relaxation is also a very helpful coping strategy for pain control, because body tension will heighten the sensation of pain. Physical relaxation can be supported by various strategies such as breathing techniques, muscle relaxation, meditation, and exercise. Chapter 16 describes some of these procedures.

Each direct-action strategy should first be explained to the client, with discussion of its purpose and procedure. Several sessions may be required to discuss and model all the possible direct-action coping methods. After the strategies have been described and modeled, the clients should select the particular methods to be used. The number of direct-action strategies used by a client will depend on the intensity of the reaction, the nature of the stress, and the client's preferences. With the helper's assistance, the client should practice using each skill in order to be able to apply it in simulated and *in vivo* situations.

Acquisition and Practice of Cognitive Coping Skills
This part of stress inoculation—the acquisition and practice of cognitive coping skills—is very similar to the cognitive restructuring strategy described earlier in this chapter. The helper models some examples of coping thoughts that the client can use during stressful phases of problem situations; then the client selects and practices substituting coping thoughts for negative or self-defeating thoughts.

Description of Four Phases of Cognitive Coping
As you remember from our discussion of information giving, the helper helps the client understand the nature of an emotional reaction by conceptualizing the reaction by phases. In helping the client acquire cognitive coping skills, the helper may first wish to review the importance of learning to cope at crucial times. The helper can point out that the client can learn a set of cognitive coping skills for each important phase: preparing for the situation, confronting and handling the situation, coping with critical moments in the situation, and rewarding himself or herself after the situation. Note that the first phase concerns coping skills *before* the situation, the second and third phases deal with coping *during* the situation, and the fourth phase concerns coping *after* the situation. The helper can describe these four phases to the client with an explanation similar to this:

> Earlier we talked about how your anger is not just one giant reaction but something that peaks at certain stressful points when you feel provoked or attacked. Now you will learn a method of cognitive control that will help you control any negative thoughts that may lead to hostility and also help you use coping thoughts at stressful points. There are four times that are important in your learning to use coping thoughts, and we'll work on each of these four phases. First is how you interpret the situation initially, and how you think about responding or preparing to respond. Second is actually dealing with the situation. Third is coping with anything that happens during the situation that *really* provokes you. After the situation, you learn to encourage yourself for dealing with your feelings in a way that is not hurtful.

Modeling Coping Thoughts

After explaining the four phases of using cognitive coping skills to the client, the helper models examples of coping statements that are especially useful for each of the four phases.

Meichenbaum (1994) and Meichenbaum and Turk (1976) have provided an excellent summary of the coping statements used by Meichenbaum and Cameron (1973) for anxiety control, by Novaco (1975) for anger control, and by Turk (1975) for pain control. These statements, presented in Table 15.3, are summarized for each of the four coping phases: preparing for the situation, confronting the situation, coping with critical moments, and reinforcing oneself for coping. The helper presents examples of coping statements for each of the four phases of a stress reaction. (Also see Learning Activity 15.3)

Client Selection of Coping Thoughts

After the helper models some possible coping thoughts for each phase, the client should add some or select those that fit. The helper should encourage the client to "try on" and adapt the thoughts in whatever way feels most natural. The client might look for coping statements that he or she has used in other stress-related situations. At this point in the procedure, the helper should be working to tailor a coping program *specifically* for this client. If the client's self-statements are too general, they may lead only to "rote repetition" and not function as effective self-instructions. Also, specific coping statements are more likely to be culturally relevant. The helper might explain the importance of the client's participation like this:

TABLE 15.3 Examples of Coping Thoughts Used in Stress Inoculation

Anxiety	Anger	Pain
I. *Preparing for a stressor* (Meichenbaum & Cameron, 1973) What is it you have to do? You can develop a plan to deal with it. Just think about what you can do about it. That's better than getting anxious. No negative self-statements; just think rationally. Don't worry; worry won't help anything. Maybe what you think is anxiety is eagerness to confront it.	*Preparing for a provocation* (Meichenbaum, 1994) This is going to upset me, but I know how to deal with it. What is it that I have to do? I can work out a plan to handle this. If I find myself getting upset, I'll know what to do. There won't be any need for an argument. Try not to take this too seriously. This could be a testy situation, but I believe in myself. Time for a few deep breaths of relaxation. Feel comfortable, relaxed, and at ease. Easy does it. Remember to keep your sense of humor.	*Preparing for the painful stressor* (Turk, 1975) What is it you have to do? You can develop a plan to deal with it. Just think about what you have to do. Just think about what you can do about it. Don't worry; worrying won't help anything. You have lots of different strategies you can call upon.
II. *Confronting and handling a stressor* (Meichenbaum & Cameron, 1973) Just "psych" yourself up—you can meet this challenge. One step at a time; you can handle the situation. Don't think about fear; just think about what you have to do. Stay relevant. This anxiety is what the doctor said you would feel. It's a reminder to use your coping exercises. This tenseness can be an ally, a cue to cope. Relax; you're in control. Take a slow deep breath. Ah, good.	*Impact and confrontation* (Meichenbaum, 1994) Stay calm. Just continue to relax. As long as I keep my cool, I'm in control. Just roll with the punches; don't get bent out of shape. Think of what you want to get out of this. You don't need to prove yourself. There is no point in getting mad. Don't make more out of this than you have to. I'm not going to let him get to me. Look for the positives. Don't assume the worst or jump to conclusions. It's really a shame that he has to act like this. For someone to be that irritable, he must be awfully unhappy. If I start to get mad, I'll just be banging my head against the wall. So I might as well relax. There is no need to doubt myself. What he says doesn't matter. I'm on top of this situation, and it's under control.	*Confronting and handling the pain* (Turk, 1975) You can meet the challenge. One step at a time; you can handle the situation. Just relax, breathe deeply, and use one of the strategies. Don't think about the pain, just what you have to do. This tenseness can be an ally, a cue to cope. Relax. You're in control; take a slow deep breath. Ah, good. This anxiety is what the trainer said you might feel. That's right; it's the reminder to use your coping skills.

(continued)

TABLE 15.3	Examples of Coping Thoughts Used in Stress Inoculation (continued)	
Anxiety	**Anger**	**Pain**
III. *Coping with the feeling of being overwhelmed* (Meichenbaum & Cameron, 1973) When fear comes, just pause. Keep the focus on the present; what is it you have to do? Label your fear from 0 to 10, and watch it change. You should expect your fear to rise. Don't try to eliminate fear totally; just keep it manageable. You can convince yourself to do it. You can reason your fear away. It will be over shortly. It's not the worst thing that can happen. Just think about something else. Do something that will prevent you from thinking about fear. Describe what is around you. That way you won't think about worrying.	*Coping with arousal* (Meichenbaum, 1994) My muscles are starting to feel tight. Time to relax and slow things down. Getting upset won't help. It's just not worth it to get so angry. I'll let him make a fool of himself. I have a right to be annoyed, but let's keep the lid on. Time to take a deep breath. Let's take the issue point by point. My anger is a signal of what I need to do. Time to instruct myself. I'm not going to get pushed around, but I'm not going haywire either. Try to reason it out. Treat each other with respect. Let's try a cooperative approach. Maybe we are both right. Negatives lead to more negatives. Work constructively. He'd probably like me to get really angry. Well, I'm going to disappoint him. I can't expect people to act the way I want them to. Take it easy, don't get pushy.	*Coping with feelings at critical moments* (Turk, 1975) When pain comes, just pause; keep focusing on what you have to do. What is it you have to do? Don't try to eliminate the pain totally; just keep it manageable. You were supposed to expect the pain to rise; just keep it under control. Just remember, there are different strategies; they'll help you stay in control. When the pain mounts, you can switch to a different strategy; you're in control.
IV. *Reinforcing self-statements* (Meichenbaum & Cameron, 1973) It worked; you did it. Wait until you tell your therapist about this. It wasn't as bad as you expected. You made more out of the fear than it was worth. Your damn ideas—that's the problem. When you control them, you control your fear. It's getting better each time you use the procedures. You can be pleased with the progress you're making. You did it!	*Reflecting on the provocation* (Meichenbaum, 1994) a. *When conflict is unresolved* Forget about the aggravation. Thinking about it only makes you upset. These are difficult situations, and they take time to straighten out. Try to shake it off. Don't let it interfere with your job. I'll get better at this as I get more practice. Remember relaxation. It's a lot better than anger. Don't take it personally. Take a deep breath. b. *When conflict is resolved or coping is successful* I handled that one pretty well. It worked! That wasn't as hard as I thought. It could have been a lot worse. I could have gotten more upset than it was worth. I actually got through that without getting angry. My pride can sure get me into trouble, but when I don't take things too seriously, I'm better off. I guess I've been getting upset for too long when it wasn't even necessary. I'm doing better at this all the time.	*Reinforcing self-statements* (Turk, 1975) Good, you did it. You handled it pretty well. You knew you could do it! Wait until you tell the trainer about which procedures worked best.

Source: From *A clinical handbook: Practical therapist manual for assessing and treating adults with post-traumatic stress disorder*, by D. Meichenbaum, pp. 407–408. Copyright 1994 by Institute Press. Originally published in "The cognitive–behavioral management of anxiety, anger, and pain," by D. Meichenbaum and D. Turk, in *The behavioral management of anxiety, depression, and pain*, by P. O. Davidson (Ed.). Copyright 1976 by Brunner/Mazel. Reprinted by permission of the author.

You know, your input in finding coping thoughts that work for you is very important. I've given you some examples. Some of these you might feel comfortable with, and there may be others you can think of too. What we want to do now is to come up with some specific coping thoughts you can and will use during these four times that fit for *you,* not me or someone else.

Client Practice of Coping Thoughts

After the client selects coping thoughts to use for each phase, the helper instructs the client to practice these self-statements by saying them aloud. This verbal practice is designed to help the client become familiar with the coping thoughts and accustomed to the words. After this practice, the client should also practice the selected coping thoughts in the sequence of the four phases. This practice helps the client learn the timing of the coping thoughts in the application phase of stress inoculation.

The helper can say something like this:

> First, I'd like you to practice using these coping thoughts just by saying them aloud to me. This will help you get used to the words and ideas of coping. Next, let's practice these coping thoughts in the sequence in which you would use them when applying them to a real situation. I'll show you. OK, first I'm anticipating the situation, so I'm going to use coping statements that help me prepare for the situation, like "I know this type of situation usually upsets me, but I have a plan now to handle it" or "I'm going to be able to control my anger even if this situation is rough." Next, I'll pretend I'm actually into the situation. I'm going to cope so I can handle it. I might say something to myself like "Just stay calm. Remember who I'm dealing with. This is her style. Don't take it personally" or "Don't overreact. Just relax."
>
> Now the person's harassment is continuing. I am going to cope with feeling more angry. I might think "I can feel myself getting more upset. Just keep relaxed. Concentrate on this" or "This is a challenging situation. How can I handle myself in a way I don't have to apologize for?" OK, now afterward I realize I didn't get abusive or revengeful. So I'll think something to encourage myself, like "I did it" or "Gee, I really kept my cool."
>
> Now you try it. Just verbalize your coping thoughts in the sequence of preparing for the situation, handling it, coping with getting really agitated, and then encouraging yourself.

Application of All Coping Skills to Problem-Related Situations

The next part of stress inoculation involves having the client apply both the direct-action and the cognitive coping skills in the face of stressful, provoking, or painful situations. Before the client is instructed to apply the coping skills *in vivo,* she or he practices applying coping skills under simulated conditions with the helper's assistance. The application phase of stress inoculation appears to be important for the overall efficacy of the procedure. Simply having a client rehearse coping skills *without* opportunities to apply them in stressful situations seems to result in an improved but limited ability to cope.

The application phase involves modeling and rehearsing to provide the client with exposure to simulations of problem-related situations. For example, the client who wanted to manage hostility would have opportunities to practice coping in a variety of hostility-provoking situations. During this application practice, the client needs to be faced with a stressful situation in which to practice the skills. In other words, the application should be arranged and conducted as realistically as possible. The hostile client can be encouraged to practice feeling very agitated and to rehearse even starting to lose control—but then applying the coping skills to gain control (Novaco, 1975). This type of application practice is viewed as the client's providing a self-model of how to behave in a stressful situation. By imagining faltering or losing control, experiencing anxiety, and then coping with this, the person practices the thoughts and feelings as they are likely to occur in a real-life situation (Meichenbaum, 1994). In the application phase of stress inoculation, the client's anxiety, hostility, or distressful emotions are used as a cue or reminder to cope.

Modeling of Application of Coping Skills

The helper should first model how the client can apply the newly acquired skills when faced with a stressful situation. Here is an example of a helper demonstration of this process with a client who is working toward hostility control (in this case, with his family):

> I'm going to imagine that the police have just called and told me that my 16-year-old son was just picked up again for breaking and entering. I can feel myself start to get really hot. Whoops, wait a minute. That's a signal [arousal cue for coping]. I'd better start thinking about

using my relaxation methods to stay calm and using my coping thoughts to prepare myself for handling this situation constructively.

OK, first of all, sit down and relax. Let those muscles loosen up. Count to 10. Breathe deeply [direct-action coping methods]. Now I'll be seeing my son shortly. What is it I have to do? I know it won't help to lash out or to hit him. That won't solve anything. So I'll work out another plan. Let him do most of the talking. Give him the chance to make amends or find a solution [cognitive coping: preparing for the situation]. Now I can see him walking in the door. I feel sort of choked up. I can feel my fists getting tight. He's starting to explain. I want to interrupt and let him have it. But wait [arousal cue for coping]. Concentrate on counting and on breathing slowly [direct-action coping]. Now just tell myself—keep cool. Let him talk. It won't help now to blow up [cognitive coping: confronting situation]. Now I can imagine myself thinking back to the last time he got arrested. Why in the hell doesn't he learn? No son of mine is going to be a troublemaker [arousal]. Whew! I'm pretty damn angry. I've got to stay in control, especially now [cue for coping]. Just relax, muscles! Stay loose [direct-action coping]. I can't expect him to live up to my expectations. I can tell him I'm disappointed, but I'm not going to blow up and shout and hit [cognitive coping: feelings of greater agitation]. OK, I'm doing a good job of keeping my lid on [cognitive coping: self-reinforcement].

Client Application of Coping Skills in Imaginary and Role-Play Practice

After the helper modeling, the client should practice a similar sequence of both direct-action and cognitive coping skills. The practice can occur in two ways: imagination and role play. We find that it is often useful to have the client first practice the coping skills while imagining problem-related situations. This practice can be repeated until the client feels very comfortable in applying the coping strategies to imagined situations. Then the client can practice the coping skills with the helper's aid in a role play of a problem situation. The role-play practice should be similar to the *in vivo* situations that the client encounters. For instance, our angry client could identify particular situations and people with whom he or she is most likely to blow up or lose control. The client can imagine each situation (starting with the most manageable one) and imagine using the coping skills. Then, with the helper taking the part of someone else such as a provoker, the client can practice the coping skills in a role play.

Application of All Coping Skills to Potential Problem Situations

Any therapeutic procedure should be designed not only to help clients deal with current concerns but also to help them anticipate constructive handling of potential concerns. In other words, an adequate therapeutic strategy should help prevent future problems in living as well as resolve current ones. The prevention aspect of stress inoculation is achieved by having clients apply the newly learned coping strategies to situations that are not problematic now but could be in the future. If this phase of stress inoculation is ignored, the effects of the inoculation may be very short-lived. In other words, if clients do not have an opportunity to apply the coping skills to situations other than the current problem-related ones, their coping skills may not generalize beyond the present problem situations.

The application of coping skills to other potentially stressful situations is accomplished in the same way as application to the present problem areas. First, after explaining the usefulness of coping skills in other areas of the client's life, the helper demonstrates the application of coping strategies to a potential, hypothetical stressor. The helper might select a situation the client has not yet encountered, one that would require active coping by anyone who might encounter it, such as not receiving a desired job promotion or raise, facing a family crisis, moving to a new place, anticipating retirement, or being very ill. After the helper has modeled application of coping skills to these sorts of situations, the client would practice applying the skills in these situations or in similar ones that she or he identifies. The practice can occur in imagination or in role-play enactments. A novel way to practice is to switch roles—the client plays the helper, and the helper plays the role of the client. The client helps or trains the helper to use the coping skills. Placing the client in the role of a helper or a trainer can provide another kind of application opportunity that may also have benefits for the client's acquisition of coping strategies and bolster the client's self-efficacy (see Chapter 18). Some version of Learning Activity 15.3 may be useful as part of training for clients as well as helpers.

Stress inoculation training is one of a number of cognitive–behavioral interventions for which computer-assisted programs have been developed and tested. Timmons and associates (2000), for example, evaluated the effectiveness of using a computer guidance program to treat male veterans with maladaptive anger. Both this and a group counseling approach were developed using Novaco's (1975) stress inoculation training. Results indicated that both venues were equally effective in reducing self-reported anger as well as anger suppression, with no differences in treatment satisfaction.

LEARNING ACTIVITY 15.3 — Stress Inoculation

Part One

Listed below are 12 examples of various direct-action coping skills. Using the coding system that precedes the examples, identify on paper the *type* of direct-action coping skill displayed in each example. Feedback follows on page 490.

Code

Information (I)

Escape route (ER)

Social support network (SSN)

Ventilation (V)

Perspective taking (PT)

Attention diversion (AD)

Imagery manipulations (IM)

Muscle relaxation (MR)

Breathing techniques (B)

Examples:

1. "Learn to take slow, deep breaths when you feel especially tense."
2. "Instead of thinking just about the pain, try to concentrate very hard on one spot on the wall."
3. "Imagine that it's a very warm day and the warmth makes you feel relaxed."
4. "If it really gets to be too much, just do the first part only—leave the rest for a while."
5. "You can expect some pain, but it is really only the result of the stitches. It doesn't mean that something is wrong."
6. "Just tighten your left fist. Hold it and notice the tension. Now relax it—feel the difference."
7. "Try to imagine a strong, normal cell attacking the weak, confused cancer cells when you feel the discomfort of your treatment."
8. "When it gets very strong, distract yourself—listen hard to the music or study the picture on the wall."
9. "If you talk about it and express your feelings about the pain, you might feel better."
10. "Your initial or intuitive reaction might cause you to see only selected features of the situation. There are also some positive aspects we need to focus on."
11. "It would be helpful to have your family and neighbors involved to provide you feedback and another perspective."
12. "Social skills are important for you to learn in order to develop the support you need from other people. Others can lessen the effects of the aversive situation."

Part Two

Listed below are eight examples of cognitive coping skills used at four phases: preparing for a situation, confronting or handling the situation, dealing with critical moments in the situation, and self-encouragement for coping. On paper, identify which phase is represented by each example. Feedback follows.

1. "By golly, I did it."
2. "What will I need to do?"
3. "Don't lose your cool even though it's tough now. Take a deep breath."
4. "Think about what you want to say—not how people are reacting to you now."
5. "Relax; it will be over shortly. Just concentrate on getting through this rough moment now."
6. "Can you feel this—the coping worked!"
7. "When you get in there, just think about the situation, not your anxiety."
8. "That's a signal to cope now. Just keep your mind on what you're doing."

> # FEEDBACK 15.3
> ## Stress Inoculation
>
> **Part One**
> 1. B
> 2. AD
> 3. IM
> 4. ER
> 5. I
> 6. MR
> 7. IM
> 8. AD
> 9. V
> 10. PT
> 11. SSN
> 12. SSN
>
> If this exercise was difficult for you, you might review the information presented in the text on direct-action coping skills.
>
> **Part Two**
> 1. Encouraging phase
> 2. Preparing for the situation
> 3. Dealing with a critical moment
> 4. Confronting the situation
> 5. Dealing with a critical moment
> 6. Encouragement for coping
> 7. Preparing for the situation
> 8. Confronting the situation
>
> If you had trouble identifying the four phases of cognitive coping skills, you may want to review Table 15.3.

Homework and Follow-Up

When the client has learned and used stress inoculation within the interviews, she or he is ready to use coping skills *in vivo*. The helper and client should discuss the potential application of coping strategies to actual situations. The helper might caution the client not to expect to cope beautifully with every problematic situation. The client should be encouraged to use a daily log to record the particular situations and the number of times that the coping strategies are used. The log data can be used in a later follow-up as one way to determine the client's progress.

In our opinion, stress inoculation training is one of the most comprehensive therapeutic treatments presently in use. Teaching clients both direct-action and cognitive coping skills that can be used in current and potential problematic situations provides skills that are under the clients' control and are applicable to future as well as current situations.

MODEL DIALOGUE: STRESS INOCULATION

Session 1

In this session, the helper will teach Joan some direct-action coping skills for mental and physical relaxation to help her cope with her physical sensations of nervousness about her math class. Imagery manipulations and slow, deep breathing will be used.

1. **Helper:** Hi, Joan. How was your week?

Client: Pretty good. You know, this, well, whatever you call it, it's starting to help. I took a test this week and got an 85—I usually get a 70 or 75.

The helper introduces the *idea of other coping skills to deal with Joan's nervousness.*

2. **Helper:** That really is encouraging. And that's where the effects of this count—on how you do in class. Because what we did last week went well for you, I believe today we might work with some other coping skills that might help you decrease your nervous feelings.

Client: What would this be?

In responses 3 and 4, the helper explains and *models possible direct-action coping skills.*

3. **Helper:** One thing we might do is help you learn how to imagine something that gives you very calm feelings, and while you're doing this to take some slow, deep breaths—like this [helper models closing eyes, breathing slowly and deeply]. When I was doing that, I thought about curling up in a chair with my favorite book—but there are many different things you could think of. For instance, to use this in your math class, you might imagine that you are doing work for which you will receive some prize or award. Or you might imagine that you are learning problems so you'll be in a position to be a helper for someone else. Do you get the idea?

Client: I think so. I guess it's like trying to imagine or think about math in a pretend kind of way.

4. **Helper:** Yes—and in a way that reduces rather than increases the stress of it for you.

Client: I think I get the idea. It's sort of like when I imagine that I'm doing housework for some famous person instead of just at my house—it makes it more tolerable.

In response 5, the helper asks Joan to *find some helpful imagery manipulations to promote calm feelings.*

5. **Helper:** That's a good example. You imagine that situation to prevent yourself from getting too bored. Here, you find a scene or scenes to think about to prevent yourself from getting too nervous. Can you take a few minutes to think about one or two things you could imagine—perhaps about math—that would help you feel calm instead of nervous?

Client (pauses): Well, maybe I could pretend that math class is part of something I need in order to do something exciting, like being an Olympic downhill skier.

In responses 6 and 7, the helper instructs Joan to *practice these direct-action coping skills.*

6. **Helper:** OK, good. We can work with that, and if it doesn't help, we can come up with something else. Why don't you try first to practice imagining this while you also breathe slowly and deeply, as I did a few minutes ago? [Joan practices.]

7. **Helper:** How did that feel?

Client: OK—it was sort of fun.

In response 8, the helper gives *homework*—asks Joan to engage in *self-directed practice* of these coping skills before the next session.

8. **Helper:** Good. Now, this week I'd like you to practice this in a quiet place two or three times each day. Keep track of your practice sessions in your log, and also rate your tension level before and after you practice. Next week we will go over this log and then work on a way you can apply what we did today—and the coping thoughts we learned in our two previous sessions. So I'll see you next week.

Session 2

In this session, the helper helps Joan integrate the strategies of some previous sessions (coping thoughts, imagery, and breathing coping skills). Specifically, Joan learns to apply all these coping skills in imagery and role-play practices of some stressful situations related to math class. Application of coping skills to problem-related situations is a part of stress inoculation and helps the client to generalize the newly acquired coping skills to *in vivo* situations as they occur.

In responses 1 and 2, the helper will *review Joan's use of the direct-action skills homework.*

1. **Helper:** How are things going, Joan?

Client: OK. I've had a hard week—one test and two pop quizzes in math. But I got 80s. I also did my imagination and breathing practice. You know, that takes a while to learn.

2. **Helper:** That's natural. It does take a lot of practice before you really get the feel of it. So it would be a good idea if you continued the daily practice again this week. How did it feel when you practiced?

Client: OK—I think I felt less nervous than before.

The helper introduces the idea of *applying all the coping skills in practice situations* **and** *presents a rationale for this application phase.*

3. **Helper:** That's good. As time goes on, you will notice more effects from it. Up to this point, we've worked on some things to help you in your math class—stopping self-defeating thoughts and using imagination and slow breathing to help you cope and control your nervousness. What I think might help now is to give you a chance to use all these skills in practices of some of the stressful situations related to your math class. This will help you use the skills when you need to during the class or related situations. Then we will soon be at a point where we can go through some of these same procedures for the other situations in which you want to express yourself differently and more frequently, such as with your folks. Does this sound OK?

Client: Yes.

Next, the helper *demonstrates (models) how Joan can practice her skills in an imaginary practice.*

4. **Helper:** What I'd like you to do is to imagine some of the situations related to your math class and try to use your coping thoughts and the imagination scene and deep breathing to control your nervousness. Let me show you how you might do this. I'm imagining that it's almost time for math class. I'm going to concentrate on thinking about how this class will help me train for the Olympic downhill program. If I catch myself thinking I wish I didn't have to go, I'm going to use some coping thoughts. Let's see—class will go pretty fast. I've been doing better. It can be a challenge. Now, as I'm in class, I'm going to stop thinking about not being able to do the work. I'm going to just take one problem at a time.

One step at a time. Oops! Mr. Lamborne just called on me. Boy, I can feel myself getting nervous. Just take a deep breath. . . . Do the best I can. It's only one moment anyway. Well, it went pretty well. I can feel myself starting to cope when I need to. OK, Joan, why don't you try this several times now? [Joan practices applying coping thoughts and direct action with different practice situations in imagination.]

In response 5, the helper *checks Joan's reaction* to applying the skills in practice through imagination.

5. **Helper:** Are you able to really get into the situation as you practice this way?

Client: Yes, although I believe I'll have to work harder to use this when it really happens.

Sometimes *role play makes the practice more real.* The helper introduces this next. Note that the helper will add a stress element by calling on Joan at unannounced times.

6. **Helper:** That's right. This kind of practice doesn't always have the same amount of stress as the "real thing." Maybe it would help if we did some role-play practice. I'll be your teacher this time. Just pretend to be in class. I'll be talking, but at an unannounced time, I'm going to call on you to answer a question. Just use your coping thoughts and your slow breathing as you need to when this happens. [Role-play practice of this and related scenarios occurs.]

The helper *assesses Joan's reaction* to role-play practice and *asks Joan to rate her level of nervousness* during the practice.

7. **Helper:** How comfortable do you feel with these practices? Could you rate the nervousness you feel as you do this on a 1-to-5 scale, with 1 being not nervous and 5 being very nervous?

Client: Well, about a 2.

The helper encourages Joan to *apply coping statements in the math-related problem situations* as they occur, assigns *homework*, and schedules a *follow-up*.

8. **Helper:** I think you are ready to use this as you need to during the week. Remember, any self-defeating thought or body tenseness is a cue to cope, using your coping thoughts and imagination and breathing skills. I'd like you to keep track of the number of times you use these on your log sheets. Also, rate your level of nervousness before, during, and after math class on the log sheet. How about coming back in two weeks to see how things are going?

Client: Fine.

SPIRITUALITY IN PRACTICE

Many of the strategies we have discussed here for managing and coping with stress are familiar to both helping professionals and the lay public. Another dimension of coping and stress management that is familiar to many, but is less clearly established in counseling-related helping services, involves spirituality. Research indicates that religion and spirituality may be important correlates of health and well-being in general, as well as how people cope with life stressors. Young, Cashwell, and Shcherbakova (2000), for example, report findings that spirituality provides a moderating effect for both depression and anxiety. George, Larson, Koenig, and McCullough (2000) identify relationships between religious practices and reduced onset of physical and mental illnesses, reduced mortality, and likelihood of recovery from or adjustment to physical and mental illness. Pursuit of spiritual comfort or guidance is commonly included as a component of coping repertoire assessment tools. Spiritual beliefs, activities (e.g., prayer; reading spiritual texts; meditation; participating in services, rituals, or traditions), and engaging in a faith community (e.g., for spiritual purposes, mutual assistance, and/or social purposes) are examples of religion or spirituality as a coping strategy. We use the term *spirituality* here to mean values, activities, and personal experiences that may include a religious base, but not necessarily so.

National surveys indicate that most Americans hold some kind of spiritual values and engage in activities such as prayer. For example, many people use prayer to help cope with many different types of problems in living and crises. This tends to be particularly true among older adults with difficulties that are more severe, and there are important cultural differences in both the importance and form of spirituality. For instance, African Americans tend to be more religiously active than European Americans (Taylor, Chatters, Jayakody, & Levin, 1996), and although there is a great deal that is common across religions of the world, there are considerable differences among the various religions and spiritual traditions (e.g., Judaism, Christianity, Islam, Buddhism, Hinduism, and Confucianism; Smart, 1993, 1994). Religious or spiritual issues constitute a recent diagnostic category in the 1994 *DSM-IV,* and helpers are likely to see an increase in the number of clients seeking help for spiritual problems or requesting inclusion of spiritual concerns as part of their work with helping professionals (see Lukoff, Lu, & Turner, 1999).

The positive potential of clients' spiritual or religious values and behaviors as resources for coping, well-being, and helping services has stimulated increased research in recent years. This has included the spiritual aspects of coping with serious illness, disabling conditions, caretaking and loss of loved ones, personal crisis, managing ongoing chronic health and mental health conditions, alcohol and other substance-use problems, goal pursuits such as athletics and sexual decision making, and professional issues such as ethics and assessment tools (see Box 15.3).

Diversity has been notably apparent in research on spirituality. As Box 15.4 illustrates, there has been increased examination of cultural group differences as well as spiritual factors relevant to gender, sexual minorities, religions, and specific cultural groups. Particularly prominent has been research with African Americans and with elders. Research has also focused on spiritual growth as a constructive consequence of highly stressful life experiences (e.g., James & Samuels, 1999). Maintaining a positive outlook and generally positive emotional state in the context of chronic and serious stressors has been significantly associated with using coping strategies that are more likely to produce good outcomes and with healing, even transformative, outcomes. It may be that spiritual values and activities foster situational appraisals or personal meanings that are emotionally comforting, help infuse ordinary events with positive meaning, and stimulate positive reframing and goal-directed problem-focused coping—important ingredients for adaptive stress management outcomes (Folkman & Moskowitz, 2000).

BOX 15.3 RESEARCH ON SPIRITUALITY

Athletics
Dillion, K. M., & Tati, J. L. (2000). Spirituality and being in the zone in team sports: A relationship? *Journal of Sport Behavior, 23*(2), 91–100.

Assessment
Belaire, C., & Young, J. S. (2000). Influences of spirituality on counselor selection. *Counseling & Values, 44*(3), 189–197.
Frame, M. W. (2000). The spiritual genome in family therapy. *Journal of Marriage & Family Counseling, 26,* 211–216.
Hatch, R. L., Burg, M. A., Naberhaus, D. S., & Hellmich, L. K. (1998). The Spiritual Involvement and Beliefs Scale: Development and testing of a new instrument. *Journal of Family Practice, 46,* 476–486.
Hodge, D. R. (2000). Spiritual ecomaps: A new diagrammatic tool for assessing marital and family spirituality. *Journal of Marriage & Family Counseling, 26,* 217–228.
Holland, J. C., Kash, K. M., Passik, S., Gronert, M. K., Sison, A., Leferberg, M., Russak, S. M., James, B. J., & Samuels, C. A. (1999). High stress life events and spiritual development. *Journal of Psychology & Theology, 27,* 250–260.
MacDonald, D. A. (2000). Spirituality: Description, measurement, and relation to the five factor model of personality. *Journal of Personality, 68*(1), 153–197.
MacDonald, D. A., Kuentzel, J. G., & Friedman, H. L. (1999). A survey of measures of spiritual and transpersonal constructs: Part two: Additional instruments. *Journal of Transpersonal Psychology, 31*(1), 155–177.
Petersen, D. M. (2000). Identity characteristics of groups with high and low spiritual self-identity. *Social Behavior & Personality, 28,* 529–538.
Standard, R. P., Sandhu, D. S., & Painter, L. C. (2000). Assessment of spirituality in counseling. *Journal of Counseling & Development, 78,* 204–210.

Death/Dying
Babler, J. E. (1997). A comparison of spiritual care provided by hospice social workers, nurses, and spiritual care professionals. *Hospice Journal, 12*(4), 15–28.
Golsworthy, R., & Coyle, A. (1999). Spiritual beliefs and the search for meaning among older adults following partner loss. *Mortality, 4*(1), 21–40.
Richards, T. A., Acree, M., & Folkman, S. (1999). Spiritual aspects of loss among partners of men with AIDS: Post-bereavement follow-up. *Death Studies, 23*(2), 103–127.
Thompson, J. E. (2000). The place of spiritual well-being in hospice patients' overall quality of life. *Hospice Journal, 15*(2), 13–27.

Disability
Byrd, E. K. (1997). Concepts related to inclusion of the spiritual component in services to persons with disability and chronic illness. *Journal of Applied Rehabilitation Counseling, 28*(4), 26–29.
Do Rozario, L. (1997). Spirituality in the lives of people with disability and chronic illness: A creative paradigm of wholeness and reconstruction. *Disability & Rehabilitation: An International Multidisciplinary Journal, 19,* 427–434.

Ethics
Frame, M. W. (2000). Spiritual and religious issues in counseling: Ethical considerations. *Counseling & Therapy for Couples & Families, 8*(1), 72–74.

Health management
Arcury, T. A., Quandt, S. A., McDonald, J., & Bell. R. A. (2000). Faith and health self-management of rural older adults. *Journal of Cross-Cultural Gerontology, 15*(1), 55–74.
Brown, C. M. (2000). Exploring the role of religiosity in hypertension management among African Americans. *Journal of Health Care for the Poor and Underserved, 11*(1), 19–32.

(continued)

> **BOX 15.3 RESEARCH ON SPIRITUALITY**
>
> *(continued)*
>
> *Illness*
>
> Baider, L., & Fox, B. (1998). A brief spiritual beliefs inventory for use in quality of life research in life-threatening illness. *Psycho-Oncology, 7,* 460–469.
>
> Cotton, S. P., Levine, E. G., Fitzpatrick, C. M., Dold, K. H., & Targ, E. (1999). Exploring the relationships among spiritual well-being, quality of life, and psychological adjustments in women with breast cancer. *Psycho-Oncology, 8,* 429–438.
>
> Dunbar, H. T., Mueller, C. W., Medina, C., & Wolf, T. (1998). Psychological and spiritual growth in women living with HIV. *Social Work, 43,* 144–154.
>
> Holland, J. C., Passik, S., Kash, K. M., Russak, S. M., Grongert, M. K., Sison, A., Lederberg, M., Fox, B., & Baider, L. (1999). The role of religious and spiritual beliefs in coping with malignant melanoma. *Psycho-Oncology, 8,* 14–26.
>
> King, M., Speck, P., & Thomas, A. (1999). The effect of spiritual beliefs on outcome from illness. *Social Science & Medicine, 48,* 1291–1299.
>
> Somlai, A. M., & Heckman, T. G. (2000). Correlates of spirituality and well-being in a community sample of people living with HIV disease. *Mental health, Religion & Culture, 3*(1), 57–70.
>
> Woods, T. E., & Ironson, G. H. (1999). Religion and spirituality in the face of illness: How cancer, cardiac, and HIV patients describe their spirituality/religiosity. *Journal of Health Psychology, 4,* 393–412.
>
> *Psychological well-being*
>
> Hawlins, R. S., Tan, S. Y., & Turk, A. A. (1999). Secular versus Christian inpatient cognitive–behavioral therapy programs: Impact on depression and spiritual well-being. *Journal of Psychology & Theology, 27,* 309–318.
>
> Young, S. J., Cashwell, C. S., & Shcherbakova, J. (2000). The moderating relationship of spirituality on negative life events and psychological adjustment. *Counseling & Values, 45*(1), 49–57.
>
> *Sexual activity*
>
> Holder, D. W., Durant, R. H., Harris, T. L., Daniel, J. H., Obeidallah, D., & Goodman, E. (2000). The association between adolescent spirituality and voluntary sexual activity. *Journal of Adolescent Health, 26,* 295–302.
>
> *Substance abuse*
>
> Borman, P. D., & Dixon, D. N. (1998). Spirituality and the 12 steps of substance abuse recovery. *Journal of Psychology & Therapy, 26,* 287–291.
>
> Carroll, J. K., McGinley, J. J., & Mack, S. E. (2000). Exploring the expressed spiritual needs and concerns of drug-dependent males in modified therapeutic community treatment. *Alcoholism Treatment Quarterly, 18*(1), 79–92.
>
> Green, L. L., Fullilove, M. T., & Fullilove, R. E. (1998). Stories of spiritual awakening: The nature of spirituality in recovery. *Journal of Substance Abuse Treatment, 15,* 325–331.
>
> Miller, W. R. (1998). Researching the spiritual dimensions of alcohol and other drug problems. *Addiction, 93,* 979–990.

Although it is not yet clear whether spirituality is exerting a direct influence or how it may be exerting indirect influence, researchers are beginning to look more closely at this subject. George and colleagues (2000) suggest three mechanisms that may be at work—specifically, that religiousness generally (1) promotes healthy behaviors, (2) is associated with stronger social supports, and (3) fosters a sense of coherence or meaning. For example, adherence to spiritual beliefs may prompt one to lifestyle and interpersonal behaviors that lead to healthy outcomes and, conversely, may discourage risky behaviors likely to result in negative outcomes. A spiritual orientation may prompt people to seek out and participate with others who share or value this orientation, which helps build a network of supportive relationships. And, as described above, spiritual beliefs and ways of relating may help people interpret negative events in ways that make sense to them or even provide solace, thus helping them to better cope with adversity, loss, and other troubling experiences. For example, in a study of African Americans diagnosed with hypertension, Brown (2000) found that a majority of participants used their religious beliefs as protective, control, and coping mechanisms in the management of their illness. They felt protected from immediate and long-term negative consequences but also felt better able to find meaning in and cope with having hypertension and to exert control over its management. Consistent with coping theory, this combination of solace, hope, and positivity in how a threat and one's ability to handle the threat are appraised may then help individuals persevere and continue the hard behavioral work of learning what they need to learn and doing what they need to do.

There is need for caution, however. Research to date has generally used a lot of different ways of assessing spirituality. This reduces our ability to generalize conclusions from findings across studies. One basic issue is that although spiritual experiences are often conceived as part of religion, spirituality is not seen as dependent on religious beliefs. A study of differences in how medically ill people define what they mean by *spiritual* and *religious* revealed some similarities but also significant differences in overall belief systems as well as interpretations of how individuals' beliefs affected their health and recovery. For example, those identifying themselves

BOX 15.4 SPIRITUALITY AND DIVERSITY

African Americans

Black, H. K. (1999). Life as a gift: Spiritual narratives of elderly African American women living in poverty. *Journal of Aging Studies, 13,* 441–455.

Campbell, M. K., Bernhardt, J. M., Waldmiller, M., Jackson, B., Potenziani, D., Weathers, B., & Demissie, S. (1999). Varying the message source in computer-tailored nutrition education. *Patient Education & Counseling, 36*(2), 157–169.

Carolan, M. T., & Allen, K. R. (1999). Commitments and constraints to intimacy for African American couples at midlife. *Journal of Family Issues, 20*(1), 3–24.

Constantine, M. G., Lewis, E. L., Conner, L. C., & Sanchez, D. (2000). Addressing spiritual religious issues in counseling African Americans: Implications for counselor training and practice. *Counseling & Values, 45*(1), 28–38.

Dunn, A. B., & Dawes, S. J. (1999). Spirituality-focused genograms: Keys to uncovering spiritual resources in African American families. *Journal of Multicultural Counseling & Development, 27*(3), 240–254.

Frame, M. G., Williams, C. B., & Green, E. L. (1999). Balm in Gilead: Spiritual dimensions in counseling African American women. *Journal of Multicultural Counseling & Development, 27*(4), 182–192.

Mattis, J. S. (1997). The spiritual well-being of African-Americans: A preliminary analysis. *Journal of Prevention & Intervention in the Community, 16*(½), 103–120.

Mattis, J. S. (2000). African American women's definitions of spirituality and religiosity. *Journal of Black Psychology, 26*(1), 101–122.

McRae, M. B., Thompson, D. A., & Cooper, S. (1999). Black churches as therapeutic groups. *Journal of Multicultural Counseling & Development, 27*(4), 207–220.

Morrison, E. F., & Thornton, K. A. (1999). Influence of southern spiritual beliefs on perceptions of mental illness. *Issues in Mental Health Nursing, 20,* 443–458.

Reese, D. J., Ahern, R. E., Nair, S., O'Faire, J. D., & Warren, C. (1999). Hospice access and use by African Americans: Addressing cultural and institutional barriers through participatory action research. *Social Work, 44,* 549–559.

Williams, C. B., & Frame, M. W. (1999). Constructing new realities: Integrating womanist traditions in pastoral counseling with African-American women. *Pastoral Psychology, 47,* 303–314.

Williams, C. B., Frame, M. W., & Green, E. (1999). Counseling groups for African American women: A focus on spirituality. *Journal for Specialists in Group Work, 24,* 260–273.

Assessment

Miller, G., Fleming, W., & Brown-Anderson, F. (1998). Spiritual well-being scale: Ethnic differences between Caucasians and African Americans. *Journal of Psychology & Theology, 26,* 358–364.

Zinnbauer, B. J., Pargament, K. I., Cole, B., Rye, M. S., Butter, E. M., Belavich, T. G., Hipp, K. M., Scott, A. B., & Kader, J. L. (1997). Religion and spirituality: Unfuzzying the fuzzy. *Journal for the Scientific Study of Religion, 36,* 549–564.

Buddhism

McGrath, P. (1998). A spiritual response to the challenge of routinization: A dialogue of discourses in a Buddhist-initiated hospice. *Qualitative Health Research, 8,* 801–812.

McGrath, P. (1998). Buddhist spirituality: A compassionate perspective on hospice care. *Mortality, 3,* 251–263.

Cross-cultural

Misra, G. (1999). Toward an indigenous psychology of cognition: Knowing in the Indian tradition. *Journal of Indian Psychology, 17*(1), 1–22.

Stanley, L. D. (1999). Transforming AIDS: The moral management of stigmatized identity. *Anthropology & Medicine, 6*(1), 103–120.

Elders

Black, H. K. (1999). A sense of the sacred: Altering or enhancing the self-portrait in older age? *Narrative Inquiry, 9,* 327–345.

Chang, B., Noonan, A. E., & Tennstedt, S. L. (1998). The role of religion/spirituality in coping with caregiving for disabled elders. *Gerontologist, 38,* 463–470.

Ingersoll, R. E. (2000). Gentle like the dawn: A dying woman's healing. *Counseling & Values, 44*(2), 129–134.

Langer, N. (2000). The importance of spirituality in later life. *Gerontology & Geriatrics Education, 20*(3), 41–50.

Meddin, J. R. (1998). Dimensions of spiritual meaning and well-being in the lives of ten older Australians. *International Journal of Aging & Human Development, 47*(3), 163–175.

Musick, M. A., Traphagan, J. W., Koenig, H. G., & Larson, D. B. (2000). Spirituality in physical health and aging. *Journal of Adult Development, 7*(2), 73–86.

Neill, C. M., & Kahn, A. S. (1999). The role of personal spirituality and religious social activity on the life satisfaction of older widowed women. *Sex Roles, 40,* 310–329.

Simmons, H. C. (1997). Spirituality and community in the last stage of life. *Journal of Gerontological Social Work, 29*(2/3), 73–91.

Filipino

Shimabukuro, K. P., Daniels, J., & D'Andrea, M. (1999). Addressing spiritual issues from a cultural perspective: The case of the grieving Filipino boy. *Journal of Multicultural Counseling & Development, 27,* 221–239.

Gender

Hall, T. A. (1997). Gender differences: Implications for spiritual formation and community life. *Journal of Psychology & Christianity, 16,* 222–232.

Hinduism

Wig, N. N. (1999). Mental health and spiritual values: A view from the East. *International Review of Psychiatry, 11*(2/3), 92–96.

Illness

Domanico, R., & Crawford, I. (2000). Psychological distress among HIV-impacted African American and Latino males. *Journal of Prevention & Intervention in the Community, 19*(1), 55–78.

(continued)

> **BOX 15.4   SPIRITUALITY AND DIVERSITY**
>
> (continued)
>
> Holt, J. L., Houg, B. L., & Romano, J. L. (1999). Spiritual wellness for clients with HIV/AIDS: Review of counseling issues. *Journal of Counseling & Development, 77,* 160–170.
>
> Simoni, J. M., & Cooperman, N. A. (2000). Stressors and strengths among women living with HIV/AIDS in New York City. *AIDS Care, 12,* 291–297.
>
> *Israeli and Jewish*
>
> Baider, L., Russak, S. M., Perry, S., Kash, K., Gronert, M., Fox, B., Holland, J., & Kaplan-Denour, A. (1999). The role of religious and spiritual beliefs in coping with malignant melanoma: An Israeli sample. *Psycho-Oncology, 81,* 27–35.
>
> Fabian, E. (1998). Concretism and identity aspects in the Jewish joke. *Psychoanalysis & Contemporary Thought, 21,* 423–441.
>
> Frank, G., Bernardo, S., Tropper, S., Noguchi, F., et al. (1997). Jewish spirituality through actions in time: Daily occupations of young Orthodox Jewish couples in Los Angeles. *American Journal of Occupational Therapy, 51*(3), 199–206.
>
> Herzbrun, M. B. (1999). Loss of faith: A qualitative analysis of Jewish nonbelievers. *Counseling & Values, 43*(2), 129–141.
>
> *Mexican Americans*
>
> Rehm, R. S. (1999). Religious faith in Mexican-American families dealing with chronic childhood illness. *IMAGE: Journal of Nursing Scholarship, 311,* 33–38.
>
> *Multi-ethnic*
>
> Brown, J. M., Ashcroft, F. G., & Miller, W. R. (1998). Purpose in life among alcoholics: A comparison of three ethnic groups. *Alcoholism Treatment Quarterly, 16*(3), 1–11.
>
> Ingersoll, R. E. (1998). Refining dimensions of spiritual wellness: A cross-traditional approach. *Counseling & Values, 42*(3), 156–165.
>
> Moadel, A., Morgan, C., Fatone, A., Grennan, J., Carter, J., Laruffia, G., Skunny, A., & Dutcher, J. (1999). Feeling meaning and hope: Self-reported spiritual and existential needs among an ethnically diverse cancer patient population. *Psycho-Oncology, 8,* 378–385.
>
> *Native Americans*
>
> Anderson, D. A., & Worthen, D. (1997). Exploring a fourth dimension: Spirituality as a resource for the couple therapist. *Journal of Marital & Family Therapy, 23*(1), 3–12.
>
> Garrett, M. T. (1999). Soaring on the wings of the eagle: Wellness of Native American high school students. *Professional School Counseling, 3*(1), 57–64.
>
> Garrett, M. T., & Wilbur, M. P. (1999). Does the worm live in the ground? Reflections on Native American spirituality. *Journal of Multicultural Counseling & Development, 27*(4), 193–206.
>
> Lewis, E. W., Duran, E., & Woodis, W. (1999). Psychotherapy in the American Indian population. *Psychiatric Annals, 29,* 474–479.
>
> *Sexual minorities*
>
> Barret, B., & Barzan, R. (1998). Gay and lesbian spirituality: A response to Donaldson. *Counseling & Values, 42*(3), 222–225.
>
> Grant, D., & Epp, L. (1998). The gay orientation: Does God mind? *Counseling & Values, 43*(1), 28–33.

as spiritual saw recovery and healing happening *through* them whereas those identifying themselves as religious were more prone to see it as happening *to* them (Hill et al., 2000; Woods & Ironson, 1999). Published work under the headings of assessment in Box 15.3 and Box 15.4 illustrate recent efforts to develop tools that remedy the fuzziness of current distinctions between spirituality and religiousness and among dimensions of spirituality, and to better understand cultural and contextual uniqueness as well as more universally shared elements. Standard, Sandhu, and Painter (2000) see spirituality as an emerging fifth force in counseling and psychotherapy and provide a review of instruments currently in use and their psychometric properties and potential uses.

Similarly, we cannot yet sufficiently determine possible confounding or other moderating factors that may be involved with spirituality and health or mental health outcomes, nor has the field yet accounted for failures to find significant outcomes (Thoresen, 1999). Although spirituality is by no means new, growth of the practice-focused research base is comparatively more recent. As with other ways of coping, there are likely to be complex relationships, individual and group differences, and situational factors that will make a difference in the roles that spirituality plays in problem development as well as problem solving and improved well-being. It would be important to know, for example, the extent to which a positive association between spirituality and well-being was due to higher levels of healthy behavior (and thus less exposure to certain risks), to family or friendship activities that yielded certain kinds of social support that buffered effects of stress, to cognitive schemas that shaped how a person viewed the world and interpreted stressors, or to some combination of the above or something entirely different. As with any factor, there are negative as well as positive potentials. Spirituality, for example, may incline a client toward rigidity, distortion, or zealotry, which would impede rather than support progress in managing stressful life circumstances or undertaking needed changes.

Paralleling the increase in research has been increased attention to spirituality in a range of medical- and counseling-related training and services (Chibnall & Duckro, 2000; Larson, Lu & Puchalski, 2000; Pellebon & Anderson, 1999; Ellis, Vinson, & Ewigman, 1999; Kilpatrick & McCullough, 1999; Hickson, Housley, & Wages, 2000; Gilbert, 2000; Taylor, Mitchell, Kenan, & Tacker, 2000; Hayworth, Patterson, Raskin, & Turner, 2000; Burke et al., 1999; Narayanasamy, 1999). There are a number of ways that spirituality may enter into practice. In addition to (1) including spirituality as part of assessment, Meador and Koenig (2000) note (2) incorporating spirituality into the treatment plan, (3) assessing the clinician's beliefs, (4) examining the clinical implications of the client's spirituality, (5) using religion or spirituality to cope with stress, (6) employing cognitive therapeutic models, and (7) avoiding clinician bias or proselytizing. Although there are competing views about the use of spirituality in professional helping, it has a longer and more widespread acceptance in some arenas than others—for example, related to death and dying, and with 12-step programs such as Alcoholics Anonymous (Tonigan, Toscova, & Connors, 1999).

Embedded throughout are ethical issues and the need for safeguards. Spirituality entails values on the part of the client, helper, and any others involved—values that may conflict, that may not be well examined or understood, that may carry costs or dangers as well as benefits. You will need to be careful with professional, ethical, and legal issues when working with spiritual values and interventions in psychotherapy. Examples include questions about (1) the nature of the helper's role and appropriate accountability oversight, (2) making helpers' and clients' values and differences explicit, (3) determining the setting and conditions of therapy, (4) how the presenting concern and goals of the client are construed and determined, (5) confronting unhealthy client values or addressing deficiencies or confusion, (6) obtaining informed consent and evaluating a helper's competency relative to spiritual dimensions, (7) maintaining professional and scientific responsibility, (8) respecting the client's religious values, (9) documenting use of spiritual interventions, (10) evaluating therapy outcome and termination, (11) making appropriate financial arrangements, and (12) treatment issues such as those that may arise in family therapy or mental health problems like dissociative disorders (e.g., ethical factors in dealing with spiritual issues such as distorted views of God or feelings of being demonized) (Chappelle, 2000; Haug, 1998; Mungadze, 2000; Richards, Rector, & Tjeltveit, 1999). Finally, it is important to be aware that differences in religious or spiritual perspectives may have substantial implications for inclusion as part of helping services.

SUMMARY

In this chapter, we examined various forms that stress takes, including cultural variations of stress as well as current models of factors that affect stress and coping. We have seen ways that stress and its management relates to many other assessment and intervention strategies described in this book. Understanding current models of stress and coping should help guide you in developing an intervention plan appropriate to specific client needs, depending on the factors that appear most important either in how stress is being experienced or what types of stress management are likely to best achieve client goals.

Specific to stress management, we presented breathing interventions to help address physiological dimensions. Clients can achieve greater awareness of their breathing and undertake breathing exercises that will help calm the central nervous system, reduce symptoms such as dizziness, and better prepare them to undertake additional steps in managing their stressful circumstances. We also described stress inoculation as an approach to teaching both physical and cognitive coping strategies. Stress inoculation training pulls together a number of strategies to increase knowledge about stress and coping, self-monitoring, cognitive change, problem solving, relaxation training, rehearsal preparation, and environmental change.

As with any intervention, you will need to assess the appropriateness of each component as well as additional ones. For example, spirituality may be an important resource to consider for use in stress management intervention. Moreover, although cultural diversity is becoming much more explicit in practice involving stress and coping, much of the research and intervention development is rooted in a Western framework—for example, that stress is viewed as a "problem" requiring the assistance of an external source such as a professional helper and some "training" in order to be alleviated or managed. For some clients, stress may be viewed more as a part of life, and self-healing practices such as meditation, movement, or one or more forms of self-management (perhaps anchored within one's personal network or community) may be attractive and relevant. We describe these topics in the following chapters.

INFOTRAC® EXPLORATIONS

1. Search for *stress* combined with a term relevant to a population of particular interest to you (e.g., *elderly, children, disabled, women, cultural* or a specific cultural group, *single parent* or *low income*). Select three to five articles and

look for ways that stressors for these groups are reflected in Table 15.1. Identify additional factors you deem important. Drawing on the stress models presented in this chapter, draw your own model of how you see stress developing and functioning for at least one of these groups.
2. Using these same articles, develop an intervention plan for each, identifying what particular components or strategies you would recommend and why. Keep in mind the need to be parsimonious, to be attentive to environmental as well as person targets of change, and to be sensitive and collaborative. Be prepared to discuss your ideas with your student colleagues.
3. Search for the term *stress management* (InfoTrac® does not presently organize under the term *stress inoculation*). Select three to five articles that report interventions, preferably examining outcomes. For each, write out the specific intervention strategies or components. From the article descriptions, see if you can ascertain if each includes an (a) educational phase, (b) a skills acquisition and rehearsal phase, and (c) an application and generalization phase.

SUGGESTED RESOURCES

Readings

Castillo, R. (1997). *Culture and mental illness.* Pacific Grove, CA: Brooks/Cole.

Davis, M., Eshelman, E. R., & McKay, M. (2000). *Relaxation and stress reduction workbook* (5th ed.). Oakland, CA: New Harbinger.

Farhi, D. (1996). *The breathing book.* New York: Holt.

Fausel, D. (1995). Stress inoculation training for stepcouples. *Marriage and Family Review, 21,* 137–155.

Fink, G. (2000). *Encyclopedia of stress.* San Diego: Academic.

Foa, E. B., Rothbaum, B. O., Riggs, D. S., & Murdock, T. B. (1991). Treatment of posttraumatic stress disorder in rape victims: A comparison between cognitive–behavioral procedures and counseling. *Journal of Consulting and Clinical Psychology, 59,* 715–723.

Greenberg, J. S. (1996). *Comprehensive stress management.* Madison, WI: Brown & Benchmark.

Humphrey, J. H. (1998). *Helping children manage stress: A guide for adults.* Washington, DC: Child & Family Press.

Laungani, P. (1993). Cultural differences in stress and its management. *Stress Medicine, 9,* 37–43.

Lehrer, P. M., & Woolfolk, R. L. (Eds.). (1993). *Principles and practice of stress management* (2nd ed.). New York: Guilford.

Leserman, J., Perkins, D., & Evans, D. (1992). Coping with the threat of AIDS: The role of social support. *American Journal of Psychiatry, 149,* 1514–1520.

McGuigan, F. J. (1999). *Encyclopedia of stress.* Boston: Allyn & Bacon.

Meichenbaum, D. (1993). Stress inoculation training: A 20-year update. In P. M. Lehrer & R. L. Woolfolk (Eds.), *Principles and practice of stress management* (2nd ed., pp. 373–406). New York: Guilford.

Meichenbaum, D. (1994). *A clinical handbook: Practical therapist manual for assessing and treating adults with post-traumatic stress disorder.* Waterloo, Ontario: Institute Press.

Rice, V. H. (Ed.). (2000). *Handbook of stress, coping, and health: Implications for nursing research, theory, and practice.* Thousand Oaks, CA: Sage.

Ross, M., & Berger, R. (1996). Effects of stress inoculation training on athletes' postsurgical pain and rehabilitation after orthopedic injury. *Journal of Consulting and Clinical Psychology, 64,* 406–410.

Walsh, F. (Ed.) (1999). *Spiritual resources in family therapy.* New York: Guilford.

Web Sites

Center for Psychospiritual Development
www.psychospiritualtherapy.com

International Stress Management Association
www.isma.org.uk

National Institute for Healthcare Research (NIHR)
www.nihr.org

Psychotherapy & Spirituality Institute
www.mindspirit.org

Stress Management: A Review of Principles
http://www.unl.edu/stress/mgmt

Stress Management and Emotional Wellness Links
http://www.imt.net/~randolfi/StressLinks.html

15 POST EVALUATION

Part One

Objective One asks you to assess your own awareness of breathing using at least 4 of 5 instructions on p. 475. Use the description under the section "Awareness of Breathing" to guide you.

Part Two

Objective Two asks you to demonstrate 10 of the 12 steps for diaphragmatic breathing. Use the checklist in Part four of the postevaluation to assess your performance.

Part Three

Objective Three asks you to describe how you would apply the five major components of stress inoculation with a client case. Using the client description below, respond to the five questions following the case description as if you were using stress inoculation with this client. Feedback follows.

Description of client: The client has been referred to you by Family Services. He is unemployed, is receiving welfare support, and has three children. He is married to his second wife; the oldest child is hers by another marriage. He has been referred because of school complaints that the oldest child, a seventh grader, has arrived at school several times with obvious facial bruises and cuts. The child has implicated the stepfather in this matter. After a long period of talking, the client reports that he has little patience with this boy and sometimes does strike him in the face as his way of disciplining the child. He realizes that maybe, on occasion, he has gone too far. Still, he gets fed up with the boy's "irresponsibility" and "lack of initiative" for his age. At these times, he reports, his impatience and anger get the best of him.

1. Explain the purpose of stress inoculation as you would to this client.
2. Briefly give an overview of the stress inoculation procedure.
3. Describe and explain one example of each of the following kinds of direct-action coping skills that might be useful to this client:
   a. Information about the situation
   b. An escape route
   c. An attention-diversion tactic
   d. An imagery manipulation
   e. Physical relaxation
   f. A palliative coping strategy (perspective taking, social support, or ventilation)
4. Explain, as you might to this client, the four phases of an emotional reaction and of times for coping. For each of the four phases, give two examples of cognitive coping skills (thoughts) that you would give to this client. The four phases are preparing for a disagreement or argument with the boy; confronting the situation; dealing with critical, very provoking times; and encouraging himself for coping.
5. Describe how you would set up practice opportunities in the interview with this client to help him practice applying the direct-action and cognitive coping skills in simulated practices of the provoking situations.

Part Four

Objective Four asks you to demonstrate 17 out of 21 steps of the stress inoculation procedure with a role-play client. Assess this activity using the Interview Checklist for Stress Inoculation on pages 500–503.

Checklist for Diaphragmatic Breathing

I. Rationale
   1. If you have doubts, check with your primary care physician before starting.
   2. Think about the purposes and benefits of abdominal breathing.

II. Comfortable position (lounge chair)
   3. Get in a comfortable position to experience and feel the movement of the abdomen.
   4. Breathe through your nose. Just notice your breath.
   5. As you inhale, notice how cool the air feels, and how much warmer the air feels when you exhale.

III. Placement of hands: visualize the movement of the diaphragm, and simulate the movement of the diaphragm with the hands
   6. Bend your arms and place the thumbs below your rib cage. Place the rest of the fingers of each hand perpendicular to your body.
   7. Visualize the movement of the diaphragm; it contracts and is drawn downward as you inhale; when you exhale, the air is pushed out of the lungs, and the diaphragm is drawn upward.
   8. Simulate the movement of the diaphragm with your fingers; the fingers straighten out as you inhale, and the fingers are curved and cone shaped.

(continued)

15 POST EVALUATION

(continued)

IV. Diaphragmatic breathing
9. Continue to breathe diaphragmatically without your hand gestures or movement; place your hands in your lap or beside your body.
10. As you breathe diaphragmatically, visualize the movement of the diaphragm as the abdomen rises and falls like the tide.

V. Daily practice and use in stressful situations
11. Select a time and place to practice daily for a week.
12. When you are in a stress situation, start breathing diaphragmatically.

Interview Checklist for Stress Inoculation

Instructions to observer: Determine which of the following steps the helper demonstrated in using stress inoculation with a client or in teaching stress inoculation to another person. Check any step the helper demonstrated in the application of the procedure.

Item	Examples of helper leads
I. Rationale	
_____ 1. Helper explains purpose of stress inoculation.	"Stress inoculation is a way to help you cope with feeling anxious so that you can manage your reactions when you're confronted with these situations."
_____ 2. Helper provides brief overview of stress inoculation procedure.	"First, we'll try to understand how your anxious feelings affect you now. Then you'll learn some coping skills that will help you relax physically—and help you use coping thoughts instead of self-defeating thoughts. Then you'll have a chance to test out your coping skills in stressful situations we'll set up."
_____ 3. Helper checks to see whether client is willing to use strategy.	"How do you feel now about working with this procedure?"
II. Information Giving	
_____ 4. Helper explains nature of client's emotional reaction to a stressful situation.	"Probably you realize that when you feel anxious, you are physically tense. Also, you may be thinking in a worried way—worrying about the situation and how to handle it. Both the physical tenseness and the negative or worry thoughts create stress for you."
_____ 5. Helper explains possible *phases* of reacting to a stressful situation.	"When you feel anxious, you probably tend to think of it as one giant reaction. Actually, you're probably anxious at certain times or phases. For example, you might feel very uptight just anticipating the situation. Then you might feel uptight during the situation, especially if it starts to overwhelm you. After the situation is over, you may feel relieved—but down on yourself, too."
_____ 6. Helper explains specific kinds of coping skills to be learned in stress inoculation and importance of client's input in tailoring coping strategies.	"We'll be learning some action kinds of coping strategies—like physical or muscle relaxation, mental relaxation, and just commonsense ways to minimize the stress of the situation. Then also you'll learn some different ways to view and

15 POST EVALUATION

STRESS MANAGEMENT STRATEGIES 501

           think about the situation. Not all these coping strategies may seem best for you, so your input in selecting the ones you feel are best for you is important."

III. Acquisition and Practice of Direct-Action Coping Skills

____ 7. Helper discusses and models direct-action coping strategies (or uses a symbolic model):

"First, I'll explain and we can talk about each coping method. Then I'll demonstrate how you can apply it when you're provoked."

    ____ a. Collecting objective or factual information about stressful situation

"Sometimes it helps to get any information you can about things that provoke and anger you. Let's find out the types of situations and people that can do this to you. Then we can see whether there are other ways to view the provocation. For example, what if you looked at it as a situation to challenge your problem-solving ability rather than as a personal attack?"

    ____ b. Identifying short-circuit or escape routes—alternative ways to deescalate stress of situation

"Suppose you're caught in a situation. You feel it's going to get out of hand. What are some ways to get out of it or to deescalate it *before* you strike out? For example, little things like counting to 60, leaving the room, using humor, or something like that."

Mental relaxation:
____ c. Attention diversion

"OK, one way to control your anger is to distract yourself—take your attention away from the person you feel angry with. If you have to stay in the same room, concentrate very hard on an object in the room. Think of all the questions about this object you can."

____ d. Imagery manipulations

"Another way you can prevent yourself from striking out at someone is to use your imagination. Think of something very calming and very pleasurable, like listening to your favorite record or being on the beach with the hot sun."

Physical relaxation:
____ e. Muscle relaxation

"Muscle relaxation can help you cope whenever you start to feel aroused and feel your face getting flushed or your body tightening up. It can help you learn to relax your body, which can, in turn, help you control your anger."

____ f. Breathing techniques

"Breathing is also important in learning to relax physically. Sometimes, in a tight spot, taking slow, deep breaths can give you time to get yourself together before saying or doing something you don't want to."

Palliative coping strategies:
____ g. Perspective taking

"Let's try to look at this situation from a different perspective—what else about the situation might you be overlooking?"

____ h. Social support network

"Let's put together some people and resources you could use as a support system."

____ i. Ventilation of feelings

"Perhaps it would be helpful just to spend some time getting your feelings out in the open."

(continued)

15 POST EVALUATION

_____ 8. Client selects most useful coping strategies and practices each under helper's direction.

"We've gone over a lot of possible methods to help you control your anger so it doesn't result in abusive behavior. I'm sure that you have some preferences. Why don't you pick the methods that you think will work best for you? We'll practice with these so you can get a feel for them."

IV. Acquisition and Practice of Cognitive Coping Skills

_____ 9. Helper describes four phases of using cognitive coping skills to deal with a stressful situation.

"As you may remember from our earlier discussion, we talked about learning to use coping procedures at important points during a stressful or provoking situation. Now we will work on helping you learn to use coping thoughts during these four important times—preparing for the situation, handling the situation, dealing with critical moments during the situation, and encouraging yourself after the situation."

_____ 10. For each phase, helper models examples of coping statements.

"I'd like to give you some ideas of some possible coping thoughts you could use during each of these four important times. For instance, when I'm trying to psych myself up for a stressful situation, here are some things I think about."

_____ 11. For each phase, client selects the most natural coping statements.

"The examples I gave may not feel natural for you. I'd like you to pick or add ones that you could use comfortably, that wouldn't seem foreign to you."

_____ 12. Helper instructs client to practice using these coping statements for each phase.

"Sometimes, because you aren't used to concentrating on coping thoughts at these important times, it feels a little awkward at first. So I'd like you to get a feel for these just by practicing aloud the ones you selected. Let's work first on the ones for preparing for a provoking situation."

_____ 13. Helper models and instructs client to practice sequence of all four phases and verbalize accompanying coping statements.

"Next I'd like you to practice verbalizing the coping thoughts aloud in the sequence that you'll be using when you're in provoking situations. For example, [helper models]. Now you try it."

V. Application of All Coping Skills to Problem-Related Situations

_____ 14. Using coping strategies and skills selected by client, helper models how to apply these in a coping manner while imagining a stressful (problem-related) situation.

"Now you can practice using all these coping strategies when confronted with a problem situation. For example, suppose I'm you and my boss comes up to me and gives me criticism based on misinformation. Here is how I might use my coping skills in that situation."

_____ 15. Client practices coping strategies while imagining problem-related stressful situations. (This step is repeated as necessary.)

"This time, why don't you try it? Just imagine this situation—and imagine that each time you start to lose control, that is a signal to use some of your coping skills."

_____ 16. Client practices coping strategies in role play of problem-related situation. (This step is repeated as necessary.)

"We could practice this in role play. I could take the part of your boss and initiate a meeting with you. Just be yourself and use your coping skills to prepare for the meeting. Then, during our meeting, practice your skills whenever you get tense or start to blow up."

15 POST EVALUATION

VI. Application of All Coping Skills to Potential Problem Situations (Generalization)

_____ 17. Helper models application of client-selected coping strategies to non-problem-related or other potentially stressful situations.

"Let's work on some situations now that aren't problems for you but could arise in the future. This will give you a chance to see how you can apply these coping skills to other situations you encounter in the future. For instance, suppose I just found out I didn't get a promotion that I believe I really deserved. Here is how I might cope with this."

_____ 18. Client practices, as often as needed, applying coping strategies to potentially stressful situations by

"OK, you try this now."

    _____ a. Imagining a potentially stressful situation

"Why don't you imagine you've just found out you're being transferred to a new place? You are surprised by this. Imagine how you would cope."

    _____ b. Taking part in a role-play practice

"This time let's role play a situation. I'll be your husband and tell you I've just found out I am very ill. You practice your coping skills as we talk."

    _____ c. Having the client be a teacher in a role play and teaching a novice how to use coping strategies for stressful situations

"This time I'm going to pretend that I have chronic arthritis and am in constant pain. It's really getting to me. I'd like you to be my trainer or helper and teach me how I could learn to use some coping skills to deal with this chronic discomfort."

VII. Homework and Follow-Up

_____ 19. Helper and client discuss application of coping strategies to *in vivo* situations.

"I believe now you could apply these coping skills to problem situations you encounter during a typical day or week. You may not find that these work as quickly as you'd like, but you should find yourself coping more and not losing control as much."

_____ 20. Helper shows client how to use log to record uses of stress inoculation for *in vivo* situations.

"Each time you use the coping skills, mark it down on the log and briefly describe the situation in which you used them."

_____ 21. Helper arranges for a follow-up.

"We could get together next week and go over your logs and see how you're doing."

Observer comments: _____
_____
_____
_____
_____
_____
_____
_____
_____

15 POSTEVALUATION FEEDBACK

PART ONE
See if you can repeat the awareness of breathing exercise without reviewing notes. That is, see if you understand sufficiently what to look for and feel in how you go about breathing to easily show it to another person. See p. 475 if you had trouble with this.

PART TWO
Use the Checklist for Diaphragmatic Breathing to assess how completely you covered each step in your demonstration.

PART THREE
1. Your rationale to this client might sound something like this:
   "You realize that there are times when your anger and impatience do get the best of you. This procedure can help you learn to control your feelings at especially hard times—when you're very upset with this child—so that you don't do something you will regret later."

2. Here is a brief overview of stress inoculation:
   "First, we'll look at the things the child can do that really upset you. When you realize you're in this type of situation, you can learn to control how upset you are—through keeping yourself calm. This procedure will help you learn different ways to keep calm and not let these situations get out of hand."

3. Information—see lead 7, part a, on the Interview Checklist for Stress Inoculation for some examples.
   Escape route—see lead 7, part b.
   Attention diversion—see lead 7, part c.
   Imagery manipulations—see lead 7, part d.
   Physical relaxation—see lead 7, parts e and f.
   Palliative coping—see lead 7, parts g, h, and i.

4. Here are some examples of a possible explanation of the four coping phases and of cognitive coping skills you might present to this client.

Phase	Explanation	Cognitive coping
Preparing for a provoking situation	Before you have a disagreement or discussion, you can plan how you want to handle it.	"What do I want to say to him that gets my point across?" "I can tell him how I feel without shouting."
Confronting a provoking situation	When you're talking to him, you can think about how to stay in control.	"Just keep talking in a normal voice, no yelling." "Let him talk, too. Don't yell a lot; it doesn't help."
Dealing with a very provoking moment	If you feel very angry, you really need to think of some things to keep you from blowing your cool.	"Wait a minute. Slow down. Don't let the lid off." "Keep those hands down. Stay calm now."
Encouraging self for coping	Recognize when you do keep your cool. It's important to do this, to give yourself a pat on the back for this.	"I kept my cool that time!" "I could feel myself getting angry, but I kept in control then."

5. Practice opportunities can be carried out by the client in imagination or by you and the client in role play. In a role-play practice, you could take the part of the child. See leads 14, 15, and 16 on the Interview Checklist for Stress Inoculation for some examples of this type of practice.

PART FOUR
Use the Interview Checklist for Stress Inoculation to assess your role-play interview.

CHAPTER 16

MEDITATION AND MOVEMENT STRATEGIES

OBJECTIVES

After completing this chapter, the student should be able to

1. Identify which step of the relaxation response is reflected by each of 9 helper responses, accurately identifying at least 7 of the 9 examples.
2. Identify which step of the mindfulness meditation procedure is reflected by at least 8 helper responses.
3. Select either mindfulness meditation or relaxation response, and teach the procedure to another person. Audiotape your teaching and assess your steps with the Interview Checklist for Mindfulness Meditation or the Interview Checklist for Relaxation Response, or have an observer evaluate your teaching, using the checklist.
4. Describe how you would apply the 7 major components of the muscle-relaxation procedure, given a simulated client case.
5. Demonstrate 13 out of 15 steps of muscle relaxation with a role-play client, using the Interview Checklist for Muscle Relaxation to assess your performance.
6. Using 1 of the 2 body scan scripts, demonstrate the body scan with a role-play client.
7. Describe at least 7 of the 10 guidelines presented for clinical application of exercise therapy and at least 5 factors that would increase risk for commencing exercise therapy.

This chapter extends the focus on stress and its management. We all know from experience that it is difficult to focus, learn, be open to and feel energized for change, or to take on the hard work involved in helping interventions when we are wound up, fragmented, overwhelmed, and exhausted from stress. Thus, strategies such as those described in this chapter are increasingly used in conjunction with the cognitively intensive strategies that are part of the cognitive–behavioral repertoire. This is especially true for stress management training and as adjuncts to other interventions when skills in self-calming, physical awareness, emotional regulation, and help with focus and presence are needed. It is important to keep in mind the value of these strategies for helpers. We have previously noted the importance of self-care, and that may be particularly so when we are relatively new to the role, anxious, and scrambling to juggle the multiple roles of student, professional helper, family, and so forth.

First, we present meditation procedures, specifically mindfulness meditation and relaxation response. In addition, we discuss two approaches to muscle relaxation training. As you will see, muscle relaxation, including body scan, can be used in combination with other interventions or as one of the components of meditation. Similarly, mindful meditating can be a useful component of muscle relaxation, helping to focus on different muscle groups and developing skills in managing the physical experience of stress. We also review recent findings and guidelines for use of exercise therapy. Exercise therapy is finding increasing use with mental health disturbances such as depression, anxiety, body dysmorphic disorder, and schizophrenia as well as a range of physical conditions such as chronic pain and across a range of populations (e.g., older adults, people with disabilities, children).

MEDITATION: PROCESSES AND USES

Meditation has long been identified as a relaxation technique and has received increasing clinical and empirical support for its use with a range of issues commonly encountered in direct service practice. What may be less well-known is the use of meditation to develop mindfulness, a potentially important intervention strategy complementary to others presented in this book. Although no one intervention strategy is a silver bullet or appropriate for all people or circumstances, meditation is becoming a common tool used in medicine, psychology, education, and self-development

(Goleman, 1988). We will review definitions of these terms before describing how to use them in practice.

Several practitioners and researchers define the meditation strategy in different ways. Fontana (1991) describes what meditation is not and what it is: "Meditation *isn't:* falling asleep, going into a trance, shutting yourself off from reality and becoming unworldly, being selfish, doing something 'unnatural,' becoming lost in thought, forgetting where you are. Meditation *is:* keeping the mind alert and attentive, keeping the mind focused and concentrated, becoming aware of the world, becoming more human, knowing where you are" (p. 17). Dean Ornish (1990) describes meditation as "concentration," "focusing your awareness," "paying attention," and "one-pointedness" (p. 238). Thich Nhat Hanh (1976) describes mindful meditation as "keeping one's consciousness alive to the present reality. . . . Mindfulness is like that—it is the miracle which can call back in a flash our dispersed mind and restore it to wholeness so that we can live each minute of life" (pp. 11, 14).

Marlatt and Kristeller (1999) also note this element of bringing one's complete attention to the present experience: of being aware of the full range of experiences that exist in the here and now. They add to this that "mindful awareness is based on an attitude of acceptance. Rather than judging one's experiences as good or bad, healthy or sick, worthy or unworthy, mindfulness accepts all personal experiences (e.g., thoughts, emotions, events) as just 'what is' in the present moment" (p. 68). One important clinical application of mindfulness is developing the capacity of an "observing self" that pays careful attention to one's own thoughts and feelings and can see thoughts as "just thinking" rather than facts or directives. One can begin to see the value of this capacity as a self-monitoring and change tool. Marlatt and Kristeller (1999) illustrate the complementarity of meditation in the following way. Whereas some cognitive interventions would focus on changing the content of clients' problematic thoughts (e.g., "I am a failure"), meditation therapy focuses on altering the client's attitude or relationship to the thought. This may include regarding thoughts as similar to the five senses in that negative thoughts are noticed as "thought stimuli" (akin to smell or hearing stimuli) and accepted as natural behavior of the mind, but not as inherently defining the self or dictating subsequent feelings or actions (see also Epstein, 1995). Thus, two main processes of meditation include an experienced perspective of the fluid, changing nature of perceived reality as well as a capacity to self-monitor as a detached, nonevaluative observer. Joan Borysenko (1988) says that "mindfulness is meditation in action and involves a 'be here now' approach that allows life to unfold without the limitation of prejudgment. It means being open to an awareness of the moment as it is and to what the moment could hold. It is a relaxed state of attentiveness to both the inner world of thoughts and feelings and the outer world of actions and perceptions" (p. 91).

Focusing on implementation, Patel (1993) describes meditation as a practice of "taking a comfortable position—either sitting, lying down, or standing, although sitting is the most usual posture. It then involves being in a quiet environment, regulating the breath, adopting a physically relaxed and mentally passive attitude, and dwelling single-mindedly upon an object. The object of meditation does not have to be physical. It can be an idea, image, or happening; it can be mental repetition of a word or phrase, as in mantra meditation; it can be observing one's own thoughts, perception, or reaction; or it can be concentrating on some bodily generated rhythm (e.g., breathing)" (p. 127).

Borysenko (1987) broadens this definition: "meditation is any activity that keeps the attention pleasantly anchored in the present moment. . . . To develop a state of inner awareness, to witness and to let go of the old dialogues, you need an observation point. If you went out in a boat to view offshore tides but neglected to put down an anchor, you would soon be carried off to sea. So it is with the mind. Without an anchor to keep the mind in place, it will be carried away by the torrent of thoughts. Your ability to watch what is happening will be lost. The practice of meditation, which calms the body through the relaxation response and fixes the mind through dropping the anchor of attention, is the most important tool of self-healing and self-regulation" (p. 36). Similarly, Snelling (1991) describes mindfulness as not being reserved for the meditative cushion, but a capacity to step back from the ongoing drama of our lives toward a more dispassionate look at the habit patterns involved and ways that we've come to identify with them.

Carrington (1993) provides a useful overview of the history of meditation as well as modern forms. Carrington reviews some of the symptoms or difficulties for which a person might benefit from meditation: "tension and/or anxiety states, psychophysiological disorders, chronic fatigue states, insomnias and hypersomnias, alcohol, drug, or tobacco abuse, excessive self-blame, chronic low-grade depressions or subacute reaction depressions, irritability, low frustration tolerance, strong submissive trends, poor developed psychological differentiation, difficulties with self-assertion, pathological bereavement reactions, separation anxiety, blocks to productivity or creativity, inadequate contact with affective life, a need to shift emphasis from client's reliance on therapist to reliance on self—of particular use when terminating psychotherapy" (pp. 150–151). Murphy and Donovan (1997) provide a thorough documentation of the physical and psychological effects of meditation. Also, as you can see from the list in Box 16.1,

BOX 16.1 RESEARCH ON MEDITATION

Academic performance
Hall, P. (1999). The effect of meditation on the academic performance of African American college students. *Journal of Black Studies, 29*, 408–415.

Anxiety reduction
Engel, L., & Anderson, L. B. (2000). Effects of body–mind training and relaxation stretching on persons with chronic toxic encephalopathy. *Patient Education & Counseling, 39*, 155–161.

Attention
Valentine, E. R., & Sweet, P. L. G. (1999). Meditation and attention: A comparison of the effects of concentrative and mindfulness meditation on sustained attention. *Mental Health, Religion, & Culture, 2*, 59–70.

Coronary disease
Helene, B., & Ford, P. (2000). Mind–body innovations—An integrative approach. *Psychiatric Quarterly, 71*, 47–58.

Depression
Teasdale, J., Segal, Z., Williams, J., & Mark, G. (1995). How does cognitive therapy prevent depressive relapse and why should attentional control (mindfulness) training help? *Behaviour Research and Therapy, 33*, 25–39.
Tloczynski, J., & Tantriella, M. (1998). A comparison of the effects of Zen breath meditation or relaxation on college adjustment. *Psychologia: An International Journal of Psychology in the Orient, 41*(1), 32–43.

Eating disorders
Kristeller, J. L., & Hallett, C. B. An exploratory study of a meditation-based intervention for binge eating disorder. *Journal of Health Psychology, 4*, 357–363.

Elderly clients
Alexander, C. N., Robinson, P., Orme-Johnson, D., & Schneider, R. H. (1994). The effects of transcendental meditation compared to other methods of relaxation and meditation in reducing risk factors, morbidity, and mortality. *Homeostasis in Health and Disease, 35*, 243–263.

Intrusive thoughts
Fabbro, F., Muzur, A., Bellen, R., Calacione, R., & Bava, A. (1999). Effects of praying and a working memory task in participants trained in meditation and controls on the occurrence of spontaneous thoughts. *Perceptual & Motor Skills, 88*, 765–770.

Relapse prevention
O'Connell, D. F. (1991). The use of transcendental meditation in relapse prevention counseling. *Alcoholism Treatment Quarterly, 8*, 58–63.
Taub, E., Steiner, S. S., Weingarten, E., & Walton, K. G. (1994). Effectiveness of broad spectrum approaches to relapse prevention in severe alcoholism: A long-term, randomized, controlled trial of transcendental meditation, EMG biofeedback and electronic neurotherapy. Special Issue: Self-recovery: Treating addictions using transcendental meditation and Maharishi Ayur-Veda: I. *Alcoholism Treatment Quarterly, 11*, 187–220.

Respiratory rehabilitation
Connolly, M. J. (1993). Respiratory rehabilitation in the elderly patient. *Reviews in Clinical Gerontology, 3*, 281–294.

School use
Laselle, K. M., & Russell, T. T. (1993). To what extent are school counselors using meditation and relaxation techniques? *School Counselor, 40*, 178–183.

Sex offenders
Derezotes, D. (2000). Evaluation of yoga and meditation trainings with adolescent sex offenders. *Child & Adolescent Social Work Journal, 17*(2), 97–113.

Stress
Alexander, C. N., Swanson, G. C., Rainforth, M. V., & Carlisle, T. W. (1993). Effects of the transcendental meditation program on stress reduction, health, and employee development: A prospective study in two occupational settings. *Anxiety, Stress and Coping: An International Journal, 6*, 245–262.
Anderson, V. L., Levinson, E. M., Barker, W., & Kiewra, K. R. (1999). The effects of meditation on teacher perceived occupational stress, state and trait anxiety, and burnout. *School Psychology Quarterly, 14*(1), 3–25.
Astin, J. A. (1997). Stress reduction through mindfulness meditation: Effects on psychological symptomatology, sense of control, and spiritual experiences. *Psychotherapy & Psychosomatics, 66*(2), 97–106.
Roth, B. (1997). Mindfulness-based stress reduction in the inner city. *Advances, 13*(4), 50–58.
Saito, Y., & Sasaki, Y. (1993). The effect of transcendental meditation training on psychophysiological reactivity to stressful situations. *Japanese Journal of Hypnosis, 38*, 20–26.
Shapiro, S. L., Schwartz, G. E., & Bonner, G. (1998). Effects of mindfulness-based stress reduction on medical and premedical students. *Journal of Behavioral Medicine, 21*, 581–599.
Staggers, F., Alexander, C. N., & Walton, K. G. (1994). Importance of reducing stress and strengthening the host in drug detoxification: The potential offered by transcendental meditation. Special Double Issue: Self-recovery: Treating addictions using transcendental meditation and Maharishi Ayur-Veda: II. *Alcoholism Treatment Quarterly, 11*, 297–331.
Winzelberg, A. J., & Luskin, F. M. (1999). The effect of a meditation training in stress levels in secondary school teachers. *Stress Medicine, 15*(2), 69–77.

recent research on meditation reflects a wide range of applications: anxiety reduction, treatment of health conditions such as coronary disease and respiratory rehabilitation, use with varying populations such as the elderly and youth in school settings, depression stress reduction in a wide range of situations, and treatment for substance abuse, eating disorders, sexual offending, and relapse prevention.

APPLICATIONS OF MEDITATION AND RELAXATION WITH DIVERSE CLIENTS

Meditation is employed world wide, and you can see in Box 16.1 examples of its use in various cultures around the world. Many of today's meditation techniques have come from long-standing Eastern traditions, and a global perspective is evident in the research from nations such as India, Thailand, and other Asian countries (e.g., Emavardhana & Tori, 1997; Vigne, 1999). Although groups used to empirically examine meditation in the United States include diversity, we have found limited instances in which meditation practices and relaxation have been explicitly used with diverse groups of clients. Ruben (1989) used relaxation training as a part of a classroom guidance program for Hispanic and black fifth-grade students. Relaxation training enhanced self esteem and reduced the dropout rate of these students. Ibanez-Ramirez, Delgado-Morales, and Pulido-Diez (1989) reported the use of relaxation training as part of a therapeutic program that was used successfully to treat impotence in young Hispanic gay men. Hall (1999) found that meditation interventions (consisting of natural breathing techniques, relaxation, and attention-focusing techniques) were associated with a significant increase in overall academic performance with African American college students. Meditation has also been used with the elderly in various ways, including the extension of longevity (Alexander, Robinson, Orme-Johnson, & Schneider, 1994), the management of respiratory problems (Connolly, 1993), and the reduction of hypertension (Alexander et al., 1994). Generally, meditation has become a significant intervention option with elderly persons, in some cases more successful than relaxation. Research has been exploring the biophysiological mechanisms through which meditation may be producing effects (Tooley, Armstrong, Norman, & Sali 2000; Lazar, Bush, Gollub, Fricchione, Khalsa, & Benson, 2000; Solberg, Halvorsen, & Holen, 2000).

BASIC MEDITATION

Patel (1993, p. 130) describes seven steps for meditation:

1. Meditate in a place free of distracting noise, movement, light, telephones, and activity of other people.
2. Make sure you are comfortable and the room is warm; wear loose clothes, empty your bladder and bowel, and do not practice for at least two hours after a meal.
3. Make sure your back is straight, your body is relaxed, and your eyes are half or fully closed.
4. Breathe through the nostrils and down into the abdomen. Make sure that your breathing is regular, slow, and rhythmical.
5. Dwell on a single object, word, phrase, or your breath.
6. Develop a passive and relaxed attitude toward distractions.
7. Practice regularly.

Two variations of meditation are illustrated in Table 16.1 and described below: (1) mindfulness and (2) relaxation responses.

STEPS IN MINDFULNESS MEDITATION

Kabat-Zinn's (1990) perception of mindfulness meditation is "to embark upon a journey of self-development, self-discovery, learning, and healing" (p. 1).

Rationale for Treatment

Jon Kabat-Zinn (1990) offers the following rationale for engaging in mindfulness meditation:

> We live immersed in a world of constant doing. Rarely are we in touch with who is doing the doing or, put otherwise, with the world of being. To get back in touch with being is not that difficult. We only need to remind ourselves to be mindful. Moments of mindfulness are moments of peace and stillness, even in the midst of activity. When your whole life is driven by doing, formal meditation practice can provide a refuge of sanity and stability that can be used to restore some balance and perspective. It can be a way of stopping the headlong momentum of all the doing and giving yourself some time to dwell in a state of deep relaxation and well-being and to remember who you are. The formal practice can give you the strength and the self-knowledge to go back to the doing and do it from out of your being. Then at least a certain amount of patience and inner stillness, clarity and balance of mind, will infuse what you are doing, and the busyness and pressure will be less onerous. In fact they might just disappear entirely [p. 60]. . . . This is why we make a special time each day for formal meditation practice. It is a way of stopping, a way of "re-minding" ourselves, of nourishing the domain of being for a change. (p. 61)*
>
> *Source: This and following quotations from *Full Catastrophe Living*, by Jon Kabat-Zinn, copyright © 1990 by J. Kabat-Zinn. Used by permission of Dell Publishing, a division of Random House, Inc.

TABLE 16.1	Steps for the Mindfulness Meditation of Kabat-Zinn (1990) and the Relaxation Response of Benson (1987) and Benson and Stuart (1992)
Mindfulness Meditation	**Relaxation Response**
1. Rationale—about nondoing, watching whatever comes up in the mind; provides energy and self-knowledge. Give overview of procedure. Confirm client's willingness to use.	1. Rationale—give purpose and overview; meditation is a way to elicit the relaxation response; sit quietly, get a focus word or phrase, and focus on breathing. Confirm willingness to try.
2. Instruct the client about attitudinal foundations for mindfulness practice: nonjudging, patience, beginner's mind, trust, nonstriving, acceptance, and letting go.	2. Instruct about when, where, and how long to practice.
3. Instruct about commitment, self-discipline, and energy.	3. Instruct about focus word, phrase, or prayer. Give examples.
4. Instruct about preparations for meditation.	4. Instruct the client about position for meditation, and eyes.
5. Do a quick body scan to relax the muscles.	5. Request the client to relax her or his muscles—or do a quick body scan.
6. Give client breathing instructions.	6. Provide instructions for breathing.
7. Instruct about a wandering mind, focus on breathing to control the mind.	7. Instruct about a passive attitude when meditating.
8. Instruct to sit quietly, close eyes, be present in the moment, 10 to 20 minutes, come out slowly.	8. Instruct the client to meditate for about 10 to 20 minutes.
9. Inquire about the just-completed meditation experience. How did it feel? How did client handle distracting thoughts?	9. Inquire about the just-completed meditation experience for the client. How did it feel? Did client handle distracting thoughts?
10. Homework—instruct client to meditate every day or 6 days a week, for 8 weeks, and about 15 to 30 minutes a day. Instruct about informal meditation.	10. Homework—instruct the client to practice meditation once or twice daily for the next week. Not within one hour after eating; use quiet place, several hours before bedtime. Instruct how to apply *in vivo*.

Mindfulness meditation is about watching or witnessing whatever comes up from one moment to the next moment. The client is told about selecting a quiet place to meditate, with eyes closed, focusing on the breath, allowing thoughts to flow freely for a period of about 10 to 20 minutes. If the mind "trips out," we can bring it back by focusing on the breath. To enhance the practice of meditation, a participant needs attitudinal foundations.

Instructions on the Attitudinal Foundations for Mindfulness Practice

Kabat-Zinn describes seven attitudinal foundations for mindfulness meditative practice:

1. *Nonjudging* means that mindfulness is aided by being an impartial witness or observer to one's own experience. We have a habit of categorizing or judging our experiences, which locks us into unaware "knee jerk" or mechanical reactions that often do not have an objective basis. For example, you can be practicing and think about all the things you have to do and how boring the practice is. These are judgments that take you away from observing whatever comes up. If you pursue these thoughts, it takes you away from moment-by-moment awareness. To remedy this, just watch your breathing.

2. *Patience* means that we often have to allow things to unfold in their own time. Practicing patience means that we don't have to fill our lives with moments of doing and activity.

3. *Expectations of the beginner's mind* are often based on our past experiences or cognitive schema, but prevent us from seeing things as they really are. It is important for beginning meditators to be open to moment-by-moment experiences without framing the moment with expectations of how we think the moment will be.

4. *Trust* is about developing trust in your feelings and intuition. Clients are instructed to trust their feelings and wisdom, not discount them. For example, if you are sitting in a particularly uncomfortable posture while meditating, change to another posture that feels better. If your intuition says do this, follow what your intuition is telling you and experiment to find a way that matches your needs. The message is to obey and trust what your body or feelings are telling you.

5. *Nonstriving* means that mindfulness meditation is about the process of practice and not about striving to achieve something or get somewhere. Instruct clients to experience the moments; they do not have to get anywhere—just attend to or be with whatever comes up.

6. *Acceptance* means don't worry about results. Instruct the client to just focus on seeing and accepting things as they are, moment by moment, and in the present.
7. *Letting go* means nonattachment or not holding on to thoughts. If, for example, a client becomes judgmental, instruct the client to let go and just observe the judging mind. (pp. 33–40)

Instruction About Commitment, Self-Discipline, and Energy

Kabat-Zinn (1990) asks his clients to make a commitment to the practice of mindfulness meditation similar to what would be required in athletic training. In addition to the seven attitudes, clients are instructed to make a strong commitment to working on themselves, to conjure up enough self-discipline to persevere, and to generate enough energy to develop a strong meditative practice and a high degree of mindfulness (p. 41). Kabat-Zinn tells his clients, "You don't have to like it; you just have to do it" (pp. 41–42). Then, after eight weeks of practice, the client can say whether the practice was useful.

Preparations for Meditation

Clients are instructed to set aside a particular *block of time* every day—at least 6 days a week and at least 8 consecutive weeks—to practice. In using mindfulness meditation, we find that a 3-week period is necessary for the practice to take hold. Clients are given instruction about making a *special place* in their homes to meditate. The place should be comfortable and free of interruptions. The recommended pose for mindfulness meditation is a *sitting posture* on either a chair or the floor. Clients are instructed to sit erect with their head, neck, and back aligned vertically; this posture allows the breath to flow easily. If sitting in a chair, sit away from the back of the chair so the spine is self-supporting (pp. 61–62). If sitting on the floor, sit on a cushion to raise the buttocks off the floor. Some clients feel more comfortable and prefer to meditate lying on their backs. We have found that some clients who meditate lying down often fall asleep. They associate relaxation with sleep, and they lose consciousness. After meditating for a period of time (a couple of weeks), these clients start to maintain awareness and decrease their urge to sleep.

Body Scan to Relax the Muscles

Kabat-Zinn (1990) describes the body scan as a purification process for different parts of the body. The body scan process helps the client to discover his or her body and to bring mind/body awareness to the moment. (We include a body scan script in the next section of this chapter, on muscle relaxation.)

Breathing Instructions

The client is instructed to observe the breath as it flows in and out (see Chapter 15). Ask the client to notice the difference in temperature of the out breath and the in breath, and to feel the sensations of the air as it goes in and out of the nostrils.

Instructions About a Wandering Mind

Attention is often carried away by thoughts cascading through the mind. Instruct clients that when this happens, they are to return their attention to the flow of breathing and let go of the thoughts. Kabat-Zinn (1990) tells his patients that thinking is not bad, nor is it even undesirable during meditation. What matters is whether you are aware of your thoughts and feelings during meditation and how you handle them (p. 69): "Meditation is not so concerned with how much thinking is going on as it is with how much room you are making for it to take place within the field of your awareness from one moment to the next" (p. 69). If the client gets stuck in a thought, feeling, sensation, sound, pain, or discomfort, instruct the client to bring his or her attention back to breathing and to let go by exhaling these distractions.

Instructions on Meditating

Instruct clients to close their eyes and to meditate for 10 to 20 minutes. After they have concluded the meditation, they may wish to sit quietly, then move or stretch, and just relax for a few moments before opening their eyes.

Discussion of the Meditation Experience

Discuss or probe the client's reaction to meditation. Clients may be unsure of themselves because they are judging the process. Discuss with them how they felt with their first meditative experience. The helper should be nonjudgmental about what clients experience. For example, if clients say that most of their experience was chasing after thoughts, encourage them to continue meditating. Every practice will be different, and it is the process of the experience that is important.

The helper should instruct the client to select a quiet place and time and to determine how often to meditate, using the instructions from the previous mindfulness meditation experience. Also, the helper should instruct the client not to meditate within 1 hour after eating; if meditation is done in the evening, it should occur several hours before bedtime.

Finally, encourage the client to bring mindful awareness throughout the day while, for example, eating, stuck in traffic, doing everyday tasks, and interacting with people. The mantra is "to be here now," "be in the moment," "be present with what you are experiencing—in feeling and thought."

Kabat-Zinn (1990) describes four other types of mindfulness meditation in addition to the breath meditation described above:

1. Sitting with the breath and the body as a whole.
2. Sitting with sound from the environment, nature, or music—it is not about listening for sounds, but hearing what is in the moment.
3. Sitting with thoughts and feelings, which means perceiving them as events in your mind and noting their content and their change.
4. Sitting with choiceless awareness—just being open and receptive to whatever comes into your field of awareness, allowing it to come and to go. (pp. 72–74)

STEPS FOR THE RELAXATION RESPONSE

The following steps illustrate the relaxation response (Benson, 1987; Benson & Stuart, 1992); they are summarized in Table 16.1.

Rationale for Treatment

Here is an example of a rationale for meditation adapted from Benson and Stuart (1992, p. 46):

> Meditation is one technique for eliciting the relaxation response. It builds upon a process of focusing the mind on an object or activity, something you naturally do most of the time. In this use of meditation, you turn your attention inward, concentrating on a repetitive focus such as a word, a phrase, a sound or breathing. Your body and your mind begin to quiet down. A state of physiological and mental rest ensues. But, as we all know too well, the mind is usually very active and difficult to focus.

Instructions About When, Where, and How Long to Practice

Benson and Stuart (1992) recommend a period before breakfast as the best time to meditate because meditating before the daily schedule begins sets a positive tone for the day; this time is usually uncluttered with events and activities. Choosing a regular time is best; this way, a routine is developed. The place where you practice is very important. Benson and Stuart (1992) recommend selecting a place that is attractive and feels safe. The place that one selects should be quiet and free from distractions and interruptions. Ideally, a person should practice 10 to 20 minutes once or twice a day. In the beginning, clients may have difficulty setting aside a routine time to meditate and committing to meditate for a particular length of time. They should experiment with different approaches to learn what works best for them.

Instructions About a Focus Word, Phrase, or Prayer

One way to focus your mind is to link the focusing to breathing, either by concentrating on the breath or by attending closely to something. You can focus on a word, phrase, or prayer. You might draw the focal word or sound from your belief system, stemming, for example from spiritual or religious views, cultural background, or a relationship to nature and the environment. A positive or calming word such as love, warm, or place or simply focusing on calm breathing.

Instructions About Position and Eyes

Any posture that is comfortable is appropriate for meditation—lying down on one's back or sitting up. We prefer to meditate while sitting up comfortably, with the back straight and having good support. Clients are requested to close their eyes because they can be in the present moment more easily this way.

Request Client to Relax Muscles

With the client focused on breathing, the helper can do a quick body scan, starting from head to feet, or from feet to head. Any of the muscle relaxation procedures described in the next section of the chapter can be used as a prelude to meditation. Basically, the client focuses on different muscle groups and breathes tension out as she or he exhales.

Breathing Instructions

When you instruct clients in breathing, ask them to notice the rising and falling of the abdomen. Have them focus on the air coming in and going out through the nostrils and notice the slightly cooler air entering the nose and the warmer air leaving. As their breathing becomes quieter and more regular, clients may notice a subtle pause when the inhalation ends and before the exhalation begins, and vice versa (Benson & Stuart, 1992, p. 43). Chapter 15 describes different breathing exercises we have used for relaxation, body awareness, and meditation.

Instructions About a Passive Attitude

Benson and Stuart (1992, p. 47) say that meditation can be like going to a movie: You can choose to become emotionally involved in the movie, or you can pull back noting that its just a movie. The practice of meditation allows people to observe or witness their thoughts, feelings, or bodily sensations. Mark Epstein (1995), in his *Thoughts Without a Thinker,* describes attention during meditation as "diminishing reactivity. . . . Separating out the reactive self from the core experience, the practice of bare attention eventually returns the meditator to a state of unconditional openness" (p. 117). It is like watching a train—just standing or sitting and looking at one car at a time go by without changing your position. You are simply witnessing or observing without using the judging part of your mind. As quickly as one car of the train enters your sight, you let it go and attend to the next car that comes into view. Also, you can instruct clients not to worry about whether the meditation is going "correctly" or how they are doing. Tell them just to maintain a passive attitude, let go, and return to their word or breath if judgmental thoughts come to mind.

Instructions About Length of Meditation

Clients are instructed to meditate for 10 to 20 minutes. The helper and client may want to select the length of time for the first meditation before the client begins. We have found that 10 minutes may be long for the first in-session meditation, but we have also found that some clients prefer a longer period.

Discussion of Meditation Experience

The helper gets the client's reaction to the just-completed meditative experience. For example, how did the client feel? How did the client handle the distractions?

Homework and Follow-Up

The helper instructs the client to meditate twice or at least once daily for the next week. The helper can help the client identify a quiet place and time to practice during the next week, reminding the client that regular meditation is an important part of the therapeutic and healing process.

CONTRAINDICATIONS AND ADVERSE EFFECTS OF MEDITATION

It is important to be aware of cautions about using meditation, realizing that it may not be appropriate for some clients. Carrington (1993) has found that some people may be "hypersensitive to meditation" and may need a shorter period of time to meditate than other people (p. 153). Some may release emotional material that is difficult for them to handle because they meditate for a very long period of time—three or four hours. For example, patients with an active psychiatric history may experience adverse effects by meditating for an extended period (Carrington, 1993, p. 154). Goleman (1988) points out that some clients with a schizoid disorder may become overly absorbed in inner realities and less connected with reality if they meditate (p. 171). People "in acute emotional states may be too agitated to begin meditation, and obsessive–compulsive clients might become overzealous with the new experience of meditation" (Goleman, 1988, pp. 171–172). Marlatt and Kristeller (1999) note that some clients may become disconcerted with sensations of dissociation (e.g., feelings of floating or of being in a trance, sometimes with disturbing thoughts flooding the mind). They also caution use of meditation with individuals with histories of obsessive–compulsive disorder or past trauma (see also Carrington, 1998), but point out that meditation may be used effectively by individuals with some types of severe psychiatric disturbance.

Finally, for some clients, the action of certain drugs may be enhanced by meditation. Carrington (1993) recommends monitoring patients practicing meditation if they are also using antianxiety, antidepressive, antihypertensive, or thyroid-regulating drugs (p. 154). The continued practice of meditation may allow some of these patients to lower their dosage of some drugs. The practitioner should be aware of any medication the client is taking and know what potential interaction might occur with a particular drug or medication and the intervention strategy. It is important for the helper to individualize the meditative process to address client needs and concerns.

MODEL EXAMPLE: MINDFULNESS MEDITATION

In this model example, we present a narrative account of how mindfulness meditation might be used with a 49-year-old Japanese American male client. Yoshi, an air traffic controller, has reported that he would like to decrease the stress he experiences in his job. He believes that decreasing his stress will help to heal his ulcer and allow him to cope better with the demands of his job. In addition to the physical signs of stress (hypertension), Yoshi also reports that he worries constantly about making mistakes at work.

1. *Rationale:* First, we explain to Yoshi that mindfulness meditation has been used to help people cope with job-related stress. We tell him that the procedure has also been used to help people with high blood pressure and anxiety as well as those who want to feel more alert. We give him an overview of mindfulness meditation, telling him that the procedure is a process of focusing on breathing in a quiet place, with eyes closed, allowing thoughts to flow freely. We explain that he should focus on breathing if his thoughts become too distracting and tell him that most people using this technique normally meditate for 10 to 20 minutes a day. We tell Yoshi that to help the practice of meditation, participants need a foundation of attitudes on which to build a meditative practice. Finally, we confirm his willingness to use meditation, and we answer any questions he may have about the process.
2. *Attitudinal Foundations for Practice:* We explain to Yoshi that there are seven attitudes that will help mindfulness meditation practice. We tell him that mindfulness is helped by being nonjudgmental, and when we meditate, we want to be an impartial witness or observer of our experience. The mind has a tendency to categorize experiences, and we want to avoid that habit. We explain to Yoshi that we don't have to fill our lives with moments of doing and activity, and we ask him to be patient by allowing things to unfold in their own time while he is meditating. We tell him that beginners in meditation usually have expectations about how they think the moments will be while meditating, but that he should just be open to the moment-by-moment experiences without injecting expectations based on past experience. We tell him to trust his feeling and intuition; there is no "right" or "correct" way to meditate. We ask him to experiment with the process to learn what fits his needs, and to obey and trust what his feelings and intuition tell him. We explain that mindfulness meditation is about the process of practice and not about striving to achieve something or get somewhere. All he has to do is experience, to be in the moment, and attend to or be with whatever comes up. We talk to him about acceptance and tell him not to worry about the outcome—just to see and accept the way things are, moment by moment, and in the present. Finally, we talk to Yoshi about letting go and experiencing nonattachment or not holding on to thoughts and feelings; we ask him just to observe whatever comes up and observe the judging mind.
3. *Instruction About Commitment, Self-Discipline, and Energy:* We tell Yoshi to commit to practicing mindfulness in much the same way an athlete would commit to training. Yoshi understands that he must make a firm commitment, discipline himself to persevere, and generate enough energy so that he can develop a strong meditative practice.
4. *Preparations for Meditation:* We ask Yoshi to set aside a block of time every day and meditate for at least six days a week, to find a quiet and special place to meditate without interruption, and to meditate in a sitting position with his back straight. We tell him to meditate for eight weeks so that he can become adjusted to the process. We instruct him not to meditate within one hour after eating and to wear comfortable clothing during the practice time.
5. *Body Scan to Relax the Muscles:* We conduct a body scan (see next section) with Yoshi and tell him that we will scan different muscle groups of his body as a purification process. We tell him that this relaxes his body and brings mind/body awareness to the moment.
6. *Breathing Instructions:* We ask Yoshi to breathe deeply and notice how his belly expands on the in breath and falls on the out breath. We ask him to feel the difference in temperature of the out breath and the in breath, and to feel the sensation of the air as it goes in and out of the nostrils.
7. *Instructions About the Mind Wandering:* Yoshi says that his attention is often carried away by cascading thoughts. We tell him that there is nothing wrong with that; when it happens, he is just to return his attention to the flow of breathing and let the thoughts go. We tell him to be aware of his thoughts and feelings during meditation. If he gets stuck in a thought, feeling, bodily sensation, sound, pain, or discomfort, he is to bring his attention back to breathing, and exhale these distractions.
8. *Instructions to Meditate:* We instruct Yoshi to sit quietly and get relaxed for about a minute. Then he is to close his eyes and focus his breathing; the air comes in and goes out. He is to just "ride" the tide of his breath. We tell Yoshi that mindfulness meditation is not an exercise and requires no effort; he can't force it. We mention to him that if distracting thoughts, feelings, sensations, or sounds occur, he should allow them to come and not try to influence them—just observe them and return to his breathing: "The air comes in and goes out." We tell Yoshi that he will meditate for 10 to 20 minutes. When the time is up, we ask him to come out of the meditation slowly by sitting with his eyes closed for about a

minute; he may want to move and stretch. We instruct Yoshi to absorb what he is experiencing and then to open his eyes slowly.

9. *Inquire About the Just-Completed Meditation Experience:* We ask Yoshi a series of questions about his experience: "How did you feel about the experience? How did you handle distractions? What are your feelings right now?"

10. *Homework:* We instruct Yoshi to meditate once a day, preferably in the morning just after he wakes up. We remind him of the things to do to prepare: find a quiet environment, select a special time, do a quick body scan, and remember the seven attitudes and commitment, discipline, and energy. We tell him not to meditate within an hour after eating and instruct him to try to be mindful and aware throughout the day, moment to moment.

Before we turn to muscle relaxation, review Learning Activity 16.1 for meditation. Try to make time for these exercises either with someone or on your own.

MUSCLE RELAXATION: PROCESS AND USES

In muscle relaxation, a person is taught to relax by becoming aware of the sensations of tensing and relaxing major muscle groups. Take a few moments to feel and to become aware of some of these sensations. Make a fist with your preferred (dominant) hand. Clench your fist of that hand. Clench it tightly, and study the tension in your hand and forearm. Feel those sensations of tension. Now let the tension go in your fist, hand, and forearm. Relax your hand and rest it. Note the difference between the tension and the relaxation. Do the exercise once more, but this time close your eyes. Clench your fist tightly, become aware of the tension in your hand and forearm, and then relax your hand and let the tension flow out. Note the different sensations of relaxing and tensing your fist.

If you did this exercise, you may have noticed that your hand and forearm *cannot* be tense and relaxed at the same time. In other words, relaxation is incompatible with tension. You may also have noted that you instructed your hand to tense up and then to relax. You sent messages from your head to your hand to impose tension and then to create relaxation. You can cue a muscle group (the hand and forearm, in this case) to perform or respond in a particular manner (tense up and relax). This exercise was perhaps too brief for you to notice changes in other bodily functions. For example, tension and relaxation can affect one's blood pressure, heart rate, and respiration rate, and can also influence covert processes and the way one performs or responds overtly:

LEARNING ACTIVITY 16.1   Meditation (Relaxation Response and Mindfulness Meditation)

Part One

Teaching mindful meditation or the relaxation response to a client is a psychoeducational process. The helper provides the instructions, and the client engages in meditation in a self-directed manner. To practice giving instructions to someone about meditation, select a partner or a role-play client, and give instructions as described in the Interview Checklist for Mindfulness Meditation or the Interview Checklist for Relaxation Response at the end of the chapter. Then assess how well your partner was able to implement your instructions. If you wish, reverse roles so that you can experience being instructed by another person.

Part Two

This learning activity provides an opportunity to try formal meditation. Do this in a quiet, restful place when you will not be interrupted for 20 minutes. Do *not* do this within one hour *after* a meal or within two hours of going to sleep.

1. Get in a comfortable sitting position, and close your eyes.
2. Relax your entire body. Think about all the tension draining out of your body.
3. Meditate for 15 to 20 minutes.
   A. Breathe easily and naturally through your nose.
   B. Focus on your breathing with the thought of a number (one) or a word. Say (think) your word silently each time you inhale and exhale.
   C. If other thoughts or images appear, don't dwell on them but don't force them away. Just relax and focus on your word or breathing.
4. Try to assess your reactions to your meditative experience:
   How do you feel about it?
   How do you feel afterward?
   What sorts of thoughts or images come into your mind?
   How much difficulty did you have with distractions?
5. Practice the relaxation response systematically—twice daily for a week, if possible.

"The long-range goal of muscle relaxation is for the body to monitor instantaneously all of its numerous control signals, and automatically to relieve tensions that are not desired" (McGuigan, 1993, p. 21).

Relaxation training is not new, but it has recently become a popular technique for dealing with a variety of client concerns. Jacobson (1929, 1964) developed an extensive procedure called "progressive relaxation." Later, Wolpe (1958) described muscle relaxation as an anxiety-inhibiting procedure in his systematic desensitization strategy (see Chapter 17). Bernstein and Borkovec (1973) wrote a thorough relaxation manual titled *Progressive Relaxation Training*.

Muscle relaxation has been used to address many emotional and physical states (see Box 16.2). Among these are aggression, anxiety, panic disorder, as part of exercise interventions, and a range of stress and health problems –asthma, cancer, headaches, HIV/AIDS, hypertension, insomnia, irritable bowel syndrome, and urinary incoordination,. Also, body scan relaxation, a technique for muscle relaxation, is an integral part of meditation and yoga training (Kabat-Zinn, 1990; LePage, 1994; Patel, 1993).

The effects of muscle relaxation, like those of any other strategy, are related to satisfactory problem assessment, client characteristics, and the helper's ability to apply the procedure competently and confidently. Practitioners should also heed other cautions: They should not apply relaxation training indiscriminately without first exploring the causes of the client's reported tension. The practitioner would probably have made a reasonable determination of these root causes during the assessment process (see Chapters 8 and 9). For example, is muscle relaxation a logical strategy for alleviating the client's discomfort? A meaningful component of a broader intervention plan? If the client is experiencing tension in a job situation, the practitioner and client may need to deal first with the client's external situation (the job). If the client is experiencing tension as a result of oppression and discrimination, this condition will need to be targeted for change. Bernstein and Borkovec (1973) point out the difference between dealing with the tension of daily hassles or difficulties and handling the tension of someone who is on the verge of financial disaster. In the latter case, combinations of therapeutic strategies may be necessary.

STEPS OF MUSCLE RELAXATION

Muscle relaxation consists of the following seven steps:
1. Rationale
2. Instructions about dress
3. Creation of a comfortable environment
4. Helper modeling of the relaxation exercises
5. Instructions for muscle relaxation
6. Posttraining assessment
7. Homework and follow-up

These steps are described in detail in the Interview Checklist for Muscle Relaxation at the end of the chapter.

Treatment Rationale

Here is an example of one way a helper might explain the *purpose* of relaxation: "This process, if you practice it regularly, can help you become relaxed. The relaxation benefits you derive can help you sleep better at night." An *overview* of the procedure might be this: "The procedure involves learning to tense and relax different muscle groups in your body. By doing this, you can compare the difference between tenseness and relaxation. This will help you to recognize tension so you can instruct yourself to relax."

In addition, the helper should explain that muscle relaxation is a *skill*. The process of learning will be gradual and will require regular practice. Finally, the helper might explain that some discomfort may occur during the relaxation process. If so, the client can just move his or her body to a more comfortable position. Finally, the client may experience some floating, warming, or heavy sensations. The helper should inform the client about these possible sensations. The explanation of the rationale for muscle relaxation should be concluded with a probing of the client's willingness to try the procedure.

Instructions About Dress

Before the actual training session, clients should be instructed about appropriate clothing. They should wear comfortable clothes such as slacks, a loose-fitting blouse or shirt, or any apparel that will not be distracting during the exercises. Clients who wear contact lenses should be told to wear their regular glasses for the training. They can take off the glasses while going through the exercises. It is uncomfortable to wear contact lenses when your eyes are closed.

Creation of a Comfortable Environment

A comfortable environment is necessary for effective muscle-relaxation training. The training environment should be quiet and free of distracting noises such as ringing telephones, street repair work outside, and airplane sounds. A padded recliner chair should be used, if possible. If the facility cannot afford one, an aluminum lawn chair or recliner covered with a foam pad may be satisfactory. If relaxation

BOX 16.2 MUSCLE RELAXATION RESEARCH

Aggression
To, M. Y. F., & Chan, S. (2000). Evaluating the effectiveness of progressive muscle relaxation in reducing the aggressive behaviors of mentally handicapped patients. *Archives of Psychiatric Nursing, 14,* 39–46.

Anxiety
Rasid, Z. M., & Parish, T. S. (1998). The effects of two types of relaxation training on students' levels of anxiety. *Adolescence, 33*(129), 99–101.

Asthma
Lehrer, P., Sargunaraj, D., & Hochron, S. M. (1992). Psychological approaches to the treatment of asthma. Special Issue: Behavioral medicine: An update for the 1990s. *Journal of Consulting and Clinical Psychology, 60,* 639–643.

Cancer
Baider, L., Uziely, B., & Kaplan De Nour, A. (1994). Progressive muscle relaxation and guided imagery in cancer patients. *General Hospital Psychiatry, 16,* 340–347.

Creativity
Krampen, G. (1997). Promotion of creativity (divergent productions) and convergent productions by systematic-relaxation exercises: Empirical evidence from five experimental studies with children, young adults, and elderly. *European Journal of Personality, 11*(2), 83–99.

Dementia disturbances
Suhr, J., Anderson, S., & Tranel, D. (1999). Progressive muscle relaxation in the management of behavioral disturbance in Alzheimer's disease. *Neuropsychological Rehabilitation, 9,* 31–44.

Headache
Arena, J., Bruno, G., Hannah, S., & Meador, K. (1995). A comparison of frontal electromyographic biofeedback training, trapezius electromyographic biofeedback training, and progressive muscle relaxation therapy in the treatment of tension headache. *Headache, 35,* 411–419.
Blanchard, E. B., Kim, M., Hermann, C. U., & Steffeck, B. D. (1993). Preliminary results of the effects on headache relief of perception of success among tension headache patients receiving relaxation. *Headache Quarterly, 4,* 249–253.
Rokicki, L. A., Holroyd, K. A., France, C. R., Lipchik, G. L., France, J. L., & Kvaal, S. A. (1997). Change mechanisms associated with combined relaxation/EMG biofeedback training for chronic tension headache. *Applied Psychophysiology & Biofeedback, 22,* 21–41.
Sartory, G., Mueller, B., Metsch, J., & Pothmann, R. (1998). A comparison of psychological and pharmacological treatment of pediatric migraine. *Behavioral Research & Therapy, 36,* 1155–1170.

HIV/AIDS
Cruess, D. G., Antoni, M. H., Kumar, M., & Schneiderman, N. (2000). Reductions in salivary cortisol are associated with mood improvement during relaxation training among HIV-seropositive men. *Journal of Behavioral Medicine, 23*(2), 107–122.
Eller, L. S. (1999). Effects of cognitive–behavioral interventions on quality of life in persons with HIV. *International Journal of Nursing Studies, 36,* 223–233.

Hypertension
Amigo, I., Gonzalez, A., & Herrera, J. (1997). Comparison of physical exercise and muscle relaxation training in the treatment of mild essential hypertension. *Stress Medicine, 13,* 59–65.
Broota, A., Varma, R., & Singh, A. (1995). Role of relaxation in hypertension. *Journal of the Indian Academy of Applied Psychology, 21,* 29–36.
Haaga, D. A. F., Davison, G. C., Williams, M. E., & Dolezal, S. L. (1994). Mode-specific impact of relaxation training for hypertensive men with Type A behavior pattern. *Behavior Therapy, 25,* 209–223.

Insomnia
Gustafson, R. (1992). Treating insomnia with a self-administered muscle relaxation training program: A follow-up. *Psychological Reports, 70,* 124–126.

Irritable bowel syndrome
Blanchard, E. B., Green, B., Scharff, L., & Schwarz-McMorris, S. P. (1993). Relaxation training as a treatment for irritable bowel syndrome. *Biofeedback and Self-Regulation, 18,* 125–132.

Panic disorder
Ost, L-G., Westling, B. E., & Hellstrom, K. (1993). Applied relaxation, exposure *in vivo* and cognitive methods in the treatment of panic disorder with agoraphobia. *Behaviour Research and Therapy, 31,* 383–394.

Physical activity
Buckelew, S. P., Conway, R., Parker, J., Deuser, W. E., Read, J., Witty, T. E., Hewett, J. E., Minor, M., Johnson, J. C., Van Male, L., McIntosh, M. J., Nigh, M., & Kay, D. R. (1998). Biofeedback/relaxation training and exercise interventions for fibromyalgia: A prospective trial. *Arthritis Care & Research, 11*(3), 196–209.

Review of abbreviated progressive muscle relaxation
Carlson, C. R., & Hoyle, R. H. (1993). Efficacy of abbreviated progressive muscle relaxation training: A quantitative review of behavioral medicine research. *Journal of Consulting and Clinical Psychology, 61,* 1059–1067.

Stress
Khasky, A. D., & Smith, J. C. (1999). Stress, relaxation states, and creativity. *Perceptual & Motor Skills, 88,* 409–416.

Urinary incoordination
Philips, H. C., Fenster, H. N., & Samsom, D. (1992). An effective treatment for functional urinary incoordination. *Journal of Behavioral Medicine, 15,* 45–63.

training is applied to groups, pads or blankets can be placed on the floor, with pillows to support each client's head. The clients can lie on the floor on their backs, with their legs stretched out and their arms along their sides with palms down.

Helper Modeling of the Relaxation Exercises

Just before the relaxation training begins, the helper should model briefly at least a few of the muscle exercises that will be used in training. The helper can start with either the right or the left hand (make a fist, then relax the hand, opening the fingers; tense and relax the other hand; bend the wrists of both arms and relax them; shrug the shoulders and relax them) and continue demonstrating some of the rest of the exercises. The helper should tell the client that the demonstration is going much faster than the speed at which the client will perform the exercises. The helper should also punctuate the demonstration with comments like "When I clench my biceps like this, I feel the tension in my biceps muscles, and now, when I relax and drop my arms to my side, I notice the difference between the tension that was in my biceps and the relative relaxation I feel now." These comments are used to show clients how to discriminate between tension and relaxation.

Instructions for Muscle Relaxation

Muscle-relaxation training can start after the helper has given the client the rationale for the procedure, answered any questions about relaxation training, instructed the client about what to wear, created a comfortable environment for the training, and modeled some of the various muscle-group exercises. In delivering (or reading) the instructions for the relaxation training exercises, the helper's voice should be conversational, not dramatic. We recommend that the helper practice along with the client during the beginning exercises. Practicing initial relaxation exercises with the client can give the helper a sense of timing for delivering the verbalizations of relaxation and tension and may decrease any awkwardness that the client feels about doing "body" exercises.

In instructing the client to tense and relax muscles, remember that you do *not* want to instruct the client to tense up as hard as possible. You do not want the client to strain a muscle. Be careful of your vocabulary when giving instructions. Do not use phrases like "as hard as you can," "sagging or drooping muscles," or "tense the muscles until they feel like they could snap." Sometimes you can supplement instructions to tense and relax with comments about the client's breathing or the experiencing of warm or heavy sensations. These comments may help the client to relax.

The various muscle groups used for client training can be categorized into 17 groups, 7 groups, or 4 groups. These sets of muscle groups, adapted from Bernstein and Borkovec (1973), are listed in Table 16.2. Generally, in initial training sessions, the helper instructs the client to go through all 17 muscle groups. When the client can alternately tense and relax any of the 17 muscle groups on command, you can abbreviate this somewhat long procedure and train the client in using 7 muscle groups. After this process, the client can practice relaxation using only 4 major muscle groups. Start with either 17 or 7 muscle groups. This may help the client to discriminate sensations of tension and relaxation in different parts of the body. Then you can gradually reduce the number of muscle groups involved. When the client gets to the point of using the relaxation *in vivo,* 4 muscle groups are much less unwieldy than 17!

The following section illustrates how the helper can instruct the client in relaxation using all 17 muscle groups. First, the helper instructs the client to settle back as comfortably as possible—either in the recliner chair or on the floor with the client's head on a pillow. The arms can be alongside the body, resting on the arms of the chair or on the floor, with the palms of the hands down. The helper then instructs the client to close her or his eyes. In some instances, a client may not wish to do this; at other times, the helper and the client may decide that it might be more therapeutic to keep the eyes open during the training. In such cases, the client can focus on some object in the room or on the ceiling. Tell the client to *listen* and to *focus* on your instructions. When presenting instructions for each muscle group, direct the client's attention to the tension, which is held for 5 to 7 seconds, and then to the feelings of relaxation that follow when the client is instructed to relax. Allow about 10 seconds for the client to enjoy the relaxation associated with each muscle group before delivering another instruction. Intermittently throughout the instructions, make muscle-group comparisons—for example, "Is your forehead as relaxed as your biceps?" While delivering the instructions, gradually lower your voice and slow the pace of delivery. Usually in initial training sessions, each muscle group is presented twice.

Here is a way the helper might proceed with initial training in muscle relaxation, using the list of 17 muscle groups in Table 16.2:

TABLE 16.2 Relaxation Exercises for 17, 7, and 4 Muscle Groups

17 muscle groups	7 muscle groups	4 muscle groups
1. Clenching *fist* of dominant *hand* 2. Clenching *fist* of nondominant *hand* 3. Bending *wrist* of one or both arms 4. Clenching *biceps* (one at a time or together) 5. Shrugging *shoulders* (one at a time or together) 6. Wrinkling *forehead* 7. Closing *eyes* tightly 8. Pressing *tongue* or clenching *jaws* 9. Pressing *lips* together 10. Pressing *head* back (on chair or pillow) 11. Pushing *chin* into chest 12. Arching *back* 13. Inhaling and holding *chest muscles* 14. Tightening *stomach* muscles 15. Contracting *buttocks*^a 16. Stretching *legs* 17. Pointing *toes* toward head	1. Hold *dominant arm* in front with elbow bent at about 45-degree angle while making a *fist* (hand, lower arm, and biceps muscles). 2. Same exercise with *nondominant arm*. 3. Facial muscle groups. Wrinkle *forehead* (or frown), squint *eyes*, wrinkle up *nose*, clench *jaws* or press *tongue* on roof of mouth, press *lips* or pull corners of mouth back. 4. Press or bury *chin* in chest (neck and throat). 5. *Chest, shoulders, upper back,* and *abdomen*. Take deep breath, hold it, pull shoulder blades back and together, while making stomach hard (pulling in). 6. *Dominant thigh, calf,* and *foot*. Lift foot off chair or floor slightly while pointing toes and turning foot inward. 7. Same as 6, with *nondominant thigh, calf,* and *foot*.	1. Right and left *arms, hands,* and *biceps* (same as 1 and 2 in 7-muscle group) 2. *Face* and *neck* muscles. Tense all *face* muscles (same as 3 and 4 in 7-muscle group) 3. *Chest, shoulders, back* and *stomach* muscles (same as 5 in 7-muscle group) 4. Both left and right upper *leg, calf,* and *foot* (combines 6 and 7 in 7-muscle group)

^aThis muscle group can be eliminated; its use is optional.
Source: Progressive Relaxation Training: A Manual for Helping Professions, by D. A. Bernstein and T. D. Borkovec. Copyright 1973 by Research Press. Used by permission.

1. *Fist of dominant hand.* "First think about your right arm, your right hand in particular. Clench your right fist. Clench it tightly and study the tension in the hand and in the forearm. Study those sensations of tension. [Pause.] Now let go. Just relax the right hand and let it rest on the arm of the chair [or floor]. [Pause.] And note the difference between the tension and the relaxation." [10-second pause.]
2. *Fist of nondominant hand.* "Now we'll do the same with your left hand. Clench your left fist. Notice the tension [5-second pause], and now relax. Enjoy the difference between the tension and the relaxation." [10-second pause.]
3. *Wrist of one or both arms.* The helper can instruct the client to bend the wrists of both arms at the same time or to bend each separately. You might start with the dominant arm if you instruct the client to bend the wrists one at a time. "Now bend both hands back at the wrists so that you tense the muscles in the back of the hand and in the forearm. Point your fingers toward the ceiling. Study the tension, and now relax. [Pause.] Study the difference between tension and relaxation." [10-second pause.]
4. *Biceps.* The helper can instruct the client to work with both biceps or just one at a time. If you train the client to do one at a time, start with the dominant biceps. The instructions for this exercise are "Now clench both your hands into fists and bring them toward your shoulders. As you do this, tighten your biceps muscles, the ones in the upper part of your arm. Feel the tension in these muscles. [Pause.] Now relax. Let your arms drop down to your sides. See the difference between the tension and the relaxation." [10-second pause.]
5. *Shoulders.* Usually the client is instructed to shrug both shoulders. However, the client could be instructed to shrug one shoulder at a time. "Now we'll move to the

shoulder area. Shrug your shoulders. Bring them up to your ears. Feel and hold the tension in your shoulders. [Pause.] Now, let both shoulders relax. Note the contrast between the tension and the relaxation that's now in your shoulders." [10-second pause.]

6. *Forehead.* This and the next three exercises are for the facial muscles. The instructions for the forehead are "Now we'll work on relaxing the various muscles of the face. First, wrinkle up your forehead and brow. Do this until you feel your brow furrow. [Pause.] Now relax. Smooth out the forehead. Let it loosen up." [10-second pause.]

7. *Eyes.* The purpose of this exercise is for the client to compare the difference between tension and relaxation for the muscles that control the movements of the eyes. "Now close your eyes tightly. Can you feel tension all around your eyes? [5-second pause.] Now relax those muscles, noting the difference between the tension and the relaxation." [10-second pause.]

8. *Tongue or jaws.* You can instruct some clients to clench their jaws: "Now clench your jaws by biting your teeth together. Pull the corners of your mouth back. Study the tension in the jaws. [5-second pause.] Relax your jaws now. Can you tell the difference between tension and relaxation in your jaw area?" [10-second pause.] This exercise may be difficult for some clients who wear dentures. An alternative exercise is to instruct them to "Press your tongue into the roof of your mouth. Note the tension within your mouth. [5-second pause.] Relax your mouth and tongue now. Just concentrate on the relaxation." [10-second pause.]

9. *Pressing the lips together.* The last facial exercise involves the mouth and chin muscles. "Now press your lips together tightly. As you do this, notice the tension all around the mouth. [Pause.] Now relax those muscles around the mouth. Enjoy this relaxation in your mouth area and your entire face. [Pause.] Is your face as relaxed as your biceps [intermuscle-group comparison]?"

10. *The head.* "Now we'll move to the neck muscles. Press your head back against your chair. Can you feel the tension in the back of your neck and in your upper back? Hold the tension. [Pause.] Now let your head rest comfortably. Notice the difference. Keep on relaxing." [10-second pause.]

11. *Chin in chest.* This exercise focuses on the muscles in the neck, particularly the front of the neck. "Now continue to concentrate on the neck area. Bring your head forward. See whether you can bury your chin into your chest. Note the tension in the front of your neck. Now relax and let go." [10-second pause.]

12. *The back.* Be careful here—you don't want the client to get a sore back. "Now direct your attention to your upper back area. Arch your back as if you were sticking out your chest and stomach. Can you feel tension in your back? Study that tension. [Pause.] Now relax. Note the difference between the tension and the relaxation." [10-second pause.]

13. *Chest muscles.* Inhaling (filling the lungs) and holding the breath focuses the client's attention on the muscles in the chest and down into the stomach area. "Now take a deep breath, filling your lungs, and hold it. Feel the tension all through your chest and into your stomach area. Hold that tension. [Pause.] Now relax and let go. Let your breath out naturally. Enjoy the pleasant sensations." [10-second pause.]

14. *Stomach muscles.* "Now think about your stomach. Tighten up the muscles in your abdomen. Hold this. Make the stomach like a knot. Now relax. Loosen those muscles now. [10-second pause.] Is your stomach as relaxed as your back and chest [muscle-group comparison]?" An alternative instruction is to tell the client to "pull in your stomach" or "suck in your stomach."

15. *The buttocks.* Moving down to other areas of the body, the helper instructs or coaches the client to tighten the buttocks. This muscle group is optional; with some clients, the helper may delete it and move on to the legs. The model instructions are "Now tighten [tense or contract] your buttocks by pulling them together and pushing them into the floor [or chair]. Note the tension. And now relax. Let go and relax." [10-second pause.]

16. *Legs.* "I'd like you now to focus on your legs. Stretch both legs. Feel tension in the thighs. [5-second pause.] Now relax. Study the difference again between tension in the thighs and the relaxation you feel now." [10-second pause.]

17. *Toes.* "Now concentrate on your lower legs and feet. Tighten both calf muscles by pointing your toes toward your head. Pretend a string is pulling your toes up. Can you feel the pulling and the tension? Note that tension. [Pause.] Now relax. Let your legs relax deeply. Enjoy the difference between tension and relaxation." [10-second pause.]

After each muscle group has been tensed and relaxed twice, the helper usually concludes relaxation training with a summary and review. The helper goes through the review by listing each muscle group and asking the client to dispel any tension that is noted as the helper names the muscle area. Here is an example:

Now I'm going to go over once more the muscle groups that we've covered. As I name each group, try to notice whether there is any tension in those muscles. If there is any, try to concentrate on those muscles and tell them to relax. Think of draining the tension completely out of your body as we do this. Now relax the muscles in your feet, ankles, and calves. [Pause.] Get rid of tension in your knees and thighs. [5-second pause.] Loosen your hips. [Pause.] Let the muscles of your lower body go. [Pause.] Relax your abdomen, waist, lower back. [Pause.] Drain the tension from your upper back, chest, and shoulders. [Pause.] Relax your upper arms, forearms, and hands. Loosen the muscles of your throat and neck. [Pause.] Relax your face. [Pause.] Let all the tension drain out of your body. [Pause.] Now just sit quietly with your eyes closed.

The practitioner can conclude the training session by evaluating the client's level of relaxation on a scale from 0 to 5 or by counting aloud to the client to instruct him or her to become successively more alert. For example:

Now I'd like you to think of a scale from 0 to 5, where 0 is complete relaxation and 5 is extreme tension. Tell me where you would place yourself on that scale now. I'm going to count from 5 to 1. When I reach the count of 1, open your eyes. 5 . . . 4 . . . 3 . . . 2 . . . 1. Open your eyes now.

Posttraining Assessment

After the session of relaxation training, the helper asks the client about the experience. The helper can ask "What is your reaction to the procedure?" "How do you feel?" "What reaction did you have when you focused on the tension?" "What about relaxation?" or "How did the contrast between the tension and relaxation feel?" The helper should be encouraging about the client's performance, praise the client, and build a positive expectancy about the training and practice.

People experiencing relaxation training may have several difficulties or stress symptoms (Bernstein & Borkovec, 1973). Some of these potential areas are cramps, excessive laughter or talking, spasms or tics, intrusive thoughts, falling asleep, inability to relax individual muscle groups, unfamiliar sensations, and holding the breath. If the client experiences muscle cramps, possibly too much tension is being created in the particular muscle group. In this case, the helper can instruct the client to decrease the amount of tension. If spasms and tics occur in certain muscle groups, the helper can mention that these occur commonly, as in one's sleep, and possibly the reason the client is aware of them now is that he or she is awake. Excessive laughter or talking would most likely occur in group-administered relaxation training. Possibly the best solution is to ignore it or to discuss how such behavior can be distracting.

A common training issue is for the client to fall asleep during relaxation training. The client should be informed that continually falling asleep can impede learning the skills associated with muscle relaxation. By watching the client throughout training, the helper can confirm whether the client is awake. The helper also can tell the client to "stay awake" during the muscle-relaxation process.

If the client has difficulty or is unable to relax a particular muscle group, the helper and client might work out an alternative exercise for that muscle group. If intrusive client thoughts become too distracting, the helper might suggest changing the focus of the thought to something less distracting or to more positive or pleasant thoughts. It might be better for some clients to gaze at a picture of their choosing placed on the wall or ceiling throughout the training. Another strategy for dealing with interfering or distracting thoughts is to help the client use task-oriented coping statements or thoughts (see Chapters 14 and 15) that would aid in focusing on the relaxation training.

Another potential difficulty is the occurrence of unfamiliar sensations, such as floating, warmth, and headiness. The helper should point out that these sensations are common and that the client should not fear them. Finally, some clients have a tendency to hold their breath while tensing a muscle. The helper needs to observe the client's breathing during muscle relaxation. If the client is holding the breath, the helper can instruct the client to breathe freely and easily. The helper can also use a variation of this procedure that we describe later.

Homework and Follow-Up

The last step in muscle relaxation is assigning homework. Four or five training sessions with two daily home practice sessions between sessions are probably sufficient. Some practitioners have found that minimal helper contact with the client and home-based relaxation training using manuals and audiotapes with telephone consultation were just as effective in reducing tension headaches as six hours of helper-assisted training. Regardless of the amount of time or number of training sessions with the client, the helper should inform the client that relaxation training, like learning any skill, requires a great deal of practice.

The more the client practices the procedure, the more proficient he or she will become in gaining control over tension, anxiety, or stress. The client should be instructed to select a quiet place for practice, free from distracting noise. The client should be encouraged to practice the muscle-relaxation exercises about 15 to 20 minutes twice a day. The exercises should be done when there is no time pressure. Some clients may not be willing to practice twice a day. The practitioner can encourage these clients to practice several times or as often as they can during the week. The exercises can be done in a recliner chair or on the floor, with a pillow supporting the head.

The client should be encouraged to complete a homework log after each practice. Figure 16.1 is an example of a homework log. Clients can rate their reactions on a scale from 1 (little or no tension) to 5 (extremely tense) before and after each practice. They can practice the relaxation exercises using a tape recording of the relaxation instructions or from memory. After client homework practices, a follow-up session should be scheduled.

A practitioner can use several techniques to promote client compliance with relaxation homework assignments. One technique is to ask the client to demonstrate during the session how the exercises for the muscles in the neck or the calf, for example, were done during last week's home practice. The helper can select randomly from four or five muscle groups for the client to demonstrate. If the exercises are demonstrated accurately, the client probably practiced.

CONTRAINDICATIONS AND ADVERSE EFFECTS OF MUSCLE RELAXATION

Generally, muscle relaxation is benign and pleasant, but for some people it can have adverse side effects—for example, clients with generalized anxiety disorder, panic disorder, or a history of hyperventilation (Bernstein & Carlson, 1993, p. 66). Some clients with certain muscles or connective tissues that have been damaged or are chronically weak will have difficulty in tensing and relaxing a particular muscle group. Also, some clients are incapable of exercising voluntary

Homework Log Sheet						
Date	Tape Number	Note Which Muscle Groups Exercised	Practice Session Number	Location of Session	Level of Tension (1–5)	
					Before Session	After Session

Note: 1 = slightly or not tense; 2 = somewhat tense; 3 = moderately tense; 4 = very tense; 5 = extremely tense.

Figure 16.1 Example of homework log sheet for relaxation training

control over all muscles in the body because of a neuromuscular disability. Finally, with some medication for diabetes or for hypertension, clients receiving relaxation training may require a change in the amount of medication they need (Bernstein & Carlson, 1993, p. 67). A medical consultation may be necessary before beginning muscle-relaxation training with clients who are taking certain types of medication. Be sure to seek such a consultation if there is a question about medications such as those described above. In cases of anxiety or panic disorders, the helping practitioner can start with the breathing exercises described in the first section of Chapter 15. If a client has difficulty with a particular muscle group, the helper can avoid that group or do a body scan. Herman (1994) notes that relaxation is often contraindicated for clients who present with severe trauma histories because of their need to maintain some degree of vigilance in order to feel safe.

VARIATIONS OF MUSCLE RELAXATION

There are several variations of the muscle-relaxation training procedure as we've described it. These variations, which include recall, counting, differential relaxation, and body scan, are arranged and designed in successive approximations, from the helper assisting the client to acquire the skills to the client applying the relaxation skills in real-life situations. The 4 muscle group exercises listed in Table 16.2 can be used in combination with the recall and counting procedures described by Bernstein and Borkovec (1973).

Recall

Recall proceeds according to the relaxation exercises for the 4 muscle groups (Table 16.2) without muscular tension. The helper first instructs the client about the rationale for using this variation of relaxation training: "To increase your relaxation skills without the need to tense up the muscles." The client is asked to focus on each muscle group. Then the helper instructs the client to focus on one of the 4 muscle groups (arms; face and neck; chest, shoulders, back, and stomach; legs and feet) and to relax and just recall what it was like when the client released the tension (in the previous session) for that particular muscle group. The helper might suggest that if there is tension in a particular muscle group, the client should just relax or send a message for the muscle to relax and should allow what tension there is to "flow out." The helper gives similar instructions for all 4 muscle groups. Again, the client is to recall what the relaxation felt like for each muscle group. Clients can generally use recall after first learning the tension/relaxation-contrast procedure for the 4 muscle groups. Gradually, the client can use recall to induce relaxation in self-directed practices. Recall can also be used in combination with counting.

Counting

The rationale for counting is that it helps the client become very deeply relaxed. Again, the helper explains the rationale for using counting. The helper says that she or he will count from 1 to 10 and that this will help the client to become more relaxed after each number. The helper might say the following slowly:

> One—you are becoming more relaxed; two—notice that your arms and hands are becoming more and more relaxed; three—feel your face and neck becoming more relaxed; four, five—more and more relaxed are your chest and shoulders; six—further and further relaxed; seven—back and stomach feel deeply relaxed; eight—further and further relaxed; nine—your legs and feet are more and more relaxed; ten—just continue to relax as you are—relax more and more.

The helper can use this counting procedure with recall. The client can also be instructed to use counting in real situations that provoke tension. For a more detailed presentation of counting, see Bernstein and Borkovec (1973). As you may remember from Chapter 15, counting is one type of direct-action coping skill used in stress inoculation. Counting can increase relaxation and decrease tension, and the client should be encouraged to practice it outside the session.

Differential Relaxation

This variation—differential relaxation—may contribute to generalization of the relaxation training from the treatment session to the client's world. The purpose of differential relaxation is to help the client recognize what muscles are needed in various situations, body positions, and activities in order to differentiate which muscle groups are used and which are not. Table 16.3 illustrates some possible levels for the differential-relaxation procedure.

As an example of differential relaxation, the helper might have the client sit in a regular chair (not a recliner) and ask the client to identify which muscles are used and which are not when sitting. If the client feels tension in muscles that are not used (face, legs, and stomach), he or she is instructed to induce and to maintain relaxation in the muscles not required for what the client is doing (sitting). The helper can instruct

TABLE 16.3	Levels of Differential-Relaxation Procedure	
Situation	Body position	Activity level
Quiet	Sitting	Low—inactive
Noisy	Standing	High—routine movements

the client to engage in different levels of the differential-relaxation procedure—for example, sitting down in a quiet place while inactive, or standing up. After several practice sessions, the client can be assigned homework in order to engage in various levels of these activities. Examples might be sitting in a quiet cafeteria, sitting in a noisy cafeteria while eating, standing in line for a ticket to some event, or walking in a busy shopping center. In practicing differential relaxation, the client tries to recognize whether any tension exists in the nonessential muscle groups. If there is tension in the nonengaged muscles, the client concentrates on dispelling it.

Body Scan

A body scan can be a powerful technique for reestablishing contact with the body because it is a way to develop concentration and flexibility of attention simultaneously (Kabat-Zinn, 1990, p. 77). The purpose of scanning your body is to feel each region or muscle group. You can focus the breath on each region of the body by breathing into the region and breathing out of the region. If the client feels tension in one region, the helper instructs the client to breathe the tension out on the exhalation. We offer two scripts for body scanning. The first provides instructions for deep muscle relaxation with little focus on breathing (Patel, 1993, pp. 123–124). The second body scan (LePage, 1994,

---

Instructions for Deep Muscle Relaxation Body Scan

1. Close your eyes. Very slowly fill your lungs, starting at the diaphragm and working right up to the top of the chest, then very slowly breathe out. After three slow breaths, allow your breathing to become normal and regular. Breathe in and out gently and rhythmically, using your diaphragm. Don't force your breath. Don't try to make it slow deliberately. Just keep your own rhythm. Be completely aware of your breathing pattern. Feel the subtle difference in the temperature of the air you are inhaling and the air you are exhaling. The air you breathe in is cooler, and the air you breathe out is warmer.
2. Now you are consciously going to relax each part of the body in turn. Relaxation means the complete absence of movement, since even the slightest movement means that some of your muscles are contracting. It also excludes holding any part rigid. Concentrate on the part you are relaxing.
3. Now take your mind to your right foot and relax your toes, instep, heel, and the ankle; stay there for a few seconds. Now move your attention slowly up, relaxing your leg, calf, knee, thigh, and the hip. Feel all the muscles, joints, and tissues of your right leg becoming completely relaxed. Relax as deeply as you can. Just keep your awareness on this feeling of deep relaxation in your right leg for a few moments.
4. Now take your mind to your left foot and repeat the process, working up the leg, knee, thigh, and the hip as before. Let all the tension ease away and enjoy the feeling of relaxation for a few seconds.
5. Next concentrate on your right hand. Relax the fingers, thumb, palm, and wrist. Move your attention up to your forearm, elbow, upper arm, and shoulder. Feel every muscle, joint, and tissue in your right arm becoming deeply relaxed. Fix your attention on the sensation of relaxation in your entire right arm for a few moments.
6. Now become aware of your left hand and relax the fingers, thumb, palm, wrist, forearm, elbow, upper arm, and the shoulder. Let all the tension ease away from the left arm.
7. Now concentrate on the base of your spine, vertebra by vertebra, relaxing each vertebra and the muscles on either side of the spine into the floor. Relax your back—first the lower back, then the middle back, and finally the upper back. Release all the tension from your back. Let the relaxation become deeper and deeper. Feel your back merging with the floor.
8. Let the muscles in your neck relax next. Let all the muscles in the front of your neck relax. Let your head rest gently and feel the back of the neck relaxing. Let the relaxation become as deep as possible.
9. Relax your chest. Every time you breathe out, relax a little more. Let your body sink into the floor a little more each time. Let all the nerves, muscles, and organs in your chest relax completely. Now relax the muscles of your stomach. Let all the nerves, muscles, and organs in your stomach relax completely. Just feel them relaxing.
10. Now concentrate on your jaw. Let it relax so that it drops slightly, your lips are just touching each other, and your teeth are apart. Relax your tongue; relax the muscles around your cheekbones. Relax your eyes and muscles around your eyes. Feel them becoming relaxed. Your eyes must become very still. Now relax your forehead; let all the muscles in your forehead become completely relaxed. There is no tension in your facial muscles at all. Now relax your scalp and all the muscles around your head.
11. Your body is now completely relaxed. Keep it relaxed for a few more minutes.

To come out of relaxation, take one deep breath, feeling the energy coming down into your arms and legs. Move your arms and legs slowly. Open your eyes without reacting to the light, and slowly sit up and stretch your body, feeling refreshed and re-energized.

(continued)

(continued)

Body Awareness Relaxation

Allow the body to begin to completely relax. . . . Inhale and feel the breath flow from the soles of the feet to the crown of the head, like a gentle slow motion wave. With each exhalation allow tension to flow out of the body. Bring your awareness to the fingers of the left hand. Inhale breath and awareness through the fingers and up the left arm. Exhale, release the arm into the support of the earth. . . . Allow relaxation to deepen with each exhalation. Now bring your awareness to the right fingertips and inhale the breath up the arm, exhale and completely relax. As you relax the arms, become more aware of all the feelings and sensations. . . . Focus all of your awareness into these sensations and then relax into them.

Now bring your awareness down to the toes of the left foot, drawing the wave of breath up to the top of the leg, and on exhalation relax the leg fully. Now bring your awareness into the right leg, and allow the wave of breath to flow up the right leg, and with the exhalation completely surrender the weight of the leg. Feel and see both legs now and with each breath become more aware of all the sensations in the legs, with each exhalation relax even more deeply. Listen to the sound of the waves as the breath flows through the body.

Now bring the breath and your awareness up into the hips, pelvis and buttocks. On the inhalation feel the pelvis area naturally expand and exhaling allow it rest down into the earth. . . . With each inhalation feel the pelvic floor being drawn gently up into the abdomen and with each exhalation allow it to completely release. Feel the wave of breath rising up from the pelvis filling the abdomen. Feel the abdomen rise and fall, and explore the abdomen with your awareness. With each exhalation the abdomen becomes softer and softer. Feel this softness touch the lower back and feel the breath there. Explore the sensations in the low back and then allow this area to soften into the earth.

Now allow breath and awareness to flow up the spine. With each inhalation, the spine fills with sensation. With each exhalation, the spine relaxes into the earth. Feeling the breath now through the entire back. Inhaling, sensing; exhaling, completely relaxing.

Now bring your awareness again to the rising and falling of the abdomen. As you inhale draw the breath up into the solar plexus filling that area fully with breath and awareness. And as you exhale, relax into the center of that awareness. Now focus the breath up into the heart and lungs, and with each exhalation relax deeper and deeper into the center of the heart.

Draw the breath into the neck and throat. Exhale, allowing any tension to be released. . . . Allow the breath to flow up through the head, with each inhalation become more aware of the sensations, with each exhalation, relax. Relax the jaw, the eyes, the forehead and the back of the head, soften the inner ears, and relax into the earth.

Feel the entire body now washed by a gentle wave of breath from the soles of the feet and the tips of the fingers, all the way to the crown of the head. Feel the peace and complete relaxation as the breath becomes softer and softer. Feel the sensations in the body becoming softer and more subtle and relax into them.

Now allow the wave of breath to be felt a little more strongly, rising up through the soles of the feet, and rising and falling in the abdomen. As the breath becomes stronger allow the sensations in the body to increase. Let the body gently begin to move with the breath. Move the toes and fingers. . . . allow the whole body to begin to gently stretch. Remaining with the eyes closed, begin to gently roll over onto the right side. Let every movement be an experience of awareness. Over the next minute come up into a seated position. And as you come to the seated position, feel the deep three part breath and experience how the body, breath and mind are in balance.

Source: Integrative Yoga Therapy Manual, by Joseph LePage, pp. 6.22–6.23. Copyright © 1994 by Integrative Yoga Therapy, Aptos, CA. Used by permission.

---

pp. 6.15–6.16) uses cues to focus on the breath throughout the instructions. Body scans are very useful variations of the traditional method of muscle relaxation for clients who tend to hold their breath while tensing muscles.

MODEL DIALOGUE: MUSCLE RELAXATION

In this dialogue, the helper demonstrates relaxation training to help Joan deal with her physical sensations of nervousness.

First, the helper gives Joan a *rationale* for relaxation. The helper explains the *purpose* of muscle relaxation and gives Joan a brief *overview* of the procedure.

1. **Helper:** Basically, we all learn to carry around some body tension. Some is OK. But in a tense spot, usually your body is even more tense, although you may not realize this. If you can learn to recognize muscle tension and relax your muscles, this state of relaxation can help to decrease your nervousness or anxiety. What we'll do is to help you recognize when your body is relaxed and when it is tense by deliberately tensing and relaxing different muscle groups in your body. We should get to the point where, later on, you can recognize the sensations that mean tension and use these as a signal to yourself to relax. Does this make sense?

Client: I think so. You'll sort of tell me how to do this?

Next, the helper *will "set up" the relaxation by attending to details about the room* and the client's comfort.

2. **Helper:** Yes. At first I'll show you so you can get the idea of it. One thing we need to do before we start is for you to get as comfortable as possible. So that you won't be distracted by light, I'm going to turn off the light. If you are wearing your contact lenses, take them out if they're uncomfortable, because you may feel more comfortable if you go through this with your eyes closed. Also, I use a special chair for this. You know the straight-backed chair you're sitting on can seem like a rock after a time. That might distract, too. So I have a padded chaise you can use for this. [Gets lounge chair out.]

Client (sits in chaise): Umm. This really is comfortable.

Next, the helper begins *to model the muscle relaxation* for Joan. This shows Joan how to do it and may alleviate any embarrassment on her part.

3. **Helper:** Good. That really helps. Now I'm going to show you how you can tense and then relax your muscles. I'll start first with my right arm. [Clenches right fist, pauses and notes tension, relaxes fist, pauses and notes relaxation; models several other muscle groups.] Does this give you an idea?

Client: Yes. You don't do your whole body?

The helper provides *further information about muscle relaxation, describes sensations* Joan might feel, and checks to see whether Joan is completely clear on the procedure before going ahead.

4. **Helper:** Yes, you do. But we'll take each muscle group separately. By the time you tense and relax each muscle group, your whole body will feel relaxed. You will feel like you are "letting go," which is very important when you tense up—to let go rather than to tense even more. Now, you might not notice a lot of difference right away—but you might. You might even feel like you're floating. This really depends on the person. The most important thing is to remain as comfortable as possible while I'm instructing you. Do you have any questions before we begin, anything you don't quite understand?

Client: I don't think so. I think that this is maybe a little like yoga.

The helper proceeds with *instructions to alternately tense and relax* each of 17 muscle groups.

5. **Helper:** Right. It's based on the same idea—learning to soothe away body tension. OK, get very comfortable in your chair, and we'll begin. [Gives Joan several minutes to get comfortable, then uses the relaxation instructions. Most of the session is spent in instructing Joan in muscle relaxation as illustrated on pp. 518–520.]

After the relaxation, the helper *queries Joan* about her feelings during and after the relaxation. It is important to find out how the relaxation affected the client.

6. **Helper:** Joan, how do you feel now?

Client: Pretty relaxed.

7. **Helper:** How did the contrast between the tensed and relaxed muscles feel?

Client: It was pretty easy to tell. I guess sometimes my body is pretty tense, and I don't think about it.

The helper assigns *relaxation practice* to Joan as *daily homework*.

8. **Helper:** As I mentioned before, this takes regular practice in order for you to use it when you need it—and to really notice the effects. I have put these instructions on this audiotape, and I'd like you to practice with this tape each day during the next week. Do the practice in a quiet place at a time when you don't feel pressured, and use a comfortable place when you do practice. Do you have any questions about the practice?

Client: No, I think I understand.

Helper *explains the use of the log*.

9. **Helper:** Also, I'd like you to use a log sheet with your practice. Mark down where you practice, how long you practice, what muscle groups you use, and your tension level before and after each practice on this 5-point scale. Remember, 0 is complete relaxation and 5 is complete or extreme tension. Let's go over an example of how you use the log. . . . Now, any questions?

Client: No. I can see this will take some practice.

Finally, the helper arranges a *follow-up*.

10. **Helper:** Right, it really is like learning any other skill—it doesn't just come automatically. Why don't

you try this on your own for two weeks and then come back, OK?

Learning Activity 16.2 outlines exercises that can help familiarize you with muscle relaxation.

EXERCISE THERAPY

Exercise has long been recognized as an important ingredient of health and has long been part of the treatment toolbelt for medically or physically related problems. What may be less well-known is the voluminous research literature on the relationship between exercise and psychological variables and, more recently, on findings showing promising effects of exercise on people with serious psychiatric disorders or problems in living. For example, a recent literature review by Tkachuk and Martin (1999) focused on the effects of exercise therapy. These findings suggest "that regular exercise is (a) a viable, cost effective, but underused treatment for mild to moderate depression that compares favorably to individual psychotherapy, group psychotherapy, and cognitive therapy, and (b) a necessary ingredient in effective behavioral treatments that reduce self-reported pain in individuals with chronic pain. Preliminary evidence also suggests that regular exercise deserves further attention as (a) a singular treatment for some anxiety disorders, for individuals suffering from body image disturbance, and for the reduction of problem behaviors of developmentally disabled persons, and (b) an adjunct in treatment programs for schizophrenia, conversion disorder, and alcohol dependence" (p. 275).

There are a variety of theories underlying these findings, although in most cases, no one theory has yet gained clear substantiation. Some of these speak to the mind/body connections (e.g., physiological mechanisms underlying depression such as thermogenic, endorphin, and monoamine neurotransmitter functioning) and others to ways that activities disrupt problematic patterns and affect our interactions with our social and physical environments in important ways (e.g., participation in exercise leads to increased perceived mastery, acts as a buffer to stress, brings people into contact with potential positive reinforcers, provides a form of meditation, and provides distraction from unpleasant cognitions, emotions, or behaviors). Also noteworthy have been findings that continued exercise beyond the period of formal intervention yields significant benefits. One illustration of this is a study of adults with major depressive disorder. Although four months of treatment with either aerobic exercise, medication (sertraline therapy), or a combination showed comparable improvement across the three conditions, those who continued exercise during the six-month period following completion of formal treatment had lower relapse rates than those in the medication group (Babyak et al., 2000).

A sampling of the research findings of exercise is presented in Box 16.3, and we have included a number of readings to further explain applications of exercise therapy with various populations and toward remediating or preventing various problems in living such as those listed in Box 16.3. The specifics of exercise therapy have taken various forms, including aerobic (e.g., walking, running, workouts) as well as nonaerobic and with varying levels of intensity, frequency, and duration. A realm of movement and exercise to consider for some clients includes yoga-based therapy. It can be modified to suit various physical restrictions and be beneficial for relaxation, conditioning, and meditative aims (LePage, 1994; Miller, 1993; Patel, 1993, provide good overviews). Rather than hard-and-fast specifics about what type of exercise is best, however, the clinical emphasis is toward developing with clients an exercise plan realistic and appropriate to them. Listed below are some guidelines to assist with this collaborative planning.

Guidelines for the Clinical Application of Exercise Therapy

Tkachuk and Martin (1999) draw from the work of Sime (1996) in listing the following as guidelines for the clinical application of exercise therapy:

1. Explore the client's exercise history to determine current exercise habits and past experiences in order to identify enjoyable activities critical to program adherence.
2. Participate in initial exercise sessions to serve as a model for appropriate client behavior.
3. Educate the client about the potential physical and mental health benefits of exercise as a commitment enhancement procedure.
4. Consider options to make exercise functional, such as commuting to work by walking, jogging, or biking or including home chores in the prescription.
5. Take advantage of the client's environment (e.g., parks, lakes, fitness trails, home equipment) in facilitating exercise activity.
6. Help the client choose enjoyable activities from a broad spectrum of choices.
7. Prescribe the type, duration, frequency, and intensity of the exercise program in terms of the client's current level of conditioning. Practitioners who are not trained or experienced in exercise physiology are advised to seek the assis-

> ## LEARNING ACTIVITY 16.2 — Muscle Relaxation
>
> Because muscle relaxation involves the alternate tensing and relaxing of a variety of muscle groups, learning the procedure well enough to use it with a client is sometimes difficult. We have found that the easiest way to learn muscle relaxation is to do it yourself. Using it not only helps you learn what is involved but also may have some indirect benefits for you—increased relaxation!
>
> In this learning activity, you will apply the muscle-relaxation procedure you've just read about to yourself. You can do this by yourself or with a partner. You may wish to try it out alone and then with someone else.
>
> ### By Yourself
>
> 1. Get in a comfortable position, wear loose clothing, and remove your glasses or contact lenses.
> 2. Use the written instructions in this chapter to practice muscle relaxation. You can do this by putting the instructions on tape or by reading the instructions to yourself. Go through the procedure quickly to get a feel for the process; then do it again slowly without trying to rely too much on having to read the instructions. As you go through the relaxation, study the differences between tension and relaxation.
> 3. Try to assess your reactions after the relaxation. On a scale from 0 to 5 (0 being very relaxed and 5 being very tense), how relaxed do you feel? Were there any particular muscle groups that were hard for you to contract or relax?
> 4. One or two times through muscle relaxation is not enough to learn it or to notice any effects. Try to practice this procedure on yourself once or twice daily over the next several weeks.
>
> ### With a Partner
>
> One of you can take the role of a helper; the other can be the person learning relaxation. Switch roles so you can practice helping someone else through the procedure and trying it out on yourself.
>
> 1. The helper should begin by giving an explanation and a rationale for muscle relaxation and any instructions about it before you begin.
> 2. The helper can read the instructions on muscle relaxation to you. The helper should give you ample time to tense and relax each muscle group and should encourage you to note the different sensations associated with tension and relaxation.
> 3. After going through the process, the helper should query you about your relaxation level and your reactions to the process.

tance of a local specialist who can supervise the ongoing prescription process.
8. Attempt to facilitate exercise within a positive social milieu.
9. Assist the client to develop behavioral self-control strategies (e.g., behavioral contracting, stimulus control, positive reinforcement) to improve program adherence.
10. Prepare the client for recidivism and reinitiation using relapse prevention strategies.

Cautions and Guidelines for Exercise Therapy

As we have stressed throughout this chapter, although the evidence to date is supportive of the various helping strategies presented here, caution should be taken in assessing risk and appropriateness. The following guidelines are adapted from Tkachuck and Martin (1999) and Leith (1994).

Considering Risk Factors

For practitioners who do not have training in exercise physiology, consultation or working liaisons with others (such as physicians or exercise physiologists) may be prudent. Medical clearance is always recommended before undertaking any formal exercise program as part of clinical practice. There are a variety of specific factors that would indicate the level of risk for negative outcomes associated with exercise therapy. Drawing from the work of King and Senn (1996), class 1 includes those individuals who are apparently healthy and require only physician clearance to commence an exercise program. Class 2 includes those who may be at higher risk for complications, and they require a limited-symptom graded exercise test prior to receiving

BOX 16.3 RESEARCH ON EXERCISE

Alzheimer's/dementia

Groene, R. II, Zapchenk, S., Marble, G., & Kantar, S. (1998). The effect of therapist and activity characteristics on the purposeful responses of probable Alzheimer's disease participants. *Journal of Music Therapy, 35,* 119–136.

Kovach, C. R., & Henschel, H. (1996). Behavior and participation during therapeutic activities on special care units. *Activities, Adaptation, and Aging, 20,* 35–45.

Anxiety

Broocks, A., Bandelow, B., Pekrun, G., George, A., Meyer, T., Bartmann, U., Hillmer-Vogel, U., & Ruther, E. (1998). Comparison of aerobic exercise, chlomipramine, and placebo in the treatment of panic disorder. *American Journal of Psychiatry, 155,* 603–609.

Kirkby, R. J., & Lindner, H. (1998). Exercise is linked to reductions in anxiety but not premenstrual syndrome in women with prospectively-assessed symptoms. *Psychology, Health, and Medicine, 3,* 211–222.

O'Connor, P. J., Raglin, J. S., & Martinsen, E. W. (2000). Physical activity, anxiety, and anxiety disorders. *International Journal of Sport Psychology, 31,* 136–155.

Parente, D. (2000). Influence of aerobic and stretching exercise on anxiety and sensation-seeking mood state. *Perceptual and Motor Skills, 90,* 347–348.

Depression

Babyak, M., Blumenthal, J. A., Herman, S., Khatri, P., Doraiswamy, M., Moore, K., Craighead, W. E., Baldewicz, T. T., & Ranga, K. K. (2000). Exercise treatment for major depression: Maintenance of therapeutic benefit at 10 months. *Psychosomatic Medicine, 62,* 633–638.

Bosscher, R. J. (1993). Running and mixed physical exercises with depressed psychiatric patients. *International Journal of Sports Psychology, 24,* 170–184.

Palenzuela, D. L., Calvo, M. G., & Avero, P. (1998). Exercise training as a protective mechanism against depression in a young population. *Psicotherma, 10,* 23–39.

Palmer, J. A., Palmer, L. K., Michiels, K., & Thigpen, B. (1995). Effects of type of exercise on depression in recovering substance abusers. *Perceptual and Motor Skills, 80,* 523–530.

Developmentally disabled clients

Bachman, J. E., & Sluyter, D. (1988). Reducing inappropriate behaviors of developmentally disabled adults using antecedent aerobic dance exercises. *Research on Developmental Disabilities, 9,* 73–83.

Croce, R., & Horvat, M. (1992). Effects of reinforcement based exercise on fitness and work productivity in adults with mental retardation. *Adapted Physical Activity Quarterly, 9,* 148–178.

Gabler-Halle, D., Halle, J. W., & Chung, Y. B. (1993). The effects of aerobic exercise on psychological and behavioral variables of individuals with developmental disabilities: A critical review. *Research in Developmental Disabilities, 14,* 359–386.

Medical/physical conditions

Burke, L. E., Dunbar-Jacob, J. M., & Hill, M. N. (1997). Compliance with cardiovascular disease prevention strategies: A review of the research. *Annals of Behavioral Medicine, 19,* 239–263.

Callahan, L. F., Rao, J., & Boutaugh, M. (1997). Arthritis and women's health: Prevalence, impact, and prevention. *American Journal of Preventive Medicine, 12,* 401–409.

Rejeski, W. J., Ettinger, W. H., Martin, K., & Morgan, T. (1998). Treating disability in knee osteoarthritis with exercise therapy: A central role for self-efficacy and pain. *Arthritis Care and Research, 11,* 94–101.

Pain

Johansson, C., Dahl, J., Jannert, M., Melin, L., & Andersson, G. (1998). Effects of a cognitive–behavioral pain management program. *Behaviour Research and Therapy, 36,* 915–930.

Stanton-Hicks, M., Baron, R., Boas, R., Gordh, T., Harden, N., Hendler, N., Kolzenburg, M., Raj, P., & Wilder, R. (1998). Complex regional pain syndromes: Guidelines for therapy. *Clinical Journal of Pain, 14,* 155–166.

Schizophrenia

Chamove, A. S. (1986). Positive short-term effects of activity on behaviour in chronic schizophrenic patients. *British Journal of Clinical Psychology, 25,* 125–133.

Faulkner, G., & Sparkes, A. (1999). Exercise as therapy for schizophrenia: An ethnographic study, *Journal of Sport and Exercise Psychology, 21,* 52–69.

Lukoff, D., Wallace, C. J., Liberman, R. P., & Burke, K. (1986). A holistic program for chronic schizophrenic patients. *Schizophrenia Bulletin, 12,* 274–282.

Substance abuse

Martin, J. E., Calfas, K. J., Pattern, C. A., Polarek, M., Hofstetter, C. R., Noto, J., & Beach, D. (1997). Prospective evaluation of three smoking interventions in 205 recovering alcoholics: One year results of projects SCRAP-Tobacco. *Journal of Consulting and Clinical Psychology, 65,* 190–194.

Palmer, J., Vacc, N., & Epstein, J. (1988). Adult inpatient alcoholics: Physical exercise as a treatment intervention. *Journal of Studies on Alcohol, 49,* 418–421.

clearance to exercise. Class 3 includes those individuals known to have risk factors such as cardiac, pulmonary, or metabolic disease, and they are required to undergo graded exercise testing, pass more stringent criteria, and be more closely monitored by medical personnel. There are also, of course, those individuals who simply should not undertake exercise therapy.

There are a variety of screening tools available for use with asymptomatic, apparently healthy adults, one being the Physical Activity Readiness Questionnaire. According to Leith (1994), the PAR-Q (British Columbia Department of Health, 1994) is highly sensitive in detecting medical contraindications to exercise and approximately 80 percent specific as referenced to the American College of Sports Medicine guidelines. The PAR-Q includes items that inquire about symptoms such as heart condition, chest pain, dizziness, bone or joint problems, and medications for blood pressure or heart condition. It is not complete, but as a minimum screening device it is appropriate for entry into low- to moderate-intensity exercise programs. Limitations include its lower sensitivity to ECG abnormalities and no detection items for pregnancy or other prescription medication. Thus, these would need to be ascertained by the practitioner. Copies of the PAR-Q can be obtained by writing to Government of Canada, Fitness and Amateur Sport, 365 Laurier Avenue West; Ottawa, Ontario, Canada K1A 0X6.

An additional screening method entails comparing the client's medical history against a list of contraindications for exercise testing and training, such as some conditions related to hypertension, cardiac functioning, metabolic disorders, and breathing (Leith, 1994). A useful resource in determining both risk factors and formulating exercise plans with people of varying conditions is the American College of Sports Medicine guidelines. They provide position statements on the recommended quantity and quality of exercise for developing and maintaining cardiorespiratory fitness, muscular fitness, and flexibility in healthy adults as well as recommendations related to older adults and conditions such as diabetes, osteoporosis, hypertension, and coronary artery disease. Contact: 401 W. Michigan St., Indianapolis, IN 46202-3233; 317-637-9200 (see Website in Suggested Resources).

SUMMARY

In this chapter we described two meditation strategies, a procedure for muscle relaxation, two scripts on scanning the body, and a review of exercise therapy. These and other meditation strategies can be used *in vivo*. Helpers must be aware that meditation, muscle relaxation, and exercise therapy can have contraindications and adverse effects for some clients. The muscle-relaxation strategy can be used with 17, 7, or 4 muscle groups. All these strategies are often used as a single treatment to prevent stress and to deal with stress-related situations. In addition, these strategies can be used as complements to other stress management interventions (Chapter 15), systematic desensitization and exposure therapies (Chapter 17), as well as other interventions (such as problem solving [Chapter 13] and self-management [Chapter 18]) in which additional aids for relaxation or mindfulness appear indicated.

INFOTRAC® EXPLORATIONS

1. Search for the term *meditation*. Of the articles retrieved, select three to five that address use of meditation as a formal intervention (e.g., as a part of professional helping practice or service). How do the procedures compare to those described in this chapter? What factors do you see as being important in determining whether meditation would be a recommended intervention for any given client?
2. Search for the term *relaxation*. Select three to five articles having to do with muscle relaxation in helping practice. How do these procedures compare to the 4, 7, and 17 muscle-group distinctions reviewed here? Would you see these articles as being appropriate resources for clients who may be interested in learning more about muscle relaxation?
3. Search for the term *exercise therapy*. Select three to five articles that describe and, ideally, evaluate the effectiveness of exercise as an intervention relevant to helping services. What guided the interventionists' judgments in selecting exercise therapy and the specific type? Are there any diversity factors (e.g., age, cultural, abledness) that you think ought to be considered in decisions to apply the described intervention?

SUGGESTED RESOURCES

Readings
Alexander, C. N., Robinson, P., Orme-Johnson, D., & Schneider, R. H. (1994). The effects of transcendental meditation compared to other methods of relaxation and meditation in reducing risk factors, morbidity, and mortality. *Homeostasis in Health and Disease, 35*, 243–263.

Arena, J., Bruno, G., Hannah, S., & Meador, K. (1995). A comparison of frontal electromyographic biofeedback training, trapezius electromyographic biofeedback training, and progressive muscle relaxation therapy in the treatment of tension headache. *Headache, 35,* 411–419.

Benson, H., & Stuart, E. M. (1992). *The wellness book: The comprehensive guide to maintaining health and treating stress-related illness.* New York: Birch Lane.

Bernstein, D. A., & Carlson, C. R. (1993). Progressive relaxation: Abbreviated methods. In P. M. Lehrer & R. L. Woolfolk (Eds.), *Principles and practice of stress management* (2nd ed., pp. 53–87). New York: Guilford.

Borysenko, J. (1997). *Meditation for inner guidance and self-healing.* (Audiotape). Niles, IL: Nightingale Conant.

Broota, A., Varma, R. & Singh, A. (1995). Role of relaxation in hypertension. *Journal of the Indian Academy of Applied Psychology, 21,* 29–36.

Carlson, C. R., & Hoyle, R. H. (1993). Efficacy of abbreviated progressive muscle relaxation training: A quantitative review of behavioral medicine research. *Journal of Counseling and Clinical Psychology, 61,* 1059–1067.

Epstein, M. (1995). *Thoughts without a thinker.* New York: Basic.

Hanh, T. N. (1991). *Peace is every step.* New York: Bantam.

Kabat-Zinn, J. (1994). *Wherever you go, there you are.* New York: Hyperion.

Kabat-Zinn, J. (1995). *Mindfulness meditation.* (Audiotape). Niles, IL: Nightingale Conant.

Lehrer, P. M., & Woolfolk, R. L. (Eds.). (1993). *Principles and practice of stress management* (2nd ed.). New York: Guilford.

Levine, S. (1991). *Guided meditations, explorations and healings.* New York: Anchor.

Long, B. (1995). *Meditation* (rev. ed.). London: Barry Long.

Murphy, M., & Donovan, S. (Eds.). (1997). *The physical and psychological effects of meditation* (2nd ed.). Sausalito, CA: Institute of Noetic Sciences.

Simpkins, C. A., & Simpkins, A. M. (1996). *Principles of meditation.* Boston: Tuttle.

Teasdale, J., Segal, Z., Williams, J., & Mark, G. (1995). How does cognitive therapy prevent depressive relapse and why should attentional control (mindfulness) training help? *Behaviour Research and Therapy, 33,* 25–39.

Weil, A. (1995). *Spontaneous healing.* New York: Ballantine.

Weil, A. (1997). *8 weeks to optimum health.* New York: Knopf.

Web Sites

American College of Sports Medicine
http://www.acsm.org

16 POSTEVALUATION

Part One

For Objective One, you will be able to identify accurately the steps of the relaxation response procedure represented by at least seven out of nine examples of helper instructive responses. On paper, for each of the following helper responses, identify which part of the meditation procedure is being implemented. There may be more than one helper response associated with a part. These examples are not in any particular order. The eight major parts of meditation are as follows:

1. Rationale
2. Instructions about when, where, and how long to practice
3. Instruction about focusing on a word, phrase, or prayer
4. Breathing instructions
5. Instruction about passive attitude
6. Meditating for 10 to 20 minutes
7. Probing about the meditative experience
8. Homework and practice

Feedback for the Postevaluation follows on page 542.

1. "It is very important that you practice this at home regularly. Usually there are no effects without regular practice—about twice daily."
2. "Find a comfortable place in your home to practice, one free of interruptions and noise."
3. "This procedure has been used to help people with high blood pressure and people who have trouble sleeping and just as a general stress-reduction process."
4. "Breathe through your nose and focus on your breathing. If you can concentrate on one word as you do this, it may be easier."
5. "Be sure to practice at a quiet time when you don't think you'll be interrupted. And do not practice within two hours after a meal or within two hours before going to bed."
6. "Just continue now to meditate like this for 10 or 15 minutes. Sit quietly then for several minutes after you're finished."
7. "How easy or hard was this for you to do?"
8. "There may be times when other images or thoughts come into your mind. Try to just maintain a passive attitude. If you're bothered by other thoughts, don't dwell on them, but don't force them away. Just focus on your breathing and your word."
9. "Pick a word like *one* or *zum* that you can focus on—something neutral to you."

Part Two

Objective Two asks you to identify accurately the steps for the mindfulness meditation procedure represented by at least 8 out of 10 helper instructive responses. Do this on paper. There may be more than one response for a given step. The helper examples are not in order. The 8 major steps of mindfulness meditation are as follows:

1. Rationale
2. Instructions about attitude
3. Preparation for meditation
4. Instructions about commitment, self-discipline, and energy
5. Breathing instructions
6. Body scan instructions
7. Discussion of client's reaction to first meditation
8. Homework and practice

Feedback follows.

1. "Meditation has benefited people by reducing tension, anxiety, stress, and headaches."
2. "Meditate for eight weeks and at the same times once or twice a day."
3. "Allow distracting thoughts to flow. Allow memories, images, and thoughts to occur. Don't try to influence them."
4. "Find a comfortable position in which to meditate."
5. "Notice as the air you breathe enters and exits your nostrils."
6. "Come out of meditation slowly. Sit with your eyes closed for two minutes. Slowly open your eyes. How do you feel?"
7. "Allow the wave of your breath to enter your body from the tip of your toes to the crown of your head."
8. "At first it will be like you are in training."

Part Three

Objective Three asks you to teach the process of meditation to another person. Select either relaxation response or mindfulness meditation to teach. You can have an observer

(continued)

16 POST EVALUATION

(continued)

evaluate you, or you can audiotape your teaching session and rate yourself. You can use the Interview Checklist for Mindfulness Meditation or the Interview Checklist for Relaxation Response that follows as a teaching guide and evaluation tool.

Part Four

Objective Four asks you to describe how you would apply the seven major parts of the muscle-relaxation procedure. Using this client description and the seven questions following it, describe how you would use certain parts of the procedure with this person. You can check your responses with the feedback that follows.

Description of client: The client is a middle-age man who is concerned about his inability to sleep at night. He has tried sleeping pills but does not want to rely on medication.

1. Give an example of a rationale you could use about the procedure. Include the purpose and an overview of the strategy.
2. Give a brief example of instructions you might give this client about appropriate dress for relaxation training.
3. List any special environmental factors that may affect the client's use of muscle relaxation.
4. Describe how you might model some of the relaxation exercises for the client.
5. Describe some of the important muscle groups that you would instruct the client to tense and relax alternately.
6. Give two examples of probes you might use with the client after relaxation to assess his use of and reactions to the process.
7. What instructions about a homework assignment (practice of relaxation) would you give to this client?

Part Five

Objective Five asks you to demonstrate 13 out of 15 steps of muscle relaxation with a role-play client. An observer or the client can assess your performance, or you can assess yourself, using the Interview Checklist for Muscle Relaxation on pages 537–541.

Part Six

Objective Six asks you to demonstrate the body scan procedure with a role-play client. An observer can assess you, or you can tape-record this activity using the script on pp. 523–524.

Interview Checklist for Mindfulness Meditation

Instructions: Determine which of the following helper leads or questions were demonstrated in the interview. Check each of the leads used by the helper. Some examples of helper leads are provided in the right column.

Item	Examples of helper leads
I. Rationale	
_____ 1. Helper describes purpose of procedure.	"I would like to teach you mindfulness meditation. This type of meditation has been used to relieve fatigue caused by anxiety, to decrease stress that leads to high blood pressure, and to bring balance and focus in your life. Meditation helps you become more relaxed and deal more effectively with your tension and stress. It may bring you new awareness about yourself and a new way of seeing and doing in your life."
_____ 2. Helper gives client an overview.	"First we will select a quiet place in which to meditate. You will then get into a relaxed and comfortable position. With your eyes closed, you will focus on your breathing, and

16 POST EVALUATION

_____ 3. Helper confirms client's willingness to use strategy.

II. Instructions About Attitudinal Foundations for Meditation

_____ 4. Helper instructs client about attitudes to help the practice of meditation.

_____ 5. Helper instructs the client about being nonjudging.

_____ 6. Helper instructs the client about patience.

_____ 7. Helper instructs the client about beginner's mind and basing moment-by-moment awareness on past experiences.

_____ 8. Helper instructs client about trusting feelings and intuition.

_____ 9. Helper instructs the client to be nonstriving.

_____ 10. Helper instructs the client about acceptance.

_____ 11. Helper instructs the client about letting go.

III. Instructions About Commitment, Self-Discipline, and Energy

_____ 12. Helper instructs client about commitment, self-discipline, and energy.

allow your thoughts to flow freely. If your mind wanders off, you can bring it back by focusing on the breath. You will meditate for 10 to 20 minutes. Then, we will talk about the experience."

"How do you feel now about practicing meditation?"

"There are seven attitudes that will help with your practice of meditation."

"First, it is best to be nonjudging. We have a tendency to categorize or judge people, things, or our experiences. These judgments take you away from observing whatever comes up while you are meditating. Judging steals energy from the moment-by-moment awareness. To remedy this, focus on your breathing."

"Second, have patience, which means just allow things to unfold in their own time. We don't have to fill our lives with moments of doing and activity."

"Third, as a beginner, what we experience in the moment is often based on our past experiences and ways of doing things. Just be open to moment-by-moment experience. Don't let past experiences judge and steal energy from moment-by-moment awareness."

"Fourth, trust your feelings and intuition while meditating. For example, if your body tells you that your posture for meditating is not comfortable, change to another posture that feels better."

"Fifth, try to be nonstriving, which means that mindfulness meditation is about the process of practice; every practice will be different. You don't want a mindset that requires you to achieve something or get somewhere. Just be in the moment, and attend to whatever comes up."

"Sixth, just focus on seeing and accepting things as they are, moment by moment, and in the present."

"Seventh, just let go, which means nonattachment or not holding on to thoughts."

"You want to make the kind of commitment required in athletic training. This strong commitment is about working on your self. You have to summon enough self-discipline to generate enough energy that you can develop a strong meditative practice and a high degree of mindfulness. You don't have to like it; you just have to do it. Then, at the end of eight weeks of practice, we can see whether the practice was useful."

(continued)

16 POST EVALUATION

(continued)

IV. **Instructions About Preparations for Meditation**

_____ 13. Helper instructs the client about time, place, and posture.

"Select a particular time every day to meditate. Meditate for at least six days a week, and for eight weeks. Find a place to meditate that will be free of interruptions and that will be comfortable. When you meditate, sit erect in a chair or on the floor. Try to have your back so that it is self-supporting."

V. **Body Scan Instructions**

_____ 14. Helper instructs client to do a body scan.

"Allow the body to begin to relax completely. Inhale and feel the breath flow from the soles of the feet to the crown of the head, like a gentle slow motion wave. With each exhalation, allow tension to flow out of the body." (Continue from the script on page 523–524.)

VI. **Breathing Instruction**

_____ 15. Helper instructs the client about breathing.

"Observe your breathing as it flows in and flows out. Notice the difference in temperature of the out breath and in breath. Feel the sensation of the air as it goes in and out of the nostrils."

VII. **Instructions About Wandering Mind**

_____ 16. Helper instructs client about what to do with cascading thoughts, feelings, sensations, sounds, pain, or discomfort.

"If you find yourself getting stuck in thoughts, feelings, sensations, sounds, pain, or discomfort, this is normal; just bring your attention to breathing, and let go by exhaling these distractions."

VIII. **Instructions to Meditate**

_____ 17. Helper instructs client about sitting quietly and relaxed for a minute. You can do a quick body scan to help with relaxation.

"Sit quietly for a while; just relax; focus on your breathing."

_____ 18. Helper instructs client to close eyes, focus on breathing, and get in a comfortable position.

"Close your eyes, get in a comfortable position, and focus on your breathing; the air comes in and flows out."

_____ 19. Helper instructs client to be in the moment, to have awareness and observe what comes up, and not give distractions any energy.

"Just be in the moment; be aware and observe whatever comes to mind. If distractions of thoughts, feelings, sounds, pain, or discomfort steal energy, just breathe them out and continue to observe and not move with the flow of these distractions."

_____ 20. Helper tells the client that she or he will meditate for 10 to 20 minutes.

"Meditate for 10 to 20 minutes. I will keep time and tell you when to stop."

_____ 21. Helper instructs client to come out of meditation slowly.

"I want you to come out of the meditation slowly. Just sit there with your eyes closed for a while; take time to absorb what you experienced. You may wish to stretch and open your eyes slowly."

IX. **Discussion of Client's Reaction to Mindfulness Meditation**

_____ 22. Helper asks client about experience with mindfulness meditation.

"What was the experience like for you?"
"How did you handle distractions?"
"How did you feel about mindfulness meditation?"

16 POST EVALUATION

X. Homework

_____ 23. Helper instructs client to meditate at home once a day and reminds client about preparation for meditation.

"Practice mindfulness meditation once a day at least 5 days a week. Remember to select a quiet environment without distractions. Do not take any alcoholic beverages or nonprescription drugs at least 24 hours before meditating. Wait for an hour before meditating after eating solid foods or drinking beverages containing caffeine. Be in the moment when you meditate; just observe what comes up without being carried away."

_____ 24. Helper instructs client about informal meditation.

"You can meditate informally when you are stressed out in stressful situations that may occur daily. Just relax and focus on your breathing; be aware and observe what is going on without giving energy to stress, and be peaceful in the situation."

Observer comments: _____
_____
_____

Interview Checklist for Relaxation Response

Instructions: Determine which of the following helper leads or questions were demonstrated in the interview. Check each of the leads used by the helper. Some examples of helper leads are provided in the right column.

Item	Examples of helper leads
I. Rationale	
_____ 1. Helper describes purpose of meditation.	"The relaxation response has been used to relieve anxiety, to decrease stress that can lead to high blood pressure, and to become more relaxed. It may give you a new focus and awareness about your self and your world."
_____ 2. Helper gives client an overview.	"You will select a focus word; then you will get in a comfortable position, relax your body, and focus on your breathing. You will maintain a passive attitude while meditating, which will elicit the relaxation response. You will meditate for 10 to 20 minutes. Then, we will talk about the experience."
_____ 3. Helper confirms client's willingness to use relaxation response.	"How do you feel about working with meditation that will elicit the relaxation response?"
II. Instructions About When, Where, and How Long to Practice	
_____ 4. Helper instructs client about when, where, and how long to practice.	"One of the best times to practice is before breakfast because it sets a positive tone for the day. This time is uncluttered with events and activities of the day. Relaxation works best if a regular time is chosen for it so that a routine is developed. Select a place to practice that is quiet and free from distractions and interruptions. Try to practice 10 to 20 minutes at least once and, better, twice a day."

(continued)

16 POST EVALUATION

(continued)

III. **Instructions About Focus Word, Phrase, or Prayer**

_____ 5. Helper provides rationale for mental word, phrase, or prayer.

_____ 6. Helper gives examples of focus word, phrase, or prayer.

"One major way to focus your mind is to link it to breathing either by concentrating on the breath or by focusing on something. You can focus on a word, phrase, or prayer."

"You might prefer a neutral calming word or phrase such as 'love' or 'peace' or 'warm'; or you can use a phrase—'the air flows in, and the air flows out.' Or you could focus on a phrase consistent with your belief system, or a sound you find calming or pleasing."

IV. **Instructions About Body Position and Eyes**

_____ 7. Helper instructs client about body posture and eyes.

"There are several ways to meditate. I'll show you one. I want you to get into a comfortable position while you are sitting there."

V. **Body Scan**

_____ 8. Helper does quick body scan with the client.

"Relax all the muscles in your body; relax [said slowly] your head, face, neck, shoulders, chest, your torso, thighs, calves, and your feet. Relax your body." (You can use the body scan script on pages 523–524).

VI. **Breathing Instructions**

_____ 9. Helper gives instructions about how to breathe.

"Breathe through your nose and focus on (or become aware of) your breathing. It is sometimes difficult to be natural when you are doing this. Just let the air come to you. Breathe easily and naturally. As you do this, say your focus word for each inhalation and exhalation. Say your focus word silently to yourself each time you breathe in and out."

VII. **Instructions About Passive Attitude**

_____ 10. Helper instructs client about passive attitude.

"Be calm and passive. If distracting thoughts or images occur, attempt to be passive about them by not dwelling on them. Return to repeating your focus word, phrase, or prayer. Try to achieve effortless breathing. After more practice, you will be able to examine these thoughts or images with greater detachment. Do not attempt to keep the thoughts out of your mind; just let them pass through. Keep your mind open; don't try to solve problems or think things over. Allow thoughts to flow smoothly into your mind and then drift out. Say your focus word and relax. Don't get upset with distracting thoughts. Just return to your focus word, phrase, or prayer."

VIII. **Instruct the Client to Meditate for About 10 to 20 Minutes**

_____ 11. Helper instructs client to meditate 10 to 20 minutes.

"Now, meditate for 10 to 20 minutes. You can open your eyes to check on the time. After you have finished, sit quietly for several minutes. You may wish to keep your eyes closed for a couple of minutes and later open them. You may not want to stand up for a few minutes."

16 POST EVALUATION

IX. Obtain Client Reaction to Relaxation Response

____ 12. Helper asks client about experience with relaxation response.

"How do you feel about the experience?"
"What sorts of thoughts or images flowed through your mind?"
"What did you do when the distracting thoughts drifted in?"
"How did you feel about your focus word, phrase, or prayer?"

X. Homework

____ 13. Helper instructs client to meditate daily for the next week.

"Practice the relaxation response two times a day. Get comfortable in your relaxation response position. Practice in a quiet place away from noise and interruptions. Do not meditate within two hours after eating or within a couple of hours before bedtime."

____ 14. Helper instructs client to apply relaxation response *in vivo*.

"Also, it would be helpful for you to apply an informal meditation in problem or stressful situations that may occur daily. You can do this by becoming detached and passive in the stressful situation. Observe yourself and focus on being calm and on your breathing. Be relaxed in situations that evoke stress."

Observer Comments: _____
_____
_____

Interview Checklist for Muscle Relaxation

Instructions: Indicate with a check mark each helper lead demonstrated in the interview. Some example leads are provided in the right column.

Item	Examples of helper leads
I. Rationale	
____ 1. Helper explains purpose of muscle relaxation.	"The name of the strategy that I believe will be helpful is *muscle relaxation*. Muscle relaxation has been used very effectively to benefit people who have a variety of concerns like insomnia, high blood pressure, anxiety, or stress, or for people who are bothered by everyday tension. Muscle relaxation will be helpful in decreasing your tension. It will benefit you because you will be able to control and to dispel tension that interferes with your daily activities."
____ 2. Helper gives overview of how muscle relaxation works.	"I will ask you to tense up and relax various muscle groups. All of us have some tensions in our bodies—otherwise, we could not stand, sit, or move around. Sometimes we have too much tension. By tensing and relaxing, you will become aware of and compare the feelings of tension and relaxation. Later we will train you to send a message to a particular muscle group to relax when nonessential tension creeps

(continued)

16 POST EVALUATION

(continued)

    ____ 3. Helper describes muscle relaxation as a skill.

    ____ 4. Helper instructs client about moving around if uncomfortable and informs client of sensations that may feel unusual.

II. Client Dress

    ____ 5. Helper instructs client about what to wear for training session.

III. Comfortable Environment

    ____ 6. Helper uses quiet environment, padded recliner chair, or floor with a pillow under client's head.

IV. Modeling the Exercises

    ____ 7. Helper models some exercises for muscle groups.

V. Instructions for Muscle Relaxation

    ____ 8. Helper reads or recites instructions from memory in conversational tone and practices along with client.

    ____ 9. Helper instructs client to get comfortable, close eyes, and listen to instructions.

    ____ 10. Helper instructs client to tense and relax alternately each of the 17 muscle groups (*two* times for each muscle group in initial training). Also occasionally makes muscle-group comparisons.
        ____ a. Fist of dominant hand

in. You will learn to control your tension and relax when you feel tension."

"Muscle relaxation is a skill. And, as with any skill, learning it well will take a lot of practice. A lot of repetition and training are needed to acquire the muscle-relaxation skill."

"At times during the training and muscle exercises, you may want to move while you are on your back on the floor [or on the recliner]. Just feel free to do this so that you can get more comfortable. You may also feel heady sensations as we go through the exercise. These sensations are not unusual. Do you have any questions concerning what I just talked about? If not, do you want to try this now?"

"For the next session, wear comfortable clothing."
"Wear regular glasses instead of your contact lenses."

"During training, I'd like you to sit in this recliner chair. It will be more comfortable and less distracting than this wooden chair."

"I would like to show you [some of] the exercises we will use in muscle relaxation. First, I make a fist to create tension in my right hand and forearm and then relax it."

"Now, get as comfortable as you can, close your eyes, and listen to what I'm going to be telling you. I'm going to make you aware of certain sensations in your body and then show you how you can reduce these sensations to increase feelings of relaxation."

"First study your right arm, your right hand in particular. Clench your right fist. Clench it tightly and study the tension in the hand and in the forearm. Study those sensations of tension. [Pause.] And now let go. Just relax the right hand and let it rest on the arm of the chair. [Pause.] And note the difference between the tension and the relaxation." [10-second pause.]

16 POST EVALUATION

_____ b. Fist of nondominant hand   "Now we'll do the same with your left hand. Clench your left fist. Notice the tension [5-second pause] and now relax. Enjoy the difference between the tension and the relaxation." [10-second pause.]

_____ c. One or both wrists   "Now bend both hands back at the wrists so that you tense the muscles in the back of the hand and in the forearm. Point your fingers toward the ceiling. Study the tension, and now relax. [Pause.] Study the difference between tension and relaxation." [10-second pause.]

_____ d. Biceps of one or both arms   "Now clench both your hands into fists and bring them toward your shoulders. As you do this, tighten your bicep muscles, the ones in the upper part of your arm. Feel the tension in these muscles. [Pause.] Now relax. Let your arms drop down again to your sides. See the difference between the tension and the relaxation." [10-second pause.]

_____ e. Shoulders   "Now we'll move to the shoulder area. Shrug your shoulders. Bring them up to your ears. Feel and hold the tension in your shoulders. Now let both shoulders relax. Note the contrast between the tension and the relaxation that's now in your shoulders. [10-second pause.] Are your shoulders as relaxed as your arms?"

_____ f. Forehead   "Now we'll work on relaxing the various muscles of the face. First, wrinkle up your forehead and brow. Do this until you feel your brow furrow. [Pause.] Now relax. Smooth out the forehead. Let it loosen up." [10-second pause.]

_____ g. Eyes   "Now close your eyes tightly. Can you feel tension all around your eyes? [5-second pause.] Now relax those muscles, noting the difference between the tension and the relaxation." [10-second pause.]

_____ h. Tongue or jaw   "Now clench your jaw by biting your teeth together. Pull the corners of your mouth back. Study the tension in the jaws. [5-second pause.] Relax your jaws now. Can you tell the difference between tension and relaxation in your jaw area?" [10-second pause.]

_____ i. Lips   "Now press your lips together tightly. As you do this, notice the tension all around the mouth. [Pause.] Now relax those muscles around the mouth. Just enjoy the relaxation in your mouth area and your entire face." [Pause.]

_____ j. Head backward   "Now we'll move to the neck muscles. Press your head back against your chair. Can you feel the tension in the back of your neck and in your upper back? Hold the tension. Now let your head rest comfortably. Notice the difference. Keep on relaxing." [Pause.]

_____ k. Chin in chest   "Now continue to concentrate on the neck area. See whether you can bury your chin into your chest. Note the

(continued)

16 POST EVALUATION

(continued)

____ l. Back

____ m. Chest muscles

____ n. Stomach muscles

____ o. Buttocks

____ p. Legs

____ q. Toes

____ 11. Helper instructs client to review and relax all muscle groups.

tension in the front of your neck. Now relax and let go." [10-second pause.]

"Now direct your attention to your upper back area. Arch your back as if you were sticking out your chest and stomach. Can you feel tension in your back? Study that tension. [Pause.] Now relax. Note the difference between the tension and the relaxation."

"Now take a deep breath, filling your lungs, and hold it. See the tension all through your chest and into your stomach area. Hold that tension. [Pause.] Now relax and let go. Let your breath out naturally. Enjoy the pleasant sensations. Is your chest as relaxed as your back and shoulders?" [10-second pause.]

"Now think about your stomach. Tighten the abdomen muscles. Hold this tension. Make your stomach like a knot. Now relax. Loosen these muscles now." [10-second pause.]

"Focus now on your buttocks. Tense your buttocks by pulling them in or contracting them. Note the tension that is there. Now relax—let go." [10-second pause.]

"I'd like you now to focus on your legs. Stretch both legs. Feel tension in the thighs. [5-second pause.] Now relax. Study the difference again between the tension in the thighs and the relaxation you feel now." [10-second pause.]

"Now concentrate on your lower legs and feet. Tighten both calf muscles by pointing your toes toward your head. Pretend a string is pulling your toes up. Can you feel the pulling and the tension? Note that tension. [Pause.] Now relax. Let your legs relax deeply. Enjoy the difference between tension and relaxation." [10-second pause.]

"Now, I'm going to go over again the different muscle groups that we've covered. As I name each group, try to notice whether there is any tension in those muscles. If there is any, try to concentrate on those muscles and tell them to relax. Think of draining any residual tension out of your body. Relax the muscles in your feet, ankles, and calves. [Pause.] Let go of your knee and thigh muscles. [Pause.] Loosen your hips. [Pause.] Loosen the muscles of your lower body. [Pause.] Relax all the muscles of your stomach, waist, and lower back. [Pause.] Drain any tension from your upper back, chest, and shoulders. [Pause.] Relax your upper arms, forearms, and hands. [Pause.] Let go of the muscles in your throat and neck. [Pause.] Relax your face. [Pause.] Let all the muscles of your body become loose. Drain all the tension from your body. [Pause.] Now sit quietly with your eyes closed."

MEDITATION AND MOVEMENT STRATEGIES   541

16   POST EVALUATION

_____ 12. Helper asks client to rate relaxation level following training session.

"Now I'd like you to think of a scale from 0 to 5, where 0 is complete relaxation and 5 extreme tension. Tell me where you would place yourself on that scale now."

VI. Posttraining Assessment

_____ 13. Helper asks client about first session of relaxation training and discusses problems with training if client has any.

"How do you feel?"
"What is your overall reaction to the procedure?"
"Think back about what we did—did you have problems with any muscle group?"
"What reaction did you have when you focused on the tension? What about relaxation?"
"How did the contrast between the tension and relaxation feel?"

VII. Homework and Follow-Up

_____ 14. Helper assigns homework and requests that client complete homework log for practice sessions.

"Relaxation training, like any skill, takes a lot of practice. I would like you to practice what we've done today. Do the exercises twice a day for 15 to 20 minutes each time. Do them in a quiet place in a reclining chair, on the floor with a pillow, or on your bed with a head pillow. Also, try to do the relaxation at a time when there is no time pressure—like arising, after school or work, or before dinner. Try to avoid any interruptions, like telephone calls and people wanting to see you. Complete the homework log I have given you. Make sure you fill it in for each practice session. Do you have any questions?"

_____ 15. Helper arranges for follow-up session.

"Why don't you practice with this over the next 2 weeks and come back then?"

Notations for problems encountered or variations used:

_____
_____
_____

Part Seven

This objective asks you to describe at least 7 of the 10 guidelines for clinical application of exercise therapy as well as at least 5 factors that would increase risk for commencing exercise therapy. First, write your responses down; then check them against the listings on pp. 526–527 in the chapter section on exercise therapy

16 POSTEVALUATION FEEDBACK

PART ONE

1. *Homework* (practice)
2. *Instruction* about where to practice
3. *Rationale*—telling the client how the procedure is used
4. *Breathing* instructions
5. *Homework*—giving the client instructions about how to carry out the practice
6. *Instructing the client to meditate* for 10 to 20 minutes
7. *Probing* about the meditative experience—assessing the client's reactions
8. *Instruction about a passive attitude*
9. *Instruction about focusing* on word or phrase

PART TWO

1. *Rationale*—reason
2. *Homework*—when to practice
3. *Instructions about attitude*
4. *Preparation* about position for meditating
5. *Breathing* instructions
6. *Discussion* about reactions to meditation
7. *Body scan*
8. *Instructions about self-discipline and commitment*

PART THREE

Use the Interview Checklist for Relaxation Response or the Interview Checklist for Mindfulness Meditation as a guide to assess your teaching.

PART FOUR

1. Rationale for client:
   a. Purpose: "This procedure, if you practice it regularly, can help you become relaxed. The relaxation benefits you derive can help you sleep better."
   b. Overview: "This procedure involves learning to tense and relax different muscle groups in your body. By doing this, you can contrast the difference between tenseness and relaxation. This will help you to recognize tension so you can instruct yourself to relax."
2. Instructions about dress: "You don't want anything to distract you, so wear comfortable, loose clothes for training. You may want to remove your glasses or contact lenses."
3. Environmental factors:
   a. Quiet room with reclining chair
   b. No obvious distractions or interruptions
4. Modeling of exercises: "Let me show you exactly what you'll be doing. Watch my right arm closely. I'm going to clench my fist and tighten my forearm, studying the tension as I do this. Now I'm going to relax it like this [hand goes limp], letting all the tension just drain out of the arm and hand and fingertips."
5. Muscle groups used in the procedure include
   a. fist of each arm
   b. wrist of each arm
   c. biceps of each arm
   d. shoulders
   e. facial muscles—forehead, eyes, nose, jaws, lips
   f. head, chin, and neck muscles
   g. back
   h. chest
   i. stomach
   j. legs and feet
6. Some possible probes are these:
   a. "On a scale from 0 to 100, 0 being very relaxed and 100 very tense, how do you feel now?"
   b. "What is your overall reaction to what you just did?"
   c. "How did the contrast between the tensed and relaxed muscles feel?"
   d. "How easy or hard was it for you to do this?"
7. Homework instructions should include
   a. practice twice daily
   b. practice in a quiet place; avoid interruptions
   c. use a reclining chair, the floor, or a bed with pillow support for your head

PART FIVE

Use the Interview Checklist for Muscle Relaxation to assess your performance.

PART SIX

Use the scripts on pp. 523–524 to assess the way you used the body scan with a role-play client.

PART SEVEN

Use the listings on pp. 526–529 to assess how complete and accurate your responses were.

CHAPTER 17

DESENSITIZATION STRATEGIES

OBJECTIVES

After completing this chapter,* the student should be able to
1. Using written examples of 4 sample hierarchies, identify at least 3 hierarchies by type (conventional or idiosyncratic).
2. Given a written client case description, identify and describe at least 9 of the following 11 procedural steps of desensitization:
   a. A rationale
   b. An overview
   c. A method for identifying client emotion-provoking situations
   d. A type of hierarchy appropriate for this client
   e. The method of ranking hierarchy items that the client could use
   f. An appropriate counterconditioning response
   g. The method of imagery assessment
   h. The method of scene presentation
   i. The method of client signaling during scene presentation
   j. A written notation method to record scene-presentation progress
   k. An example of a desensitization homework task
3. Demonstrate at least 22 out of 28 steps of systematic desensitization in several role-play interviews.

Consider the following case:

> A high school student gets good grades on homework and self-study assignments, but whenever he takes a test, he "freezes." Some days, if he can, he avoids or leaves the class because he feels so anxious about the test, even the day before. When he takes a test, he feels overcome with anxiety; he cannot remember very much, and his resulting test grades are quite low.

*Material on systematic desensitization was developed in part by Cynthia R. Kalodner, Department of Psychology, Towson University.

This case description reflects an instance in which a person has learned an anxiety response to a situation. According to Bandura (1969), anxiety is a persistent, learned, maladaptive response resulting from stimuli that have acquired the capacity to elicit very intense emotional reactions. In addition, the student described in this case felt fear in a situation where there was no obvious external danger (sometimes called a *phobia;* Morris, 1991, p. 161). Further, to some degree, he managed to avoid the nondangerous feared situation (sometimes called a *phobic reaction;* p. 161). Individuals with phobias often need counseling or therapy.

In contrast, in the next two cases, a person is prevented from learning an anxiety response to a certain situation:

> A child is afraid to learn to swim because of a prior bad experience with water. The child's parent or teacher gradually introduces the child to swimming, first by visiting the pool, dabbling hands and feet in the water, getting in up to the knees, and so on. Each approach to swimming is accompanied by a pleasure—being with a parent, having a toy or an inner tube, or playing water games.

> A person has been in a very bad car accident. The person recovers and learns to get back in a car by sitting in it, going for short distances first, often accompanied by a friend or hearing pleasant music on the radio.

In these two descriptions, the situation never got out of hand; that is, it never acquired the capacity to elicit a persistent anxiety response, nor did the persons learn to avoid the situation continually. Why? See whether you can identify common elements in these situations that prevented these two persons from becoming therapy candidates. Go over the last two cases again. Do you notice that in each one, some type of

543

stimulus or emotion was present that counteracted the fear or anxiety? The parent used pleasurable activities to create enjoyment for the child while swimming; the person in the car took a friend or listened to music. In addition, these persons learned gradually to become more comfortable with a potentially fearful situation. Each step of the way represented a larger or more intense dose of the feared situation.

In a simplified manner, these elements reflect some of the counterconditioning processes that seem to occur in the procedure of exposure therapy. There are a variety of desensitizing exposure methods, varying in (1) the exposure medium used—via imagination/imaginal or actual situations *in vivo*, (2) whether exposure to the troubling cues or stimuli is in an intensive or graduated manner, (3) the extent to which response prevention methods are employed (blocking habitual avoidance responses), and (4) the extent to which emotional reprocessing is applied (adding cognitive methods to revise or reinterpret underlying ideas and associations that are fueling the emotional distress); see Prochaska and Norcross (1999) and Himle (2000) for brief overviews of various exposure therapies as well as other effective change strategies. You should be aware that although there are a number of therapies that use exposure techniques (imagined, vicarious, *in vivo*, recalled), many people use the term *exposure therapy* to refer to actual situation or *in vivo* forms of exposure in particular. In general, therapies that use exposure techniques are often used in combination with other intervention strategies, such as relaxation and breathing or rebreathing training (breathing air already exhaled through cupped hands into a paper bag to reduce symptoms of hyperventilation), stress inoculation training, problem-solving training, modeling, modeling and visualization, reframing, and various self-monitoring, stimulus control, and self-efficacy enhancing strategies. Anxiety, phobias, and obsessive–compulsive disorders are among the most common problems for which exposure therapies are applied, but effective outcomes have also been achieved with other problematic emotions such as anger, grief, and posttraumatic stress disorder (PTSD).

In this chapter we will focus on detailed implementation of systematic desensitization, for this will provide you with broadly generalizable tools that can be adjusted to the needs of specific cases—for example, choosing to use more intensive versus gently graduated exposure, using *in vivo* versus imaginal methods, or amplifying the extent to which cognitive methods to accelerate emotional processing are used. We will end with attention to exposure variations—*in vivo* desensitization, eye movement desensitization and reprocessing, and working with PTSD.

SYSTEMATIC DESENSITIZATION

According to Wolpe (1990, p. 150),

> Systematic desensitization is one of a variety of methods used to break down neurotic anxiety-response habits in piecemeal fashion. . . . After a physiological state inhibiting anxiety has been induced in the patient by means of muscle relaxation, the patient is exposed to a weak anxiety-arousing stimulus for a few seconds. If the exposure is repeated, the stimulus progressively loses its ability to evoke anxiety. Successively stronger stimuli are then similarly treated.

REPORTED USES OF DESENSITIZATION

Systematic desensitization was used widely as early as 1958 by Wolpe. In 1961, Wolpe reported its effectiveness in numerous case accounts, which were substantiated by successful case reports cited by Lazarus (1967). Since 1963, when Lang and Lazovik conducted the first controlled study of systematic desensitization, its use as a therapy procedure has been the subject of numerous empirical investigations and case reports.

Systematic desensitization using imaginal exposure has been used to treat various kinds of phobias—distinctions between simple and social phobias, generalized agoraphobia, as well as very specific phobias such as dogs, spiders, and enclosed spaces. Not surprisingly, anxiety is another very common application, again across a wide range of situations or life domains such as math, testing, performance, public speaking, and dietary restraint. Systematic desensitization has also been used to treat obsessive–compulsive disorder (Cox, Swinson, Morrison, & Lee, 1993), addiction, anger, and trauma. Increasingly, desensitization is being used in behavioral medicine—in areas such as preparing patients for invasive medical procedures (Horne, Vatmanidis, & Careri, 1994; Korth, 1993) and for troubling symptoms such as headaches (see Box 17.1).

Desensitization using *in vivo* exposure has been used widely for anxiety and phobia problems with children and adults. A significant area of development has included the use of computer-assisted and virtual environments and tools in implementing exposure therapies. Box 17.2 provides examples of exposure therapy research, including computer-assisted and virtual reality methods. There is yet a great deal to learn about the strengths and limitations of such technological applications, but results to date are largely promising, and applications are likely to grow. Another growth area is application of desensitization for trauma and posttraumatic stress disorder (PTSD). Many of the studies listed in Box 17.1 and Box 17.2 combine desensitization methods with other change

BOX 17.1 RESEARCH ON SYSTEMATIC DESENSITIZATION

Addiction
Piane, G. (2000). Contingency contracting and systematic desensitization for heroin addicts in methadone maintenance programs. *Journal of Psychoactive Drugs, 32,* 311–319.

Anger/aggression
Tyson, P. D. (1998). Physiological arousal, reactive aggression, and the induction of an incompatible relaxation response. *Aggression & Violent Behavior, 3,* 143–158.

Anxiety
Dietary restraint anxiety
Pitre, A., & Nicki, R. (1994). Desensitization of dietary restraint anxiety and its relationship to weight loss. *Journal of Behavioral Therapy and Experimental Psychiatry, 25,* 153–154.
Math anxiety
Foss, D., & Hadfield, O. (1993). A successful clinic for the reduction of mathematics anxiety among college students. *College Student Journal, 27,* 157–165.
Schneider, W., & Nevid, J. (1993). Overcoming math anxiety: A comparison of stress inoculation training and systematic desensitization. *Journal of College Student Development, 34,* 283–288.
Speech anxiety
Freeman, T., Sawyer, C. R., & Behnke, R. R. (1997). Behavioral inhibition and the attribution of public speaking state anxiety. *Communication Education, 46*(3), 175–187.
Motley, M., & Molloy, J. (1994). An efficacy test of a new therapy for public speaking anxiety. *Journal of Applied Communication Research, 22,* 48–58.
Test anxiety
Kennedy, D. V., & Doepke, K. J. (1999). Multicomponent treatment of a test anxious college student. *Education & Treatment of Children, 22,* 203–217.
Strumpf, J., & Fodor, I. (1993). The treatment of test anxiety in elementary school-age children: Review and recommendations. *Child and Family Behavior Therapy, 15,* 19–42.

Behavioral medicine
Horne, D., Vatmanidis, P., & Careri, A. (1994). Preparing patients for invasive medical and surgical procedures: II. Using psychological interventions with adults and children. *Behavioral Medicine, 20,* 15–21.
Korth, E. (1993). Psychological operation-preparation with children: Preparation of a five-year old boy for the amputation of his left leg with play, family, and behavior therapy. *Zeitschrift fur Klinische Psychologie, 22,* 62–76.

Headache
Devi, S. G., & Kaliappan, K. V. (1997). Improvement of psychosomatic disorders among tension headache subjects using behavior therapy and Somatic Inkblot Series. *Journal of Projective Psychology & Mental Health, 4*(2), 113–120.
Martin, P. R. (2000). Headache triggers: To avoid or not to avoid, that is the question. *Psychology & Health, 15,* 801–809.

Obsessive–compulsive disorder
Cox, B., Swinson, R., Morrison, B., & Lee, P. (1993). Clomipramine, fluoxetine, and behavior therapy in the treatment of obsessive–compulsive disorder: A meta-analysis. *Journal of Behavior Therapy and Experimental Psychiatry, 24,* 149–153.

Phobias
Acrophobia
Menzies, R., & Clarke, J. (1995). Individual response patterns, treatment matching, and the effects of behavioural and cognitive interventions for acrophobia. *Anxiety, Stress, and Coping, 8,* 141–160.
Childhood phobias
King, N. (1993). Simple and social phobias. *Advances in Clinical Child Psychology, 15,* 305–341.
Claustrophobia
Hoffman, S., Herzog-Bronsky, R., & Zim, S. (1994). Dialectical psychotherapy of phobias: A case study. *International Journal of Short Term Psychotherapy, 9,* 229–233.
Dog phobia
Freeman, S. (1997). Treating a dog phobia in a person with Down's syndrome by use of systematic desensitization and modelling. *British Journal of Learning Disabilities, 25*(4), 154–157.
Social phobia and agoraphobia
Kelly, C., & Cooper, S. (1993). Panic and agoraphobia associated with a cerebral arteriovenous malformation. *Irish Journal of Psychological Medicine, 10,* 94–96.
Yang, K., Yang, M., & Liu, H. (1999). Comparative study of the effects of accompanied systematic desensitization in the treatment of social phobia. *Chinese Mental Health Journal, 13,* 238–239.

Stress
Cary, M., & Dua, J. (1991). Cognitive–behavioral and systematic desensitization procedures in reducing stress and anger in caregivers for the disabled. *International Journal of Stress Management, 6*(2), 75–87.

Trauma
Frueh, B. C., de Arellano, M. A., & Turner, S. M. (1997). Systematic desensitization as an alternative exposure strategy for PTSD. *American Journal of Psychiatry, 154,* 287–288.
Nayak, M. B., Resnick, H. S., & Holmes, M. M. (1999). Treating health concerns within the context of childhood sexual assault: A case study. *Journal of Traumatic Stress, 12,* 101–109.
Pantalon, M. V., & Motta, R. W. (1998). Effectiveness of anxiety management training in the treatment of posttraumatic stress disorder: A preliminary report. *Journal of Behavior Therapy & Experimental Psychiatry, 29,* 21–29.
Schwartz, C., Houlihan, D., Krueger, K. F., & Simon, D. A. (1997). The behavioral treatment of a young adult with post traumatic stress disorder and a fear of children. *Child & Family Behavior Therapy, 19,* 37–49.

BOX 17.2 RESEARCH ON EXPOSURE THERAPY

Alcohol dependence
Staiger, P. K., Greeley, J. D., & Wallace, S. D. (1999). Alcohol exposure therapy: Generalisation and changes in responsivity. *Drug & Alcohol Dependence, 57,* 2–40.

Anxiety
Carter, M. M., Marin, N. W., & Murrell, K. L. (1999). The efficacy of habituation in decreasing subjective distress among high anxiety-sensitive college students. *Journal of Anxiety Disorders, 13,* 575–589.

Childhood phobias
Silverman, W. K., Kurtines, W. M., Ginsburg, G. S., Weems, C. F., Rabian, S., & Lourdes, T. (1999). Contingency management, self-control, and education support in the treatment of childhood phobic disorders: A randomized clinical trial. *Journal of Consulting & Clinical Psychology, 67,* 675–687.

Computer-assisted and virtual
Boutelle, K. N. (1998). The use of exposure with response prevention in a male anorexic. *Journal of Behavior Therapy & Experimental Psychiatry, 29,* 79–84.
Clark, A., Kirkby, K. C., Daniels, B. A., & Marks, I. M. (1998). A pilot study of computer-aided vicarious exposure for obsessive–compulsive disorder. *Australian & New Zealand Journal of Psychiatry, 32,* 268–275.
Coldwell, S. E., Getz, T., Milgrom, P., Prall, C. W., Spadafora, A., & Ramsay, D. S. (1998). CARL: A LabView 3 computer program for conducting exposure therapy for the treatment of dental injection fear. *Behaviour Research & Therapy, 36,* 429–441.
Foa, E. B., Dancu, C. V., Hembree, E. A., Jaycox, L. H., Meadows, E. A., & Street, G. P. (1999). A comparison of exposure therapy, stress inoculation training, and their combination for reducing posttraumatic stress disorder in female assault victims. *Journal of Consulting & Clinical Psychology, 67,* 194–200.
Hodges, L. F., Rothbaum, B. O., Alacron, R., Ready, D., Shahar, F., Graap, K., Pair, J., Herbert, P., Gotz, D., Wills, B., & Baltzell, D. (1999). A virtual environment for the treatment of chronic combat-related post-traumatic stress disorder. *CyberPsychology & Behavior, 2,* 7–14.
Huang, M. P., Himle, J., & Alessi, N. E. (2000). Vivid visualization in the experience of phobia in virtual environments: Preliminary results. *CyberPsychology & Behavior, 3,* 315–320.
Jang, D., P., Ku-Jeong, H., Shin, M. B., Choi, Y. H., & Kim, S. I. (2000). Objective validation of the effectiveness of virtual reality psychotherapy. *CyberPsychology & Behavior, 3,* 365–374.
Kahan, M. (2000). Integration of psychodynamic and cognitive–behavioral therapy in a virtual environment. *CyberPsychology & Behavior, 3,* 179–183.
Kahan, M., Tanzer, J., Darvin, D., & Borer, F. (2000). Virtual reality-assisted cognitive–behavioral treatment for fear of flying: Acute treatment and follow-up. *CyberPsychology & Behavior, 3,* 387–392.
Kirkby, K. C., Berrios, G. E., Daniels, B. A., Menzies, R. G., Clark, A., & Romano, A. (2000). Process-outcome analysis in computer-aided treatment of obsessive–compulsive disorder. *Comprehensive Psychiatry, 41,* 259–265.
Rothbaum, B. O., Hodges, L., Alacron, R., Ready, D., Shahar, F., Graap, K., Pair, J., Herbert, P., Gotz, D., Wills, B., & Baltzell, D. (1999). Virtual reality exposure for PTSD Vietnam veterans: A case study. *Journal of Traumatic Stress, 12,* 263–271.
Rothbaum, B. O., & Hodges, L. F. (1999). The use of virtual reality exposure in the treatment of anxiety disorders. *Behavior Modification, 23,* 507–525.

Context change
Mineka, S., Mystkowski, J. L., Hladek, D., & Rodriguez, B. I. (1999). The effects of changing contexts on return of fear following exposure therapy for spider fear. *Journal of Consulting & Clinical Psychology, 67,* 599–604.

Eating disorder
Bulik, C. M., Sullivan, P. F., Carter, F. A., McIntosh, V. V., & Joyce, P. R. (1998). The role of exposure with response prevention in the cognitive–behavioural therapy for bulimia nervosa. *Psychological Medicine, 28,* 611–623.

Guided threat reappraisal
Kamphius, J. H., & Telch, M. J. (2000). Effects of distraction and guided threat reappraisal on fear reduction during exposure-based treatments for specific fears. *Behavior Research & Therapy, 38,* 1163–1181.

Obsessive–compulsive disorder
de Haan, E., Hoogduin, K. A., Buitelaar, J. K., & Keijsers, G. P. J. (1998). Behavior therapy versus clomipramine for the treatment of obsessive–compulsive disorder. *Journal of the American Academy of Child & Adolescent Psychiatry, 37,* 1022–1029.
Franklin, M. E., Abramowitz, J. S., Kozak, M. J., Levitt, J. T., & Foa, E. B. (2000). Effectiveness of exposure and ritual prevention for obsessive compulsive disorder: Randomized compared with nonrandomized samples. *Journal of Consulting & Clinical Psychology, 68,* 594–602.
Marks, I. M., O'Dwyer, A.M., Meehan, O., Greist, J., Baer, L., & McGuire, P. (2000). Subjective imagery in obsessive–compulsive disorder before and after exposure therapy: Pilot randomised controlled trial. *British Journal of Psychiatry, 176,* 387–391.
Wetzel, C., Bents, H., & Florin, I. (1999). High-density exposure therapy for obsessive–compulsive inpatients: A 1-year follow-up. *Psychotherapy & Psychosomatics, 68*(4), 186–192.

Panic and agoraphobia
Bakker, A., van Balkom, A. J. L. M., & van Dyck, R. (2000). Selective serotonin reuptake inhibitors in the treatment of panic disorder and agoraphobia. *International Clinical Psychopharmacology, 15* (Suppl. 2), S25–S30.
de Beurs, E., van Balkom, A. J. L. M., van Dyck, R., & Lange, A. (1999). Long-term outcome of pharmacological and psychological treatment for panic disorder with agoraphobia: A 1-year naturalistic follow-up. *Acta Psychiatrica Scandinavica, 99,* 59–67.
Murphy, M. T., Michelson, L. K., Marchione, K., Marchione, N., & Testa, S. (1998). The role of self-directed in vivo exposure in combination with cognitive therapy, relaxation training, or therapist-assisted exposure in the treatment of panic disorder with agoraphobia. *Journal of Anxiety Disorders, 12,* 117–138.
Rowe, M. K., & Craske, M. G. (1998). Effects of an expanding-spaced vs massed exposure schedule on fear reduction and return of fear. *Behaviour Research & Therapy, 36,* 701–711.

> **BOX 17.2 RESEARCH ON EXPOSURE THERAPY** *CONTINUED*
>
> Teusch, L., & Boehme, H. (1999). Is the exposure principle really crucial in agoraphobia? The influence of client-centered "nonprescriptive" treatment on exposure. *Psychotherapy Research, 9,* 115–123.
>
> *Social phobia*
> Coles, M. E., & Heimberg, R. G. (2000). Patterns of anxious arousal during exposure to feared situations in individuals with social phobia. *Behaviour Research & Therapy, 38,* 405–424.
> Hoffman, S. G. (2000). Self-focused attention before and after treatment of social phobia. *Behavior Research & Therapy, 38,* 717–725.
>
> *Trauma*
> Abrahams, S., & Udwin, O. (2000). Treatment of post-traumatic stress disorder in an eleven-year-old boy using imaginal and in vivo exposure. *Clinical Child Psychology & Psychiatry, 5,* 387–401.
> Bryant, R. A., Sackville, T., Dang, S. T., Moulds, M., & Guthrie, R. (1999). Treating acute stress disorder: An evaluation of cognitive behavior therapy and supporting counseling techniques. *American Journal of Psychiatry, 156,* 1780–1786.
> Fahy, T. J. (2000). Imaginal exposure or cognitive therapy in the treatment of post-traumatic stress disorder. *British Journal of Psychiatry, 176,* 597.
> Fecteau, G., & Nicki, R. (1999). Cognitive behavioural treatment of post traumatic stress disorder after motor vehicle accident. *Behavioural & Cognitive Psychotherapy, 27,* 201–214.
> Foa, E. B. (2000). Psychosocial treatment of posttraumatic stress disorder. *Journal of Clinical Psychiatry, 61* (Suppl. 5), 43–51.
> Glynn, S. M., Eth, S., Randolph, E. T., Foy, D. W., Urbaitis, M., Boxer, L., Paz, G. G., Leong, G. B., Firman, G., Salk, J. D.,
>
> Katzman, J. W., & Crothers, J. (1999). A test of behavioral family therapy to augment exposure for combat-related posttraumatic stress disorder. *Journal of Consulting & Clinical Psychology, 67,* 243–251.
> Hembree, E. A., & Foa, E. B. (2000). Posttraumatic stress disorder: Psychological factors and psychological interventions. *Journal of Clinical Psychiatry, 61* (Suppl. 7), 33–39.
> Marks, I., Lovell, K., Noshirvani, H., Livanou, M., & Thrasher, S. (1998). Treatment of posttraumatic stress disorder by exposure and/or cognitive restructuring: A controlled study. *Archives of General Psychiatry, 55,* 317–325.
> Pantalon, M. V., & Motta, R. W. (1998). Effectiveness of anxiety management training in the treatment of posttraumatic stress disorder: A preliminary report. *Journal of Behavior Therapy & Experimental Psychiatry, 29,* 21–29.
> Tarrier, N., & Humphreys, L. (2000). Subjective improvement in PTSD patients with treatment by imaginal exposure or cognitive therapy: Session by session changes. *British Journal of Clinical Psychology, 39,* 27–34.
> Tarrier, N., Pilgrim, H., Sommerfield, C., Faragher, B., Reynolds, M., Graham, E., & Barrowclough, C. (1999). A randomized trial of cognitive therapy and imaginal exposure in the treatment of chronic posttraumatic stress disorder. *Journal of Consulting & Clinical Psychology, 67,* 13–18.
> Tarrier, N., Sommerfield, C., & Pilgrim, H. (1999). Relatives' expressed emotion and PTSD treatment outcome. *Psychological Medicine, 29,* 801–811.
> Tarrier, N., Sommerfield, C., Pilgrim, H., & Humphreys, L. (1999). Cognitive therapy or imaginal exposure in the treatment of post-traumatic stress disorder. *British Journal of Psychiatry, 175,* 571–575.

strategies (e.g., cognitive therapy, family therapy, social skills training, stress management) or test the relative effectiveness of desensitizing exposure to other methods or of one form of exposure to another. Also growing is application of desensitization through eye movement desensitization and reprocessing (EMDR; Shapiro, 1995) as well as cognitive–behavioral emotional processing of fear methods (Foa & Meadows, 1997).

Of course, one should not apply desensitization automatically whenever a client reports "anxiety." In some cases, the anxiety may be the logical result of another issue. For example, a person who continually procrastinates on work deadlines may feel anxious. Using this procedure would only help the person become desensitized or numb to the possible consequences of continued procrastination. A more logical approach might be to help the client reduce the procrastination behavior that is clearly the antecedent for the experienced anxiety. This illustration reiterates the importance of thorough assessment (Chapters 8 and 9) as a prerequisite for selecting and implementing helping strategies.

Generally, desensitization is the superior treatment for phobias and is most appropriate when a client has the capability or the skills to handle a situation or perform an activity but avoids the situation or performs less than adequately because of anxiety (Kleinknecht, 1991). For example, in the case described at the beginning of this chapter, the high school student had the ability to do well and possessed adequate study skills, yet his performance on tests was not up to par because of his response. In contrast, if a person avoids a situation because of skill deficits, then desensitization will be inappropriate and ineffective (Rimm & Masters, 1979).

As you may recall from Chapters 12 and 13, modeling and problem-solving procedures work very well with many kinds of skill-deficit problems. People with many fears or with general, pervasive anxiety may benefit more from stress management strategies (Chapters 15 and 16) or from combinations of strategies in which desensitization may play some role. In addition, some anxiety may be maintained by the client's maladaptive self-verbalizations. In such instances, cognitive restructuring or targeted schema change (Chapter 14) may be a first treatment choice or may be used in conjunction with desensitization (see Berman, Miller, & Massman, 1985). Van Hout, Emmelkamp, and Scholing (1994) evaluated the role of negative self-statements during *in vivo* desensitization of eight adult clients with phobia and agoraphobia. Four of the clients were most improved, and four were least improved. Results showed that the total frequency of negative self-statements at the beginning, middle, and end of desensitization differentiated best between the most and least improved clients. These authors suggest that, therapeutically, it seems wise to continue desensitization not only until both subjective and physiological measures of anxiety are reduced but also until the frequency of negative self-statements is reduced to zero (Van Hout, Emmelkamp, & Scholing, 1994). Desensitization should not be used when the client's anxiety is nonspecific or free-floating (Foa, Steketee, & Ascher, 1980). Biofeedback, meditation, and muscle relaxation may also be useful supplemental strategies, as may assertiveness or related social skills training (Meyer & Deitsch, 1996).

At the same time, desensitization should not be overlooked as a possible treatment strategy for client problems that do not involve anxiety. Marquis, Morgan, and Piaget (1973) suggest that desensitization can be used with any conditioned emotion such as anger and loss. Box 17.1 and Box 17.2 illustrate additional promising directions for systematic desensitization and exposure therapy.

MULTICULTURAL VARIATIONS OF ANXIETY AND USE OF SYSTEMATIC DESENSITIZATION

To date, explicit attention to the use of desensitization with diverse groups of clients has been limited. Clinical samples and research with nonclinical samples (samples following disasters and college samples) have included diversity, but our review yields limited findings. Diversity is evident with respect to gender and age—from young children to older adults. Racial and cultural diversity is more illustrative, including case examples as well as groups—for instance, use of desensitization to treat Japanese undergraduates with test phobia and speech anxiety (Kamimura & SaSaki, 1991), a Latina with multiple phobias (Acierno, Tremont, Last, & Montgomery, 1994), and an African American man with a 10-year history of PTSD (Frueh, de Arellano, & Turner, 1997). Eye movement desensitization and reprocessing has been used to treat PTSD for a 68-year-old World War II Native American veteran and also several African American Vietnam combat veterans (Lipke & Botkin, 1992; Thomas & Gafner, 1993).

All these cases report the successful use of desensitization—either imagined, in real situations, or through EMDR. Note, however, that although anxiety by and large appears to be a universal phenomenon, "the specific social events antecedent to many emotional states and the responses to those events are, in part, culture-specific" (Kleinknecht, Dinnel, Tanouye-Wilson, & Lonner, 1994, p. 175). Kleinknecht and associates (1994), for example, distinguish between social phobia as described in Western countries and *Taijin Kyofusho* (TKS), a Japanese condition referred to as social phobia—although this condition has been reported in China and Korea as well as Japan. The Western version of social phobia, described in the *DSM-IV* (American Psychiatric Association, 1994), begins in childhood or early adolescence and appears to be equal across genders; the anxiety begins with the concern that the person will embarrass *himself* or *herself*. In TKS, which affects more males than females, the concern is that the person will do something that in some way will embarrass or offend *someone else* (Kleinknecht et al., 1994). This difference reflects the variation in cultural values between some Western cultures that focus on independence and individuality ("The squeaky wheel gets the grease") and some Asian cultures that focus on interdependence or collectivity ("The nail that sticks out gets pounded down") (Triandis, 1990).

As Kleinknecht and associates (1994) observe, different cultural values affect how anxiety is presented by the client, what the client's major concern about the anxiety is, and what cognitive and behavioral patterns the helper must focus on (p. 178). In many respects, emotions are part of cultural systems, and their meaning is at least partly derivative of these systems as well as the historical context. This may be evident at an individual or family level as well as at a collective level, such as shared trauma among war victims and veterans, those subjected to community violence, victims of disasters, persecution, or historical colonial injustices. Practitioners who are not aware of these variations may miss the crucial component of an anxiety-related client issue and focus the intervention on a secondary rather than the primary area. In Chapter 15 we discussed some other cultural variations of stress and anxiety. In some cases, the use of cultural consultants, interpreters, or traditional healers may be an important adjunct to more appropriately understand the nature of the distress, relevant symptoms, and how to work with the individual and her or his family system (Friedman, 1997).

EXPLANATIONS OF DESENSITIZATION

Although desensitization has enjoyed substantial empirical support, a great deal of controversy surrounds its current status. There is general agreement that desensitization is effective in reducing fears and neurotic behavior. The controversy centers on how and why the procedure works, or what processes surrounding desensitization are responsible for its results. Connor-Greene (1993) found that nonspecific factors such as the therapeutic alliance and the client's expectations of change appeared to account for some of the therapeutic effects of desensitization. Ford (cited in Wolpe, 1990) asserts that there is evidence to the contrary to indicate that expectations of change are not a reliable predictor of long-term improvement.

We briefly summarize here two of the possible theoretical explanations of the desensitization procedure. This discussion should help you understand the theoretical basis of both the counterconditioning and the extinction rationales for implementing desensitization.

Desensitization by Reciprocal Inhibition

In 1958, Wolpe explained the way in which desensitization works by the principle of *reciprocal inhibition*. When reciprocal inhibition occurs, a response such as fear is inhibited by another response or activity that is stronger than and incompatible with the fear response (or any other response to be inhibited). In other words, if an incompatible response occurs in the presence of fear of a stimulus situation and if the incompatible response is stronger than the fear, desensitization occurs, and the stimulus situation loses its capacity to evoke fear. The reciprocal inhibition theory is based on principles of classical conditioning. For desensitization to occur, according to the reciprocal inhibition principle, three processes are required:

1. A strong anxiety-competing or counterconditioning response must be present. Usually, this competing or inhibiting response is deep muscle relaxation. Although other responses (such as eating, assertion, and sexual responses) can be used, Wolpe (1990) believes that relaxation is most helpful.
2. A graded series of anxiety-provoking stimuli is presented to the client. These stimulus situations are typically arranged in a hierarchy, with low-intensity situations at the bottom and high-intensity situations at the top.
3. Contiguous pairing must occur involving one of these aversive stimulus situations and the competing or counterconditioning response (relaxation). This pairing is usually accomplished by having the client achieve a state of deep relaxation and then imagine an aversive stimulus (presented as a hierarchy item) while relaxing. The client stops imagining the situation whenever anxiety (or any other emotion to be inhibited) occurs. After additional relaxation, the situation is presented again several times.

In recent years, some parts of the reciprocal inhibition principle have been challenged, both by personal opinion and by empirical explorations. There is some doubt that relaxation behaves in the manner suggested by Wolpe—as a response that is inherently antagonistic to anxiety. As Kazdin and Wilcoxon (1976) observe, some research indicates that desensitization is not dependent on muscle relaxation, a hierarchical arrangement of anxiety-provoking stimuli, or the pairing of these stimuli with relaxation as an incompatible response (p. 731). These research results have led some people to abandon a reciprocal inhibition explanation for desensitization.

Desensitization by Extinction

Lomont (1965) proposed that extinction processes account for the results of desensitization. In other words, anxiety responses diminish when conditioned stimuli are presented repeatedly without reinforcement. This theory is based on principles of operant conditioning. Wolpe (1990) agrees that desensitization falls within this operational definition of extinction and that extinction may play a role in desensitization. Similarly, Wilson and Davison (1971) have argued that desensitization reduces a client's anxiety level enough that the client gradually approaches the feared stimuli, and the fear is then extinguished. Figure 17.1 shows the seven major components of systematic desensitization. A summary of the procedural steps associated with each component is included in the Interview Checklist for Systematic Desensitization at the end of the chapter.

COMPONENTS OF DESENSITIZATION

Treatment Rationale

The purpose and overview given to the client about desensitization are important because they introduce the client to the principles of desensitization. Further, the outcomes of desensitization may be enhanced when the client is given very clear instructions and a positive expectancy set.

Rationale and Overview of Counterconditioning Model

With the counterconditioning model, you would present a rationale that explains how the client's fear or other conditioned emotion can be counterconditioned using desensitization.

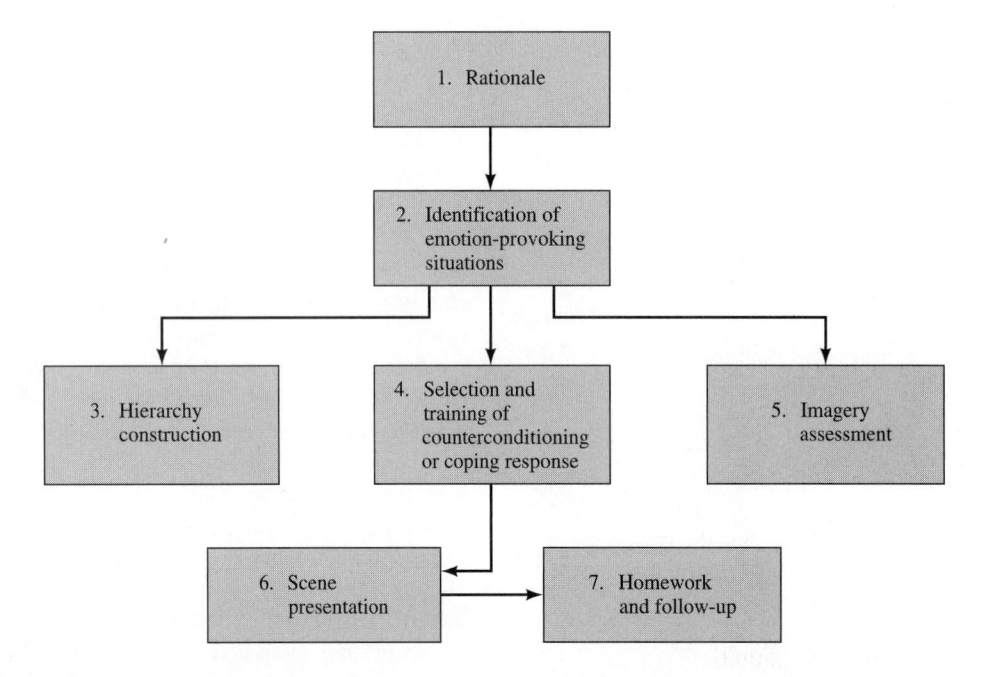

Figure 17.1 Components of systematic desensitization procedure

Your overview of the procedure would emphasize the use of an anxiety-free response to replace the conditioned emotion, the construction of a hierarchy consisting of a graduated series of items representing the emotion-provoking situations, and the pairing of these hierarchy items with the anxiety-free response (such as relaxation).

MODEL DIALOGUE: RATIONALE FOR DESENSITIZATION

Here is an example of a rationale the therapeutic practitioner or helper could use to explain to Joan how desensitization can help her with her fear and avoidance of math class:

> Joan, we've talked about how you get very nervous before and during your math class. Sometimes you try to skip it. But you realize you haven't always felt this way about math. You've *learned* to feel this way. There is a procedure called desensitization that can help you replace your tension with relaxation. Eventually, the things about math class you now fear will not be tense situations for you. This procedure has been used very successfully to help other people reduce their fear of a certain situation.
>
> In desensitization, you will learn how to relax. After you're relaxed, I'll ask you to imagine some things about your math class—starting with not too stressful things and gradually working with more stressful things. As we go along, the relaxation will start to replace the anxiety. These stressful situations then will no longer seem so stressful to you.
>
> What questions do you have about this?

Identification of Emotion-Provoking Situations

If the helper and client have defined the problem thoroughly, there will already be some indications about the dimensions or situations that provoke anxiety (or any other emotional arousal) in the client. However, the helper and client must be sure to isolate the most crucial situations in which the client needs to become less anxious or upset (Goldfried & Davison, 1976, p. 114). This is not always an easy task, as first appearances can be deceiving. Wolpe (1990) describes a case in which the initial theme seemed to be fear of social places but was determined actually to be fear of rejection or criticism. In another case, an unexpected source of anxiety concerning impotence was found to be a fear of inflicting physical trauma. Goldfried and Davison recommend that helpers ask themselves and their clients what the consequences may be of desensitization to one thing or another (p. 115).

The emotion-provoking situations must be defined idiosyncratically for each client. Marquis, Ferguson, and Taylor (1980) observe that, even among clients who have the same type of fear or phobia, the specific anxiety-provoking situations associated with the fear can vary greatly.

Helpers can use at least three ways to try to identify past and present situations that are anxiety provoking to the client. These three methods are the interview assessment, client self-monitoring, and client completion of related self-report questionnaires.

Interview Assessment

The interview assessment will be similar to the one proposed in Chapters 8 and 9 on problem assessment. The helper should use leads that will establish the particular circumstances and situations that elicit the conditioned emotion. For instance, does the client feel anxious in all social situations or only those with strangers present? Does the client's anxiety vary with the number of people present? With whether the client is accompanied or alone? Does the client experience more anxiety with people of the same sex or the other sex? These are examples of the kind of information the interview assessment could provide about a client's anxiety in certain social situations.

Client Self-Monitoring

In addition to the information obtained during the session, the helper may obtain even more data by having the client observe and record on a log the emotion-provoking situations as they occur during the week. The client would observe and note what was going on, where, with whom, and when the emotion, such as anxiety, was detected. The client also might rate the level of anxiety felt during the situation on a scale of 1 (low) to 10 (high) or on a scale of 0 (no anxiety) to 100 (panic).

Self-Report Questionnaires

Some helpers find that additional data about particular emotion-provoking situations can be gained by having the client complete one or more self-report questionnaires. A commonly used questionnaire is the Wolpe and Lang (1964) Fear Survey Schedule (FSS), which contains 87 items that may cause fear or unpleasant feelings. The FSS is available in Appendix C of the Wolpe (1990) text. Also available in the Wolpe book is the Willoughby questionnaire, which lists anxiety responses in interpersonal contexts.

The helper should persist in this process until specific emotion-provoking situations are identified. Marquis and colleagues (1973, p. 2) indicate that information gathering is not complete until the helper knows the factors related to the onset and maintenance of the client's concern and until the client believes that all pertinent information has been shared with the helper. At this point, the helper and client are ready to construct a hierarchy.

MODEL DIALOGUE: IDENTIFYING EMOTION-PROVOKING SITUATIONS

Helper: Joan, we've already discussed some of the situations about your math class that make you feel anxious. What are some of these?

Client: Before class, just thinking about having to go bothers me. Sometimes at night I get anxious—not so much doing math homework but studying for tests.

Helper: OK. Can you list some of the things that happen during your math class that you feel anxious about?

Client: Always when I take a test. Sometimes when I am doing problems and don't know the answers—having to ask Mr. Lamborne for help. And, of course, when he calls on me or asks me to go to the board.

Helper: Good. And I believe you said before that you feel nervous about volunteering answers, too.

Client: Right—that, too.

Helper: Yet these sorts of situations don't seem to upset you in your other classes?

Client: No. And really math class has never been as bad as it is this year. I guess part of it is the pressure of getting closer to graduating, and, well, my teacher makes me feel dumb. I felt scared of him the first day of class. And I've always felt somewhat nervous about working with numbers.

Helper: So some of your fear centers on your teacher, too—and then perhaps there's some worry about doing well enough to graduate.

Client: Right. Although I know I won't do *that* badly.

Helper: OK, good. You realize that, even with not liking math and worrying about it, you won't get a bad grade.

Client: Not worse than a C.

Helper: There's one thing I'd like you to do this week. Could you make a list of anything about the subject of math—and your math class—that has happened and has made you nervous? Also, write down anything about math or your class that *could* happen that you would feel anxious about.

Client: OK.

Helper: Earlier, too, you had mentioned that sometimes these same feelings occur in situations with your parents, so after we work with math class, we'll come back and work on the situations with you and your parents.

Hierarchy Construction

A *hierarchy* is a list of stimulus situations to which the client reacts with graded amounts of anxiety or some other emotional response (Wolpe, 1990). Hierarchy construction can consume a good deal of interview time because of the various factors involved in constructing an adequate hierarchy. These factors include selection of a type of hierarchy, the number of hierarchies (single or multiple), identification of hierarchy items, identification of control items, and ranking and spacing of items. (See Learning Activity 17.1)

Types of Hierarchies

On the basis of the stimulus situations that evoke anxiety (or any emotion to be counterconditioned), the helper should select an appropriate type of hierarchy in which to cast individual items or descriptions of the aversive situations. Wolpe (1990) distinguishes between conventional and idiosyncratic hierarchies. Conventional hierarchies are unidimensional and incremental in terms of time or distance from a feared object. Most simple phobias can be treated with the development of a conventional hierarchy. On the other hand, idiosyncratic hierarchies are highly individualized because they are based on the past conditioning of an individual. The type of hierarchy used will depend on the nature of the client's problem. A conventional hierarchy is developed by using items that represent physical or time dimensions, such as distance from one's house or time before taking an exam. In either case, anxiety seems to vary with proximity to the feared object or situation. Someone who is afraid to leave the house will become more anxious as the distance from the house increases. A client who is

---

LEARNING ACTIVITY 17.1 — Hierarchy Construction

This learning activity is designed to give you some practice in constructing hierarchies. You can do this activity by yourself or with another person.

Part One

Conventional Hierarchy

Think of for yourself, or have your partner identify, a situation that you fear and avoid. This should be a situation in which the fear increases as the distance or time proximity toward the feared object or situation gets closer. For example, you might fear and avoid approaching certain kinds of animals or high places (distance). Or you might get increasingly anxious as the time before an exam, a speech, or an interview diminishes (time). For this situation, identify the specific situations that are anxiety provoking. Try to identify all the relevant parameters of the situation.

For example, does your anxiety vary if you're alone or with another person, if you're taking a midterm or a quiz, if you're speaking before a large or a small group? List each anxiety-provoking situation that could be a hierarchy item on a separate index card. Also, list one control (pleasant) item on a card. After you or your partner believes all the relevant items are listed, take the cards and assign a sud value to each item. The control item will be at the bottom, followed by items that evoke successively greater anxiety. Check to make sure that there are no differences that exceed 10 units between sud values.

Part Two

Idiosyncratic Hierarchy

See whether you or your partner can identify a situation about which you have painful or unpleasant memories. Such situations might include loss of a prized object, loss of a job or friend, or termination of a close relationship. Generate emotion-provoking situations associated with pleasant memories and unpleasant memories. List each situation on a separate card. When all the items are identified and listed, assign sud values to each. Check the sud values to make sure that there are no differences that exceed 10 units between sud values.

anxious about an exam will become more anxious as the exam draws closer.

Here is an example of a conventional hierarchy used with a client who was anxious about taking a test. You will see that the items are arranged according to time:

1. Your instructor announces on the first day of class that the first exam will be held in one month. You know that the month will go quickly.
2. A week before the exam, you are sitting in class, and the instructor reminds the class of the exam date. You realize you have a lot of studying to do during the week.
3. You are sitting in the class, and the instructor mentions the exam, scheduled for the next class session, two days away. You realize you still have a lot of pages to read.
4. Now it is one day before the exam. You are studying in the library. You wonder whether you have studied as much as everyone else in the class.
5. It is the night before the test. You are in your room studying. You think about the fact that this exam grade is one-third of your final grade.
6. It is the night before the exam—late evening. You have just finished studying and have gone to bed. You're lying awake going over your reading in your mind.
7. You wake up the next morning, and your mind flashes that this is exam day. You wonder how much you will remember of what you read the night and day before.
8. It is later in the day, one hour before the exam. You do some last-minute scanning of your lecture notes. You start to feel a little hassled—even a little sick. You wish you had more time to prepare.
9. It is 15 minutes before the class—time to walk over to the classroom. As you're walking over, you realize how important this grade will be. You hope you don't "blank out."
10. You go into the building, stop to get a drink of water, and then enter the classroom. You look around and see people laughing. You think that they are more confident and better prepared than you.
11. The instructor is a little late. You are sitting in class waiting for the teacher to come and pass out the tests. You wonder what will be on the test.
12. The instructor has just passed out tests. You receive your copy. Your first thought is that the test is so long—will you finish in time?
13. You start to work on the first portion of the test. There are some questions you aren't sure of. You spend time thinking and then see that people around you are writing. You skip these questions and go on.
14. You look at your watch. The class is half over—only 25 minutes left. You feel you have dawdled on the first part of the test. You wonder how much your grade will be pulled down if you don't finish.
15. You continue to work as fast as you can; occasionally, you worry about the time. You glance at your watch—five minutes left. You still have a lot of unanswered questions.
16. Time is just about up. There are some questions you had to leave blank. You worry again because this test accounts for one-third of your grade.

An idiosyncratic hierarchy focuses on a particular issue that is associated with anxiety for an individual client. For example, Wolpe (1990) describes several cases of clients who are concerned about illnesses in themselves and others. Items on the "Illness in Others" list include the sight of a physical deformity, the sight of bleeding, automobile accidents, and nurses in uniform. A list of "Illnesses in Self" includes a tight sensation in the head, clammy feet, perspiring hands, dizziness, and rapid breathing. These items are developed with each client individually and pertain to individual fears and concerns. There is no sequential ordering; rather, the helper and the client must work together to develop a hierarchy that contains the feared items in increasing increments of fear-producing potential. Here is an example of this kind of hierarchy (Wolpe, 1990, p. 167):

External Series (Illness in Others)

1. Child with two short legs
2. Man walking slowly—short of breath owing to a weak heart
3. Blind man working elevator
4. Child with one leg longer than another
5. A hunchback
6. A person groaning with pain
7. A man with a club foot
8. A one-armed man
9. A one-legged man
10. A person with a high temperature owing to a relatively nondangerous disease such as influenza

Number of Hierarchies

Whether you use one or several hierarchies also depends on the client's issue and preferences and on your preferences. Some helpers believe that separate hierarchies should be constructed for different themes or different parameters of one theme. Using multiple hierarchies may be less confusing but can require more time for hierarchy construction and presentation. Generally, up to four different hierarchies can be used in an individual desensitization session (Wolpe, 1990).

Identification of Hierarchy Items

The helper must initiate a method of generating the items for the hierarchy. The client's role in this process is extremely important. Generally, the helper can ask the client to aid in identifying hierarchy items by interview questions or by a homework assignment. The helper can question the client about particular emotion-provoking scenes during the interview. However, questioning the client about the scenes should not occur simultaneously with the client's relaxation training. If the client is queried about hierarchy items after engaging in a period of deep relaxation, her or his responses may be altered.

If the client has difficulty responding concretely to interview questions, the helper can assign homework for item identification. The helper can give the client a stack of blank 3×5 index cards. The client is asked to generate items during the week and to write down each item on a separate note card. Often, this homework assignment is useful even with clients who respond very thoroughly to the interview questions. During the week, the client has time to add items that were not apparent during the session.

The helper should continue to explore and generate hierarchy items until a number have been identified that represent a range of aversive situations and varying degrees of emotional arousal. A hierarchy typically contains 10 to 20 items. Goldfried and Davison (1976) and Marquis and colleagues (1973) suggest some criteria to use in constructing adequate hierarchy items:

1. Some of the items should represent situations that, if carried out by the client *in vivo,* are under the client's control (do not require instigation from others).
2. An item must be concrete and specific. Embellishing the item description with sufficient details may help the client obtain a clear and vivid visualization of the item during scene presentation. As an example, an item that reads "Your best friend disapproves of you" is too general. A more concrete item would be "Your best friend disapproves of your boyfriend and tells you that you are stupid for going out with him."
3. Items should be similar to or represent actual situations the client has faced or may have to face in the future. If dialogue is written into an item, the language used should be adapted to the client.
4. Items selected should reflect a broad range of situations in which the client's fear (or other emotion) does or could occur.
5. Items should be included that reflect all different levels of the emotion, ranging from low to high intensity.

After the hierarchy items are identified, the client and helper can identify several control items.

Identification of Control Items

A control item consists of a relaxing or neutral scene to which the client is not expected to have any strong emotional reaction. Control scenes are placed at the bottom of the hierarchy and represent a zero or "no anxiety" ranking. Some examples of control items are to "imagine a colored object," "imagine you're sitting in the sun on a day with a completely blue sky," or "imagine you're looking at a field of vivid yellow daffodils." A control item is often used to test the client's ability to visualize anxiety-free material and to give the client a relaxing or pleasant scene to imagine during scene presentation in order to enhance the level of relaxation. After all the hierarchy and control items have been identified, the client can arrange the items in order of increasing emotional arousal through a ranking method.

Ranking and Spacing of Hierarchy Items

The helper and client work together to identify an appropriate order for the items in the hierarchy. Generally, the client plays the major role in ranking, but the helper must ensure that the spacing between items is satisfactory. The hierarchy items are ranked in order of increasing difficulty, stress, or emotional arousal. The control items are placed at the bottom of the hierarchy, and each item that represents more difficulty or greater anxiety is placed in a successively higher position in the hierarchy. Items at the top of the hierarchy represent the situations that are most stressful or anxiety producing for the client.

The helper should explain how the hierarchy items are arranged before asking the client to rank them. The helper should also explain the purpose of this type of hierarchy arrangement so the client fully understands the necessity of spending time to rank the items. The helper can point out that desensitization occurs gradually and that the function of a hierarchy is to identify low-stress items to which the client will be desensitized before higher-stress items. The client's learning to face or cope with a feared situation will begin with more manageable situations first and gradually extend to more difficult situations. The helper may emphasize that at no point will the client be asked to imagine or cope with a scene or situation that is very stressful before learning to deal successfully with less stressful scenes. This point is often reassuring to an occasional client whose anxiety is so great that the desensitization procedure itself is viewed with great trepidation.

The *sud* scale is used to quantify the items on the hierarchies. A sud is a *subjective unit of disturbance* (Wolpe, 1990) and can be explained to clients in the following way: "Think of the worst anxiety you can imagine and assign it the number 100. Then think of being absolutely calm—that is, no anxiety at all—and call this 0. Now you have a scale of anxiety. At every waking moment of your waking life you must be somewhere between zero and 100. How do you rate yourself at this moment?" (Wolpe, 1990, p. 91).

When a client uses the sud scale to arrange items, each item is assigned a number representing the amount of stress it generates for the client. If the item doesn't generate much stress, the client may assign it 10, 15, or 20 suds. Average amounts of stress might be assigned 35, 40, 45, or 50, whereas 85, 90, 95, and 100 suds represent situations that produce great anxiety or stress.

After the items are arranged according to the assigned suds, the helper should make sure that no item is separated from the previous item by more than 10 suds; at the high end of the scale, spacing of no more than 5 suds between items is often necessary (Wolpe, 1990). If there are large gaps (greater than 10 or 5 suds), the helper and client should write additional, intermediate items to fill in. If there are too many items around the same level, particularly at the lower end of the hierarchy, some may be deleted. The sud system makes it easy to determine whether there is too much or too little space between items. Second, the use of the sud scale at this point in desensitization introduces the client to a way to discriminate and label varying degrees of relaxation and tension. This kind of labeling system is often useful during relaxation training and scene presentation.

Although we have described how to construct a hierarchy for an individual client, hierarchy construction can also be adapted for groups of clients. For some clients, standardized hierarchies may work as well as individualized ones.

It is even possible to have machines conduct the desensitization process. Lang, Melamed, and Hart (1970) described the use of two tape recorders, one with the hierarchy items and one with relaxation items, to treat snake phobia. Others have also described the use of tape-recorded material instead of the helper's participation (Denholtz & Mann, 1974; Kahn & Baker, 1968). The use of tapes may be especially helpful in cases when the client is too anxious to relax in the presence of the helper (Wolpe, 1990). Recent developments also present hierarchies on computers using "virtual realities" (Nelissen, Muris, & Merckelbach, 1995).

MODEL DIALOGUE: HIERARCHY CONSTRUCTION USING THE SUD SCALE

Helper: Hi, Joan. I see you brought your list with you. That's great, because today we're going to work on a list that's called a hierarchy, which is like a staircase or a ladder. In your case, it will center on the theme or the idea of math anxiety. It's a list of all the situations about math that are anxiety producing for you. We'll list these situations, and then I'll ask you to assign each one a sud value. A sud is a number that describes how anxious you feel. The higher the sud, the more anxious you feel. It works like this. Think of the worst anxiety you can imagine, and assign it the number 100. Then think of being absolutely calm—that is, having no anxiety at all—and call this 0. Now you have a scale of anxiety. At every waking moment of your waking life you must be somewhere between 0 and 100. Now we are going to go through your list and assign suds to each item. Does this seem clear?

Client: Yes. Actually I did something like that this week in making my list, didn't I?

Helper: Right, you did. Now what we want to do is take your list, add any other stressful situations that aren't on here, and make sure each item on this list is specific. We may need to add some details to some of the items. The idea is to get a close description of the way the situation actually is or actually does or could happen. Let's take a look at your list now.

1. Sitting in English thinking about math class
2. On way to math class
3. At home, doing math homework
4. At home, studying for a math test
5. In math class, teacher giving out test
6. In math class, taking test
7. In math class, teacher asking me question
8. In math class, at board, having trouble
9. In math class, working problems at desk, not knowing some answers
10. Asking teacher for help
11. Volunteering an answer
12. Getting test or assignment back with low grade
13. Hearing teacher tell me I'll flunk or barely pass
14. Doing anything with numbers, even outside math class, like adding up a list of numbers
15. Talking about math with someone

It looks like you've really worked hard at putting down some math situations that are stressful for you and indicating just how stressful they are. OK, let's go over this list and fill in some details. For each item here, can you write in one or two more details about the situation? What exactly happens that you feel nervous about? For instance, when you're sitting in English, what is it you're thinking that makes you nervous?

Client: I see what you mean.

Helper: Let's go over each item here, and as you tell me the details, I'll jot these down. [This step proceeds until a concrete description is obtained for each item. Helper checks them to see whether items meet necessary criteria, which, with added details, these do. The criteria are these: some items are under client's control; items are concrete; items represent past, present, or future anxiety-provoking scenes; items sample a broad range of situations; items represent varying levels of anxiety.]

Helper: What else can you think of about math that is or could be stressful?

Client: Nothing right now. Not everything on my list has happened, but like, if my teacher did tell me I was going to flunk, that would be very tense.

Helper: You've got the idea. Now can you think of something not related to math that would be pleasant or relaxing for you to think about—like skiing down a slope or lying on the beach?

Client: Well, what about sitting in front of a campfire roasting marshmallows?

Helper: Good. Now later on, as we proceed, I might ask you to relax by imagining a pleasant scene. Then you could imagine something like that.

Client: OK.

Helper: I'd like you to take a look at the items we've listed on these cards and assign a sud value to each item. We can start with the pleasant item having to do with the campfire at the bottom of the list and assign a sud score of 0. Now we have to assign a sud value to each of the other situations we described.

Client: So the next thing should be something that only bothers me a little bit, right? Then I'll pick the one about me sitting at home and doing problems that are pretty easy. A sud score could be 10.

Helper: Great! You have the right idea. Which one would be next on the hierarchy?

Client: I think that when I think about going to math class, I get anxious, so I'll pick the one about being in English class and knowing that math class is next, and I'll give it a sud of 20.

Helper: OK, so what would be next?

Client: On the way to math class. Going in and having the teacher look at homework. This makes me more anxious. I'll give it a sud of 30.

Helper: You are doing great. We have more items to rate. Which would be next?

Client: Talking to my friend about a test that is coming up. Worrying that I might not pass it. This is a sud of about 35. And the next one would have to be the one about seeing a long list of numbers and having to see if the addition is right. That would be about 40 on the sud scale.

Helper: OK. What would be next?

Client: I get anxious thinking about being in math class, at my desk, and having trouble doing my work. That one would be a sud of 50. The next one would also be in math class and would involve not being able to do some of the problems. I'd have to ask my teacher for help. That would be 60.

Helper: Looks like we are about half done. Let's finish the list and continue to assign sud values to each item. [The process continues until each of the 16 cards has been assigned a sud value.] Now it seems as if you have ordered each of these situations in terms of the sud value. We can see that there are no large gaps between items, so we can begin with this hierarchy. Later we can move items around or reassign sud values, if we need to do so. I'm going to lay each card out to see what you've got here, starting at the bottom.

Card 1:

(sud 0) Sitting in front of a campfire on a cool night with friends, singing songs and roasting marshmallows [control item].

Card 2:

(sud 10) Sitting in my room at my desk doing routine math homework over fairly easy material.

Card 3:

(sud 20) Sitting in English about 10 minutes before the bell. Thinking about going to math class next and wondering if I can hide or if I'll get called on.

Card 4:
(sud 30) Walking down the hall with a couple of classmates to math class. Walking in the door and seeing the teacher looking over our homework. Wondering how I did.

Card 5:
(sud 35) A girlfriend calls up and talks about our upcoming test in math—wonder if I'll pass it.

Card 6:
(sud 40) Seeing a big list of numbers, like on a store receipt, and having to check the total to make sure it's OK.

Card 7:
(sud 50) In math class, sitting at my desk: having to work on problems and coming across some that are confusing. Don't have much time to finish.

Card 8:
(sud 60) Working on problems at my desk. I'm stumped on a couple. Nothing I try works. Having to go up and ask Mr. Lamborne for help. He tries to do it for me; I feel dumb.

Card 9:
(sud 65) Sitting in my room at home the night before a big math test: studying for the test and wondering if I'll blank out on it.

Card 10:
(sud 75) In math class taking a test and coming across some problems I don't know how to do.

Card 11:
(sud 80) Waiting to get a test or an assignment back and worrying about a low grade.

Card 12:
(sud 85) Sitting in math class and the teacher asks for the answer: raising my hand to volunteer it and I wonder if it's right.

Card 13:
(sud 90) Sitting in math class waiting for a big test to be passed out. Wondering what's on it and if I'll be able to remember things.

Card 14:
(sud 95) Sitting in math class and suddenly the teacher calls on me and asks me for an answer. I feel unprepared.

Card 15:
(sud 98) Sitting in math class and the teacher sends me to the board. I'm at the board trying to work a problem in front of the class. I'm getting stuck.

Card 16:
(sud 100) The teacher calls me in for a conference after school. Mr. Lamborne is telling me I'm in big trouble and barely passing. There's a good chance I could flunk math.

Helper: OK, now it seems like each of these items represents a somewhat more stressful situation. Do you feel that there are any large jumps between items—like going from a very low-stress situation to a higher-stress one suddenly?

Client (looks over list): No, I don't think so.

Helper: Then we'll stick with this list and this order for now. Of course, this is tentative. Later on, if we feel that something needs to be moved around or added, we will do so.

Selection and Training of Counterconditioning Response

According to the principles of reciprocal inhibition and counterconditioning, for desensitization to take place, the client must respond in a way that inhibits (or counterconditions) the anxiety or other conditioned emotion. The helper selects, and trains the client to use, a response that can be considered either an alternative to anxiety or incompatible with anxiety.

Selection of a Response

The helper's first task is to select an appropriate counterconditioning response for the client to use. Typically, the anxiety-inhibiting or counterconditioning response used in desensitization is deep muscle relaxation (Wolpe, 1990). Muscle relaxation has some advantages. Levin and Gross (1985) found that relaxation heightens the vividness of imagery. Also, as you may remember from Chapter 16, its use in anxiety reduction and management is well documented. Wolpe (1990) prefers muscle relaxation because it doesn't require any sort of motor activity to be directed from the client toward the sources of anxiety (p. 154). Muscle relaxation is easily learned by most clients and easily taught in the interview. It is also adaptable for daily client practice. However, an occasional client may have difficulty engaging in relaxation. Further, relaxation is not always applicable to *in vivo* desensitization, in which the client carries out rather than imagines the hierarchy items.

When deep muscle relaxation cannot be used as the counterconditioning response, the helper may decide to proceed without this sort of response or to substitute an alternative response. In some cases, clients have been desensitized without relaxation. However, with a client who is very anxious, it may be risky to proceed without any response to counteract the anxiety.

If muscle relaxation is not suitable for a client, guided imagery (Chapter 12), meditation (Chapter 16), and coping thoughts (Chapters 14 and 15) may be reasonable substitutes that are practical to use in the interview and easy to teach. For example, if the helper selects guided imagery, the client can focus on pleasant scenes during desensitization. If meditation is selected, the client can focus on breathing and counting. In the case of coping thoughts, the client can whisper or subvocalize coping statements.

Explanation of Response to the Client

The client will be required to spend a great deal of time in the session and at home learning the response. Usually a large amount of client time will result in more payoffs if the client understands how and why this sort of response should be learned.

In emphasizing that the response is for counterconditioning, the helper can explain that one of the ways desensitization can help the client is by providing a substitute for anxiety (or other emotions). The helper should emphasize that this substitute response is incompatible with anxiety and will minimize the felt anxiety so that the client does not continue to avoid the anxiety-provoking situations.

Training in the Response

The helper will need to provide training for the client in the particular response to be used. The training in muscle relaxation or any other response may require at least portions of several sessions to complete. The training in a counterconditioning response can occur simultaneously with hierarchy construction. Half the interview can be used for training; the rest can be used for hierarchy construction. Remember, though, that identifying hierarchy items should not occur simultaneously with relaxation. The helper can follow portions of the interview protocol for cognitive restructuring (Chapter 14) for training in coping statements; the interview checklists for guided imagery (Chapter 12), muscle relaxation, and meditation (Chapter 16) can be used to provide training in these responses.

Before and after each training session, the helper should ask the client to rate the felt level of stress or anxiety. This is another time the sud scale is very useful. The client can use the 0–100 scale and assign a numerical rating to the level of anxiety. Generally, training in the counterconditioning response should be continued until the client can discriminate different levels of anxiety and can achieve a state of relaxation after a training session equivalent to 10 or less on the 100-point sud scale. If, after successive training sessions, the client has difficulty using the response in a nonanxious manner, another response may need to be selected.

After the client has practiced the response with the helper's direction, daily homework practice should be assigned. An adequate client demonstration of the counterconditioning response is one prerequisite for actual scene presentation. A second prerequisite involves a determination of the client's capacity to use imagery.

MODEL DIALOGUE: SELECTION OF AND TRAINING IN COUNTERCONDITIONING RESPONSE

Helper: Joan, perhaps you remember that when I explained desensitization to you, I talked about replacing anxiety with something else, like relaxation. What I'd like to do today is show you a relaxation method you can learn. How does that sound?

Client: OK, is it like yoga?

Helper: It's carried out differently from yoga, but it is a skill you can learn with practice, and it has effects similar to those of yoga. This is a process of body relaxation. It involves learning to tense and relax different muscle groups in your body. Eventually you will learn to recognize when a part of you starts to get tense, and you can signal to yourself to relax.

Client: Then how do we use it in desensitization?

Helper: After you learn this, I will ask you to imagine the items on your hierarchy—but only when you're relaxed, like after we have a relaxation session. You'll be imagining something stressful, only you'll be relaxed. After you keep working with this, the stressful situations become less and less anxiety provoking for you.

Client: That makes sense to me, I think. The relaxation can help the situation to be less tense.

Helper: Yes, it plays a big role—which is why I consider the time we'll spend on learning the relaxation skill so important. Now, one more thing, Joan. Before and after each relaxation session, I'll ask you to tell me how tense or how relaxed you feel at that moment. You can do this by using a number from 0 to 100—0 would be total relaxation, and 100 would be total anxiety or tenseness. How do you feel right now, on that scale?

Client: Not totally relaxed, but not real tense. Maybe around a 30.

Helper: OK. Would you like to begin with a relaxation-training session now?

Client: Sure. [Training in muscle relaxation following the interview checklist presented in Chapter 16 is given to Joan. An abbreviated version of this is also presented in the model dialogue on scene presentation later in this chapter.]

Imagery Assessment

The typical administration of desensitization relies heavily on client imagery. The relearning (counterconditioning) achieved in desensitization occurs during the client's visualization of the hierarchy items. This, of course, assumes that imagination of a situation is equivalent to a real situation and that the learning that occurs in the imagined situation generalizes to the real situation. Mahoney and Thoresen (1974) note evidence that there may be considerable variability in the degree to which these assumptions about imagery really operate. Still, if desensitization is implemented, the client's capacity to generate images is vital to the way that this procedure is typically used.

Explanation to the Client

The helper can explain that the client will be asked to imagine the hierarchy items as if the client were a participant in the situation. The helper might say that imagining a feared situation can be very similar to actually being in the situation. If the client becomes desensitized while imagining the aversive situation, then the client will also experience less anxiety when actually in the situation. The helper can suggest that because people respond differently to using their imaginations, it is a good idea to practice visualizing several situations.

Assessment of Client Imagery

The client's capacity to generate clear and vivid images can be assessed by use of practice (control) scenes or by a questionnaire, as described in Chapter 12. Generally, it is a good idea to assess the client's imagery for desensitization at two times—when the client is deliberately relaxed and when the client is not deliberately relaxed. According to Wolpe (1990), imagery assessment of a scene under relaxation conditions serves two purposes. First, it gives the helper information about the client's ability to generate anxiety-free images. Second, it suggests whether any factors are present that may inhibit the client's capacity to imagine anxiety-free material. For example, a client who is concerned about losing self-control may have trouble generating images of a control item (Wolpe, 1990). After each visualization, the helper can ask the client to describe the details of the imagined scene aloud. Clients who cannot visualize scenes may have to be treated with an alternative strategy for fear reduction that does not use imagery, such as participant modeling or *in vivo* desensitization (see also the section on *in vivo* desensitization).

Criteria for Effective Imagery

In the typical administration of desensitization, the client's use of imagery plays a major role. A client who is unable to use imagery may not benefit from a hierarchy that is presented in imagination. From the results of the client's imagery assessment, the helper should determine whether the client's images meet the criteria for effective therapeutic imagery. These four criteria have been proposed by Marquis and associates (1973, p. 10):

1. The client must be able to imagine a scene concretely, with sufficient detail and evidence of touch, sound, smell, and sight sensations.
2. The scene should be imagined in such a way that the client is a participant, not an observer.
3. The client should be able to switch a scene image on and off upon instruction.
4. The client should be able to hold a particular scene as instructed without drifting off or changing the scene.

If during imagery assessment it becomes clear that the client cannot meet some or all of these criteria, the helper may decide to continue to use imagery and provide imagery training or to add a dialogue or a script; to present the hierarchy in another manner (slides, role plays, or actual experience); or to terminate desensitization and use an alternative therapeutic strategy. Whenever the client is able to report clear, vivid images that meet most of the necessary criteria, the helper can initiate the nuts and bolts of desensitization—presentation of the hierarchy items.

MODEL DIALOGUE: IMAGERY ASSESSMENT

The following assessment should be completed two times: once after a relaxation session and once when Joan is not deliberately relaxed.

Helper: Joan, I will be asking you in the procedure to imagine the items we've listed in your hierarchy. Sometimes people use their imaginations differently, so it's a good idea to see how you react to imagining something. Could you just sit back, close your eyes, and relax? Now get a picture of a winter snow scene in your mind. Put yourself in the picture, doing something. [Pauses.] Now can you describe exactly what you imagined?

Client: Well, it was a cold day, but the sun was shining. There was about a foot of snow on the ground. I was on a toboggan with two friends going down a big hill very fast. At the bottom of the hill we rolled off and fell in the snow. That was cold!

Helper: So you were able to imagine sensations of coldness. What colors do you remember?

Client: The hill, of course, was real white, and the sky was blue. The sun kind of blinded you. I had on a bright red ski jacket.

Helper: Good. Let's try another one. I'll describe a scene and ask you to imagine it for a certain amount of time. Try to get a clear image as soon as I've described the scene. Then, when I say "Stop the image," try to erase it from your mind. OK, here's the scene. It's a warm, sunny day with a good breeze. You're out on a boat on a crystal-clear lake. Now imagine this—put in your own details. [Pauses.] OK, Joan, stop the image. Can you tell me what you pictured? [Joan describes the images.] How soon did you get a clear image of the scene after I described it?

Client: Oh, not long. Maybe a couple of seconds.

Helper: Were you able to erase it when you heard me say *stop*?

Client: Pretty much. It took me a couple of seconds to get completely out of it.

Helper: Did you always imagine being on a boat, or did you find your imagination wandering or revising the scene?

Client: No, I was on the boat the entire time.

Helper: How do you feel about imagining a scene now?

Client: These are fun. I don't think imagination is hard for me anyway.

Helper: Well, you do seem pretty comfortable with it, so we can go ahead.

Joan's images meet the criteria for effective imagery: The scenes are imagined concretely, she sees herself in a scene as a participant, she is able to turn the image on and off fairly well on instruction, she holds a scene constant, and there is no evidence of any other difficulties.

Hierarchy Scene Presentation and Signaling Method

Scenes in the hierarchy are presented after the client has been given training in a counterconditioning response and after the client's imagery capacity has been assessed. Each scene presentation is paired with the counterconditioning response so that the client's anxiety (or other emotion) is counterconditioned, or decreased. There are different ways to present scenes to the client. Wolpe (1990) described the following method. The person is instructed to imagine the scene as described by the helper and is told to raise an index finger to indicate to the helper that the scene is clear. The helper allows the client to hold the image of the scene for five to seven seconds and terminates it by saying "Stop the scene." Next, the helper asks the client how much anxiety was generated in terms of suds; the helper might ask, "How much did imagining this scene increase your sud level?"

In the signaling method suggested by Wolpe (1990), the client raises a finger to inform the helper that the scene is clear. Other signaling methods have been described elsewhere (Marquis et al., 1973).

Format of a Scene-Presentation Session

Scene presentation follows a fairly standardized format. Each scene-presentation session should be preceded by a training session involving the designated counterconditioning response. As you will recall, the idea is to present the hierarchy items concurrently with some counterconditioning or coping response. For example, the helper can inform the client that the first part of the session will be a period of relaxation, after which the helper will ask the client to imagine a scene from the hierarchy. Each desensitization session should begin with a brief period of muscle relaxation, meditation, or guided imagery. The client's relaxation rating following this period should be 10 or less on the 100-point sud scale before the helper presents a hierarchy item.

At this point, the helper begins by describing a hierarchy item to the client and instructing the client to evoke the scene in imagination. The initial session begins with the first (least anxiety-provoking) item in the hierarchy. Successive scene presentations always begin with the last item successfully completed at the preceding session. This helps to make a smooth transition from one session to the next and checks on the client's learning retention. Starting with the last successfully completed item may also prevent spontaneous recovery of the anxiety response (Marquis et al., 1973, p. 11). Sometimes, relapse between two scene-presentation sessions does occur, and this procedure is a way to check for it.

In presenting the item, the helper should describe it and ask the client to imagine it. The helper usually presents an item for a specified amount of time before asking the client to stop the image. The duration of a scene is usually five to seven seconds. There are reasons to vary the amount of time that a scene is imagined by a client. First, if the client indicates that he or she is experiencing strong anxiety, the scene should be stopped. If the helper believes that the client might have a large increase in anxiety with a particular scene, the helper might limit the time imagining that scene to less than two seconds. Wolpe (1990) indicates that early presentations of scenes tend to be shorter and that later ones tend to be longer.

If the client holds the scene for the specified duration and does not report any tension, the helper can instruct the client to stop the scene and to take a little time to relax. This relaxation time serves as a breather between item presentations. During this time, the helper can cue the onset of relaxation with descriptive words such as "let all your muscles relax" or with the presentation of a control item. There is no set time for a pause between items. Generally, a pause of 10 to 30 seconds is sufficient, although some clients may need as much as 2 or 3 minutes (Wolpe, 1990). It is suggested that the helper check with the client regarding the sud level between scene presentations.

If the client experienced anxiety during the visualization, the helper will instruct the client to imagine the scene again and check on the level of anxiety generated. It is often necessary to present a scene three or four times until the presentation of the scene does not lead to an increase in anxiety. Wolpe (1990) indicates that at times as many as 10 presentations are necessary to reduce the anxiety to 0. Anxiety must be reduced to 0 suds with each item before the next item in the hierarchy is presented.

An item that continues to elicit anxiety after three presentations may indicate some trouble and a need for adjustment. Continued anxiety for one item may indicate a problem in the hierarchy or in the client's visualization. There are at least three things a helper can try to alleviate continual anxiety resulting from the same item: A new, less anxiety-provoking item can be added to the hierarchy; the same item can be presented to the client more briefly; or the client's visualization can be assessed to determine whether the client is drifting from or revising the scene.

The helper should be careful to use standardized instructions at all times during scene-presentation sessions. Standardized instructions are important regardless of whether the client signals anxiety or reports a high or a low anxiety rating on the sud scale. Rimm and Masters (1979) observe that a helper can inadvertently reinforce a client for not signaling anxiety by saying "Good." The client, often eager to please the helper, may learn to avoid giving reports of anxiety because these are not similarly reinforced.

Each scene-presentation session should end with an item that evokes no anxiety or receives a low sud rating, as the last item of a series is well remembered. At times, the helper may need to return to a lower item on the hierarchy so that a non-anxiety-provoking scene can end the session. Systematic desensitization sessions should be terminated after 15 to 30 minutes (Wolpe, 1990), although some clients may be able to work longer, especially after the first few sessions have been completed. Limiting the presentation may allow time for up to 10 scene presentations, and at advanced stages of the process, some clients will be able to go through more than 30 scenes in a single session. A session may be terminated sooner if the client seems restless. Desensitization requires a great deal of client concentration, and the helper should not try to extend a session beyond the client's concentration limits.

Identify Notation Method

Desensitization also requires some concentration and attention on the helper's part. Just think about the idea of conducting perhaps four or five scene-presentation sessions with one client and working with one or more hierarchies with 10 to 20 items per hierarchy! The helper has a great deal of information to note and recall. Most helpers use some written recording method during the scene-presentation sessions. There are several ways to make notations of the client's progress in each scene-presentation session. We describe two. These methods are only suggestions; you may discover a notation system that parallels more closely your own procedural style of desensitization.

Marquis and associates (1973) use a "Desensitization Record Sheet" to record the hierarchy item numbers and the anxiety or sud rating associated with each item presentation. Their record sheet is shown in Figure 17.2, with a sample notation provided at the top of the sheet.

Subject's Name: Jane Doe				Time needed to relax at the beginning of the session: 15 minutes
Theme of Hierarchy: Criticism				Time needed to visualize the scene presented: 10 sec./8 sec./9 sec./5 sec.

Date and Total Time Spent in Session	Item Hierarchy Number	Anxiety + or − or Sud Rating		Time Between Items	Comments, Observations, Changes in Procedure, or Other Special Treatment
7-14-02 45 minutes	4	+8 +20	−15 +30	60 sec./ 60 sec./ 30 sec./ 60 sec./	

Figure 17.2 Desensitization record sheet
Source: A Guidebook for Systematic Desensitization, (3rd ed.), by J. Marquis, W. Morgan, and G. Piaget, 1973. Veterans' Workshop, Palo Alto, CA. Reprinted with permission of the authors.

Goldfried and Davison (1994) use a notation system written on a 3 × 5 index card that contains the description of the hierarchy item and the item number. Under the item description is space for the helper to note the duration of the item presentations and whether item presentation elicited anxiety. An example is presented in Figure 17.3. In this example, the numbers refer to the time in seconds that the client visualized each presentation of the item. The plus sign indicates a no-anxiety or low-sud visualization, and the minus sign indicates an anxiety or high-sud visualization. Note that there were two successive no-anxiety visualizations (+5 and +7) before the item was terminated.

MODEL DIALOGUE: SCENE PRESENTATION

Helper: Joan, after our relaxation session today, we're going to start working with your hierarchy. I'd like to explain how this goes. After you've relaxed, I'll ask you to imagine the first item on the low end of your hierarchy—that is, the pleasant one. It will help you relax even more. Then I'll describe the next item. I will show you a way to let me know if you feel any anxiety while you're imagining it. If you do, I'll ask you to stop or erase the image and to relax. You'll have some time to relax before I give you an item again. Does this seem clear?

Client: I believe so.

Helper: One more thing. If at any point during the time you're imagining a scene you feel nervous or anxious about it, just raise your finger. This will signal that to me. I'll also ask you to report the sud level that you feel after each scene is imagined.

Client: OK.

Helper: Just to make sure we're on the same track, could you tell me what you believe will go on during this part of desensitization?

Client: Well, after relaxation you'll ask me to imagine an item at the bottom of the hierarchy. If I feel any anxiety, I'll raise my finger, and you'll ask me to erase the scene and relax. And I'll also tell you how anxious I feel then.

Helper: Good. And even if you don't signal anxiety after a little time of imagining an item, I'll tell you to stop and relax. This gives you a sort of breather. Ready to begin?

Client: Yep.

Helper: First we'll begin with some relaxation. Just get in a comfortable position and close your eyes and relax. . . . Let the tension drain out of your body. . . . Now, after the word *relax,* just let your arms go limp. . . . Now relax your face. . . . Loosen up your face and neck muscles. . . . As I name each muscle group, just use the word *relax* as the signal to let go of all the tension. . . . Joan, you'll feel even more relaxed by thinking about a pleasant situation. . . . Just imagine you're sitting around a campfire on a cool winter night. . . . You're with some good friends, singing songs and roasting marshmallows. [Presentation of Item 1, or control item, giving Joan about 30 seconds for this image.] Now I'd like you to imagine you're sitting in your room at your desk doing math homework that's pretty routine and is fairly easy. [Presenta-

```
                                              Item No. 6
                                              Date 7-14-02
ITEM DESCRIPTION
You are walking to class thinking about the
upcoming exam. Your head feels crammed full of details.
You are wondering whether you've studied the right material.


+5  −7  +5  +7
```

Figure 17.3 Notation card
Source: Adapted from *Clinical Behavior Therapy* (expanded edition), by M. R. Goldfried and G. C. Davison. Copyright © 1994 by Wiley Interscience. Reprinted by permission of the authors.

tion of Item 2 in hierarchy, with helper noting duration of presentation on stopwatch. Helper allows the scene to be imagined for five to seven seconds and watches to see whether Joan signals any anxiety by raising her finger. Joan does not respond, indicating that she is not feeling anxious while imagining this item.] OK, Joan, stop that image and erase it from your mind. Just concentrate on feeling very relaxed. [Pauses 10 to 30 seconds.] Now I'd like you to again imagine you're in your room sitting at your desk doing math homework that is routine and fairly simple. [Second presentation of Item 2, with helper allowing the scene to be imagined again for five to seven seconds and watching to see whether Joan signals any anxiety by raising her finger. Joan does not respond, indicating that she is not feeling anxious while imagining this item.] Joan, now just erase the image from your mind and relax. Let go of all your muscles. [Pause 10 to 30 seconds. As two successive presentations of this item did not elicit any anxiety, the helper will move on to Item 3.] Now I'd like you to imagine you're sitting in English class. It's about ten minutes before the bell. Your mind drifts to math class. You wonder if anything will happen, like getting called on. [Presentation of Item 3 in hierarchy, with helper noting duration of presentation with stopwatch. Helper allows the scene to be imagined again for 5 to 7 seconds and watches to see whether Joan signals any anxiety by raising her finger. This time, Joan raises her finger at 6 seconds, indicating that she is feeling anxious while imagining this item.] Joan, what is the sud level that you are feeling right now?

Client: I feel about 20 suds thinking about this.

Helper: Joan, just erase that image from your mind. . . . Now relax. Let relaxation flood your body. . . . Think again about being in front of a campfire. [Pauses for 10 to 30 seconds for relaxation.] Now I'd like you to again imagine you're sitting in English class. It's almost time for the bell. You think about math class and wonder if you'll be called on. [Second presentation of Item 3 in the hierarchy. Helper notes duration with stopwatch. Helper allows the scene to be imagined again for five to seven seconds and watches to see whether Joan signals any anxiety by raising her finger. Joan does not respond, indicating that she is not feeling anxious while imagining this item.] Joan, now just erase that image and concentrate on relaxing. [Pauses 10 to 30 seconds.] OK, again imagine yourself sitting in English class. It's just a few minutes before the bell. You think about math class and wonder if you'll be called on. [Third presentation of Item 3. Helper allows the scene to be imagined again for 5 to 7 seconds and watches to see whether Joan signals any anxiety by raising her finger. Joan does not respond, indicating that she is not feeling anxious while imagining this item.] As the last two presentations of this item did not evoke anxiety, the helper can move on to item 4. Joan, stop imagining that scene. Think about a campfire. . . . Just relax. [Another control item can be used for variation. After 10 to 30 seconds, item 4 is presented or session is terminated.]

If this session had been terminated after the successful completion of item 3, the next scene-presentation session would begin with item 3. Other hierarchy items would be presented in the same manner as in this session. If Joan reported anxiety for three successive presentations of one item, the session would be interrupted, and an adjustment in the hierarchy would be made. (See Learning Activity 17.2.)

Homework and Follow-Up

Homework is essential to the successful completion of desensitization. Homework may include daily practice of the selected relaxation procedure, visualization of the items completed in the previous session, and exposure to *in vivo* situations.

Assignment of Homework Tasks

Most helpers instruct clients to practice once or twice daily the relaxation method being used. Practice is especially critical in the early sessions, in which training in the counterconditioning response occurs. In addition, a helper can assign the client to practice visualizing the items covered in the last session after the relaxation session. Cassette tapes or computerized "virtual realities" can also be used for this purpose. Gradually, *in vivo* homework tasks can be added. As desensitization progresses, the client should be encouraged to participate in real-life situations that correspond to the situations covered in hierarchy-item visualization during the sessions. The shift to real life is very important in aiding generalization from imagined to real anxiety-producing situations. However, there may be some risk in the client's engaging in a real situation corresponding to a hierarchy item that has not yet been covered in the scene-presentation sessions.

Homework Log Sheets and Follow-Up

The client should record completion of all homework assignments on daily log sheets. After all desensitization sessions are completed, a follow-up session or contact should be arranged.

MODEL DIALOGUE: HOMEWORK AND FOLLOW-UP

Helper: Joan, you've been progressing through the items on your list very well in our session. I'd like you to try some practice on your own similar to what we've been doing.

Client: OK, what is it?

Helper: I'm thinking of an item that's near the middle of your list. It's something you've been able to imagine last

---

LEARNING ACTIVITY 17.2 — Scene Presentation

This learning activity is designed to familiarize you with some of the procedural aspects of scene presentation. You can complete this activity by yourself or with a partner who can serve as your client.

1. Select one of the hierarchies you or your partner developed in Learning Activity 17.1 (on hierarchy construction).
2. Administer relaxation or imagery to yourself or to your partner.
3. If you have a partner to act as a role-play client, tell the client to signal anxiety by raising a finger and mention that the sud numbers will be used to indicate anxiety when the client raises a finger.
4. By yourself or with your partner, start by presenting the lowest item in the hierarchy. If no anxiety is signaled after a specified duration, instruct your partner to remove the image and relax; then re-present the same scene. Remember, two successive no-anxiety presentations are required before the next item is presented. If anxiety is signaled, instruct yourself or your partner to remove the image and relax. After 10 to 30 seconds, re-present the same item.
5. Select a notation system to use. Record at least the number of times each item was presented, the duration of each presentation, and whether each presentation did or did not evoke anxiety. If anxiety was indicated, be sure to use the sud scale to note the amount of anxiety that the client felt.

week and this week without reporting any nervousness. It's the one on your volunteering an answer in class.

Client: You think I should do that?

Helper: Yes, although there is something I'd like to do first. I will put this item and the two before it on tape. Each day after you practice your relaxation, I'd like you to use the tape and go over these three items just as we do here. If this goes well for you, then next week we can talk about your actually starting to volunteer a bit more in class.

Client: OK with me.

Helper: One more thing. Each time you use the tape this week, make a notation on a blank log sheet. Also note your tension level before and after the practice on the 0-to-100 scale. Then I'll see you next week.

Figure 17.4 summarizes all the components of systematic desensitization. You may find this summary to be a useful review of procedural aspects of this strategy.

PROBLEMS ENCOUNTERED DURING DESENSITIZATION

Although desensitization can be a very effective therapeutic procedure, problems are occasionally encountered that make it difficult or impossible to administer. Sometimes these problems can be minimized or alleviated. At other times, a problem may require the helper to adopt an alternative strategy.

Wolpe (1990) identifies three major barriers to effective implementation of desensitization. These include difficulties of relaxation, misleading or irrelevant hierarchies, and

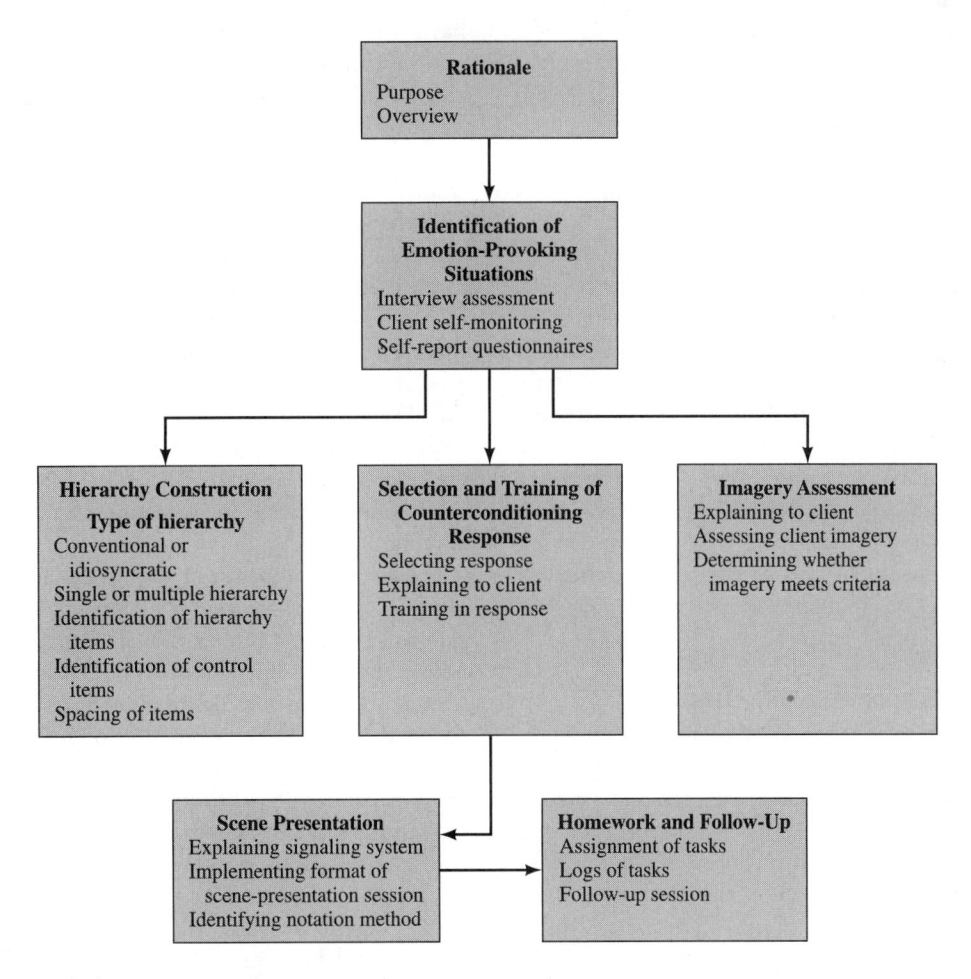

Figure 17.4 Expanded components of systematic desensitization.

inadequacies of imagery (p. 181). When a client is unable to lower anxiety to less than 10 suds, relaxation is not working well. According to Wolpe (1990), it may be effective to use a medication before the systematic desensitization session. An additional alternative is to try inducing relaxation through hypnosis. Another reason that desensitization may not proceed is related to the hierarchies being used. Sometimes, despite the time spent developing the hierarchies, the client and helper have missed the core problem, and the hierarchy does not address the issue. In this case, the solution is to consider redeveloping the hierarchy. Finally, a client may be unable to visualize adequately the images that are required for the procedure to work. In this case, the helper and client can work together to develop more complete and vivid descriptions of the items on the hierarchy. Another possibility to consider is that the item is generating so much anxiety that the client detaches from the imagery. Additional hierarchy items may be necessary before moving on to the item that preceded an inability to visualize.

Occasionally, clients will benefit from a different form of desensitization. Two of the possible variations of desensitization are discussed in the next section.

VARIATIONS OF SYSTEMATIC DESENSITIZATION

The desensitization procedure described in this chapter reflects a broadly applicable procedure applied over a series of sessions to an individual client by a helping professional, using an individualized hierarchy imagined by the client. As we mentioned previously, actual or *in vivo* exposure methods can be used instead of or in addition to imaginal exposure methods. This section briefly describes two possible variations of desensitizing exposure: *in vivo* desensitization (often referred to as exposure therapy) and eye movement desensitization and reprocessing (EMDR). For more detailed information, we encourage you to consult the references mentioned in this section and those listed in the suggested readings at the end of the chapter.

In Vivo Desensitization/Exposure Therapy

In vivo desensitization involves actual client exposure to the situations in the hierarchy. The client engages in the graded series of situations instead of imagining each item. For example, rather than imagining a feared stimulus such as a spider, type of place, or type of situation, that item or circumstance would either be brought to the client or the client to it or to some comparable facsimile. This variation might be used when a client has difficulty using imagery, when a client does not experience anxiety during imagery, or when a client's actual exposure to the situations will have more therapeutic effects. If the client can actually be exposed to the feared stimuli, then *in vivo* desensitization may be preferable to imagined exposure because it will produce more rapid results and will foster greater generalization.

A practitioner may accompany the client to the feared situation, particularly at earlier points in the intervention with clients experiencing higher levels of distress. (Self-controlled exposure or exposure with trained others such as family or group members may also be used, particularly at later points in the intervention or as homework.) *In vivo* desensitization resembles participant modeling (Chapter 12), in which the client performs a graduated series of difficult tasks with the help of induction aids. A sample of recent research involving *in vivo* desensitization or exposure therapy is listed in Box 17.2. Anxiety, panic, and phobias are prominent clinical targets, as are trauma and clients struggling with obsessive–compulsive disorders. The field use of exposure techniques has also seen a considerable increase in the use of computer-aided treatment, including the use of virtual stimuli to help create effective, achievable environments appropriate to the nature of the originating issue.

One procedural problem associated with *in vivo* desensitization involves adequate use and control of a counterconditioning response. Sometimes it is difficult for a client to achieve a state of deep relaxation while simultaneously performing an activity. McGrath, Tsui, Humphries, and Yule (1990) reported using conversation and a play therapy environment as counterconditioning responses when using *in vivo* desensitization for a nine-year-old girl. However, it is not always necessary to use a counterconditioning response to decrease the client's anxiety in threatening situations. Often, exposure alone will result in sufficient anxiety reduction, particularly if the exposure occurs in graduated amounts and with induction aids.

Nelissen and colleagues (1995) suggest that during *in vivo* exposure, information that is discordant with the irrational elements of anxiety is more available and more easily incorporated by the client, resulting in a reduction of the feared stimuli. This begins to point to the increasing attention to cognitive methods supplementing what is otherwise a predominantly behavioral intervention. One example of the combined use of desensitization and cognitive change methods (and, not uncommonly, other methods related to stress management) is in work by Foa and colleagues (Foa & Kozak, 1986; Foa & Meadows, 1997; Hembree & Foa, 2000). Recall the discussion in Chapter 14 regarding schemas and how information—be it descriptive, values, goals, feelings, other sensory states—gets structured in cognitive structures and networks. The combination of exposure and cognitive methods thus allows for activation of the feeling structure (e.g., anxiety, fear, loss) accompanied by presentation of information corrective or reconstructive of problematic aspects of the feeling structure. Examples of this include clients realizing that being in apparently safe situations that remind them of trauma or their distress are not dangerous, that experiencing the feeling state (fear, anxiety) does not lead to loss of control (Foa & Meadows, 1997).

Eye Movement Desensitization and Reprocessing (EMDR)

EMDR is more recent in origin; rather than deriving from a specific theory base, it arose from observation by proposal of an "accelerated information-processing" (AIP) model developed by Francine Shapiro to account for resolution of traumatic memories. According to the AIP model, when a person has neurological balance, he or she processes information with appropriate associations and integrates the experience into a positive emotional and cognitive schema (Shapiro, 1995). Traumatic events are seen to create an *imbalance* or a *block* in the nervous system with respect to processing the information. Traumatic memories are at least partly isolated from the broader neuro-network and held neurologically in a disturbed state that includes images, sounds, emotions, cognitions, and physical sensations associated with the event. Shapiro (1995) hypothesizes a self-healing capacity within people that, if stimulated, helps reintegrate traumatic memories into a nondisturbed form. Eye movements or other stimuli such as taps or tones are believed to trigger this self-healing mechanism. Related beliefs and evaluations about oneself become stored along with other cognitive, affective, and physiological aspects of the traumatizing experience. Negative self-representations deriving from the trauma are seen to play a central role in preserving distortions related to the traumatic memory. After blocks to the imbalanced information processing system are removed, the information, including self-representations, can be adapted and integrated into more functional and positive emotional and cognitive schemas consistent with the client's goals.

EMDR provides an illustration of some of the ongoing tensions and issues to be considered by helping professionals. There are strong proponents and equally strong critics. Considerable concern has been voiced over commercial promotion of a technique before it has undergone rigorous review or testing of its demonstrated effectiveness, generalizability, maintenance, or causal linkage of observed effects to theorized mechanisms (Herbert et al., 2000; Kaplan & Manicavasager, 1998; Lohr, Lilienfeld, Tolin, & Herbert, 1999; Muris & Merckelbach, 1999; Rosen, 1999). Others, on the other hand, believe that clinical findings are promising and that some critiques have been unfair (de Jongh, Ten, & Renssen, 1999; Smyth, Greenwald, de Jongh, & Lee, 2000; VanEtten & Taylor, 1998; Zabukovec, Lazrove, & Shapiro, 2000). Some have stressed the importance of formal training as through Shapiro's EMDR Institute, close adherence to protocol, and potentially misleading emphasis on eye movements in the treatment's name (Shapiro, 1999; Greenwald, 1996). Cautions have been raised about ethical and legal issues in using EMDR without proper training and supervision (Stevens, 2000). And there are efforts to sort out strengths and limitations, concluding with a mixed picture (Cahill, Carrigan, & Frueh, 1999; Feske, 1998; Shephard, Stein, & Milne, 2000; Spector & Read, 1999).

In a recent review of research on the use of EMDR for PTSD under the auspices of the PTSD Treatment Guidelines Task Force, Chemtob, Tolin, van der Kolk, and Pitman (2000) summarize this mixed picture. They indicate that there is growing evidence that some components of EMDR do reliably produce favorable outcomes compared to wait-list, routine-care, and active-treatment controls. There is considerable question about whether all EMDR components are necessary or contribute meaningfully to outcomes. For greater confidence in EMDR's efficacy, what is particularly needed now is research specifically comparing EMDR to other independently tested PTSD-focused treatments, using more extensive controls addressing limitations of prior research, with larger and more diverse samples, and with designs that allow clearer testing of the proposed theory for how this approach works. Empirical support thus far does not necessarily imply support for the proposed theory of EMDR, indicating that claims that the technique is working in ways identified by its developers presently exceed the body of empirical support. Nonetheless, this body of research is highlighting questions about traditional theories such as the need for prolonged, continuous exposure and necessary dosage or sequence of intervention components that may help deepen understanding of trauma mechanisms and treatment.

We present EMDR despite the controversy and uncertainty about its evidence base to provide you some insight into issues involved with any emerging line of intervention development. Polarizations and questions are by no means unique to EMDR and reflect the importance of the converging skills and capacities that make up the practice nexus. These tensions and debates illustrate, for example, the value of a preparedness to pose penetrating questions of critical thinking and of critical consciousness, to carefully attend to ethical responsibilities and safeguards, and to present to clients and colleagues in a balanced manner the mixed analysis to date as part of honest, collaborative practice. New and evolving interventions will always be present, and we see value in maintaining an open-mindedness about innovation, along with responsible caution, expectations of evidence, and forthrightness with clients. Although it is beyond the scope of this book to detail, we direct readers interested in treatments for PTSD to the compiled practice guidelines from the International Society for Traumatic Stress Studies (Foa, Keane, & Friedman, 2000). In addition to EMDR and cognitive–behavioral therapy, guidelines for group therapy, pharmacotherapy, marital and family therapy, and others are presented.

Concerns to Consider with Exposure-Based Methods

Exposure-based therapies have a robust clinical and empirical base of support for their effectiveness in reducing emotional responses that can be seriously disabling to individuals and their families. Thus, we see these as important clinical tools. However, we urge perhaps more than ever that such techniques be undertaken with great care. These strategies are explicitly anxiety evoking, undertaken with individuals struggling with terribly frightening, distressing disorders not uncommonly stemming from disempowering, traumatizing experiences. Although intervention descriptions are not necessarily specific about the nature of the therapeutic relationship, we see issues of earned trust, honest communication, empathy, and collaboration in design and implementation to be essential. Prochaska and Norcross (1999) likened the therapeutic relationship associated with exposure therapies as having elements of "tough love that says, 'Don't run away from your problems. Soon you will master it and have a future free from conditioned fears'" (p. 255). This kind of courage and firm guidance may be a critical ingredient to helping others better understand and learn to manage their otherwise overwhelming feelings.

In addition, we emphasize the need to appreciate the contexts people live within that give rise to such struggles (such as insensitivity, violence, oppression) and to the courage and support needed to undertake strategies that will place one face to face with emotional pain. Similarly, critical and effectiveness commitments (ethics in practice, critical thinking, evidence base) as well as the mindfulness of diversity central to the practice nexus call for caution as new or variant methods evolve.

SUMMARY

Systematic desensitization is one of the oldest of the behavioral strategies developed to alleviate anxiety. There does not seem to be a great deal of ongoing research testing this procedure, perhaps because research conducted until the 1970s demonstrated the effectiveness of desensitization through repeated studies (Wolpe, 1990). Although desensitization is time-consuming to implement, it is clearly an effective way to help clients alleviate anxiety and specifically to treat phobias. In practice, many helpers find that the combination of desensitization and other strategies may be used to help clients lessen disabling emotions such as anxiety and learn new ways of handling situations that are anxiety provoking. Clients seem to benefit most when they have multiple ways of controlling anxiety and fear through desensitization, and additional strategies that they can continue to use after the helping process has ended.

Desensitization has been used in limited ways with diverse groups of clients who present with phobias and anxiety as well as other emotional problems such as anger and loss. Remember that although anxiety seems to be a universal phenomenon, the specific presentation of it as well as the cues surrounding it are often very culturally specific and may vary as a function of other diversity factors (e.g., age, gender, disability characteristics).

There are a variety of exposure and desensitization methods that require careful assessment to make choices well suited for clients, their circumstances, and their needs. *In vivo* exposure versus imaginal process is one such distinction. *In vivo* exposure and eye movement desensitization and reprocessing (EMDR) are increasingly being tested with posttraumatic stress disorders. The empirical and clinical track record with exposure methods generally supports their use. We add the caveat to undertake such change strategies with particular sensitivity and recognition of support needs.

INFOTRAC® EXPLORATIONS

1. Search for the term *phobia*, and select three to five articles that report interventions. Assess the extent to which each covers the components identified in this chapter (see Figure 17.4 for an overview). If components are missing (different, added, modified), does the article provide a sufficient rationale and evidence base for what is being used? Does the package appear appropriate to the client(s) in question?
2. Search for the term *trauma*, and select three to five articles that directly address use of interventions. This chapter

notes strategy differences in type of exposure, such as imaginal, virtual, and *in vivo*. Desensitization strategies are often combined with other intervention techniques such as cognitive restructuring, relaxation, and emotional reprocessing. Write out what you see to be the central differences in the types of treatments in the articles. Does each article provide, in your judgment, a sufficient rationale for why that intervention or set of interventions was selected?

3. Search for the term *EMDR*, and select three to five articles that directly address the use of this treatment strategy, two or three that are generally positive in their assessments and two or three that raise serious criticisms. Briefly list the pros and cons as you see them in the articles. Keep in mind the practice nexus factors reviewed in Chapters 1 and 2 (e.g., ethical obligations, critical thinking, attentiveness to diversity and environmental factors, evidence support, open-mindedness to new ideas and challenges). Based on your assessment, how might you describe the intervention to a client?

SUGGESTED RESOURCES

Readings

Antony, M. M., & Swinson, R. P. (2000). *Phobic disorders and panic in adults: A guide to assessment and treatment.* Washington, DC: American Psychological Association.

Cahill, S. P., Carrigan, M. H., & Frueh, B. C. (1999). Does EMDR work? and if so, why?: A critical review of controlled outcome and dismantling research. *Journal of Anxiety Disorders, 13,* 5–33.

Foa, E. B., Keane, T., & Friedman, M. J. (Eds.). (2000). Effective treatments for PTSD. New York: Guilford.

Friedman, S. (Ed.). (1997). *Cultural issues in the treatment of anxiety.* New York: Guilford.

Hembree, E. A., & Foa, E. B. (2000). Posttraumatic stress disorder: Psychological factors and psychosocial interventions. *Journal of Clinical Psychiatry, 61,* 33–39.

Himle, J. A. (2000). Affective change: Depression and anxiety disorders. In P. Allen-Meares & C. Garvin (Eds.), *The handbook of social work direct practice* (pp. 217–240). Thousand Oaks, CA: Sage.

Menzies, R., & Clarke, J. (1993). A comparison of *in vivo* and vicarious exposure in the treatment of childhood water phobia. *Behavior Research and Therapy, 31,* 9–15.

Mineka, S., Mystkowski, J. L., Hladek, D., & Rodriguez, B. I. (1999). The effects of changing contexts on return of fear following exposure therapy for spider fear. *Journal of Consulting & Clinical Psychology, 67,* 599–604.

Morris, R. J. (1991). Fear reduction methods. In F. H. Kanfer & A. P. Goldstein (Eds.), *Helping people change* (4th ed., pp. 161–201). New York: Pergamon.

Roth, W. T. (Ed.). (1997). *Treating anxiety disorders.* San Francisco: Jossey-Bass.

Rothbaum, B. O., & Hodges, L. F. (1999). The use of virtual reality exposure in the treatment of anxiety disorders. *Behavior Modification, 23,* 507–525.

Tarrier, N., & Humphreys, L. (2000). Subjective improvement in PTSD patients with treatment by imaginal exposure or cognitive therapy: Session by session changes. *British Journal of Clinical Psychology, 39,* 27–34.

VanEtten, M. L., & Taylor, S. (1998). Comparative efficacy of treatments for post-traumatic stress disorder: A meta analysis. *Clinical Psychology and Psychotherapy, 5,* 126–144.

Wolpe, J. (1990). *The practice of behavior therapy* (4th ed.). New York: Pergamon.

Web Sites

EMDR Institute
http://www.emdr.com

International Society for Traumatic Stress Studies
http://www.istss.org

National Center for PTSD
http://www.ncptsd.org

NIMH: *Anxiety Disorders*
http://www.nimh.nih.gov/anxiety

17 POSTEVALUATION

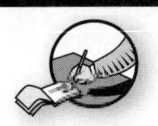

Part One

Objective One states that you should be able to identify accurately at least 3 out of 4 hierarchies by type. Read each hierarchy carefully, and then identify on a piece of paper whether the hierarchy is conventional or idiosyncratic. Feedback is provided at the end of the postevaluation.

Hierarchy 1 (fear of heights)

1. You are walking along the sidewalk. It is on a completely level street.
2. You are walking along the sidewalk, ascending. At the top of the street, you look down and realize you've climbed a hill.
3. You are climbing a ladder to a second-story window.
4. You are riding in a car, and the road curves higher and higher.
5. You are riding in a car, and you look outside. You notice you are driving on the edge of a good-sized hill.
6. You are starting to climb to the top of a fire tower. You are halfway up. You look down and see how far you've climbed.
7. You are climbing a ladder to the roof of a three-story house.
8. You have climbed to the top of a fire tower and look down.
9. You are riding in a car and are at the edge of a cliff on a mountain.
10. You are at the very top of a mountain, looking down into the surrounding valley.

Hierarchy 2 (fear of being rejected)

1. You speak to a stranger on the street. He doesn't hear you.
2. You go into a department store and request some information from one of the clerks. The clerk snaps at you in response.
3. You ask a stranger to give you change. She gives you a sarcastic reply.
4. You ask a casual acquaintance to lend you a book. He refuses.
5. You ask a friend over to dinner. The friend is too busy to come.
6. You apply for a membership in a social club, and your application is denied.
7. You are competing for a job. You and another person are interviewed. The other person is hired; you are not chosen.
8. You have an argument with your best friend. She leaves suddenly. You don't hear from her for a while.
9. You have an argument with your partner. Your partner says he would rather do things alone than with you.
10. Your partner says he doesn't love you anymore.

Hierarchy 3 (loss of a close relationship)

1. You remember a warm, starry night. You ask this woman you love to marry you. She accepts. You are very happy.
2. The two of you are traveling together soon after your marriage, camping out and traveling around in a van.
3. The two of you are running in the water together at the beach and having a good time being together.
4. You and this person are eating dinner together at home.
5. The two of you are disagreeing over how to spend money. She wants to save it; you are wanting to use some of it for camping supplies.
6. The two of you are arguing over your child. She wants the child to go with you on all trips; you want a babysitter occasionally.
7. The two of you are starting to eat some meals apart. You are working late to avoid coming home for dinner.
8. She is wrapped up in her social activities; you are caught up in your work. On the weekends you go your separate ways.
9. You have a discussion about your relationship and separate activities. You start sleeping on the couch.
10. The two of you go to see a lawyer to initiate discussion about a separation.

Hierarchy 4 (fear of giving speeches)

1. Your instructor casually mentions a required speech to be given by the end of the course.
2. Your instructor passes around a sign-up sheet for the speeches. You sign up.
3. You talk about the speech with some of your classmates. You aren't sure what to say.

17 POSTEVALUATION

4. You go to the library to look up some resource material for your speech. You don't find too much.
5. Some of your classmates start to give speeches. You think about how good their speeches are and wonder how yours will be.
6. It is a week before the speech. You're spending a lot of time working on it.
7. It is the day before the speech. You're going over your notes religiously.
8. It is the night before the speech. You lie awake thinking about it.
9. It is the next morning. You wake up and remember it is speech day. You don't feel hungry at breakfast.
10. Later that morning, you're walking to speech class. A classmate comes up and says "Well, I guess you're on today."
11. You're sitting in speech class. The instructor will call on you at any moment. You keep going over your major points.

Part Two

Objective Two asks you to identify and describe at least 9 out of 11 procedural steps of desensitization, using a written client case description. Read this case description carefully; then respond by identifying and describing the 11 items listed after the description.

Your client is a fifth-grade boy at a local elementary school. This year, the client's younger sister has entered first grade at the same school. After a few weeks at school, your client, Ricky, began to complain about school to his teacher and parents. He would come to school and get sick. His parents would come and take him home. After a medical check-up, the doctor can find nothing physically wrong with Ricky. Yet Ricky continues either to get sick at school or to wake up sick in the morning. He appears to be better on weekends. He says he hates school and it makes him sick to his stomach to have to go. On occasion, he has vomited in the morning. The parents report that it is getting harder and harder to get Ricky to attend school. Suppose you were to use desensitization as one strategy in this case to help Ricky overcome his tension and avoidance of school. Identify and describe how you would implement the following 11 steps of desensitization with Ricky. Adapt your language to words that a 10-year-old can understand.

1. Your rationale of desensitization
2. Your description of an overview of desensitization
3. A method for helping Ricky identify the anxiety-provoking situations about school
4. The type of hierarchy that would be used with Ricky
5. The sud method that Ricky would use to arrange the hierarchy items
6. An appropriate counterconditioning response that you could train Ricky to use
7. The method of assessing Ricky's imagery capacity
8. The method of scene presentation that you would use with Ricky
9. The method that Ricky could use for signaling during scene presentation
10. A notation method that you might use to keep track of hierarchy presentation
11. An example of one homework task associated with desensitization that you might assign to Ricky to complete

Feedback follows the Postevaluation.

Part Three

Objective Three asks you to demonstrate at least 22 out of 28 steps of systematic desensitization with a role-play client. Several role-play interviews may be required for you to include all the major procedural components of desensitization. Use the Interview Checklist for Systematic Desensitization on pages 573–579 as an assessment tool.

POST EVALUATION FEEDBACK

PART ONE

1. *Conventional.* Items are arranged by increasing height off the ground.
2. *Idiosyncratic.* Items are arranged around the theme of rejection.
3. *Idiosyncratic.* Items are arranged from pleasant to unpleasant memories of an ex-spouse.
4. *Conventional.* Items are arranged by time; as the time approaching the situation diminishes, the fear intensifies.

PART TWO

Here are some possible descriptions of the 11 procedural steps of desensitization you were asked to identify and describe. See whether your responses are in some way similar to these:

1. *Rationale:* "Ricky, it seems that it's very hard for you to go to school now or even think about school without feeling sick. There are some things about school that upset you this much. We can work together to find out what bothers you, and I can help you learn to be able to go to school without feeling so upset or sick to your stomach, so you can go to school again and feel OK about it. How does that sound?"

2. *Overview:* "There are several things you and I will do together. First, we'll talk about the things about school that upset you. I'll ask you to think about these situations, only instead of feeling upset when you do, I'll show you a way to stay calm and keep the butterflies out of your stomach. It will take a lot of practice in this room, but after a while you will be able to go back to your class and feel calm and OK about it!"

3. *Method* for identifying the anxiety-provoking situations:
   a. Use of interview leads, such as "Ricky, what do you do in school that makes you feel sick? What about school makes you want to stay at home? What happens at school that bothers you? When do you feel most upset about school?"
   b. Use of client self-monitoring, such as "Ricky, could you keep a chart for me this week? Each time you feel upset about school, mark down what has happened or what you're thinking about that makes you feel upset or sick."

4. *Type of hierarchy:* An idiosyncratic hierarchy would be used. One hierarchy might consist of school-related anxiety-provoking situations. Depending on the anxiety-provoking situations identified, another idiosyncratic hierarchy may emerge, dealing with jealousy. It is possible that the avoidance of school is a signal that Ricky really fears being upstaged by his younger sister.

5. *Ranking method:* The sud method can be used with Ricky. The helper will need to take additional time to explain the method to Ricky and provide examples of things that might be as high as 90 suds and items that would be as low as 10 suds.

6. *Counterconditioning response:* Muscle relaxation can be used easily with a child Ricky's age as long as you show him (by modeling) the different muscle groups and the way to tighten and relax a muscle.

7. *Method of imagery assessment:* Ask Ricky to tell you some daydreams he has or some things he loves to do. Before and after a relaxation-training session, ask him to imagine or pretend he is doing one of these things. Then have him describe the details of his imagined scene. Children often have a capacity for more vivid and descriptive imagery than adults.

8. *Scene presentation:* Ricky is told to imagine the scene as described by the helper and to raise an index finger to indicate to the helper that the scene is clear in his mind. The helper should allow Ricky to hold the image of the scene for five to seven seconds and terminate it by saying "Stop the scene." Next, the helper asks Ricky how much anxiety was generated in terms of suds; the helper might ask "How much did imagining this scene increase your sud level?"

9. *Signaling method:* The helper should tell Ricky to raise a finger to inform the helper that he sees the scene clearly.

10. *Notation method:* The easiest notation method might be to use each hierarchy card and note the number of times each item is presented, the duration of each presentation, and an indication of whether Ricky did or did not report being "tense" during or after the item. This notation system looks like this:

    Item No.____ Date____
    Item description
    +5 −7 +5 +7

The item was presented four times; the numbers 5, 7, 5, and 7 refer to the duration of each presentation; the + indicates no anxiety report; the − indicates a "tense" signal.

17 POST EVALUATION FEEDBACK

11. Examples of possible homework tasks:
    a. A list of anxiety-related situations
    b. Practice of muscle relaxation
    c. Practice of items covered in the interview
    d. Exposure to certain school-related *in vivo* situations

PART THREE

You or an observer can rate your desensitization interviews using the Interview Checklist for Systematic Desensitization that follows.

Interview Checklist for Systematic Desensitization

Instructions to observer: Listed below are some procedural steps of systematic desensitization. Check which of these steps were used by the helper in implementing this procedure. Some possible examples of these leads are described in the right column of the checklist.

Item	Examples of helper leads
I. Rationale	
_____ 1. Helper gives client rationale for desensitization, clearly explaining how it works.	"This procedure is based on the idea that you can learn to replace your fear (or other conditioned emotion) in certain situations with a better or more desirable response, such as relaxation or general feelings of comfort." "You have described some situations in which you have learned to react with fear (or some other emotion). This procedure will give you skills to help you cope with these situations so they don't continue to be so stressful."
_____ 2. Helper describes brief overview of desensitization procedure.	"There are three basic things that will happen—first, training you to relax; next, constructing a list of situations in which you feel anxious; and finally, having you imagine scenes from this list, starting with low-anxiety scenes, while you are deeply relaxed." "First you will learn how to relax and how to notice tension so you can use it as a signal to relax. Then we'll identify situations that, to varying degrees, upset you or make you anxious. Starting with the least discomforting situations, you will practice the skill of relaxation as a way to cope with the stress."
_____ 3. Helper checks to see whether client is willing to use strategy.	"Are you ready to try this now?"
II. Identification of Emotion-Provoking Situations	
_____ 4. Helper initiates at least one of the following means of identifying anxiety-provoking stimulus situations:	
_____ a. Interview assessment through problem leads	"When do you notice that you feel most _____?" "Where are you when this happens?" "What are you usually doing when you feel _____?" "What types of situations seem to bring on this feeling?"
_____ b. Client self-monitoring	"This week I'd like you to keep track of any situation that seems to bring on these feelings. On your log, write down where you are, what you're doing, whom you're with, and the intensity of these feelings."

(continued)

POSTEVALUATION FEEDBACK

(continued)

    ____ c. Self-report questionnaires

"One way that we might learn more about some of the specific situations that you find stressful is for you to complete this short questionnaire. There are no right or wrong answers—just describe how you usually feel or react in the situations presented."

____ 5. Helper continues to assess anxiety-provoking situations until client identifies some specific situations.

"Let's continue with this exploration until we get a handle on some things. Right now you've said that you get nervous and upset around certain kinds of people. Can you tell me some types or characteristics of people that bother you or make you anxious almost always?"

"OK, good, so you notice you're always very anxious around people who can evaluate or criticize you, like a boss or teacher."

III. Hierarchy Construction

____ 6. Helper identifies a type of hierarchy to be constructed with client:

"Now we're going to make a list of these anxiety-provoking situations and fill in some details and arrange these in an order, starting with the least anxiety-provoking situation all the way to the most anxiety-provoking one."

    ____ a. Conventional

"Because you get more and more anxious as the time for the speech gets closer and closer, we'll construct these items by closer and closer times to the speech."

    ____ b. Idiosyncratic

"We'll arrange these items according to the different kinds of situations in which people criticize you—depending on who does it, what it's about, and so on."

____ 7. Helper identifies the number of hierarchies to be developed:

    ____ a. Single hierarchy

"We will take all these items that reflect different situations that are anxiety producing for you and arrange them in one list."

    ____ b. Multiple hierarchies

"Because you find several types of situations stressful, we'll construct one list for situations involving criticism and another list for situations involving social events."

____ 8. Helper initiates identification of hierarchy items through one or more methods:

    ____ a. Interview questions (*not* when client is engaged in relaxation)

"I'd like us to write down some items that describe each of these anxiety-provoking scenes with quite a bit of detail."

"Describe for me what your mother could say that would bother you most. How would she say it? Now who, other than your mother, could criticize you and make you feel worse? What things are you most sensitive to being criticized about?"

    ____ b. Client completion of note cards (homework)

"This week I'd like you to add to this list of items. I'm going to give you some blank index cards. Each time you think of another item that makes you get anxious or upset about criticism, write it down on one card."

17 POSTEVALUATION FEEDBACK

_____ 9. Helper continues to explore hierarchy items until items are identified that meet the following criteria:

_____ a. Some items, if carried out *in vivo,* are under the client's control (do not require instigation from others).

"Can you think of some items that, if you actually were to carry them out, would be things you could initiate without having to depend on someone else to make the situation happen?"

_____ b. Items are concrete and specific.

"OK, now just to say that you get nervous at social functions is a little vague. Give me some details about a social function in which you might feel pretty comfortable and one that could make you feel extremely nervous."

_____ c. Items are similar to or represent past, present, or future situations that *have* provoked or *could* provoke the emotional response from client.

"Think of items that represent things that have made you anxious before or currently—and things that could make you anxious if you encountered them in the future."

_____ d. Items have sampled broad range of situations in which emotional response occurs.

"Can you identify items representing different types of situations that seem to bring on these feelings?"

_____ e. Items represent different levels of emotion aroused by representative stimulus situations.

"Let's see if we have items here that reflect different amounts of the anxiety you feel. Here are some items that don't make you too anxious. What about ones that are a little more anxiety provoking, up to ones where you feel panicky?"

_____ 10. Helper asks client to identify several control items (neutral, non-emotion-arousing).

"Sometimes it's helpful to imagine some scenes that aren't related to things that make you feel anxious. Could you describe something you could imagine that would be pleasant and relaxing?"

_____ 11. Helper explains purpose of ranking and spacing items according to increasing levels of arousal.

"It may take a little time, but you will rank these hierarchy items from least anxiety producing to most anxiety producing. This gives us an order to the hierarchy that is gradual so we can work just with more manageable situations before moving on to more stressful ones."

_____ 12. Helper asks client to arrange hierarchy items in order of increasing arousal, using sud method, and explains method to client.

"Now I would like you to take the items and arrange them in order of increasing anxiety, using the following method."

_____ a. Sud scale

"I'd like you to arrange these items using a 0-to-100 scale. 0 represents total relaxation, and 100 is complete panic. If an item doesn't give you any anxiety, give it a 0. If it is just a little stressful, maybe a 15 or 20. Very stressful items would get a higher number, depending on how stressful they are."

_____ 13. Helper adds or deletes items if necessary to achieve reasonable spacing of items in hierarchy.

"Let's see, at the lower end of the hierarchy you have many items. We might drop out a few of these. But you have only three items at the upper end, so we have some big gaps here. Can you think of a situation provoking a little bit more anxiety than this item but not quite as much as this next one? We can add that in here."

(continued)

POST EVALUATION FEEDBACK

(continued)

IV. Selection and Training of Counterconditioning Response

____ 14. Helper selects appropriate counterconditioning response to use to countercondition anxiety (or other conditioned emotion):
    ____ a. Deep muscle relaxation   (contrasting tensed and relaxed muscles)
    ____ b. Guided imagery   (evoking pleasurable scenes in imagination)
    ____ c. Meditation   (focusing on breathing and counting)
    ____ d. Coping thoughts or statements   (concentrating on coping or productive thoughts incompatible with self-defeating ones)

____ 15. Helper explains purpose of particular response selected and describes its role in desensitization.

"This response is like a substitute for anxiety. Learning it will take time, but it will help to decrease your anxiety so that you can face rather than avoid these feared situations."

"This training will help you recognize the onset of tension. You can use these cues you learn as a signal to relax away the tension."

____ 16. Helper trains client in use of counterconditioning response and suggests daily practice of this response.

"We will spend several sessions learning this so you can use it as a way to relax. This relaxation on your part is a very important part of this procedure. After you practice this here, I'd like you to do this at home two times each day over the next few weeks. Each practice will make it easier for you to relax."

____ 17. Helper asks client before and after each training session to rate felt level of anxiety or arousal.

"Using a scale from 0 to 100, with 0 being complete relaxation and 100 being intense anxiety, where would you rate yourself now?"

____ 18. Helper continues with training until client can discriminate different levels of anxiety and can use nonanxiety response to achieve 10 or lower rating on 0–100 scale.

"Let's continue with this until you feel this training really has an effect on your relaxation state after you use it."

V. Imagery Assessment

____ 19. Helper explains use of imagery in desensitization.

"In this procedure, I'll ask you to imagine each hierarchy item as if you were actually there. We have found that imagining a situation can be very similar to actually being in the situation. Becoming desensitized to anxiety you feel while imagining an unpleasant situation will transfer to real situations, too."

____ 20. Helper assesses client's capacity to generate vivid images by
    ____ a. Presenting control items when client is using a relaxation response

"It might be helpful to see how you react to using your imagination."

"Now that you're relaxed, get a picture in your mind of sitting in the sun on a warm day. The sky is very blue, not a cloud in it. The grass and trees are green. You can feel the warmth of the sun on your body."

    ____ b. Presenting hierarchy items when client is not using a relaxation response

"OK, just imagine that you're at this party. You don't know anyone. Get a picture of yourself and the other people there. It's a very large room."

17

POST EVALUATION FEEDBACK

      ____ c. Asking client to describe imagery evoked in *a* and *b*

"Can you describe what you imagined? What were the colors you saw? What did you hear or smell?"

____ 21. Helper, with client's assistance, determines whether client's imagery meets the following criteria and, if so, decides to continue with desensitization:

      ____ a. Client is able to imagine scene concretely with details.

"Were you able to imagine the scene clearly? How many details can you remember?"

      ____ b. Client is able to imagine scene as participant, not onlooker.

"When you imagined the scene, did you feel as if you were actually there and involved—or did it seem as if you were just an observer, perhaps watching it happen to someone else?"

      ____ c. Client is able to switch scene on and off when instructed to.

"How soon were you able to get an image after I gave it to you? When did you stop the image after I said *stop?*"

      ____ d. Client is able to hold scene without drifting off or revising it.

"Did you ever feel as if you couldn't concentrate on the scene and started to drift off?"

"Did you ever change anything about the scene during the time you imagined it?"

      ____ e. Client shows no evidence of other difficulties.

"What else did you notice that interfered with getting a good picture of this in your mind?"

VI. Hierarchy Scene Presentation

____ 22. Helper explains method of scene presentation.

"I am going to present an item in the hierarchy, and I'd like you to imagine the scene as clearly as you can. I will wait while you imagine the scene and watch to see whether you signal any anxiety."

____ 23. Helper checks client's anxiety level, allows the client to hold the image of the scene for five to seven seconds, and terminates it by saying, "Stop the scene."

"How much did imagining this scene increase your sud level?"

____ 24. For each session of scene presentation:

      ____ a. Helper precedes scene presentation with muscle relaxation or other procedures to help client achieve relaxation before scenes are presented.

"Let your whole body become heavier and heavier as all your muscles relax. . . . Feel the tension draining out of your body. . . . Relax the muscles of your hands and arms. . . ."

      ____ b. Helper begins initial session with lowest (least-anxiety-provoking) item in hierarchy and for successive sessions begins with last item successfully completed at previous session.

"I'm going to start this first session with the item that is at the bottom of the hierarchy."

"Today we'll begin with the item we ended on last week for a review."

      ____ c. Helper describes item and asks client to imagine it for five to seven seconds.

"Just imagine you are sitting in the classroom waiting for the test to be passed to you, wondering how much you can remember." [Counts 5 to 7 seconds.]

          ____ (1) If client held image and did not signal anxiety, helper instructs client to stop image and relax for 10 to 30 seconds.

"Now stop visualizing this scene and just take a little time to relax. Think of sitting in the sun on a warm day, with blue sky all around you."

(continued)

(continued)

        _____ (2) If client indicated anxiety during or after visualizing scene, helper asks for a sud rating and tells the client to erase the scene and relax for 10 to 30 seconds. Helper then represents that same scene for 5 to 7 seconds and watches to see whether the client signals any anxiety by raising her finger.   "What is your sud rating?"

    _____ d. After pause of 10 to 30 seconds between items, helper presents each item to client a second time.   "Now I want you to imagine the same thing. Concentrate on being very relaxed; then imagine that you are sitting in the classroom waiting for the test to be passed to you, wondering how much you can remember."

    _____ e. Each item is successfully completed (with no anxiety) at least two successive times (more for items at top of hierarchy) before new item is presented.   "I'm going to present this scene to you once more now. Just relax; then imagine that. . . ."

    _____ f. If an item elicits anxiety after three presentations, helper makes some adjustments in hierarchy or in client's visualization process.   "Let's see what might be bogging us down here. Do you notice that you are drifting away from the scene while you're imagining it—or revising it in any way? Can you think of a situation we might add here that is just a little bit less stressful for you than this one?"

    _____ g. Standardized instructions are used for each phase of scene presentation; reinforcement of *just* the no-anxiety items is avoided.   "OK, I see that was not stressful for you. Just concentrate on relaxing a minute."

"What was your feeling of anxiety on the 0-to-100 scale? 20. OK, I want you to just relax for a minute; then I'll give you the same scene."

    _____ h. Each scene-presentation session ends with a successfully completed item (no anxiety for at least two successive presentations).   "OK, let's end today with this item we've just been working on, since you reported 5 suds during the last two presentations."

    _____ i. Each session is terminated
        _____ (1) After 15 to 20 minutes of scene presentation   "We've done quite a bit of work today. Just spend a few minutes relaxing, and then we will stop."
        _____ (2) After indications of client restlessness or distractibility

_____ 25. Helper uses written recording method during scene presentation to note client's progress through hierarchy.   "As we go through this session, I'm going to make some notes about the number of times we work with each item and your anxiety rating of each presentation."

VII. Homework and Follow-Up

    _____ 26. Helper assigns homework tasks that correspond to treatment progress of desensitization procedure: "There is something I'd like you to do this week on a daily basis at home."

17 POST EVALUATION FEEDBACK

_____ a. Daily practice of selected relaxation procedure
"Practice this relaxation procedure two times each day in a quiet place."

_____ b. Visualization of items successfully completed at previous session
"On this tape there are three items we covered this week. Next week at home, after your relaxation sessions, practice imagining each of these three items."

_____ c. Exposure to *in vivo* situations corresponding to successfully completed hierarchy items.
"You are ready now to actually go to a party by yourself. We have gotten to a point where you can imagine doing this without any stress."

_____ 27. Helper instructs client to record completion of homework on daily log sheets.
"Each time you complete a homework practice, record it on your log sheet."

_____ 28. Helper arranges for follow-up session or check-in.
"Check in with me in two weeks to give me a progress report."

Observer comments: _____
_____
_____

CHAPTER 18

SELF-MANAGEMENT STRATEGIES:
SELF-MONITORING, STIMULUS CONTROL, SELF-REWARD, SELF-AS-A-MODEL, AND SELF-EFFICACY

OBJECTIVES

After completing this chapter, the student should be able to:
1. Given a written client case description, describe the use of self-monitoring and stimulus control for the client.
2. Teach another person how to engage in self-monitoring as a self-change strategy.
3. Given a written client case description, be able to describe the use of a culturally relevant self-management program for the client.
4. Teach another person how to use self-monitoring, stimulus control, self-reward, and self-as-a-model.

In self-management, the helping professional aids the client to better understand naturally occurring processes (predominantly behavioral and psychological) that are believed to exert considerable influence over behaviors or responses that have become problematic for the client. Self-management is a very teaching-oriented approach—that is, teaching clients *during* formal sessions about processes that are fueling problems and about processes that will lead to desired changes after clients undertake stages of activities *outside* formal sessions to achieve sustainable changes. Thus, the client does most of the work *between* sessions. One of the major goals of self-management intervention is to assist clients in gaining a greater capacity for self-determined initiative or "agency" relative to their goals and to achieve increasing independence in their desired functioning (Kanfer & Gaelick-Buys, 1991).

In several respects, self-management draws on a very wide range of tools and interventions, with a meaningful set pulled together by the client and helper depending on assessment, goals, and conditions. Consistent with the practice nexus, it is a strongly collaborative, environmentally attentive strategy that has been used across a wide range of specific problems in living and with varying clientele (e.g., age groups, disability status, problem severity, cultural heritage). We do urge caution in that self-management strategies can be presented or approached in a decontextualized manner—inattentive, for example, to current or historical environmental inequities or stressors that are as much if not more the true source of the issues that the client is struggling with. We see the emphasis on "self" here to be valuable toward empowering, goal-achieving awareness, and skill building, not as a question of approaching clients as selves that need to be managed to accommodate flawed circumstances.

Definitions of self-management can vary in part because different theorists emphasize different processes and strategies, and in part because of overlap among related terms that are sometimes used interchangeably and can be confusing. For example, self-change methods have been referred to as self-control (Cautela, 1969; Thoresen & Mahoney, 1974), self-regulation (Kanfer & Gaelick-Buys, 1991), and self-management (Mahoney, 1971, 1972). We focus on *self-management* in part because it conveys the notion of handling one's life within a set of life conditions and because literature searches on this term will glean you applications of change techniques more than basic research on underlying processes. Also, the term *self-management* avoids the concepts of inhibition and restriction often associated with the words *control* and *regulation* (Thoresen & Mahoney, 1974)—although these associations can be misleading as in some self-regulatory applications that are more about insight, opening up new options, and integrative linkages among physiology, psychology, and social phenomena.

In spite of differing emphases, self-management tends to be anchored in social learning and social cognitive theories underlying cognitive–behavioral models. According to Bandura (1977, 1986, 1989, 1991, 1997), for example, the social cognitive theory holds that human behavior is extensively motivated and regulated by the ongoing exercise of self-influence. The major self-management processes operate through four principal subfunctions: (1) self-monitoring of one's behavior, its components, and its effects; (2) judgment of one's behavior; (3) affective self-reactions; and (4) self-efficacy. Self-efficacy plays a central role in the exercise of personal agency by its strong impact on thought, affect, motivation, and action. Self-efficacy is very important in helping clients achieve treatment goals and enhancing their confidence and ability to execute the self-management strategies. The therapeutic alliance between the client and helper is necessary to support the client "as a cooperative observer, reporter and change agent" (Kanfer & Gaelick-Buys, 1991, p. 306). Behavioral change is very often challenging and frequently not pleasant. If clients are involved in negotiating treatment planning and setting goals, they are much more likely to implement the strategies and to achieve the change goals successfully. Finally, as Kanfer and Gaelick-Buys (1991) maintain, situation difficulties or symptoms often cannot be readily changed; the client must then learn coping strategies to handle these intractable situations as effectively as realistically possible.

Self-management strategies have several client outcomes that may include the following: (1) to use more effective task, interpersonal, cognitive, and emotional behaviors; (2) to alter perceptions of and judgmental attitudes toward problematic situations or persons; and (3) either to change or learn to cope with a stress-inducing situation (Kanfer & Gaelick-Buys, 1991, p. 307). This chapter describes four self-management strategies:

Self-monitoring—observing and recording your own particular behaviors (thoughts, feelings, and actions) about yourself and your interactions with environmental events

Stimulus control—prearranging antecedents or cues to increase or decrease your performance of a target behavior

Self-reward—giving yourself a positive stimulus following a desired response

Self-as-a-model—using yourself as the model; seeing yourself performing the goal behavior in the desired manner

These four strategies may be viewed as self-management because in each procedure the client, in a self-directed fashion, monitors, alters, rewards, models, and possesses self-efficacy to perform a specific task to produce the desired behavioral changes. We address self-efficacy more fully later in this chapter. As we have indicated so often in previous chapters, none of these strategies is entirely independent of the client's personal history, gender, age, culture, ethnicity, and environmental variables. In fact, because self-management treatment planning is so greatly dependent on careful assessment not only of concerns and needs but also on the client's ability to take on a self-manager role, diversity and contextualizing factors are particularly important considerations.

In addition to these four self-management procedures, a wide range of other change strategies are often found in the clinical literature (e.g., problem solving, coping, stress management). Broadly speaking, a client can use virtually any helping strategy in a self-directed manner. For example, a client could apply relaxation training to manage anxiety by using a relaxation-training audiotape without the assistance of a helper. In fact, some degree of client self-management may be a necessary component of many significant change efforts. For example, in all the other helping strategies described in this book, some elements of self-management are suggested in the procedural guidelines for strategy implementation. However, not all change strategies are predicated on the same degree of understanding the learning principles underlying processes that self-management is. These self-managed aspects of any formal change procedure typically include the following:

1. Client self-directed practice in the interview
2. Client self-directed practice in the *in vivo* setting (often through homework tasks)
3. Client self-observation and recording of target behaviors or of homework
4. Client self-reward (verbal or material) for successful completion of action steps and homework assignments

CLINICAL USES OF SELF-MANAGEMENT STRATEGIES

Self-management strategies have been used for a wide range of clinical concerns (see Box 18.1). They have been applied to many health problems, including arthritis, asthma, cancer, cardiac disease, diabetes, epilepsy, headaches, vision loss, nutrition, and self-health care. Among the psychological problems for which self-management strategies have been applied are autism, mood disorders, behavior disorders, eating disorders, depression, emotional disturbance, and insomnia. Self-management, in combination with social support, has been used to manage pain, to decrease substance and alcohol abuse, to help compensate for developmental disabilities, and to improve effectiveness in learning and nondisruptive classroom behavior. Measures of self-management, self-regulation, and self-efficacy have been developed and are available for use in practice.

BOX 18.1 RESEARCH ON SELF-MANAGEMENT

Anger
Medd, J., & Tate, R. L. (2000). Evaluation of an anger management therapy programme following acquired brain injury: A preliminary study. *Neuro-Psychological Rehabilitation, 10,* 185–201.
Rossiter, R., Hunjiset, E., & Pulsford, M. (1998). Anger management training and people with moderate to severe learning disabilities. *British Journal of Learning Disabilities, 26,* 67–74.

Arthritis
Barlow, J. H., Williams, B., & Wright, C. C. (1997). Improving arthritis self-management among older adults: "Just what the doctor didn't order." *British Journal of Health Psychology, 2*(2), 175–186.
Barlow, J. H., Williams, B., & Wright, C. C. (1997). The reliability and validity of the arthritis self-efficacy scale in an UK context. *Psychology, Health, & Medicine, 2,* 3–17.
Lorig, K., Gonzalez, V. M., Larunet, D. D., Morgan, L., & Laris, B. A. (1998). Arthritis self-management program variations: Three studies. *Arthritis Care & Research, 11,* 448–454.

Asthma
Allen, R., & Jones, M. P. (1998). The validity and reliability of an asthma knowledge questionnaire used in the evaluation of a group asthma education self-management program for adults with asthma. *Journal of Asthma, 35,* 537–545.
Bartholomew, L. K., Gold, R. S., Parcel, G. S., Czyewski, D. I., Sockrider, M. M., Fernandez, M., Shegog, R., & Swank, P. (2000). Watch, discover, think, and act: Evaluation of computer-assisted instruction to improve asthma self-management in inner-city children. *Patient Education & Counseling, 39,* 269–280.
Belloch, A., Perpiona, M., Pacual, L. M., de Diego, A., & Creer, T. L. (1997). The revised asthma problem behavior checklist: Adaptation for use in Spanish asthma patients. *Journal of Asthma, 43,* 31–41.
Buston, K. M., & Wood, S. F. (2000). Noncompliance amongst adolescents with asthma: Listening to what they tell us about self-management. *Family Practice, 17,* 134–138.
Jones, A., Pill, R., & Adams, S. (2000). Qualitative study of views of health professionals and patients on guided self-management plans for asthma. *British Medical Journal, 321,* 1507–1510.
Perez, M. G., Feldman, L., & Caballero, F. (1999). Effects of a self-management educational program for the control of childhood asthma. *Patient Education & Counseling, 36,* 47–55.

Cancer
Cunningham, A. J., Phillips, C., Lockwood, G. A., Hedley, D. W., & Edmonds, C. V. I. (2000). Association of involvement in psychological self-regulation with longer survival in patients with metastatic cancer: An exploratory study. *Advances in Mind-Body Medicine, 16,* 276–286.

Cardiology
Clark, N. M., Janz, N. K., Dodge, J. A., Schlork, M. A., Fingerlin, T. E., Wheeler, J. R. C., Liang, J., Keteyian, S. J., & Santinga, J. T. (2000). Changes in functional health status of older women with heart disease: Evaluation of a program based on self-regulation. *Journal of Gerontology, 55B*(2), S117–S126.
Clark, N. M., Janz, N. K., Dodge, J. A., Schlork, M. A., Wheeler, J. R. C., Liang, J., Keteyian, S. J., & Santinga, J. T. (1997). Self-management of heart disease by older adults. *Research on Aging, 19,* 362–382.

Chronically mentally ill
Corrigan, P. W., & Basit, A. (1997). Generalization of social skill straining for persons with severe mental illness. *Cognitive & Behavioral Practice, 4,* 191–206.
Kennedy, M. G., Schlepp, K. G., & O'Connor, F. W. (2000). Symptoms of self-management and relapse in schizophrenia. *Archives of Psychiatric Nursing, 14,* 266–275.

Classroom behavior
Davies, S., & Witte, R. (2000). Self-management and peer-monitoring within a group-contingency to decrease uncontrolled verbalizations of children with attention-deficit/hyperactivity disorder. *Psychology in the Schools, 37,* 135–147.
Peterson, L. D., Young, K. R., West, R. P., & Peterson, M. H. (1999). Construction and validation of four childhood asthma self-management scales: Parent barriers, child and parent self-efficacy, and parent belief in treatment efficacy. *Education & Treatment of Children, 22,* 357–372.

Creative writing
Albertson, L. R., & Billingsley, F. F. (2001). Using strategy instruction and self-regulation to improve gifted students' creative writing. *Journal of Secondary Gifted Education, 12,* 90–101.

Depression
Rokke, P. D., Timhave, J. A., & Jocic, Z. (1999). The role of client choice and target selection in self-management therapy for depression in older adults. *Psychology & Aging, 14,* 155–169.
Rokke, P. D., Timhave, J. A., & Jocic, Z. (2000). Self-management therapy and educational group therapy for depressed elders. *Cognitive Therapy & Research, 24,* 99–119.

Diabetes
Clark, M., & Hampson, S. E. (2000). Implementing a psychological intervention to improve lifestyle self-management in patients with Type 2 diabetes. *Patient Education & Counseling, 42,* 242–256.
Paterson, B., & Thorne, S. (2000). Development evolution of expertise in diabetes self-management. *Clinical Nursing Research, 9,* 402–419.

Disability-related
Autism
Koegel, L. K., Koegel, R. L., Harrower, J. K., & Carter, C. M. (1999). Pivotal response intervention 1: Overview of approach. *Journal of the Association for Persons with Severe Handicaps, 24*(3), 174–185.

Down syndrome
Cuskelly, M., Zhang, A., & Gilmore, L. (1998). The importance of self-regulation in young children with Down syndrome. *International Journal of Disability, Development, & Education, 45,* 331–341.

Education settings
Cavalier, A. R., Ferrettie, R. P., & Hodges, A. E. (1997). Self-management within a classroom token economy for students with learning disabilities. *Research in Developmental Disabilities, 18*(3), 167–178.
Koegel, L. K., Harrower, J. K., & Koegel, R. L. (1999). Support for children with developmental disabilities in full inclusion classrooms through self-management. *Journal of Positive Behavior Interventions, 1,* 26–34.

BOX 18.1   RESEARCH ON SELF-MANAGEMENT

McDougall, D. (1998). Research on self-management techniques used by students with disabilities in general education settings: A descriptive review. *Remedial & Special Education, 18,* 310–320.

Snyder, M. C., & Bambara, L. M. (1997). Teaching secondary students with learning disabilities to self-manage classroom survival skills. *Journal of Learning Disabilities, 30,* 534–543.

Health care
O'Hara, L., DeSouza, L. H., & Ide, L. (2000). A Delphi study of self-care in a community population of people with multiple sclerosis. *Clinical Rehabilitation, 14*(1), 62–71.

Hygiene
Garff, J. T., & Storey, K. (1998). The use of self-management strategies for increasing the appropriate hygiene of persons with disabilities in supported employment settings. *Education & Training in Mental Retardation & Developmental Disabilities, 33,* 179–188.

Epilepsy
Schmid-Schoenbein, C. (1998). Improvement of seizure control by psychological methods in patients with intractable epilepsy. *Seizure, 7,* 261–270.

Headaches
Acury, T. A., Quandt, S. A., McDonald, J., & Bell, R. A. (2000). Faith and health self-management of rural older adults. *Journal of Cross-Cultural Gerontology, 15,* 55–74.

Olness, K., Hall, H., Rozniecki, J. J., Schmidt, W., & Theroharides, T. C. (1999). Mast cell activation in children with migraine before and after training in self-regulation. *Headache, 39,* 101–107.

Health care
Lorig, K. R., Sobel, D. S., Stewart, A. L., Brown, B. W., Jr., Bandura, A., Ritter, P., Gonzalez, V. M., Laurent, D. D., & Holman, H. R. (1999). Evidence suggesting that a chronic disease self-management program can improve health status while reducing hospitalization. *Medical Care, 37,* 5–14.

HIV/AIDS
Gifford, A. L., & Sengupta, S. (1999). Self-management health education for chronic HIV infection. *AIDS Care, 11*(1), 115–130.

Homework
Carrington, P., Lehrer, P. M., & Wittenstrom, K. (1997). A children's self-management system for reducing homework-related problems: Parent efficacy ratings. *Child & Family Behavior Therapy, 19,* 1–22.

Nutrition
Quandi, S. A., McDonald, J., Acury, T. A., Bell, R. A., & Vitolins, M. Z. (2000). Nutritional self-management of elderly widows in rural communities. *Gerontologist, 40,* 86–96.

Pain
Kerns, R. D., Rosenberg, R., Jamison, R. N., Caudill, M. A., & Haythornthwaire, J. (1997). Readiness to adopt a self-management approach to chronic pain: The pain stages of change questionnaire. *Pain, 72,* 227–234.

LeFort, S. M., Gray-Donald, K., Powat, K. M., & Jeans, M. E. (1998). Randomized controlled trial of a community-based psycho-education program for the self-management of chronic pain. *Pain, 74,* 287–306.

Self-management regulation measures
Ownsworth, T. L., McFarland, K., & Young, R. McD. (2000). Development and standardization of the self-regulation skills interview (SRSI): A new clinical assessment tool for acquired brain injury. *Clinical Neuropsychologist, 14,* 76–92.

Self-management skills
Kern, L., Marder, T. J., Boyajian, A. E., Elliot, C., et al. (1997). Augmenting the independence of self-management procedures by teaching self-initiation across setting and activities. *School Psychology Quarterly, 12,* 23–32.

Yamamoto, J., Kunieda, Y., & Kakutani, A. (1999). Acquisition and generalization of self-management skills among students with developmental disabilities. *Japanese Journal of Developmental Psychology, 10,* 209–219.

Self-regulated learning
Bockaerts, M. (1997). Self-regulated learning: A new concept embraced by researchers, policy makers, educators, teachers, and students. *Learn & Instruction, 7,* 161–186.

Social behavior
Embregts, P. J. M. (2000). Effectiveness of video feedback and self-management on inappropriate social behavior of youth with mild mental retardation. *Research in Developmental Disabilities, 21,* 409–423.

Substance abuse
Brichcin, M., Cadova, I., & Zyka, J. (1997). Objective manifestations of will factors in adolescents abusing drugs. *Ceskoslovenka Psychologie, 41,* 1–29.

Copeland, J. (1997). A qualitative study of barriers to formal treatment among women who self-manage change in addictive behavior. *Journal of Substance Abuse Treatment, 14,* 183–190.

Horvath, A. T., & Velten, E. (2000). SMART Recovery®: Addiction recovery support from a cognitive–behavioral perspective. *Journal of Rational–Emotive & Cognitive Behavior Therapy, 18*(3), 181–191.

Vision loss
Brody, B. L., Williams, R. A., Thomas, R. G., Kaplan, R. M., Chu, R. M., & Brown, S. I. (1999). Age-related macular degeneration: A randomized clinical trial of a self-management intervention. *Annals of Behavioral Medicine, 21,* 322–329.

Lanfaloni, G. A., Baglioni, A., & Tafi, L. (1997). Self-regulation training programs for subjects with mental retardation and blindness. *Developmental Brain Dysfunction, 10,* 231–239.

Weight loss
Braet, C. (1999). Treatment of obese children: A new rationale. *Clinical Child Psychology & Psychiatry, 4,* 579–591.

Kitsantas, A. (2000). The role of self-regulation strategies and self-efficacy perceptions in successful weight loss maintenance. *Psychology & Health, 15,* 811–820.

MULTICULTURAL APPLICATIONS OF SELF-MANAGEMENT

Self-management has recently been used with diverse groups of clients in areas such as health management, school success, relationship conflict, and HIV intervention. Jacob, Penn, Kulik, and Spieth (1992) researched the effects of self-management and positive reinforcement on the self-reported compliance rate of African American women who performed breast self-examinations over a nine-month period. Both self-management and positive reinforcement were associated with high compliance rates, especially for women who were designated initially as "monitors" (e.g., more likely to "track" things about themselves).

Roberson (1992) also explored the role of compliance and self-management in adult rural African Americans who had been diagnosed with chronic health conditions. She found that the patients and their health professionals had different notions of compliance and also different treatment goals. The patients defined compliance in terms of apparent "good health" and wanted a treatment that was manageable, viable, and effective. They developed systems of self-management to cope with their illness that were suitable to their lifestyles, belief patterns, and personal priorities. They believed they were managing their illness and treatment regimen effectively. Roberson (1992) suggested that as professionals we need to focus less on noncompliance rates per se and more on understanding differing perspectives and enhancing clients' efforts to manage their own illnesses and to live effectively with them.

Asthma has been a health focus. Haire-Joshu, Fisher, Munro, and Wedner (1993) explored attitudes toward asthma care within a sample of low-income African American adults receiving services at a public acute care facility versus patients receiving services at a private setting that stressed preventive self-management. Those persons in the acute care setting were more likely to engage in self-treatment (such as relying on over-the-counter medication) or to avoid or delay care, compared to the patients who had learned preventive asthma self-management techniques—findings that urge attention to factors such as access to resources and differential histories with service providers in planning interventions. An innovative computer-assisted instructional program (the main character in the game could match the subject on gender and ethnicity; the protagonist's asthma could be tailored similarly to the subjects) to improve asthma self-management in inner-city children has achieved promising initial results in both self-management behaviors and health outcomes (Bartholomew, Gold, Parcel, Czyzewski, Sockrider, Fernandez, Shegog, & Swank, 2000). Rao and Kramer (1993) found self-control to be an important aspect of stress reduction and coping among African American mothers who had infants with sickle cell conditions. Notably, other strategies complementary to self-control (positive reappraisal, seeking social support, problem solving) were also found useful.

Self-management has also been found to be an effective component of HIV-infection risk-reduction training with gay men (Kelly & St. Lawrence, 1990; Martin, 1993). In a study of several hundred African American youth, self-management was part of an eight-week HIV-risk-reduction program that compared receiving either information or skills training versus both information and skills training (St. Lawrence, Brasfield, Jefferson, Alleyne, O'Bannon, & Shirley, 1995). Youth who received both information and skills training lowered their risk to a greater degree, maintained risk reduction changes better, and deferred the onset of sexual activity to a greater extent than those who received only one component of training. However, issues of drop-out and perceived self-relevance have also been raised in HIV-prevention interventions for inner-city heterosexual African American men (Kalichman, Rompa, & Coley, 1997).

Recent research has indicated the utility of broadening the view of resources to be included in self-management interventions—to draw upon environmental resources such as social support people and networks, spirituality, and opportunities to work with families or communities to develop culturally relevant approaches. A computer-assisted program applied to asthma self-management is one such example. In addition to research findings, Bartholomew and colleagues (2000) also offer an overview of applying theory (e.g., about self-efficacy and self-regulatory processes) to a self-management need in a culturally sensitive manner. Wang and Abbott (1998) describe a project to work with a Chinese community group toward developing a culturally sensitive community-based self-management program for chronic diseases such as diabetes and hypertension. Faith, prayer, and religious activities were demonstrated to be importantly associated with health management among a racially diverse group of rural older adults (Arcury, Quandt, McDonald, & Bell, 2000), arguing for the need to consider such factors in developing self-management plans. In related work, factors that need to be considered in working with rural populations, particularly among vulnerable elders such as those widowed, has been addressed relative to nutritional self-management (Quandt, McDonald, Arcury, Bell, & Vitolins, 2000).

It would seem that self-management could be incorporated as a culturally effective intervention with many clients from diverse groups, especially as self-management is time limited, deals with the present, and focuses on pragmatic problem resolution (Sue & Sue, 1999). Similarly, focus on behavioral patterns as well as beliefs or orientations to promote action and not just "talk" and self-exploration would be consistent with the use of a self-management intervention. However, we would note that self-management need not be construed to be a "lone ranger" or nonreflective method, but rather one that can sensibly build on environmental resources and cultural perspectives about self and problem solving. Self-management may also appeal to some clients who do not like or feel comfortable with traditional mental health services. Keep in mind that in self-management efforts, the work is client managed, and most of it occurs outside helping sessions. Values and belief systems (e.g., that self-reliance, faith, and inclusion in community are important general strategies for living) as well as characteristics of the client's environment—social, material, informational, sociopolitical—can be important dimensions of assessment to guide appropriate self-management intervention planning.

However, caution must be used in selecting self-management as an appropriate intervention for all clients from diverse cultural groups. McCafferty (1992) has suggested that the process of self-regulation varies among cultures and societies. Some of the notions involved in self-management strategies are decidedly Eurocentric. Casas (1988) asserts that the basic notion underlying self-management may "not be congruent with the life experiences of many racial/ethnic minority persons. More specifically, as a result of life experiences associated with racism, discrimination, and poverty, people may have developed a cognitive set (e.g., an external locus of control, an external locus of responsibility, and learned helplessness) that . . . is antithetical to any self-control approaches" (pp. 109–110). Recall from the discussion of world views in Chapter 11 that there are four quadrants of Sue and Sue's (1999) cultural identity model based on the dimensions of locus of control and the locus of responsibility (IC-IR, IC-ER, EC-IR, EC-ER); these quadrants range from internal control to external control and from internal responsibility to external responsibility. Thus, locus of control and locus of responsibility seem to be mediating variables that affect the appropriateness of using self-management for some women clients and for some clients of color. In an innovative study conducted by St. Lawrence (1993), African American female and male youth completed measures of knowledge related to AIDS, attitudes toward the use of condoms, vulnerability to HIV infection, peer sexual norms, personal sexual behavior, contraceptive preferences, and locus of control. Condom use as prevention was associated with greater internal locus of control, which was higher for the African American girls than for the boys. In addition to the mediating variables of locus of control and locus of responsibility, the client's identification with his or her cultural (collective) identity, acculturation status, and assimilation may also be mediating variables that affect the use of self-management for non-Euro-American clients.

Guidelines for Using Self-Management with Diverse Groups of Clients

We recommend the following guidelines in using self-management approaches with diverse groups of clients:

1. Consider the client's lifestyle, beliefs, behavioral patterns, and personal priorities in assessing the usefulness of self-management. For example, if the client is interested in following the progress of events, a strategy such as self-monitoring may be relevant to his or her personal and cognitive style. For clients who have no interest in such tracking, self-monitoring may appear to be a waste of time, an activity that is personally and culturally irrelevant.
2. Adapt the intervention to the client's culture and background. Some clients have been socialized to be very private and would feel most uncomfortable in publicly displaying their self-monitoring data. Other clients would be unlikely to discipline themselves to go to one place to obtain stimulus control, such as using a smoking chair to help control smoking. And, depending on the client's history, the idea of using self-rewards may be awkward or benefit from reframing. At the very least, the rewards must be tailored to the client's gender, age, and culture.
3. Discover the client's world view (see Chapter 11) and consider the relevance of self-management based on this perception of the world. For clients whose cultural identity or the targeted issue is shaped by external locus of control and external locus of responsibility, self-management may not be a good match or may need to be discussed as an option with such factors in mind.
4. Consider the relevance of self-management against the client's goals for helping intervention and also the context of the client's life. If the client is also struggling with multiple problems in living, aversive external structures and discrimination, serious vulnerabilities, or overwhelming pressures, self-management would have a limited role, if

deemed appropriate at all. Consider, for example, how it might feel if you were a low-income mother with no social support and few resources and were regularly beaten by your live-in male partner—and your helping practitioner told you to engage in some form of self-management. On the other hand, one or more self-management strategies may provide some concrete relief—perhaps in better managing a health problem or in helping her child better manage troubling classroom behavior—that can be a meaningful part of a larger set of goals.

CHARACTERISTICS OF AN EFFECTIVE SELF-MANAGEMENT PROGRAM

Well-constructed and well-executed self-management programs have some advantages over helper-administered procedures. For instance, the use of a self-management procedure may increase a person's perceived control over the environment and decrease dependence on the helper or others. Perceived control over the environment often motivates and supports a person to take some action. Second, self-management approaches are practical—inexpensive and portable (Thoresen & Mahoney, 1974, p. 7). Third, such strategies are usable. By this we mean that a person will occasionally refuse to go "into therapy" or formalized helping to stop drinking or to lose weight but will agree to use the self-administered instructions that a self-management program provides. This may be particularly advantageous with some clients who are mistrustful of therapy or related forms of professional helping. Finally, self-management strategies may enhance generalization of learning—both from the interview to the environment and from problematic to nonproblematic situations (Thoresen & Mahoney, 1974, p. 7). These are some of the possible advantages of self-management that have spurred both researchers and practitioners to apply and explore some of the components and effects of successful self-management programs.

Although many questions remain unanswered, we can tentatively say that the following factors may be important in an effective self-management program:
1. A combination of strategies, some focusing on antecedents of behavior and others on consequences
2. Consistent use of strategies over a period of time
3. Evidence of client self-evaluation, goal setting, and self-efficacy
4. Use of covert, verbal, or material self-reinforcement
5. Some degree of external or environmental support

Combination of Strategies

We have mentioned that self-management is often combined with other change strategies and that a combination of self-management strategies is usually more useful than a single strategy. In a weight-control study, Mahoney, Moura, and Wade (1973) found that the addition of self-reward significantly enhanced the procedures of self-monitoring and stimulus control, and that those who combined self-reward and self-punishment lost more weight than those who used just one of the procedures. Stress inoculation training (see Chapter 15) includes application of self-management principles within a multicomponent package, with considerable support across a variety of concerns (Meichenbaum & Deffenbacher, 1988; Meichenbaum, 1994) and with children and adolescents (Maag & Kotlash, 1994; Ollendick & King, 2000). Issues for which combinations of self-management components have been used include weight control (Mahoney & Mahoney, 1976); interpersonal skills training (McFall & Dodge, 1982); developmental disabilities (Litrownik, 1982); anxiety (Deffenbacher & Suinn, 1982); addictive disorders (Marlatt & Parks, 1982); depression among children, adults, and elders (Rehm, 1982; Rehm & Sharp, 1996; Rokke, Tomhave, & Jocic, 1999); insomnia (Bootzin, 1977); and academic performance (Neilans & Israel, 1981). The research tables in this chapter provide current examples across a range of life domains and concerns.

Consistent Use of Strategies

Consistent, regular use of the strategies is a very important component of effective self-management. Seeming ineffectiveness may be due not to the impotence of the strategy but to its inconsistent or sporadic application (Thoresen & Mahoney, 1974, p. 107). It is probable that successful self-controllers use strategies more frequently and more consistently than unsuccessful self-controllers. Similarly, "failures" in a self-management program may be lax in using the procedures. Also, if self-management efforts are not used over a certain period of time, their effectiveness may be too limited to produce any change.

Self-Evaluation, Standard Setting, and Self-Efficacy

Self-evaluation in the form of standard setting (or goal setting) and intention statements seems to be an important component of a self-management program. Some evidence also suggests that self-selected stringent standards affect performance more positively than do lenient standards (Bandura, 1971). It is important to distinguish outcome expectations—one's beliefs about whether a certain behavior or event will produce a particular outcome—from self-efficacy expectations—the belief or level of confidence a person has in his or her ability to develop intentions, set behavioral goals, and successfully execute the behavior(s) in question. A client may have confidence that she or he can manage a certain action but not undertake it due to a belief that it will not accomplish the desired outcome (or that obstacles will intervene to prevent the desired outcome). In some cases, these may be realistic readings of a situation, underscoring the importance of careful assessment of a client's circumstances and other agents or factors that may have significant roles in the desired outcome. In general, however, perceived self-efficacy is seen by many as a centrally important component—without this, it is difficult at best to build an intervention program that requires substantial client involvement or to achieve incrementally successful, reinforcing outcomes along the way. On the other hand, strengthening efficacy expectations can augment an internal resource crucial to subsequent successes in a self-management intervention. For example, successful self-controllers usually set higher goals and criteria for change than unsuccessful self-controllers do. However, the standards set should be realistic and within reach, or it is unlikely that self-reinforcement will ever occur.

Bandura (1997) offers a discussion of sources through which self-efficacy expectations are typically influenced: (1) one's own performance accomplishments, (2) vicarious experience (e.g., observing others, reading stories, imagining), (3) verbal persuasion, and (4) physiological and affective states (e.g., strategies to pair positive mood and a relaxed state with conditions under which self-efficacy is needed).

Use of Self-Reinforcement

Self-reinforcement, whether covert, verbal, or material, appears to be an important ingredient of an effective self-management program. Being able to praise oneself covertly or to note positive improvement seems to be correlated with self-change. In contrast, self-criticism (covert and verbal) seems to mitigate against change (Mahoney & Mahoney, 1976). It is important to consider what any given client will experience as genuinely reinforcing. For example, some people may find that material self-reward (such as money or valued items) may be more effective than either self-monitoring or self-punishment; others may find various forms of social support or pride to be more effective. Self-reinforcement must also be relevant to the client's gender and culture.

Environmental Support

Some degree of external support is necessary to effect and maintain the changes resulting from a self-management program. For example, public display of self-monitoring data and the help of another person provide opportunities for social reinforcement that often augment behavior change. Successful self-controllers may report receiving more positive feedback from others about their change efforts than do unsuccessful self-controllers. To maintain any self-managed change, there must be some support from the social and physical environment, although how this is best achieved may vary for clients from different cultural backgrounds, age cohorts, or life circumstances. We previously used examples to illuminate variability in how "self" may be conceptualized differently among people and how self-management may be embedded for some within networks, communities, historical legacies, or current conditions that should be considered. The examples illustrated ways that faith and spirituality may be important along with support networks and cultural identities (Gartett, 1999, provides an example for Native American youth).

STEPS IN DEVELOPING A CLIENT SELF-MANAGEMENT PROGRAM

We have incorporated these five characteristics of effective self-management into a description of the steps associated with a self-management program. The steps are applicable to any program in which the client uses stimulus control, self-monitoring, or self-reward. Figure 18.1 summarizes the steps associated with developing a self-management program; the characteristics of effective self-management reflected in the steps are noted in the left column of the figure.

For developing a self-management program, steps 1 and 2 both involve aspects of standard setting and self-evaluation. In step 1, the client identifies and records the target behavior and its antecedents and consequences. This step involves self-monitoring, in which the client collects baseline data about the behavior to be changed. If baseline data have not been collected as part of assessment (see Chapter 9), it is imperative that such data be collected now, before using any self-management strategies. In step 2, the client explicitly identifies the desired behavior, conditions, and level of change. As you may remember from Chapter 10, the behavior, conditions, and level of change are the three parts of a counseling outcome goal. Defining the goal is an important part of self-management because of the possible motivating effects of standard setting. Establishing goals may

588 CHAPTER 18

Characteristics of an Effective Self-Management Program

Standard setting, self-evaluation, and self-efficacy

Standard setting, self-evaluation, and self-efficacy

Combination of strategies

Combination of strategies

Client commitment and consistent use of strategies

Consistent use of strategies

Consistent use of strategies

Consistent use of strategies

Self-evaluation
Self-reinforcement
Environmental support

Steps in Developing a Self-Management Program

Step 1
Client identifies and records target behavior, controlling antecedents, and consequences (baseline); estimates confidence in achieving target behavior

Step 2
Client identifies desired behavior and direction of change (goals); estimates confidence in achieving goals

Step 3
Helper explains possible self-management strategies

Step 4
Client selects one or more self-management strategies

Step 5
Client verbally commits to carry out step 4

Step 6
Helper instructs and models selected strategies

Step 7
Client rehearses selected strategies

Step 8
Client uses selected strategies *in vivo*

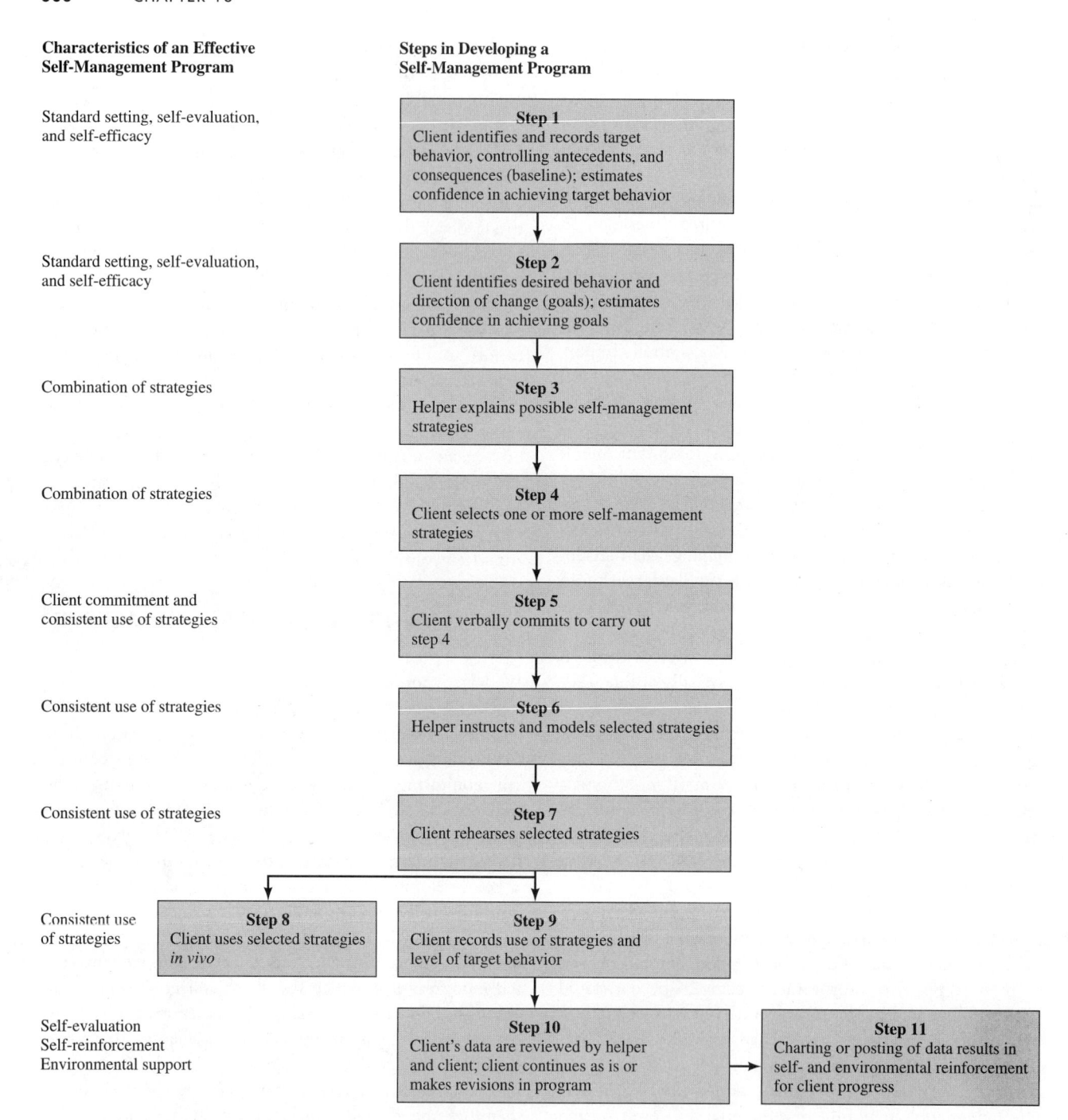

Step 9
Client records use of strategies and level of target behavior

Step 10
Client's data are reviewed by helper and client; client continues as is or makes revisions in program

Step 11
Charting or posting of data results in self- and environmental reinforcement for client progress

Figure 18.1 Developing an effective self-management program

interact with some of the self-management procedures and contribute to the desired effects.

Steps 3 and 4 are directed toward helping the client select a combination of self-management strategies to use. The helper will need to explain all the possible self-management strategies to the client (step 3). The helper should emphasize that the client should select some strategies that involve prearrangement of the antecedents and some that involve manipulation and self-administration of consequences. Ultimately, the client is responsible for selecting which self-management strategies should be used (step 4). Client selection of the strategies is an important part of the overall *self-directed* nature of self-management, although this step may benefit from assistance from the professional helper or others involved in supporting the client's efforts in sorting through the choices.

Steps 5–9 all involve procedural considerations that may strengthen client commitment and may encourage consistent use of the strategies over time. First, the client commits himself or herself verbally by specifying what and how much change is desired and the action steps (strategies) the client will take to produce the change (step 5). Next, the helper will instruct the client in how to carry out the selected strategies (step 6). (The helper can follow the guidelines listed later in the chapter for self-monitoring, those for stimulus control, and those for self-reward.) Explicit instructions and modeling by the helper may encourage the client to use a procedure more accurately and effectively. The instructional set given by a helper may contribute to some degree to the overall treatment outcome. The client also may use the strategies more effectively if there is an opportunity to rehearse the procedures in the interview under the helper's direction (step 7). Finally, the client applies the strategies *in vivo* (step 8) and records (monitors) the frequency of use of each strategy and the level of the target behavior (step 9). Some of the treatment effects of self-management may also be a function of the client's self-recording.

Steps 10 and 11 involve aspects of self-evaluation, self-reinforcement, and environmental support. The client has an opportunity to evaluate progress toward the goal by reviewing the self-recorded data collected during strategy implementation (step 10). Review of the data may indicate that the program is progressing smoothly or that some adjustments are needed. When the data suggest that some progress toward the goal is being made, the client's self-evaluation may set the occasion for self-reinforcement. Charting or posting the data (step 11) can enhance self-reinforcement and can elicit important environmental support for long-term maintenance of client change.

The following section describes how self-monitoring can be used to record the target behavior. Such recording can occur initially for problem assessment and goal setting, or it can be introduced later as a self-change strategy. We will discuss how self-monitoring can be specifically used to promote behavior change.

SELF-MONITORING: PURPOSES, USES, AND PROCESSES

Purposes of Self-Monitoring

In Chapter 9 we defined self-monitoring as a process in which clients observe and record things about themselves and their interactions with environmental situations. Self-monitoring is a useful adjunct to assessment because the observational data can verify or change the client's verbal report about the target behavior. We recommend that clients record their daily self-observations over a designated time period on a behavior log. Usually, the client observes and records the target behavior, the controlling antecedents, and the resulting consequences. Thoresen and Mahoney (1974) assert that self-monitoring is a major *first* step in any self-change program (as in any change program). The client must be able to discover what is happening *before* implementing a self-change strategy, just as the helper must know what is going on before using any other therapeutic procedure. In other words, any self-management strategy, like any other strategy, should be preceded by a baseline period of self-observation and recording. During this period, the client collects and records data about the behavior to be changed (B), the antecedents (A) of the behavior, and the consequences (C) of the behavior. In addition, the client may wish to note how much or how often the behavior occurs. For example, a client might record the daily amount of study time or the number of times he or she left the study time and place to do something else. The behavior log presented in Chapter 9 for assessment data can also be used by a client to collect baseline data before implementing a self-management program. If the helper introduces self-management strategies *after* assessment, these self-observation data should be already available.

As we discussed in Chapter 10, self-monitoring is also very useful for evaluation of goals or outcomes. When a client self-monitors the target behavior either before or during a treatment program, "the primary utility of self-monitoring lies in its assessment or data collection function" (Ciminero et al., 1977, p. 196). In recent years, however, practitioners and researchers have realized that the mere act of self-observation can produce change. As one collects data about oneself, the

> ### LEARNING ACTIVITY 18.1 Self-Monitoring
>
> This learning activity is designed to help you use self-monitoring yourself. The instructions describe a self-monitoring plan for you to try out.
>
> 1. *Discrimination of a target response:*
>   a. Specify one target behavior you would like to change. Pick either the positive or the negative side of the behavior to monitor—depending on which you value more and whether you want to increase or decrease this response.
>   b. Write down a definition of this behavior. How clear is your definition?
>   c. Can you write some examples of this behavior? If you had trouble with these, try to tighten up your definition—or contrast positive and negative instances of the behavior.
> 2. *Recording of the response:*
>   a. Specify the *timing* of your self-recording. Remember the rules of thumb:
>   (1) Use prebehavior monitoring to decrease an undesired response.
>   (2) Use postbehavior monitoring to increase a desired response.
>   (3) Record immediately—don't wait.
>   (4) Record when there are no competing responses.
>
>   Write down the timing you choose.
>   b. Select a *method* of recording (frequency, duration, and so on). Remember:
>   (1) Frequency counts for clearly separate occurrences of the response.
>   (2) Duration or latency measures for responses that occur for a period of time.
>   (3) Intensity measures to determine the severity of a response.
>   c. Select a *device* to assist you in recording. Remember that the device should be
>   (1) Portable
>   (2) Accessible
>   (3) Economical
>   (4) Obtrusive enough to serve as a reminder to self-record
>   d. After you have made these determinations, engage in self-monitoring for at least a week (preferably two). Then complete steps 3, 4, and 5.
> 3. *Charting of response:* Take your daily self-recording data and chart them on a simple line graph for each day that you self-monitored.
> 4. *Displaying of data:* Arrange a place (that you feel comfortable with) to display your chart.
> 5. *Analysis of data:* Compare your chart with your stated desired behavior change. What has happened to the behavior?

data collection may influence the behavior being observed. We now know that self-monitoring is useful not only to collect data but also to promote client change. If properly structured and executed, self-monitoring can be used as one type of self-management strategy. (See Learning Activity 18.1.)

Clinical Uses of Self-Monitoring

A number of research reports and clinical studies have explored self-monitoring as a major change strategy. Box 18.2 indicates a variety of subjects for which self-monitoring has been used. These include alcohol use, classroom behaviors, social and relationship dynamics, pain, anxiety and panic, problem solving, learning, eating and weight loss, stress, and a range of health concerns. Self-monitoring has been used with many different populations, including those with disabilities, with chronic mental illness, children, elders, caregivers, and across cultures.

Factors Influencing the Reactivity of Self-Monitoring

As you may recall from Chapter 10, two issues involved in self-monitoring are the reliability of the self-recording and its reactivity. Reliability, the accuracy of the self-recorded data, is important when self-monitoring is used to evaluate the goal behaviors. However, when self-monitoring is used as a change strategy, the accuracy of the data is less crucial. From a helping perspective, the reactivity of self-monitoring makes it suitable for a change strategy. As an example of reactivity, Kanfer and Gaelick-Buys (1991) noted that a married or partnered couple using self-monitoring to observe their frequent arguments reported that whenever the

BOX 18.2 RESEARCH ON SELF-MONITORING

Alcohol consumption
Walitze, K. S., & Connors, G. J. (1999). Treating problem drinking. *Alcohol Research & Health, 23,* 138–143.

Autism
Akane, A. (1998). Self-monitoring of autistic behavior. *Psychology: A Journal of Human Behavior, 35,* 23–29.
Strain, P. S., Kohler, F. W., Storey, K., & Danko, C. D. (1994). Teaching preschoolers with autism to self-monitor their social interactions: An analysis of results in home and school settings. *Journal of Emotional and Behavioral Disorders, 2,* 78–88.

Blood glucose
Bernbaum, M., Albert, S. G., McGinnis, J., & Brusca, S. (1994). The reliability of self blood glucose monitoring in elderly diabetic patients. *Journal of the American Geriatrics Society, 42,* 779–781.

Classroom
Todd, A. W., Horner, R. H., & Sugai, G. (1999). Self-monitoring and self-recruited praise: Effects on problem behavior, academic engagement, and work completion in a typical classroom. *Journal of Positive Behavior Interventions, 1*(2), 66–76.
VanLeuvan, P., & Wang, M. C. (1997). An analysis of students' self-monitoring in first- and second-grade classrooms. *Journal of Educational Research, 90*(3), 132–143.
Wood, S. J., Murdock, J. Y., Cronin, M. E., Dawson, N. M., & Kirby, P. C. (1998). Effects of self-monitoring on on-task behaviors of at-risk middle school students. *Journal of Behavioral Education, 8,* 263–279.

Cultural factors
Goodwin, R., & Soon, A. P. Y. (1994). Self-monitoring and relationship adjustment: A cross-cultural analysis. *Journal of Social Psychology, 134,* 35–39.
Weierter, S. J. M., Ashkanasy, N. M., & Callan, V. J. (1997). Effect of self-monitoring and national culture on follower perceptions of personal charisma and charismatic message. *Australian Journal of Psychology, 49,* 101–105.

Developmentally disabled workers
Kaplan, H., Hemmes, N. S., Motz, P., & Rodriguez, H. (1996). Self-reinforcement and persons with developmental disabilities. *Psychological Record, 46,* 161–178.

Hair pulling
Rogers, P., & Darnley, S. (1997). Self-monitoring, competing response, and response cost in the treatment of trichotillomania: A case report. *Behavioural and Cognitive Psychotherapy, 25,* 281–290.
Stoylen, I. J. (1996). Treatment of trichotillomania by habit reversal. *Scandinavian Journal of Behaviour Therapy, 25*(¾), 149–153.

Immune system
Greene, B. R., Blanchard, E. B., & Wan, C. K. (1994). Long-term monitoring of psychosocial stress and symptomatology in inflammatory bowel disease. *Behaviour Research and Therapy, 32,* 217–226.

Obsessive–compulsive disorder
McKay, D., Todaro, J. F., Neziroglu, F., & Yaryura, T. J. A. (1996). Evaluation of a naturalistic maintenance program in the treatment of obsessive compulsive disorder: A preliminary investigation. *Journal of Anxiety Disorders, 10,* 211–217.

Pain perception
Dar, R., & Leventhal, H. (1993). Schematic processes in pain perception. *Cognitive Therapy and Research, 17,* 341–357.

Panic attacks
de Beurs, E., Garssen, B., Buikhuisen, M., & Lange, A. (1994). Continuous monitoring of panic. *Acta Psychiatrica Scandinavica, 90,* 38–45.

Performance of children with learning disabilities
Jitendra, J. K., Cole, C. L., Hoppes, M. K., & Wilson, B. (1998). Effects of a direct instruction main idea summarization program and self-monitoring on reading comprehension of middle school students with learning disabilities. *Reading and Writing Quarterly: Overcoming Learning Difficulties, 14,* 379–396.
Jitendra, A. K., Hoppes, M. K., & Xin, Y. P. (2000). Enhancing main idea comprehension for students with learning problems: The role of a summarization strategy and self-monitoring instruction. *Journal of Special Education, 34*(3), 127–139.
Reid, R. (1996). Research in self-monitoring with students with learning disabilities: The present, the prospects, the pitfalls. *Journal of Learning Disabilities, 29,* 317–331.

Problem solving
Lan, W., Repman, J., & Chyung, S. Y. (1998). Effects of practicing self-monitoring of mathematical problem-solving heuristics on impulsive and reflective college students' heuristics knowledge and problem-solving ability. *Journal of Experimental Education, 67,* 32–52.

Schizophrenia/delusions
Brebion, G., Amador, X., David, A., Mapaspina, D., Sharif, Z., & Gorman, J. M. (2000). Positive symptomatology and source-monitoring failure in schizophrenia: An analysis of symptom-specific effects. *Psychiatry Research, 95,* 119–131.
Dayus, B., & van den Broek, M. D. (2000). Treatment of stable delusional confabulations using self-monitoring training. *Neuropsychological Rehabilitation, 10,* 415–427.
Stirling, J. D., Hellewell, J. S. E., & Quraishi, N. (1998). Self-monitoring dysfunction and the schizophrenic symptoms of alien control. *Psychological Medicine, 281,* 675–683.

Self-efficacy
Zimmerman, B. J., & Kitsantas, A. (1996). Self-regulated learning of a motoric skill: The role of goal setting and self-monitoring. *Journal of Applied Sport Psychology, 8,* 60–75.

Smoking
Becona, E., & Vasquez, F. L. (1997). Does using relapse prevention increase the efficacy of a program for smoking cessation? An empirical study. *Psychological Reports, 81,* 291–296.

(continued)

> **BOX 18.2** **RESEARCH ON SELF-MONITORING** CONTINUED
>
> *Suicide ideation*
> Clum, G. A., & Curtin, L. (1993). Validity and reactivity of a system of self-monitoring suicide ideation. *Journal of Psychopathology and Behavioral Assessment, 15,* 375–385.
>
> *Weight loss*
> Foreyt, J. P., & Goodrick, G. K. (1994). Attributes of successful approaches to weight loss and control. *Applied and Preventive Psychology, 3,* 209–215.
>
> *Workers' health*
> Fox, M. L., & Dwyer, D. (1995). Stressful job demands and worker health: An investigation of the effects of self-monitoring. *Journal of Applied Social Psychology, 25,* 1973–1995.

monitoring device (a tape recorder) was turned on, the argument was avoided.

Although the reactivity of self-monitoring can be a dilemma in data collection, it can be an asset when self-monitoring is used intentionally as a helping strategy. In using self-monitoring as a change strategy, try to maximize the reactive effects of self-monitoring—at least to the point of producing desired behavioral changes. Self-monitoring for *long* periods of time maintains reactivity.

A number of factors seem to influence the reactivity of self-monitoring. A summary of these factors suggests that self-monitoring is most likely to produce positive behavioral changes when change-motivated subjects continuously monitor a limited number of discrete, positively valued target behaviors; when performance feedback and goals or standards are made available and are unambiguous; and when the monitoring act is both salient and closely related in time to the target behaviors.

Nelson (1977) has identified eight variables that seem to be related to the occurrence, intensity, and direction of the reactive effects of self-monitoring:

1. *Motivation.* Clients who are interested in changing the self-monitored behavior are more likely to show reactive effects when they self-monitor.
2. *Valence of target behaviors.* Behaviors that a person values positively are likely to increase with self-monitoring; negative behaviors are likely to decrease; neutral behaviors may not change.
3. *Type of target behaviors.* The nature of the behavior that is being monitored may affect the degree to which self-monitoring procedures effect change.
4. *Standard setting (goals), reinforcement, and feedback.* Reactivity is enhanced for people who self-monitor in conjunction with goals and the availability of performance reinforcement or feedback.
5. *Timing of self-monitoring.* The time when the person self-records can influence the reactivity of self-monitoring. Results may differ depending on whether self-monitoring occurs before or after the target response.
6. *Devices used for self-monitoring.* More obtrusive or visible recording devices seem to be more reactive than unobtrusive devices.
7. *Number of target responses monitored.* Self-monitoring of only one response increases reactivity. As more responses are concurrently monitored, reactivity decreases.
8. *Schedule for self-monitoring.* The frequency with which a person self-monitors can affect reactivity. Continuous self-monitoring may result in more behavior change than intermittent self-recording.

Three factors may contribute to the reactive effects of self-monitoring:

1. *Client characteristics.* Client intellectual and physical abilities may be associated with greater reactivity when self-monitoring.
2. *Expectations.* Clients seeking help may have some expectations for desirable behavior changes. However, it is probably impossible to separate client expectations from implicit or explicit therapeutic "demands" to change the target behavior.
3. *Behavior change skills.* Reactivity may be influenced by the client's knowledge and skills associated with behavior change. For example, the reactivity of addictive behaviors may be affected by the client's knowledge of simple, short-term strategies such as fasting or abstinence. These are general guidelines, and their effects may vary with the gender, class, race, and ethnicity of each specific client.

STEPS OF SELF-MONITORING

Self-monitoring involves at least six important steps: *rationale* for the strategy, *discrimination* of a response, *recording* of a response, *charting* of a response, *display* of data, and *analysis* of data (Thoresen & Mahoney, 1974, pp. 43–44). Each

TABLE 18.1	Steps of Self-Monitoring
1. *Rationale* for self-monitoring	A. Purpose
	B. Overview of procedure
2. *Discrimination* of a response	A. Selection of target response to monitor
	1. Type of response
	2. Valence of response
	3. Number of responses
3. *Recording* of a response	A. Timing of recording
	1. Prebehavior recording to decrease a response; postbehavior recording to increase a response
	2. Immediate recording
	3. Recording when no competing responses distract recorder
	B. Method of recording
	1. Frequency counts
	2. Duration measures
	a. Continuous recording
	b. Time sampling
	C. Devices for recording
	1. Portable
	2. Accessible
	3. Economical
	4. Somewhat obtrusive
4. *Charting* of a response	A. Charting and graphing of daily totals of recorded behavior
5. *Displaying* of data	A. Chart for environmental support
6. *Analysis* of data	A. Accuracy of data interpretation
	B. Knowledge of results for self-evaluation and self-reinforcement

of these six steps and guidelines for their use are discussed here and summarized in Table 18.1. Remember that the steps are all interactive and that the presence of all of them may be required for a person to use self-monitoring effectively. Also, remember that any or all of these steps may need to be adapted, depending on the client's gender and culture.

Treatment Rationale

First, the practitioner explains the rationale for self-monitoring. Before using the strategy, the client should be aware of what the self-monitoring procedure will involve and how the procedure will help with the client's concern. An example, adapted from Benson and Stuart (1992), follows:

> The purpose of self-monitoring is to increase your awareness of your sleep patterns. Research has demonstrated that people who have insomnia benefit from keeping a self-monitoring diary. Each morning for a week you will record the time you went to bed the previous night; approximately how many minutes it took you to fall asleep; if you awakened during the night, how many minutes you were awake; the total number of hours you slept; and the time you got out of bed in the morning. Also, on a scale you will rate how rested you feel in the morning, how difficult it was to fall asleep the previous night, the quality of sleep, your level of physical tension when you went to bed the previous night, your level of mental activity when you went to bed, and how well you think you were functioning the previous day. The diary will help us evaluate your sleep and remedy issues. This kind of awareness helps in correcting factors that might contribute to your insomnia. How does that sound?

Discrimination of a Response

When a client engages in self-monitoring, an observation, or discrimination, of a response is required first. For example, a client who is monitoring fingernail biting must be able to discriminate instances of nail biting from instances of other behavior. Discrimination of a response occurs when the client is able to identify the presence or absence of the behavior and whether it is overt, like nail biting, or covert, like a positive self-thought. Thoresen and Mahoney (1974, p. 43) point out that making behavioral discriminations can be thought of as the "awareness" facet of self-monitoring.

Discrimination of a response involves helping the client identify *what* to monitor. This decision will often require helper assistance. The type of the monitored response may affect the results of self-monitoring. For example, self-monitoring may produce greater weight loss for people who recorded their daily weight and daily caloric intake than for those who recorded only daily weight. As McFall (1977) has observed, it is not very clear why some target responses seem to be better ones to self-monitor than others; at this point, the selection of target responses remains a pragmatic choice. Mahoney (1977, pp. 244–245) points out that there may be times when self-monitoring of certain responses could detract from intervention effectiveness, as in asking a suicidal client to monitor depressive thoughts.

The effects of self-monitoring also vary with the valence of the target response. There are always "two sides" of a behavior that could be monitored—the positive and the negative (Mahoney & Thoresen, 1974, p. 37). There also seem to be times when one side is more important for self-monitoring than the other (Mahoney & Thoresen, 1974, p. 37).

Unfortunately, there are very few data to guide a decision about the exact type and valence of responses to monitor. Because the reactivity of self-monitoring is affected by the value assigned to a behavior (Watson & Tharp, 2002), one guideline might be to have the client monitor the behavior that she or he cares *most* about changing. Generally, it is a good idea to encourage the client to limit monitoring to one response, at least initially. If the client engages in self-monitoring of one behavior with no difficulties, then more items can be added.

Recording of a Response

After the client has learned to make discriminations about a response, the helper can provide instructions and examples about the method for recording the observed response. Most clients have probably never recorded their behavior *systematically*. Systematic recording is crucial to the success of self-monitoring, so it is imperative that the client understand the importance and methods of recording. The client needs instructions about when and how to record and about devices for recording. The timing, method, and recording devices can all influence the effectiveness of self-monitoring.

Timing of Self-Monitoring: When to Record

One of the least understood processes of self-monitoring involves timing, or the point when the client actually records the target behavior. Instances have been reported of both prebehavior and postbehavior monitoring. In prebehavior monitoring, the client records the intention or urge to engage in the behavior *before* doing so. In postbehavior monitoring, the client records each completed instance of the target behavior—*after* the behavior has occurred. Kazdin (1974, p. 239) points out that the precise effects of self-monitoring may depend on the point at which monitoring occurs in the chain of responses relative to the response being recorded. Kanfer and Gaelick-Buys (1991) conclude that existing data are insufficient to judge whether pre- or postbehavior monitoring will have maximal effects. Nelson (1977) indicates that the effects of the timing of self-monitoring may depend partly on whether other responses are competing for the person's attention at the time the response is recorded. Another factor influencing the timing of self-monitoring is the amount of time between the response and the actual recording. Most people agree that delayed recording of the behavior weakens the efficacy of the monitoring process (Kanfer & Gaelick-Buys, 1991; Kazdin, 1974).

We suggest four guidelines that may help the helper and client decide when to record. First, if the client is using monitoring as a way to *decrease* an undesired behavior, prebehavior monitoring may be more effective, for this seems to interrupt the response chain early in the process. An example for self-monitoring an undesired response would be to record whenever you have the urge to smoke or to eat. Prebehavior monitoring may result in more change than postbehavior monitoring. If the client is using self-monitoring to *increase* a desired response, then postbehavior monitoring may be more helpful. Postbehavior monitoring can make a person more aware of a low-frequency, desirable behavior. Third, recording instances of a desired behavior as it occurs or immediately after it occurs may be most helpful. The guideline is to "record *immediately* after you have the urge to smoke—or *immediately* after you have covertly praised yourself; do not wait even for 15 or 20 minutes, as the impact of recording may be lost." Fourth, the client should be encouraged to record the response when not distracted by the situation or by other competing responses. The client should be instructed to record the behavior *in vivo* as it occurs, if possible, rather than at the end of the day, when he or she is dependent on recall. *In vivo* recording may not always be feasible, and in some cases the client's self-recording may have to be performed later.

Method of Self-Monitoring: How to Record

The helper also needs to instruct the client in a *method* for recording the target responses. McFall (1977) points out that the method of recording can vary in a number of ways:

> It can range from a very informal and unstructured operation, as when subjects are asked to make mental notes of any event that seems related to mood changes, to something fairly formal and structured, as when subjects are asked to fill out a mood-rating sheet according to a time-sampling schedule. It can be fairly simple, as when subjects are asked to keep track of how many cigarettes they smoke in a given time period; or it can be complex and time-consuming, as when they are asked to record not only how many cigarettes they smoke, but also the time, place, circumstances, and affective response associated with lighting each cigarette. It can be a relatively objective matter, as when counting the calories consumed each day; or it can be a very subjective matter, as when recording the number of instances each day when they successfully resist the temptation to eat sweets. (p. 197)

Ciminero and associates (1977, p. 198) suggest that the recording method should be "easy to implement, must produce a representative sample of the target behavior, and must be sensitive to changes in the occurrence of the target behavior." Keep the method informal and unstructured for clients who are not "monitors" or who do not value "tracking" in such a systematic way.

As you may remember from our description of outcome evaluation in Chapter 10, frequency, duration, and intensity can be recorded with either a continuous recording or a time-sampling method. Selection of one of these methods will depend mainly on the type of target response and the frequency of its occurrence. To record the *number* of target responses, the client can use a frequency count. Frequency counts are most useful for monitoring responses that are discrete, do not occur all the time, and are of short duration (Ciminero et al., 1977, p. 190). For instance, clients might record the number of times they have an urge to smoke or the number of times they praise or compliment themselves covertly.

Other kinds of target responses are recorded more easily and accurately by duration. Anytime a client wants to record the amount or length of a response, a duration count can be used. Ciminero and associates (1977, p. 198) recommend the use of a duration measure whenever the target response is not discrete and it varies in length. For example, a client might use a duration count to note the amount of time spent reading textbooks or practicing a competitive sport. Or a client might want to keep track of the length of time spent in a "happy mood."

Sometimes a client may want to record two different responses and use both the frequency and duration methods. For example, a client might use a frequency count to record each urge to smoke and a duration count to monitor the time spent smoking a cigarette. Watson and Tharp (2002) suggest that the helper can recommend frequency counts whenever it is easy to record clearly separate occurrences of the behavior and duration counts whenever the behavior continues for long periods.

Clients can also self-record the intensity of responses whenever data are desired about the relative severity of a response. For example, a client might record the intensity of happy, anxious, or depressed feelings or moods.

Format of Self-Monitoring Instruments

There are many formats of self-monitoring instruments that a client can use to record the frequency, duration, or severity of the target response as well as information about contributing variables. The particular format of the instrument can affect reactivity and can increase client compliance with self-monitoring. The format of the instrument should be tailored to the client situation and goal and to the client. Figure 18.2 shows examples of formats for monitoring instruments. Example 1 in the figure illustrates a thought record, which could be used for a variety of client concerns, particularly those that have a strong mood component (Greenberger & Padesky, 1995). The client records episodes of situations, moods, automatic thoughts and images, evidence that supports the hot thoughts, evidence that does not support the hot thoughts, alternative or balanced thoughts, and a new rating of moods.

Example 2 shows a format useful for relatively frequent recordings—for example, with couples for self-monitoring of the content and quality of their interactions. In this format, each person records the content of the interaction with the partner (for example, having dinner together, talking about finances, discussing work, going to movies, dealing with a parenting issue) and rates the quality of that interaction.

Example 3 shows a format useful when more detail is needed and the client is likely to benefit from having her or his attention directed to components (e.g., what was I saying to myself just then?), to connections (e.g., the types of events that seem to systematically trigger certain reactions), and to the level of one's reaction and views about how it was handled. This format works well with anxiety responses. This format can also be adapted to other covert (internal) responses. Each of these formats can use a variety of self-recording devices.

Example 4 shows a format that may be particularly useful for people with limited verbal skills—for example, young children, people for whom English is not a first language, and individuals with developmental disabilities. The Family SCAMIN (Self-Concept and Motivation Inventory) asks the question "What face would you wear?" to assist clients in indicating their feelings about certain conditions such as how they feel at home (Farrah, Milchus, & Reitz, 1968). Part of the point here is that monitoring tools can used in a range of mediums appropriate to the client and the informational needs.

Devices for Self-Monitoring

Clients often report that one of the most intriguing aspects of self-monitoring involves the device or mechanism used for recording. For recording to occur systematically and accurately, the client must have access to some recording device. A variety of devices have been used to help clients keep accurate records. Note cards, daily log sheets, and diaries can be used to make written notations. A popular self-recording device is a wrist counter, such as a golf counter. The golf counter can be used for self-recording in different settings. If several behaviors are being counted simultaneously, the client can wear several wrist counters or use knitting tallies. A wrist

Example 1
Thought record

1. Situation Who? What? When? Where?	2. Moods a. What did you feel? b. Rate each mood (0–100%).	3. Automatic Thoughts (Images) a. What was going through your mind just before you started to feel this way? Any other thoughts? Images? b. Circle the hot thought.	4. Evidence That Supports the Hot Thought	5. Evidence That Does Not Support Hot Thought	6. Alternative/ Balanced Thoughts a. Write an alternative or balanced thought. b. Rate how much you believe in each alternative or balanced thought (0–100%).	7. Rate Moods Now Rerate moods listed in column 2 as well as any new moods (0–100%).

Figure 18.2 Four examples of formats for self-monitoring instruments

Source: From *Mind over Mood: A Cognitive Therapy Treatment Manual for Clients,* by D. Greenberger and C. A. Padesky, p. 37. Copyright 1995 by The Guilford Press. Reprinted by permission.

Example 2
Content and quality of marital interactions
Record the type of interaction under "Contents." For each interaction, circle one category that best represents the quality of that interaction.

Time	Content of interaction	Quality of interaction				
		Very pleasant	Pleasant	Neutral	Unpleasant	Very unpleasant
6:30 A.M.		++	+	0	−	− −
7:00		++	+	0	−	− −
7:30		++	+	0	−	− −
8:00		++	+	0	−	− −

Example 3
Self-monitoring log for recording anxiety responses
Instructions for recording:

Date and time	Frequency of anxiety response	External events	Internal dialogue (self-statements)	Behavioral factors	Degree of arousal	Skill in handling situation
Record day and time of incident	Describe each situation in which anxiety occurred	Note what triggered the anxiety	Note your thoughts or things you said to yourself when this occurred	Note how you responded— what you did	Rate the intensity of the anxiety: (1) a little intense (2) somewhat intense (3) very intense (4) extremely intense	Rate the degree to which you handled the situation effectively: (1) a little (2) somewhat (3) very (4) extremely

Figure 18.2 Four examples of formats for self-monitoring instruments (continued)

Example 4

Family SCAMIN (Self-Concept and Motivation Inventory)

Name: __Mrs. Lee__

Date: __10/28/90__

Father's Family Surname: __Smith__   Mother's Family Surname: __Jones__

Paternal Grandparents   Maternal Grandparents

Dad   Mom
                68

You and Your Siblings: Me 42, Sis 47, Brother 38

Your Spouse (Current and Past): Lee 42

Your Children: Daughter 16, Son 6

Supportive Friends: Edna 44

Figure 18.2 Four examples of formats for self-monitoring instruments (continued)

Source: From *Clinical Assessment for Social Workers: Quantitative and Qualitative Methods*, by C. Jordan and C. Franklin, p. 419. Copyright 1995 by Lyceum Books, Inc. Reprinted by permission.

counter with rows of beads permits the recording of several behaviors. Audio- and videotapes, toothpicks, or small plastic tokens can also be used as recording devices. Watson and Tharp (2002) report the use of coins: A client can carry coins in one pocket and transfer one coin to another pocket each time a behavior occurs. Children can record frequencies by pasting stars on a chart or by using a countoon, which has pictures and numbers for three recording columns: "What do I do," "My count," and "What happens." Clocks, watches, and kitchen timers can be used for duration counts. The nature of the device depends, of course, on what kind of observations are most useful (e.g., notes about thoughts, feelings, circumstances, and reactions require different devices than those needed for frequency or duration).

Not surprisingly, information technology is opening up new mediums. Many if not most paper-and-pencil formats can be used via a computer and a common word processing program, and some of the multimedia capabilities of computers allow for more engaging devices (such as an art-based program—see McLeod, 1999). For some people, this is a quicker and more accessible approach. As an example, the form can be sent electronically as can responses (aiding with communication between client and helper between sessions, a particularly important issue for people living in more remote or rural locations or with transportation constraints) and is always available in a file or at a Web site. A computer-based format may be easier to keep up with than a piece of paper that's gotten lost in the pile on the dining room table. As with computer-assisted assessment tools, there is some evidence that computers can have a positive impact. For example, Calam and associates (2000) discuss benefits for children and for people with disabilities. McGuire and colleagues (2000) describe advantages of using touchscreen technology that does not require keyboard use. Newman and colleagues (Newman, Consoli, & Taylor, 1997; Newman, Kenardy, Herman, & Taylor, 1997) review the advantages and disadvantages of a number of computer tools in this regard, including the use of palmtop computers that are sufficiently small to be carried at all times (and, thus, more likely to be available in target situations relevant to intervention).

In earlier chapters, we addressed the use of computer-assisted information in practice (Chapter 7), as assessment tools (Chapter 9), and in practice monitoring and evaluation (Chapter 10). Bloom, Fischer, and Orme (1999), Nurius and Hudson (1993), and Nugent, Sieppert, and Hudson (2001) discuss at length computer tools available for use in a variety of direct human service activities as well as for access to evaluation software via the Web (Chapter 10 describes a number of rapid-assessment instruments in paper-and-pencil as well as computer-assisted formats).

The helper and client select a recording device. Here is an opportunity to be inventive! There are several practical criteria to consider in helping a client. The device should be portable and accessible so that it is present whenever the behavior occurs (Watson & Tharp, 2002). It should be easy, convenient, and economical. The obtrusiveness of the device should also be considered. The recording device can function as a cue (discriminative stimulus) for the client to self-monitor, so it should be noticeable enough to remind the client. However, a device that is too obtrusive may draw attention from others who could reward or punish the client for self-monitoring (Ciminero et al., 1977, p. 202). Finally, the device should be capable of giving cumulative frequency data so that the client can chart daily totals of the behavior (Thoresen & Mahoney, 1974). Many of the devices used for practice assessment may be useful for ongoing self-monitoring (see Chapter 10).

After the client has been instructed in the timing and method of recording, and after a recording device has been selected, the client should practice using the recording system. Breakdowns in self-monitoring often occur because a client does not understand the recording process clearly. Rehearsal of the recording procedures may ensure that the client will record accurately. Generally, a client should engage in self-recording for three to four weeks. Usually, the effects of self-monitoring are not apparent in only one or two weeks' time.

Charting of a Response

The data recorded by the client should be translated onto a more permanent storage record such as a chart or graph that will enable the client to inspect the self-monitored data visually. This type of visual guide may provide the occasion for client self-reinforcement (Kanfer & Gaelick-Buys, 1991), which, in turn, can influence the reactivity of self-monitoring. The data can be charted by days, using a simple line graph. For example, a client counting the number of urges to smoke a cigarette could chart these by days, as in Figure 18.3. A client recording the amount of time spent studying each day could use the same sort of line graph to chart duration of study time. The vertical axis would be divided into time intervals such as 15 minutes, 30 minutes, 45 minutes, or 1 hour.

The client should receive either oral or written instructions on a way to chart and graph the daily totals of the recorded response. The helper can assist the client in interpreting the chart in the sessions on data review and analysis. If a client is using self-monitoring to increase a behavior, the line on the graph should go up gradually if the self-monitoring is having the desired effect; if self-monitoring is influencing an

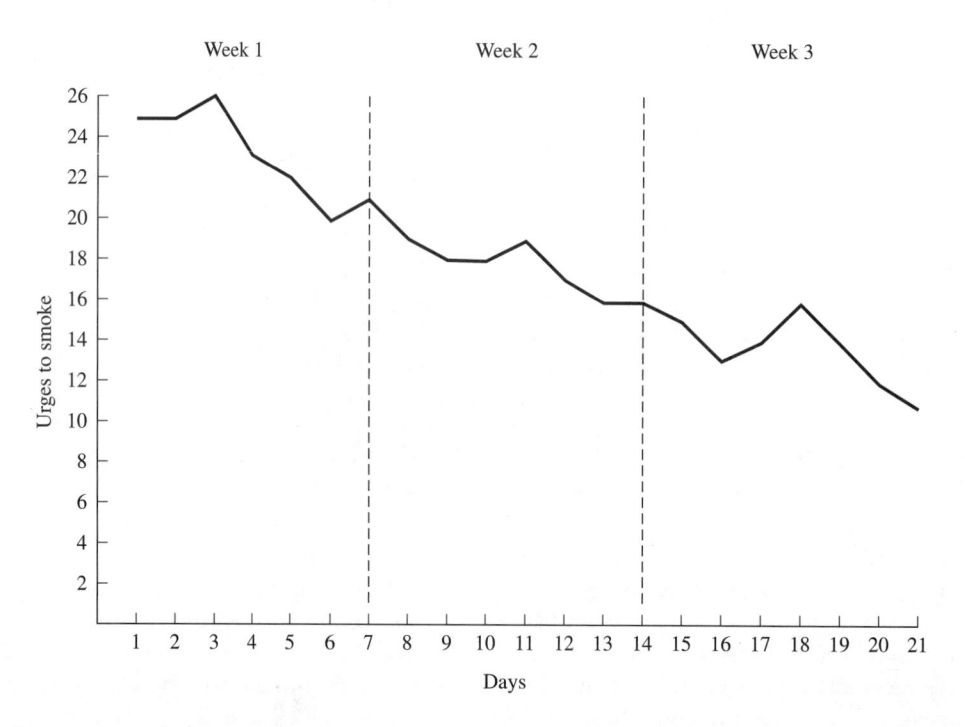

Figure 18.3 Self-monitoring chart

undesired response to decrease, the line on the graph should go down gradually.

Display of Data

After the graph has been made, the client has the option of displaying the completed chart. If the chart is displayed in a "public" area, this display may prompt environmental reinforcement, a necessary part of an effective self-management program. The effects of self-monitoring are usually augmented when the data chart is displayed as a public record. However, some clients will not want to make their data public for reasons of confidentiality or shame avoidance.

Analysis of Data

If the client's recording data are not reviewed and analyzed, the client may soon feel as if he or she was told to make a graph just for practice in drawing straight lines! A very important facet of self-monitoring is the information that it can provide to the client. There is some evidence that people who receive feedback about their self-recording change more than those who do not. The recording and charting of data should be used *explicitly* to provide the client with knowledge of results about behavior or performance. Specifically, the client should bring the data to weekly sessions for review and analysis. In these sessions, the helper can encourage the client to compare the data with the desired goals and standards. The client can use the recorded data for self-evaluation and determine whether the data indicate that the behavior is within or outside the desired limits. The helper can also aid in data analysis by helping the client interpret the data correctly. As Thoresen and Mahoney observe, "Errors about what the charted data represent can seriously hinder success in self-control" (1974, p. 44). Guidance on ways to meaningfully display and analyze client self-monitoring data has been growing in sophistication over the years. Many of the methods and guidelines presented in Chapter 10 for use by helpers can be adapted for client self-monitoring.

MODEL EXAMPLE: SELF-MONITORING

As you may recall from Joan's goal chart in Chapter 10, one of Joan's goals was to increase her positive thoughts (and simultaneously decrease her negative thoughts) about her ability to do well with math. This goal lends itself well to application of self-management strategies for several reasons. First, the goal represents a covert behavior (positive thoughts), which is observable only by Joan. Second, the flip side of the goal (the negative thoughts) represents a very well-learned habit. Probably most of these negative thoughts occur *outside* the sessions. To change this thought pattern, Joan will need to use strategies she can apply frequently (as needed) *in vivo,* and she will need to use strategies that she can administer to herself.

Here is a description of the way that self-monitoring could be used to help Joan achieve this goal:

1. *Treatment rationale.* The helper would provide an explanation of what Joan will self-monitor and why, emphasizing that this is a strategy she can apply herself, can use with a "private" behavior, and can use as frequently as possible in the actual setting.
2. *Discrimination of a response.* The helper would need to help Joan define the target response explicitly. One definition could be "Anytime I think about myself doing math or working with numbers successfully." The helper should provide some possible examples of this response, such as "Gee, I did well on my math homework today" or "I was able to balance my checkbook today." Joan should also be encouraged to identify some examples of the target response. Because Joan wants to increase this behavior, the target response would be stated in the "positive."
3. *Recording of a response.* The helper should instruct Joan in timing, a method, and a device for recording. In this case, because Joan is using self-monitoring to increase a desired behavior, she would use postbehavior monitoring. Joan should be instructed to record *immediately* after a target thought has occurred. She is interested in recording the *number* of such thoughts, so she could use a frequency count. A tally on a note card or a wrist counter could be selected as the device for recording. After these instructions, Joan should practice recording before actually doing it. She should be instructed to engage in self-monitoring for about four consecutive weeks.
4. *Charting of a response.* After each week of self-monitoring, Joan can add her daily frequency totals and chart them by days on a simple line graph, as shown in Figure 18.4. Joan is using self-monitoring to increase a behavior; as a result, if the monitoring has the desired effect, the line on her graph should gradually rise. It is just starting to do so here; additional data for the next few weeks should show a greater increase if the self-monitoring is influencing the target behavior in the desired direction.
5. *Display of data.* After Joan has made a data chart, she may wish to post it in a place such as her room, although this is a very personal decision.
6. *Analysis of data.* During the period of self-monitoring, Joan should bring in her data for weekly review sessions with the helper. The helper can provide reinforcement and

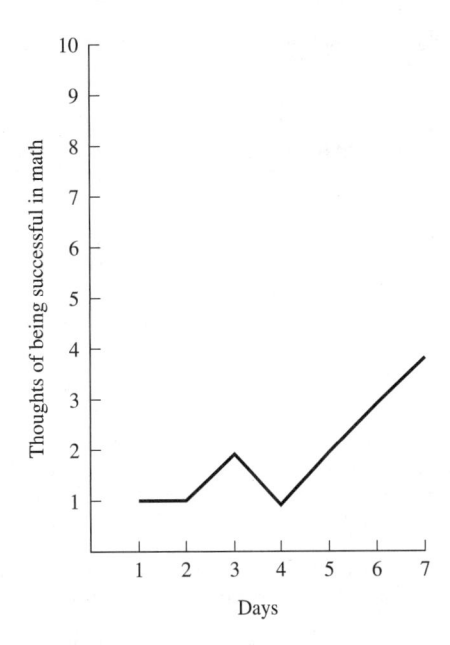

Figure 18.4 Simple line graph for self-monitoring

help Joan interpret the data accurately. Joan can use the data for self-evaluation by comparing the "story" of the data with her stated desired behavior and level of change.

STIMULUS CONTROL

Kanfer and Gaelick-Buys (1991, p. 335) define *stimulus control* as the predetermined arrangement of environmental conditions that makes it impossible or unfavorable for an undesired behavior to occur. Stimulus-control methods emphasize rearranging or modifying environmental conditions that serve as cues or antecedents of a particular response. As you may recall from the discussion of the ABC model of behavior in Chapter 8, a behavior is often guided by certain things that precede it (antecedents) and is maintained by positive or negative events that follow it (consequences). Remember also that both antecedents and consequences can be external (overt) or internal (covert). For example, an antecedent could be a situation, an emotion, a cognition, or an overt or covert verbal instruction.

Clinical Uses of Stimulus Control

Stimulus-control procedures have been used for a wide range of concerns; see Box 18.3 for a sample of recent research on stimulus control. This procedure has been used to treat eating disorders, obesity, fitness activities, toilet training,

> **BOX 18.3 RESEARCH ON STIMULUS CONTROL**
>
> *Bulimia*
> Viens, M. J., & Hranchuk, K. (1992). The treatment of bulimia nervosa following surgery using a stimulus control procedure: A case study. *Journal of Behavior Therapy and Experimental Psychiatry, 23,* 313–317.
>
> *Disability-related*
> Asmus, J. M., Wacker, D. P., Harding, J., Berg, W. K., Derby, K. M., & Kocis, E. (1999). Evaluation of antecedent stimulus parameters for the treatment of escape-maintained aberrant behavior. *Journal of Applied Behavior Analysis, 32,* 495–513.
> Carr, E. G., Yarborough, S. C., & Langdon, N. A. (1997). Effects of idiosyncratic stimulus variables on functional analysis outcomes. *Journal of Applied Behavior Analysis, 30,* 673–686.
> Graff, R. B., Libby, M. E., & Green, G. (1998). The effects of reinforcer choice on rates of challenging behavior and free operant responding in individuals with severe disabilities. *Behavioral Interventions, 13,* 249–268.
> Hanley, G. P., Piazza, C. C., Fisher, W. W., & Adelinis, J. D. (1997). Stimulus control and resistance to extinction in attention-maintained SIB. *Research in Developmental Disabilities. 18,* 251–260.
> Ray, K. P., Skinner, C. H., & Watson, T. S. (1999). Transferring stimulus control via momentum to increase compliance in a student with autism: A demonstration of collaborative consultation. *School Psychology Review, 28,* 622–628.
>
> *Effective teaching*
> Martens, B. K., & Kelly, S. Q. (1993). A behavioral analysis of effective teaching. *School Psychology Quarterly, 8,* 10–26.
>
> *Fitness*
> Estabrooks, P., Courneya, K., & Nigg, C. (1996). Effect of a stimulus control intervention on attendance at a university fitness center. *Behavior Modification, 20,* 202–215.
>
> *Insomnia*
> Jacobs, G. D., Benson, H., & Friedman, R. (1993). Home-based central nervous system assessment of a multifactor behavioral intervention for chronic sleep-onset insomnia. *Behavior Therapy, 24,* 159–174.
> Lichstein, K. L., Wilson, N. M., & Johnson. C. T. (2000). Psychological treatment of secondary insomnia. *Psychology & Aging, 15,* 232–240.
> Reidel, B. W., Lichstein, K. L., Peterson, B. A., Epperson, M. T., Means, M. K., & Aguillard, R. N. (1998). A comparison of the efficacy of stimulus control for medicated and nonmedicated insomniacs. *Behavior Modification, 22,* 3–28.
>
> *Obesity*
> Haddock, C. K., Shadish, W. R., Klesges, R. C., & Stein, R. J. (1994). Treatments for childhood and adolescent obesity. *Annals of Behavioral Medicine, 16,* 235–244.
>
> *Pelvic examination*
> Williams, J. G., Park, L. I., & Kline, J. (1992). Reducing distress associated with pelvic examinations: A stimulus control intervention. *Women and Health, 18,* 41–53.
>
> *Social influence*
> Weatherly, J. N., Miller, K., & McDonald, T. W. (1999). Social influence as stimulus control. *Behavior & Social Issues, 9,* 25–45.
>
> *Toilet training*
> Taylor, S., Cipani, E., & Clardy, A. (1994). A stimulus control technique for improving the efficacy of an established toilet training program. *Journal of Behavior Therapy and Experimental Psychiatry, 25,* 155–160.
>
> *Writing tasks*
> Stromer, R., MacKay, H., Howell, S., & McVay, A. (1996). Teaching computer-based spelling to individuals with developmental and hearing disabilities. Transfer of stimulus control to writing tasks. *Journal of Applied Behavior Analysis, 29,* 25–42.

anxiety, effectiveness in teaching, and resistance and compliance responses. If the number of studies is an indicator, an important use of stimulus control is in the treatment of insomnia. Also notable is the proportion of very recent research with people with learning and related disabilities.

How Antecedents Acquire Stimulus Control

When antecedents are consistently associated with a behavior that is reinforced in the *presence* (not the absence) of these antecedent stimuli, they gain control over the behavior. You might think of this as an antecedent working as a stimulus for a certain response. When an antecedent gains stimulus control over the response, there is a high probability that the response will be emitted in the presence of these particular antecedent events. For example, most of us automatically slow down, put our foot on the brake, and stop the car when we see a red traffic light. The red light is a stimulus that has gained control over our stopping-the-car behavior. Generally, the fact that antecedents exert stimulus control is helpful, as it is in driving: We go when we see a green light and stop at the sight of a red light.

Inappropriate Stimulus Control in Troubling Behavior

Behaviors that trouble clients may occur because of *inappropriate* stimulus control. Inappropriate stimulus control may be related to obesity. Eating responses of overweight people tend to be associated with many environmental cues. If a person eats something not only at the dining table but

TABLE 18.2	Principles and Examples of Stimulus-Control Strategies
Principle of change	

To decrease a behavior:
 Example
	Reduce or narrow the frequency of cues associated with the behavior.
	 1. Prearrange or alter cues associated with the place of the behavior:
	   a. Prearrange cues that make it hard to execute the behavior. Place fattening foods in high, hard-to-reach places.
	   b. Prearrange cues so that they are controlled by others. Ask friends or family to serve you only one helping of food and to avoid serving fattening foods to you.
	 2. Alter the time or sequence (chain) between the antecedent cues and the resulting behaviors:
	   a. Break up the sequence. Buy and prepare food only on a full stomach.
	   b. Change the sequence. Substitute and engage in nonfood activities when you start to move toward snacking (toward refrigerator, cupboard, or candy machine).
	   c. Build pauses into the sequence. Delay second helpings of food or snacks for a predetermined amount of time.

To increase a behavior: Example	Increase or prearrange the cues associated with the response. 1. Seek out these cues deliberately to perform the desired behavior. Initially arrange only one room with a desk to study. When you need to study, go to this place. 2. Concentrate on the behavior when in the situation. Concentrate only on studying in the room. If you get distracted, get up and leave. Don't mix study with other activities, such as listening to records or talking. 3. Gradually extend the behavior to other situations. When you have control over studying in one room, extend the behavior to another conducive room or place. 4. Promote the occurrence of helpful cues by other people or by self-generated reminders. Ask your roommate to remind you to leave the desk when you are talking or distracted; remind yourself of good study procedures by posting a list over your study desk or by using verbal or covert self-instructions.

also when working in the kitchen, watching television, walking by the refrigerator, and stopping at a Dairy Queen, the sheer number of eating responses could soon result in obesity. Too many environmental cues are often related to other client difficulties, particularly "excesses" such as substance use. In these cases, the primary aim of a self-management stimulus-control method is to reduce the number of cues associated with the undesired response, such as eating or smoking.

Other troubling behaviors have been observed that seem to involve excessively narrow stimulus control. At the opposite pole from obesity are people who eat so little that their physical and psychological health suffers (anorexia nervosa). For these people, there are too few eating cues, among other elements involved with this issue. Lack of exercise can be a function of too narrow stimulus control. For some people, the paucity of environmental cues associated with exercise results in very little physical activity. In these cases, the primary aim of a stimulus-control strategy is to establish or increase the number of cues that will elicit the desired behavior.

To summarize, stimulus-control self-management involves reducing the number of antecedent stimuli associated with an undesirable behavior and simultaneously increasing the antecedent cues associated with a desirable response (Mahoney & Thoresen, 1974; Thoresen & Mahoney, 1974). Table 18.2 shows the principal methods of stimulus control and some examples.

Using Stimulus Control to Decrease Behavior

To decrease the rate of a behavior, the antecedent cues associated with the behavior should be reduced in frequency or altered in terms of time and place of occurrence. When cues are separated from the habitual behavior by alteration or elimination, the old, undesired habit can be terminated (Mahoney & Thoresen, 1974, p. 42). Many behavioral "excesses," such as eating, smoking, drinking, or self-criticism, are tied to a great number of antecedent situations. Reducing these cues can restrict the occurrence of the undesired behavior. Existing cues can be prearranged to make the target behavior so hard to execute that the person is unlikely to do it. An example would be altering the place of smoking by moving one's smoking chair to an inconvenient place like the basement. The smoker would have to go downstairs each time she or he wanted a cigarette. Cues can also be prearranged by placing their control in the hands of another person. Giving your pack of cigarettes to a friend is an example of this method. The friend should agree to help you reduce smoking and should agree not to reinforce or punish any instances of your smoking behavior (the undesired response).

A behavior can also be reduced through stimulus control by interrupting the learned pattern or sequence that begins with one or more antecedent cues and results in the undesired response. This sequence may be called a *chain*. A troubling behavior is often the result of a long chain of events. For example, a variety of behaviors make up the sequence of smoking. Before puffing on a cigarette, a person has to go to a store, buy cigarettes, take out one cigarette from the pack, and light the cigarette.

This chain might be interrupted in a number of ways—e.g., breaking up or unlinking the chain of events, changing the chain, or building pauses into the chain (Watson & Tharp, 2002). All these methods involve prearranging or altering the nature of the sequence and how the behavior in question is tied to stimuli events and patterned ways of responding. A chain of events can be broken up by discovering and interrupting an event early in the sequence or by scrambling the typical order of events. For example, the smoker could break up the chain by not going to stores that sell cigarettes. Or, if the smoker typically smokes at certain times, the usual order of events leading to smoking could be mixed up. The smoker could also change the typical chain of events. People who start to light up a cigarette whenever they are bored, tense, or lacking something to do with their hands could perform a different activity at this point, such as calling a friend when bored, relaxing when tense, or knitting or playing cards to provide hand activity. Finally, smokers could interrupt the chain by deliberately building pauses into it. As you may recall, when antecedents exert control over a behavior, the behavior occurs almost automatically. One way to deal with this automatic quality is to pause before responding to a cue. For instance, whenever the smoker has an urge to light up in response to a stress cue, a deliberate pause of ten minutes can be built in before the person actually does light up. Gradually, this time interval can be increased. Deliberately building in pauses to make a record (in a journal, computer notebook, or other monitoring tool) can be useful toward building in reflection—for example, about how one is feeling, thoughts in the moment, environmental conditions of the moment—which can help in breaking behavior chains. Sometimes you can even strengthen the pause procedure by covertly instructing yourself on what you want to do or by thinking about the benefits of not smoking. The pause itself can then become a new antecedent.

Using Stimulus Control to Increase Behavior

Stimulus-control methods can also be used to increase a desired response. As noted in Table 18.2, to increase the rate of a response, a person increases or prearranges the antecedent cues associated with the desired behavior. The person deliberately seeks out these cues to perform the behavior and concentrates only on this behavior when in the situation. Competing or distracting responses must be avoided. Gradually, as stimulus control over the behavior in one situation is achieved, the person can extend the behavior by performing it in another, similar situation. This process of stimulus generalization means that a behavior learned in one situation can be performed in different but similar situations (Watson & Tharp, 2002). The person can promote the occurrence of new antecedent cues by using reminders from others, self-reminders, or overt or covert self-instructions. The rate of a desired response is increased by increasing the times and places in which the person performs the response.

As an example, suppose that you are working with a client who wants to increase his or her amount of daily exercise. First, more cues would be established to which the person would respond with isometric or physical activity. For example, the person might perform isometric activities whenever sitting in a chair or waiting for a traffic light. Or the person might perform physical exercises each morning and evening on a special exercise mat. The client would seek out these prearranged cues and concentrate on performing the activity while in the situation. Other behaviors should not be performed while in these situations, as a competing response could interfere with the exercise activity (Watson & Tharp, 2002). Gradually, the client could extend the exercise activities to new but similar situations—for example, doing isometrics while sitting on the floor or waiting for a meeting to start. The person could also promote exercise behavior in these situations by reminders—posting an exercise chart on the wall or carrying it around in a pocket or wallet, displaying an exercise list, and so forth.

Stimulus-control instructions have also been used to increase sleep. For example, clients were instructed as follows: (1) Go to bed or lie down to sleep only when sleepy. (2) Do not read, watch TV, or eat in bed—use the bed only for sleeping and/or sexual activities. (3) If unable to fall asleep after 10 to 20 minutes, get out of bed and engage in some activity. Return to bed only when sleepy—and continue this procedure throughout the night as necessary. (4) Set the alarm clock and get up at the same time every morning regardless of the amount of sleep obtained during the night. (5) Do not take naps during the day.

According to Kanfer and Gaelick-Buys (1991, p. 335), one advantage of stimulus control is that only minimal self-initiated steps are required to trigger environmental changes that effect desired or undesired responses. However, stimulus-control methods are often insufficient to modify behavior without the support of other strategies. As Mahoney and Thoresen (1974) observe, stimulus-control methods are usually not sufficient for long-term self-change unless accompanied by other self-management methods that exert control over the *consequences* of the target behavior. One self-management method that involves self-presented consequences is discussed in the following section, and illustrated in Learning Activity 18.2.

MODEL EXAMPLE: STIMULUS CONTROL

This model example will illustrate how stimulus control can be used as one way to help Joan achieve her goal of increasing positive thoughts about her math ability. Recall that the principle of change in using stimulus control to increase a behavior is to increase the cues associated with the behavior. Here's how we would implement this principle with Joan:

1. Establish at least one cue that Joan could use as an antecedent for positive thoughts. We might suggest something like putting a piece of tape over her watch.
2. Develop a list of several positive thoughts about math. Each thought could be written on a blank card that Joan could carry with her.
3. Instruct Joan to read or think about a thought on one card *each* time that she looks at her watch. Instruct her to seek out the opportunity deliberately by looking at her watch frequently and then concentrating on one of these positive thoughts.
4. When Joan gets to the point that she automatically thinks of a positive thought after looking at her watch, other cues can be established that she can use in the same way. For instance, she can put a smiley face ☺ on her math book. Each time she gets out her math book and sees the "smiley face," she can use this cue to concentrate on another positive thought.
5. She can promote more stimulus control over these thoughts by using reminders. For instance, Joan could put a list of positive thoughts on the mirror or on the closet door in her room. Each time she sees the list, it serves as a reminder. Or she can ask a friend or classmate to remind her to "think positively" whenever the subject of math or math class is being discussed.

LEARNING ACTIVITY 18.2 Stimulus Control

The emphasis in this chapter is on self-management, so the learning activities are designed to help you use these strategies yourself. The purpose of this learning activity is to help you reduce an unwanted behavior, using stimulus-control methods.

1. Specify a behavior that you find undesirable and you wish to decrease. It can be an overt one, such as smoking, eating, biting your nails, or making sarcastic comments, or it can be a covert behavior, such as thinking about yourself in negative ways or thinking how great food or smoking tastes.
2. Select one or more stimulus-control methods to use for behavior reduction from the list and examples given in Table 18.2. Remember, you will be reducing the number of cues or antecedent events associated with this behavior by altering the times and places the undesired response occurs.
3. Implement these stimulus-control methods daily for two weeks.
4. During the two weeks, engage in self-monitoring of your target response. Record the type and use of your method and the amount of your target behavior, using frequency or duration methods of recording.
5. At the end of two weeks, review your recording data. Did you use your selected method consistently? If not, what contributed to your infrequent use? If you used it consistently, did you notice any gradual reduction in the target behavior by the end of two weeks? What problems did you encounter in applying a stimulus-control method with yourself? What did you learn about stimulus control that might help you when using it with clients?

SELF-REWARD: PROCESSES AND USES

Self-monitoring and stimulus-control procedures may be enough to maintain the desired goal behavior for many people. However, for some people with low self-esteem, depression, strong emotional reactions, environmental consequences, or low self-efficacy, self-monitoring may not always be effective in regulating behavior (Kanfer & Gaelick-Buys, 1991). In such cases, self-reward procedures are used to help clients regulate and strengthen their behavior with the aid of self-produced consequences. Many actions of an individual are controlled by self-produced consequences as much as by external consequences.

According to Bandura (1971), there are several necessary conditions of self-reinforcement, or self-reward:

1. The individual (rather than someone else) determines the criteria for adequacy of her or his performance and for resulting reinforcement.
2. The individual (rather than someone else) controls access to the reward.
3. The individual (rather than someone else) is his or her own reinforcing agent and administers the rewards.

Note that self-reward involves *both* the self-determination and the self-administration of a reward. This distinction has, at times, been overlooked in self-reinforcement research and application. Nelson, Hayes, Spong, Jarrett, and McKnight (1983, p. 565) propose that "self-reinforcement is effective primarily because of its stimulus properties in cuing natural environmental consequences."

As a self-management procedure, self-reward is used to strengthen or increase a desired response. The operations involved in self-reward are assumed to parallel those that occur in external reinforcement. In other words, a self-presented reward, like an externally administered reward, is defined by the function it exerts on the target behavior. A reinforcer (self or external) is something that when administered following a target response, tends to maintain or increase the probability of that response in the future. A major advantage of self-reward over external reward is that a person can use and apply this strategy independently.

Self-rewards can be classified into two categories: positive and negative. In positive self-reward, one presents oneself with a positive stimulus (to which one has free access) *after* engaging in a specified behavior. Examples of positive reward include praising yourself after you have completed a long and difficult task, buying yourself a new compact disk after you have engaged in a specified amount of piano practice, or imagining that you are resting on your favorite spot after you have completed your daily exercises. Negative self-reward involves the removal of a negative stimulus after execution of a target response. For example, taking down an uncomplimentary picture or chart from your wall after performing the target response is an example of negative self-reward.

Our discussion of self-reward as a therapeutic strategy is limited to the use of positive self-reward for several reasons. First, there has been very little research to validate the negative self-reward procedure. Second, by definition, negative self-reward involves an aversive activity. It is usually unpleasant for a person to keep suet in the refrigerator or to put an ugly picture on the wall. Many people will not use a strategy that is aversive. Second, we do not recommend that helpers suggest strategies that seem aversive, because the client may feel that terminating the helping relationship is preferable to engaging in an unpleasant change process.

Research on Self-Reward

As with other management strategies, self-reward has been used in many clinical applications. Recent research illustrates some of those uses. In some instances, self-reward is part of a cluster of interventions—for example, as one component used with developmental disabilities (Harchik, Sherman, & Sheldon, 1992), promoting physical activity and behavioral control with elementary-age children (Cromie & Baker, 1997; Marcoux et al., 1999), enhancing the academic productivity of secondary students with learning problems (Seabaugh & Schumaker, 1994), and treating an 11-year-old girl fearful of AIDS infection, other diseases, and poisoning (Hagopian, Weist, & Ollendick, 1990). Research has reported the effective use of self-reward to help with weight loss, improve study skills, enhance dating skills, and increase the activity levels of depressed persons. Other research has explored moderating variables and alternative reward sources. For example, Enzle, Roggeveen, and Look (1991) found that ambiguous standards of performance coupled with self-administration of rewards reduced intrinsic motivation whereas clear standards with self-administration of rewards maintained high levels of intrinsic motivation. Solomon and colleagues (1998) found that external monetary rewards appeared more compelling than self-reward suggestions in fostering breast self-exams. Research has also examined factors that may interfere with one's capacity to productively use self-reward. This includes people with depression and self-defeating attitudes and those with persistent pain (Kaoly & Lecci, 1997; Schill & Kramer, 1991). Finally, variables have recently been examined relative to their likely support of self-reward. This includes Field and Steinhardt's (1992) findings that a lower external locus of control score was associated with higher positive self-reinforcement and the importance of explicit goals (preferably self-chosen) as part of change strategies involving self-reward (Fuhrmann & Kuhl, 1998; Kuhl & Baumann, 2000). Collectively, this work indicates the importance of client state variables and environmental demand characteristics in the application of a self-reward strategy.

Some of the clinical effects typically attributed to the self-reinforcement procedure may also be due to certain external factors, including a client's previous reinforcement history, client goal setting, the role of client self-monitoring, surveillance by another person, external contingencies in the client's environment, and the instructional set given to the client about the self-reward procedure. The exact role that these external variables may play in self-reward is still relatively unknown. However, a helper should acknowledge and perhaps try to capitalize on some of these factors to heighten the clinical effects of a self-reward strategy.

COMPONENTS OF SELF-REWARD

Self-reward involves planning by the client of appropriate rewards and of the conditions in which they will be used. Self-reward can be described by four major components: (1) selection of appropriate self-rewards, (2) delivery of self-rewards, (3) timing of self-rewards, and (4) planning for self-change maintenance. These components are described in this portion of the chapter and are summarized in the following list. Although these components are discussed separately, remember that all of them are integral parts of an effective self-reward procedure.

1. Selection of appropriate rewards
   a. Individualize the reward.
   b. Use accessible rewards.
   c. Use several rewards.
   d. Use different types of rewards (verbal/symbolic, material, imaginal, current, potential).
   e. Use potent rewards.
   f. Use rewards that are not punishing to others.
   g. Match rewards to target response.
   h. Use rewards that are relevant to the client's culture, gender, age, class, and so on.
2. Delivery of self-rewards
   a. Self-monitor for data of target response.
   b. Specify what and how much is to be done for a reward.
   c. Specify frequent reinforcement in small amounts for different levels of target response.
3. Timing of self-reward
   a. Reward should come after, not before, behavior.
   b. Rewards should be immediate.
   c. Rewards should follow performance, not promises.
4. Planning for self-change maintenance
   a. Enlist help of others in sharing or dispensing rewards (if desired).
   b. Review data with helper.

Selection of Appropriate Rewards

In helping a client to use self-reward effectively, some time and planning must be devoted to selecting rewards that are appropriate for the client and the desired target behavior. Selecting rewards can be time-consuming. However, effective use of self-reward is somewhat dependent on the availability of events that are truly reinforcing to the client. The helper can assist the client in selecting appropriate self-rewards; however, the client should have the major role in determining the specific contingencies.

Rewards can take many different forms. A self-reward may be verbal/symbolic, material, or imaginal. One verbal/symbolic reward is self-praise, such as thinking or telling oneself "I did a good job." This sort of reward may be especially useful with a very self-critical client (Kanfer & Gaelick-Buys, 1991). A material reward is something tangible—an event (such as a movie), a purchase (such as a banana split), or a token or point that can be exchanged for a reinforcing event or purchase. An imaginal reinforcer is the covert visualization of a scene or situation that is pleasurable and produces good feelings. Imaginal reinforcers might include picturing yourself as a thin person after losing weight or imagining that you are waterskiing on a lake you have all to yourself.

Self-rewards can also be classified as current or potential. A current reward is something pleasurable that happens routinely or occurs daily, such as eating, talking to a friend, or reading a newspaper. A potential reward is something that would be new and different if it happened, something that a person does infrequently or anticipates doing in the future. Examples of potential rewards include going on a vacation or buying a "luxury" item (something you love but rarely buy for yourself, not necessarily something expensive). Engaging in a "luxury" activity—something you rarely do—can be a potential reinforcer. For a person who is very busy and constantly working, "doing nothing" might be a luxury activity that is a potential reinforcer.

In selecting appropriate self-rewards, a client should consider the availability of these various kinds of rewards. We believe that a well-balanced self-reward program involves a *variety* of types of self-rewards. A helper might encourage a client to select *both* verbal/symbolic and material rewards.

Relying only on material rewards may ignore the important role of positive self-evaluations in a self-change program. Further, material rewards have been criticized for overuse and misuse. Imaginal reinforcers may not be so powerful as verbal/symbolic and material ones. However, they are completely portable and can be used to supplement verbal/symbolic and material rewards when it is impossible for an individual to use these other types (Watson & Tharp, 2002).

In selecting self-rewards, a client should also consider the use of both current and potential rewards. One of the easiest ways for a client to use current rewards is to observe what daily thoughts or activities are reinforcing and then to rearrange these so that they are used in contingent rather than noncontingent ways (Watson & Tharp, 2002). However, whenever a client uses a current reward, some deprivation or self-denial is involved. For example, agreeing to read the newspaper only after cleaning the kitchen involves initially denying oneself some pleasant, everyday event in order to use it to reward a desired behavior. As Thoresen and Mahoney (1974) point out, this initial self-denial introduces an aversive element into the self-reward strategy. Some people do not respond well to any aversiveness associated with self-change or self-directed behavior. One of the authors, in fact, consistently "abuses" the self-reward principle by doing the reward before the response (reading the paper before cleaning the kitchen)—precisely as a reaction against the aversiveness of this "programmed" self-denial. One way to prevent self-reward from becoming too much like programmed abstinence is to have the client select novel or potential reinforcers to use in addition to current ones.

There are several ways that a helper can help a client identify and select various kinds of self-rewards. One way is simply with verbal report. The helper and client can discuss current self-reward practices and desired luxury items and activities (Kanfer & Gaelick-Buys, 1991). The client can also identify rewards by using *in vivo* observation. The client should be instructed to observe and list current consequences that seem to maintain some behaviors. Finally, the client can identify and select rewards by completing preference and reinforcement surveys. A preference survey is designed to help the client identify preferred and valued activities. Here is an example of one that Watson and Tharp (2002, p. 203) recommend:

1. What will be the rewards of achieving your goal?
2. What kind of praise do you like to receive, from yourself or from others?
3. What kinds of things do you like to have?
4. What are your major interests?
5. What are your hobbies?
6. What people do you like to be with?
7. What do you like to do with those people?
8. What do you do for fun?
9. What do you do to relax?
10. What do you do to get away from it all?
11. What makes you feel good?
12. What would be a nice present to receive?
13. What kinds of things are important to you?
14. What would you buy if you had an extra $20? $50? $100?
15. On what do you spend your money each week?
16. What behaviors do you perform every day? (Don't overlook the obvious or the commonplace.)
17. Are there any behaviors that you usually perform instead of the target behavior?
18. What would you hate to lose?
19. Of the things you do every day, which would you hate to give up?
20. What are your favorite daydreams and fantasies?
21. What are the most relaxing scenes you can imagine?

The client can complete this sort of preference survey in writing or in a discussion. Clients who find it difficult to identify rewarding events might also benefit from completing a more formalized reinforcement survey, such as the Reinforcement Survey Schedule or the Children's Reinforcement Survey Schedule, written by Cautela (1977). The client can be given homework assignments to identify possible verbal/symbolic and imaginal reinforcers. For instance, the client might be asked to make a daily list for a week of positive self-thoughts or of the positive consequences of desired change. Or the client could make a list of all the things about which she or he likes to daydream or of some imagined scenes that would be pleasurable (Watson & Tharp, 2002).

Sometimes a client may seem thwarted in initial attempts to use self-reward because of difficulties in identifying rewards. Watson and Tharp (2002) note that people whose behavior consumes the reinforcer (such as smoking or eating), whose behavior is reinforced intermittently, or whose avoidance behavior is maintained by negative reinforcement may not be able to identify reinforcing consequences readily. Individuals who are locked into demanding schedules may not be able to find daily examples of reinforcers. Depressed people sometimes have trouble identifying reinforcing events. In these cases, the helper and client have several options that can be used to overcome difficulties in selecting effective self-rewards.

A client who does not have the time or money for material rewards might use imaginal rewards. Imagining pleasant scenes following a target response has been described by Cautela (1970) as *covert positive reinforcement* (CPR). In the CPR procedure, the client usually imagines performing a desired behavior, followed by imagination of a reinforcing scene. A helper might consider use of imaginal reinforcers only when other kinds of reinforcers are not available.

A second available option is to use a client's everyday activity as a self-reward. Some clinical cases have used a mundane activity such as answering the phone or opening the daily mail as the self-reward. (Actually, such an activity may work more as a cuing device than a reinforcer—see Thoresen and Mahoney, 1974). If a frequently occurring behavior is used as a self-reward, it should be a desirable or at least a neutral activity. As Watson and Tharp (2002) note, clients should not use as a self-reward any high-frequency behavior that they would stop immediately if they could. Using a negative high-frequency activity as a reward may seem more like punishment than reinforcement.

With depressed clients, selecting self-rewards is often difficult because many events lose their reinforcing value for someone who is depressed. Before using self-reward with a depressed client, it might be necessary to increase the reinforcing value of certain events. Anton, Dunbar, and Friedman (1976) describe the procedure of "anticipation training" designed to increase depressed clients' positive anticipations of events. In anticipation training, a client identifies and schedules several pleasant events to perform and then constructs three positive anticipation statements for each activity. The client imagines engaging in an activity and imagines the anticipation statements associated with the activity. An example adapted from Anton and colleagues of some anticipation statements for one activity appears below:

Activity planned: *Spending an afternoon at the lake*
Date to be carried out: *Tuesday; Wednesday if it rains Tuesday*
I will enjoy: *sitting on the beach reading a book*
I will enjoy: *getting in the water on a hot day*
I will enjoy: *getting fresh air*

No thought, event, or imagined scene is reinforcing for everyone. Often, what one person finds rewarding is very different from the rewards selected by someone else. In using self-reward, it is important to help clients choose rewards that will work well for *them*—not for the helper, a friend, or a spouse. Kanfer and Gaelick-Buys (1991) note the importance of considering the client's history and also of taking into account the client's gender, culture, age, class, and personal preferences.

The helper should use the following guidelines to help the client determine some self-rewards that might be used effectively.
1. *Individualize* the reward to the client.
2. The reward should be *accessible* and *convenient* to use after the behavior is performed.
3. *Several* rewards should be used interchangeably to prevent satiation (a reward can lose its reinforcing value because of repeated presentations).
4. Different *types* of rewards should be selected (verbal/symbolic, material, imaginal, current, potential).
5. The rewards should be *potent* but not so valuable that an individual will not use them contingently.
6. The rewards should not be *punishing* to others. Watson and Tharp (2002) suggest that if a reward involves someone else, the other person's agreement should be obtained.
7. The reward should be *compatible* with the desired response (Kanfer & Gaelick-Buys, 1991). For instance, a person losing weight might use new clothing as a reward or thoughts of a new body image after weight loss. Using eating as a reward is not a good match for a weight-loss target response.
8. The rewards should be relevant to the client's values and circumstances as well as appropriate to her or his culture, gender, age, socioeconomic status, and any other salient features (e.g., personality and personal philosophy).

Delivery of Self-Reward

The second part of working out a self-reward strategy with a client involves specifying the conditions and method of delivering the self-rewards. First, a client cannot deliver or administer a self-reward without some data. Self-reward delivery is dependent on systematic data gathering; self-monitoring is an essential first step.

Second, the client should determine the precise conditions under which a reward will be delivered. The client should, in other words, state the rules of the game. The client should know *what* and *how much* has to be done before administering a self-reward. Self-reward is usually more effective when clients reward themselves for small steps of progress. In other words, performance of a subgoal should be rewarded. Waiting to reward oneself for demonstration of the overall goal usually introduces too much of a delay between responses and rewards.

Finally, the client should indicate how much and what kind of reward will be given for performing various responses or different levels of the goals. The client should specify that doing so much of the response results in one type of reward and how much of it. Reinforcement is usually more effective when broken down into smaller units that are self-administered more frequently. The use of tokens or points provides for frequent, small units of reinforcement; these can be exchanged for a "larger" reinforcer after a certain amount of points or tokens are accumulated. Learning Activity 18.3 walks you through a self-reward exercise with questions to consider.

Timing of Self-Reward

The helper also needs to instruct the client about the timing of self-reward—when a self-reward should be administered. There are three ground rules for the timing of a self-reward:

1. A self-reward should be administered *after* performing the specified response, not before.
2. A self-reward should be administered *immediately* after the response. Long delays may render the procedure ineffective.
3. A self-reward should follow *actual performance,* not promises to perform.

Planning for Self-Change Maintenance

Self-reward, like any self-change strategy, needs environmental support for long-term maintenance of change (Kanfer & Gaelick-Buys, 1991; Mahoney & Thoresen, 1974). The last part of using self-reward involves helping the client find ways to plan for self-change maintenance. First, the helper can give the client the option of enlisting the help of others in a self-reward program. Other people can share in or dispense some of the reinforcement if the client is comfortable with this idea (Watson & Tharp, 2002). Some evidence indicates that certain people may benefit more from self-reward if initially in the program they have received their rewards from others (Mahoney & Thoresen, 1974). Second, the client should plan to review with the helper the data collected during self-reward. The review sessions give the helper a chance to reinforce the client and to help the client make any necessary revisions in the use of the strategy. Helper expectations and approval for client progress may add to the overall effects of the self-reward strategy if the helper serves as a reinforcer to the client.

Some Cautions in Using Rewards

The use of rewards as a motivational and informational device is a controversial issue (Eisenberger & Cameron, 1996). Using rewards, especially material ones, as incentives has been criticized on the grounds that tangible rewards are overused, are misused, and often discourage rather than encourage the client.

As a change strategy, self-reward should not be used indiscriminately. Before suggesting self-reward, the helper should carefully consider the individual client, the client's previous reinforcement history, and the client's desired change. Self-reward may not be appropriate for clients from cultural backgrounds in which the use of rewards is considered "undesirable or immodest" (Kanfer & Gaelick-Buys, 1991, p. 338). When a helper and client do decide to use self-reward, two cautionary guidelines should be followed. First, material rewards should not be used solely or indiscriminately. The helper should seek ways to increase a person's intrinsic satisfaction in performance before automatically resorting to extrinsic rewards as a motivational technique. Second, the helper's role in self-reward should be limited to providing instructions about the procedure and encouragement for progress. The client should be the one who selects the rewards and determines the criteria for delivery and timing of reinforcement. When the target behaviors and the contingencies are specified by someone other than the person using self-reward, the procedure can hardly be described accurately as a self-change operation.

MODEL EXAMPLE: SELF-REWARD

This example will illustrate how self-reward could be used to help Joan increase her positive thoughts about her ability to do well in math:

1. *Selection of rewards:* First, the helper would help Joan select some appropriate rewards to use for reaching her predetermined goal. The helper would encourage Joan to identify some self-praise she could use to reward herself symbolically or verbally ("I did it"; "I can gradually see my attitude about math changing"). Joan could give herself points for daily positive thoughts. She could accumulate and exchange the points for material rewards, including current rewards (such as engaging in a favorite daily event) and potential rewards (such as a purchase of a desired item). These are suggestions; Joan should be responsible for the actual selection. The helper could suggest that Joan identify possible rewards through observation or completion of a preference survey. The helper should make sure that the rewards that Joan selects are accessible and easy to use. Several rewards should be selected to prevent satiation. The helper should also make sure that the rewards selected are potent, compatible with Joan's goal, not punishing to anyone else, and relevant to Joan.
2. *Delivery of rewards:* The helper would help Joan determine guidelines for delivery of the rewards selected. Joan

> ### LEARNING ACTIVITY 18.3 Self-Reward
>
> This learning activity is designed to have you engage in self-reward.
>
> 1. Select a target behavior you want to increase. Write down your goal (the behavior to increase, desired level of increase, and conditions in which behavior will be demonstrated).
> 2. Select several types of self-rewards to use, and write them down. The types to use are verbal/symbolic, material (both current and potential), and imaginal. See whether your selected self-rewards meet the following criteria:
>   a. Individually tailored to you?
>   b. Accessible and convenient to use?
>   c. Several self-rewards?
>   d. Different types of self-rewards?
>   e. Potent rewards?
>   f. Rewards not punishing to others?
>   g. Rewards compatible with your desired goal?
>   h. Rewards relevant to your gender and culture?
> 3. Set up a plan for delivery of your self-reward: What type of reinforcement and how much will be administered? How much and what demonstration of the target behavior are required?
> 4. When do you plan to administer a self-reward?
> 5. How could you enlist the aid of another person?
> 6. Apply self-reward for a specified time period. Did your target response increase? To what extent?
> 7. What did you learn about self-reward that might help you in suggesting its use to diverse groups of clients?

might decide to give herself a point for each positive thought. This allows for reinforcement of small steps toward the overall goal. A predetermined number of daily points, such as 5, might result in delivery of a current reward, such as watching TV or going over to her friend's house. A predetermined number of weekly points could mean delivery of a potential self-reward, such as going to a movie or purchasing a new item. Joan's demonstration of her goal beyond the specified level could result in the delivery of a bonus self-reward.

3. *Timing of rewards:* The helper would instruct Joan to administer the reward *after* the positive thoughts or after the specified number of points is accumulated. The helper can emphasize that the rewards follow performance, not promises. The helper should encourage Joan to engage in the rewards as soon as possible after the daily and weekly target goals have been met.
4. *Planning for self-change maintenance:* The helper can help Joan find ways to plan for self-change maintenance. One way is to schedule periodic "check-ins" with the helper. In addition, Joan might select a friend who could help her share in the reward by watching TV or going shopping with her or by praising Joan for her goal achievement.

SELF-AS-A-MODEL

The self-as-a-model procedure uses the client as the model. The procedure as we present it in this chapter has been developed primarily by Hosford (1974). Hosford and de Visser (1974) have described self-modeling as a procedure in which the client sees himself or herself as the model—performing the goal behavior in the desired manner. The client also practices with an audiotape. Successful practices are rewarded, and errors are corrected. Note that this procedure involves not only modeling but also practice and feedback.

Why have the client serve as the model? The literature indicates that such model characteristics as prestige, status, age, sex, and ethnic identification have differential influence on clients (Bandura, 1969, 1971). For some people, observing another person—even one with similar characteristics—may produce negative reactions. Some people may attend and listen better when they hear or see themselves on tape or on video (Hosford, Moss, & Morrell, 1976). For example, when we perform in front of a video camera or a tape recorder, we have to admit there is a little exhibitionist or "ham" in each of us.

Dowrick (1999) reviewed studies on self-as-a-model, noting its use from toddlers to grandparents and across a range of targets such as physical skills (rehabilitation and sports), academic and vocational goals, communication, and personal and social adjustment. In general, Dowrick suggests that self-as-a-model using images of one's future success may be more fruitful than other approaches (e.g., as an extension of peer modeling). Recent research has applied self-as-a-model to decrease issues such as disruptive behavior (Possell, Kehle, McLoughlin, & Bray, 1999), stuttering (Bray & Kehle, 1998), mutism (Kehle, Madaus, Baratta, & Bray, 1998), inappropriate sexual behavior (Dowrick & Ward,

1997), and fear responses (Schwartz, Houlihan, Kreuger, & Simon, 1997). Self-as-a-model has also been found successful to increase targeted goals, such as task behavior (Clare, Jenson, Kehle, & Bray, 2000), appropriate responding with autistic children (Buggey, Toombs, Gardener, & Cervetti, 1999), performance success in young gymnasts (Winfrey & Weeks, 1993), focus and math performance in ADHD children (Woltersdorf, 1992), classroom participation (Hartley, Bray, & Kehle, 1998), and how to request needed assistance among preschoolers with developmental disabilities (Hepting & Goldstein, 1996).

The behavior to be modeled should cohere with the client's age, gender, and culture. We have adopted five steps associated with the self-as-a-model procedure from Hosford and de Visser (1974). These five components, which are illustrated in the Checklist for Self-As-a-Model on p. 613, are the following:

1. Rationale about the strategy
2. Recording the desired behaviors on tape
3. Editing the tape
4. Demonstrating with the edited tape
5. Homework: client self-observation and practice

Treatment Rationale

After the client and helper have reviewed the troubling behaviors and the goal behaviors, the helper presents a treatment rationale for the self-as-a-model procedure to the client. The helper might say something like this:

> The procedure we are going to use is based on the idea that people learn new habits or skills by observing other people in various situations [reason]. The way this is done is that people watch other people doing things or they observe a film or tape of people doing things. What we are going to do is vary this procedure a little by having you observe yourself rather than someone else. The way we can do this is to videotape [or audiotape] your desired behavior, and then you can see [hear] yourself on the tape performing the behavior. After that, you will practice the behavior that you saw [heard] on the tape, and I will give you feedback about your practice performance. I think that seeing yourself perform and practice these behaviors will help you acquire these skills [overview]. How does this sound to you? [client's willingness]

Of course, this is only one version of the rationale for the self-as-a-model procedure that a helper might use. A helper could add "Seeing yourself perform these behaviors will give you confidence in acquiring these skills." This statement emphasizes the cognitive component of the self-as-a-model strategy: By using oneself as the model, one sees oneself coping with a formerly anxiety-arousing or difficult situation.

Recording the Desired Behaviors

The desired goal behaviors are recorded on audio- or videotape first. For example, one particular client may need to acquire several assertion skills, such as expression of personal opinions using a firm and strong voice tone, delivery of opinions without errors in speech, and delivery of the assertive message without response latency (within 5 seconds after the other person's message). For this example, the helper and client might start with voice tone and record the client expressing opinions to another person in a firm, strong voice. The helper might have to coach the client so that at least some portion of the taped message reflects this desired response. The tape should be long enough that the client will later be able to hear himself or herself expressing opinions in a firm voice throughout several verbal exchanges with the other person. The helper might have to spend a great deal of time staging the recording sessions in order to obtain tapes of the client's goal behavior. A dry run might be helpful before the actual tape is made.

Sometimes the helper can instruct clients to obtain recordings of their behavior *in vivo*. For example, clients who stutter could be asked to audiotape their interactions with others during designated times of the week. We have also suggested such recordings to people who felt incompetent in talking with those of the other sex. The advantage of *in vivo* recordings is that examples of the client's actual behavior in real-life situations are obtained. However, it is not always possible or desirable to do this, particularly if the client's baseline level of performing the desired skill is very low. Whether tapes are made *in vivo* or in the session, the recording is usually repeated until a sample of the desired behavior is obtained.

Editing the Tape

Next, the helper will edit the audio- or videotape recordings so that the client will see or hear *only* the appropriate (goal) behavior. Hosford and colleagues (1976) recommend that the "inappropriate" behaviors be deleted from the tape, leaving a tape of only the desired responses. The purpose in editing out the inappropriate behaviors is to provide the client with a positive, or self-enhancing, model. It is analogous to weeding out the dandelions in a garden and leaving the daffodils. In our example, we would edit out portions of the tape when the client did not express opinions in a strong voice and leave in all the times when the client did use a firm voice. For the stutterer, the stuttering portions of the tape would be deleted so that the edited tape included only portions of conversations in which stuttering did not occur.

Demonstrating with the Edited Tape

After the tape has been edited, the helper plays it for the client. First, the client is told what to observe on the tape. For our examples of stuttering and assertion training, the helper might say "Listen to the tape and notice that, in these conversations you have had, you are able to talk without stuttering" or "Note that you are maintaining eye contact when you are delivering a message to the other person."

After these instructions, the helper and client play back the tape. If the tape is long, it can be stopped at various points to obtain the client's reaction. At these points, or after the tape playback, it is important for the helper to give encouragement or positive feedback to the client for demonstrating the desired behavior.

After the tape playback, the client should practice behaviors that were demonstrated on the tape. The helper can prompt successful practice by coaching, rewarding successes, and correcting errors. This component of self-as-a-model relies heavily on practice and feedback.

Homework: Client Self-Observation and Practice

The client may benefit more from the self-as-a-model strategy when the edited tape is used in conjunction with practice outside the interview. The helper can instruct the client to use a self-model audiotape as a homework aid by listening to it daily. (For homework purposes, the use of a videotape may not be practical.) After each daily use of the taped playback, the client should practice the target behavior covertly or overtly. The client could also be instructed to practice the behavior without the tape. Gradually, the client should be instructed to use the desired responses in actual instances outside the interview setting. In addition, the client should record the number of practice sessions and the measurement of the goal behaviors on a log sheet. And, as with any homework assignment, the helper should arrange for a follow-up after the client completes some portion of the homework. The following checklist for self-as-a-model illustrates these steps.

Checklist for Self-As-a-Model

Rationale About Strategy

_____ 1. Helper provides rationale about strategy.
_____ 2. Helper provides overview of strategy.
_____ 3. Helper determines client's willingness to try strategy.

Recording Desired Behaviors

_____ 4. Helper breaks desired behaviors into subskills.
_____ 5. For each subskill, helper coaches client about ways to perform successfully.
_____ 6. Client performs skill, using helper or tape for feedback.
_____ 7. Client records self demonstrating skill on video- or audiotape. Recording occurs in the interview or *in vivo* situation outside the session. Recording is repeated until sample of desired behavior is obtained.

Editing the Tape

_____ 8. Helper edits tape so that a clear picture of client's desired behavior is evident and instances of undesired behavior are deleted.

Demonstrating with the Edited Tape

_____ 9. Client is instructed about what to look or listen for during tape playback.
_____ 10. Helper initiates playback of edited tape for client observation.
_____ 11. Helper provides positive feedback to client for demonstration of desired behavior on tape.
_____ 12. Helper initiates client practice of taped behaviors; successes are rewarded and errors corrected.

Homework: Client Self-Observation and Practice

_____ 13. Client is requested to observe or listen to the model tape and to practice the goal responses daily—both overtly and covertly—for a certain period of time.
_____ 14. Helper gives some kind of self-directed prompts, such as cue cards.
_____ 15. Helper asks client to record number of practice sessions and to rate performance of goal behaviors on a homework log sheet.
_____ 16. Helper initiates a face-to-face or telephone follow-up to assess client's use of homework and to provide encouragement.

MODEL DIALOGUE: SELF-AS-A-MODEL

To assist you in identifying the steps of a self-as-a-model strategy, the following dialogue is presented with our client Joan. In this dialogue, the strategy is used to help Joan achieve one of her goals described in Chapter 10: increasing her initiating skills in her math class.

Session 1

In response 1, the helper provides Joan with a *rationale* for the self-as-a-model strategy. One initiating skill, that of volunteering answers to questions, will be targeted using this strategy. Note that the helper presents a *rationale* and also confirms the *client's willingness* to try the strategy.

1. **Helper:** One of the things we discussed that is a concern for you now in your math class is that you rarely volunteer answers or make comments during class. As we talked about before, you feel awkward doing this and unsure about how to do it in a way that makes you feel confident. One thing we might try that will help you build up your skills for doing this is called "self-as-a-model." It's sort of a fun thing because it involves not only you but also this tape recorder. It's a way for you to actually hear how you come across when volunteering answers. It can help you do this the way you want to and can also build up your confidence about this. What do you think about trying this?

Client: Well, I've never heard myself on tape too much before. Other than that, it sounds OK.

In response 2, the helper *responds to Joan's concern* about the tape recorder and initiates a period of using it so it doesn't interfere with the strategy.

2. **Helper:** Sometimes the tape recorder does take a little time to get used to, so we'll work with it first so you are accustomed to hearing your voice on it. We might spend some time doing that now. [Joan and the helper spend about 15 minutes recording and playing back their conversation.]

In response 3, the helper gives Joan an *overview* of what is involved in the self-as-a-model strategy.

3. **Helper:** You seem to feel more comfortable with the recorder now. Let me tell you what this involves so you'll have an idea of what to expect. After we work out the way you want to volunteer answers, you'll practice this and we'll tape several practice sessions. Then I'll give you feedback, and we'll use the tape as feedback. We'll take the one practice that really sounds good to you, and you can take that and the recorder home so you can listen to it each day. Does that seem pretty clear?

Client: I think so. I guess the tape is a way for me to find out how I really sound.

In response 4, the helper emphasizes the cognitive or *coping part* of self-as-a-model.

4. **Helper:** That's right. The tape often indicates you can do something better than you think, which is the reason that it does help.

Client: I can see that. Just hearing myself a little while ago helped. My voice doesn't sound as squeaky as I thought.

In this case, the client's verbal participation has already been defined by three behaviors. One behavior, volunteering answers, will be worked with at this point. The other two can be added later. In response 5, the helper will *coach* Joan on ways to perform this skill.

5. **Helper:** OK, Joan, let's talk about what you might do to volunteer answers in a way that you would feel good about. What comes to your mind about this?

Client: I just hardly ever volunteer in the class now. I just wait until Mr. Lamborne calls on me. It's not that I don't know the answer, because lots of times I do. I guess I just need to raise my hand and give out the answer. See, usually he'll say, "OK, who has the answer to this problem?" So all I need to do is raise my hand and give the answer, like 25 or 40 or whatever. I don't know why I don't do it. I guess I'm afraid I will sound silly or maybe my voice will sound funny.

In the next response, the helper uses a *clarification* to determine Joan's particular concern about this skill.

6. **Helper:** So are you more concerned with the way you sound than with what you have to say?

Client: I think so.

In response 7, the helper continues to *coach* Joan about ways to perform the desired skill, volunteering answers, and also initiates a *trial practice*.

7. **Helper:** Let's try this. Why don't I pretend to be Mr. Lamborne, and then you raise your hand and give me an answer? Just try to speak in a firm voice that I can easily hear. Maybe even take a deep breath at first. OK? [Helper turns on tape recorder.] (as Mr. Lamborne) Who has the answer to this problem?

[Joan raises her hand.]

Helper (as Mr. Lamborne, looks around room, pauses): Joan?

Client (in a fairly audible voice): 25. After the dry run, the helper, in responses 8–10, gives *feedback* (using tape playback) about Joan's performance of the target behavior.

8. **Helper:** OK, let's stop. What did you think about that?

Client: Well, it wasn't really that hard. I took a deep breath.

9. **Helper:** Your voice came across pretty clear. Maybe it could be just a little stronger. OK. Let's hear this on tape [playback of tape.]

10. **Helper:** How do you feel about what you just heard?

Client: Well, I sound fine. I mean, my voice didn't squeak.

In response 11, the helper initiates *tape recordings* of Joan's demonstration of the skill (volunteering answers). This tape will be edited and used as a modeling tape.

11. **Helper:** No, it was pretty strong. Let's do this several times now. Just take a deep breath and speak firmly. [Practice ensues and is recorded.]

In response 12, the helper explains the *tape-editing process*; the tape is edited before their next session.

12. **Helper:** I'm going to need to go over this tape before we use it for feedback. So maybe that's enough for today. We can get together next week, and I'll have this tape ready by then. Basically, I'm just going to edit it so you can hear the practice examples in which your voice sounded clear and firm. [Before the next session, the helper erases any portions of the tape in which Joan's answers were inaudible or high-pitched, leaving only audible, firm, level-pitched answers.]

Session 2

After a brief warm-up period in this session, the helper *instructs* Joan about what to listen for in the *demonstration with the edited tape playback*.

1. **Helper:** Joan, I've got your tape ready. I'd like to play back the tape. When I do, I'd like you to note how clearly and firmly you are able to give the answers. [Tape is played.]

2. **Helper:** What did you think?

Client: You're right. I guess I don't sound silly, at least not on that tape.

In response 3, the helper gives *positive feedback* to Joan about demonstrating the skill.

3. **Helper:** You really sounded like you felt very confident about the answers. It was very easy to hear you.

Client: But will I be able to sound like that in class?

In response 4, the helper instructs Joan on how to use the tape as *daily homework* in conjunction with practice. Note that the homework assignment specifies *what* and *how much* Joan will do.

4. **Helper:** Yes, and we'll be working on that as our next step. In the meantime, I'd like you to work with this tape during the week. Could you set aside a certain time each day when you could listen to the tape, just like we did today? Then after you listen to the tape, practice again. Imagine Mr. Lamborne asking for the answer. Just raise your hand, take a deep breath, and speak firmly. Do you understand how to use this now?

Client: Yes, just listen to it once a day and then do another round of practice.

In response 5, the helper asks Joan to *record her use of homework on log sheets*.

5. **Helper:** As you do this, I'd like you to use these log sheets and mark down each time you do this homework. Also, rate on this five-point scale how comfortable you feel in doing this before and each time you practice.

Client: That doesn't sound too difficult, I guess.

In response 6, the helper encourages Joan to *reinforce herself* for progress and *arranges for follow-up* on homework at their next session.

6. **Helper:** This recording on your log sheet will help you see your progress. You've made a lot of progress, so give yourself a pat on the back after you hear the tape this week. Next week we can talk about how this worked out, and then we'll see whether we can do the same type of thing in your classes.

The next step would be to obtain some tape-recorded samples of Joan's volunteering in a class situation. A nonthreatening class in which Joan presently does volunteer might be used first, followed by her trying this out in math class. A challenge in this step is to arrange for tape-recorded samples in a way that is not embarrassing to Joan in the presence of her classmates. (See Learning Activity 18.4).

SELF-EFFICACY

Self-efficacy is described by Bandura, Adams, and Beyer (1977) as a cognitive process that mediates behavioral change. Self-efficacy refers to our judgments and subsequent beliefs of how capable we are of performing certain things under specific situations. This includes but is not limited to overt behaviors—for example, how capable we believe we

LEARNING ACTIVITY 18.4 — Self-As-a-Model

You may recall from the case of Ms. Weare and Freddie that Ms. Weare wants to eliminate the assistance she gives Freddie in getting ready for school in the morning. One of Ms. Weare's concerns is to find a way to tell Freddie about the new ground rules—mainly that she will not help him get dressed and will not remind him when the bus is five minutes away. Ms. Weare is afraid that after she does this, Freddie will either pout or talk back to her. She is concerned that she will not be able to follow through with her plan or will not be firm in the way she delivers the ground rules to him.

Describe how you could use the five components of the self-as-a-model strategy to help Ms. Weare accomplish these four things:

1. Deliver clear instructions to Freddie.
2. Talk in a firm voice.
3. Maintain eye contact while talking.
4. Avoid talking down, giving in, or changing her original instructions.

Feedback follows below.

FEEDBACK 18.4 — Self-As-a-Model

1. **Rationale for strategy:** First, the helper explains to Ms. Weare how the self-as-a-model procedure could help her (rationale) and what is involved in the procedure (overview). Then the helper asks Ms. Weare how she feels about trying this procedure (client's willingness).
2. **Recording the desired behavior:** According to the case description, there are four things Ms. Weare wants to do in talking to Freddie. The helper will probably need to coach Ms. Weare on a successful way to perform the skills before recording her demonstration of it, and a dry run may be necessary. When the helper believes Ms. Weare can demonstrate the skills at least sometimes, a video or audio recording will be made. (For eye contact, a videotape would be necessary.) Because Ms. Weare presently is not engaging in these behaviors with Freddie, an in-session tape would be more useful than an *in vivo* tape at this point. The helper can role play the part of Freddie during the taping. The taping should continue until an adequate sample of each of the four skills is obtained.
3. **Editing the tape:** After the tape has been recorded, the helper will edit it. Only inappropriate examples of the skill will be deleted. For example, instances when Ms. Weare looks away will be erased from the tape. The edited tape will consist only of times when she maintains eye contact. A final tape in which she uses all four skills will consist only of times when she is using the desired skills.
4. **Demonstrating with the edited tape:** After the edited tape is ready, it will be used for demonstration and practice with Ms. Weare. The helper will instruct Ms. Weare about what to look for and then play back the tape. The helper will give positive feedback to Ms. Weare for instances of demonstrating eye contact and the other three skills. After the playback, Ms. Weare will practice the skill and receive feedback from the helper about the practice performance.
5. **Homework: Client self-observation and practice:** After Ms. Weare is able to practice the skills with the helper, she can use the self-modeling tape as homework. Specifically, the helper will instruct her to listen to or view the tape on her own if possible. She can also practice the skills—first covertly and later overtly—with Freddie. This practice can occur with or without the tape. A follow-up should be arranged to check on her progress.

are in managing our thoughts or feelings in specific situations as well as how capably we can undertake particular actions. Our self-efficacy beliefs can be broad in that we think we can accomplish something in most situations (like walking, being able to communicate in our native language) or may be situation specific (we may believe we can be assertive or resist temptation in some situations, but not others).

There are some important distinctions to keep in mind. Self-efficacy beliefs foster expectations of our personal abilities to accomplish something. This is related to but different from *outcome* expectations—that is, our beliefs that these actions of ours will result in desired outcomes (Bandura, 1986). We may feel that we have the ability to accomplish a task, say at school or work, and thus have high self-efficacy in this regard. But if we believe that this alone is not sufficient for achieving the desired outcome—like succeeding in a change or recognition of a job well done—then we have low outcome expectations (due perhaps to beliefs that the outcome is dependent on other people, events, or forces that are not predictable or are not likely to be efficacious). Including outcome expectations and factors likely to affect the outcome of an attempted task is clearly important to assessment. As important as self-efficacy is to fueling people's pursuits of what is important to them, so too is realistic consideration of whether this is enough: of barriers that can thwart success regardless of the skills and beliefs that an individual can bring to the effort.

Self-efficacy is not the same thing as self-esteem. For example, we can have high self-efficacy beliefs about certain tasks or abilities, but low overall self-esteem. This can be due to a lot of reasons, such as not valuing things we do well as much as things we believe we are not able to successfully accomplish, or input from others that devalues what we believe we can do well. In general, however, self-esteem is enhanced when our self-efficacy is high in domains of life that we care most about and in which we desire to exert personal control—when we feel capable of doing what is required to achieve success, or when we realize that we have reached our goal. Underlying self-efficacy is optimism and hope that yield high efficacy, or helplessness and despair that contribute to low efficacy.

We can have high self-efficacy in some life domains but low in others, like believing we are capable of being successful at work but are lousy at parenting. In general, efficacy beliefs also build on experience, whether vicarious or actual, and draw from our cognitive schemas about who we are (e.g., my experiences with and input from others about my academic ability incline me to have high or low self-efficacy about mastering an academic challenge, depending on the nature of that experience and input). Thus, self-efficacy is not fixed, but is largely learned and shaped by life experience, and can be relearned and reshaped through focused intervention. Part of the reason that self-efficacy is so important is that it has been found to be a significant component in many issues germane to well-being, like tackling versus avoiding challenges and opportunities, degree of effort expended, persistence with the task, problem solving, coping, performance, confidence, determination, optimism, hopefulness, and enthusiasm.

Over the last several years, research about self-efficacy has flourished. Box 18.4 lists a selected sample of these studies. Here we see wide-ranging life domains and clinical concerns such as abortion, substance use, health conditions (asthma, cancer, cardiovascular, dental health, diabetes, multiple sclerosis, HIV/AIDS), achievement and performance, vocational and work issues, dietary behavior, eating disorders, coping, computer-related, maternity and parenting, anxiety, and trauma. The list of self-efficacy research is far greater than we can present here. Thus, we encourage you to undertake your own literature searches on problems, goals, or populations of particular relevance to you.

Several sources contribute to self-efficacy and to similar concepts in the constellation of one's personality or personal constructs. According to Bandura (1977, 1986, 1997), four primary sources influence efficacy expectations: (1) actual performance accomplishments, (2) mind/body states such as emotional arousal, (3) environmental experiences such as vicarious learning, and (4) verbal installation—as a prelude to treatment. Verbal installation is the persuasion process that the helper uses to enhance a client's confidence or self-efficacy expectations about performing specific tasks. A helping professional might foster positive self-efficacy by talking with the client about his or her past success in performing similar or related tasks. Or the helper can attempt to build confidence by discussing any of the client's successful experiences if the client has not engaged in tasks for which self-confidence or efficacy was needed.

Performance Accomplishments

There is huge variability in how people perform. People who have a high degree of self-efficacy recoup very quickly from failure. At one extreme are people who are motivated, energized, and risk taking despite the possibility of failure—partly because they do not anticipate failure or are able to interpret failure in ways that do not significantly diminish their future self-efficacy expectations. At the other extreme are those people who fall into a state of learned helplessness (Seligman, 1990). These people are plagued with depressed feelings that contribute to pessimism, a low level of energy, negative internal dialogue, vulnerability, and hopelessness, thus resulting in low levels of attempted performance.

BOX 18.4   RESEARCH ON SELF-EFFICACY

Abortion
Cozzarelli, C. (1993). Personality and self-efficacy as predictors of coping with abortion. *Journal of Personality and Social Psychology, 65,* 1224–1236.

Alcohol use
Aas, H., Klepp, K., Laberg, J., & Edvard, L. (1995). Predicting adolescents' intentions to drink alcohol: Outcome expectancies and self-efficacy. *Journal of Studies on Alcohol, 156,* 293–299.
Greenfield, S. J., Hufford, M. R., Vagge, L. M., Muenz, L. R., Costello, M. E., & Weiss, R. D. (2000). The relationship of self-efficacy expectancies to relapse among alcohol dependent men and women: A prospective study. *Journal of Studies on Alcohol, 61,* 345–351.
Maisto, S. A., Connors, G. J., & Zwiak, W. H. (2000). Alcohol treatment changes in coping skills, self-efficacy, and levels of alcohol use and related problems one year following treatment initiation. *Psychology of Addictive Behaviors, 14,* 257–266.

Asthma
Alaniz, K. L., & Nordstrand, J. (1999). Camp superteens: An asthma education program for adolescents. *American Journal of Maternal/Child Nursing, 24*(3), 133–137.

Athletics
Escarti, A., & Guzman, J. F. (1999). Effects of feedback on self-efficacy, performance, and choice in an athletic task. *Journal of Applied Sport Psychology, 11*(1), 83–96.

Battered women
Lerner, C. F., & Kennedy, L. T. (2000). Stay–leave decision-making in battered women: Trauma, coping, and self-efficacy. *Cognitive Therapy & Research, 24*(2), 215–232.

Cancer
Eiser, C., Hill, J., & Blacklay, A. (2000). Surviving cancer: What does it mean for you? An evaluation of a clinic-based intervention for survivors of childhood cancer. *Psycho-Oncology, 9*(3), 214–220.
McCormick, L. K., Masse, L., Cunnings, S. S., & Burke, C. (1999). Evaluation of skin cancer prevention module for nurses: Change in knowledge, self-efficacy, and attitudes. *American Journal of Health Promotion, 13*(5), 282–289.

Cardiovascular
Lox, C. L., & Freehill, A. J. (1999). Impact of pulmonary rehabilitation on self-efficacy, quality of life, and exercise tolerance. *Rehabilitation Psychology, 44,* 208–221.
Ng, J. Y. Y., Tam, S. F., Yew, W. W., & Lam, W. K. (1999). Effects of video modeling on self-efficacy and exercise performance of COPD patients. *Social Behavior & Personality, 27,* 475–486.
Wright, R. A., Wadley, V. G., Pharr, R. P., & Butler, M. (1994). Interactive influence of self-reported ability and avoidant task demand on anticipatory cardiovascular responsivity. *Journal of Research in Personality, 28,* 68–86.

Career
Betz, N. E. (2000). Self-efficacy theory as a basis for career assessment. *Journal of Career Assessment, 8,* 205–222.
Donnay, D. A. C., & Borgen, F. H. (1999). The incremental validity of vocational self-efficacy: An examination of interest, self-efficacy, and occupation. *Journal of Counseling Psychology, 46,* 432–447.
Kraus, L. J., & Hughey, K. F. (1999). The impact of an intervention on career decision-making self-efficacy and career indecision. *Professional School Counseling, 2,* 384–390.
Ryan, N., Solberg, V., & Brown, S. (1996). Family dysfunction, parental attachment, and career search self-efficacy among community college students. *Journal of Counseling Psychology, 43,* 84–89.
Sullivan, K. R., & Mahalik, J. R. (2000). Increasing career self-efficacy for women: Evaluating a group intervention. *Journal of Counseling & Development, 78*(1), 54–62.

Child abuse prevention
Dumont, H., Hebert, M., & Lavoie, F. (1999). The contribution of individual characteristics to children's learning in a workshop on abuse prevention. *Canadian Journal of Community Mental Health, 18*(1), 39–56.

Chronic mental disorders
Carpinello, S. E., Kenight, E. L., Markowitz, F. E., & Pease, E. A. (2000). The development of the Mental Health Confidence Scale: A measure of self-efficacy in individuals diagnosed with mental disorders. *Psychiatric Rehabilitation Journal, 23,* 236–243.

Computer related
Decker, C. A. (1999). Technical education transfer: Perceptions of employee computer technology self-efficacy. *Computers in Human Behavior, 15*(2), 161–172.
Eastin, M., & LaRose, R. (2000). Internet self-efficacy and the psychology of the digital divide. *Journal of Computer-Mediated Communication, 6,* np.
Hollis-Sawyer, L. A., & Sterns, H. L. (1999). A novel goal-oriented approach for training older adult computer novices: Beyond the effects of individual-difference factors. *Educational Gerontology, 25,* 661–684.
Klein, B., & Richards, J. C. (2001). A brief Internet-based treatment for panic disorder. *Behavioral and Cognitive Psychotherapy, 29*(1), 113–117.
Staples, D. S., Hulland, J. S., & Higgins, C. A. (1999). A self-efficacy theory explanation for the management of remote workers in virtual organizations. *Organizational Science, 10,* 758–776.

Coping
Aspinwall, L. G., & Richter, L. (1999). Optimism and self-mastery predict more rapid disengagement from unsolvable tasks in the presence of alternatives. *Motivation & Emotion, 23*(3), 221–245.
Benight, C. C., Swift, E., Sanger, J., Smith, A., & Zeppelin, D. (1999). Coping self-efficacy as a mediator of distress following a natural disaster. *Journal of Applied Social Psychology, 29,* 2443–2464.

Dental health
Maupome, G., Borges, A., Ramirez, L. E., & Diez-de-Bonilla, J. (1999). Perceptions of tooth loss and peridontal problems in an independent elderly population: Content-analysis of interview discourse. *Journal of Cross-Cultural Gerontology, 14*(1), 43–63.

BOX 18.4 RESEARCH ON SELF-EFFICACY CONTINUED

Diabetes
Griva, K., Myers, L. B., & Newman, S. (2000). Illness perceptions and self-efficacy beliefs in adolescents and young adults with insulin dependent diabetes mellitus. *Psychology & Health, 15,* 733–750.
Piette, J. D., Weinberger, M., & McPhee, S. J. (2000). The effect of automated calls with telephone nurse follow-up on patient-centered outcomes of diabetes care: A randomized, controlled trial. *Medical Care, 38,* 218–230.

Dietary behavior
Povey, R., Conner, M., Sparks, P., James, R., & Shepherd, R. (2000). Application of the theory of planned behaviour to two dietary behaviours: Roles of perceived control and self-efficacy. *British Journal of Health Psychology, 5*(2), 121–139.

Eating disorders
Smalec, J. L., & Klingle, R. S. (2000). Bulimia interventions via interpersonal influence: The role of threat and efficacy in persuading bulimics to seek help. *Journal of Behavioral Medicine, 23*(1), 37–57.

Exercise
Dawson, K., & Brawley, L. R. (2000). Examining the relationship between exercise goals, self-efficacy, and overt behavior with beginning exercisers. *Journal of Applied Social Psychology, 30,* 315–329.
Rodgers, W., & Brawley, L. (1996). The influence of outcome expectancy and self-efficacy on the behavioral intentions of novice exercisers. *Journal of Applied Social Psychology, 26,* 618–634.
Sullum, J., Clark, M. M., & King, T. K. (2000). Predictors of exercise relapse in a college population. *Journal of American College Health, 48*(4), 175–180.

Gender issues
Betz, N. E., & Schifano, R. S. (2000). Evaluation of an intervention to increase realistic self-efficacy and interests in college women. *Journal of Vocational Behavior, 56*(1), 35–52.
Chaplain, R. P. (2000). Beyond exam results? Differences in the social and psychological perceptions of young males and females at school. *Educational Studies, 26*(2), 177–190.
Dickerson, A., & Taylor, M. A. (2000). Self-limiting behavior in women: Self-esteem and self-efficacy as predictors. *Group and Organization Management, 25*(2), 191–210.
Lapan, R. T., Adams, A., Turner, S., & Hinkelman, J. M. (2000). Seventh graders' vocational interest and efficacy expectation patterns. *Journal of Career Development, 26,* 215–229.
Weitlauf, J. C., Smith, R. E., & Cervone, D. (2000). Generalization effects of coping-skills training: Influence of self-defense training on women's efficacy beliefs, assertiveness, and aggression. *Journal of Applied Psychology, 85,* 625–633.

Headache
French, D. J., Holroyd, K. A., Pinell, C., Malinoski, P. T., O'Donnell, F., & Hill, K. R. (2000). Perceived self-efficacy and headache-related disability. *Headache, 40,* 647–656.
Martin, N. J., Holroyd, K. A., & Rokicki, L. A. (1993). The headache self-efficacy scale: Adaptation to recurrent headaches. *Headache, 33,* 244–248.

Health
Eachus, P. (1993). Development of the health student self-efficacy scale. *Perceptual and Motor Skills, 77,* 670.
Schwartzer, R., & Renner, B. (2000). Social–cognitive predictors of health behavior: Action self-efficacy and coping self-efficacy. *Health Psychology, 19,* 487–495.

HIV/AIDS
Denson, D. R., Voight, R., & Eisenman, R. (1994). Self-efficacy and AIDS prevention for university students. *International Journal of Adolescence and Youth, 5*(½), 105–113.
Semple, S. J., Petterson, T. L., & Grant, I. (2000). The sexual negotiation behavior of HIV-positive gay and bisexual. *Journal of Consulting & Clinical Psychology, 68,* 934–937.
Weeks, K., Levy, S., Zhu, C., & Perhats, C. (1995). Impact of a school-based AIDS prevention program in young adolescents' self-efficacy skills. *Health Education Research, 10,* 329–344.

Job-related
Brouwers, A. T., & Tomic, W. (2000). A longitudinal study of teacher burnout and perceived self-efficacy in classroom management. *Teaching & Teacher Education, 16,* 239–253.
Friedman, I. A. (2000). Burnout in teachers: Shattered dreams of impeccable professional performance. *Journal of Clinical Psychology, 56,* 595–606.
Gregoire, J., & Suddith, C. (1999). The relationship between self-efficacy beliefs and two indicators of training effectiveness in an applied setting: A meta-analytical procedure. *Science et Comportment, 28*(1), 39–54.
King, R., LeBas, J., & Spooner, D. (2000). The impact of caseload on the personal efficacy of mental health case managers. *Psychiatric Services, 51,* 364–368.
Krieshok, T. S., Ulven, C., Hecox, J. L., & Wettersten, K. (2000). Resume therapy and vocational test feedback: Tailoring interventions to self-efficacy outcomes. *Journal of Career Assessment, 8,* 267–281.
Prieto, L. R., & Meyers, S. A. (1999). Effects of training and supervision on the self-efficacy of psychology graduate teaching assistants. *Teaching of Psychology, 26,* 264–266.
Washington. O. (1999). Effects of cognitive and experiential group therapy on self-efficacy and perceptions of employability of chemically dependent women. *Issues in Mental Health Nursing, 20*(3), 181–198.

Learning
Cassidy, S., & Eachus, P. (2000). Learning style, academic belief systems, self-report student proficiency, and academic achievement in higher education. *Educational Psychology, 20,* 307–320.
Fall, M., Balanz, J., Johnson, L., & Nelson, L. (1999). A play therapy intervention and its relationship to self-efficacy and learning behaviors. *Professional School Counseling, 2*(3), 194–204.
Moriarty, B., Douglas, G., Punch, K., & Hattie, J. (1995). The importance of self-efficacy as a mediating variable between learning environments and achievement. *British Journal of Educational Psychology, 65,* 73–84.
Shea, C., & Howell, J. M. (2000). Efficacy–performance spirals: An empirical test. *Journal of Management, 26,* 791–812.

(continued)

> **BOX 18.4 RESEARCH ON SELF-EFFICACY** *CONTINUED*
>
> *Maternal self-efficacy*
> Gross, D., Conrad, B., Fogg, L., & Wothke, W. (1994). A longitudinal model of maternal self-efficacy, depression, and difficult temperament during toddlerhood. *Research in Nursing and Health, 17,* 207–215.
>
> *Math self-efficacy*
> Randhawa, B. S. (1994). Self-efficacy in mathematics, attitudes, and achievement of boys and girls from restricted samples of two countries. *Perceptual and Motor Skills, 79,* 1011–1018.
>
> *Multiple sclerosis*
> Wingerson, N. W., & Wineman, N. M. (2000). The mental health, self-efficacy, and satisfaction outcomes of a community counseling demonstration project for multiple sclerosis patients. *Journal of Applied Rehabilitation Counseling, 3*(2), 11.
>
> *Opiate addicts relapse risk*
> Reilly, P., Sees, K., Shopshire, M., & Hall, S. (1995). Self-efficacy and illicit opoid use in a 180-day methadone detoxification treatment. *Journal of Consulting and Clinical Psychology, 63,* 158–162.
>
> *Pain*
> Arnstein, P., Caudill, M., Mandle, C. L., Norris, A., & Beasley, R. (1999). Self-efficacy as a mediator of the relationship between pain intensity, disability, and depression in chronic pain patients. *Pain, 80,* 483–491.
> Ellis, J. A., Blouin, R., & Lockett, J. (1999). Patient-controlled analgesia: Optimizing the experience. *Clinical Nursing Research, 8,* 283–294.
> Stevens, M. J., Ohlwein, A. L., & Catanzaro, S. J. (2000). Further evidence that self-efficacy predicts acute pain. *Imagination, Cognition, & Personality, 19*(2), 185–194.
>
> *Parenting*
> Jackson, A. P., & Huang, C. C. (2000). Parenting stress and behavior among single mothers of preschoolers: The mediating role of self-efficacy. *Journal of Social Service Research, 26*(4), 29–42.
>
> *Perfectionism*
> LoCicero, K., & Ashby, J. S. (2000). Multidimensional perfectionism and self-reported self-efficacy in college students. *Journal of College Student Psychotherapy, 15*(2), 47–56.
>
> *Phobia*
> Zoeller, L. A., Echiverri, A., & Craske, M. G. (2000). Processing of phobic stimuli and its relationship to outcome. *Behaviour Research & Therapy, 38,* 921–931.
>
> *Relapse for substance abuse*
> Rawson, R. A., Obert, J. L., McCann, M. J., & Marinelli-Casey, P. (1993). Relapse prevention models for substance abuse treatment. *Psychotherapy, 30,* 284–298.
>
> *Shyness*
> Kuzuu, S. (1994). The effects of self-observation on self-efficacy of shy students. *Japanese Journal of Counseling Science, 27,* 97–104.
>
> *Smoking*
> Dijkstra, A., & de Vries, H. (2000). Self-efficacy expectations with regard to different tasks in smoking. *Psychology & Health, 15,* 501–511.
> Mudde, A., Kok, G., & Strecher, V. (1995). Self-efficacy as a predictor for the cessation of smoking. *Psychology and Health, 10,* 353–367.
> Pederson, L. L., Ahluwalia, J. S., Harris, K. J., & McGrady, G. A. (2000). Smoking cessation among African Americans: What we know and do not know about interventions and self-quitting. *Preventive Medicine: An International Journal Devoted to Practice & Theory, 31*(1), 23–38.
>
> *Social anxiety*
> Nicastro, R., Luskin, F., Raps, C., & Benisovich, S. (1999). The relationship of imperatives and self-efficacy to indices of social anxiety. *Journal of Rational–Emotive & Cognitive Behavior Therapy, 17,* 249–265.
>
> *Trauma*
> Benight, C. C., Freyaldenhoven, R. W., Highes, J., Ruiz, J. M., Zoschke, T. A., & Lovallo, W. R. (2000). Coping self-efficacy and psychological distress following the Oklahoma City bombing. *Journal of Applied Social Psychology, 30,* 1331–1344.
> Saigh, P., Mroueh, M., Zimmerman, B., & Fairbank, J. (1995). Self-efficacy expectations among traumatized adolescents. *Behaviour Research and Therapy, 33,* 701–704.

When these people experience failure, they are more likely to interpret it as further evidence that they are not capable ("It's my fault," "I always screw things up," "This is just another example that I can never do anything right."), thus further deepening future low efficacy expectations. You can see the cognitive underpinnings of self-efficacy and ways that self-schemas, cognitive processing habits, and interactions with the world can contribute either positively or negatively to self-efficacy beliefs (see Chapter 14).

Most of us fall somewhere between these two extremes. Perceived self-efficacy is a major determinant in whether people engage in a task, the amount of effort they exert if they do engage, and how long they will persevere with the task if they encounter adverse circumstances. For example, people who frequently surf the Internet on their personal computers in search of a particular Web page feel competent in performing this task. They may feel quite confident in their abilities and persevere for some time in their search, even when they are unsuccessful in locating a specific Web page. However, the same people may feel less competent in programming software and may avoid programming tasks. Sometimes people feel competent at performing a task, but do not perform it because there is no incentive for doing so. Also, some people may have unrealistic expectations about performing a task simply because they are unfamiliar with the task. For example, some people may feel *overconfident* about doing something, and others may experience *less* confidence. Generally, when we develop competence of any kind, we enhance and strengthen our self-efficacy, confidence, self-esteem, willingness to take risks, and ability to perform the task.

Mind/Body Link to Self-Efficacy

As we have learned in prior chapters, what we are feeling emotionally and the bodily sensations and phenomena accompanying differing emotions have important implications for what cognitions we are likely to access from memory and to generate in that context. If we are feeling highly anxious, for example, we will have a different set of cognitions salient to our information processing in the moment than if we are feeling calm or excited. Thus, if we are feeling anxious in a situation, it will be difficult to access memories of when we were successful in the past or to focus on aspects of the situation that address how we might be successful, which, in turn, will result in a set of schemas and perceptions active in that situation that are unlikely to support high self-efficacy expectations. Thus, one's ability to be aware of and manage one's emotional state (e.g., to shift from a high level of emotional arousal to a lower level, from anxiety more toward determination) is a valuable tool toward managing self-efficacy beliefs and expectations.

Similarly, we are becoming increasingly aware of the ways that not only our thoughts, feelings, and behaviors interact, but how these also affect and are affected by many bodily systems, such as biochemistry and neurological processes. For example, there are chain reactions and interaction within the mind/body information processing system. Some of this work involves the information molecules, peptides, and receptors that serve as biochemicals of emotion (Pert, 1993) and ways that messenger molecules or neuropeptides influence self-efficacy. As we've noted, a person who has a high degree of self-confidence and higher perceptions of personal control, compared with someone of lower self-confidence, is inclined to attempt more difficult tasks, use more energy, persevere longer at solutions when faced with adversity, and refuse to blame himself or herself when encountering failure. One hypothesis here is that the production of endogenous morphine (endorphins) in the brain is high and that the production of catecholamines (stress hormones) is low—relevant because production of endorphins is positively correlated with confidence. It has an analgesic effect, which spreads throughout the body and reduces sensitivity to pain (Bandura, Cioffi, Taylor, & Brouillard, 1988; Pert, 1993).

In contrast, those people without feelings of control have low levels of perceived self-efficacy, avoid difficult tasks, have lower expectancies, and have a weak commitment to achieving a goal. They are more vulnerable to dwelling on their personal inadequacies, allowing negative self-talk, putting forth less effort, having little energy for a task, and taking longer to recover from failure on some task. They are very susceptible to stress and depression. For these people, who feel that they are not in control, their feelings of low self-efficacy can possibly increase the production of catecholamines (Bandura, Taylor, Williams, Mefford, & Barchas, 1985). Our emotional state affects our perceived level of self-efficacy; this state, in turn, causes information molecules or neuropeptides to produce either stress hormones or brain opioids, depending on our emotional state. The degree of perceived self-efficacy and biochemical reactivity have many contributors, including origins in the family (on both a genetic and social basis) and the environmental and cultural context in which the family resides. Needless to say, this is but one small part of the complex relationships of our psychoneuroendocrinology, thoughts, feelings, and actions (Zillmann & Zillmann, 1996). Although self-efficacy fundamentally refers to beliefs, it, as with other cognitions, is far from being "all in the head."

Environmental Influences

A person's self-efficacy is influenced by reciprocal interactions of cognitive, affective, behavioral, relational, and environmental and/or cultural variables (Bandura, 1989). Family of origin, culture, and environmental setting mold a person's perceived self-efficacy, which contributes to cognitive development and functioning. Bandura (1993) proposed that perceived self-efficacy exerts a powerful influence on four major developmental processes: cognitive, motivational, affective, and perceptual selection. For example, Bandura (1993) asserts that there are four different levels at which perceived self-efficacy operates as an important contributor to academic development: (1) students' beliefs in their efficacy to regulate their own learning and to master academic activities determine their level of motivation and academic accomplishments, (2) teachers' beliefs in their efficacy to motivate and promote learning affect the types of learning environments they create and the degree of their students' academic progress, (3) faculties' beliefs in their collective instructional efficacy contribute significantly to their schools' level of achievement, and (4) student body characteristics influence school-level achievement more strongly by altering faculties' beliefs in their collective efficacy.

Note that these four levels of perceived self-efficacy are also affected by the client's world view. Bandura and others have begun to explore self-efficacy from a cultural perspective (Bandura, 1995). Oettingen (1995), for example, examines cultural effects on self-efficacy relative to differences based on individualism versus collectivism, power differential, masculinity, and avoidance of uncertainty. In collectivist cultures, core group members are likely to be a primary source of efficacy information for each individual as contrasted to higher reliance on one's own evaluations and emotional reactions in individualistic cultures. Cultures or social conditions in which there are large power differentials are likely to find those with greater power as stronger sources or environmental influences relative to efficacy appraisals, as opposed to conditions with less power disparity, in which individuals may be more inclined to see their actions and outcomes as more closely tied to themselves and, thus, efficacy belief and expectations to be more anchored in themselves. There are many dimensions of vicarious learning, including the availability of successful and relevant models to literally demonstrate the abilities in question. Chapter 12 offers background on modeling relevant in this regard.

Self-Efficacy As a Prelude for Treatment

A client's expectations, based on his or her perceived self-efficacy, determine the underlying cognitive process that accounts for changes in therapeutic outcomes and achievement of treatment goals. Clients must acquire self-efficacy (confidence) to perform the specific skills associated with a particular therapeutic strategy so that they can achieve their therapeutic goals. Bandura (1982) has demonstrated that there is a strong relationship between an individual's level of perceived self-efficacy and his or her later level of performance. Self-efficacy is a mental precondition that has a striking influence on the successful application of treatment. We believe that if the helper can maximize the client's perceived self-efficacy and expectancies about treatment, the client will be confident about using the specific steps associated with the treatment protocol and enhance the potential benefits and effectiveness of treatment. Rosenthal and Steffek (1991) say that "all psychotherapies—whatever techniques they comprise—must raise patients' self-efficacy if patients are to attempt, or persist at, activities they formerly avoided or inhibited" (p. 80).

The strength of self-efficacy assessment involves the specification of the goals for change discussed in Chapter 10. Clients can be provided with a series of specific goal behaviors or outcome goals for treatment. They can be asked to rate how much they believe they can perform these behaviors and how confident they are of their judgment. These ratings are usually measured on a scale ranging from 0 (uncertain) to 100 (certain). For example, Ozer and Bandura (1990) offered 45 women volunteers a program to deal effectively with the risk of sexual assault. All the women had limited their cultural, educational, and social activities because they lacked a sense of ability (self-efficacy) to handle potential dangers that might occur to them when going out alone. Self-efficacy training was assessed in several areas: (1) competence in self-defense was measured on scales of perceived capacity to retaliate with disabling blows, for example, if assaulted; (2) ability to increase activities was measured on scales of perceived comfort in resuming nighttime outdoor recreation, attending concerts, and going to restaurants and nightclubs—all activities that take place after dark; (3) efficacy for interpersonal encounters was measured on scales of the women's perceived capacity for assertive response if they were threatened or harassed in social contexts such as at work, on dates, on public transportation, or at parties; (4) efficacy to control troublesome cognitions was measured by a scale of perceived capacity to stop ruminating about possible attacks; and (5) a variety of ratings of thoughts about, vulnerability to, risk of facing, and fear concerning sexual assault were measured (Ozer & Bandura, 1990). The success of achieving therapeutic goals may be largely a function of a client's self-efficacy, with each strategy designed to reach a specific goal. Also, the client's age, gender, social class, and cultural and ethnic background will influence the degree of efficacy or confidence he or she feels in performing a specific task.

MULTICULTURAL APPLICATIONS OF SELF-EFFICACY

Increasingly, self-efficacy is being investigated with diverse groups of clients and research participants. As is evident in Box 18.5, the topics on which self-efficacy has been empirically studied with diverse groups are varied. In the area of prevention and risk reduction, for example, self-efficacy has been examined as a factor relative to drug and alcohol use, smoking, HIV and other sexually transmitted diseases, cardiovascular disease, and other health conditions. As we noted in Chapter 16, exercise and physical activity are increasingly a target of clinical focus, and self-efficacy is part of that line of research. Depression, social support, mental distress, and other dimensions of emotional and psychological well-being include self-efficacy as a factor. Studies of academic performance and various aspects of job seeking, work, and career have long implicated self-efficacy, and continue with diverse

BOX 18.5 DIVERSITY APPLICATION OF SELF-EFFICACY

Academic performance and career selection

Boileau, L., Bouffard, T., & Vezeau, C. (2000). The examination of self, goals, and their impact on school achievement in sixth grade students. *Canadian Journal of Behavioural Science, 32*(1), 6–17.

Bong, M. (1999). Personal factors affecting the generality of academic self-efficacy judgments: Gender, ethnicity, and relative expertise. *Journal of Experimental Education, 67,* 315–331.

Bong, M. (2001). Between- and within-domain relations of academic motivation among middle and high school students: Self-efficacy, task value, and achievement goals. *Journal of Educational Psychology, 93*(1), 23–24.

Bong, M., & Clark, R. E. (1999). Comparison between self-concept and self-efficacy in academic motivation research. *Educational Psychologist, 34*(3), 139–153.

Gloria, A. M., & Robinson Kurpius, S. E. (2001). Influences of self-beliefs, social support, and comfort in the university environment on the academic persistence decisions of American Indian undergraduates. *Cultural Diversity & Ethnic Minority Psychology, 7*(1), 88–102.

Gutman, L. M., et al. (2000). The role of protective factors in supporting the academic achievement of poor African American students during the middle school transition. *Journal of Youth & Adolescence, 29,* 223–248.

Kremer-Hayon, L., & Tillema, H. H. (1999). Self-regulated learning in the context of teacher education. *Teaching & Teacher Education, 15,* 507–522.

Lee, J., & Cramond, B. (1999). The positive effects of mentoring economically disadvantaged students. *Professional School Counseling, 2*(3), 172–178.

Morrow, S., Gore, P., & Campbell, B. (1996). The application of a socio-cognitive framework to the career development of lesbian women and gay men. *Journal of Vocational Behavior, 48,* 136–148.

O'Brien, K. M., Dukstein, R. D., Jackson, S. L., Tomlinson, M. J., & Kamatuka, N. A. (1999). Broadening career horizons for students in at-risk environments. *Career Development Quarterly, 47*(3), 215–229.

O'Brien, V., Martinez-Pons, M., & Kopala, M. (1999). Mathematics self-efficacy, ethnic identity, gender, and career interests related to mathematics and science. *Journal of Educational Research, 92*(4), 231–235.

Panagos, R. J., & Dubois, D. L. (1999). Career self-efficacy development and students with learning disabilities. *Learning Disabilities Research & Practice, 14*(1), 25–34.

Shih, S. S., & Alexander, J. M. (2000). Interacting effects of goal setting and self- or other-referenced feedback on children's development of self-efficacy and cognitive skills within the Taiwanese classroom. *Journal of Educational Psychology, 92,* 536–543.

Stewart, S. M., Bond, M. H., Deeds, O., Westrick, J., & Wong, C. M. (1999). Predictors of high school achievement in a Hong Kong international school. *International Journal of Psychology, 34*(3), 163–174.

Assessment

Cheung, S. K., & Sun. S. Y. K. (1999). Assessment of optimistic self-beliefs: Further validation of the Chinese version of the General Self-Efficacy Scale. *Psychological Reports, 85*(3, Pt. 2) 1221–1224.

Jeffreys, M. R. (2000). Development and psychometrics evaluation of the Transcultural Self-Efficacy Tool: A synthesis of findings. *Journal of Transcultural Nursing, 11*(2), 127–136.

Kawauchi, K. (1999). Construction of the Campus Interaction Self-Efficacy Scale for students with visual impairments. *Japanese Journal of Educational Psychology, 47,* 471–479.

Resnick, B. (1999). Reliability and validity testing of the self-efficacy for functional activities scale. *Journal of Nursing Measurement, 7*(1), 5–20.

Cardiovascular disease prevention

Winkleby, M., Flora, J., & Kraemer, H. (1994). A community-based heart disease intervention: Predictors of change. *American Journal of Public Health, 84,* 767–772.

Condom use

Barkley, T. W., Jr., & Burns, J. L. (2000). Factor analysis of the Condom Use Self-Efficacy Scale among multicultural college students. *Health Education Research, 15,* 485–489.

Bogart, L. M., Cecil, H., & Pinkerton, S. D. (2000). Intentions to use the female condom among African American adults. *Journal of Applied Social Psychology, 30,* 1923–1953.

Kvalem, I. L., & Traeen, B. (2000). Self-efficacy, scripts of love, and intention to use condoms among Norwegian adolescents. *Journal of Youth & Adolescence, 29,* 337–353.

Cultural differences

Brown, C., Darden, E. E., Shelton, M. C., & Dipoto, M. C. (1999). Career exploration and self-efficacy of high school students: Are there urban/suburban differences? *Journal of Career Assessment, 7,* 227–237.

Durndell, A., Haag, Z., & Laithwaite, H. (2000). Computer self-efficacy and gender: A cross-cultural study of Scotland and Romania. *Personality & Individual Differences, 28,* 1037–1044.

Earley, P. C., Gibson, C. B., & Chen, C. C. (1999). "How did I do?" versus "How did we do?" Cultural contrasts of performance feedback use and self-efficacy. *Journal of Cross-Cultural Psychology, 30,* 594–619.

Mau, W. C. (2000). Cultural differences in career decision-making styles and self-efficacy. *Journal of Vocational Behavior, 57,* 365–378.

Piontkowski, U., Florack, A., Hoelker, P., & Obdrzalek, P. (2000). Predicting acculturation attitudes of dominant and non-dominant groups. *International Journal of Intercultural Relations, 24*(1), 1–26.

Randhwawa, B. S., & Gupta, A. (2000). Cross-national gender differences in mathematics achievement, attitude, and self-efficacy within a common intrinsic structure. *Canadian Journal of School Psychology, 15*(2), 51–66.

Schaubroeck, J., Lam, S. S., & Xie, J. L. (2000). Collective efficacy versus self-efficacy in coping responses to stressors and control: A cross-cultural study. *Journal of Applied Psychology, 85,* 512–525.

Tafarodi, R. W., & Walters, P. (1999). Individualism-collectivism, life events, and self-esteem: A test of two trade-offs. *European Journal of Social Psychology, 29,* 797–814.

(continued)

BOX 18.5   DIVERSITY APPLICATION OF SELF-EFFICACY *CONTINUED*

Troth, G., & Grainger, J. (2000). The psychological impact of custody on the Aboriginal adolescent. *Psychiatry, Psychology, & Law, 7*(1), 89–96.

Depression

Casten, R. J., Rovner, B. W., Pasternak, R. E., & Pelchat, R. (2000). A comparison of self-reported function assessed before and after depression treatment among depressed geriatric patients. *International Journal of Geriatric Psychiatry, 15,* 813–818.

Ennis, N. E., Hobfoll, S. E., & Schroeder, K. E. E. (2000). Money doesn't talk: How economic stress and resistance resources impact inner-city women's depressive mood. *American Journal of Community Psychology, 28*(2), 149–173.

Makaremi, A. (2000). Self-efficacy and depression among Iranian college students. *Psychological Reports, 86,* 386–388.

Disability and disorders

Brody, B. L., Williams, R. A., Thomas, R. G., Kaplan, R. M., Chu, R. M., & Brown, S. I. (1999). Age-related macular degeneration: A randomized clinical trial of a self-management intervention. *Annals of Behavioral Medicine, 21,* 322–329.

Hampton, N. Z. (2000). Self-efficacy and quality of life in people with spinal cord injuries in China. *Rehabilitation Counseling Bulletin, 43*(2), 66–74.

Heller, T., Miller, A. B., & Hseich, K. (1999). Impact of a consumer-directed family support program on adults with developmental disabilities and their family caregivers. *Family Relations: Interdisciplinary Journal of Applied Family Studies, 48,* 419–427.

Kempen, G. I. J. M., van Heuvelen, M. J. G., van Sonderen, E., van den Brink, R. H., Kooijman, A. C., & Ormel, J. (1999). The relationship of functional limitations to disability and the moderating effects of psychological attributes in community-dwelling older persons. *Social Sciences & Medicine, 48,* 1161–1172.

Kempen, G. I. J. M., van Sonderen, E., & Ormel, J. (1999). The impact of psychological attributes on changes in disability among low-functioning older persons. *Journals of Gerontology: Series B: Psychological Sciences & Social Sciences, 54B*(1), P23–P29.

Lackner, J., Carosella, A., & Feuerstein, M. (1996). Pain expectancies, pain, and functional self-efficacy expectancies as determinants of disability in patients with chronic low back disorders. *Journal of Consulting and Clinical Psychology, 64,* 212–220.

Rumrill, P. D., Jr. (1999). Effects of social competence training program on accommodation request activity, situational self-efficacy, and Americans with Disabilities Act knowledge among employed people with visual impairments and blindness. *Journal of Vocational Rehabilitation, 12*(1), 25–31.

Drug/alcohol use

Allsop, S., Saunders, B., & Phillips, M. (2000). The process of relapse in severely dependent male problem. *Addiction, 95*(1), 95–106.

Epstein, J., Botvin, G., Diaz, T., & Toth, V. (1995). Social and personal factors in marijuana use and intentions to use drugs among inner city minority youth. *Journal of Developmental and Behavioral Pediatrics, 16,* 14–20.

Epstein, J. A., Griffin, K. W., & Botvin, G. J. (2000). Role of general and specific competence skills in protecting inner-city adolescents from alcohol use. *Journal of Studies on Alcohol, 81,* 379–386.

Guthrie, B. J., & Low, L. K. (2000). A substance use prevention framework: Considering the social context for African American girls. *Public Health Nursing, 17,* 363–373.

Taylor, M. J. (2000). The influence of self-efficacy on alcohol use among American Indians. *Cultural Diversity & Ethnic Minority Psychology, 6*(2), 152–167.

Wills, T. A., Gibbons, F. X., Gerrard, M., & Brody, G. H. (2000). Protection and vulnerability processes relevant for early onset of substance use: A test among African American children. *Health Psychology, 19,* 253–263.

Ethnic identity

Bennett, M. D., Jr., & Fraser, M. W. (2000). Urban violence among African-American males: Integrating family, neighborhood, and peer perspectives. *Journal of Sociology & Social Welfare, 27*(3), 93–117.

Smith, E. P., Walker, K., Fields, L., Brookins, C. C., & Seay, R. C. (1999). Ethnic identity and its relationship to self-esteem, perceived efficacy, and prosocial attitudes in early adolescence. *Journal of Adolescence, 22,* 867–880.

Ying, Y. W., Lee, P. A., & Tsai, J. L. (2000). Cultural orientation and racial discrimination: Predictors of coherence in Chinese American young adults. *Journal of Community Psychology, 28,* 427–442.

Exercise/physical activity

Booth, M. L., Owen, N., Bauman, A., Clavisi, O., & Leslie, E. (2000). Socio–cognitive and perceived environmental influences associated with physical activity in older Australians. *Preventive Medicine, 31,* 15–22.

Castro, C. M., Sallis, J. F., Hickman, S. A., Lee, R. E., & Chen, A. H. (1999). A prospective study of psychosocial correlates of physical activity for ethnic minority women. *Psychology & Health, 14,* 277–293.

Clark, D. O. (1999). Physical activity and its correlates among urban primary care patients aged 55 years or older. *Journals of Gerontology: Series B: Psychological Sciences & Social Sciences, 54B*(1), S41–S48.

Clark, D. O., & Nothwehr, F. (1999). Exercise self-efficacy and its correlates among socioeconomically disadvantaged older adults. *Health Education & Behavior, 26,* 535–546.

Clark, D. O., Patrick, D., Grembowski, D., & Durham, M. (1995). Socio-economic status and exercise self-efficacy in late life. *Journal of Behavioral Medicine, 18,* 355–376.

Fang, Y., & Zhu, P. (2000). The relationship of middle school students' perception of motivational climate in physical training classes and intrinsic motivation, self-efficacy, and physical performance. *Psychological Science, 23,* 236–237, 229 (China).

Heesch, K. C., Massey, L. C., & Aday, L. A. (2000). Perceptions of sedentary African-American women about continuous versus intermittent walking. *Women & Health, 30*(4), 43–59.

Katula, J. A., Blissner, B. J., & McAuley, E. (1999). Exercise and self-efficacy effects on anxiety reduction in healthy, older adults. *Journal of Behavioral Medicine, 22,* 233–247.

Lafferty, S. C. (2000). Physical activity among older Mexican American women. *Research in Nursing & Health, 23,* 383–392.

BOX 18.5   DIVERSITY APPLICATION OF SELF-EFFICACY

McAuley, E., Blissner, B., Katula, J., & Duncan. T. E. (2000). Exercise environment, self-efficacy, and affective response to acute exercise in older adults. *Psychology & Health, 15,* 341–355.

McAuley, E., Katula, J., Mihalko, S. L., Blissner, B., Duncan. T., Pena, M., & Dunn, E. (1999). Mode of physical activity and self-efficacy in older adults: A latent growth curve analysis. *Journals of Gerontology Series B: Psychological Sciences & Social Sciences, 54B*(5), P283–P252.

Peterson, E., Howland, J., Kielhofner, G., Lachman, M. E., Assmann, S., Cote, J., & Jette, A. (1999). Falls self-efficacy and occupational adaptation among elders. *Physical & Occupational Therapy in Geriatrics, 16*(½), 1–16.

Stevens, M., Lemmink, K. A. P. M., Greef, M. H. G. de, & Rispens, P. (2000). Stimulating physical activity in sedentary older adults: First results. *Preventive Medicine: An International Journal Devoted to Practice & Theory, 31,* 547–553.

Health

Hartman, C. A., Manos, T. M., Winter, C., Hartman, D. M., Li, B., & Smith, J. C. (2000). Effects of T'ai Chi training on function and quality of life indicators in older adults with osteoarthritis. *Journal of the American Geriatrics Society, 48,* 1553–1559.

Rosengren, K. S., McAuley, E., Woods, D., & Mihalko, S. (2000). Gait, balance, and self-efficacy in older black and white American women. *Journal of American Geriatrics Society, 48,* 707–709.

Siero, F. W., Broer, J., Bemelmans, W. J. E., & Meyboom-de Jong, B. M. (2000). Impact of group nutrition education and surplus value of Prochaska-based stage-matched information on health-related cognitions and on Mediterranean nutrition behavior. *Health Education Research, 15,* 635–647.

HIV risk prevention

Belgrave, F., Randolph, S., Carter, C., & Braithwaire, N. (1993). The impact of knowledge, norms, and self-efficacy on intentions to engage in AIDS-preventive behaviors among young incarcerated African-American males. *Journal of Black Psychology, 19,* 155–168.

Bowleg, L., Belgrave, F. Z., & Reisen, C. A. (2000). Gender roles, power strategies, and precautionary sexual self-efficacy: Implications for black and Latina women's HIV/AIDS protective behaviors. *Sex Roles, 42,* 613–635.

Colon, R. M., Wiatrek, D. E., & Evans, R. I. (2000). The relationship between psychosocial factors and condom use among African-American adolescents. *Adolescence, 35,* 559–569.

Faryna, E. L., & Morales, E. (2000). Self-efficacy and HIV-related risk behaviors among multiethnic adolescents. *Cultural Diversity & Ethnic Minority Psychology, 6*(1), 42–56.

Malow, R., Corrigan, S., Cunningham, S., & West, J. (1993). Psychosocial factors associated with condom use among African American drug abusers in treatment. *AIDS Education and Prevention, 5,* 244–253.

Rotherman-Borus, M. J., Roasario, M., Reid, H., & Koopman, C. (1995). Predicting patterns of sexual acts among homosexual and bisexual youths. *American Journal of Psychiatry, 152,* 555–595.

Yzer, M. C., Siero, F. W., & Buunk, B. P. (2000). Can public campaigns effectively change psychological determinants of safer sex? An evaluation of three Dutch campaigns. *Health Education Research, 15,* 339.

Job seeking and performance

Bikos, L. H., & Furry, T. S. (1999). The job search club for international students: An evaluation. *Career Development Quarterly, 48*(1), 31–44.

Davidson, O. B., & Eden, D. (2000). Remedial self-fulfilling prophecy: Two field experiments to prevent Golem effects among disadvantaged women. *Journal of Applied Psychology, 85,* 386–398.

Keim, J., & Strauser, D. R. (2000). Job readiness, self-efficacy, and work personality: A comparison of trainee and instructor perceptions. *Journal of Vocational Rehabilitation, 14*(1), 13–21.

Kneipp, S. M. (2000). The health of women in transition from welfare to employment. *Western Journal of Nursing Research, 22,* 656–674.

Nesdale, D., & Pinter, K. (2000). Self-efficacy and job-seeking activities in unemployed ethnic youth. *Journal of Social Psychology, 140,* 608–614.

Orpen, C. (1995). Self-efficacy beliefs and job performance among black managers in South Africa. *Psychology Reports, 76,* 649–650.

Watkins, D. (2000). Hong Kong student teachers' personal construction of teaching efficacy. *Educational Psychology, 20,* 212–235.

Low income

Boardman, J. D., & Robert, S. A. (2000). Neighborhood socioeconomic status and perceptions of self-efficacy. *Sociological Perspectives, 43*(1), 117–136.

Brekke, M., Hjordahl, P., Telle, D. S., & Kvien, T. K. (1999). Disease activity and severity in patients with rheumatoid arthritis: Relations to socioeconomic inequality. *Social Science & Medicine, 48,* 1743–1750.

Epel, E. S., Bandura, A., & Zimbardo, P. G. (1999). Escaping homelessness: The influence of self-efficacy and time perspective on coping with homelessness. *Journal of Applied Social Psychology, 29,* 575–596.

Kunz, J., & Kalil, A. (1999). Self-esteem, self-efficacy, and welfare use. *Social Work Research, 23*(2), 119–126.

Moldofsky, Z. (2000). Meals made easy: A group program at a food bank. *Social Work with Groups, 23*(1), 83–96.

Raver, C. C., & Leadbeater, B. J. (1999). Mothering under pressure: Environmental, child, and dyadic correlates of maternal self-efficacy among low-income women. *Journal of Family Psychology, 13,* 523–534.

Todd, J. L., & Worell, J. (2000). Resilience in low-income, employed, African American women. *Psychology of Women Quarterly, 24*(2), 119–128.

Mental health/well-being

Bisconti, T. L., & Bergeman, C. S. (1999). Perceived social control as a mediator of the relationships among social support, psychological well-being, and perceived health. *Gerontologist, 39*(1), 94–103.

(continued)

> **BOX 18.5** **DIVERSITY APPLICATION OF SELF-EFFICACY** CONTINUED
>
> Cheung, S. K., & Sun, S. Y. K. (2000). Effects of self-efficacy and social support on the mental health condition of mutual-aid organization members. *Social Behavior & Personality, 28,* 413–422.
>
> Chou, K. R., LaMontagne, L. L., & Hepworth, J. T. (1999). Burden experienced by caregivers of relatives with dementia in Taiwan. *Nursing Research, 48*(4), 206–214.
>
> Gillespie, A., Peltzer, K., & MacLachlan, M. (2000). Returning refugees: Psychosocial problems and mediators of mental health among Malawian returnees. *Journal of Mental Health (UK), 8*(2), 165–178.
>
> Houston, D. M., McKee, K. J., & Wilson, J. (2000). Attributional style, efficacy, and the enhancement of well-being among housebound older people. *Basic & Applied Social Psychology, 22,* 309–317.
>
> Mizell, C. A. (1999). African American men's personal sense of mastery: The consequences of the adolescent environment, self-concept, and adult achievement. *Journal of Black Psychology, 25*(2), 210–230.
>
> Peltzer, K., Cherian, V. L., & Cherian, L. (1999). Minor psychiatric morbidity in South African secondary school pupils. *Psychological Reports, 85,* 397–402.
>
> Nyamathi, A. M., Stein, J. A., & Bayley, L. J. (2000). Predictors of mental distress and poor physical health among homeless women. *Psychology & Health, 15,* 483–500.
>
> Zimmerman, M. A., Ramirez-Valles, J., & Malton, K. L. (1999). Resilience among urban African American male adolescents: A study of the protective effects of sociopolitical control on their mental health. *American Journal of Community Psychology, 27,* 733–751.
>
> *Parenting*
>
> Brody, G. H., Flor, D. L., & Gibson, N. M. (1999). Linking maternal efficacy beliefs, developmental goals, parenting practices, and child competence in rural single-parent African American families. *Child Development, 70,* 1197–1208.
>
> Izzo, C., Weiss, L., Shanahan, T., & Rodriguez-Brown, F. (2000). Parental self-efficacy and social support as predictors of parenting practices and children's socioemotional adjustment in Mexican immigrant families. *Journal of Prevention & Intervention in the Community, 20*(½), 197–213.
>
> Jackson, A. P. (2000). Maternal self-efficacy and children's influence on stress and parenting among single black mothers in poverty. *Journal of Family Issues, 21*(1), 3–16.
>
> Jung, L. P., & Silbereisen, R. K. (1999). Supportive parenting and adolescent adjustment across time in former East and West Germany. *Journal of Adolescence, 22,* 719–736.
>
> Kwok, S., & Wong, D. (2000). Mental health of parents with young children in Hong Kong: The roles of parenting stress and parenting self-efficacy. *Child & Family Social Work, 5*(1), 57–65.
>
> Weber, J. L., & O'Brien, M. (1999). Latino children's responses to simulated interparental conflict. *Cognitive Therapy & Research, 23*(3), 247–270.
>
> *Prostate cancer*
>
> Boehm, S., Coleman-Burns, P., Schlenk, E., & Funnell, M. (1995). Prostate cancer in African American men: Increasing knowledge and self-efficacy. *Journal of Community Health Nursing, 12,* 161–169.
>
> *Smoking*
>
> Epstein, J. A., Griffin, K. W., & Botvin, G. J. (2000). A model of smoking among inner-city adolescents: The role of personal competence and perceived social benefits of smoking. *Preventive Medicine: An International Journal Devoted to Practice & Theory, 31*(2, Pt. 1), 107–114.
>
> *Social functioning*
>
> Heberlein, W., Licht, M. H., & Licht, B. G. (1999). Older adults' perceptions of control in social situations. *Social Behavior & Personality, 27*(1), 29–37.
>
> *STDs*
>
> Nuwaha, F., Faxelid, E., Neema, S., Eriksson, C., & Hoejer, B. (2000). Psychosocial determinants for sexual partner referral in Uganda: Qualitative results. *International Journal of STD & AIDS, 11*(3), 156–161.

client samples. Increasingly, older adults, people with disabilities, and those struggling with poverty are included in self-efficacy research, in addition to examination of cultural differences, both in the United States and elsewhere.

The concept of resilience is gaining attention, and self-efficacy appraisals are a part of that analysis. Zimmerman, Ramirez-Valles, and Maton (1999), for example, tested the protective effects of African American male adolescents' beliefs about their efficacy in social and political systems (termed sociopolitical control) on the link between helplessness and mental health (psychological symptoms and self-esteem). They found that high sociopolitical self-efficacy beliefs limited the negative consequences of helplessness on mental health, suggesting the value of this form of self-efficacy in buffering or protecting youth from negative consequences of feeling helplessness.

One of the premises behind self-efficacy theory is that its effect is often one of mediating the relationship of background variables to outcomes. Using statistical models to test these kind of relationships has become more possible in recent years. Smith, Walker, Fields, Brookins, and Seay (1999) found support for this among a sample of male and female early adolescents from different racial/ethic backgrounds. Specifically, they found that, although related, ethnic identity and self-esteem were distinct from each other and that both contributed to prosocial attitudes about goal attainment operating through (and mediated by) self-efficacy of their ability to achieve. This type of finding supports the argument that, although critically important, efforts to foster healthy identity and positive self-esteem may not be sufficient in supporting achievement of outcome goals if self-efficacy beliefs do not correspond.

Attention has also been directed to environmental and contextual factors, for these influence or interact with self-efficacy. Boardman and Robert (2000) focused on people's socioeconomic status, questioning whether neighborhood socioeconomic characteristics were related to individuals' self-efficacy. Their findings showed that lower socioeconomic status corresponded with lower self-efficacy. Of particular note was the finding that neighborhood indicators of lower SES (high proportions of unemployment and public assistance) were associated with lower self-efficacy above and beyond the relationship of individual-level SES to self-efficacy. Consistent with today's practice nexus, findings such as these remind us that helping efforts with individuals and their families are best pursued with the critical awareness that people are always embedded in many types of environments—social, material, cultural, political—that are important considerations in assessment and intervention.

Considerable research on HIV/AIDS continues, including diverse samples relative to race, sexual orientation, and socioeconomic status. Self-efficacy has emerged as a significant component of HIV prevention (Antoni, 1991; Aspinwall, Kemeny, Taylor, & Schneider, 1991; Belgrave, Randolph, Carter, & Braithwaite, 1993; Malow, Corrigan, Cunningham, & West, 1993; Rotheram-Borus, Rosario, Reid, & Koopman, 1995). The bulk of research continues to suggest the importance of self-efficacy to predict HIV-related risk behaviors. However, findings are also indicating complexities, including the need for theoretical models of behavior change to include dimensions of diversity and identity. To illustrate, Faryna and Morales (2000) found within an ethnically diverse sample of high school students that ethnicity consistently appeared a stronger predictor of HIV-related risk behaviors than did gender, self-efficacy, or knowledge, attitudes, and beliefs regarding sexual activity and substance use. Cochran and Mays (1993) discuss some potential issues in the application of current models to predict risk behaviors, in this instance focusing on African Americans. They note that these models emphasize the importance of individualistic, direct control of behavioral choices and deemphasize external factors such as racism and poverty that are particularly relevant to those within the African American community at highest risk of HIV infection. They contend that applications of these models without consideration of the unique issues associated with behavioral choices within the African American community may not capture the most relevant determinants of risk behaviors. Others have also discussed the need for AIDS education and prevention that mobilize the will of members of the African American community (Gasch, Poulson, Fullilove, & Fullilove, 1991). These authors note that such a prevention program is based on three assumptions:

1. The environment plays a critical role in conditioning behavior.
2. The experiences of community deterioration differ between African American men and women.
3. African Americans in urban areas are struggling to make sense of the threatening ecological and social environment with which they come into contact on a daily basis.

Gasch and associates propose a model of AIDS education that focuses on social responsibility for African American men and *contextual* self-efficacy for African American women.

Self-efficacy was examined as a predictor in marijuana use and in intentions to use drugs among African American and Hispanic seventh-grade, low-income youth (Epstein, Botvin, Diaz, & Toth, 1995). Social influences, including tolerance of marijuana use by adults, friends, and role models, predicted marijuana use. Lack of self-efficacy and low academic performance were related to the youths' intentions to use cocaine, crack, and other drugs. Self-efficacy figured in another drug use study—one of African American adults who used drugs through needle injections (Krepcho, Fernandez-Esquer, Freeman, & Magee, 1993). Specifically, self-efficacy was explored as one of a number of predictor variables for cleaning needles with bleach during drug use. Out of all ten predictor variables, the best predictors of bleach use were self-efficacy, expectations about bleach use, and age of the adult. Focusing on preventing drug use, Van-Hasselt, Hersen, Null, and Ammerman (1993) describe a drug use prevention program for African American children that focuses on the development of family-based alternative activities to promote self-efficacy, achievement, and self-esteem.

Winkleby, Flora, and Kraemer (1994) examined self-efficacy as one of a number of factors related to changes in cardiovascular disease risk-factor scores (RFSS) of adult men and women of varied racial and ethnic groups who had received a six-year cardiovascular disease risk-reduction educational program. The subgroup with the highest proportion of positive changes was composed of people over 55 years of age with the highest perceived risk, highest health media use, and highest blood pressure and cholesterol levels. The subgroup with the lowest proportion of positive changes consisted of those who were less educated, reported less health knowledge, and had lower self-efficacy scores.

Self-efficacy is also an important variable in academic success. Bryan and Bryan (1991) found self-efficacy and positive mood induction to be related to performance of both junior high and high school students with a learning disability. At the postsecondary level, college self-efficacy—or the degree of confidence that one can successfully complete college—was an important determinant of student adjustment for Mexican American and Latino American college students (Solberg, O'Brien, Villareal, & Kennel, 1993).

Bandura's (1986) self-efficacy model has also been applied to career selection. Morrow, Gore, and Campbell (1996) investigated the effects of self-efficacy on the career development patterns of lesbian women and gay men. With an ethnically mixed group of high school equivalency students (predominantly Hispanic and Native American girls and boys) from seasonal farm work backgrounds, students' interests, perceived incentives, and self-efficacy expectations (beliefs about their ability to learn to engage in an occupation successfully) predicted their willingness to consider future occupations (Church, Teresa, Rosebrook, & Szendre, 1992). Among an ethnically mixed high school population of over 800 rural girls and boys (Hispanic, Native American, and white youth), Lauver and Jones (1991) found differences in self-efficacy estimates for career choice among varied ethnic groups, with efficacy lowest for 7 of the 18 occupations studied among the Native American youth.

Gender is also a variable that affects self-efficacy in career selection. Church and associates (1992) found that both Hispanic and Native American male and female high-school-equivalency students reported greater willingness to consider occupations dominated by their own gender, with the women students showing a greater tendency to reject occupations dominated by the opposite gender. This finding suggests less self-efficacy related to expectations of success in nontraditional occupations. In the Lauver and Jones (1991) study of Hispanic, Native American, and white rural youth, gender differences were found in both interest and self-efficacy estimates for same-gender and cross-gender occupations, with the boys considering fewer cross-gender options than the girls. Self-efficacy has also been explored as a contributing variable in the exercise habits and physical activity of elderly persons (McAuley, Shaffer, & Rudolph, 1995—see also Box 18.5).

Guidelines for Using Self-Efficacy with Diverse Groups of Clients

From a multicultural standpoint, the goal of strengthening self-efficacy, when used alone, suffers from some of the criticisms we have made of the relevance of self-management approaches for clients of color. As Cochran and Mays (1993) previously noted, the self-efficacy model generally emphasizes the importance of individualistic, direct control of behavioral choices. This reflects a world view that is high in both internal locus of control and internal locus of responsibility. People from cultures that stress collectivity and unity may not feel comfortable with this model, as may individuals who have experienced unjust societal conditions such as racism and poverty. Increasingly, self-efficacy is being researched and approached from a lifespan perspective and in a more contextualized manner. This includes more attention to historical, cultural, developmental, linguistic, social network, privilege, and other environmental factors that are likely to exert influence on individuals' evolving sense of self-efficacy as well as how their self-efficacy schemas and appraisals are activated or interpreted in specific situations. For example, in outlining a substance use prevention framework targeting African American females, Guthrie and Low (2000) emphasize the need to attend to the influences of factors such as racism, sexism, classism, and ageism toward developing ethnically meaningful and efficacious interventions.

The growth of positive findings with diverse people does argue that improved self-efficacy is useful as an intervention target and empowerment tool if it is sought within the context of additional change processes. Schulz and Heckhausen (1999) argue that although striving for control within one's life is a human universal across historical time and cultural settings, the expression of control striving and related beliefs is shaped in part by culture. They emphasize the importance of a lifespan perspective, particularly toward increasing our understanding of how self-efficacy changes late in life and the implications of these changes to how a helper may conceptualize self-efficacy and devise an intervention plan. This is very consistent with the themes we urge in this book: to include attention to environmental and diversity factors and to a collaborative approach to service that takes the context, strengths, and realistic limitations of people and their circumstances into account. In a related vein, Epel, Bandura, and Zimbardo (1999) report findings of self-efficacy and time perspective of homeless adults relative to their coping strategies regarding housing and employment. They report that those high on future orientation had shorter periods of homelessness, were more likely to enroll in training, and reported gaining more positive benefits from their situation, whereas those high in present orientation used more avoidant coping strategies yet had greater success in getting temporary housing. Despite the predictive power of self-efficacy and time orientation, there were no predictors of stable housing—reflective of the scarce resources and limitations of individual efforts to change fundamental conditions. Growing attention to empowerment recognizes these and other limitations to the concept and power of individual self-efficacy. Gutierrez (1990), for example, proposes that an empowerment process for women, people of color, and others with limiting or marginalizing conditions include not only ways to increase self-efficacy but also the development of group and cultural consciousness and the reduction of personal and self-blame. We see this perspective as highly useful because it focuses on external social–contextual factors as well as the sense of confidence in oneself.

MODEL EXAMPLE: SELF-EFFICACY

In Chapter 10, we presented the goals for Joan. The first goal—asking questions and making reasonable requests—had four subgoals: (1) to decrease anxiety ratings associated with anticipation of failure in math class and rejection by parents, (2) to increase positive self-talk and thoughts that "girls are capable" in math class and other competitive situations from zero or two times a week to four or five times a week over the next two weeks, (3) to increase attendance in math class from two or three times a week to four or five times a week during treatment, and (4) to increase verbal participation and initiation in math class and with her parents from none or once a week to three or four times a week over the next two weeks during treatment. Verbal participation is defined as asking and answering questions posed by teachers or parents, volunteering answers or offering opinions, or going to the chalkboard.

The helper can determine the extent of Joan's self-efficacy (confidence) for each of the goal behaviors. Self-efficacy can be measured by asking Joan to give a verbal rating of her confidence for each goal on a scale from 0 (no confidence) to 100 (a great deal of confidence). Alternatively, the helper can design a rating scale and ask Joan to circle her rating of confidence for each goal. (See Learning Activity 18.5). Possible scales for all the goals are shown below:

Goal One for Math Class:

Confidence in *decreasing anxiety* (from 70 to 50) about possible failure in *math class*

0   10   20   30   40   50   60   70   80   90   100
Uncertain   Total Certainty

Goal One for Parents:

Confidence in *decreasing anxiety* (from 70 to 50) about possible *rejection by parents*

0   10   20   30   40   50   60   70   80   90   100
Uncertain   Total Certainty

Goal Two for Math Class:

Confidence to *increase positive self-talk and thoughts*—"girls are capable"—to four or five times a week in *math class*

0   10   20   30   40   50   60   70   80   90   100
Uncertain   Total Certainty

Goal Two for Other Situations:

Confidence to *increase positive self-talk and thoughts*—"girls are capable"—to four or five times a week in *other competitive situations*

0   10   20   30   40   50   60   70   80   90   100
Uncertain   Total Certainty

LEARNING ACTIVITY 18.5 Self-Efficacy

In this learning activity, you are to determine and assess your self-efficacy.

1. Review Chapter 10 and select some goals you would like to achieve. Your general goal may have to be divided into subgoals.
2. Write down your goals and/or subgoals. Make sure that your written goals comply with the guidelines presented in Chapter 10.
3. For the goal you would like to achieve, make a scale (0 to 100) to measure your self-efficacy (confidence) in performing your goal behaviors, thoughts, or feelings for each subgoal, and for each person with whom and setting in which the goal is to be performed.
4. Assess your self-efficacy by circling the number on each scale that reflects your degree of uncertainty or certainty (confidence) in performing each goal.
5. You might wish to use the self-efficacy scales to self-monitor your confidence over a period of time as you gain more experience in performing the goal behaviors.

Goal Three:

Confidence to *increase attendance* in *math class* to four or five times a week

0   10   20   30   40   50   60   70   80   90   100
Uncertain   Total Certainty

Goal Four for Math Class:

Confidence in *asking* questions in *math class*

0   10   20   30   40   50   60   70   80   90   100
Uncertain   Total Certainty

Confidence in *answering* questions in *math class*

0   10   20   30   40   50   60   70   80   90   100
Uncertain   Total Certainty

Confidence in *volunteering answers* in *math class*

0   10   20   30   40   50   60   70   80   90   100
Uncertain   Total Certainty

Confidence in *going to the chalkboard* in *math class*

0   10   20   30   40   50   60   70   80   90   100
Uncertain   Total Certainty

Goal Four for Parents:

Confidence in *asking parents questions*

0   10   20   30   40   50   60   70   80   90   100
Uncertain   Total Certainty

Confidence in *answering questions asked by parents*

0   10   20   30   40   50   60   70   80   90   100
Uncertain   Total Certainty

Confidence in *offering opinions to parents*

0   10   20   30   40   50   60   70   80   90   100
Uncertain   Total Certainty

There are seven different behaviors and settings listed in Objective Four. We are very specific about assessing the degree of Joan's self-efficacy for each *behavior* and *setting* described in Objective Four. As Joan becomes more successful in achieving her goal behaviors, measures of her self-efficacy or confidence will increase.

SUMMARY

Self-management is a process in which clients direct their own behavior change using any one change intervention strategy or a combination of strategies. The self-monitoring strategy provides a method by which a client can become more aware of his or her overt behavior or internal responses such as thoughts or feelings. Self-monitoring may also provide information about the social and environmental context that influences these behaviors. Stimulus-control procedures require predetermined arrangement of environmental conditions that are antecedents of a target behavior, or cues to increase or decrease that behavior. As a self-management strategy, self-reward involves presenting oneself with a positive stimulus *after* engaging in a specified behavior. Self-modeling is a method in which the client can acquire desired behaviors by using himself or herself as a model. These four strategies are typically classified as self-management because in each procedure the client prompts, alters, or controls antecedents and consequences to produce desired changes in behavior in a self-directed fashion. Promoting client commitment to use self-management strategies can be achieved by introducing these strategies later in the helping process, assessing the client's motivation for change, creating a social support system to aid the client in the use of the strategy, and maintaining contact with the client while self-management strategies are being used. All of these self-management strategies, as well as other interventions we describe in this book, are affected by self-efficacy, a cognitive process that mediates behavioral change. These change strategies and tools can—and, we argue, *should*—be applied collaboratively with clients and in the service of building on strengths, supporting empowerment and self-determination, and being critically attentive to environmental factors that may be relevant targets of change as well as potential resources.

Self-management interventions have been used with diverse groups of clients both within the United States and elsewhere, including diversity with respect to gender, age, disability status, sexual orientation, socioeconomic level, and race and ethnicity. As the research summaries show, recent empirical work in general and that specific to diversity has varied across the four components of self-management included here, with self-efficacy being most extensively researched. Given the "self" emphasis among these strategies, it may be the case that self-management interventions will appeal most to clients who value self-reliance and who desire interventions that are time limited, focused on the present, and designed to resolve identified concerns. However, processes involved in self-regulation appear to vary across cultures and societies, and many of the notions underlying self-management are decidedly Eurocentric, such as the notions of internal locus of control and internal locus of responsibility. These as well as variables such as the client's cultural or collective identity and acculturation and assimilation status may affect the appropriateness of self-management or ways in which these tools and interventions are applied. We concur with Gutierrez (1990), who proposes that an empowerment process for clients from diverse groups include not only ways to increase the client's sense of self-efficacy but also ways to develop group and cultural consciousness, the reduction of personal self-blame and denigration, and access to resources and opportunities inherent to goal achievement.

A Final Note

As we terminate this journey, we would like to leave you with a few thoughts. First, set careful and realistic personal and professional limits for yourself as a helping practitioner. Learn what you can and cannot do for and with clients. A critical part of effective help giving is to know when to back off and assess the process: Is it time to redefine roles and responsibilities? To bring in additional helping resources or prepare to transition to a different helping context?

Second, examine your expectations for yourself and your clients. Helping practitioners often find that their expectations for change differ markedly from those of clients, particularly reluctant or pessimistic clients. In such instances, practitioners are often meeting more of their own needs for change and success than pursuing the needs and issues of clients. Effective practice is endangered when the helper wants more (or something different) for clients than the clients want for themselves. In such cases, the practitioner's efforts are at odds with the client's, and limited progress is likely. Recognize that change efforts by all of us are difficult, especially with long-standing behavior patterns. Also, remember that clients' efforts to resist change are often positive because they are protective and reflect underlying strengths. Seeming resistance may provide signals of elements that the client is not experiencing as relevant or consistent with his or her values, goals, perspective, personality, context, or other dimensions of "where the client is"—signals to pay attention to in respectful, collaborative, ethical practice.

Bear in mind that the work of professional helping is tough—at times, really tough. Recently, there has been a focus in the help-giving professions on "compassion fatigue"—a state of physical and/or mental exhaustion that occurs in professional helpers when they don't have good boundaries for themselves, care too much for others at the expense of themselves, and just get worn out by the stresses and frustrations of working within today's complex and constrained system of care. Fortunately, there has also been attention to the great rewards of a career in the helping professions. This includes sustainable "passionate commitment" and factors that help practitioners maintain high levels of personal accomplishment and a sense of being energized rather than drained by their professional work.

There are some themes associated with the successful experience of passionate commitment over the course of a career that may be constructive parts of your own practice nexus. These themes include (Dlugos & Friedlander, 2001): (1) balance (maintaining boundaries, seeking diversity within work activities, using leisure activities to provide relief), (2) adaptiveness/openness (viewing obstacles as challenges to be met with creativity, active pursuit of feedback about one's work), (3) intentional learning (deliberate learning from struggles, continued depth in learning from work with clients), and (4) transcendence and humility (acknowledging spiritual dimensions of helping, appreciating the social justice and community dimensions of our lives).

Finally, above all, be flexible. The skills and strategies offered in this book are simply methodology that is more or less effective depending on the creativity and intuition of the user. Remember that there is great variance among individual clients—not only in terms of cultural and gender factors but also in terms of covert and overt behavioral patterns, life and developmental histories, and sociopolitical milieus. We have spoken a great deal in this book about subgroups of clients—men, women, young, old, gay, lesbian, learning disabled, physically challenged, and people of all different races and ethnic groups. However, remember that each subgroup is made up of individuals who cannot and should not be categorized or stereotyped by their status in a group. Helping professionals who are flexible regard each client as unique and regard each helping strategy as a tool to be used or set aside depending on its effectiveness in producing client-generated outcomes.

INFOTRAC® EXPLORATIONS

1. Search for the term *self-management*. Select two to four articles that describe intervention outcomes with one or more issues of interest to you. Write out the intervention components involved for each issue/article. What aspects are common across all articles? What are points of difference with respect to the intervention strategies or how these are explained or applied?
2. Search for the term *self-monitoring*, and select two to four articles on different client populations. Take a careful look at the self-monitoring tool or procedure(s) described in each article. Write your understanding of what these involve, how the tools are similar or common, how useful or engaging you deem them to be for that population, and any recommendations you might make (e.g., about the tool or procedure, how it is explained or used, ways to record or display results).

3. Search for the combined terms *self-efficacy* and some problem in living of particular interest to you. Select two to four articles on conceptual or clinical descriptions of how self-efficacy plays an important role either in problem development or in supporting the change goals and interventions. Briefly write out your description of how you understand this to work. (For example, what exactly does self-efficacy do? What promotes or undermines it? Are there contextual or diversity factors to be sensitive to in this regard?)

SUGGESTED RESOURCES

Readings

Self-Management

Arcury, T. A., Quandt, S. A., McDonald, J., & Bell, R. A. (2000). Faith and health self-management of rural older adults. *Journal of Cross-Cultural Gerontology, 15,* 55–74.

Bartholomew, L. K., Gold, R. S., Parcel, G. S., Czyewski, D. I., Sockrider, M. M., Fernandez, M., Shegog, R., & Swank, P. (2000). Watch, discover, think, and act: Evaluation of computer-assisted instruction to improve asthma self-management in inner-city children. *Patient Education & Counseling, 39,* 269–280.

Bockaerts, M. (1997). Self-regulated learning: A new concept embraced by researchers, policy makers, educators, teachers, and students. *Learning & Instruction, 7,* 161–186.

Davies, S., & Witte, R. (2000). Self-management and peer-monitoring within a group-contingency to decrease uncontrolled verbalizations of children with attention-deficit/hyperactivity disorder. *Psychology in the Schools, 37,* 135–147.

Gifford, A. L., & Sengupta, S. (1999). Self-management health education for chronic HIV infection. *AIDS Care, 11*(1), 115–130.

Marks, I. M. (1994). Behavior therapy as an aid to self-care. *Current Directions in Psychological Science, 3,* 19–22.

McDougall, D. (1998). Research on self-management techniques used by students with disabilities in general education settings: A descriptive review. *Remedial & Special Education, 18,* 310–320.

Parcel, G. S., Swank, P. R., Mariotto, M. J., & Bartholomew, L. K. (1994). Self-management of cystic fibrosis: A structural model for educational and behavioral variables. *Social Science and Medicine, 38,* 1307–1315.

Rokke, P. D., Tomhave, J. A., & Jocic, Z. (2000). Self-management therapy and educational group therapy for depressed elders. *Cognitive Therapy & Research, 24,* 99–119.

Smith, L. L., Smith, J. N., & Beckner, B. M. (1994). An anger-management workshop for women inmates. *Families in Society, 75,* 172–175.

Watson, D. L., & Tharp, R. G. (2002). *Self-directed behavior* (8th ed.). Pacific Grove, CA: Brooks/Cole.

Williams, R. L., Moore, C. A., Pettibone, T. J., & Thomas, S. P. (1992). Construction and validation of a brief self-report scale of self-management practices. *Journal of Research in Personality, 26,* 216–234.

Weiss, D. H. (1999). *The self-management workshop: Helping people take control of their lives and their work (A trainer's guide).* New York: American Management Association.

Self-Monitoring

Cole, C. L., & Bambara, L. M. (2000). Self-monitoring: Theory and practice. In E. S. Shapiro and T. R. Kratochwill (Eds.), *Behavioral assessment in schools: Theory, research, and clinical foundations.* New York: Guilford.

Dayus, B., & van den Broek, M. D. (2000). Treatment of stable delusional confabulations using self-monitoring training. *Neuropsychological Rehabilitation, 10,* 415–427.

Fox, M., & Deyer, D. (1995). Stressful job demands and worker health: An investigation of the effects of self-monitoring. *Journal of Applied Social Psychology, 25,* 1973–1995.

Goodwin, R., & Soon, A. P. Y. (1994). Self-monitoring and relationship adjustment: A cross-cultural analysis. *Journal of Social Psychology, 134,* 35–39.

Halford, W. K., Gravestock, F. M., Lowe, R., & Scheldt, S. (1992). Toward a behavioral ecology of stressful marital interactions. *Behavioral Assessment, 14,* 199–217.

Harris, K. R., Graham, S., Reid, R., & McElroy, K. (1994). Self-monitoring of attention versus self-monitoring of performance: Replication and cross-task comparison studies. *Learning Disability Quarterly, 17,* 121–139.

Jordan, C., and Franklin, C. (1995). *Clinical assessment for social workers: Quantitative and qualitative methods.* Chicago: Lyceum.

Madsen, J., Sallis, J. F., Rupp, J. W., & Senn, K. L. (1993). Relationship between self-monitoring of diet and exercise change and subsequent risk factor changes in children and adults. *Patient Education and Counseling, 21,* 61–69.

McDougall, D., & Brady, M. (1995). Using audio-cued self-monitoring for students with severe behavior disorders. *Journal of Educational Research, 88,* 309–317.

Reid, R. (1996). Research in self-monitoring with students with learning disabilities: The present, the prospects, the pitfalls. *Journal of Learning Disabilities, 29,* 317–331.

Reynolds, M., & Salkovskis, P. M. (1992). Comparison of positive and negative intrusive thoughts and experimental investigation of the differential effects of mood. *Behaviour Research and Therapy, 30,* 273–281.

Todd, A. W., Horner, R. H., & Sugai, G. (1999). Self-monitoring and self-recruited praise: Effects on problem behavior, academic engagement, and work completion in a typical classroom. *Journal of Positive Behavior Interventions, 1*(2), 66–76.

Walitze, K. S., & Connors, G. J. (1999). Treating problem drinking. *Alcohol Research & Health, 23,* 138–143.

Stimulus Control

Estabrooks, P., Courneya, K., & Nigg, C. (1996). Effects of a stimulus control intervention on attendance at a university fitness center. *Behavior Modification, 20,* 202–215.

Graff, R. B., Libby, M. E., & Green, G. (1998). The effects of reinforcer choice on rates of challenging behavior and free operant responding in individuals with severe disabilities. *Behavioral Interventions, 13,* 249–268.

Haddock, C. K., Shadish, W. R., Klesges, R. C., & Stein, R. J. (1994). Treatments for childhood and adolescent obesity. *Annals of Behavioral Medicine, 16,* 235–244.

Hauri, P. J. (2000). The many faces of insomnia. In D. I. Mostofsky and D. H. Barlow (Eds.), *The management of stress and anxiety in medical disorders* (pp. 143–159). Needham Heights, MA: Allyn & Bacon.

Lichstein, K. L., Wilson, N. M., & Johnson. C. T. (2000). Psychological treatment of secondary insomnia. *Psychology & Aging, 15,* 232–240.

Poulson, C. L., & Effie, K. (1996). Arranging the development of conceptual behavior: A technology for stimulus control. In S. W. Bijou & E. Ribes (Eds.), *New directions in behavior development.* Reno, NV: Context.

Ray, K. P., Skinner, C. H., & Watson, T. S. (1999). Transferring stimulus control via momentum to increase compliance in a student with autism: A demonstration of collaborative consultation. *School Psychology Review, 28,* 622–628.

Stromer, R., MacKay, H., Howell, S., & McVay, A. (1996). Teaching computer-based spelling to individuals with developmental and hearing disabilities. *Journal of Applied Behavior Analysis, 29,* 25–42.

Taylor, S., Cipani, E., & Clardy, A. (1994). A stimulus control technique for improving the efficacy of an established toilet training program. *Journal of Behavior Therapy and Experimental Psychiatry, 25,* 155–160.

Weatherly, J. N., Miller, K., & McDonald, T. W. (1999). Social influence as stimulus control. *Behavior & Social Issues, 9,* 25–45.

Williams, J. G., Park, L. I., & Kline, J. (1992). Reducing distress associated with pelvic examinations: A stimulus control intervention. *Women and Health, 18,* 41–53.

Self-Reward

Cromie, S. D., & Baker, L. J. V. (1997). The behavioural self-control of study in third-level students: A review. In K. Dillenburger, M. F. O'Reilly, et al. (Eds.), *Advances in behaviour analysis* (pp. 113–133). Dublin, Ireland: University College Dublin Press.

Eisenberger, R., & Cameron, J. (1996). Detrimental effects of reward: Reality or myth? *American Psychologist, 51,* 1153–1166.

Field, L. K., & Steinhardt, M. A. (1992). The relationship of internally directed behavior to self-reinforcement, self-esteem, and expectancy values for exercise. *American Journal of Health Promotion, 7,* 21–27.

Fuhrmann, A., & Kuhl, J. (1998). Maintaining a healthy diet: Effects of personality and self-reward versus self-punishment on commitment to and enactment of self-chosen and assigned goals. *Psychology and Health, 13,* 651–686.

Kanfer, F. H., & Gaelick-Buys, L. (1991). Self-management methods. In F. H. Kanfer & A. P. Goldstein (Eds.), *Helping people change* (4th ed., pp. 305–360). New York: Pergamon.

Karoly, P., & Lecci, L. (1997). Motivational correlates of self-reported persistent pain in young adults. *Clinical Journal of Pain, 13,* 104–109.

Lecci, L., Karoly, P. R., Ruehlman, L. S., & Lanyon, R. I. (1996). Goal-relevant dimensions of hypochondriacal tendencies and their relation to symptom manifestation and psychological distress. *Journal of Abnormal Psychology, 105,* 42–52.

Marcoux, M. F., Sallis, J. F., McKenzie, T. L., Marshall, S., Armstrong, C. A., & Goggin, K. J. (1999). Process evaluation of a physical self-management program for children: SPARK. *Psychology and Health, 14,* 659–677.

Schill, T., & Kramer, J. (1991). Self-defeating personality, self-reinforcement, and depression. *Psychological Reports, 69,* 137–138.

Solomon, L. J., Flynn, B. S., Worden, J. K., Mickey, R. M., Skelly, J. M., Geller, B. M., Peluso, N. W., & Webster, J. A. (1998). Assessment of self-reward strategies for maintenance of breast self-examination. *Journal of Behavioral Medicine, 21,* 83–102.

Self-As-a-Model

Bray, M. A., & Kehle, T. J. (1998). Self-modeling as an intervention for stuttering. *School Psychology Review, 27,* 587–598.

Brown, G. W., & Middleton, H. (1998). Use of self-as-a-model to promote generalization and maintenance of the reduction of self-stimulation in a child with mental retardation. *Education & Training in Mental Retardation & Developmental Disabilities, 33,* 76–80.

Buggey, T., Toombs, K., Gardener, P., & Cervetti, M. (1999). Training responding behaviors in students with autism: Using videotaped self-modeling. *Journal of Positive Behavior Interventions, 1,* 205–214.

Clare, S. K., Jenson, W. R., Kehle, T., J., & Bray, M. A. (2000). Self-modeling as a treatment for increasing on-task behavior. *Psychology in the Schools, 37,* 517–522.

Dowrick, P. W. (1999). A review of self-modeling and related interventions. *Applied and Preventive Psychology, 8,* 23–39.

Hartley, E. T., Bray, M. A., & Kehle, T. J. (1998). Self-modeling as an intervention to increase student classroom participation. *Psychology in the Schools, 35,* 363–372.

Kehle, T. J., Madaus, M. R., Baratta, V. S., & Bray, M. A. (1998). Augmented self-modeling as a treatment for children with selective mutism. *Journal of School Psychology, 36,* 247–260.

Possell, L. E., Kehle, T. J., McLoughlin, C. S., & Bray, M. A. (1999). Self-modeling as an intervention to reduce disruptive classroom behavior. *Cognitive and Behavioral Practice, 6,* 99–105.

Reamer, R. B., Brady, M. P., & Hawkins, J. (1998). The effects of video self-modeling on parents' interactions with children with developmental disabilities. *Education and Training in Mental Retardation and Developmental Disabilities, 33,* 131–143.

Schunk, D. H., & Zimmerman, B. J. (1997). Social origins of self-regulatory competence. *Educational Psychologist, 32,* 195–208.

Self-Efficacy

Arnstein, P., Caudill, M., Mandle, C. L., Norris, A., & Beasley, R. (1999). Self-efficacy as a mediator of the relationship between pain intensity, disability, and depression in chronic pain patients. *Pain, 80,* 483–491.

Bandura, A. (1977). Self-efficacy: Toward a unifying theory of behavioral change. *Psychological Review, 84,* 191–215.

Bandura, A. (1982). Self-efficacy mechanism in human agency. *American Psychologist, 37,* 122–147.

Bandura, A. (1989). Human agency in social cognitive theory. *American Psychologist, 44,* 1175–1185.

Bandura, A. (1997). *Self-efficacy: The exercise of self-control.* New York: Freeman.

Benight, C. C., Swift, E., Sanger, J., Smith, A., & Zeppelin, D. (1999). Coping self-efficacy as a mediator of distress following a natural disaster. *Journal of Applied Social Psychology, 29,* 2443–2464.

Betz, N. E. (2000). Self-efficacy theory as a basis for career assessment. *Journal of Career Assessment, 8,* 205–222.

Dickerson, A., & Taylor, M. A. (2000). Self-limiting behavior in women: Self-esteem and self-efficacy as predictors. *Group and Organization Management, 25*(2), 191–210.

Friedman, I. A. (2000). Burnout in teachers: Shattered dreams of impeccable professional performance. *Journal of Clinical Psychology, 56,* 595–606.

Friedman, L. C., Nelson, D. ., Webb, J. A., & Hoffman, L. P. (1994). Dispositional optimism, self-efficacy, and health beliefs as predictors of breast self-examination. *American Journal of Preventive Medicine, 10,* 130–135.

Kraus, L. J., & Hughey, K. F. (1999). The impact of an intervention on career decision-making self-efficacy and career indecision. *Professional School Counseling, 2,* 384–390.

Lerner, C. F., & Kennedy, L. T. (2000). Stay–leave decision-making in battered women: Trauma, coping, and self-efficacy. *Cognitive Therapy & Research, 24*(2), 215–232.

Maisto, S. A., Connors, G. J., & Zwiak, W. H. (2000). Alcohol treatment changes in coping skills, self-efficacy, and levels of alcohol use and related problems one year following treatment initiation. *Psychology of Addictive Behaviors, 14,* 257–266.

Applications with Diverse Groups of Clients

Barkley, T. W., Jr., & Burns, J. L. (2000). Factor analysis of the Condom Use Self-Efficacy Scale among multicultural college students. *Health Education Research, 15,* 485–489.

Bong, M. (1999). Personal factors affecting the generality of academic self-efficacy judgments: Gender, ethnicity, and relative expertise. *Journal of Experimental Education, 67,* 315–331.

Bowleg, L., Belgrave, F. Z., & Reisen, C. A. (2000). Gender roles, power strategies, and precautionary sexual self-efficacy: Implications for black and Latina women's HIV/AIDS protective behaviors. *Sex Roles, 42,* 613–635.

Clark, D. O., & Nothwehr, F. (1999). Exercise self-efficacy and its correlates among socioeconomically disadvantaged older adults. *Health Education & Behavior, 26,* 535–546.

Ennis, N. E., Hobfoll, S. E., & Schroeder, K. E. E. (2000). Money doesn't talk: How economic stress and resistance resources impact inner-city women's depressive mood. *American Journal of Community Psychology, 28*(2), 149–173.

Gutman, L. M., et al. (2000). The role of protective factors in supporting the academic achievement of poor African American students during the middle school transition. *Journal of Youth & Adolescence, 29,* 223–248.

Izzo, C., Weiss, L., Shanahan, T., & Rodriguez-Brown, F. (2000). Parental self-efficacy and social support as predictors of parenting practices and children's socioemotional adjustment in Mexican immigrant families. *Journal of Prevention & Intervention in the Community, 20*(½), 197–213.

Jeffreys, M. R. (2000). Development and psychometrics evaluation of the Transcultural Self-Efficacy Tool: A synthesis of findings. *Journal of Transcultural Nursing, 11*(2), 127–136.

Lee, J., & Cramond, B. (1999). The positive effects of mentoring economically disadvantaged students. *Professional School Counseling, 2*(3), 172–178.

Panagos, R. J., & Dubois, D. L. (1999). Career self-efficacy development and students with learning disabilities. *Learning Disabilities Research & Practice, 14*(1), 25–34.

Schaubroeck, J., Lam, S. S., & Xie, J. L. (2000). Collective efficacy versus self-efficacy in coping responses to stressors and control: A cross-cultural study. *Journal of Applied Psychology, 85,* 512–525.

Smith, E. P., Walker, K., Fields, L., Brookins, C. C., & Seay, R. C. (1999). Ethnic identity and its relationship to self-esteem, perceived efficacy, and prosocial attitudes in early adolescence. *Journal of Adolescence, 22,* 867–880.

Taylor, M. J. (2000). The influence of self-efficacy on alcohol use among American Indians. *Cultural Diversity & Ethnic Minority Psychology, 6*(2), 152–167.

Web Sites

Technology

Computers in Mental Health
http://www.ex.ac.uk/cimh/software/htm

HUSITA/CUSSN (Computer Use in Social Services Network)
http://www2.uta.edu/cussn/cussn.html

New Technology in the Human Services
http://www.chst.soton.ac.uk/nths/

World Wide Web Resources for Social Works
http://www.nyu.edu/socialwork/wwwrsw/

18 POST EVALUATION

PART ONE

For Objective One, describe the use of self-monitoring and stimulus control for the following client case.

Case Description

The client, Maria, is a thirty-something Puerto Rican woman who was physically separated from her husband of 15 years when they came to the United States in separate trips. Although they were reunited about a year ago, she reports that during the last year she has had "*ataques de nervios*"—which she describes as trembling and faintness. She worries that her husband will die young and she will be left alone. Her history reveals no evidence of *early* loss or abandonment; however, she has experienced losses with her immigration. Also, she seems to be self-sacrificing and dependent on Juan, her husband. She reports being a very religious person and praying a lot about this.

She asks assistance in gaining some control over these "*ataques de nervios*." How would you use self-monitoring and stimulus control to help her decrease the "*ataques de nervios*"?

What else would you focus on in addition to the use of these two strategies, given her cultural background and the case description?

Feedback follows.

PART TWO

Objective Two asks you to teach someone else how to engage in self-monitoring. Your teaching should follow the six guidelines listed in Table 18.1: rationale, response discrimination, self-recording, data charting, data display, and data analysis. Feedback follows.

PART THREE

Objective Three asks you to describe the application of a culturally relevant self-management program for a given client case (self-efficacy, self-modeling, self-monitoring, self-reward, and stimulus control).

Case Description

The client, Thad, is a young African American man who has recently identified himself as gay. Thad has been working with you in coming to terms with his sexual orientation and now is at a point where he has visited some gay bars and has participated in some gay activities. However, he has not asked anyone out and wants to find a way to do so. You have discussed the use of self-monitoring and self-reward as possible interventions for this goal. Thad is interested in this and would like to go out at least once a week with a male partner.

How would you use and adapt the interventions of self-monitoring, self-reward, self-modeling, stimulus control, and self-efficacy with this particular client?

Feedback follows.

PART FOUR

Objective Four asks you to teach someone else how to use self-reward, self-monitoring, self-control, and self-as-a-model. You can use the steps of self-monitoring on page 593, the stimulus-control principles on page 603, the components for self-reward on page 607, and the checklist for self-as-a-model on page 613.

18 POSTEVALUATION FEEDBACK

PART ONE
Self-Monitoring

1. In the rationale, you would lemphasize how this strategy xould help obtain information about the client's direction. You would also explain that she would be recording defined *ataques de nervios in vivo* on a a daily basis for several weeks. You need to be careful to frame the rationale in a way that respects her cultural values.
2. Response-discrimination training would involve selecting, defining, and giving examples of the response to be monitored. The helper should model some examples of the defined behavior and elicit some others from the client. Specifically, you would help the client define the nature and content of the behaviors she would be recording, such as feeling faint.
3. *Timing of the recording:* Because this client is using self-monitoring to decrease an undesired behavior, she would engage in prebehavior monitoring: Each time she felt faint or worried, she would record.
Method of recording: The client would be instructed to use a frequency count and record the number of times she felt faint or worried. If she was unable to discern when these started and ended, she could record with time sampling. For example, she could divide a day into equal time intervals and use the "all or none" method. If such thoughts occurred during an interval, she would record yes; if they did not, she would record no. Or, during each interval, she could rate the approximate frequency of these behaviors on a numerical scale, such as 0 for "never occurring," 1 for "occasionally," 2 for "often," and 3 for "very frequently."
Device for recording: There is no one right device to assist this client in recording. She could count the frequency using a tally on a note card, golf wrist counter, or hand-held computer. Or she could use a daily log sheet to keep track of interval occurrences.
4. A simple chart might have days along the horizontal axis and frequency of behaviors along the vertical axis.
5. This client may not wish to display the data in a public place at home. She could carry the data in her purse or backpack.
6. The client could engage in data analysis by reviewing the data with the helper or by comparing the data with the baseline or with her goal (desired level of behavior change). The latter involves self-evaluation and may set the stage for self-reinforcement.

Stimulus Control
You can explain the use of stimulus control as another way to help her gain some feeling of personal control surrounding these "ataques de nervios" by confining them to particular places and times so that they don't occur so randomly and unpredictably. You could suggest the use of a worry spot or worry chair that she goes to at a designated time to do her worrying and that she is to stop worrying when she leaves this place or chair.

Also, in addition to these two self-management interventions, it would be useful to explore her feelings of loss and safety surrounding her immigration experience, the adaptations she is having to make to a different culture, and the conflicts she may be experiencing between the two cultures.

PART TWO
Use Table 18.1 as a guide to assist your teaching. You might also determine whether the person you taught implemented self-monitoring accurately.

PART THREE
First, you would need to determine how well the use of self-management "fits" with Thad's beliefs, values, world view, and lifestyle. Assuming that Thad is receptive to the use of self-management and that he is oriented more toward an internal than an external locus of control and responsibility, you can proceed. (However, it is also important to explore whether there may be any external social factors that are contributing to his sense of discomfort.) You may first wish to assess and work with self-efficacy, or Thad's confidence in himself and the contacts he will make with other men. Note that in this case his sense of self-efficacy is related to both his identity development as a gay male and as an African American. We anticipate that as Thad uses various self-management tools, his sense of self-efficacy will increase.

Self-modeling could be used to videotape or audiotape role plays in which Thad initiates social contacts with other men.
Self-reward can be used in conjunction with times he actually makes social contacts with men and goes out with a man.

1. The *verbal symbolic rewards* used by Thad could consist of self-praise or covert verbalizations about the positive consequences of his behavior. Here are some examples:
   "I did it! I asked him out."
   "I did just what I wanted to do."
   "Wow! What a good time I'll have with _____."

Material rewards would be things or events that Thad indicates he prefers or enjoys. These might include watching TV, listening to music, or playing sports. Both current and potential rewards should be used. Of course, these activities are only possibilities; he has to decide whether they are reinforcing.

Examples of an imaginal reward may include either pleasant scenes or scenes related to going out:
   Imagining oneself on a raft on a lake
   Imagining oneself on a football field
   Imagining oneself with one's partner at a movie
   Imagining oneself with one's partner lying on a warm beach

(continued)

POSTEVALUATION FEEDBACK

(continued)

Self-monitoring can be used to help Thad track the number of social contacts he has with other men.

Stimulus control can be used to help Thad increase the number of cues associated with increasing his social contacts with other men. For example, he might start in one place or with one activity where he feels most comfortable; gradually, he can increase his visits to other places and activities where he will find other gay men.

PART FOUR

Use the following:
Self-monitoring steps on page 593
Principles of stimulus control on page 603
Components of self-reward on page 607
Checklist for self-as-a-model on page 613

APPENDIX

Codes of ethics and related standards of professional practice can be found on Web sites for the following helping professions. This is not an exhaustive list. If you seek details about standards or guidelines for other professional groups, we have additional Web sites listed in Chapters 1 and 2. Online resources such as Grohol (2002) and Norcross and colleagues (2000) may be useful in your search. We also include a Web site to review available manuals for empirically validated treatments.

American Association of Marriage and Family Therapy (http://www.aamft.org/about/revisedcodeethics.htm)

American Counseling Association (http://www.counseling.org)

American Psychological Association (http://www.apa.org)

American Psychological Society (http://www.psychologicalscience.org)

Code of Professional Ethics for Rehabilitation Counselors (http://crccertification.com)

International Society for Mental Health Online (http://www.ismo.org)

National Association of Social Workers (http://www.naswdc.org)

National Board for Certified Counselors Standards for the Ethical Practice of WebCounseling (http://www.nbcc.org)

Manuals for Empirically Validated Treatments (http://www.apa.org/divisions/div12/est)

Grohol, J. M. (2002). *The insider's guide to mental health resources online.* New York: Guilford.

Norcross, J. C., et al. (2000). *Authoritative guide to self-help resources in mental health.* New York: Guilford.

REFERENCES

Abell, N., & Hudson, W. (2000). Pragmatic applications of single-case and group designs in social work practice evaluation and research. In P. Allen-Meares & C. Garvin (Eds.), *Handbook of social work direct practice,* (pp. 535–550). Thousand Oaks, CA: Sage.

Achterberg, J. (1985). *Imagery in healing: Shamanism and modern medicine.* Boston: Shambhala.

Acierno, K., Tremont, G., Last, C., & Montgomery, D. (1994). Tripartite assessment of the efficacy of eye-movement desensitization in a multi-phobic patient. *Journal of Anxiety Disorders, 8,* 259–276.

Adler, A. (1964). *Social interest: A challenge to mankind.* New York: Capricorn.

Agency for Health Care Policy and Research (AHCPR). (1990). *Clinical guideline development.* (AHCPR Program Note, Publication No. 0m90–0086). Silver Springs, MD: AHCPR Publications Clearinghouse.

Agency for Health Care Policy and Research (AHCPR). (1993). *Clinical practice guideline quick reference guide for clinicians: Depression in primary care, detection, diagnosis and treatment.* AHCPR Publication No. 93–0552. Rockville, MD: AHCPR Publications.

Ahijevych, K., & Wewers, M. (1993). Factors associated with nicotine dependence among African American women cigarette smokers. *Research in Nursing and Health, 16,* 283–292.

Alexander, C. N., Robinson, P., Orme-Johnson, D. W., & Schneider, R. (1994). The effects of transcendental meditation compared to other methods of relaxation and meditation in reducing risk factors, morbidity, and mortality. *Homeostasis in Health and Disease, 35,* 243–263.

Alferi, S. M., Carver, C. S., Antoni, M. H., Weiss, S., & Duran, R. E. (2001). An exploratory study of social support, distress, and life disruption among low-income Hispanic women under treatment for early stage breast cancer. *Health Psychology, 20,* 41–46.

Allison, K., Crawford, I., Echemendia, R., Robinson, L., & Knepp, D. (1994). Human diversity and professional competence. *American Psychologist, 49,* 792–796.

Alvarez, J., & Jason, L. (1993). The effectiveness of legislation, education, and loaners for child safety in automobiles. *Journal of Community Psychology, 21,* 280–284.

American Counseling Association. (1995). *Code of ethics.* Alexandria, VA: Author.

American Psychiatric Association. (1994). *Diagnostic and statistical manual of mental disorders* (4th ed.). Washington, DC: Author.

American Psychological Association. (1992). *Ethical principles of psychologists.* Washington, DC: Author.

American Psychological Association. (1993). *Guideline for providers of psychological services to ethnic, linguistic, and culturally diverse populations.* Washington, DC: Author.

American Psychological Association. (1995b, July). *Services by telephone, teleconferences and Internet.* A statement by the Ethics Committee of the American Psychological Association. www.apa.org/ethics/stmnt01.html.

American Psychological Association, Task Force on the Promotion & Dissemination of Psychological Procedures. (1995a). *Template for developing guidelines: Interventions for mental disorders and psychological aspects of physical disorders.* Washington, DC: American Psychological Association.

Anderson, C. M., & Stewart, S. (1983). *Mastering resistance: A practical guide to family therapy.* New York: Guilford.

Anderson, R., & McMillion, P. (1995). Effects of similar and diversified modeling on African American women's efficacy expectations and intentions to perform breast self-examination. *Health Communication, 7,* 327–343.

Andrada, P., & Korte, A. (1993). *En aquellas tiempos:* A reminiscing group with Hispanic elderly. *Journal of Gerontological Social Work, 20,* 25–42.

Ankuta, G., & Abeles, N. (1993). Client satisfaction, clinical significance, and meaningful change in psychotherapy. *Professional Psychology, 24,* 70–74.

Anton, J. L., Dunbar, J., & Friedman, L. (1976). Anticipation training in the treatment of depression. In J. D. Krumboltz & C. E. Thoresen (Eds.), *Counseling methods* (pp. 67–74). New York: Holt, Rinehart and Winston.

Antoni, M. (1991). Psychosocial stressors and behavioral interventions in gay men with HIV infection. *International Review of Psychiatry, 3,* 383–399.

Antoni, M. H., Lehman, J. M., Kilbourn, K. M., Boyers, A. E., Culver, J. L., Alferi, S. M., Yount, S. E., McGregor, B. A., Arena, P. L., Harris, S. D., Price, A. A., & Carver, C. S. (2001). Cognitive–behavioral stress management intervention decreases the prevalence of depression and enhances benefit finding among women under treatment for early-stage breast cancer. *Health Psychology, 20,* 20–32.

Antonuccio, D., Danton, W., & DeNelsky, G. (1995). Psychotherapy versus medication for depression: Challenging the conventional wisdom with data. *Professional Psychology, 26,* 574–585.

Arbuthnott, K. D., Arbuthnott, D. W., & Rossiter, L. (2001a). Guided imagery and memory: Implications for psychotherapists. *Journal of Counseling Psychology, 48,* 123–132.

Arbuthnott, K. D., Arbuthnott, D. W., & Rossiter, L. (2001b). Laboratory research, treatment innovation, and practice guidelines: A reply to Enns (2001) and Courtois (2001). *Journal of Counseling Psychology, 48,* 140–143.

Arcury, T. A., Quandt, S. A., McDonald, J., & Bell, R. A. (2000). Faith and health self-management of rural older adults. *Journal of Cross-Cultural Gerontology, 15,* 55–74.

Arean, P. A. (1993). Cognitive behavioral therapy with older adults. *The Behavior Therapist, 16,* 236–239.

Armour-Thomas, E., Bruno, K., & Allen, B. (1992). Toward an understanding of higher-order thinking among minority students. *Psychology in the Schools, 29,* 273–280.

Arredondo, P., Toporek, R., Brown, S. P., Jones, J., Locke, D. C., Sanchez, J., & Stadler, H. (1996). Operationalization of the multicultural counseling competencies. *Journal of Multicultural Counseling and Development, 24,* 42–78.

Aspinwall, L., Kemeny, M., Taylor, S., & Schneider, S. (1991). Psychosocial predictors of gay men's AIDS risk-reduction behavior. *Health Psychology, 10,* 432–444.

Atkinson, D. R., Brown, M. T., Parham, T. A., Matthews, L. G., Landrum-Brown, J., & Kim, A. U. (1996). African American client skin tone and clinical judgments of African American and European American psychologists. *Professional Psychology, 27,* 500–505.

Atkinson, D. R., & Hackett, G. (1998). *Counseling diverse populations* (2nd ed). Boston: McGraw-Hill.

Atkinson, D. R., Morten, G., & Sue, D. W. (1998). *Counseling American minorities* (5th ed). Boston: McGraw-Hill.

Atkinson, D. R., Thompson, C. E., & Grant, S. K. (1993). A three-dimensional model for counseling racial/ethnic minorities. *The Counseling Psychologist, 21,* 257–277.

Axelson, J. A. (1999). *Counseling and development in a multicultural society* (3rd ed.). Pacific Grove, CA: Brooks/Cole.

Babyak, M., Blumenthal, J. A., Herman, S. Khatri, P., Doraiswamy, M., Moore, K., Craighead, W. E., Baldewicz, T. T., & Ranga, K. K. (2000). Exercise treatment for major depression: Maintenance of therapeutic benefit at 10 months. *Psychosomatic Medicine, 62,* 633–638.

Baer, J., Kivlahan, D., & Donovan, D. (1999). Integrating skills training and motivational therapies. *Journal of Substance Abuse Treatment, 17,* 15–23.

Baker, J., & Krugh, M. (1996, April). *Do I say Hispanic or Latino/Latina?* Paper presented at the Ohio University Multicultural Counselor Education Conference, Athens, OH.

Baker, S. B. (1981). *Cleaning up our thinking: A unit in self-improvement.* Unpublished manuscript, Division of Counseling and Educational Psychology, Pennsylvania State University, University Park.

Bandura, A. (1969). *Principles of behavior modification.* New York: Holt, Rinehart & Winston.

Bandura, A. (1971). Vicarious and self-reinforcement processes. In R. Glaser (Ed.), *The nature of reinforcement.* New York: Academic.

Bandura, A. (1976). Effecting change through participant modeling. In J. D. Krumboltz & C. E. Thoresen (Ed.), *Counseling methods* (pp. 248–265). New York: Holt, Rinehart & Winston.

Bandura, A. (1977). Self-efficacy: Toward a unifying theory of behavior change. *Psychological Review, 84,* 191–215.

Bandura, A. (1982). Self-efficacy mechanism in human agency. *American Psychologist, 37,* 122–147.

Bandura, A. (1986). *Social foundations of thought and action: A social cognitive theory.* Englewood Cliffs, NJ: Prentice-Hall.

Bandura, A. (1989). Human agency in social cognitive theory. *American Psychologist, 44,* 1175–1185.

Bandura, A. (1991). Social cognitive theory of self-regulation. Special Issue: Theories of cognitive self-regulation. *Organizational Behavior and Human Decision Processes, 50* (2), 248–287.

Bandura, A. (1993). Perceived self-efficacy in cognitive development and functioning. *Educational Psychologist, 28,* 117–148.

Bandura, A. (Ed.). (1995). *Self-efficacy in changing societies.* New York: Cambridge University Press.

Bandura, A. (1997). *Self-efficacy: The exercise of self-control.* New York: Freeman.

Bandura, A., Adams, N. E., & Beyer, J. (1977). Cognitive processes mediating behavioral change. *Journal of Personality and Social Psychology, 35,* 125–139.

Bandura, A., Cioffi, D., Taylor, C., & Brouillard, M. E. (1988). Perceived self-efficacy in coping with cognitive stressors and opioid activation. *Journal of Personality and Social Psychology, 55,* 477–488.

Bandura, A., & Simon, K. (1977). The role of proximal intentions in self-regulation of refractory behavior. *Cognitive Therapy and Research, 1,* 177–193.

Bandura, A., Taylor, C., Williams, S. L., Mefford, I. N., & Barchas, J. D. (1985). Catecholamine secretion as function of perceived coping self-efficacy. *Journal of Consulting and Clinical Psychology, 53,* 406–415.

Barak, A., Patkin, J., & Dell, D. M. (1982). Effects of certain counselor behaviors in perceived expertness and attractiveness. *Journal of Counseling Psychology, 29,* 261–267.

Barlow, D. H., & Durand, V. M. (1995). *Abnormal psychology: An integrative approach.* Pacific Grove, CA: Brooks/Cole.

Barron, J. (Ed.). (1998). *Making diagnosis meaningful.* Washington, DC: American Psychological Association.

Bartholomew, L. K., Gold, R. S., Parcel, G. S., Czyewski, D. I., Sockrider, M. M., Fernandez, M., Shegog, R., & Swank, P. (2000). Watch, discover, think, and act: Evaluation of computer-assisted instruction to improve asthma self-management in inner-city children. *Patient Education and Counseling, 39,* 269–280.

Basic Behavioral Science Research for Mental Health. (1995). Emotion and motivation. *American Psychologist, 50,* 838–845.

Basic Behavioral Science Task Force of the National Advisory Mental Health Council. (1996). Thought and communication. *American Psychologist, 51,* 181–189.

Basoglu, M. (1997). Torture as a stressful life event: A review of the current status of knowledge. In T. W. Miller (Ed.), *Clinical disorders and stressful life events* (pp. 45–69). Madison, CT: International Universities Press.

Baucom, D. H., & Epstein, N. (1990). *Cognitive–behavioral marital therapy.* New York: Brunner/Mazel.

Bauermeister, J., Berrios, B., Jiminez, A., Acevedo, L., & Gordon, M. (1990). Some issues and instruments for the assessment of attention-deficit hyperactivity disorder in Puerto Rican children. *Journal of Clinical Child Psychology, 19,* 9–16.

Beck, A., Rush, A., Shaw, B., & Emery, G. (1979). *Cognitive therapy of depression.* New York: Guilford.

Beck, A. T. (1967). *Depression.* New York: Hoeber.

Beck, A. T. (1976). *Cognitive therapy and the emotional disorders.* New York: International Universities Press.

Beck, A. T. (1993). Cognitive therapy: Past, present, and future. *Journal of Consulting and Clinical Psychology, 62,* 194–198.

Beck, A. T., Steer, R. A., & Brown, G. K. (1996). *The Beck Depression Inventory II.* San Antonio: The Psychological Corporation, Harcourt Brace.

Beck, J. S. (1995). *Cognitive therapy.* New York: Guilford.

Becker, D., & Lamb, S. (1994). Sex bias in the diagnosis of borderline personality disorders and post-traumatic stress disorder. *Professional Psychology, 25,* 55–61.

Belenky, M. F., Clinchy, B. M., Goldbeyer, N. R., & Tarule, J. M. (1986). *Women's ways of knowing.* New York: Basic.

Belgrave, F., Randolph, S., Carter, C., & Braithwaite, N. (1993). The impact of knowledge, norms, and self-efficacy on intentions to engage in AIDS-preventive behaviors among young incarcerated African American males. *Journal of Black Psychology, 19,* 155–168.

Bell, Y., Brown, R., & Bryant, A. (1993). Traditional and culturally relevant presentations of a logical reasoning task and performance among African-American students. *Western Journal of Black Studies, 17,* 173–178.

Benjamin, L. (2000). Scientific discipline can enhance clinical effectiveness. In S. Soldz & L. McCullough (Eds.), *Reconciling empirical knowledge and clinical experience* (pp. 197–220). Washington, DC: American Psychological Association.

Bennett, B. E., Bryant, B. K., VandenBos, G. R., & Greenwood, A. (1990). *Professional liability and risk management.* Washington, DC: American Psychological Association.

Benson, H. (1976). *The relaxation response.* New York: Avon.

Benson, H. (1987). *Your maximum mind.* New York: Avon.

Benson, H., & Stuart, E. M. (Eds.). (1992). *The wellness book: The comprehensive guide to maintaining health and treating stress-related illness.* New York: Birch Lane.

Berg, I., & Jaya, A. (1993). Different and same: Family therapy with Asian-American families. *Journal of Marital and Family Therapy, 19,* 31–38.

Berg-Cross, L., & Chinen, R. T. (1995). Multicultural training models and the person-in-culture interview. In J. G. Ponterotto, J. M. Casas, L. A. Suzuki, & C. M. Alexander (Eds.). *Handbook of multicultural counseling* (pp. 333–357). Thousand Oaks, CA: Sage.

Berlin, S. (2001). *Clinical social work: A cognitive–integrative perspective.* New York: Oxford University Press.

Berman, J. S., Miller, R. C., & Massman, P. J. (1985). Cognitive therapy vs. systematic desensitization: Is one treatment superior? *Psychological Bulletin, 97,* 451–461.

Bernstein, D. A., & Borkovec, T. D. (1973). *Progressive relaxation training: A manual for helping professions.* Champaign, IL: Research Press.

Bernstein, D. A., & Carlson, C. R. (1993). Progressive relaxation: Abbreviated methods. In P. M. Lehrer & R. L. Woolfolk (Eds.), *Principles and practice of stress management* (2nd ed., pp. 53–87). New York: Guilford.

Beutler, L. (2000). David and Goliath: When empirical and clinical standards of practice meet. *American Psychologist, 55,* 997–1007.

Beutler, L., & Clarkin, J. (1990). *Systematic treatment selection.* New York: Brunner/Mazel.

Beutler, L., Clarkin, J., & Bongar, B. (2000). *Guidelines for the systematic treatment of the depressed patient.* New York: Oxford University Press.

Beutler, L., & Harwood, T. (2000). *Prescriptive psychotherapy: A practical guide to systematic treatment selection.* New York: Oxford University Press.

Bijou, S. W., & Baer, D. M. (1976). *Child development I: A systematic and empirical theory.* Englewood Cliffs, NJ: Prentice-Hall.

Birch, B. B. (1995). *Power yoga.* New York: Fireside.

Birdwhistell, R. L. (1970). *Kinesics and context.* Philadelphia: University of Pennsylvania Press.

Bloom, J. (2000). Technology and Web counseling. In H. Hackney (Ed.), *Practice issues for the beginning counselor* (pp. 183–202). Needham Heights, MA: Allyn & Bacon.

Bloom, M., Fischer, J., & Orme, J. (1999). *Evaluating practice: Guidelines for the accountable professional* (3rd ed.). Needham Heights, MA: Allyn & Bacon.

Bly, R. (1996). *The sibling society.* Reading, MA: Addison-Wesley.

Blythe, B., & Reithoffer, A. (2000). Assessment and measurement issues in direct practice in social work. In P. Allen-Meares & C. Garvin (Eds.), *Handbook of social work direct practice* (pp. 551–564). Thousand Oaks, CA: Sage.

Boardman, J. D., & Robert, S. A. (2000). Neighborhood socioeconomic status and perceptions of self-efficacy. *Sociological Perspectives, 43,* 117–136.

Boehnlein, J. K., & Kinzie, J. D. (1997). In T. W. Miller (Ed.), *Clinical disorders and stressful life events* (pp. 19–43). Madison, CT: International Universities Press.

Bohart, A. T., & Greenberg, L. (1997). *Empathy reconsidered.* Washington, DC: American Psychological Association.

Bootzin, R. R. (1977). Effects of self-control procedures for insomnia. In R. B. Stuart (Ed.), *Behavioral self-management: Strategies, techniques, and outcomes* (pp. 176–195). New York: Brunner/Mazel.

Bordin, E. S. (1979). The generalizability of the psychoanalytic concept of the working alliance. *Psychotherapy: Theory, Research and Practice, 16,* 256–260.

Borysenko, J. (1987). *Minding the body, mending the mind.* New York: Bantam.

Botvin, G., Baker, E., Botvin, E., & Dusenbury, L. (1993). Factors promoting cigarette smoking among black youth: A causal modeling approach. *Addictive Behaviors, 18,* 397–405.

Bowlby, J. (1988). *A secure base: Parent-child attachments and healthy human development.* New York: Basic.

Bracho-de-Carpio, A., Carpio-Cedraro, F., & Anderson, L. (1990). Hispanic families and teaching about AIDS: A participatory approach at the community level. *Hispanic Journal of Behavioral Sciences, 12,* 165–176.

Brammer, L. M., Abrego, P. J., & Shostrom, E. L. (1993). *Therapeutic psychology: Fundamentals of counseling and psychotherapy* (6th ed.). Englewood Cliffs, NJ: Prentice-Hall.

Brammer, L. M., & MacDonald, G. (1999). *The helping relationship* (6th ed.). Needham Heights, MA: Allyn & Bacon.

Bray, M. A., & Kehle, T. J. (1998). Self-modeling as an intervention for stuttering. *School Psychology Review, 27,* 587–598.

Breggin, P. (1999). *The heart of being helpful: Empathy and the creation of a healing presence.* New York: Springer.

Brehm, J. W. (1966). *A theory of psychological reactance.* New York: Academic.

Brehm, S. S. (1976). *The application of social psychology to clinical practice.* Washington, DC: Hemisphere.

Brems, C. (2000). *Dealing with challenges in psychotherapy and counseling.* Belmont, CA: Brooks/Cole.

Brems, C. (2001). *Basic skills in psychotherapy and counseling.* Belmont, CA: Brooks/Cole.

Brigham, D. (1994). *Imagery for getting well.* New York: Norton.

Brothers, D. (1995). *Falling backwards: An exploration of trust and self-experience.* New York: Norton.

Brown, C. M. (2000). Exploring the role of religiosity in hypertension management among African Americans. *Journal of Health Care for the Poor and Underserved, 11,* 19–32.

Brown, D., Scheflin, A., & Hammond, C. (1998). *Memory, trauma, treatment, and the law*. New York: Norton.

Brown, J. (1997). The question cube: A model for developing repertoire in training couple and family therapists. *Journal of Marital and Family Therapy, 23*, 27–40.

Brown, L. (2000). Feminist therapy. In C. Snyder & R. Ingram (Eds.), *Handbook of psychological change* (pp. 358–379). New York: Wiley.

Brown, L. M., & Gilligan, C. (1992). *Meeting at the crossroads*. New York: Ballantine.

Brown, L. S. (1992). Introduction. In L. S. Brown & M. Ballou (Eds.), *Personality and psychopathology: Feminist reappraisals* (pp. 111–115). New York: Guilford.

Brown, L. S. (1994). *Subversive dialogues: Theory in feminist therapy*. New York: Basic.

Brown, L. S., & Ballou, M. (1992). *Personality and psychopathology: Feminist reappraisals*. New York: Guilford.

Bryan, T., & Bryan, J. (1991). Positive mood and math performance. *Journal of Learning Disability, 24*, 490–494.

Buggey, T., Toombs, K., Gardener, P., & Cervetti, M. (1999). Training responding behaviors in students with autism: Using videotaped self-modeling. *Journal of Positive Behavior Interventions, 1*, 205–214.

Burke, M. T., Hackney, H., Hudson, P., Miranti, J., Watts, G. A., & Epp, L. (1999). Spirituality, religion, and CACREP curriculum standard. *Journal of Counseling and Development, 77*, 251–257.

Burnett, J. W., Anderson, W. P., & Heppner, P. P. (1995). Gender roles and self-esteem: A consideration of environmental factors. *Journal of Counseling and Development, 73*, 323–326.

Cahill, S. P., Carrigan, M. H., & Frueh, B. C. (1999). Does EMDR work? and if so, why?: A critical review of controlled outcome and dismantling research. *Journal of Anxiety Disorders, 13*, 5–33.

Calam, R., Cox, A., Glasgow, D., Jimmieson, P., & Larsen, S. G. (2000). Assessment and therapy with children: Can computers help? *Clinical Child Psychology and Psychiatry, 5*, 329–343.

Calhoun, L. G., & Tedeschi, R. G. (1998). Beyond recovery from trauma: Implications for clinical practice and research. *Journal of Social Issues, 54*, 357–371.

Calhoun, L. G., & Tedeschi, R. G. (1999). *Facilitating posttraumatic growth: A clinician's guide*. Mahweh, NJ: Erlbaum.

Callaghan, G. (2001). Demonstrating clinical effectiveness for individual practitioners and clinics. *Professional Psychology, 32*, 289–297.

Canino, I., & Spurlock, J. (2000). *Culturally diverse children and adolescents: Assessment, diagnosis, and treatment* (2nd ed.). New York: Guilford.

Carkhuff, R. R. (1969a). *Helping and human relations*. Vol. 1: *Practice and research*. New York: Holt, Rinehart and Winston.

Carkhuff, R. R. (1969b). *Helping and human relations*. Vol. 2: *Practice and research*. New York: Holt, Rinehart and Winston.

Carkhuff, R. R. (1987). *The art of helping* (6th ed.). Amherst, MA: Human Resource Development Press.

Carkhuff, R. R. (1993). *The art of helping* (8th ed.). Amherst, MA: Human Resource Development Press.

Carkhuff, R. R., & Pierce, R. M. (1975). *Trainer's guide: The art of helping*. Amherst, MA: Human Resource Development Press.

Carkhuff, R. R., Pierce, R. M., & Cannon, J. R. (1977). *The art of helping III*. Amherst, MA: Human Resource Development Press.

Carlson, C. R., & Hoyle, R. H. (1993). Efficacy of abbreviated progressive muscle relaxation training: A quantitative review of behavioral medicine research. *Journal of Consulting and Clinical Psychology, 61*, 1059–1067.

Carrington, P. (1993). Modern forms of meditation. In P. M. Lehrer & R. L. Woolfolk (Eds.), *Principles and practice of stress management* (2nd ed., pp. 139–168). New York: Guilford.

Carrington, P. (1998). *The book of meditation*. Boston: Element.

Casas, J. M. (1988). Cognitive behavioral approaches: A minority perspective. *The Counseling Psychologist, 16*, 106–110.

Caspar, F. (1995). *Plan analysis: Toward optimizing psychotherapy*. Seattle: Hogrefe & Huber.

Cass, V. C. (1979). Homosexual identity formation: A theoretical model. *Journal of Homosexuality, 4*, 219–235.

Castillo, R. J. (1997). *Culture and mental illness*. Pacific Grove, CA: Brooks/Cole.

Cautela, J. R. (1966). The treatment of compulsive behavior by covert sensitization. *Psychological Record, 16*, 33–41.

Cautela, J. R. (1969). Behavior therapy and self-control: Techniques and implications. In C. Franks (Ed.), *Behavior therapy: Appraisal and status* (pp. 323–340). New York: McGraw-Hill.

Cautela, J. R. (1970). Covert reinforcement. *Behavior Therapy, 1*, 33–50.

Cautela, J. R. (1977). *Behavior analysis forms for clinical intervention* (Vol. 2). Champaign, IL: Research Press.

Cavaliere, F. (October, 1995). Payers demand increased provider documentation. *American Psychological Association Monitor*, p. 41.

Chambless, D. L., & Hollon, S. D. (1998). Defining empirically supported therapies. *Journal of Consulting and Clinical Psychology, 66*, 7–18.

Chappelle, W. (2000). A series of progressive legal and ethical decision-making steps for using Christian spiritual interventions in psychotherapy. *Journal of Psychology and Theology, 28,* 43–53.

Cheatham, H., Ivey, A., Ivey, M. B., & Simek-Morgan, L. (1993). Multicultural counseling and therapy. In A. Ivey, M. B. Ivey, & L. Simek-Morgan (Eds.), *Counseling and psychotherapy: A multicultural perspective* (pp. 114–115). Needham Heights, MA: Allyn & Bacon.

Cheatham, H., & Stewart, J. (1990). *Black families: Interdisciplinary perspective.* New Brunswick, NJ: Transactional.

Chemtob, C. M., Tolin, D. F., van der Kolk, B. A., & Pitman, R. K. (2000). Eye movement desensitization and reprocessing. In E. B. Foa, T. Keane, & M. J. Friedman, (Eds.). *Effective treatments for PTSD* (pp. 333–335). New York: Guilford.

Chenneville, T. (2000). HIV, confidentiality, and duty to protect: A decision-making model. *Professional Psychology: Research and Practice, 31,* 661–670.

Cheston, S. E. (1991). *Making effective referrals: The therapeutic process.* New York: Gardner.

Chibnall, J. T., & Duckro, P. N. (2000). Does exposure to issues of spirituality predict medical students' attitudes towards spirituality in medicine? *Academic Medicine, 67,* 661.

Chiu, M. L. (1997). The influence of anticipatory fear on foreign student adjustment: An exploratory study. *International Journal of Intercultural Relationships, 19,* 1–44.

Chojnacki, J. T., & Gelberg, S. (1995). The facilitation of gay/lesbian/bisexual support-therapy group by heterosexual counselors. *Journal of Counseling and Development, 73,* 352–354.

Church, A., Teresa, J., Rosebrook, R., & Szendre, D. (1992). Self-efficacy for careers and occupational consideration in minority high school equivalency students. *Journal of Counseling Psychology, 39,* 498–508.

Ciminero, A. R., Nelson, R. O., & Lipinski, D. P. (1977). Self-monitoring procedures. In A. R. Ciminero, K. S. Calhoun, & H. E. Adams (Eds.), *Handbook of behavioral assessment* (pp. 195–232). New York: Wiley.

Cisneros, S. (1984). *The house on Mango Street.* New York: Random House.

Claiborn, C. D. (1982). Interpretation and change in counseling. *Journal of Counseling Psychology, 29,* 439–453.

Claiborn, C. D., & Dowd, E. T. (1985). Attributional interpretations in counseling: Content versus discrepancy. *Journal of Counseling Psychology, 32,* 188–196.

Claiborn, C. D., Ward, S. R., & Strong, S. R. (1981). Effects of congruence between counselor interpretations and client beliefs. *Journal of Counseling Psychology, 28,* 101–109.

Clancy, S. M., McNally, R. J., & Schacter, D. L. (1999). Effects of guided imagery on memory distortion in women reporting recovered memories of childhood sexual abuse. *Journal of Traumatic Stress, 12,* 559–569.

Clare, S. K., Jenson, W. R., Kehle, T. J., & Bray, M. A. (2000). Self-modeling as a treatment for increasing on-task behavior. *Psychology in the Schools, 37,* 517–522.

Clark, A. J. (1998). Reframing: A therapeutic technique in group counseling. *Journal for Specialists in Group Work, 23,* 66–73.

Clark, C. C. (1996). *Wellness practitioner: Concepts, research, and strategies.* New York: Springer.

Clark, D. M., & Salkovskis, P. M. (1989). *Cognitive therapy for panic and hypochondriasis.* New York: Pergamon.

Cochran, S., & Mays, V. (1993). Applying social psychological models to predicting HIV-related sexual risk behaviors among African Americans. *Journal of Black Psychology, 19,* 142–154.

Cohen, D., & Cohen, G. (1999). *The virtuous therapist: Ethical practice of counseling and psychotherapy.* Belmont, CA: Wadsworth.

Cohen, J. A., & Welch, L. M. (2000). Attitudes, beliefs, values, and culture as mediators of stress. In V. H. Rice (Ed.), *Handbook of stress, coping, and health: Implications for nursing research, theory, and practice* (pp. 335–366). Thousand Oaks, CA: Sage.

Coleman, E., & Remafedi, G. (1989). Gay, lesbian and bisexual adolescents: A critical challenge to counselors. *Journal of Counseling and Development, 68,* 36–40.

Coleman, H. (1995). Strategies for coping with cultural diversity. *The Counseling Psychologist, 23,* 722–740.

Committee on Lesbian, Gay, and Bisexual Concerns Joint Task Force on Guidelines for Psychotherapy with Lesbian, Gay, and Bisexual Clients (2000). Guidelines for psychotherapy with lesbian, gay, and bisexual clients. *American Psychologist, 55,* 1440–1451.

Connolly, M. J. (1993). Respiratory rehabilitation in the elderly patient. *Reviews in Clinical Gerontology, 3,* 281–294.

Connor-Greene, P. (1993). The therapeutic context: Preconditions for change in psychotherapy. *Psychotherapy, 30,* 375–382.

Constantine, M. (2000). Social desirability attitudes, sex, and affective and cognitive empathy as predictors of self-reported multicultural counseling competence. *The Counseling Psychologist, 28,* 857–872.

Consumer Reports. (1995, November). Does therapy help? (pp. 734–739).

Cook, D. A., & Helms, J. E. (1988). Visible racial/ethnic group supervisors' satisfaction with cross-cultural supervision as predicted by relationship characteristics. *Journal of Counseling Psychology, 35,* 268–273.

Cooper, C., & Gottlieb, M. C. (2000). Ethical issues with managed care: Challenges facing counseling psychology. *The Counseling Psychologist, 28,* 179–236.

Cooper, J. F. (1995). *A primer of brief therapy.* New York: Norton.

Corcoran, K., & Fischer, J. (2000). *Measures for clinical practice* (3rd ed.). New York: Free Press.

Corey, G., Corey, M., & Callanan, P. (1998). *Issues and ethics in the helping professions* (5th ed.). Pacific Grove, CA: Brooks/Cole.

Cormier, S., & Hackney, H. (1999). *Counseling strategies and interventions* (5th ed.). Needham Heights, MA: Allyn & Bacon.

Corrigan, J. D., Dell, D. M., Lewis, K. N., & Schmidt, L. D. (1980). Counseling as a social influence process: A review. *Journal of Counseling Psychology, 27,* 395–441.

Courtois, C. (1996). *Healing the incest wound: Adult survivors in therapy.* New York: Norton.

Courtois, C. (1999). *Recollections of sexual abuse: Treatment principles and guidelines.* New York: Norton.

Courtois, C. A. (2001). Commentary on "Guided imagery and memory": Additional considerations. *Journal of Counseling Psychology, 48,* 133–135.

Cowger, C. D. (1994). Assessing client strengths: Clinical assessment for client empowerment. *Social Work, 39,* 262–267.

Cox, B., Swinson, R., Morrison, R., & Lee, P. (1993). Clomipramine, fluoxetine, and behavior therapy in the treatment of obsessive–compulsive disorder: A meta-analysis. *Journal of Behavior Therapy and Experimental Psychiatry, 24,* 149–153.

Cozzarelli, C. (1993). Personality and self-efficacy as predictors of coping with abortion. *Journal of Personality and Social Psychology, 65,* 1224–1236.

Crawford, M., & Unger, R. (2000). *Women and gender: A feminist psychology* (3rd ed.). Boston: McGraw-Hill.

Cromie, S. D., & Baker, L. J. V. (1997). The behavioural self-control of study in third-level students: A review. K. Dillenburger, M. F. O'Reilly, et al. (Eds.). *Advances in behaviour analysis* (pp. 113–133). Dublin, Ireland: University College Dublin Press.

Cronbach, L. J. (1990). *Essentials of psychological testing* (5th ed.). New York: Harper & Row.

Cross, W. E. (1971). The Negro-to-black conversion experience: Toward a psychology of black liberation. *Black World, 20,* 13–27.

Crum, A. (2000). *The 10-step method of stress relief: Decoding the meaning and significance of stress.* Boca Raton, FL: CRC.

Csikszentmihalyi, M. (1990). *Flow: The psychology of optimal experience.* New York: HarperPerennial.

Cuéllar, I., & Paniagua, F. (Eds.). (2000). *Handbook of multicultural mental health: Assessment and treatment of diverse populations.* San Diego, CA: Academic.

Cullen, C. (1983). Implications of functional analysis. *British Journal of Clinical Psychology, 22,* 137–138.

Cummings, N., Budman, S., & Thomas, J. (1998). Efficient psychotherapy as a viable response to scarce resources and rationing of treatment. *Professional Psychology, 29,* 460–469.

Cushman, P., & Gilford, P. (2000). Will managed care change our way of being? *American Psychologist, 55,* 985–996.

D'Augelli, A. R., & Patterson, C. J. (Eds.), (1995). *Lesbian, gay, and bisexual identities over the lifespan: Psychological perspectives* (pp. 165–189). New York: Oxford University Press.

Dalenberg, C. (2000). *Countertransference and the treatment of trauma.* Washington, DC: American Psychological Association.

Das, A. K. (1995). Rethinking multicultural counseling: Implications for counselor education. *Journal of Counseling and Development, 74,* 45–74.

Davidson, G. N. S., & Horvath, A. O. (1997). Three sessions of brief couples therapy: A clinical trial. *Journal of Family Psychology, 11,* 422–435.

Davis, C. G., Nolen-Hoeksema, S., & Larson, J. (1998). Making sense of loss and benefiting from the experience: Two construals of meaning. *Journal of Personality and Social Psychology, 75,* 561–574.

Davis, S., & Meier, S. (2001). *The elements of managed care.* Belmont, CA: Wadsworth.

Day, J. (1995). Obligation and motivation: Obstacles and resources for counselor well-being and effectiveness. *Journal of Counseling and Development, 73,* 108–110.

Day, R. W., & Sparacio, R. T. (1980). Structuring the counseling process. *Personnel and Guidance Journal, 59,* 246–250.

DeAngelis, T. (1994, August). Women less likely to pursue technology-related careers. *American Psychological Association Monitor,* p. 30.

De Jongh, A., Ten Broeke, E., & Renssen, M. R. (1999). Treatment of specific phobias with Eye Movement Desensitization and Reprocessing (EMDR): Protocol, empirical status, and conceptual issues. *Journal of Anxiety Disorders, 13,* 69–85.

Deffenbacher, J. L., Oetting, E. R., & DiGiuseppe, R. A. (2002) Principles of empirically supported interventions applied to anger management. *The Counseling Psychologist, 30,* 262–280.

Deffenbacher, J. L., & Suinn, R. M. (1982). The self-control of anxiety. In P. Karoly & F. H. Kanfer (Eds.), *Self-management and behavior change* (pp. 393–442). New York: Pergamon.

DeJong, W. (1994). Relapse prevention. *International Journal of the Addictions, 29,* 681–705.

Denholtz, M., & Mann, E. (1974). An audiovisual program for group desensitization. *Journal of Behavior Therapy and Experimental Psychiatry, 5,* 27–29.

Derogatis, L. R. (1983). *SCL-90 R administration, scoring and procedures manual-II.* Towson, MD: Clinical Psychometric Research.

Devore, W., & Schlesinger, E. (1999). *Ethnic-sensitive social work practice* (5th ed). Needham Heights, MA: Allyn & Bacon.

Dixon, D. N., & Glover, J. A. (1984). *Counseling: A problem-solving approach.* New York: Wiley.

Dixon, W. A. (2000). Problem-solving appraisal and depression: Evidence for a recovery model. *Journal of Counseling and Development, 78,* 87–91.

Dlugos, R. F., & Friedlander, M. L. (2001). Passionately committed psychotherapists: A qualitative study of their experience. *Professional Psychology: Research and Practice, 32,* 298–304.

Dobson, K. S. (Ed.). (2001). *Handbook of cognitive-behavioral therapies* (2nd ed.). New York: Guilford.

Dobson, K. S., & Dozois, D. J. A. (2001). Historical and philosophical bases of the cognitive–behavioral therapies. In K. S. Dobson (Ed.), *Handbook of cognitive–behavioral therapies* (2nd ed., pp. 3–39). New York: Guilford.

Dorn, F. J. (1984). The social influence model: A social psychological approach to counseling. *Personnel and Guidance Journal, 62,* 342–345.

Dorn, F. J., & Day, B. J. (1985). Assessing change in self-concept: A social psychological approach. *American Mental Health Counselors Association Journal, 7,* 180–186.

Dorris, M. (1995, Spring). Heroic possibilities. *Teaching tolerance* (pp. 11–15).

Dossey, L. (1993). *Healing words.* New York: Harper/Collins.

Dowrick, P. W. (1999). A review of self-modeling and related interventions. *Applied and Preventive Psychology, 8,* 23–39.

Dowrick, P. W., & Ward, K. M. (1997). Video feedforward in the support of a man with intellectual disability and inappropriate sexual behaviour. *Journal of Intellectual and Developmental Disability, 22,* 147–160.

Draycott, S., & Dabbs, A. (1998). Cognitive dissonance 2: A theoretical grounding of motivational interviewing. *British Journal of Clinical Psychology, 37,* 355–364.

Duan, C., & Hill, C. (1996). The current state of empathy research. *Journal of Counseling Psychology, 43,* 261–274.

Duhl, F. J., Kantor, D., & Duhl, B. S. (1973). Learning, pace and action in family therapy: A primer of sculpture. In D. A. Bloch (Ed.), *Techniques of family psychotherapy.* New York: Grune & Stratton.

Duke, L: (1994, August 28). This harrowed ground. The Washington Post Magazine, pp. 8–13, 20–25.

Duley, S. M., Cancelli, A. A., Kratochwill, T. R., Bergan, J. R., & Meredith, K. E. (1983). Training and generalization of motivational analysis interview assessment skills. *Behavioral Assessment, 5,* 281–293.

Dunbar, E. (2001). Counseling practices to ameliorate the effects of discrimination and hate events: Toward a systematic approach to assessment and intervention. *The Counseling Psychologist, 29,* 276–307.

D'Zurilla, T. J. (1986). *Problem-solving therapy: A social competence approach to clinical intervention.* New York: Springer.

D'Zurilla, T. J. (1988). Problem-solving therapies. In K. D. Dobson (Ed.), *Handbook of cognitive–behavioral therapies* (pp. 85–135). New York: Guilford.

D'Zurilla, T. J., & Goldfried, M. R. (1971). Problem-solving and behavior modification. *Journal of Abnormal Psychology, 78,* 107–126.

D'Zurilla, T. J., & Nezu, C. M. (Eds.). (1990). Development and preliminary evaluation of the Social Problem-Solving Inventory (SPSI). *Psychological Assessment: A Journal of Consulting and Clinical Psychology, 2,* 156–163.

D'Zurilla, T. J., & Nezu, C. M. (1999). *Problem-solving therapy: A social competence approach to clinical intervention* (2nd ed.). New York: Springer.

Eckert, P. (1994). Cost control through quality improvement: The new challenge for psychology. *Professional Psychology, 25,* 3–8.

Edelstein, B. A., Drozdick, L. W., & Kogan, J. N. (1998). Assessment of older adults. In A. S. Bellack & M. Hersen (Eds.), *Behavioral assessment: A practical handbook* (4th ed., pp. 378–407). Boston: Allyn & Bacon.

Edelstein, B., & Semenchuk, E. (1996). Interviewing older adults. In L. Carstensen, B. Edelstein, & L. Dornbrand (Eds.), *The practical handbook of clinical gerontology* (pp. 153–173). Thousand Oaks, CA: Sage.

Edwards, C., & Murdock, N. (1994). Characteristics of therapist self-disclosure in the counseling process. *Journal of Counseling and Development, 72,* 384–389.

Egan, G. (1998). *The skilled helper* (6th ed.). Pacific Grove, CA: Brooks/Cole.

Eisenberger, R., & Cameron, J. (1996). Detrimental effects of reward: Reality or myth? *American Psychologist, 51,* 1153–1166.

Ekman, P. (1964). Body position, facial expression and verbal behavior during interviews. *Journal of Abnormal and Social Psychology, 68,* 295–301.

Ekman, P. (1982). Methods for measuring facial action. In K. R. Scherer & P. Ekman (Eds.), *Handbook of methods in nonverbal behavior research* (pp. 45–135). New York: Cambridge University Press.

Ekman, P. (1993). Facial expression and emotion. *American Psychologist, 48,* 384–392.

Ekman, P., & Friesen, W. V. (1967). Head and body cues in the judgment of emotion: A reformulation. *Perceptual and Motor Skills, 24,* 711–724.

Eliot, G. R., & Eisdorfer, C. (1982). *Stress and human health.* New York: Springer-Verlag.

Eliot, S. (1994). *Group activities for counselors.* Spring Valley, CA: Inner Choice Publishing.

Eller, L. S. (1999). Effects of cognitive–behavioral interventions on quality of life in persons with HIV. *International Journal of Nursing Studies, 36,* 223–233.

Ellis, A. (1962). *Reason and emotion in psychotherapy.* New York: Lyle Stuart.

Ellis, A. (1984). *Rational–emotive therapy and cognitive behavior therapy.* New York: Springer.

Ellis, A., & Harper, R. A. (1975). *A new guide to rational living.* Englewood Cliffs, N.J.: Prentice-Hall.

Ellis, M. R., Vinson, D. C., & Ewigman, B. (1999). Addressing spiritual concerns of patients: Family physicians' attitudes and practices. *Journal of Family Practice, 48,* 105–109.

Emavardhana, T., & Tori, C. D. (1997). Changes in self-concept, ego defense mechanisms, and religiosity following seven-day Vipassana meditation retreats. *Journal for the Scientific Study of Religion, 36,* 194–206.

Enns, C. (1993). Twenty years of feminist counseling and therapy. *The Counseling Psychologist, 21,* 33–87.

Enns, C. Z. (2000). Gender issues in counseling. In S. D. Brown & R. W. Lent (Eds.), *Handbook of counseling psychology* (3rd ed., pp. 601–638). New York: Wiley & Sons, Inc.

Enns, C. Z. (2001). Some reflections on imagery and psychotherapy implications. *Journal of Counseling Psychology, 48,* 136–139.

Enzle, M. E., Roggeveen, J. P., & Look, S. C. (1991). Self- versus other-reward administration and intrinsic motivation. *Journal of Experimental Social Psychology, 27,* 468–479.

Epel, E. S., Bandura, A., & Zimbardo, P. G. (1999). Escaping homelessness: The influence of self-efficacy and time perspective on coping with homelessness. *Journal of Applied Social Psychology, 29,* 575–596.

Epstein, J., Botvin, G., Diaz, T., & Toth, V. (1995). Social and personal factors in marijuana use and intentions to use drugs among inner city minority youth. *Journal of Developmental and Behavioral Pediatrics, 16,* 14–20.

Epstein, M. (1995). *Thoughts without the thinker.* New York: Basic.

Erickson, M. H., Rossi, E., & Rossi, S. (1976). *Hypnotic realities.* New York: Irvington.

Estes, C. (1992). *Women who run with the wolves.* New York: Ballantine.

Exline, R. V. & Winters, L. C. (1965). Affective relations and mutual glances in dyads. In S. S. Thompkins & C. E. Izard (Eds.), *Affect cognition, and personality.* New York: Springer.

Faiver, C., Ingersoll, R., O'Brien, E., & McNally, C. (2001). *Explorations in counseling and spirituality.* Belmont, CA: Wadsworth.

Faludi, S. (1991). *Backlash: The undeclared war against American women.* New York: Crown.

Farrah, G. A., Milchus, N. J., & Reitz, W. (Eds.). (1968). *The self-concept and motivation inventory: What face would you wear? SCAMIN manual of direction.* Dearborn Heights, MI: Person-O-Metrics.

Farrell, A. D., & McCullough-Vaillant, L. (1996). Computerized assessment system for psychotherapy evaluation and research (CASPER): Development and current status. In M. J. Miller, K. W. Hammond, & M. M. Hile (Eds.), *Mental health computing* (pp. 34–53). New York: Springer.

Faryna, E. L., & Morales, E. (2000). Self-efficacy and HIV-related behaviors among multiethnic adolescents. *Cultural Diversity and Ethnic Minority Psychology, 6,* 42–56.

Fassinger, R. E. (2000). Gender and sexuality in human development: Implications for prevention and advocacy in counseling psychology. In S. D. Brown & R. W. Lent (Eds.), *Handbook of counseling psychology* (3rd ed., pp. 346–378). New York: Wiley.

Faust, J., Olson, R., & Rodriguez, H. (1991). Same-day surgery preparation: Reduction of pediatric patient arousal and distress through participating modeling. *Journal of Consulting and Clinical Psychology, 59,* 475–478.

Fensterheim, H. (1983). Basic paradigms, behavioral formulation and basic procedures. In H. Fensterheim & H. Glazer (Eds.), *Behavioral psychotherapy: Basic principles and case studies in an integrative clinical model* (pp. 40–87). New York: Brunner/Mazel.

Feske, U. (1998). Eye movement desensitization and reprocessing treatment for posttraumatic stress disorder. *Clinical Psychology: Science and Practice, 5,* 171–181.

Field, L. K., & Steinhardt, M. A. (1992). The relationship of internally directed behavior to self-reinforcement, self-esteem, and expectancy values for exercise. *American Journal of Health Promotion, 7,* 21–27.

Fink, G. (2000). *Encyclopedia of stress.* San Diego, CA: Academic.

Finn, J., & Holden, G. (Eds.). (2000). Human services on-line: A new area for service delivery (Special issue). *Journal of Technology in Human Services, 17,* (1, 2, 3).

Fisch, R., Weakland, J., & Segal, L. (1982). *The tactics of change: Doing therapy briefly.* San Francisco: Jossey-Bass.

Fishelman, L. (1991, March). Algorithm construction and use. In *Developing algorithms and treatment guidelines in mental health.* Institute sponsored by Harvard Community Health Plan and Harvard Medical School, Boston.

Fishman, S. T., & Lubetkin, B. S. (1983). Office practice of behavior therapy. In M. Hersen (Ed.), *Outpatient behavior therapy: A clinical guide.* New York: Grune & Stratton.

Fitzgerald, L. F., & Nutt, R. (1986). The Division 17 Principles Concerning the Counseling/Psychotherapy of Women: Rationale and implementation. *The Counseling Psychologist, 14,* 180–216.

Foa, E. B., Keane, T., & Friedman, M. J. (Eds.). (2000). *Effective treatments for PTSD: Practice guidelines from the International Society for Stress Studies.* New York: Guilford.

Foa, E. B., & Kozak, M. J. (1986). Emotional processing of fear and exposure to corrective information. *Psychological Bulletin, 99,* 20–35.

Foa, E. B., & Meadows, E. A. (1997). Psychosocial treatments for post-traumatic stress disorder: A critical review. In J. Spence (Ed.), *Annual review of psychology* (pp. 449–480). Vol. 48. Palo Alto, CA: Annual Reviews.

Foa, E. B., Steketee, G. S., & Ascher, L. M. (1980). Systematic desensitization. In A. Goldstein & E. B. Foa (Eds.), *Handbook of behavioral interventions: A clinical guide* (pp. 38–91). New York: Wiley.

Fodor, I. G. (1992). The agoraphobic syndrome: From anxiety neurosis to panic disorder. In L. S. Brown & M. Ballou (Eds.), *Personality and psychopathology: Feminist reappraisals* (pp. 177–205). New York: Guilford.

Folkman, S. (1997). Positive psychological states and coping with severe stress. *Social Science and Medicine, 38,* 309–316.

Folkman, S., & Moskowitz, J. T. (2000). Positive affect and the other side of coping. *American Psychologist, 55,* 647–654.

Follette, W., & Hayes, S. (2000). In C. Snyder & R. Ingram (Eds.), *Handbook of psychological change* (pp. 381–408). New York: Wiley.

Fong, M. L., & Cox, B. G. (1983). Trust as an underlying dynamic in the counseling process: How clients test trust. *Personnel and Guidance Journal, 62,* 163–166.

Fontana, D. (1991). *The elements of meditation.* New York: Element.

Ford, M., & Widiger, T. A. (1989). Sex bias in the diagnosis of histrionic and antisocial personality disorders. *Journal of Consulting and Clinical Psychology, 57,* 301–305.

Fouad, N. A., & Brown, M. T. (2000). Role of race and social class in development: Implications for counseling psychology. In S. D. Brown & R. W. Lent (Eds.), *Handbook of counseling psychology* (3rd ed., pp. 379–408). New York: Wiley.

Foulks, E. F. (1982). Therapeutic interventions with urban black adolescents. In E. Jones & S. Korchin (Eds.), *Minority mental health* (pp. 267–295). New York: Praeger.

Freeman, E. (2000). Direct practice in fields related to development tasks: A life-span perspective. In P. Allen-Meares & C. Garvin (Eds.), *Handbook of social work direct practice* (pp. 415–435). Thousand Oaks, CA: Sage.

Freiberg, P. (1995, May). Older people thrive with the right therapy. *American Psychological Association Monitor,* p. 38.

Freire, P. (1972). *Pedagogy of the oppressed.* New York: Herder & Herder.

Fretz, B. R., Corn, R., Tuemmler, J. M., & Bellet, W. (1979). Counselor nonverbal behaviors and client evaluations. *Journal of Counseling Psychology, 26,* 304–311.

Fried, R. (1993). The role of respiration in stress and stress control: Toward a theory of stress as a hypoxic phenomenon. In P. M. Lehrer & R. L. Woolfolk (Eds.), *Principles and practice of stress management* (2nd ed., pp. 301–331). New York: Guilford.

Friedman, S. (Ed.). (1997). *Cultural issues in the treatment of anxiety.* New York: Guilford.

Frueh, B. C., de Arellano, M. A., & Turner, S. M. (1997). Systematic desensitization as an alternative exposure strategy for PTSD. *American Journal of Psychiatry, 154,* 287–288.

Fuhrmann, A., & Kuhl, J. (1998). Maintaining a healthy diet: Effects of personality and self-reward versus self-punishment on commitment to and enactment of self-chosen and assigned goals. *Psychology and Health, 13,* 651–686.

Gaines, R., & Price-Williams, P. (1990). Dreams and imaginative processes in American and Balinese artists. *Psychiatric Journal of the University of Ottawa, 15,* 107–110.

Gambrill, E. D. (1977). *Behavior modification: Handbook of assessment, intervention, and evaluation.* San Francisco: Jossey-Bass.

Gambrill, E. D. (1990). *Critical thinking in clinical practice.* San Francisco: Jossey-Bass.

Gambrill, E. D. (1999). Evidence based practice: An alternative to authority based practice. *Families in Society, 80,* 342–350.

Gammon, E. A. (2000). Examining the needs of culturally diverse rural caregivers who have adults with severe developmental disabilities living with them. *Families in Society, 81,* 174–185.

Gartett, M. T. (1999). Soaring on the wings of the eagle: Wellness of Native American high school students. *Professional School Counseling, 3,* 57–64.

Garvin, C., & Seabury, B. (1997). *Interpersonal practice in social work: Promoting competence and social justice* (2nd ed.). Needham Heights, MA: Allyn & Bacon.

Gasch, H., Poulson, D., Fullilove, R., & Fullilove, M. (1991). Shaping AIDS education and prevention programs for African Americans amidst community decline. *Journal of Negro Education, 60,* 85–96.

Gazda, G. M., Asbury, F. S., Balzer, F., Childers, W. C., Phelps, R. E., & Walters, R. P. (1999). *Human relations development: A manual for educators* (6th ed.). Needham, MA: Allyn & Bacon.

Gelso, C. J., & Carter, J. A. (1985). The relationship in counseling and psychotherapy: Components, consequences, and theoretical antecedents. *The Counseling Psychologist, 13,* 155–243.

Gelso, C. J., & Carter, J. A. (1994). Components of the psychotherapy relationship: Their interaction and unfolding during treatment. *Journal of Counseling Psychology, 41,* 296–306.

Gelso, C. J., & Fretz, B. R. (1992). *Counseling psychology.* New York: Harcourt.

Gelso, C. J., Fassinger, R., Gomez, M., & Latts, M. (1995). Countertransference reactions to lesbian clients. *Journal of Counseling Psychology, 42,* 356–364.

Gelso, C. J., & Hayes, J. A. (1998). *The psychotherapy relationship.* New York: Wiley.

Gelso, C. J., Hill, C. E., Mohr, J., Rochlen, A., & Zack, J. (1999). Describing the face of transference: Psychodynamic therapists' recollections about transference in cases of successful long-term therapy. *Journal of Counseling Psychology, 46,* 257–267.

Gendlin, E. T. (1996). *Focusing-oriented psychotherapy: A manual of the experiential method.* New York: Guilford.

George, L. K., Larson, D. B., Koenig, H. G., & McCullough, M. E. (2000). Spirituality and health: What we know, what we need to know. *Journal of Social and Clinical Psychology, 19,* 102–116.

Geyman, J. P., Deyo, R. A., & Ramsey, S. D. (2000). *Evidence-based clinical practice: Concepts and approaches.* Boston: Butterworths/Heinemann.

Gibbs, L. (in press). *Evidence-based practice for social workers.* Pacific Grove, CA: Brooks/Cole.

Gibbs, L., & Gambrill, E. (1999). *Critical thinking for social workers: Exercises for the helping profession* (2nd ed.). Thousand Oaks, CA: Pine Forge Press.

Gilbert, L. A., & Scher, M. (1999). *Gender and sex in counseling and psychotherapy.* Boston: Allyn & Bacon.

Gilbert, M. C. (2000). Spirituality in social work groups: Practitioners speak out. *Social Work with Groups, 22,* 67–84.

Gilliland, B. E. & James, R. K. (1998). *Theories and Strategies of Counseling and Psychotheraphy.* Boston: Allyn and Bacon.

Gladstein, G. (1983). Understanding empathy: Integrating counseling, development, and social psychology perspectives. *Journal of Counseling Psychology, 30,* 467–482.

Glauser, A., & Bozarth, J. (2001). Person-centered counseling: The culture within. *Journal of Counseling and Development, 79,* 142–147.

GlenMaye, L. (1998). Empowerment of women. In L. M. Gutiérrez, R. J. Parsons, & E. O. Cox (Eds.), *Empowerment in social work practice: A sourcebook* (pp. 29–51). Pacific Grove, CA: Brooks/Cole.

Goldfried, M. R. (1983). The behavior therapist in clinical practice. *Behavior Therapy, 6,* 45–46.

Goldfried, M. R. (1995). *From cognitive behavior therapy to psychotherapy integration.* New York: Springer.

Goldfried, M. R., & Davison, G. C. (1976). *Clinical behavior therapy.* New York: Holt, Rinehart and Winston.

Goldfried, M. R., & Davison, G. C. (1994). *Clinical behavior therapy* (expanded ed.). New York: Wiley Interscience.

Goldfried, M. R., Greenberg, L. S., & Marmer, C. (1990). Individual psychotherapy: Process and outcome. *Annual Review of Psychology, 41,* 659–688.

Goldiamond, I., & Dyrud, J. E. (1967). Some applications and implications of behavioral analysis in psychotherapy. In J. Schlein (Ed.), *Research in psychotherapy* (Vol. 3). Washington, DC: American Psychological Association.

Goldstein, A. P., & Higginbotham, H. N. (1991). Relationship-enhancement methods. In F. H. Kanfer & A. P. Goldstein (Eds.), *Helping people change* (4th ed., pp. 20–69). New York: Pergamon.

Goleman, D. (1988). *The meditative mind.* New York: Jeremy P. Tarcher/Perigee.

Gollwitzer, P. (1999). Implementation intentions. *American Psychologist, 54,* 493–503.

Gomory, T. (1999). Programs of assertive community treatment (PACT): A critical review. *Ethical Human Sciences and Services, 1,* 147–163.

Goodwin, R., & Soon, A. P. Y. (1994). Self-monitoring and relationship adjustment: A cross-cultural analysis. *Journal of Social Psychology, 134,* 35–39.

Goodyear, R., & Schumate, J. (1996). Perceived effects of therapist self-disclosure of attraction to clients. *Professional Psychology, 27,* 613–616.

Gorrell, J. (1993). Cognitive modeling and implicit rules: Effects on problem-solving performance. *American Journal of Psychology, 106,* 51–65.

Gorski, P. C. (2001). *Multicultural education and the Internet: Intersections and integrations.* Boston: McGraw-Hill.

Gottleib, L. (1991, March). Algorithm-based clinical quality improvement. *Developing algorithm and treatment guidelines in mental health.* Institute sponsored by Harvard Community Health Plan and Harvard Medical School, Boston.

Gottman, J. M., & Leiblum, S. R. (1974). *How to do psychotherapy and evaluate it.* New York: Holt, Rinehart and Winston.

Graves, J. R., & Robinson, J. D. (1976). Proxemic behavior as a function of inconsistent verbal and nonverbal messages. *Journal of Counseling Psychology, 23,* 333–338.

Gray-Little, B., & Kaplan, D. (2000). Race and ethnicity in psychotherapy research. In C. Snyder & R. Ingram (Eds.), *Handbook of psychological change* (pp. 591–613). New York: Wiley.

Greenberg, J. S. (1996). *Comprehensive stress management.* Madison, WI: Brown & Benchmark.

Greenberg, L. S., & Goldman, R. L. (1988). Training in experiential therapy. *Journal of Consulting and Clinical Psychology, 56,* 696–702.

Greenberg, L. S., Rice, L. N., & Elliott, R. (1993). *Facilitating emotional change.* New York: Guilford.

Greenberger, D., & Padesky, C. A. (1995). *Mind over mood: A cognitive therapy treatment manual for clients.* New York: Guilford.

Greenson, R. R. (1967). *The technique and practice of psychoanalysis* (Vol. 1). Madison, CT: International University Press.

Greenwald, R. (1996). The information gap in the EMDR controversy. *Professional Psychology: Research and Practice, 27,* 67–72.

Grohol, J. M. (2000). *The insider's guide to mental health resources.* New York: Guilford.

Guidano, V. F. (1995). Self-observation in constructivist psychotherapy. In R. A. Neimeyer & M. J. Mahoney (Eds.), *Constructivism in psychotherapy* (pp. 155–168). Washington, DC: American Psychological Association.

Guralnick, M. (1993). Developmentally appropriate practice in the assessment and intervention of children's peer relations. *Topics in Early Childhood Special Education, 13,* 344–371.

Guralnick, M., & Neville, B. (1997). Designing early intervention programs to promote children's social competence. In M. J. Guralnick (Ed.), *The effectiveness of early intervention* (pp. 579–610). Baltimore: Brookes.

Guthrie, B. J., & Low, L. K. (2000). A substance use prevention framework: Considering the social context for African American girls. *Public Health Nursing, 17,* 363–373.

Gutierrez, L. (1990). Working with women of color: An empowerment perspective. *Social Work, 35,* 149–153.

Gutkin, T. B. (1993). Cognitive modeling: A means for achieving prevention in school-based consultation. *Journal of Educational and Psychological Consultation, 4,* 179–183.

Hackney, H., & Cormier, L. S. (2001). *The professional counselor* (4th ed.). Needham Heights, MA: Allyn & Bacon.

Haddock, C. K., Shadish, W. R., Klesges, R. C., & Stein, R. J. (1994). Treatment of childhood and adolescent obesity. *Annals of Behavioral Medicine, 16,* 235–244.

Hagopian, L. P., Weist, M. D., & Ollendick, T. H. (1990). Cognitive–behavior therapy with an 11-year-old girl fearful of AIDS infection, other diseases, and poisoning: A case study. *Journal of Anxiety Disorders, 4,* 257–265.

Hains, A. (1989). An anger-control intervention with aggressive delinquent youths. *Behavioral Residential Treatment, 4,* 213–230.

Haire-Joshu, D., Fisher, E., Munro, J., & Wedner, J. (1993). A comparison of patient attitudes toward asthma self-management among acute and preventive care settings. *Journal of Asthma, 30,* 359–371.

Hall, E. T. (1966). *The hidden dimension.* Garden City, NY: Doubleday.

Hall, E. T. (1976). *Beyond culture.* New York: Anchor Press.

Hall, P. D. (1999). The effect of meditation on the academic performance of African-American college students. *Journal of Black Studies, 29,* 408–415.

Hammond, R., & Yung, B. (1991). Preventing violence in at-risk African American youth. *Journal of Health Care for the Poor and Underserved, 2,* 359–373.

Hanh, T. N. (1976). *The miracle of mindfulness.* Boston: Beacon.

Hanna, F. J., & Ritchie, M. H. (1995). Seeking the active ingredients of psychotherapeutic change: Within and outside the context of therapy. *Professional Psychology, 26,* 176–183.

Hansen, J. C., Rossberg, R., & Cramer, S. (1994). *Counseling theory and process* (5th ed.). Needham Heights, MA: Allyn & Bacon.

Hansen, N. D., & Goldberg, S. G. (1999). Navigating the nuances: A matrix of considerations for ethical–legal dilemmas. *Professional Psychology: Research and Practice, 30,* 495–503.

Hansen, N. D., Pepitone-Arreola-Rockwell, F., & and Greene, A. F. (2000). Multicultural competence: Criteria and case examples. *Professional Psychology: Research and Practice, 31*(6), 652–660.

Harchik, A. E., Sherman, J. A., & Sheldon, J. B. (1992). The use of self-management procedures by people with developmental disabilities: A brief review. *Research in Developmental Disabilities, 13,* 211–227.

Harris, S., & Busby, D. (1998). Therapist physical attractiveness: An unexplored influence on client disclosure. *Journal of Marital and Family Therapy, 24,* 251–257.

Hartley, E. T., Bray, M. A., & Kehle, T. J. (1998). Self-modeling as an intervention to increase student classroom participation. *Psychology in the Schools, 35,* 363–372.

Hatch, M., & Paradis, C. (1993). Panic disorder with agoraphobia. A focus on group treatment with African Americans. *The Behavior Therapist, 16,* 240–242.

Haug, I. (1998). Including a spiritual dimension in family therapy: Ethical considerations. *Contemporary Family Therapy: An International Journal, 20,* 181–194.

Hayes, J., McCracken, J., McClanahan, M., Hill, C., Harp, J., & Carozzoni, P. (1998). Therapist perspectives on countertransference: Qualitative data in search of a theory. *Journal of Counseling Psychology, 45,* 468–482.

Hayes, S., Barlow, D., & Nelson-Gray, R. (1999). *The scientist practitioner: Research and accountablity in the age of managed care* (2nd ed.). Boston: Allyn & Bacon.

Haynes, S. N. (1998). The changing nature of behavioral assessment. In A. S. Bellack & M. Hersen (Eds.). (1998). *Behavioral assessment: A practical handbook* (4th ed., pp. 1–22). Boston: Allyn & Bacon.

Hays, K. F. (1995). Putting sport psychology into (your) practice. *Professional Psychology: Research and Practice, 26,* 33–40.

Hays, P. A. (2001). *Addressing cultural complexities in practice.* Washington, DC: American Psychological Association.

Helms, J., & Cook, D. (1999). *Using race and culture in counseling and psychotherapy.* Needham Heights, MA: Allyn & Bacon.

Helms, J. E. (Ed.). (1990a). *Black and white racial identity: Theory, research and practice.* New York: Greenwood.

Helms, J. E. (1990b). Counseling attitudinal and behavioral predispositions: The black/white interaction model. In J. E. Helms (Ed.), *Black and white racial identity: Theory, research, and practice* (pp. 145–163). New York: Greenwood.

Helms, J. E. (1994a). The conceptualization of racial identity and other "racial" concepts. In E. Trickett, R. Watts, & D. Birman (Eds.), *Human diversity: Perspectives on people in context* (pp. 285–311). San Francisco: Jossey-Bass.

Helms, J. E. (1994b). How multiculturalism obscures racial factors in the therapy process: Comment on Ridley et al. (1994), Sodowsky et al. (1994), Ottavi et al. (1994), and Thompson et al. (1994). *Journal of Counseling Psychology, 41,* 162–165.

Hembree, E. A., & Foa, E. B. (2000). Posttraumatic stress disorder: Psychological factors and psychosocial interventions. *Journal of Clinical Psychiatry, 61,* 33–39.

Hendricks, G. (1995). *Conscious breathing.* New York: Bantam.

Heppner, P., & Frazier, P. (1992). Social psychological processes in psychotherapy: Extrapolating basic research to counseling psychology. In S. D. Brown & R. W. Lent (Eds.), *Handbook of counseling psychology* (3rd ed., pp. 141–176). New York: Wiley.

Heppner, P. P. (1988). *The problem solving inventory.* Palo Alto, CA: Consulting Psychologist Press.

Heppner, P. P., & Claiborn, C. D. (1989). Social influence research in counseling: A review and critique. *Journal of Counseling Psychology, 36,* 365–387.

Heppner, P. P., & Heesacker, M. (1982). Interpersonal influence process in real-life counseling: Investigating client perceptions, counselor experience level, and counselor power over time. *Journal of Counseling Psychology, 29,* 215–223.

Hepting, N. H., & Goldstein, H. (1996). Requesting by preschoolers with developmental disabilities: Videotaped self-modeling and learning of new linguistic structures. *Topics in Early Childhood Special Education, 16,* 407–427.

Hepworth, D., Rooney, R., & Larsen, J. A. (1997). *Direct social work practice: Theory and skills* (5th ed.). Pacific Grove, CA: Brooks/Cole.

Herbert, J. D., Lilienfeld, S. O., Lohr, J. M., Montgomery, R. W., O'Donohue, W. T., Tosen, G. M., & Tolin, D. F. (2000). Science and pseudoscience in the development of eye movement desensitization and reprocessing: Implications for clinical psychology. *Clinical Psychology Review, 20,* 945–971.

Herman, J. L. (1994, April). *Women's pathways to healing.* Paper presented at the Learning from Women Conference, Boston.

Hermansson, G. L., Webster, A. C. & McFarland, K. (1988). Counselor deliberate postural lean and communication of facilitative conditions. *Journal of Counseling Psychology, 35,* 149–153.

Herring, R., & Meggert, S. (1994). The use of humor as a counselor strategy with Native American Indian children. *Elementary School Guidance and Counseling, 29,* 67–76.

Herron, W. G., Javier, R. A., Primavera, L. H., & Schultz, C. L. (1994). The cost of psychotherapy. *Professional Psychology, 25,* 106–110.

Hickson, J., Housley, W., & Wages, D. (2000). Counselors' perceptions of spirituality in the therapeutic process. *Counseling and Values, 45,* 58–66.

Hill, C., & Nutt Williams, E. (2000). The process of individual therapy. In S. D. Brown & R. W. Lent (Eds.), *Handbook of counseling psychology* (3rd ed., pp. 670–710). New York: Wiley.

Hill, C. E., Siegelman, L., Gronsky, B. R., Sturniolo, F., & Fretz, B. R. (1981). Nonverbal communication and counseling outcome. *Journal of Counseling Psychology, 28,* 203–212.

Hill, P. C., Pargament, K. I., Hood, R. W., Jr., McCullough, M. E., Swyers, J. P., Larson, D. B., & Zinnbauer, B. J. (2000). Conceptualizing religion and spirituality: Points of commonality, points of departure. *Journal for the Theory of Social Behaviour, 30,* 51–77.

Hill, R., Thorn, B., & Packard, T. (2000). Counseling older adults: Theoretic and empirical issues in prevention and intervention. In S. Brown & R. Lent (Eds.), *Handbook of counseling psychology* (pp. 499–531). Thousand Oaks, CA: Sage.

Himle, J. A. (2000). Affective change: Depression and anxiety disorders. In P. Allen-Meares & C. Garvin (Eds.), *The handbook of social work direct practice* (pp. 217–240). Thousand Oaks, CA: Sage.

Ho, D. Y. F. (1995). Internalized culture, culturocentrism, and transcendence. *The Counseling Psychologist, 23,* 4–24.

Hodges, K. (1997). *Child and adolescent functional assessment scale.* Ann Arbor, MI: Functional Assessment System.

Hohmann, M. (1998). Motivational interviewing: An intervention tool for child welfare use when working with substance-abusing parents. *Child Welfare, LXXVII,* 275–289.

Hollon, S. D., & Kendall, P. C. (1981). In vivo assessment techniques for cognitive-behavioral processes: In P. C. Kendall & S. D. Hollon (Eds.), *Assessment strategies for cognitive-behavioral interventions* (pp. 319–362). New York: Academic.

Homme, L. E. (1965). Perspectives in psychology: XXIV. Control of coverants, the operants of the mind. *Psychological Record, 15,* 505–511.

Horne, D., Vatmanidis, P., & Careri, A. (1994). Preparing patients for invasive medical and surgical procedures: II. Using psychological interventions with adults and children. *Behavioral Medicine, 20,* 15–21.

Horvath, A. O., & Symonds, B. D. (1991). Relation between working alliance and outcome in psychotherapy: A meta-analysis. *Journal of Counseling Psychology, 38,* 139–149.

Hosford, R. E. (1974). *Counseling techniques: Self-as-a-model film.* Washington, DC: American Personnel and Guidance Press.

Hosford, R. E., & de Visser, L. (1974). *Behavioral approaches to counseling: An introduction.* Washington, DC: American Personnel and Guidance Press.

Hosford, R. E., Moss, C., & Morrell, G. (1976). The self-as-a-model technique: Helping prison inmates change. In J. D. Krumboltz & C. E. Thoresen (Eds.), *Counseling methods* (pp. 487–495). New York: Holt, Rinehart and Winston.

Howard, K., Brill, P., Lueger, R., & O'Mahoney, M. (1995). *Integra outpatient tracking* system. Philadelphia: Compass Information Services.

Howard, K. I., Kopta, S. M., Krause, M. S., & Orlinsky, D. E. (1986). The dose–effect relationship in psychotherapy. *American Psychologist, 41,* 159–164.

Hoyt, W. T. (1996). Antecedents and effects of perceived therapist credibility: A meta-analysis. *Journal of Counseling Psychology, 43,* 430–447.

Huang, L. N. (1994). An integrative approach to clinical assessment and intervention with Asian-American adolescents. *Journal of Clinical Child Psychology, 23,* 21–31.

Hubble, M., Duncan, B., & Miller, S. (1999). Directing attention to what works. In M. Hubble, B. Duncan, & S. Miller (Eds.), *The heart and soul of change* (pp. 407–448). Washington, DC: American Psychological Association.

Hudson, W. W. (1996a). *Computer assisted assessment package.* Tallahassee, FL: WALMYR.

Hudson, W. W. (1996b). *Computer assisted social services.* Tallahassee, FL: WALMYR.

Hughes, D. (1990). Participant modeling as a classroom activity. *Teaching of Psychology, 17,* 238–240.

Hull, C. L. (1980). *A behavior system.* New Haven, CT: Yale University Press.

Humphrey, J. H. (1998). *Helping children manage stress: A guide for adults.* Washington, DC: Child & Family Press.

Hurd, E., Moore, C., & Rogers, R. (1995). Quiet success: Parenting strengths among African Americans. *Families in Society, 76,* 434–443.

Hutchins, D., & Cole Vaught, C. (1997). *Helping relationships and strategies* (3rd ed.). Pacific Grove, CA: Brooks/Cole.

Hutchins, J. (1995). AAMFT readers meet, set agenda. *Family Therapy News,* June 5.

Ibanez-Ramirez, M., Delgado-Morales, F., & Pulido-Diez, J. (1989). Secondary situational impotence in case of homosexuality. *Analisis y Modificacion de Conducta, 15,* 297–304.

Iglesias, E., & Cormier, S. (In press). The transformation of girls to women: Finding voice and developing strategies for liberation. *Journal of Multicultural Counseling and Development.*

Ilacqua, G. E. (1994a). Migraine headaches: Coping efficacy of guided imagery training. *Headache, 34,* 99–102.

Ingram, R., Hayes, A., & Scott, W. (2000). Empirically supported treatments: A critical analysis. In C. Snyder & R. Ingram (Eds.), *Handbook of psychological change* (pp. 40–60). New York: Wiley.

Irvin, J., Bowers, C., Dunn, M., & Wang, M. (1999). Efficacy of relapse prevention: A meta-analytic review. *Journal of Consulting and Clinical Psychology, 67,* 563–570.

Itai, G., & McRae, G. (1994). Counseling older Japanese American clients: An overview and observation. *Journal of Counseling and Development, 72,* 373–377.

Ivey, A. E. & Ivey, M. B. (1999b). International interviewing and counseling (4th ed.). Pacific Grove, CA: Brooks/Cole.

Ivey, A. E., Gluckstern, N. B., & Ivey, M. B. (1993). *Basic attending skills* (3rd ed.). North Amherst, MA: Microtraining Associates.

Ivey, A. E., Ivey, M. B., & Simek-Downing, L. (1987). *Counseling and psychotherapy: Skills, theories, and practice* (2nd ed.). Englewood Cliffs, NJ: Prentice-Hall.

Ivey, A. E., Ivey, M. B., & Simek-Morgan, L. (1997). *Counseling and psychotherapy: A multicultural perspective* (4th ed.). Needham Heights, MA: Allyn & Bacon.

Iwamasa, G. Y. (1993). Asian Americans and cognitive behavioral therapy. *The Behavior Therapist, 16,* 233–235.

Jackson, G. G. (1987). Cross-cultural counseling with Afro-Americans. In P. Pedersen (Ed.), *Handbook of cross-cultural counseling and therapy* (pp. 231–237). New York: Praeger.

Jacob, T., Penn, N., Kulik, J., & Spieth, L. (1992). Effects of cognitive style and maintenance strategies of breast self-examination (BSE) practice by African American women. *Journal of Behavioral Medicine, 15,* 589–609.

Jacobs, E. (1994). *Impact therapy.* Odessa, FL: Psychological Assessment Resources.

Jacobson, E. (1929). *Progressive relaxation.* Chicago: University of Chicago Press.

Jacobson, E. (1964). *Anxiety and tension control.* Philadelphia: Lippincott.

Jacobson, N., & Hollon, S. (1996). Cognitive behavior therapy vs. pharmacotherapy: Now that the jury's returned its verdict, it is time to present the rest of the evidence. *Journal of Consulting and Clinical Psychology, 64,* 74–80.

Jacobson, N., Roberts, L., Berns, S., & McGlinchey, J. (1999). Methods for defining and determining clinical significance of treatment effects: Description, application, and alternatives. *Journal of Consulting and Clinical Psychology, 67,* 300–307.

Jacobson, N. S., Follette, W. C., & Revenstorf, D. (1984). Psychotherapy outcome research: Methods of reporting variability and evaluating clinical significance. *Behavior Therapy, 15,* 336–352.

Jacobson, N. S., & Truax, P. (1991). Clinical significance: A statistical approach to defining meaningful change in psychotherapy research. *Journal of Consulting and Clinical Psychology, 59,* 12–19.

James, B. J., & Samuels, C. A. (1999). High stress life events and spiritual development. *Journal of Psychology and Theology, 27,* 250–260.

Jiang, T., Sun, C., & Wu, Z. (1999). Difference in problem solving between elderly diabetics and elderly healthy people. *Chinese Journal of Clinical Psychology, 7,* 204–207.

Johanson, J. & Kurtz, R. (1991). *Grace unfolding: Psychotherapy in the spirit of the Tao-te Ching.* New York: Bell Tower, Division of Crown.

Johnson, D. W. (2000). *Reaching out: Interpersonal effectiveness and self-actualization* (7th ed.). Needham Heights, MA: Allyn & Bacon.

Johnson, K. (1998). *Trauma in the lives of children: Crisis and stress management techniques for counselors, teachers, and other professionals.* Alameda, CA: Hunter House.

Johnson, W. B., & Ridley, C. R. (1992). Brief Christian and non-Christian rational–emotive therapy with depressed Christian clients: An exploratory study. *Counseling and Values, 36,* 220–229.

Jones, E. E. (1993). Introduction to special section: Single-case research in psychotherapy. *Journal of Consulting and Clinical Psychology, 61,* 371–372.

Jones, E. E., Kanouse, D., Kelley, H. H., Wisbett, R. E., Valins, S., & Weiner, B. (Eds.). (1972). *Attribution: Perceiving the causes of behavior.* Morristown, NJ: General Learning Press.

Josselson, R. (1992). *The space between us.* San Francisco: Jossey-Bass.

Kabat-Zinn, J. (1990). *Full catastrophe living.* New York: Dell.

Kabat-Zinn, J. (1993). Meditation. In B. Moyers (Ed.), *Healing and the mind* (pp. 115–144). New York: Doubleday.

Kabat-Zinn, J. (1994). *Wherever you go there you are.* New York: Hyperion.

Kadushin, A., & Kadushin, G. (1997). *The social work interview: A guide for human service professionals* (4th ed.). New York: Columbia University Press.

Kahn, M. (1991). *Between therapist and client.* New York: W. H. Freeman.

Kahn, M., & Baker, B. L. (1968). Desensitization with minimal therapist contact. *Journal of Abnormal Psychology, 73,* 198.

Kalichman, S. C., Rompa, D., & Coley, B. (1997). Lack of positive outcomes from a cognitive–behavioral HIV and AIDS prevention intervention for inner-city men: Lessons from a controlled pilot study. *AIDS Education and Prevention, 9,* 299–313.

Kamimura, E., & SaSaki, Y. (1991). Fear and anxiety reduction in systematic desensitization and imaging strategies: A comparison of response and stimulus oriented imaging. *Japanese Journal of Behavior Therapy, 17,* 29–38.

Kanfer, F. H., & Gaelick-Buys, L. (1991). Self-management methods. In F. H. Kanfer & A. P. Goldstein (Eds.), *Helping people change* (4th ed., pp. 305–360). New York: Pergamon.

Kanfer, F. H., & Saslow, G. (1969). Behavioral diagnosis. In C. M. Franks (Ed.), *Behavior therapy: Appraisal and status* (pp. 417–444). New York: McGraw-Hill.

Kantor, J. R. (1970). An analysis of the experimental analysis of behavior (TEAB). *Journal of the Experimental Analysis of Behavior, 13,* 101–108.

Kantrowitz, R., & Ballou, M. (1992). A feminist critique of cognitive–behavioral therapy. In L. S. Brown & M. Ballou (Eds.), *Personality and psychopathology: Feminist reappraisals* (pp. 70–87). New York: Guilford.

Kaplan, H. I., & Sadock, B. J. (1998). *Synopsis of psychiatry: Behavioral sciences, clinical psychiatry* (8th ed.). Baltimore: Williams, Lippincott & Wilkins.

Kaplan, R., & Manicavasagar, V. (1998). Adverse effect of EMDR: A case report. *Australia and New Zealand Journal of Psychiatry, 32,* 731–732.

Karasu, T., Docherty, J., Gelenberg, A., Kupfer, D., Merriam, A., & Shadoan, R. (1993). Practice guidelines for major depressive disorder in adults. *American Journal of Psychiatry, 150* (Supplement), 1–26.

Karenga, M. (1980). *Kawaida theory.* Los Angeles: Kawaida.

Karoly, P. & Lecci, L. (1997). Motivational correlates of self-reported persistent pain in young adults. *Clinical Journal of Pain, 13,* 104–109.

Kazdin, A. (1993). Psychotherapy for children and adolescents: Current progress and future research directions. *American Psychologist, 48,* 644–657.

Kazdin, A. E. (1974). Self-monitoring and behavior change. In M. J. Mahoney & C. E. Thoresen (Eds.), *Self-control: Power to the person* (pp. 218–246). Pacific Grove, CA: Brooks/Cole.

Kazdin, A. E. & Wilcoxon, L. A. (1976). Systematic desensitization and non-specific treatment effects: A method logical evaluation. *Psychological Bulletin, 83,* 729–758

Kazdin, A. E. (1977). Assessing the clinical or applied importance of behavior change through social validation. *Behavior Modification, 1,* 427–452.

Kazdin, A. E. (1993). Evaluation in clinical practice: Clinically sensitive and systematic methods of treatment delivery. *Behavior Therapy, 24,* 11–15.

Kazdin, A. E. (1997). Practitioner review: Psychosocial treatments for conduct disorder in children. *Journal of Child Psychology and Psychiatry and Allied Disciplines, 38,* 161–178.

Kazdin, A. E., & Wilcoxon, L. A. (1976). Systematic desensitization and nonspecific treatment effects: A methodological evaluation. *Psychological Bulletin, 83,* 729–758.

Keel, L., & Brown, S. (1999, July). Professional disclosure statements. *Counseling Today,* 14–15.

Kehle, T. J., Madaus, M. R., Baratta, V. S., & Bray, M. A. (1998). Augmented self-modeling as a treatment for children with selective mutism. *Journal of School Psychology, 36,* 247–260.

Kelly, C., & Cooper, S. (1993). Panic and agoraphobia associated with a cerebral arteriovenous malformation. *Irish Journal of Psychological Medicine, 10,* 94–96.

Kelly, J., & St. Lawrence, J. (1990). The impact of community-based groups to help persons reduce HIV infection risk behaviors. *AIDS Care, 2,* 25–36.

Kemp, S., Whittaker, J., & Tracy, E. (1997). *Person–environment practice: The social ecology of interpersonal helping.* New York: Aldine de Gruyter.

Kendall, P., Marrs-Garcia, A., Nath, S., & Sheldrick, R. (1999). Normative comparisons for the evaluation of clinical significance. *Journal of Consulting and Clinical Psychology, 67,* 285–299.

Kendall, P. C. (Ed.). (2000). *Child and adolescent therapy: Cognitive behavioral procedures* (2nd ed.). New York: Guilford.

Kenyan, P. (1999). *What would you do? An ethical case workbook for human service professionals.* Pacific Grove, CA: Brooks/Cole.

Kiesler, D. J. (1966). Some myths of psychotherapy research and the search for a paradigm. *Psychological Bulletin, 65,* 110–136.

Killick, S., & Allen, C. (1997). Shifting the balance—motivational interviewing to help behavior change in people with bulimia nervosa. *European Eating Disorders Review, 5,* 33–41.

Kilpatrick, S. D., & McCullough, M. E. (1999). Religion and spirituality in rehabilitation psychology. *Rehabilitation Psychology, 44,* 388–402.

King, C. N. & Senn, M. D. (1996). Exercise testing and prescription: Practical recommendations for the sedentary. *Sports Medicine, 21,* 326–336.

King, J. (1998). Contact and boundaries: A psychology of relationship. *Proceedings of the United States Association of Body Process Conference,* 267–272.

Kiresuk, T. J., & Sherman, R. E. (1968). Goal attainment scaling: A general method for evaluating comprehensive mental health programs. *Community Mental Health Journal, 4,* 443–453.

Kirst-Ashman, K., & Hull, G. (2002). *Understanding generalist practice.* Pacific Grove, CA: Brooks/Cole–Wadsworth Group.

Kitchener, K. S. (1984). Intuition, critical evaluation and ethical principles: The foundation for ethical decisions in counseling psychology. *The Counseling Psychologist, 12,* 43–55.

Kitchener, K. S. (1988). Dual role relationships: What makes them so problematic? *Journal of Counseling and Development, 67,* 217–221.

Kitchener, K. S. (1999). *The foundations of ethical practice, research, and teaching in psychology.* Mahweh, NJ: Erlbaum.

Kitchener, K. S., & Anderson, S. K. (2000). Ethical issues in counseling psychology: Old themes—new problems. In S. D. Brown & R. W. Lent (Eds.), *Handbook of counseling psychology* (3rd ed., pp. 50–82). New York: Wiley.

Kivlighan, D., Jr., Patton, M., & Foote, D. (1998). Moderating effects of client attachment on the counselor experience–working alliance relationship. *Journal of Counseling Psychology, 45,* 274–278.

Kleinknecht, R. (1991). *Mastering anxiety: The nature and treatment of anxious conditions.* New York: Plenum.

Kleinknecht, R., Dinnel, D., Tanouye-Wilson, S., & Lonner, W. (1994). Cultural variation in social anxiety and phobia: A study of *Taijin Kyofusho. The Behavior Therapist, 17,* 175–178.

Kliewer, W., & Lewis, H. (1995). Family influences on coping processes in children and adolescents with sickle cell disease. *Journal of Pediatric Psychology, 20,* 511–525.

Knapp, M. L., & Hall, J. (1997). *Nonverbal communication in human interaction* (5th ed.). Orlando, FL: Holt, Rinehart & Winston.

Kohut, H. (1971a). *The analysis of the self.* New York: International Universities Press.

Kohut, H. (1971b). *The restoration of the self.* New York: International Universities Press.

Kohut, H. (1984). *How does analysis cure?* Chicago: University of Chicago Press.

Korth, E. (1993). Psychological operation-preparation with children: Preparation of a five-year old boy for the amputation of his left leg with play, family, and behavior therapy. *Zeitschrift fur Klinische Psychologie, 22,* 62–76.

Kottler, J. A., & Brown, R. W. (1992). *Introduction to therapeutic counseling* (2nd ed.). Pacific Grove, CA: Brooks/Cole.

Kremer, T. G., & Gesten, E. L. (1998). Confidentiality limits of managed care and clients' willingness to self-disclose. *Professional Psychology: Research and Practice, 29,* 553–558.

Krepcho, M., Fernandez-Esquer, M., Freeman, A., & Magee, E. (1993). Predictors of bleach use among current African-American injecting drug users: A community study. *Journal of Psychoactive Drugs, 25,* 135–141.

Krieger, N. (1999). Embodying inequality: A review of concepts, measures, and methods for studying health consequences of discrimination. *International Journal of Social Welfare, 29,* 295–352.

Krivonos, P. D., & Knapp, M. L. (1975). Initiating communication: What do you say when you say hello? *Central States Speech Journal, 26,* 115–125.

Kuehlwein, K. T. (1992). Working with gay men. In A. Freeman & F. M. Dattillio (Eds.), *Comprehensive casebook of cognitive therapy* (pp. 249–255). New York: Plenum.

Kuhl, J. & Baumann, N. (2000). Self-regulation and rumination: Negative affect and impaired self-accessibility. In W. J. Perrig & A. Grob (Eds.), *Control of human behavior, mental processes, and consciousness: Essays in honor of the 60th birthday of August Frammer* (pp. 283–305). Mahweh, NJ: Erlbaum.

LaCrosse, M. B. (1980). Perceived counselor social influence and counseling outcomes: Validity of the counselor rating form. *Journal of Counseling Psychology, 27,* 320–327.

LaFromboise, T., Coleman, H. L. K., & Gerton, J. (1993). Psychological impact of biculturalism: Evidence and theory. *Psychological Bulletin, 114,* 395–412.

LaFromboise, T., & Dixon, D. N. (1981). American Indian perception of trustworthiness in a counseling interview. *Journal of Counseling Psychology, 28,* 135–139.

LaFromboise, T., & Low, K. (1989). American Indian adolescents. In J. Gibbs & L. Hwang (Eds.), *Children of color* (pp. 114–147). San Francisco: Jossey-Bass.

Lam, D. J., & Palsane, M. N. (1997). Research on stress and coping: Contemporary Asian approaches. In H. S. R. Kao & D. Sinha (Eds.), *Asian perspectives on psychology* (pp. 265–281). Thousand Oaks, CA: Sage.

Lambert, M., & Bergin, A. (1992). Achievements and limitations of psychotherapy research. In D. K. Freedheim (Ed.), *History of psychotherapy: A century of change* (pp. 360–390). Washington, DC: American Psychological Association.

Lambert, M., Hansen, N., Umphress, V., Lunnen, K., Okiishi, J., Burlingame, G., & Reisinger, C. (1996). *Administration and scoring manual for the Outcome Questionnaire (OQ-45:2).* Stevenson, MD: American Professional Credentialing Services.

Lambert, M., & Hill, C. (1994). Assessing psychotherapy outcomes and processes. In A. Bergin & S. Garfield (Eds.), *Handbook of psychotherapy and behavior change* (4th ed., pp. 72–113). New York: Wiley.

Lambert, M., Okiishi, J., Finch, A., & Johnson, L. (1998). Outcome assessment: From conceptualization to implementation. *Professional Psychology, 29,* 63–70.

Lambert, M. J., Ogles, B. M., & Masters, K. S. (1992). Choosing outcome assessment devices: An organizational and conceptual scheme. *Journal of Counseling and Development, 70,* 527–532.

Lang, P. J., & Lazovik, A. (1963). Experimental desensitization of a phobia. *Journal of Abnormal and Social Psychology, 66,* 519–525.

Lang, P. J., Melamed, B. G., & Hart, J. (1970). A psychophysiological analysis of fear modification using an automated desensitization procedure. *Journal of Abnormal Psychology, 76,* 221.

Lankton, S. R. (1980). *Practical magic: A translation of basic neurolinguistic programming into clinical psychotherapy.* Cupertino, CA: Meta.

Larson, E. (1998). Reframing the meaning of disability to families: The embrace of paradox. *Social Science and Medicine, 47,* 865–875.

Laungani, P. (1993). Cultural differences in stress and its management. *Stress-Medicine, 9,* 37–43.

Lauver, P., & Jones, R. (1991). Factors associated with perceived career options in American Indian, white and Hispanic rural high school students. *Journal of Counseling Psychology, 38,* 159–166.

Lawendowski, L. (1998). A motivational intervention for adolescent smokers. *Preventive Medicine, 27,* A39–A46.

Lazar, S. W., Bush, G., Gollub, R. L., Fricchione, G. L., Khalsa, G., & Benson, H. (2000). Functional brain mapping of the relaxation response and meditation. *Neuroreport: For Rapid Communication of Neuroscience Research, 11,* 1581–1585.

Lazarus, A., & Fay, A. (1982). Resistance or rationalization? A cognitive–behavioral perspective. In P. L. Wachtel (Ed.), *Resistance: Psychodynamic and behavioral approaches* (pp. 115–132). New York: Plenum.

Lazarus, A. A. (1967). In support of technical eclecticism. *Psychological Reports, 21,* 415–416.

Lazarus, A. A. (1976). *Multimodal behavior therapy.* New York: Springer.

Lazarus, A. A. (1984). *In the mind's eye: The power of imagery for personal enrichment.* New York: Guilford.

Lazarus, A. A. (1989). *The practice of multimodal therapy.* Baltimore: Johns Hopkins University Press.

Lazarus, A. A. (1997). *Brief but comprehensive psychotherapy: The multimodal way.* New York: Springer.

Lazarus, R. S. (1990). Theory-based stress measurement. *Psychological Inquiry, 1,* 3–13.

Lazarus, R. S., & Folkman, S. (1984). *Stress, appraisal, and coping.* New York: Springer.

Leahy, R. (1996). *Cognitive therapy: Basic principles and implications.* Northvale, NJ: Aronson.

Leahy, R., & Holland, S. (2000). *Treatment plans and interventions for depression and anxiety disorders.* New York: Guilford.

Lecomte, C., Bernstein, B. L., & Dumont, F. (1981). Counseling interactions as a function of spatial–environmental conditions. *Journal of Counseling Psychology, 28,* 536–539.

Lehrer, P. M., & Woolfolk, R. (1982). Self-report assessment of anxiety: Somatic, cognitive, and behavioral modalities. *Behavioral Assessment, 4,* 167–177.

Lehrer, P. M., & Woolfolk, R. L. (Eds.). (1993). *Principles and practice of stress management* (2nd ed.). New York: Guilford.

Leininger, M. M. (1988). Leininger's theory of nursing: Culture care diversity and universality. *Nursing Science Quarterly, 1,* 152–160.

Leith, L. M. (1994). *Foundations of exercise and mental health.* Morgantown, WV: Fitness Information Technology.

LePage, J. (1994). *Integrative yoga therapy manual.* Aptos, CA: Integrative Yoga Therapy.

Lerman, H. (1992). The limits of phenomenology: A feminist critique of the humanistic personality theories. In L. S. Brown & M. Ballou (Eds.), *Personality and psychotherapy: Feminist reappraisals.* New York: Guilford.

Leserman, J., Perkins, D., & Evans, D. (1992). Coping with the threat of AIDS: The role of social support. *American Journal of Psychiatry, 149,* 1514–1520.

LeShan, L. (1974). *How to meditate.* New York: Bantam.

LeShan, L. (1995). Mobilizing the life force, treating the individual. *Alternative Therapies, I,* 63–69.

Levin, R., & Gross, A. (1985). The role of relaxation in systematic desensitization. *Behaviour Research and Therapy, 23,* 187–196.

Levitov, J. E., Fall, K. A., & Jennings, M. C. (1999). Counselor clinical training with client-actors. *Counselor Education and Supervision, 38,* 249–259.

Lin, M. J., Kelly, K. R., & Nelson, R. C. (1996). A comparative analysis of the interpersonal process in school-based counseling and consultation. *Journal of Counseling Psychology, 43,* 389–393.

Linscott, J., & DiGiuseppe, R. (1998). Cognitive assessment. In A. Bellack & M. Hersen (Eds.), *Behavioral assessment* (pp. 104–125). Needham Heights, MA: Allyn & Bacon.

Lipke, H., & Botkin, A. (1992). Case studies of eye movement desensitization and reprocessing (EMDR) with chronic post-traumatic stress disorder. *Psychotherapy, 29,* 591–595.

Litrownik, A. J. (1982). Special considerations in the self-management training of the developmentally disabled. In P. Karoly & F. H. Kanfer (Eds.), *Self-management and behavior change* (pp. 315–352). New York: Pergamon.

Locke, D. C. (1990). A not so provincial view of multicultural counseling. *Counselor Education and Supervision, 30,* 18–25.

Lohr, J. M., Lilienfeld, S. O., Tolin, D. F., & Herbert, J. D. (1999). Eye movement desensitization and reprocessing: An analysis of specific versus nonspecific treatment factors. *Journal of Anxiety Disorders, 13,* 185–207.

Lomont, J. F. (1965). Reciprocal inhibition or extinction? *Behaviour Research and Therapy, 3,* 209–219.

Long, L. & Prophit, P. (1981). *Understanding/responding: A communication manual for nurses.* Monterey, CA: Wadsworth Health Sciences.

Lopez, M., & Mermelstein, R. (1995). A cognitive–behavioral program to improve geriatric rehabilitation outcome. *Gerontologist, 35,* 696–700.

Luborsky, L. (1984). *Principles of psychoanalytic psychotherapy: A manual for supportive expressive treatment.* New York: Basic.

Lukoff, D., Lu, F., & Turner, R. (1999). From spiritual emergency to spiritual problem: The transpersonal roots of the new *DSM-IV* category. *Journal of Humanistic Psychology, 38,* 21–50.

Lum, D. (1996). *Social work practice and people of color.* Pacific Grove, CA: Brooks/Cole.

Lum, D. (2000). *Social work practice and people of color* (4th ed.). Pacific Grove, CA: Brooks/Cole.

Lum, L. C. (1976). The syndrome of habitual chronic hyperventilation. In O. Hill (Ed.), *Modern trends in psychosomatic medicine* (Vol. 3). Boston: Butterworth.

Lyddon, W. J. (1995). First- and second-order change: Implications for rationalist and constructivist cognitive therapies. *Journal of Counseling and Development, 69,* 122–127.

Maag, J. W., & Kotlash, J. (1994). Review of stress inoculation training with children and adolescents: Issues and recommendations. *Behavior Modification, 18,* 443–469.

MacKay, P., & Marlatt, G. (1990). Maintaining sobriety. *International Journal of the Addictions, 25,* 1257–1276.

Maddux, J. E. (Ed.). (1995). *Self-efficacy, adaptation, and adjustment.* New York: Plenum.

Mahoney, K., & Mahoney, M. J. (1976). Cognitive factors in weight reduction. In J. D. Krumboltz & C. E. Thoresen (Eds.), *Counseling methods* (pp. 99–105). New York: Holt, Rinehart and Winston.

Mahoney, M. (2000). A changing history of efforts to understand and control change: The case of psychotherapy. In C. Snyder & R. Ingram (Eds.), *Handbook of psychological change* (pp. 3–12). New York: Wiley.

Mahoney, M. J. (1971). The self-management of covert behavior: A case study. *Behavior Therapy, 2,* 575–578.

Mahoney, M. J. (1972). Research issues in self-management. *Behavior Therapy, 3,* 45–63.

Mahoney, M. J. (1974). *Cognition and behavior modification.* Cambridge, MA: Ballinger.

Mahoney, M. J. (1977). Some applied issues in self-monitoring. In J. Cone & R. Hawkins (Eds.), *Behavioral assessment: New directions in clinical psychology* (pp. 241–254). New York: Brunner/Mazel.

Mahoney, M. J. (1995). Theoretical developments in the cognitive psychotherapies. In M. J. Mahoney (Ed.), *Cognitive and constructive psychotherapies* (pp. 3–19). New York: Springer.

Mahoney, M. J., Moura, N. G., & Wade, T. C. (1973). Relative efficacy of self-reward, self-punishment, and self-monitoring techniques for weight loss. *Journal of Consulting and Clinical Psychology, 40,* 404–407.

Mahoney, M. J., & Thoresen, C. E. (Eds.). (1974). *Self-control: Power to the person.* Pacific Grove, CA: Brooks/Cole.

Maibach, E., & Flora, J. A. (1993). Symbolic modeling and cognitive rehearsal: Using video to promote AIDS prevention self-efficacy. Special Issue: The role of communication in health promotion. *Communication Research, 20,* 517–545.

Mail, P. (1995). Early modeling of drinking behavior by Native American elementary school children playing drunk. *International Journal of the Addictions, 30,* 1187–1197.

Malgady, R., Rogler, T., & Costantino, G. (1990). Culturally sensitive psychotherapy for Puerto Rican children and adolescents: A program of treatment outcome research. *Journal of Consulting and Clinical Psychology, 58,* 704–712.

Mallinckrodt, B. (1991). Clients' representations of childhood emotional bonds with parents, social support, and formation of working alliance. *Journal of Counseling Psychology, 38,* 401–409.

Mallinckrodt, B. (1993). Session impact, working alliance, and treatment outcome in brief counseling. *Journal of Counseling Psychology, 40,* 25–32.

Mallinckrodt, B., Coble, H., & Gantt, D. (1995). Working alliance, attachment memories, and social competencies of women in brief therapy. *Journal of Counseling Psychology, 42,* 79–84.

Mallinckrodt, B., Gantt, D., & Coble, H. (1995). Attachment patterns in the psychotherapy relationship: Development of the client attachment to therapist scale. *Journal of Counseling Psychology, 42,* 307–317.

Mallinckrodt, B., King, J., & Coble, H. (1998). Family dysfunction, alexithymia, and client attachment to therapist. *Journal of Counseling Psychology, 45,* 497–504.

Malow, R., Corrigan, S., Cunningham, S., & West, J. (1993). Psychosocial factors associated with condom use among African American drug abusers in treatment. *AIDS Education and Prevention, 5,* 244–253.

Manning, S. S. (1998). Empowerment in mental health programs: Listening to the voices. In L. M. Gutiérrez, R. J. Parsons, & E. O. Cox (Eds.), *Empowerment in social work practice: A sourcebook* (pp. 89–109). Pacific Grove, CA: Brooks/Cole.

Marcoux, M. F., Sallis, J. F., McKenzie, T. L., Marshall, S., Armstrong, C. A., & Goggin, K. J. (1999). Process evaluation of a physical self-management program for children: SPARK. *Psychology and Health, 14,* 659–677.

Marks, L. (1998). Deconstructing locus of control: Implications for practitioners. *Journal of Counseling and Development, 76,* 251–260.

Markus, H. R., Kitayama, S., & Heiman, R. J. (1996). Culture and basic psychological principles. In E. T. Higgens & A. W. Kruglanski (Eds.), *Social psychology: Handbook of basic principles* (pp. 857–914). New York: Guilford.

Marlatt, G., & Gordon, J. R. (1985). *Relapse prevention.* New York: Guilford.

Marlatt, G., & Parks, G. A. (1982). Self-management of addictive behaviors. In P. Karoly & F. H. Kanfer (Eds.), *Self-management and behavior change* (pp. 443–448). New York: Pergamon.

Marlatt, G. A., & Kristeller, J. L. (1999). Mindfulness and meditation. In W. R. Miller (Ed.), *Integrating spirituality into treatment: Resources for practitioners* (pp. 67–84). Washington, DC: American Psychological Association.

Marquis, J., Ferguson, J. M., & Taylor, C. B. (1980). Generalization of relaxation skills. *Journal of Behavior Therapy and Experimental Psychiatry, 11,* 95–99.

Marquis, J. N., Morgan, W., & Piaget, G. (1973). *A guidebook for systematic desensitization* (3rd ed.). Palo Alto, CA: Veterans' Workshop.

Marsella, A., Friedman, M., Gerrity, E., & Scarsfield, R. C. (1996). *Ethnocultural aspects of posttraumatic stress disorder.* Washington, DC: American Psychological Association.

Marsella, A. J. (1998). Toward a "global-community" psychology. *American Psychologist, 53,* 1282–1291.

Marten, P., & Heimberg, R. (1995). Toward an integration of independent practice and clinical research. *Professional Psychology, 26,* 48–53.

Martin, D. (1993). Coping with AIDS-risk reduction efforts among gay men. *AIDS Education and Prevention, 5,* 104–120.

Martin, K., & Hall, C. (1995). Using mental imagery to enhance intrinsic motivation. *Journal of Sport and Exercise Psychology, 17,* 54–65.

Matson, J. (1985). Modeling. In A. S. Bellack & M. Hersen (Eds.), *Dictionary of behavior therapy techniques,* (pp. 150–151). New York: Pergamon.

Maurer, R. E., & Tindall, J. H. (1983). Effect of postural congruence on client's perception of empathy. *Journal of Counseling Psychology, 30,* 158–163.

McAuley, E., Shaffer, S., & Rudolph, D. (1995). Affective responses to acute exercise in elderly impaired males: The moderating effects of self-efficacy and age. *International Journal of Aging and Human Development, 41,* 13–27.

McAuliffe, G. J., & Eriksen, K. P. (1999). Toward a constructivist and developmental identity for the counseling profession: The context–phase–stage–style model. *Journal of Counseling and Development, 77,* 267–280.

McCafferty, S. (1992). The use of private speech by adult second language learners: A cross-cultural study. *Modern Language Journal, 76,* 179–189.

McCarthy, P. (1982). Differential effects of counselor self-referent responses and counselor status. *Journal of Counseling Psychology, 29,* 125–131.

McFall, R. M. (1977). Parameters of self-monitoring. In R. B. Stuart (Ed.), *Behavioral self-management: Strategies, techniques and outcomes* (pp. 196–214). New York: Brunner/Mazel.

McFall, R. M., & Dodge, K. A. (1982). Self-management and interpersonal skills learning. In P. Karoly & F. H. Kanfer (Eds.), *Self-management and behavior change* (pp. 353–392). New York: Pergamon.

McGill, D. W. (1992). The cultural story in multicultural family therapy. *Families in Society, 73,* 339–349.

McGrath, T., Tsui, E., Humphries, S., & Yule, W. (1990). Successful treatment of a noise phobia in a nine-year-old girl with systematic desensitization in vivo. *Educational Psychology, 10,* 79–83.

McGuigan, F. J. (1993). Progressive relaxation: Origins, principles, and clinical applications. In P. M. Lehrer & R. L. Woolfolk (Eds.), *Principles and practice of stress management* (pp. 17–52). New York: Guilford.

McGuigan, F. J. (1999). *Encyclopedia of stress.* Boston: Allyn & Bacon.

McGuire, M., Bakst, K., Fairbanks, L., McGuire, M., Sachinvala, N., Von Scotti, H., & Brown, N. (2000). Cognitive, mood, and functional evaluations using touchscreen technology. *Journal of Nervous and Mental Disease, 188,* 813–817.

McLeod, C. (1999). Empowering creativity with computer-assisted art therapy: An introduction to available programs and techniques. *Art Therapy, 16,* 201–205.

McMinn, M. R., Buchanan, T., Ellens, B. M., & Ryan, M. K. (1999). Technology, professional practice, and ethics: Survey findings and implications. *Professional Psychology: Research and Practice, 30,* 165–172.

McNeill, B. W., May, R. J., & Lee, V. J. (1987). Perceptions of counselor source characteristics by premature and successful terminators. *Journal of Counseling Psychology, 34,* 86–89.

McNeill, B. W., Stoltenberg, C. D. (1989). Reconceptualizing social influence in counseling. The elaboration likelihood model. *Journal of Counseling Psychology, 36,* 24–33.

Meador, B., & Rogers, C. (1984). Person-centered therapy. In R. J. Corsini (Ed.), *Current psychotherapies* (pp. 142–195). Itasca, IL: Peacock.

Meador, K. G., & Koenig, H. G. (2000). Spirituality and religion in psychiatric practice: Parameters and implications. *Psychiatric Annals, 30,* 549–555.

Meara, N., Schmidt, L., & Day, J. (1996). A foundation for ethical decisions, policies, and character. *The Counseling Psychologist, 24,* 4–77.

Mehan, H., Hubbard, L., & Villanueva, I. (1994). Forming academic identities: Accommodations without assimilation among involuntary minorities. *Anthropology and Education Quarterly, 25,* 91–117.

Mehrabian, A. (1976). *Public places and private spaces.* New York: Basic.

Meichenbaum, D. (1977). *Cognitive-behavior modification.* New York: Plenum.

Meichenbaum, D. H. (1985). *Stress-inoculation training.* New York: Pergamon.

Meichenbaum, D. H. (1993). Stress inoculation training: A 20-year update. In P. M. Lehrer & R. L. Woolfolk (Eds.), *Principles and practice of stress management* (2nd ed., pp. 373–406). New York: Guilford.

Meichenbaum, D. H. (1994). *A clinical handbook/practical therapist manual for assessing and treating adults with posttraumatic stress disorder (PTSD).* Waterloo, Ontario, Canada: Institute Press.

Meichenbaum, D. H., & Cameron, R. (1973). *Stress inoculation: A skills training approach to anxiety management.* Unpublished manuscript, University of Waterloo, Waterloo, Ontario, Canada.

Meichenbaum, D. H., & Cameron, R. (1983). Stress inoculation training: Toward a general paradigm on training coping skills. In D. H. Meichenbaum & M. E. Jaremko (Eds.), *Stress reduction and prevention* (pp. 115–157). New York: Plenum.

Meichenbaum, D. H., & Deffenbacher, J. L. (1988). Stress inoculation training. *Counseling Psychologist, 16,* 69–90.

Meichenbaum, D. H., & Goodman, J. (1971). Training impulsive children to talk to themselves: A means of developing self-control. *Journal of Abnormal Psychology, 77,* 115–126.

Meichenbaum, D. H., & Turk, D. (1976). The cognitive–behavioral management of anxiety, anger, and pain. In P. O. Davidson (Ed.), *The behavioral management of anxiety, depression and pain.* New York: Brunner/Mazel.

Melchert, T. P., & Patterson, M. M. (1999). Duty to warn and interventions with HIV-positive clients. *Professional Psychology: Research and Practice, 30,* 180–186.

Mesquita, B., & Frijda, N. (1992). Cultural variations in emotions: A review. *Psychological Bulletin, 112,* 179–204.

Meyer, R. G., & Deitsch, S. E. (1996). *The clinician's handbook: Integrated diagnostics, assessment, and intervention in adult and adolescent psychopathology* (4th ed.). Needham Heights, MA: Allyn and Bacon.

Middleton, M., & Cartledge, G. (1995). The effects of social skills instruction and parental involvement on the aggressive behavior of African American males. *Behavior Modification, 19,* 192–210.

Miller, J. B. (1991). The development of women's sense of self. In J. Jordan, A. Kaplan, J. B. Miller, I. Stiver, & J. Surrey (Eds.), *Women's growth in connection* (pp. 11–26). New York: Guilford.

Miller, R. C. (1993). Working with the breath. In G. Feuerstein & S. Bodian (Eds.), *Living yoga* (pp. 27–39). New York: Tarcher/Perigee–Putnam.

Miller, W. R. (1996). Motivational interviewing: Research, practice and puzzles. *Addictive Behaviors, 21,* 835–842.

Miller, W. R. (1998). Why do people change addictive behavior? *Addiction, 93,* 163–172.

Miller, W. R. (Ed.), (1999). *Integrating spirituality into treatment: Resources for practitioners.* Washington, DC: American Psychological Association.

Miller, W. R. (2000). Rediscovering fire: Small interventions, large effects. *Psychology of Addictive Behaviors, 14,* 6–18.

Milne, C. R., & Dowd, E. T. (1983). Effect of interpretation style on counselor social influence. *Journal of Counseling Psychology, 51,* 603–606.

Miranda, J., & Dwyer, E. V. (1993). Cognitive behavioral therapy for disadvantaged medical patients. *The Behavior Therapist, 16,* 226–228.

Mischel, W. (1973). *Personality and assessment* (2nd ed.). New York: Wiley.

Mitchell, K., Levin, A., & Krumboltz, J. (1999). Planned happenstance: Constructing unexpected career opportunities. *Journal of Counseling and Development, 77,* 115–124.

Mitchell, R. W. (2001). *Documentation in counseling records.* Washington, DC: American Counseling Association.

Moncher, M., & Schinke, S. (1994). Group intervention to prevent tobacco use among Native American youth. *Research on Social Work Practice, 4,* 160–171.

Moorey, S., Hughes, P., Knynenberg, P., & Michaels, A. (2000). The Problem Solving Scale in a sample of patients referred for cognitive therapy. *Behavioural and Cognitive Psychotherapy, 28,* 131–138.

Moos, R. H., & Schaefer, J. A. (1993). Coping resources and processes: Current concepts and measures. In L. Goldberger & S. Breznitz (Eds.), *Handbook of stress: Theoretical and clinical aspects* (2nd ed., pp. 234–257). New York: Free Press.

Moras, K., Telfer, L. A., & Barlow, D. H. (1993). Efficacy and specific effects data on new treatments: A case study strategy with mixed anxiety-depression. *Journal of Consulting and Clinical Psychology, 61,* 412–420.

Morgan, D., & Morgan, R. (2001). Single-participant research design. *American Psychologist, 56,* 119–127.

Morran, D. K., Kurpius, D. J., Brack, G., & Rozecki, T. G. (1994). Relationship between counselors' clinical hypotheses and client ratings of counselor effectiveness. *Journal of Counseling and Development, 72,* 655–660.

Morran, K., Kurpius, D., Brack, C., & Brack, G. (1995). A cognitive-skills model for counselor training and supervision. *Journal of Counseling and Development, 73,* 384–389.

Morris, R. J. (1991). Fear reduction methods. In F. H. Kanfer & A. P. Goldstein (Eds.), *Helping people change* (4th ed., pp. 161–201). New York: Pergamon.

Morrison, J. (1995). *DSM-IV made easy.* New York: Guilford.

Morrison, J. (1995). *The first interview: A guide for clinicians.* New York: Guilford.

Morrison, J. (1999). *When psychological problems mask medical disorders.* New York: Guilford.

Morrison, J., & Anders, T. (1999). *Interviewing children and adolescents.* New York: Guilford.

Morrow, S., Gore, P., & Campbell, B. (1996). The application of a socio-cognitive framework to the career development of lesbian women and gay men. *Journal of Vocational Behavior, 48,* 136–148.

Morse, G. G. (1997). Effects of positive reframing and social support on perception of perimenstrual changes among women with premenstrual syndrome. *Health Care for Women International, 18,* 175–193.

Motenko, A. K., & Greenberg, S. (1995). Reframing dependence in old age. *Social Work, 40,* 382–390.

Motley, M., & Molloy, J. (1994). An efficacy test of a new therapy for public-speaking anxiety. *Journal of Applied Communication Research, 22,* 48–58.

Mungadze, J. (2000). Is it dissociation or demonization? Sorting out spiritual and clinical issues in the treatment of dissociative disorders. *Journal of Psychology and Christianity, 19,* 139–143.

Muris, P., & Merckelbach, H. (1999). Traumatic memories, eye movements, phobia, and panic: A critical note on the proliferation of EMDR. *Journal of Anxiety Disorders, 13,* 209–223.

Murphy, M., & Donovan, S. (Eds.). (1997). *The physical and psychological effects of meditation* (2nd ed.). Sausalito, CA: Institute of Noetic Sciences.

Mwaba, K., & Pedersen, P. (1990). Relative importance of intercultural, interpersonal, and psychopathological attributions in judging critical incidents by multicultural counselors. *Journal of Multicultural Counseling and Development, 18,* 107–117.

Myrick, R. D., & Myrick, L. S. (1993). Guided imagery: From mystical to practical. Special Issue: Counseling and children's play. *Elementary School Guidance and Counseling, 28,* 62–70.

Nagae, N., Nedate, K., & Sekiguchi, Y. (1999). Self-instructional training for shyness: Differences in improvements produced by different types of coping self-statements. *Japanese Journal of Counseling Science, 32,* 32–42.

Narayanasamy, A. (1999). A review of spirituality as applied to nursing. *International Journal for Nursing Studies, 36*(2), 117–125.

Nathan, P. (1998). Practice guidelines: Not yet ideal. *American Psychologist, 53,* 250–299.

National Association of Social Workers. (1996). *Code of ethics.* Washington, DC: Author.

Neilans, T. H., & Israel, A. C. (1981). Towards maintenance and generalization of behavior change: Teaching children self-regulation and self-instructional skills. *Cognitive Therapy and Research, 5,* 189–195.

Neill, K. (1993). Ethnic pain styles in acute myocardial infarction. *Western Journal of Nursing Research, 15,* 531–543.

Neimeyer, R. A., & Raskin, J. D. (2001). Varieties of constructivism in psychotherapy. In K. S. Dobson (Ed.), *Handbook of cognitive–behavioral therapies* (2nd ed., pp. 393–430). New York: Guilford.

Nelissen, I., Muris, P., & Merckelback, H. (1995). Computerized exposure and in vivo exposure treatments of spider fear in children: Two case reports. *Journal of Behavior Therapy and Experimental Psychiatry, 26,* 153–156.

Nelson, R. O. (1977). Methodological issues in assessment via self-monitoring. In J. D. Cone & R. P. Hawkins (Eds.), *Behavioral assessment: New directions in clinical psychology* (pp. 217–254). New York: Brunner/Mazel.

Nelson, R. O. (1983). Behavioral assessment: Past, present, and future. *Behavioral Assessment, 5,* 195–206.

Nelson, R. O., & Barlow, D. H. (1981). Behavioral assessment: Basic strategies and initial procedures. In D. H. Barlow (Ed.),

Behavioral assessment of adult disorders (pp. 13–43). New York: Guilford.

Nelson, R. O., Hayes, S. C., Spong, R. T., Jarrett, R. B., & McKnight, D. L. (1983). Self-reinforcement: Appealing misnomer or effective mechanism. *Behaviour Research and Therapy, 21,* 557–566.

Newman, M. G., Consoli, A., & Taylor, C. B. (1997). Computers in assessment and cognitive behavioral treatment of clinical disorders: Anxiety as a case in point. *Behavior Therapy, 28,* 211–235.

Newman, M. G., Kenardy, J., Herman, S., & Taylor, C. B. (1997). Comparison of palmtop-computer-assisted brief cognitive–behavioral treatment to cognitive–behavioral treatment for panic disorder. *Journal of Consulting and Clinical Psychology, 65,* 178–183.

Nezu, A. M., & Nezu, C. M. (Eds.). (1989). *Clinical decision making in behavior therapy: A problem-solving perspective.* Champaign, IL: Research Press.

Nezu, A. M., Nezu, C. M., Friedman, S. H., Faddis, S., & Houts, P. S. (1998). *Helping cancer patients cope: A problem-solving approach.* Washington, DC: American Psychological Association.

Nezu, A. M., Nezu, C. M., & Perri, M. B. (1989). *Problem-solving therapy for depression: Theory, research, and clinical guidelines.* New York: Wiley.

Nichols, M. P. (1995). *The lost art of listening.* New York: Guilford.

Nickerson, K., Helms, J., & Terrell, F. (1994). Cultural mistrust, opinions about mental illness, and black students' attitudes toward seeking psychological help from white counselors. *Journal of Counseling Psychology, 41,* 378–385.

Nickerson, R. S. (1986). *Reflections on reasoning.* Hillsdale, NJ: Erlbaum.

Nolen-Hoeksema, S., Girgus, J. S., & Seligman, M. (1992). Predictors and consequences of childhood depressive symptoms: A 5-year longitudinal study. *Journal of Abnormal Psychology, 101,* 405–422.

Norcross, J. C. (Ed.). (in press). Empirically supported therapy relationships: Report of the Division 29 Task Force. *Psychotherapy, 38*(4).

Norcross, J. C. (Ed.). (in press). *Psychotherapy relationships that work: Therapist contributions and responsiveness to patient needs.* New York: Oxford University Press.

Norcross, J. C., Alford, B. A., & DeMichele, J. T. (1992). The future of psychotherapy: Delphi data and concluding observations. *Psychotherapy, 29,* 150–158.

Norcross, J. C., Santrock, J. W., Smith, T., Campbell, L. F., & Smith, T. P. (2000). *Authoritative guide to self-help resources in mental health.* New York: Guilford.

Novaco, R. W. (1975). *Anger control: The development and evaluation of an experimental treatment.* Lexington, MA: Heath.

Nugent, W., Sieppert, J., & Hudson, W. (2001). *Practice evaluation for the 21st century.* Pacific Grove, CA: Brooks/Cole–Wadsworth Group.

Nurius, P. S. (1995). Critical thinking: A meta-skill for integrating practice and information technology training. *Computers in Human Services, 12,* 109–126.

Nurius, P. S. (1999). Three online books—*Psych Online, Psychological Resources on the WWW,* & *The Insider's Guide to Mental Health Resources. Journal of Technology in Human Services, 16,* 57–64.

Nurius, P. S. (2000). Coping. In P. Allen-Meares & C. Garvin (Eds.), *The handbook of social work direct practice* (pp. 349–372). Thousand Oaks, CA: Sage.

Nurius, P. S., & Hudson, W. W. (1993). *Human services: Practice evaluation and computers.* Pacific Grove, CA: Brooks/Cole.

Oettingen, G. (1995). Cross-cultural perspectives on self-efficacy. In A. Bandura (Ed.), *Self-efficacy in changing societies* (pp. 149–176). New York: Cambridge University Press.

Ogles, B., Lambert, M., & Masters, K. (1996). *Assessing outcome in clinical practice.* Boston: Allyn & Bacon.

Okun, B., Fried, J., & Okun, M. (1999). *Understanding diversity.* Pacific Grove, CA: Brooks/Cole.

Okun, B. F. (1997). *Effective helping* (5th ed.). Pacific Grove, CA: Brooks/Cole.

O'Leary, K. D., & Wilson, G. T. (1987). *Behavior therapy* (2nd ed.). Englewood Cliffs, NJ: Prentice-Hall.

Ollendick, T. H., & King, N. J. (2000). Empirically supported treatments for children and adolescents (pp. 386–425). In P. C. Kendall (Ed.), *Child and adolescent therapy: Cognitive behavioral procedures* (2nd ed.). New York: Guilford.

Omizo, M. M., Omizo, S. A., & Kitaoka, S. K. (1998). Guided affective and cognitive imagery to enhance self-esteem among Hawaiian children. *Journal of Multicultural Counseling and Development, 26,* 52–62.

Oppenheimer, M. (1992). Alma's bedside ghost: Or the importance of cultural similarity. *Hispanic Journal of Behavioral Sciences, 14,* 496–501.

Organista, K., Dwyer, E. V., & Azocar, F. (1993). Cognitive behavioral therapy with Latino outpatients. *The Behavior Therapist, 16,* 229–232.

Ornish, D. (1990). *Reversing heart disease.* New York: Ballantine.

Ostaseski, F. (1994). Stories of lives lived and now ending. *The Sun,* Dec. #228, 10–13.

Ottens, A., Shank, G., & Long, R. (1995). The role of abductive logic in understanding and using advanced empathy. *Counselor Education and Supervision, 34,* 199–211.

Overholser, J. C. (1990). Passive relaxation training with guided imagery: A transcript for clinical use. *Phobia Practice and Research Journal, 3,* 107–122.

Overholser, J. C. (1991). The use of guided imagery in psychotherapy: Modules for use with passive relaxation training. *Journal of Contemporary Psychotherapy, 21,* 159–172.

Oyserman, D., Gant, L., & Ager, J. (1995). A socially contextualized model of African American identity: Possible selves and school persistence. *Journal of Personality and Social Psychology, 69,* 1216–1232.

Oz, S. (1995). A modified balance-sheet procedure for decision making in therapy: Cost-cost comparison. *Professional Psychology, 25,* 78–81.

Ozer, R. L., & Bandura, A. (1990). Mechanisms governing empowerment effects: A self-efficacy analysis. *Journal of Personality and Social Psychology, 58,* 472–486.

Paddock, J. R., Joseph, A. L., Chan, F. M., Terranova, S., Manning, C., & Loftus, E. F. (1998). When guided visualization procedures may backfire: Imagination inflation and predicting individual differences in suggestibility. *Applied Cognitive Psychology, 12* (Special issue): S63–S75.

Paddock, J. R., Noel, M., Terranova, S., Eber, H. W., Manning, C., & Loftus, E. F. (1999). Imagination inflation and the perils of guided visualization. *Journal of Psychology, 133,* 581–595.

Papp, P. (1976). Family choreography. In P. J. Guerin, Jr. (Ed.), *Family therapy: Theory and practice* (pp. 465–479). New York: Gardner.

Passons, W. R. (1975). *Gestalt approaches in counseling.* New York: Holt, Rinehart and Winston.

Patel, C. (1993). Yoga-based therapy. In P. M. Lehrer & R. L. Woolfolk (Eds.), *Principles and practice of stress management* (2nd ed., pp. 89–137). New York: Guilford.

Patterson, J., Hayworth, M., Turner, C., & Raskin, M. (2000). Spiritual issues in family therapy: A graduate-level course. *Journal of Marriage and Family Counseling, 2,* 199–210.

Patterson, L. E., & Welfel, E. R. (2000). *The counseling process* (5th ed.). Pacific Grove, CA: Brooks/Cole.

Patton, M. (2000). Counseling psychology training: A matter of good teaching. *The Counseling Psychologist, 28,* 701–711.

Paul, R. (1993). *Critical thinking: What every person needs to know to survive in a rapidly changing world.* Santa Rosa, CA: Foundation for Critical Thinking.

Paulson, B., Truscott, D., & Stuart, J. (1999). Clients' perceptions of helpful experiences in counseling. *Journal of Counseling Psychology, 46,* 317–324.

Peck, M. S. (1978). *The road less traveled.* New York: Simon & Schuster.

Pedersen, P. B., & Ivey, A. (1993). *Culture-centered counseling and interviewing skills.* New York: Praeger.

Pekarik, G., & Guidry, L. (1999). Relationship of satisfaction to symptom change, follow-up adjustment, and clinical significance in private practice. *Professional Psychology, 30,* 474–478.

Pellebon, D. A., & Anderson, S. C. (1999). Understanding the life issues of spiritually-based clients. *Families in Society, 80,* 229–238.

Perls, F. S. (1973). *The Gestalt approach and eyewitness to therapy.* Palo Alto, CA: Science and Behavior Books.

Persons, J. B., & Davidson, J. (2001). Cognitive–behavioral case formulation. In K. S. Dobson (Ed.), *Handbook of cognitive–behavioral therapies* (2nd ed., pp. 86–110). New York: Guilford.

Pert, C. (1993). The chemical communicators. Interview by B. Moyers with C. Pert, in *Healing and the mind* (pp. 177–193). New York: Doubleday.

Peterson, D. B., Murray, G. C., & Chan, F. (1998). Ethics and technology. In R. Cottone & V. Tarvydas (Eds.), *Ethical and professional issues in counseling* (pp. 196–235). Upper Saddle River, NJ: Prentice Hall.

Petry, N., Tennen, H., & Affleck, J. (2000). Stalking the elusive client variable in psychotherapy research. In C. Snyder & R. Ingram (Eds.), *Handbook of psychological change* (pp. 89–107). New York: Wiley.

Picucci, M. (1992). Planning an experiential weekend workshop for lesbians and gay males in recovery. *Journal of Chemical Dependency Treatment, 5,* 119–139.

Pietrofesa, J. J., Hoffman, A., Splete, H. H., & Pinto, D. V. (1978). *Counseling: Theory, research, and practice.* Chicago: Rand McNally.

Pilkington, N. W., & Cantor, J. M. (1996). Perceptions of heterosexual bias in professional psychology programs: A survey of graduate students. *Professional Psychology, 27,* 604–612.

Pinsof, W., & Wynne, L. (Eds.). (1995). Family therapy effectiveness: Current research and theory. (Special issue). *Journal of Marital and Family Therapy, 21*(4).

Pipher, M. (1994). *Reviving Ophelia: Saving the selves of adolescent girls.* New York: Putnam.

Pollard, D. (1993). Gender, achievement, and African-American students' perceptions of their school experience. *Educational Psychologist, 28,* 341–356.

Possell, L. E., Kehle, T. J., McLoughlin, C. S., & Bray, M. A. (1999). Self-modeling as an intervention to reduce disruptive classroom behavior. *Cognitive and Behavioral Practice, 6,* 99–105.

Pressly, P., and Heesacker, M. (2001). The physical environment and counseling: A review of theory and research. *Journal of Counseling and Development, 79,* 148–160.

Prochaska, J. (1999). How do people change, and how can we change to help many more people? In M. Hubble, B. Duncan, & S. Miller (Eds.), *The heart and soul of change* (pp. 227–258). Washington, DC: American Psychological Association.

Prochaska, J. (2000). Change at differing stages. In C. Snyder & R. Ingram (Eds.), *Handbook of psychological change* (pp. 109–127). New York: Wiley.

Prochaska, J., & DiClemente, C. (1982). Transtheoretical therapy: Towards a more integrative model of change. *Psychotherapy, 19,* 276–278.

Prochaska, J., & DiClemente, C. (1985). Common processes of self-change of smoking: Toward an integrative model of change. *Journal of Consulting and Clinical Psychology, 51,* 390–395.

Prochaska, J., DiClemente, C., & Norcross, J. (1992). In search of how people change: Applications to addictive behaviors. *American Psychologist, 47,* 1102–1114.

Prochaska, J. O., & Norcross, J. C. (1999). *Systems of psychotherapy: A transtheoretical analysis* (4th ed.). Pacific Grove, CA: Brooks/Cole.

Project MATCH Research Group. (1997). Matching alcoholism treatment to client heterogeneity: Project MATCH post-treatment drinking outcomes. *Journal of Studies in Alcohol, 58,* 7–29.

Puchalski, C. M., Larson, D. B., & Lu, F. G. (2000). Spirituality courses in psychiatry residency programs. *Psychiatric Annals, 30,* 543–548.

Pulos, L. (1996). *The power of visualization.* (Audiotapes). Niles, IL: Nightingale/Conant.

Quandt, S. A., McDonald, J., Arcury, T. A., Bell, R. A., & Vitolins, M. Z. (2000). Nutritional self-management of elderly widows in rural communities. *Gerontologist, 40,* 86–96.

Quintana, S., and Atkinson, D. R. (2002). A multicultural perspective on principles of empirically supported interventions. *The Counseling Psychologist, 30,* 281–290.

Rao, R., & Kramer, L. (1993). Stress and coping among mothers of infants with a sickle cell condition. *Children's Health Care, 22,* 169–188.

Raskin, N., & Rogers, C. (1995). Person-centered therapy. In J. Corsini & D. Wedding (Eds.), *Current psychotherapies* (5th ed., pp. 128–161). Itasca, IL: Peacock.

Rath, S. (1998). Verbal self-instructional training: An examination of its efficacy, maintenance, and generalization. *European Journal of Psychology of Education, 13,* 399–409.

Reed, B. G., Newman, P. A., Suarez, Z. E., & Lewis, E. A. (1997). Interpersonal practice beyond diversity and toward social justice: The importance of critical consciousness. In C. D. Garvin & B. A. Seabury *Interpersonal practice in social work: Promoting competence and social justice* (pp. 44–78). Boston: Allyn & Bacon.

Reed, J. R., Patton, M. J., & Gold, P. B. (1993). Effects of turn-taking sequences in vocational test interpretation interviews. *Journal of Counseling Psychology, 40,* 144–155.

Rehm, L. P. (1982). Self-management in depression. In P. Karoly & F. H. Kanfer (Eds.), *Self-management and behavior change* (pp. 522–567). New York: Pergamon.

Rehm, L. P., & Sharp, R. N. (1996). Strategies in the treatment of childhood depression. In M. A. Reinecke, F. M. Dattilio, & A. Freeman (Eds.), *Cognitive therapy with children and adolescents: A casebook for clinical practice* (pp. 103–123). New York: Guilford.

Reichelova, E., & Baranova, E. (1994). Training program for the development of prosocial behavior in children. *Psychologia a Patopsychologia Dietata, 29,* 41–50.

Reid, W., & Misener, E. (2000). Adult change. In P. Allen-Meares & C. Garvin (Eds.), *Handbook of social work direct practice* (pp. 241–259). Thousand Oaks, CA: Sage.

Reid, W. H. (1995). *Treatment of the DSM-IV psychiatric disorders.* New York: Brunner/Mazel.

Remen, N. (1996). *Kitchen table wisdom: Stories that heal.* New York: Riverhead Books.

Renfrey, G. S. (1992). Cognitive–behavior therapy and the Native American client. *Behavior Therapy, 23,* 321–340.

Resnick, R. J. (1995). How come outcome? *American Psychological Association Monitor, 26,* 2.

Reyes, M., Routh, D., Jean-Gilles, M., & Sanfilippo, M. (1991). Ethnic differences in parenting children in fearful situations. *Journal of Pediatric Psychology, 16,* 717–726.

Rhodes, F., & Humfleet, G. (1993). Using goal-oriented counseling and peer support to reduce HIV/AIDS risk among drug users not in treatment. *Drugs and Society, 7,* 185–204.

Rice, V. H. (Ed.). (2000). *Handbook of stress, coping, and health: Implications for nursing research, theory, and practice.* Thousand Oaks, CA: Sage.

Richards, P. S., Rector, J. M., & Tjeltveit, A. C. (1999). Values, spirituality, and psychotherapy. In W. R. Miller (Ed.), *Integrating spirituality into treatment: Resources for practitioners* (pp. 133–160). Washington, DC: American Psychological Association.

Richardson, B., & Stone, G. L. (1981). Effects of cognitive adjunct procedure within a microtraining situation. *Journal of Counseling Psychology, 28,* 168–175.

Richmond, M. E. (1917). *Social diagnosis.* New York: Russell Sage Foundation.

Ridley, C., Li, L., & Hill, C. (1998). Multicultural assessment. *The Counseling Psychologist, 26,* 827–910.

Riley, W., Barenie, J., Mabe, P., & Myers, D. (1990). Smokeless tobacco use in adolescent females: Prevalence and psychosocial factors among racial/ethnic groups. *Journal of Behavioral Medicine, 13,* 207–220.

Riley, W., Barenie, J., Mabe, P., & Myers, D. (1991). The role of race and ethnic status on the psychosocial correlates of smokeless tobacco use in adolescent males. *Journal of Adolescent Health, 12,* 15–21.

Rimm, D. C., & Masters, J. C. (1979). *Behavior therapy: Techniques and empirical findings* (2nd ed.). New York: Academic.

Ritchie, E. C. (1992). Treatment of gas mask phobia. *Military Medicine, 157,* 104–106.

Roberson, M. (1992). The meaning of compliance: Patient perspectives. *Qualitative Health Research, 2,* 7–26.

Roberts, M., Vernberg, E., & Jackson, Y. (2000). Psychotherapy with children and families. In C. Snyder & R. Ingram (Eds.), *Handbook of psychological change* (pp. 500–519). New York: Wiley.

Robinson, T., & Ward, J. (1991). A belief in self far greater than anyone's disbelief: Cultivating resistance among African American female adolescents. In C. Gilligan, A. Rogers, & D. Tolman (Eds.), *Women, girls and psychotherapy: Reframing resistance* (pp. 87–104). Binghamton, NY: Haworth.

Robinson, T. L., & Howard-Hamilton, M. (2000). *The convergence of race, ethnicity, and gender: Multiple identities in counseling.* Upper Saddle River, NJ: Prentice Hall.

Rogers, C. (1942). *Counseling and psychotherapy.* Boston: Houghton Mifflin.

Rogers, C. (1951). *Client-centered therapy.* Boston: Houghton Mifflin.

Rogers, C. (1957). The necessary and sufficient conditions of therapeutic personality change. *Journal of Consulting Psychology, 21,* 95–103.

Rogers, C. (1977). *Carl Rogers on personal power.* New York: Delacorte Press.

Rogers, C., Gendlin, E., Kiesler, D., & Truax, C. (1967). *The therapeutic relationship and its impact: A study of psychotherapy with schizophrenics.* Madison, WI: University of Wisconsin Press.

Rogers, R. (2001). *Handbook of diagnostic and structured interviewing.* New York: Guilford.

Rogoff, B., & Chavajay, P. (1995). What's become of research on the cultural basis of cognitive development? *American Psychologist, 50,* 859–877.

Rohrbaugh, M., Tennen, H., Press, S., & White, L. (1981). Compliance, defiance and therapeutic paradox: Guidelines for strategic use of paradoxical interventions. *American Journal of Orthopsychiatry, 51,* 454–467.

Rokke, P. D., Tomhave, J. A., & Jocic, Z. (1999). The role of client choice and target selection in self-management therapy for depression in older adults. *Psychology and Aging, 14,* 155–169.

Rollnick, S., Heather, N., & Bell, A. (1992). Negotiating behavioral change in medical settings: The development of brief motivational interviewing. *Journal of Mental Health, 1,* 25–37.

Rollnick, S., Mason, P., & Butler, C. (1999). *Health behavior change: A guide for practitioners.* Philadelphia: Churchill Livingstone.

Rollnick, S., & Miller, W. R. (1995). What is motivational interviewing? *Behavioral and Cognitive Psychotherapy, 23,* 325–334.

Root, M. P. (1992). Reconstructing the impact of trauma on personality. In L. S. Brown & M. Ballou (Eds.), *Personality and psychopathology: Feminist reappraisals* (pp. 229–265). New York: Guilford.

Rosado, J. W., Jr., & Elias, M. J. (1993). Ecological and psychocultural mediators in the delivery of services for urban, culturally diverse Hispanic clients. *Professional Psychology, 24,* 450–459.

Rose, S. D., & LeCroy, C. W. (1991). Group methods. In F. H. Kanfer & A. P. Goldstein (Eds.), *Helping people change* (pp. 422–453). New York: Pergamon.

Rosen, G. M. (1999). Treatment fidelity and research on eye movement desensitization and reprocessing (EMDR). *Journal of Anxiety Disorders, 13,* 173–184.

Rosenthal, T. L. (1993). To soothe the savage beast. *Behaviour Research and Therapy, 31,* 439–462.

Rosenthal, T. L., & Steffek, B. D. (1991). Modeling methods. In F. H. Kanfer & A. P. Goldstein (Eds.), *Helping people change* (4th ed., pp. 70–121). New York: Pergamon.

Ross, C. A. (1990). *Multiple personality disorder: Diagnosis, clinical features and treatment.* New York: Wiley.

Rotherman-Borus, M. J., Rosario, M., Reid, H., & Koopman, C. (1995). Predicting patterns of sexual acts among homosexual and bisexual youths. *American Journal of Psychiatry, 152,* 588–595.

Rotter, J. B. (1966). Generalized expectancies for internal versus external control of reinforcement. *Psychological Monographs: General and Applied, 80*(1, Whole No. 609).

Ruben, A. (1989). Preventing school dropouts through classroom guidance. *Elementary School Guidance and Counseling, 24,* 21–29.

Ruiz, A. S. (1990). Ethnic identity: Crisis and resolution. *Journal of Multicultural Counseling and Development, 18,* 29–40.

Ryan, C., & Futterman, D. (1998). *Lesbian and gay youth: Care and counseling.* New York: Columbia University Press.

Safran, J. (1990). Towards a refinement of cognitive therapy in light of interpersonal theory. *Clinical Psychology Review, 10,* 87–105.

Safran, J., & Muran, J. (2000). *Negotiating the therapeutic alliance: A relational treatment guide.* New York: Guilford.

Salkovskis, P., & Clark, D. (1993). Panic disorder and hypochondriasis. *Advances in Behavioral Research and Therapy, 15,* 23–48.

Salkovskis, P. M. (Ed.). (1996). *Frontiers in cognitive therapy.* New York: Guilford.

Santiago-Rivera, A. (1995). Developing a culturally sensitive treatment modality for bilingual Spanish-speaking clients. *Journal of Counseling and Development, 74,* 12–17.

Sarwer, D. B., & Sayers, S. L. (1998). Behavioral interviewing. In A. S. Bellack & M. Hersen (Eds.), *Behavioral assessment: A practical handbook* (4th ed., pp. 63–79). Boston: Allyn & Bacon.

Saunders, T., Driskell, J. E., Johnston, J. H., & Salas, E. (1996). The effect of stress inoculation training on anxiety and performance. *Journal of Occupational Health Psychology, 1,* 170–186.

Scheel, M., Seaman, S., Roach, K., Mullin, T., & Blackwell Mahoney, K. (1999). Client implementation of therapist recommendations predicted by client perceptions of fit, difficulty of implementation, and therapist influence. *Journal of Counseling Psychology, 46,* 308–316.

Schill, T., & Kramer, J. (1991). Self-defeating personality, self-reinforcement, and depression. *Psychological Reports, 69,* 137–138.

Schinke, S., Botvin, G., Orlandi, M., & Schilling, R. (1990). African American and Hispanic American adolescents, HIV infection, and prevention intervention. *AIDS Education and Prevention, 2,* 305–312.

Schinke, S., Orlandi, M., Gordon, A., & Weston, E. (1989). AIDS prevention via computer-based intervention. *Computers in Human Services, 5,* 147–156.

Schlossberger, E., & Hecker, L. (1996). HIV and family therapist's duty to warn: A legal and ethical analysis. *Journal of Marital and Family Therapy, 22,* 27–40.

Schneider, R., Casey, J., & Kohn, R. (2000). Motivational vs. confrontational interviewing: A comparison of substance abuse assessment practices at employee assistance programs. *Journal of Behavioral Health Services and Research, 27,* 60–74.

Schoech, D. (1999). *Human services technology* (2nd ed.). New York: Haworth.

Schoefield, W. (1964). *Psychotherapy: The purchase of friendship.* Englewood Cliffs, NJ: Prentice-Hall.

Schulz, R., & Barefoot, J. (1974). Nonverbal responses and affiliative conflict theory. *British Journal of Social and Clinical Psychology, 13,* 237–243.

Schulz, R., & Heckhausen, J. (1999). Aging, culture, and control: Setting a new research agenda. *Journals of Gerontology: Series B: Psychological Sciences and Social Sciences, 54B,* 139–145.

Schwartz, C., Houlihan, D., Krueger, K. F., & Simon, D. A. (1997). The behavioral treatment of a young adult with post traumatic stress disorder and a fear of children. *Child and Family Behavior Therapy, 19,* 37–49.

Seabaugh, G. O., & Schumaker, J. B. (1994). The effects of self-regulation training on the academic productivity of secondary students with learning problems. *Journal of Behavioral Education, 4,* 109–133.

Sedney, M., Baker, J., & Gross, E. (1994). "The story" of a death: Therapeutic considerations with bereaved families. *Journal of Marital and Family Therapy, 20,* 287–296.

Seligman, L. (1998). *Selecting effective treatments.* San Francisco: Jossey-Bass.

Seligman, M. (1982). *Helplessness: On depression, development and death.* San Francisco: Freeman.

Seligman, M. (1990). *Learned optimism.* New York: Pocket.

Senour, M. (1982). How counselors influence clients. *Personnel and Guidance Journal, 60,* 345–350.

Sexton, T. L., and Alexander, J. F. (2002). Family-based empirically supported interventions. *The Counseling Psychologist, 30,* 238–261.

Sexton, T. L., & Whiston, S. C. (1994). The status of the counseling relationship: An empirical review, theoretical implications, and research directions. *The Counseling Psychologist, 22,* 6–78.

Shainberg, D. (1993). *Healing in psychotherapy.* Langhorne, PA: Gordon & Breach.

Shapiro, F. (1995). *Eye movement desensitization and reprocessing: Basic principles, protocols and procedures.* New York: Guilford.

Shapiro, F. (1999). Eye movement desensitization and reprocessing (EMDR) and the anxiety disorders: Clinical and research implications of an integrated psychotherapy treatment. *Journal of Anxiety Disorders, 13,* 35–67.

Sharma, S., & Sud, A. (1990). Examination stress and test anxiety: A cross-cultural perspective. *Psychology and Developing Societies, 2,* 183–201.

Shepherd, J., Stein, K., & Milne, R. (2000). Eye movement desensitization and reprocessing in the treatment of post-traumatic stress disorder: A review of an emerging therapy. *Psychological Medicine, 30,* 863–871.

Shiang, J. (2000). Research & practice: Does culture make a difference? In S. Soldz & L. McCullough (Eds.), *Reconciling empirical knowledge and clinical experience* (pp. 167–196). Washington, DC: American Psychological Association.

Shoham, V., Bootzin, R., Rohrbaugh, M., & Urry, H. (1996). Paradoxical versus relaxation treatment for insomnia: The moderating role of reactance. *Sleep Research, 24a,* 365.

Shuman, D. W., & Foote, W. (1999). *Jaffee v. Redmond's* impact: Life after the Supreme Court's recognition of a psychotherapist-patient privilege. *Professional Psychology: Research and Practice, 30,* 479–487.

Silverman, W. K., & Serafini, L. T. (1998). Assessment of child behavior problems: Internalizing disorders. In A. S. Bellack & M. Hersen (Eds.), *Behavioral assessment: A practical handbook* (4th ed., pp. 342–361). Boston: Allyn & Bacon.

Sime, W. (1996). Guidelines for clinical applications of exercise therapy for mental health. In J. L. Van Raalte & B. W. Brewer (Eds.), *Exploring sport and exercise psychology* (pp. 159–187). Washington, DC: American Psychological Association.

Simon, R. I. (1999). Therapist–patient sex. *Forensic Psychiatry, 22,* 31–47.

Simon, S. (1995). *Values clarification* (2nd ed.). New York: Warner.

Simone, D. H., McCarthy, P., & Skay, C. (1998). An investigation of client and counselor variables that influence likelihood of counselor self-disclosure. *Journal of Counseling and Development, 76,* 174–182.

Simpkinson, A., & Simpkinson, C. (1998). Feeding one another. *Common Boundary,* Nov.–Dec., 20–26.

Sinacore-Guinn, A. L. (1995). The diagnostic window: Culture- and gender-sensitive diagnosis and training. *Counselor Education and Supervision, 35,* 18–31.

Singer, J. L. (1975). Navigating the stream of consciousness: Research in daydreaming and related inner experience. *American Psychologist, 30,* 727–738.

Skovholt, T. (2001). *The resilient practitioner.* Needham Heights, MA: Allyn & Bacon.

Skovholt, T., & Ronnestad, M. (1995). *The evolving professional self.* New York: Wiley.

Sloane, D., & Gleason, C. (1999). Behavior management planning for problem behaviors in dementia: A practical model. *Professional Psychology, 30,* 27–36.

Smart, D. W., & Smart, J. F. (1997). *DSM-IV* and culturally sensitive diagnosis: Some observations for counselors. *Journal of Counseling and Development, 75,* 392–398.

Smart, J. F., & Smart, D. (1995). Acculturative stress of Hispanics: Loss and challenge. *Journal of Counseling and Development, 73,* 390–396.

Smart, N. (1993). *Religions of Asia.* Englewood Cliffs, NJ: Prentice Hall.

Smart, N. (1994). *Religions of the West.* Englewood Cliffs, NJ: Prentice Hall.

Smith, B. (1992). Raising a resister. In C. Gilligan, A. Rogers, & D. Tolman (Eds.), *Women, girls and psychotherapy: Reframing resistance* (pp. 137–148). Binghamton, NY: Haworth.

Smith, D., & Fitzpatrick, M. (1995). Patient–therapist boundary issues. *Professional Psychology, 26,* 499–506.

Smith, E. P., Walker, K., Fields, L., Brookins, C. C., & Seay, R. C. (1999). Ethnic identity and its relationship to self-esteem, perceived efficacy, and prosocial attitudes in early adolescence. *Journal of Adolescence, 22,* 867–880.

Smith, K. J., Subich, L., & Kalodner, C. (1995). The transtheoretical model's stages and processes of change and their relation to premature termination. *Journal of Counseling Psychology, 42,* 34–39.

Smyth, N. J., Greenwald, R., de Jongh, A., & Lee, C. (2000). The expert consensus guideline series: Treatment of posttraumatic stress disorder: Commentary. *Journal of Clinical Psychiatry, 61,* 784.

Snelling, J. (1991). *The Buddhist handbook.* Rochester, VT: Inner Traditions.

Snowden, L. R., & Cheung, F. K. (1990). Use of inpatient mental health services by members of ethnic minority groups. *American Psychologist, 45,* 347–355.

Snyder, C. R. (1995). Conceptualizing, measuring and nurturing hope. *Journal of Counseling and Development, 73,* 355–360.

Solberg, E. E., Halvorsen, R., & Holen, A. (2000). Effect of meditation on immune cells. *Stress Medicine, 16,* 185–190.

Solberg, V., O'Brien, K., Villareal, P., & Kennel, R. (1993). Self-efficacy and Hispanic college students: Validation of the College Self-Efficacy Instrument. *Hispanic Journal of Behavioral Sciences, 15,* 80–95.

Solomon, L. J., Flynn, B. S., Worden, J. K., Mickey, R. M., Skelly, J. M., Geller, B. M., Peluso, N. W., & Webster, J. A. (1998). Assessment of self-reward strategies for maintenance of breast self-examination. *Journal of Behavioral Medicine, 21,* 83–102.

Sommers-Flanagan, J., & Sommers-Flanagan, R. (in press). *Clinical interviewing* (3rd ed.). New York: Wiley.

Soo-Hoo, T. (1998). Applying frame of reference and reframing techniques to improve school consultation in multicultural settings. *Journal of Educational and Psychological Consultation, 9,* 325–345.

Spector, J., & Read, J. (1999). The current status of eye movement desensitization and reprocessing (EMDR). *Clinical Psychology and Psychotherapy, 6,* 165–174.

Spiegel, S. B., & Hill, C. E. (1989). Guidelines for research on therapist interpretation: Toward greater methodological rigor and relevance to practice. *Journal of Counseling Psychology, 36,* 121–129.

Spitzer, R. L., Gibbon, M., Skodol, A. E., Williams, J. B., & First, M. B. (1994). *DSM IV casebook.* Washington, DC: American Psychiatric Association.

Spivack, G., Platt, J. J., & Shure, M. B. (1976). *The problem-solving approach to adjustment.* San Francisco: Jossey-Bass.

St. Lawrence, J. (1993). African American adolescents' knowledge, health-related attitudes, sexual behavior, and contraceptive decisions: Implications for the prevention of adolescent HIV infection. *Journal of Consulting and Clinical Psychology, 61,* 104–112.

St. Lawrence, J., Brasfield, T., Jefferson, K., Alleyne, E., O'Bannon, R., & Shirley, A. (1995). Cognitive–behavioral intervention to reduce African American adolescents' risk for HIV infection. *Journal of Consulting and Clinical Psychology, 63,* 221–237.

Stamps, R., & Barach, P. (2001). *The therapist's Internet handbook.* New York: Norton.

Steenbarger, B. N. (1994). Duration and outcome of psychotherapy: An integrative review. *Professional Psychology, 25,* 111–119.

Stevens, P. (2000). Practicing within our competence: New techniques create new dilemmas. *Family Journal Counseling and Therapy for Couples and Families, 8,* 278–280.

Stevenson, H. C., & Renard, G. (1993). Trusting ole wise ones: Therapeutic use of cultural strengths in African-American families. *Professional Psychology, 24,* 433–442.

Strong, S. R. (1968). Counseling: An interpersonal influence process. *Journal of Counseling Psychology, 15,* 215–224.

Strong, S. R., Welsh, J., Corcoran, J., & Hoyt, W. (1992). Social psychology and counseling psychology: The history, products, and promise of an interface. *Journal of Counseling Psychology, 39,* 139–157.

Strupp, H. H., & Binder, J. L. (1984). *Psychotherapy in a new key.* New York: Basic.

Sue, D., & Sue, D. W. (1993). Ethnic identity: Cultural factors in the psychological development of Asians in America. In D. Atkinson, G. Morten, & D. W. Sue (Eds.), *Counseling American minorities* (pp. 199–210). Madison, WI: Brown & Benchmark.

Sue, D. W. (1994). Asian-American mental health and help-seeking behavior. *Journal of Counseling Psychology, 41,* 292–295.

Sue, D. W., Arredondo, P., & McDavis, R. (1992). Multicultural counseling competencies and standards: A call to the profession. *Journal of Counseling and Development, 70,* 477–487.

Sue, D. W., Carter, R. T., Casas, J. M., Fouad, N. A., Ivey, A. E., Jensen, M., LaFromboise, T., Manese, J. E., Ponterotto, J. G., & Vazquez-Nutall, E. (1998). *Multicultural counseling competencies: Individual and organizational development.* Thousand Oaks, CA: Sage.

Sue, D. W., Ivey, A. E., & Pedersen, P. B. (1996). *A theory of multicultural counseling and therapy.* Pacific Grove, CA: Brooks/Cole.

Sue, D. W., & Sue, D. (1990). *Counseling the culturally different* (2nd ed.). New York: Wiley.

Sue, D. W., & Sue, D. (1999). *Counseling the culturally different* (3rd ed.). New York: Wiley.

Sue, S. (1991). Ethnicity and culture in psychological research and practice. In J. D. Goodchilds (Ed.), *Psychological perspectives on human diversity in America* (pp. 51–85). Washington, DC: American Psychological Association.

Sue, S., & Sue, D. W. (1971). Chinese-American personality and mental health. *Amerasia Journal, 1,* 36–49.

Suinn, R. M. (1986). *Seven steps to peak performance: The mental training manual for athletes.* Lewiston, NY: Huber.

Suinn, R. M., & Richardson, F. (1971). Anxiety management training: A nonspecific behavior therapy program for anxiety control. *Behavior Therapy, 3,* 308–310.

Summers, N. (2001). *Fundamentals of case management practice.* Belmont, CA: Wadsworth.

Sweeney, M. A., Cottle, W. C., & Kobayashi, M. J. (1980). Nonverbal communication: A cross-cultural comparison of American and Japanese counseling students. *Journal of Counseling Psychology, 27,* 150–156.

Swenson, L. C. (1997). *Psychology and law* (2nd ed.). Pacific Grove, CA: Brooks/Cole.

Szapocznik, J., & Kurtines, W. (1980). Acculturation, biculturalism and adjustment among Cuban Americans. In A. Padilla (Ed.), *Recent advances in acculturation research: Theory, models, and some new findings* (pp. 139–157). Boulder, CO: Westview.

Szapocznik, J., & Kurtines, W. (1993). Family psychology and cultural diversity. *American Psychologist, 48,* 400–407.

Tallman, K. & Bohard, A. C. (1999). The client as a common factor: Clients as self healers. In M. A. Hubble, B. L. Duncan,

& Miller, S. D. *The Heart and Soul of Change* (pp. 91–132) Washington D.C.: American Psychological Association.

Taylor, E., Mitchell, J. E., Kenan, S., & Tacker, R. (2000). Attitudes of occupational therapists toward spirituality in practice. *American Journal of Occupational Therapy, 54,* 421–428.

Taylor, I., & O'Reilly, M. F. (1997). Toward a functional analysis of private verbal self-regulation. *Journal of Applied Behavior Analysis, 30,* 43–58.

Taylor, J., Gilligan, C., & Sullivan, A. (1995). *Between voice and silence: Women and girls, race and relationships.* Cambridge, MA: Harvard University Press.

Taylor, R. J., Chatters, L. M., Jayakody, R., & Levin, J. S. (1996). Black and white differences in religious participation: A multisample comparison. *Journal for the Scientific Study of Religion, 35,* 403–410.

Taylor, S., Cipani, E., & Clardy, A. (1994). A stimulus control technique for improving the efficacy of an established toilet training program. *Journal of Behavior Therapy and Experimental Psychiatry, 25,* 155–160.

Taylor, S. E., & Pham, L. B. (1996). Mental simulation, motivation, and action. In P. M. Gollwitzer & J. A. Bargh (Eds.), *The psychology of action* (pp. 219–235). New York: Guilford.

Taylor, S. E., Pham, L. B., Rivkin, I., & Armor, D. A. (1998). Harnessing the imagination: Mental simulation and self-regulation of behavior. *American Psychologist, 53,* 429–439.

Tedeschi, R. G., & Calhoun, L. G. (1995). *Trauma and transformation: Growing in the aftermath of suffering.* Thousand Oaks, CA: Sage.

Terr, L. (1990). *Too scared to cry: Psychic trauma in childhood.* New York: Harper & Row.

Teyber, E. (2000). *Interpersonal processes in psychotherapy* (4th ed.). Pacific Grove, CA: Brooks/Cole.

Thase, M. (2000). Psychopharmacology in conjunction with psychotherapy. In C. Snyder & R. Ingram (Eds.), *Handbook of psychological change* (pp. 475–497). New York: Wiley.

Thomas, R., & Gafner, G. (1993). PTSD in an elderly male: Treatment with eye movement desensitization and reprocessing (EMDR). *Clinical Gerontologist, 14,* 57–59.

Thompson, C., & Rudolph, L. (2000). *Counseling children* (5th ed.). Pacific Grove, CA: Brooks/Cole.

Thompson, L. W. (1996). Cognitive–behavioral therapy and treatment for late-life depression. *Journal of Clinical Psychiatry, 57,* 29–37.

Thoresen, C. E. (1999). Spirituality and health: Is there a relationship? *Journal of Health Psychology, 43,* 291–300.

Thoresen, C. E., & Mahoney, M. J. (1974). *Behavioral self-control.* New York: Holt, Rinehart and Winston.

Thyer, B., & Myers, L. (2000). Approaches to behavior change. In P. Allen-Meares & C. Garvin, (Eds.), *Handbook of social work direct practice* (pp. 197–216). Thousand Oaks, CA: Sage.

Timmons, P. L., Oehlert, M. E., Sumerall, S. W., Timmons, C. W., et al. (2000). Stress inoculation training for maladaptive anger: Comparison of group counseling versus computer guidance. *Computers in Human Behavior, 13,* 51–64.

Tix, A. P., & Frazier, P. A. (1998). The use of religious coping during stressful life-events: Main effects, moderation, and mediation. *Journal of Consulting and Clinical Psychology, 66,* 411–422.

Tkachuk, G. A., & Martin, G. L. (1999). Exercise therapy for patients with psychiatric disorders: Research and clinical implications. *Professional Psychology: Research and Practice, 30,* 275–282.

Tonigan, J. S., Toscova, R. T., & Connors, G. J. (1999). Spirituality and the 12-step programs: A guide for clinicians. In W. R. Miller (Ed.), *Integrating spirituality into treatment: Resources for practitioners* (pp. 111–131). Washington, DC: American Psychological Association.

Tooley, G. A., Armstrong, S. M., Norman, T. R., & Sali, A. (2000). Acute increases in night-time plasma melatonin levels following a period of meditation. *Biological Psychology, 53,* 69–78.

Tracey, E. M., & Whittaker, J. K. (1990). The social network map: Assessing social support in clinical social work practice. *Families in Society, 71,* 461–470.

Trager, G. L. (1958). Paralanguage: A first approximation. *Studies in Linguistics, 13,* 1–12.

Treasure, J., & Ward, A. (1997). A practical guide to the use of motivational interviewing in anorexia nervosa. *European Eating Disorders Review, 5,* 102–114.

Treviño, J. (1996). Worldview and change in cross-cultural counseling. *The Counseling Psychologist, 24,* 198–215.

Triandis, H. (1990). Cross-cultural studies of individualism and collectivism. In J. Berry, J. Draguns, & M. Cole (Eds.), *Cross-cultural perspectives.* Lincoln, NE: University of Nebraska Press.

Triandis, H. C. (1994). *Culture and social behavior.* New York: McGraw-Hill.

Truax, C. B., & Mitchell, K. M. (1971). Research on certain therapist interpersonal skills in relation to process and outcome. In A. Bergin & S. Garfield (Eds.), *Handbook of psychotherapy and behavior change: An empirical analysis* (pp. 299–344). New York: Wiley.

Turk, D. (1975). *Cognitive control of pain: A skills training approach for the treatment of pain.* Unpublished master's thesis, University of Waterloo. Waterloo, Ontario, Canada.

Turner, W. L. (1993). Identifying African-American family strengths. *Family Therapy News, 24,* 9, 14.

Uhlemann, M., Lee, Y. D., & Martin, J. (1994). Client cognitive responses as a function of quality of counselor verbal responses. *Journal of Counseling and Development, 73,* 198–203.

Underwood, P. W. (2000). Social support: The promise and the reality. In V. H. Rice (Ed.), *Handbook of stress, coping, and health: Implications for nursing research, theory, and practice* (pp. 367–391). Thousand Oaks, CA: Sage.

Unger, R., & Crawford, M. (1996). *Women and gender: A feminist psychology* (2nd ed.). Boston: McGraw-Hill.

Ussher, J. (1990). Cognitive behavioral couples therapy with gay men referred for counseling in an AIDS setting: A pilot study. *AIDS-Care, 2,* 43–51.

Van Hasselt, V., Hersen, M., Null, J., & Ammerman, R. (1993). Drug abuse prevention for high risk African American children and their families: A review and model program. *Addictive Behaviors, 18,* 213–234.

Van Vlaenderen, H. (1999). Problem solving: A process of reaching common understanding and consensus. *South African Journal of Psychology, 29,* 166–177.

VandenBos, G. R. (Ed.). (1996). Outcome assessment of psychotherapy (Special issue). *American Psychologist, 51*(10).

VanEtten, M. L., & Taylor, S. (1998). Comparative efficacy of treatments for post-traumatic stress disorder: A meta analysis. *Clinical Psychology and Psychotherapy, 5,* 126–144.

VanHout, W., Emmelkamp, P., & Scholing, A. (1994). The role of negative self-statements during exposure in vivo: A process study of eight panic disorder patients with agoraphobia. *Behavior Modification, 18,* 389–410.

Vargas, A. M., & Borkowski, J. G. (1982). Physical attractiveness and counseling skills. *Journal of Counseling Psychology, 29,* 246–255.

Vasquez, M. (1993). The 1992 ethics code: Implications for the practice of psychotherapy. *Texas Psychologist, 45,* 11.

Vasquez, M. (1994). Implications of the 1992 ethics code for the practice of individual psychotherapy. *Professional Psychology, 25,* 321–328.

Vasquez, M. J. T. (2000). Advancing the study of Chicana/o psychology. *The Counseling Psychologist, 29,* 118–127.

Vigne, J. (1999). Meditation and mental health. *Indian Journal of Clinical Psychology, 24,* 46–51.

Wachtel, P. L. (1993). *Therapeutic communication: Principles and effective practice.* New York: Guilford.

Waehler, C., Kalodner, C., Wampold, B., & Lichtenberg, J. (2000). Empirically supported treatments (ESTS) in perspective. *The Counseling Psychologist, 28,* 657–671.

Waehler, C. A., & Lenox, R. A. (1994). A concurrent (versus stage) model for conceptualizing and representing the counseling process. *Journal of Counseling and Development, 73,* 17–22.

Wahler, R. G., & Fox, J. J. (1981). Setting events in applied behavior analysis: Toward a conceptual and methodological expansion. *Journal of Applied Behavior Analysis, 14,* 327–338.

Walters, R. P. (1980). *Amity: Friendship in action.* Boulder, CO: Christian Helpers.

Wampold, B. (2000). Outcomes of individual counseling and psychotherapy: Empirical evidence addressing two fundamental questions. In S. D. Brown & R. W. Lent (Eds.), *Handbook of Counseling Psychology* (pp. 711–739). New York: Wiley.

Wampold, B., Lichtenberg, J., & Waehler, C. (2002). Principles of empirically supported interventions in counseling psychology. *The Counseling Psychologist, 30,* 197–217.

Wang, C., & Abbott, L. J. (1998). Development of a community-based diabetes and hypertension preventive program. *Public Health Nursing, 15,* 406–414.

Watson, B., Bell, P., & Chavez, E. (1994). Conflict handling skills used by Mexican American and white non-Hispanic students in the educational system. *High School Journal, 78,* 35–39.

Watson, D. L., & Tharp, R. G. (2002). *Self-directed behavior* (8th ed.). Pacific Grove, CA: Brooks/Cole.

Watson, O. M. (1970). *Proxemic behavior: A cross-cultural study.* The Hague: Mouton.

Watts-Jones, D. (1990). Toward a stress scale for African-American women. *Psychology of Women Quarterly, 14,* 271–275.

Weeks, G. R., and L'Abate, L. (1982). *Paradoxical psychotherapy: Theory and practice with individuals, couples, and families.* New York: Brunner/Mazel.

Weiss, J. (1995). Cognitive therapy and life-review therapy. *Journal of Mental Health Counselors, 17,* 157–172.

Welfel, E. (2002). *Ethics in counseling and psychotherapy.* Pacific Grove, CA: Brooks/Cole.

Wells, M., & Glickauf-Hughes, C. (1986). Techniques to develop object constancy with borderline clients. *Psychotherapy, 23,* 460–468.

Werner-Wilson, R., Zimmerman, T., & Price, S. (1999). Are goals and topics influenced by gender and modality in the initial marriage and family therapy session? *Journal of Marital and Family Therapy, 25,* 253–262.

Whaley, A. (2001). Cultural mistrust and mental health services for African Americans: A review and meta-analysis. *The Counseling Psychologist, 29,* 513–529.

Whiston, S., & Sexton, T. (1993). An overview of psychotherapy outcome research: Implications for practice. *Professional Psychology, 24,* 43–51.

Whiston, S. C. (2002). Application of the principles: Career counseling and interventions. *The Counseling Psychologist, 30,* 218–237.

White, M., & Epston, P. (1990). *Narrative means to therapeutic ends.* New York: Norton.

Whitfield, K. E., Baker-Thomas, T., Heyward, K., Gatto, M., & Williams, Y. (1999). Evaluating a measure of everyday problem solving for use in African Americans. *Experimental Aging Research, 25,* 209–221.

Williams, J. G., Park, L. I., & Kline, J. (1992). Reducing distress associated with pelvic examinations: A stimulus control intervention. *Women and Health, 18,* 41–53.

Williams, O. (1994). Group work with African American men who batter: Toward more ethnically sensitive practice. *Journal of Comparative Family Studies, 25,* 91–103.

Wilson, G. T. (1995). Behavior therapy. In R. J. Corsini & D. Wedding (Eds.), *Current psychotherapies* (pp. 197–228). Itasca, IL: Peacock.

Wilson, G. T., & Davison, G. C. (1971). Processes of fear reduction in systematic desensitization: Animal studies. *Psychological Bulletin, 76,* 1–14.

Wilson, L. L., & Stith, S. M. (1993). Culturally sensitive therapy with black clients. In D. R. Atkinson, G. Morten, & D. W. Sue (Eds.), *Counseling American minorities* (pp. 101–122). Madison, WI: Brown & Benchmark.

Winfrey, M. L., & Weeks, D. L. (1993). Effects of self-modeling on self-efficacy and balance beam performance. *Perceptual and Motor Skills, 77,* 907–913.

Winkleby, M., Flora, J., & Kraemer, H. (1994). A community-based heart disease intervention: Predictors of change. *American Journal of Public Health, 84,* 767–772.

Winnicott, D. W. (1958). *The maturational processes and the facilitating environment.* New York: International Universities Press.

Wirth, L. (1945). The problem of minority groups. In R. Linton (Ed.), *The science of man in the world crisis* (pp. 347–372). New York: Columbia University Press.

Wolfe, J. L. (1992). Working with gay women. In A. Freeman & F. M. Dattilio (Eds.), *Comprehensive casebook of cognitive therapy* (pp. 249–255). New York: Plenum.

Wolpe, J. (1958). *Psychotherapy by reciprocal inhibition.* Stanford, CA: Stanford University Press.

Wolpe, J. (1990). *The practice of behavior therapy* (4th ed.). New York: Pergamon.

Wolpe, J., & Lang, P. J. (1964). A fear survey schedule for use in behavior therapy. *Behaviour Research and Therapy, 2,* 27–30.

Woltersdorf, M. A. (1992). Videotape self-modeling in the treatment of attention-deficit hyperactivity disorder. *Child and Family Behavior Therapy, 14,* 53–73.

Woodman, M. (1992). *Leaving my father's house.* Boston: Shambhala.

Woodman, M. (1993). The eternal feminine: Mirror and container. *New Dimensions, 20,* 8–13.

Woods, T. E., & Ironson, G. H. (1999). Religion and spirituality in the face of illness: How cancer, cardiac, and HIV patients describe their spirituality/religiosity. *Journal of Health Psychology, 4,* 393–412.

Woody, R. H. (1999). Domestic violations of confidentiality. *Professional Psychology: Research and Practice, 30,* 607–610.

Wright, J., & Davis, D. (1994). The therapeutic relationship in cognitive–behavioral therapy: Patient perceptions and therapist responses. *Behavior Therapy, 24,* 25–45.

Wurtele, S. K., Marrs, S. R., & Miller-Perrin, C. L. (1987). Practice makes perfect? The role of participant modeling in sexual abuse prevention programs. *Journal of Consulting and Clinical Psychology, 55,* 599–602.

Wynd, C. A. (1992). Personal power imagery and relaxation techniques used in smoking cessation programs. *American Journal of Health Promotion, 6,* 184–189, 196.

Yang, B., & Clum, G. (1994). Life stress, social support, and problem-solving skills predictive of depression symptoms, hopelessness, and suicide ideation in an Asian student population: A test model. *Suicide and Life Threatening Behavior, 24,* 127–139.

Yeh, C. J., & Hwang, M. Y. (2000). Interdependence in ethnic identity and self: Implications for theory and practice. *Journal of Counseling and Development, 78,* 420–429.

Yoder, J. D. (1999). *Women and gender: Transforming psychology.* Upper Saddle River, NJ: Prentice Hall.

Youell, K. J., & McCullough, J. P. (1975). Behavioral treatment of mucous colitis. *Journal of Consulting and Clinical Psychology, 43,* 740–745.

Young, J. E. (1999). *Cognitive therapy for personality disorders: A schema-focused approach* (3rd ed.). Sarasota, FL: Professional Resource Press.

Young, J. E., Beck, A. T., & Weinberger, A. (1998). Depression. In D. H. Barlow (Ed.), *Clinical handbook of psychological disorders: A step-by-step treatment manual* (3rd ed.). New York: Guilford.

Young, J. S., Cashwell, C. S., & Shcherbakova, J. (2000). The moderating relationship of spirituality on negative life events and psychological adjustment. *Counseling and Values, 45,* 49–57.

Young-Eisendrath, P. (1984). *Hags and heroes: A feminist approach to Jungian psychotherapy with couples.* Toronto, Ontario Canada: Inner City.

Zabukovec, J., Lazrove, S., & Shapiro, F. (2000). Self-healing aspects of EMDR: The therapeutic change process and perspectives of integrated psychotherapies. *Journal of Psychotherapy Integration, 10,* 189–206.

Zalaquett, C. P., & Wood, R. J. (Eds.). (1997). *Evaluating stress: A book of resources.* Lanham, MA: Scarecrow.

Zamostny, K. P., Corrigan, J. D., & Eggert, M. A. (1981). Replication and extension of social influence processes in counseling: A field study. *Journal of Counseling Psychology, 28,* 481–489.

Zarit, S., & Zarit, J. (1998). *Mental disorders in older adults.* New York: Guilford.

Zastrow, C. H. (1999). *The practice of social work* (6th ed.). Pacific Grove, CA: Brooks/Cole.

Zeidner, M., & Endler, N. (Eds.). (1996). *Handbook of coping: Theory, research, applications.* New York: Wiley.

Zillmann, D., & Zillmann, M. (1996). Psychoneuroendocrinology of social behavior. In E. T. Higgins & A. W. Kruglanski (Eds.), *Social psychology: Handbook of basic principles* (pp. 39–71). New York: Guilford.

Zimmerman, M. A., Ramirez-Valles, J., & Maton, K. I. (1999). Resilience among urban African American male adolescents: A study of protective effects of sociopolitical control on their mental health. *American Journal of Community Psychology, 27,* 733–751.

Zlotlow, S. F., & Allen, G. J. (1981). Comparison of analogue strategies for investigating the influence of counselors' physical attractiveness. *Journal of Counseling Psychology, 28,* 194–202.

NAME INDEX

Abbott, L. J., 584
Abeles, N., 283
Abell, N., 281, 289
Abrego, P. J., 16, 34, 65, 77, 120
Achterberg, J., 361
Acierno, K., 548
Adams, N. E., 615
Adler, A., 176
Affleck, J., 287
Ager, J., 446
AHCPR, 311
Ahijevych, K., 438
Alexander, C. N., 508
Alferi, S. M., 471
Alford, B. A., 7
Allen, B., 410
Allen, C., 261
Allen, G. J., 119
Alleyne, E., 584
Allison, K., 33
Alper, T., 50
Alvarez, J., 352
American Counseling Association, 22, 34, 120
American Counselors Association, 33
American Psychiatric Association, 192, 195, 548
American Psychological Association, 22, 23, 33, 34, 120, 147-148
Ammerman, R., 627
Anders, T., 190, 208, 209
Anderson, C. M., 79, 80, 309
Anderson, L., 412
Anderson, R., 351

Anderson, S. C., 497
Anderson, S. K., 34, 37, 38
Anderson, W. P., 257
Andrada, P., 359
Ankuta, G., 283
Anton, J. L., 609
Antoni, M., 627
Antoni, M. H., 470, 479
Antonuccio, D., 311, 312
Arbuthnott, D. W., 358
Arbuthnott, K. D., 358
Arcury, T. A., 584
Arean, P. A., 439
Armor, D. A., 348
Armour-Thomas, E., 410
Armstrong, S. M., 508
Arredondo, P., 31
Ascher, L. M., 548
Aspinwall, L., 627
Atkinson, D. R., 22, 23, 27, 28, 29, 106, 194-195, 311, 327, 328, 329
Axelson, J. A., 25, 180, 326
Azocar, F., 440

Babyak, M., 526
Baer, D. M., 187
Baer, J., 261
Baker, B. L., 555
Baker, E., 351
Baker, J., 24, 85
Baker, L. J. V., 606
Baker, S. B., 217
Ballou, M., 194, 226, 230, 342, 343, 437, 438

Bandura, A., 217, 221, 255, 256, 273, 275, 277, 280, 297, 348, 349, 351, 435, 543, 580, 586, 587, 606, 611, 615, 617, 621, 622, 628
Barach, P., 190
Barak, A., 117
Baranova, E., 352
Baratta, V. S., 611
Barchas, J. D., 621
Barlow, D., 281
Barlow, D. H., 194, 281, 471
Barron, J., 192
Bartholomew, L. K., 584
Basic Behavioral Science Task Force of the National Advisory Mental Health Council, 147, 216
Basoglu, M., 471
Bauermeister, J., 195
Baumann, N., 607
Beck, A., 435
Beck, A. T., 286, 433, 434, 442, 446, 447
Beck, J., 434
Beck, J. S., 361, 435, 455
Becker, D., 194
Belenky, M. F., 230
Belgrave, F., 627
Bell, A., 261
Bell, P., 411
Bell, R. A., 584
Bell, Y., 410
Bellack, A., 185
Bellet, W., 56
Belwood, M., 281, 286, 288

Benjamin, L., 310
Bennett, B. E., 37
Benson, H., 467, 508, 509, 511, 512, 593
Berg, I., 75, 147, 257, 330
Berg-Cross, L., 212
Bergan, J. R., 208
Bergin, A., 65
Berlin, S., 435
Berman, J. S., 548
Bernstein, B. L., 52
Bernstein, D. A., 515, 517, 518, 520, 521, 522
Beutler, L., 266, 308, 309-310, 313, 314, 315, 317-319, 321, 342
Beyer, J., 615
Bijou, S. W., 187
Binder, J. L., 317
Birch, B. B., 477
Birdwhistell, R. L., 45
Blackwell Mahoney, K., 113
Bloom, J., 147
Bloom, M., 275, 276, 281, 282, 287, 288, 289, 290, 291, 599
Bly, R., 419
Blythe, B., 281, 283
Boardman, J. D., 627
Boehnlein, J. K., 471
Bohart, A., 65, 277
Bongar, B., 308, 315
Bootzin, R. R., 586
Bordin, E. S., 74
Borkovec, T. D., 515, 517, 518, 520, 522
Borkowski, J. G., 119

673

Borysenko, J., 467, 506
Botkin, A., 548
Botvin, E., 351
Botvin, G., 351, 412, 627
Bowlby, J., 445
Bracho de-Carpio, A., 412
Brack, C., 9, 84
Brack, G., 9, 84
Braithwaite, N., 627
Brammer, L. M., 16, 34, 65, 77, 120, 139, 142, 143
Brasfield, T., 584
Bray, M. A., 611, 612
Brehm, J. W., 77, 309
Brehm, S., 309
Brehm, S. S., 77
Brems, C., 17, 18, 20, 21, 55-56
Brigham, D., 359
British Columbia Department of Health, 529
Bronfenbrenner, U., 180
Brookins, C. C., 626
Brothers, D., 124
Brouillard, M. E., 621
Brown, C. M., 494
Brown, D., 358
Brown, G. K., 286
Brown, L., 324, 325
Brown, L. M., 201
Brown, L. S., 24, 180, 194, 226, 257, 312, 322, 324, 331, 333, 342, 396, 437
Brown, M. T., 31
Brown, R., 410
Brown, R. W., 18
Brown, S., 331
Bruno, K., 410
Bryan, J., 628
Bryan, T., 628
Bryant, A., 410
Bryant, B. K., 37
Buchanan, T., 39, 40
Budman, S., 322
Buggey, T., 612
Burke, M. T., 497
Burnett, J. W., 225
Burnett, R., 271
Busby, D., 119
Bush, G., 508
Butler, C., 261

Cahill, S. P., 567
Calam, R., 599
Calhoun, L. G., 470
Callaghan, G., 285, 286, 287, 288, 291
Callanan, P., 22
Cameron, J., 610
Cameron, R., 227, 485, 486
Campbell, B., 628
Cancelli, A. A., 208
Canino, I., 211, 212, 221, 226, 227
Cannon, J. R., 101
Cantor, J. M., 24
Careri, A., 544
Carkhuff, R. R., 64, 96, 101, 161, 276, 277, 278
Carlson, C. R., 521, 522
Carpio-Cedraro, F., 412
Carrigan, M. H., 567
Carrington, P., 506, 512
Carter, C., 627
Carter, J. A., 63, 74, 75
Casas, J. M., 585
Casey, J., 161
Cashwell, C. S., 492
Caspar, F., 307, 310
Cass, V. C., 29
Castillo, R. J., 184, 196, 470, 471
Cautela, J. R., 434, 580, 608, 609
Cavaliere, F., 286, 288
Cervetti, M., 612
Chambless, D. L., 311
Chan, F., 40
Chappelle, W., 497
Chatters, L. M., 492
Chavajay, P., 180
Chavez, E., 411
Cheatham, H., 331, 332-333
Chemtob, C. M., 567
Chenneville, T., 36, 37
Cheston, S. E., 38
Cheung, F. K., 27, 194
Chibnall, J. T., 497
Chinen, R. T., 212
Chiu, M. L., 481
Chojnacki, J. T., 257
Church, A., 628
Ciminero, A. R., 282, 589, 595, 599

Cioffi, D., 621
Cisneros, S., 280
Claiborn, C. D., 114, 141, 142
Clancy, S. M., 358
Clare, S. K., 612
Clark, C. C., 467
Clark, D., 313
Clarkin, J., 266, 308, 310, 314, 315, 318, 319, 320, 321, 342
Clinchy, B. M., 230
Clum, G., 411
Coble, H., 74, 75
Cochran, S., 627, 628
Cohen, D., 122-123
Cohen, G., 122-123
Cohen, J. A., 470
Cole-Vaught, C., 88, 98
Coleman, E., 23
Coleman, H., 27
Coleman, H. L. K., 27
Coley, B., 584
Committee on Lesbian, Gay, and Bisexual Concerns Joint Task Force, 23-24
Cone, J. D., 283, 286, 287, 288, 291
Connolly, M. J., 508
Connor, K., 497
Connor-Greene, P., 549
Consoli, A., 599
Constantine, M., 65
Cook, D., 129
Cook, D. A., 24, 29, 30, 68, 73, 75, 103, 107, 120, 122, 129, 155
Cooper, C., 37, 39
Cooper, J. F., 226, 260
Corcoran, J., 6, 113
Corcoran, K., 282, 283, 285, 288
Corey, G., 18, 22, 35, 36-37, 71
Corey, M., 18, 22
Cormier, L. S., 6, 52, 68, 89, 137, 211, 266, 267, 280, 315, 317, 335, 338
Corn, R., 56
Corrigan, J. D., 115, 117, 120
Corrigan, S., 627
Costantino, G., 352
Cottle, W. C., 58
Courtois, C., 329

Courtois, C. A., 358
Cowger, C. D., 181
Cox, B., 544
Cox, B. G., 124, 126, 128
Cramer, S., 122
Crawford, I., 33
Crawford, M., 24, 29
Cromie, S. D., 606
Cronbach, L. J., 282
Cross, W. E., 28
Crum, A., 467
Csikszentmihalyi, M., 256
Cullen, C., 189
Cummings, N., 322
Cunningham, S., 627
Cushman, P., 312, 321, 322, 324-325, 343
Czyewski, D. I., 584

Dabbs, A., 262
Danton, W., 311
Das, A. K., 27, 31
D'Augelli, A. R., 31
Davidson, J., 444
Davis, C. G., 469
Davis, D., 64
Davis, S., 286, 331, 335
Davison, G. C., 550-551, 554, 562, 563
Day, 17
Day, B. J., 116
Day, J., 34, 646
Day, R. W., 120, 121, 122
de Arellano, M. A., 548
de Jongh, A., 567
de Visser, L., 611, 612
Deffenbacher, J. L., 586
Deitsch, S. E., 548
DeJong, W., 260
Delgado-Morales, F., 508
Dell, D. M., 117
DeMichele, J. T., 7
DeNelsky, G., 311
Denholtz, M., 555
Derogatis, L. R., 286
Devore, W., 145
Diaz, T., 627
DiClemente, C., 258, 308-309
DiGiuseppe, R., 218

NAME INDEX

Dinnel, D., 548
Dixon, D. N., 123, 256, 264, 272, 275, 279
Dixon, W. A., 410
Dlugos, R. F., 631
Dobson, K. S., 434, 435
Docherty, J., 311
Dodge, K. A., 586
Donovan, D., 261
Donovan, S., 506
Dorn, F. J., 113, 116
Dorris, M., 28
Dossey, L., 334
Dowd, E. T., 142
Dowrick, P. W., 611
Dozois, D. J. A., 434
Draycott, S., 262
Driskell, J. E., 479
Duan, C., 65
Duckro, P. N., 497
Duhl, B. S., 54
Duhl, F. J., 54
Duke, L., 30, 647
Duley, S. M., 208
Dumont, F., 52
Dunbar, E., 330
Dunbar, J., 609
Duncan, B., 63, 260
Durand, V. M., 471
Dusenbury, L., 351
Dwyer, E. V., 440
Dyrud, J. E., 187
D'Zurilla, T. J., 406, 409, 410, 413, 414, 415, 416, 417, 418, 419, 434

Echemendia, R., 33
Eckert, P., 284
Edelstein, B. A., 123, 208
Edwards, C., 120, 156
Egan, G., 6, 8, 18, 64, 65, 69, 70, 96, 106, 116, 117, 134, 135, 139, 141, 145, 146, 151, 153, 155, 156, 157, 159, 160, 161-162
Eggert, M. A., 115
Eisdorfer, C., 479
Eisenberger, R., 610
Ekman, P., 45, 46, 48, 49, 51
Elias, M. J., 180, 181, 228, 257, 330-331

Eliot, G. R., 479
Ellens, B. M., 39, 40
Eller, L. S., 359
Elliott, R., 156
Ellis, A., 217, 434, 435
Ellis, M. R., 497
Emavardhana, T., 508
Emery, G., 435
Emmelkamp, P., 548
Endler, N., 469
Enns, C., 26
Enns, C. Z., 24, 358
Enzle, M. E., 606
Epel, E. S., 628
Epstein, J., 627
Epstein, M., 506, 512
Epston, P., 85
Erickson, M. H., 46
Eriksen, K. P., 181, 182
Estes, C., 359
Evans, D., 396
Ewigman, B., 497
Exline, 48, 648

Faiver, C., 192
Fall, K. A., 9
Faludi, S., 22
Farrah, G. A., 596
Farrell, A. D., 208
Faryna, E. L., 627
Fassinger, R. E., 29
Fay, A., 77
Fensterheim, H., 215
Ferguson, J. M., 551
Fernandez, M., 584
Fernandez-Esquer, M., 627
Feske, U., 567
Field, L. K., 606-607
Fields, L., 626
Fink, G., 467, 469
Finn, J., 148
First, M. B., 190
Fisch, R., 77, 78, 80, 228, 309
Fischer, J., 275, 276, 281, 282, 283, 285, 288, 599
Fishelman, L., 311
Fisher, E., 584
Fishman, S. T., 188, 225
Fitzgerald, L. F., 24
Fitzpatrick, M., 37, 38, 71, 156

Flora, J., 627
Foa, E. B., 329, 547, 548, 566, 567, 568
Fodor, I. G., 186, 193, 194
Folkman, S., 468, 470, 493
Follette, W., 178
Follette, W. C., 286
Fong, M. L., 124, 126, 128
Fontana, D., 506
Foote, W., 36, 74
Ford, 549
Ford, M., 194
Fouad, N. A., 31
Foulks, E. F., 211
Fox, J. J., 187
Franklin, C., 598
Frazier, P., 116
Frazier, P. A., 439
Freeman, A., 627
Freeman, E., 181
Freiberg, P., 439
Freire, P., 28, 330, 332
Fretz, B. R., 56, 57, 64
Fricchione, G. L., 508
Fried, R., 472, 474, 478
Friedlander, M. L., 631
Friedman, L., 609
Friedman, M., 312
Friedman, M. J., 329, 568
Friedman, S., 548
Friesen, W. V., 45, 46
Frijda, N., 49, 95
Frueh, B. C., 548, 567
Fuhrmann, A., 607
Fullilove, M., 627
Fullilove, R., 627
Futterman, D., 31

Gaelick-Buys, L., 580, 581, 590, 594, 599, 601, 605, 606, 607, 608, 609, 610
Gafner, G., 548
Gaines, R., 359
Gambrill, E., 4, 19, 314
Gambrill, E. D., 4, 221, 265, 274, 277, 279
Gammon, E. A., 412
Gant, L., 446
Gantt, D., 74, 75
Gardener, P., 612

Gartett, M. T., 587
Garvin, C., 147, 180, 222, 226
Gasch, H., 627
Gazda, G. M., 56, 58, 64, 71, 107, 138, 148, 152
Gelberg, S., 257
Gelenberg, A., 311
Gelso, C. J., 6, 63, 64, 72, 73, 74, 75
Gendlin, E., 64
Gendlin, E. T., 392, 396, 467
George, L. K., 492, 494
Gerrity, E., 312
Gerton, J., 27
Gesten, E. L., 36
Gibbon, M., 190
Gibbs, L., 4, 19, 311, 314
Gilbert, L. A., 26
Gilbert, M. C., 497
Gilford, P., 312, 321, 322, 324-325, 343
Gilligan, C., 201, 329, 351, 396
Gilliland, 64, 650
Girgus, J. S., 446
Gladstein, G., 65
Gleason, C., 208, 228
GlenMaye, L., 32
Glickauf-Hughes, C., 67
Glover, J. A., 256, 264, 272, 275, 279
Gluckstern, N. B., 84, 95, 101, 156
Gold, R. S., 584
Goldberg, S. G., 3, 5-6
Goldbeyer, N. R., 230
Goldfried, M. R., 215, 286, 434, 435, 443, 549, 550-551, 554, 562, 563
Goldiamond, I., 187
Goldman, R. L., 317
Goldstein, A. P., 16, 70, 113
Goldstein, H., 612
Goleman, D., 506, 512
Gollub, R. L., 508
Gollwitzer, P., 272, 277, 278
Goodman, J., 402, 434
Goodyear, R., 156
Gordon, A., 412
Gordon, J. R., 260
Gore, P., 628

Gorski, P. C., 147
Gottleib, L., 311
Gottlieb, M. C., 37, 39
Gottman, J. M., 266
Grant, S. K., 327
Graves, J. R., 58
Gray-Little, B., 312
Greenberg, J. S., 467, 468, 469, 472
Greenberg, L., 65
Greenberg, L. S., 156, 286, 317
Greenberg, S., 396
Greenberger, D., 595, 596
Greene, A. F., 31
Greenson, R. R., 73-74
Greenwald, R., 567
Greenwood, A., 37
Grohol, J. M., 148
Gronsky, B. R., 57
Gross, A., 557
Gross, E., 85
Guidano, V. F., 443
Guidry, L., 283, 284
Guralnick, M., 435
Guthrie, B. J., 628
Gutierrez, L., 629, 631

Hackett, G., 22, 23
Hackney, H., 6, 52, 68, 89, 137, 211, 266, 267, 315, 317, 335, 338
Hagopian, L. P., 606
Hains, A., 400
Haire-Joshu, D., 584
Hall, C., 359
Hall, E. T., 46, 52
Hall, J. A., 45, 46-47, 48, 49, 50, 51
Hall, P. D., 508
Halvorsen, R., 508
Hammond, C., 358
Hammond, R., 412
Hanh, T. N., 506
Hanna, F. J., 257
Hansen, J. C., 122
Hansen, N. D., 3, 5-6, 31
Harchik, A. E., 606
Harper, R. A., 435
Harris, S., 119
Hart, J., 555

Hartley, E. T., 612
Harwood, T., 308, 309, 310, 314, 315, 317-319
Hatch, M., 438
Haug, I., 497
Hayes, A., 308
Hayes, J. A., 6, 73
Hayes, S., 178, 281, 288
Hayes, S. C., 606
Haynes, S. N., 242
Hays, K. F., 342, 343, 437, 438, 440
Hays, P. A., 184
Hayworth, M., 497
Heather, 261
Hecker, L., 36
Heckhausen, J., 628
Heesacker, M., 114, 116, 117, 118
Heiman, R. J., 435
Heimberg, R., 285
Helms, J., 128
Helms, J. E., 24, 29, 30, 68, 73, 75, 103, 107, 120, 122, 129, 155
Hembree, E. A., 566
Hendricks, G., 475, 478
Heppner, P., 116
Heppner, P. P., 114, 115-116, 117, 118, 257, 409
Hepting, N. H., 612
Hepworth, D., 6, 8, 65, 76, 96, 135, 137, 139, 151, 152, 153, 155, 156, 159, 161, 162, 181, 220, 227, 241, 266, 267, 335
Herbert, J. D., 567
Herman, J. L., 522
Herman, S., 599
Hermansson, G. L., 119, 652
Herring, R., 358-359
Herron, W. G., 320-321, 322
Hersen, M., 185, 627
Heslin, R., 50
Hickson, J., 497
Higginbotham, H. N., 16, 70, 113
Hill, C., 65, 161, 183, 307
Hill, C. E., 57, 58, 72, 141, 142
Hill, P. C., 496
Hill, R., 209
Himle, J. A., 544
Ho, D. Y. F., 24, 26-27

Hodges, K., 208, 286
Hoffman, A., 122
Hohmann, M., 261
Holden, G., 148
Holen, A., 508
Holland, S., 218, 335, 435, 443, 444
Hollon, S., 311
Hollon, S. D., 254, 311
Homme, L. E., 434
Horne, D., 544
Horvath, A. O., 74
Hosford, R. E., 611, 612
Houlihan, D., 612
Housley, W., 497
Howard, K., 286
Howard, K. I., 322
Howard-Hamilton, M., 31, 119
Hoyt, W., 6, 113
Hoyt, W. T., 114, 115, 116, 117
Huang, L. N., 396
Hubbard, L., 410
Hubble, M., 63, 260
Hudson, W., 281, 287, 289, 599
Hudson, W. W., 13, 286-287, 599
Hull, C. L., 189
Hull, G., 266, 338
Humfleet, G., 351
Humphrey, J. H., 467
Humphries, S., 566
Hurd, E., 351
Hutchins, D., 88, 98
Hutchins, J., 280-281, 284
Hwang, M. Y., 27

Ibanez-Ramirez, M., 508
Iglesias, E., 280
Ingersoll, R., 192
Ingram, R., 308, 311, 312-313
Ironson, G. H., 496
Irvin, J., 260
Israel, A. C., 586
Itai, G., 55, 147, 195
Ivey, A., 331, 332-333
Ivey, A. E., 8, 31, 47, 64, 65, 71, 84, 85, 89, 92, 94, 95, 101, 106, 134, 137, 156, 159, 160, 161, 180, 181, 226, 228, 437, 654

Ivey, M. B., 8, 47, 64, 84, 85, 89, 92, 94, 95, 101, 134, 137, 156, 159, 160, 161, 180, 181, 226, 228, 331, 332-333, 437, 654
Iwamasa, G. Y., 438

Jackson, G. G., 230
Jackson, Y., 322
Jacob, T., 584
Jacobson, E., 467, 515
Jacobson, N., 311
Jacobson, N. S., 286
Jaffee v. Redmond
James, 64
James, B. J., 493
Jarrett, R. B., 606
Jason, L., 352
Javier, R. A., 320
Jaya, A., 75, 147, 257, 330
Jayakody, R., 492
Jean-Gilles, M., 352
Jefferson, K., 584
Jennings, M. C., 9
Jenson, W. R., 612
Jiang, T., 411
Jocic, Z., 586
Johanson, J., 70
Johnson, D. W., 70, 71, 123-124, 129, 141, 161
Johnson, K., 467
Johnson, W. B., 438
Johnston, J. H., 479
Jones, E. E., 281, 326
Jones, R., 628
Jordan, C., 598
Josselson, R., 68-69

Kabat-Zinn, J., 86, 467, 508, 509-510, 511, 515, 523
Kadushin, A., 31
Kadushin, G., 31
Kahn, M., 66, 67, 72, 73, 555
Kalichman, S. C., 584
Kalodner, C., 258
Kalodner, C. R., 543
Kamimura, E., 548
Kanfer, F. H., 175, 580, 581, 590, 594, 599, 601, 605, 606, 607, 608, 609, 610
Kantor, D., 54

Kantor, J. R., 187
Kantrowitz, R., 230, 342, 343, 437, 438
Karoly, 606
Kaplan, D., 312
Kaplan, H. I., 209
Kaplan, R., 567
Karasu, T., 311
Karenga, M., 397
Kazdin, A., 365, 655
Kazdin, A. E., 281, 286, 312, 409, 549, 594, 655
Keane, T., 329, 568
Keel, L., 331
Kehle, T. J., 611, 612
Kelly, J., 412, 584
Kelly, K. R., 145
Kemeny, M., 627
Kemp, S., 182, 219, 221, 222, 227
Kenan, S., 497
Kenardy, J., 599
Kendall, P., 286
Kendall, P. C., 254, 435
Kennel, R., 628
Kenyan, P., 34, 35, 39
Khalsa, G., 508
Kiesler, D., 64
Kiesler, D. J., 65
Killick, S., 261
Kilpatrick, S. D., 497
King, C. N., 529
King, J., 74, 80-81
King, N. J., 435, 438, 586
Kinzie, J. D., 471
Kiresuk, T. J., 273, 285
Kirst-Ashman, K., 266, 338
Kitaoka, S. K., 359
Kitayama, S., 435
Kitchener, K. S., 34, 37, 38
Kivlahan, D., 261
Kivlighan, D., Jr., 74, 75
Kleinknecht, R., 547, 548
Kliewer, W., 351
Knapp, M. L., 45, 46-47, 48, 49, 50, 51
Knepp, D., 33
Kobayashi, M. J., 58
Koenig, H. G., 492, 497
Kohn, R., 161
Kohut, H., 65-67, 72

Koopman, C., 627
Kopta, S. M., 322
Korte, A., 359
Korth, E., 544
Kotlash, J., 586
Kottler, J. A., 18
Kozak, M. J., 566
Kraemer, H., 627
Kramer, J., 606
Kramer, L., 410, 584
Kratochwill, T. R., 208
Krause, M. S., 322
Kremer, T. G., 36
Krepcho, M., 627
Krieger, N., 471-472
Kristeller, J. L., 506, 512
Krivonos, P. D., 50
Krueger, K. F., 612
Krugh, M., 24
Krumboltz, J., 279
Kuehlwein, K. T., 439
Kuhl, J., 607
Kulik, J., 584
Kupfer, D., 311
Kurpius, D., 9
Kurpius, D. J., 84
Kurtines, W., 26-27
Kurtz, R., 70

L'Abate, L., 79
LaCrosse, M. B., 114
LaFromboise, T., 27, 123, 180-181
Lam, D. J., 471
Lamb, S., 194
Lambert, M., 65, 273, 281, 283, 285, 286, 287, 307
Lang, P. J., 551, 555
Lankton, S. R., 118
Larsen, J., 220, 227, 241
Larsen, J. A., 6, 8, 65
Larson, D. B., 492, 497
Larson, E., 397
Larson, J., 469
Last, C., 548
Laungani, P., 470
Lauver, P., 628
Lawendowski, L., 261
Lazar, S. W., 508
Lazarus, A., 358

Lazarus, A. A., 77, 175-176, 177, 181, 213, 214, 216, 217, 227, 228, 544
Lazarus, R. S., 468
Lazrove, S., 567
Leahy, R., 218, 335, 435, 443, 444, 446, 463
Lecci, 606
Lecomte, C., 52
LeCroy, C. W., 406
Lee, C., 567
Lee, P., 544
Lee, V. J., 116
Lee, Y. D., 87
Lehrer, P. M., 286, 291, 467
Leiblum, S. R., 266
Leininger, M. M., 470
Leith, L. M., 527, 529
Lenox, R. A., 7
LePage, J., 515, 523-524, 526
Lerman, H., 64
Leserman, J., 396
LeShan, L., 226
Levin, A., 279
Levin, J. S., 492
Levin, R., 557
Levitov, J. E., 9
Lewis, H., 351
Lewis, K. N., 117
Li, L., 183
Lichtenberg, J., 311
Lilienfeld, S. O., 567
Lin, Meei-Ju, 145
Linscott, J., 218
Lipinski, D. P., 282
Lipke, H., 548
Litrownik, A. J., 586
Locke, D. C., 24
Lohr, J. M., 567
Lomont, J. F., 549
Long, L., 95
Long, R., 65
Lonner, W., 548
Look, S. C., 606
Lopez, M., 439
Low, K., 180-181
Low, L. K., 628
Lu, F., 493
Lu, F. G., 497
Lubetkin, B. S., 188, 225

Luborsky, L., 317
Lukoff, D., 493
Lum, D., 22, 31, 37, 125-126, 147, 156, 324, 327, 328, 329, 342
Lum, L. C., 179
Lundervold, D., 281, 286, 288
Lyddon, W. J., 257

Maag, J. W., 586
MacKay, P., 260
Madaus, M. R., 611
Maddux, J. E., 280
Magee, E., 627
Mahoney, K., 586, 587
Mahoney, M. J., 258, 259, 282, 434, 435, 559, 580, 586, 587, 589, 592, 594, 599, 600, 603, 605, 608, 609, 610
Mail, P., 351
Malgady, R., 352, 353
Mallinckrodt, B., 74, 75
Malow, R., 627
Manicavasagar, V., 567
Mann, E., 555
Manning, S. S., 32-33
Marcoux, M. F., 606
Marks, L., 326
Markus, H. R., 435
Marlatt, G., 260, 586
Marlatt, G. A., 506, 512
Marmer, C., 286
Marquis, J. M., 548, 551, 554, 559, 560, 561, 562
Marsella, A., 312
Marsella, A. J., 13
Marshak, M., 73, 74
Marten, P., 285
Martin, D., 584
Martin, G. L., 526-527
Martin, J., 87
Martin, K., 359
Mason, P., 261
Massman, P. J., 548
Masters, J. C., 178, 547, 561
Masters, K., 273, 285
Maton, K. I., 626
Matson, J., 346
Maurer, R. E., 58
May, R. J., 116
Mays, V., 627, 628

McAuley, E., 628
McAuliffe, G. J., 181, 182
McCafferty, S., 585
McCarthy, P., 120, 155, 156
McCullough, J. P., 274
McCullough, M. E., 492, 497
McCullough-Vaillant, L., 208
McDavis, R., 31
McDonald, J., 584
McFall, R. M., 586, 594, 595
McFarland, K., 119
McGill, D. W., 96
McGrath, T., 566
McGuigan, F. J., 467, 515
McGuire, M., 599
McKnight, D. L., 606
McLeod, C., 599
McLoughlin, C. S., 611
McMillion, P., 351
McMinn, M. R., 39, 40
McNally, C., 192
McNally, R. J., 358
McNeill, B. W., 116
McRae, G., 55, 147, 195
Meador, B., 64
Meador, K. G., 497
Meadows, E. A., 547, 566, 567
Meara, N., 34
Mefford, I. N., 621
Meggert, S., 358-359
Mehan, H., 410
Mehrabian, A., 53
Meichenbaum, D. H., 214, 227, 329, 402, 434, 435, 479, 482, 483, 485, 486, 487, 586
Meier, S., 286, 331, 335
Melamed, B. G., 555
Melchert, T. P., 37
Merckelbach, H., 555, 567
Meredith, K. E., 208
Mermelstein, R., 439
Merriam, A., 311
Mesquita, B., 49, 95
Meyer, R. G., 548
Milchus, N. J., 596
Miller, J. B., 26
Miller, R. C., 526, 548
Miller, S., 63, 260
Miller, W. R., 84, 161, 260-261
Milne, C. R., 142

Milne, R., 567
Miranda, J., 440
Mischel, W., 180, 187
Misener, E., 258, 275, 277, 330
Mitchell, J. E., 497
Mitchell, K., 279, 280
Mitchell, K. M., 64
Mitchell, R. W., 241, 242
Mohr, J., 72
Moncher, M., 412
Montgomery, D., 548
Moore, C., 351
Moorey, S., 409-410
Moos, R. H., 469
Morales, E., 627
Moras, K., 281
Morgan, W., 548, 562
Morran, D. K., 84, 175
Morran, K., 9
Morrell, G., 611
Morris, R. J., 543
Morrison, J., 190, 208, 209
Morrison, R., 544
Morrow, S., 628
Morten, G., 29
Moskowitz, J. T., 493
Moss, C., 611
Motenko, A. K., 396
Moura, N. G., 586
Mullin, T., 113
Mungadze, J., 497
Munro, J., 584
Muran, J., 6, 75, 76, 309
Murdock, N., 120, 156
Muris, P., 555, 567
Murphy, M., 506
Murray, G. C., 40
Mwaba, K., 195
Myers, L., 178

Nagae, N., 400
Narayanasamy, A., 497
Nathan, P., 311
National Association of Social Workers, 22, 34, 120
National Board for Certified Counselors Standards for the Ethical Practice of WebCounseling, 34
National Organization for Human Service Education, 34

Nedate, K., 400
Neilans, T. H., 586
Neimeyer, R. A., 433
Nelissen, I., 555, 566
Nelson, R. C., 145
Nelson, R. O., 194, 207, 282, 592, 594, 606
Nelson-Gray, R., 281
Neville, B., 435
Newman, M. G., 599
Nezu, A. M., 413, 414, 415, 416, 417, 418, 419
Nezu, C. M., 409, 415, 419
Nichols, M. P., 84, 85
Nickerson, K., 128
Nickerson, R. S., 18-19
Nolen-Hoeksema, S., 446, 469
Norcross, J., 258
Norcross, J. C., 7-8, 63, 64, 143, 433, 544, 568
Norman, T. R., 508
Novaco, R. W., 485, 487, 488
Nugent, W., 287, 288, 290, 599
Null, J., 627
Nurius, P. S., 13, 147, 286, 469, 599
Nutt, R., 24
Nutt-Williams, E., 161

O'Bannon, R., 584
O'Brien, E., 192
O'Brien, K., 628
Oettingen, G., 622
Ogles, B., 273, 285
Okun, B. F., 22
O'Leary, K. D., 185
Ollendick, T. H., 435, 438, 586, 606
Omizo, M. M., 359
Omizo, S. A., 359
Oppenheimer, M., 396
O'Reilly, M. F., 400
Organista, K., 440
Orlandi, M., 412
Orlinsky, D. E., 322
Orme, J., 275, 276, 281, 599
Orme-Johnson, D. W., 508
Ornish, D., 467, 506
Ostaseski, F., 85, 86
Ottens, A., 65

Overholser, J. C., 361
Oyserman, D., 446
Oz, S., 264
Ozer, R. L., 622

Packard, T., 209
Paddock, J. R., 358
Padesky, C. A., 595, 596
Painter, L. C., 496
Palsane, M. N., 471
Papp, P., 54
Paradis, C., 438
Parcel, G. S., 584
Parks, G. A., 586
Passons, W. R., 46, 55
Patel, C., 474, 506, 508, 515, 523, 526
Patkin, J., 117
Patterson, C. J., 31
Patterson, J., 497
Patterson, L. E., 152, 160, 161
Patterson, M. M., 37
Patton, M., 74, 311
Paul, R., 3, 19, 314
Paulson, B., 64
Peck, S., 414
Pedersen, P. B., 31, 195
Pekarik, G., 283, 284
Pellebon, D. A., 497
Penn, N., 584
Pepitone-Arreola-Rockwell, F., 31
Perkins, D., 396
Perls, F. S., 46
Perri, M. B., 419
Persons, J. B., 444
Pert, C., 621
Peterson, D. B., 40
Petry, N., 287, 308, 309
Pham, L. B., 348, 365
Piaget, G., 548, 562
Picucci, M., 351
Pierce, R. M., 96, 101
Pietrofesa, J. J., 122
Pilkington, N. W., 24
Pinsof, W., 320
Pinto, D. V., 122
Pipher, M., 201
Pitman, R. K., 567
Platt, J. J., 434
Pollard, D., 410

Possell, L. E., 611
Poulson, D., 627
Price, S., 257
Price-Williams, P., 359
Primavera, L. H., 320
Prochaska, J., 258, 259, 260, 262, 272, 308-309
Prochaska, J. O., 7-8, 433, 544, 568
Project MATCH, 261
Prophit, P., 95
Puchalski, C. M., 497
Pulido-Diez, J., 508
Pulos, L., 361

Quandt, S. A., 584
Quintana, S., 311

Ramirez-Valles, J., 626
Randolph, S., 627
Rao, R., 410, 584
Raskin, J. D., 433
Raskin, M., 497
Raskin, N., 64
Rath, S., 400
Read, J., 567
Rector, J. M., 497
Reed, B. G., 20
Rehm, L. P., 586
Reichelova, E., 352
Reid, H., 627
Reid, W., 258, 275, 277, 330
Reithoffer, A., 281, 283
Reitz, 596
Remafedi, G., 23
Remen, N., 107
Renard, G., 23, 128
Renfrey, G. S., 440
Renssen, M. R., 567
Resnick, R. J., 281
Revenstorf, D., 286
Reyes, M., 351-352
Rhodes, F., 351
Rice, L. N., 156
Rice, V. H., 467, 469
Richards, P. S., 497
Richardson, B., 99, 100
Richardson, F., 434
Richmond, M. E., 175
Ridley, C., 183, 213

Ridley, C. R., 438
Riley, W., 351
Rimm, D. C., 178, 547, 561
Ritchie, M. H., 257
Rivkin, I., 348
Roach, K., 113
Roberson, M., 584
Robert, S. A., 627
Roberts, M., 322
Robinson, J. D., 58
Robinson, L., 33
Robinson, P., 508
Robinson, T., 396-397
Robinson, T. L., 31, 119
Rochlen, A., 72
Rogers, C., 6, 64, 65-66, 69, 96
Rogers, R., 208, 351
Roggeveen, J. P., 606
Rogler, T., 352
Rogoff, B., 180
Rohrbaugh, M., 309
Rokke, P. D., 586
Rollnick, H. N., 261
Rollnick, S., 84, 260, 261
Rompa, D., 584
Ronnestad, M., 7
Rooney, R., 6, 8, 65, 220, 227, 241
Root, M. P., 184, 194
Rosado, J. W., Jr., 180, 181, 228, 257, 330-331
Rosario, M., 627
Rose, S. D., 406
Rosebrook, R., 628
Rosen, G. M., 567
Rosenthal, T. L., 346, 347, 622
Ross, C. A., 194
Rossberg, R., 122
Rossi, E., 46
Rossi, S., 46
Rossiter, E., 358
Rotherman-Borus, M. J., 627
Rotter, J. B., 326
Routh, D., 352
Ruben, A., 508
Rudolph, D., 628
Rudolph, L., 99, 106
Ruiz, A. S., 28
Rush, A., 435

Ryan, C., 31
Ryan, M. K., 39, 40

Sadock, B. J., 209
Safran, J., 6, 75, 76, 309
Salas, E., 479
Sali, A., 508
Salkovskis, P., 313
Salkovskis, P. M., 435
Samuels, C. A., 493
Sanderson, W., 311
Sandhu, D. S., 496
Sanfilippo, M., 352
Santiago-Rivera, A., 315, 325-326, 330
Sarwer, D. B., 207, 208
SaSaki, Y., 548
Saslow, G., 175
Saunders, T., 479
Sayers, S. L., 207, 208
Scarsfield, R. C., 312
Schacter, D. L., 358
Schaefer, J. A., 469
Scheel, M., 113
Scheflin, A., 358
Scher, M., 26
Schill, T., 606
Schilling, R., 412
Schinke, S., 412
Schlesinger, E., 145
Schlossberger, E., 36
Schmidt, L., 34
Schmidt, L. D., 117
Schneider, R., 161, 508
Schneider, S., 627
Schoech, D., 39, 147, 148
Schoefield, W., 33
Scholing, A., 548
Schultz, C. L., 320
Schulz, R., 628
Schumaker, J. B., 606
Schumate, J., 156
Schwartz, C., 612
Scott, W., 308
Seabaugh, G. O., 606
Seabury, B., 147, 180, 222, 226
Seaman, S., 113
Seay, R. C., 626
Sedney, M., 85
Segal, L., 77

Sekiguchi, Y., 400
Seligman, L., 315, 316
Seligman, M., 329, 446, 617
Semenchuk, E., 123, 208
Senn, M. D., 529
Senour, M., 113
Serafini, L. T., 242
Sexton, T. L., 63, 73, 74, 114, 117
Shadoan, R., 311
Shaffer, S., 628
Shainberg, D., 137, 138
Shank, G., 65
Shapiro, F., 547, 567
Sharma, S., 471
Sharp, R. N., 586
Shaw, B., 435
Shcherbakova, J., 492
Shegog, R., 584
Sheldon, J. B., 606
Shepherd, J., 567
Sherman, J. A., 606
Sherman, R. E., 273, 285
Shiang, J., 257
Shirley, A., 584
Shoham, V., 309
Shostrom, E. L., 16, 34, 65, 77, 120
Shuman, D. W., 36
Shure, M. B., 434
Siegelman, L., 57
Sieppert, J., 287, 599
Silverman, W. K., 242
Sime, W., 526
Simek-Downing, L., 92
Simek-Morgan, L., 47, 85, 89, 94, 101, 137, 180, 181, 331, 332-333, 437
Simon, D. A., 612
Simon, K., 273, 275, 277
Simon, R. I., 49
Simon, S., 21
Simone, D. H., 155, 156, 157
Simpkinson, A., 84
Simpkinson, C., 84
Sinacore-Guinn, A. L., 183-184, 185, 192, 194, 195, 226
Singer, J. L., 48
Skay, C., 155, 156
Skodol, A. E., 190
Skovholt, T., 7

Sloane, D., 208, 228
Smart, D., 27
Smart, D. W., 196
Smart, J. F., 27, 196
Smart, N., 492
Smith, B., 396
Smith, D., 37, 38, 71, 156
Smith, E. P., 626
Smith, K. J., 258, 259
Smith, M. J., 473
Smyth, N. J., 567
Snelling, J., 506
Snowden, L. R., 27, 194
Snyder, C. R., 256
Sockrider, M., 584
Solberg, E. E., 508
Solberg, V., 628
Solomon, L. J., 606
Sommers-Flanagan, J., 107
Sommers-Flanagan, S., 107
Soo-Hoo, T., 397
Sparacio, R. T., 120, 121, 122
Spector, J., 567
Spiegel, S. B., 141, 142
Spieth, L., 584
Spitzer, R. L., 190
Spivack, G., 434
Splete, H. H., 122
Spong, R. T., 606
Spurlock, J., 211, 212, 221, 226, 227
St. Lawrence, J., 412, 584, 585
Stamps, R., 190
Standard, R. P., 496
Steenbarger, B. N., 63
Steer, R. A., 286
Steffek, B. D., 346, 347, 622
Stein, K., 567
Steinhardt, M. A., 606-607
Steketee, G. S., 548
Stevens, P., 567
Stevenson, H. C., 23, 128
Stewart, S., 79, 80, 309
Stith, S. M., 33
Stone, G. L., 99, 100
Strong, S. R., 6, 113-114, 142
Strupp, H. H., 317
Stuart, E. M., 467, 509, 511, 512, 593

Stuart, J., 64
Sturniolo, F., 57
Subich, L., 258
Sud, A., 471
Sue, D., 27, 28, 45, 47, 48, 49, 50, 51, 52, 54, 55, 58, 65, 85, 95, 106-107, 114-115, 117, 119, 126, 128, 129, 130, 134, 142, 155, 161, 163, 168, 195, 230, 256-257, 326, 327, 328, 329, 330, 341, 585
Sue, D. W., 27, 28, 29, 31, 45, 47, 48, 49, 50, 51, 52, 54, 55, 58, 65, 85, 95, 106-107, 114-115, 117, 119, 126, 128, 129, 130, 134, 142, 155, 161, 163, 168, 195, 230, 256-257, 326, 327, 328, 329, 330, 341, 585
Sue, S., 195
Suinn, R. M., 359, 434, 586
Sullivan, A., 329, 351, 396
Summers, N., 181, 182, 183
Sun, C., 411
Swank, P., 584
Sweeney, M. A., 58
Swenson, L. C., 242
Swinson, R., 544
Symonds, B. D., 74
Szapocznik, J., 26-27
Szendre, D., 628

Tacker, R., 497
Tallman, 277
Tallman, K., 277
Tanouye-Wilson, S., 548
Tarule, J. M., 230
Taylor, C., 621
Taylor, C. B., 551, 599
Taylor, E., 497
Taylor, I., 400
Taylor, J., 329, 351, 396
Taylor, R. J., 492
Taylor, S., 567, 627
Taylor, S. E., 348, 365
Tedeschi, R. G., 470
Telfer, L. A., 281
Ten Broeke, E., 567
Tennen, H., 287
Teresa, J., 628
Terr, L., 85

Terrell, F., 128
Teyber, E., 67, 68, 94, 95, 152
Tharp, R. G., 594, 595, 599, 604, 608, 609, 610
Thase, M., 320, 322
Thomas, J., 322
Thomas, R., 548
Thompson, C., 99, 106
Thompson, C. E., 327
Thompson, L. W., 439
Thoresen, C. E., 282, 434, 496, 559, 580, 586, 589, 592, 594, 599, 600, 603, 605, 608, 609, 610
Thorn, B., 209
Thyer, B., 178
Timmons, P. L., 488
Tindall, J. H., 58
Tix, A. P., 439
Tjeltveit, A. C., 497
Tkachuck, G. A., 526-527
Tolin, D. F., 567
Tomhave, J. A., 586
Tonigan, J. S., 497
Tooley, G. A., 508
Toombs, K., 612
Tori, C. D., 508
Toscova, R. T., 497
Toth, V., 627
Tracey, E. M., 221
Tracy, E., 182
Trager, G. L., 45
Treasure, J., 261
Tremont, G., 548
Treviño, J., 326, 330
Triandis, H., 548
Triandis, H. C., 181
Truax, C., 64
Truax, C. B., 64
Truax, P., 286
Truscott, D., 64
Tsui, E., 566
Tuemmler, J. M., 56
Turk, D., 485, 486
Turner, C., 497
Turner, R., 493
Turner, S. M., 548
Turner, W. L., 23

Uhlemann, M., 87
Underwood, P. W., 469

Unger, R., 24, 29
Ussher, J., 439

van der Kolk, B. A., 567
Van Hasselt, V., 627
Van Hout, W., 548
Van Vlaenderen, H., 411
VandenBos, G. R., 37, 311
VanEtten, M. L., 567
Vargas, A. M., 119
Vasquez, M. J. T., 31, 35, 39
Vatmanidis, P., 544
Vernberg, E., 322
Vigne, J., 508
Villanueva, I., 410
Villareal, P., 628
Vinson, D. C., 497
Vitolins, M. Z., 584

Wachtel, P. L., 392
Wade, T. C., 586
Waehler, C., 311, 312
Waehler, C. A., 7
Wages, D., 497
Wahler, R. G., 187
Walker, K., 626
Walters, R. P., 57
Wampold, B., 308, 311
Wang, C., 584
Ward, A., 261
Ward, J., 396-397
Ward, K. M., 611
Watson, B., 411
Watson, D. L., 594, 595, 599, 604, 608, 609, 610
Watson, O. M., 47, 52
Watts-Jones, D., 286
Weakland, J., 77
Webster, 119
Wedner, J., 584
Weeks, D. L., 612
Weeks, G. R., 79
Wehrly, B., 169
Weinberger, A., 446, 447
Weiss, J., 439
Weist, M. D., 606
Welch, L. M., 470
Welfel, E., 266
Welfel, E. R., 152, 160, 161
Wells, M., 67

Welsh, J., 6, 113
Werner-Wilson, R., 257
West, J., 627
Weston, E., 412
Wewers, M., 438
Whaley, A., 129
Whiston, S. C., 63, 73, 74, 114, 117
White, M., 85
Whitfield, K. E., 411
Whittaker, J., 182
Whittaker, J. K., 221
Widiger, T. A., 194
Wilcoxon, L. A., 549
Williams, J. B., 190
Williams, O., 351
Williams, S. L., 621

Wilson, G. T., 185, 226, 549
Wilson, L. L., 33
Winfrey, M. L., 612
Winkleby, M., 627
Winnicott, D. W., 66, 68
Winters, 48
Wirth, L., 28
Wolfe, B., 440
Wolpe, J., 515, 544, 548, 549, 550, 551, 552, 553, 554, 555, 557, 559, 560, 561, 565-566, 568
Woltersdorf, M. A., 612
Wood, R. J., 467
Woodman, M., 20, 68
Woods, T. E., 496
Woody, R. H., 37

Woolfolk, R., 286, 291
Woolfolk, R. L., 467
Wright, J., 64
Wu, Z., 411
Wynne, L., 320

Yang, B., 411
Yeh, C. J., 27
Yoder, J. D., 24
Youell, K. J., 274
Young, J. E., 446, 447, 448-450, 463
Young, J. S., 492
Young-Eisendrath, P., 328, 329
Yule, W., 566
Yung, B., 412

Zabukovec, J., 567
Zack, J., 72
Zalaquett, C. P., 467
Zamostny, K. P., 115
Zarit, J., 179
Zarit, S., 179
Zastrow, C., 123, 129
Zeidner, M., 469
Zillmann, D., 621
Zillmann, M., 621
Zimbardo, P. G., 628
Zimmerman, M. A., 626
Zimmerman, T., 257
Zlotlow, S. F., 119

SUBJECT INDEX

ABC model of behavior, 190. *See also* Client issues, conceptualizing
    antecedents, 187, 223
    behavior, 186, 215
    consequences, 187, 224
Acculturation 325
    management of diversity, 26
    psychology of oppression, 27
Action steps, 275. *See also* Subgoals
Advanced empathy, 139.
Affect, 176, 215
American Counseling Association, 15, 42, 639
American Psychiatric Association, 15, 190 (*DSM IV*)
American Psychological Association, 15; ethical standards, 42, 639
Assessment. *See* Client issues, categories for assessing. *See also* Defining client issues, Interview assessment
Attractiveness, 118-122
Axis, 192-193. *See also* DSM-IV

BASIC ID, 175-178. *See also* Client issues, conceptualizing
Behavior. *See also* Cognitive change, cognitive restructuring
    ABC model, 186-190
    affect and mental state, 178-179, 215
    cognitions, 216
    context, 218
    goal behavior, 255
    overt, 216
    relationships, 220
    somatic sensation, 216
Behavior logs, 242-245, 589, 594-599
Body scan, 510, 518, 523
Breathing
    and meditation, 510
    and relaxation, 511
    awareness, 475
    contraindications and adverse effects, 478
    diaphragmatic, 476
    model example, 478
    physiology, 472
    rationale, 476

Change processes and models. *See also* Treatment strategies; Resistance
    practice nexus, 2

    interviewing overview, 8
    level of change, 273
    outcome goals, 257
    Prochaska change model, 258-260
Clarification, 88-91
Client issues, categories
    ascertaining the frequency, duration, and severity, 229
    explaining the purpose of assessment, 212
    exploring the client's perception of the concern, 228
    exploring previous solutions, 226
    identifying antecedents, 223
    identifying the client's coping skills, strengths, 226-227
    identifying concerns, 213
    identifying consequences, 224
    identifying the range of issues, 213
    identifying secondary gains, 225
    prioritizing and selecting issues, 214
    understanding the present behaviors, 215
Client issues, conceptualizing
    ABC model, 185-190
    assumptions, 178-179
    BASIC ID model, 175-178
    model case, 196
    person-in-environment model, 181-185
Client issues, defining. *See also* Interview assessment
    client self-monitoring assessment, 242-245
    gender and multicultural factors in assessment, 230
    limitations of interview leads in problem assessment, 230
    notes and record keeping, 241
Client nonverbal behavior
    cultural patterns, 47
    environment, 53
    how to work with, 54-56
    paralinguistics, 51
    proxemics, 52
    time, 53
Client self-monitoring assessment, 242-245, 589-601
Cognitions, 176, 217. *See also* Cognitive change, therapy, and restructuring
Cognitive modeling with cognitive self-instructional training
    covert self-guidance, 403
    homework and follow-up, 403
    interview checklist

SUBJECT INDEX

model dialogue, 403
model of task and self-guidance, 401
overt external guidance, 402
overt self-guidance, 403
rationale, 401

Cognitive change, therapy, and restructuring. *See also* Cognitive restructuring, six components
categories of distorted thoughts, 443
client monitoring of thoughts, 447
developments in cognitive therapy, 397
early maladaptive schemas, 448-450
guidelines for using cognitive restructuring with diverse clients, 404
model dialogue, 454
multicultural applications, 513
rationale, 441
terminology, 433
uses, 435

Cognitive restructuring, six components, 440-441
contrast of self-defeating and self enhancing thoughts, 441
identification of client thoughts in problem situations, 442
introduction and practice of coping thoughts, 451
introduction and practice of self-statements, 453
shifting from self-defeating to coping thoughts, 452
rationale, 441

Competence, 18. *See also* Expertness, Multicultural counseling competence; Resistance
Confidentiality, 35
Confrontation
client reactions, 161
ground rules, 160
steps, 162

Contextual issues. *See also* Environment
assessment, 218
person-in-environment model, 181-185
self-efficacy, 627
social context, 180
reframes, 396

Coping skills and strategies, 483
Counseling theory. *See* Facilitative conditions, Helper nonverbal behavior
Cost effectiveness in treatment, 320
Couple therapy treatment, 319-321
Covert modeling
applications, 368
homework and follow-up, 370
model dialogue, 370
practice scenes, 365
rationale, 365
treatment scenes, 365

Critical thinking, 19
treatment selection, 311-314

Cross-cultural issues. *See also* Guidelines for use with diverse groups
biases in diagnosis, 194
cultural competence, 31
cultural identity development, 26-28
intake and interviewing, 211-212
minority identity, 29
nonverbal behavior, 47

outcome goals, 256
stress, 470
testing trust, 128-129
white identity, 30

DSM-IV (Diagnostic and Statistical Manual of Mental Disorders), 190-196
Decision making, 34-35, 266. *See also* Treatment selection factors
Descriptive logs, 242-245
Desensitization
by extinction, 549
by reciprocal inhibition, 549
concerns about exposure therapy, 568
EDMR, 567
hierarchies, 552-557
homework and follow-up, 564
identification of emotion-provoking situations
imagery assessment, 559
in-vivo, 566
multicultural applications, 546
problems, 565
rationale, 549
scene presentation, 560
selection and training of counter-conditioning response, 557
uses, 544

Diagnostic labeling/classification of client problems, limitations of, 194-196 *See also* DSM-IV
Diaphragmatic breathing, 476
Diversity and multicultural competence. *See also* Guidelines for use with diverse groups, Multicultural counseling, Multicultural issues
acculturation and the management of diversity, 26
acculturation and the psychology of oppression, 27
cultural identity development, 28
cultural issues in intake and mental status interviews, 230
evidence-based treatments, 311
gender and multicultural biases in diagnosis, 194
spirituality, 495
stress, 470
treatment planning and selection, 323

Drugs, 176

Ecomaps and social network maps, 220-222, 241
EMDR, 567
Empathy, 65-71. *See also* Advanced empathy
Empirically supported treatments. *See* Evidence-based treatments
Empowered consent, 331
Environment. *See also* Contextual factors.
assessment, 218, 227
facilitative conditions, 68
muscle relaxation, 515
nonverbal behavior, 53
person-in-environment model, 181-185
self-efficacy, 621
self-management, 587

Ethical issues
client rights, 38
client welfare, 34
confidentiality, 35
decision making, 34-35

Ethical issues, *(cont.)*
  emerging issues, 39
  multiple relationships, 37
  referral, 38
  technology use, 40
Evaluation of outcome goals
  baseline, 288
  client satisfaction, 283
  duration, 282
  during treatment, 289
  follow-up, 290
  frequency, 281
  intensity, 282
  measures, 284-285
  occurrence, 283
  post-treatment, 290
Evidence-based treatment and critical thinking, 3-5, 63, 311-314
Exercise therapy
  cautions, 527
  guidelines, 526
Expertness, 116-119
Exposure therapy. *See* Desensitization
Eye movement desensitization and reprocessing (EMDR), 567

Facilitative conditions
  empathy (accurate understanding), 65
  genuineness and positive regard, 69
  limit-setting responses, 67
  nonverbal cues, 71
  the holding environment, 68
  validation of clients' experience, 66

Genuineness in the helping relationship, 69
Goal attainment scaling, 273-274, 285, 295
Goals. *See* Outcome goals.
Guided imagery. *See also* Covert modeling
  client imagery assessment, 356
  client imagery potential, 362
  homework and follow-up, 363
  imagery scenes, 362
  model example, 363
  multicultural applications, 358
  rationale, 361
Guidelines for use with diverse groups. *See also* Diversity and multicultural competence, Multicultural counseling, Multicultural issues
  cognitive therapy, 404
  cultural competence, 31
  in treatment planning, 322
  listening response, 106
  meditation, 508
  participant modeling, 352
  problem-solving, 412
  self-efficacy, 628
  self-management, 585

Helper nonverbal behavior, 56-58
  cultural patterns, 47
  genuineness, 69
  warmth, 70-71
Helping. *See also* Interpersonal influence, Facilitative conditions, Guidelines for use with diverse groups, Nonverbal behavior, Resistance, Transference and countertransference, Working alliance and ruptures
  competence, 18
  ethical issues, 34
  influencing responses, 134
  interpersonal awareness, 21
  intimacy, 20
  listening, 85
  multicultural competence, 24-33
  overview, 6
  power, 19
  self-awareness, 17
  values, 21, 26
History-taking
  cultural issues, 211
  identifying antecedents and consequences, 223-225
  model dialogue, 230
  previous solutions, 226
  sensitive subjects, 209
Homosexuality, 23

Imagery, 176. *See also* Guided imagery.
Immediacy
  ground rules for, 152
  steps, 153
In vivo desensitization, 566
Influencing responses
  confrontation, 159-165
  immediacy, 151-155
  interpretation, 139-145
  information giving, 143-150
  questions, 137-141
  self-disclosure, 155-159
Information giving
  differences between advice and, 145
  ground rules, 146
  steps, 145
  technology, 147
Information technology
  and ethics, 40
  influencing responses, 147
  information giving, 147
  practice nexus, 13-14
Intake interviews and client history
  cultural issues in intake and mental-status interviews, 211
  handling sensitive subjects, 209
  history taking content, 208
Interpersonal awareness, 21
Interpersonal influence
  attractiveness, 118-122
  expertness, 116-119
  interaction, 114, 116
  Strong's model, 74
  trustworthiness, 122-129
Interpersonal relationships, 176
Interpretation. *See also* Advanced empathy, Questions, Self-disclosure

SUBJECT INDEX

client reactions, 142
ground rules, 141
steps, 143
Interview assessment. *See also* Client issues, categories; Client issues, defining.
   assessing client environments, 218
   assessing client strengths, 226-227
   client self-monitoring assessment, 242
   cultural issues, 211
   ecomaps, 220-222, 241
   gender and multicultural factors in interview assessment, 230
   intake interviews and history, 208-211
   limitations, 230
   mental status examination, 209-211
   model dialogue, 230
   notes and record-keeping, 241
Interview leads for
   defining goals, 272-279
   identifying goals, 262-271
   obstacles, 279
   subgoals, 278-279
   resources, 280
Involuntary clients, 79, 260, 309, 319

Kinesics, 45, 48-49. *See* Exercise therapy, Muscle relaxation

Lazarus model of case conceptualization (the BASIC ID), 175-178
Listening responses
   barriers, 106
   clarification, 88-91
   clients' stories, 85
   diverse clients, 106
   paraphrasing, 89-94
   reflection, 92-102
   responses, 86-87
   requirements for helpers, 85
   summarization, 101-106
Logs, use in assessment, 242-245.

Marriage (couple) therapy treatment, 319-321
Measurement. *See* Evaluation of outcome goals
Meditation
   applications with diverse clients, 508
   body scan, 510
   contraindications and adverse effects, 512
   mindfulness, 508
   model example, 512
   rationale, 508
   relaxation response, 511
   uses, 505
Mental relaxation. *See* Meditation.
Mental-status examination, 209-211
Modeling. *See* Cognitive modeling, Covert modeling, Participant modeling
Motivational interviewing, 261
Movement. *See* Exercise therapy, Muscle relaxation
Multicultural counseling: *See also* Diversity and multicultural competence, Guidelines for use with diverse groups, Multicultural issues.
   acculturation and diversity, 26
   acculturation and oppression, 27
   competence, 24
   cultural identity development, 28
   multicultural competence, 24-26
Multicultural issues
   assessment, 320
   cognitive therapy, 373
   desensitization, 548
   diagnosis, 194
   imagery, 358
   interview assessment, 230
   outcome goals, 256
   participant modeling, 351
   problem-solving, 410
   reframing, 396
   self-efficacy, 622
   self-management, 584
   treatment, 322-336
Muscle relaxation
   muscle groups, 518
   body scan, 518, 523
   contraindications and adverse effects of, 521
   helper modeling of the relaxation exercises, 517
   creation of a comfortable environment, 515
   homework and follow-up, 520
   instructions about dress, 515
   instructions for muscle relaxation, 517
   model dialogue, 525
   posttraining assessment, 520
   rationale, 515
   variations, 522

National Association of Social Workers, 15; ethical standards, 42; 639
Nonverbal behavior. *See* Client nonverbal behavior, Helper nonverbal behavior.
Notes and record keeping, 241

Occupational stress evolution grid, 473
Outcome goals
   change issues, 257
   cultural issues, 256
   evaluation, 280-290
   goal definition, 271-276
   goal identification, 262-271
   model goal identification, 267
   model example, 291
   purposes, 255
   resistance issues, 260
   subgoals, 277-280
Outcome measures. *See* Evaluation of outcome goals

Paralinguistics, 51
Paraphrasing, 89-94
Participant modeling
   guided participation, 349
   guidelines for using with diverse clients, 352
   model dialogue, 353

Participant modeling, *(cont.)*
    modeling, 348
    multicultural applications, 351
    success, or reinforcing, experiences, 351
    rationale, 348
Person-in-environment model, 181-185
Positive regard, 69-71
Practice evaluation. *See* Evaluation of outcome goals
Practice nexus, 1
    central components, 2-5
    managed care context, 5
Problem identification. *See* Client issues, defining
Problem-solving therapy, 406
    cautions, 417
    decision making, 415
    emotions, 416
    generation of alternative solutions, 415
    guidelines for using with diverse groups of clients, 412
    maintenance and generalization, 417
    model example, 419
    multicultural applications, 410
    problem definition and formulation, 414
    rationale, 413
    six stages of, 413
    solution implementation and verification, 416
Prochaska change model, 258-260
Proxemics, 52

Questions
    guidelines, 137
    open and closed, 137
    steps, 138

Referral issues, 266
Reflection, 92-102
Reframing
    context reframes, 396
    deliberate enactment of selected perceptual features, 396
    homework and follow-up, 396
    identification of alternative perceptions, 396
    identification of client perceptions and feelings, 395
    meaning reframes, 395
    model case, 398
    modification of perceptions in problem situations, 396
    multicultural applications, 396
    process, 391
    rationale, 395
    uses, 392
Relabeling. *See* Reframing
Relationship enhancers
    attractiveness, 118-122
    expertness, 116-119
    trustworthiness, 122-129
Relaxation and meditation, 510. *See also* Muscle relaxation.
Resistance
    client participation, 77
    client position, 77
    compassion fatigue, 79
    competence anxiety, 79
    outcome goals, 260
    personalizing, 76
    reframing, 397
    timing and pacing, 77
    treatment directiveness, 319
    treatment selection, 309

Secondary gains, 225
Self-as-a-model, 612-614
Self-disclosure
    cultural issues in intake and mental-status interviews, 230
    cultural patterns, 47
    ground rules, 135
    steps, 157
Self-efficacy
    as a prelude for treatment, 622
    distinctions, 615
    environmental influences, 621
    guidelines for using with diverse groups of clients, 628
    mind/body link, 621
    model example, 619
    multicultural applications, 622
    performance accomplishments, 617
Self-management
    developing programs, 587
    guidelines for using with diverse groups of clients, 585
    multicultural applications, 584
    self-as-a-model, 611
    self-efficacy, 165
    self-evaluation, 586
    self-monitoring, 589
    self-reinforcement, 587
    self-reward, 606
    stimulus control, 601
    strategies, 586
    uses, 581
Self-monitoring
    charting of response, 589
    discrimination of response, 593
    factors, 590
    model example, 600
    purposes, 589
    rationale, 593
    recording of responses, 594
Self-reward
    cautions, 610
    delivery, 609
    model example, 610
    maintenance, 610
    research, 606
    selection of appropriate rewards, 607
    timing, 610
    uses, 606
Sensation, 176, 216
Silence, 45, 51
Social network maps, 220-222
Spirituality in practice, 492, 495

Stimulus control
  antecedents, 602
  inappropriate in troubling behavior, 602
  model example, 605
  to decrease behavior, 603
  to increase behavior, 604
  uses, 601
Strengths of clients, 226-227
Stress inoculation
  acquisition and practice of cognitive coping skills, 484
  acquisition and practice of direct-action coping skills, 483
  application of all coping skills to potential problem situations, 488
  application of all coping skills to problem-related situations, 487
  homework and follow-up, 496
  information giving, 481
  model dialogue, 491
  rationale, 491
  uses, 479
Stress management
  breathing and stress, 472
  cultural and life-course variations in stress, 470
  hyperventilation syndrome, 474
  occupational stress evolution grid, 473
  spirituality and stress, 495
  stress inoculation, 479
  stress and coping, 467
Strong's model, 113
Subgoals (action steps)
  sequencing, 275
  obstacles, 279
  resources, 280
Summarization, 101-106
Symbolic modeling, 346-347
Systematic desensitization. *See* Desensitization.

Termination issues, 335
Time
  environment, 53
  timing influencing responses, 134
  timing and resistance, 77
  timing and self-reward, 610
Transference and countertransference, 71
Treatment. *See also* Evidence-based treatment
  cost effectiveness, 320

  decision rules, 314-320
  empowered consent, 331-335
  model dialogue, 338
  multicultural and gender issues, 322
  termination issues, 335-338
  treatment selection factors, 308-314
Treatment decision rules. *See also* Treatment selection factors
  cost effectiveness, 320
  duration, 319
  mode, 319
  type, 315
Treatment goals. *See* Outcome goals
Treatment rationales
  breathing exercises, 476
  cognitive modeling, 401
  cognitive restructuring, 441
  covert modeling, 365
  desensitization, 549
  guided imagery, 361
  meditation, 508
  muscle relaxation, 515
  participant modeling, 348
  problem solving, 413
  reframing, 395
  relaxation, 511
  self-as-a-model, 612
  self-monitoring, 593
  stress inoculation, 481
Treatment selection factors. *See also* Treatment decision rules
  client characteristics, 308-310
  documentation and practice guidelines, 311
  helper preferences and flexibility, 310
Treatment strategies, Chapters 12-18. *See also* Change processes and models, Treatment selection factors.
Trustworthiness
  client tests, 123-128
  cross-cultural helping, 128-129

Values, 21, 26
Visualization. *See* Guided imagery.

Warmth, 70
Working alliance and ruptures, 73-76

TO THE OWNER OF THIS BOOK:

We hope that you have found *Interviewing and Change Strategies for Helpers,* Fifth Edition, useful. So that this book can be improved in a future edition, would you take the time to complete this sheet and return it? Thank you.

School and address: _____

Department: _____

Instructor's name: _____

1. What I like most about this book is: _____

_____

_____

2. What I like least about this book is: _____

_____

_____

3. My general reaction to this book is: _____

_____

4. The name of the course in which I used this book is: _____

_____

5. Were all of the chapters of the book assigned for you to read? _____

   If not, which ones weren't? _____

6. In the space below, or on a separate sheet of paper, please write specific suggestions for improving this book and anything else you'd care to share about your experience in using the book.

_____

_____

_____

_____

_____

Optional:

Your name: _____ Date: _____

May Brooks/Cole quote you, either in promotion for *Interviewing and Change Strategies for Helpers, Fifth Edition*, or in future publishing ventures?

Yes: _____ No: _____

Sincerely,

Sherry Cormier
Paula S. Nurius

- -
FOLD HERE

BUSINESS REPLY MAIL
FIRST CLASS   PERMIT NO. 358   PACIFIC GROVE, CA

POSTAGE WILL BE PAID BY ADDRESSEE

ATT: HELPING PROFESSIONS EDITOR: LISA GEBO

Brooks/Cole Publishing Company
511 Forest Lodge Road
Pacific Grove, California 93950-9968

NO POSTAGE
NECESSARY
IF MAILED
IN THE
UNITED STATES

- -
FOLD HERE

IN-BOOK SURVEY

At Brooks/Cole, we are excited about creating new types of learning materials that are interactive, three-dimensional, and fun to use. To guide us in our publishing/development process, we hope that you'll take just a few moments to fill out the survey below. Your answers can help us make decisions that will allow us to produce a wide variety of videos, CD-ROMs, and Internet-based learning systems to complement standard textbooks. If you're interested in working with us as a student Beta-tester, be sure to fill in your name, telephone number, and address. We look forward to hearing from you!

In addition to books, which of the following learning tools do you currently use in your counseling/human services/social work courses?

_____ **Video** _____ in class _____ school library _____ own VCR

_____ **CD-ROM** _____ in class _____ in lab _____ own computer

_____ **Macintosh disk** _____ in class _____ in lab _____ own computer

_____ **Windows disk** _____ in class _____ in lab _____ own computer

_____ **Internet** _____ in class _____ in lab _____ own computer

How often do you access the Internet? _____

My own home computer is a:

_____

The computer I use in class for counseling/human services/social work courses is a:

_____

If you are NOT currently using multimedia materials in your counseling/human services/social work courses, but can see ways that video, CD-ROM, Internet, or other technologies could enhance your learning, please comment below:

_____

_____

_____

Other comments (optional): _____

_____

Name _____ Telephone _____

Address _____

School _____

Professor/Course _____

You can fax this form to us at (650) 592-9081 or detach, fold, secure, and mail.

FOLD HERE

BUSINESS REPLY MAIL
FIRST CLASS   PERMIT NO. 358   PACIFIC GROVE, CA

POSTAGE WILL BE PAID BY ADDRESSEE

ATT: *Marketing*

The Wadsworth Group
10 Davis Drive
Belmont, CA 94002

NO POSTAGE
NECESSARY
IF MAILED
IN THE
UNITED STATES

FOLD HERE

Attention Professors:

Brooks/Cole is dedicated to publishing quality publications for education in the social work, counseling, and human services fields. If you are interested in learning more about our publications, please fill in your name and address and request our latest catalogue, using this prepaid mailer. Please choose one of the following:

☐ social work   ☐ counseling   ☐ human services

Name: _____

Street Address: _____

City, State, and Zip: _____

FOLD HERE

BUSINESS REPLY MAIL
FIRST CLASS   PERMIT NO. 358   PACIFIC GROVE, CA

POSTAGE WILL BE PAID BY ADDRESSEE

ATT: *Marketing*

**The Wadsworth Group
10 Davis Drive
Belmont, CA 94002**

NO POSTAGE
NECESSARY
IF MAILED
IN THE
UNITED STATES

FOLD HERE